W9-AJO-257

Frommer's®
Australia

My Australia

by Lee Mylne
photo captions by Lee Mylne & Marc Llewellyn

HOW TO SUM UP AUSTRALIA IN JUST A FEW WORDS? IMPOSSIBLE.
How to nominate a favorite place? Equally difficult. The only thing I can say
with certainty is that preconceptions of this vast continent and the people
who call it home are sure to be challenged once you get here.

Australians are a mixed bunch; for more than two hundred years, people have come from all over the world to settle here. I'm one of those people
and although I may have lived in and visited more places than most native
Australians, I still find something new and surprising every time I travel in this
country. If I had to choose, Melbourne—with its European style, unpre-
dictable weather and rattling green trams—is my pick (sorry, Sydney). But my
other love is the dusty red earth of the Outback. It's harsh and bright, and
unlike any other place. Everyone should experience the brooding, mystical
presence of Uluru (Ayers Rock) at least once.

Whatever you're looking for—beaches, rainforest, desert, mountains,
smart cities, quiet country towns, or outdoor adventure, you'll find it somewhere in Australia.

The pictures in the following pages showcase this diverse, unique country at its best.

© Bruno Perousse/AGE Fotostock

© William Harrigan/Stephen Frink Collection/Alamy

I'm always bowled over when I see the **SYDNEY OPERA HOUSE (left)** with the Harbour Bridge behind it. It must be one of the most impressive sights in the world. This particular view is taken from Mrs. Macquarie's Chair, in the Royal Botanic Gardens.

When the sun is shining (and it almost always is here), the colors of the **GREAT BARRIER REEF (above)** are beyond belief. Snorkelers on the day cruise boats may feel crowded in their commercial reef enclosures, but divers can get away from it all and commune with the deep . . . reef sharks, turtles, rays and a myriad of tiny vivid fish. It's no wonder the boats take hundreds of people each day and they all come back longing for more.

First page: top, © Penny Tweedie/Alamy; bottom, © APL/J. Carnemolla/Masterfile

© Jack Sullivan/Alamy

CLIMBING AYERS ROCK (left) is frowned upon by the Aboriginal guardians of Uluru (its Aboriginal name), but tourists do it every day. It's easy to see why local Aborigines refer to these intruders as *minga*—or little ants. Watching the sun go down on **ULURU (right)**, is one of the most magical experiences I've had in Australia. The colors turn from pink, to orange, to purple and red—it's like one giant rocky sunset in itself. They've come a long way from a basement in Kuranda in 1987, and there's no looking back for the **TJAPUKAI DANCERS (below)**. Now a much slicker, sophisticated show, the Tjapukai Aboriginal Cultural Park on the outskirts of Cairns is more theme park than theater, but still one of the best opportunities many visitors will have to meet and talk to Aborigines in Queensland. No, you've not been abducted by aliens. You're in northern Australia, where the land is an ocher moonscape and the insects are building towers. Litchfield National Park, a day trip from Darwin, is home to these amazing **TERMITE MOUNDS (below right)**. Spookily, they are all aligned with each other and on a north-south axis.

© Dave Levitt/Lonely Planet Images

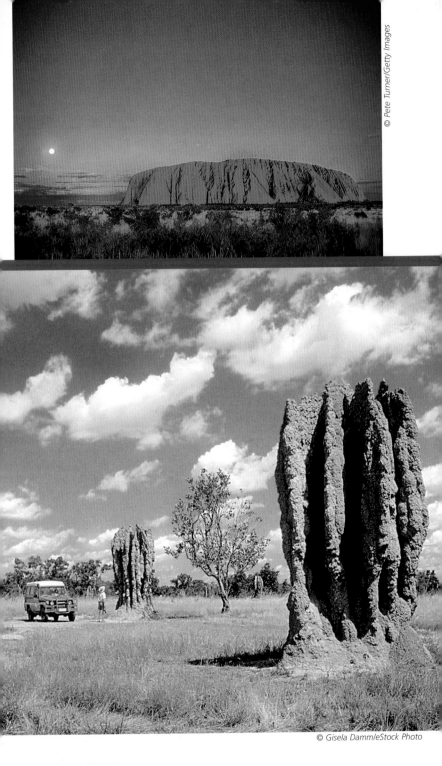

© Pete Turner/Getty Images

© Gisela Damm/eStock Photo

© Glen Allison/AGE Fotostock

Walk on this side of the Brisbane River for the best views of the city. Once derelict, the land under Kangaroo Point cliffs is now one of my favorite Brisbane parks. Walk from South Bank Parklands to the Story Bridge, and you'll find sculptures like these **RED GYMNASTS (above)**, families picnicking, bikes whizzing by . . . and watch out for those inline skaters!

The annual **SYDNEY GAY AND LESBIAN MARDI GRAS (right)** is a huge event and I've lost count of the times I've stood on milk crates to watch the procession swing by. It's all color and sequins, and fun for all the family.

Opposite page: © Jeff Yates/Lonely Planet Images

© Greg Elms/Lonely Planet Images

A day out at cricket—with a rulebook in hand—is one of the quintessential Aussie experiences. The sound of leather against willow, the roar of the crowd as a ball's hit for six, the sun beating down on the **MELBOURNE CRICKET GROUND (MCG)**. They also play Australian Rules football here before packed houses.

© Sean Davey/Australian Picture Library/Corbis

Tasmania's so beautiful that you might never know it once hosted one of the harshest penal colonies in the old British Empire. I'm always struck by **PORT ARTHUR**'s **(left)** peacefulness when I visit, despite the horrors that the convicts endured. **KANGAROO ISLAND (below)**, in South Australia, is my favorite place to spot native animals. It's not all seals and koalas though, as these weather-shaped rocks attest. Aboriginal **ROCK ART (right)** is a reminder of how ancient this culture is. Aboriginal legends and Creation stories are told in these simple outlines, so if you can take a guide who can explain the meanings, do so. Because it is so stunning in its beauty and its wildlife, I fell in love with **HERON ISLAND (below right)** more than a decade ago. It is one of my favorite places in the world for its laid-back style, away-from-the-world on the edge of the Continental shelf. The gently sighing, weeping turtles lay their eggs starting in November and in February their tiny hatchlings scuttle across the sand to start a life that will eventually—if they survive—bring them home again.

© Richard I'Anson/Lonely Planet Images

© Charles & Josette Lenars/Corbis

© Cousteau Society/Getty Images

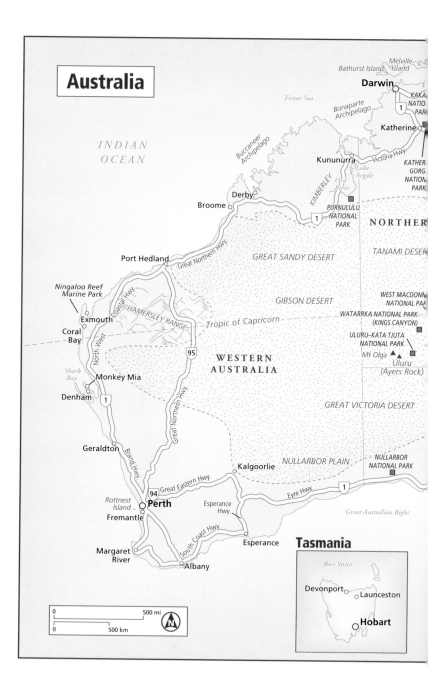

Australia

INDIAN
OCEAN

Timor Sea

Bathurst Island *Melville Island*

Darwin

Bonaparte Archipelago

KAKA NATIO PARK

1

Katherine

Buccaneer Archipelago

Kununurra

Lake Argyle

KATHER GORG NATION PARK

Victoria Hwy.

KIMBERLEY

Ord River

Derby

Broome

1

PURNULULU NATIONAL PARK

NORTHER

Great Northern Hwy.

Port Hedland

GREAT SANDY DESERT

TANAMI DESER

Ningaloo Reef Marine Park

Coastal Hwy.

HAMERSLEY RANGE

GIBSON DESERT

WEST MACDONN NATIONAL PAR

Exmouth

Tropic of Capricorn

WATARRKA NATIONAL PARK (KINGS CANYON)

Coral Bay

North West Hwy.

95

ULURU–KATA TJUTA NATIONAL PARK

Mt Olga

Uluru (Ayers Rock)

Shark Bay

Monkey Mia

WESTERN AUSTRALIA

Denham

1

GREAT VICTORIA DESERT

Great Northern Hwy.

Geraldton

Brand Hwy.

NULLARBOR PLAIN

NULLARBOR NATIONAL PARK

Kalgoorlie

Great Eastern Hwy.

1

Eyre Hwy.

Rottnest Island

94

Perth

Fremantle

Esperance Hwy.

Great Australian Bight

Margaret River

South Coast Hwy.

Esperance

Tasmania

Albany

Bass Strait

Devonport

Launceston

Hobart

0   500 mi

0   500 km

N

Sydney Transportation Systems

⊠ Post Office
ⓘ Information

Area of Detail

North Sydney

Sydney

Bondi Junction

Port Jackson

0   1/4 mi
0   1/4 km

Port Jackson/
Sydney Harbour

BENNELONG POINT

Man O' War Wharf

Farm Cove

ROYAL BOTANIC GARDENS

POTTS POINT

Woolloomooloo Bay

Cowper Wharf Roadway

Government House

Mrs Macquarie's Rd

State Library of NSW

THE DOMAIN

Cahill Expressway

Sydney Harbour Bridge

Sydney Harbour Tunnel

The Rocks Visitors Centre

Campbells Cove

Circular Quay West

DAWES POINT

To North Sydney

Hickson Rd

Lower Fort St

Bradfield Highway

Upper Fort St

MILLERS POINT

THE ROCKS

Argyle St

Cumberland

George St

Playfair St

Sydney Cove

Manly JetCat Wharf

Manly Ferry Wharf

Circular Quay East

CIRCULAR QUAY

Circular Quay

Cahill Expressway

Albert St

Alfred St

Young St

Loftus St

Phillip St

Bent St

Macquarie St

Phillip

Bligh St

Hunter St

Martin Place

Elizabeth

Martin Place

General Post

Gloucester St

Harrington St

Bridge St

Pitt St

George St

York St

Carrington St

Margaret St

Western Distributor

Wynyard

Hickson Rd.

Darling Harbour

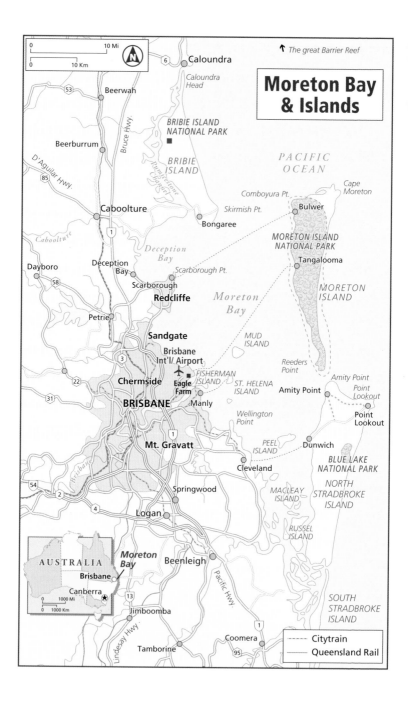

Moreton Bay & Islands

Frommer's®

Australia

2006

by Marc Llewellyn & Lee Mylne

Here's what the critics say about Frommer's:

"A major publishing challenge for any travel guide is keeping it up to date, and when travelers pick up one on a destination as big as Australia, they want to know that what the writers are giving them is accurate . . . Australian-based writers, including Brisbane-based Lee Mylne, are on the ball."
—*Courier Mail*

"Detailed, accurate, and easy-to-read information for all price ranges."
—*Glamour Magazine*

"Hotel information is close to encyclopedic."
—*Des Moines Sunday Register*

"Frommer's Guides have a way of giving you a real feel for a place."
—*Knight Ridder Newspapers*

WILEY
Wiley Publishing, Inc.

Published by:

Wiley Publishing, Inc.

111 River St.
Hoboken, NJ 07030-5774

Copyright © 2006 Wiley Publishing, Inc., Hoboken, New Jersey. All rights reserved. No part of this publication may be reproduced, stored in a retrieval system or transmitted in any form or by any means, electronic, mechanical, photocopying, recording, scanning or otherwise, except as permitted under Sections 107 or 108 of the 1976 United States Copyright Act, without either the prior written permission of the Publisher, or authorization through payment of the appropriate per-copy fee to the Copyright Clearance Center, 222 Rosewood Drive, Danvers, MA 01923, 978/750-8400, fax 978/646-8600. Requests to the Publisher for permission should be addressed to the Legal Department, Wiley Publishing, Inc., 10475 Crosspoint Blvd., Indianapolis, IN 46256, 317/572-3447, fax 317/572-4355, or online at http://www.wiley.com/go/permissions.

Wiley and the Wiley Publishing logo are trademarks or registered trademarks of John Wiley & Sons, Inc. and/or its affiliates. Frommer's is a trademark or registered trademark of Arthur Frommer. Used under license. All other trademarks are the property of their respective owners. Wiley Publishing, Inc. is not associated with any product or vendor mentioned in this book.

ISBN-13: 978-0-7645-9594-3
ISBN-10: 0-7645-9594-6

Editor: Kathleen Warnock
Production Editor: Ian Skinnari
Cartographer: Nicholas Trotter
Photo Editor: Richard Fox
Production by Wiley Indianapolis Composition Services

Front cover photo: Northern territory: Gum Tree & Devil's Marbles
Back cover photo: Competitors in Bondi Beach lifeguard race

For information on our other products and services or to obtain technical support, please contact our Customer Care Department within the U.S. at 800/762-2974, outside the U.S. at 317/572-3993 or fax 317/572-4002.

Wiley also publishes its books in a variety of electronic formats. Some content that appears in print may not be available in electronic formats.

Manufactured in the United States of America

5 4 3 2 1

Contents

List of Maps   viii

What's New in Australia   1

1   The Best of Australia   4

by Marc Llewellyn & Lee Mylne

1 The Top Travel Experiences 4

2 The Best Outdoor Adventures 8

3 The Best Places to View Wildlife 9

4 The Best Places to Experience the Outback 11

5 The Best Beaches 12

6 The Best Diving & Snorkeling Sites 13

7 The Best Places to Bushwalk (Hike) 14

8 The Best Places to Learn About Aboriginal Culture 15

9 The Best of Small-Town Australia 16

10 The Best Museums 17

11 The Best Luxury Accommodations 18

12 The Best Moderately Priced Accommodations 19

13 The Best Alternative Accommodations 20

14 The Best B&Bs & Guesthouses ...21

15 The Best Restaurants 22

16 The Best Reasonably Priced Restaurants 23

2   Planning Your Trip to Australia   25

by Lee Mylne

1 The Regions in Brief 25

2 Visitor Information 29

   Australia: Red Alert Checklist 30

3 Entry Requirements & Customs 30

4 Money 34

   The Australian Dollar, the U.S. Dollar & the British Pound 35

5 When to Go 37

   Australia Calendar of Events 39

6 Travel Insurance 41

7 Health & Safety 43

8 Specialized Travel Resources 45

9 Planning Your Trip Online 49

   Frommers.com: The Complete Travel Resource 50

10 The 21st-Century Traveler 51

   Online Traveler's Toolbox 54

11 Getting There 55

   Flying with Film & Video 60

12 Packages for the Independent Traveler 60

13 Escorted General-Interest Tours 62

14 The Active Traveler 63
15 Getting Around Australia 68
16 Tips on Accommodations 80

17 Recommended Books & Films 84
Fast Facts: Australia 85

3 Suggested Itineraries 91

by Marc Llewellyn & Lee Mylne

1 Australia in 1 Week 91
2 Australia in 2 Weeks 96
3 Australia for Families (Starting in Sydney) 97

4 An Inland Odyssey: Driving from Sydney to Melbourne 99
5 A Few Days in Margaret River, WA 101

4 Sydney 103

by Marc Llewellyn

1 Orientation 104
Neighborhoods in Brief 108
2 Getting Around 111
Fast Facts: Sydney 117
3 Where to Stay 120
4 Where to Dine 136
What to Know about BYO 136
Something Fishy 148

5 What to See & Do in Sydney 153
Great Deals on Sightseeing 153
6 Harbor Cruises & Organized Tours 171
7 Staying Active 173
8 Spectator Sports 176
9 Shopping 176
10 Sydney After Dark 183

5 New South Wales 190

by Marc Llewellyn

1 The Blue Mountains 192
2 The Hunter Valley: Wine Tasting & More .202
Bunking Down in a Caravan, Man 207
Something Special: A Cattle Station in the Upper Hunter 209
3 Port Stephens: Dolphin- & Whale-Watching 211

4 North of Sydney along the Pacific Highway: Australia's Holiday Coast 214
5 South of Sydney along the Princes Highway 224
6 The Snowy Mountains: Australia's Ski Country 231
7 Outback New South Wales 234

6   Brisbane   241

by Lee Mylne

1 Orientation 241

Neighborhoods in Brief 245

2 Getting Around 245

Fast Facts: Brisbane 249

3 Where to Stay 250

4 Where to Dine 253

5 Exploring Brisbane 256

6 Organized Tours 259

7 Enjoying the Great Outdoors 260

Brisbane's Bridge Climb 261

8 The Shopping Scene 262

9 Brisbane After Dark 263

Brisbane's Historic Pubs 265

10 Brisbane's Moreton Bay
& Islands 266

7   Queensland & the Great Barrier Reef   270

by Lee Mylne

1 Exploring the Great
Barrier Reef 274

2 Cairns 284

3 Port Douglas, Daintree &
the Cape Tribulation Area 304

4 The North Coast: Mission Beach,
Townsville & the Islands 315

5 The Whitsunday Coast &
Islands 330

Come Sail with Me 334

6 The Capricorn Coast &
the Southern Reef Islands 343

Up Close & Personal
with a Turtle 350

7 Fraser Island: Ecoadventures
& Four-Wheel-Drive Fun 353

8 The Sunshine Coast 357

9 The Gold Coast 365

10 The Gold Coast Hinterland:
Back to Nature 374

8   The Red Centre   379

by Marc Llewellyn

1 Exploring the Red Centre 379

2 Alice Springs 382

3 Road Trips from Alice Springs 395

Road Trips to the East &
West Macs 396

4 Kings Canyon 398

5 Uluru–Kata Tjuta National
Park (Ayers Rock/The Olgas) 399

Dinner in the Desert 403

9   The Top End   409

by Lee Mylne

1 Exploring the Top End 409

2 Darwin 412

Cheap Eats & More! 421

3 Kakadu National Park 424

*Never Smile at a You-
Know-What!* 427

A Side Trip to a Tiwi Island 428

4 Katherine 432

10 Perth & Western Australia   436

by Lee Mylne

*Tiptoeing through
the Wildflowers* 439

1 Perth 440

Neighborhoods in Brief 443

Take a Free Ride 444

Fast Facts: Perth 445

2 Side Trips from Perth 462

3 Margaret River & the Southwest:
Wine Tasting in the Forests 469

Taking a Dip with Flipper 470

4 The Goldfields 476

5 The Midwest & the Northwest:
Where the Outback Meets
the Sea .479

6 The Kimberley: A Far-Flung
Wilderness 486

11 Adelaide & South Australia   501

by Marc Llewellyn

1 Adelaide 502

*The Adelaide & WOMADelaide
Festivals* 506

Fast Facts: Adelaide 508

2 Side Trips from Adelaide 520

So Much Wine, So Little Time 522

3 Kangaroo Island 529

*Culling Koalas—A National
Dilemma* 535

4 Outback South Australia 538

*A Fabulous Four-Wheel-Drive
Adventure* 543

5 The Coorong 544

12 Melbourne   546

by Marc Llewellyn

1 Orientation 546

Neighborhoods in Brief 549

2 Getting Around 551

Fast Facts: Melbourne 553

3 Where to Stay 554

4 Where to Dine 561

5 Seeing the Sights 568

6 Enjoying the Great Outdoors
or Catching an Aussie Rules
Football Match 574

7 Shopping 576

Death by Chocolate 578

8 Melbourne After Dark 579

9 Side Trips from Melbourne 584

(13) Victoria   593

by Marc Llewellyn

1 Ballarat: Gold-Rush City 594
2 The Great Ocean Road: One of
the World's Most Scenic Drives 598
3 The Murray River 602

Ned Kelly Country 604
4 The High Country 607
5 The Northwest: Grampians
National Park 612

(14) Canberra   615

by Marc Llewellyn

1 Orientation 615
2 Getting Around 618
Fast Facts: Canberra 619
3 Where to Stay 620
4 Where to Dine 623
5 Seeing the Sights 624

Up, Up & Away... 625
*Boat & Ghost Tours
in Canberra* 626
6 Outdoor Pursuits 628
7 Canberra After Dark 629

(15) Tasmania   630

by Marc Llewellyn

1 Exploring Tasmania 630
2 Hobart 634
3 Port Arthur: Discovering
Tasmania's Convict Heritage 646
4 Freycinet National Park 648

5 Launceston 651
6 Cradle Mountain & Lake
St. Clair National Park 656
Hiking the Overland Track 658
7 The West Coast 659

Appendix A: Australia in Depth   662

by Marc Llewellyn

1 Australia's Natural World 662
2 The People Down Under 664
3 Australian History 101 666
Dateline 666

4 Aussie Eats & Drinks 669
*Witchetty Grubs, Lilli-Pillies
& Other Good Eats* 670

Appendix B: Useful Toll-Free Numbers & Websites   672

Index   674

General Index 674
Accommodations Index 687

Restaurant Index 690

List of Maps

Australia   6

Suggested Australia Itineraries   92

Greater Sydney   105

Sydney Harbour   109

Sydney Ferries   115

Where to Stay in Central Sydney   122

Where to Dine in Sydney   138

Where to Dine in The Rocks   143

Central Sydney Attractions   154

New South Wales   191

The Blue Mountains   193

The Hunter Valley   203

Greater Brisbane   243

Brisbane Accommodations,
  Dining & Attractions   246

Queensland   272

The Great Barrier Reef   275

Cairns   285

Port Douglas, Daintree &
  Cape Tribulation   305

The North Coast   317

Magnetic Island   328

The Whitsunday Region   331

The Central Queensland Coast   345

The Sunshine Coast   359

The Gold Coast   367

The Red Centre   381

Alice Springs   383

The Northern Territory   411

Darwin   413

Western Australia   437

Perth   441

The Kimberley Region   487

South Australia   503

Adelaide   505

The Barossa   521

Adelaide Hills   527

Kangaroo Island   530

Greater Melbourne   547

Where to Stay in Central
  Melbourne   555

Where to Dine in Central
  Melbourne   563

Where to Stay & Dine
  in St. Kilda   567

Melbourne Attractions   569

Side Trips from Melbourne   585

Victoria   595

Canberra   617

Tasmania   631

Hobart   635

An Invitation to the Reader

In researching this book, we discovered many wonderful places—hotels, restaurants, shops, and more. We're sure you'll find others. Please tell us about them, so we can share the information with your fellow travelers in upcoming editions. If you were disappointed with a recommendation, we'd love to know that, too. Please write to:

Frommer's Australia 2006
Wiley Publishing, Inc. • 111 River St. • Hoboken, NJ 07030-5774

An Additional Note

Please be advised that travel information is subject to change at any time—and this is especially true of prices. We therefore suggest that you write or call ahead for confirmation when making your travel plans. The authors, editors, and publisher cannot be held responsible for the experiences of readers while traveling. Your safety is important to us, however, so we encourage you to stay alert and be aware of your surroundings. Keep a close eye on cameras, purses, and wallets, all favorite targets of thieves and pickpockets.

About the Authors

Sydney resident **Marc Llewellyn** is one of Australia's premier travel writers and the winner of the several travel writing awards, including the Australian Society of Travel Writer's Travel Writer of the Year award 2001/2002. His latest travelogue, *Riders to the Midnight Sun,* tells of his cycle journey from the Ukrainian Black Sea to Arctic Russia—in a bid to escape the Australian heat. He is co-author of *Frommer's Australia from $50 a Day* and *Frommer's Australia from $60 a Day.*

Lee Mylne writes for a broad range of consumer and travel trade publications around Australia. Born and raised in New Zealand, she has worked in newspapers, magazines, and radio, and traveled widely before finally figuring out she could make a living out of it. She has lived in Australia since 1986 and is a Full Member of the Australian Society of Travel Writers. Her books include *Frommer's Portable Australia's Great Barrier Reef.* She is co-author of *Frommer's Australia from $50 a Day* and *Frommer's Australia from $60 a Day.*

Other Great Guides for Your Trip:

Frommer's Australia from $60 a Day
Frommer's Portable Australia's Great Barrier Reef
Frommer's New Zealand
Frommer's South Pacific

Frommer's Star Ratings, Icons & Abbreviations

Every hotel, restaurant, and attraction listing in this guide has been ranked for quality, value, service, amenities, and special features using a **star-rating system.** In country, state, and regional guides, we also rate towns and regions to help you narrow down your choices and budget your time accordingly. Hotels and restaurants are rated on a scale of zero (recommended) to three stars (exceptional). Attractions, shopping, nightlife, towns, and regions are rated according to the following scale: zero stars (recommended), one star (highly recommended), two stars (very highly recommended), and three stars (must-see).

In addition to the star-rating system, we also use **seven feature icons** that point you to the great deals, in-the-know advice, and unique experiences that separate travelers from tourists. Throughout the book, look for:

Finds	Special finds—those places only insiders know about
Fun Fact	Fun facts—details that make travelers more informed and their trips more fun
Kids	Best bets for kids and advice for the whole family
Moments	Special moments—those experiences that memories are made of
Overrated	Places or experiences not worth your time or money
Tips	Insider tips—great ways to save time and money
Value	Great values—where to get the best deals

The following **abbreviations** are used for credit cards:

AE	American Express	DISC	Discover	V	Visa
DC	Diners Club	MC	MasterCard		

Frommers.com

Now that you have the guidebook to a great trip, visit our website at **www.frommers.com** for travel information on more than 3,000 destinations. With features updated regularly, we give you instant access to the most current trip-planning information available. At Frommers.com, you'll also find the best prices on airfares, accommodations, and car rentals—and you can even book travel online through our travel booking partners. At Frommers.com, you'll also find the following:

- Online updates to our most popular guidebooks
- Vacation sweepstakes and contest giveaways
- Newsletter highlighting the hottest travel trends
- Online travel message boards with featured travel discussions

What's New in Australia

The land Down Under continues to change in exciting ways. Travelers have new possibilities for getting to and around the country, and a greater choice of things to do once they are here. Here's a brief summary of the latest happenings. You'll find more detail in each of the regional chapters.

PLANNING YOUR TRIP/GETTING AROUND The past year has seen a greater measure of stability over the Australian skies. After the upheavals of the recent past, Australian carriers have settled in to a period of consolidation, with some expansion. All offer good Internet deals.

Competition is tough, with no-frills carrier **Virgin Blue** (© 13 67 89 in Australia, or 07/3295 2296; www.virginblue.com.au) battling it out with Qantas-owned **Jetstar** (© 13 15 38 in Australia; www.jetstar.com.au). Qantas international subsidiary **Australian Airlines** (© 1300/799 798 in Australia) continues to provide an option for visitors from Asia, and an alternative link between Cairns, Sydney, and the Gold Coast.

Virgin offshoot **Pacific Blue** (© 13 16 45 in Australia; www.virginblue.com.au), launched in 2004, now services a growing number of Australian cities from Auckland, Wellington, and Christchurch in New Zealand. It also flies to a few Pacific islands, including Fiji, Vanuatu, and the Cook Islands.

Regional Express (© 13 17 13 in Australia; www.regionalexpress.com.au) serves regional New South Wales, South Australia, Victoria, and northern Tasmania.

SYDNEY Accommodations Vibe Hotels has rapidly expanded into Sydney, buying and renovating three hotels: **Vibe Rushcutters** (© 02/8353 8988) in Rushcutters Bay near Kings Cross; **Vibe Goulburn** (© 02/9282 0988) in Goulburn Street, near Central Station; and **Vibe North Sydney** (© 02/9955 1111), across the Harbour Bridge at Milsons Point. The hotels offer pleasant business-class accommodations at very reasonable prices. Book online (www.vibehotels.com.au) and find rooms from as little as A$182 (US$146) a night.

Attractions A new, exciting addition to Sydney Tower is **Skytour** (© 02/9223 0933), a series of interactive exhibits where you can sit in a room lit by hurricane lamps and listen to Australian yarns, watch moving models and holograms of Australian landscapes, visit a reconstruction of an Aboriginal cave with appropriate sounds and melodies, and in a big-screen simulator, go virtual white-water rafting in Queensland, climb Uluru (Ayers Rock), and have a close encounter with a saltwater crocodile.

NEW SOUTH WALES New on the hotel scene in Byron Bay is the **Byron at Byron** (© 1300 554 362 in Australia; www.thebyronatbyron.com.au). The hotel is on an 18-hectare (45-acre) site under a canopy of rainforest and beside some beautiful wetlands about 5 minutes by car from the town itself. There are 92 guest

Tips Butt Out Down Under . . .

Smokers traveling to Australia will find greater restrictions on the number of places you can light up. Smoking is banned or heavily restricted in most public places, such as museums, cinemas, theaters, and airport terminals. From early 2006, a total ban on smoking will apply in pubs and clubs in Tasmania, followed by Queensland and Western Australia in July 2006. Victoria and New South Wales will go the same way in 2007.

rooms in all, with lots of wood features, a dining area, and a contemporary galley kitchen. The main building offers a restaurant and a spa.

BRISBANE After several years in the planning-and-permission stages, the **Story Bridge Adventure Climb** (© 07/3514 6900; www.storybridgeadventureclimb. com.au) has launched tours, becoming the world's third bridge climb (after Sydney and Auckland). Visitors can now "climb" the Story Bridge to a 44m-high (143-ft.) viewing platform overlooking the city, the river, and Moreton Bay and its islands.

QUEENSLAND Accommodations After several years of catering to the 18-to-35 market, Great Keppel Island's popular resort has returned to what it has always done best: family holidays. Rebranded as **Mercure Resort Great Keppel Island** (© 1800/245 658 in Australia, or 07/ 4939 5044; www.greatkeppelresort.com. au), under the Accor umbrella, it has been completely refurbished and now has family-friendly features such as a kids' club.

Attractions Visitors to Bundaberg's **Mon Repos Conservation Park** (© 07/ 4159 1652 for the visitor center), one of the two largest loggerhead-turtle rookeries in the South Pacific, will find waiting to watch turtles nesting (Nov–Mar) much less stressful after the introduction of a new booking system for turtle-watching tours. Access to the beach is by ticket only, and you must book your visit through the **Coral Coast Visitor Information Centre** (© 07/4153 8888).

THE TOP END Skycity Darwin, Gilruth Avenue, Mindil Beach, Darwin (© 1800/891 118 in Australia, or 08/ 8943 8888; www.skycitydarwin.com.au), has been taken over by the Skycity Entertainment Group and completed a A$10-million (US$8-million) refurbishment of the whole resort, and added 10 new AAA-rated five-star Superior Rooms, which have cool marble bathrooms with spa baths and full-length glass windows that provide uninterrupted views of the beachfront, and private balconies.

PERTH & WESTERN AUSTRALIA Guests at **El Questro Wilderness Park,** Gibb River Road, approximately 100km (62 miles) southwest of Kununurra (© 1300/656 565 in Australia, or 08/ 9169 1777; www.elquestro.com.au), can now stay overnight in the new luxury **Mt. Cockburn Lodge,** on the rugged and isolated Kimberley coastline. There are six funky double *goondis* (Aboriginal for "shelter") complete with goose-feather pillows, luxurious showers, and slate floors for guests to stay in. The lodge is only for guests at El Questro Homestead, Emma Gorge Resort, or the Station Township Bungalows, who take part in the Mount Cockburn Safari. The all-inclusive cost is A$900 (US$720) for adults and A$450 (US$360) for children under 12.

TASMANIA The **West Coast Wilderness Railway** (© 1800/ 130 002 in Australia; www.federalresorts.com.au) between Queenstown and Strahan in Tasmania took the Significant Tourist Attractions award at the Australian Tourism Awards in February 2005. Passengers can travel one-way along the 35km (22-mile) route, through Tasmanian wilderness, or a full 6-hour return trip. The railway began life as the Mt. Lyell Mining and Railway Co. Ltd. in 1896, and was used to transport copper and mineral concentrates from Queenstown to Strahan port, using a novel "third track" rack-and-pinion system to enable its locomotives to negotiate 1:16 gradients.

1

The Best of Australia

by Marc Llewellyn & Lee Mylne

Maybe we're biased because we live here, but Australia has a lot of bests—world bests, that is. It has some of the best natural scenery, the weirdest wildlife, the most brilliant scuba diving and snorkeling, the best beaches (shut up, California), the oldest rainforest (110 million years and counting), the oldest human civilization (some archaeologists say 40,000 years, some say 120,000; whatever—it's old), the best wines (come see what we mean), the best weather (give or take the odd Wet season in the north), the most innovative East-meets-West-meets-someplace-else cuisine—all bathed in sunlight that brings everything up in Technicolor.

"Best" means different things to different people, but scarcely a visitor lands on these shores without having the Great Barrier Reef at the top of the "Things to See" list. So they should, because it really is a glorious natural masterpiece. Also high on most folks' lists is Ayers Rock. This monolith must have some kind of magnet inside it designed to attract planeloads of tourists. We're not saying the Rock isn't special, but we think the vast Australian desert all around it is even more so. The third attraction on most visitors' lists is Sydney, the Emerald City that glitters in the antipodean sunshine on—here we go with the "bests" again—the best harbor, spanned by the best bridge in the world (yes it is, San Francisco).

But as planes zoom overhead delivering visitors to the big three attractions, Aussies in charming country towns, on far-flung beaches, on rustic sheep stations, in rainforest villages, and in mountain lodges shake their heads and say sadly, "They don't know what they're missin'." Well, that's the aim of this chapter—to show you what you're missin'. Read on, and consider taking the road less traveled.

1 The Top Travel Experiences

- **Hitting the Rails on the *Indian Pacific* Train:** This 3-day journey across the Outback regularly makes it onto travel magazines' "Top Rail Journeys in the World" lists. The desert scenery ain't all that magnificent—it's the unspoiled, empty vastness that passengers appreciate. It includes the longest straight stretch of track in the world, 478km (296 miles) across the treeless Nullarbor Plain. Start in Sydney and end in Perth, or vice versa, or just do a section. See "Getting Around Australia" in chapter 2.

- **Experiencing Sydney** (NSW): Sydney is more than just the magnificent Harbour Bridge and Opera House. No other city has beaches in such abundance, and few have such a magnificently scenic harbor. Our advice is to board a ferry, walk from one side of the bridge to the other, and try to spend a week here, because you're going to need it. See chapter 4, "Sydney."

Tips   **A Note on Abbreviations**

In the listings below, NSW stands for New South Wales, QLD for Queensland, NT for the Northern Territory, WA for Western Australia, SA for South Australia, VIC for Victoria, TAS for Tasmania, and ACT for the Australian Capital Territory.

- **Seeing the Great Barrier Reef** (QLD): It's a glorious 2,000km-long (1,240-mile) underwater coral fairyland with electric colors and bizarre fish life—and it comes complete with warm water and year-round sunshine. This is what you came to Australia to see. When you're not snorkeling over coral and giant clams almost as big as you, scuba diving, calling at tropical towns, or lazing on deserted island beaches, you'll be trying out the sun lounges or enjoying the first-rate food. See chapter 7, "Queensland & the Great Barrier Reef."

- **Exploring the Wet Tropics Rainforest** (QLD): Folks who come from skyscraper cities like Manhattan and Los Angeles can't get over the moisture-dripping ferns, the neon-blue butterflies, and the primeval peace of this World Heritage rainforest stretching north, south, and west from Cairns. Hike it, four-wheel-drive it, or glide over the treetops in the Skyrail gondola. See "Cairns" in chapter 7.

- **Bareboat Sailing in the Whitsundays** (QLD): Bareboat means unskippered—that's right, even if you think port is an after-dinner drink, you can charter a yacht, pay for a day's instruction from a skipper, and then take over the helm yourself and explore these 74 island gems. It's easy. Anchor in deserted bays, snorkel over dazzling reefs, fish for coral trout, and feel the wind in your sails. See "The Whitsunday Coast & Islands" in chapter 7.

- **Exploring Kata Tjuta (the Olgas) & Uluru (Ayers Rock)** (NT): Just why everyone comes thousands of miles to see the big red stone of Ayers Rock is a mystery, and that's probably why they come—because the Rock is a mystery. Just 50km (31 miles) from Ayers Rock are the round red heads of the Olgas, a second rock formation more significant to Aborigines and more intriguing to many visitors. See "Uluru–Kata Tjuta National Park (Ayers Rock/The Olgas)" in chapter 8.

- **Taking an Aboriginal Culture Tour** (Alice Springs, NT): Eating female wasps, contemplating a hill as a giant resting caterpillar, and imagining that the stars are your grandmother smiling down at you will give you a new perspective on Aboriginal culture. See what we mean on a half-day tour from the Aboriginal Art & Culture Centre. See p. 388.

- **Discovering the Kimberley** (WA): Australia's last frontier, the Kimberley is a romantic cocktail of South Sea pearls, red mountain ranges, aqua seas, deadly crocodiles, Aboriginal rock art, and million-acre farms in a never-ending wilderness. Cross it by four-wheel-drive, stay in safari tents on a cattle ranch, swim under waterfalls, ride a camel along the beach in Broome, and more. See chapter 9, "The Top End."

- **Rolling in Wildflowers** (WA): Imagine Texas three times over and covered in wildflowers. That's what much of Western Australia looks like every spring, from around August through October, when pink, mauve, red, white, yellow, and blue wildflowers bloom. Aussies flock here for this spectacle, so book ahead. See the box

Australia

THE TOP END
See Chapter 9

QUEENSLAND
See Chapter 7

HE RED CENTRE
See Chapter 8

See Chapter 6

SOUTH
AUSTRALIA
See Chapter 11

See Chapter 11

See Chapter 14

See Chapter 4

VICTORIA
See Chapter 13

See Chapter 12

Thursday
Island

Coral
Sea

Gulf
of
Carpentaria

CAPE
YORK
PENINSULA

nhem
Land

SOUTH
PACIFIC
OCEAN

Cooktown

DAINTREE
NATIONAL
PARK

Port Douglas

Cairns
Mission
Beach

RRITORY

66

ennant
Creek

Barkly Hwy.

Mt. Isa

Landsborough Hwy.

Flinders Hwy.

78

Townsville

Whitsunday
Islands
National
Park

Proserpine

Mackay

CDONNELL RANGES

Alice Springs

SIMPSON DESERT

QUEENSLAND

Longreach

66

Capricorn Hwy.

1

Rockhampton

Gladstone

Bundaberg

Fraser
Island

SOUTH
USTRALIA

Coober Pedy

87

Stuart Hwy.

FLINDERS RANGES
NATIONAL PARK

Barrier Hwy.

Broken Hill

32

Port Pirie

Adelaide

Kangaroo
Island

Princes Hwy.

Dukes Hwy.

Mt. Gambier

Darling River

15

Brisbane

Sunshine
Coast

LAMINGTON
NAT'L. PK.

Gold
Coast

1

71

Lightning
Ridge

Coffs
Harbour

Oxley Hwy.

Tamworth

Dubbo

NEW
SOUTH WALES

Mildura

20

Murray River

Newell Hwy.

39

Wodonga

31

Albury

8

Ballarat

Geelong

Melbourne

VICTORIA

Apollo Bay

Mt. Kosciuszko

SNOWY
MOUNTAINS

BLUE MTNS.
NAT'L. PK.

New England Hwy.

Pacific Hwy.

32

Port
Macquarie

Newcastle

Sydney

Hume Hwy.

Princes Hwy.

CANBERRA

1

A.C.T.

Tasman Sea

To Tasmania (see inset)

"Tiptoeing Through the Wildflowers" in chapter 10.

- **Drinking in the Barossa Valley** (SA): One of Australia's four largest wine-producing areas, this German-speaking region less than an hour's drive from Adelaide is also the prettiest. Adelaide's restaurants happen to be some of the country's best, too, so test out your wine purchases with the city's terrific food. See "Side Trips from Adelaide" in chapter 11.
- **Getting Dusty in the Desert** (SA): Head inland from Adelaide to the Outback to visit remote pubs and settlements, the craggy ridges of the Flinders Ranges, dry salt lakes, and deserts. See chapter 11, "Adelaide & South Australia."
- **Seeing the Sights along the Great Ocean Road** (VIC): This 106km (66-mile) coastal road carries you past wild and stunning beaches, forests, and dramatic cliff-top scenery—including the Twelve Apostles, a dozen pillars of red rock standing in isolation in the foaming Southern Ocean. See "The Great Ocean Road: One of the World's Most Scenic Drives" in chapter 13.

2 The Best Outdoor Adventures

- **Sea Kayaking:** Kayaking is a great way to explore Queensland's Whitsunday Islands as well as Dunk Island off Mission Beach in Queensland. **Rivergods** (© **08/9259 0749;** www.rivergods.com.au) in Perth even takes you on a sea-kayaking day trip to snorkel with wild sea lions and watch penguins feeding. This Western Australian company also runs multiday expeditions past whales, dolphins, and sharks in Shark Bay, and over coral at Ningaloo Reef on the Northwest Cape. For details on the Whitsunday Islands and Dunk Island, see chapter 7. For information about Perth and Western Australia, see chapter 10.
- **Horse Trekking in the Snowy Mountains** (NSW): Ride the ranges like the man from Snowy River, staying in bush lodges or camping beneath the stars. See "In the Footsteps of the Man from Snowy River" in chapter 5.
- **Abseiling (Rappelling) in the Blue Mountains** (NSW): Careering backward down a cliff face with the smell of eucalyptus in your nostrils is not everyone's idea of fun, but you sure know you're alive. Several operators welcome both novices and the more experienced. See "The Blue Mountains" in chapter 5.
- **White-Water Rafting on the Tully River** (Mission Beach, QLD): The Class III to IV rapids of the Tully River swoosh between lush, rainforested banks. The guides are professional, and the rapids are just hairy enough to be fun. It's a good choice for first-time rafters. See "The North Coast: Mission Beach, Townsville & the Islands" in chapter 7.
- **Four-Wheel-Driving on Fraser Island** (QLD): Burning down 75-Mile Beach in a 4×4 on the biggest sand island in the world is liberating, if not great for the environment. Paradoxically, the island is ecologically important and popular with nature lovers. Hike its eucalyptus forests and rainforests, swim its clear lakes, and fish off the beach. See "Fraser Island: Ecoadventures & Four-Wheel-Drive Fun" in chapter 7.
- **Game Fishing:** Battle a black marlin off Cairns and you might snare the world record; that's how big they get down there. Marlin and other game catches run around much of the Australian coastline—Exmouth on the

Northwest Cape in Western Australia (see chapter 10), and Broome and Darwin in the Top End (see chapter 9) are two other hot spots.

- **Canoeing the Top End** (NT): Paddling between the sun-drenched ocher walls of Katherine Gorge sharpens the senses, especially when a (harmless) freshwater crocodile pops up! **Gecko Canoeing** (© **1800/634 319** in Australia, or 08/8972 2224; www.geckocanoeing.com.au) will take you downriver to the rarely explored Flora and Daly River systems to visit Aboriginal communities, shower under waterfalls, hike virgin bushland, and camp in swags on the banks. See "Katherine" in chapter 9.

- **Surfing in Margaret River** (WA): A 90-minute surf lesson with four-time Western Australia surf champ Josh Palmateer is a great introduction to the sport—if only to hear Josh's Aussie accent! In July and August, Josh shifts his classes to Cable Beach in Broome. See chapter 10.

- **Skiing in the Victorian Alps** (VIC): Skiing in Australia? Sure. When you've had enough coral and sand, you can hit the slopes in Victoria. Where else can you swish down the mountain between gum trees? See "The High Country" in chapter 13.

3 The Best Places to View Wildlife

- **Pebbly Beach** (NSW): The eastern gray kangaroos that inhabit Murramarang National Park, 20 minutes south of Ulladulla on the south coast of New South Wales, tend to congregate along this beach and the adjoining dunes. See "South of Sydney along the Princes Highway" in chapter 5.

- **Montague Island** (Narooma, NSW): This little island just offshore from the seaside town of Narooma, on the south coast, is a haven for nesting seabirds, but the water around it is home to the main attractions. Dolphins are common; fairy penguins, too. In whale-watching season, you're sure to spot southern right and humpback whales. See "South of Sydney along the Princes Highway" in chapter 5.

- **Jervis Bay** (NSW): This is probably the closest place to Sydney where you're certain to see kangaroos in the wild—and where you can pet them, too. The national park here is home to hundreds of bird species, including black cockatoos, as well as plenty of possums. See "South of Sydney along the Princes Highway" in chapter 5.

- **Lone Pine Koala Sanctuary** (Brisbane, QLD): Cuddle a koala (and have your photo taken doing it) at this park, the world's first and largest koala sanctuary. Apart from some 130 koalas, lots of other Aussie wildlife—including wombats, Tasmanian devils, 'roos (which you can hand-feed), and colorful parakeets—are on show. See p. 256.

- **Hervey Bay** (QLD): The warm waters off Hervey Bay, and in particular the lovely Platypus Bay, on the Queensland coast, are where the humpback whales come each year between June and October in increasing numbers to give birth. The long journey from Antarctica brings them up the coast to frolic with their young for several months before making the return trip. Hervey Bay's many cruises can bring you closer to these gentle giants than you'll ever come elsewhere. See "Fraser Island: Ecoadventures & Four-Wheel-Drive Fun" in chapter 7.

- **Australian Butterfly Sanctuary** (Kuranda, near Cairns, QLD): Walk through the biggest butterfly "aviary" in Australia and see some of Australia's most gorgeous butterflies, including the electric-blue Ulysses. See many species of butterfly feed, lay eggs, and mate, and inspect caterpillars and pupae. Wearing pink, red, or white encourages the butterflies to land on you. See p. 295.
- **Wait-a-While Rainforest Tours** (QLD): Head into the World Heritage–listed Wet Tropics Rainforest behind Cairns or Port Douglas with this ecotour operator to spotlight possums, lizards, pythons, even a platypus, so shy that most Aussies have never seen one in the wild. About once a month, a group will spot the rare, bizarre Lumholtz's tree kangaroo. See "Cairns" in chapter 7.
- **Heron Island** (off Gladstone, QLD): There's wonderful wildlife on this "jewel in the reef" any time of year, but the best time to visit is November to March, when the life cycle of giant green loggerhead and hawksbill turtles is in full swing. From November to January, the turtles come ashore to lay their eggs. From late January to March, the hatchlings emerge and head for the water. You can see it all by strolling down to the beach, or join a university researcher to get the full story. See "The Capricorn Coast & the Southern Reef Islands" in chapter 7. Mon Repos Turtle Rookery, near Bundaberg in Queensland (see "Up Close & Personal with a Turtle," p. 350) and the Northwest Cape in Western Australia (see "The Midwest & the Northwest: Where the Outback Meets the Sea" in chapter 10) are two other good turtle-watching sites.
- **Currumbin Wildlife Sanctuary** (The Gold Coast, QLD): Tens of thousands of unbelievably pretty red, blue, green, and yellow rainbow lorikeets have been screeching into this park for generations to be hand-fed by delighted visitors every morning and afternoon. The sanctuary has 'roos and other Australian animals, too, but the birds steal the show. See p. 371.
- **Kakadu National Park** (NT): One-third of Australia's bird species live in Kakadu; so do lots of saltwater crocs. A cruise on the Yellow Water Billabong, or aboard the Original Jumping Crocodiles cruise en route to the park, are some of the best ways to see them in the wild. See "Kakadu National Park" in chapter 9.
- **The Northwest Cape** (WA): For the thrill of a lifetime, go snorkeling with a whale shark. No one knows where they come from, but these mysterious monsters (up to 18m/60 ft. long) surface in the Outback waters off Western Australia every year from March to early June. A mini-industry takes snorkelers out to swim alongside the sharks as they feed (on plankton, not snorkelers). See "The Midwest & the Northwest: Where the Outback Meets the Sea" in chapter 10.
- **Tangalooma** (QLD), **Bunbury** (WA) **& Monkey Mia** (WA): In several places, you can see, hand-feed, or swim with wild dolphins. At Bunbury, south of Perth, you can swim with them or join cruises to see them (they come right up to the boat). If you want an almost guaranteed dolphin sighting, head to Tangalooma Wild Dolphin Resort on Moreton Island, off Brisbane, where you can hand-feed them, or to Monkey Mia on the lonely Outback coast, where they cruise past your legs. Even better is a cruise on the *Shotover* catamaran to see some of the area's 10,000 dugongs (manatees), plus turtles, sea

snakes, sharks—and more. See chapters 6 and 10.

- **Kangaroo Island** (SA): You're sure to see more native animals here—including koalas, wallabies, birds, echidnas, reptiles, seals, and sea lions—than anywhere else in the country, apart from a wildlife park. Another plus: The distances between major points of interest are not great, so you won't spend half the day just getting from place to place. See "Kangaroo Island" in chapter 11.

4 The Best Places to Experience the Outback

- **Broken Hill** (NSW): There's no better place to experience real Outback life than in Broken Hill. There's the city itself, with its thriving art scene and the Royal Flying Doctor service; a historic ghost town on its outskirts; a national park with Aboriginal wall paintings; an opal mining town nearby; and plenty of kangaroos, emus, and giant wedge-tailed eagles. See "Outback New South Wales" in chapter 5.

- **Lightning Ridge** (NSW): This opal-mining town is as rough and ready as the stones the miners pull out of the ground. Meet amazing characters, share in the eccentricity of the place, and visit opal-rush areas with mole-hill scenery made by the old sun-bleached mine tailings. See "Outback New South Wales" in chapter 5.

- **Uluru–Kata Tjuta National Park** (Ayers Rock, NT): Sure, Ayers Rock will enthrall you with its eerie beauty, but the nearby Olgas are more soothing, more interesting, and taller than the Rock, so make the time to wander through them, too. Hike the Rock's base, burn around it on a Harley-Davidson, saunter up to it on a camel, climb it if you must. Don't go home until you've felt the powerful heartbeat of the desert. See "Uluru–Kata Tjuta National Park (Ayers Rock/The Olgas)" in chapter 8.

- **The MacDonnell Ranges** (NT): The Aborigines say these red rocky hills were formed by the Aboriginal "Caterpillar Dreaming" that wriggled from the earth here. To the west of Alice Springs are dramatic gorges, idyllic (and bloody cold) water holes, and cute wallabies. To the east are Aboriginal rock carvings and the Ross River Homestead, where you can crack a cattle whip, throw a boomerang, feast on damper and billy tea, and ride a horse or camel in the bush. See "Road Trips from Alice Springs" in chapter 8.

- **Kings Canyon** (NT): Anyone who saw the cult flick *The Adventures of Priscilla, Queen of the Desert* will remember the scene in which the transvestites climb a soaring orange cliff and survey the desert floor. That was Kings Canyon, about 320km (198 miles) from Alice Springs in one direction, with Ayers Rock in the other. Trek the dramatic rim or take the easier shady route along the bottom. Don't forget your lipstick, guys. See "Kings Canyon" in chapter 8.

- **The Northwest Cape** (WA): This treeless moonscape of red anthills, spiky spinifex, and blazing heat seems to go on forever, so it's all the more amazing to find a beautiful coral reef offshore. Drive the rugged hills in a four-wheel-drive vehicle, dodging kangaroos on the way; swim with giant manta rays; snorkel right off the beach; scuba dive coral outcroppings; and laze on blindingly white beaches. This is where the Outback meets the sea. See "The Midwest & the Northwest: Where the Outback Meets the Sea" in chapter 10.

- **Coober Pedy** (SA): It may be hot and dusty, but you'll get a true taste of the Outback when you tag along with the local mail carrier as he makes his rounds to the area's remote cattle stations (ranches). It's a 12-hour, 600km (372-mile) journey along sun-baked dirt roads. See "Outback South Australia" in chapter 11.

5 The Best Beaches

- **Palm Beach** (Sydney): At the end of a string of beaches stretching north from Sydney, Palm Beach is long and white, with good surfing and a golf course. See chapter 4, "Sydney."
- **Hyams Beach** (Jervis Bay, NSW): This beach in off-the-beaten-path Jervis Bay is said to be the whitest in the world. You need to wear sunblock if you decide to stroll along it, because the reflection from the sun, even on a cloudy day, can give you a nasty sunburn. The beach squeaks as you walk. See "South of Sydney along the Princes Highway" in chapter 5.
- **Four Mile Beach** (Port Douglas, QLD): The sea is turquoise, the sun is warm, the palms sway, and the low-rise hotels starting to line this country beach can't spoil the feeling that it is a million miles from anywhere. But isn't there always a serpent in paradise? In this case the "serpents" are north Queensland's seasonal, potentially deadly marine stingers. Come from June through September to avoid them, or confine your swimming to the stinger net the rest of the year. See "Port Douglas, Daintree & the Cape Tribulation Area" in chapter 7.
- **Mission Beach** (QLD): Azure water, islands dotting the horizon, and white sand edged by vine forests make this beach a real winner. The bonus is that hardly anyone comes here. Cassowaries (giant emulike birds) hide in the rainforest, and the tiny town of Mission Beach makes itself invisible behind the leaves. Visit from June through September to avoid marine stingers. See "The North Coast: Mission Beach, Townsville & the Islands" in chapter 7.
- **Whitehaven Beach** (Whitsunday Island, QLD): It's not a surf beach, but this 6km (3¾-mile) stretch of white silica sand on uninhabited Whitsunday Island is pristine and peaceful. Bring a book, curl up under the rainforest lining its edge, and fantasize that the cruise boat is going to leave without you. See "The Whitsunday Coast & Islands" in chapter 7.
- **Surfers Paradise Beach** (Gold Coast, QLD): Actually, all 35 of the beaches on the 30km (19-mile) Gold Coast strip in south Queensland are worthy of inclusion here. Every one has sand so clean it squeaks, great surf, and fresh breezes—ignore the tacky high-rises. Surfers will like Burleigh Heads. See "The Gold Coast" in chapter 7.
- **Cable Beach** (Broome, WA): Is it the South Sea pearls pulled out of the Indian Ocean, the camels loping along the sand, the sunsets, the surf, or the red earth meeting the green sea that gives this beach its exotic appeal? Maybe it's the 26km (16 miles) of white sand. The only time to swim here is June through September, when deadly marine stingers aren't around. See "The Kimberley: A Far-Flung Wilderness" in chapter 10.
- **Cottesloe Beach** (Perth, WA): Perth has 19 great beaches, but this petite crescent is the prettiest. After you've checked out the scene, join the

fashionable set for brunch in the Indiana Tea House, a mock-Edwardian bathhouse fronting the sea.

Surfers head to Scarborough and Trigg. See chapter 10, "Perth & Western Australia."

6 The Best Diving & Snorkeling Sites

- **Port Douglas** (QLD): Among the fabulous dive sites off Port Douglas, north of Cairns, are Split-Bommie, with its delicate fan corals and schools of fusiliers; Barracuda Pass, with its coral gardens and giant clams; and the swim-through coral spires of the Cathedrals. Snorkelers can glide over the coral and reef fish life of Agincourt Reef. See "Port Douglas, Daintree & the Cape Tribulation Area" in chapter 7.

- **Lizard Island** (QLD): Snorkel over 150-year-old giant clams—as well as gorgeous underwater coral—in the Clam Garden, off this exclusive resort island northeast of Cairns. Nearby is the famous Cod Hole, where divers can hand-feed giant potato cod. See p. 301.

- **Cairns** (QLD): Moore, Norman, Hardy, Saxon, and Arlington reefs and Michaelmas and Upolu cays—all about 90 minutes off Cairns—offer great snorkeling and endless dive sites. Explore on a day trip from Cairns or join a live-aboard adventure. See "Cairns" in chapter 7.

- **Coral Sea** (QLD): In this sea east of the Great Barrier Reef off north Queensland, you'll see sharks feeding at Predator's Playground; 1,000m (3,280 ft.) drop-offs in the Abyss; reefs covering hundreds of square miles; and tropical species not found on the Great Barrier Reef. This is not a day-trip destination; many dive operators run multiday trips on live-aboard vessels. Visibility is excellent—up to 100m (328 ft.). See "The North Coast: Mission Beach, Townsville & the Islands" in chapter 7.

- **Yongala wreck** (QLD): Sunk by a cyclone in 1911, the 120m (394-ft.) SS *Yongala* lies in the Coral Sea off Townsville. Schools of trevally, kingfish, barracuda, and batfish surround the wreckage; giant Queensland grouper live under the bow, lionfish hide under the stern, turtles graze on the hull, and hard and soft corals make their home on it. It's too far for a day trip; live-aboard trips run from Townsville and Cairns. See "The North Coast: Mission Beach, Townsville & the Islands" in chapter 7.

- **The Whitsunday Islands** (QLD): As well as Blue Pearl Bay, these 74 breathtaking islands offer countless dive sites both among the islands and on the Outer Great Barrier Reef, 90 minutes away. Bait Reef on the Outer Reef is popular for its drop-offs. Snorkelers can explore not just the Outer Reef, but also patch reefs among the islands and rarely visited fringing reefs around many islands. See "The Whitsunday Coast & Islands" in chapter 7.

- **Heron Island** (QLD): Easily the number-one snorkel and dive site in Australia. If you stayed in the water for a week, you couldn't snorkel all the acres of coral stretching from shore. Take your pick of 22 dive sites: the Coral Cascades, with football trout and anemones; the Blue Pools, favored by octopus, turtles, and sharks; Heron Bommie, with its rays, eels, and Spanish dancers; and more. Absolute magic. See "The Capricorn Coast & the Southern Reef Islands" in chapter 7.

- **Lady Elliot Island** (QLD): Gorgeous coral lagoons, perfect for snorkeling, line this coral cay island off the town of Bundaberg. Boats take you farther out to snorkel above manta rays, plate coral, and big fish. Divers can swim through the blow hole, 16m (52 ft.) down, and see Gorgonian fans, soft and hard corals, sharks, barracudas, and reef fish. See "The Capricorn Coast & the Southern Reef Islands" in chapter 7.

- **Rottnest Island** (WA): Just 19km (12 miles) off Perth, this former prison island has excellent snorkeling and more than 100 dive sites. Wrecks, limestone overhangs, and myriad fish will keep divers entertained. There are no cars, so snorkelers should rent a bike and snorkel gear, buy a visitor-center map of suggested snorkel trails, and head off to

find their own private coral garden. The sunken grotto of Fishhook Bay is great for fish life. See "Side Trips from Perth" in chapter 10.

- **Ningaloo Reef** (WA): A well-kept secret is how we'd describe Australia's second great barrier reef, stretching 260km (161 miles) along the Northwest Cape halfway up Western Australia. Coral starts right on shore, not 90 minutes out to sea as at the Great Barrier Reef. You can snorkel or dive with manta rays, and dive to see sharks, angelfish, turtles, eels, grouper, potato cod, and much more. Snorkel with whale sharks up to 18m (59 ft.) long from March to early June. See "The Midwest & the Northwest: Where the Outback Meets the Sea" in chapter 10.

7 The Best Places to Bushwalk (Hike)

- **Blue Mountains** (NSW): Many bushwalks in the Blue Mountains National Park offer awesome views of valleys, waterfalls, cliffs, and forest. All are easy to reach from Sydney. See "The Blue Mountains" in chapter 5.

- **Whitsunday Islands** (QLD): Most people think of snorkeling and watersports when they come to these subtropical national-park islands clad in dense rainforest and bush, but every resort island we recommend has hiking trails. Some are flat, some hilly. Wallabies and butterflies are common sights. South Molle has the best network of trails and 360-degree island views from its peak. See "The Whitsunday Coast & Islands" in chapter 7.

- **Lamington National Park** (QLD): Few other national parks in Australia have such a well-marked network of trails (160km/99 miles in all) as this one, just 90 minutes from the Gold Coast. Revel in dense subtropical rainforest, marvel at mossy 2,000-year-old

Antarctic beech trees, delight in the prolific wallabies and birds, and soak up the cool mountain air. See "The Gold Coast Hinterland: Back to Nature" in chapter 7.

- **Larapinta Trail** (The Red Centre, NT): You can start from Alice Springs and walk the entire 250km (155-mile) semidesert trail, which winds through the stark crimson McDonnell Ranges. You don't have to walk the entire length—plenty of day-length and multiday sections are possible. This one's for the cooler months only (Apr–Oct). See "Alice Springs" in chapter 8.

- **Kakadu National Park** (NT): Whether a wetlands stroll or an overnight hike in virgin bushland, you can find it in this World Heritage–listed park. You'll see red cliffs, cycads, waterfalls, lily-filled lagoons hiding man-eating crocodiles, what sometimes looks like Australia's entire bird population, and Aboriginal rock art. See "Kakadu National Park" in chapter 9.

- **Cape-to-Cape** (WA): Rugged sea cliffs, a china-blue sea, eucalyptus forest, white beaches, and coastal heath are what you will find as you hike between Cape Naturaliste and Cape Leeuwin, in the southwest corner of Western Australia. In season, you'll see whales and wildflowers. See "Margaret River & the Southwest: Wine Tasting in the Forests" in chapter 10.

- **Freycinet National Park** (TAS): The trek to Wine Glass Bay passes pink-granite outcrops, with views over an ocean sliced by a crescent of icy sand. It's prehistorically beautiful. See "Freycinet National Park" in chapter 15.

- **Cradle Mountain & Lake St. Clair National Park** (TAS): The 80km (50-mile) Overland Track is the best hike in Australia. The trek, from Lake St. Clair to Cradle Mountain, takes 5 to 10 days, depending on your fitness level. Shorter walks, some lasting just half an hour, are also accessible. See "Cradle Mountain & Lake St. Clair National Park" in chapter 15.

8 The Best Places to Learn About Aboriginal Culture

- **The Umbarra Aboriginal Cultural Centre** (Wallaga Lake, near Narooma, NSW): This center offers boomerang- and spear-throwing instruction, painting with natural ochers, discussions on Aboriginal culture, and guided walking tours of Aboriginal sacred sites. See p. 230.

- **Tjapukai Aboriginal Cultural Park** (Cairns, QLD): This multimillion-dollar center showcases the history of the Tjapukai people—their Dreamtime creation history and their often-harrowing experiences since the white man arrived—using a film, superb theatrical work, and a dance performance. Its Aboriginal art and crafts gift shop is one of the country's best. See p. 289.

- **Aboriginal Art & Culture Centre** (Alice Springs, NT): You'll taste bush food, see a dance, throw boomerangs and spears, and learn about Aboriginal family values in one half-day tour of this Aborigine-owned center in Alice Springs. Be sure to hang around for the 1-hour didgeridoo lesson at the end. See p. 386.

- **Anangu Tours** (Ayers Rock, NT): The Anangu are the owners of Ayers Rock or, in their native tongue, Uluru. Join them for walks around the Rock as you learn about the poisonous "snake men" who fought battles here, pick bush food off the trees, throw spears, visit rock paintings, and watch the sun set over the monolith. Their Cultural Centre near the base of the Rock has displays about the Aboriginal Dreamtime. See "Uluru–Kata Tjuta National Park (Ayers Rock/The Olgas)" in chapter 8.

- **Manyallaluk: The Dreaming Place** (Katherine, NT): This Aboriginal community welcomes visitors and teaches them to paint, weave, throw boomerangs, and perform other tasks of daily life. A low-key day and the chance to chat one-on-one with Aboriginal people in their bush home. See "Katherine" in chapter 9.

- **Mangarrayi People** (Katherine, NT): Mike Keighley of **Far Out Adventures** (© **0427/152 288;** www. farout.com.au) takes tours to beautiful Elsey Station (a ranch) near Katherine, where you visit with the children of the local Mangarrayi people. Sample bush tucker, learn a little bush medicine, and swim in a natural "spa-pool" in the Roper River. See "Katherine" in chapter 9.

- **Yamatji Bitja Aboriginal Bush Tours** (Kalgoorlie, WA): Geoffrey Stokes (② **08/9021 5862** or 0407/378 602), brought up the traditional Aboriginal way in the bush, takes you out to track emus, forage for bush food, and maybe even hunt a 'roo for dinner (with a gun, not a boomerang!). Explore the bush, learn about Aboriginal Dreamtime creation myths, and find out more about his childhood. See "The Goldfields" in chapter 10.

- **Tandanya Aboriginal Cultural Institute** (Adelaide, SA): This is a great place to experience life through Aboriginal eyes. You might catch one of the dances or other performances, and you'll have plenty of other opportunities to find out more about Aboriginal culture. See p. 517.

9 The Best of Small-Town Australia

- **Central Tilba** (NSW): Just inland from Narooma on the south coast, this historic hamlet is one of the cutest you'll see, complete with blacksmiths and leatherwork outlets. The ABC Cheese Factory offers free tastings, and you can spend hours browsing antiques stalls or admiring the period buildings. See "South of Sydney along the Princes Highway" in chapter 5.

- **Broken Hill** (NSW): Known for its silver mines, the quirky town of Broken Hill has more pubs per capita than just about anywhere else. It's the home of the School of the Air—a "classroom" that transmits lessons by radio to communities spread over thousands of miles of Outback. Here you'll also find the Palace Hotel, made famous in *The Adventures of Priscilla, Queen of the Desert,* as well as plenty of colonial mansions and heritage homes. See "Outback New South Wales" in chapter 5.

- **Port Douglas** (QLD): What happens when Sydneysiders and Melbournites discover a one-street fishing village in tropical north Queensland? Come to Port Douglas and find out. A strip of groovy restaurants and a championship golf course have not diminished "Port's" old-fashioned air. Four Mile Beach is at the end of the street, and boats depart daily for the Great Barrier Reef. See "Port Douglas, Daintree & the Cape Tribulation Area" in chapter 7.

- **Mission Beach** (QLD): You'd never know this tidy village existed (it's hidden in lush rainforest off the highway) if you weren't well informed. Aussies know it's here, but few bother to patronize its dazzling beach, offshore islands, and rainforest trails, so you'll have the place to yourself. There's great white-water rafting on the nearby Tully River, too. See "The North Coast: Mission Beach, Townsville & the Islands" in chapter 7.

- **Broome** (WA): This romantic pearling port on the far-flung Kimberley coast on the Indian Ocean blends Aussie corrugated-iron architecture with red pagoda roofs left by Chinese pearl divers. The town fuses a sophisticated international ambience with Outback attitude. Play on Cable Beach (see "The Best Beaches," earlier in this chapter) and stay at glamorous Cable Beach Club Resort. This is the place to add to your South Sea pearl collection. See "The Kimberley: A Far-Flung Wilderness" in chapter 10.

- **Kalgoorlie** (WA): This is it, the iconic Australian country town. Vibrant Kalgoorlie sits on what used to be the richest square mile of gold-bearing earth ever. It still pumps around 2,000 ounces *a day* out of the ground. Have a beer in one of the gracious 19th-century pubs, peer into the world's biggest open-cut gold mine, and wander the ghost-town streets of its sister town, Coolgardie. See "The Goldfields" in chapter 10.

- **Hahndorf** (SA): A group of Lutheran settlers founded this German-style town in the Adelaide Hills in the 1830s. You'll love the churches, the wool factory and crafts shops, and the delicious German food at the local cafes, restaurants, and bakeries. See "Side Trips from Adelaide" in chapter 11.

- **Coober Pedy** (SA): For an Outback experience that's fair-dinkum (genuine), few places are as weird and wonderful as this opal-mining town in the middle of nowhere. Visit mines, see wacky museums, and stay in a hotel underground—not all that unusual, considering that the locals live like moles anyway. See "Outback South Australia" in chapter 11.

- **Launceston** (TAS): Tasmania's second city is not much larger than your average European or American small town, but it's packed with Victorian and Georgian architecture and remnants of Australia's convict past. Spend a few days and discover the scenery; splurge a little on a stay in a historic hotel. See "Launceston" in chapter 15.

10 The Best Museums

- **Australian National Maritime Museum** (Sydney, NSW): The best things about this museum are the ships and submarines often docked in the harbor out front. You can climb aboard and experience what it's like to be a sailor. Inside are some fascinating displays relating to Australia's dependence on the oceans. See p. 159.

- **Alice Springs Telegraph Station Historical Reserve** (NT): It's not called a museum, but that's what this restored telegraph-repeater station out in the picturesque hills by a spring—Alice Springs—really is. From the hot biscuits turned out of the wood-fired oven to the old telegraph equipment, this 1870s settlement is as real as history can get. See p. 387.

- **Australian Aviation Heritage Centre** (Darwin, NT): The pride of this hangar is a B-52 bomber on permanent loan from the U.S. But there's loads more, and not just planes, engines, and other aviation paraphernalia—there are stories, jokes, and anecdotes associated with the exhibits that will appeal even if you don't have avgas (aviation fuel) running in your veins. See "Darwin" in chapter 9.

- **Warradjan Aboriginal Cultural Centre** (NT): "Memorable and moving" were the words used by one reader to describe her visit to this small, stylish museum in Kakadu National Park. Learn about Dreamtime myths and daily life of Aboriginal people in Kakadu. See "Kakadu National Park" in chapter 9.

- **Western Australian Maritime Museum** and the adjacent **Shipwreck Galleries** (Perth, WA): Housed in the historic port precinct of Fremantle, Perth, this museum tells tales of the harsh Western Australian coastline since the Dutch first bumped into it and abandoned it as useless in the 1600s. Anyone who ever dreamed of finding a shipwreck laden with pieces of eight will relish the displays of treasure recovered from the deep. See p. 458.

- **New Norcia Museum & Art Gallery** (New Norcia, WA): This tiny museum in the Spanish Benedictine monastery town of New Norcia holds a mind-boggling collection of European

Renaissance art. The museum has all kinds of memorabilia: the monks' manuscripts, clothing, instruments, and gifts from Queen Isabella of Spain. See "Side Trips from Perth" in chapter 10.

- **The Migration Museum** (Adelaide, SA): This museum gives visitors insight into the people who came to Australia, how and where they settled, and how many suffered getting here. Don't expect a lot of musty displays—this museum is full of hands-on activities. See p. 516.

- **Australian War Memorial** (Canberra, ACT): Given its name, you might think this museum is a bleak place, but you'd be wrong. It gives important insight into the Anzac (Australian and New Zealand Army Corps) spirit, including an exhibit on the tragic battle of Gallipoli. There's also a pretty good art collection. See p. 624.

- **National Museum of Australia** (ACT): Using state-of-the-art technology and hands-on exhibits, Australia's newest and most impressive museum concentrates on Australian society and its history since 1788, the interaction of people with the Australian environment, and Aboriginal and Torres Strait Islander cultures and histories. See p. 626.

11 The Best Luxury Accommodations

- **Sir Stamford at Circular Quay, Sydney** (℡ **1300/301 391** in Australia, or 02/9252 4600): This AAA-rated five-star hotel combines old-world luxury with a wonderful bar and nice views. I like the top-hatted doorman who valet-parked my rusting 1976 Toyota without a comment. See p. 125.

- **Park Hyatt Sydney** (℡ **800/633-7313** in the U.S. and Canada, or 02/9241 1234 in Australia): You'll have to book well in advance to snag a room at Sydney's best-situated property, at the edge of the city's historic Rocks district. Many rooms have fabulous views across the harbor to the Sydney Opera House. See p. 124.

- **The Sebel Reef House & Spa Palm Cove** (Cairns, QLD; ℡ **1800/079 052** in Australia): Everyone who stays here says the same thing: "It feels like home." Airy rooms look into tropical gardens, waterfalls cascade into the pools, mosquito nets drape over the beds, and you could swear pith-helmeted colonial officers will be back any minute to finish their gin-and-tonics in the Brigadier Bar. Idyllic Palm Cove Beach is just across the road. See p. 299.

- **Lizard Island** (off Cairns, QLD; ℡ **1300/134 044** in Australia, or 02/8296 8010): Lizard Island has long been popular with Americans for its game fishing, wonderful coral and diving, smart food, and simple upscale lodge accommodations. See p. 301.

- **Bedarra Island** (off Mission Beach, QLD; ℡ **1300/134 044** in Australia, or 02/8296 8010): Presidents and princesses in need of a little time out come to this small rainforest island ringed by beaches. The timber villas are cozy, and the discreet staff assures privacy. Best of all, though, is the extravagant 24-hour open bar. See p. 322.

- **Orpheus Island Resort** (off Townsville or Cairns, QLD; ℡ **07/4777 7377** in Australia): Beloved of film stars and others who relish privacy, this resort has simple, attractive rooms; good food; a marvelous sense of seclusion; and a beautiful location in the curve of a palm-lined bay. The only way in is by seaplane. See p. 330.

- **Hayman** (Whitsunday Islands, QLD; ✆ **1800/075 175** in Australia, or Leading Hotels of the World, 800/745-8883 in the U.S. and Canada, 0800/1010-1111 in the U.K. and Ireland, or 0800/44 1016 in New Zealand): On Hayman Island in the Whitsundays, this is Australia's most glamorous resort. It has classy rooms, excellent restaurants, a staff that's keen to please, a superb hexagonal swimming pool, and a fleet of charter boats waiting to spirit you off to the Reef or your own deserted isle. See p. 340.

- **Longitude 131** (Uluru/Ayers Rock, Red Centre, NT; ✆ **08/8957 7888**): A newcomer to the Ayers Rock resort scene, Longitude 131 is an African-style luxury safari camp set in the sand dunes, with great views of Uluru (Ayers Rock). It's very exclusive and very expensive, but you experience the Outback in style. See p. 406.

- **El Questro Homestead** (The Kimberley, WA; ✆ **1300/656 565** in Australia, 800/221-4542 in the U.S. and Canada, 020/8283 4500 in the U.K., 0800/44 4422 in New Zealand, or 08/9169 1777): Charming country decor spiced up with Indonesian antiques, good cooking, and a dramatic gorge location make this glamorous homestead on a million-acre cattle station popular with jet-setters. Cruise wild gorges, heli-fish for barramundi, and hike to Aboriginal rock art while you're here. See p. 492.

- **Cable Beach Club Resort Broome** (Broome, WA; ✆ **1800/099 199** in Australia, or 08/9192 0400): Chinatown meets the Outback at this elegant corrugated-iron-and-pagoda-studded resort lying low along glorious Cable Beach in the romantic pearling port of Broome. Three to-die-for suites, decorated with superb Asian antiques and paintings by luminaries of the Australian art world. See p. 498.

- **The Hotel Como** (Melbourne, VIC; ✆ **1800/033 400** in Australia, or 03/9825 2222): Great service, nice rooms, and free plastic ducks make this one of our favorite top-flight Australian hotels. See p. 561.

- **Hyatt Hotel Canberra** (Canberra, ACT; ✆ **800/233-1234** in the U.S. and Canada, or 02/6270 1234): Visiting heads of state and pop stars make this their residence when staying in Canberra. It's a 2-minute drive from the central shopping district, and a stone's throw from Lake Burley Griffin and the Parliamentary Triangle. See p. 620.

12 The Best Moderately Priced Accommodations

- **Explorers Inn Hotel** (✆ **1800/623 288** in Australia) and **Hotel George Williams** (✆ **1800/064 858** in Australia), both in Brisbane, QLD: These two hotels around the corner from each other are shining examples of what affordable hotels should be—trendy, clean, and bright, with useful facilities like a 24-hour front desk, hair dryers, helpful staff, and a pleasant, inexpensive restaurant attached. See p. 251 and p. 252.

- **The Reef Retreat** (Cairns, QLD; ✆ **07/4059 1744**): It's not often you find so much decorating taste—wooden blinds, teak furniture, and colorful upholstery—at a price you want to pay, but that's what you get at the apartments in trendy Palm Cove, one of Cairns's most desirable beach-front suburbs. There's a pool on the lovely landscaped grounds, but the beach is just a block away. See p. 301.

- **Archipelago Studio Apartments** (Port Douglas, QLD; ℂ **07/4099 5387**): They may be tiny, but these pretty apartments have a homey atmosphere and are seconds from Four Mile Beach. Some units have sea views. The solicitous proprietor is a font of advice on things to see and do. See p. 312.
- **Miss Maud Swedish Hotel** (Perth, WA; ℂ **1800/998 022** in Australia): Staying here is like staying at Grandma's—just as she's finished a major redecoration job. You're right in the heart of Perth, and the friendly staff and huge buffet breakfasts (included in the room rate) complete the picture. See p. 447.
- **North Adelaide Heritage Group** (Adelaide, SA; ℂ **08/8272 1355**):

These accommodations consist of 18 fabulous properties in North Adelaide and Eastwood. The former Friendly Meeting Chapel Hall resembles a small church stocked with Victorian antiques. Another memorable place is the George Lowe Esq. Apartment, done in the style of a 19th-century gentleman's bachelor pad. See p. 512.

- **York Mansions** (Launceston, TAS; ℂ **03/6334 2933**): If you feel that where you stay is as important to your visit as what you see, then don't miss on a night or two here. This National Trust–classified building has five spacious apartments, each with a distinct character. It's like living the high life in the Victorian age. See p. 653.

13 The Best Alternative Accommodations

- **Underground Motel** (White Cliffs, NSW; ℂ **1800/021 154** in Australia, or 08/8091 6677): All but two of this motel's rooms are underground. Rooms are reached by a maze of spacious tunnels dug out of the rock beneath this opal-mining town. See p. 238.
- **South Long Island Nature Lodge** (The Whitsunday Islands, QLD; ℂ **07/4946 9777**): The five comfy beachfront cabins are basic, but your vacation at this island ecoretreat will be anything but. Sea kayak, sail, snorkel, hike rainforest trails, dine with other guests outside under the Milky Way, and maybe even swim with Myrtle, the pet kangaroo. Considering you'll only shell out for wine and maybe a seaplane trip to the Reef, this is a great value for its exclusivity. See p. 341.
- **Kingfisher Bay Resort** (Fraser Island, QLD; ℂ **1800/072 555** in Australia): If it weren't for the ranger station and natural-history videos in

the lobby, the wildlife walks, the guided four-wheel-drive safaris, and the other ecoactivities, you'd hardly know that this comfortable, modern hotel is an ecoresort. See p. 356.

- **Binna Burra Mountain Lodge** (ℂ **1800/074 260** in Australia) **& O'Reilly's Rainforest Guesthouse** (ℂ **1800/688 722** in Australia), both in the Gold Coast Hinterland, QLD: Tucked almost 1,000m (3,280 ft.) up on rainforested ridges, these cozy retreats offer fresh mountain air, activities, and instant access to the hiking trails of Lamington National Park. At O'Reilly's you can hand-feed brilliantly colored rainforest birds every morning. See p. 377 and p. 378.
- **Emma Gorge Resort** (The Kimberley, WA; ℂ **800/221-4542** in the U.S. and Canada, or 08/9169 1777): At this spick-and-span little safari camp on the 400,000-hectare (1-million-acre) El Questro cattle station, guests stay in cute tents with wooden floors and electric lights, eat at a rustic

gourmet restaurant, and join in the many hikes, bird-watching tours, river cruises, and more. See p. 493.

- **Prairie Hotel** (Flinders Ranges, SA; ℰ **08/8648 4844**): This remarkable tin-roofed, stone-walled Outback pub in the Flinders Ranges has quaint rooms, a great bar out front where you can meet the locals, and some of the best food in Australia. See p. 541.
- **Freycinet Lodge** (Freycinet National Park, Coles Bay, TAS; ℰ **03/6257 0101**): These ecofriendly bush cabins

are right next to one of the nation's best walking trails. The ocean views from the magnificent restaurant and the surrounding balconies are spectacular. See p. 649.

- **Cradle Mountain Lodge** (Cradle Mountain, TAS; ℰ **13 24 69** in Australia, or 03/6492 1303): Just minutes from your comfortable cabin are 1,500-year-old trees, moss forests, craggy mountain ridges, limpid pools and lakes, and hordes of scampering marsupials. See p. 657.

14 The Best B&Bs & Guesthouses

- **The Russell** (The Rocks, Sydney; ℰ **02/9241 3543**): This B&B, wonderfully positioned in the city's old quarter, is the coziest place to stay in Sydney. It has creaky floorboards, a ramshackle feel, brightly painted corridors, and rooms with immense character. See p. 125.
- **Echoes Hotel & Restaurant, Blue Mountains** (Katoomba, NSW; ℰ **02/4782 1966**): Echoes is right on the edge of a dramatic drop into the Jamison Valley. The views from the balconies are breathtaking. See p. 197.
- **Barrington Guest House** (Barrington Tops National Park, The Hunter, NSW; ℰ **02/4995 3212**): Nestled in a valley just outside the Barrington Tops National Park, this charming guesthouse and luxury cabin property offers magnificent rainforest walks, plenty of native animals, and excellent activities, such as horseback riding through the bush. See p. 209.
- **Ulladulla Guest House** (Ulladulla, NSW; ℰ **02/4455 1796**): Works of art on the walls, fabulous food, and a lagoonlike pool among the palm trees—all this and lovely rooms, with hosts who can't do enough for you. See p. 228.

- **Waverley** (Brisbane, QLD; ℰ **07/3369 8973**): This gorgeous old timber Queenslander house has pretty rooms and a cool deck within earshot of rainbow lorikeets chirping in the mango trees. And the cute shops and galleries of fashionable Paddington are right outside your door. See p. 252.
- **Lilybank Bed & Breakfast** (Cairns, QLD; ℰ **07/4055 1123**): This rambling 1890s homestead used to be the Cairns mayor's residence. Today, owners Pat and Mike Woolford welcome guests to its comfy rooms, wide verandas, and blooming gardens. You can also stay in the renovated gardener's cottage. See p. 299.
- **Marae** (near Port Douglas, QLD; ℰ **07/4098 4900**): Lush bushland full of butterflies and birds is the setting for this gorgeous contemporary Queenslander house with hip rooms and an outdoor plunge pool. Owners John and Pam Burden promise a warm welcome and a wonderful breakfast. See p. 313.
- **The Rocks** (Townsville, QLD; ℰ **07/4771 5700**): The owners have poured Victorian charm into this old Queenslander, with stylish, not frilly,

results. Eat off antique china in the old dining room, bathe in a claw-foot tub in the main bathroom, and meet other guests for sherry on the wide old veranda at dusk. See p. 326.

- **The Summer House** (Darwin, NT; ℰ **08/8981 9992**): Groovy guest rooms with hip furniture, funky bathrooms, louvered windows, and tropical gardens make this converted apartment block an oasis of cool—in both senses of the word. See p. 419.

- **Hansons Swan Valley** (near Perth, WA; ℰ **08/9296 3366**): Good-bye faded lace, hello Art Deco—here is a B&B with cutting-edge style for young sophisticates. Jon and Selina Hanson have created a stylish retreat nestled among the Swan Valley vineyards, an easy drive from Perth. See p. 466.

- **Heritage Trail Lodge** (Margaret River, WA; ℰ **08/9757 9595**): How many B&Bs do you know that provide a double Jacuzzi in every room? These salmon-pink cabins abut tall karri forest where parrots flit. 'Roos hop into the parking lot on occasion, and the fabulous Margaret River wineries surround you. See p. 474.

- **Collingrove Homestead** (Angaston, the Barossa Valley, SA; ℰ **08/8564 2061**): This country house, built in 1856, has an air of colonial manor farm living, with hunting trophies, rifles, and oil paintings festooning the walls, and plenty of oak paneling and antiques scattered about. See p. 524.

15 The Best Restaurants

- **Rockpool** (Sydney, NSW; ℰ **02/9252 1888**): with the chefs on view and designer chairs to sit on, Rockpool is a consistent favorite, not least for its fabulous, inventive food. See p. 142.

- **Mezzaluna** (Sydney, NSW; ℰ **02/ 9357 1988**): Come here for exquisite food, flawless service, and a great view across the city's western skyline. The main dining room opens onto an all-weather terrace kept warm in winter by giant, overhead fan heaters. Don't miss it. See p. 147.

- **Quay** (Sydney, NSW; ℰ **02/9251 5600**): Sydney's best seafood restaurant offers perhaps the loveliest view in town. Gaze through the large windows toward the Opera House, the city skyline, the North Shore suburbs, and the Harbour Bridge. See p. 141.

- **Tetsuya's** (Sydney, NSW; ℰ **02/9267 2900**): Chef Tetsuya Wakuda is arguably Sydney's most famous chef, and his nouveau Japanese creations are imaginative enough to guarantee that this hip eatery is a constant number one in Australia. See p. 145.

- **e'cco bistro** (Brisbane, QLD; ℰ **07/ 3831 8344**): Simple food, elegantly done, has won this small but elegant bistro a stack of awards, and you'll soon see why. Not least among its titles is Australia's top restaurant award, the Remy Martin Cognac/ Gourmet Traveller Restaurant of the Year. Booking ahead is essential. See p. 253.

- **Fishlips Bar & Bistro** (Cairns, QLD; ℰ **07/4041 1700**): Clever ways with fresh seafood and other Aussie ingredients—think crocodile—make this cheerful blue beach house a real winner, the pick of the bunch in Cairns. See p. 303.

- **Fraser's** (Perth, WA; ℰ **08/9481 7100**): The city center and Swan River sparkling in the sunshine seem so close that you can almost reach out and touch them from the terrace of this parkland restaurant. Come here for sensationally good Modern Australian food turned out with flair and flavor; seafood is a specialty. See p. 450.

- **Newtown House** (Vasse, near Margaret River, WA; ✆ **08/9755 4485**): Chef Stephen Reagan makes intelligent, flavorsome food that beautifully partners with premium Margaret River wines. Stay in his homestead B&B overnight and explore the wineries the next day. See p. 475.
- **Prairie Hotel** (Flinders Ranges, SA; ✆ **08/8648 4844**): Chef Darren ("Bart") Brooks serves high-class cuisine in the middle of nowhere. His "feral" foods, such as kangaroo tail soup and a mixed grill of emu

sausages, camel steak, and kangaroo, is remarkable. See p. 541.
- **Flower Drum** (Melbourne, VIC; ✆ **03/9662 3655**): Praise pours in for this upscale eatery serving Cantonese food. The food is exquisite and the service impeccable. See p. 562.
- **The Tryst** (Canberra, ACT; ✆ **02/6239 4422**): Canberra has far grander and more expensive restaurants, but this place has found a spot in our hearts for its constantly delicious food. It's also relaxed, feeling almost communal on busy nights. See p. 623.

16 The Best Reasonably Priced Restaurants

- **Phillip's Foote** (Sydney, NSW; ✆ **02/9241 1485**): In the heart of the historic neighborhood known as The Rocks, this barbecue restaurant serves fish, meat, and poultry. Pick your own protein and throw it on the "barbie" in the courtyard behind a historic pub. See p. 144.
- **Green Papaya** (East Brisbane, QLD; ✆ **07/3217 3599**): Owner and chef Lien Yeoman offers flavorful North Vietnamese cuisine in a cheerful setting—a simple formula that draws enthusiastic crowds. If you need advice as you contemplate the menu, the helpful staff will offer as much guidance as you need. See p. 255.
- **Salsa Bar & Grill** (Port Douglas, QLD; ✆ **07/4099 4922**): The animated atmosphere and attractive surroundings set the scene for an excellent dining experience. Appetizers and main courses run the gamut from simple fare to sophisticated tropical creations; desserts are fantastic. See p. 315.
- **Zouí Alto** (Townsville, QLD; ✆ **07/4721 4700**): The reasonable prices belie the quality of the Modern Australian food at this 14th-floor establishment. The husband-and-wife team of Mark and Eleni Edwards (he's the

chef) presides over one of the best restaurants in the country. See p. 327.
- **Ricky Ricardo's** (Sunshine Coast, QLD; ✆ **07/5447 2455**): The breathtaking view of the Noosa River is just one delightful element of this restaurant, which serves seasonal Modern Australian cuisine that relies heavily on fresh seafood and local produce. Incidentally, the restaurant gets its name from a relative of one of the co-owners, not the Cuban-American TV pioneer. See p. 364.
- **Season** (Sunshine Coast, QLD; ✆ **07/5447 3747**): A great location right on the beach, a chef who made a name for himself in Sydney, and flavorful Modern Australian cuisine combine to make Season one of the area's most popular restaurants. See p. 364.
- **Red Ochre Grill** (Alice Springs, NT; ✆ **08/8950 6666**): "Gourmet bush tucker" might sound like a contradiction, but this restaurant (part of an upscale chain) pulls it off. The kitchen combines native ingredients and international techniques to exceptionally good effect. See p. 394.
- **Hansons** (Henley Brook, WA; ✆ **08/9296 3366**): In the wine country just outside Perth, Hansons serves Modern Australian dishes indoors and

outdoors. The elegant restaurant is part of Hansons Swan Valley, a sleek, contemporary B&B. See p. 467.

- **Bamboo House** (Melbourne, VIC; © 03/9662 1565): A favorite with both local businesspeople and the Chinese community, Bamboo House offers superb service as well as excellent Cantonese and northern Chinese cuisine. Top choices on the extensive menu include duck in plum sauce, chicken with shallot sauce, and the

signature Szechuan smoked duck. See p. 562.

- **Mures Upper Deck** (Hobart, TAS; © 03/6231 2121): Views of the water make a perfect backdrop for ultrafresh seafood and scrumptious desserts. The menu relies heavily on the catch that comes in on the restaurant's own fishing boat. Lower Deck, in the same complex, is a reasonably priced self-service family restaurant. See p. 643.

2

Planning Your Trip to Australia

by Lee Mylne

This chapter aims to answer all the practical questions that may pop up as you're planning your trip: how will you get there, how much will it cost, what are the ins and outs of traveling Down Under, and myriad other details. We've done the legwork—ferreting out deals on airfares, listing package companies, locating outdoor adventure operators, and more—so you won't have to.

1 The Regions in Brief

About 84% of Australia's 20 million people huddle in cities around the coast covering a mere 1% of this vast continent. The reason is simple: Much of Australia is harsh Outback country, characterized by savanna land, spectacular rocky outcrops, shifting deserts, and dry salt lakes. In these parts of the country, the soil is poor and the rainfall scarce, and some rivers don't even make it to the ocean. The roads that traverse the interior are sometimes barely distinguishable, and most people choose air travel or stick to the coastal fringe.

In spectacular contrast, on the coast—particularly in the east, where most people live—Nature's bounty has almost overdone it. Here, Australia is blessed with one of the greatest natural attractions in the world: the Great Barrier Reef. There are also rainforests in Queensland, alpine scenery in Tasmania, wildflowers in Western Australia, rolling wine country in South Australia, a great coastal drive in Victoria, bird-filled wetlands in the Northern Territory, and countless sand beaches more or less everywhere.

Australia consists of six states—New South Wales (NSW), Queensland (QLD), Victoria (VIC), South Australia (SA), Western Australia (WA), and Tasmania (TAS)—and two internal territories, the Australian Capital Territory (ACT) and the Northern Territory (NT). The national capital is Canberra, in the ACT.

See the map in the color insert at the front of this book to visualize the regions described here.

NEW SOUTH WALES Australia's most populated state is also the most visited by tourists. They come to see Sydney—and who can blame them? It's one of the most glamorous and beautiful cities in the world, with dozens of harbor and ocean beaches in and around it, and a mixture of bushland and city development around Sydney Harbour. Sydney is also a good base for day trips or overnight excursions inland, especially to the scenic Blue Mountains and the wineries of the Hunter Valley.

Farther afield, a string of quaint beachside towns stretches down the southern coast to Victoria. Along the north coast are remnant areas of rainforest and a more tropical air in the laid-back hangout of Byron Bay.

The inland is dry and sparsely forested. Highlights include the mining town of Broken Hill (known for wildlife, art galleries, and Aboriginal influences), and Outback opal-mining towns White Cliffs and Lightning Ridge, which exist in a wacky underground world of their own.

QUEENSLAND   Without a doubt, the biggest draw for visitors to Queensland is the Great Barrier Reef. Ogling the tropical fish, sea creatures, and rainbow-hued corals is a holiday highlight for most people. The Reef stretches more than 2,000km (1,240 miles) along Queensland's coast, as far south as Bundaberg, 384km (238 miles) north of Brisbane, the state capital. Alluring island resorts dot the coast; while most are expensive, we've found a few that won't break the bank.

Queensland is also known for its white-sand beaches. Many of the best are on the Gold Coast in the state's south (about an hour's drive from Brisbane), and the Sunshine Coast (a 2-hr. drive north of Brisbane). Cairns and Port Douglas in the north have their fair share of beaches, too, but be warned: Swimming in their waters can be *very* hazardous to your health. Deadly box jellyfish, or "stingers," halt all ocean swimming at beaches in the northern third of the country from October through May. In Queensland, stingers may be found in all coastal waters north of Gladstone. Most patrolled beaches in these areas have "stinger nets," which aim to keep the little blighters out, but the thimble-sized Irakandji jellyfish is small enough to sneak through the mesh, and its sting can be fatal. All patrolled beaches have warning signs, and the lifeguards do regular net drags to see if there are any in the water. If they find any, they promptly close the beach. But to be absolutely sure, at this time of year you should stick to the waterfront lagoons at Airlie Beach and Cairns, or to your hotel pool. The jellyfish are mainly found in coastal waters and do not interfere with Great Barrier Reef activities like snorkeling or diving, which are out of the habitat of marine stingers.

Island swimming is mostly stinger-free, but be careful and take advice from the lifeguards before plunging into that inviting water.

One of the most appealing of Queensland's destinations is the aquatic playground made up of the 74 Whitsunday Islands in the Great Barrier Reef Marine Park. These mostly uninhabited islands are a paradise for kayaking, snorkeling, diving, fishing, hiking, watersports, birding, and bareboat sailing.

Another big attraction is the lush 110-million-year-old Daintree rainforest, just north of Port Douglas.

Brisbane has Australia's largest koala sanctuary (you can cuddle one if you like), and you can hand-feed wild dolphins on a day trip across Brisbane's Moreton Bay. In the Gold Coast hinterland is Lamington National Park, a rainforested mountain region great for hiking and spotting wildlife.

THE RED CENTRE   The eerie silence of Uluru, also known as Ayers Rock, is what draws everyone to the sprawling ocher sands of the Red Centre, the heart of the Northern Territory. Many visitors make the delightful discovery that the lesser-known nearby domes of Kata Tjuta, or "the Olgas," are even more

---

⌒Tips Size Does Matter

When planning your trip, keep in mind that Australia is as big as western Europe and about the same size as the 48 contiguous U.S. states. Melbourne and Brisbane are a long day's drive from Sydney, and driving from Sydney to Perth takes the better part of a week.

spectacular (if that's possible). A half-day's drive from the Rock brings you to Kings Canyon, an awesomely lovely desert gorge popular with hikers. If you visit the Red Centre, try to spend at least a few days in Alice Springs. This laid-back Outback town has the best Aboriginal arts and crafts shopping in Australia, Aboriginal tours, a world-class desert wildlife park, stunning scenery, hikes through the stark MacDonnell Ranges, an Outback ranch to stay at, and even camel rides along a dry riverbed.

THE TOP END The northwest reaches of the country (from the rocky red ranges of the Kimberley in Western Australia to the northern third of the Northern Territory) encompass what Aussies eloquently dub "the Top End." This is Crocodile Dundee territory, a remote, vast, semidesert region where the cattle probably outnumber the people. In this book, we have concentrated on the Northern Territory section of the "Top End." (The Kimberley appears in the Western Australia chapter.)

Near the tropical city of Darwin, the territory's capital, is Kakadu National Park, where you can cruise past crocodiles on inland billabongs (ponds), bird-watch, and visit ancient Aboriginal rock-art sites. Closer to Darwin is Litchfield National Park, where you can take a dip in fern-fringed swimming holes surrounded by red cliffs—stuff straight from Eden. You can cruise the waterways of Katherine Gorge, a few hours' drive south of Darwin, or explore them by canoe. Near Katherine you can canoe rarely explored, croc-infested inland rivers and learn to make your own didgeridoo (a large wooden traditional Aboriginal musical instrument).

WESTERN AUSTRALIA Distance and high airfares work against Western Australia's tourism industry, which is a shame, because this is one of Australia's most wild and beautiful regions. The seas

teem with whales in season, and thrill-seekers can swim alongside gigantic but gentle whale sharks on the Northwest Cape every fall (Mar–June). This cape is home to one of Australia's best-kept secrets, a second barrier reef called Ningaloo Marine Park, which runs for 260km (161 miles). It's one of the few reefs in the world to grow on a western coast. You can snorkel with manta rays here or try the fantastic diving. Just 19km (12 miles) off Perth, snorkelers can gaze at corals and fish on Rottnest Island, and in Shark Bay at Monkey Mia, tourists can greet wild dolphins (or is it the other way around?).

In the southwest "hook" of the continent lies the Margaret River wine region. Wild forests, thundering surf, dramatic cliffs, rich bird life, and wild 'roos make it one of the country's most attractive wine regions. The state's capital, Perth, has surf beaches and a restored 19th-century port with a fun atmosphere and some great museums. One or 2 hours' drive from the city brings you to some cute towns, like the Spanish Benedictine monastery town of New Norcia. Inland, the state is mostly wheat fields and desert, but if you have the inclination, head 600km (372 miles) east of Perth to the gold-mining town of Kalgoorlie, where you'll find the world's largest open-cast gold mine. With its gracious old pubs lining the wide bustling streets, it's what an Aussie country town should look like.

In the Kimberley, you can visit the ancient Geikie and Windjana gorges, farms where the world's best South Sea pearls grow, and the charming (in a corrugated-iron sort of way) beachside frontier town of Broome. This tract of the country is so little populated and so underexplored that most Aussies never contemplate coming here. Getting around is expensive, because the region is so vast. Near Kununurra, on the eastern edge of the Kimberley, is a 400,000-hectare (1-million-acre) cattle station, El

---

Fun Fact **Where to Cuddle a Koala**

Koalas might look soft and cuddly, but the reality is a bit different. They are wild animals with sharp claws, and you should treat them with caution. Koalas in the wild are not safe to approach—even if you could reach them. Most of your encounters with them will be at a distance, looking on as they rest high in the branches of a tree, or in a wildlife park where "controlled cuddling" is allowed. Cuddling is allowed only in Queensland, South Australia, and Western Australia. In Victoria, New South Wales, and Tasmania, holding a koala is not allowed, but in some places you can pose beside one and have your photo taken. There are no koalas in the Northern Territory.

In southeast Queensland you can join a **Wild Koala Eco Tour** run by the Australian Koala Foundation (AKF) to see koalas in their natural habitat. You are guided by local scientists whose expert eyes will find even the most concealed koalas. The A$89 (US$71) tour includes a half-day guided koala walk, transfers to and from your Brisbane accommodations, and lunch at Queensland's oldest licensed pub, The Grand View Hotel at Cleveland, overlooking beautiful Moreton Bay. All profits go to AKF's koala conservation and restoration projects. Tours operate daily. Bookings are essential: © **1800 4KOALA;** www.savethe koalas.com; after hours or weekends © 07 5520 7238, or mobile phone 0413/085 858.

Questro, where you can camp in safari tents (or stay in an upmarket—read "expensive"—homestead). From Kununurra you can fly over or hike into the beehive-shaped rock formation of the Bungle Bungles, cruise on the bird-rich, croc-infested Ord River, and tour the Argyle Diamond Mine, the world's biggest.

SOUTH AUSTRALIA Stretched between Western Australia and Victoria is the nation's breadbasket, South Australia. The capital, Adelaide, is a stately place known for its conservatism, parks, and churches. It makes an ideal base for exploring Australia's illustrious wine region, the Barossa Valley. Big labels like Penfolds, Seppelts, and Wolf Blass are here, but take time to sniff out the many smaller, though no less outstanding, vineyards. And it's less than an hour from the city!

Bring your binoculars to the massive water-bird sanctuary, the Coorong. Stay in an underground hotel in the offbeat opal-mining town of Coober Pedy (it's too hot above ground), or order a 'roo-burger at the historic Prairie Hotel in the craggy, ancient lands of the Flinders Ranges in the South Australian Outback.

The greatest of South Australia's attractions—apart from wine, of course—is Kangaroo Island, the best place in Australia to see native animals. In a day you can spot wallabies, kangaroos, koalas, oodles of birds (from black swans to kookaburras), echidnas, and penguins. The beach teems with sea lions.

VICTORIA Australia's second-largest city, Melbourne, is the capital of Victoria. Melbourne is more stately and "Old World" than Sydney, and offers an exciting mix of ethnicities and the country's best fashion shopping. Nearby Phillip Island is famous for its Penguin Parade, during which hundreds of tiny penguins dash up the beach to their burrows at dusk. The historic gold-mining city of Ballarat is not far away. Victoria is also the site of one of Australia's great road trips, the Great Ocean Road. It stretches for 106km (66 miles) along the southern coast, where the eroded rock towers named the Twelve Apostles stand tall in the sea. Then there's the inland "high country," the stomping ground of the title character in Banjo Patterson's 1890 poem "The Man from Snowy River."

AUSTRALIAN CAPITAL TERRITORY (ACT)   Surrounded entirely by New South Wales is the Australian Capital Territory. The ACT is made up of bushland and the nation's capital, Canberra, a planned city similar in architectural concept to Washington, D.C. Many Australians consider the capital boring, but Canberra will surprise you. It has some of the country's best museums and great restaurants, so don't automatically exclude it from your itinerary.

TASMANIA   Last stop before Antarctica is the island state of Tasmania. Visit the Apple Isle for its beautiful national parks, stretches of alpine wilderness and gloomy forests, fruit and lavender farms, the world's best trout fishing, and an exquisitely slow pace of life rarely experienced anywhere else. If you're up to it, you could tackle the Overland Track, an 85km (53-mile) hiking trail between Cradle Mountain and Lake St. Clair that passes through highland moors, dense rainforests, and several mountains. A more leisurely option is a visit to the picturesque stone ruins of Port Arthur, Australia's version of Devil's Island, where thousands of convicts brought in to settle the new British colony were imprisoned and died. All of Tasmania is spectacular, but you haven't seen anything until you've experienced Freycinet National Park, with its pink granite outcrops set against an emerald-green sea.

2 Visitor Information

The **Australian Tourist Commission** is the best source of information on traveling Down Under. Its website, **www.australia.com**, has more than 10,000 pages of listings of tour operators, hotels, car-rental companies, special travel outfitters, holidays, maps, distance charts, suggested itineraries, and much more. The site provides information tailored to travelers from your country of origin, including packages and deals. By signing up for the free online Travel Club, you will receive e-mail news of hot deals, events, and the like on a regular basis. You can also order brochures online. The ATC operates a website only, no telephone lines. Other good sources are the websites of Australia's state tourism marketing offices. They are:

- **Canberra Tourism:** www.canberra tourism.com.au.
- **Northern Territory Tourist Commission:** www.travelnt.com or (for international visitors) www.australias outback.com.

Tips Get Help from the ATC

The Australian Tourist Commission (ATC) maintains a network of "Aussie Specialist" travel agents in hundreds of cities across the United States, Canada, the United Kingdom, New Zealand, and other countries. The agents are trained on the best destinations, hotels, deals, and tours Down Under. Get a referral to the nearest two Aussie Specialists by clicking on "Talk to an Aussie Specialist" on the home page on the ATC's website, **www.australia.com**.

> ### *Tips* Australia: Red Alert Checklist
>
> - Don't forget that you will need a visa to enter Australia (unless you are a New Zealand citizen).
> - Do any theater, restaurant, or travel reservations need to be booked in advance?
> - Did you make sure your favorite attraction is open? Check ahead for opening and closing times.
> - If you purchased traveler's checks, have you recorded the check numbers, and stored the documentation separately from the checks?
> - Did you pack your camera and an extra set of camera batteries, and purchase enough film? If you packed film in your checked baggage, did you invest in protective pouches to shield film from airport X-rays?
> - Do you have a safe, accessible place to store money?
> - Did you bring ID cards that could entitle you to discounts, such as AAA and AARP cards, student IDs, and the like?
> - Did you bring enough prescription medication to last through your trip? Australian pharmacists may fill only prescriptions written by Australian doctors.
> - Did you bring extra glasses or contact lenses?
> - Did you find out your daily ATM withdrawal limit?
> - Do you have your credit card PIN? Is there a daily withdrawal limit on credit card cash advances?
> - If you have an e-ticket, do you have documentation? To check in at a kiosk, you'll need the credit card you bought your ticket with or a frequent-flyer card.
> - Did you leave a copy of your itinerary with someone at home?
> - Did you check to see if any travel advisories have been issued by the U.S. State Department (http://travel.state.gov) regarding your destination?
> - Do you have the address and phone number of your country's embassy or consulate with you?

- **South Australian Tourism Commission:** www.southaustralia.com.
- **Tourism New South Wales:** www.visit nsw.com.au or www.sydneyaustralia.com.
- **Tourism Queensland:** www.queens landholidays.com.au or (for North Americans) www.destinationqueens land.com.
- **Tourism Tasmania:** www.discover tasmania.com.
- **Tourism Victoria:** www.visitvictoria.com.
- **Western Australian Tourism Commission:** www.westernaustralia.com.

3 Entry Requirements & Customs

ENTRY REQUIREMENTS

Along with a current passport valid for the duration of your stay, the Australian government requires a visa from visitors of every nation, except New Zealand, to be issued before you arrive. If you are short-term visitor or business traveler, the process is easy and can be done in a few minutes on the Internet, using the Australian government's **Electronic Travel Authority (ETA).** This is an electronic visa that takes the place of a stamp in your passport.

Tourists should apply for a **Visitor ETA.** The visa itself is free, though there is a service charge for getting it via the Internet, and valid for as many visits to Australia of up to 3 months each within a 1-year period. Tourists may not work in Australia, so if you are visiting for business, you have two choices: Apply for a **Short Validity Business ETA,** which covers a single visit of 3 months within a 1-year period, or pay A$65 (US$52) to apply for a **Long Validity Business visa,** which entitles you to as many 3-month stays in Australia as you like for the life of your passport but cannot be done online.

You can apply for an ETA yourself, or have your travel agent or airline do it when you book your plane ticket. (This service may incur an additional fee from the airline or travel agent.) To apply online, visit **www.eta.immi.gov.au**; the A$20 (US$16) charge is payable by credit card (Amex, Diners Club, MasterCard, or Visa). Assuming you do not have a criminal conviction and are in good health, your ETA should be approved quickly. You can also apply for the visa at Australian embassies, high commissions, and consulates (see below for their locations). Children traveling on their parent's passport must have their own ETA.

Fees mentioned in this section are in Australian dollars; the exact amount charged by the Australian embassy, consulate, or high commission in your country will depend on the foreign currency exchange rate.

If your travel agent or airline is not connected to the ETA system, you will need to apply for a visa the old-fashioned way—by taking or mailing your passport, a completed visa application form, and the appropriate payment to your nearest Australian embassy or consulate.

In the United States, Canada, the United Kingdom, Ireland, and many other countries, most agents and airlines are ETA-compatible. You will also need to go the old-fashioned route if you are someone other than a tourist or a business traveler—for example, a student studying in Australia; a businessperson staying longer than 3 months; a long-term resident; an athlete going for a competition; a member of the media on assignment; a performer; or a member of a social group or cultural exchange. If you fall into one of these categories, you will need to apply for a **Temporary Residence visa.** There is a A$65 (US$52) fee for non-ETA tourist and business visas for stays of up to 3 months, and A$165 (US$132) for business visas for stays between 3 months and 4 years. Non-ETA visa application fees for other kinds of travelers vary, from free to thousands of dollars. Contact the nearest Australian embassy, consulate, or high commission to check the forms of payment they accept.

Apply for non-ETA visas at Australian embassies, consulates, and high commissions. In the United States, apply to the Australian Embassy, 1601 Massachusetts Ave. NW, Washington, DC 20036 (© **202/797-3000;** dimia-washington @dfat.gov.au). The website of the Australian Embassy in North America is www.austemb.org.

In Canada, contact the Australian High Commission, 50 O'Connor St., No. 710, Ottawa, ON K1P 6L2 (© **888/ 990-8888;** www.ahc-ottawa.org). For business-visa inquiries in the United States and Canada, call © **800/579-7664.**

In the United Kingdom and Ireland, contact the Australian High Commission, Australia House, The Strand, London WC2B 4LA (© **020/09065 508900** for 24-hr. recorded information; www. australia.org.uk). There is no counter service at the High Commission in London, and you should obtain an application form for a non-ETA visa by post or over the Internet at the Australian Department of Immigration and Multicultural Affairs website (www.immi.gov.au). This site also has a good explanation of the ETA system.

Allow at least a month for processing of non-ETA visas.

For information on how to get a passport, go to "Passports" in the "Fast Facts" section of this chapter—the websites listed provide downloadable passport applications as well as the current fees for processing passport applications. For an up-to-date country-by-country listing of passport requirements around the world, go to the "Foreign Entry Requirement" Web page of the U.S. State Department at **http://travel.state.gov/foreignentry reqs.html**.

CUSTOMS
WHAT YOU CAN BRING INTO AUSTRALIA

The duty-free allowance in Australia is A$900 (US$720) or, for those under 18, A$450 (US$360). Anyone over 18 can bring in up to 250 cigarettes or 250 grams of cigars or other tobacco products, 2.25 liters (41 fluid oz.) of alcohol, and "dutiable goods" to the value of A$900 (US$720), or A$450 (US$360) if you are under 18.

"Dutiable goods" are luxury items such as perfume, watches, jewelry, furs, plus gifts of any kind. Keep this in mind if you intend to bring presents for family and friends in Australia; gifts given to you also count toward the dutiable limit. Personal goods that you're taking with you are usually exempt from duty, but if you are returning with valuable goods that you already own, file form B263. Customs officers do not collect duty of less than A$50 (US$40) as long as you declared the goods in the first place.

A helpful brochure, available from Australian consulates or Customs offices, as well as online, is *Know Before You Go.* For more information, contact Australian Customs Services, Locked Bag 3000, Sydney International Airport, NSW 2020 (✆ **02/8339 6714**), or check out www.customs.gov.au.

You need not declare cash in any currency, and other currency instruments, such as traveler's checks, under a value of A$10,000 (US$8,000). Firearms in Australia are strictly controlled; contact the nearest Australian diplomatic post for advice on importing a handgun.

Australia is a signatory to the Convention on International Trade in Endangered Species (CITES), which restricts or bans the import of products made from protected wildlife. Examples of the restricted items are coral, giant clam, wild cats, monkey, zebra, crocodile or alligator, bear, some types of caviar, American ginseng, and orchid products. Banned items include ivory, tortoise (marine turtle)

Tips **Passport Savvy**

Allow plenty of time before your trip to apply for a passport; processing normally takes 3 weeks but can take longer during busy periods (especially spring). And keep in mind that if you need a passport in a hurry, you'll pay a higher processing fee. When traveling, safeguard your passport in an inconspicuous, inaccessible place like a money belt, and keep a copy of the critical pages with your passport number in a separate place. If you lose your passport, visit the nearest embassy or consulate of your native country as soon as possible for a replacement.

shell, rhinoceros or tiger products, and sturgeon caviar. Bear this in mind if you stop in other countries en route to Australia where souvenirs made from items like these may be sold. Australian authorities may seize these items.

Because Australia is an island, it is free of many agricultural and livestock diseases. To keep it that way, strict quarantine applies to importing plants, animals, and their products, including food. "Sniffer" dogs at Australian airports detect these products (as well as drugs). Some items may be held for treatment and returned to you; others may be confiscated; and others may be held over for you to take with you when you leave the country. Amnesty trash bins are available before you reach the immigration counters in airport arrivals halls for items such as fruit. Don't be alarmed if, just before landing, the flight attendants spray the aircraft cabin (with products approved by the World Health Organization) to kill potentially disease-bearing insects. For more information on what is and is not allowed, contact the nearest Australian embassy or consulate, or Australia's Department of Agriculture, Fisheries, and Forestry, which runs the Australian Quarantine and Inspection Service (© 02/ 6272 3933; www.affa.gov.au). Its website has a list of restricted or banned foods, animal and plant products, and other items.

WHAT YOU CAN TAKE HOME FROM AUSTRALIA

Returning **U.S. citizens** who have been away for at least 48 hours are allowed to bring back, once every 30 days, $800 worth of merchandise duty-free. You'll be charged a flat rate of duty on the next $1,000 worth of purchases. Any dollar amount beyond that is dutiable at whatever rates apply. On mailed gifts, the duty-free limit is $200. Be sure to have your receipts or purchases handy to expedite the declaration process. *Note:* If you

owe duty, you are required to pay on your arrival in the United States, by cash, personal check, government or traveler's check, or money order. Some locations accept Visa and MasterCard.

To avoid having to pay duty on foreign-made personal items you owned before you left on your trip, bring along a bill of sale, insurance policy, jeweler's appraisal, or receipts of purchase. Or you can register items that can be readily identified by a permanently affixed serial number or marking—think laptop computers, cameras, and CD players—with Customs before you leave. Take the items to the nearest Customs office or register them with Customs at the airport from which you're departing. You'll receive, at no cost, a Certificate of Registration, which allows duty-free entry for the life of the item.

With some exceptions, you cannot bring fresh fruits and vegetables and some meat products into the United States. For specifics on what you can bring back, download the invaluable free pamphlet *Know Before You Go* online at **www.cbp. gov.** (Click on "Travel," then "Know Before You Go! Online Brochure.") Or contact **U.S. Customs & Border Protection (CBP),** 1300 Pennsylvania Ave. NW, Washington, DC 20229 (© **202/ 354-1000**), and request the pamphlet.

For a clear summary of **Canadian** rules, write for the booklet *I Declare,* issued by the **Canada Customs and Revenue Agency** (© **800/461-9999** in Canada, or 204/983-3500; www.cbsa-asfc.gc.ca). Canada allows its citizens a C$750 exemption, and you're allowed to bring back duty-free 200 cigarettes, 200 tobacco sticks, 40 imperial ounces of liquor, and 50 cigars. In addition, you're allowed to mail gifts to Canada valued at less than C$60 a day, provided they're unsolicited and don't contain alcohol or tobacco (write on the package "Unsolicited gift, under $60 value"). All valuables should be declared on the Y-38 form before departure from Canada, including serial numbers of valuables you already own, such as expensive foreign cameras. *Note:* The $750 exemption can only be used once a year and only after an absence of 7 days.

U.K. citizens returning from **a non-E.U. country** have a Customs allowance of: 200 cigarettes; 50 cigars; 250 grams of smoking tobacco; 2 liters of still table wine; 1 liter of spirits or strong liqueurs (over 22% volume); 2 liters of fortified wine, sparkling wine or other liqueurs; 60cc (ml) perfume; 250cc (ml) of toilet water; and £145 worth of all other goods, including gifts and souvenirs. People under 17 cannot have the tobacco or alcohol allowance. For more information, contact **HM Customs & Excise** (© **0845/010-9000,** or 020/8929-0152 from outside the U.K.; www.hmce.gov.uk).

The duty-free allowance for **New Zealand** is NZ$700. Citizens over 17 can bring in 200 cigarettes, 50 cigars, or 250 grams of tobacco (or a mixture of all three if their combined weight doesn't exceed 250g); plus 4.5 liters of wine and beer, or 1.125 liters of liquor. New Zealand currency does not carry import or export restrictions. Fill out a certificate of export, listing the valuables you are taking out of the country; that way, you can bring them back without paying duty. Most questions are answered in a free pamphlet, *Advice to Travellers,* available at New Zealand consulates and Customs offices or online. For more information, contact **New Zealand Customs,** The Customhouse, 17–21 Whitmore St., Box 2218, Wellington (© **0800/428-786** or 04/473-6099; ww.customs.govt.nz).

4 Money

For American and European travelers, Australia is very affordable because of the perilous state of the Australian dollar during the past few years. Most travelers will find money matters relatively easy in Australia, but beware the small town where traveler's checks may not be readily accepted.

CURRENCY

The Australian dollar is divided into 100¢. Coins are 5¢, 10¢, 20¢, and 50¢ pieces (silver) and $1 and $2 pieces (gold). Prices often end in a variant of 1¢ and 2¢ (for example, 78¢ or $2.71), a relic from the days before 1-cent and 2-cent pieces were phased out. Prices are rounded to the nearest 5¢—so 77¢ rounds down to 75¢, and 78¢ rounds up to 80¢). Bank notes come in denominations of $5, $10, $20, $50, and $100.

The Universal Currency Converter (www.xe.com/ucc) will give you up-to-the-minute conversions for your dollar or pound in dozens of countries.

It's a good idea to exchange at least some money—just enough to cover airport incidentals and transportation to

---

⌐Tips A Note About the Exchange Rate

As you budget your trip, bear in mind the extreme volatility of the Australian dollar against the U.S. dollar. In recent years, we've seen the value fluctuate between US62¢ and US81¢, with some experts predicting that it might go as high as US85¢. (As noted in the table titled "The Australian Dollar, the U.S. Dollar & the British Pound," below, in calculating prices in this book we valued the Australian dollar at US80¢ when calculating conversions.)

The Australian Dollar, the U.S. Dollar & the British Pound

For U.S. Readers   The rate of exchange used to calculate the dollar values given in this book was US$1 = approximately A$1.25 (or A$1 = US80¢).

For British Readers   The rate of exchange used to calculate the pound values in the accompanying table was £1 = A$2.45 (or A$1 = 40p).

Note: International exchange rates for the Australian dollar can fluctuate markedly. Check the latest rate when you plan your trip. The table below, and all the prices in this book, should be used only as a guide.

A$	US$	UK£	A$	US$	UK£
0.25	0.20	0.10	30.00	24.00	12.00
0.50	0.40	0.20	35.00	28.00	14.00
1.00	0.80	0.40	40.00	32.00	16.00
2.00	1.60	0.80	45.00	36.00	18.00
3.00	2.40	1.20	50.00	40.00	20.00
4.00	3.20	1.60	55.00	44.00	22.00
5.00	4.00	2.00	60.00	48.00	24.00
6.00	4.80	2.40	65.00	52.00	26.00
7.00	5.60	2.80	70.00	56.00	28.00
8.00	6.40	3.20	75.00	60.00	30.00
9.00	7.20	3.60	80.00	64.00	32.00
10.00	8.00	4.00	85.00	68.00	34.00
15.00	12.00	6.00	90.00	72.00	36.00
20.00	16.00	8.00	95.00	76.00	38.00
25.00	20.00	10.00	100.00	80.00	40.00

your hotel—before you leave home (though don't expect the exchange rate to be ideal), so you can avoid lines at airport ATMs (automated teller machines). You can exchange money at your local American Express or Thomas Cook office or your bank. If you're far away from a bank with currency-exchange services, **American Express** offers traveler's checks and foreign currency, though with a $15 order fee and additional shipping costs, at www.americanexpress.com or © **800/807-6233.**

ATMs

The easiest and best way to get cash away from home is from an ATM (automated teller machine). The **Cirrus** (© **800/424-7787;** www.mastercard.com) and **PLUS** (© **800/843-7587;** www.visa.com) networks span the globe; look at the back of your bank card to see which network you're on, then call or check online for ATM locations at your destination. Be sure you know your personal identification number (PIN) before you leave home, and be sure to find out your daily withdrawal limit before you depart. Also keep in mind that many banks impose a fee every time a card is used at a different bank's ATM, and that fee can be higher for international transactions (up to US$5 or more) than for domestic ones (where they're rarely more than US$1.50). On top of this, the bank from which you withdraw cash may charge its own fee. For international withdrawal fees, ask your bank.

You can also get cash advances on your credit card at an ATM. Keep in mind that credit card companies try to protect themselves from theft by limiting the funds someone can withdraw outside their home country, so call your credit card company before you leave home. And keep in mind that you'll pay interest from the moment of your withdrawal, even if you pay your monthly bills on time.

Most ATMs in Australia will be linked to a network that likely includes your bank at home. In Outback areas, carry cash and a credit card, because ATMs can be hard to find in small country towns, and shopkeepers in remote parts may not cash traveler's checks.

TRAVELER'S CHECKS

Traveler's checks are something of an anachronism from the days before the ATM made cash accessible at any time. Traveler's checks used to be the only sound alternative to traveling with dangerously large amounts of cash. They were as reliable as currency, but, unlike cash, could be replaced if lost or stolen.

These days, traveler's checks are less necessary because most cities have 24-hour ATMs that allow you to withdraw small amounts of cash as needed. However, keep in mind that you will likely be charged an ATM withdrawal fee if the bank is not your own, so if you're withdrawing money every day, you

might be better off with traveler's checks—provided that you don't mind showing identification every time you want to cash one.

However, be warned that traveler's checks are not as widely accepted in Australia as in many other countries. If you do opt for them, get them in Australian dollars. Checks in U.S. dollars are accepted at banks, big hotels, currency exchanges, and some shops in major tourist regions, but smaller shops, restaurants, and other businesses will have no idea what the exchange rate is when you present a U.S. check. Another advantage of Australian-dollar checks is that the two largest Aussie banks, ANZ and Westpac, cash them free; it will cost you around A$5 to A$11 (US$4–US$8.80) to cash checks denominated in foreign currency at most Australian banks.

You can get traveler's checks at almost any bank. **American Express** offers denominations of $20, $50, $100, $500, and (for cardholders only) $1,000. You'll pay a service charge ranging from 1% to 4%. Cardholders can also get American Express traveler's checks over the phone by calling ✆ **800/221-7282;** Amex gold and platinum cardholders who use this number are exempt from the 1% fee.

Visa offers traveler's checks at Citibank locations nationwide, as well as at several other banks. The service charge ranges between 1.5% and 2%; checks come in denominations of $20, $50, $100, $500, and $1,000. Call ✆ **800/227-6811** for information. AAA members can obtain

---

(*Tips* **Small Change**

When you change money, ask for some small bills or loose change. Petty cash will come in handy for tipping and public transportation. Consider keeping the change separate from your larger bills, so that it's readily accessible and you'll be less of a target for theft.

> **Tips Dear Visa: I'm Off to Kununurra!**
>
> Some credit card companies recommend that you notify them of any impending trip abroad so that they don't become suspicious when the card is used numerous times in a foreign destination and block your charges. Even if you don't call your credit card company in advance, you can always call the card's toll-free emergency number (see "Fast Facts: Australia," later in this chapter) if a charge is refused—a good reason to carry the phone number with you. But perhaps the important lesson here is to carry more than one card with you on your trip; a card might not work for any number of reasons, so having a backup is the smart way to go.

Visa checks without a fee at most AAA offices or by calling © **866/339-3378.**

Both companies offer checks in Australian dollars. You'll pay the rate of exchange at the time of your purchase (so it's a good idea to monitor the rate before you take the plunge), and probably a transaction fee per order, plus a shipping fee if you order online.

If you choose to carry traveler's checks, be sure to keep a record of their serial numbers separate from your checks in the event that they are stolen or lost. You'll get a refund faster if you know the numbers.

CREDIT CARDS

Credit cards are a safe way to carry money; they also provide a convenient record of all your expenses, and they generally offer relatively good exchange rates. You can also withdraw cash advances from your credit cards at banks or ATMs, provided you know your PIN. If you've forgotten yours, or didn't even know you had one, call the number on the back of your credit card and ask the bank to send

it to you. It usually takes 5 to 7 business days, though some banks will provide the number over the phone if you tell them your mother's maiden name or some other personal information. When you use your credit card abroad, most banks assess a 2% fee above the 1% fee charged by American Express, MasterCard, or Visa for currency conversion on credit charges. But credit cards still may be the smart way to go when you factor in things like exorbitant ATM fees and higher traveler's check exchange rates (and service fees).

Visa and MasterCard are universally accepted in Australia; American Express and Diners Club are considerably less common, and Discover is not used. Always carry a little cash, because many merchants will not take cards for purchases under A$15 (US$12) or so.

For tips and telephone numbers to call if your wallet is stolen or lost, go to "Lost & Found" in the "Fast Facts: Australia" section, later in this chapter.

5 When to Go

When it is winter in the Northern Hemisphere, Australia is basking in the Southern Hemisphere's summer, and vice versa. Midwinter in Australia is July and August, and the hottest months are November through March. Remember, unlike in the Northern Hemisphere, the

farther south you go in Australia, the colder it gets.

THE TRAVEL SEASONS

Airfares to Australia offered by U.S. airlines are lowest from mid-April to late August—the best time to visit the Red

Centre, the Top End, and the Great Barrier Reef.

HIGH SEASON The peak travel season in the most popular parts of Australia is the Aussie winter. In much of the country—Queensland from around Townsville and northward, all of the Top End and the Red Centre, and most of Western Australia—the most pleasant time to travel is April through September, when daytime temperatures are 66° to 88°F (19°–31°C) and it rarely rains. June, July, and August are the busiest months in these parts; you'll need to book accommodations and tours well in advance, and you will pay higher rates then, too.

On the other hand, Australia's summer is a nice time to visit the southern states—New South Wales, Victoria, South Australia, Western Australia from Perth to the south, and Tasmania. Even in winter, temperatures rarely dip below freezing, and snow falls only in parts of Tasmania, in the ski fields of Victoria, and in the Snowy Mountains of southern New South Wales.

The best months to visit Australia, I think, are September and October, when it's often still warm enough to hit the beach in the southern states, it's cool enough to tour Uluru (Ayers Rock), and the humidity and rains have not come to Cairns and the Top End (although it will be very hot by Oct). And the wildflowers are in full bloom in Western Australia.

LOW SEASON October through March (summer) it is just too hot, too humid, too wet—or all three—to tour the Red Centre, the Top End, and anywhere in Western Australia except Perth and the southwest. The Top End, the Kimberley, and North Queensland, including Cairns, suffer an intensely hot, humid wet season from November or December through March or April. In the Top End and Kimberley, this is preceded by an even stickier "build-up" in October and November. Some attractions and tour companies close, floodwaters render others off-limits, and hotels drop their rates, often dramatically. So if you decide to travel in these areas at this time—and lots of people do—be prepared to take the heat, the inconvenience of floods, and, in tropical coastal areas, the slight chance of encountering cyclones.

HOLIDAYS

In addition to the period from December 26 to the end of January, when Aussies take their summer vacations, the 4 days at Easter (from Good Friday to Easter Monday) and all school holidays are very busy, so book ahead. The school year in Australia is broken into four semesters, with 2-week holidays around Easter, the last week of June and the first week of July, and the last week of September and the first week of October. Some states break at slightly different dates. There's a 6-week summer (Christmas) vacation from mid-December to the end of January.

Almost everything shuts down on Good Friday, Christmas Day, and Boxing Day (Dec 26), and much is closed January 1, Easter Sunday, and Easter Monday. Most establishments close until 1pm, if

---

Tips Steer Clear of the Vacation Rush

Try to avoid Australia from Boxing Day (Dec 26) to the end of January, when Aussies take their summer vacations. In popular seaside holiday spots, hotel rooms and airline seats get scarce as hen's teeth, and it's a rare airline or hotel that will discount full rates by even a dollar.

not all day, on Anzac Day (Apr 25), a World War I commemorative day.

Among the major public holidays are: New Year's Day (Jan 1); Australia Day (Jan 26); Labor Day (second Mon in Mar, WA); Eight Hours Day (first Mon in Mar, TAS); Labor Day (second Mon in Mar, VIC); Canberra Day (third Mon in Mar, ACT); Good Friday; Easter Sunday; Easter Monday; Anzac Day (Apr 25); May Day (first Mon in May, NT); Labour Day (first Mon in May, QLD); Adelaide Cup (third Mon in May, SA); Foundation Day (first Mon in June, WA); Queen's Birthday (second Mon in June, except WA); Royal National Show Day (second or third Wed in Aug, QLD); Queen's Birthday (Mon in late Sept/early Oct, WA); Labour Day (first Mon in Oct, NSW and SA); Melbourne Cup Day (first Tues in Nov, Melbourne); Christmas (Dec 25); and Boxing Day (Dec 26). If December 26 falls on a weekend, the following Monday is a holiday.

AUSTRALIA CALENDAR OF EVENTS

January

Sydney Festival. Highlights of Sydney's visual and performing arts festival are free jazz or classical music concerts held outdoors on 2 Saturday nights near the Royal Botanic Gardens. (Take a picnic and arrive by 4pm to get a place.) Call © **02/8248 6500** or go to www.sydneyfestival.org.au. Three weeks in January.

Hyundai Hopman Cup, Perth. Tennis greats from the world's nine top tennis nations battle it out in a 7-day mixed-doubles competition. Contact the booking agent, BOCS Ticketing (© **1800/193 300** in Australia, or 08/9484 1133), or check www.hopmancup.com.au. December 31, 2005 to January 7, 2006.

Tamworth Country Music Festival, Tamworth (459km/285 miles northwest of Sydney), New South Wales. It may look like an Akubra Hat Convention, but this gathering of rural folk and city folk who would like to be rural folk is Australia's biggest country music festival. The Tamworth Information Centre (© **02/6755 4300;** www.tamworth.nsw.gov.au) takes bookings. January 20 to January 29, 2006.

Australia Day. Australia's answer to Fourth of July marks the landing of the First Fleet of convicts at Sydney Cove in 1788. Every town puts on some kind of celebration; in Sydney, there are ferry races and Tall Ships on the harbor, food and wine stalls in Hyde Park, open days at museums and other attractions, and fireworks in the evening. January 26.

March

Sydney Gay & Lesbian Mardi Gras. A month of events, culminating in a spectacular parade of costumed dancers and decorated floats, watched by several hundred thousand onlookers, followed by a giant warehouse party (by invitation only). Contact Sydney Gay & Lesbian Mardi Gras (© **02/9568 8600;** www.mardigras.org.au). Parade is usually the last Saturday in February or first Saturday in March.

XVIII Commonwealth Games, Melbourne. The best athletes in the Commonwealth—made up of 71 countries around the world—will meet to battle it out in a contest of elite sports held only every 4 years. The main venue will be the Melbourne Cricket Ground. Tickets are available only by lottery, but there are special arrangements for visitors to Australia from Commonwealth and other countries. See the Games website, www.commonwealthgames.com.au, for more details. March 15 to March 26, 2006.

Australian Formula One Grand Prix, Melbourne. The first Grand Prix of the year on the international FIA Formula One World Championship circuit is battled out on one of its fastest circuits, in Melbourne. For tickets, contact Ticketmaster (© **13 16 41** in Australia) or order online at http://cars.grandprix.com.au. Four days in the first or second week of March.

Australian Surf Life Saving Championships, Kurrawa Beach, Gold Coast, Queensland. Up to 6,000 bronzed Aussie and international men and women swim, ski paddle, sprint relay, pilot rescue boats, parade past admiring crowds, and resuscitate "drowning" swimmers in front of 10,000 spectators. Contact Surf Life Saving Australia (© **02/9130 7370;** www.slsa.asn.au).

June

Sydney Film Festival. World and Australian premieres of Aussie and international movies take place in the State Theatre and other venues. Contact the Sydney Film Festival (© **02/9280 0511;** www.sydneyfilmfestival.org). Two weeks from first or second Friday in June.

August

***Sun-Herald* City to Surf,** Sydney. Fifty thousand Sydneysiders pound the pavement (or walk or wheelchair it) in this 14km (8¾-mile) "fun run" from the city to Bondi Beach, which has been run for the past 35 years. For entry details, visit www.city2surf.sunherald.com.au (from June onward) or call © **1800/555 514** in Australia. If slots are available, you can enter the day of the race. The fee is around A$25 (US$20). Second Sunday in August.

September

Floriade, Canberra. A million tulips, daffodils, hyacinths, and other blooms carpet the banks of Canberra's Lake Burley Griffin in stunning themed flower-bed designs at this celebration, which features performing arts and other entertainment. Contact Canberra Visitors Centre (© **1300/554 114** in Australia; www.canberratourism.com.au) or the Floriade team (© **02/6205 0666;** www.floriadeaustralia.com). September 16 to October 15, 2006.

Henley-on-Todd Regatta, Alice Springs. Sounds sophisticated, doesn't it? It's actually a harum-scarum race down the dry bed of the Todd River in homemade "boats" made from anything you care to name—an old four-wheel-drive chassis, say, or beer cans lashed together. The only rule is the vessel has to look *vaguely* like a boat. Contact the organizers at © **08/8952 4061;** www.henleyontodd.com.au. Third Saturday in September.

October

Lexmark Indy 300 Carnival, Surfers Paradise, Queensland. The world's best Indy-car drivers race a street circuit around Surfers Paradise on the glitzy Gold Coast, as part of the international FedEx Championship champ car motor-sport series. Contact Ticketek (© **13 19 31** in Australia or 07/3404 6700 in Brisbane; www.ticketek.com), or check the event's website (www.indy.com.au). Four days in mid- or late October.

November

Melbourne Cup, Flemington racecourse. They say the whole nation stops to watch this horse race. That's about right. If you're not actually at the A$3.5-million (US$2.8-million) race, you're glued to the TV—or, well, you're probably not an Australian. Women wear hats to the office, files on desks all over the country make way for a late chicken and champagne lunch, and don't even think about flagging a cab at the 3:20pm race time. For tickets, contact Ticketmaster (© **13 16 41**

in Australia); for information, visit www.vrc.net.au. First Tuesday in November.

December

Sydney-to-Hobart Yacht Race. Find a cliff-top spot near the Heads to watch the glorious show of spinnakers as 100 or so yachts leave Sydney Harbour for this grueling world-class event. The organizer is the Sydney-based Cruising Yacht Club of Australia (© **02/9363** **9731;** www.cyca.com.au). Starts December 26.

New Year's Eve. Watching the Sydney Harbour Bridge light up with fireworks is a treat. The main show is at 9pm, not midnight, so young kids don't miss out. Pack a picnic and snag a Harbour-side spot by 4pm, or even earlier at the best vantage point—Mrs. Macquarie's Chair in the Royal Botanic Gardens. December 31.

6 Travel Insurance

Check your existing insurance policies and credit card coverage before you buy travel insurance. You may already be covered for lost luggage, canceled tickets, or medical expenses.

The cost of travel insurance varies widely, depending on the cost and length of your trip, your age and health, and the type of trip you're taking, but expect to pay between 5% and 8% of the vacation itself.

TRIP-CANCELLATION INSURANCE

Trip-cancellation insurance helps you get your money back if you have to back out of a trip, if you have to go home early, or if your travel supplier goes bankrupt. Allowed reasons for cancellation can range from sickness to natural disasters to the State Department declaring your destination unsafe for travel. (Insurers usually won't cover vague fears, though, as many travelers discovered who tried to cancel their trips in Oct 2001 because they were wary of flying.) In this unstable world, trip-cancellation insurance is a good buy if you're getting tickets well in advance—who knows what the state of the world, or of your airline, will be in 9 months? Insurance policy details vary, so read the fine print—and make sure that your airline or cruise line is on the list of carriers covered in case of bankruptcy. A good resource is **"Travel Guard Alerts,"** a list of companies considered high-risk by Travel Guard International (see website below). Protect yourself further by paying for the insurance with a credit card—by law, consumers can get their money back on goods and services not received if they report the loss within 60 days after the charge is listed on their credit card statement.

Note: Many tour operators, particularly those offering trips to remote or high-risk areas, include insurance in the cost of the trip or can arrange insurance policies through a partnering provider, a convenient and often cost-effective way for the traveler to obtain insurance. Make sure the tour company is a reputable one, however: Some experts suggest you avoid buying insurance from the tour or cruise company you're traveling with, saying it's better to buy from a "third party" insurer than to put all your money in one place.

For more information, contact one of the following recommended insurers: **Access America** (© 866/807-3982; www.accessamerica.com); **Travel Guard International** (© 800/826-4919; www.travelguard.com); **Travel Insured International** (© 800/243-3174; www.travelinsured.com); and **Travelex Insurance Services** (© 888/457-4602; www.travelexinsurance.com).

MEDICAL INSURANCE
For travel overseas, most health plans (including Medicare and Medicaid) do not provide

Tips   Quick ID

Tie a colorful ribbon or piece of yarn around your luggage handle, or slap a distinctive sticker on the side of your bag. This makes it less likely that someone will mistakenly appropriate it. And if your luggage gets lost, it will be easier to find.

coverage, and the ones that do often require you to pay for services upfront and reimburse you only after you return home. Even if your plan does cover overseas treatment, most out-of-country hospitals make you pay your bills upfront, and send you a refund only after you've returned home and filed the necessary paperwork with your insurance company.

In a worst-case scenario, there's the high cost of emergency evacuation. Australia's immense distances mean you can sometimes be a long way from a hospital or a doctor. Make sure your policy covers medical evacuation by helicopter or Australia's Royal Flying Doctor Service airlift. (You might well need this if you become sick or injured in the Outback.)

One of the most potentially financially ruinous situations arising from getting sick in Australia is evacuation to your home country. Your policy should cover the cost to fly you back home in a stretcher, along with a nurse, should that be necessary. A stretcher takes up three coach-class seats, and you may need extra seats for a nurse and medical equipment.

Australia has a reciprocal medical-care agreement with Great Britain and a limited agreement with Ireland and New Zealand. It covers travelers for medical expenses for immediately necessary treatment in a public hospital (but not evacuation to your home country, ambulances, funerals, and dental care) by Australia's national health system, called Medicare, which is similar to the program by the same name in the United States. It's crucial to buy insurance, though, because medical care in Australia is expensive, and the national health-care system typically

covers only 85%, sometimes less, of treatment; you will not be covered for treatment in a private hospital; and evacuation insurance is a must. Most foreign students must take out the Australian government's Overseas Student Health Cover as a condition of entry.

If you require additional medical insurance, try **MEDEX Assistance** (© 410/453-6300; www.medexassist.com) or **Travel Assistance International** (© 800/821-2828; www.travelassistance.com; for general information on services, call the company's Worldwide Assistance Services, Inc., at © 800/643-5525).

LOST-LUGGAGE INSURANCE   On international flights (including U.S. portions of international trips), baggage coverage is limited to approximately $9.07 per pound, up to approximately $635 per checked bag. If you plan to check items more valuable than the standard liability, see if your valuables are covered by your homeowner's policy, get baggage insurance as part of your comprehensive travel-insurance package, or buy Travel Guard's "BagTrak" product. Don't buy insurance at the airport, where it's usually overpriced. Be sure to take any valuables or irreplaceable items with you in your carry-on luggage, because airline policies don't cover many valuables (including books, money, and electronics).

If your luggage is lost, immediately file a lost-luggage claim at the airport, detailing the luggage contents. For most airlines, you must report delayed, damaged, or lost baggage within 4 hours of arrival. The airlines are required to deliver luggage, once found, directly to your house or destination free of charge.

7 Health & Safety

STAYING HEALTHY

You don't have to worry much about health issues on a trip to Australia. Hygiene standards are high, hospitals are modern, and doctors and dentists are well qualified. Because of the continent's size, you can sometimes be a long way from a hospital or a doctor, but help is never far away, thanks to the Royal Flying Doctor Service. However, standard medical travel insurance may be advisable (see the previous section).

GENERAL AVAILABILITY OF HEALTH CARE

No vaccinations are needed to enter Australia unless you have been in a yellow fever danger zone—that is, South America or Africa—in the past 6 days.

Australian pharmacists may only fill prescriptions written by Australian doctors, so carry enough medication with you for your trip. Doctors are listed under "M," for "Medical Practitioners," in the Yellow Pages, and most large towns and cities have 24-hour clinics. Failing that, go to the local hospital's emergency room.

BUGS, BITES & OTHER WILDLIFE CONCERNS Snake and spider bites may not be as common as the hair-raising stories you will hear would suggest, but it pays to be wary. Australia's two deadly spiders are the large hairy funnel web and the tiny red-back, which has a distinctive red slash on its back. Snakes are common throughout Australia. You are most likely to see one if you are in the bush or hiking. If you are bitten, keep calm; moving as little as possible may save your life. Demobilize the limb and wrap that whole section of the limb tightly (but not tight enough to restrict blood flow) with a wide cloth or bandage (not a narrow tourniquet). Then send someone to the nearest hospital, where antivenin should be available.

If you go bushwalking (hiking through the bush), check your whole body for ticks, which are common. If you find one, dab it with methylated spirits or some other noxious chemical. Wait for awhile, and then gently pull the tick out with tweezers, carefully ensuring that you don't leave its head buried inside the wound.

Many Aussie marine creatures are deadly. Avoid stingrays, stonefish (which look like stones, so don't walk on underwater "rocks"), lionfish, and puffer fish. Never touch a blue-ringed octopus (it has blue circles all over its body) or a cone shell (a large shellfish shaped like a blunt cone). Marine stingers, or box jellyfish, inhabit the coastal waters of the northern third of the country in summer. Their sting is very painful and can cause heart failure and death. If you are stung, pour vinegar over the affected site immediately—local authorities leave bottles of vinegar on the beach specifically for this purpose. On beaches in Sydney and other areas, you might come across "blue bottles" (which are sometimes also called "stingers" but are not the same as the jellyfish that plague swimmers and divers in the waters farther north). These long-tentacled blue jellyfish (also known as Portuguese man-of-war) inflict a generally harmless but painful sting that can last for hours. Sometimes you'll see warning signs on patrolled beaches. The best remedy if you are stung is to rinse the area liberally in seawater or fresh water to remove any tentacles stuck to the skin. For intense pain, apply heat or cold, whichever feels better. If you experience breathing difficulties or disorientation following a jellyfish sting, seek medical attention immediately.

There are two types of crocodiles in Australia: the freshwater crocodile, which grows to almost 3m (10 ft.), and the highly dangerous estuarine (or saltwater) crocodile, which reaches 5 to 7m (17–23 ft.). Freshwater crocs are considered harmless; unfortunately, estuarine crocs aren't. They are called "saltwater" crocs but live mostly in freshwater rivers, wetlands, gorges, and billabongs (ponds). They are very dangerous, move at lightning speed, and can remain unseen even an inch beneath the water; few people survive an attack. *Never* swim in, or stand near the bank of, any river, swamp, or pool in the northern third of Australia, unless you know for certain it's croc-free, and don't swim at beaches near stream or river mouths.

SUN/ELEMENTS/EXTREME WEATHER EXPOSURE Australians have the world's highest death rate from skin cancer because of the country's intense sunlight. Limit your exposure to the sun, especially during the first few days of your trip, and from 11am to 3pm in summer and 10am to 2pm in winter. Remember that UV rays reflected off walls, water, and the ground can burn you even when you're not in direct sunlight. Use a broad-spectrum sunscreen with a high protection factor (SPF 30 or higher).

Wear a broad-brimmed hat that covers the back of your neck, ears, and face (a baseball cap won't do it), and a long-sleeved shirt. Remember that children need more protection than adults do. Don't even think about traveling without sunglasses, or you'll spend your entire vacation squinting against Australia's "diamond light."

Cyclones occasionally affect tropical areas such as Darwin and Queensland's coastal regions, from about Gladstone north, during January and February, but serious damage is relatively rare.

WHAT TO DO IF YOU GET SICK AWAY FROM HOME

In most cases, your existing health plan will provide the coverage you need. But double-check; you may want to buy **travel medical insurance** instead. (See "Travel Insurance," above.) Bring your insurance ID card with you when you travel.

If you suffer from a chronic illness, consult your doctor before your departure. For conditions like epilepsy, diabetes, or heart problems, wear a **Medic Alert identification tag** (© 888/633-4298; www.medicalert.org), which will immediately alert doctors to your condition and give them access to your records through Medic Alert's 24-hour hot line.

Tips Avoiding "Economy-Class Syndrome"

Deep vein thrombosis, or, as it's known in the world of flying, "economy-class syndrome," is a blood clot that develops in a deep vein. It's a potentially deadly condition that can be caused by sitting in cramped conditions—such as an airplane cabin—for too long. During your flight, get up, walk around, and stretch your legs every 60 to 90 minutes to keep your blood flowing. Other preventive measures include frequent flexing of the legs while sitting, drinking lots of water, and avoiding alcohol and sleeping pills. If you have a history of deep vein thrombosis, heart disease, or another condition that puts you at high risk, some experts recommend wearing compression stockings or taking anticoagulants when you fly; always ask your physician about the best course for you. Symptoms of deep vein thrombosis include leg pain, leg swelling, and even shortness of breath.

Pack **prescription medications** in your carry-on luggage, and carry prescription medications in their original containers, with pharmacy labels—otherwise they won't make it through airport security. *Remember:* Australian pharmacists may fill only prescriptions written by an Australian doctor. Don't forget an extra pair of contact lenses or prescription glasses.

Contact the **International Association for Medical Assistance to Travelers** (© 716/754-4883, or 416/652-0137 in Canada; www.iamat.org) for tips on travel and health concerns in Australia, and lists of local doctors. The United States **Centers for Disease Control and Prevention** (© 800/311-3435; www.cdc.gov) provides up-to-date information on necessary vaccines and health hazards by region or country.

If you get sick, consider asking your hotel concierge to recommend a local doctor—even his or her own.

STAYING SAFE

Driving probably poses one of the greatest risks to visitors to Australia. Australians drive on the left, something that North American and European visitors often have difficulty remembering. Drivers and passengers, including taxi passengers, must wear a seat belt at all times, by law. Avoid driving between dusk and dawn in country areas, because this is when kangaroos are most active, and a collision with a 'roo is something to be avoided at all costs. Road trains—as many as three big truck carriages linked together, which can be up to 54m (177 ft.) long—are another danger, particularly in the Outback. *Warning:* If you break down or get lost, never leave your vehicle. Most people who get lost do so in Outback spots, and those who wander off to look for help or water usually die in the attempt. If it happens to you, stay with your car. See "Getting Around Australia," p. 68.

8 Specialized Travel Resources

TRAVELERS WITH DISABILITIES

Most disabilities shouldn't stop anyone from traveling. There are more options and resources out there than ever before. Most hotels, major stores, attractions, and public restrooms in Australia have wheelchair access. Many smaller lodges and even B&Bs are starting to cater to guests with disabilities, and some diving companies cater to scuba divers with disabilities. National parks make an effort to include wheelchair-friendly pathways, too. Taxi companies in bigger cities can usually supply a cab equipped for wheelchairs.

TTY facilities are still limited largely to government services. For information on all kinds of facilities and services (not just travel-related organizations) for people with disabilities, contact **National Information Communication Awareness Network,** P.O. Box 407, Curtin, ACT 2605 (© 1800/806 769 voice and TTY in Australia, or 02/6285 3713; www.nican.com.au). This free service can put you in touch with accessible accommodations and attractions throughout Australia, as well as with travel agents and tour operators who understand your needs.

Many travel agencies offer customized tours and itineraries for travelers with disabilities. **Flying Wheels Travel** (© 507/451-5005; www.flyingwheelstravel.com) offers escorted tours and cruises that emphasize sports and private tours in minivans with lifts. **Access-Able Travel Source** (© 303/232-2979; www.access-able.com) offers extensive access information and advice for traveling around the world with disabilities. **Accessible Journeys** (© 800/846-4537 or 610/521-0339; www.disabilitytravel.com) caters specifically to slow walkers and wheelchair travelers and their families and friends.

Organizations that offer assistance to travelers with disabilities include **Moss-Rehab** (② 800/CALL-MOSS; www.mossresourcenet.org), which provides a library of accessible-travel resources online; **SATH,** the Society for Accessible Travel and Hospitality (② 212/447-7284; www.sath.org; annual membership fees: $45 adults, $30 seniors and students), which offers a wealth of travel resources for all types of disabilities and informed recommendations on destinations, access guides, travel agents, tour operators, vehicle rentals, and companion services; and the **American Foundation for the Blind** (② 800/232-5463; www.afb.org), a referral resource for the blind and visually impaired that includes information on traveling with Seeing Eye dogs.

For more information specifically targeted to travelers with disabilities, the community website **iCan** (www.icanonline.net/channels/travel/index.cfm) has destination guides and several regular columns on accessible travel. Also check out the quarterly magazine *Emerging Horizons* ($15 per year, $20 outside the U.S.; www.emerginghorizons.com); and *Open World* magazine, published by SATH (see above; subscription: $13 per year, $21 outside the U.S.).

GAY & LESBIAN TRAVELERS

Sydney is one of the most gay-friendly cities in the world, and across most of Australia, the gay community has a high profile and lots of support services. There are plenty of gay and lesbian bars, and most Saturday nights see a privately operated gay dance party taking place in an inner-city warehouse somewhere. The cafes and pubs of Oxford Street in Darlinghurst, a short cab ride or long stroll from Sydney's downtown area, are the liveliest gay spots. The annual Sydney Gay & Lesbian Mardi Gras, culminating in a huge street parade and party in late February or early March, is a high point on the city's calendar.

In rural areas of Australia, you may still encounter a little conservative resistance to gays and lesbians, but Australians everywhere are generally tolerant. Noosa, on Queensland's Sunshine Coast, is a favored destination for revelers after the Sydney Mardi Gras, and a couple of resorts in north Queensland cater to gay and lesbian travelers. One of the best known is **Turtle Cove Resort** (② 1300/727 979 in Australia, or 07/4059 1800; www.turtlecove.com.au), on a private beach between Cairns and Port Douglas.

Some services you may find useful are the **Gay & Lesbian Counselling Service** of NSW (② 02/8594 9500 for the administration office), which runs a hot line (② 1800/184 527 in Australia, or 02/8594 9596) from 7:30 to 10pm daily. Its website, www.glccs.org.au, has contact information for each state. In Sydney, the **Albion Street Centre** (② 02/9332 9600 for administration, 1800/451 600 in Australia outside Sydney, or 02/9332 9700 in Sydney for the information line) is an AIDS clinic and information service.

The **International Gay and Lesbian Travel Association** (② 800/448-8550 or 954/776-2626; www.iglta.org) is the trade association for the gay and lesbian travel industry, and offers an online directory of gay- and lesbian-friendly travel businesses; go to the IGLTA website and click on "Members." Gay & Lesbian Tourism Australia (www.galta.com.au) also has listings of useful businesses in each state.

Many agencies offer tours and travel itineraries specifically for gay and lesbian travelers. **Above and Beyond Tours** (② 800/397-2681; www.abovebeyondtours.com) specializes in gay and lesbian travel to Australia. **Now, Voyager** (② 800/255-6951; www.nowvoyager.com) is a well-known San Francisco–based gay-owned and -operated travel service. *Fellow Traveller* (② 03/9429 6110; www.fellowtraveller.com.au), Australia's only free gay and lesbian accommodations guide, is produced annually by Melbourne's weekly gay and lesbian newspaper, *MCV*. It is distributed nationally. The following travel guides are available at most travel bookstores and gay and lesbian bookstores, or you can order them online: *Spartacus International Gay Guide* (Bruno Gmünder Verlag; www.spartacusworld.com/gayguide) and *Odysseus: The International Gay Travel Planner* (Odysseus Enterprises Ltd.), both good, annual English-language guidebooks focused on gay men; the *Damron* guides (www.damron.com), with separate, annual books for gay men and lesbians; and *Gay Travel A to Z: The World of Gay & Lesbian Travel Options at Your Fingertips*, by Marianne Ferrari (Ferrari International; Box 35575, Phoenix, AZ 85069), a very good gay and lesbian guidebook series.

Gay.com Travel (© 800/929-2268 or 415/644-8044; www.gay.com/travel or www.outandabout.com) is online resource that's a successor to the popular *Out & About* print magazine.

It provides regularly updated information about gay-owned, gay-oriented, and gay-friendly lodging, dining, sightseeing, nightlife and shopping establishments, in every important destination worldwide, and trip-planning information for gay and lesbian travelers for more than 50 destinations and along different themes ranging from Sex & Travel to Vacations for Couples.

SENIOR TRAVEL

Mention the fact that you're a senior when you make your travel reservations.

Seniors—often called "pensioners" in Australia—from other countries don't always qualify for the discounted entry prices to tours, attractions, and events that Australian seniors enjoy, but mostly they do. Always inquire about discounts when booking hotels, flights, and train or bus

tickets. The best ID to bring is something that shows your date of birth or something that marks you as an "official" senior, like a membership card from AARP.

Members of **AARP** (formerly known as the American Association of Retired Persons), 601 E St. NW, Washington, DC 20049 (© 888/687-2277; www.aarp.org), get discounts on hotels, airfares, and car rentals. AARP offers members a wide range of benefits, including *AARP: The Magazine* and a monthly newsletter. Anyone over 50 can join.

Many reliable agencies and organizations target the 50-plus market. **Elderhostel** (© 877/426-8056; www.elderhostel.org) arranges study programs for those 55 and over (and a spouse or companion of any age) in the U.S. and in more than 80 countries around the world. Most international courses last 2 to 4 weeks, and many include airfare, accommodations in university dormitories or modest inns, meals, and tuition. **ElderTreks** (© 800/741-7956; www.eldertreks.com) offers small-group tours to off-the-beaten-path or adventure-travel locations, restricted to travelers 50 and older. **INTRAV** (© 800/456-8100; www.intrav.com) is a high-end tour operator that caters to the mature traveler, not specifically seniors, with trips around the world that include guided safaris, polar expeditions, private-jet adventures, and small-boat cruises down jungle rivers.

Recommended publications offering travel resources and discounts for seniors include: the quarterly magazine *Travel 50 & Beyond* (www.travel50andbeyond.com) and *Travel Unlimited: Uncommon Adventures for the Mature Traveler* (Avalon).

FAMILY TRAVEL

If you have enough trouble getting your kids out of the house in the morning, dragging them thousands of miles away may seem like an insurmountable challenge. But family travel can be immensely rewarding, giving you new ways of seeing the world through smaller pairs of eyes.

Australians travel widely with their own kids, so facilities for families, including family passes to attractions, are common.

A great accommodations option for families is Australia's huge stock of serviced or unserviced apartments (with or without daily maid service). Often less expensive than a hotel room, they offer a living room, a kitchen, a bathroom or two, and the privacy of a separate bedroom for adults. "Tips on Accommodations," later in this chapter, has details on the major apartment chains. Most Australian hotels will arrange babysitting given a day's notice.

International airlines and domestic airlines in Australia charge 75% of the adult fare for kids under 12. Most charge 10% for infants under 2 not occupying a seat. Australian transport companies, attractions, and tour operators typically charge half price for kids under 12 or 14 years.

Many Australian resorts have "kids' clubs" with extensive programs designed for under-12s and, in some cases, teenagers. The French-owned Accor chain of hotels and resorts, which is Australia's largest chain, has kids' clubs, kids' menus designed by a nutritionist (and not just the same boring fodder you get everywhere else), and other family-friendly facilities including family rooms. Other resorts, such as Hamilton Island, have "kids stay, eat, and play free" offers, particularly during holiday periods. Many hotels will offer connecting units or "family rooms." Ask when booking, and look out for our "kid friendly" icon in this book.

Don't forget that children entering Australia on their parent's passport still need their own visa. See "Entry Requirements," earlier in this chapter.

Rascals in Paradise (© 415/921-7000; www.rascalsinparadise.com) sells family vacation packages to Australia.

Familyhostel (© 800/733-9753; www.learn.unh.edu/familyhostel) takes the whole family, including kids 8 to 16, on moderately priced domestic and international learning vacations. A team of academics guides lectures, field trips, and sightseeing.

You can find good family-oriented vacation advice on the Internet from sites like **Family Travel Forum** (www.familytravelforum.com), a comprehensive site that offers customized trip planning; the **Family Travel Network** (www.familytravelnetwork.com), an award-winning site that offers travel features, deals, and tips; **Traveling Internationally with Your Kids** (www.travelwithyourkids.com), a comprehensive site offering sound advice for long-distance and international travel with children; and **Family Travel Files** (www.thefamilytravelfiles.com), which offers an online magazine and a directory of off-the-beaten-path tours and tour operators for families.

WOMEN TRAVELERS

Women Welcome Women World Wide (5W; www.womenwelcomewomen.org.uk) works to foster international friendships by enabling women of different countries to visit one another (men can come along on the trips; they just can't join the club). It's a big, active organization, with more than 3,500 members from all walks of life in some 70 countries.

Check out the award-winning website **Journeywoman** (www.journeywoman.com), a "real life" women's travel information network where you can sign up for a free e-mail newsletter and get advice on everything from etiquette and dress to safety; or the travel guide *Safety and Security for Women Who Travel,* by Sheila Swan Laufer and Peter Laufer (Travelers' Tales, Inc.), offering common-sense advice and tips on safe travel.

STUDENT TRAVEL

If you're planning to travel to Australia, you'd be wise to arm yourself with an **International Student Identity Card**

(ISIC), which offers substantial savings on rail passes, plane tickets, and entrance fees. It also provides you with basic health and life insurance and a 24-hour help line. The card is available for $22 from **STA Travel** (© **800/781-4040,** and outside North America there's probably a local number in your country; www.sta.com or www.statravel.com), the biggest student travel agency in the world. If you're no longer a student but are under 26, you can get an **International Youth Travel Card (IYTC)** for the same price from the same people, which entitles you to some discounts (but not on museum admissions).

Travel CUTS (© **800/592-2887;** www.travelcuts.com) offers similar services for both Canadians and U.S. residents. Irish students should turn to **USIT** (© **01/602-1904;** www.usit.ie).

SINGLE TRAVELERS

Many people prefer traveling alone, and for independent travelers, solo journeys offer infinite opportunities to make friends and meet locals. Unfortunately, if you like resorts, tours, or cruises, you're likely to get hit with a "single supplement" to the base price. Single travelers can avoid these supplements by agreeing to room with other single travelers on the trip. An even better idea is to find a compatible roommate before you go from one of the many roommate locator agencies. **Travel Buddies Singles Travel Club** (© **800/998-9099;** www.travelbuddies worldwide.com), based in Canada, runs small, intimate, single-friendly group trips to a range of destinations, including Australia, and will match you with a roommate free of charge. **TravelChums** (© **212/787-2621;** www.travelchums. com) is an Internet-only travel-companion matching service with elements of an online personals-type site, hosted by the respected New York–based Shaw Guides travel service. Many reputable tour companies offer singles-only trips. **Backroads** (© **800/462-2848;** www.backroads.com) offers more than 130 active trips to 90 destinations worldwide, including Australia.

For more information, check out the latest edition of Eleanor Berman's *Traveling Solo: Advice and Ideas for More Than 250 Great Vacations* (Globe Pequot), a guide with advice on traveling alone, whether on your own or on a group tour. Or turn to the **Travel Alone and Love It** website (www.travelalone andloveit.com), designed by former flight attendant Sharon Wingler, the author of the book of the same name. Her site is full of tips for single travelers.

9 Planning Your Trip Online

SURFING FOR AIRFARES

The "big three" online travel agencies— **Expedia.com, Travelocity.com,** and **Orbitz.com**—sell most of the air tickets bought on the Internet. (Canadian travelers should try expedia.ca and Travelocity.ca; U.K. residents can go for expedia. co.uk and opodo.co.uk.) Each has different business deals with the airlines and may offer different fares on the same flights, so it's wise to shop around. Expedia and Travelocity will also send you **e-mail notification** when a cheap fare to your favorite destination becomes available. Of the smaller travel agency websites, **SideStep** (www.sidestep.com) has gotten the best reviews from Frommer's authors. It's a browser add-on that purports to "search 140 sites at once," but in reality only beats competitors' fares as often as other sites do.

Also remember to check **airline websites.** Even with major airlines, you can often shave a few bucks from a fare by booking directly through the airline and avoiding a travel agency's transaction fee. But you'll get these discounts only by **booking online:** Most airlines now

> **Tips** **Frommers.com: The Complete Travel Resource**
>
> For an excellent travel-planning resource, we highly recommend **Frommers.com** (www.frommers.com), voted Best Travel Site by *PC Magazine*. We're a little biased, of course, but we guarantee that you'll find the travel tips, reviews, monthly vacation giveaways, bookstore, and online-booking capabilities thoroughly indispensable. Among the special features are our popular **Destinations** section, where you'll get expert travel tips, hotel and dining recommendations, and advice on the sights to see for more than 3,500 destinations around the globe; the **Frommers.com Newsletter,** with the latest deals, travel trends, and money-saving secrets; our **Community** area featuring **Message Boards,** where Frommer's readers post queries and share advice (sometimes even our authors show up to answer questions); and our **Photo Center,** where you can post and share vacation tips. When your research is done, the **Online Reservations System** (www.frommers.com/book_a_trip) takes you to Frommer's preferred online partners for booking your vacation at affordable prices.

offer online-only fares that even their phone agents know nothing about. For the websites of airlines that fly to and from Australia, go to "Getting There," later in this chapter.

Great **last-minute deals** are available through free weekly e-mail services provided directly by the airlines. Most of these are announced on Tuesday or Wednesday and must be purchased online. Most are only valid for travel that weekend, but some can be booked weeks or months in advance. Sign up for weekly e-mail alerts at airline websites or check megasites that compile comprehensive lists of last-minute specials, such as **Smarter Travel** (smartertravel.com). For last-minute trips, **site59.com** and **lastminutetravel.com** in the U.S. and **lastminute.com** in Europe often have better air-and-hotel package deals than the major-label sites. A website listing numerous bargain sites and airlines around the world is **www.itravelnet.com**.

If you're willing to give up some control over your flight details, use a so-called **"opaque" fare service** like **Priceline** (www.priceline.com; www.priceline.co.uk for Europeans) or its smaller competitor **Hotwire** (www.hotwire.com). Both offer rock-bottom prices in exchange for travel on a "mystery airline" at a mysterious time of day, often with a mysterious change of planes en route. The mystery airlines are all major, well-known carriers—but your chances of getting a 6am or 11pm flight are pretty high. Hotwire tells you flight prices before you buy; Priceline usually has better deals than Hotwire, but you have to play their "name our price" game. If you're new at this, the helpful folks at **BiddingForTravel** (www.biddingfortravel.com) do a good job of demystifying Priceline's prices.

Priceline and Hotwire are great for flights within North America and between the U.S. and Europe. But for flights to other parts of the world, consolidators will almost always beat their fares. *Note:* In 2004, Priceline added non-opaque service to its roster. You now have the option to pick exact flights, times, and airlines from a list of offers—or opt to bid on opaque fares as before.

For much more about airfares and savvy air-travel tips and advice, pick up a copy of *Frommer's Fly Safe, Fly Smart* (Wiley Publishing, Inc.).

SURFING FOR HOTELS

Shopping online for hotels is generally done by booking one of two ways: through the hotel's own website or through an independent booking agency (or a fare-service agency like Priceline; see below). Regardless of how you book, it's a good idea to **get a confirmation number** and **make a printout** of any online booking transaction.

Internet hotel agencies have multiplied in mind-boggling numbers of late, competing for the business of millions of consumers surfing for accommodations around the world.

This competitiveness can be a boon to consumers who have the patience and time to shop and compare the online sites for good deals—but shop they must, for prices can vary considerably from site to site. And keep in mind that hotels at the top of a site's listings may be there for no other reason than that they paid for the placement.

Shopping online for hotels is much easier in the U.S., Canada, and certain parts of Europe than it is in the rest of the world, but Australian hotels—even the small ones—are pretty Internet savvy, as are B&Bs. Of the "big three" sites, **Expedia** offers a long list of special deals and "virtual tours" or photos of available rooms so you can see what you're paying for (a feature that helps counter the claims that the best rooms are often held back from bargain-booking websites). **Travelocity** runs a close second and posts unvarnished customer reviews. Also reliable are Hotels.com and Quikbook.com. An excellent free program, **TravelAxe** (www.travelaxe.com), can help you search multiple hotel sites at once, even ones you may never have heard of—and conveniently lists the total price of the room, including the taxes and service charges.

Another booking site, **Travelweb** (www.travelweb.com), is partly owned by the hotels it represents (including the Hilton, Hyatt, and Starwood chains) and is therefore plugged directly into the hotels' reservations systems—unlike independent online agencies, which have to fax or e-mail reservation requests to the hotel, a good portion of which get misplaced in the shuffle. More than once, travelers have arrived at the hotel, only to be told that they have no reservation. To be fair, many of the major sites are undergoing improvements in service and ease of use, and Expedia will soon be able to plug directly into the reservations systems of many hotel chains—none of which can be bad news for consumers.

SURFING FOR RENTAL CARS

For booking rental cars online, the best deals are usually found at rental-car company websites, although all the major online travel agencies also offer rental-car reservations services. Priceline and Hotwire work well for rental cars, too; the only "mystery" is which major rental company you get, and for most travelers the difference between Hertz, Avis, and Budget is negligible.

10 The 21st-Century Traveler

INTERNET ACCESS AWAY FROM HOME

Travelers have any number of ways to check their e-mail and surf the Internet on the road. Of course, using your own laptop—or PDA (personal digital assistant) or electronic organizer with a modem—gives you the most flexibility. But even if you don't have a computer, you can still check your e-mail and even use your office computer from cyber-cafes.

WITHOUT YOUR OWN COMPUTER

It's hard nowadays to find a city that *doesn't* have a few cybercafes, and that certainly applies in Australia. Although there's no definitive directory for cybercafes—these are independent businesses, after all—two places to start looking are at **www.cybercaptive.com** and **www.cybercafe.com**. In major tourist cities like Cairns and Darwin, there are whole streets full of cybercafes. Aside from formal cybercafes, most **youth hostels** nowadays have at least one computer with Internet access. And most **public libraries** offer Internet access free or for a small charge. Avoid **hotel business centers** unless you're willing to pay exorbitant rates.

Most major airports now have **Internet kiosks** scattered throughout their gates. These kiosks, which you'll also see in shopping malls, hotel lobbies, and tourist information offices around the world, give you basic Web access for a per-minute fee that's usually higher than cybercafe prices. The kiosks' clunkiness and high price means they should be avoided whenever possible.

To retrieve your e-mail, ask your **Internet service provider (ISP)** if it has a Web-based interface tied to your existing e-mail account. If your ISP doesn't have such an interface, you can use the free **mail2web** service (www.mail2web.com) to view and reply to your home e-mail. For more flexibility, you may want to open a free, Web-based e-mail account with **Yahoo! Mail** (mail.yahoo.com). (Microsoft's Hotmail is another popular option, but Hotmail has severe spam problems.) Your home ISP may be able to forward your e-mail to the Web-based account automatically.

If you need access to files on your office computer, look into a service called **GoToMyPC** (www.gotomypc.com). It provides a Web-based interface for you to manipulate a distant PC from any-where—even a cybercafe—provided your "target" PC is on and has an always-on connection to the Internet (such as with Road Runner cable). The service offers top-quality security, but if you're worried about hackers, use your own laptop rather than a cybercafe computer to log onto the GoToMyPC system.

WITH YOUR OWN COMPUTER

Wi-Fi (wireless fidelity) is the buzzword in computer access, and more and more hotels, cafes, and retailers are signing on as wireless "hot spots" from which you can establish a high-speed connection without cable wires, networking hardware, or a phone line (see below). You can get Wi-Fi connection one of several ways. Many laptops sold recently have built-in Wi-Fi capability (an 802.11b wireless Ethernet connection). Mac owners have their own networking technology, Apple AirPort. For those with older computers, an 802.11b/**Wi-Fi card** (around $50) can be plugged into your laptop. You sign up for wireless access service much as you do for cellphone service, through a plan offered by one of several commercial companies that have made wireless service available in airports, hotel lobbies, and coffee shops, primarily in the U.S. (followed by the U.K. and Japan). **Boingo** (www.boingo.com) and **Wayport** (www.wayport.com) have set up networks in airports and high-class hotel lobbies. IPass providers (see below) also give you access to a few hundred wireless hotel lobby setups. Best of all, you don't need to be staying at the hotel to use the its network; just set yourself up on a nice couch in the lobby. The companies' pricing policies can be byzantine, with a variety of monthly, per-connection, and per-minute plans, but in general you pay around $30 a month for limited access—and as more and more companies jump on the wireless bandwagon, prices are likely to get even more competitive.

Cities around the world also have places that provide **free wireless networks.** To locate them, go to **www.personaltelco.net/index.cgi/Wireless Communities**.

In addition, major Internet service providers (ISPs) have **local access numbers** around the world, allowing you to go online by simply placing a local call. Check your ISP's website or call its toll-free number and ask how you can use your current account away from home, and how much it will cost.

If you're traveling outside the reach of your ISP, the **iPass** network has dial-up numbers in most of the world's countries. You'll have to sign up with an iPass provider, which will then tell you how to set up your computer for your destination(s). For a list of iPass providers, go to www.ipass.com and click on "Individual Purchase." One solid provider is **i2roam** (www.i2roam.com; ℂ **866/811-6209** or 920/233-5863).

Wherever you go, bring a **connection kit** of the right power and phone adapters, a spare phone cord, and a spare Ethernet network cable—or find out whether your hotel supplies them to guests. Australia's electricity supply is 240 volts, 50 Hz. North Americans and Europeans will need to buy a converter before they leave home, because Australian stores usually only stock converters for Aussie appliances to fit American and European outlets.

USING A CELLPHONE IN AUSTRALIA

The three letters that define much of the world's **wireless capabilities** are GSM (Global System for Mobiles), a big, seamless network that makes for easy cross-border cellphone use throughout Europe and dozens of other countries worldwide. In the U.S., T-Mobile, AT&T Wireless, and Cingular use this quasi-universal system; in Canada, Microcell, and some Rogers customers are GSM, and all Europeans and most Australians use GSM.

If your cellphone is on a GSM system, and you have a world-capable multiband phone such as many (but not all) Sony Ericsson, Motorola, or Samsung models, you can make and receive calls across civilized areas on much of the globe. Just call your wireless operator and ask for "international roaming" to be activated on your account. Unfortunately, per-minute charges can be high.

That's why it's important to buy an "unlocked" world phone from the get-go. Many companies sell "locked" phones that restrict you from using any other removable computer memory phone chip (called a **SIM card**) other than the ones they supply. Having an unlocked phone allows you to install a cheap, prepaid SIM card (found at a local retailer) in your destination country. (Show your phone to the salesperson; not all phones work on all networks.) You'll get a local phone number—and much, much lower calling rates. Getting an already locked phone unlocked can be a complicated process, but it can be done; just call your cellular operator and say you'll be going abroad for several months and want to use the phone with a local provider.

For many, **renting** a cellphone is a good idea. In Australia—reputed to have one of the world's highest per-capita rates of ownership of "mobile" telephones, as they are known here—they are available for daily rental at major airports and in big cities, and increasingly from car- and motor-home-rental companies. The cell network is digital, not analog. Calls to or from a mobile telephone are generally more expensive than calls to or from a fixed telephone—A60¢ (US40¢) a minute is a ballpark guide, although the price varies depending on the telephone company, the time of day, the distance between caller and recipient, and the telephone's pricing plan.

An advantage of renting the phone before you leave home is that way you can give loved ones and business associates your new number, make sure the phone works, and take the phone wherever you go—especially helpful for overseas trips through several countries, where local phone-rental agencies often bill in local currency and may not let you take the phone to another country.

In Australia, mobile phone company **Vodafone** (www.vodarent.com.au) has outlets at Brisbane, Cairns, Perth, and Melbourne international airports, Sydney international and domestic airports and at stores in Surfers Paradise on the Gold Coast. They cost A$6 to A$10 (US$4.80–US$8) a day, plus call charges and insurance, depending on the kind of phone and coverage you want. You can rent a SIM card for A$1 (US80¢) a day.

Two good wireless rental companies are **InTouch USA** (© 800/872-7626;

www.intouchglobal.com) and **RoadPost** (© 888/290-1616 or 905/272-5665; www.roadpost.com). Give them your itinerary, and they'll tell you what wireless products you need. InTouch will also, for free, advise you on whether your existing phone will work overseas; simply call © 703/222-7161 between 9am and 4pm Eastern Standard Time, or go to http://in touchglobal.com/travel.htm.

For trips of more than a few weeks spent in one country, **buying a phone** becomes economically attractive, because many nations have cheap, no-questions-asked prepaid phone systems. Once you arrive at your destination, stop by a local cellphone shop and get the cheapest package; you'll probably pay less than US$100 for a phone and a starter calling card. Local calls may be as low as US10¢ per minute, and in many countries incoming calls are free.

Tips Online Traveler's Toolbox

Veteran travelers usually carry some essential items to make their trips easier. Following is a selection of handy online tools to bookmark and use.

- **Visa ATM Locator** (www.visa.com), for locations of Plus ATMs worldwide, or **MasterCard ATM Locator** (www.mastercard.com), for locations of Cirrus ATMs worldwide.
- **Intellicast** (www.intellicast.com) and **Weather.com** (www.weather.com). Gives weather forecasts for all 50 states and for cities around the world.
- **Mapquest** (www.mapquest.com). This best of the mapping sites lets you choose a specific address or destination, and in seconds, it will return a map and detailed directions.
- **Universal Currency Converter** (www.xe.com/ucc). See what your dollar or pound is worth in more than 100 other countries.
- **Time and Date** (www.timeanddate.com). See what time (and day) it is anywhere in the world.
- **Travel Warnings** (http://travel.state.gov, www.voyage.gc.ca, www.smartraveller.gov.au). These sites report on places where health concerns or unrest might threaten American, British, Canadian, and Australian travelers. Generally, U.S. warnings are the most paranoid; Australian warnings are the most relaxed.

True wilderness adventurers, or those planning on spending time in the Outback or other remote areas, should consider renting a **satellite phone**. "Satphones" are different from cellphones in that they connect to satellites rather than ground-based towers. A satphone is more costly than a cellphone but works where there's no cellular signal and no towers. You can rent satellite phones from **RoadPost** (ⓒ **888/290-1616** or 905/272-5665; www.roadpost.com). InTouch USA (see above) offers a wider range of satphones but at higher rates. Per-minute call charges can be even cheaper than roaming charges with a regular cellphone, but the phone itself is more expensive (up to US$150 a week), and depending on the service you choose, people calling you may incur high long-distance charges. As of this writing, satphones were very expensive to buy.

11 Getting There

BY PLANE

Australia is a long, long haul from anywhere except New Zealand. Sydney is a nearly 15-hour nonstop flight from Los Angeles, longer if you come via Honolulu. From the East Coast, add 5½ hours. If you're coming from the States via Auckland, add transit time in New Zealand plus another 3 hours for the Auckland-Sydney leg. If you are coming from the United Kingdom, brace yourself for a flight of 12 hours, more or less, from London to Asia; then possibly a long day in transit, because flights to Australia have a habit of arriving in Asia early in the morning and departing around midnight; and finally the 8- to 9-hour flight to Australia.

Sydney, Cairns, Melbourne, Brisbane, Adelaide, Darwin, and Perth are all international gateways, but most airlines fly only into Sydney. A few fly to Melbourne and Brisbane.

THE MAJOR CARRIERS

Here are toll-free reservations numbers and websites for the major international airlines serving Australia. The "13" prefix in Australia means that the number incurs the same cost as a local call from anywhere in the country.

CARRIERS FLYING FROM NORTH AMERICA

- **Air Canada** (ⓒ **888/247-2262** in the U.S. and Canada, 02/8248 5757 in Sydney, or 1300/655 767 from elsewhere in Australia; www.aircanada.com).
- **Air New Zealand** (ⓒ **800/262-1234** in the U.S., 310/615-1111 in the Los Angeles area, 800/663-5494 in Canada, or 13 24 76 in Australia; www.airnewzealand.com).
- **Qantas** (ⓒ **800/227-4500** in the U.S. and Canada, or 13 13 13 in Australia; www.qantas.com.au).
- **United Airlines** (ⓒ **800/538-2929** in the U.S. and Canada, or 13 17 77 in Australia; www.united.com or www.united.ca).

CARRIERS FLYING FROM THE UNITED KINGDOM

- **British Airways** (ⓒ **0870/850 9850** in the U.K., 1890/626 747 in Ireland, or 1300/767 177 in Australia; www.britishairways.com).
- **Cathay Pacific** (ⓒ **020/8834 8888** in the U.K., or 13 17 47 in Australia; www.cathaypacific.com/uk).
- **Malaysia Airlines** (ⓒ **0870/607 9090** in the U.K. and Ireland, or 13 26 27 in Australia; www.malaysiaairlines.com.my or www.malaysiaairlineseurope.com).
- **Qantas** (ⓒ **0845/774 7767** in the U.K., or 13 13 13 in Australia; www.qantas.com.au).
- **Singapore Airlines** (ⓒ **0870/608 8886** in the U.K., or 13 10 11 in Australia; www.singaporeair.com/uk).

• **Thai Airways International** (© **0870/6060 911** in the U.K., or 1300/651 960 in Australia; www.thaiair.com).

GETTING THROUGH THE AIRPORT

With the federalization of airport security, security procedures at U.S. airports are more stable and consistent than ever. Generally, you'll be fine if you arrive **1 hour** before a domestic flight and **2 hours** before an international flight; if you show up late, tell an airline employee and you'll probably be whisked to the front of the line.

Bring a **current, government-issued photo ID** such as a driver's license or passport. Keep your ID ready to show at check-in, the security checkpoint, and sometimes the gate. If you have an e-ticket, print out the **official confirmation page;** you'll need to show your confirmation at the security checkpoint. (Children under 18 do not need government-issued photo IDs for domestic flights, but they do for international flights to most destinations.)

In 2003, the TSA phased out **gate check-in** at all U.S. airports. And **e-tickets** have made paper tickets nearly obsolete. Passengers with e-tickets can beat ticket-counter lines by using airport **electronic kiosks** or even **online check-in** from your home computer. Online check-in involves logging on to the airline website, finding your reservation, and printing out your boarding pass—and the airline may even offer you bonus miles to do so! If you're using a kiosk at the airport, bring the credit card you used to book the ticket or your frequent-flier card. Print out your boarding pass from the kiosk and simply proceed to the security checkpoint with your pass and a photo ID. If you're checking bags or looking to snag an exit-row seat, you will be able to do so using most airline kiosks. Even the smaller airlines are employing the kiosk

system, but always call your airline to make sure these alternatives are available. **Curbside check-in** is also a good way to avoid lines, although a few airlines still ban curbside check-in; call before you go.

Security lines are getting shorter, but some doozies remain. If you have trouble standing for long periods, tell an airline employee; the airline will provide a wheelchair. Speed up security by **not wearing metal objects** such as big belt buckles or clanky earrings. If you have metallic body parts, a note from your doctor can prevent a long chat with the security screeners. Keep in mind that only **ticketed passengers** are allowed past security, except for folks escorting passengers with disabilities or children.

Federalization has stabilized **what you can carry on** and **what you can't.** The general rule is that sharp things are out, nail clippers are okay, and food and beverages must be passed through the X-ray machine—but that security screeners can't make you drink from your coffee cup. Bring food in your carry-on rather than checking it, as explosive-detection machines used on checked luggage have been known to mistake food (especially chocolate, for some reason) for bombs. Travelers in the U.S. are allowed one carry-on bag, plus a "personal item" such as a purse, briefcase, or laptop bag. Carry-on hoarders can stuff all sorts of things into a laptop bag; as long as it has a laptop in it, it's still considered a personal item. The Transportation Security Administration (TSA) has issued a list of restricted items; check its website (www.tsa.gov/public/index.jsp) for details. Airport screeners may decide that your checked luggage needs to be searched by hand. You can purchase luggage locks that allow screeners to open and relock a checked bag if hand-searching is necessary. Look for Travel Sentry certified locks at luggage or travel shops and Brookstone stores (you can buy them online at www.brookstone.com). These locks, approved by the TSA, can be opened by luggage inspectors with a special code or key. For more information on the locks, visit www.travelsentry.org. If you use something other than TSA-approved locks, your lock will be cut off your suitcase if a TSA agent needs to hand-search your luggage.

FLYING FOR LESS: TIPS FOR GETTING THE BEST AIRFARE

If you're flying from the U.S., keep in mind that the airlines' low season is from mid-April to the end of August—and this happens to be the best time to visit most parts of Australia. High season is December through February; shoulder season is March to mid-April and September through November.

Keep an eye out for special deals throughout the year. Unexpectedly low passenger loads often lead airlines to put cheap offers on the market. The catch is these usually have a short lead time, requiring you to travel in the next 6 weeks or so. Some deals involve taking a circuitous route, via Fiji or Japan, for instance.

Some travel agents specializing in cheap fares include **Austravel** (© **0870/166 2020** in the U.K.; www.austravel.net); **Downunder Direct,** a division of Swain Australia (© **800/642-6224** in the U.S. and Canada; www.downunderdirect. com); and **Goway** (© **800/387-8850** in the U.S. and Canada; www.goway.com).

Here are some other ways to keep your airfare costs down.

- Passengers who can book their ticket **long in advance,** who can **stay over Saturday night,** or who **fly midweek** or **at less-trafficked hours** may pay a fraction of the full fare. If your schedule is flexible, say so, and ask if you can secure a cheaper fare by changing your flight plans.

- You can also save on airfares by keeping an eye out in local newspapers for **promotional specials** or **fare wars,** when airlines lower prices on their most popular routes. You rarely see fare wars offered for peak travel times, but if you can travel in the off-months, you may snag a bargain.

- **Search the Internet** for cheap fares (see "Planning Your Trip Online," earlier in this chapter).

- Try to book a ticket **in its country of origin.** For instance, if you're planning a one-way flight from Sydney to Auckland, an Australia-based travel agent such as Flight Centres will probably have the lowest fares. For multileg trips, book in the country of

---

Tips Don't Stow It—Ship It

If ease of travel is your main concern and money is no object, you can ship your luggage and sports equipment with one of the growing number of luggage-service companies that pick up, track, and deliver your luggage (often through couriers such as Federal Express) with minimum hassle for you. Traveling luggage-free may be ultraconvenient, but it's not cheap: One-way overnight shipping can cost from $100 to $200, depending on what you're sending. Still, for some people, especially the elderly or the infirm, it's a sensible solution to lugging heavy baggage. Specialists in door-to-door luggage delivery are **Virtual Bellhop** (www.virtualbellhop.com), **SkyCap International** (wwww.skycap international.com), **Luggage Express** (www.usxpluggageexpress.com), and **Sports Express** (www.sportsexpress.com).

> **Tips** **Travel in the Age of Bankruptcy**
>
> Airlines can go bankrupt, so protect yourself by **buying your tickets with a credit card.** The Fair Credit Billing Act guarantees that you can get your money back from the credit card company if a travel supplier goes under (and if you request the refund within 60 days of the bankruptcy). **Travel insurance** can also help, but make sure it covers "carrier default" for your specific travel provider. And be aware that if a U.S. airline goes bust midtrip, a 2001 federal law requires other carriers to take you to your destination (albeit on a space-available basis) for a fee of no more than $25, provided you rebook within 60 days of the cancellation.

the first leg; for example, book Melbourne–Auckland–Los Angeles in Australia.

- **Consolidators,** also known as bucket shops, are great sources for international tickets. Start by looking in Sunday newspaper travel sections; U.S. travelers should focus on the *New York Times, Los Angeles Times,* and *Miami Herald.* **Beware:** Bucket shop tickets are usually nonrefundable or rigged with stiff cancellation penalties, often as high as 50% to 75% of the ticket price, and some put you on charter airlines, which may leave at inconvenient times or experience delays. Several reliable consolidators are worldwide and available on the Net. **STA Travel** (© **800/781-4040;** www.statravel.com) is now the world's leader in student travel, thanks to its purchase of Council Travel. It also offers good fares for travelers of all ages.
- Join **frequent-flier clubs.** Accrue enough miles, and you'll be rewarded with free flights and elite status. It's free, and you'll get the best choice of seats, faster response to phone inquiries, and prompter service if your luggage is stolen, your flight is canceled or delayed, or if you want to change your seat. You don't need to fly to build frequent-flier miles—**frequent-flier credit**

cards can provide thousands of miles for doing your everyday shopping.

- For many more tips about air travel, including a rundown of the major frequent-flier credit cards, pick up a copy of *Frommer's Fly Safe, Fly Smart* (Wiley Publishing, Inc.).

LONG-HAUL FLIGHTS: HOW TO STAY COMFORTABLE

Long flights can be trying; stuffy air and cramped seats can make you feel as if you're being sent parcel post in a small box. But with a little advance planning, you can make an otherwise unpleasant experience almost bearable.

- Your choice of airline and airplane will definitely affect your legroom. Research firm Skytrax has posted a list of average seat pitches for international airlines at www.airlinequality.com.
- Emergency-exit seats and bulkhead seats typically have the most legroom. Emergency-exit seats are usually held back to be assigned the day of a flight (to ensure that the seat is filled by someone able-bodied); it's worth getting to the ticket counter early to snag one of these spots for a long flight. Many passengers find that bulkhead seats (in the row facing the wall at the front of the cabin) offer more legroom, but keep in mind that bulkheads are where airlines often

put baby bassinets, so you may be sitting next to an infant.

- To have two seats for yourself in a three-seat row, try for an aisle seat in a center section toward the back of coach. If you're traveling with a companion, book an aisle and a window seat. Middle seats are usually booked last, so chances are good you'll end up with three seats to yourselves. And in the event that a third passenger is assigned the middle seat, he or she will probably be more than happy to trade for a window or an aisle.

- Ask about entertainment options. Many airlines offer seat-back video systems where you get to choose your movies or play video games—but only on some of their planes. (Boeing 777s are your best bet.)

- To sleep, avoid the last row of any section or a row in front of an emergency exit, as these seats are the least likely to recline. Avoid seats near highly trafficked toilet areas. Avoid seats in the back of many jets—they can be narrower than those in the rest of coach class. You also may want to reserve a window seat so that you can rest your head and avoid being bumped in the aisle.

- Get up, walk around, and stretch every 60 to 90 minutes to keep your blood flowing. This helps avoid **deep vein thrombosis,** or "economy-class syndrome," a potentially deadly condition that can be caused by sitting in cramped conditions for too long (see the box "Avoiding 'Economy-Class Syndrome,'" earlier in this chapter). Other preventive measures include drinking lots of water and avoiding alcohol (see next paragraph).

- Drink water before, during, and after your flight to combat the lack of humidity in airplane cabins—which

---

Tips Coping with Jet Lag

Jet lag is a pitfall of traveling across time zones. If you're flying north-south, say from Canada to Australia, and you feel sluggish when you touch down, your symptoms will be caused by dehydration and the general stress of air travel. When you travel east to west or vice-versa, however, your body becomes thoroughly confused about what time it is, and everything from your digestion to your brain gets knocked for a loop. Traveling east is more difficult on your internal clock than traveling west, as most people's bodies find it more acceptable to stay up late than to fall asleep early.

Here are some tips for combating jet lag:

- **Reset your watch** to your destination time before you board the plane.
- **Drink lots of water** before, during, and after your flight. Avoid alcohol.
- **Exercise and sleep well** for a few days before your trip.
- If you have trouble sleeping on planes, **fly eastward on morning flights.**
- **Daylight** is the key to resetting your body clock. At the website for **Outside In** (www.bodyclock.com), you can get a customized plan of when to seek and avoid light.
- If you need help getting to sleep earlier than you usually would, some doctors recommend taking either the hormone **melatonin** or the sleeping pill **Ambien**—but not together. Some recommend that you take 2 to 5 milligrams of melatonin about 2 hours before your planned bedtime—but again, always check with your doctor on the best course of action for you.

Tips **Flying with Film & Video**

Never pack film—developed or undeveloped—in checked bags, as the new, more powerful scanners in U.S. airports can fog film. The film you carry with you can be damaged by scanners as well. X-ray damage is cumulative; the faster the film and the more times you put it through a scanner, the more likely the damage. Film under 800 ASA is usually safe for up to five scans. If you're taking your film through additional scans, U.S. regulations permit you to demand hand inspections. In international airports, you're at the mercy of airport officials. On international flights, store your film in transparent bags, so you can remove it easily before you go through scanners. Keep in mind that airports are not the only places where your camera may be scanned: Highly trafficked attractions are X-raying visitors' bags with increasing frequency.

Most photo supply stores sell protective pouches designed to block damaging X-rays. The pouches fit both film and loaded cameras. They should protect your film in checked baggage, but they also may raise alarms and result in a hand inspection.

You'll have little to worry about if you are traveling with a **digital camera**. Unlike film, which is sensitive to light, the digital camera and storage cards are not affected by airport X-rays, according to Nikon. Still, if you plan to travel extensively, you may want to play it safe and hand-carry your digital equipment or ask that it be inspected by hand. See "Digital Photography on the Road," p. 61.

An organization called **Film Safety for Traveling on Planes (FSTOP;** ℂ **888/301-2665;** www.f-stop.org) can provide additional tips for traveling with film and equipment.

Carry-on scanners will not damage **videotape** in video cameras, but the magnetic fields emitted by the walk-through security gateways and hand-held inspection wands will. Always place your loaded camcorder on the screening conveyor belt or have it hand-inspected. Be sure your batteries are charged, because you may be required to turn the device on to ensure that it's what it appears to be.

---

can be drier than the Sahara. Bring a bottle of water on board. Avoid alcohol, which will dehydrate you.
• If you're flying with kids, don't forget to carry on toys, books, pacifiers, and

chewing gum to help them relieve ear pressure buildup during ascent and descent. Let each child pack his or her own backpack with favorite toys.

12 Packages for the Independent Traveler

Before you start your search for the lowest airfare, you may want to consider booking your flight as part of a travel package. Package tours are not the same

thing as escorted tours. Package tours are simply a way to buy the airfare, accommodations, and other elements of your trip (such as car rentals, airport transfers, and sometimes even activities) at the same time and often at discounted prices—kind of like one-stop shopping. Tour operators buy packages in bulk and resell them to the public at a cost that usually undercuts standard rates.

Several big **online travel agencies**—Expedia, Travelocity, Orbitz, Site59, and Lastminute.com—also do a brisk business in packages. If you're unsure about the pedigree of a smaller packager, check with the Better Business Bureau in the city where the company is based, or go online at www.bbb.org. If a packager won't tell you where it's based, don't fly with it.

Austravel (© **0870/166-2020** in the U.K.; www.austravel.net) offers independent packages Down Under. The following companies offer both independent and escorted tours: **ATS Tours** (© **888/781-5170** in the U.S. and Canada; www.ats tours.com); **Collette Vacations** (© **401/727-9000** in the U.S., 800/468-5955 in Canada, or 0800/0921-888 in the U.K.; www.collettevacations.com); **Goway** (© **800/387-8850** in the U.S. and Canada; www.goway.com); **Maupintour** (© **800/255-4266** in the U.S. and Canada; www.maupintour.com); **Qantas Vacations** (© **800/348-8145** in the U.S., or 800/348-8137 in Canada; www.qantas vacations.com); **Sunbeam Tours** (© **800/955-1818** in the U.S. and Canada; www.sunbeamtours.com); **Swain Australia Tours** (© **800/22-SWAIN** in the U.S. and Canada; www.swainaustralia. com); Swain Australia's budget-travel division, **Downunder Direct** (© **800/642-6224** in the U.S. and Canada; www.down underdirect.com); and **United Vacations** (© **800/377-1816** in the U.S. and Canada; www.unitedvacations.com). Swain Australia is operated and largely staffed by Aussies. Collette Vacations, Sunbeam Tours, Swain Australia, and Goway have offices in Australia.

Travel packages are also listed in the travel section of your local Sunday newspaper. Or check ads in the national travel magazines such as *Arthur Frommer's Budget Travel Magazine, Travel & Leisure, National Geographic Traveler,* and *Condé Nast Traveler.*

Package tours can vary by leaps and bounds. Some offer a better class of hotels than others. Some offer the same hotels for lower prices. Some offer flights on

---

Tips Digital Photography on the Road

Many travelers are going digital these days when it comes to taking vacation photographs. Not only are digital cameras relatively unaffected by airport X-rays, but with digital equipment you don't need to lug armloads of film as you travel. In fact, nowadays you don't even need to carry your laptop to download the day's images to make room for more. With a **media storage card,** sold by all major camera dealers, you can store hundreds of images in your camera. These "memory" cards come in different configurations—from memory sticks to flash cards to secure digital cards—and different storage capacities (the more megabytes of memory, the more images a card can hold). They range in price from $30 to over $200. (*Note:* Each camera model works with a specific type of card, so you'll need to determine which storage card is compatible with your camera.) When you get home, you can print the images on your color printer or take the storage card to a camera store, drugstore, or chain retailer. Or have the images developed online with a service like **Snapfish** (www.snapfish.com) for something like 25¢ a shot. See "Flying with Film & Video," p. 60.

scheduled airlines, while others book charters. Some limit your choice of accommodations and travel days. You are often required to make a large payment upfront. On the plus side, packages can save you money, offering group prices but allowing for independent travel. Some even let you add a few guided excursions or escorted day trips (also at prices lower than if you booked them yourself) without booking an entirely escorted tour.

Before you invest in a package tour, get some answers. Ask about the **accommodations choices** and prices for each.

Then look up the hotels' reviews in your Frommer's guide and check their rates online for your specific dates of travel. You'll also want to find out what **type of room** you get. If you need a certain type of room, ask for it; don't take whatever is thrown your way. Request a nonsmoking room, a quiet room, a room with a view, or whatever you fancy.

Finally, look for **hidden expenses.** Ask whether airport departure fees and taxes, for example, are included in the total cost.

13 Escorted General-Interest Tours

Escorted tours are structured group tours, with a group leader. The price usually includes everything from airfare to hotels, meals, tours, admission costs, and local transportation.

Connections Adventures (call Australian Pacific Touring ⓒ **800/290-8687** in the U.S.; Goway ⓒ **800/387-8850** in the U.S. and Canada, or 02/9262 4755 in Australia; www.connections1835.com. au), and **Contiki** (ⓒ **866/CONTIKI** in the U.S. and Canada, 09/300 1601 in New Zealand, or 02/9511 2200 in Australia; www.contiki.com) specialize in escorted tours for 18- to 35-year-olds. These trips attract a lot of Australians, too, so they are a good way to meet locals. **Premier Vacations** (ⓒ **800/321-6720** in the U.S. and Canada; www.premierdownunder. com) is another reliable escorted tour operator.

Many people derive a certain ease and security from escorted trips. Escorted tours—whether by bus, motorcoach, train, or boat—let travelers sit back and enjoy their trip without having to spend lots of time behind the wheel or worrying about details. You know your costs upfront; and there are few surprises. Escorted tours can take you to the maximum number of sights in the minimum amount of time with the least amount of

hassle—you don't have to sweat over the plotting and planning of a vacation schedule. Escorted tours are particularly convenient for people with limited mobility. They can also be a great way to make new friends.

On the downside, an escorted tour often requires a big deposit upfront, and lodging and dining choices are predetermined. You'll get little opportunity for serendipitous interactions with locals. The tours can be jam-packed with activities, leaving little room for individual sightseeing, whim, or adventure—plus they also often focus only on the heavily touristed sites, so you miss out on the lesser-known gems.

Before you invest in an escorted tour, ask about the **cancellation policy:** Is a deposit required? Can the company cancel the trip if it doesn't get enough people? Do you get a refund if the company cancels? If *you* cancel? How late can you cancel if you are unable to go? When do you pay in full? *Note:* If you choose an escorted tour, think strongly about purchasing trip-cancellation insurance, especially if the tour operator asks you to pay upfront. See the section on "Travel Insurance," p. 41.

You'll also want to get a complete **schedule** of the trip to find out how much sightseeing is planned each day and whether enough time has been allotted for relaxing or wandering solo.

The **size** of the group is also important to know upfront. Generally, the smaller the group, the more flexible the itinerary, and the less time you'll spend waiting for people to get on and off the bus. Find out the **demographics** of the group as well. What is the age range? What is the gender breakdown? Is this mostly a trip for couples or singles?

Discuss what is included in the **price.** You may have to pay for transportation to and from the airport. A box lunch may be included in an excursion, but drinks might cost extra. Tips may not be included. Find out if you will be charged if you decide to opt out of certain activities or meals.

Finally, if you plan to travel alone, you'll need to know if a **single supplement** will be charged and if the company can match you up with a roommate.

14 The Active Traveler

Australia's wide-open spaces and great weather cry out to even the most dedicated lazybones. Most operators and outfitters listed below specialize in adventure vacations for small groups. Meals, accommodations, equipment rental, and guides are usually included in their packages, though international airfares are not. Where you end up spending the night varies depending on the package you select—on a sea-kayaking trip, you almost always camp on the beach; on a hiking expedition you may stay at a wilderness lodge; and on a biking trip you often stop over at B&B-style lodgings. More information on the outdoor activities discussed below appears in the relevant regional chapters. *Tip:* Before you hit the outdoors, review the safety tips in the "Health & Safety" section, p. 43.

SCUBA DIVING

Diving Down Under is one of the best travel experiences in the world. There are good dive sites all around the coastline, not just on the Great Barrier Reef. A second barrier reef in Ningaloo Reef Marine Park stretches 260km (161 miles) off the coast of Western Australia. (See chapter 10 or Exmouth Diving Centre's website at www.exmouthdiving.com.au for a good description of dive sites there.) Not all the good sites are on coral. In Tasmania, for instance, you can dive kelp beds

popular with seals, and in South Australia you can cage-dive with great white sharks. For a rundown on the country's outstanding dive areas, see "The Best Diving & Snorkeling Sites" in chapter 1.

Wherever you find coral in Australia, you'll find dive companies offering learn-to-dive courses, day trips, and, in some cases, extended journeys on live-aboard vessels. Most international dive certificates, including PADI, NAUI, SSI, and BSAC, are recognized. It's easy to rent gear and wet suits wherever you go, or you can bring your own.

Beginners' courses are known as "open-water certification" and usually require 2 days of theory in a pool at the dive company's premises, followed by 2 or 3 days on a live-aboard boat where you make between four and nine dives, including a night dive if you opt for the 5-day course. Open-water certification courses range from an intensive 3 to 5 days, for which you can expect to pay about A$350 to A$600 (US$280–US$480). A 5-day course is seen as the best. When comparing the value offered by dive schools, keep in mind that if the practical section of your course does not take place on a live-aboard boat, you will have to budget for accommodations and meals. Most operators offer courses right up to instructor level. If you're pressed for time, a PADI Referral course might suit you. It allows you to do your theory work at home, do a few hours of pool work at a PADI dive center in your home country, and then spend 2 or 3 days in the Australian ocean doing your qualifying dives.

Remember to allow time in your itinerary for a medical exam in Australia (see the next paragraph), and expect the dive instructor to grill you on your theory again before you hit the water.

If you're already a certified diver, remember to bring your "C" card and log book. If you're going to do a dive course, you'll need a medical certificate from an Australian doctor that meets Australian standard AS4005.1, stating that you are fit for scuba diving. (An all-purpose physical is not enough.) Virtually all dive schools will arrange the medical exam for you; expect to pay around A$50 (US$40) for it. Remember, you must complete your last dive 24 hours before you fly in an aircraft. This catches a lot of people off guard when they are preparing to fly to their next destination the day after a visit to the Reef. You won't be able to helicopter off the Reef back to the mainland, either. Check to see if your travel insurance covers diving. **The Divers Alert Network** (© 800/446-2671; www.divers alertnetwork.org) sells diving insurance and has diving and nondiving medical emergency hot lines, and an information line for dive-related medical questions.

If you've never been diving and don't plan to become qualified, you can see what all the fuss is about on an "introductory" dive that lets you dive in the company of an instructor on a one-time basis, with a briefing beforehand. Most dive operators on the Great Barrier Reef and other dive locations offer introductory dives.

See "Exploring the Great Barrier Reef" in chapter 7 for more information.

For information on dive regions and operators, try the state tourism marketing boards' websites (see "Visitor Information," earlier in this chapter). Tourism Queensland's website (www.queensland holidays.com.au) has information on most dive operators working the Great Barrier Reef. If you know where you want to dive, you may obtain an even more detailed list of operators by bypassing the big tourism boards and contacting the local tourist office for a list of local dive operators. **Dive Queensland** (the Queensland Dive Tourism Association; © **07/4051 1510;** fax 07/4051 1519; www.dive-queensland. com.au) requires its member operators to abide by a code of ethics. Its website has a list of members and the services they offer. It includes a few in other states, too. Another good source is **Diversion Dive Travel & Training** (© **07/4039 0200;** www.diversionoz.com), a Cairns-based travel agent that specializes in dive holidays on the Great Barrier Reef, as well as in other good dive spots in Australia. It books day trips and extended diving excursions on a choice of live-aboard vessels, as well as dive courses, island resorts with diving, accommodations, and nondiving tours. It also sells diving insurance. Its proprietors are both dive instructors, and one of them is trained as a handicapped diving instructor for divers with disabilities.

Peter Stone's Dive Australia is a 608-page guidebook to more than 2,000 dive sites all over Australia. It by no means lists every site, but it does contain many sites off the dive-tourist trail (many not on the Great Barrier Reef), so divers in search of new territory may find it handy. It also contains

---

(Tips **Peak Time on the Reef**

August through January is peak visibility time on the Great Barrier Reef, but the marine life will amaze you any time of year.

a lot of background such as dive operators and associations, a chapter on Australian diving law, the nearest hyperbaric chambers, and travel tips. Order from the publisher, Oceans Enterprises (© **03/5182 5108;** www.oceans.com.au). The book costs A$42 (US$34) plus postage.

BUSHWALKING (HIKING)

With so much unique scenery and many rare animals and plants, it's not surprising that Australia is full of national parks crisscrossed with hiking trails. You're never far from a park with a bushwalk, whether it's an easy stroll, or a 6-day odyssey on the Cape-to-Cape trail in Western Australia.

A good Australian bushwalking Web page is **www.bushwalking.org.au**. The best place to get information about bushwalking is the National Parks & Wildlife Service, or its equivalent in each state; sources include:

- **Environmental Protection Agency** (QLD Parks & Wildlife Service; © **07/3227 7111;** www.epa.qld.gov. au).
- **NSW National Parks & Wildlife Service** (www.npws.nsw.gov.au). It has a visitor information center at 102 George St., The Rocks, Sydney (© **1300/361 967** in Australia, or 02/9253 4600).
- **Parks & Wildlife Commission of the Northern Territory** (© **08/8999 5511;** www.nt.gov.au/ipe/pwcnt). The Northern Territory Tourist Commission (see "Exploring the Red Centre," in chapter 8) is the official source of information on parks and wildlife matters.
- **Parks Victoria** (© **13 19 63;** www. parkweb.vic.gov.au).
- **South Australian Department for Environment and Heritage** (© **08/ 8204 9010;** www.denr.sa.gov.au).
- **Tasmania Parks and Wildlife Service** (© **1300/368 550;** www.dpiwe. tas.gov.au).

- **Western Australian Department of Conservation and Land Management (CALM;** © **08/9334 0333;** www.calm.wa.gov.au).

Some parks charge an entry fee, often ranging from A$6 to A$18 (US$4.80–US$14).

MORE ACTIVE VACATIONS FROM A TO Z

ABSEILING Rappelling is another name for this sport that involves backing down vertical cliff faces on a rope and harness. The rugged, beautiful Blue Mountains near Sydney are Australia's abseiling capital. In the Margaret River region in Western Australia, you can do it as mighty breakers crash on the cliffs below. You can even do it in the heart of Brisbane on riverside cliffs.

BIKING Much of Australia's countryside is flat and ideal for cycling, as Aussies call biking, but consider the heat and vast distances before setting out. There are plenty of biking trails. The rainforest hills behind Cairns hosted the world mountain-biking championships in 1996, and Sydney's Blue Mountains have good mountain-biking trails. On Rottnest Island off Perth, it's the only mode of transport from one coral-filled bay to the next. All major towns and most resort centers rent regular bikes and mountain bikes.

If you're interested in taking an extended trip, you may find a copy of *Cycling Australia: Bicycle Touring Throughout the Sunny Continent,* by Australian Ian Duckworth (Motorbooks, 1996) useful. This 224-page guide outlines short trips and eight long trips with maps and route descriptions. Any bookstore can order it, or it is often available used for under US$5 from www.amazon. com or for £9.95 from the Quayside Bookshop in the United Kingdom (© **01626/77 5436;** quaybook@aol. com).

Fun Fact   **Something Different: Camel Trekking**

Camels Down Under? You bet. Australia has one of the world's largest camel populations, and even exports racing camels to the Middle East. Camels were imported to negotiate waterless deserts in the 1900s but were later set free. They are now a popular way to trek the country. Short rambles of an hour or two in Alice Springs and at Uluru (Ayers Rock) are a novel way to see the Outback, or you can join extended camel treks through Outback deserts offered by a number of operators. Several companies in Broome lead guided rides along beautiful Cable Beach.

Remote Outback Cycle Tours (© 08/9279 6969; www.cycletours.com.au) takes novice and expert riders, young and old, on extended tours across the country. The distances are vast, but the trip combines cycling with four-wheel-drive travel. Itineraries include the Red Centre, the historic Oodnadatta Track cattle-driving route from Alice Springs to Adelaide via the underground opal-mining town of Coober Pedy in South Australia, and from Adelaide to Perth across the Nullarbor Plain desert and through the pretty Margaret River wine region in southern Western Australia.

BIRDING Australia's unique geography as an island continent means it has species you won't see anywhere else. It is probably best known for its brilliant parrots, but you will see species from the wetlands, savanna, mulga scrub, desert, oceans, dense bushland, rainforest, mangroves, rivers, and other habitats. More than half of the country's species have been spotted in the Daintree Rain Forest area in north Queensland, and one-third live in wetlands-rich Kakadu National Park in the Top End. The Coorong in South Australia and Broome in the Top End are home to marvelous waterfowl populations.

To get in touch with birding clubs all over Australia, contact **Birds Australia** (© 03/9882 2622; www.birdsaustralia.com.au).

Kirrama Wildlife Tours (© 07/4065 5181; www.kirrama.com.au) operates birding expeditions to remote regions in northern Australia from a base in north Queensland. Broome-based ornithologist George Swann of **Kimberley Birdwatching, Wildlife & Natural History Tours** (© 08/9192 1246; www.kimberley birdwatching.com.au) leads extended birding trips throughout the Kimberley and the Northern Territory. Fine Feather Tours (© 07/4094 1199; www.finefeather tours.com.au), based near Port Douglas near the Daintree Rain Forest, operates bird-watching day trips and afternoon river cruises.

CANOEING & SEA KAYAKING Katherine Gorge in the Northern Territory offers some spectacular flat canoeing. You'll find delightful canoeing on the bird-rich Ord River in the Top End. Katherine Gorge and the Ord are full of generally harmless freshwater crocodiles, but *never* canoe in saltwater-crocodile territory. White-water canoeing can be found in Barrington Tops National Park north of Sydney.

A growing number of operators all around the coastline rent kayaks and lead guided expeditions. Popular spots are the Whitsunday Islands in north Queensland, the cold southern seas around Tasmania, and Byron Bay, where you can take a 3-hour "dolphin kayaking" trip to see wild dolphins (and whales June–Oct) and "kayak-surf" the waves.

Rivergods (© **08/9259 0749;** www.rivergods.com.au) conducts multiday sea-kayaking, canoeing, and white-water-rafting adventures throughout Western Australia's pristine ocean and rivers, in which whales, sharks, dugongs (manatees), sea snakes, turtles, and dolphins abound. The company also runs a "sea kayak with wild seals" day outing from Perth. **Gecko Canoeing** (© **08/8972 2224;** www.geckocanoeing.com.au) leads canoeing trips of 1 to 18 days from Katherine along remote Top End rivers between April and September.

CAVING Australia doesn't have a lot of caves, but the ones it has are spectacular. The best spots are in the Blue Mountains west of Sydney and the Margaret River region in southwest Western Australia. For tourists who want to see caves and stay clean and safe (as opposed to spelunkers), the best caves are the spectacular Jenolan Caves in the Blue Mountains, a honeycomb of caverns bursting with intricate stalactites and stalagmites, and the 350 limestone caves in Margaret River, of which five are open to the public. Two are "adventure caves," which any novice caver (as opposed to an experienced spelunker) can explore on a 2- or 3-hour tour. You can also go caving at Olssen's Capricorn Caverns, near Rockhampton, in Central Queensland.

FISHING Reef, game, deep sea, beach, estuary, and river fishing—Australia's massive coastline lets you do it all. Drop a line for coral trout on the Great Barrier Reef; go for the world-record black marlin off Cairns; hook a fighting "barra" (barramundi) in the Northern Territory or the Kimberley; or cast for trout in Tasmania's highland lakes. Charter boats will take you out for the day from most towns all around the coast.

GOLF Australians are almost as passionate about golf as they are about football and cricket—after all, Greg Norman started life as an Aussie! Queensland has the lion's share of the stunning resort courses, such as the Sheraton Mirage in Port Douglas, Laguna Quays Resort near the Whitsundays, and the Hyatt Regency Sanctuary Cove Resort on the Gold Coast. The Gold Coast has more than 40 courses. Joondaloop Country Club in Western Australia was voted Number One Resort Course in Australia by *Golf Australia* magazine for 2003. One of the world's best desert courses is at Alice Springs.

Most courses rent clubs for around A$30 (US$24). Greens fees start at around A$20 (US$16) for 18 holes but average A$65 (US$52) or more on a championship course. **Koala Golf** (© **1300/301 686;** www.koalagolf.com) offers escorted day trips and package tours to excellent golf courses in major cities and holiday areas around Australia. It has offices in Sydney, Melbourne, Brisbane, Perth, Cairns, and Queensland's Gold and Sunshine coasts.

HORSEBACK RIDING Horseback-riding operators are everywhere in Australia. A particularly pleasant vacation is a multiday riding and camping trek in "The Man from Snowy River" country, the Snowy Mountains in New South Wales.

SAILING The 74 islands of the Whitsundays in Queensland are an out-of-this-world backdrop for sailing. And you don't have be an expert—the Whitsunday region is Australia's "bareboating" capital. Bareboating means you can charter an unskippered yacht and sail yourself. Even those without a scrap of experience can do it, although it's best to have someone on board who knows aft from fore. Perth and Sydney are mad about sailing; experienced sailors can head to the nearest yacht club to offer themselves as crew, especially during summer twilight races. The clubs are often short of sailors, and most will welcome out-of-towners.

SURFING   You'll have no trouble finding a good surf beach along the Australian coast. Perth and Sydney are blessed with loads right in the city. Other popular spots include the Gold and Sunshine coasts in Queensland, the legendary Southern Ocean swells along Victoria's southern coast, and magnificent sets off Margaret River in Western Australia. Don't take your board much north of the Sunshine Coast—the Great Barrier Reef puts a stop to the swell from there all the way to the northern tip of Queensland. Loads of companies rent surf gear. Beginner lessons are offered at many surf beaches. Remember, surf only at patrolled beaches, and never surf alone.

WHITE-WATER RAFTING   The best rapids are the Class V torrents on the Nymboida and Gwydir rivers behind Coffs Harbour in New South Wales. More Class V rapids await you on the Johnstone River in north Queensland, where access is by helicopter. Loads of tourists who have never held a paddle hurtle down the Class III to IV Tully River or the gentler Class II to III Barron River on a day trip from Cairns. The Snowy River National Park in Victoria and the Franklin River in the wilds of Tasmania are other popular spots. See also "Canoeing & Sea Kayaking," above.

AUSTRALIA-BASED OUTFITTERS & OPERATORS

Auswalk (© **02/6457 2220;** www. auswalk.com.au) offers self-drive or escorted/accommodated walking tours through picturesque parts of Australia such as the Great Ocean Road in Victoria,

tropical Magnetic Island in Queensland, and the Fraser Island wilderness.

Tasmanian Expeditions (© **03/6339 3999;** www.tas-ex.com) conducts day trips and extended expeditions featuring hiking, cycling, rafting, abseiling, canoeing, sea kayaking, and rock-climbing throughout Tasmania's national parks and unspoiled rural areas.

World Expeditions (© **888/464-TREK** or 415/989-2212 in the U.S., 020/8870-2600 in the U.K., 09/368 4161 in New Zealand, or 02/8270 8400 or 1300/720 000 in Australia; www. worldexpeditions.com.au) runs expeditions in many parts of Australia. Destinations include places less traveled, such as Hinchinbrook Island in the Great Barrier Reef Marine Park, and the long-distance Bibbulmun Track in Western Australia's southwest. Some trips incorporate other pursuits, like rafting, sailing, or biking.

U.S.-BASED OUTFITTERS & OPERATORS

The **Great Outdoor Recreation Pages (GORP)** site (**http://gorp.away.com**) not only has links to adventure-tour operators to Australia, but also contains articles, sells books and maps, and has links to heaps of sites on Australia with an action slant.

Outer Edge Expeditions (© **800/322-5235** or 517/552-5300; www.outer edge.com) and **The World Outdoors** (© **800/488-8483** or 303/413-0938; www.theworldoutdoors.com) both offer ecologically minded multisport diving, hiking, mountain-biking, canoeing, and kayaking packages to the Great Barrier Reef and North Queensland rainforest.

15 Getting Around Australia

Lesson number one: You won't be able to see Uluru (Ayers Rock) from your Sydney hotel room window. It's 2,841km (1,761 miles) away. Possibly the biggest mistake tourists make Down Under (apart from

getting horribly sunburned) is failing to comprehend the distances between popular locations. One of the urban legends that grew up around the 2000 Olympics was the tale of the tourist who asked where in Sydney Harbour he could catch the boat to the Great Barrier Reef. That's a mere 2,800km (1,736 miles) north. Don't try to cram too much into your trip.

Traveling overland may make sense in Europe or North America, but in Australia flying is the best way between most points. People who go by train, bus, or car are often disappointed at Australia's flat vistas of desert, wheat fields, and gum trees—the same landscape can go on for days. A good compromise is to take to the air for long trips and save the land travel for short hops of a few hours. Try not to backtrack, which eats up valuable time and money.

BY PLANE

Australia is a big country with a small population to support its air routes. Airfares are high. This section contains some tips to help you save.

Most domestic air travel is operated by **Qantas** (✆ **800/227-4500** in the U.S. and Canada, 020/8600 4307 in the U.K., 09/357 8900 in Auckland, 0800/808 767 in New Zealand, or 13 13 13 in Australia; www.qantas.com.au). You may get a cheaper fare with the no-frills airlines **Virgin Blue** (✆ **13 67 89** in Australia, or 07/3295 2296; www.virginblue.com.au), its sibling company **Pacific Blue** (✆ **13 16 45** in Australia, or 07/3295 2284; www.virginblue.com.au), or Qantas-owned newcomer **Jetstar** (✆ **13 15 38** in Australia; www.jetstar.com.au).

Another Qantas subsidiary, **Australian Airlines** (book through Qantas or ✆ **1300/799 798** in Australia for general inquiries; www.australianairlines.com.au), flies from Cairns to Sydney and the Gold Coast, as well as to ports in Asia. Newcomer **Regional Express** (✆ **13 17 13** in Australia; www.regionalexpress.com.au) serves regional New South Wales, South Australia, Victoria, and northern Tasmania.

Virgin flies to every capital, as well as Cairns, Townsville, Mackay, Proserpine, Rockhampton, Hervey Bay, the Gold Coast, and the Sunshine Coast, all in Queensland; Broome and Kalgoorlie in Western Australia; Alice Springs in the Red Centre; several coastal towns in New South Wales; and Launceston in Tasmania. Jetstar serves only the eastern states, South Australia and Tasmania, flying to Cairns, the Whitsundays, Mackay, Rockhampton, the Sunshine Coast, the Gold Coast, Brisbane, Sydney, Newcastle, Adelaide, Hobart, Launceston, and Melbourne. (Melbourne has two airports: the main international terminal at Tullamarine, and Avalon Airport, about 50km/31 miles from the city. Make sure you check which one your flight leaves from before you book.) Competition is hot, so it's likely that both Virgin Blue and Jetstar will have added to their route networks before you get to Australia.

Australia's air network is not as well developed as that of North America or Europe, so don't assume there is a direct flight to your chosen destination, or that there is a flight every hour or even every day. *Note:* All flights in Australia are nonsmoking.

FARES FOR INTERNATIONAL TRAVELERS Qantas typically offers international travelers a discount of around 30% off the full fares that Australians pay for domestic flights bought within Australia. To qualify, quote your passport number and international ticket number when reserving. Don't assume the fare for international travelers is the best deal, though—the latest deal in the market that day (or even better, perhaps, a package deal with accommodations thrown in) may be cheaper still.

AIR PASSES If you plan on whipping around to more than one city, purchasing a Qantas **Boomerang Pass** is much cheaper than buying regular fares. You must buy the minimum-size pass before you arrive in Australia, and you can extend it to other cities once you get there. Residents of Australia and New Zealand cannot purchase this pass.

With Qantas's Boomerang Pass, for example, you must purchase a minimum of two coupons (with a maximum of 10), priced differently depending on where you travel and whether the flights are in high demand. Fares are sold in zones: Zone A prices start at A$160 (US$128) for flights of up to 1,200km (750 miles); Zone B at A$295 (US$236) for those between 1,201 and 1,840km (751 and 1,150 miles); and Zone C at A$360 (US$288) for travel more than 1,840km (1,150 miles). Travel to Cairns from Melbourne and Sydney is at Zone B rates, as is travel to Alice Springs and Uluru (Ayers Rock) from anywhere in Australia. There is a A$175 (US$140) surcharge each way on flights to luxury Hayman Island in the Whitsundays. Fares may be higher depending on the availability of seats, so your coupons may cost more depending on the day you buy them and how many seats are available on the flight you book.

Passes are a great value when you consider that a fully flexible one-way fare from Melbourne to Cairns—a 2,254km (1,400-mile), 2-hour journey—is slightly more than A$800 (US$640), compared with the Boomerang pass fare of A$295 (US$236).

Coupons are also good for travel to and from New Zealand and to the most popular South Pacific nations, and can also be used with Air Pacific and Air Vanuatu. You must book your first two coupon destinations before you arrive; you can book the rest as you go, by phoning or visiting any Qantas office. Another great thing about these fares is that they are changeable and the unused portion is refundable; you will incur a A$50 (US$40) fee to change destinations after the coupons have been issued. Many small towns and short flight sectors, some island resorts, and some airports served by subsidiaries of Qantas are not covered by the passes, but most times you can find local fares to these places that are just as good a value as the Boomerang pass.

AERIAL TOURS   The great thing about aerial touring is that it allows you to whiz around the vast Australian continent to see many highlights, and you get to skip all the featureless countryside that typically separates Australia's most fascinating bits. Much of the landscape (such as the weird Bungle Bungles formations in the Kimberley) is best seen from the air, anyhow. **Aircruising Australia** ★ (② **1800/252 053** in Australia, or 02/9693 2233; www.aircruising.com.au) operates upscale aerial tours of 8 to 14 days in a private aircraft, usually a 38-passenger Dash 8, which is nimble enough to "flight-see" as low as 300m (1,000 ft.). One factor you may regard as a plus is that the company mainly markets within Australia, so your fellow passengers are likely to be Aussies. Perhaps because the tours are expensive for Australians, most passengers are over 55. Those who have taken these tours recommend them, saying they are extremely well organized, with lots of time for the land-based sightseeing, some free time, and a maximum 2 hours in the air most days. Accommodations are usually the best available, and the itineraries include "fun extras." Fares in 2005 ranged from A$8,549 to A$11,745 (US$6,839–US$9,396) per person sharing a double or twin room.

You may not think of Antarctica as part of your Australian vacation, but **Antarctica Sightseeing Flights** (② **1800/ 633 449** in Australia, or 03/9725 8555; www.antarcticaflights.com.au) offers once-in-a-lifetime visits to the icy continent. The 12-hour journey offers spectacular viewing over the frozen beauty of Antarctica—a truly memorable experience that comes at a high price for a day trip. Flights are seasonal (Nov–Feb) and include a New Year's Eve flight. Most leave from Sydney or Melbourne, with connections from Brisbane, Canberra, and Adelaide. The tours have been running for 11 years, operated by Croydon Travel with chartered Qantas jumbo jets carrying 350 passengers. You reach the Antarctic coastline after about 4 hours flying and spend the next 4 hours above some of the world's most pristine and spectacular territory. Below are magnificent glaciers, mountain ranges, soaring coastal cliffs, and ice floes. There's no problem viewing all this, despite the fact that you might not have a window seat—everyone moves around and takes turns, and a rotating seating system works well. In 2005 and 2006, fares ranged from A\$899 (US\$719) in an economy center seat to A\$5,199 (US\$4,159) in first class—but this is unlike any other flight you've been on.

BY TRAIN

Australia's trains are clean, comfortable, and safe, and for the most part service standards and facilities are perfectly adequate. The rail network in Australia links Perth to Adelaide, and continues on to Melbourne and north to Canberra, Sydney, Brisbane, and right up the coast to Cairns. There's also a line from Adelaide to Alice Springs and Darwin. Some rural towns, such as Broken Hill, also have rail service. Trains generally cost more than buses but are still reasonably priced. The exceptions are two trains promoted as "experiences" rather than a mere mode of transport—the *Indian Pacific* and the *Ghan* (described below)—that can be frightfully expensive.

Most long-distance trains have sleepers with big windows, air-conditioning, electric outlets, wardrobes, sinks, and fresh sheets and blankets. First-class sleepers have en-suite (attached private) bathrooms, and fares often include meals. Second-class sleepers use shared shower facilities, and meals are not included. Some second-class sleepers are private

cabins; on other trains you share with strangers. Single cabins are usually of broom-closet dimensions but surprisingly comfy, with their own toilet and basin. The food ranges from mediocre to pretty good. Smoking is usually banned, or allowed only in the club cars or special "smoking rooms."

Different entities manage Australia's rail routes. They are the private enterprise **Great Southern Railway** (℃ 13 21 47 in Australia, or 08/8213 4592; www.gsr.com. au), which runs the *Indian Pacific*, the *Overland,* and the *Ghan,* and these government bodies: **Traveltrain,** the long-distance train division of Queensland Rail (℃ 13 22 32 in Australia; www.travel train.qr.com.au), which handles rail within that state; **Countrylink** (℃ 13 22 32 in Australia; www.countrylink.nsw. gov.au), which manages travel within New South Wales and from Sydney to Canberra, Melbourne, and Brisbane; and the **Public Transport Authority,** or PTA (℃ 1300/662 205 in Western Australia, or 08/9326 2600; www.transwa.wa.gov. au), which operates trains in Western Australia.

Outside Australia, the umbrella organization **Rail Australia** (www.railaustralia. com.au) handles inquiries and makes reservations for all long-distance trains, with the exception of PTA routes, through its overseas agents: **ATS Tours** (℃ 310/643-0044) in the U.S.; **Goway** (℃ 416/322-1034) in Canada; **International Rail** (℃ 0870/751-5000) in the U.K.; and **Tranz Scenic** (℃ 03/339 3809) in New Zealand.

Great Southern Railway's *Indian Pacific* ✪ is a glamorous train linking Sydney, Broken Hill, Adelaide, and Perth in a 3-day Outback run twice a week. Slightly less posh but still comfortable, the *Ghan* (named after Afghani camel trainers who traveled the Outback in the 19th c.) travels between Sydney, Melbourne, Adelaide, and Alice Springs twice a week, with connections from Sydney and Perth on the *Indian Pacific* and from Melbourne on the *Overland* (see below). In early 2004, a new rail line opened linking Alice Springs and Darwin, with twice-weekly round-trips between Adelaide and Darwin and between Adelaide and Alice Springs. Both the *Ghan* and the *Indian Pacific* offer a choice of economy seats and second- or first-class sleepers.

Great Southern Railway's third train, the *Overland,* provides a more prosaic journey between Adelaide and Melbourne twice a week. Countrylink runs daily trains from Sydney to Melbourne, Canberra, and Brisbane, and to a number of New South Wales country towns.

Queensland Rail's Traveltrain operates two trains on the Brisbane–Cairns route: The *Sunlander* runs twice a week from Brisbane to Cairns, offering a choice of the premium, all-inclusive Queenslander Class; single-, double-, or triple-berth sleepers; or economy seats. Two services also run as far as Townsville on this route without Queenslander Class. The high-speed **Tilt Train** operates three weekly trips on the same route in less time—by about 8 hours—with business-class–style seating. Tilt Trains also serve Rockhampton daily from Brisbane. Traveltrain also operates trains to Outback towns. All Traveltrain and most Countrylink long-distance trains stop at most towns en route, so they're useful for exploring the eastern states.

PACKAGES   Great Southern Railway, Countrylink, and Queensland Rail Traveltrain (see above) offer rail packages that include accommodations and sightseeing.

RAIL PASSES   National, East Coast, New South Wales, Queensland, and Great Southern Railway rail passes are available from Rail Australia (see above) at its overseas agents. National passes must be bought before you arrive and are available only to holders of non-Australian passports. East Coast (Melbourne-

Sydney-Brisbane-Cairns) and Queensland passes can be purchased before or after you arrive in Australia. Passes are not valid for first-class travel, but upgrades are available.

The national **Austrail Flexipass** is good for economy seats and second-class sleepers on all long-distance trains (except PTA service in Western Australia) and is even good for suburban city train networks. It allows you to travel for 15 or 22 days, consecutive or not, within a 6-month period. Prices are A$862 (US$690) for a 15-day Flexipass to A$1,210 (US$968) for a 22-day Flexipass.

BY BUS

Bus travel in Australia is a big step up from the low-rent affair it can be in the United States. Terminals are centrally located and well lit, the buses—called "coaches" Down Under—are clean and air-conditioned, you sit in adjustable seats, videos play on board, and the drivers are polite and sometimes even point out places of interest along the way. Some buses have restrooms. Unlike Australia's train service, the extensive bus network will take you almost everywhere. Buses are all nonsmoking.

Australia has one national coach operators: **Greyhound Australia** (© **13 14 99** in Australia, or 07/4690 9888; www.greyhound.com.au; no relation to Greyhound in the U.S.). The company does not operate within Tasmania, which is serviced by **Redline Coaches** (© **1300/360 000** in Australia; www.redline coaches.com.au). In addition to point-to-point services, Greyhound Australia also offers a limited range of tours at popular locations on its networks, including Uluru, Kakadu, Monkey Mia in Western Australia, and the Great Ocean Road in Victoria.

Note: Fares and some passes are considerably cheaper for seniors, students, backpacker cardholders, and Hostelling International/YHA members.

BUS PASSES Bus passes are a great value. There are several kinds—Day passes, Pre-set Itinerary passes, and Kilometre passes. Look into the one that suits you best. Note that even with a pass, you may still need to book the next leg of your trip 12 or 24 hours ahead as a condition of the pass; during school vacation periods, which are always busy, booking as much as 7 days ahead may be smart.

If you know where you are going and are willing to obey a "no backtracking" rule, consider Greyhound Australia's **Aussie Explorer** predetermined itinerary pass. These passes allow unlimited stops in a generous time frame on a preset one-way route (you are permitted to travel the route in either direction). There is a huge range of itineraries to choose from. As an example, the **Aussie Reef and Rock** pass takes in Alice Springs, Katherine, Darwin, Mount Isa, Cairns, and the whole east coast down to Sydney. The pass is valid for 6 months and costs A$1,131 (US$905) from Sydney, including tours to Uluru (Ayers Rock), Kakadu National Park, and Kings Canyon. You don't have to start in Sydney; you can start at any point along any of the pass routes, in which case the pass may be cheaper. In the case of the Reef and Rock pass, that means you could start farther up the track, at Brisbane (in which case the pass costs A$1,046/US$837) or Cairns (from where the pass costs A$698/US$558). The **All Australian Pass** costs A$2,458 (US$1,966) and is valid for a year.

The **Aussie Kilometre Pass** allows unlimited stops in any direction within the mileage you buy. Passes are available in increments of 1,000km (620 miles). Prices range from A$328 (US$262) for 2,000km (1,240 miles)—enough to get you from Cairns to Brisbane—to A$2,310 (US$1,848) for a whopping 20,000km (6,200 miles).

SAMPLE TRAVEL TIMES & BUS FARES

Here are some sample bus fares and travel times, to give you an idea of what you're getting yourself into as you step aboard. All fares and travel times are one-way.

Route	Travel Time (Approx.)	Fare
Broome-Darwin	27 hr.	A$302 (US$242)
Sydney-Brisbane	17 hr.	A$100 (US$80)
Cairns-Brisbane	29 hr.	A$201 (US$161)

BY CAR

Australia's roads sometimes leave a bit to be desired. The taxes of 19 million people get spread pretty thin when it comes to maintaining roads across a continent. Most highways are two-lane affairs with the occasional rut and pothole, often no outside line markings, and sometimes no shoulders to speak of.

When you are poring over the map of Australia, remember that what looks like a road may be an unsealed (unpaved) track suitable for four-wheel-drive vehicles only. Many roads in the Top End are passable only in the dry season (about Apr–Nov). If you plan long-distance driving, get a road map (see below for sources) that marks paved and unpaved roads.

You cannot drive across the middle of the country (except along the north-south Stuart Hwy. linking Adelaide and Darwin) because most of it is desert. In most places you must travel around the edge on Highway 1. The map inside the back cover of this book marks the major highways.

You can use your current driver's license or an international driver's permit in every state of Australia. By law, you must carry your license with you when driving. The minimum driving age is 16 or 17, depending on which state you visit, but some car-rental companies require you to be 21, or sometimes 26, if you want to rent a four-wheel-drive vehicle.

CAR RENTALS

Think twice about renting a car in tourist hot spots such as Cairns. In these areas most tour operators pick you up and drop you back at your hotel door, so having a car may not be worth the expense.

The "big four" car-rental companies all have networks across Australia:

- **Avis** (© **13 63 33** in Australia, www.avis.com.au; 800/230-4898 in the U.S., www.avis.com; 800/272-5871 in Canada; 0870/6060-100 in the U.K. and Ireland, www.avis.co.uk; 0800/655 111 in New Zealand, www.avis.co.nz).
- **Budget** (© **1300/794 344** in Australia, www.budget.com.au; 800/527-0700 in the U.S., www.budget.com; 800/268-8900 in Canada, www.budget.ca; 0134/4484-100 in the U.K., www.budget-uk.com; 906/627-711 in Ireland, www.budget-ireland.com; 0800/283 438 in New Zealand, www.budget.co.nz).
- **Hertz** (© **13 30 39** in Australia, www.hertz.com.au; 800/654-3131 in the U.S., www.hertz.com; 800/263-0600 in English or 800/263-0678 in French in Canada, or 416/620-9620

in Toronto, www.hertz.ca; 020/7026-0077 in the U.K., www.hertz.co.uk; 1/676-7476 in Ireland; 0800/654 321 in New Zealand).
- **Thrifty** (© **1300/367 227** in Australia, www.thrifty.com.au; 800/229-0984 in the U.S. and Canada, www.thrifty.com; 0800/783-0405 in the U.K., www.thrifty.co.uk; 1800/51-5800 in Ireland, www.thrifty.ie; 0800/73 7070 in New Zealand, www.thrifty.co.nz).

Two other large companies with offices around Australia are:

- **Europcar** (© **1300/13 13 90** in Australia or 03/9330 6160, www.deltaeuropcar.com.au; 877/940-6900 in the U.S. and Canada; 0870/607-5000 in the U.K., www.europcar.co.uk; 1/614-2800 in Ireland, www.europcar.ie; 0800/628 227 in New Zealand). Europcar has the third-largest fleet in Australia.
- **Red Spot Car Rentals** (© **1300/668 810** in Australia, or 02/9211 1144; www.redspotrentals.com.au). It has depots in Sydney, Melbourne, Brisbane, Perth, Cairns, and the Gold Coast.

SAMPLE DRIVING DISTANCES & TIMES

Here are a few sample road distances between popular points and the minimum time it takes to drive between them.

Route	Distance	Approx. Driving Time
Cairns-Sydney	2,495km (1,547 miles)	29 hr. (allow 4–5 days)
Sydney-Melbourne	873km (541 miles)	15 hr. (allow 1–2 days)
Sydney-Perth	4,131km (2,561 miles)	51 hr. (allow 6–7 days)
Adelaide-Darwin	3,024km (1,875 miles)	31 hr. (allow 4–6 days)
Perth-Darwin	4,163km (2,581 miles)	49 hr. (allow 6–8 days)

A small sedan for zipping around a city or touring a wine region will cost about A$45 to A$80 (US$36–US$64) a day. A feistier vehicle with enough grunt to get you from state to state will cost around A$70 to A$100 (US$56–US$80) a day.

Rentals of a week or longer usually reduce the price by A$5 (US$4) a day or so.

A regular car will get you to most places in this book, but because the country has many unpaved roads, it can make sense to rent a four-wheel-drive vehicle. All of the major car-rental companies rent them. They are more expensive than a regular car, but you can get them for as little as A$75 (US$60) per day if you shop around, cheaper for rentals of a week or longer.

The rates quoted here are only a guide. Many smaller local companies—and the big guys, too—offer competitive specials, especially in tourist areas with distinct off seasons. Advance purchase rates, usually 7 to 21 days, can offer significant savings.

INSURANCE   Insurance for loss of, or damage to, the car, and third-party property insurance are usually included, but read the agreement carefully, because the fine print contains information the front-desk staff may not tell you. For example, damage to the car body may be covered, but not damage to the windshield or tires, or damage caused by water or driving too close to a bushfire.

The deductible, known as "excess" in Australia, on insurance may be as high as A$2,000 (US$1,600) for regular cars and up to A$5,500 (US$4,400) on four-wheel-drives and motor homes. You can reduce it, or avoid it altogether, by paying a premium of between about A$20 to A$50 (US$16–US$40) per day on a car or four-wheel-drive, and around A$25 to A$50 (US$20–US$40) per day on a motor home. The amount of the excess reduction premium depends on the vehicle type and the extent of reduction you choose. Your rental company may bundle personal accident insurance and baggage insurance into this premium. And again, check the conditions; some excess reduction payments do not reduce excesses on single-vehicle accidents, for example.

ONE-WAY RENTALS   Australia's distances often make one-way rentals a necessity, for which car-rental companies can charge a hefty penalty amounting to hundreds of dollars. A one-way fee usually applies to motor-home renters, too—usually around A$200 to A$220 (US$160–US$176), more for remote outback areas such as Broome and Alice Springs. And there's a 7-day rental minimum.

MOTOR HOMES   Motor homes (Aussies call them camper vans) are popular in Australia. Generally smaller than the RVs in the United States, they come in two-, three-, four-, or six-berth versions, and usually have everything you need, such as a minifridge/freezer (icebox in the smaller versions), microwave, gas stove, cooking and cleaning utensils, linens, and touring information including maps and campground guides. All have showers and toilets, except some two-berthers. Most have air-conditioned driver's cabins, but not all have air-conditioned living quarters, a necessity in most parts of the country from November through March. Four-wheel-drive campers are available, but they tend to be small, and some lack hot water, toilet, shower, and air-conditioning. Minimum driver age for motor homes is usually 21.

(*Tips*   **Insurance Alert**

Damage to a rental car caused by an animal (hitting a kangaroo, for instance) is not covered by car-rental companies' insurance policies. Nor is driving on an unpaved road—and Australia has a lot of those.

Australia's biggest national motor-home-rental companies are **Apollo Motorhome Holidays** (② **1800/777 779** in Australia, or 07/3260 5466; www.apollocamper.com.au), **Britz Camper-van Rentals** (② **1800/331 454** in Australia, or 03/8379 8890; www.britz.com), **Hertz Campervans** (② **1800/33 5888** in Australia, or 08/8261 8833; www.hertz campervans.com), and **Maui** (② **1300/363 800** in Australia, or 03/8379 8891; www.maui-rentals.com).

For a two-berth motor home with shower and toilet, Britz's 2005 and 2006 rates range from A$50 to A$190 (US$40–US$152) per day, over a 5- to 20-day rental period. For a four-berth with shower and toilet over the same period, you are looking at A$120 to A$270 (US$96–US$216) per day. Rates vary with the seasons. May and June are the slowest months; December and January are the busiest. It's sometimes possible to get better rates by booking in your home country before departure. Renting for longer than 3 weeks knocks a few dollars off the daily rate. Most companies will demand a minimum 4- or 5-day rental. Give the company your itinerary before booking, because some routes, such as the ferry across to Tasmania—or, in the case of a four-wheel-drive motor home, the Gibb River Road in the Kimberley—may need the company's permission. Companies may not permit you to drive their two-wheel-drive motor home on unpaved roads; Apollo and Hertz do not, while Britz and Maui do allow two-wheel-drive campers to travel on unsealed access roads to recognized campgrounds.

Frustratingly, most local councils take a dim view of "free camping," the practice of pulling over by the roadside to camp for the night. Instead, you will likely have to stay in a campground.

ON THE ROAD

GAS The price of petrol (gasoline) will probably elicit a cry of dismay from Americans and a whoop of delight from Brits. Prices go up and down, but roughly, you're looking at around A90¢ a liter (or US$2.72 per U.S. gal.) for unleaded petrol in Sydney, and A$1.20 a liter (or US$3.62 per U.S. gal.), or more, in the Outback. One U.S. gallon equals 3.78 liters. Most rental cars take unleaded gas, and motor homes run on diesel, which costs around A90¢ to A$1.20 a liter (US$2.72–US$3.62 per U.S. gal.), depending on your location.

DRIVING RULES Australians drive on the left, which means you give way to the right. Left turns on a red light are not permitted unless a sign says so.

Roundabouts (traffic circles) are common at intersections; approach these slowly enough to stop if you have to, and give way to all traffic on the roundabout. Flash your indicator as you leave the roundabout (even if you're going straight, because technically that's a left turn).

The only strange driving rule is Melbourne's requirement that drivers turn right from the left lane at certain intersections in the city center. This allows the city's trams to carry on uninterrupted in the right lane. Pull into the left lane opposite the street you are turning into, and make the turn when the traffic light in the street you are turning into becomes green. These intersections are signposted.

The maximum permitted blood alcohol level when driving is 0.05%, which equals approximately two 200-milliliter (6.6-oz.) drinks in the first hour for men, one for women, and one drink per hour for both sexes after that. The police set up random breath-testing units (RBTs) in cunningly disguised and unlikely places all the time, so getting caught is easy. You will face a court appearance if you do.

The speed limit is 50kmph (31 mph) or 60kmph (37 mph) in urban areas and 100kmph (62 mph) or 110kmph (68 mph) in most country areas. Speed-limit signs are black numbers circled in red on a white background.

Drivers and passengers, including taxi passengers, must wear a seat belt at all times when the vehicle is moving forward, if the car is equipped with a belt. Young children are required to sit in the rear seat in a child-safety seat or harness; car-rental companies will rent these to you, but be sure to book them. Tell the taxi company you have a child when you book a cab so that it can send a car with the right restraints.

MAPS   The maps published by the state automobile clubs listed below in "Auto Clubs" will likely be free if you are a member of an affiliated auto club in your home country. None will mail them to you overseas; pick them up on arrival. Remember to bring your auto-club membership card to qualify for discounts or free maps.

Two of the biggest map publishers in Australia are **HEMA Maps** (℗ **07/3340 0000;** www.hemamaps.com.au) and **Universal Publishers** (℗ **1800/021 987** in Australia, or 02/9857 3700; www. universalpress-online.com). Both publish an extensive range of national, state, regional, and city maps. HEMA has a strong list of regional maps ("Gold Coast and Region" and "The Red Centre" are just a few), while Universal produces a complete range of street directories by city, region, or state under the "UBD" and "Gregory's" labels. HEMA produces four-wheel-drive and motorbike road atlases and many regional four-wheel-drive maps—good if you plan to go off the trails—an atlas of Australia's national parks, and maps to Kakadu and Lamington national parks.

Both companies produce a range of national road atlases. Universal's UBD *Motoring Atlas of Australia* helpfully publishes street maps of small regional towns in each state. Australia is so big that a national atlas is good for overall trip planning and long-distance or interstate journeys, but sometimes of limited use on day trips or short journeys, because it is not detailed enough. You may find it worthwhile to purchase a map to the local area—say, a "Cairns to Cooktown" map if you want to explore Cairns, Kuranda, Port Douglas, and other towns within an hour or two of Cairns.

HEMA and Universal Press maps are distributed in the United States by **Map Link** (℗ **800/962-1394;** www.maplink. com). HEMA maps are also distributed in Canada, by **ITMB**, or International Travel Maps and Books (℗ **604/879- 3621;** www.itmb.com), and in the U.K. by **Estate Publications** (℗ **01580/76 4225;** www.estate-publications.co.uk).

In Australia, auto clubs (see below), bigger newsdealers, and bookstores are your best sources for maps. Gas stations stock a limited range relating to their location, and visitor information centers sometimes stock a range of maps to the area and the whole state.

ROAD SIGNS   Australians navigate by road name, not road number. The easiest way to get where you're going is to familiarize yourself with the major towns along your route and follow the signs toward them.

AUTO CLUBS   Every state and territory in Australia has its own auto club. Your auto association back home probably has a reciprocal agreement with Australian clubs, which may entitle you to free maps, accommodations guides, and emergency roadside assistance. Don't forget to bring your membership card.

Even if you're not a member, the clubs are a good source of advice on local traffic regulations, touring advice, road conditions, traveling in remote areas, and any other motoring questions you may have. They sell maps, accommodations guides, and camping guides to nonmembers at reasonable prices. They share a website: **www.aaa.asn.au**. You can drop into numerous regional offices as well as the head office locations listed here.

- **New South Wales & ACT: National Roads and Motorists' Association (NRMA),** 74–76 King St. (at George St.), Sydney, NSW 2000 (✆ **13 11 22** in New South Wales, or 02/9292 9222).

- **Victoria: Royal Automobile Club of Victoria (RACV),** 550 Princes Hwy., Noble Park, VIC 3174 (✆ **13 19 55** in Australia, or 03/9790 2211). A more convenient city office is at 422 Little Collins St., Melbourne.

- **Queensland: Royal Automobile Club of Queensland (RACQ),** 300 St. Pauls Terrace, Fortitude Valley, QLD 4006 (✆ **13 19 05** in Australia, or 07/3872 8429). A more convenient city office is in the General Post Office (GPO) building, 261 Queen St., Brisbane (✆ **07/3872 8465**).

- **Western Australia: Royal Automobile Club of WA (RAC),** 228 Adelaide Terrace, Perth, WA 6000 (✆ **13 17 03** or 08/9421 4444).

- **South Australia: Royal Automobile Association of South Australia (RAA),** 41 Hindmarsh Sq., Adelaide, SA 5000 (✆ **08/8202 4600**).

- **Northern Territory: Automobile Association of the Northern Territory (AANT),** 79–81 Smith St., Darwin, NT 0800 (✆ **08/8981 3837**).

- **Tasmania: Royal Automobile Club of Tasmania (RACT),** corner of Murray and Patrick streets, Hobart, TAS 7000 (✆ **13 27 22** in Tasmania, or 03/6232 6300).

ROAD CONDITIONS & SAFETY

Here are some common motoring dangers and ways to avoid them:

FATIGUE Fatigue is a killer on Australia's roads. The rule is to take a 20-minute break every 2 hours, even if you don't feel tired. In some states, "driver reviver" stations operate on major roads during holiday periods. They serve free tea, coffee, and cookies, and are often at roadside picnic areas that have restrooms.

KANGAROOS & OTHER WILDLIFE

It's a sad fact, but kangaroos are a road hazard. Avoid driving in country areas between dusk and dawn, when 'roos are most active. If you hit one, always stop and check its pouch for live joeys (baby kangaroos), because females usually have one in the pouch. Wrap the joey tightly in a towel or old sweater, don't feed or overhandle it, and take it to a vet in the nearest town or call one of the following wildlife care groups: **Wildlife Information & Rescue Service (WIRES)** in New South Wales (✆ 02/8977 3333); **Wildlife Victoria** (✆ 0500/540 000 or 03/9663 9211); **Wildlife Rescue** in Queensland (✆ 0418/792 598); **RSPCA Wildlife** in the ACT (✆ 02/6287 8100 or 0413/495 031); **Wildcare** in Western Australia (✆ 08/9474 9055); **Wildlife Rescue** in the Northern Territory (✆ 08/8999 4536); **Fauna Rescue of S.A.** in South Australia (✆ 08/8289 0896); or **Wildcare** in Tasmania (✆ 03/6233 2852). Most vets will treat native wildlife for free.

Some highways run through unfenced stations (ranches), where sheep and cattle pose a threat. Cattle like to rest on the warm bitumen road at night, so put your lights on high to spot them. If an animal does loom up, slow down—but never swerve, or you may roll. If you have to, hit it. Tell ranchers within 24 hours if you have hit their livestock.

Car-rental companies will not insure for animal damage to the car, which should give you an inkling of how common an occurrence this is.

ROAD TRAINS Road trains consist of as many as three big truck carriages linked together to make a "train" up to 54m (177 ft.) long. If you're in front of one, give the driver plenty of warning when you brake, because the trains need a lot of distance to slow down. Allow at least 1 clear kilometer (over ½ mile) before you pass one, but don't expect the driver to make it easy—"truckies" are notorious for their lack of concern for motorists.

UNPAVED ROADS Many country roads are unsealed (unpaved). They are usually bone-dry, which makes them more slippery than they look, so travel at a moderate speed—35kmph (22 mph) is not too cautious, and anything over 60kmph (37 mph) is dangerous. Don't overcorrect if you veer to one side. Keep well behind any vehicles, because the dust they throw up can block your vision.

FLOODS Floods are common in the Top End and north of Cairns from November or December through March or April (the wet season). Never cross a flooded road unless you are sure of its depth. Crocodiles may be in the water, so do not wade in to test it! Fast-flowing water is dangerous, even if it's very shallow. When in doubt, stay where you are and wait for the water to drop; most flash floods subside in 24 hours. Check the road conditions ahead at least once a day in the wet season.

RUNNING OUT OF GAS Gas stations (also called "roadhouses" in rural areas) can be few and far between in the Outback, so fill up at every opportunity.

WHAT IF YOUR VEHICLE BREAKS DOWN?

Warning: If you break down or get lost, never leave your vehicle. Many a motorist—often an Aussie who should have known better—has died wandering off on a crazy quest for help or water, knowing full well that neither is to be found for maybe hundreds of miles. Most people who get lost do so in Outback spots; if that happens to you, conserve your body moisture by doing as little as possible and staying in the shade of your car. Put out distress signals in patterns of three—three yells, three columns of smoke, and so on. The traditional Outback call for help is "Coo-*ee*," with the accent on the "ee" and yodeled in a high pitch; the sound travels a surprisingly long way.

The state auto clubs listed above provide free breakdown emergency assistance to members of many affiliated automobile associations around the world.

EMERGENCY ASSISTANCE

The emergency breakdown assistance telephone number for every Australian auto club is *Ⓒ* **13 11 11** from anywhere in Australia. It is billed as a local call. If you are not a member of an auto club at home that has a reciprocal agreement with the Australian clubs, you'll have to join the Australian club on the spot before the club will tow or repair your car. This usually costs only around A$80 (US$64), not a big price to pay when you're stranded—although in the Outback, the charge may be considerably higher. Most car-rental companies also have emergency assistance numbers.

TIPS FOR FOUR-WHEEL DRIVERS

Always keep to the four-wheel-drive track. Going off-road causes soil erosion, a significant environmental problem in Australia. Leave gates as you found them. Obtain permission from the owners before venturing onto private station (ranch) roads. On an extended trip or in remote areas, carry 5 liters (1.3 gal.) of drinking water per person per day (dehydration occurs fast in the Australian heat); enough food to last 3 or 4 days more than you think you will need; a first-aid kit; spare fuel; a jack and two spare tires; spare fan belts, radiator hoses, and air-conditioner hoses; a tow rope; and a good map that marks all gas stations. In seriously remote areas outside the scope of this book, carry a high-frequency and CB radio. (A cellphone may not work in the Outback.) Advise a friend, your hotel manager, the local tourist bureau, or a police station of your route and your expected time of return or arrival at your destination.

16 Tips on Accommodations

Accommodations properties in Australia carry star ratings given by AAA Tourism, which has been awarding ratings since the 1950s. This independent assessment is based on facilities, amenities, maintenance, and cleanliness. Ratings run from one to five stars. Stars are featured in AAA Tourism guides, and recent research shows 70% of travelers use the star ratings when choosing their accommodations (these star ratings are noted below using asterisks). The rating scheme covers over 18,000 accommodations throughout every state and territory.

 * Offers a basic standard of accommodations, simply furnished, with a resident manager.
 ** Similar standard to one star but offers more comfort and value with additional features. These are well-maintained properties offering an average standard of accommodations with average furnishings, bedding, and floor coverings.
 *** Well appointed, with a comfortable standard of accommodations, and above-average furnishings and floor coverings.
 **** Exceptionally well-appointed establishments with high-quality furnishings, a high degree of comfort, high standard of presentation, and guest services.
 ***** International standard establishments offering superior appointments, furnishings, and decor, with an extensive range of first-class guest services. Reception, room service, and housekeeping available 18 hours a day, with restaurant/bistro facilities available 7 nights a week. A number and variety of room styles, suites, or both are available. Choice of dining facilities, 24-hour room service, housekeeping, and valet parking. Porter and concierge service available, as well as a dedicated business center and conference facilities.

Note: All accommodations listed in this book have private bathrooms unless otherwise noted.

HOTELS   It's a rare hotel room that does not have reverse-cycle air-conditioning for heating and cooling, a telephone, a color TV, a clock radio, a minifridge (if not a minibar), an iron and ironing board, and self-serve coffee and tea. Private bathrooms are standard, although they often have only a shower, not a tub.

The largest hotel group in Australia is the French chain Accor, which has more than 100 properties (that's about 15,000 rooms) under its Sofitel, Novotel, Mercure, All Seasons, Ibis, and Formule 1 brands. Many other international chains, such as Marriott, Sheraton, and Hilton, have properties in Australia.

SERVICED APARTMENTS   Serviced apartments are favored by many Aussie families and business travelers. You get a fully furnished apartment with one, two, or three bedrooms, a living room, a kitchen or kitchenette, a laundry, and often two bathrooms—in other words, all the facilities of a hotel suite and more, often for less than the cost of a four-star hotel room. (Not every apartment kitchen has a dishwasher, so check if that's important to you.) A nice two-bedroom apartment can cost anywhere from around

A$165 to A$695 (US$132–US$556) a night, depending on your location and the season. Australia's apartment inventory is enormous and ranges from clean and comfortable, if a little dated, to luxurious. Most apartments can be rented for 1 night, especially in cities, but in popular vacation spots, some proprietors will insist on a minimum 3-night stay, or even a week in high season.

Medina Serviced Apartments (© **1300/300 232** in Australia, or 02/9356 1000; www.medinaapartments.com.au) has a chain of midrange to upscale properties in Sydney, Melbourne, Brisbane, Canberra, Adelaide, and Perth. Australia's biggest apartment chain is **Quest Serviced Apartments** (© **1800/334 033** in Australia, or 03/9645 7566, 0800/944 400 in New Zealand; www.questapartments.com.au). It has four brands: the upscale Quest Establishments, the midrange Quest Inns, Quest Lodgings for longer stays, and Quest Resorts, in every state and territory.

MOTELS & MOTOR INNS Australia's plentiful motels are neat and clean, if often a little dated. You can count on them to provide air-conditioning, a telephone, a color TV, a clock radio, a minifridge or minibar, and self-serve tea and coffee. Most have only showers, not bathtubs. Some have restaurants attached, and many have swimming pools. Motor inns offer a greater range of facilities and a generally higher standard of rooms than motels. Rates average A$70 to A$110 (US$56–US$88) double.

BED & BREAKFAST INNS B&Bs are cheap and plentiful in Australia. It is easy to find charming rooms for around A$80 (US$64) for a double. Bathroom facilities are often shared, although more properties now offer private, if not always en-suite (attached), bathrooms.

Travel agents rarely list B&Bs because the establishments are not big enough to pay a commission, so they can be hard to find. A good source is *The Australian Bed & Breakfast Book* (www.bbbook.com.au; published in the U.S. by Pelican USA), which lists more than 500 B&Bs across Australia. Although the B&Bs pay to be in the book, they have to meet standards set by the editors. The entire book is posted on the website, and in Australia, it's widely available in bookshops and newsdealers, or you can order it direct (© **02/6658 5701**) for A$20 (US$16) plus A$15 (US$12) for overseas postage.

Orangewood, a Northern Territory B&B, provides an index of Australian B&B directories at this address: **www.bed-and-breakfast.au.com/dir dir.htm**.

What Next? Productions Pty. Ltd. (© **0438/600 696** mobile phone; www.beautifulaccommodation.com) publishes a color guide, *Beautiful B&Bs & Small Hotels,* listing 190 exquisite properties in Victoria, South Australia, and Tasmania, many in charming country areas. They also publish *Beautiful Accommodation in Queensland* and *Beautiful Accommodation in New South Wales.* The properties listed are more upscale than most, roughly in the A$150 to A$300 (US$120–US$240) range. Each book sells for A$30 (US$24) in Australian bookstores and can be ordered online.

PUBS Aussie pubs are really made for drinking, not spending the night, but many offer rooms upstairs, usually with shared bathroom facilities. Because most pubs are decades old, the rooms may be either old-fashioned or just plain old. Pub accommodations are dying out in the cities but still common in the country. Australians are rowdy drinkers, so sleeping over the bar can be hellishly noisy, but the pub's saving grace is incredibly low rates. Most charge per person, not per room, and you will rarely pay more than A$50 (US$40) per person a night.

HOUSE SWAPS Many international visitors to Australia have happily swapped homes with locals using the Internet to find their "perfect match." A plethora of sites can help you make your search. Two that list up to 100 Australian homes each are www.holi-swaps.com/swapsau.htm and www.homebase-hols.com. You can browse the listings free, but it costs around US$40 to view the contact details or to list your own home.

FARM STAYS   The Aussie answer to the dude ranch is a farm stay. Australian farm stays are rarely as well set up for tourists as the dude ranch Billy Crystal's character visited in *City Slickers*. Most are farms first, tourist operations second, so you may have to find your own fun and know how to take care of yourself, at least to a degree.

Accommodations on farms can be anything from a basic bunkhouse (ask if it's air-conditioned, because most farms are in very hot areas) to rustically luxurious digs. Do some research on your farm—a lot of activities are seasonal, some farmers will not allow you to get involved in dangerous work, not all will offer horseback riding, and *farm* means different things in different parts of Australia. If you like green fields and dairy cows, Victoria may be the place for you. If checking fences on a dusty 500,000-hectare (200,000-acre) Outback station (ranch) sounds wildly romantic, head to Western Australia or the Northern Territory.

Australian Farm & Country Tourism (✆ **1800/803 007** or 02/9493 9955 in Australia) is a cooperative marketing organization for farm-stay properties. Its website has information on about 40 properties in Queensland, New South Wales, and Victoria. Another good contact is **Bed & Breakfast and Farmstay Victoria** (✆ **1300/132 358** or 03/9431 5417; www.agv.net.au). Rates vary, but you will find many properties charging under A$200 (US$160) for a double, which sometimes includes breakfast. Meals are often available as an optional extra.

SAVING ON YOUR HOTEL ROOM

The **rack rate** is the maximum rate that a hotel charges for a room. Hardly anybody pays this price, however, except during high season or holidays. To lower the cost of your room:

- **Ask about special rates or other discounts.** Always ask whether a room less expensive than the first one quoted is available, or whether any special rates apply to you. You may qualify for corporate, student, military, senior, or other discounts. Mention membership in AAA, AARP, frequent-flier programs, or trade unions, which may entitle you to special deals as well. Find out the hotel policy on children—do kids stay free in the room or is there a special rate?
- **Dial direct.** When booking a room in a chain hotel, you'll often get a better deal by calling the individual hotel's reservation desk rather than the chain's main number.
- **Book online.** Many hotels offer Internet-only discounts, or supply

---

Tips   **Meet the People Down Under**

If you want to see an Australian Rules football game in the company of a knowledgeable local in Melbourne or swim at Bondi Beach with a Sydneysider, contact **Friends Overseas—Australia** (✆ **718/261-0534**; www.friendsoverseas.org). This program is designed to match visitors with friendly Aussies of like age and interests, so you can spend time with them. The membership fee is US$25.

rooms to Priceline, Hotwire, or Expedia at rates much lower than the ones you can get through the hotel itself. Shop around. And if you have special needs—a quiet room, a room with a view—call the hotel directly and make your needs known after you've booked online.

- **Remember the law of supply and demand.** Resort hotels are most crowded and therefore most expensive on weekends, so discounts are usually available for midweek stays. Business hotels in downtown locations are busiest during the week, so you can expect big discounts over the weekend. Many hotels have high-season and low-season prices, and booking the day after high season ends can mean big discounts.

- **Look into group or long-stay discounts.** If you come as part of a large group, you should be able to negotiate a bargain rate, since the hotel can then guarantee occupancy in a number of rooms. Likewise, if you're planning a long stay (at least 5 days), you might qualify for a discount. As a general rule, expect 1 night free after a 7-night stay.

- **Avoid excess charges and hidden costs.** When you book a room, ask whether the hotel charges for parking. Use your own cellphone, pay phones, or prepaid phone cards instead of dialing direct from hotel phones, which usually have exorbitant rates. And don't be tempted by the room's minibar offerings: Most hotels charge through the nose for water, soda, and snacks. Finally, ask about local taxes and service charges, which can increase the cost of a room by 15% or more. If a hotel insists upon tacking on a surprise "energy surcharge" that wasn't mentioned at check-in or a "resort fee" for amenities you didn't use, you can often make a case for getting it removed.

- **Consider the pros and cons of all-inclusive resorts and hotels.** The term "all-inclusive" means different things at different hotels. Many all-inclusive hotels will include three meals daily, sports equipment, spa entry, and other amenities; others may include all or most drinks. In general, you'll save money going the "all-inclusive" way—as long as you use the facilities provided. The down side is that your choices are limited and you're stuck eating and playing in one place for the duration of your vacation.

- **Book an efficiency.** A room with a kitchenette allows you to shop for groceries and cook your own meals. This is a big money saver, especially for families on long stays.

LANDING THE BEST ROOM

Somebody has to get the best room in the house. It might as well be you. You can start by joining the hotel's frequent-guest program, which may make you eligible for upgrades. A hotel-branded credit card usually gives it owner "silver" or "gold" status in frequent-guest programs for free. Always ask about a corner room. They're often larger and quieter, with more windows and light, and they often cost the same as standard rooms. When you make your reservation, ask if the hotel is renovating; if it is, request a room away from the construction. Ask about nonsmoking rooms; rooms with views; rooms with twin, queen-, or king-size beds. If you're a light sleeper, request a quiet room away from vending machines, elevators, restaurants, bars, and discos. Ask for a room that has been renovated or redecorated most recently.

If you aren't happy with your room when you arrive, ask for another one. Most lodgings will be willing to accommodate you.

In resort areas, particularly in warm climates, ask the following questions before you book a room:

Tips   Dial E for Easy

For quick directions on how to call Australia, see the "Telephones" listing in the "Fast Facts: Australia" section at the end of this chapter or check out the "Telephone Tips" on the inside front cover of the book.

- What's the view like? Cost-conscious travelers may be willing to pay less for a back room facing the parking lot, especially if they don't plan to spend much time in their room.
- Does the room have air-conditioning or ceiling fans? Do the windows open? If they do, and the nighttime entertainment takes place alfresco, you may want to find out when show time is over.

- What's included in the price? Your room may be moderately priced, but if you're charged for beach chairs, towels, sports equipment, and other amenities, you could end up spending more than you bargained for.
- How far is the room from the beach and other amenities? If it's far, is there transportation to and from the beach, and is it free?

17 Recommended Books & Films

Australian literature has come a long way since the days when the bush poets A. B. "Banjo" Paterson and Henry Lawson penned their odes to a way of life now largely lost. The best known of these is Paterson's epic *The Man from Snowy River* (Buccaneer Books, 1996), which first hit the bestseller list in 1895 and was made into a film. But the literary scene has always been lively, and Australia has a wealth of classics, many of them with the Outback at their heart.

Miles Franklin wrote *My Brilliant Career* (HarperCollins, 2001), the story of a young woman faced with the dilemma of choosing between marriage and a career, in 1901; Colleen McCullough's *Thorn Birds* (Avon, 1996) is a romantic epic about forbidden love between a Catholic priest and a young woman; *We of the Never Never* (Avon, 1984) by Mrs. Aeneas Gunn, tells the story of a young woman who leaves the comfort of her Melbourne home to live on a cattle station in the Northern Territory; and *Walkabout* (Sundance, 1984) by James V. Marshall explores the relationship between an Aborigine and two lost children in the bush. It was later made into a powerful film.

If you can find it, *The Long Farewell* (Penguin Books, 1983) by Don Charlwood presents firsthand diary accounts of long journeys from Europe to Australia in the last century. A good historical account of the early days is Geoffrey Blainey's *The Tyranny of Distance* (Pan Macmillan, 1977), first published in 1966. Robert Hughes's *The Fatal Shore: The Epic of Australia's Founding* (Vintage Books, 1988) is a best-selling nonfiction study of the country's early days. For a contemporary, if somewhat dark, take on the settlement and development of Sydney, delve into John Birmingham's *Leviathan* (Random House, 1999). From an Aboriginal perspective, *Follow the Rabbit-Proof Fence* (University of Queensland Press, 1997) by Doris Pilkington tells the true story of three young girls from the "Stolen Generation" who ran away from a mission school to return to their families (a movie version was released in 2002).

Modern novelists include David Malouf, Elizabeth Jolley, Helen Garner, Sue

Woolfe, and Peter Carey, whose *True History of the Kelly Gang* (Vintage Books, 2001), a fictionalized autobiography of the outlaw Ned Kelly, won the Booker Prize in 2001. West Australian Tim Winton evokes his part of the continent in stunning prose; his latest novel, *Dirt Music* (Scribner, 2002), is no exception.

Outsiders who have tackled Australia include Jan Morris and Bill Bryson. Morris's *Sydney* (Viking) was published in 1992, and Bryson's *In a Sunburned Country* (Broadway Books, 2001), while not always a favorite with Australians, may appeal to American readers.

FAST FACTS: Australia

American Express For all travel-related customer inquiries regarding any American Express service, including reporting a lost card, call ℂ **1300/132 639.** To report lost or stolen traveler's checks, call ℂ **1800/251 902.**

Area Codes See "Telephones," below.

ATM Networks See "Money," p. 34.

Business Hours Banks are open Monday through Thursday from 9:30am to 4pm, Friday 9:30am to 5pm. General business hours are Monday through Friday from 8:30am to 5:30pm. Shopping hours are usually 8:30am to 5:30pm weekdays and 9am to 4 or 5pm on Saturday. Many shops close on Sunday, although major department stores and shops in tourist precincts are open 7 days.

Car Rentals See "Getting Around Australia," p. 68.

Currency See "Money," p. 34.

Dates Australians write their dates day/month/year; so March 6, 1958, is 06/03/58.

Driving Rules See "Getting Around Australia," p. 68.

Drugstores These are called "chemist shops" or "pharmacies." Australian pharmacists are permitted to fill only prescriptions written by Australian doctors.

Electricity The current is 240 volts AC, 50 hertz. Sockets take two or three flat, not rounded, prongs. North Americans and Europeans will need to buy a converter before they leave home (don't wait until you get to Australia, because Australian stores are likely to stock only converters for Aussie appliances to fit American and European outlets). Some large hotels have 110V outlets for electric shavers (or dual voltage), and some will lend converters, but don't count on it in smaller, less expensive hotels, motels, or B&Bs. Power does not start automatically when you plug in an appliance; you need to flick the switch beside the socket to the "on" position.

Embassies & Consulates Most diplomatic posts are in Canberra: **British High Commission,** Commonwealth Avenue, Canberra, ACT 2600 (ℂ 02/6270 6666); **Embassy of Ireland,** 20 Arkana St., Yarralumla, ACT 2600 (ℂ 02/6273 3022); **High Commission of Canada,** Commonwealth Avenue, Yarralumla, ACT 2600 (ℂ 02/6270 4000); **New Zealand High Commission,** Commonwealth Avenue, Canberra, ACT 2600 (ℂ 02/6270 4211); and the **United States Embassy,** 21 Moonah Place, Yarralumla, ACT 2600 (ℂ 02/6214 5600). Embassies or consulates with posts in state capitals are listed in "Fast Facts" in the relevant state chapters of this book.

Emergencies Dial ✆ **000** anywhere in Australia for police, ambulance, or the fire department. This is a free call from public and private telephones and needs no coins. The TTY emergency number is ✆ **106.**

Holidays See "Australia Calendar of Events," earlier in this chapter.

Information See "Visitor Information," earlier in this chapter. For telephone directory assistance within Australia, call ✆ **12455.**

Internet Access Internet access is available just about everywhere, including some of the smallest Outback towns, which generally have at least one cyber-cafe, coin-operated machines, or both. Coin-op terminals are also available at larger airports. Major tourist towns such as Darwin and Cairns sometimes have whole streets full of cybercafes.

Liquor Laws Hours vary from pub to pub, but most are open daily from around 10am or noon, to 10pm or midnight. The minimum drinking age is 18. Random breath tests to catch drunk drivers are common, and drunk-driving laws are strictly enforced. Getting caught drunk behind the wheel will mean a court appearance, not just a fine. The maximum permitted blood alcohol level is 0.05%. Alcohol is sold in liquor stores, in the "bottle shops" attached to every pub, and in some states in supermarkets.

Lost & Found Be sure to contact your credit card companies the minute you discover that your wallet has been lost or stolen, and file a report at the nearest police precinct. Your credit card company or insurer may require a police report number or record of the loss. Most credit card companies have an emergency toll-free number to call if your card is lost or stolen; they may be able to wire you a cash advance immediately or deliver an emergency credit card in a day or two. In Australia, call toll-free: **American Express** (✆ **1300/132 639**), **MasterCard** (✆ **1800/120 113**), and **Visa** (✆ **1800/125 440**). Visa's U.S. emergency number is ✆ **800/847-2911** or 410/581-9994. American Express cardholders and traveler's check holders should call ✆ **800/992-3404.** Master-Card holders should call ✆ **800/MC-ASSIST** or 636/722-7111. For other credit cards, call the toll-free number directory at ✆ **800/555-1212.**

If you need emergency cash over the weekend when all banks and American Express offices are closed, you can have money wired to you through **Western Union** (✆ **800/325-6000;** www.westernunion.com).

Identity theft and fraud are potential complications of losing your wallet, especially if you've lost your driver's license along with your cash and credit cards. Notify the major credit-reporting bureaus immediately; placing a fraud alert on your records may protect you against liability for criminal activity. The three major U.S. credit-reporting agencies are **Equifax** (✆ **800/766-0008;** www.equifax.com), **Experian** (✆ **888/397-3742;** www.experian.com), and **Trans Union** (✆ **800/479-8660;** www.transunion.com). Finally, if you've lost all forms of photo ID, call your airline and explain the situation; it might allow you to board the plane if you have a copy of your passport or birth certificate and a copy of the police report you've filed.

Mail A postcard costs A$1.10 (US88¢) to the United States, Canada, the United Kingdom, or New Zealand.

Maps Newsdealers, auto clubs, and bookstores are your best sources for maps (see "Getting Around Australia," p. 68).

Newspapers & Magazines The national daily newspaper is *The Australian,* which publishes an expanded edition with a color magazine on Saturday. Most capital cities have their own daily papers, usually a tabloid and a broadsheet. The Australian current-affairs magazine, *The Bulletin with Newsweek,* is published weekly, and there is an Australian edition of *Time.*

Passports **For Residents of the United States:** Whether you're applying in person or by mail, you can download passport applications from the U.S. State Department website at **http://travel.state.gov/passport_services.html**. To find your regional passport office, either check the U.S. State Department website or call the **National Passport Information Center** toll-free number (© **877/ 487-2778**) for automated information.

For residents of Canada: Passport applications are available at travel agencies throughout Canada or from the central **Passport Office,** Department of Foreign Affairs and International Trade, Ottawa, ON K1A 0G3 (© **800/567-6868;** www.ppt.gc.ca).

For residents of the United Kingdom: To pick up an application for a standard 10-year passport (5-year passport for children under 16), visit your nearest passport office, major post office, or travel agency, or contact the 24-hour hot line at the **United Kingdom Passport Service** (© **0870/521-0410;** www.ukpa.gov.uk).

For residents of Ireland: You can apply for a 10-year passport at the **Passport Office,** Setanta Centre, Molesworth Street, Dublin 2 (© **01/671-1633;** www.irl gov.ie/iveagh). Those under age 18 must apply for a 5-year passport (infants under 3 get a 3-year passport). You can also apply at 1A S. Mall, Cork (© **021/ 494-4700**), or at most main post offices.

For residents of New Zealand: You can pick up a passport application at any New Zealand Passports Office or download it from the website. Contact the **Passports Office** at © **0800/225 050** in New Zealand, or 04/474 8100, or log on to www.passports.govt.nz.

Pets Leave 'em at home. You will be back home planning your next vacation before Fluffy clears quarantine Down Under.

Pharmacies See "Drugstores," above.

Police Dial © **000** anywhere in Australia. This is a free call from public and private telephones and requires no coins.

Safety Violent crime is uncommon, and the political situation is stable. Guns are strictly controlled. Purse-snatchers are the same threat they are all over the world. See "Health & Safety," earlier in this chapter.

Smoking Smoking in most public areas, such as museums, cinemas, and theaters, is restricted or banned. Smoking in restaurants may be limited—Western Australia and New South Wales ban it altogether, and in many other states, restaurants have smoking and nonsmoking sections. Pubs and clubs, for a long time the last bastion for smokers, are also heading for total bans. These will be introduced from January 2006 in Tasmania and from July 2006 in Queensland and Western Australia. Victoria and New South Wales will go the same way in 2007. Australian aircraft on all routes are completely nonsmoking, as are all airport buildings.

Taxes Australia applies a 10% Goods and Services Tax (GST) on most products and services. Your international airline tickets to Australia are not taxed, nor are domestic airline tickets for travel within Australia *if you bought them outside Australia.* If you buy Australian airline tickets once you arrive in Australia, you will pay GST on them.

Through the Tourist Refund Scheme (TRS), Australians and international visitors can claim a refund of the GST (and of a 14.5% wine tax called Wine Equalisation Tax, or WET) paid on a purchase of more than A$300 (US$240) from a single outlet, within the last 30 days before you leave. More than one item may be included in that A$300. For example, you can claim the GST you paid on 10 T-shirts each worth A$30 (US$24), as long as they were bought from a single store. Do this as you leave by presenting your receipt or "tax invoice" to the Australian Customs Service's TRS booths, located beyond passport control in the International Terminal departure areas at most airports. If you buy several things on different days from one store, which together add up to A$300 or more, you must ask the store to total all purchases on one tax invoice (or receipt)—now there's a nice piece of bureaucracy to remember Australia by! Pack the items in your carry-on baggage, because you must show them to Customs. You can use the goods before you leave Australia and still claim the refund, but you cannot claim a refund on things you have consumed (film you use, say, or food). You cannot claim a refund on alcohol other than wine. Allow an extra 15 minutes to stand in line at the airport and get your refund.

You can also claim a refund if you leave Australia as a cruise passenger from Circular Quay or Darling Harbour in Sydney, Cairns, Darwin, Hobart, or Fremantle (Perth). If your cruise departs from elsewhere in Australia, or if you are flying out from an airport other than Sydney, Melbourne, Brisbane, Adelaide, Cairns, Perth, Darwin or the Gold Coast, telephone the **Australian Customs Service** (© **1300/363 263** in Australia, or 02/6275 6666) to see if you can still claim the refund.

Items bought in duty-free stores will not be charged GST. Nor will items you export—such as an Aboriginal painting that you buy in a gallery in Alice Springs and have shipped straight to your home outside Australia.

Basic groceries are not GST-taxed, but restaurant meals are.

Other taxes include departure tax of A$38 (US$30) for every passenger 12 years and over, included in the price of your airline ticket when you buy it in your home country; landing and departure taxes at some airports, also included in the price of your ticket; and "reef tax," officially dubbed the Environmental Management Charge, of A$4.50 (US$3.60) for every person over the age of 4 every time he or she enters the Great Barrier Reef Marine Park. (This charge goes toward park upkeep.)

Telephones The primary telecommunications network in Australia is Telstra (www.telstra.com).

To call Australia: If you're calling Australia from the United States:

1. Dial the international access code 011.
2. Dial the country code 61.
3. Dial the city code (drop the 0 from any area code given in this book) and then the number. So, if you're calling Sydney, the whole number you'd dial would be 011-61-2-0000-0000.

To make international calls: To make international calls from Australia, first dial 0011 and then the country code (U.S. or Canada 1, U.K. 44, Ireland 353, New Zealand 64). Next dial the area code and number. For example, if you wanted to call the British Embassy in Washington, D.C., you would dial 0011-1-202-588-7800. For other country codes, call ℂ **1222** or look in the back of the Australian White Pages.

For directory assistance: Dial ℂ **12455** if you're looking for a number inside Australia, or ℂ **1225** for numbers to all other countries.

For operator assistance: If you need operator assistance in making a call, dial ℂ **1234**. To make a collect call, dial ℂ **12550**. To find a number, call Directory Assistance at ℂ **1223** for numbers in Australia and ℂ **1225** for international numbers.

Toll-free numbers: Numbers beginning with 1800 in Australia are toll-free, but calling a U.S. 1-800 (or 1-888, 1-877, or 1-866) number from Australia is not toll-free; it costs the same as an overseas call.

Other numbers: Numbers starting with 13 or 1300 in Australia are charged at the local fee of A25¢ anywhere in Australia. Numbers beginning with 1900 (or 1901 or 1902 and so on) are pay-for-service lines, and you will be charged as much as A$5 (US$4) a minute.

Time Zone Eastern Standard Time (EST, sometimes also written as AEST) covers Queensland, New South Wales, the Australian Capital Territory, Victoria, and Tasmania. Central Standard Time (CST) is used in the Northern Territory and South Australia, and Western Standard Time (WST) is the standard in Western Australia. When it's noon in New South Wales, the ACT, Victoria, Queensland, and Tasmania, it's 11:30am in South Australia and the Northern Territory, and 10am in Western Australia. All states except Queensland, the Northern Territory, and Western Australia observe daylight saving time, usually from the last Sunday in October (the first Sun in Oct in Tasmania) to the last Sunday in March. However, not all states switch over to daylight saving on the same day or in the same week.

The east coast of Australia is GMT (Greenwich Mean Time) plus 10 hours. When it is noon on the east coast, it is 2am in London that morning, and 6pm in Los Angeles and 9pm in New York the previous night. These times are based on standard time, so allow for daylight saving in the Australian summer, or in the country you are calling. New Zealand is 2 hours ahead of the east coast of Australia, except during daylight saving, when it is 3 hours ahead of Queensland.

Tipping Tipping is not expected in Australia. It is usual to tip around 5% or round up to the nearest A$10 (US$8) for a substantial meal in a restaurant.

Some passengers round up to the nearest dollar in a cab, but it's okay to insist on every bit of change back. Tipping bellboys and porters is sometimes done, but no one tips bar staff, barbers, or hairdressers.

Useful Phone Numbers **U.S. Dept. of State Travel Advisory** (© 202/647-5225; staffed 24 hr.); **U.S. Passport Agency** (© 202/647-0518); **U.S. Centers for Disease Control International Traveler's Hotline** (© 877/FYI-TRIP).

Water Water is fine to drink everywhere. In the Outback, the taps may carry warm brackish water from underground, called "bore water," for showers and laundry, while drinking water is collected in rainwater tanks.

3

Suggested Itineraries

by Marc Llewellyn & Lee Mylne

Australia's size and its distance from Northern Hemisphere destinations are the two most daunting things about planning a visit. It's a long way to come for just a week, but if that's all you can spare, you still want to see as much as possible. While our inclination is to immerse ourselves in one spot, we're aware that not everyone wants to do that. Seeing as much as you can is often a priority.

Australia is a complex and fascinating place, merging ancient Aboriginal culture with modern life. You'll learn a lot in a week or two, but will have just scraped the surface of this vast nation.

If you're a first-time visitor, with only 1 or 2 weeks, you may find these two itineraries most helpful: **Australia in 1 Week** or **Australia in 2 Weeks.** These itineraries can be shifted around to suit your needs; you could substitute the Cairns section of Australia in 1 Week for the Uluru/Red Centre suggestions in Australia in 2 Weeks, flying from Sydney to Uluru.

If you've been to Australia before, or have already visited our major icons—Sydney, the Great Barrier Reef, or Uluru (Ayers Rock)—you might want to focus on another aspect of the country. You may even want to head out west to see the lesser-known, but very rewarding, parts of the country. If you're bringing your family with you, our Australia for Kids itinerary may give you some ideas to keep the young ones occupied (at the same time entertaining their parents).

You might also review our "Best of" chapter to see what experiences or sights have special appeal to you, and adjust the itineraries to suit your own interests.

Getting around this vast continent, where the major attractions are thousands of miles apart, is daunting and time-consuming. **Flying** is the only way to cover long distances efficiently, but unfortunately it can also be expensive. Remember to allow flying time in your itineraries and don't try to pack too much in on the days you fly—even domestic flights can be around 3 hours, and can be draining. See "Getting Around Australia" in chapter 2 for information about air passes and getting the best rate on Australia's domestic carriers.

Our best advice is to take a tip from Australians: If the pace gets too hectic, just chill out and reorder your sightseeing priorities. Take time to meet the locals and ask their advice on what you should see as well.

1 Australia in 1 Week

Impossible! Australia is so vast that in 1 week, only a small corner of it—perhaps one city or a few of the natural wonders—will be all you get in such a short time. It will be memorable, nevertheless, and careful planning will maximize your time and allow you to see some of the major sights.

Suggested Australia Itineraries

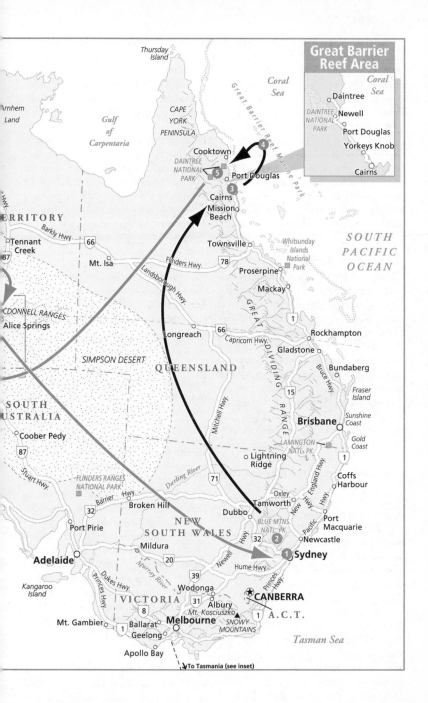

Use the following itinerary to make the most out of a week in Australia, but make sure you don't exhaust yourself trying to cram everything in. Australians are a laid-back lot, generally, and in some places the pace is relaxed. And that's just the way to enjoy it. One week provides barely enough time to see the best of Sydney, which for most people is the entry point to Australia. Your first view of the **Sydney Harbour Bridge** and the **Opera House** may well be from the air as your plane comes in. It's a spectacular introduction to a great city.

If you have only a week and want to head farther afield, there are two main choices, depending on your interests. The **Great Barrier Reef** is a "must" for divers, but don't forget that you must allow time either side of your reef trip before flying. There are no such problems with Australia's other icon, **Uluru (Ayers Rock),** in the heart of the **Red Centre.** This triangle, of course, is something of a cliché, but still gives you a complete Australian experience. Realistically, you will have to choose between the Reef and the Rock, or choose not to scuba dive while you are in Queensland.

Days ❶ & ❷: Arrive in Sydney ★★★

Check into your hotel and spend whatever time you have after arrival recovering from almost-guaranteed jetlag. If you arrive in the morning and have a full day ahead of you, try to stay up and hit the nearest cafe for a shot of caffeine to keep you going. Head to **Circular Quay** and from there get a fantastic view of **Sydney Harbour Bridge,** before strolling to the **Sydney Opera House** and soaking up some history at **The Rocks.** If you have time, you can take the ferry from Circular Quay to Manly beach to round off a fairly easy day with fish and chips, then head to bed for some much-needed sleep.

Start **Day 2** with a ride to the top of the Sydney AMP Tower, for stunning 360-degree views of the city, stretching as far as the Blue Mountains. The 295m (984-ft.) tower has several attractions, including the Great Australian Exhibition Ride—a simulator ride the kids will love. For an introduction to Australia's wildlife, head to Taronga Zoo or the Sydney Aquarium. If you enjoy museums, put the Australia Museum, the Australian National Maritime Museum at Darling Harbour, and the interactive Powerhouse Museum on your list for the day. For an insight into Sydney's beginnings as a convict settlement, visit the Hyde Park Barracks

Museum, a convict-built prison. Finish off your day with a twilight (or later at weekends) **Bridge-Climb** ★ or take the kids to **Luna Park,** a small and fairly traditional amusement park that's at its best at night.

Day ❸: A Day Trip to the Blue Mountains ★★★

Take the train from Central Station to Katoomba for a day, exploring the beauty of the Blue Mountains, 2 hours from Sydney. Once there, jump on the Blue Mountains Explorer Bus, which allows you to hop on and off wherever you please. There are also many day-tour operators running to the Blue Mountains from Sydney. Whichever mode of transport you use, don't miss the spectacular Three Sisters rock formations, best viewed from Echo Point Road at Katoomba.

The adventurous might prefer to take a tour from Katoomba to the **Jenolan Caves,** about a 90-minute drive southwest. Nine caves are open for exploration, and you can take canyoning tours of between 3 hours and a full day. Head back to Sydney and have dinner somewhere with a view of the harbor.

Day ❹: Cairns, gateway to the Great Barrier Reef

On **Day 4,** take the earliest flight you can from Sydney to Cairns—flight time is 3 hours—and check into a hotel in the city, which on such a tight schedule will make getting to the major attractions quicker and easier than staying on the northern beaches, out of town. Explore the city a little and to see some wildlife—including a massive saltwater crocodile—in the bizarre setting of the **Cairns Rainforest Dome,** atop the Hotel Sofitel **Reef Casino.** You will have time the rest of the day to head out to visit the **Tjapukai Aboriginal Cultural Park** ✦. If you are not going to the Red Centre, this is a great place to learn about Aboriginal culture and life, albeit in a theme-park kind of way. You could spend several hours here, or save the visit for the evening, when **Tjapukai by Night** tours give a different look at traditional ceremonies, including dinner and a fire-and-water outdoor show.

Day ❺: A day trip to the Reef ★★★

Day trips to the Great Barrier Reef leave from the Reef Fleet Terminal. The trip to the outer reef takes about 2 hours, and once there you will spend your day on a pontoon with about 300 people. Experienced divers may prefer to take a day trip with one of the dive charter companies who take smaller groups and visit two or three reefs. The pontoons of the big operators also offer the chance to take a scenic flight—a truly spectacular experience. Divers must spend another 24 hours in Cairns before flying. If you are content to snorkel, ride the glass-bottom boats, and soak up the sun, you will be able to fly the next day. After returning to Cairns, take a stroll along the Esplanade and eat at one of the busy cafes and restaurants that line the strip.

Day ❻: Kuranda or the Daintree ★★

Waiting out the day after diving (you can't fly for 24 hours after you've been on a dive) can be spent discovering another aspect to Australia—the rainforest. Take a trip to the mountain village of **Kuranda** aboard the steam train along the **Kuranda Scenic Railway,** past waterfalls and gorges. In Kuranda, explore the markets and the nature parks, and maybe take a **Kuranda Riverboat Tour,** which runs about 45 minutes. Make your return journey on the **Skyrail** cableway, which carries you over the rainforest (you can get to ground level at a couple of stations on the way) to the edge of Cairns. The views are sensational.

Another option is to head to the World Heritage–listed **Daintree rainforest** ✦, 2 hours' drive north of Cairns. Many tour operators, including Port Douglas–based Heritage & Interpretive Tours, run day tours into the Daintree and Cape Tribulation National Parks. If you are exploring on your own, make time for a 1-hour cruise on the **Daintree River** with **Dan Irby's Mangrove Adventures,** where you will travel in a small open boat and see lots of fascinating wildlife. Both day and night tours are highly recommended.

If you choose the Daintree option, overnight in the lovely resort town of **Port Douglas** and head to one of its great restaurants—try **Nautilus** for fine dining or **Salsa Bar & Grill** for a more relaxed and lively atmosphere.

Day ❼: Cairns to Sydney

Drive back to Cairns in the morning, and head to the airport for your flight to Sydney. Unless you have a flight directly out of Cairns, you will spend most of your last day in Australia returning to Sydney. With the time you have left in Sydney, treat yourself to dinner at a restaurant overlooking the harbor, with its bridge and Opera House illuminated. It's a sight you'll carry home with you.

2 Australia in 2 Weeks

With 2 weeks, your visit to Australia will be much more relaxed and you will get a greater sense of the diversity of Australia, its landscape, and its people. You will get to see all three icons—Sydney, the Great Barrier Reef, and Uluru—in more depth, and maybe even have time to go outside those areas, especially if you limit your icons to two instead of three.

Days ❶ through ❻: Follow itineraries as outlined above

Day ❼: Cairns to Uluru

On **Day 7,** leave Cairns as early as you can (this will probably mean spending the night in Cairns rather than Port Douglas). Your flight to Ayers Rock Airport will take around 3 hours, sometimes more, depending on the type of aircraft you are on. Make sure you book a direct flight, and not one that goes via Sydney! Try to get a window seat for the spectacular views as you fly over the Outback.

If you take the early flight, you can be in **Uluru** by around 9am, which gives you the whole day to take in the enormity of this fabulous monolith. Take the shuttle from Ayers Rock Resort (which is the only place to stay, but offers many accommodations choices) to the Rock. If you decide to **climb** Uluru (remembering that the Aboriginal traditional owners would prefer you didn't), make sure you don't do it at the hottest time of day. A climb will take you between 2 and 4 hours, depending on your fitness. An alternative is to join **Anangu Tours** for a walk around it; one of the best is the late-afternoon Kuniya walk, which concludes with watching sunset over Uluru—an unforgettable sight. Spend some time in the impressive and interesting **Uluru-Kata Tjuta Cultural Centre** near the base of Uluru. And after doing all that in a day, you'll be ready for a quiet dinner at whatever hotel you've chosen.

Day ❽: Exploring Uluru ★★★

Sunrise is one of the magic times at Uluru, so make the effort to get up early on Day 8. This is also a great time to do the 9.6km (6-mile) Base Walk circumnavigating Uluru, which takes 2 to 3 hours. There are a range of other ways to experience Uluru, including camel rides, Harley-Davidson tours, and helicopter joy-flights, but walking up close to the Rock beats them all, in my opinion.

You will also have time today to head to **Kata Tjuta** (also called The Olgas) where you will see there is much more to the Red Centre than just one Rock. Kata Tjuta is about 48km (30 miles) west of Uluru, but plenty of tours go there if you do not have your own wheels.

End your day in the desert with the Sounds of Silence dinner, run by Ayers Rock Resort. Sip champagne as the sun sets over Uluru, to the eerie music of the didgeridoo, then tuck into kangaroo, barramundi, and other native foods. But it's not the food you're here for—it's the silence and the stars. A short stargazing session with an astronomer ends a memorable evening.

Day ❾: Uluru to Kings Canyon

Hire a 4WD and tackle the long Outback drive from Uluru to Alice Springs, stopping for a night at **Kings Canyon**. It is 306km (190 miles) from Uluru to Kings Canyon (also known as **Watarrka National Park**), which offers another unbeatable look at Outback Australia. You can spend the afternoon walking up the side of the canyon and around the rim. It is very steep, and will take you around 4 hours. A gentler walk is the short and shady canyon floor walk. Stay overnight at Kings Canyon Resort.

Day ⑩: Kings Canyon to Alice Springs

Get an early start for Alice Springs, and take the unpaved but interesting Mereenie Loop Road, which will take you through the Glen Helen Gorge or the historic Hermannsburg mission settlement. Whichever road you take, the scenery is like nowhere else in Australia. You will probably spend most of the day driving to Alice, making a few stops along the way.

On arrival check into a hotel and head out to one of the local restaurants, several of which offer sophisticated versions of "bush tucker" including kangaroo, emu, and crocodile dishes.

Day ⑪: Alice Springs

If you can stand another early start, take a **dawn balloon flight** over the desert, usually followed by a champagne breakfast. If you don't head back to bed immediately for a few hours catch-up sleep, there are plenty of attractions to discover, including the **Alice Springs Desert Park** for a look at some unusual Australian creatures, the **School of the Air,** and the **Royal Flying Doctor Service** base. In the afternoon, take a half-day tour with an Aboriginal guide at the **Aboriginal Art & Culture Centre.** Alternatively, visit the **Alice Springs Telegraph Station historical reserve** set in an oasis just outside town for a look at early settler life. Finish the day with a **sunset camel ride**

down the dry Todd River bed and have dinner at the camel farm.

Day ⑫: Alice Springs to Sydney

Direct flights from Alice Springs to Sydney leave in the early afternoon, so you have all morning to explore more of the town and perhaps buy some Aboriginal art (this is one of the best places to get it).

On arrival in Sydney after an almost 3-hour flight, book into your hotel and spend the night discovering some of the city's nightlife.

Day ⑬: A day at Bondi Beach

For sands of a different kind to those you've experienced in recent days, take the bus to Sydney's most famous beach, **Bondi,** and spend it lazing on the sand or—in summer, at least—taking a dip in the surf. Take the Bondi Explorer bus from Circular Quay, which gives you a choice of harborside bays and coastal beaches, or take the train to Bondi Junction and then a bus to the beach. The scenic cliff-top walk to **Bronte Beach** is worth doing, or you can continue farther to **Coogee.**

Day ⑭: Sydney

Your final day in Australia can be spent on last-minute shopping and seeing those Sydney sights that you haven't had time for so far. Cap it all off with a slap-up seafood dinner somewhere with a fantastic view of the Harbour Bridge.

3 Australia for Families (Starting in Sydney)

Australia is an unbelievable destination for kids—and not just for the kangaroos and koalas that almost every child (and parent!) is desperate to see. Our suggestion is to explore Sydney for 2 days with family in tow, then head up to the beautiful Blue Mountains on a day trip to ride the cable car and the world's steepest railway. The climax comes with a few days exploring the Barrier Reef and the rainforest around Port Douglas.

Days ① & ②: Sydney

First off, head to Circular Quay to see the Sydney Opera House. A tour inside might be a bit much for younger kids, but you can walk around a fair bit of it

and take the obligatory photos of Australia's most famous landmark. To stretch your legs, head from here into the Royal Botanic Gardens to spot long-beaked ibises wandering around the grass and hundreds of fruit bats squabbling among the treetops in the jungle section in the middle of the gardens.

Walk back past the Opera House and the ferries to The Rocks, where you can take a quick stroll through the historic streets, stopping off for a look at The Puppet Shop at the Rocks, where you can get up close to a (puppet) kangaroo or emu with strings attached.

There are plenty of places to eat lunch, but a filling prospect is pasta or ravioli or the likes at Rossini, opposite the ferry terminals, where you can sit outside and watch the world go by. Portions are large, so you might want to split a meal between younger kids.

After lunch take a ferry to Taronga Zoo, where a cable car takes you up the hill to the main entrance. All the kids' favorites are here, from kangaroos and koalas to platypuses, located in a nocturnal house. A farmyard section edges onto a playground of sorts with lots of water features to give your kids a sprinkle on a hot day.

On **Day 2** head to the city center for an elevator ride up to the top of Sydney Tower, where you can look right across Sydney as far as the Blue Mountains in the distance. Entry includes admission to Skytour, which features a darkened storytelling room where the kids can learn a little about Australian legends and Aborigines, and there's also a thrilling simulator ride that takes you on adventures throughout Australia.

It's a short walk from here to Darling Harbour, where you can cap off the morning with a visit to Sydney Aquarium. The sharks are huge here, and they swim right above your head, but the real attraction is the amazing Barrier Reef section, where tens of thousands of colorful fish swim by in huge tanks to the sound of classical music.

Eat lunch at one of the many cheap eateries on the other side of the bridge

before either taking the monorail back to Town Hall or taking another ferry from near the Aquarium back to Circular Quay.

If it's a hot day, or you just want to go to the beach, you have two main choices: From Circular Quay you can take a half-hour ferry ride, or a 15-minute high-speed JetCat to Manly. Here you can laze the afternoon away, and can even rent a surfboard, body board, or in-line skates. Or, take a CityRail train from Town Hall to Bondi, then a bus to Bondi Beach, where you can reward your efforts with ice cream or a late afternoon pizza from Pompei's, on the main drag.

Day ❸: The Blue Mountains

You could easily spend a couple more days with the kids having fun in Sydney, but you shouldn't miss a trip the mountains. Several companies run tour buses to the area, stopping off at an animal park along the way. The best one to visit is Featherdale, where you can get up close to more kangaroos, koalas, and Tasmanian Devils. The tour will also stop at Scenic World, where you can take the short ride on the Scenic Railway. It's very steep, so hold on tight. At the bottom you'll find yourselves among an ancient tree fern forest—it's truly remarkable. A short walk takes you to the Skyway, a cable car that travels 300m (984 ft.) above the Jamison Valley.

Elsewhere in the mountains there are fabulous views across craggy bluffs and deep bowls of gum trees. It's a long day, so pack plenty of snacks and a few favorite toys.

Days ❹, ❺ & ❻: The Reef and the Rainforest

Now it's time to head north, up the tropics. You'll need to fly, of course, otherwise it would take you several days to drive up the coast. Most people base themselves in Port Douglas rather than Cairns, because the beach is huge and uncrowded and some of the best trips originate from here.

After the flight, relax on the beach, but remember to swim inside the nets off the sand; the "stingers" (box jellyfish) around here can cause life-threatening stings, especially where kids are concerned.

The next day, it's time to visit the reef. Thankfully, once on the reef itself, the dangerous jellyfish are very uncommon. Cruise boats take around 90 minutes to get from Port Douglas to the outer reef, but once there you are in for some amazing snorkeling. Expect to see numerous species of corals and fish, and even an occasional turtle. A good seafood lunch is generally served onboard so you won't go hungry!

On **Day 6,** it's time for a real jungle experience. Tours leave Port Douglas daily for the Daintree National Park and the Cape Tribulation Rainforests. Usually included in the tour is a boat trip among the local crocodiles, a stroll along an isolated beach, and, of course, walks in the rainforest, where you emerge into a dripping world of palms, strangler figs, staghorns, pythons, frogs, and electric-blue butterflies.

On the 7th day, fly back to Sydney. If you have time, take the kids by ferry to Luna Park, just across from Circular Quay, or walk there across the Harbour Bridge. The fun park is small, with a few rides suitable for younger kids, but it does boast a magnificent view across to the Harbour Bridge and Opera House, which look glorious after the sun's gone down.

4 An Inland Odyssey: Driving from Sydney to Melbourne

When Sydneysiders get tired of the city they often dream of "going bush." If they could, they'd head west into the setting sun and out into the Outback. Not many local city slickers ever get to realize their dream, but you can do it for them on this 7-day inland odyssey from Sydney to Melbourne.

Day ❶: The Blue Mountains

Armed with your road map, leave Sydney via Parramatta Road, by the M4 motorway and the Great Western Highway. Two hours should see you safely in the cool of the Blue Mountains. Drive into the little town of Katoomba, where you could stop for a quick coffee break or early lunch at the historic Paragon Café before taking a short spin to see the incredible views across to the Three Sisters rock formation from Echo Point. From here, follow the signs to Scenic World, where you can take the world's steepest railway into an enchanting world of tree ferns—it will take just a couple of minutes to get down. Take the cable car up and continue on your journey.

Keep following the Great Western Highway as it heads west for 39km (24 miles), through Blackheath, Mount Victoria, and Hartley, and then downhill toward the old mining town of Lithgow. The most famous attraction around here is the **Zig-Zag Railway** ★★, a former coal route that crosses the valleys on impressive viaducts and winds around the eucalyptus-covered hills. A steam train runs the 18km (11-mile) back-and-forth route on Wednesdays, Saturdays, Sundays, and school holidays, and a diesel train does the route on other days. It costs A$20 (US$16) for adults round-trip and A$10 (US$8) for kids, and takes 1½ hours. Call ✆ 02/6355 2955 for details.

The highway leads from here down onto the plains and into **Bathurst** ★, approximately 200km (124 miles) west of Sydney, and 5km (3 miles) west of Lithgow. Bathurst, which was proclaimed a city in 1815, is the oldest inland settlement in Australia. Its 19th-century architecture is beautifully preserved, and makes for pleasant wandering. Stay here for the night.

Day ❷: Canowindra to Dubbo

It's a 56km (34-mile) drive along the Mitchell Highway from Bathurst to Orange. Highly recommended is a 58km (36-mile) sidetrack down through a landscape of spare trees and orange soil to **Canowindra,** to visit the Age of Fishes Museum (www.ageoffishes.org.au). A chance discovery in 1955 near here revealed an extensive fossil bed dating back 360 million years, and containing over 3,500 fish, some with armored shells, lungs, and huge jaws like crocodiles. The fish are well displayed, many still in their muddy-looking rock shelves.

Make your way back to the Mitchell Highway for the 150km (93-mile) trek northwest to Dubbo, which has that beginning-of-the-Outback feel, with plenty of Akubra hats around. Five kilometers (3 miles) south of town is the **Western Plains Zoo,** set in over 300 hectares (741 acres) of bushland and home to more than 1,000 animals, which roam large outdoor enclosures. The zoo has paths for walking, cycling, and vehicles, and is worth visiting if you have the time.

Day ❸: Mount Grenfell and Wilcannia

From Dubbo continue for 166km (103 miles) along the highway to Nyngan, a small township on the edge of the true Outback where you can while away a short time in the local museum or spot birds among the rivergums at Rotary Park.

From here the Barrier Highway scoots across dusty arid red plains for 597km (370 miles) to Broken Hill. The best place to stop for the night is Cobar, 133km (83 miles) from Nyngan. There's an excellent rural museum here, and some fascinating local pubs and historic buildings.

You'll find some of the best Aboriginal art in NSW at **Mount Grenfell,** 40km (25 miles) farther along the Barrier Highway

from Cobar—a signpost directs you off the main road and it's another 32km (19 miles) to three rock overhangs where 1,300 richly colored stencils and drawings cover the surfaces.

It's a 265km (164-mile) drive from here to **Wilcannia,** across a landscape scuttling with giant lizards and emus (the 'roos usually come out at dusk). Wilcannia can seem a bit threatening because of the Aborigines who tend to cluster around in the streets, but they love to talk, so don't worry too much.

From Wilcannia you can veer north along a bitumen road for 97km (60 miles) to the opal-mining town of **White Cliffs** (p. 237), where most people live underground.

Day ❹: White Cliffs on the way to Broken Hill

It's worth spending most of the day discovering the fascinating sights of White Cliffs before making your way back to the highway and completing the 197km (122-mile) journey to **Broken Hill** (p. 234).

Day ❺: Opal Mining in Broken Hill

Rest up in **Broken Hill** ⭐ for the day, and make sure you take a tour of the town with a local tour company; you won't regret it. Sights to see include the School of the Air and the Royal flying Doctor Service base, as well as popping out to **Silverton** (p. 236).

Days ❻ & ❼: Down to Mildura and the Murray Valley

A long, 295km (183-mile) drive takes you south along the Silver City Highway to Mildura, where you can stop for lunch. It's another 544km (337 miles) from here to Melbourne, but there are good highways much of the way. A good stopover for the night is **Echuca** (p. 602), 210km (130 miles) north of Melbourne, reached by the Murray Valley Highway, where you can spend the morning on a paddle steamer on the Murray River.

5 A Few Days in Margaret River, WA

Getting to see more of Australia than its most famous icons and the east-coast beaches is not always easy. But if you have the time, there are many wonderful places to discover off the beaten track, which will give another dimension to your image and memories of Australia. Here, we suggest a few days in the Margaret River region, just a few hours' drive south of the Western Australia capital, Perth. You can add it on to the end of a week or so in the east, or change it with the latter part of the 1- or 2-week itineraries above.

Note that each year from August to mid-November, the southern half of Western Australia is blessed with a carpet of 12,000 species of white, yellow, mauve, pink, red, and blue **wildflowers** ✿. Wildflower shows and festivals in country towns throughout the state accompany the annual blossoming. September and October are the peak months.

Starting from the pleasant, sunny city of Perth, you can tailor your trek for wildlife watching, winery tours, and the chance to see unique small villages.

Fly to Perth from any of the other destinations above; for specific information on getting there from the other capitals or overseas (if you choose to start in the west and head east), see chapter 10, "Perth & Western Australia."

Day ❶: Welcome to Perth

The capital of Western Australia, **Perth** ✿, has great food, a fabulous outdoor life of biking and beaches, plenty of smallish museums well worth a look, and a beautiful historic port, Fremantle. If you'd like to spend a day or so getting over your jet lag as well as getting to know the city, you can overnight here before taking off on your exploration of WA. A relaxing way to spend the day is at the port of **Fremantle** ✿, about 19km (12 miles) south of Perth's downtown at the mouth of the Swan River.

"Freo" is a bustling district of 150 National Trust buildings, alfresco cafes, museums, galleries, pubs, markets, and shops in a masterfully preserved historical atmosphere. It's still a working port, so you will see fishing boats unloading and yachts gliding in and out of the harbor. Perth's population makes a beeline for the place every weekend, resulting in a wonderful hubbub of buzzing shoppers, merchants, java drinkers, yachties, tourists, and fishermen. You can enjoy the parade as you knock back a beer or two on the veranda of a gorgeous old pub.

Day ❷: Perth to Margaret River

A leisurely 4-hour drive southwest from Perth will put you on the edge of the vineyards of Margaret River, a compact region which is easy to find your way around. En route, stop off at the town of Bunbury, where you may be lucky enough to see the **wild dolphins,** which regularly come in to "play" with visitors. Make the township of Margaret River your base for a few days' touring which will take you to your choice of around 40 wineries, as well as art galleries and many other gourmet produce outlets. Have dinner at one of the gourmet restaurants in Margaret River's main street—perhaps try the local seafood specialty, marron (a crustacean), with a bottle of Margaret River wine.

Day ❸: South to Cape Leeuwin

Spend the rest of the day traveling the winding country roads of the southwest "hook" of Western Australia. Caves Road runs from Margaret River south to Augusta and the historic lighthouse at **Cape Leeuwin,** where the Indian and Southern oceans meet. Augusta is also one of the best places in the south to see migrating whales in season and there are many tours available. Your trip will take you through stands of massive karri and jarrah trees. Don't miss Boranup Drive, a scenic detour that will take you to the coast for a view of the Indian Ocean. For the adventurous, there is a maze of caves, some of which are open to the public. Have lunch at one of the winery restaurants or picnic in their lovely gardens. Wind your way back to Margaret River, with the car stocked with some new wines to try, as well as local cheeses, olive oil, and more. Remember to designate a driver before setting out if you are planning to wine taste; Australia's drink-driving laws are strictly enforced and carry heavy penalties.

Day ❹: North to Cape Naturaliste and Perth

Caves Road runs north from Margaret River heading for Cape Naturaliste. Northwest of the town of **Cowaramup** you will find clusters of wineries including some of Australia's big names, as well as the **Margaret River Chocolate Company.** Take your time through the tree-lined country roads and take time to explore some of the local galleries and enjoy the wildlife. At Yallingup, you will swing northeast for Dunsborough, where—between June and November— you can go whale-watching as the majestic humpbacks migrate. Another stop on your way back to Perth should be at the seaside town of Busselton, where a visit to the underwater observatory on the jetty is well worthwhile.

Sydney

by Marc Llewellyn

Sunny, sexy, and sophisticated, Sydney (pop. 4.1 million) basks in its worldwide recognition as the shining star of the Southern Hemisphere. The "Emerald City" is one of the most attractive on earth. Some people compare it to San Francisco—it certainly has that relaxed feel—but the gateway to Australia is very much its own unique city.

First, of course, there's the Sydney Opera House, one of the most recognized buildings in the world. This white-sailed construction on Sydney Cove, designed by Danish architect Jørn Utzon, is the pride of the city—but there's far more on offer.

For example, you can walk across that other great icon, the Sydney Harbour Bridge, on the pathway beside the trains and traffic and catch the CityRail train back into town. Those with a daredevil spirit can join a Bridge Climb tour across catwalks and ladders to the top of the main arch for 360-degree views across the Opera House and the ferries and boats below.

Sydney is one of the biggest cities in the world—but fortunately most of the interesting things are concentrated in a relatively compact area around one of the finest urban harbors in the world.

There's so much to do in Sydney that you could easily spend a week here and still find yourself crashing into bed at night exhausted by trying to see all the main attractions.

Sydney's greatest summer experience is on the beaches—and with over 20 strung along the city's oceanfront and dozens more around the harbor, you'll be spoiled for choice. The most famous is Bondi, a strip of golden sand legendary for its Speedo-clad Lifesavers and surfboard riders. From here a "must do" is the 3.2km (2-mile) coastal path that leads off across the cliff tops, via cozy Tamarama Beach (dubbed "Glamourama" for its chic sun worshippers), to glorious Bronte Beach, where you can cool down in the crashing waves of the Pacific.

Another beach favorite is Manly, a 30-minute ferry trip from Circular Quay. Pick up some fish and chips and head for the main beach, flanked by a row of giant pines that chatter with hundreds of colorful lorikeets at dusk.

The best time to return is in the early evening, when the lights of the skyscrapers around Circular Quay streak like rainbows across the water of the harbor, and the sails of the Opera House and the girders of the Harbour Bridge are lit up—it's magical.

History is enshrined in its many museums and art galleries, while modern Sydney comes alive in the more recent developments around Darling Harbour and the restaurant and entertainment area nearby at Cockle Bay and Kings Wharf. At Darling Harbour you'll find the world-class Sydney Aquarium. You can also start your gourmet tour of Sydney's Modern Australian cooking style, which encompasses the best of freshness with spices from Asia and flavors from the Mediterranean.

Add to all this the side trips to the gorges and cliffs of the Blue Mountains, the wineries of the Hunter Valley, and the dolphin- and whale-watching around Port Stephens (see "Port Stephens: Dolphin- & Whale-Watching" in chapter 5), and you'll see why Sydney gets so much praise.

The frugal traveler will find that, compared to other major international cities, Sydney offers good value. Food and public transport are cheap, and attractions are generally not prohibitively expensive. (Senior and student prices are almost always available if you have identification.) The price of a hotel room is far cheaper than in other major population centers such as New York and London.

1 Orientation

ARRIVING

BY PLANE **Sydney International Airport** is 8km (5 miles) from the city center. Free shuttle buses link the international and domestic terminals. In both terminals, you'll find luggage carts, wheelchairs, a post office (open Mon–Fri 9am–5pm), mailboxes, currency exchange, duty-free shops (including one before you go through Customs on arrival, selling alcohol and perfume), restaurants, bars, stores, showers, luggage lockers, a Baggage Held Service for larger items, ATMs, and tourist information desks. You can rent mobile phones in the international terminal. There is also a Sydney Visitors Centre bookings desk (© **02/9667 6050**) offering cheap deals on hotels (see "Where to Stay," later in this chapter), as well as car rental, phone cards, and maps and brochures. Here you can also buy the SydneyPass (see section 2, "Getting Around"). The airport is efficient, has extremely strict quarantine procedures—you must declare all food—and is completely nonsmoking. On arrival, pick up a copy of *Sydney The Official Guide,* from the rack just before passport control, which contains tear-out discount tickets for some of Sydney's major attractions. Luggage trolleys are free in the international arrival terminal but cost A$3 (US$2.40) outside the departure terminal (you'll need coins). *Tip:* Duty-free alcohol and perfumes are available on arrival in Sydney from an international flight. You can take two bottles of standard alcohol through Customs without declaring them.

GETTING INTO TOWN The **Sydney Airport Train Link** connects the international and domestic airports to the city stations of Central, Museum, St. James, Circular Quay, Wynyard, and Town Hall. You'll need to change trains for other Sydney stations. Unfortunately, the line has no dedicated luggage areas and, because it's on a scheduled route into the city from the suburbs, it gets very crowded during rush hours (approx. 7–9am and 4–6:30pm). If you have lots of luggage and you're traveling into

---

Tips Tourist Refund Scheme

Visitors to Australia are entitled to claim any Goods and Services Tax (GST) on purchases over A$300 (US$240) per store. The GST component is 10% of the sale price. Do this at the refund booth located past Customs. After doing the paperwork—you need to have the goods and receipt with you, not in your checked luggage—you will receive your refund by check on the spot. You can convert this to cash at any foreign exchange booth at Sydney Airport.

St. Albans

YENGO NATIONAL PARK

Wiseman's Ferry

DHARUG NATIONAL PARK

36

Spencer

Gunderman

Old Sydney Town

Australian Reptile Park

Wamberal

Gosford

Terrigal

Avoca Beach

83

Brisbane Water

1

BRISBANE WATER NAT'L PARK

Woy Woy

Killcare Heights

BOUDDI NATIONAL PARK

Maroota

65

36

MARRAMARRA NATIONAL PARK

Mooney Mooney

Brooklyn

Broken Bay

Barrenjoy Head

Palm Beach

Cattai

Hawkesbury

Old Northern Rd.

Glenorie

83

KU-RING-GAI CHASE NATIONAL PARK

Avalon

Newport

14

Pitt Town

Berowra

Elanora Heights

Mona Vale

Windsor

2

Pacific Hwy.

Berowra Creek

Sydney-Newcastle Fwy.

3

Oxford Falls

Narrabeen

Collaroy

See "Sydney Harbour" Map

Dee Why

Hornsby

1

Brookvale

Dural

1

14

Manly

Pennant Hills

Koala Park

Epping

Chatswood

2

Mosman

Watsons Bay

Windsor Rd.

7

2

3

2

76

40

Baulkham Hills

Ryde

Sydney

Bondi

Featherdale Wildlife Park

Parramatta

Sydney Olympic Park, Homebush Bay

Randwick

Rooty Hill

Blacktown

4

Strathfield

4

Randwick Racecourse

Prospect Reservoir

5

64

70

4

7

Western Motorway

Australian Wildlife Park

Wonderland Sydney

Fairfield

Hume Hwy.

Bankstown

Sydney Int'l Airport

69

Cabramatta

31

Warwick Raceway

5

Botany Bay

BOTANY BAY NATIONAL PARK

Liverpool

MS Motorway

1

7

Cronulla

69

Camden Valley Way

Hume Hwy.

Sutherland

Bundeena

Princes Hwy.

ROYAL NATIONAL PARK

AUSTRALIA

Sydney
Canberra

31

0   1000 Mi
0   1000 Km

Campbelltown

69

0   15 mi
0   15 km

> ### *Tips* Taxi Savvy
>
> Especially in busy periods, taxi queues can be long, and drivers may try to cash in by insisting you share a cab with other passengers in line at the airport. Here's the scam: After dropping off the other passengers, the cab driver will attempt to charge you the full price of the journey, despite the fact that the other passengers paid for their sections. You certainly won't save any money sharing a cab if this happens, and your journey will be a long one. I find it's often better to wait until you can get your own cab, or catch an airport bus to the city center (and then take a taxi from there to your hotel, if necessary). If you are first in line in the taxi stand, the law states that you can refuse to share the cab.

the city at these times, it's probably best to take an airport bus (below) or a taxi. Otherwise walk to the end of the platform, and there should be more room onboard. There are elevators at the Airport Train Link stations and some at the city train stations (but the crowds and lack of staff and signs mean you'll probably end up lugging it all up loads of steps anyway). The train takes 10 minutes to reach the Central Railway Station and continues to Circular Quay. Trains leave every 15 minutes or so and cost A$11 (US$8.80) one-way for adults and A$7.30 (US$5.80) for children. Round-trip fares are A$16 (US$13) for adults (A$14/US$11 off-peak—for travel before 9am weekdays, and all day on weekends and public holidays), and A$11 (US$8.80) for children. Adults can take advantage of the **City Hopper ticket** which means you can travel to the city from the airport and use CityRail trains all day within the city center (bounded by North Sydney, Kings Cross, and Redfern stations). Tickets cost A$18 (US$15) for travel in peak time and A$16 (US$13) for off-peak travel.

Another option is a **Group Ticket,** which allows up to three adults to travel into the city together for a set price of A$27 (US$21). You can only buy this ticket at the airport.

Finally, a **Family Fare** ticket allows a second child (or more) to travel for free with an adult. The first child pays the standard child fare.

The **Kingsford Smith Airport Coach** operates to the city center from bus stops outside the terminals. This service will drop you off (and pick you up) at your hotel (pickups require at least 1 hr. advance notice; call © **02/9667 3221**). Tickets cost A$7 (US$5.60) one-way and A$11 (US$8.80) round-trip. The return portion can be used at any time in the future.

A **taxi** from the airport to the city center costs about A$27 (US$22). In 2005 a A$2 (US$1.60) surcharge was added to taxi fares from the airport. An expressway, the Eastern Distributor, is the fastest way to reach the city from the airport. There's a A$3.50 (US$2.80) toll from the airport to the city (the taxi driver pays the toll and adds the cost to your fare), but there is no toll to the airport. A 10% credit card charge applies. The flag-fall rate is A$2.75 (US$2.15) and a booking fee (not necessary at the airport) is A$1.15 (US90¢).

BY TRAIN   Central Station (© **13 15 00** for CityRail, or 13 22 32 for Countrylink interstate trains) is the main city and interstate train station. It's at the top of George Street in downtown Sydney. All interstate trains depart from here, and it's a major CityRail hub. Many city buses leave from neighboring Railway Square for places like Town Hall and Circular Quay.

BY BUS   **Greyhound** coaches operate from the **Sydney Coach Terminal** (✆ 02/9281 9366), on the corner of Eddy Avenue and Pitt Street, bordering Central Station.

BY CRUISE SHIP   Cruise ships dock at the **Overseas Passenger Terminal** in The Rocks, opposite the Sydney Opera House, or in Darling Harbour if The Rocks facility is already occupied.

BY CAR   Drivers enter Sydney from the north on the Pacific Highway, from the south on the M5 and Princes highways, and from the west on the Great Western Highway.

VISITOR INFORMATION

The **Sydney Visitor Centre,** 106 George St., The Rocks (✆ **1800 067 676** in Australia, or 02/9255 1788; www.sydneyvisitorcentre.com), is a good place to pick up maps, brochures, YHA cards, and general tourist information about Sydney as well as towns in New South Wales; it also has two floors of displays on The Rocks. The office is open daily from 9am to 6pm. There's another visitor center in Darling Harbour (33 Wheat St.). It's open from 10am to 6pm daily.

   Also in The Rocks is the **National Parks & Wildlife Centre,** in Cadmans Cottage, 110 George St. (✆ **02/9247 5033**). This place has lots of national park information and runs boat tours to some of the islands in Sydney Harbour. Elsewhere, there's a **City Host information kiosk,** located at Martin Place (between Elizabeth and Castlereagh sts.). It's open daily from 9am to 5pm. There's also a Visitor Centre at the International Terminal. If you want to inquire about destinations and holidays in Sydney or the rest of New South Wales, call **Tourism New South Wales**'s help line (✆ **13 20 77** in Australia).

   Electronic information on cinema, theater, exhibitions, and other events is available through **Talking Guides** (✆ **13 16 20** in Australia). You'll need a code number for each topic, which you can find on page 3 of the A–K section of the *Sydney Yellow Pages.* The service costs the same as a local call.

   A good website is **CitySearch Sydney** (www.sydney.citysearch.com.au), for events, entertainment, dining, and shopping.

CITY LAYOUT

Sydney is one of the largest cities in the world by area, covering more than 1,730 sq. km (675 sq. miles) from the sea to the foothills of the Blue Mountains. Thankfully, the city center is compact. The jewel in Sydney's crown is its harbor, which empties into the South Pacific Ocean through headlands known simply as North Head and South Head. On the southern side of the harbor are the high-rises of the city center; the Sydney Opera House; a string of beaches, including Bondi; and the inner-city suburbs. The Sydney Harbour Bridge and a tunnel connect the city center to the high-rises of the North Sydney business district and the affluent northern suburbs and beautiful ocean beaches beyond.

MAIN ARTERIES & STREETS   The city's main thoroughfare, **George Street,** runs up from **Circular Quay** (pronounced "key"), past Wynyard CityRail station and Town Hall, to Central Station. A whole host of streets run parallel to George, including Pitt, Elizabeth, and Macquarie streets. **Macquarie Street** runs up from the Sydney Opera House, past the Royal Botanic Gardens and Hyde Park. **Martin Place** is a pedestrian thoroughfare that stretches from Macquarie to George streets. It's about halfway between Circular Quay and Town Hall—in the heart of the city center. The easy-to-spot Sydney Tower (also known as Centrepoint Tower), facing onto pedestrian-only **Pitt Street Mall** on Pitt Street, is the main city-center landmark. Next to Circular Quay and across from the Opera House is **The Rocks,** a cluster of small streets that was once slums and is now a tourist attraction. Roads meet at Town Hall from Kings Cross in one direction and Darling Harbour in the other. From Circular Quay to The Rocks it's a 5- to 10-minute stroll, to Wynyard about 10 minutes, and to Town Hall about 20 minutes. From Town Hall to the near side of Darling Harbour it's about a 10-minute walk.

NEIGHBORHOODS IN BRIEF

South of the Harbour

Circular Quay This transport hub for ferries, buses, and CityRail trains is tucked between the Harbour Bridge and the Sydney Opera House. The Quay, as it's called, is a good spot for a stroll, and its outdoor restaurants and street performers are popular. The Rocks, the Royal Botanic Gardens, the Contemporary Art Museum, and the start of the main shopping area (centered on Pitt and George sts.) are a short walk away. To reach the area on public transport, take a CityRail train, ferry, or city-bound bus to Circular Quay.

The Rocks This small historic area, a short stroll west of Circular Quay, is packed with colonial stone buildings, intriguing back streets, boutiques, pubs, tourist stores, and top-notch restaurants and hotels. It's the most exclusive place to stay in the city because of its beauty and its proximity to the Opera House and harbor. Shops are geared toward Sydney's yuppies and wealthy Asian tourists—don't expect bargains. On weekends a portion of George Street is blocked off for The Rocks Market, with stalls selling souvenirs and crafts. To reach the area on public transport, take any bus for Circular Quay or The Rocks (on George St.) or a CityRail train or ferry to Circular Quay.

Town Hall In the heart of the city, this area is home to the main department stores and two Sydney landmarks, the Town Hall and a historic shopping mall called the Queen Victoria Building (QVB). In this area are Sydney Tower and the boutique-style chain stores of Pitt Street Mall. Farther up George Street are major movie houses, the entrance to Sydney's Spanish district (around Liverpool St.), and the city's Chinatown. To reach the area on public transportation, take any bus from Circular Quay on George Street, or a CityRail train to the Town Hall stop.

Darling Harbour Designed as a tourist precinct, Darling Harbour features Sydney's main convention, exhibition, and entertainment centers; a waterfront promenade; the Sydney Aquarium; the Panasonic IMAX Theatre; the Australian Maritime Museum; the Powerhouse Museum; Star City, Sydney's casino; a major food court; and plenty of shops. Nearby are the funky restaurants of Cockle Bay and Kings Wharf. To reach Darling Harbour by public transport, take a ferry from Circular Quay (Wharf 5), the monorail from Town Hall, or the light rail (tram) from Central Station.

Kings Cross & the Suburbs Beyond "The Cross," as it's known, is the city's red-light district—though it's also

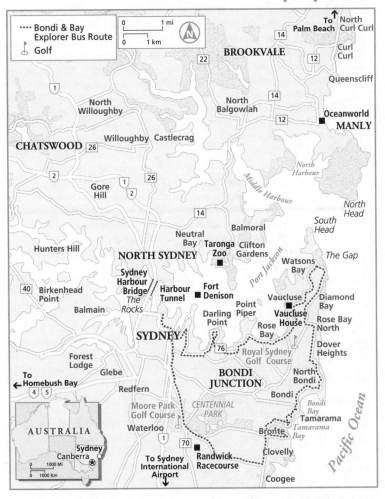

Bondi & Bay Explorer Bus Route

Golf

0   1 mi
0   1 km

To North
Palm Beach   Curl Curl

14

BROOKVALE

Curl
Curl

12

22

Queenscliff

14

1

North
Willoughby

North
Balgowlah

12

Oceanworld
MANLY

CHATSWOOD   26

Willoughby   Castlecrag

North
Harbour

2

1   26

Gore
Hill

2

Middle Harbour

North
Head

14

Hunters Hill

Balmoral

South
Head

Neutral
Bay   Taronga   Clifton
Zoo   Gardens

NORTH SYDNEY

Port Jackson

The Gap

Watsons
Bay

40   Birkenhead
Point

Sydney
Harbour
Bridge
The
Rocks

Harbour
Tunnel

Fort
Denison

Balmain

Point
Piper

Vaucluse

Diamond
Bay

Darling
Point

Vaucluse
House

Rose Bay
North

SYDNEY

Rose
Bay

Dover
Heights

Forest
Lodge

76

Royal Sydney
Golf Course

To
← Homebush Bay

Glebe

BONDI
JUNCTION

North
Bondi

4   5

Redfern

Bondi

Bondi
Bay

Moore Park
Golf Course

CENTENNIAL
PARK

Tamarama

Pacific Ocean

AUSTRALIA

Waterloo

Tamarama
Bay

1

Bronte
Bronte
Bay

Sydney
Canberra

70

Clovelly

1000 Mi
1000 Km

To Sydney
International
Airport

Randwick
Racecourse

Coogee

home to some of Sydney's best-known nightclubs and restaurants. The area has plenty of backpacker hostels, a few bars, and some upscale hotels. The main drag, Darlinghurst Road, is short but crammed with strip joints, prostitutes, addicts, drunks, and such. Also here are cheap e-mail centers that offer discount overseas phone rates. Fortunately, there's a heavy police presence, but do take care. Beyond the strip clubs and glitter, the suburbs of Elizabeth

Bay, Double Bay, and Rose Bay hug the waterfront. To reach the area on public transport, take a CityRail train to Kings Cross. From the next stop, Edgecliff, it's a short walk to Double Bay and a longer one to Rose Bay along the coast.

Paddington/Oxford Street This inner-city suburb, centered on trendy Oxford Street, is known for its expensive terrace houses, off-the-wall boutiques and bookshops, and restaurants, pubs, and nightclubs. It's also the heart of Sydney's large gay community and has a liberal scattering of gay bars and dance spots. To reach the area by public transport, take bus no. 380 or 382 from Circular Quay (on Elizabeth St.); no. 378 from Railway Square, Central Station; or no. 380 or 382 from Bondi Junction. The lower end of Oxford Street is a short walk from Museum CityRail Station (take the Liverpool St. exit).

Darlinghurst Between grungy Kings Cross and upscale Oxford Street, this extroverted, grimy terraced suburb is home to some of Sydney's best cafes. It's probably not wise to wander around at night. Take the CityRail train to Kings Cross and head right from the exit.

Central The congested and polluted crossroads around Central Station, the city's main train station, has little to recommend it. Buses run from here to Circular Quay, and it's a 20-minute walk to Town Hall. The Sydney Central YHA (youth hostel) is here.

Newtown This popular student area centers on car-clogged King Street, which is lined with alternative shops, bookstores, and ethnic restaurants. People-watching is the thing to do—see how many belly-button rings, violently colored hairdos, and Celtic arm tattoos you can spot. To reach the area on public transport, take a CityRail train to Newtown Station.

Glebe Young professionals and students come to this inner-city suburb for the cafes, restaurants, pubs, and shops along the main thoroughfare, Glebe Point Road. All this, plus a location 15 minutes from the city and 30 minutes from Circular Quay, makes it a good place for budget-conscious travelers. To reach Glebe, take bus no. 431, 433, or 434 from Millers Point, The Rocks (on George St.), or bus no. 459 behind Town Hall.

Bondi & the Southern Beaches Some of Sydney's most glamorous surf beaches—Bondi, Bronte, and Coogee—lie along the South Pacific coast southeast of the city center. Bondi has a wide sweep of beach (crowded in summer), some interesting restaurants and bars, plenty of attitude and beautiful bodies—and no CityRail station. To reach Bondi by public transport, ride bus no. 380 or 382 to Bondi Beach from Circular Quay—it takes up to an hour—or (a quicker alternative) a CityRail train to Bondi Junction to connect with the same buses. Bus no. 378 from Railway Square, Central Station, goes to Bronte, and bus no. 373 or 374 travels to Coogee from Circular Quay.

Watsons Bay Watsons Bay is known for The Gap—a section of dramatic sea cliffs—as well as several good restaurants, such as Doyles on the Beach, and the Watsons Bay Hotel beer garden, also run by Doyles. It's a terrific spot to spend a sunny afternoon. To reach it on public transportation, take bus no. 324 or 325 from Circular Quay. There's limited ferry service daily from Circular Quay (Wharf 2), starting at 10:15am on weekdays, 9:15am on weekends and holidays.

North of the Harbour

North Sydney Across the Harbour Bridge, the high-rises of North Sydney attest to its prominence as a business area. There's little for tourists here, except the possibility of being knocked over on a busy thoroughfare. Chatswood (take a CityRail train from Central or Wynyard station) has some good suburban-type shopping, and Milsons Point has a decent pub, the Kirribilli Hotel, as well as Luna Park, an amusement park that recently reopened despite complaints from wealthy locals who complained it was too noisy—you can see the giant smiling clown face from Circular Quay.

The North Shore Ferries and buses provide access to these wealthy neighborhoods across the Harbour Bridge. Gorgeous Balmoral Beach, Taronga Zoo, and upscale boutiques are the attractions in Mosman. Take a ferry from Circular Quay (Wharf 2) to Taronga Zoo—10 minutes—and a bus to Balmoral Beach (another 10 min.).

Manly & the Northern Beaches Half an hour away by ferry, or 15 minutes by the faster JetCat, Manly is famous for its ocean beach—it gives Bondi a run for its money—and scores of cheap food outlets. Farther north are more beaches popular with surfers. CityRail train lines do not go to the northern beaches. The farthest beach from the city, Palm Beach, has magnificent surf and lagoon beaches, walking paths, and a golf course. To reach the area by public transport, take the ferry or JetCat from Circular Quay (Wharves 2 and 3) to Manly. Change at Manly interchange (transfer point) for various buses to the northern beaches, nos. 148 and 154 through 159. You can also take bus no. L90 from Wynyard station.

West of the City Center

Balmain West of the city center, a short ferry ride from Circular Quay, Balmain was once Sydney's main shipbuilding area. In the last few decades, the area has become trendy and expensive. The suburb has a village feel to it, abounds with restaurants and pubs, and stages a popular Saturday market at the local church. Take bus no. 441, 442, or 432 from Town Hall or George Street, or a ferry from Circular Quay (Wharf 5), and then a short bus ride up the hill to the main shopping area.

Homebush Bay Sydney Olympic Park was the main site of the 2000 Olympic Games. You'll find Stadium Australia, the Aquatic Center, and Homebush Bay Information Centre, parklands, and a water-bird reserve. To reach the area by public transport, take a CityRail train from Circular Quay to the Olympic Park station.

2 Getting Around

BY PUBLIC TRANSPORTATION

State Transit operates the city's buses and the ferry network, CityRail runs the urban and suburban trains, and Sydney Ferries runs the public passenger ferries. Some private bus lines operate buses in the outer suburbs. In addition, a monorail connects the city center to Darling Harbour, and a light rail (tram) line runs between Central Station and Wentworth Park in Pyrmont.

MONEY-SAVING TRANSIT PASSES Several passes are available for visitors who will be using public transportation frequently. All work out to be much cheaper than buying individual tickets.

Tips **A Colorful Public Transit Map**

You'll find a two-page, full-color map of the major public transit systems in the color insert at the front of this book; you can see the layout of the CityRail, Monorail, Sydney Explorer Bus, and Light Rail.

> **_Tips_ Transit Information**
>
> For bus, ferry, and train timetable information, call **Infoline** (© **13 15 00** in Australia) daily from 6am to 10pm. Otherwise check the website for Sydney buses and ferries (www.sydneybuses.nsw.gov.au) or CityRail (www.cityrail.info). Pick up a **Sydney Transport Map** (a guide to train, bus, and ferry services) at any rail, bus, or ferry office.

The **SydneyPass** includes unlimited travel on Sydney Explorer coaches, Bondi & Bay Explorer coaches, three Sydney Harbour cruises, the JetCat to Manly, the high-speed RiverCat to Parramatta (linking the city center to this important heritage and business center along a historic waterway), Sydney buses, Sydney Ferries, and CityRail trains (within the "Red TravelPass" travel zone, which includes the entire city center, as well as to Bondi Junction). The SydneyPass costs A$100 (US$80) for adults and A$50 (US$40) for children for 3 days of travel over a 7-day period; A$130 (US$104) for adults and A$65 (US$52) for children for 5 days over a 7-day period; and A$150 (US$120) for adults and A$75 (US$60) for children for 7 consecutive days. Family fares are also available. Buy tickets at the information desk at the airport, at the TransitShop at Circular Quay (outside McDonald's), from the Sydney Ferries ticket offices at Circular Quay, and from Explorer bus drivers.

A **Weekly Travel Pass** allows unlimited travel on buses, trains, and ferries. There are six different passes (each a different color) depending on the distance you need to travel. The passes visitors most commonly use are the Red Pass and the Green Pass. The Red Pass costs A$32 (US$26) for adults and A$16 (US$13) for kids and covers all transportation within the city center and near surroundings. This pass will get you aboard inner harbor ferries, for example, but not the ferry to Manly. The Green Pass, which costs A$40 (US$32) for adults and A$20 (US$16) for kids, will take you to more distant destinations, including Manly (aboard the ferry but not the JetCat before 7pm). You can buy either pass at newsdealers or bus, train, and ferry ticket outlets.

The **Day Tripper** ticket gives you unlimited bus, train, and ferry travel for 1 day. Tickets cost A$15 (US$12) for adults and A$7.50 (US$6) for children. The pass is available at all bus, train, and ferry ticket outlets.

A **CityHopper** ticket allows unlimited all-day travel on CityRail trains bounded by Kings Cross, North Sydney, and Redfern. Peak-time tickets cost A$6.80 (US$5.40) for adults and A$3.40 (US$2.70) for children, and off-peak tickets cost A$4.80 (US$3.80) for adults and A$2.40 (US$1.90) for children. If you're coming from farther out you can still ask for a CityHopper. It will cost an extra A$2 (US$1.60) for adults and A$1 (US80¢) for children on top of your return rail ticket.

A **Travelten ticket** offers 10 bus rides for a discounted price. A Blue Travelten covers two sections on the bus route and costs A$13 (US$10) for adults and A$6.30 (US$5) for children; a Brown Travelten covers up to nine sections and costs A$21 (US$17) for adults and A$11 (US$8.50) for children. The **Travelten ferry ticket** costs A$30 (US$24) for adults and A$15 (US$12) for kids and is good for 10 trips within the inner harbor (this excludes Manly). The Manly ferry Travelten costs A$45 (US$36) for adults and A$23 (US$18) for children, and the JetCat Travelten to Manly (before 7pm) costs A$66 (US$53) for adults (no kids' price). Buy Travelten tickets at newsdealers, bus depots, or the Circular Quay ferry terminal. Tickets are transferable, so if two or more people travel together, you can use the same ticket.

BY PUBLIC BUS   Buses are frequent and reliable and cover a wide area of metropolitan Sydney—though you might find the system a little difficult to navigate if you're visiting some of the outer suburbs. The minimum fare (which covers most short hops in the city) is A$1.60 (US$1.30) for adults and A80¢ (US65¢) for children for a 4km (2½-mile) "section." The farther you go, the cheaper each section is. For example, the 44km (27-mile) trip to Palm Beach, way past Manly, costs A$5.20 (US$4.15) for adults and A$2.60 (US$2) for kids. Sections are marked on bus-stand signs, but most Sydneysiders are as confused about the system as you will be—when in doubt, ask the bus driver.

Most buses bound for the northern suburbs, including night buses to Manly and the bus to Taronga Zoo, leave from Wynyard Park on Carrington Street, behind the Wynyard CityRail station on George Street. Buses to the southern beaches, such as Bondi and Bronte, and the western and eastern suburbs leave from Circular Quay. Buses to Balmain leave from behind the QVB.

Call the **Transport Info Line** (𝄐 **13 15 00**) for information, or ask the staff at the bus information kiosk on the corner of Alfred and Loftus streets, behind Circular Quay CityRail station (𝄐 **02/9219 1680**). The kiosk is open Monday through Saturday from 8am to 8pm and Sunday from 8am to 6pm. Buses run from 4am to around midnight during the week, less frequently on weekends and holidays. Some night buses to outer suburbs run after midnight and throughout the night. You can purchase single tickets onboard; exact change is not required.

BY SYDNEY EXPLORER BUS   These bright red buses operate every day, traveling a 28km (18-mile) circuit and stopping at 26 places of interest. These include the Sydney Opera House, the Royal Botanic Gardens, the State Library, Mrs. Macquarie's Chair, the Art Gallery of New South Wales, Kings Cross, Elizabeth Bay House, Wynyard CityRail station, the QVB, Sydney AMP Tower, the Australian Museum, Central Station, Chinatown, Darling Harbour, and The Rocks. Buses depart from Circular Quay at 18-minute intervals starting at 8:40am, with the last "round-trip" service departing Circular Quay at 5:20pm (and returning to Circular Quay at 7pm). Board anywhere along the route where you see the distinctive red Sydney Explorer sign, and leave at any attraction along the way. If you want to stay on the bus from start to finish, the full circuit takes 1½ hours. Your Sydney Explorer ticket entitles you to free travel on regular "blue and white" Sydney Buses within the same zone covered by your Sydney Explorer Ticket until midnight. When planning your itinerary for the day, remember that some attractions, such as museums, close at 5pm. Tickets cost A$36 (US$28) for adults, A$18 (US$14) for children 4 to 16, and A$90 (US$72) for a family. Buy tickets onboard the bus. You can also buy a 2-day Twin Ticket for both the Sydney Explorer Bus and the Bondi Explorer Bus (see below). This ticket costs A$62 (US$50) for adults, A$31 (US$25) for children, and A$155 (US$124) for a family.

BY BONDI EXPLORER BUS   The Bondi Explorer operates every day, traveling a 30km (19-mile) circuit around the eastern harborside bays and coastal beaches. Stops along the way include Kings Cross, Double Bay, Watsons Bay, Bondi Beach, Bronte Beach, Coogee Beach, Paddington, Oxford Street, and Martin Place. The bus departs from Circular Quay at 25-minute intervals starting at 9:15am, with the last "round-trip" service departing Circular Quay at 4:20pm (and returning to Circular Quay at

5:55pm). Board anywhere along the route where you see the Bondi & Bay Explorer sign, and get off at any attraction along the way. If you wish to stay on board from start to finish without making any stops, the entire circuit takes 1½ hours. Your ticket entitles you to free travel on regular "blue and white" Sydney Buses within the same zone covered by your Bondi & Bay Explorer ticket until midnight. The 1-day fare is A$36 (US$29) for adults, A$18 (US$14) for children 4 to 16, and A$90 (US$72) for families. Buy the ticket onboard.

BY FERRY & JETCAT   The best way to get a taste of a city that revolves around its harbor is to jump aboard a ferry. The main ferry terminal is at Circular Quay. Machines at each wharf dispense tickets. (There are also change machines.) For ferry information, call ℂ **13 15 00** or visit the ferry information office opposite Wharf 4. Timetables are available for all routes.

   One-way journeys within the inner harbor (virtually everywhere except Manly and Parramatta) cost A$4.80 (US$3.80) for adults and A$2.40 (US$1.90) for children. The ferry to Manly takes 30 minutes and costs A$6 (US$4.80) for adults and A$3 (US$2.40) for children. It leaves from Wharf 3. The rapid JetCat service to Manly takes 15 minutes and costs A$7.50 (US$6) for both adults and children. After 7pm all trips to and from Manly are by JetCat at ferry prices. Ferries run from 6am to midnight.

BY CITYRAIL   Sydney's publicly owned train system is a good news/bad news way to get around. The good news is that it can be a cheap and efficient way to see the city, the bad news is that the system is limited; many tourist areas—including Manly, Bondi Beach, and Darling Harbour—are not connected to the network. In the last couple of years, it's become even more problematic. While trains tend to run regularly, the idea of some sort of timetable went out of the window in 2004 and 2005 when safety issues relating to a crash forced the state government to institute strict medical tests on its train drivers. The result, compounded with decades of underinvestment, meant drastic cuts to services—particularly on weekends. CityRail timetables should be viewed as basic guides only. Single tickets within the city center cost A$3 (US$2.40) for adults and A$1.50 (US$1.20) for children. Return tickets cost A$6 (US$4.80) for adults and A$3 (US$2.40) for children in peak time, and A$3.60 (US$2.90) for adults and A$2.40 (US$1.90) for children in off-peak.

   Prices regularly increase. Information is available from **Infoline** (ℂ **13 15 00** in Australia).

BY COUNTRYLINNK   Comfortable and efficient **Countrylink** trains out of Central Station link the city with the far suburbs and beyond. For reservations, call ℂ **13 22 32** in Australia between 6:30am and 10pm, or visit the **Countrylink Travel Center** (ℂ **02/9224 2742;** www.countrylink.info), Station Concourse, Wynyard CityRail station, for brochures and bookings.

BY METRO MONORAIL   The metro monorail, with its single overhead line, is seen by many as a blight and by others as a futuristic addition to the city. The monorail connects the central business district to Darling Harbour—though it's only a 15-minute walk from Town Hall. The system operates Monday through Thursday from 7am to 10pm, Friday and Saturday from 7am to midnight, and Sunday from 8am to 10pm. Tickets are A$4 (US$3.20), free for children under 5. An all-day monorail pass costs A$8 (US$6.40) for adults and A$22 (US$18) for a family; it may be worth buying—it comes with vouchers offering 25% off entrance fees to some local attractions. The trip from the city center to Darling Harbour takes around 12 minutes. Look for the gray

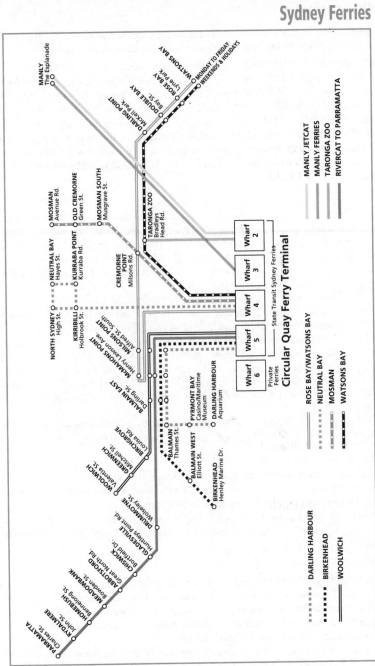

Sydney Ferries

Circular Quay Ferry Terminal

- Wharf 2
- Wharf 3
- Wharf 4
- Wharf 5
- Wharf 6

State Transit Sydney Ferries

Private Ferries

MANLY The Esplanade

MONDAY TO FRIDAY
WEEKENDS & HOLIDAYS

ROSE BAY Lyne Park
DOUBLE BAY Bay St.
DARLING POINT McKell Park

WATSONS BAY

MOSMAN Avenue Rd.
OLD CREMORNE Green St.
MOSMAN SOUTH Musgrave St.
NEUTRAL BAY Hayes St.
KURRABA POINT Kurraba Rd.
CREMORNE POINT Milsons Rd.
TARONGA ZOO Bradleys Head Rd.
NORTH SYDNEY High St.
KIRRIBILLI Holbrook St.
MILSONS POINT Alfred St. South
McMAHONS POINT Henry Lawson Ave.
BALMAIN EAST Darling St.
PYRMONT BAY Casino/Maritime Museum
DARLING HARBOUR Aquarium
BALMAIN Thames St.
BIRCHGROVE Louisa Rd.
BALMAIN WEST Elliott St.
BIRKENHEAD Henley Marine Dr.
DRUMMOYNE Wolseley St.
GREENWICH Mitchell St.
WOOLWICH Valentia St.
GLADESVILLE Bortfield Dr.
HUNTLEYS POINT Hunters Rd.
CHISWICK Great North Rd.
ABBOTSFORD Bowden St.
MEADOWBANK Bennelong St.
HOMEBUSH John St.
RYDALMERE Charles St.
PARRAMATTA

MANLY JETCAT
MANLY FERRIES
TARONGA ZOO
RIVERCAT TO PARRAMATTA

ROSE BAY/WATSONS BAY
NEUTRAL BAY
MOSMAN
WATSONS BAY

DARLING HARBOUR
BIRKENHEAD
WOOLWICH

115

overhead line and the plastic tubelike structures that are the stations. Call **Metro Monorail** (© 02/8584 5288; www.metrolightrail.com.au) for more information.

BY METRO LIGHT RAIL   A system of trams runs on a route that traverses a 3.6km (2¼-mile) track between Central Station and Wentworth Park in Pyrmont. It provides good access to Chinatown, Paddy's Markets, Darling Harbour, the Star City casino, and the Sydney Fish Markets. The trams run every 10 minutes. The one-way fare is A$2.90 to A$3.90 (US$2.30–US$3.10) for adults and A$1.40 to A$3.80 (US$1.10–US$3) for children 4 to 15, depending on distance. A day pass costs A$8.40 (US$6.70) for adults, A$6.30 (US$5) for children, and A$20 (US$16) for a family of five. Contact **Metro Light Rail** (© 02/8584 5288; www.metrolight rail.com.au) for details.

BY TAXI

Taxis are a relatively economical way to get around. Several companies serve the city center and suburbs. All journeys are metered. If you cross either way on the Harbour Bridge or through the Harbour Tunnel, it will cost you an extra A$3 (US$2.40)—a rip-off considering there's only an official toll on the way into the city. If you take the Eastern Distributor from the airport, it's A$3.50 (US$2.80). An extra 10% will be added to your fare if you pay by credit card.

Taxis line up at stands in the city, such as those opposite Circular Quay and Central Station. They are also frequently found in front of hotels. A yellow light on top of the cab means it's vacant. Cabs can be hard to get on Friday and Saturday nights and between 2 and 3pm every day, when cabbies are changing shifts after 12 hours on the road. Tipping is not necessary, but it's appreciated—a dollar or so is plenty. Some people prefer to sit up front, but it's certainly not considered rude if you don't. Passengers must wear seat belts in the front and back seats. The **Taxi Complaints Hotline** (© 1800/648 478 in Australia) deals with problem taxi drivers. Taxis are licensed to carry four people.

The main cab companies are **Taxis Combined Services** (© 02/9332 8888); **RSL Taxis** (© 02/9581 1111); **Legion Cabs** (© 13 14 51); and **Premier** (© 13 10 17).

BY WATER TAXI

Harbour Taxis, as they are called, operate 24 hours a day and are a quick, convenient way to get to waterfront restaurants, harbor attractions, and some suburbs. They can also be chartered for private cruises. A journey from Circular Quay to Watsons Bay, for example, costs about A$145 (US$116) for the boat (it holds 10, so the more people the cheaper it is). The main operator is **Water Taxis Combined** (© 1300/666 484 in Australia).

BY CAR

Traffic restrictions, parking, and congestion can make getting around by car frustrating, but if you plan to visit some of the outer suburbs or take excursions elsewhere in New South Wales, then renting a car will give you more flexibility. The National Roads and Motorists' Association (NRMA) is the New South Wales auto club; for emergency breakdown service, call © 13 11 11.

Car-rental agencies in Sydney include **Avis,** 214 William St., Kings Cross (© 1800/ 225 553); **Budget,** 93 William St., Kings Cross (© 13 27 27 in Australia, or 02/9339 8888); **Hertz,** corner of William and Riley streets, Kings Cross (© 13 30 39 in Australia); and **Thrifty,** 75 William St., Kings Cross (© 02/9380 5399). Avis, Budget,

Hertz, and Thrifty also have desks at the airport. Rates average about A$60 (US$48) per day for a small car. One of the best-value operations is **Bayswater Car Rentals,** 180 William St., Kings Cross (✆ 02/9360 3622), which has small cars for A$48 (US$38) a day, A$25 (US$20) a day for 6 days or more.

You can rent a motor home (called a camper van by some Aussies) from **Britz Campervans,** 653 Gardeners Rd., Mascot, NSW 2020 (✆ **1800/331 454** in Australia, or 02/9667 0402; www.britz.com). Plan to pay about A$105 (US$84) a day for a two-person van in winter and around A$145 (US$116) in summer. You can drop off your van at most state capitals and in Cairns, a convenience that costs an extra A$200 (US$160).

FAST FACTS: Sydney

American Express The main Amex office is at Level 3, 130 Pitt St., near Martin Place (✆ **02/9236 4200**). It cashes traveler's checks and acts as a travel-booking service. It's open Monday through Friday from 8:30am to 5pm and Saturday from 9am to noon. Another foreign exchange office is on the walkway leading up to the Sydney Opera House (✆ **02/9251 1970**). If you've lost your traveler's checks, go to the head office, 175 Liverpool St. (✆ **02/9271 1111**). It's a locked security building so you'll need to call ahead.

Babysitters **Dial an Angel** (✆ **02/9416 7511** or 02/9362 4225) is a well-regarded babysitting service.

Business Hours General office and banking hours are Monday through Friday from 9am to 5pm. Many banks, especially in the city center, are open from around 9:30am to 12:30pm on Saturday. Shopping hours are usually from 8:30am to 5:30pm daily (9am–5pm Sat), and most stores stay open until 9pm on Thursday. Most city-center stores are open from around 10am to 4pm on Sunday.

Currency Exchange Most major bank branches offer currency exchange services. Small foreign-currency exchange offices are clustered at the airport and around Circular Quay and Kings Cross. **Thomas Cook** has offices at the airport; at 175 Pitt St. (✆ **02/9231 2877**), open Monday through Friday from 6:45am to 5:15pm and Saturday from 10am to 2pm; and on the lower ground floor of the QVB (✆ **02/9264 1133**), open Monday through Friday from 9am to 6pm (until 9pm Fri), Saturday from 9am to 6pm, and Sunday from 11am to 5pm.

Dentist A well-respected office in the city is **City Dental Practice,** Level 2, 229 Macquarie St., near Martin Place (✆ **02/9221 3300**). For dental problems after hours, call **Dental Emergency Information** (✆ **02/9369 7050**).

Doctor The **Park Medical Centre,** Shop 4, 27 Park St. (✆ **02/9264 4488**), in the city center near Town Hall, is open Monday through Friday from 8am to 6pm; consultations cost A$40 (US$32) for 15 minutes. (*Note:* If you plan to take a dive course in Australia, get your medical exam done here. It costs A$70/US$56, about the cheapest in Australia.) The **Kings Cross Travelers' Clinic,** Suite 1, 13 Springfield Ave., Kings Cross, just off Darlinghurst Road (✆ **1300/369 359** in Australia, or 02/9358 3066), is great for travel medicines and emergency contraception pills, among other things. Hotel visits in the Kings Cross area cost

A$80 (US$64); consultations cost A$40 (US$32). The **Travelers' Medical & Vacci-nation Centre,** Level 7, 428 George St., in the city center (© **02/9221 7133**), stocks and administers travel-related vaccinations and medications.

Embassies & Consulates All foreign embassies are based in Canberra. You'll find the following consulates in Sydney: **United Kingdom,** Level 16, Gateway Building, 1 Macquarie Place, Circular Quay (© **02/9247 7521**); **New Zealand,** 55 Hunter St. (© **02/9223 0144**); **United States,** Level 59, MLC Centre, 19–29 Martin Place (© **02/9373 9200**); and **Canada,** Level 5, 111 Harrington St., The Rocks (© **02/9364 3000**).

Emergencies Dial © **000** to call police, the fire service, or an ambulance. Call the **Emergency Prescription Service** (© **02/9235 0333**) for emergency drug prescriptions, and the NRMA for car breakdowns (© **13 11 11**).

Eyeglass Repair **Perfect Vision,** Shop C22A, in the Sydney AMP Tower, 100 Market St. (© **02/9221 1010**), is open Monday through Friday from 9am to 6pm (until 9pm Thurs) and Saturday from 9am to 5pm. It's the best place to replace lost contact lenses; bring your prescription.

Holidays See "When to Go" in chapter 2. New South Wales also observes Labour Day on the first Monday in October.

Hospitals Make your way to **Sydney Hospital,** Macquarie Street, at the top end of Martin Place (© **02/9382 7111** for emergencies). **St. Vincents Hospital** is at Victoria and Burton streets in Darlinghurst, near Kings Cross (© **02/9339 1111**).

Hot Lines Call the **Poisons Information Center** (© **13 11 26**); the **Gay and Lesbian Counseling Line** (© 02/9207 2800; 4pm–midnight); the **Rape Crisis Center** (© 02/9819 6565); or the **Crisis Center** (© 02/9358 6577).

Internet Access Several Internet and e-mail centers are scattered around Kings Cross, Bondi, and Manly.

Lost Property There is no general lost property bureau in Sydney. Contact the nearest police station if you think you've lost something. For items lost on trains, contact the **Lost Property Office,** 494 Pitt St., near Central Railway Station (© **02/9379 3000**). The office is open Monday through Friday from 8:30am to 4:30pm. For items left behind on planes or at the airport, go to the Federal Airport Corporation's administration office on the top floor of the International Terminal at Sydney International Airport (© **02/9667 9583**). For stuff left behind on buses or ferries, call © **02/9245 5777**. Each taxi company has its own lost property office.

Luggage Storage You can leave your bags at the International Terminal at the airport. A locker costs A$5 (US$4) per day; the storage room charges around A$9 (US$7.20) per day per piece. The room is open from 4:30am to the last flight of the day. Call © **02/9667 0926** for information. Otherwise, leave luggage at the cloakroom at Central Station, near the front of the main building (© **02/9219 4395**). Storage at the rail station costs A$5 (US$4) per article per day. The **Travelers Contact Point,** 7th floor, 428 George St., above the Dymocks bookstore (© **02/9221 8744**), stores luggage for A$15 (US$12) per piece per month. It also operates a general delivery service; has Internet access, a travel agency, and a jobs board; and ships items to the U.K. and Ireland.

My, what an inefficient way to fish.

Ring toss, good. Horseshoes, bad.

Faster! Faster! Faster!

We take care of the fiddly bits, from providing over 43,000 customer reviews of hotels, to helping you find our best fares, to giving you 24/7 customer service. So you can focus on the only thing that matters. Goofing off.

travelocity®

You'll never roam alone.™

©2005 Travelocity.com LP. All rights reserved. CST # 2056372-50.

travelocity.com   1-888-TRAVELOCITY   AOL Keyword: Travel

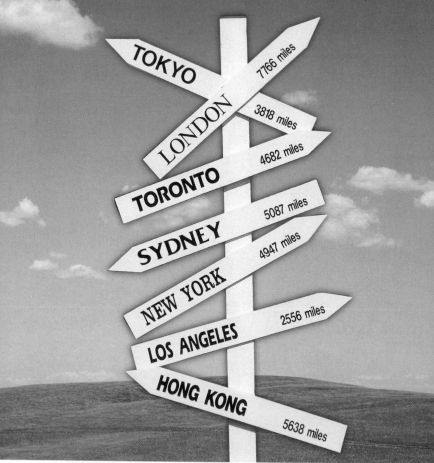

Newspapers The *Sydney Morning Herald* is considered one of the world's best newspapers—by its management, at least—and is available throughout metropolitan Sydney. The equally prestigious *Australian* is available nationwide. The metropolitan *Daily Telegraph* is a more casual read and publishes a couple of editions a day. The *International Herald Tribune, USA Today,* the British *Guardian Weekly,* and other U.K. newspapers can be found at Circular Quay newspaper stands and most newsdealers.

Pharmacies (Chemist Shops) Most suburbs have pharmacies that are open late. For after-hours referral, contact the **Emergency Prescription Service (℃ 02/9235 0333).**

Police In an emergency, dial ℃ **000.** Make nonemergency police inquiries through the Sydney Police Centre (℃ **02/9281 0000).**

Post Office The General Post Office (GPO) is at 130 Pitt St., not far from Martin Place (℃ **13 13 18** in Australia). It's open Monday through Friday from 8:30am to 5:30pm and Saturday from 10am to 2pm. General-delivery letters can be sent c/o Poste Restante, G.P.O., Sydney, NSW 2000, Australia (℃ **02/9244 3733**), and collected at 310 George St., on the third floor of the Hunter Connection shopping center. It's open Monday through Friday from 8:15am to 5:30pm. For directions to the nearest post office, call ℃ **1800/043 300.**

Restrooms These can be found in the QVB (second floor), at most department stores, at Central Station and Circular Quay, near the escalators by the Sydney Aquarium, and in the Harbourside Festival Marketplace in Darling Harbour.

Safety Sydney is an extremely safe city, but as anywhere else, it's good to keep your wits about you and your wallet hidden. If you wear a money belt, keep it under your shirt. Be wary in Kings Cross and Redfern at all hours and around Central Station and the cinema strip on George Street near Town Hall station in the evening—the latter is a hangout for local gangs, though they're usually busy holding each other up for their sneakers. Other places of concern are the back lanes of Darlinghurst, around the naval base at Woolloomooloo, and along the Bondi restaurant strip when the drunks spill out after midnight. Several people have reported thieves at the airport on occasion. If traveling by train at night, travel in the carriages next to the guard's van, marked with a blue light on the outside.

Taxes Australia imposes a 10% Goods and Services Tax (GST) on most goods sold in Australia and most services. The GST applies to most travel-related goods and services, including transport, hotels, tours, and restaurants. By law, the tax has to be included in the advertised price of the product, though it doesn't have to be displayed independently of the pretax price. See the box "Tourist Refund Scheme," p. 104.

Taxis See "Getting Around," earlier in this chapter.

Telephones Sydney's public phone boxes take coins, and many also accept credit cards and A$10 (US$8) phone cards available from newsdealers. Local calls cost A40¢ (US25¢).

Transit Information Call the **Infoline** (℃ **13 15 00** in Australia) daily from 6am to 10pm.

Useful Telephone Numbers For news, dial ✆ **1199**; for the time, ✆ **1194**; for Sydney entertainment, ✆ **11 688**; for directory assistance, ✆ **12 455**; for Travelers Aid Society, ✆ **02/9211 2469**.
Weather For the local forecast, call ✆ **1196**.

3 Where to Stay

The 2000 Sydney Olympics, and the exposure the city received, led to more visitors to the city and more hotels to cater to them. Unfortunately, the worldwide threat of terrorism has had an adverse effect, too. Although it's unlikely you'll find the city's hotels completely booked if you turn up looking for a bed for the night, it's probably wise to reserve rooms in advance.

DECIDING WHERE TO STAY The best location for lodging in Sydney is in The Rocks and around Circular Quay—a short stroll from the Sydney Opera House, the Harbour Bridge, the Royal Botanic Gardens, and the ferry terminals.

Hotels around Darling Harbour offer good access to the local facilities, including museums, the Sydney Aquarium, and the Star City casino. Most Darling Harbour hotels are a 10- to 15-minute walk, or a short monorail or light rail trip, from Town Hall and the central shopping district in and around the AMP Sydney Tower and Pitt Street Mall.

Another way to hunt for discounted hotel rooms is through an independent hotel search site. The two most popular are **www.lastminute.com.au** and **www.wotif.com**. Lastminute.com allows you to check prices of various room categories at least a month in advance. Wotif.com allows you to search for a room up to 14 days in the future. Hotels also provide both sites with special deals for rooms for the next couple of days.

More hotels are grouped around Kings Cross, Sydney's red-light district. Some of the hotels here are among the city's best, and you'll also find a range of cheaper lodgings, including several backpacker hostels. Kings Cross can be unnerving at any time, but especially on Friday and Saturday nights when the area's strip joints and nightclubs are jumping. Staying here does have its advantages: You get a real inner-city feel, and it's close to excellent restaurants and cafes around the Kings Cross, Darlinghurst, and Oxford Street areas.

Glebe, with its ethnic restaurants, is another inner-city suburb popular with tourists. It's well served by local buses.

Value Last-Minute Room Deals

If you turn up in town without a reservation, you should definitely use the Sydney Visitors Centre bookings desk (✆ **02/9667 6050**), in the arrivals hall of the airport's International Terminal. It negotiates deals with many of Sydney's hotels (but not hostels) and offers exceptional discounts on rooms that haven't been filled that day. You can save up to 50% on a room. The desk is open from 6am to the last flight of the day. It also offers discounts on tours (to the Blue Mountains, for example) and cheap tickets for flights within Australia.

If you want to stay near the beach, check out the options in Manly and Bondi, though you should consider their distance from the city center and the lack of CityRail trains to these areas. A taxi to Manly from the city will cost around A$35 (US$28) and to Bondi around A$26 (US$21).

MAKING A DEAL   The prices given below for very expensive and expensive hotels are mostly the **rack rates,** the recommended retail price, which guests can pay at the busiest periods if they book at short notice. Always ask about discounts, package deals, and any other special offerings when booking a hotel, especially if you are traveling in winter when hotels are less likely to be full. Ask about weekend discounts, corporate rates, and family plans.

Booking direct through a hotel's website can also yield savings. For instance, a search of the website for Accor, a company that manages 31 quality hotels in and around Sydney, shows that you could save up to 50% of the rack rate. A double room at the four-star Mercure Hotel Sydney on Broadway, for example, can cost A$157 (US$125), including breakfast. The rack rate is A$220 (US$176) a night. A night at the four-star All Seasons Premier Menzies Hotel, near Wynyard, costs A$148 (US$118) for a double room, including breakfast. The rack rate is A$300 (US$240). On the Accor website (www.accor.com), you can check rates months in advance.

Serviced apartments are also well worth considering because you can save a bundle by cooking your own meals; many also have free laundry facilities.

Almost all hotels offer nonsmoking rooms; inquire when you make a reservation if it's important to you. Most moderately priced to very expensive rooms will have tea- and coffeemaking facilities, and an iron. Like hotels elsewhere, some of Sydney's lodgings are in on the increasing trend to rip off guests with pay-per-view movie channels (around A$16/US$13 per movie), rather than to provide full access to a range of free cable TV channels.

The price categories used below are defined as follows: Very Expensive, A$250 (US$200) and up; Expensive, A$150 to A$250 (US$120–US$200); Moderate, A$80 to A$150 (US$64–US$120); Inexpensive, below A$80 (US$64). Prices are for a double room. In Australia, a "double" room means you get one double, queen-size, or king-size bed in a room.

THE ROCKS/CIRCULAR QUAY
VERY EXPENSIVE
Observatory Hotel ★★★   This exclusive hotel, a 10-minute walk uphill from The Rocks and George Street, is a turn-of-the-20th-century beauty competing for top-hotel-in-Sydney honors. It's fitted with antiques, objets d'art, and the finest carpets, wallpapers, and draperies. Plus, it's renowned for its personalized service. Rooms are plush and quiet, with huge bathrooms. Some rooms have city views; others look out over the harbor. The pool here is one of the best in Sydney: Note the Southern Hemisphere constellations on the roof. The health club offers a free float in the flotation tank for early arrivals coming in from overseas.

89–113 Kent St., Sydney, NSW 2000. ⓒ **1800/806 245** in Australia, or 02/9256 2222. Fax 02/9256 2233. www. observatoryhotel.com.au. 100 units. A$415–A$450 (US$332–US$360) double; from A$510 (US$408) suite. Extra person A$66 (US$53). Children under 14 stay free in parent's room. AE, DC, MC, V. Parking A$30 (US$24). Bus: 339, 431, or 433 to Millers Point. **Amenities:** Restaurant; bar; chemical-free heated indoor pool; floodlit tennis court; health club w/flotation tank; sauna; concierge; business center; 24-hr. room service; laundry service; dry cleaning. *In room:* A/C, TV w/pay movies, VCR, CD player, dataport, minibar, hair dryer, safe.

Bernly Private Hotel **23**
DeVere Hotel **25**
The Grace Hotel Sydney **11**
Hotel 59 **21**
The Hughenden **20**
The Kirketon **22**
The Lord Nelson
Brewery Hotel **3**
Medina Grand,
Harbourside **12**
Observatory Hotel **4**
Park Hyatt Sydney **1**
Park Regis Sydney **15**
Quay Grand Suites Sydney **7**
The Russell **6**
The Sebel Pier One Sydney **2**
Shangri-la Hotel Sydney **8**
Sir Stamford
at Circular Quay **9**
The Stafford **5**
Star City Hotel **13**
Sullivans Hotel **19**
Sydney Central YHA **16**
Travelodge Hotel Sydney **17**
Victoria Court Sydney **24**
Wattle Private Hotel **18**
Westin Sydney **10**
Wool Brokers Arms **14**

To Double
Bay
& Rose Bay

Roslyn Gardens Rd.

Greenknowe Ave.
Elizabeth Bay
Mac
Greenknowe Ave.
Hughes St.
Orwell St.
Macleay St.
Roslyn St.
Ward Ave.
Bayswater Rd.
Kellett St.
Kings Cross Rd.
Craigend St.

KINGS CROSS

Victoria St.
Darlinghurst Rd.

McElho... St.
Brougham St.

WOOLLOOMOOLOO

Dowling St.

Plunkett St.

Sir John Young Cr.

THE DOMAIN

Art Gallery of NSW

Prince Albert Rd.

St. Mary's Rd.
Boomerang
Haig Ave.

St. Mary's Cathedral

College St.

St. James Rd.

Australian Museum

Stanley St.

William St.

Riley St.
Liverpool St.
Yurong St.
Forbes St.
Bourke St.
Palmer St.
Burton St.

DARLINGHURST

Barcom Ave.
Glenview St.
Glenmore
Brown St.

PADDINGTON

Greens
Oxford St.
Napier St.
Dowling

Moore Park Rd.

To Bondi →

N

1/4 mi
1/4 km

Darlinghurst Rd.
Flinders St.

Crown St.
Fitzroy St.
Riley St.
Waterloo St.

SURRY HILLS

Oxford St.
Pelican St.
Hunt St.
Campbell St.
Foster St.
Albion St.
Foveaux St.

To Sydney Airport →

BELMORE PARK

Eddy Ave.
Central Station
Rawson Pl.
Pitt St.
Lee St.
George St.
Hay St.
Campbell St.

To Newtown →

Park St.

HYDE PARK

Anzac War Memorial

Elizabeth St.
Castlereagh St.

Sydney Tower

Pitt Street Mall

Mall
King St.
George St.
Market St.
York St.
Clarence St.
Kent St.
Sussex St.

Queen Victoria Building

Town Hall

TOWN HALL

St. Andrew's Cathedral

Druitt St.
Bathurst St.
Pitt St.
Liverpool St.
George St.
Goulburn St.

DARLING HARBOUR

CHINESE GARDENS

Harbour St.
Ultimo Rd.
Thomas St.
Quay St.

Entertainment Centre

Sydney Aquarium

PYRMONT

Pyrmont Bridge

Cockle Bay

Harbourside Festival Marketplace

Convention Centre

Western Distributor

TUMBALONG PARK

Exhibition Centre

Pier St.

Powerhouse Museum

Her Majesty's Theatre

National Maritime Museum

Pyrmont St.
Darling Dr.
Harris St.
Mary Ann St.
Thomas St.
Macarthur St.
Wattle St.
Bulwara Rd.

To Glebe →

11
12
13
14
15
16
17
18
20
21
22
23
24
2

123

Park Hyatt Sydney ★★   This artistically curving property on The Rocks foreshore is the best-positioned hotel in Sydney. It's right on the water, and some rooms have fantastic views across the harbor to the Sydney Opera House. Its location and general appeal mean it's usually full and frequently has to turn guests away. The room rates have skyrocketed in recent years, and unless you have money to burn, plenty of other places are far cheaper and just as nice.

The building itself is a pleasure to look at, and from a ferry on the harbor it looks like a wonderful addition to the toy-town landscape of The Rocks. The good-size rooms incorporate every possible luxury. Room rates here depend on views; the least expensive units have only glimpses of the harbor. (The most expensive rooms look over the Opera House.) Each of the 33 executive suites has two balconies with a telescope.

The **Verandah on the Park** restaurant offers good buffet food indoors or outside on the edge of the harbor, and is worth a visit even if you don't stay here.

7 Hickson Rd., The Rocks, Sydney, NSW 2000. ℭ **800/633-7313** in the U.S. and Canada, or 02/9241 1234. Fax 02/9256 1555. www.sydney.hyatt.com. 158 units. A$650–A$700 (US$520–US$560) double; A$820–A$920 (US$656–US$736) executive studio; from A$1,000 (US$800) suite. Extra person A$55 (US$44). Children under 18 stay free in parent's room. Ask about weekend discounts and packages. AE, DC, MC, V. Parking A$22 (US$17). CityRail, bus, or ferry: Circular Quay. **Amenities:** 2 restaurants; bar and lounge; heated outdoor pool; health club and spa; concierge; business center; 24-hr. room service; babysitting; laundry service. *In room:* A/C, TV, dataport, minibar, coffeemaker, hair dryer, iron/ironing board, safe.

Quay Grand Suites Sydney ★★   The best serviced-apartment complexes, like this one, can outdo superior AAA-rated five-star hotels—even in price. This building, on the pedestrian concourse leading up to the Sydney Opera House, also houses private apartments costing upward of A$750,000 (US$600,000)—so you know you are in exclusive territory. The spacious, ultramodern apartments either face the Botanic Gardens or have fantastic views across the ferry terminals and the Sydney Harbour Bridge. The fully equipped units have balconies so you can admire the views. The noises from the CityRail station (including train announcements) and the ferry horns are captivating but can easily be shut out. Bathrooms are large and feature a good-size Jacuzzi. You might want to eat at the hotel's **Quadrant** restaurant, which serves Modern Australian food; two separate excellent eateries—Aqua Luna and Aria—are on the promenade down below. The Dendy cinema, in the same strip, has good art-house movies.

61 Macquarie St., E. Circular Quay, Sydney, NSW 2000. ℭ **1800/091 954** in Australia, or 02/9256 4000. Fax 02/9256 4040. www.mirvachotels.com.au. A$335–A$507 (US$268–US$405) 1-bedroom apt. Extra person A$35 (US$28). Ask about weekend packages and long-term discounts. AE, DC, MC, V. Valet parking A$20 (US$16). CityRail, bus, or ferry: Circular Quay. **Amenities:** Restaurant; bar (the trendy ECQ); small health club; concierge; 24-hr. room service; massage; babysitting; laundry service; dry cleaning; nonsmoking rooms. *In room:* A/C, TV w/pay movies, dataport, kitchen, minibar, coffeemaker, hair dryer, iron/ironing board, washing machine, dryer.

Shangri-la Hotel Sydney ★★   For a room with a view, you're not going to do better than this ultramodern landmark hotel a 5-minute walk from Circular Quay. All rooms look out onto Darling Harbour or across the Opera House and Harbour Bridge. Try to book a room on the 20th floor or above: From here Sydney is laid out at your feet, with ferries buzzing around below you like bathtub toys. If you really want to splurge, book a corner room for an extraordinary vista. Rooms are comfortably furnished and decorated to blend with sky, city, and sea. The hotel is popular with tour groups, particularly from Japan, hence the great Japanese restaurants here.

176 Cumberland St., The Rocks, Sydney, NSW 2000. ℭ **1800/801 088** in Australia, or 02/9250 6000. Fax 02/9250 6250. www.shangri-la.com. 563 units. A$450–A$500 (US$360–US$400) double; A$750 (US$600) corner room; A$550–A$4,900 (US$440–US$3,920) suite. Extra person A$60 (US$48). Children stay free in parent's room. Ask

about packages. AE, DC, MC, V. Parking A$21 (US$17). CityRail or ferry: Circular Quay. **Amenities:** 2 restaurants; lounge; 2 bars; heated indoor pool; exercise room; Jacuzzi; sauna; concierge; business center; salon; 24-hr. room service; babysitting; laundry service; currency exchange; early-arrivals/late-departures lounge. *In room:* A/C, TV w/pay movies, dataport, minibar, hair dryer, iron/ironing board, safe.

Sir Stamford at Circular Quay ★★★

Talk about plush! This is Sydney's most deluxe hotel—from the moment the doorman doffs his top hat to you, you enter the world of aristocracy, complete with the slight scent of cigar smoke and aged brandy in the air. This hotel, formally the Ritz-Carlton, has a prime location, just a short walk from Circular Quay and the Opera House, and just across the road from the Royal Botanic Gardens. Rooms are exceptionally large and luxurious, with good-size marble bathrooms. Most rooms have a small balcony. The rooms on the east side of the hotel have the best views across the Botanic Gardens. Most rooms are accessible to wheelchairs.

93 Macquarie St., Sydney, NSW 2000. ✆ **1300/301 391** in Australia, or 02/9252 4600. Fax 02/9252 4286. www. stamford.com.au. 105 units. A$540 (US$432) double; A$580 (US$464) deluxe harbor-view double; A$705–A$3,000 (US$564–US$2,400) Sir Stamford presidential suite. AE, DC, MC, V. Parking A$40 (US$32). CityRail, bus, or ferry: Circular Quay. **Amenities:** Restaurant; bar; solar-heated outdoor pool; exercise room; sauna; concierge; business center; 24-hr. room service; babysitting; laundry service; currency exchange. *In room:* A/C, TV w/pay movies, fax, dataport, minibar, hair dryer, iron/ironing board, safe.

EXPENSIVE

The Russell ★★ *Finds*

This is the coziest place to stay in The Rocks, and perhaps in all of Sydney. It's more than 100 years old, and it shows its age wonderfully in the creaks of the floorboards and the ramshackle feel of the brightly painted corridors. Every room is different in style, size, and shape; all come with a queen-size bed, and most have cable TV. (Others can have a TV moved in if requested.) All rooms have immense character, including a series of rooms added on in 1990 above the Fortune of War Hotel next door. There are no harbor views, but from some rooms you can see the tops of the ferry terminals at Circular Quay. Guests have the use of a comfortable sitting room, a living room with magazines and books, and a rooftop garden. The apartment is a large, open-plan unit with a king-size bed and small kitchen; it's suitable for three people (there's a double sofa bed). It overlooks Circular Quay.

143A George St., The Rocks, Sydney, NSW 2000. ✆ **02/9241 3543.** Fax 02/9252 1652. www.therussell.com.au. 29 units, 19 with bathroom. A$140–A$195 (US$112–US$156) double without bathroom; A$235–A$290 (US$188–US$232) double with bathroom; A$320 (US$256) suite or apt. Extra person A$15 (US$12). Rates include continental breakfast. AE, DC, MC, V. No parking available. CityRail or ferry: Circular Quay. **Amenities:** Restaurant; lounge. *In room:* TV, coffeemaker, iron/ironing board.

The Sebel Pier One Sydney ★ *Finds*

A premier waterfront hotel, the Sebel is in the historic Woolloomooloo Wharf complex and has been painstakingly renovated, leaving as much of the original structure intact as possible. It's a wonderfully intoxicating blend of old wooden beams and tasteful modern art. The only drawback to staying in one of the tastefully appointed waterfront rooms is that the harbor views—through windows that run all the way to the floor—could make you want to stay in for the rest of the day. Or perhaps the cocktail bar, touted as one of the trendiest in town, is more your scene.

11 Hickson Rd., Walsh Bay, Sydney NSW 2000. ✆ **1800/780 485** in Australia. Fax 02/8298 9777. www.mirvac hotel.com.au. 161 units. A$235 (US$188) double; A$290 (US$232) waterfront room. Rates include breakfast. AE, DC, MC, V. CityRail or ferry: Circular Quay. Bus: George St. **Amenities:** Restaurant; bar; gym; Jacuzzi; outdoor terrace. *In room:* A/C, TV, dataport, minibar, hair dryer, iron/ironing board, safe.

The Stafford The Stafford offers some of the best-positioned serviced apartments in Sydney, right in the heart of The Rocks, very close to the harbor and Circular Quay, and a short stroll from the central business district. The property consists of modern apartments in a six-story building (the best units, for their harbor and Opera House views, are on the top three floors) and seven two-story terrace houses dating from 1870 to 1895. The Stafford is highly recommended for its location, spacious rooms, and fully equipped kitchen.

75 Harrington St., The Rocks, Sydney, NSW 2000. © **02/9251 6711.** Fax 02/9251 3458. www.rendezvoushotels.com. 61 units. A$235–A$275 (US$188–US$220) studio double; A$280 (US$225) 1-bedroom apt; A$320 (US$256) executive 1-bedroom apt; A$295 (US$236) terrace house; A$370 (US$295) 1-bedroom penthouse. Extra person A$15 (US$12). Children under 12 stay free in parent's room. Ask about weekly discounts. AE, DC, MC, V. Parking A$15 (US$12). CityRail or ferry: Circular Quay. **Amenities:** Small outdoor pool; exercise room; Jacuzzi; sauna; tour desk; car-rental desk; business center; limited room service; babysitting; laundry service; dry cleaning. *In room:* A/C, TV, dataport, kitchen, minibar, coffeemaker, hair dryer, iron/ironing board.

MODERATE

The Lord Nelson Brewery Hotel Sydney's oldest pub was established in 1841 after serving as a private residence since its construction in 1836. It's an attractive, three-story sandstone building with a busy pub on the ground floor, a good brasserie on the second, and hotel accommodations on the third. The rooms were totally renovated in 1999. They're compact, but spacious enough to swing your bags around without hitting the walls. From its creaky floorboards and bedroom walls made from convict-hewn sandstone blocks, to the narrow corridors, the wood fire, and the homemade beer in the bar, The Lord Nelson positively wallows in colonial atmosphere.

At the corner of Kent and Argyle sts., The Rocks, Sydney, NSW 2000. © **02/9251 4044.** Fax 02/9251 1532. www.lord nelson.com.au. 9 units, 8 with bathroom. A$120 (US$96) double without bathroom; A$180 (US$144) double with bathroom. Extra person A$30 (US$24). Rates include continental breakfast. AE, DC, MC, V. No parking available. CityRail or ferry: Circular Quay. **Amenities:** 2 restaurants; bar. *In room:* TV, fax, coffeemaker, hair dryer, iron/ironing board.

CITY CENTER
VERY EXPENSIVE

The Grace Hotel Sydney ★★ The centrally located Grace occupies the historic Grace Building, a replica of the *Chicago Tribune* Building in the United States and one of Australia's finest examples of commercial Gothic architecture. The 11-story building's L-shaped lobby has marble flagstones, stained-glass windows, a lace ironwork balcony, Art Deco furniture and light fittings, and high ceilings supported by marble columns. Guest rooms vary in size (the more expensive doubles are "deluxe," the cheaper "executive"), with king-size beds or a pair of doubles; they open off almost surreally wide corridors. Three rooms are suitable for travelers with disabilities.

77 York St., Sydney, NSW 2000. © **1800/682 692** in Australia, or 02/9299 8777. Fax 02/9299 8189. www.grace hotel.com.au. 382 units. A$374–A$396 (US$299–US$317) double; A$572 (US$458) suite. Extra person A$50 (US$40). Children under 17 stay free in parent's room. AE, DC, MC, V. Parking A$28 (US$22). CityRail: Wynyard. **Amenities:** 2 restaurants; bar; heated outdoor pool; gym; sauna; concierge; business center; 24-hr. room service; massage; babysitting; laundry service; currency exchange. *In room:* A/C, TV, dataport, minibar, coffeemaker, hair dryer, iron/ironing board, safe.

Westin Sydney ★ One of Sydney's most celebrated AAA-rated five-star hotels, the Westin is in the center of the city, in the Martin Place pedestrian mall. Integrated into a former post office from the 19th century, the Westin's charm is modern and classic all at once. The large rooms have comfortable beds and floor-to-ceiling windows. The hotel is home to several bars, restaurants, and clothing shops. Just steps from the central shopping streets and the QVB, and a 10- to 15-minute walk to both the Sydney Opera House and Darling Harbour, the hotel features an impressive seven-story atrium, a wonderful two-level health club, and an exclusive day spa.

1 Martin Place, Sydney, NSW 2000. © **800/WESTIN-1** in the U.S., or 02/8223 1111. Fax 02/8223 1222. www.westin. com.au. 416 units. A$286 (US$229) double. AE, DC, MC, V. Parking A$25 (US$20). **Amenities:** Cafe; bar; day spa; massage; babysitting; laundry service; currency exchange. *In room:* A/C, TV, dataport, minibar, coffeemaker, hair dryer, iron/ironing board, safe.

EXPENSIVE

Park Regis Sydney This hotel occupies the top 15 floors of a 45-story building and is well placed in the central business district, just 2 blocks from Hyde Park and Town Hall. There's nothing spectacular about it, but the rooms are light, modern, and practical. Many of the guests are business travelers, which gives the hotel a corporate feel. Nevertheless, it's a relatively good value considering the location. Rooms at the front have views over the city and park.

27 Park St. (at Castlereagh St.), Sydney, NSW 2000. © **1800/221 138** in Australia, or 02/9267 6511. Fax 02/9264 2252. www.parkregissydney.com.au. 120 units (all with shower only). A$165 (US$132) double; A$198 (US$154) suite. Extra person A$22 (US$18). Children under 14 stay free in parent's room. Aussie auto club discounts available. AE, DC, MC, V. Parking A$20 (US$16). CityRail: Town Hall. Monorail: Park Plaza. **Amenities:** Small heated outdoor pool; concierge; tour desk; 24-hr. room service; babysitting; laundry service; dry cleaning; nonsmoking rooms. *In room:* A/C, TV, fridge, coffeemaker, hair dryer.

MODERATE

Travelodge Hotel Sydney *★* This business-oriented hotel is cheap for Sydney, comfortable, and well located—making it a good option for some travelers. The rooms are motel-like in appearance, with a queen-size bed or twin beds. Many come with a sofa. From here it's a short walk to Oxford Street, Town Hall, Hyde Park, and the monorail to Darling Harbour.

27–33 Wentworth Ave., Sydney, NSW 2000. © **02/8267 1700.** Fax 02/8267 1800. www.travelodge.com.au. 406 units. A$119 (US$95) double or twin. Extra person A$16 (US$13). AE, DC, MC, V. Parking around corner A$17 (US$14). CityRail: Museum. **Amenities:** Restaurant; massage; babysitting; nonsmoking rooms. *In room:* A/C, TV, dataport, kitchenette, fridge, coffeemaker, hair dryer, iron/ironing board.

INEXPENSIVE

Sydney Central YHA *★★* *Value* This multiple-award-winning hostel is one of the biggest and busiest in the world. With a 98% year-round occupancy rate, you'll have to book early. It's in a historic nine-story building, and offers far more than standard basic accommodations. In the basement is the Scu Bar, a popular drinking hole with pool tables and occasional entertainment. There's also an entertainment room with more pool tables and e-mail facilities, TV rooms on every floor, and an audiovisual room that shows movies. Rooms are clean and basic. Three dorm rooms hold eight people each; 24 sleep up to six; and 70 accommodate four. The YHA is accessible to travelers with disabilities.

A new hostel, the Railway Square YHA (8–10 Lee St., at the corner of Upper Carriage Lane and Lee St., or enter via the Henry Dean Plaza, Sydney, NSW 2000; © **02/9281 9666;** fax 02/9281 9688) opened in 2004. The 64-bed hostel offers four-to-eight-bed dorms and 10 double rooms in a historic 1904 building adjoining "Platform Zero" at Central Railway Station. Some dorm rooms are even located in railway carriages. There's a spa pool, Internet cafe, tour desk, indoor and outdoor communal areas, and a self-catering kitchen. Dorm rooms cost from A$27 to A$33 (US$22–US$26) a night, doubles with shared bathroom are A$78 (US$62), and doubles with bathroom are A$88 (US$70).

There are more than 140 YHA hostels in Australia. Check the website for the full list, which includes other hostels in Sydney, such as the **Glebe Point YHA,** the **Sydney Beachhouse YHA** in the beachside suburb of Collaroy, and **Pittwater YHA** in Ku-ring-gai Chase National Park (accessible only by boat, and a fabulous way to experience the "bush" around Sydney).

11 Rawson Place (at Pitt St., outside Central Station), Sydney, NSW 2000. ℂ 02/9281 9111. Fax 02/9281 9199. www.yha.com.au. 97 dorm units with 448 beds; 54 twin units, 43 with bathroom. A$28–A$33 (US$22–US$26) dorm bed; A$82 (US$66) twin without bathroom; A$94 (US$75) twin with bathroom. Non-YHA members are charged an extra A$3.50 (US$2.80) per night. MC, V. Parking A$12 (US$9.60). CityRail: Central. **Amenities:** Restaurant; bar; small heated outdoor pool; sauna; 2 kitchens; TV room. *In room:* No phone.

AT DARLING HARBOUR

VERY EXPENSIVE

Star City Hotel ★★ Opened in 1997, this A$900-million (US$720-million) gambling and entertainment complex includes an AAA-rated five-star hotel, with rooms overlooking Darling Harbour and the architecturally interesting Pyrmont Bridge. Although the four split-level Royal Suites are spectacular—each with three TVs, a giant Jacuzzi, a full kitchen, two bathrooms, its own sauna, and the services of the former butler to the governor of Queensland—the standard rooms are somewhat small and sterile. Executive suites are very nice. If you stay here, pay the extra money for a room with spectacular views over Darling Harbour.

80 Pyrmont St., Pyrmont, Sydney, NSW 2009. ℂ 1800/700 700 in Australia, or 02/9777 9000. Fax 02/9657 8344. www.starcity.com.au. 491 units. A$350–A$370 (US$280–US$296) double; from A$510 (US$408) and way up suite. Extra person A$40 (US$32). Ask about special packages. AE, DC, MC, V. Parking A$15 (US$12). Ferry: Pyrmont Bay. Monorail: Harbourside. Light Rail: Star City. **Amenities:** 4 restaurants; large heated outdoor pool; Jacuzzi; sauna; gaming rooms; concierge; free shuttle bus from central business district; business center; shopping arcade; salon; 24-hr. room service; massage; laundry service; 2 theaters; currency exchange. *In room:* A/C, TV, dataport, minibar, coffeemaker, hair dryer.

EXPENSIVE

Medina Grand, Harbourside ★★ This impressive serviced hotel (which is essentially a furnished apartment with maid service) offers modern, very comfortable rooms at competitive prices. It's a little oddly placed—reached by an offshoot road and a short, unattractive walk from the Sydney Aquarium in Darling Harbour—but it makes up for it by being close to all of the Darling Harbour, Cockle Bay, and Town Hall attractions and shops. You can choose between studio and one-bedroom apartments, which all come with Italian designer furniture, large windows, and balconies (some with good harbor views). Studio units come with a kitchenette, and one-bedroom units come with a fully equipped kitchen and a second TV. All have dataports. Medina offers very good package and weekend rates, which means this place can work out to be a real bargain. Higher prices in the ranges below are for water-view units.

Corner of Shelley and King sts., King St. Wharf, Sydney, NSW 2000. ℂ 1300/300 232 in Australia, or 02/9249 7000. Fax 02/9249 6900. www.medinaapartments.com.au. 114 units. A$238–A$254 (US$190–US$203) studio; A$265–A$330 (US$212–US$264) 1-bedroom apt. AE, DC, MC, V. CityRail: Town Hall. **Amenities:** Small heated indoor pool; exercise room; concierge; tour desk; business center; laundry service; nonsmoking rooms. *In room:* A/C, TV, dataport, kitchenette, minibar, coffeemaker, hair dryer, iron/ironing board.

Tips **Homes Away from Home**

Medina, the company behind the Medina Grand, Harbourside, operates several other serviced-apartment complexes in Sydney. They include the **Medina Executive,** Sydney Central (✆ **02/8396 9800**), in a historic building near Central station; the pleasant **Medina Classic** in Martin Place (✆ **02/9224 6400**); coastal **Medina Executive,** near Coogee Beach (✆ **02/9578 6000**); and the AAA-rated five-star **Medina Grand,** Sydney (✆ **02/9274 0000**), between Town Hall and Darling Harbour. Check the website (www.medinaapartments.com.au) for prices and details about these highly recommended properties. Rates range from A$165 to A$488 (US$132–US$390), with many prices and combinations in between.

MODERATE

Wool Brokers Arms   You'll find this friendly 1886 heritage building on the far side of Darling Harbour, next to the prominent AAA-rated four-star Novotel hotel and hidden behind a monstrous aboveground parking garage. It's on a noisy road, so unless you're used to traffic, avoid the rooms at the front. Rooms are simply furnished, with a double bed and a sink. Room no. 3 is one of the nicer ones. Family rooms have a king-size bed, a set of bunks, and two singles through an open doorway. There are 19 shared bathrooms. It's adequate for a few nights.

22 Allen St., Pyrmont, Sydney, NSW 2009. ✆ **02/9552 4773.** Fax 02/9552 4771. www.ozemail.com.au/~wool brokers. 26 units, none with bathroom. A$89 (US$71) double; A$110 (US$88) triple; A$130 (US$104) family room for 4. Rates include continental breakfast. Extra person A$20 (US$16). AE, MC, V. Parking A$11 (US$8.80) nearby. Bus: 501 from central business district or Central Station. Light Rail: Convention Centre. **Amenities:** Tour desk; coin-op laundry; nonsmoking rooms. *In room:* TV.

IN KINGS CROSS & THE SUBURBS BEYOND

EXPENSIVE

The Kirketon ★   If you want to stay somewhere a bit offbeat and class yourself as a hip, fashionable type, then this boutique hotel in Darlinghurst is a fascinating option. Rooms come with king-size, queen-size, double, or twin beds, and are lightly stocked with modernist furniture and custom-made fittings, including mirrored headboards, sleek bathrooms hidden away behind mirrored doors, and interestingly textured bedspreads and areas of wallpaper. All in all, the decor is fun if you like this sort of thing, although I found it jarred with my more conventional taste. Junior rooms are quite compact, and some Premium rooms come with a tub as well as shower. Executive rooms are quite large and have a VCR; some have a small balcony overlooking the main road (the road can be noisy at night). The inside scoop is that the best Junior room is no. 330, the best Premium room no. 340, and the best executive room no. 323. I would definitely ask for a room away from the main road. The same company operates another stylish boutique hotel, **Medusa,** 267 Darlinghurst Rd. (✆ **02/9331 1000**).

229 Darlinghurst Rd., Darlinghurst, NSW 2010. ✆ **02/9332 2011.** Fax 02/9332 2499. www.kirketon.com.au. 40 rooms. A$139 (US$111) junior room; A$169 (US$135) premium double; A$189 (US$151) executive double. Book these rates over the Internet. Maximum 2 people per room. AE, DC, MC, V. Free parking in garage around corner. **Amenities:** Restaurant; bar. *In room:* A/C, TV, dataport, minibar, hair dryer.

MODERATE

DeVere Hotel   The DeVere has been recommended by several readers who commented on the friendly staff and the bargain-basement prices when booked at the Tourism New South Wales Travel Centre at the Sydney airport. Although the rooms are very modern, they are a little too standard gray for my liking (although the owner says some are now yellow). Superior rooms are a bit larger, and the executive room is larger still and comes with nicer furniture. They are certainly a bargain compared to similar, but far more expensive, rooms elsewhere in Sydney. The suites have views of Elizabeth Bay, a Jacuzzi, and a king-size bed rather than a queen-size. Some suites have a kitchenette with no cooking facilities. Some standard rooms have an extra single bed. Breakfast is available; prices start at A$8 (US$6.40).

44–46 Macleay St., Potts Point, NSW 2011. © **1800/818 790** in Australia, 0800/441 779 in New Zealand, or 02/9358 1211. Fax 02/9358 4685. www.devere.com.au. 100 units. A$150 (US$120) double; A$195 (US$152) superior room; A$225 (US$180) executive room or studio; A$280 (US$224) suite. Extra person A$45 (US$36). Check website for packages. Children under 12 stay free in parent's room. AE, DC, MC, V. Parking at nearby Landmark Hotel A$12 (US$9.60) per exit. CityRail: Kings Cross. Bus: 311 from Circular Quay. **Amenities:** Tour desk; car-rental desk; business center; laundry service; dry cleaning. *In room:* A/C, TV, fridge, coffeemaker, hair dryer.

Hotel 59 *Kids*   This popular and friendly B&B is well worth considering if you want to be near the Kings Cross action, but far enough away to get a decent night's sleep. Deluxe rooms have a queen- or king-size bed and a tub/shower, while the smaller standard rooms come with a double bed and a shower. The two large superior rooms come with a separate living room, two single beds, and two more that can be locked together to form a king-size. One comes with a small kitchen with a microwave and hot plates. All rooms are well kept and comfortable, with private bathrooms. The cafe below serves breakfast. A flight of stairs and the lack of an elevator might make this a bad choice for travelers with disabilities.

59 Bayswater Rd., Kings Cross, NSW 2011. © **02/9360 5900.** Fax 02/9360 1828. www.hotel59.com.au. 8 units (some with shower only). A$115 (US$92) standard double; A$125 (US$100) deluxe double; A$135 (US$108) superior room. Extra person A$15 (US$12); extra child 2–12 A$10 (US$8). Rates include cooked breakfast. MC, V. No parking. CityRail: Kings Cross. **Amenities:** Cafe; TV lounge; tour desk; car-rental desk; nonsmoking rooms. *In room:* A/C, TV, kitchen, fridge, coffeemaker, hair dryer, iron/ironing board.

INEXPENSIVE

Bernly Private Hotel *Finds*   This place, tucked just off Darlinghurst Road, is a find. It's a rabbit warren of rooms run by a friendly staff, catering to everyone from short-term travelers to newly arrived immigrants. All rooms are new and clean. The more expensive rooms are superior to most others of their price in the area. Budget rooms are a bit scruffier and smaller than the standards, but are perfectly livable. Some come with a microwave oven, and all have a small TV. Backpacker rooms have two sets of bunk beds, though just two people seem to occupy most. Some of the backpacker rooms have a shower. There's a rooftop sun deck and a lounge with cable TV. Five family rooms come with double beds and two singles.

15 Springfield Ave., Potts Point, NSW 2011. © **02/9358 3122.** Fax 02/9356 4405. www.bernlyprivatehotel.com.au. 95 units, 12 with bathroom. A$66 (US$53) budget double with shared bathroom; A$99 (US$79) double with bathroom; A$132 (US$106) triple with bathroom; A$154 (US$123) family room with bathroom; A$25 (US$20) dorm bed. Extra person A$22 (US$18). AE, DC, MC, V. Metered street parking. CityRail: Kings Cross. **Amenities:** TV lounge. *In room:* A/C, TV, fridge, coffeemaker, iron/ironing board.

Victoria Court Sydney ★ *Value*   This cute, well-priced place is made up of two 1881 terrace houses joined together. It's near a string of backpacker hostels and popular cafes on a leafy street running parallel to sleazy Darlinghurst Road. The glass-roofed breakfast room on the ground floor is a work of art, decked out with hanging ferns, giant bamboo, wrought-iron tables and chairs, and a trickling fountain. Just off this space is a peaceful guest lounge stacked with books and newspapers. The very plush rooms come with either king- or queen-size beds, but lack a tub in the bathroom. There's a coin-op laundry just down the road.

122 Victoria St., Potts Point, NSW 2011. © **1800/630 505** in Australia, or 02/9357 3200. Fax 02/9357 7606. www.victoriacourt.com.au. 22 units. A$75–A$115 (US$60–US$92) double; A$165 (US$132) deluxe double with sun deck; A$250 (US$200) honeymoon suite with balcony. Extra person A$20 (US$16). Rates include buffet breakfast. AE, DC, MC, V. Free secure parking. CityRail: Kings Cross. **Amenities:** Guest lounge. *In room:* A/C, TV.

OXFORD STREET/DARLINGHURST

MODERATE

Sullivans Hotel   About half of this boutique hotel's guests come from overseas, mainly from the United Kingdom, Europe, and the United States. There's also a small corporate following. Sullivans is right in the heart of the action in one of Sydney's most popular shopping, entertainment, restaurant, and gay pub and club areas. The hotel is particularly popular with Americans during Gay and Lesbian Mardi Gras. All rooms are simple and compact, but good for a few nights. They come with an attached shower. Standard rooms have two single beds, and the garden rooms have a queen-size bed and pleasant garden views.

21 Oxford St., Paddington, NSW 2021. © **02/9361 0211.** Fax 02/9360 3735. www.sullivans.com.au. 64 units. A$135 (US$108) standard double; A$150 (US$120) garden room double and triple; A$150 (US$120) family room; A$210 (US$168) 2 connecting rooms. AE, DC, MC, V. Limited free parking. Bus: 378 from Central Station or 380 from Circular Quay. **Amenities:** Breakfast cafe; small heated outdoor pool; free use of bikes; coin-op laundry; free Internet access. *In room:* A/C, TV w/free movies, fridge, hair dryer, iron/ironing board.

Wattle Private Hotel *(Finds)*   This attractive Edwardian-style house built between 1900 and 1910 offers basic to very pleasant accommodations in the increasingly fashionable inner-city suburb of Darlinghurst, known for its great cafes, nightlife, and restaurants. The hotel was renovated and refurbished in early 2004 and has changed a lot. Double rooms are rather basic and quite small, but large windows open them. Nicer and larger queen rooms have a queen-size bed, king rooms have a king-size bed (some have harbor views), while a deluxe twin room has two king-size beds. There's also a family room that sleeps up to six people. Expect period features, such as high ceilings and ornate moldings. Rooms are on four stories, but there's no elevator, so if you don't fancy too many stairs, try to get a room on a lower floor. There's a rooftop garden with harbor and city views. The hotel was undergoing continued minor refurbishment in 2005.

108 Oxford St. (at corner of Palmer St.), Darlinghurst, NSW 2010. © **02/9332 4118.** Fax 02/9331 2074. www.the wattle.com 11 units. A$99–A$159 (US$79–US$127) double; A$110–A$179 (US$88–US$143) queen; A$120–A$239 (US$96–US$191) king; A$140–A$239 (US$112–US$191) king with harbor views; A$140–A$239 (US$112–US$191) deluxe twin; A$200–A$350 (US$160–US$280) family unit. More expensive rates are for peak times and discounts are available year-round. Extra person A$29 (US$23). Rates include continental breakfast. MC, V. No parking. Bus: Any to Taylor Sq. from Circular Quay. **Amenities:** Coin-op laundry. *In room:* A/C, TV, minibar.

IN NEWTOWN

INEXPENSIVE

Billabong Gardens   For that inner-city feel, you can't beat Newtown, with its busy street happenings, cheap restaurants, and grunge look. It's also easy to get to by bus or CityRail. Billabong Gardens is just off the main drag, King Street, and earned a five-star backpackers' rating from the National Roads and Motorists' Association. Rooms are simply furnished in pine and have exposed brickwork. Besides the dormitory accommodations, you might consider the double or twin rooms, which offer pretty good value. The more expensive rooms have their own bathrooms. It's a friendly place with lots of native plants scattered around, and a pool in a pleasant courtyard. On the property are a comfortable TV lounge, a large kitchen, and a barbecue. It's very secure and offers 24-hour access. Motel-style rooms are also available.

5–11 Egan St., Newtown, NSW 2042. ℂ **02/9550 3236.** Fax 02/9550 4352. www.billabonggardens.com.au. 37 units. A$20–A$26 (US$16–US$21) dorm bed; A$66–A$88 (US$53–US$70) double or twin. Motel rooms: A$88 (US$70) double; A$105 (US$84) triple. Family rooms available. MC, V. Parking A$5 (US$4). CityRail: Newtown. Bus: 422, 423, 426, or 428. **Amenities:** Small heated outdoor pool; Jacuzzi; game room; coin-op laundry; free Internet access. In room: No phone.

IN GLEBE
EXPENSIVE
Tricketts Luxury Bed & Breakfast ★★　As soon as I walked into this atmospheric old place, I wanted to ditch my modern Sydney apartment and move in. Your first impression as you enter the tessellated, tiled corridor of the 1880s Victorian mansion is the jumble of plants and ornaments, the high ceilings, the Oriental rugs, and the leaded windows. Guests relax over a decanter of port or with a magazine on wicker furniture on the veranda overlooking fairly busy Glebe Point Road. The guest rooms are quiet and homey. My favorites are no. 2, with its wooden floorboards and king-size bed, and no. 8—The Honey Room Suite—with a 1820s king-size four-poster bed. There's a nice courtyard out back. The owner, Liz Tricketts, is a delight and is a rich source of Sydney's history.

270 Glebe Point Rd., Glebe (the water end), NSW 2037. ℂ **02/9552 1141.** Fax 02/9692 9462. www.tricketts.com.au. 7 units (all with shower only). A$198 (US$158) double; A$220 (US$176) honeymoon suite. Rates include continental breakfast. MC, V. Free parking. Bus: 431 from George St. **Amenities:** Tour desk; massage; nonsmoking rooms. In room: A/C, TV, hair dryer.

MODERATE
Alishan International Guest House　The Alishan is a quiet place with a real Aussie feel. It's at the city end of Glebe Point Road, just 10 minutes by bus from the shops around Town Hall. It's a mixture of upmarket youth hostel and typical guesthouse. Standard dorm rooms are spotless, light, and bright, and come with two sets of bunks. Doubles have a double bed, a sofa and armchair, and a shower. Grab room no. 9 if you fancy sleeping on one of two single mattresses on the tatami mat floor, Japanese style.

100 Glebe Point Rd., Glebe, NSW 2037. ℂ **02/9566 4048.** Fax 02/9525 4686. www.alishan.com.au. 19 units. A$27–A$33 (US$22–US$26) dorm bed; A$99–A$115 (US$79–US$92) double; A$154 (US$123) family room. Extra person A$16 (US$13). AE, MC, V. Secured parking for 6 cars; metered street parking. Bus: 431 or 433 from George St., or Kingsford Smith Shuttle from airport. **Amenities:** Coin-op laundry; Internet access. In room: TV, fridge.

IN BONDI
Bondi Beach is a good place to stay if you want to be close to the surf and sand, though if you're getting around by public transport you'll need to catch a bus to Bondi Junction, then a train to the city center. (You can stay on the bus all the way, but it takes forever.)

In addition to the properties recommended below, there are two good backpacker hostels. **Indy's,** 35a Hall St. (ℂ **02/9365 4900;** www.indysbackpackers.com.au), offers four- to eight-person dorm rooms for A$18 (US$14) in winter and A$22

(US$18) in summer, and double rooms in a separate building opposite North Bondi Surf Club for the same price per person. **Noah's,** 2 Campbell Parade (© **02/9365 7100**), has a great ambience and offers modern four- to eight-person dorm rooms for A$24 to A$25 (US$19–US$20) as well as doubles for A$55 (US$44) and beach doubles for A$65 (US$52). Weekly rates range from A$144 to A$330 (US$115–US$264).

VERY EXPENSIVE

Swiss-Grand Hotel ★★   Right on Bondi Beach, overlooking the Pacific, the Swiss-Grand is the best hotel in Bondi. It occupies a unique position overlooking the waves and sand of one of Australia's most famous cultural icons. The lobby is grand indeed, with high ceilings and stylish furniture. A renovation in 2002 made each room into a suite, with separate bedroom and living room. All suites are spacious, and each comes with a rather luxurious bathroom. All rooms have two TVs; some have Jacuzzis. All oceanfront units have balconies. The general sumptuousness of the accommodations and a terrific day spa help make this a fine place to stay. It's popular with American and European travelers with a bit of money to spend.

Corner of Campbell Parade and Beach Rd. (P.O. Box 219, Bondi Beach, NSW 2026). © **800/344-1212** in the U.S., 1800/655 252 in Australia, 0800/951 000 in the U.K., 0800/056 666 in New Zealand, or 02/9365 5666. Fax 02/9365 9710. www.swissgrand.com.au. 230 units. A$308 (US$246) standard double; A$352 (US$281) oceanview double; from A$396 (US$317) suite. Packages are available on their website. Extra person A$44 (US$35). AE, DC, MC, V. Free parking. Bus: 380 from Circular Quay. **Amenities:** 2 restaurants; rooftop and indoor heated pools; fitness center; Jacuzzi, tour desk. *In room:* A/C, TV, coffeemaker, hair dryer, iron/ironing board.

MODERATE

Bondi Beachside Inn ★ *Kids*   With such a great location, right on the beachfront, you can't get much better value than this. A modern seven-story hotel, which prides itself on being family-friendly, the Beachside Inn has quite large rooms with compact bathrooms. The more expensive rooms have balconies with ocean views. It's well loved by return travelers, so it's advisable to book well ahead, especially during the summer.

152 Campbell Parade, Bondi Beach, NSW 2026. © **02/9130 5311**. Fax 02/9365 2646. www.bondiinn.com.au. 70 units. A$120–A$140 (US$96–US$112) double. Extra person A$25 (US$20); extra child A$10 (US$8). AE, DC, MC, V. Free parking. Bus: 380 or 382 from Circular Quay. *In room:* A/C, TV, fridge, coffeemaker.

Bondi Serviced Apartments   If you plan on staying a week or more, these pleasant, privately owned apartments could be ideal. They're on busy Bondi Road, a 5-minute walk to the beach, and opposite a post office (with phones—the apartment complex doesn't have any), an Internet parlor, and a 24-hour supermarket. The studio rooms at the front of the hotel suffer from traffic noise, but are larger than the quieter ones in the back. That said, all are good-size and have a nice feel about them. Each has a double bed (the front rooms also have an extra single) and a full kitchen. There's no air-conditioning (though the sea breeze does tend to cool Bondi down a bit in summer). The owner describes it as a "no frills" complex—hence the lack of phones, Internet address, fax number, and credit card payments, and the cleaning service is weekly rather than daily if you book for a week or more.

164–166 Bondi Rd., Bondi Beach, NSW 2026. © **02/9363 5529**. www.bondi-serviced-apartments.com.au. 12 units. A$450–A$750 (US$360–US$600) apt per week. More expensive rate is for summer. Daily rates A$105 (US$84) for budget studio and A$120 (US$96) for a standard studio. Ask about long-term discounts. No credit cards. Free parking. Bus: 380 or 382 from city center or Bondi Junction. **Amenities:** Coin-op laundry. *In room:* TV, kitchen, iron/ironing board.

Ravesi's on Bondi Beach ★★   Right on Australia's most famous golden sands, this boutique property reopened in May 2002 after major renovations to the restaurant, bar, and many rooms. The AAA-rated three-star hotel offers modern minimalist rooms with white marble bathrooms—all very chic, with African tribal wall hangings. Standard doubles are spacious; there's a one-bedroom suite, and a split-level one-bedroom option with the bedroom upstairs. Room nos. 5 and 6 and the split-level suite have the best views of the ocean. All rooms have Juliet balconies, and the split-level suite has its own terrace. If you're a light sleeper, request a room on the top floor, because the popular **Ravesi's Restaurant** can be quite noisy on busy nights. An attractive glass-sided ground-floor bar is the in place on the Bondi scene, with lounge, house, and "chill" music every evening. The bar is a great place to watch the outside street scene.

Corner of Hall St. and Campbell Parade, Bondi Beach, NSW 2026. (℃) **02/9365 4422.** Fax 02/9365 1481. www.ravesis. com.au. 16 units. A$125 (US$100) standard double; A$230 (US$184) double with side view; A$295 (US$236) beachfront room; A$275 (US$220) 1-bedroom suite; A$275–A$350 (US$220–US$280) split-level suite with terrace. Extra person A$30 (US$24). 2 children under 12 stay free in parent's room. AE, DC, MC, V. Parking at the Swiss-Grand Hotel nearby A$8 (US$6.40). CityRail: Bondi Junction; then bus 380. Bus: 380 from Circular Quay. **Amenities:** Restaurant; bar; tour desk; 24-hr. room service; laundry service; dry cleaning. *In room:* AC, TV, minibar, hair dryer, iron/ironing board, safe.

IN MANLY

If you decide to stay in my favorite beachside suburb, be aware that ferries from the city stop running at midnight. If you get stranded, you'll be facing an expensive taxi ride (around A$40/US$32), or you'll need to make your way to the bus stand behind Wynyard CityRail station to catch a night bus. Consider buying a multiple-ride ticket, which will save you quite a bit of money if you're staying in Manly for a few days.

Manly has several backpacker places that are worth checking out. The best is **Manly Backpackers Beachside,** 28 Ragland St. ((℃) **02/9977 3411;** fax 02/9977 4379; www. manlybackpackers.com.au), which offers dorm beds from A$22 to A$27 (US$18–US$21), double from A$52 to A$62 (US$42–US$49). The hostel charges a A$30 (US$24) key deposit.

VERY EXPENSIVE

Manly Pacific Parkroyal ★★   If you could bottle the views from this top-class hotel—across the sand and through the Norfolk Island Pines to the Pacific Ocean—you'd make a fortune. Standing on your private balcony in the evening with the sea breeze in your nostrils and the chirping of hundreds of lorikeets is nothing short of heaven. The Manly Pacific is the only hotel of its class in this wonderful beachside suburb. There's nothing claustrophobic here, from the broad expanse of glittering foyer to the wide corridors and spacious accommodations. Each standard room is light and modern, with two double beds, a balcony, limited cable TV, and all the necessities. Views over the ocean are really worth the extra money. The hotel is a 10-minute stroll, or a A$4 (US$3.20) taxi ride, from the Manly ferry.

55 North Steyne, Manly, NSW 2095. (℃) **02/9977 7666,** or 800/835-7742 in the U.S. and Canada. Fax 02/9977 7822. www.sixcontinentshotels.com. 169 units. A$283–A$327 (US$226–US$261) double; A$512 (US$409) suite. Extra person A$32 (US$26). AE, DC, MC, V. Parking A$10 (US$8). Ferry or JetCat: Manly. **Amenities:** 2 restaurants; 2 bars; heated rooftop pool; exercise room; Jacuzzi; sauna; concierge; tour desk; 24-hr. room service; laundry service. *In room:* A/C, TV, dataport, minibar, coffeemaker, hair dryer, iron/ironing board.

MODERATE

Manly Lodge ★ *Kids*   At first sight this ramshackle building halfway between the main beach and the harbor doesn't look like much. But don't let the tattiness—especially the cramped, hostel-like foyer bristling with tourist brochures—put you off. Some of the rooms are lovely, and the whole place has a nice atmosphere and plenty of character. Double rooms are not exceptional. They come with a double bed, stone or carpet floors, a TV and VCR, and either a Jacuzzi or a tub/shower combination. Some of the standard doubles and all of the deluxe doubles have a kitchen. Family rooms have a set of bunk beds and a double in one room, and a shower. Family suites are very classy; each has a Jacuzzi, a small kitchen area, one double and three singles in the bedroom, and two sofa beds in the living area. The lodge also has table tennis and even an Olympic-size trampoline. For purposes of setting room rates, peak season is defined as Christmas, Easter, and school holidays.

22 Victoria Parade, Manly, NSW 2095. ℭ 02/9977 8655. Fax 02/9976 2090. www.manlylodge.com.au. 24 units. Standard double A$132–A$154 (US$105–US$123) peak season, A$108–A$132 (US$86–US$105) off season; deluxe double A$154–A$198 (US$123–US$158) peak season, A$132–A$154 (US$105–US$123) off season; family suite A$264–A$330 (US$211–US$264) peak season, A$187–A$262 (US$149–US$209) off season. Extra person A$30 (US$24); extra child under 10 A$17 (US$14). Ask about weekly rates and off-season discounts. Rates include continental breakfast. AE, MC, V. Free parking. Ferry or JetCat: Manly. **Amenities:** Exercise room; Jacuzzi; sauna; coin-op laundry. In room: A/C, TV.

Manly Paradise Motel and Beach Plaza Apartments ✦

I walked into this place after taking a look around the modern Manly Waterfront Apartment Hotel next door and immediately felt more at home here. The motel and apartment complex are separate, but share a reception area. The irregularly shaped rooms are big yet cozy, and come with a shower and a springy double bed. Though there is no restaurant, you can get breakfast in bed; a simple breakfast costs about A$10 (US$8). My only concern is that the traffic can make it a little noisy during the day (but you'll probably be on the beach then, anyway). Some rooms have glimpses of the sea. Residents of the apartment complex share the swimming pool (with views) on the roof.

The apartments are magnificent—very roomy, with thick carpets. They're stocked with everything you need, including a washing machine and dryer, a full kitchen with dishwasher, and two bathrooms (one with a tub). The sea views from the main front balcony are heart-stopping.

54 N. Steyne, Manly, NSW 2095. ℭ 1800/815 789 in Australia, or 02/9977 5799. Fax 02/9977 6848. www.manly paradise.com.au. 40 units (some with shower only). A$105–A$165 (US$84–US$132) double motel unit; A$295 (US$236) 2-bedroom apt. Extra person A$25 (US$20). Ask about long-term discounts. AE, DC, MC, V. Free secured parking. Ferry or JetCat: Manly. **Amenities:** Indoor heated pool; dry cleaning; nonsmoking rooms. In room: A/C, TV, dataport, hair dryer, iron/ironing board.

Periwinkle–Manly Cove Guesthouse

Nicely positioned across the road from one of Manly's two harbor beaches, the Periwinkle is a short walk from the ferry, the shops along the Corso, and the main ocean beach. Rooms are small and come with a double bed. Some have a shower and toilet (these go for the higher prices noted below), but otherwise you'll have to make do with one of four separate bathrooms (one has a tub). A full kitchen next to a pleasant-enough communal lounge means you could save money by not eating out. Room nos. 5 and 10 are the nicest and have screened balconies overlooking the harbor (but no bathrooms). For atmosphere, I prefer the Manly Lodge (see above). No smoking inside.

18–19 E. Esplanade, Manly, NSW 2095. ℭ 02/9977 4668. Fax 02/9977 6308. www.periwinkle.citysearch.com.au. 18 units, 12 with bathroom. A$135 (US$108) double without bathroom; A$165 (US$132) double with bathroom. Units with harbor views A$10 (US$8) extra. Extra person A$25 (US$20). Rates include continental breakfast. MC, V. Free parking. Ferry or JetCat: Manly. **Amenities:** Coin-op laundry; nonsmoking rooms. In room: TV, fridge.

AT THE AIRPORT

Stamford Sydney Airport ★★   This is the best airport hotel. Opened in 1992, it has the largest rooms, each with a king-size bed or two doubles, access to airport information, and a good-size bathroom with tub. The location is 7 minutes from the airport, and pickup service is free. Day-use rates are A$85 (US$68) for 2 to 4 hours and A$115 (US$92) for 4 to 8 hours.

Corner of O'Riordan and Robey sts. (P.O. Box 353, Mascot, Sydney, NSW 2020). ℂ **1300/301 391** in Australia, or 02/9317 2200. Fax 02/9317 3855. www.stamford.com.au. 314 units. A$270 (US$216) double; from A$370 (US$296) suite. Extra person A$25 (US$20). Children under 17 stay free in parent's room. Ask about discount packages and weekend rates. AE, DC, MC, V. A$5 (US$4) self-parking for up to 10 days. **Amenities:** 2 restaurants; bar; good-size outdoor pool; fitness center; Jacuzzi; sauna; concierge; business center; 24-hr. room service; babysitting; laundry service; currency exchange; nonsmoking rooms; executive rooms. *In room:* A/C, TV, minibar, dataport, coffeemaker, hair dryer, iron/ironing board.

4 Where to Dine

Sydney is a gourmet paradise, with an abundance of fresh seafood, a vast range of vegetables and fruit always in season, prime meats at inexpensive prices, and top-quality chefs making international names for themselves. Asian and Mediterranean cooking have had a major influence on Australian cuisine, with spices and herbs finding their way into most dishes. Immigration has brought with it almost every type of cuisine you can imagine, from African to Tibetan, from Russian to Vietnamese. Some areas of the city are dedicated to one type of food, while other areas are melting pots of styles.

Sydney is a great place to try Modern Australian, or "Mod Oz," cuisine, which has been applauded by chefs and food critics around the world. Modern Australian cuisine emphasizes fresh ingredients and a creative blend of European styles with Asian

---

Value **What to Know about BYO**

Most moderate and inexpensive restaurants in Sydney are **BYO,** as in "bring your own" bottle, though some places also have extensive wine and beer lists. More moderately priced restaurants are introducing corkage fees, which mean you pay anywhere from A$2 to A$4 (US$1.60–US$3.20) per person for the privilege of the waiter opening your bottle of wine. Very expensive restaurants discourage BYO.

Sydney's **cheap eats** congregate in inner-city areas such as along King Street in Newtown, Crown Street in Darlinghurst, and Glebe Point Road in Glebe. There are also inexpensive joints scattered among the more upscale restaurants in Kings Cross and along trendy Oxford Street.

I would avoid the takeout booths along the ferry wharves at Circular Quay, after revelations that some of them harbored nasty bugs. The fish-and-chip shop opposite the "bottle shop" (liquor store) is an exception—it serves some of the best french fries in Sydney.

Smoking is banned in all Sydney restaurants, except if you're eating at a sidewalk table.

influences. (Some foodies complain that some restaurants use the label "Modern Australian" as an excuse to serve skimpy portions—like one lamb chop atop a tiny mound of mashed potatoes sprinkled with curry sauce.) At its best, Modern Australian food is world-class, but you'll probably have to go to the best of Sydney's restaurants to see what the scene is all about.

Australians think American-style coffee tastes like ditch water and favor a range of Italian-style coffee creations. Ask for a latte if you just want coffee with milk. "Bottomless" cups of coffee are rare in Australia. By the way, in Australia, the first course is called the entree and the second course the main.

NEAR CIRCULAR QUAY
VERY EXPENSIVE

Forty One ★★ MODERN AUSTRALIAN   Powerful people, international celebrities, and average Sydneysiders out for a special celebration all come here to feel exclusive. It's won plenty of awards. The 41st-floor views over the city and the harbor are terrific, the service is fun, the cutlery is the world's best, and Swiss chef and owner Dietmar Sawyere has given the food a wickedly good Asian slant. In all, it's a glamorous place to experience the best of Australian cuisine. The signature dish is roast wild hare, with celeriac and potato purée, Viennese carrots, and chartreuse jus. The menu changes every 2 weeks to keep up with seasonal produce.

Level 41, Chifley Tower, 2 Chifley Sq. ℂ **02/9221 2500**. forty.one@chifleytower.com.au. Reservations required. 3-course menu A$120 (US$96); 3-course menu with matched wine A$140 (US$112); 6 courses with wine A$200 (US$160). AE, DC, MC, V. Tues–Fri noon–4pm; Mon–Sat 7–10pm. CityRail: Wynyard.

Guillaume at Bennelong ★ FRENCH   If you go to Bondi, you have to swim in the Pacific; if you see the Harbour Bridge, you have to walk across it; if you visit the Opera House, you must eat at Guillaume at Bennelong. The restaurant is as uniquely designed as the building itself, with tall glass windows that furrow around in an arch and grab the harbor and Circular Quay by the throat. Renowned French chef Guillaume Brahini's offerings could include sealed veal sweetbreads with broad beans, asparagus, peas, and shiitake mushrooms; or confit of Atlantic salmon on braised endive with red-wine sauce. It's hardly innovative, but sometimes tradition wins. Many would rather miss the first half of the opera they've paid a fortune to see than leave before dessert. The best bar in town is upstairs, where you can see over the water to the bridge and up to the other "sails." Good bar food is available until 11:30pm.

In the Sydney Opera House, Bennelong Point. ℂ **02/9241 1999**. Fax 02/9241 3795. enquiries@guillaumeatbennelong.com.au. Reservations recommended. Main courses A$35 (US$28). AE, DC, MC, V. Thurs–Fri noon–3pm; Mon–Sat 5:30–10:30pm. CityRail, bus, or ferry: Circular Quay.

EXPENSIVE

Botanic Gardens Restaurant MODERN AUSTRALIAN   You couldn't ask for a better walk to a restaurant than through the Royal Botanic Gardens, next to the Sydney Opera House. Enjoying lunch on the wisteria-covered balcony in the middle of Sydney's most beautiful park is a treat every visitor should enjoy. Main courses include the very popular white sausage (boudin blanc) with lentils and braised fennel. Try perfect crème brûlée with underlying plum purée for dessert (A$12/US$9.20).

In the Royal Botanic Gardens. ℂ **02/9241 2419**. Reservations recommended. Main courses A$22–A$28 (US$18–US$22). AE, DC, MC, V. Daily noon–3pm. Bus or ferry: Circular Quay.

Where to Dine in Sydney

Ashiana **30**
Bar Coluzzi **33**
bel mondo **3**
Bill's **34**
Botanic Gardens
   Restaurant **19**
Bourbon & Beefsteak
   Bar **38**
Café Sydney **14**
Capitan Torres **31**
Chinta Ria (The Temple
   of Love) **27**
City Extra **15**
Doyles at the Quay **7**
Edna's Table **26**
Forty One **21**
G'Day Café **5**
Govindas **35**
Guillaume at
   Bennelong **16**
The Gumnut Café **9**
Hard Rock Cafe **32**
Hernandez **36**
The Italian Village **1**

Level Two Revolving
   Restaurant **25**
The Löwenbräu Keller **4**
Mezzaluna **38**
The Old Coffee Shop **23**
Otto Ristorante **20**
Pancakes Licensed
   Café **2**
Phillip's Foote **10**
Portobello Caffé **17**
Quay **8**
Quay Deli **12**
Rockpool **11**
Rossini **13**
Sailors Thai **11**
Supreme View Café **22**
Sushi Roll **24**
Sydney Cove Oyster
   Bar **18**
Tetsuya's **29**
Waterfront Restaurant **1**
Wolfie's Grill **1**
Zaaffran **28**
Zia Pina **6**

Finds **A Great Place for Picnic Grub**

If you're looking for something to take with you on a harbor cruise or on a stroll through the Royal Botanic Gardens, you can't go wrong with **Quay Deli,** E5 Alfred St., next to the pharmacy under the Circular Quay CityRail station, facing the road (*C* **02/9241 3571**). You'll find all sorts of goodies, including gourmet sandwiches and takeout foods such as olives, Greek dishes, pasta, salads, meat pies, and the best English-style custard tarts around. Everything is fresh and tasty. Lunch items go for A$1.80 to A$4.50 (US$1.45–US$3.60). It's open Monday through Friday from 5am to 6:45pm, Saturday from 9am to 4pm. No credit cards.

City Extra ITALIAN/AUSTRALIAN   Because this place stays open 24 hours, it's convenient if you get the munchies at a ridiculous hour. It's also nicely placed, right next to the Manly ferry terminal. The plastic chairs and outdoor tables make it a pleasant spot to while away an inexpensive meal. A range of pastas are available, as well as salads, pies, steaks, ribs, fish, and Asian-influenced dishes. There's also a fat selection of desserts. The food is much nicer and a better value next door at Rossini (see below).

Shop E4, Circular Quay. *C* **02/9241 1422.** Reservations not accepted. Main courses A$13–A$26 (US$10–US$21). 10% surcharge midnight–6am, Sun, public holidays. AE, DC, MC, V. Daily 24 hr. CityRail, bus, or ferry: Circular Quay.

Sydney Cove Oyster Bar SEAFOOD   Just before you reach the Sydney Opera House, you'll notice a couple of small shedlike buildings with tables and chairs set up to take in the stunning views of the harbor and the Harbour Bridge. The first is a Sydney institution, serving some of the best oysters in town. Light meals such as Asian-style octopus and seared tuna steak are also on the menu.

No. 1 Eastern Esplanade, Circular Quay East. *C* **02/9247 2937.** www.sydneycoveoysterbar.com. Main courses A$25–A$35 (US$20–US$28). 10% surcharge weekends and public holidays. AE, DC, MC, V. Mon–Sat 11am–11pm; Sun 11am–8pm. CityRail, bus, or ferry: Circular Quay.

MODERATE

Rossini ★ *Kids* ITALIAN   This cafeteria-style Italian restaurant opposite Ferry Wharf 5 at Circular Quay is wonderfully positioned for people-watching. The outside tables are perfect for breakfast or a quick bite before a show at the Opera House. Breakfast croissants, Italian doughnuts, muffins, and gorgeous Danish pastries cost A$2 (US$1.60), and bacon and eggs A$8 (US$6.40). Wait to be seated for lunch or dinner, make your choice, pay at the counter, take a ticket, and then pick up your food. Meals, including veal parmigiana, cannelloni, ravioli, chicken crepes, and octopus salad, are often huge. You could easily get away with one meal for two people—ask for an extra plate—and while it's not the best Italian you'll ever eat, it is tasty. Coffee fanatics rate the Rossini brew as average.

Shop W5, Circular Quay. *C* **02/9247 8026.** Main courses A$10–A$15 (US$8–US$12). No credit cards. Daily 7am–10pm. CityRail, bus, or ferry: Circular Quay.

INEXPENSIVE

Portobello Caffé PIZZA/SANDWICHES   Sharing the address of the Sydney Cove Oyster Bar (and the same priceless views), the Portobello Caffé offers first-class gourmet sandwiches on Italian wood-fired bread, small but delicious gourmet pizzas, breakfast croissants, snacks, cakes, and hot and cold drinks. Walk off with sensational ice cream in a cone for around A$3 (US$2.40).

No. 1 Eastern Esplanade, Circular Quay East. 🕐 **02/9247 8548**. Main courses A$8 (US$6.40). 10% surcharge Sun and public holidays. AE, DC, MC, V. Minimum credit card purchase A$30 (US$24). Daily 8am–11:50pm. CityRail, bus, or ferry: Circular Quay.

THE ROCKS
VERY EXPENSIVE

bel mondo ✦✦ NORTHERN ITALIAN   With its uncomplicated cuisine, bel mondo has deservedly positioned itself alongside the best of Sydney's upscale restaurants. At this family-run affair, chef Stefano Manfredi is helped out in the kitchen by his mum, Franca, a pasta diva in her own right. The restaurant is large and long, with high ceilings, and the energetic pace and the banging and clashing coming from the open kitchen give the place a New York feel. Standout appetizers include grilled sea scallops with soft polenta and pesto. Favorite main courses include roast lamb with rosemary and roast potatoes, and potato gnocchi with burnt butter and Parmesan. The wine list is extensive. bel mondo's **Antibar** is cheaper and more relaxed; it offers some of the best antipasto I've tasted in Australia, as well as light meals (A$14–A$22/US$11–US$18) and features jazz on Friday evenings from 5:30 to 7:30pm.

In the Argyle Department Store, 3rd floor, 18–24 Argyle St., The Rocks. 🕐 **02/9241 3700**. reservations@belmondo.com.au. Reservations recommended. Main courses A$27–A$46 (US$22–US$37). 10% surcharge Sun and public holidays. AE, DC, MC, V. Tues–Fri 12:30–2:30pm; Mon–Thurs 6:30–10:30pm; Fri–Sat 6:30–11pm; Sun 6:30–10pm. CityRail, bus, or ferry: Circular Quay.

Café Sydney MODERN AUSTRALIAN   Located in the historic Customs House—the building with the clock tower across the square and behind the ferry wharfs at Circular Quay—Café Sydney is a fabulous spot to watch the world go by on the harbor. It has spectacular views of the Sydney Harbour Bridge. The interior design is fresh and modern, with lots of wood and soft lighting, and the menu features plenty of European-style classics and others with a distinct Asian influence and an emphasis on seafood. A couple of options are tandoori roast salmon with *chana masala* (curried chickpeas, Indian-style) and coconut sambol (a hot side dish from Sri Lanka), and wood-grilled veal with figs, Gorgonzola, and speck (bits of bacon, German-style). The Havana Bar here offers cozy wood cubicles and great cocktails. Downstairs in the courtyard is an informal cafe, which is also nice for cocktails or a quick lunch.

Level 5, Customs House, corner of Loftus and Alfred sts., Circular Quay. 🕐 **02/9251 8683**. Reservations recommended in restaurant. Main courses A$23–A$30 (US$18–US$24). AE, DC, MC, V. Daily 12:30–2:30pm; Mon–Sat 6:30–10:30pm. CityRail, bus, or ferry: Circular Quay.

Quay ✦✦✦ MODERN AUSTRALIAN   With its enviable location on top of the cruise-ship terminal, Quay offers perhaps the loveliest view in the city, and some feel

---

What's the Restaurant Surcharge?
Some Australian restaurants charge surcharges on public holidays and Sundays. Typically this can amount to an extra A$2 to up to A$6 (US$1.60–US$4.80) or more per person. Restaurants argue that it's difficult to get staff to work on these days, so they need to provide a cash incentive not to call in with a hangover from the previous night.

that it's Sydney's best restaurant (though I prefer Tetsuya's). In good weather, the sun sparkles off the water and through the large windows; the Opera House, city skyline, North Shore suburbs, and Harbour Bridge all look magnificent. At night, when the city lights wash over the harbor and bridge and the Opera House's sails are lit up, the view is even better. Chef Peter Gilmore's menu is a revelation of French, Italian, and Australian ideas. Signature dishes include crisped pressed duck with garlic purée and porcini mushrooms, and seared yellowfin tuna with tomato jelly, roasted eggplant, and basil oil. This restaurant has tempted all the big-name visitors to Sydney. Quay was named Restaurant of the Year in 2003 and 2004 by the *Sydney Morning Herald's Good Food Guide.*

On the upper level of the Overseas Passenger Terminal, Circular Quay West, The Rocks. ℭ 02/9251 5600. www. quay.com.au. Reservations recommended well in advance. Main courses A$38 (US$30). A$6 (US$4.80) per-person surcharge on public holidays. AE, DC, MC, V. Mon–Fri noon–2:30pm; Daily 6–10pm. CityRail, bus, or ferry: Circular Quay.

Rockpool ★★ MODERN AUSTRALIAN   The Rockpool is an institution in Sydney and is known for its inventive food. It's approached by a steep ramp and opens up into two stories of ocean-green carpet, designer chairs, and stainless steel. Along with the bar, the kitchen—with its busy chefs and copper pots and pans—is very much at the center of things. Menus change regularly, but you can expect to find anything from a dozen fresh oysters and spanner crab with lemon ravioli to fish cooked with coconut milk and Indian garam masala and served with snow peas and semolina noodles. On my last visit, the desserts were a letdown after the fabulous main courses.

109 George St., The Rocks. ℭ 02/9252 1888. Reservations required. Main courses A$38 (US$30). AE, DC, MC, V. Mon–Sat 6–11pm. CityRail, bus, or ferry: Circular Quay.

Sailors Thai ★ THAI   With a reputation as hot as the chiles in its jungle curry, Sailors Thai canteen attracts lunchtime crowds who come to eat great-tasting noodles and the likes of pork and prawn wonton soup, red curry with litchis, and Thai salads at its one stainless steel table with some 40 chairs. Four other tables overlook the cruise-ship terminal and the quay. Downstairs, the a la carte restaurant serves inventive food that's a far cry from the fare at your average Thai restaurant, such as stir-fried pineapple curry with chiles and cashew nuts, and wonderfully glutinous coconut ash pudding, made from the ash of burnt coconuts cooked with licorice root, coconut water, rice flour, and sugar.

106 George St., The Rocks. ℭ 02/9251 2466. Reservations required well in advance in restaurant, not accepted in canteen. Main courses A$26–A$32 (US$21–US$26) in restaurant, A$15–A$23 (US$12–US$18) in canteen. AE, DC, MC, V. Restaurant Mon–Fri noon–2pm; Mon–Sat 6–10pm. Canteen daily noon–9pm. CityRail, bus, or ferry: Circular Quay.

EXPENSIVE

Doyles at the Quay *Overrated* SEAFOOD   Just below Quay (see above) is Doyles, a name synonymous with seafood in Sydney. Most customers sit outside to enjoy the fabulous views across the harbor, though thick green railings do somewhat interrupt the view of the Opera House. Businesspeople and tourists come here if they don't want to lay out the cash for Quay or if they fancy a more relaxed style. The most popular dish is basically pricey fish and chips (with a choice of ocean trout, garfish, John Dory, swordfish, whiting, and salmon). You can also get a dozen oysters for A$20 (US$16) or a lobster for A$65 (US$52).

Doyles on the Beach ★★ (ℭ 02/9337 2007), at Watsons Bay, is a much better option, with lovely beach and water views. Food here includes Tasmanian "Atlantic" salmon cutlets (A$34/US$27), and lobster and prawn salad (A$63/US$50). Nearby is **Doyles Fisherman's Wharf** (ℭ 02/9337 1572), on the ferry wharf; it used to be a

Where to Dine in The Rocks

bel mondo **3**
Café Sydney **13**
Doyles at the Quay **7**
G'Day Café **5**
The Gumnut Café **9**
The Italian Village **1**
The Löwenbräu Keller **4**
Pancakes Licensed Café **2**
Phillip's Foote **10**
Quay **8**
Rockpool **12**
Sailors Thai **11**
Waterfront Restaurant **1**
Wolfie's Grill **1**
Zia Pina **6**

Church ✝
Pedestrian Walkway •••••
Stairs ▥

0 ———— 1/10 Mi
0 ———— 100 Meters

DAWES PT. PARK
Campbells Cove
Hickson Rd.
Pottinger St.
Downshire St.
Lower Fort St.
Trinity Ave.
Bradfield Hwy.
Hickson Rd.
Circular Quay West
George St.
Gloucester Walk
Cumberland St.
THE ROCKS
ARGYLE PLACE PARK
Watson Rd.
OBSERVATORY PARK
Kent St.
Argyle
Playfair St.
Kendall Plaza
St.
Cambridge St.
Suez Canal
Gloucester St.
Harrington St.
Longs Ln.
Globe St.
George St.
Cahill Expy.
Overseas Passenger Terminal
Sydney Cove
Museum of Contemporary Art
Circular Quay Ferry Terminal

takeout joint and now also has sit-down service. Doyles also runs the food service at the wonderful Watsons Bay Hotel nearby. Ferries run to Watsons Bay from Circular Quay in time for lunch at 10:30am, 11:30am, and 12:30pm Monday through Friday, and at 11:15am and 1:15pm on Saturday, Sunday, and public holidays. On weekdays the last ferry returns at 3:50pm, and on weekends at 4:15 and 6:10pm.

Overseas Passenger Terminal, Circular Quay. ℂ **02/9252 3400**. Main courses A$20–A$33 (US$16–US$26). DC, MC, V. Daily 11:30am–3pm; Mon–Sat 5:30–10:30pm; Sun 5:30–9:30pm. CityRail, bus, or ferry: Circular Quay.

The Löwenbräu Keller ⭐ BAVARIAN   Renowned for celebrating Oktoberfest every day for the past 20 years, this is the place to watch Aussies let their hair down. Come for lunch and munch a club sandwich or focaccia in the glassed-off atrium while watching the daytime action of The Rocks. For a livelier scene, head here on Friday or Saturday night, when mass beer-sculling (chugging) and yodeling are accompanied by a brass band, and costumed waitresses ferry foaming beer steins about the atmospheric, cellarlike space. Options include hearty southern German and Austrian fare and no fewer than 17 varieties of German beers in bottle or on draught (tap). There's a good wine list, and, surprisingly, vegetarians have a few choices, too.

18 Argyle St. (at Playfair St.), The Rocks. ℂ **02/9247 7785**. Reservations recommended. Main courses A$15–A$22 (US$12–US$18). AE, DC, MC, V. Daily 9:30am–2am (kitchen closes at 11pm). CityRail, bus, or ferry: Circular Quay.

Pancakes Licensed Café AMERICAN/PANCAKES   Buttermilk and chocolate pancakes; French crepes filled with seafood, chicken, and mushrooms; vegetables in basil-cream sauce; and smoked ham and cheese are the most popular dishes served in this old warehouse done up in Art Deco style. Beef ribs, pastas, and pizzas are also good sellers. Breakfast is always available.

10 Hickson Rd. (enter from Hickson Rd. or George St.), The Rocks. ⓒ **02/9247 6371.** Reservations not accepted. Main courses A$13–A$22 (US$10–US$18); breakfast A$8.95–A$12 (US$7–US$9.60). AE, DC, MC, V. Daily 24 hr. CityRail, bus, or ferry: Circular Quay.

Phillip's Foote �’ BARBECUE   Venture behind this historic pub and you'll find a courtyard strung with tables, benches, and large barbecues. Choose your own steak, lemon sole, trout, chicken, or pork, and throw it on the "barbie." It's fun, it's filling, and you might even make some new friends while your meal's sizzling.

101 George St., The Rocks. ⓒ **02/9241 1485.** Main courses A$23 (US$18). AE, DC, MC, V. Mon–Sat noon–midnight; Sun noon–10pm. CityRail, bus, or ferry: Circular Quay.

Waterfront Restaurant ⚑ MODERN AUSTRALIAN   You can't help but notice the mast, rigging, and sails that mark this restaurant in a converted stone warehouse. It's one of four in a row (though a Chinese restaurant was closing at the time of writing) right next to the water below the main spread of The Rocks. It's very popular at lunchtime, when businesspeople snap up the best seats outside in the sunshine. At night, with the colors of the city washing over the harbor, it can be magical. You get a choice of such things as steaks, mud crab, fish filets, or prawns. The seafood plate (A$53/US$42) includes lobsters, Balmain bugs (small, odd-looking crayfish), prawns, scallops, baby squid, fish pieces, and octopus. The food is simple and fresh, at prices that reflect the glorious position and views.

In the same building you'll find sister restaurants **Wolfie's Grill** (ⓒ **02/9241 5577**), which serves good chargrilled beef and seafood dishes for A$22 to A$26 (US$18–US$21), and **The Italian Village** (ⓒ **02/9247 6111**), which serves regional Italian cuisine for A$22 to A$30 (US$18–US$24). All three restaurants offer fantastic water views and indoor and outdoor dining.

In Campbell's Storehouse, 27 Circular Quay West, The Rocks. ⓒ **02/9247 3666.** Reservations recommended. Main courses A$26–A$29 (US$21–US$23). A$3.30 (US$2.60) per-person surcharge weekends and public holidays. AE, DC, MC, V. Daily noon–10:30pm. CityRail, bus, or ferry: Circular Quay.

MODERATE

The Gumnut Café 𝘒𝘪𝘥𝘴 MODERN AUSTRALIAN   A hearty lunch in a courtyard shaded from the sun by giant umbrellas—ah, heaven. With a great location in the heart of The Rocks, this 1890 sandstone cottage restaurant also has an extensive indoor seating area, so it's a perfect place to take a break from all that sightseeing. On weekends live jazz sets the mood. The breakfast specials (A$8.50/US$6.80) are popular with guests from surrounding hotels, and at lunchtime the cafe bustles with tourists and local office workers. Lunchtime blackboard specials cost A$11 (US$8.80). More regular fare includes the disappointing Ploughman's Lunch (why spoil a traditional English meal of bread, cheese, and pickles by limiting the bread and adding unappealing vegetables and salad?), the better chicken and leek pies, and good pasta and noodle dishes. Filling Turkish sandwiches cost A$7.70 to A$9 (US$6.20–US$7.20). The courtyard is heated in winter, making it quite cozy. BYO; no corkage fee.

28 Harrington St., The Rocks. ⓒ **02/9247 9591.** Main courses A$8.50–A$14 (US$6.80–US$11). AE, DC, MC, V. Sun–Wed 8am–5pm; Thurs–Sat 8am–10:30pm. CityRail, bus, or ferry: Circular Quay.

INEXPENSIVE

G'Day Café *Value* CAFE   According to the manager, about half the tourists who visit Sydney eat at this little place in the heart of The Rocks. That's not surprising, considering it offers simple, satisfying food at around half the price you'd expect to pay in such a tourist precinct. The interior is uninspiring, but in back there's a leafy courtyard. Among the offerings are focaccia sandwiches, hearty soups, salads, burgers, lasagna, chili con carne, and beef curry.

83 George St., The Rocks. 🅒 **02/9241 3644.** Main courses A$3–A$7 (US$2.40–US$5.60). AE. Sun–Thurs 5am–midnight; Fri–Sat 5am–3am. CityRail, bus or ferry: Circular Quay.

Zia Pina PIZZA/PASTA   With 10 tables crammed downstairs and another 24 upstairs, there's not much room to breathe in this cramped traditional pizzeria and spaghetti house. But squeeze in between the bare-brick walls and wallow in the clashes and clangs coming from the hardworking chefs in the kitchen. Pizzas come in two sizes; the larger feeds two people. Servings of delicious gelato go for a cool A$4 (US$3.20).

93 George St., The Rocks. 🅒 **02/9247 2255.** Reservations recommended well in advance. Main courses A$9–A$22 (US$7.20–US$18). AE, DC, MC, V. Daily noon–3pm; Sun–Mon 5–9pm; Tues–Thurs 5–10:30pm; Fri–Sat 5–11:30pm. CityRail, bus, or ferry: Circular Quay.

NEAR TOWN HALL
VERY EXPENSIVE

Level Two Revolving Restaurant *Overrated* GRILLS/ROASTS/SEAFOOD/ASIAN   For those not scared of heights, Level Two offers a self-service all-you-can-eat buffet—ideal if you don't want to pay for the a la carte goodies a floor down at its sister restaurant, **Level One.** This place, in the dome at the top of the Sydney AMP Tower, is popular with tourists, who come here for the stupendous views across Sydney and, on a clear day, as far as the Blue Mountains. The dining area takes about an hour to fully rotate, but even going this slowly, I find it a bit off-putting—especially when you're some 250m (820 ft.) up. You can heap your plate with a selection of five appetizers, then choose from 15 main courses, including steaks, roasts, pork knuckles, beef Stroganoff, seafood, and Asian dishes. There are also five desserts to choose from. The prices are as sky-high as the views.

Sydney AMP Tower, Market St. (between Pitt and Castlereagh sts.). 🅒 **02/9233 3722.** reservations@sydney-tower restaurant.com. Reservations recommended. Lunch Mon–Sat A$40 (US$32), Sun A$49 (US$39); dinner A$49 (US$32). Children 3–12 A$20 (US$13) lunch and early dinner. 10% surcharge on drinks weekends and public holidays. AE, DC, MC, V. Daily 11:30am–3:30pm and 5–11:45pm. CityRail: St. James. Monorail: City Centre.

Tetsuya's ⭐⭐⭐ MODERN JAPANESE   Chinese chef Tetsuya Wakuda is arguably Sydney's most famous chef, and his food is certainly cutting edge. This is not Japanese food as you might know it, but a fusion of Eastern and Western styles that has made him the darling of Australian gastronomy. Everybody who is anybody wants to eat in the tranquil Japanese garden that serves as the restaurant space—getting a table is difficult. To have a chance, you need to book when reservations become available, 4 weeks in advance. The restaurant is stylish and light, and the food mind-blowing. The menu changes constantly, but to give you an idea, think tofu with duck foie gras and sherry vinegar; marinated roast breast of duck with coffee; tartare of tuna with olive oil and wasabi jelly; and seared filet of veal with porcini mushrooms, sautéed green beans, and asparagus.

529 Kent St., Sydney. 🅒 **02/9267 2900.** Reservations required; accepted 4 weeks ahead. 8-course lunch A$100 (US$80); 12-course dinner A$155 (US$124). AE, DC, MC, V. Fri noon–3pm; Tues–Sat 6–10pm. CityRail: Town Hall.

EXPENSIVE

Capitan Torres SPANISH   Sydney's Spanish quarter, around Liverpool Street (a 10-min. walk from Town Hall station on your right just past Sydney's main cinema strip), offers some great restaurants, of which Capitan Torres is my favorite. Downstairs is a tapas bar with traditional stools, Spanish staff, and lots of authentic dark oak. Upstairs on two floors is a fabulous restaurant with heavy wooden tables and an atmosphere thick with sangria and regional food. The garlic prawns are incredible, and the whole snapper a memorable experience. The tapas are better at **Asturiana** (© **02/ 9264 1010**), another Spanish restaurant a couple of doors down. Make sure·you insist on eating at the bar for that authentic experience. *Warning:* Spanish serving staff in Sydney can be a bit gruff, so come armed with your sense of humor.

73 Liverpool St. (just past the cinema strip on George St., near Town Hall). © **02/9264 5574**. Fax 02/9283 2292. Main courses A$18–A$23 (US$14–US$18); tapas A$8–A$11 (US$6–US$8.80). AE, DC, MC, V. Daily noon–3pm; Mon–Sat 6–11pm, Sun 6–10pm. CityRail: Town Hall.

INEXPENSIVE

Supreme View Café ★ *Finds* CAFE   If you happen to be in the city center, this fabulous, largely undiscovered restaurant and cafe is a must for the great value and the absolutely fantastic views reaching over Hyde Park and even to the harbor. It's very large inside, has panoramic windows, and serves meals from the counter. Hearty breakfasts include bacon and eggs, omelets, and cereals. All-day dishes run to sandwiches, Caesar salad, homemade pies, pastas, and lasagna. Even if you're not hungry, it's well worth popping in for a coffee. It's particularly handy if you are staying in the lower Oxford Street area.

Level 14, Law Courts Bldg., 184 Phillip St. (Queens Sq.). © **02/9230 8224**. Main courses A$8–A$13 (US$6–US$10); coffee and cake A$5 (US$4). No credit cards. Mon–Fri 7am–5pm. CityRail or bus: Museum.

Sushi Roll ★ SUSHI   The fresh, simple food at this bargain-basement takeout is a healthy alternative to the greasy edibles with which many travelers end up satisfying their hunger. A large range of sushi and nori rolls peek out from behind the counter if you turn up at lunchtime, and you can eat at the tables opposite. The gourmet sandwiches and meals available at other establishments in the food court here make it a good stopover after a morning's shopping and sightseeing.

Sydney Central Plaza (downstairs in the food court next to Myer department store on Pitt St. Mall). © **02/9233 5561**. Sushi rolls A$1.70 (US$1.40) each. No credit cards. Mon–Wed and Sat 8am–7pm; Thurs 8am–10pm; Sun 10am–6pm. CityRail or bus: Town Hall.

DARLING HARBOUR

EXPENSIVE

Zaaffran ★★ CONTEMPORARY INDIAN   Sydney certainly hasn't seen an Indian restaurant like this one before. Forget the dark interiors and Indian murals. Here you find white surfaces, a glass-fronted wine cellar, and magnificent views of the water and the Sydney skyline from the far side of Darling Harbour. (An outdoor terrace provides the best views.) The restaurant started when two brothers from Bombay joined forces with chef Vikrant Kapoor, formerly the chef de cuisine at Raffles in Singapore. Together, they've revolutionized classic Indian cuisine. Expect such delights as chicken breast morsels in yogurt-onion sauce with mustard seeds, curry leaf, and mountain chiles; or scallops, calamari, and tiger prawns in a ragout of puréed onions, tomato, and green coconut cream infused with Kashmiri chile, green cardamom, and cloves. Even fans of traditional Indian food are impressed by the creations here. It's a world away from almost anything you'd find on the subcontinent.

Level 2, 345 Harbourside Shopping Centre, Darling Harbour. ✆ **02/9211 8900**. Reservations recommended. Main courses A$20–A$25 (US$16–US$20). AE, DC, MC, V. Daily noon–2:30pm and 6–11pm. Ferry or monorail: Darling Harbour.

MODERATE
Chinta Ria (The Temple of Love) ⭐ MALAYSIAN   Cockle Bay's star attraction for those who appreciate good food and fun ambience without paying a fortune, Chinta Ria is on the roof of the three-story development. In a round building dominated by a giant golden Buddha in the center, Chinta Ria serves fairly good "hawker-style" (read: cheap and delicious) Malaysian food. While the food is good, the atmosphere is even more memorable. The service is slow, but who cares in such an interesting space, with plenty of nooks, crannies, and society folk to look at. There are seats outside (some within range of the noise of the highway), but the best views unfold inside. Hot-and-sour soup—with tofu, mushrooms, bamboo shoots, and preserved cabbage—makes an interesting starter, and I recommend chile prawns and *hokkeien char* (soft-cooked egg noodles with extras) as main dishes.

Cockle Bay Wharf Complex. ✆ **02/9264 3211**. Main courses A$11–A$28 (US$8.80–US$22). AE, DC, MC, V. Daily noon–2:30pm and 6–11pm. Ferry or monorail: Darling Harbour.

WOOLLOOMOOLOO WHARF
EXPENSIVE
Otto Ristorante ⭐⭐ MODERN ITALIAN   Recognized as one of Sydney's premier restaurants, Otto boasts lush designer appointments and dim lighting that make it popular with local celebrities and socialites alike. You must book well ahead to taste the delectable taleggio and cauliflower panna cotta or twice-roasted duck in rich lentil and red-wine sauce. For dessert I recommend the Campari and grenadine poached pear, which is simply out of this world.

8 the Wharf Woolloomooloo, 6 Cowper Wharf Rd. ✆ **02/9368 7488**. Reservations required. Main courses A$30–A$36 (US$24–US$29). AE, DC, MC, V. Tues–Sun noon–3:30pm; Mon 6–10:30pm; Tues–Sat 6pm–midnight; Sun 6–9pm. Limited street parking. Bus: 311 from Circular Quay. Water taxi: Berth 53.

KINGS CROSS/DARLINGHURST
EXPENSIVE
Mezzaluna ⭐⭐ MODERN ITALIAN   Exquisite food, flawless service, and an almost unbeatable view across the city's western skyline have all helped Mezzaluna position itself firmly among Sydney's top restaurants. A cozy, candlelit place with white walls and polished wooden floorboards, the main dining room opens onto a huge all-weather terrace kept warm in winter by giant overhead fan heaters. The restaurant's owner, Sydney culinary icon Beppi Polesi, provides an exceptional wine list to complement a menu that changes daily. There's always a fabulous risotto on the menu. Other delights may include rack of lamb roasted with olives and oregano and served with baked baby eggplant, or roasted Muscovy duck breast served with figs and pomegranate. Whatever you choose, you can't really go wrong.

123 Victoria St., Potts Point. ✆ **02/9357 1988**. Fax 02/9357 2615. www.mezzaluna.com.au. Reservations recommended. Main courses A$20–A$45 (US$16–US$36). AE, DC, MC, V. Mon–Fri noon–3pm; Mon–Sat 6–11pm. CityRail: Kings Cross.

MODERATE
Bourbon & Beefsteak Bar INTERNATIONAL   Extensively renovated in 2003, Bourbon & Beefsteak has been a Kings Cross institution for more than 30 years. It

---

Moments **Something Fishy**

If you like fresh seafood at cheap prices, then saunter down to the **Sydney Fishmarket** ⨕, on the corner of Bank Street and Pyrmont Bridge Road, Pyrmont (ⓒ **02/9660 1611**). The major retailers here sell sashimi at the cheapest prices in Sydney. If you prefer your seafood cooked, then stay for lunch at one of the eateries scattered along the boardwalk and inside the main building. You can also call the **Fishline** (ⓒ **02/9552 2180**) for information on special events such as seafood cooking classes.

To get to the Fishmarket, take the light rail (tram) from Central Station, Chinatown, or Darling Harbour to the Fishmarket stop, or walk from Darling Harbour. (Follow the signs.)

---

still attracts everyone from visiting U.S. sailors and tourists to businesspeople and ravers. The fact that it's open 24 hours means many people never seem to leave—occasionally you'll find someone taking a nap in the bathroom. The American-themed restaurant is always busy, churning out steaks, seafood, salads, Tex-Mex dishes, ribs, and pasta, under the supervision of award-winning chef Colin Holt.

Every night there's live music in the **Piano Bar** from 5 to 9pm, followed by a mixture of jazz, Top 40, and rock 'n' roll until 5am. A disco downstairs starts at 11pm every night, finishing at 6am. The music is geared toward the 18-to-25 crowd of locals and tourists.

24 Darlinghurst Rd., Kings Cross. ⓒ 02/9358 1144. Reservations recommended Fri–Sun. Main courses A$13–A$28 (US$10–US$22). A$2 (US$1.60) surcharge weekends and public holidays. AE, DC, MC, V. Daily 24 hr. (breakfast 6–11am; happy hour 4–7pm). CityRail: Kings Cross.

Hard Rock Cafe AMERICAN   The obligatory half-Cadillac through the wall beckons you into this shrine to rock 'n' roll. Among the items on display are costumes worn by Elvis, John Lennon, and Elton John, as well as guitars from Sting and the Bee Gees, drums from Phil Collins and the Beatles, and one of Madonna's bras. The mainstays here are the burgers, with ribs, chicken, fish, salads, and T-bone steaks on the menu, too. Most meals come with french fries or baked potatoes and a salad. It's really busy on Friday and Saturday evenings from around 7:30 to 10:30pm, when you might have to line up to get a seat.

121–129 Crown St., Darlinghurst. ⓒ 02/9331 1116. Reservations not accepted. Main courses A$9.95–A$22 (US$7.80–US$18). 10% surcharge weekends and public holidays. AE, DC, MC, V. Daily noon–midnight. Shop daily 10am–midnight. Closed Dec 25. CityRail: Museum, then walk across Hyde Park, head down the hill past the Australian Museum on William St., and turn right onto Crown St. Sydney Explorer Bus: Stop no. 7.

INEXPENSIVE

Govindas VEGETARIAN   When I think of Govindas, I can't help smiling. Perhaps it's because I'm recalling the happy vibe from the Hare Krishna center it's based in, or maybe it's because the food is so cheap! Or maybe it's because they even throw in a decent movie with the meal. (The movie theater is on a different floor.) The food is simple vegetarian, served buffet style and eaten in a basic room off black-lacquer tables. Typical dishes include pastas and salads, lentil dishes, soups, and casseroles. It's BYO and doctrine-free.

112 Darlinghurst Rd., Darlinghurst. 𝒞 **02/9380 5155**. Dinner A$16 (US$13), including movie. AE, MC, V. Daily 6–11pm. CityRail: Kings Cross.

GLEBE
VERY EXPENSIVE

The Boathouse on Blackwattle Bay ★★ *Finds* SEAFOOD
Located above Sydney University's rowing club and overlooking a working area of Sydney Harbour, this converted boat shed offers water views across to the city and the Anzac Bridge. It serves terrific French-inspired seafood in an elegant, yet informal, atmosphere of white tablecloths and natural lighting. The service is good, and you can see the chefs at work in the open-plan kitchen. You can't go wrong with the signature dish, the fabulous snapper fish pie with roasted tomatoes and mashed potatoes. There are usually nine varieties of oysters on the menu. A good wine list and delicious desserts cap off a truly memorable experience. I highly recommend The Boathouse, particularly as a lunchtime treat. Catch a taxi—it's a little hard to find.

End of Ferry Rd., Glebe. 𝒞 **02/9518 9011**. www.boathouse.net.au. Main courses A$36–A$41 (US$29–US$33). AE, DC, MC, V. Tues–Sun noon–2:30pm and 6:30–10pm. Bus: 431, 433, or 434 from Millers Point, The Rocks (on George St.), or 459 from behind Town Hall.

PADDINGTON

The top end of Oxford Street, which runs from Hyde Park in central Sydney toward Bondi, has a profusion of trendy bars and cafes and a scattering of cheaper eateries among the more glamorous ones.

Bistro Lulu ☆ FRENCH/AUSTRALIAN
Gabrielle, my delightful French friend, raves about Bistro Lulu. "It's the worn floorboards and smell of coffee—it's like being back in Paris," she says. But Gabrielle won't find the same Australian influence in the food back home. Here chef Luke Mangan serves undemanding yet elegant food. To me the menu seems a little ho-hum international, the sort of stuff you might find in good hotel restaurants worldwide. Duck confit and vegetarian artichoke & fig gallette were Gabrielle's favorites, but the menu changes frequently. Such a long list of good wines by the glass is pleasing and rare to find in Sydney. The place is always busy.

257 Oxford St., Paddington 𝒞 **02/9380 6888**. Main courses A$25–A$26 (US$20–US$21). AE, DC, MC, V. Thurs–Sat noon–3pm; Mon–Sat 6–11pm; Sun 6–10pm. Bus: Oxford St.

CAFE CULTURE

Debate rages over which cafe serves the best coffee in Sydney, which has the best atmosphere, and which has the tastiest snacks. The main cafe scenes center on **Victoria Street** in Darlinghurst, **Stanley Street** in East Sydney, and **King Street** in Newtown. Other places, including Balmoral Beach on the North Shore, Bondi Beach, and Paddington, all have their own favored hangouts.

Note: Americans will be sorry to learn that, unlike in the States, free refills of coffee are rare in Australian restaurants and cafes. Sip slowly. Expect a cup of coffee to cost A$2.50 to A$3 (US$2–US$2.40); main courses run A$8 to A$15 (US$6.40–US$12)

This section includes my favorite cafes around town.

Balmoral Boatshed Kiosk ☆ *Finds*
A real discovery, this beautiful rustic cafe is right on the water beside the dinghies and sailing craft of the wooden Balmoral Boatshed (located to the far right of the central beach as you look at the water). It's a heavenly place for enjoying a breakfast muffin or a ham-and-cheese croissant while basking

in the sun. This place is popular with families on weekend mornings, so if you hate kids, find somewhere else. (The nearby Sandbar has the best takeout food and coffee.)

2 The Esplanade, Balmoral Beach. © **02/9968 4412**. Summer daily 8am–6pm; winter daily 8am–5pm. Ferry to Taronga Zoo, then bus to Balmoral Beach.

Bar Coluzzi   Although it may no longer offer the best coffee in Sydney, this café's claim to fame is that long ago it served real espresso when the rest of the city was drinking Nescafé. People-watching is a favorite hobby at this fashionably worn-around-the edges spot in the heart of Sydney's cafe district.

322 Victoria St., Darlinghurst. © **02/9380 5420**. MC, V. Daily 5am–8pm. CityRail: Kings Cross.

Bill's   This bright and airy place, strewn with flowers and magazines, serves nouveau cafe-style food. It's so popular you might have trouble finding a seat. The signature breakfast dishes—including ricotta hotcakes with honeycomb butter and banana, and sweet corn fritters with roast tomatoes and bacon—are the stuff of legend. Last time I was here I asked for fried instead of scrambled eggs and was brusquely told I had to stick to the menu—a response that is really unforgivable.

433 Liverpool St., Darlinghurst. © **02/9360 9631**. Fax 02/9360 7302. AE, MC, V. Mon–Sat 7:30am–3pm. CityRail: Kings Cross.

Café Hernandez ⭐ *Finds*   The walls of this tiny, cluttered cafe are crammed with eccentric fake masterpieces, and the aroma of 20 types of coffee roasted and ground on the premises permeates the air. It's almost a religious experience for discerning inner-city coffee addicts. The Spanish espresso is a treat.

60 Kings Cross Rd., Potts Point. © **02/9331 2343**. www.cafehernandez.com.au. MC, V, AE. Daily 24 hr. CityRail: Kings Cross.

The Old Coffee Shop ⭐   Sydney's oldest coffee shop opened in the Victorian Strand Arcade in 1891. The shop may or may not serve Sydney's best java, but the old-world feel of the place and the sugary snacks, cakes, and pastries make up for it. It's a good spot to take a break from shopping and sightseeing.

Ground floor, Strand Arcade. © **02/9231 3002**. MC, V. Mon–Fri 7:30am–5pm; Sat 8:30am–5pm; Sun 10:30am–4pm. CityRail: Town Hall.

IN NEWTOWN: GREAT ETHNIC EATS

Inner-city Newtown is three stops from Central Station on CityRail, and 10 minutes by bus from central Sydney. On Newtown's main drag, **King Street,** many inexpensive restaurants offer food from all over the world.

Le Kilimanjaro AFRICAN   With so many excellent restaurants in Newtown—they close down or improve quickly enough if they're bad—I picked Kilimanjaro because it's the most unusual. It's a tiny place, with limited seating on two floors. Basically, you enter, you choose a dish off the blackboard menu (while standing), and a waiter escorts you to your seat. On a recent visit I had couscous, African bread (similar to Indian chapati), and *saussou-gor di guan* (tuna in a rich sauce). Another favorite dish is *yassa* (chicken in a rich sauce). All meals are served on traditional wooden plates.

280 King St., Newtown. © **02/9557 4565**. Reservations not accepted. Main courses A$8.50–A$9.50 (US$7–US$7.60). No credit cards. CityRail: Newtown.

Old Saigon *Value* VIETNAMESE   I highly recommend this place for a cheap night out. Bursting with atmosphere, Old Saigon was owned until 1998 by a former American Vietnam War correspondent who loved Vietnam so much he ended up living there and marrying a local before coming to Australia. Just to make sure you knew his history, he put up his photos on the walls and scattered homemade tin helicopters around the place. His Vietnamese brother-in-law has taken over, but the food is still glorious; the spicy squid dishes are among my favorites. A popular pastime is grilling your own strips of venison, beef, wild boar, kangaroo, or crocodile over a burner at your table, then wrapping the meat in rice paper with lettuce and mint, and dipping it in chile sauce. BYO.

107 King St., Newtown. (©) 02/9519 5931. Reservations recommended. Main courses A$12–A$43 (US$9.60–US$34); most dishes around A$18 (US$14). AE, DC, MC, V. Wed–Fri noon–3pm; Tues–Sun 6–11pm. CityRail: Newtown.

BONDI BEACH
EXPENSIVE
Bondi Icebergs/Icebergs Dining Room & Bar ★★★ SEAFOOD/MEDITER-RANEAN   This revamped old swimming club complex overlooking Bondi Beach is a truly fabulous place to hang out. From its corner position on the cliffs, the Icebergs Bar looks directly across the beach and water, and its floor-to-roof windows make sure you get to experience what's probably the best view in Sydney.

The bar features lots of cushions and even hammocks, and the views stretch on across the balcony and into the restaurant. Inside this highly recommended eating place it's all frosted glass dividers (to match the colour of the ocean), and crisp white tablecloths and napkins (to resemble the surf). Not surprisingly, seafood features highly on the menu. You may well find wild scallops; risotto with coral trout and oregano; a fish stew from Livorno; and spaghetti with clams.

Here too is the Sundeck Café, which boasts a variety of light snacks and meals ranging from focaccia, salads and burgers to fresh local seafoods and pasta, all swerved out on a terrace with fantastic views.

1 Notts Ave., Bondi Beach .(©) 02/9365 9000. Reservations essential. Main courses A$36–A$44 (US$29–US$35) AE, DC, MC, V. Tues–Sat 12–3pm; 6.30–10:30pm. Sun 12–3pm, 6:30-9pm.). Bus: 380 to Bondi Beach.

MODERATE
Thai Terrific ★ THAI   Thai Terrific by name, terrific Thai by nature. This superb place around the corner from the Bondi Hotel is run with flair and efficient service. The large back room can be noisy, so if you prefer less din with your dinner, sit at one of the sidewalk tables. The servings are enormous—three people could fill up on just two main courses. The *tom yum* (hot and sour) soups and spicy prawn or seafood laksa noodle soups (made with coconut milk) are the best I've tasted in Australia and very filling. I also highly recommend the red curries.

Equally nice (and quieter) is the Bangkok-style **Nina's Ploy Thai Restaurant** ★, 132 Wairoa Ave. ((©) 02/9365 1118), at the corner of Warners Avenue at the end of the main Campbell Parade strip. Main courses here cost A$8 to A$13 (US$6.40–US$10); cash only.

147 Curlewis St., Bondi Beach. (©) 02/9365 7794. Reservations recommended Fri–Sat night. Main courses A$11–A$20 (US$8.80–US$16). AE, DC, MC, V. Daily noon–11pm. Bus: 380 to Bondi Beach.

INEXPENSIVE
Pompei's ★★ *Finds* PIZZA/PASTA/ICE CREAM   The recipe is simple: Use good ingredients and you'll get good pizzas—regulars swear they are the best in Sydney. Toppings include figs, prosciutto, fresh goat cheese, and pumpkin. Pompei's also has a selection of pizzas without cheese. And leave some room for the homemade gelati,

---

Finds Sydney's Best Fries

If you're looking for the best french fries in Sydney, head to **Manly Ocean Foods,** three shops down from the beach on the Corso. Avoid the fish and chips here (the shark is not the best, in my opinion), and spend a few dollars extra on barramundi, salmon, perch, or snapper.

---

the best in Sydney by far. The last time I had anything so good was recently in Pompeii, Italy, itself, and I swore then it was the best I'd ever eaten. Try dense raspberry, thick chocolate, tiramisu, or lemoncello. The water views and outside tables are another plus.

126–130 Roscoe St. at Gould St., Bondi Beach. ℭ **02/9365 1233.** Reservations recommended. Pizza A$13–A$17 (US$10–US$14). AE, DC, MC, V. Tues–Sun 11am–11pm.

Turenne's at Bondi ✸ _Finds_ CARIBBEAN   Being greeted by the owner, Turenne himself, armed with his delicious complimentary punch and welcoming smile, makes you feel at home the moment you enter this beautifully understated restaurant. The menu includes such creations as prawns, cashews, and crispy coconut served on fresh betel leaf; I recommend court bouillon of a whole snapper with lentils, and crème brûlée with fresh fruit. The service is attentive and professional. Caribbean music rounds off this relaxed experience perfectly.

49 Hall St. ℭ **02/9363 7609.** Reservations recommended. Main courses A$15–A$24 (US$12–US$19). AE, DC, MC, V. Daily 6–11pm. Closed Tues in winter.

MANLY

Manly is 30 minutes from Circular Quay by ferry, or 15 minutes by JetCat. The takeout shops that line **the Corso,** as well as the **pedestrian mall** that runs between the ferry terminal and the main Manly Beach, offer everything from Turkish kabobs to Japanese noodles.

INEXPENSIVE

Ashiana ✸ INDIAN   You'll be hard pressed to find a better cheap Indian restaurant in the Sydney area. Tucked away up a staircase next to the Steyne Hotel (just off the Corso and near the main beach), Ashiana has won prizes for its traditional spicy cooking. I've eaten there for years. Portions are large and filling, and the service is very friendly. The butter chicken is magnificent, while _malai kofta_ (cheese and potato dumplings in mild, creamy sauce) is the best this side of Bombay. Beer is the best drink with everything. Work off the heavy load in your stomach with a beachside stroll afterward.

Corner of Sydney Rd. and the Corso, Manly. ℭ **02/9977 3466.** Reservations recommended. Main courses A$8.50–A$18 (US$6.80–US$14). AE, MC, V. Daily 5:30–11pm. Ferry or JetCat: Manly.

Green's Eatery VEGETARIAN   Of the many eateries in Manly, this nice little vegetarian place, just off the Corso on the turnoff before the Steyne Hotel, does the best lunchtime business. The food is healthy and good quality. The menu includes 11 different vegetarian burgers, vegetable curries and noodle dishes, patties and salads, soups, smoothies, and wraps. Green's serves some exceptionally nice cakes, too, which despite being incredibly wholesome are surprisingly tasty. On a nice day you can sit outside.

1–3 Sydney Rd., Manly. ℭ **02/9977 1904.** Menu items A$1.20–A$7.40 (US95¢–US$5.95). No credit cards. Daily 8am–7pm. Ferry or JetCat: Manly.

5 What to See & Do in Sydney

The only problem with visiting Sydney is fitting in everything you want to do and see. Of course, you won't want to miss the iconic attractions: the **Opera House** and the **Harbour Bridge.** Everyone seems to be climbing over the arch of the bridge these days on the Bridge Climb Tour, so look up for the tiny dots of people waving to the ferry passengers below.

You should also check out the native wildlife in **Taronga Zoo** and the **Sydney Aquarium,** stroll around the tourist precinct of **Darling Harbour,** and get a dose of Down Under culture at the not-too-large **Australian Museum.** Also try to take time out to visit one of the nearby national parks for a taste of the Australian bush. If it's hot, take your "cozzie" (swimsuit) and towel to **Bondi Beach** or **Manly.**

I also recommend a quick trip out of town. Go bushwalking in the **Blue Mountains,** wine tasting in the **Hunter Valley,** or dolphin spotting at **Port Stephens** (see chapter 5 for details on all three).

Whatever you decide to do, you won't have enough time. Don't be surprised if you start planning your next visit before your first is even finished.

THE OPERA HOUSE & SYDNEY HARBOUR

Officially called Port Jackson, **Sydney Harbour** is the focal point of Sydney and one of the features—along with the beaches and easy access to surrounding national parks—that makes this city so special. It's entered through **the Heads,**

Value Great Deals on Sightseeing

The **Privileges Card** (☏ 02/6161 1999 in Australia; www.privilegescard.com) is a great way to save money if you plan to visit Sydney's biggest attractions. The card costs A$35 (US$28), is good for up to 1 month, and can be used in Sydney, Canberra, and Melbourne. In Sydney, all the major attractions offer some sort of discount, like two-for-one admission or reduced-price if you're traveling alone, and buy-one-get-one-free deals. When you show the card you'll also get discounts (typically 20%) on harbor cruises and at certain restaurants (sometimes a free main course if two of you are dining, or a 20% rebate off the total bill for the cardholder and three others). To get a card, fill out an application, available on the Internet and at tourist information centers in Sydney; you'll receive a booklet with details on where you can save. If you book in advance, the company can arrange to have the card sent to your hotel.

The **See Sydney & Beyond** card (☏ 02/9247 6611; www.seesydneycard. com), a cashless smart card packaging more than 40 of the city's main attractions and tours, is valuable for avoiding lines and saving money, although you'll have to plan well to get the most out of it. The card can be purchased for a 1-, 2-, 3-, or 7-day period; the 1-day pass costs A$65 (US$52) for adults and A$45 (US$36) for children. You can also purchase cards including public transportation; a 1-day card with this option costs A$80 (US$24) for adults and A$53 (US$42) for children.

Central Sydney Attractions

Art Gallery of New South Wales **10**
Australian Museum **12**
Australian National Maritime Museum **18**
Chinese Garden **20**
Customs House **4**
Elizabeth Bay House **9**
Hyde Park Barracks Museum **14**
IMAX Theatre Sydney **19**
Museum of Contemporary Art **3**
Museum of Sydney **5**
Powerhouse Museum **21**
Royal Botanic Gardens **7**
State Library of NSW **8**
St James Church **15**
St. Mary's Cathedral **13**
Sydney Aquarium **17**
Sydney Harbour Bridge **1**
Sydney Jewish Museum **11**
Sydney Observatory **2**
Sydney Opera House **6**
Sydney Tower **16**

two bush-topped outcrops (you'll see them if you take a ferry or JetCat to Manly), beyond which the harbor laps at some 240km (149 miles) of shoreline before stretching out into the Parramatta River. Visitors are often awestruck by the harbor's beauty, especially at night, when the sails of the Opera House and the girders of the Harbour Bridge are lit up, and the waters are swirling with the reflection of lights from the abutting high-rises—reds, greens, blues, yellows, and oranges. During the day, it buzzes with green-and-yellow ferries pulling in and out of busy Circular Quay, sleek tourist craft, fully rigged Tall Ships, giant container vessels making their way to and from the wharves of Darling Harbour, and hundreds of white-sailed yachts.

The greenery along the harbor's edges is a surprising feature, thanks to the **Sydney Harbour National Park,** a haven for native trees and plants, and a feeding and breeding ground for lorikeets and other nectar-eating bird life. In the center of the harbor is a series of islands; the most impressive is the tiny isle supporting **Fort Denison,** which once housed convicts and acted as part of the city's defense.

THE HARBOR ON THE CHEAP   The best way to see Sydney Harbour is from the water. Several companies operate tourist craft (see "Harbor Cruises & Organized Tours," later in this chapter), but it's easy enough just to hop on a regular passenger ferry (see "Getting Around," earlier in this chapter). The best ferry excursions are over the beachside suburb of **Manly** (come back after dusk to see the lights ablaze around The Rocks and Circular Quay); to **Watsons Bay,** where you can have lunch and wander along the cliffs; to **Darling Harbour,** for all the area's entertainment and the fact that you travel right under the Harbour Bridge; and to **Mosman Bay,** just for the ride and to see the grand houses that overlook exclusive harbor inlets.

FAST ACTION ON THE HARBOR   For a thrill ride, you can board a 420-horsepower jet boat, which zooms about on three high-speed waterway tours at speeds of up to 40 knots (about 80kmph/50 mph), with huge 240-degree turns and instant stops. **Harbour Jet** (© 1300/887 373 in Australia, or 02/9212 3555; www.harbourjet.com) offers a 35-minute Jet Blast Adventure costing A$60 (US$48) for adults, A$40 (US$32) for kids under 15, and A$180 (US$144) for a family. A 50-minute Sydney Harbour Adventure costs A$75 (US$60) for adults, A$50 (US$40) for kids, and A$225 (US$180) for a family; an 80-minute Middle Harbour Adventure cruise costs A$95 (US$76) for adults, A$65 (US$52) for kids, and A$288 (US$230) for a family. Rides are fast and furious and pump with rock music. The boat leaves from the Convention Jetty, between the Convention Centre and the Harbourside Shopping complex on the far side of Darling Harbour. These trips don't operate every day, so check beforehand.

Another option is **Oz Jet Boat** (© 02/9808 3700; www.ozjetboating.com), which departs every hour from the Eastern Pontoon at Circular Quay (on the walkway to the Opera House). These large red boats are a bit more powerful than the blue Harbour Jet ones, but you might not notice the difference. This company offers a 30-minute ride for A$50 (US$40) for adults, A$35 (US$28) for kids, and A$150 (US$120) for a family; and a 1-hour trip out to Sydney Heads on weekends for A$90 (US$72) for adults, A$60 (US$48) for children, and A$270 (US$216) for a family.

Sydney Harbour Bridge ✸✸✸ (Moments)   One thing few tourists do, although it only takes an hour or so, is to walk across the Harbour Bridge. The bridge, completed in 1932, is 1,150m (3,772 ft.) long and spans 503m (1,650 ft.) from the south shore to the north. It accommodates pedestrian walkways, two railway lines,

Moments A Walk on the Wild Side: Climbing the Harbor Bridge

At one time, only bridge workers had the opportunity to view Sydney from the top of the main bridge arch. But since October 1998, Sydneysiders and tourists have been able to experience the spectacular view and the exhilarating achievement of climbing to the top of one of Australia's icons. The experience takes 3 hours from check-in at the **BridgeClimb** ★★ base, 5 Cumberland St., The Rocks (✆ **02/9240 1100** or 02/8274 7777; fax 02/9240 1122; www.bridge climb.com), to completion. The office is open daily from 8am to 6pm, and climbers leave in small groups every 10 minutes or so. Climbers wear "Bridge Suits" and are harnessed to a line. Participants are also breath-tested for alcohol and are banned from carrying anything, including cameras. Climbs cost A$160 (US$128) for adults and A$100 (US$80) for children 12 to 16 on weekdays during the day and for night climbs Monday to Thursday; and A$185 (US$148) for adults and A$125 (US$100) for children for climbs on Friday, Saturday, and Sunday. Daily Twilight climbs cost A$225 (US$180) for adults and A$175 (US$140) for kids. Children under 12 are not allowed to climb.

and an eight-lane road. The 30-minute stroll from one end to the other offers excellent harbor views. From the other side, you can take a CityRail train from Milsons Point back to the city (to Wynyard—change there for Circular Quay, Town Hall, or Central).

As you walk across, stop off at the **Pylon Lookout** (✆ **02/9247 3408**), at the southeastern pylon. Admission is A$8.50 (US$6.80) for adults, A$3 (US$2.40) for children over 7. From the top of this bridge support, 89m (292 ft.) above the water, you get panoramic views of Sydney Harbour, the ferry terminals of Circular Quay, and beyond. An interesting museum charts the building of the bridge. The Pylon Lookout is open daily from 10am to 5pm (closed Dec 25). Reach the pylon by walking to the far end of George Street in The Rocks toward the Harbour Bridge. Just past The Mercantile pub, you'll see some stone steps that take you onto Cumberland Street. From there, it's a 2-minute walk to the steps underneath the bridge on your right. Climb four flights of stairs to reach the bridge's Western Footway, and then walk along to the first pylon. *Note:* Climbing up inside the pylon involves 200 steps.

Sydney Opera House ★★★   Only a handful of buildings around the world are as architecturally and culturally significant as the Sydney Opera House. But what sets it apart from, say, the Taj Mahal and the Great Pyramids of Egypt is that this white-sailed construction caught midbillow over the waters of Sydney Cove is a working building. Most visitors are surprised to learn it's not just an opera house, but a full-scale performing-arts complex with five major performance spaces. The biggest and grandest is the 2,690-seat **Concert Hall,** which has the best acoustics of any building of its type in the world. Come here to experience opera, chamber music, symphonies, dance, choral performances, and even rock 'n' roll. The **Opera Theatre** is smaller, seating 1,547, and books operas, ballets, and dance. The **Drama Theatre,** seating 544, and the **Playhouse,** seating 398, specialize in plays and smaller-scale performances. The **Boardwalk,** seating 300, is used for dance and experimental music.

The history of the building is as intriguing as the design. The New South Wales Government raised the construction money with a lottery. Danish Architect Jørn Utzon won an international competition to design it. From the start, the project was controversial, with many Sydneysiders believing it was a monstrosity. Following a disagreement, Utzon returned home without ever seeing his finished project. The interior fell victim to a compromise design, which, among other things, left too little space to perform full-scale operas. And the cost? Initially the project was budgeted at a cool A$7 million (US$5.6 million), but by the time it was finished in 1973 it had cost a staggering A$102 million (US$82 million), most raised through a series of lotteries. Since then, continual refurbishment and the major task of replacing the asbestos-laden grouting between the hundreds of thousands of white tiles that make up its shell has cost many millions more.

But now that long-overdue reconstruction is in progress, aimed at putting into practice what Jørn Utzon has long visualized. The tatty old reception hall has already been transformed into an impressive welcome room. Its centerpiece is Utzon's first foray into visual art: a glorious floor-to-ceiling tapestry inspired by Bach's Hamburg Symphonies and Raphael's painting, *Procession to Calvary*.

Preliminary work has also started on the Western Loggia, or colonnade, which will open up the foyers of The Playhouse, Drama Theatre, and The Studio to harbor views and create spaces for cafes and functions. Eventually, all three western foyers will be combined into one, and their box offices and bars will be centralized, too. Investigations are also going ahead into refurbishing the Opera Theatre and improving the acoustics in the Concert Hall.

Tours & Tickets: Guided tours of the Opera House last about an hour and are conducted daily from 9am to 5pm, except Good Friday and December 25. Though guides try to take groups into the main theaters and around the foyers, if you don't get to see everything you want, it's because the Opera House is not a museum but a workplace. There's almost always some performance, practice, or setting up to be done. Reservations are essential. Tour sizes are limited, so be prepared to wait. Tours include approximately 200 stairs. (Tours for people with disabilities can be arranged.) Specialized tours, focusing on the building's architecture and engineering, for example, can also be arranged.

The Tourism Services Department at the Sydney Opera House can book **combination packages,** including dinner and a show; a tour, dinner, and a show; or a champagne interval performance. Prices vary depending on shows and dining venues. Visitors from overseas can buy tickets by credit card and pick them up at the box office on arrival, or contact a local tour company specializing in Australia. Advance ticket purchases are a good idea, because performances are very popular. The views from the back rows are hardly worth the effort and expense if you turn up on the day of performance. Tickets for performances vary from as little as A$12 (US$9.60) for children's shows to A$180 (US$144) for good seats at the opera. Plays average A$40 to A$60 (US$32–US$48).

Free performances take place outside on the Opera House boardwalks on Sunday afternoons and during festival times. The artists range from musicians and performance artists to school groups.

Bennelong Point. ℂ **02/9250 7250** for guided tours and information, or 02/9250 7777 box office. Fax 02/9251 3943. www.sydneyoperahouse.com. Box office Mon–Sat 9am–8:30pm; Sun 2 hr. before performance. Tours A$23 (US$18). Tours daily 9am–5pm (every 30 min.), subject to theater availability. Backstage Tour A$140/US$112 (starts daily at 7am, for 2 hr., with breakfast). CityRail, bus, or ferry: Circular Quay. Sydney Explorer bus. Parking: Daytime A$7 (US$5.60) per hour; evening A$23 (US$18) flat rate.

Luna Park *(Kids)*   The huge smiling clown face and the fairground attractions, which are easily visible from Circular Quay, make up one of Australia's iconic attractions. Opened in 1935 and closed for many years since, it reopened in 2004. It's small but fun, with traditional theme-park amusements rather than high-tech rides. It has a carousel, dodge-'em cars, a Ferris wheel, and the like. Several rides are suitable for small children, too. You buy tickets—or "lunas," as they're called—at booths inside the park.

1 Olympic Dr., Milsons Point (across the harbor from the Sydney Opera House). © 02/9922 6644. www.luna parksydney.com. Free admission. Rides A$3–A$5 (US$2.40–US$4); family day pass with unlimited rides A$95 (US$76). Sun–Thurs 11am–7:30pm; Fri–Sat 10am–midnight. Ferry or CityRail: Milsons Point.

ATTRACTIONS AT DARLING HARBOUR

Many tourists head to Darling Harbour for the Harbourside Festival Marketplace, a huge structure beside the Pyrmont pedestrian and monorail bridge that's crammed full of cheap eateries and a few interesting shops. However, Sydney's tourist precinct has a lot more to offer.

Australian National Maritime Museum ★ *(Kids)*   Modern Australia owes almost everything to the sea, so it's not surprising that there's a museum dedicated to ships, from Aboriginal vessels to submarines. You'll find ships' logs, things to pull and tug at, and the fastest boat in the world, the *Spirit of Australia.* Docked in the harbor are several ships and launches, including an Australian Navy destroyer, the *Vampire,* and an Oberon Class submarine. You can clamber over many of them. Allow 2 hours.

Darling Harbour. © 02/9298 3777. www.anmm.gov.au. Free admission to main exhibition. Admission to all ships A$18 (US$14) adults, A$9 (US$7.20) children 5–15, A$35 (US$28) families. Navy Package (includes museum, *Vampire,* and submarine *Onslow*) A$10 (US$8) adults, A$6 (US$4.80) children, A$25 (US$20) families. Admission to single vessels available. Daily 9:30am–5pm (until 6:30pm in Jan). Ferry: Darling Harbour. Monorail: Harbourside. Sydney Explorer bus.

Chinese Garden   The largest Chinese garden of its type outside China offers a pleasant escape from the city concrete. Expert gardeners from China's Guangdong Province designed the garden according to principles of garden design dating to the 5th century. Allow 30 minutes.

Darling Harbour (adjacent to the Entertainment Centre). © 02/9281 6863. Admission A$6 (US$4.80) adults, A$3 (US$2.40) children, A$15 (US$12) families. Daily 9:30am–dusk. Ferry: Darling Harbour. Monorail: Convention. Sydney Explorer bus.

IMAX Theatre Sydney   Four different IMAX films are usually showing on the gigantic eight-story-high screen. Each flick lasts about 50 minutes or so. If you've ever been to an IMAX theater before, you know what to expect. As you watch, your mind is tricked into feeling that it's right in the heart of the action. Also shown are 3-D movies, which cost A$1 (US80¢) extra.

Southern Promenade, Darling Harbour. © 02/9281 3300. Admission A$16 (US$13) adults, A$11 (US$8.80) children 3–15, A$45 (US$36) families. Sun–Thurs 10am–10pm; Fri–Sat 10am–11:30pm. Ferry: Darling Harbour. Monorail: Convention. Sydney Explorer bus.

Powerhouse Museum *(Kids)*   Sydney's most interactive museum is also one of the largest in the Southern Hemisphere. In the postmodern industrial interior you'll find all sorts of displays and gadgets relating to the sciences, transportation, human achievement, decorative art, and social history. The many hands-on exhibits make this fascinating museum worthy of a couple of hours of your time.

500 Harris St., Ultimo (near Darling Harbour). ℭ **02/9217 0111.** Admission A$10 (US$8) adults, A$5 (US$4) students and children 5–15, A$24 (US$19) families. Free admission 1st Sat of every month. Daily 10am–5pm. Ferry: Darling Harbour. Monorail: Harbourside. Sydney Explorer bus.

Sydney Aquarium ★★ *Kids*   This is one of the world's best aquariums and should be near the top of any Sydney itinerary. The main attractions are the underwater walkways through two enormous tanks—one full of giant rays and gray nurse sharks and the other where you can see the seals in action (nearby building work throughout 2005 and possibly into 2006 may mean the seals won't be on display). Other excellent exhibits include a giant Plexiglas room suspended inside a pool patrolled by rescued seals, and a magnificent section on the Great Barrier Reef, where thousands of colorful fish school around coral outcrops. Also on display are two saltwater crocodiles and some fairy penguins. Try to visit during the week, when it's less crowded. Allow around 2 hours.

Aquarium Pier, Darling Harbour. ℭ **02/9262 2300.** Admission A$24 (US$19) adults, A$12 (US$9.60) children 3–15, A$56 (US$45) families. Daily 9am–10pm. Seal Sanctuary closes at 7pm in summer. CityRail: Town Hall. Ferry: Darling Harbour. Sydney Explorer bus.

OTHER TOP ATTRACTIONS: A SPECTACULAR VIEW, SYDNEY'S CONVICT HISTORY & MORE

Hyde Park Barracks Museum ★   These Georgian-style barracks were designed in 1819 by the convict and architect Francis Greenway. They were built by convicts and inhabited by fellow prisoners. These days they house relics from those early days in interesting, modern displays, including log books, early settlement artifacts, and a room full of ships' hammocks in which visitors can lie and listen to fragments of prisoner conversation. If you are interested in Sydney's early beginnings, I highly recommend a visit. The displays are far more straightforward that those at the Museum of Sydney (see listing later in this chapter). The courtyard cafe is excellent. Allow 1 hour or more.

Queens Sq., Macquarie St. ℭ **02/9223 8922.** Admission A$7 (US$5.60) adults, A$3 (US$2.40) children, A$17 (US$14) families. Daily 9:30am–5pm. CityRail: St. James or Martin Place. Sydney Explorer bus.

Museum of Contemporary Art (MCA)   This imposing sandstone museum set back from the water on The Rocks side of Circular Quay offers wacky, entertaining, inspiring, and befuddling displays of what's new (and dated) in modern art. It houses the J. W. Power Collection of more than 4,000 pieces, including works by Andy Warhol, Christo, Marcel Duchamp, and Robert Rauschenberg, as well as temporary exhibits. It's relatively new and still building up its collection, so this museum isn't as impressive as major modern art museums in, say, London or New York. Still, it's worth at least 1 hour.

140 George St., Circular Quay W. ℭ **02/9252 4033.** www.mca.com.au. Free general admission. Daily 10am–6pm (5pm in winter). CityRail, bus, or ferry: Circular Quay. Sydney Explorer bus.

Sydney AMP Tower ★ *Kids*   The tallest building in the Southern Hemisphere is not hard to miss—it resembles a giant steel pole skewering a golden marshmallow. Standing more than 300m (984 ft.) tall, the tower offers stupendous 360-degree views across Sydney and as far as the Blue Mountains. Fortunately, an elevator takes you to the indoor viewing platform on the top floor; if you were to walk up the fire escape, you'd have to climb 1,504 steps. The general ticket price includes admission to Sky-tour, a fascinating experience in several different surroundings. The settings include a storytelling room (you sit in a room lit by hurricane lamps and listen to some stories); a room with a small stage flickering with moving models of Australian landscapes and holograms; and a fake Aboriginal cave with appropriate sounds and melodies. The final stop is the Great Australian Exhibition Ride, where visitors are strapped into moving chairs in front of a 180-degree screen. On this simulator ride, you white-water raft in Queensland, climb Uluru (Ayers Rock), and have a close encounter with a salt-water crocodile. It's great fun, and kids love it. Don't be too concerned if you feel the building tremble slightly, especially in a stiff breeze—I'm told it's perfectly natural. Below the tower are three floors of stores and restaurants. Allow 1 hour.

Pitt and Market sts. ⒸⒸ 02/9223 0933. Admission A$22 (US$18) adults, A$13 (US$11) children 5–16, A$46 (US$37) families (up to 3 kids). Daily 9am–10:30pm. CityRail: St. James or Town Hall. Sydney Explorer bus.

Sydney Olympic Park ⭐   The site of the 2000 Olympic Games is still very much a tourist attraction as well as a major sporting venue. Most of the Olympic venues are at this dedicated Olympic precinct at Homebush Bay, which also has plenty of bars and restaurants. Start at the **Homebush Bay Information Centre,** which has displays, walking maps, and tour tips. It's open daily from 9am to 5pm.

Nearby is **Telstra Stadium** (ⒸⒸ 02/8765 2300; www.telstrastadium.com.au), the site of the opening and closing ceremonies, the track and field events, and some Olympic soccer games. It was called Stadium Australia back then. Today it schedules Australian Rules games and rugby league, rugby union, and soccer matches. A 30-minute tour of the stadium costs A$15 (US$12) for adults, A$7.50 (US$6) for children, and A$42 (US$34) for a family. A 1-hour behind-the-scenes tour is A$26 (US$14) for adults, A$13 (US$10) for children, and A$60 (US$48) for a family. Tours leave hourly from 10:30am to 3:30pm.

Also at the Olympic Park is the **Sydney International Aquatic Centre** (ⒸⒸ 02/ 9752 3666; www.sydneyaquaticcentre.com.au), which comprises the Olympic pool, diving pool, and training facilities. A 50-minute tour of the aquatic center, including a swim and a spa afterward, costs A$17 (US$14) for adults, A$8.50 (US$6.80) for kids 4 to 15, and A$47 (US$37) for families. Call ahead to make an appointment. Just a swim costs A$5.80 (US$4.60) adults, A$4.60 (US$3.70) kids, A$19 (US$15) families.

There are wonderful views of the Sydney Olympic Park and the city from Level 17 of the **Novotel hotel** (ⒸⒸ 02/8762 1111), located in the park. Entry to the observation area costs A$4 (US$3.20) for adults and A$2 (US$1.60) for children over 7. You can purchase a SuperPass covering entry to the Observation Center at the Novotel and a guided tour of Stadium Australia and the Sydney Aquatic Center (including swimming). Tickets are available from participating venues or the visitor center for A$40 (US$32) for adults, A$20 (US$16) for children, and A$79 (US$63) for a family.

One of the best ways to get to the Olympic Site is on the Sydney Explorer bus.

Sydney Olympic Site, Olympic Park, Homebush Bay. ⒸⒸ 02/9714 7888 Homebush Bay Information Centre. www.sydneyolympicpark.nsw.gov.au. CityRail: Olympic Park. Sydney Explorer bus.

'ROOS, KOALAS & OTHER AUSSIE WILDLIFE

The Sydney Aquarium is discussed on p. 160.

Australian Reptile Park   What started as a one-man operation supplying snake antivenin in the early 1950s has become a nature park teeming with the slippery-looking creatures. But it's not all snakes and lizards; you'll also find saltwater crocodiles and American alligators, as well as plenty of somewhat cuddlier creatures, such as koalas, platypuses, wallabies, dingoes, and flying foxes. The park is on beautiful bushland crossed by nature trails. A devastating fire burned down the entire park in mid-2000, killing all of the animals. The staff has worked valiantly to start up a new collection. The park is a short detour off the route heading up to the Hunter Valley, Barrington Tops, and Port Stephens. Somersby is near Gosford, 84km (52 miles) north of Sydney.

Pacific Hwy., Somersby. ✆ 02/4340 1022. www.reptilepark.com.au. Admission A$18 (US$14) adults, A$12 (US$9.20) children, A$46 (US$37) families. Daily 9am–5pm. Closed Dec 25. CityRail: Gosford (trains leave Central Station every 30 min.). By car: Take the Pacific Hwy. and the Sydney-Newcastle Fwy. (F3); the trip takes about 1 hr.

Featherdale Wildlife Park ★★ *Kids*   If you have time to visit only one wildlife park in Sydney, make it this one. The selection of Australian animals is excellent, and, most important, the animals are very well cared for. You could easily spend a couple of hours here despite the park's compact size. You'll have the chance to hand-feed friendly kangaroos and wallabies, and get a photo taken next to a koala. (There are many here, both the New South Wales variety and the larger Victorian type.) The park's newest addition is the **Reptilian Pavilion.** It houses 30 different native species of reptiles in 26 realistic exhibits.

217 Kildare Rd., Doonside. ✆ 02/9622 1644. Fax 02/9671-4140. www.featherdale.com.au. Admission A$18 (US$14) adults, A$8.50 (US$6.80) children 3–15, A$45 (US$36) families. Daily 9am–5pm. CityRail: Blacktown, then bus 725 (ask driver to tell you when to get off). By car: Take the M4 motorway to Reservoir Rd., turn off, travel 4km (2½ miles), then turn left at Kildare Rd.

Koala Park   This is probably the only place in the country (unless you travel all the way to Kangaroo Island in South Australia) where you'll be able to spot this many koalas in one place. In all, around 55 koalas roam within the park's leafy boundaries. Free koala cuddling sessions take place at 10:20 and 11:45am, and 2 and 3pm daily. There are wombats, dingoes, kangaroos, wallabies, emus, and native birds here, too. You can hire a private guide to take you around for A$70 (US$56) for a 2-hour session, or hitch onto one of the free "hostess" guides who wander around the park like Pied Pipers.

84 Castle Hill Rd., West Pennant Hills. ✆ 02/9484 3141 or 02/9875 2777. www.koalapark.com. Admission A$18 (US$14) adults, A$8 (US$6.40) children, A$46 (US$37) families. Daily 9am–5pm. Closed Dec 25. CityRail: Pennant Hills station via North Strathfield (45 min.), then bus 651, 652, 653, 654, or 655 to park.

Oceanworld Manly *Kids*   Though not as impressive as the Sydney Aquarium, Oceanworld can be combined with a visit to Manly Beach (see "North of Sydney Harbour," below) for a nice day's outing. There's a decent display of Barrier Reef fish, as well as giant sharks. Also here are the five most venomous snakes in the world. Shark feeding is at 11am on Monday, Wednesday, and Friday. There is also a **"dive with the sharks"** ★★★ program, where you can dive in the tanks with giant gray nurse sharks. It costs A$165 (US$132) for qualified divers, A$195 (US$156) for qualified divers who have logged less than 15 dives or haven't dived in the last 6 months, or A$220 (US$176) for nonqualified divers (includes an introduction to scuba diving course). You must download an application form from the website.

West Esplanade, Manly. ✆ 02/8251 7877. www.oceanworld.com.au. Admission A$17 (US$14) adults, A$8.95 (US$7) children, A$42 (US$70) families. Daily 10am–5:30pm. Ferry or JetCat: Manly.

Taronga Zoo ★ *Kids*   Taronga has the best view of any zoo in the world. Set on a hill, it looks out over Sydney Harbour, the Opera House, and the Harbour Bridge. It's easiest on the legs to explore the zoo from the top down. The main attractions are the fabulous chimpanzee exhibit, the gorilla enclosure, and the Nocturnal Houses, where you can see some of Australia's many nighttime marsupials, including the platypus and the cuter-than-cute bilby (the official Australian Easter bunny), out and about. There's an interesting reptile display, a couple of impressive Komodo dragons, a scattering of indigenous beasties—including a few koalas, echidnas, kangaroos, dingoes, and wombats—and lots more. The kangaroo and wallaby exhibit is unimaginative; you'd be better off going to Featherdale Wildlife Park (see above). Animals are fed at various times during the day. The zoo can get crowded on weekends, so I strongly advise visiting during the week or early in the morning on weekends. Annoying major renovation work will continue into 2006. Interestingly, the three sun bears near the lower ferry entrance and exit were rescued by an Australian businessman, John Stephens, from a restaurant in Cambodia, where they were to have their paws cut off and served in soup. There's a lot of redevelopment going on at the zoo, so expect some annoying renovations when you visit. Allow around 3 hours.

Bradley's Head Rd., Mosman. © 02/9969 2777. Admission A$27 (US$21) adults, A$14 (US$11) children 4–15, A$70 (US$56) family. Admission includes a trip on the Aerial Safari cable car. Daily 9am–5pm (until 9pm Jan). Ferry: Taronga Zoo. Lower zoo entrance is at ferry terminal.

HITTING THE BEACH

One of the big bonuses of visiting Sydney in the summer (Dec–Feb) is that you get to experience the beaches in their full glory.

Most major city beaches, such as Manly and Bondi, have lifeguards on patrol, especially during the summer. They check the water conditions and are on the lookout for **"rips"**—strong currents that can pull a swimmer far out to sea. Safe places to swim are marked by red and yellow flags. You must always swim between these flags. If you are using a foam or plastic body board or "boogie board," it's advisable to use it between the flags. Fiberglass surfboards must be used outside the flags. (Expect a warning from the beach loudspeakers and an A$100/US$80 fine if you fail to take notice.)

WHAT ABOUT SHARKS & OTHER NASTIES?   One of the first things visitors wonder when they hit the water in Australia is: *Are there sharks?* The answer is yes, but fortunately they are rarely spotted inshore—you are far more likely to spy a migrating whale. In reality, sharks have more reason to be scared of us than we of them; most of them end up as the fish in your average packet of fish and chips. (Shark filets are often sold as "flake.") Though some beaches—such as the small beach next to the Manly ferry wharf and a section of Balmoral Beach in Mosman—have permanent shark nets, most rely on portable nets that are moved from beach to beach.

Another common problem off Sydney's beaches are **"blue bottles"**—small blue jellyfish, often called "stingers" in Australia and "Portuguese-men-o'-war" elsewhere. You'll often find these creatures (which are not the same as the stingers around the Great Barrier Reef) washed up along the beach; they become a hazard for swimmers when there's a strong breeze coming off the ocean and they're blown in to shore (watch out for warning signs erected on the shoreline). Minute individual stinging cells often break off the main body of the creature, and they can cause minor itching or stinging. Or you might be hit by the full force of a blue bottle, which will often stick to your skin and wrap its tentacles around you. Blue bottles deliver a hefty punch from their many stinging cells, causing a severe burning sensation almost immediately. Wearing a T-shirt in the water reduces the risk somewhat (though a pair of waterlogged jeans isn't a good idea). If you are stung, rinse the area liberally with seawater or fresh water to remove any tentacles stuck in the skin. For intense pain, apply heat or cold, whichever feels better. If you experience breathing difficulties or disorientation, seek medical attention immediately.

SOUTH OF SYDNEY HARBOUR

Sydney's most famous beach is **Bondi** ★★. In many ways it's a raffish version of a California beach, with plenty of tanned skin and in-line skaters. Though the beach is nice, it's cut off from the cafe and restaurant strip that caters to beachgoers by a road that pedestrians have to funnel across in order to reach the sand. On summer weekend evenings it's popular with souped-up cars and groups of disaffected youths. To reach Bondi Beach, take the CityRail train to Bondi Junction, then transfer to bus no. 380 (a 15-min. bus journey). You can also catch bus no. 380 directly from Circular Quay (but it can take an hour or so at peak times).

If you follow the water along to your right at Bondi, you'll come across a scenic cliff-top trail that takes you to **Bronte Beach** (a 20-min. walk), via gorgeous little **Tamarama,** nicknamed "Glamourama" for its trendy sun-worshippers. This boutique beach is known for its dangerous rips. Bronte has better swimming than Bondi. To go straight to Bronte, catch bus no. 378 from Circular Quay, or pick up the bus at the Bondi Junction CityRail station.

Clovelly Beach, farther along the coast, is blessed with a large rock pool carved into a rock platform and sheltered from the force of the Tasman Sea. This beach is accessible for visitors in wheelchairs on a series of ramps. To reach Clovelly, take bus no. 339 from Circular Quay.

The cliff walk from Bondi will eventually bring you to **Coogee,** which has a pleasant strip of sand with a couple of hostels and hotels nearby. To reach Coogee, take bus no. 373 or 374 from Circular Quay (on Pitt, George, and Castlereagh sts., and Taylor Sq. on Oxford St.) or bus no. 314 or 315 from Bondi Junction.

NORTH OF SYDNEY HARBOUR

On the North Shore you'll find **Manly** ★★, a long curve of golden sand edged with Norfolk Island pines. Follow the crowds shuffling through the pedestrian Corso to the main ocean beach. (Don't be fooled by the two small beaches on either side of the ferry terminal, as some people have—including the novelist Arthur Conan Doyle, who traveled to Manly by ferry and, presuming the small beach near the ferry station was the best the suburb had to offer, did not bother to disembark.)

Fun Fact Grin & Bare It

If getting an all-over tan is your scene, you have a couple of options in Sydney. The nudist beach at **Lady Jane Bay** is a short walk from Camp Cove Beach. You get there from Cliff Street in Watsons Bay, reached by walking along the strip of sand—to the right as you look at the sea—at the back of the Watsons Bay Hotel. Or you can try **Cobblers Beach,** off the short, but steep, bush track that leads from the far side of the playing field oval next to the main HMAS *Penguin* naval base at the end of Bradley's Head Road in Mosman. (Follow the procession of men in shorts.) Be prepared for a largely male-oriented scene—as well as the odd boatload of beer-swigging peeping toms.

You'll find one of Sydney's nicest walks here, too. Looking at the ocean, head to your right along the beachfront and follow the coastal path to small and sheltered **Shelly Beach** ⋆, a nice area for snorkeling and swimming. (A small takeout outlet that sells drinks and snacks sits next to the good, but pricey, Le Kiosk beachfront restaurant.) Follow the bitumen path up the hill to the car park. Here, a track cuts up into the bush and leads toward a firewall, which marks the entrance to the Sydney Harbour National Park. Around here you'll have spectacular ocean views across to Manly and the northern beaches (the headland farther in the distance is Palm Beach). The best way to reach Manly is on a ferry or JetCat from Circular Quay.

Farther north along the coast are a string of ocean beaches. (See the "Greater Sydney" map earlier in this chapter for a map of this area.) They include the surf spots of **Curl Curl, Dee Why, Narrabeen, Mona Vale, Newport, Avalon,** and finally **Palm Beach** ⋆, a long and beautiful strip of sand separated from the calmer waters of **Pittwater** by sand dunes and a golf course. Here you'll find the Barrenjoey Lighthouse, which offers fine views along the coast. Take bus no. 136 or 139 from Manly to Curl Curl. Bus no. 190 runs from Wynyard to Newport and then via the other northern beaches as far as Palm Beach.

The best harbor beach is at **Balmoral** ⋆, a wealthy North Shore hangout with some good cafes (the Sandbar is the best for food) and two good, upmarket beach-view restaurants—the **Bathers Pavillion** (𝄽 02/9969 5050) and **The Watermark** (𝄽 02/ 9968 3433). The beach itself is split into three parts. As you look toward the sea, the middle section is the most popular with sunbathers, and the wide expanse to your left and the sweep of surreally beautiful sand to your right have a mere scattering. There's a caged pool area for swimming. Reach Balmoral on the ferry to Taronga Zoo and then a 5-minute ride on a connecting bus from the ferry wharf, or catch the bus from the stop outside the zoo's top entrance.

MUSEUMS, GALLERIES, HISTORIC HOUSES & MORE

Art Gallery of New South Wales ⋆   The numerous galleries here present some of the best of Australian art and many fine examples by international artists, including good displays of Aboriginal and Asian art. You enter from The Domain parklands (across the road from the Royal Botanic Gardens) on the third floor of the museum. On the fourth floor you will find an expensive restaurant and a gallery that often mounts free photography displays. On the second floor is a wonderful cafe overlooking the wharves and warships of Woolloomooloo. Every January and February there is a fabulous display of the best work created by school students throughout the state. Allow at least 1 hour.

Art Gallery Rd., The Domain. 𝄽 02/9225 1744. www.artgallery.nsw.gov.au. Free admission to most galleries. Special exhibitions vary; usually around A$12 (US$9.60) adults, A$7 (US$5.60) children. Thurs–Tues 10am–5pm; Wed 10am–9pm. Tours of general exhibits Sat–Sun 11am, 1pm, and 2pm; Mon 1pm and 2pm; Tues–Fri 11am, noon, 1pm, and 2pm. Tours of Aboriginal galleries Tues–Sun 11am. Free Aboriginal performance Tues–Sat noon. CityRail: St. James. Sydney Explorer bus.

Australian Museum   Though nowhere near as impressive as, say, the Natural History Museum in London, Sydney's premier natural history museum is still worth a look. Displays are presented thematically, the best being the Aboriginal section with its traditional clothing, weapons, and everyday implements. There are some sorry examples of stuffed Australian wildlife, too. Temporary exhibits run from time to time. Allow 1 to 2 hours.

6 College St. ✆ **02/9320 6000.** www.austmus.gov.au. Admission A$8 (US$6.40) adults, A$3 (US$2.40) children, A$19 (US$15) families. Special exhibits extra. Daily 9:30am–5pm. Closed Dec 25. CityRail: Museum, St. James, or Town Hall. Sydney Explorer bus.

Customs House   This museum, in the sandstone building with the clock and flags across the large square opposite the Circular Quay CityRail station and the ferry wharves, opened in December 1998. It's worth a look inside if you're interested in architecture. You might be hooked by the series of modern-art objects displayed on the ground floor, and the traveling exhibits on the third floor—though often you won't be. Outside in the square is a popular cafe selling reasonably priced coffee, cakes, sandwiches, and the like. Allow 15 minutes.

Alfred St., Circular Quay. ✆ **02/9320 6429.** Free general admission; extra charge for some exhibits. Daily 9:30am–5pm. CityRail, bus, or ferry: Circular Quay.

Done Sydney Observatory ⭐   The city's only major museum of astronomy offers visitors a chance to see the southern skies through modern and historic telescopes. The best time to visit is during the night on a guided tour, when you can take a close-up look at some of the planets. However the introduction of a new **Space Theatre 3D ride,** which takes you zooming through the stars during the day is worth doing, too. During the day you can still see the fascinating telescopes. The Space Theatre starts at 2:30pm and 3:30pm Mondays to Fridays, and 11am, noon, 2pm, and 3:30pm on weekends and daily during school holidays. Night tours go from 6:15 to 8pm and 8:15 to 10pm April to September; 8:15 to 10pm October and November; 8:30 to 10:15pm December and January; and 8:15 to 10pm February and March. Schedules are subject to change, so be sure to check the times when you book your tour. The planetarium and hands-on exhibits are also interesting.

Observatory Hill, Watson Rd., Millers Point. ✆ **02/9217 0485.** Daytime A$6 (US$4.80) adults, A$4 (US$3.20) children, A$16 (US$13) family. Guided night tours (reservations required) A$15 (US$12) adults, A$10 (US$8) children, A$40 (US$32) families. Daily 10am–5pm. CityRail, bus, or ferry: Circular Quay.

Elizabeth Bay House   A good example of colonial architecture, this house was built in 1835 and was described at the time as the "finest house in the colony." Visitors can tour the whole house and get a real feeling of the history of the fledgling settlement. The house is on a headland and has some of the best harbor views in Sydney. Allow 1 hour.

7 Onslow Ave., Elizabeth Bay. ✆ **02/9356 3022.** Admission A$7 (US$5.60) adults, A$3 (US$2.40) children, A$17 (US$14) families. Tues–Sun 10am–4:30pm. Closed Good Friday and Dec 25. Bus: 311 from Circular Quay or Sydney Explorer.

Museum of Sydney   You'll need to have your brain in full working order to make the most of the contents of this three-story postmodern building near Circular Quay, which encompasses the remnants of Sydney's first Government House. The place is far from a conventional showcase of history; instead, it houses a rather minimalist collection of first-settler and Aboriginal objects and multimedia displays that "invite" the museum-goer to discover Sydney's past for him- or herself. Some Frommer's readers have criticized the place, saying it's not just minimalist—it's simply unfathomable. By the way, that forest of poles filled with hair, oyster shells, and crab claws in the courtyard adjacent to the industrial-design cafe tables is called *Edge of Trees*. It's a metaphor for the first contact between Aborigines and the British. There's a reasonable cafe out front. Allow anywhere from an hour to a lifetime to understand.

37 Phillip St. © **02/9251 5988**. Admission A$7 (US$5.60) adults, A$3 (US$2.40) children under 15, A$17 (US$14) families. Daily 9:30am–5pm. CityRail, bus, or ferry: Circular Quay. Sydney Explorer bus.

St. James Church   Sydney's oldest surviving colonial church, begun in 1822, was designed by the government architect, and former convict, Francis Greenway. At one time the church's spire served as a landmark for ships coming up the harbor, but today it looks totally lost amid the skyscrapers. It's well worth seeking out, though, especially for the plaques on the wall, which pay testament to the hard early days of the colony when people were lost at sea, were "speared by blacks," and died while serving the British Empire overseas.

Queens Sq., Macquarie St. © **02/9232 3022**. Daily 8am–5pm.

St. Mary's Cathedral   Sydney's most impressive place of worship is a giant sandstone construction between The Domain and Hyde Park. The original St. Mary's was built in 1821, but the chapel was destroyed by fire. Work on the present cathedral began in 1868, but due to lack of funds, it remained unfinished until construction of the two spires began in 1999. The stained-glass windows inside are impressive. St. Mary's is Roman Catholic and was built for Sydney's large population of Irish convicts. In perhaps Sydney's worst pre-Olympic planning, the beautiful brown sandstone building was marred by a wide stretch of dark gray paving outside—now the battleground contested by skateboarders and city council types. The two spires were completed in extraquick time for the Olympics, too.

College and Cathedral sts. © **02/9220 0400**. Mon–Fri 6:30am–6:30pm; Sat 8am–7:30pm; Sun 6:30am–7:30pm.

State Library of New South Wales   The state's main library consists of two side-by-side sections, the Mitchell and Dixon libraries. A newer reference-library complex nearby has two floors of reference materials, local newspapers, and microfiche viewers. Leave your bags in the free lockers downstairs. (You'll need a A$2 coin, which is refundable.) I highly recommend the library's leafy **Glasshouse Café,** in my opinion one of the best walk-in lunch spots in Sydney. The older building contains many older books on the ground floor, and often mounts free art and photography displays in the upstairs galleries. A small library section in the Sydney Town Hall building has international newspapers.

Macquarie St. © **02/9273 1414**. Free admission. Mon–Fri 9am–5pm; Sat–Sun and selected holidays 11am–5pm. Closed Jan 1, Good Friday, and Dec 25–26. CityRail: Martin Place. Sydney Explorer bus.

Sydney Jewish Museum   Harrowing exhibits here include documents and objects relating to the Holocaust and the Jewish culture, mixed with soundscapes, audiovisual displays, and interactive media. There's also a museum shop, a resource center, a small theater, and a traditional kosher cafe. It's considered one of the best museums of its type in the world. Allow 1 to 2 hours.

148 Darlinghurst Rd., Darlinghurst. © **02/9360 7999**. Fax 02/9331 4245. www.sjm.com.au. Admission A$10 (US$8) adults, A$6 (US$4.80) children, A$22 (US$18) families. Sun–Thurs 10am–4pm; Fri 10am–2pm. Closed Jewish holidays, Good Friday, and Dec 25. CityRail: Kings Cross.

Vaucluse House   Overlooking Sydney Harbour, this house has lavish entertainment rooms and impressive stables and outbuildings. It was constructed in 1803 and was the home of Charles Wentworth, the architect of the Australian Constitution. It's set in 11 hectares (27 acres) of gardens, bushland, and beach frontage—perfect for picnics. Allow 1 hour.

Wentworth Rd., Vaucluse. © 02/9337 1957. www.hht.nsw.gov.au. Admission A$7 (US$5.60) adults, A$3 (US$2.40) children. House Tues–Sun 10am–4:30pm; grounds daily 7am–5pm. Free guided tours. Closed Good Friday and Dec 25. Bus: 325 from Circular Quay, or Bondi & Bay Explorer.

PARKS & GARDENS
IN SYDNEY

ROYAL BOTANIC GARDENS   If you are going to spend time in one of Sydney's green spaces, then make it the **Royal Botanic Gardens** ⚹ (© 02/9231 8111), next to the Sydney Opera House. The gardens were laid out in 1816 on the site of a farm dedicated to supplying food for the colony. They're informal in appearance, with a scattering of duck ponds and open spaces, though several areas are dedicated to particular plant species. These include the rose garden, the cacti and succulent display, and the central palm and rainforest groves (watch out for the thousands of large fruit bats, which chatter and argue among the rainforest trees). **Mrs. Macquarie's Chair,** along the coast path, offers superb views of the Opera House and the Harbour Bridge. The "chair" is a step cut out of sandstone with a huge stone plaque on top. It bears the name of Elizabeth Macquarie (1788–1835), the wife of Gov. Lachlan Macquarie. (It's a favorite stop for tour buses.) The sandstone building dominating the gardens nearest to the Opera House is the **Government House,** once the official residence of the governor of New South Wales. (He moved out in 1996 in the spirit of republicanism.) The pleasant gardens are open to the public daily from 10am to 4pm, and the house is open Friday through Sunday from 10am to 3pm. Entrance to both is free. If you plan to park around here, note that parking meters cost upwards of A$4 (US$3.20) per hour, and you need A$1 coins.

A popular walk takes you through the Royal Botanic Gardens to the **Art Gallery of New South Wales.** The gardens are open daily from 7am to dusk. Admission is free.

HYDE PARK   In the center of the city is Hyde Park, a favorite with lunching businesspeople. Of note here are the **Anzac Memorial** to Australian and New Zealand troops killed in the wars, and the **Archibald Fountain,** complete with spitting turtles and sculptures of Diana and Apollo. At night, twinkling lights illuminate avenues of trees, giving the place a magical appearance.

MORE CITY PARKS   Another Sydney favorite is giant **Centennial Park** (© 02/9339 6699), usually entered from the top of Oxford Street. It opened in 1888 to celebrate the centenary of European settlement, and today encompasses huge areas of lawn, several lakes, picnic areas with outdoor grills, cycling and running paths, and a cafe. It's open from sunrise to sunset. To get there, take bus no. 373, 374, 378, 380, or 382 from the city, or the Bondi & Bay Explorer.

A hundred years later, **Bicentennial Park,** at Australia Avenue, in Homebush Bay, came along. Forty percent of the park's total 100 hectares (247 acres) is general parkland reclaimed from a city dump; the rest is the largest existing remnant of wetlands on the Parramatta River and is home to many species of local and migratory wading birds, cormorants, and pelicans. Follow park signs to the **visitor information office** (© 02/9763 1844), open Monday through Friday from 10am to 4pm, and Saturday and Sunday from 9:30am to 4:30pm. To reach the park, take a CityRail train to Homebush Bay station.

BEYOND SYDNEY

SYDNEY HARBOUR NATIONAL PARK   You don't need to go far to experience Sydney's nearest national park. The Sydney Harbour National Park stretches around parts of the inner harbor and includes several small islands. (Many first-time visitors are surprised at the amount of bushland remaining in prime real-estate territory.) The best walk through the Sydney Harbour National Park is the **Manly to Spit Bridge Scenic Walkway** (© 02/9977 6522). This 10km (6-mile) track winds its way from Manly (it starts near the Oceanarium) via Dobroyd Head to Spit Bridge, where you can catch a bus back to the city. The walk takes around 3 hours at a casual pace, and the views across busy Sydney Harbour are fabulous. There are a few Aboriginal stone carvings, which are signposted along the route. Maps are available from the **Manly Visitors Information Bureau** (© 02/9977 1088), opposite the main beach.

Other access points to the park include tracks around Taronga Zoo (ask the zoo staff to point you toward the obscured entrances) and above tiny Shelly Beach, opposite the main beach at Manly.

Also part of the national park is recently restored **Fort Denison,** in the middle of the harbor between Circular Quay and Manly. The fort was built during the Crimean War in response to fears of a Russian invasion, and was later used as a penal colony. One- to 2-hour **Heritage Tours** of the island leave from Cadmans Cottage, 110 George St., in The Rocks (© 02/9247 5033). They cost A$22 (US$18) for adults and A$18 (US$14) for students and children. Call ahead for times and bookings. Pick up maps of the Sydney Harbour National Park at Cadmans Cottage.

Another great walk in Sydney can be combined with lunch or a drink at Watsons Bay. A 15-minute bush stroll to **South Head** starts from the small beach outside the Watsons Bay Hotel. Walk to the end of the beach (to your right as you look at the water), up the flight of steps to Short Street, then left along Cliff Street to the end of Camp Cove Beach. Continue along the coast past the nudist Lady Bay Beach to the lighthouse at South Head, where there are some great views (of the coastline, not the nudists). Across the road in front of the Watsons Bay Hotel is another section of the national park, known for its cliff-top views. Here you'll find The Gap, a sheer cliff popular for suicides, sadly. Ferries from Circular Quay and the Bondi & Bay Explorer go to Watsons Bay.

MORE NATIONAL PARKS   Forming a semicircle around the city are Sydney's biggest parks of all. To the west is the **Blue Mountains National Park** (see chapter 5); to the northeast is **Ku-ring-gai Chase National Park;** and to the south is the magnificent **Royal National Park.** All three parks are home to marsupials such as echidnas and wallabies, numerous bird and reptile species, and a broad range of native plant life. Walking tracks, which take as little as half an hour to as long as a few days to cover, make each park accessible to the visitor.

Ku-ring-gai Chase National Park (© 02/9457 9322 or 02/9457 9310) is a great place to take a bushwalk through gum trees and rainforest on the lookout for wildflowers, sandstone rock formations, and Aboriginal art. There are plenty of tracks through the park; one of my favorites is a relatively easy 2.5km (1.5-mile) tramp to **The Basin** (Track 12). The well-graded dirt path takes you down to a popular estuary with a beach and passes some significant Aboriginal engravings. There are also wonderful water views over Pittwater from the picnic areas at **West Head.** Pick up a free walking guide at the park entrance, or gather maps and information in Sydney at the National Parks & Wildlife Service's center at **Cadmans Cottage,** 110 George St., The Rocks (© 02/9247 8861).

The park is open from sunrise to sunset, and admission is A$10 (US$8) per car. You can either drive to the park or catch a ferry from Palm Beach to The Basin (from there, you can walk up Track 12 and back). Ferries run on the hour (except at 1pm) from 9am to 5pm daily and cost A$4 (US$3.20) one-way; call ℂ **02/9918 2747** for details. Shorelink bus no. 577 runs from the Turramurra CityRail station to the nearby park entrance every hour on weekdays and every 2 hours on weekends; call ℂ **02/9457 8888** for details. There is no train service to the park. Camping is allowed only at The Basin (ℂ **02/9457 9853**) and costs A$12 (US$9.60) for two people booked in advance.

If you have a car you could visit the **Ku-ring-gai Wildflower Garden,** 420 Mona Vale Rd., St. Ives (ℂ **02/9440 8609**), which is essentially a huge area of natural bush-land and a center for urban bushland education. There are plenty of bushwalking tracks, self-guided walks, and a number of nature-based activities. It's open daily from 8am to 4pm. Admission is A$2.50 (US$2) for adults, A$1 (US80¢) for children, and A$6 (US$4.80) for families.

South of Sydney is the remarkable **Royal National Park,** Farrell Avenue, Suther-land (ℂ **02/9542 0648**). It's the world's oldest national park, declared in 1879. (The main competitor to the title is Yellowstone in the United States, which was set aside for conservation in 1872 but not designated a national park until 1883.) Severe bush-fires almost destroyed the whole lot in early 1994, but the trees and bush plants have recovered remarkably. There's no visitor center, but you can get information at park entrances, where you'll have to pay an A$11 (US$8.80) per-car entry fee.

There are several ways to reach the park, but my favorites are the little-known access points from Bundeena and Otford. To get to **Bundeena,** take a CityRail train from Central Station to the seaside suburb of Cronulla (around 1 hr.). Just below the train station, through an underpass, you'll find Cronulla Wharf. From there, hop on the delightful ferry run by **National Park Ferries** (ℂ **02/9523 2990**) to Bundeena, which I highly recommend you visit. There are three stunning beaches here. Ferries run on the half-hour (except 12:30pm on weekdays) and stop at around 7pm. After you get off the ferry, the first turn on your left just up the hill will take you to won-derful Jibbon Beach. Walk along the beach to the end, hop up some rocks, and follow the track (about 20 min.) through the park to Jibbon Head, for some stunning ocean views. Look out for the Aboriginal rock carvings off to your right before you reach it (the sign's a little obscured). It's around a 3-hour round-trip walk to Marley Beach (which has strong surf and dangerous rips) and a 6-hour round-trip to beautiful Wat-tamolla, where there's safe swimming for children in the salty lagoon. The ferry returns to Cronulla from Bundeena hourly on the hour (except 1pm). The fare is A$4.50 (US$3.60) each way.

An alternative way to reach the park is to take the train from Central Station to **Otford,** then climb the hill up to the sea cliffs. If you're driving, you might want to follow the scenic cliff-edge road down into Wollongong. The entrance to the national park is a little tricky to find, so you might have to ask directions—but roughly, it's just to the left of a cliff top popular for hang-gliding, radio-controlled airplanes, and kites. A 2-hour walk from the sea cliffs through beautiful and varying bushland and a palm forest will take you to Burning Palms Beach. There is no water along the route. The walk back up is steep, so attempt this trek only if you're reasonably fit. Trains to the area are irregular, and the last one departs around 4pm, so give yourself at least 2½ hours for the return trip to the train station to make sure you don't get stranded. It's possible to walk the memorable 26km (16 miles) from Otford to Bundeena, or vice versa, in 2 days. (Take all your food, water, and camping gear.) The track sticks to the coast, crosses several beaches, and is relatively easy to follow.

Tips **A Stroll on The Rocks**

Sydney is relatively compact, so it's a wonderful city for exploring on foot. I particularly recommend a wander through The Rocks, site of the oldest settlement in Australia, a rough-and-tumble place where prostitutes, gang members, and other shady characters loitered more than a century ago. **The Rocks Walking Tour (© 02/9247 6678)** has an organized stroll (see "Walking Tours," below).

ESPECIALLY FOR KIDS

Kids can have fun at plenty of places in Sydney, but my choices below are particularly suitable for youngsters. (All are reviewed in full above.)

At **Taronga Zoo** (p. 162), an all-time favorite with kids, the barnyard animals, surprisingly, get as much attention as the koalas. If your kids want hands-on contact with the animals, though, you'd better head to **Featherdale Wildlife Park** (p. 162), where they can get their photo taken next to a koala, and hand-feed and stroke kangaroos and wallabies. You can't stroke koalas in New South Wales. Even more interactive are the exhibits just crying out to be touched and bashed at the **Powerhouse Museum** (p. 159).

The sharks at **Oceanworld** (p. 162) in Manly and at the **Sydney Aquarium** (p. 160) in Darling Harbour are big lures for kids, too, and the thrill of walking through a long Plexiglas tunnel as giant manta rays perch over their heads will lead to more squeals of excitement.

Another outing for both adults and children is to crawl around inside boats and submarines at the **Australian National Maritime Museum** (p. 159).

And what kid wouldn't enjoy a day at the beach? Sydney's got plenty to choose from, like **Bondi** and **Manly.**

6 Harbor Cruises & Organized Tours

For details on the **Sydney Explorer** bus, see "Getting Around," earlier this chapter.

HARBOR CRUISES

The best thing about Sydney is the harbor, and you shouldn't leave without taking a harbor cruise. **Sydney Ferries (© 13 15 00** in Australia, or 02/9245 5600; www.sta. nsw.gov.au) offers a 1-hour morning harbor cruise with commentary departing Circular Quay, Wharf 4, daily at 10am and 11:15am. It costs A$15 (US$12) for adults, A$7.50 (US$6) for children under 16, and A$38 (US$30) for families (with any number of children). A 2½-hour afternoon cruise explores more of the harbor; it leaves from Wharf 4 at 1pm on weekdays and 1:30pm on weekends and public holidays. This tour costs A$22 (US$18) for adults, A$11 (US$8.80) for children, and A$55 (US$44) for families. The highly recommended 1½-hour **Evening Harbour Lights tour,** which takes in the city lights as far east as Double Bay and west to Goat Island, leaves Monday through Saturday at 8pm from Wharf 5. The evening tour costs A$19 (US$15) for adults, A$9.50 (US$7.60) for children, and A$48 (US$38) for families.

Captain Cook Cruises, departing jetty no. 6, Circular Quay (© **02/9206 1111;** www.captaincook.com.au), offers several harbor excursions on its sleek vessels, with commentary along the way.

Examples include a 2-hour-20-minute **Coffee Cruise** departing from Jetty 6, Circular Quay, at 10am and 2:15pm daily. It costs A$44 (US$35) for adults, A$24 (US$19) for kids, and A$99 (US$80) for a family. Another is a Seafood Buffet Lunch cruise, departing Circular Quay at 12:30pm daily, and costing A$57 (US$45.60) for adults and A$30 (US$24) for children.

Its **Sydney Harbour Explorer** cruise is popular and stops off at The Rocks, Watson's Bay, Taronga Zoo and Darling Harbour. You get on and off when you want. It costs A$27 (US$22) for adults, A$14 (US$11) for kids, and A$65 (US$52) for a family, and leaves Circular Quay at 9:45am, 11:30am, 1:30pm, and 3:30pm daily.

Another favourite is the 1 hour-15 minute **Harbour Highlights Cruise**, which costs A$22 (US$18) for adults, A$11 (US$8.80) for kids and A$59 (US$47) for adults. It leaves Circular Quay at 9:30am, 11am, 12:45pm, 2:30pm, 4pm, 6pm, and 7:30pm. The first and last cruises are only offered if there are sufficient passengers for a trip.

The company also offers a range of dinner cruises.

Captain Cooke cruises have ticket booths at Jatty 6, Circular Quay (open from 8:30am to 7pm) and at 1 King Street Wharf, darling harbour (near the Sydney Aquarium).It has limited opening hours of 11am to 4pm daily.

Matilda Cruises (© 02/9264 7377; www.matilda.com.au) offers a 1-hour **Rocket Harbour Explorer** narrated sightseeing tour leaving the pontoon at the far end of Sydney Aquarium at Darling Harbour eight times daily beginning at 9:30am (six times daily in winter, Apr–Sept, beginning at 10:30am). You can stay on for the full hour, or get off and on again at Circular Quay, the Opera House, Watsons Bay, and Taronga Zoo. The last boat leaves Taronga Zoo at 5:10pm in summer (4:10pm in winter). There's tea and coffee on board. The cruise costs A$24 (US$19) for adults, A$14.50 (US$11.60) for children 5 to 12, and A$55 (US$) for a family.

A new service is the **Manly Rocket Express Service**, leaving Darling Harbour and stopping off at Circular Quay, Rose Bay and Manly, before returning. You can get on and off again when you want. There's commentary and coffee and tea. The cruise departs every 90 minutes each day from 9:15am. From Darling Harbour to Manly it takes 45 minutes and costs the same as the Rocket Harbour Explorer above.

The company also runs morning and afternoon cruises, and lunch and dinner cruises with good food. One example is the **Seafood Lunch** cruise, with a seafood buffet. It leaves Darling Harbour at noon and Jetty 6 at Circular Quay at 12:30pm. The one-and-a-half-hour crise cost A$62 (US$50) for adults and A$37 (US$30) for kids aged six to 12.

Matilda Cruises have a ticket booth at Jetty 6 at Circular Quay, and a ticket office next to the Sydney Aquarium at Darling Harbour.

⟮Tips⟯ Top Gun

If you have time and money to spare, you might want to try riding in a real-life jet fighter over trees and water on Sydney's outskirts. There are several options, including a 20-minute aerobatic and patrol run costing A$1,595 (US$1,275); a 30-minute low-level simulated attack run for A$1,995 (US$1,596); and a dogfight (bring along a rich friend) for A$2,495 (US$1,996). Contact **Jet Fighter Flights** (© 1800/880 501 in Australia; www.jetfighterflights.com).

HARBOR CRUISE TICKETS & INFO

The one-stop shop for tickets and information on all harbor cruises is the **Australian Travel Specialists** (✆ **02/9247 5151**; www.atstravel.com.au). It's a good idea to check websites before you come to Australia, or pop into a ticket office at Darling harbour or Circular Quay, because cruise options, departure times, and prices change frequently. You can book on the Net, too.

WALKING TOURS

The center of Sydney is compact, and you can see a lot in a day on foot. If you want to learn more about Sydney's early history, then book a guided tour with **The Rocks Walking Tour** (✆ **02/9247 6678**), based at the Shop K4, Kendall Lane (off Argyle St., The Rocks). Excellent walking tours leave Monday through Friday at 10:30am, 12:30pm, and 2:30pm, and Saturday and Sunday at 11:30am and 2pm (in Jan only 10:30am and 2:30pm on weekdays). The 1½-hour tour costs A$16 (US$13) for adults, A$11 (US$8.80) for children 10 to 16, A$41 (US$33) for families, free for accompanied children under 10.

For other historical walks, contact **Sydney Guided Tours** (✆ **02/9660 7157**). The company's owner, Maureen Fry, has been in the business for over 13 years and employs trained guides qualified in disciplines such as history, architecture, and botany. She offers a range of tours, including an introductory tour of Sydney, a tour of Macquarie Street, and many others. Call in advance to find out what's available. Walking tours cost A$17 (US$14) for 2 hours as part of a group.

A journey with a difference is **Weird Sydney Ghost and History Tours** (✆ **02/ 9555 2700**; www.destinytours.com.au). The tour—in a hearse—is fascinating and fun. It explores a section of historic Sydney and more modern additions, including a former VD clinic, the Sydney Opera House, and some buildings along Macquarie Street. It costs A$149 (US$119) for the 1½- to 2-hour trip.

MOTORCYCLE TOURS

Blue Thunder Motorcycle Tours (✆ **02/9977 7721** or 0414/278 983) runs Harley-Davidson tours of Sydney, the Blue Mountains, and places around New South Wales. A 1-hour ride (you sit on the back of the bike) around the city costs A$90 (US$72). A half-day trip to the northern beaches or down the south coast through the Royal National Park costs A$265 (US$212), including lunch. Full-day trips cost A$370 (US$296) including lunch and snacks, and go to the Hunter Valley, the south coast, Bathurst, or the Blue Mountains.

If you love motorbikes and want to take one out on your own for a self-guided or guided tour, contact **Bikescape** (✆ **02/9356 2453**; www.bikescape.com.au). It will rent you a bike to go around Sydney, or as far afield as Byron Bay or the Great Ocean Road in Victoria.

7 Staying Active

BIKING   The best place to cycle in Sydney is Centennial Park. Rent bikes from **Centennial Park Cycles,** 50 Clovelly Rd., Randwick (✆ **02/9398 5027**), which is 200m (656 ft.) from the Musgrave Avenue entrance. (The park has five main entrances.) Mountain bikes cost A$9 (US$7.20) for the first hour, A$13 (US$10) for 2 hours, and A$20 (US$16) for 4 hours.

Bicycles in The City, 722 George St., near Central Station (✆ **02/9280 2229**), rents mountain bikes; prices start at A$5 (US$4) per hour, or A$25 (US$20) per day.

You can rent in-line skates for the same daily rate with all protective clothing. Helmets are compulsory in Australia.

FITNESS CLUBS The **City Gym,** 107 Crown St., East Sydney (✆ **02/9360 6247**), is a busy 24-hour gym near Kings Cross. Drop-in visits are A$10 (US$8).

GOLF Sydney has over 90 golf courses and plenty of fine weather. The 18-hole championship course at **Moore Park Golf Club,** Cleveland Street and Anzac Parade, Waterloo (✆ **02/9663 1064**), is the nearest to the city. Visitors are welcome every day except all day Friday and Sunday mornings. Greens fees are A$24 (US$19) Monday through Friday, and A$27 (US$22) Saturday and Sunday.

One of my favorite courses is **Long Reef Golf Club,** Anzac Avenue, Collaroy (✆ **02/9982 2943**). This northern beaches course is surrounded by the Tasman Sea on three sides and has gorgeous views. Greens fees are A$25 (US$20) midweek, and A$35 (US$28) on weekends.

For general information on courses, call the **New South Wales Golf Association** (✆ **02/9264 8433**).

IN-LINE SKATING The best places to skate are along the beachside promenades at Bondi and Manly beaches and in Centennial Park. **Manly Blades,** 49 N. Steyne (✆ **02/9976 3833**), rents skates for A$12 (US$9.60) for the first hour and A$6 (US$2.40) for each subsequent hour, or A$25 (US$20) per day. Lessons are A$25 (US$20), including 1-hour skate rental and a half-hour lesson. **Bondi Boards & Blades,** 148 Curlewis St., Bondi Beach (✆ **02/9365 6555**), rents skates for A$11 (US$8.80) for the first hour, A$5.50 (US$4.40) for each subsequent hour, and A$20 (US$16) for 24 hours. Ask about a free lesson. **Total Skate,** 36 Oxford St., Paddington, near Centennial Park (✆ **02/9380 6356**), rents skates for A$10 (US$8) for the first hour, A$5 (US$4) for subsequent hours, and A$30 (US$24) for 24 hours. Ask about a free lesson.

JOGGING The **Royal Botanic Gardens, Centennial Park,** and any **beach** are the best places to kick-start your body. You can also run across the Harbour Bridge, though you'll have to put up with the car fumes. Another popular spot is along the sea cliffs from Bondi Beach to Bronte Beach.

PARASAILING If being strapped to a parachute 100m (328 ft.) above Sydney Harbour while being towed by a speedboat is your idea of fun, contact **Sydney Harbour Parasailing and Scenic Tours** (✆ **02/9977 6781**). A regular flight will put you in the air for 8 to 10 minutes at the end of a 100m (328-ft.) line. Flights cost A$55 (US$44) per adult. Tandem rides (for children and adults) are also available. The boat departs from next to the Manly ferry wharf in Manly.

SCUBA DIVING Plenty of people learn to dive in Sydney before taking off for the Barrier Reef. Don't expect coral reefs, though. **Pro Dive,** 27 Alfreda St., Coogee (✆ **02/9665 6333**), offers a 4-day learn-to-dive program costing A$345 (US$276). A day of diving for registered divers costs A$105 (US$84).

SURFING **Bondi Beach** and **Tamarama** are the best surf beaches on the south side of Sydney Harbour. **Manly, Narrabeen, Bilgola, Collaroy, Long Reef,** and **Palm** beaches are the most popular on the north side. Most beach suburbs have surf shops where you can rent a board. At Bondi Beach, the **Bondi Surf Co.,** 72 Campbell Parade (✆ **02/9365 0870**), rents surfboards for A$45 (US$36) for 4 hours or A$60 (US$48) all day. Body boards cost A$20 (US$16) for 2 hours and A$60 (US$48) all day. In Manly, **Aloha Surf,** 44 Pittwater Rd. (✆ **02/9977 3777**), rents surfboards.

Finds **A Surf Adventure**

If you've always fancied learning to surf, then head for **Waves Surf School** (© **1800/851 101** in Australia, or 0414/682 228 mobile; www.wavessurf school.com.au). It takes budding surfers on 1-day trips from Sydney to the Royal National Park. Trips cost A$69 (US$55), including equipment and lunch. If you're young enough to spend the night in a "double-decker party bus," then you might consider a 2-day surfing trip to Seal Rocks, north of Sydney, for A$189 (US$151). The company also takes adventurous travelers on a 4-day surfing trip from Sydney to Byron Bay for A$399 (US$319).

Manly Surf School (© **02/9977 6977**) offers 2-hour surf classes for A$40 (US$32), 2-day sessions for A$70 (US$56), and 3-day classes for A$90 (US$72). **Wave Action Surf School** (© **02/9970 6813,** or 0413/177 242 mobile) charges the same rates as Manly Surf School, on the breakers at Palm Beach. Also, it offers a 1-day surf tour from central Sydney to Palm Beach and other northern Sydney beaches with sight-seeing and lunch for A$100 (US$80).

SWIMMING   The best place to swim indoors in Sydney is the **Sydney Aquatic Centre,** at Olympic Park, Homebush Bay (© **02/9752 3666**). It's open Monday through Friday from 5am to 9:45pm, and Saturday, Sunday, and public holidays from 6am to 7:45pm (6:45pm May–Oct), and charges A$5.80 (US$4.60) adults, A$4.60 (US$3.70) children 4 to 15, A$19 (US$15) families.

The most central of Sydney's pools is **Cook and Phillip Park,** 4 College St., at William Street (© **02/9326 0444**). The center has three pools: one for serious swimmers, another with a wave machine, and a hydrotherapy pool with easy ramp access and bubble jets. Entry is A$5.50 (US$4.40) for adults and A$4 (US$3.20) for kids. To find it, walk to the cathedral across Hyde Park, and continue for a couple of minutes along the dark paved area outside the cathedral's front entrance (keeping Hyde Park on your right). Look for signs directing you down some stairs to the entrance.

Another good bet is the **North Sydney Olympic Pool,** Alfred South Street, Milsons Point (© **02/9955 2309**). It's just over the Harbour Bridge, near the amusement park, so why not have a swim after a walk over from the city? Swimming here costs A$3.50 (US$2.80) for adults and A$1.65 (US$1.30) for children. More world records have been broken in this outdoor pool than in any other. There's a separate indoor pool, too.

The **Bondi Icebergs Club,** 1 Notts Ave. (© **02/9130 3120**), at Bondi Beach, on the rocks to the right of the beach as you look at the sea, has an Olympic-size pool and a children's pool. Entrance costs A$3.30 (US$2.60) and includes a sauna. (And an excellent restaurant; see review p. 151.)

TENNIS   There are hundreds of places around the city to play one of Australia's most popular sports. A nice spot is the **Miller's Point Tennis Court,** Kent Street, The Rocks (© **02/9256 2222**). It's run by the Observatory Hotel and is open daily from 7:30am to 10pm. The court costs A$25 (US$20) per hour. The **North Sydney Tennis Centre,** 1A Little Alfred St., North Sydney (© **02/9371 9952**), has three courts available daily from 6am to 10pm. They cost A$16 (US$13) until 5pm on weekdays and A$20 (US$16) at other times.

WINDSURFING   My favorite spot to learn to windsurf or to set out onto the harbor is **Balmoral Beach,** in Mosman on the North Shore. Rent boards at **Balmoral Windsurfing, Sailing and Kayaking School & Hire,** 3 The Esplanade, Balmoral Beach (© **02/9960 5344**). Windsurfers cost A$27 (US$22) per hour for beginners and A$38 (US$30) for advanced windsurfing equipment. Lessons cost A$175 (US$140) for 5 hours of instruction over a weekend for beginners, and A$195 (US$156) for advanced lessons. This place also rents fishing boats.

YACHTING   **Balmoral Boat Shed,** Balmoral Beach (© **02/9969 6006**), rents catamarans, 3.5m (11-ft.) aluminum runabouts, canoes, and surf skis. The catamarans and runabouts cost A$35 (US$28) for the first hour (with a A$80/US$64 deposit); a full day costs A$120 (US$96). Other vessels, such as canoes, cost A$12 (US$9.60) per hour with a A$10 (US$8) deposit.

   Sydney by Sail (© **02/9280 1110,** or 0419/367 180 mobile) offers sailing courses on Sydney Harbour. A long, 1-day introductory course costs A$450 (US$360).

8 Spectator Sports

CRICKET   The **Sydney Cricket Ground,** at the corner of Moore Park and Driver Avenue, is famous for its 1-day and test matches, played October through March. Phone the **New South Wales Cricket Association** (© **02/9339 0999**) for match details, and **Sportspace Tours** (© **02/9380 0383**) for stadium tours.

FOOTBALL   In this city, "football" means rugby league. If you want to see burly chaps pound into each other while chasing an oval ball, then be here between May and September. The biggest venue is the **Sydney Football Stadium,** Moore Park Road, Paddington (© **02/9360 6601,** or 1900/963 133 for match information). Buy tickets through **Ticketek** (© **02/9266 4800**).

HORSE RACING   Sydney has four horse-racing tracks: Randwick, Canterbury, Rosehill, and Warwick Farm. The most central and best known is **Randwick Racecourse,** Alison Street, Randwick (© **02/9663 8400**). The biggest race day of the week is Saturday. Entry costs A$9 (US$7.20). Call the **Sydney Turf Club** (© **02/9930 4000**) with questions about Rosehill and Canterbury, and the Randwick number for Warwick Farm.

SURFING CARNIVALS   Every summer these uniquely Australian competitions bring large crowds to Sydney's beaches to watch surf clubs compete in various watersports. Contact the **Surf Lifesaving Association** (© **02/9597 5588**) for times and locations. Other beach events include Iron Man and Iron Woman competitions, during which Australia's fittest struggle it out in combined swimming, running, and surfing events.

YACHT RACING   Sailing competitions take place on the harbor most summer weekends, but the start of the **Sydney to Hobart Yacht Race** on Boxing Day (Dec 26) is something not to be missed. The race starts from the harbor near the Royal Botanic Gardens.

9 Shopping

You'll find plenty of places to keep your credit cards in action in Sydney. Most shops of interest to the visitor are in **The Rocks** and along **George and Pitt streets** (including the shops below the Sydney AMP Tower and along Pitt Street Mall). Other shopping precincts worth checking out are **Mosman** on the North Shore and **Double Bay** in the eastern suburbs for exclusive boutique shopping, **Chatswood** for its general shopping centers, the **Sydney Fishmarket** for the sake of it, and the various **weekend markets** (listed below). *Note:* At the time of writing, there was talk about major renovations at the Sydney AMP Tower, which may be closed by the time you arrive.

Don't miss the **Queen Victoria Building (QVB)**, on the corner of Market and George streets. This Victorian shopping arcade is one of the prettiest in the world and has some 200 boutiques—mostly men's and women's fashion—on four levels. The arcade is open 24 hours, but the shops do business Monday through Saturday from 9am to 6pm (Thurs to 9pm) and Sunday from 11am to 5pm.

Several other arcades in the city center also have potential, including the **Sydney Central Plaza,** beside the Myer department store on Pitt Street Mall; and the **Skygarden Arcade,** which runs from Pitt Street Mall to Castlereagh Street. The **Strand Arcade** (between Pitt St. Mall and George St.) was built in 1892 and is interesting for its architecture and small boutiques, food stores, and cafes, and the Down Town Duty Free store on the basement level.

On **Pitt Street Mall** you'll find record shops, including HMV, a branch of The Body Shop, and boutiques such as Just Jeans, Jeans West, Katies, and Esprit.

Oxford Street runs from the city to Bondi Junction through Paddington and Darlinghurst and is home to countless clothing stores for the style conscious. You could easily spend anywhere from 2 hours to a whole day making your way from one end to the other. Detour down William Street once you get to Paddington to visit the headquarters of celebrated international Australian designer Collette Dinnigan. On the same street are the trendy boutiques Belinda and Corner Store (cutting-edge designs), and Pelle and Di Nuovo (luxury recycled goods).

Tip: American Express cards seem to be unpopular with many shop owners.

SHOPPING HOURS Regular shopping hours are generally Monday through Wednesday and Friday from 8:30 or 9am to 6pm, Thursday from 8:30 or 9am to 9pm, Saturday from 9am to 5 or 5:30pm, and Sunday from 10 or 10:30am to 5pm. Exceptions are noted in the store listings below.

SYDNEY SHOPPING FROM A TO Z
ABORIGINAL ARTIFACTS & CRAFTS

Aboriginal & Tribal Art Centre   This center carries a wide range of desert paintings and bark paintings, mostly of very high quality. Collectibles such as didgeridoos, fabrics, books, and boomerangs are on sale, too. Open daily from 10am to 5pm. 1st floor, 117 George St., The Rocks. (C) **02/9247 9625.** Fax 02/9247 4391.

Coo-ee Aboriginal Art Gallery and Shop   The proprietors of Coo-ee collect artifacts and fine art from more than 30 Aboriginal communities and dozens of individual artists throughout Australia. The gallery also stocks the country's largest collection of limited-edition prints. Also here are plenty of hand-painted fabrics, T-shirts, didgeridoos, boomerangs, sculpture, bark paintings, jewelry, music, and books. Don't expect bargain prices, though; you pay for the quality here. Open Monday through Saturday from 10am to 6pm and Sunday from 11am to 5pm. 98 Oxford St., Paddington. (C) **02/9332 1544.**

Didj Beat Didjeridoo's   Here you'll find the most authentic and well-priced didgeridoos in Sydney. Open daily from 10am to 6:30pm. Shop 2, The Clock Tower Sq., corner of Argyle and Harrington sts. (C) **02/9251 4289.**

Gavala Aboriginal Art & Cultural Education Centre   I'd head here first if I were in the market for a decent boomerang or didgeridoo. Gavala is entirely owned and operated by Aborigines, and it stocks plenty of authentic Aboriginal crafts, including carved emu eggs, grass baskets, cards, and books. A first-rate painted didgeridoo will cost anywhere from A$100 to A$450 (US$80–US$360). Gavala also sponsors cultural talks, didgeridoo-making lessons, and story-telling sessions. Open daily from 10am to 9pm. Shop 377, Harbourside Festival Marketplace, Darling Harbour. © 02/9212 7232.

ART PRINTS & ORIGINALS

Done Art and Design   Ken Done is well known for having designed his own Australian flag, which he hopes to raise over Australia should it abandon its present one following the formation of a republic. The art here is his. The clothing designs—which feature printed sea- and beachscapes, the odd colorful bird, and lots of pastels—are by his wife, Judy. Open daily from 10am to 5:30pm. 1 Hickson Rd., off George St., The Rocks. © 02/9247 2740.

Ken Duncan Gallery   This photographer-turned-salesman is making a killing from his exquisitely produced large-scale photographs of Australian scenery. Open daily from 9am to 8pm (to 9pm Thurs) in summer, 9am to 7pm in winter. 73 George St., The Rocks (across from The Rocks Visitor Centre). © 02/9241 3460. Fax 02/9241 3462.

BOOKS

You'll find a good selection of specialized books on Sydney and Australia for sale at the **Art Gallery of New South Wales,** the Garden Shop in the **Royal Botanic Gardens,** the **Museum of Sydney,** the **Australian Museum,** and the **State Library of New South Wales.** See listings earlier in this chapter.

Abbey's Bookshop   This interesting, centrally located shop specializes in literature, history, and mystery, and has a whole floor on language and education. 131 York St., behind the QVB. © 02/9264 3111.

Angus & Robertson Bookworld   One of Australia's largest bookshops, with two stories of books—including a good guidebook and Australiana section—and games. 168 Pitt St., Pitt Street Mall. © 02/9235 1188.

Dymocks   One of the largest book department stores in the city, Dymocks has three levels of general books and stationery. There's a good travel section with plenty of guides. Open Monday through Wednesday and Friday from 9am to 6pm, Thursday

---

Finds **A World-Class Gallery of Aboriginal Art**

Quality Aboriginal art from some of Australia's best-known painters is on sale at **Original & Authentic Aboriginal Art** at 79 George St., The Rocks (© 02/9251 4222). Artists whose work is represented include Paddy Fordham Wainburranga, whose paintings hang in the White House in Washington, and Janet Forrester Nangala, whose work has been exhibited in the Australian National Gallery in Canberra. Expect to pay in the range of A$1,000 to A$4,000 (US$800–US$3,200) for the larger paintings. There are some nice painted pots here, too, costing A$30 to A$80 (US$24–US$64). Open daily from 10am to 6:30pm.

from 9am to 9pm, Saturday from 9am to 5pm, and Sunday from 10am to 5pm. 424–428 George St. (just north of Market St.). ℂ 02/9235 0155.

Gleebooks Bookshop Specializing in art, general literature, psychology, sociology, and women's studies, Gleebooks also has a secondhand store (with a large children's department) down the road at 191 Glebe Point Rd. Open daily 8am to 9pm. 49 and 191 Glebe Point Rd., Glebe. ℂ 02/9660 2333.

Goulds Book Arcade Come here to search for unusual dusty volumes. Located about a 10-minute walk from the Newtown CityRail station, the place is bursting at the seams with many thousands of secondhand and new books, all in a very rough order. You can browse for hours here. Open daily from 8am to midnight. 32–38 King St., Newtown. ℂ 02/9519 8947.

Travel Bookshop Hundreds of travel guides, maps, Australiana titles, coffee-table books, and accessories line the shelves of this excellent bookshop. There's also an Amex counter. Open Monday through Friday from 9am to 6pm and Saturday from 10am to 5pm. Shop 3, 175 Liverpool St. (across from the southern end of Hyde Park, near the Museum CityRail station). ℂ 02/9261 8200.

CRAFTS

Australian Craftworks This place showcases some of Australia's best arts and crafts, collected from some 300 artists from around the country. It's all displayed in a former police station built in 1882, a time of economic depression when mob riots and clashes with police were common in this area. The cells and administration areas are now gallery spaces. Open daily from 8:30am to 7pm. 127 George St., The Rocks. ℂ 02/9247 7156.

The Puppet Shop at the Rocks ✹ *Finds* I can't believe I kept walking past the sign outside this place for so many years without looking in. Deep down in the bowels of a historic building, I eventually came across several cramped rooms absolutely packed with puppets, costing a couple of dollars to a couple of hundred. The owners make their own puppets—mostly Australian in style (emus, koalas, that sort of thing)—and import things from all over the world. Wooden toys abound, too. It's the best shop in Sydney! Open daily from 10am to 5:30pm. 77 George St., The Rocks. ℂ 02/9247 9137.

Telopea Gallery The New South Wales Society of Arts and Crafts runs this shop, which exhibits works by its members, all of whom are New South Wales residents. There are some wonderful glass, textile, ceramic, jewelry, metal, and wood-turned items for sale. Open daily from 9:30am to 5:30pm. Shop 2, Metcalfe Arcade, 80–84 George St., The Rocks. ℂ 02/9241 1673.

DEPARTMENT STORES

The two big names in Sydney shopping are David Jones and Myer. Both stores are open Monday through Wednesday and Friday through Saturday from 9am to 6pm, Thursday from 9am to 9pm, and Sunday from 11am to 5pm.

David Jones (ℂ 02/9266 5544) is the city's largest department store, selling everything from fashion to designer furniture. You'll find the women's section on the corner of Elizabeth and Market streets, and the men's section on the corner of Castlereagh and Market streets.

Myer (ℂ 02/9238 9111), formally Grace Brothers, is similar to David Jones, but the building is newer and flashier. It's on the corner of George and Market streets.

DUTY-FREE SHOPS

Sydney has several duty-free shops selling goods at a discount. To take advantage of the bargains, you need a passport and a flight ticket, and you must export what you buy. The duty-free shop with the best buys is **Downtown Duty Free,** which has two city outlets, one on the basement level of the Strand Arcade, off Pitt Street Mall (*© **02/9233 3166**), and one at 105 Pitt St. (*© **02/9221 4444**). Five more stores are at Sydney International Airport and are open from the first to the last flight of the day.

FASHION

The best places to shop for fashion are the **QVB** and the **Sydney Central Plaza** (on the ground floor of the mall next to the Myer department store on Pitt St. Mall). The major **Pitt Street Mall** outlets will also keep you up-to-date. For really trendy clothing, head to **Paddington,** and for alternative clothes, go to **Newtown.**

Australian Outback Clothing

R.M. Williams   Moleskin trousers may not be the height of fashion at the moment, but you never know. R.M. Williams boots are famous for being both tough and fashionable. You'll find Akubra hats, Driza-bone coats, and kangaroo-skin belts here, too. 389 George St. (between Town Hall and Central CityRail stations). *© **02/9262 2228.**

Thomas Cook Boot & Clothing Company   Located between Town Hall and Central CityRail stations, this place specializes in Australian boots, Driza-bone coats, and Akubra hats. There's another shop at 129 Pitt St., near Martin Place (*© **02/9232 3334**). 790 George St., Haymarket. *© **02/9212 6616.** www.thomascookclothing.com.au.

Men's Fashion

Esprit Mens   Not so cheap but certainly colorful clothes come out of this designer store where bold hues and fruity patterns are the in thing. Quality shirts cost around A$60 (US$48). Shop 10G, Sydney Central Plaza, 450 George St. *© **02/9233 7349.**

Gowings ✦   Probably the best all-round men's clothing store in Sydney, Gowings sells quality clothing on several levels. There's also an eclectic mix of gardening equipment, gourmet camping gear, odds and ends for the extrovert, a good range of Australian bush hats, and R.M. Williams boots (at around A$250/US$200 a pair). If you want to risk it, you can even get a cheap haircut here. There's a similar store at 319 George St., near Wynyard CityRail station (*© **02/9262 1281**). 45 Market St. *© **02/9264 6321.**

Outdoor Heritage   Quality clothing with a yachting influence is what you'll find at this good-looking store specializing in casual, colorful gear. Shop 13G, Sydney Central Plaza, 450 George St. *© **02/9235 1560.**

Unisex Fashion

Country Road   This chain has outlets all across Australia as well as in the United States. The clothes, for both men and women, are good quality but tend to be quite expensive (though you might find something smart). Other branches are in the QVB, the Skygarden Arcade, Bondi Junction, Darling Harbour, Double Bay, Mosman, and Chatswood. 142–146 Pitt St. *© **02/9394 1818.**

Mostrada   If you're looking for good-quality leather items at very reasonable prices, then this is your place. Leather jackets for men and women go for A$199 to A$899 (US$159–US$719), with an average price of around A$400 (US$320). There are also bags, belts, and other leather accessories. Store 15G, Sydney Central Plaza, 450 George St. *© **02/9221 0133.**

Women's Fashion

In addition to the places listed below, head to **Oxford Street** (particularly Paddington) for more avant-garde designers.

Carla Zampatti   Some 30 Carla Zampatti stores around Australia offer stylish fashions at hard-to-swallow prices. Open Monday through Saturday from 10am to 5pm. 143 Elizabeth St. ✆ **02/9264 3257.**

Dorian Scott   Probably the best place to go for hand-knit sweaters—called "jumpers" in Australia—Dorian Scott has a wide range of colorful garments from more than 200 leading Australian designers. While some items go for A$80 (US$64), others will set you back several hundred. You'll also find accessories for men, women, and children in this two-story emporium, including Hot Tuna surf wear and Thomas Cook adventure clothing. Open Monday through Saturday from 9:30am to 7pm and Sunday from 10am to 6pm. There are two Dorian Scott stores at Sydney International Airport (✆ **02/9667 3255**) and another at the Inter-Continental Sydney hotel, 117 Macquarie St. (✆ **02/ 9247 1818**). 105 George St., The Rocks. ✆ **02/9221 8145.** Fax 02/9251 8553.

FOOD

The goodies you'll find in the food section of **David Jones** department store on Castlereagh Street (the men's section) are enough to tempt anyone. The store sells the best local and imported products to the rich and famous.

Coles   One of the few supermarkets in the city center, this place is a good bet if you want to cook for yourself or are after ready-made food (including tasty sandwiches) and cheap soft drinks. There's another Coles beneath the giant Coca-Cola sign on Darlinghurst Road, Kings Cross. Open daily from 6am to midnight. Wynyard station, Castlereagh St., Wynyard (opposite the Menzies Hotel and the public bus stands). ✆ **02/9299 4769.**

Darrell Lea Chocolates   This is the oldest location of Australia's most famous chocolate shop. Pick up some wonderful handmade chocolates as well as other unusual candies, including the best licorice this side of the Kasbah. At the corner of King and George sts. ✆ **02/9232 2899.**

Sydney Fishmarket   Finding out what people eat can be a good introduction to a new country and, in my opinion, nowhere is this more fascinating than at the local fish market. Here you'll find seven major fish retailers selling everything from shark to Balmain bugs (small crayfish), with hundreds of species in between. Watch out for the local pelicans being fed the fishy leftovers. There's also a Doyles restaurant (p. 142) and a sushi bar, a couple of cheap seafood eateries, a fruit market, and a good deli. The retail sections are open daily from 7am to 4pm. Get here by light rail (get off at the Fishmarket stop), or walk from Darling Harbour. Parking costs A$2 (US$1.60) for the first 3 hours. At the corner of Bank St. and Pyrmont Bridge Rd., Pyrmont. ✆ **02/9660 1611.**

GIFTS & SOUVENIRS

The shops at **Taronga Zoo,** the **Oceanarium** in Manly, the **Sydney Aquarium,** and the **Australian Museum** are all good sources for gifts and souvenirs. Many shops around **The Rocks** are worth browsing, too.

Australian Geographic   A spinoff of the Australian version of *National Geographic* magazine, this store sells good-quality crafts and Australiana. On hand are camping gadgets, telescopes, binoculars, garden utensils, scientific oddities, books, calendars, videos, music, toys, and lots more. Harbourside Festival Marketplace, Darling Harbour. ✆ **02/ 9212 6539.** Sydney AMP Tower, Pitt St. ✆ **02/9231 5055.**

Ikonstore   This interesting little store on the pedestrian pathway to the Sydney Opera House from Circular Quay has a fascinating collection of watches and gadgets for the gourmet collector. 16, Opera Quays, East Circular Quay. ✆ 02/9252 6352.

National Trust Gift and Bookshop   You can pick up some nice souvenirs, including books, Australiana crafts, and indigenous foodstuffs here. An art gallery on the premises presents changing exhibits of paintings and sculpture by Australians. There's also a cafe. Closed Monday. Observatory Hill, The Rocks. ✆ 02/9258 0154.

The Wilderness Society Shop   Australiana is crawling out of the woodwork at this cute little crafts emporium dedicated to spending all its profits on saving the few remaining untouched forests and wilderness areas of Australia. You'll find some quality crafts items, cute children's clothes, books, cards, and knickknacks. Sydney AMP Tower, Castlereagh St. ✆ 02/9233 4674.

MARKETS

Balmain Market   Active from 8:30am to 4pm every Saturday, this market has some 140 vendors selling crafts, jewelry, and knickknacks. Take the ferry to Balmain (Darling St.); the market is a 10-minute walk up Darling Street. On the grounds of St. Andrew's Church, Darling St., Balmain ✆ 02/9555 1791.

Bondi Markets   A nice place to stroll around on Sunday after your brunch on Campbell Parade and discover the upcoming young Australian designers. This market specializes in clothing and jewelry, new, secondhand, and retro. It's open Sunday from 9am to 5pm. Bondi Beach School, Campbell Parade. ✆ 02/9398 5486.

Paddington Bazaar   At this Saturday-only market you'll find everything from essential oils and designer clothes to New Age jewelry and Mexican hammocks. Expect things to be busy from 10am to 4pm. Take bus no. 380 or 389 from Circular Quay and follow the crowds. On the grounds of St. John's Church, Oxford St., on the corner of Newcome St. ✆ 02/9331 2646.

Paddy's Markets   A Sydney institution, Paddy's Markets has hundreds of stalls selling everything from cheap clothes and plants to chickens. It's open Friday through Sunday from 9am to 4:30pm. Above Paddy's Markets is **Market City** (✆ 02/9212 1388), which has three floors of fashion stalls, food courts, and specialty shops. Of particular interest is the largest Asian-European supermarket in Australia, on level 1, and the **Kam Fook Yum Cha** Chinese restaurant on level 3, also the largest in Australia. At the corner of Thomas and Hay sts., Haymarket, near Chinatown. ✆ 1300/361 589 in Australia, or 02/9325 6924.

The Rocks Market   Held every Saturday and Sunday, this touristy market has more than 100 vendors selling everything from crafts, housewares, and posters to jewelry and curios. The main street is closed to traffic from 10am to 4pm to make it easier to stroll around. George St., The Rocks. ✆ 02/9255 1717.

MUSIC

Birdland   This is the best store in Sydney for jazz and blues, and it stocks a sizable collection of rare items. The staff is very knowledgeable. 3 Barrack St. ✆ 02/9299 8527. www.birdland.com.au.

HMV   This is one of the best music stores in Sydney. The jazz section is impressive. CDs in Australia are not cheap, with most new releases costing around A$30 to A$35 (US$24–US$28). Pitt St. Mall. ✆ 02/9221 2311.

Red Eye Records   These two shops, tucked away downstairs in a small arcade not far from Pitt Street Mall and the Strand Arcade, are directly across from one another. The larger store sells a wide range of modern CDs, and the smaller store stocks a great collection of quality secondhand and end-of-the-line CDs for around A$20 (US$16) each. Tank Stream Arcade (downstairs), at the corner of King and Pitt sts. (near Town Hall). ✆ 02/9233 8177 (new recordings), or 02/9233 8125 (secondhand CDs). www.redeye.com.au.

Sounds Australian   You can find anything you've ever heard that sounds Australian here. From rock and pop to didgeridoo and country, it's all here. And if you haven't a clue what's good and what's bad, you can spend some time listening before you buy. The management is quite knowledgeable. In the Argyle Stores department store, The Rocks. ✆ 02/9247 7290. Fax 02/9241 2873.

OPALS
There are plenty of opal shops around in Sydney, but don't expect to walk away with any bargains. Best just to choose one you like and haggle.

Altman & Cherny   A good selection of opals—black, white, and boulder varieties— as well as jewelry is on sale here. Ask to see "The Aurora Australis," the world-famous black opal valued at A$1 million (US$800,000). 19–31 Pitt St. (near Circular Quay). ✆ 02/ 9251 4717.

Australian Opal Cutters   Learn more about opals before you buy at this shop. The staff will give you lessons about opals to help you compare pieces. Suite 10, Level 4, National Building, 250 Pitt St. ✆ 02/9261 2442.

WINE
Australian Wine Centre   This is one of the best places in the country to pick up Australian wines by the bottle or the case. The shop stocks a wide range of wines from all over Australia, including bottles from small boutique wineries you're unlikely to find anywhere else. Individual tastings are possible at any time, and there are formal tastings every Thursday and Friday from 4 to 6pm. Wine is exported all over the world from here, so if you want to send home a crate of your favorite, you can be assured it will arrive in one piece. The center owns the wine bar and bistro next door, which is open Monday through Saturday from 6am until 10pm. You can drink here without dining. 1 Alfred St., Shop 3 in Goldfields House, Circular Quay. ✆ 02/9247 2755.

10 Sydney After Dark

Australians are party animals when they're in the mood; whether it's a few beers around the barbecue with friends or an all-night rave at a trendy dance club, they're always on the lookout for the next event. You'll find that alcohol plays a big part in the Aussie culture.

WHERE TO FIND OUT WHAT'S ON
The best way to find out what's on is to get hold of the "Metro" section of the Friday *Sydney Morning Herald* or the "Seven Days" pullout from the Thursday *Daily Telegraph*.

THE PERFORMING ARTS
If you have an opportunity to see a performance in the **Sydney Opera House,** jump at it. The "House" is actually not that impressive inside, but the walk back after the show toward the ferry terminals at Circular Quay, with the Sydney Harbour Bridge lit up and the crowd all around you debating the best part of this play or who dropped

---

Tips It's a Festival!

If you happen to be in Australia in January, plan to attend one of the many events that are part of the annual **Sydney Festival.** The festival kicks off just after New Year's and continues through the month, with recitals, plays, films, and performances at venues throughout the city, including Town Hall, the Royal Botanic Gardens, the Sydney Opera House, and Darling Harbour. Some events are free. "Jazz in The Domain" and "Symphony in The Domain" are two free outdoor performances held in the Royal Botanic Gardens, generally on the third and fourth weekends in January; each event attracts thousands of Sydneysiders. For more information, contact **Festival Ticketek** (✆ **02/9266 4111;** fax 02/9267 4460). Buy tickets and find out about performances on the Web at **www.sydneyfestival.org.au.**

---

a beat in that performance—well, it's like hearing Gershwin on the streets of New York. You'll want the moment to stay with you forever. For details on Sydney's most famous performing-arts venue, see "What to See & Do in Sydney," earlier in this chapter.

THE OPERA, SYMPHONY & BALLET

Australian Ballet Based in Melbourne, the Australian Ballet tours the country with its performances. The Sydney season, at the Opera House, is from mid-March until the end of April. A second Sydney season runs November through December. Level 15, 115 Pitt St. ✆ **02/9223 9522.** www.australianballet.com.au.

Australian Chamber Orchestra Based in Sydney, this well-known company performs at various venues around the city, from nightclubs to specialized music venues, including the Concert Hall in the Sydney Opera House. Opera Quays, 2 East Circular Quay. ✆ **02/9357 4111,** or 02/8274 3888 box office. www.aco.com.au.

Opera Australia Opera Australia performs at the Sydney Opera House's Opera Theatre. The opera runs January through March and June through November. 480 Elizabeth St., Surry Hills. ✆ **02/9699 1099,** or 02/9319 1088 bookings. www.opera-australia.org.au.

Sydney Symphony Orchestra The renowned Edo de Waart conducts Sydney's finest symphony orchestra. It performs throughout the year in the Opera House's Concert Hall. The main symphony season runs March through November, and there's a summer season in February. Level 5, 52 William St., East Sydney. ✆ **02/9334 4644,** or 02/9334 4600 box office. www.symphony.org.au.

THEATER

Sydney's blessed with plenty of theaters, many more than I have space for here—check the *Sydney Morning Herald,* especially the Friday edition, for information on what's currently in production.

Belvoir Street Theatre The hallowed boards of the Belvoir are home to Company B, which pumps out powerful local and international plays upstairs in a wonderfully moody main theater, formerly part of a tomato-sauce factory. Downstairs, a smaller venue generally shows more experimental productions, such as Aboriginal performances and dance. 25 Belvoir St., Surry Hills. ✆ **02/9699 3444.** Tickets around A$34 (US$27).

Capital Theatre Sydney's grandest theater plays host to major international and local productions like (cough) Australian singing superstar Kylie Minogue. It's also been the Sydney home of musicals such as *Miss Saigon* and *My Fair Lady*. 13–17 Campbell St., Haymarket, near Town Hall. ℂ **02/9320 5000**. Ticket prices vary.

Her Majesty's Theatre A quarter of a century old, this large theater is still trawling in the big musicals. Huge productions that have run here include *Evita* and *Phantom of the Opera*. 107 Quay St., Haymarket, near Central Station. ℂ **02/9212 3411**. Ticket prices average A$55–A$75 (US$44–US$60).

Wharf Theatre This wonderful theater is on a refurbished wharf on the edge of Sydney Harbour, just beyond the Harbour Bridge. The long walk from the entrance of the pier to the theater along old creaky wooden floorboards builds up excitement for the show. Based here is the Sydney Theatre Company, a group well worth seeing, whatever the production. Dinner before the show at the Wharf's restaurant offers special views of the harbor. Pier 4, Hickson Rd., The Rocks. ℂ **02/9250 1777**. www.sydneytheatre. com.au. Ticket prices vary.

THE CLUB & MUSIC SCENE
JAZZ, FOLK & BLUES

The Basement ☆ Australia's hottest jazz club also manages to squeeze in plenty of blues, folk, and funk. Acts appear every night, and it's best to book ahead. Call for the schedule, pick up one at the club, or visit the website. 29 Reiby Place, Circular Quay. ℂ **02/ 9251 2797**. www.thebasement.com.au/club_info.htm. Cover A$15–A$20 (US$12–US$16) for local acts, A$20–A$40 (US$16–US$32) for international performers.

side-on café Known by locals as one of the few live venues in Sydney to showcase deliciously diverse jazz nearly every night of the week, this surprisingly decent restaurant is part of an arts complex and serves a two-course meal for A$27 (US$22). Patrons are a blend of artists, musicians, and jazz lovers. The side-on endeavors to promote upcoming local talent as well as established acts, and is also home to an art gallery upstairs. Located just over 5km (3 miles) from the center of town, it's not all that central but is easily reached by public transport and well worth the detour. Daily 7pm until late. 83 Paramatta Rd., Anandale, near Anandale Hotel. www.side-on.com.au. Cover A$13 (US$10).

ROCK

Metro A medium-size rock venue with space for 1,000, the Metro is the best place in Sydney to see local and international acts. Tickets sell out quickly. 624 George St. ℂ **02/9264 2666**.

DANCE CLUBS

Clubs come and go, and change names and music, so check the latest with a phone call. You can also check the "Metro" section in the Friday *Sydney Morning Herald;* free giveaway newspapers available in some bars along Oxford Street have info about the latest clubs.

Nightclub entrance charges change regularly, but generally are A$10 to A$15 (US$8–US$12). The Bourbon & Beefsteak Bar, with its A$5 (US$4) cover charge, is an oddity.

Bourbon & Beefsteak Bar Right in the middle of Sydney's red-light district, this 24-hour restaurant and nightspot has a small dance floor. Bands play on the ground level Friday and Saturday nights. It's popular with a whole range of ages, from 18 to 60. 24 Darlinghurst Rd., Kings Cross. ℂ **02/9358 1144**. Cover A$5 (US$4).

Chinese Laundry A couple of dance floors, one with rock walls to enhance the beat of the hip-hop, trance, and dance. What to wear? Dress like you want to *un*-impress. Open Friday and Saturday from 11pm to 4am. Below the Slip Inn bar (see "The Bar Scene," below), Sussex St. (turn right as you face the bridge from Cockle Bay across to Darling Harbour, and it's a 2-min. walk). ℭ **02/9299 4777.**

Home Cavelike in shape and feel, with a balcony to look down upon the throng, Home has a reputation for bad bouncers—the *Sydney Morning Herald* newspaper had a Christmas party here, and even the influential journalists were abused. Still, it's managed to survive—hope you can. DJs spin funk and heavy drum-and-bass-style music, good for the serious clubber. Cockle Bay Wharf, Darling Harbour. ℭ **02/9266 0600.** Cover A$25 (US$20).

Mister Goodbar A young, trendy crowd of locals fills Mister Goodbar's two good-size dance floors, where they can groove to a range of rap, funk, and hip-hop music Wednesday through Saturday. 11a Oxford St., Paddington. ℭ **02/9360 6759.**

Tantra "Upmarket nightclubbing for the likes of models and beautiful people from the [affluent] North Shore of Sydney," is how the manager describes this place. The interior is pseudo-Roman with lots of pillars. The club offers hard-core club and dance music: "'70s Boogie Wonderland" night Friday, commercial house music Saturday, and "funky" house music Sunday. Dress code is fashionable, with a shirt collar required for men, and no sneakers. 169 Oxford St., Darlinghurst. ℭ **02/9331 7729.**

GAY & LESBIAN CLUBS

Sydney has a huge gay community, so there's a very happening scene. The center of it all is Oxford Street, though Newtown has established itself as a major gay hangout, too. For information on events, pick up a copy of the *Sydney Star Observer* or *Lesbians on the Loose,* available at art-house cinemas, cafes, and stores around Oxford Street. Nightclub entrance charges generally range from A$10 to A$15 (US$8–US$12).

Arq This 24-hour club has an amazing light show and the best DJs in town. A very big place specializing in the latest dance tunes. Daily 24 hours. 16 Flinders St., Darlinghurst. ℭ **02/9380 8700.**

Civic This original Art Deco hotel has been tastefully spruced up to accommodate three levels of entertainment. There's a theater on the lower first floor (basement), a

---

Tips **Sydney Gay & Lesbian Mardi Gras**

Each March Sydney lights up to the biggest carnival this side of Rio. Some 450,000 people pack into the city center, concentrated on Oxford Street to watch as members of Sydney's GLBT communities pack a punch with colorful floats and frocks. The crowd is diverse, from kids to grannies, and those in the know bring a stepladder or milk crate to get a better view. Sydney's hotels are at their busiest during Mardi Gras, particularly anything with a view of the route. The postparade party is an affair not for the faint-hearted! Sequins, tight pants, and anything outrageously glamorous goes. Some 19,000 revelers attend. For more information check out the official Mardi Gras website: www.mardigras.org.au.

saloon bar on the ground floor, and an Australian restaurant with live jazz upstairs, as well as an outdoor cocktail terrace. Great bands. Corner of Pitt and Goulburn sts., Sydney ℂ 02/8267 3181.

Gilligan's & Ginger's A cocktail bar on the first floor of the Oxford Hotel, Gilligan's & Ginger's is home to a thriving social scene and great views of Oxford Street and the city skyline. DJs spin the latest handbag hits for the drag queens. 134 Oxford St., Darlinghurst, corner of Taylor Sq. ℂ 02/9331 3467.

The Stonewall Hotel An institution with three levels of entertainment and many special nights. Don't miss Sydney's Diva, Ricca Paris, at the pickup night Malebox on Wednesdays. Daily noon to 5am. 175 Oxford St., Darlinghurst. ℂ 02/9360 1963. Free entry most nights.

Taxi Club "Tacky Club," as it's affectionately known, is a Sydney institution good for "handbag music"—or old pop and new pop. 40 Flinders St., Darlinghurst (near Taylor Sq., Oxford St.). ℂ 02/9331 4256.

THE BAR SCENE

Most of Australia's drinking holes are known as "hotels," after the tradition of providing room and board alongside a good drink in the old days. Occasionally you might hear them referred to as pubs. The term *bar* tends to apply in upscale hotels and trendy establishments. Bars close at various times, generally from midnight to around 3am. Unless the listing says otherwise, these bars do not charge a cover.

Bondi Hotel This huge conglomerate across the road from Bondi Beach offers pool upstairs, a casual beer garden outside, and a resident DJ Thursday through Sunday from 8pm to 4am. There's also a free nightclub on Friday nights. Watch yourself; too much drink and sun turns some people nasty here. 178 Campbell Parade, Bondi Beach. ℂ 02/9130 3271.

Cargo Bar & Lounge This split-level waterfront bar on the city side of Darling Harbour (past the Sydney Aquarium) has a large ground-floor bar with access to an outdoor beer garden. The lounge upstairs features trendy leather and red footstools (apparently you sit on them). Cocktails and cigars are upstairs and more casual beers downstairs. Some nice pizzas here, too—if you like them topped with emu, crocodile, or kangaroo. 52–60 The Promenade, King St. Wharf. ℂ 02/9262 1777.

The Establishment A trendy night out is in store if you set foot in this restored historic building with its 42m (138-ft.) bar, lots of floor-to-ceiling columns, and pressed-metal ceilings. It's fashionable, and the food downstairs—fish and chips and the like—is nice but unadventurous. There's better eating upstairs in the fine-dining restaurant. 252 George St., City. ℂ 02/9240 3000.

The Friend in Hand In the same location as the fantastically cheap Caesar's No Names spaghetti house, The Friend in Hand offers cheap drinks, poetry readings on Tuesday at 8:30pm, a trivia night on Thursday at 8:30pm, and the distinctly unusual Crab Racing Party every Wednesday at around 8pm. Crab fanciers buy a crustacean for around A$4 (US$3.20), give it a name, and send it off to do battle in a race against about 30 others. There are heats and finals, and victorious crustaceans win their owners prizes. 58 Cowper St., Glebe. ℂ 02/9660 2326.

Henry the Ninth Bar This mock-Tudor drinking hole gets very busy on Friday and Saturday nights. It serves some good ales in an oaky atmosphere. An Irish band whips up the patrons on Thursday and Friday nights, and a cover band does the same on Wednesday and Saturday nights. A good-value happy hour brings beer prices tumbling Monday through Thursday from 5:30 to 7:30pm, Friday 5:30 to 8:30pm, and Saturday 8 to 10pm. In the Sydney Hilton, 259 Pitt St. ℭ **02/9266 2000.**

Hero of Waterloo Hotel ★   This sandstone landmark, built in 1845, was once reputedly the stalking ground of press gangs, who'd whack unsuspecting landlubbers on the head, push them down a trapdoor, and cart them out to sea. Today, the strangely shaped drinking hole is popular with the locals. It schedules old-time jazz bands (the musicians are often in their 70s and 80s) on Saturday and Sunday from 1:30 to 6:30pm, and Irish and cover bands Friday to Sunday at 8:30pm. 81 Lower Fort St., The Rocks. ℭ **02/9252 4553.**

Jacksons on George   A popular drinking spot, this place has four floors of drinking, eating, dancing, and pool playing, and is a popular haunt of tourists and after-work office staff. Pool is expensive here at A$3 (US$2.40) a game (you'll need to ask the rules—Australians have their own), and drinks have a nasty habit of going up in price without warning as the evening wears on. The nightclub plays dance music, and there's a smart-casual dress code. During happy hour (Mon–Fri 5–7pm), drinks cost around one-third less than normal. 178 George St., The Rocks. ℭ **02/9247 2727.** Cover A$10 (US$8) for nightclub Fri–Sat after 10pm.

Lord Dudley Hotel   This great English-style pub has the best atmosphere of just about any drinking hole in Sydney, with log fires in winter, couches to relax on, three bars, and a restaurant. The best way to get to this is from the Edgecliff CityRail station (between Kings Cross and Bondi Junction). From there, bear right along the edge of the bus station, walk up the hill for 5 minutes, then take a right onto Jersey Road—ask the railway staff for the correct exit if you can find anyone working. 236 Jersey Rd., Woollahra. ℭ **02/9327 5399.**

Lord Nelson Hotel ★ *(Value)*   A Sydney sandstone landmark, the Lord Nelson rivals the Hero of Waterloo (above) for the title of Sydney's oldest pub. The drinks are sold English-style, in pints and half-pints, and the landlord even makes his own prize-winning beers. Of those, Three Sheets is the most popular—but if you can't handle falling over on your way home, you might want to try a drop of Quail (a pale beer), Victory (based on an English bitter), and a dark beer called Admiral. You can get some good pub grub here, too. Upstairs there's a more formal brasserie. Kent and Argyle sts., The Rocks. ℭ **02/9251 4044.**

Marble Bar   Once part of a hotel demolished in the 1970s, the Marble Bar is unique: the only grand cafe–style drinking hole in Australia. With oil paintings, marble columns, and brass everywhere, it's the picture of 15th-century Italian Renaissance architecture, a tourist attraction in itself. Live music, generally jazz or soul, plays here Tuesday through Saturday beginning at 8:30pm. Dress smart on Friday and Saturday evenings. Drinks are normally very expensive, but the happy hour (daily 7–9pm) cuts prices down to what you'd pay during normal drinking hours elsewhere. In the Sydney Hilton, 259 Pitt St. ℭ **02/9266 2000.**

The Mercantile   Sydney's original Irish bar is scruffy and loud when the Irish music's playing in the evening, but it's an essential stop on any pub-crawl in The Rocks. The Guinness is some of the best you'll taste in Sydney. Irish bands kick off every night around 8pm. 25 George St., The Rocks. ℭ **02/9247 3570.**

Slip Inn This multifunction bar and bistro setup is a popular place to drink and meet. There's a garden bar downstairs in a courtyard, along with a trattoria selling pizzas. Upstairs there's a Thai bistro that's open for lunch, and a large square bar. It's crowded on Friday evenings, but you'll never feel like a sardine. Sussex St., Darling Harbour. ℭ 02/9299 4777. A 2-min. walk toward the city from the Town Hall/Cockle Bay side of the pedestrian bridge across to Darling Harbour.

Watsons Bay Hotel ★★ *Finds* If it's a sunny afternoon, get over to Watsons Bay for the best food you'll find in the sun anywhere. The beer garden serves good seafood and barbecue meat dishes, while you sip your expensive wine or beer overlooking the harbor. Nearby are the fabulous Doyles Wharf Restaurant and Doyles at the Beach takeout. 1 Military Rd., Watsons Bay. ℭ 02/9337 4299.

MOVIES

The city's major movie houses, **Hoyts** (ℭ 13 27 00 in Australia), **Greater Union** (ℭ 02/9267 8666), and **Village** (ℭ 02/9264 6701), are right next to each other on George Street just past Town Hall. They tend to show big-budget movie releases. Other options are the **Dendy Cinemas,** 19 Martin Place (ℭ 02/9233 8166); 261–263 King St., Newtown (ℭ 02/9550 5699); and 2 East Circular Quay, just before you reach the Opera House (ℭ 02/9247 3800). All show art-house movies; the Dendy Quay allows wine and beer bought on the premises to be consumed in the cinema. In Paddington, the **Verona,** 17 Oxford St. (ℭ 02/9360 6099), and the **Academy Twin,** 2 Oxford St. (ℭ 02/9361 4455), conveniently located next to each other, always screen the best local and foreign films in Sydney.

Another exceptional art house and recent-blockbuster cinema is the **Hayden Orpheum Picture Palace,** 380 Military Rd., Cremorne (ℭ 02/9908 4344). This eight-screen Art Deco gem is an experience in itself, especially on Saturday and Sunday evenings when a Wurlitzer pops up from the center of the Cinema 2 stage, and a musician in a tux gives a stirring rendition of times gone by. Eat "Jaffas," round candy-coated chocolates, if you want to fit in.

Movie prices hover around A$15 (US$12), with half-price night generally on Tuesday.

THE CASINO

Star City This huge entertainment complex has 15 main bars, 12 restaurants, 2 theaters—the Showroom, which presents Las Vegas–style revues, and the Lyric, Sydney's largest theater—as well as a huge complex of retail shops. All the usual gambling tables are here, in four main gambling areas. In all, there are 2,500 slot machines to gobble your change. You must be over 18 to gamble. Open 24 hours. 80 Pyrmont St., Pyrmont (adjacent to Darling Harbour). ℭ 02/9777 9000. Ferry: Pyrmont (Darling Harbour). Monorail: Casino.

5

New South Wales

by Marc Llewellyn

With so much to experience in a state as big as New South Wales, you're not going to see all the major attractions in one hit, so you must prioritize. If you have just a few days to spare, you should certainly head out to the Blue Mountains, part of the Great Dividing Range that separates the lush eastern coastal strip from the more arid interior. Although these mountains are more like hills, they are spectacular, with tall eucalyptus trees, deep river valleys, waterfalls, and craggy cliffs. Or spend a day in the vineyards of the lower Hunter (also known as the Hunter Valley). If you have a few more days, I recommend heading to Barrington Tops National Park, north of the Hunter, for the rainforest and native animals, or down to the pristine beaches of Jervis Bay for gorgeous scenery and great bushwalks.

For longer trips, you can head north toward the Queensland border on the 964km (598-mile) route to Brisbane. You'll pass pretty seaside towns, deserted beaches, and tropical hinterland. Another option is to travel along the south coast 1,032km (640 miles) to Melbourne. Along the way are some of the country's most spectacular beaches, quaint hamlets, opportunities to spot dolphins and whales, and extensive national parks. If you want to experience the Outback, then head west across the Blue Mountains. You are sure to see plenty of kangaroos, emus, reptiles, and giant wedge-tailed eagles. The main Outback destination is the extraordinary opal-mining town of Lightning Ridge, where you can meet some of the most eccentric fair-dinkum (that means "authentic" or "genuine") Aussies you'll come across anywhere.

EXPLORING THE STATE

VISITOR INFORMATION The **Sydney Visitors Centre,** 106 George St., The Rocks (✆ **13 20 77** in Australia; www.tourism.nsw.gov.au), will give you general information on what to do and where to stay throughout the state. **Tourism New South Wales** (✆ **02/9931 1111**) will direct you to the regional tourist office in the town or area you are interested in.

GETTING AROUND **By Car** From Sydney, the **Pacific Highway** heads along the north coast into Queensland, and the **Princes Highway** hugs the south coast and runs into Victoria. The **Sydney-Newcastle Freeway** connects Sydney with its industrial neighbor and the vineyards of the Hunter. The **Great Western Highway** and the **M4 motorway** head west to the Blue Mountains. The **M5 motorway, Hume Highway,** is the quickest way to get to Melbourne (via Canberra).

The state's automobile association, the **National Roads and Motorists' Association (NRMA),** 151 Clarence St., Sydney (✆ **13 11 22** in Australia), offers free maps

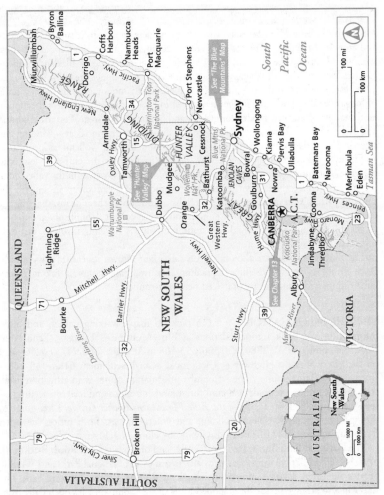

and touring guides to members of overseas motoring associations, including AAA in the United States, CAA in Canada, AA and RAC in the United Kingdom, and NZAA in New Zealand.

By Train Countrylink (© **13 22 32** in Australia) trains travel to most places of interest in the state and as far south as Melbourne in Victoria and across the border into southern Queensland. Countrylink also has special rates for car rental through Thrifty.

By Plane Qantas (© **13 13 13** in Australia) and **Eastern Australia Airlines** (book through Qantas) fly to most major cities and towns in the state.

1 The Blue Mountains ★★

Although the **Blue Mountains** are where Sydneysiders go now to escape the humidity and crowds of the city, in the early days of the colony, the mountains kept at bay those who would explore the interior. In 1813, three explorers—Gregory Blaxland, William Charles Wentworth, and William Lawson—managed to conquer the cliffs, valleys, and dense forest, and cross the mountains (which are hardly mountains, but rather a series of hills covered in bush and ancient fern trees) to the plains beyond. There they found land the colony urgently needed for grazing and farming. The **Great Western Highway** and **Bells Line of Road** are the access roads through the region today—winding and steep in places, they are surrounded by the Blue Mountains and Wollemi national parks.

The area is known for its spectacular scenery, particularly the cliff-top views into the valleys of gum trees and across to craggy outcrops that tower from the valley floor. It's colder up here than down on the plains, and clouds can sweep in and fill the canyons with mist in minutes, while waterfalls cascade down sheer drops, spraying the dripping fern trees that cling to the gullies. You'll need at least a couple of days up here to get the best out of it—a single-day tour, with all the traveling involved, can only just scratch the surface.

The Blue Mountains are also one of Australia's best-known adventure playgrounds. Rock climbing, caving, abseiling (rappelling), bushwalking, mountain biking, horse-back riding, and canoeing are practiced here year-round.

BLUE MOUNTAIN ESSENTIALS

VISITOR INFORMATION   You can pick up maps, walking guides, and other information and book accommodations at **Blue Mountains Tourism,** Echo Point Road, Katoomba, NSW 2780 (© **1300/653 408** in Australia, or 02/4739 6266); and on the Great Western Highway at Glenbrook, a small settlement 61km (38 miles) from Sydney (same phone). The Katoomba information center is an attraction itself, with glass windows overlooking a gum forest, and cockatoos and lorikeets feeding on seed dispensers. Pick up a copy of the *Blue Mountains Pocket Guide,* a free guide to dining, accommodations, bushwalking, and entertainment. Both offices are open from 9am to 5pm daily (the office at Glenbrook closes at 4:30pm Sat–Sun).

The **National Park Shop,** Heritage Centre, end of Govetts Leap Road, Blackheath (© **02/4787 8877;** www.npws.nsw.gov.au), is run by the National Parks and Wildlife Service and offers detailed information about the Blue Mountains National Park. The staff can also arrange personalized guided tours of the mountains. It's open daily from 9am to 4:30pm (closed Dec 25).

Check the website, www.bluemts.com.au, for more information on the area.

GUIDED TOURS FROM SYDNEY   Many private bus operators offer day trips from Sydney, but it's important to shop around. Some offer a guided coach tour during which you just stretch your legs occasionally, while others let you get your circulation

---

Fun Fact **Color Me Blue**

The Blue Mountains derive their name from the ever-present blue haze that is caused by light striking the droplets of eucalyptus oil that evaporate from the leaves of the dense surrounding forest.

going with a couple of longish bushwalks. One highly recommended operator is **Oz Trek Adventure Tours** (© 02/9360 3444; www.oztrek.com.au). Its trips include a tour of the Olympic site, a visit to Glenbrook National Park (where you'll see kangaroos and wallabies in the wild), tours of all the major Blue Mountain sites, and a 1½-hour bush-walk. It costs A$54 (US$43) for adults and A$43 (US$34) for kids. You can add overnight packages, horseback riding, and abseiling.

Sydney Tours-R-Us (© 02/9498 4084; sydneytoursrus@yahoo.com.au) runs minicoaches to the Blue Mountains, stopping off at the Telstra Stadium (where the Sydney Olympics were held) and Featherdale Wildlife Park. Then you see all the major sights in the mountains and get to sing Aussie folk music on the way back home. Brochures are all over town. The trip costs A$79 (US$63).

Visitours (© 02/9909 0822; www.visitours.com.au) runs a fabulous minibus trip to the mountains, also stopping at Featherdale Wildlife Park and the Olympic site. You get to see all the usual 1-day sights, learn to throw a boomerang and play the didgeridoo, and take a ferry ride down the Parramatta River back to Circular Quay in Sydney. The trip costs A$82 (US$66) with lunch.

Wonderbus (© 1800/669 800 in Australia, 1300/556 357, or 02/9555 9800; www.wonderbus.com.au) offers tours that run to the Blue Mountains and also to Jenolan Caves. Trips start at A$155 (US$124) including all entry fees and lunch.

Tips   Timing Is Everything: When to Visit

If you can, try to visit the Blue Mountains on **weekdays,** when most Syd-neysiders are at work and prices are lower. Note that the colder winter months (June–Aug) are the busiest season. This period is known as **Yuletide**—the locals' version of the Christmas period, when most places offer traditional Christmas dinners and roaring log fires.

Grayline (**1300/858 687** in Australia; www.grayline.com) offers several Blue Mountains trips in large coaches from A$100 (US$80). A combined Blue Moun-tains/Jenolan Caves trip costs A$123 (US$98) for adults and A$62 (US$49) for kids. If you hate big-group travel, choose another option.

BUSHWALKING & OTHER ACTIVE ENDEAVORS

Almost every other activity costs money, but bushwalking (hiking) is the exception to the rule that nothing in life is free. There are some 50 walking trails in the Blue Moun-tains, ranging from routes you can cover in 15 minutes to the 3-day **Six Foot Track** ✦ that starts outside Katoomba and finishes at Jenolan Caves. If you are planning on some bushwalking, I highly recommend picking up *Sydney and Beyond—Eighty-Six Walks in NSW* by Andrew Mevissen (Macstyle Publishing). It features eight walks in the Blue Mountains, from easy 1-hour treks to 6-hour tramps. Buy it at bookshops and tourist information centers. The staff at the tourist offices and national park office will be happy to point you in the right direction, whether it be for an hour's stroll or a full day's hike.

Great Australian Walks, 81 Elliot St., Balmain, NSW 2041 (© **1300/360 499** in Australia, or 02/9555 7580; www.greatwalks.com.au), is a superb operator offering walks in the Blue Mountains. I had great fun on their 3-day "Six Foot Track Walk" from Katoomba to Jenolan Caves. Though not a wilderness trek, it goes through pockets of rainforest and gum forests and traverses farming country.

One of the best adventure operators in the area, **High 'n' Wild,** 3/5 Katoomba St., Katoomba, NSW 2780 (© **02/4782 6224;** www.high-n-wild.com.au), offers a series of canyoning expeditions, taking in scenic rainforest gullies and caverns made up of dramatic rock formations and fern-lined walls. There's a bit of swimming and plenty of walking, wading, and squeezing through tight spaces involved—and sometimes rappelling (called "abseiling" in Australia)—but fortunately, being double-jointed is not a prerequisite.

If you really want to test your head for heights, try High 'n' Wild's 150m (492-ft.) "Mega Jump"—the highest continuous rappel in the Southern Hemisphere. This heart-pumping descent down a sheer cliff is suitable for the fearless beginner, but the staff assures me you soon settle in by learning the ropes on the 10-story-high junior slopes beforehand.

If that's too much to handle, you could always try a day on an inflatable raft between huge towering rock walls on the Wollangambe River. There are a few minor rapids to navigate, and the bushwalk down to the river and back up again can be a lit-tle testing, but it's certainly suitable for a family outing. Prices start at A$69 (US$55) for rappelling and A$85 (US$68) for canyoning. Raft adventures cost A$169 (US$135).

Other excellent adventure operators are the **Blue Mountains Adventure Company,** 84a Bathurst Rd. (P.O. Box 242), Katoomba, NSW 2780 (© **02/4782 1271;** bmac@bmac.com.au), located above the Summit Gear Shop; and the **Australian School of Mountaineering,** 166 Katoomba St., Katoomba, NSW 2780 (© **02/4782 2014**). Both offer rock climbing, rappelling, and canyoning trips. The Adventure Company also offers caving and mountain biking, and the School of Mountaineering offers bushcraft and survival training. Expect to pay around A$100 (US$80) for a day-long introductory rock-climbing course, including rappelling, and A$99 to A$125 (US$79–US$100) for a day's canyoning.

If you feel like some adventure on your own, you can rent a mountain bike from **Cycletech,** 182 Katoomba St., Katoomba (© **02/4782 2800**). Standard mountain bikes cost A$19 (US$15) for a half-day and A$28 (US$22) for a full day; superior front-suspension mountain bikes cost A$28 (US$22) for a half-day and A$50 (US$40) for a full day.

KATOOMBA: GATEWAY TO THE BLUE MOUNTAINS
114km (71 miles) W of Sydney

Katoomba (pop. 11,200) is the largest town in the Blue Mountains and the focal point of the Blue Mountains National Park. It's an easy 1½- to 2-hour trip from Sydney by train, bus, or car. The town is a low-socioeconomic pocket in a very affluent region, with one of the highest unemployment rates in the state.

GETTING THERE   By car from central Sydney, travel along Parramatta Road and turn off onto the M4 motorway (around 2 hr. to Katoomba). Another route is via the Harbour Bridge to North Sydney, along the Warringah Freeway (following signs to the M2). Then take the M2 to the end and follow signs to the M4 and the Blue Mountains. This takes around 1½ hours.

Frequent rail service connects Sydney to Katoomba from Central Station; contact **CityRail** (© **13 15 00**) or **Countrylink** (© **13 22 32**) for details. The train trip takes 2 hours. Trains leave almost hourly from platform nos. 12 and 13, stopping at Katoomba, and then at Mount Victoria and Lithgow. An adult same-day round-trip ticket costs around A$12 (US$10) off-peak, and A$20 (US$16) during commuter hours. A child's ticket costs A$3 (US$2.40).

GETTING AROUND   The best way to get around the Blue Mountains without your own transport is the **Blue Mountains Explorer Bus** (© **02/4782 4807;** www.explorerbus.com.au). The double-decker bus leaves from outside Katoomba train station every hour from 9:30am until 4:30pm and stops at 27 attractions, resorts, galleries, and tearooms in and around Katoomba and Leura. You can get on and off as often as you want. Tickets cost A$25 (US$20) for adults, A$13 (US$10) for children, and A$63 (US$50) for a family; prices include discounts on the Scenic Railway and the Skyway (see "Exploring the Area," below), and at some other attractions and restaurants. You can also link this tour bus with the CityRail train from Sydney. The **Blue Mountains Explorer Link Ticket,** available from CityRail stations, includes round-trip train fare and Explorer Bus tickets and costs A$39 (US$31) for adults, A$15 (US$12) for children, and A$62 (US$50) for a family.

Another option is **Trolley Tours** (© **1800/801 577** in Australia; www.trolley tours.com.au), which is a kind of tram on wheels with commentary. An all-day pass costs A$12 (US$10) and includes stops at various attractions around Katoomba and

Leura, too. The trolley leaves Katoomba Station each hour, connecting with the trains from Sydney.

Fantastic Aussie Tours (© 02/4782 1866; www.fantastic-aussie-tours.com.au) is based in the Blue Mountains and runs excursions in the area, These include guided walks from A$39 to A$85 (US$31–US$68); a Rocks and Rainforest tour by four-wheel-drive, costing A$92 (US$74) for adults and A$46 (US$37) for kids; and a basic Blue Mountains tour combined with a trip to Jenolan caves (with entry to one cave). See the Jenolan caves section below.

EXPLORING THE AREA

The most visited and photographed attractions in the Blue Mountains are the rock formations known as the **Three Sisters** ★★. For the best vantage point, head to **Echo Point Road,** across from the Blue Mountains Tourism office. Or try Evans Lookout, Govetts Leap, and Hargreaves Lookout, all at Blackheath (see "Blackheath," later in this chapter)—none of which is on the Blue Mountains Explorer Bus or Trolley Tours route.

One thing you have to do in the Blue Mountains is ride the **Scenic Railway,** the world's steepest—follow the road signs to Scenic World. It consists of a carriage on rails that is lowered 415m (1,361 ft.) into the Jamison Valley at a maximum incline of 52 degrees. It's *very* steep and quite a thrill. Originally the rail line was used to transport coal and shale from the mines below in the 1880s. The trip takes only a few minutes; at the bottom are some excellent walks through forests of ancient tree ferns. Another popular attraction is the **Skyway,** a cable car that travels 300m (984 ft.) above the Jamison Valley. The round-trip takes 6 minutes. The Scenic Railway and the Skyway (© 02/4782 2699) each cost A$14 (US$11) round-trip for adults, A$7 (US$5.60) for children, and A$35 (US$28) for a family. They operate from 9am to 5pm daily (last trip at 4:50pm). They depart from the ticket office at 1 Violet St., Katoomba (follow the signs). I'd advise taking the Scenic Railway down, going for a walk, and taking the cable car back up.

Canyons, waterfalls, underground rivers—the Blue Mountains has them all, and before you experience them in person you can catch them on the (giant) screen at the **MAXVISION Cinema,** 225–237 Great Western Hwy., Katoomba (© 02/4782 8900). The special effects shown on the screen, 18m (59 ft.) high and 24m (79 ft.) wide, make you feel like you're part of the action. At the time of writing, the 38-minute film *The Edge* was being shown every day at 10:20am, 11:05am, 12:10pm, 1:30pm, 2:13pm, and 5:30pm. It would be worth ringing ahead as these times seem to change from time to time. Tickets cost A$13 (US$10) for adults, A$11 (US$8.80) for students, and A$7.50 (US$6) for children. The cinema is a 5- to 10-minute walk from the train station. Recently released movies play part of the giant screen in the evening. There are a restaurant and a snack bar on the premises.

Tips **Seeing the Blue Mountains from the Back of a Harley**

A thrilling way to see the Blue Mountains is on the back of a chauffeur-driven Harley-Davidson. **Blue Thunder Bike Tours** (© 1800/800 184 in NSW, or mobile 0408 618 982; www.bluethunder.com.au) leaves from Manly Wharf in Sydney (but will pick you up anywhere in the city). Rides cost A$345 (US$276) for a full day with lunch to the Blue Mountains. The company offers lots of cheaper Sydney rides.

To get back to Sydney, I highly recommend taking the Bells Line of Road through Bilpin. This route takes up to 3 hours, but you can stop off at the wonderful **Mount Tomah Botanic Gardens** ☆. (You can't miss the large sign on your right about 10 min. before you get to Bilpin.) An adjunct of the Royal Botanic Gardens in Sydney, Mount Tomah is dedicated to cold-climate plants. It's compact and has a very good cafe serving lunch daily. Allow around 2 hours for a stop here.

WHERE TO STAY
Very Expensive
Echoes Hotel & Restaurant, Blue Mountains ☆ *Finds*   Lilianfels (see below) might be more expensive, but Echoes, just across the road on a cliff overlooking the Jamison Valley, has superior views. Large windows, balconies, and a sizeable deck allow guests to soak up the fantastic scenery. Rooms are simply furnished and smaller than those at Lilianfels; all have underfloor heating and are recommended if you're cashed up.

3 Lilianfels Ave., Katoomba, NSW 2780. 𝒞 02/4782 1966. Fax 02/4782 3707. www.echoeshotel.com.au. 12 units. A$833 (US$666) 2-night weekend double, including breakfast; A$950 (US$760) 2-night weekend suite; A$335 (US$268) weekday double, A$385 (US$308) weekday suite. Packages are available. AE, DC, MC, V. Free parking. **Amenities:** Restaurant; bar; Jacuzzi; sauna; nonsmoking rooms. *In room:* A/C, TV, minibar, coffeemaker, hair dryer, iron/ironing board.

Lilianfels Blue Mountains ☆☆   Set just over a road from Echo Point, this Victorian country-house hotel—a member of the Small Luxury Hotels of the World—is a full-service yet cozy establishment. Rooms are spacious, expensive, and furnished with antiques. Most have king-size beds. Those with views are more expensive. The living areas are just as grand, with roaring log fires and more antiques. Views are impressive, especially from the lounge, which overlooks the Jamison Valley. On the grounds is an 1889 cottage. Meant for two, it has a sitting room, a bedroom with a four-poster bed, a Jacuzzi, an intimate fireplace, and its own gardens. Among the other offerings at Lilianfels are a billiards room, a library and reading room, and a lawn for French boules.

Lilianfels Ave., Katoomba, NSW 2780. 𝒞 1800/024 452 in Australia, or 02/4780 1200. Fax 02/4780 1300. www.slh. com. 85 units, 1 cottage. A$530–A$630 (US$448–US$504) double; A$635–A$870 (US$508–US$696) suite. Extra person A$55 (US$44). Ask about off-season packages. AE, DC, MC, V. Free parking. **Amenities:** 2 restaurants; small indoor pool; health club w/flotation tank; exercise room; Jacuzzi; sauna; bike rental; tour desk; secretarial services; 24-hr. room service; massage; laundry service; dry cleaning; nonsmoking rooms. *In room:* A/C, TV, minibar, coffeemaker, hair dryer, iron/ironing board.

Moderate
The Carrington Hotel ☆☆ *Finds*   Construction started on this grand Victorian hotel in 1880, and it reopened in 2000 after a major renovation. A ramshackle structure, The Carrington is a must-stay if you're into buildings of the British Raj style. Downstairs are a restaurant and breakfast room (once a ballroom), a couple of lounges with antiques, and a gorgeous wood-paneled billiard room. Chandeliers and 1930s-style lamps reflecting off silver trophies won by the local Rifle Club give everything a warm glow. Unfortunately, heavy Plexiglas doors greet you as you enter each of the many corridors—a necessary fire precaution. All the rooms are delightful, with royal gold and blue carpets and drapes that would probably be gaudy if they didn't fit in with the overall style. Traditional rooms share bathrooms; colonial rooms come with a deep tub in the bathroom (with a noisy fan) and no view to speak of; deluxe colonial rooms have a balcony and mountain views; premier rooms have Jacuzzis and great views; and the suites are fit for a duke and duchess. Dinner here costs A$100 (US$80) per person, and the breakfast is one of the best I've encountered.

15–47 Katoomba St. (P.O. Box 28), Katoomba, NSW 2780. ✆ **02/4782 1111.** Fax 02/4782 1421. www.thecarrington. com.au. 63 units. Traditional double A$119 (US$95) Sun–Thurs, A$139 (US$111) Fri–Sat; colonial double A$170 (US$136) Sun–Thurs, A$190 (US$152) Fri–Sat; deluxe colonial double A$205 (US$164) Sun–Thurs, A$225 (US$180) Fri–Sat; premier double (no view) A$205 (US$164) Sun–Thurs, A$225 (US$180) Fri–Sat; premier double (with view) A$245 (US$196) Sun–Thurs, A$265 (US$212) Fri–Sat; suite A$315–A$445 (US$252–US$356) Sun–Thurs, A$335–A$465 (US$268–US$372) Fri–Sat. Ask about weekend packages. Rates include full breakfast. AE, DC, MC, V. **Amenities:** Restaurant; bar. *In room:* TV, coffeemaker, iron/ironing board.

Echo Point Holiday Villas ★ These are the closest self-contained accommoda-
tions to the Three Sisters Lookout. The two front-facing villas are the best because of their beautiful mountain views. Some villas have one double and two single beds, plus a foldout double bed in the lounge room. There are barbecue facilities in the backyard. The two cottages are also fully self-contained, sleeping up to eight, and have a tub, central heating, and access to nice gardens.

36 Echo Point Rd., Katoomba, NSW 2780. ✆ **02/4782 3275.** Fax 02/4782 7030. www.echopointvillas.com.au. 5 villas (all with shower only), 2 cottages. Villa A$140 (US$112) Fri–Sat and public holidays, A$110 (US$88) Sun–Thurs; A$160 (US$128) cottage for 2. Cottage 2-night minimum. Extra person A$12 (US$10). AE, DC, MC, V. *In room:* TV, kitchen, fridge, hair dryer, iron/ironing board.

Inexpensive

Katoomba Mountain Lodge This AAA-rated two-star property is quite cozy,
with rooms looking out across the mountains. Doubles are basic and lack a TV, but are adequate for a couple of nights. All share bathrooms. On the premises you'll find a TV lounge with a log fire, a BYO dining room, and a game room. The staff can arrange tour packages.

31 Lurline St., Katoomba, NSW 2780. ✆/fax **02/4782 3933.** www.bluemts.com.au/kmtlodge. 23 units, none with bathroom. A$58 (US$46) double Sun–Thurs, A$78 (US$62) double Fri–Sat (2-night minimum). Ask about packages. AE, DC, MC, V. **Amenities:** Game room; tour desk; coin-op laundry. *In room:* No phone.

WHERE TO DINE

Katoomba Street has many ethnic dining choices, whether you're hungry for Greek, Chinese, or Thai. Restaurants in the Blue Mountains are generally more expensive than equivalent places in Sydney.

Expensive

Lindsay's ★★ INTERNATIONAL Swiss chef Beat Ettlin has been making waves in
Katoomba ever since he left some of the best European restaurants behind to try his hand at dishes such as pan-fried crocodile nibbles on pumpkin scones with ginger dipping sauce. The food in this upscale, New York–style speakeasy is as glorious as its decor—Tiffany lamps, sketches by Australian artist Norman Lindsay, and booths lining the walls. The three-level restaurant is warmed by a cozy fire surrounded by an antique lounge stage and resounds every night to piano, classical music, or a jazz band. The menu changes every few weeks, but a recent popular dish was grilled veal medallions topped with Balmain bugs (small, saltwater crayfish), with potato and béarnaise sauce.

122 Katoomba St., Katoomba. ✆ **02/4782 2753.** Reservations recommended. Main courses A$14–A$24 (US$11–US$19). AE, MC, V. Wed–Sun 6pm–midnight.

TrisElies GREEK Perhaps it's the belly dancers, the plate smashing, or the smell of
moussaka, but as soon as you walk through the door of this lively eatery you feel as if you've been transported to an authentic Athenian *taverna*. The restaurant folds out onto three tiers of tables, all with a good view of the stage where Greek or international performances take place every night. The food is solid Greek fare—souvlakia,

traditional dips, fried haloumi cheese, Greek salads, casseroles like Mother could have made, whitebait (tiny fried fish), and sausages in red wine—with a few Italian and Spanish extras. In winter, warm up beside one of two log fires.

287 Bathurst Rd., Katoomba. © 02/4782 4026. Fax 02/4782 1128. www.triselies.com.au. Reservations recommended. Main courses A$17–A$26 (US$14–US$21). AE, DC, MC, V. Sun–Thurs 5pm–midnight; Fri–Sat 5pm–3am.

Inexpensive

Chork Dee Thai Restaurant THAI   Loved by the locals, Chork Dee offers good Thai food in a pleasant but modest setting. It serves the usual Thai fare, including satay, spring rolls, and fish cakes to start, followed by lots of curries, noodles, and sweet-and-sour dishes. While vegetarians won't find any starters without meat or fish, plenty of veggie and tofu dishes are available as main courses. BYO.

216 Katoomba St., Katoomba. © 02/4782 1913. Main courses A$7.70–A$17 (US$6.15–US$14). AE, MC, V. Sun–Thurs 5:30–9pm; Fri–Sat 5:30–10pm.

Paragon Café *Value* CAFE   The Paragon has been a Blue Mountains institution since it opened for business in 1916. Inside, it's decked out with dark-wood paneling, bas-relief figures guarding the booths, and chandeliers. The homemade soups are delicious. The cafe also serves pies, pastas, grills, seafood, waffles, cakes, and a Devonshire tea of scones and cream.

65 Katoomba St., Katoomba. © 02/4782 2928. Menu items A$3–A$10 (US$2.40–US$8). AE, MC, V. Tues–Fri 10am–3:30pm; Sat–Sun 10am–4pm.

LEURA

107km (66 miles) W of Sydney; 3km (2 miles) E of Katoomba

The fashionable capital of the Blue Mountains, Leura is known for its gardens, its attractive old buildings (many holiday homes for Sydneysiders), and its cafes and restaurants. The National Trust has classified Leura's main street as an urban conservation area. Just outside Leura is the **Sublime Point Lookout,** which has spectacular views of the Three Sisters in Katoomba. From the southern end of **Leura Mall,** a cliff drive takes you all the way back to Echo Point in Katoomba; along the way you'll enjoy spectacular views across the Jamison Valley.

WENTWORTH FALLS ★★

103km (64 miles) W of Sydney; 7km (4½ miles) E of Katoomba

This pretty town has numerous crafts and antiques shops, but the area is principally known for its 281m (922-ft.) waterfall, situated in **Falls Reserve.** On the far side of the falls is the **National Pass Walk**—one of the best in the Blue Mountains. It's cut into a cliff face with overhanging rock faces on one side and sheer drops on the other. The views over the Jamison Valley are spectacular. The track takes you down to the base of the falls to the **Valley of the Waters.** Climbing up out of the valley is quite a bit more difficult, but just as rewarding.

A NICE SPOT FOR LUNCH

Conservation Hut Café CAFE   This pleasant cafe is in the national park on top of a cliff overlooking the Jamison Valley. It's a good place for a bit of lunch on the balcony after the Valley of the Waters walk, which leaves from outside. It serves the usual cafe fare—burgers, salads, sandwiches, and pastas. There are vegetarian options, too. There's a nice log fire inside in winter.

At the end of Fletcher St., Wentworth Falls. © 02/4757 3827. Menu items A$6–A$15 (US$4.80–US$12). AE, MC, V. Daily 9am–5pm.

MEDLOW BATH

150km (93 miles) W of Sydney; 6km (3¾ miles) NW of Katoomba

Between Katoomba and Blackheath, Medlow Bath is a cozy place, with its own rail-way station, a secondhand bookstore, and a few properties hidden between the trees. Its one claim to fame is the **Hydro Majestic Hotel** (② 02/4788 1002), a must-do stop for any visitor to the Blue Mountains. The historic Hydro Majestic has fabulous views over the Megalong Valley; the best time to appreciate the views is at sunset with a drink on the terrace. Otherwise, it sells Devonshire tea all day, and plenty of cakes, snacks, coffee, and tea.

WHERE TO STAY

Mercure Grand Hydro Majestic Hotel ★★   The most famous hotel in the Blue Mountains was built in 1904 by Mark Foy, a retail baron, world traveler, sportsman, and hypochondriac. Once called "A Palace in the Wilderness," this former health resort underwent a huge renovation and reopened in 2001 in the style Mr. Foy might have liked. The long, whitewashed building, with great bushland views from the restaurant and many of its more expensive rooms, is reminiscent of the grand hotels of Queen Victoria's time. The property even has a croquet lawn and English lawn bowls. The standard Heritage rooms are furnished in Art Deco style and have views of the garden. The similar Gallery rooms have slightly better views, some with valley glimpses. Cloister rooms, mostly in another wing, are decorated in both Art Deco and Edwardian (think country style), and have valley views. Some of these have Jacuzzis. Rooms in the Del-monte Wing, decorated in French Provincial style, also have views. The suites are sumptuous. Higher rates in the ranges below apply on Friday and Saturday.

Medlow Bath, NSW 2780. ② 02/4788 1002. Fax 02/4788 1063. www.hydromajestic.com.au. 84 units. A$250–A$290 (US$200–US$232) Heritage double; A$290–A$330 (US$232–US$264) Gallery double; A$330–A$370 (US$264–US$296) Cloister double; A$370–A$410 (US$296–US$328) Cloister double with Jacuzzi; A$830–A$1,070 (US$664–US$856) suite. Rates include breakfast. Extra person A$30 (US$24). Check the website for great details, such as a A$150 (US$120) per-night double room. AE, MC, V. **Amenities:** Restaurant; bar; 2 outdoor lit tennis courts; health club; tour desk; limited room service. *In room:* TV, minibar, coffeemaker, hair dryer.

BLACKHEATH

114km (71 miles) W of Sydney; 14km (8¾ miles) NW of Katoomba

Blackheath is the highest town in the Blue Mountains at 1,049m (3,441 ft.). The **Three Brothers** at Blackheath are not as big or as famous as the Three Sisters in Katoomba, but you can climb two of them for fabulous views. Or you could try the **Cliff Walk** from **Evans Lookout** to **Govetts Leap** (named after a surveyor who mapped the region in the 1830s), where there are magnificent views over the **Grose Valley** and **Bridal Veil Falls.** The 1½-hour tramp passes through banksia, gum, and wattle forests, with spectacular views of peaks and valleys. If you want a guide in the area, contact **Blue Mountains Magic** (② 02/4787 6354; www.bluemts.com.au), based in Blackheath. The guide, Phil Foster, is a trained botanist.

Blackheath has some interesting tearooms and antiques shops.

GETTING THERE   The Great Western Highway takes motorists from Katoomba to Blackheath. CityRail trains also stop at Blackheath.

VISITOR INFORMATION   The **Heritage Centre** (② 02/4787 8877; www.npws. nsw.gov.au), operated by the National Parks and Wildlife Service, is close to Govetts Leap Lookout on Govetts Leap Road. It has information on guided walks, camping, and hiking, as well as information on local European and Aboriginal historic sites. It's open daily from 9am to 4:30pm.

EXPLORING THE AREA ON HORSEBACK

One of the nicest ways to get around is on horseback. **Werriberri Trail Rides** (© 02/ 4787 9171; fax 02/4787 6680), at the base of the Blue Mountains, 10km (6 miles) from Blackheath on Megalong Road in the Megalong Valley, offers guided multiday rides through the Megalong Valley and beyond. Suitable for beginners to advanced riders.

WHERE TO STAY

Jemby-Rinjah Lodge ★   The Blue Mountains National Park is just a short walk away from this interesting alternative accommodations option. There are nine standard cabins (seven two-bedroom cabins, and two one-bedroom loft cabins), one deluxe cabin called Treetops Retreat, and three pole-frame lodges good for groups. The well-spaced cabins are right in the bush and can sleep up to six people. Each has a slow-combustion heater, carpets, a bathroom, a fully equipped kitchen, and a lounge and dining area. There are laundry and barbecue areas nearby. The lodges have five bedrooms, two bathrooms, and a common lounge area with a circular fireplace. You can rent linens, but bring your own food. Free pickup can be arranged from Blackheath train station. Treetops Retreat has a Japanese hot tub, TV, VCR, stereo, and three private balconies with bush views. It sleeps two, making it a perfect romantic getaway. The nearby walking trails take you to the spectacular Grand Canyon; the Grose Valley Blue Gum forests; and Walls Cave, a resting place for local Aborigines 10,000 years ago.

336 Evans Lookout Rd., Blackheath, NSW 2785. © 02/4787 7622. Fax 02/4787 6230. www.jembyrinjahlodge. com.au. 10 cabins, 3 lodges. Standard 1- and 2-bedroom cabins A$130 (US$104) Mon–Thurs, A$159 (US$159) Fri–Sun; deluxe cabins A$199 (US$159) Mon–Thurs, A$250 (US$200) Fri–Sun; Ecolodges (8 adults/group booking) A$79 (US$63) per person Mon–Thurs, A$95 (US$76) per person Fri–Sun. Extra adult A$30 (US$24), extra child A$22 (US$18). Linen A$14 (US$11) per bed. AE, DC, MC, V. **Amenities:** Restaurant w/lounge area; coin-op laundry; non-smoking rooms. *In room:* TV, kitchenette, fridge, coffeemaker.

JENOLAN CAVES ★

182km (113 miles) W of Sydney; 70km (43 miles) SW of Katoomba

The winding road from Katoomba eventually takes you to a spur of the Great Dividing Range and a series of underground limestone caves considered some of the world's best. Known to the local Aborigines as Binoomea, meaning "dark place," the caves are an impressive amalgamation of stalactites, stalagmites, and underground rivers and pools. They have been open to the public since 1866.

GETTING THERE   It's a 1½-hour drive from Katoomba to the caves. CityRail trains run to Katoomba and link up with daily Jenolan Caves excursions run by **Fantastic Aussie Tours** (© 02/4782 1866, or 1300/300 915 in Sydney; www.fantastic-aussie-tours.com.au). The day tour departs Katoomba at 10:30am and returns at 5:15pm. It costs A$75 (US$60) for adults, A$38 (US$30) for children, and A$200 (US$160) for a family. The company also runs transfers to Jenolan from Katoomba, departing at 10:30am and leaving Jenolan at 3:45pm daily. They cost A$85 (US$68) for adults and A$43 (US$34) for kids. The company can transfer you to Jenolan Caves for A$50 (US$40) for adults and A$25 (US$20) for kids. Ask about family fares.

EXPLORING THE CAVES

Nine caves are open for exploration, with guided tours operated by **Jenolan Caves Reserves Trust** (*C* **02/6359 3311;** www.jenolancaves.org.au). The first cave tour starts at 10am weekdays and 9:30am weekends and holidays. The final tour departs at 4:30pm (5pm in warmer months). Tours last 1 to 2 hours, and each costs A$15 to A$22 (US$12–US$18) for adults, A$10 to A$15 (US$8–US$12) for children under 15. Family rates and multiple cave packages are available. The best all-around cave is **Lucas Cave; Imperial Cave** is best for seniors. Adventure Cave Tours, which include canyoning, last 3 hours to a full day and cost A$55 to A$188 (US$44–US$150) per person.

WHERE TO STAY

The Gatehouse Jenolan   The Gatehouse is a cozy budget-style lodge with a separate cottage nearby. It's opposite the caves. The Gatehouse sleeps 66 people in all, in seven six-bed rooms and six four-bed rooms in the main building. The cottage can accommodate up to four couples. There are two common rooms, lockers, washing machines and dryers, and kitchen facilities. There are outdoor barbecues on the premises, and apparently at least one ghost.

Jenolan Caves Village, NSW 2790. *C* **02/6359 3322.** Fax 02/6359 3227. 13 units, 1 cottage. Weekend A$90 (US$72) 4-person dorm room; A$120 (US$96) 6-person dorm room; A$121 (US$97) cottage. Weekday A$60 (US$48) 4-person dorm room, A$80 (US$64) 6-person dorm room; A$89 (US$71) cottage. Linen A$3.30 (US$2.60) per person. AE, MC, V. **Amenities:** Coin-op laundry.

Jenolan Caves House ⟨★⟩   This heritage-listed hotel built between 1888 and 1906 is one of the most outstanding structures in New South Wales. The main part of the enormous three-story building is made of sandstone and fashioned in Tudor-style black and white. Around it are several cottages and former servants' quarters. Accommodations within the main house vary, from simple "traditional" rooms with shared bathrooms to "classic" rooms with private bathrooms. The traditional and classic rooms are old-world and cozy, with heavy furniture and views over red-tile rooftops or steep slopes. Classic rooms have views of Jenolan Caves Valley and gardens; "grand classic" rooms have spectacular views across the hills and countryside. "Mountain lodge" rooms, in a building behind the main house, are more motel-like. The 2-night weekend rates show why you should avoid this place on weekends.

Jenolan Caves Village, NSW 2790. *C* **02/6359 3322.** Fax 02/6359 3227. www.jenolancaves.com. 101 units, 87 with bathroom. A$190–A$250 (US$152–US$200) traditional double; A$280–A$380 (US$224–US$304) classic double; A$330–A$450 (US$264–US$360) grand classic double, A$370–A$450 (US$296–US$360) classic suite; A$400–A$560 (US$320–US$448) grand classic suite; A$210–A$280 (US$168–US$224) mountain lodge double. Rates include dinner. Higher rates are for Fri, Sat, Sun, and public holidays. 2-night minimum on weekends. Extra person A$60 (US$48). AE, DC, MC, V. **Amenities:** 2 restaurants; bar; tour desk; nonsmoking rooms. *In room:* TV, coffeemaker, hair dryer.

2 The Hunter Valley: Wine Tasting & More ⟨★⟩

Cessnock: 190km (118 miles) N of Sydney

The Hunter Valley (or "the Hunter," as it's also called) is the oldest commercial wine-producing area in Australia, as well as a major site for coal mining. Internationally acclaimed wines have poured out of the Hunter since the early 1800s. Though the region falls behind the major wine-producing areas of Victoria in terms of volume, it has the advantage of being just 2 hours from Sydney.

People come here to visit the vineyards' "cellar doors" for free wine tasting, to enjoy the scenery, to sample the area's highly regarded cuisine, or to escape from the city for a romantic weekend. The whole area is dedicated to the grape and the plate, and you'll find many superb restaurants amid the vineyards and farmland.

In the **Lower Hunter,** centered on the towns of Cessnock and Pokolbin, are around 110 wineries and cellar doors, including well-known producers such as Tyrell, Rothbury, Lindemans, Draytons, McGuigans, and McWilliams. Many varieties of wine are produced here, including semillon, shiraz, chardonnay, cabernet sauvignon, and pinot noir.

Farther north, the **Upper Hunter** represents the very essence of Australian rural life, with its sheep and cattle farms, historic homesteads, more wineries, and rugged bushland. The vineyards here tend to be larger than those in the south, and they produce more aromatic varieties, such as traminers and Rieslings. February through March is harvest time.

The Upper Hunter gives way to the forested heights of the World Heritage–listed Barrington Tops National Park. The ruggedly beautiful park is home to some of the highest Antarctic beech trees in the country. It abounds with animals, including several marsupial species and a profusion of birds.

HUNTER VALLEY ESSENTIALS

GETTING THERE   To get to the wine-producing regions of the Hunter, leave Sydney by the Harbour Bridge or Harbour Tunnel and follow the signs for Newcastle. Just

---

Tips A Wine-Buying Tip

The best years ever for red wines in this part of Australia were 1998 and 2000, and 2004 when long, hot summers produced fewer but more intensely flavored grapes. Stock up on anything you can find from those vintages. At the other end of the scale, 1997 was a bad year, and 1996, 1999, 2001, and 2002 produced average vintages. The year 2003 was good but not as outstanding as 1998 and 2000.

---

before Hornsby, turn off the highway and head up the National 1/F3 freeway. After around an hour, take the Cessnock exit and follow signs to the vineyards. The trip will take about 2½ hours. Barrington Tops National Park is reached via the Upper Hunter town of Dungog.

A rental car should cost at least A$45 (US$36) a day from Sydney, and you might put in around A$40 (US$32) worth of gas for a couple of days of touring (the price hovers around A$1 a liter, or US$3 a gal.). In the Hunter, contact **Hertz,** 1A Aberdare Rd., Cessnock (© **13 30 39** in Australia, or 02/4991 2500).

ORGANIZED TRIPS FROM SYDNEY   Several companies offer **day trips** to the Hunter Valley from Sydney.

Visitours (© **02/9909 0822;** www.visitours.com.au) takes small groups to the Hunter to visit up to six wineries as well as cheese and fudge producers. The trip costs A$85 (US$68), or A$95 (US$76) with lunch.

Grayline (© **1300/858 687;** www.grayline.com.au) offers coach trips to the vineyards every Tuesday, Wednesday, Friday, and Sunday costing A$152 (US$121) for adults and A$76 (US$61) for kids. It visits three wineries and includes lunch.

VISITOR INFORMATION   **Wine Country Visitors Information Centre,** Main Road, Pokolbin, NSW 2325 (© **02/4990 4477;** fax 02/4991 4518; www.winecountry. com.au), is open Monday through Friday from 9am to 5pm, Saturday from 9:30am to 5pm, and Sunday from 9:30am to 3:30pm. The staff can make accommodations bookings and answer any questions. The **Dungog Visitors Information Centre,** Dowling Street, Dungog (© **02/4992 2212**), has plenty of information on the Barrington Tops area. A good general website is www.winecountry.com.au.

VISITING THE WINERIES

Many people start their journey through the Hunter by popping into the **Hunter Valley Wine Society,** at the corner of Broke and Branxton roads, Pokolbin (© **1300/303 307** in Australia, or 02/4941 3000). The club basically acts as a Hunter Valley wine clearinghouse, sending bottles and cases to members all over Australia, and some overseas. It's also a good place to talk to experts about the area's wines, and to taste a few of them. It's open daily from 9am to 5pm.

You might also like to visit the **Small Winemakers Centre,** McDonalds Road, Pokolbin (© **02/4998 7668**). At any one time it represents around six of the region's smaller producers.

Most of the wineries in the region are open for cellar-door tastings, and it's perfectly acceptable just to turn up, taste a couple of wines or more, and then say your goodbyes without buying anything. Though you will come across some unusual vintages, especially at the boutique wineries, don't expect to find any bargains—city bottle shops buy in bulk and at trade price, which means you can probably get the same bottle of wine for less in Sydney than at the cellar door in the Hunter.

If you're not traveling by car, see the following section for information about day tours of the wineries.

Drayton Family Wines   Drayton's produces some spectacular shiraz. Oakey Creek Rd., Pokolbin. ℭ **02/4998 7513.** Mon–Fri 9am–5pm; Sat–Sun 10am–5pm.

Hunter Estate Winery   The Hunter's largest winery crushes some 6,500 tons of grapes a year. Come here for excellent semillon and shiraz. Hermitage Rd., Pokolbin. ℭ **02/ 4998 7777.** Daily 10am–5pm. Tours daily 11am and 2pm.

Lindemans Hunter River Winery   This famous winery offers an interesting sparkling red shiraz. McDonald Rd., Pokolbin. ℭ **02/4998 7684.** Mon–Fri 9am–4:30pm; Sat–Sun 10am–4:30pm.

McGuigan Brothers Winery   A winery worth visiting, McGuigan Brothers also has a cheese factory and bakery on the site. McDonald Rd., Pokolbin. ℭ **02/4998 7402.** Daily 9:30am–5pm. Tours daily at noon.

McWilliams Mount Pleasant Winery   Famous for its Elizabeth Semillon, which has won 39 trophies and 214 gold medals since 1981, and its Lovedale Semillon, which has won 39 trophies and 74 gold medals since 1984. Marrowbone Rd., Pokolbin. ℭ **02/4998 7505.** Daily 10am–4:30pm. Tours daily 11am.

Mount View Estate   The Australian pioneer of Verdelho wines—a grape attributed to Portugal, also grown in small quantities in Italy and France. It's a very crisp and dry white wine, which I like with seafood. Mount View Rd., Mount View. ℭ **02/4990 3307.** Daily 10am–5pm.

Peterson's Champagne House   This is the only specialist champagne winery in the Hunter. At the corner of Broke and Branxton roads, Pokolbin. ℭ **02/4998 7881.** Daily 9am–5pm.

Peterson's Vineyard   Peterson's produces fine chardonnay, semillon, and shiraz. Mount View Rd., Mount View. ℭ **02/4990 1704.** Mon–Sat 9am–5pm; Sun 10am–5pm.

Rothbury Estate ⭐   This very friendly winery produces the magnificent Brokenback Shiraz and the nice Mudgee Shiraz. Broke Rd., Pokolbin. ℭ **02/4998 7555.** Daily 9:30am–4:30pm.

Tamburlaine Winery   Don't miss this boutique winery, the winner of many wine and tourism awards. McDonald Rd., Pokolbin. ℭ **02/4998 7570.** Daily 9:30am–5pm.

Tinklers   If you want to taste grapes in season, head to Tinklers. It sells some 30 different varieties of eating grapes between December and March, and nectarines, plums, peaches, and vegetables at other times of the year. It also offers wine tasting and free

---

Tips **Remember a Designated Driver!**

Australia's drunk-driving laws are strict and rigidly enforced. Both easily identifiable and unmarked police cars patrol the vineyard regions. If you are interested in tasting some grapes in the Hunter Valley, choose a designated driver or take a guided tour (see above).

> **Tips** A Wine-Tasting Tip
>
> Some wineries routinely offer some of their inferior wines for tastings. I've made a habit of asking for a list of their premium wines available for tasting. Most wineries usually have a bottle or two of their better wines uncorked for those with a serious interest.

---

vineyard walks at 11am Saturday and Sunday. Pokolbin Mountains Rd., Pokolbin. ℂ **02/4998 7435.** Daily 10am–4pm.

Tyrell's Tyrell's has produced some famous wines and exports all over the world. Broke Rd., Pokolbin. ℂ **02/4993 7000.** Tours daily 1:30pm.

DAY TOURS, HOT-AIR BALLOON RIDES & OTHER FUN STUFF

If you don't have a car, you'll have to get around as part of a tour, because no public transport runs between the wineries.

Trekabout Tours (ℂ **02/4990 8277**) offers half-day and full-day winery tours for a maximum of six people. Half-day tours cost A$28 (US$22), with visits to five or six wineries; full-day tours cost A$44 (US$35) and take in up to nine wineries. The company can pick you up from your hotel in Cessnock or Pokolbin.

Also offering local pickup is **Hunter Vineyard Tours** (ℂ **02/4991 1659**), which has a full-day tour on a 12- or 21-seat bus, taking in five wineries. It costs A$38 (US$30), or A$55 (US$44) with a two-course meal.

A tranquil way to see the wineries is from above. **Balloon Aloft,** in Cessnock (ℂ **1800/028 568** in Australia, or 02/4938 1955; www.balloonaloft.com.au), offers year-round dawn balloon flights that include postflight champagne and optional breakfast costing A$16 (US$13). Flights last about an hour and cost A$280 (US$224) for adults and A$170 (US$136) for kids ages 8 to 12.

If you like adventure, try **Grapemobile Bicycle and Walking Tours** (ℂ **0500/ 804 039** in Australia, or ℂ/fax 02/4991 2339). This company supplies you with a mountain bike, helmet, guide, and support bus, and takes you on a peaceful meander through the wineries. Tours cost A$98 (US$78), including lunch in a restaurant. The firm also rents bicycles—A$22 (US$18) for a half-day and A$30 (US$24) for a full day.

WHERE TO STAY

The Hunter Valley is far more expensive on weekends and during public holidays than on weekdays. Room prices jump significantly, and some properties insist on a 2-night stay. It's worth checking out the information board in the Wine Country Visitors Information Centre (see "Visitor Information," above) for special deals, including self-contained accommodations, cottages, resorts, and guesthouses.

IN CESSNOCK

Staying in Cessnock is a good idea if you don't have a car and are relying on local tour companies to pick you up and show you around the area.

Cessnock Heritage Inn This 1920s building, built as a pub, is right in the center of Cessnock, so there's easy access to pubs and restaurants. All the rooms are done in country style, with dried grasses, floral bedspreads, and the like. All are quite large, with high ceilings, but differ greatly—the smallest room has a double bed, others have queen-size beds and singles, and there are two family rooms (sleeping five). There's a guest lounge where you can chat with the owners.

Vincent St. (P.O. Box 714), Cessnock, NSW 2325. © 02/4991 2744. Fax 02/4991 2720. www.hunterweb.com.au/heritageinn.html. 13 units. Weekend A$120 (US$96) double; A$200 (US$160) 2-night package. Weekday A$90 (US$72) double. Rates include breakfast. AE, MC, V. **Amenities:** Tour desk; nonsmoking rooms. *In room:* A/C, ceiling fan, TV w/free videos, minibar, coffeemaker.

IN POKOLBIN
Very Expensive

Casuarina Restaurant and Country Inn ★★ *(Finds*   Now, this place is really an oddity. Each of its very different suites has an unusual theme. Just naming them will give you an idea: the Moulin Rouge, the Oriental, the Bordello, Casanova's Loft, the Mariners Suite, British Empire, Out of Africa, Edwardian, Palais Royale, and Romeo's Retreat. The most popular is the Bordello, with a pedestaled king-size bed, voluptuous pink curtains, and strategically placed mirrors. To get the full picture, it's well worth roaming around the website before you book. The award-winning **restaurant** serves Mediterranean-style food.

Hermitage Rd., Pokolbin, NSW 2321. © 02/4998 7888. Fax 02/4998 7692. www.casuarinainn.com.au. 10 units. A$265 (US$212) weekday; A$310 (US$248) weekend. 2-night minimum on weekends. AE, DC, MC, V. **Amenities:** Restaurant (see "Where to Dine," below); large heated outdoor pool; laundry service; nonsmoking rooms. *In room:* A/C, TV, coffeemaker, hair dryer.

Peppers Convent Hunter Valley ★★   Originally a convent for Brigidine nuns in the early part of the 20th century, this building was transported some 600km (372 miles) from Coonamble in central New South Wales to its present location in 1990. A year later, it opened as a hotel. Rooms are elegant and spacious, with baroque decor, including plaster frieze ceilings and thick, rich drapes. French doors open onto private verandas overlooking patches of bushland. King rooms are larger and have wicker lounge areas. There is an elegant sitting area where drinks are served, and a light and airy breakfast room serving the best breakfasts in the Hunter (A$28/US$22). The Pepper Tree Complex includes Pepper Tree Wines and the excellent Robert's Restaurant.

Tips   **Bunking Down in a Caravan, Man**

Two trailer (caravan) parks offer reasonably comfortable accommodations in trailers and cabins. **Cessnock Cabins and Caravan Park** (© 02/4990 5819; fax 02/4991 2944), Allandale/Branxton Road, Nulkaba (2km/1¼ miles north of Cessnock), has four on-site vans for A$30 to A$40 (US$24–US$32), and a double and 12 cabins with shower for A$48 to A$69 (US$38–US$55)—the more expensive prices for weekends. There are also camping sites for A$14 (US$11) and powered sites for A$16 (US$13).

The **Valley Vineyard Tourist Park** (©/fax 02/4990 2573) on Mount View Road (on the way to the vineyards) has five trailers for A$35 (US$28) and 12 cabins with shower for A$55 (US$44). Two two-bedroom units cost A$75 (US$60). Powered sites cost A$16 to A$20 (US$13–US$16), and a camping site A$12 (US$10). There are a BYO restaurant, a campers' kitchen, and a swimming pool on-site.

In the Pepper Tree Complex, Halls Rd., Pokolbin, NSW 2320. ℭ **02/4998 7764.** Fax 02/4998 7323. www.peppers. com.au. 17 units. Weekend A$323–A$387 (US$258–US$309) double; weekday A$291–A$332 (US$233–US$265) double. Extra adult A$44 (US$35). Extra child 5–15 A$22 (US$18). Children under 5 stay free in parent's room. 2-night minimum on weekends. Ask about packages and check website the week before for specials. AE, DC, MC, V. **Amenities:** Restaurant (see "Where to Dine," below); medium-size heated outdoor pool; outdoor lit tennis court; Jacuzzi; free use of bikes; concierge; tour desk; car-rental desk; business center; massage; babysitting; laundry service; dry cleaning; nonsmoking rooms. *In room:* A/C, TV, minibar, coffeemaker, hair dryer, iron/ironing board.

Peppers Guest House   This tranquil escape is set in beautiful bush gardens. The spot is so peaceful that kangaroos hop up to the veranda in the evenings looking for treats. The "classic" rooms downstairs have French doors that you can fling open; upstairs rooms have just a tad more old-fashioned charm and come with air-conditioning. All rooms have king-size beds and are furnished with colonial antiques. Guests don't come here for action; they come to relax. The Pampering Place offers massages and facials, and a gentle 30-minute trail winds through the bush. There's a pleasant guest lounge with an open fireplace and a bar. The restaurant, **Chez Pok,** is an upscale establishment with mismatched china and pretty good country food.

Ekerts Rd., Pokolbin, NSW 2321. ℭ **02/4998 7596.** Fax 02/4998 7739. www.peppers.com.au. 47 units, 1 cottage. Weekend A$277 (US$221) colonial double; A$303 (US$242) classic double; A$315 (US$252) vintage double; A$347 (US$277) heritage suite. Weekday A$273 (US$218) colonial double; A$283 (US$226) classic double; A$292 (US$233) vintage double; A$327 (US$261) heritage suite. 2-night minimum on weekends. Weekday rates include buffet breakfast. AE, DC, MC, V. **Amenities:** Restaurant (see "Where to Dine," below); small heated indoor pool; outdoor lit tennis court; bike rental; laundry service; nonsmoking rooms. *In room:* A/C, TV, minibar, coffeemaker, hair dryer, iron/ ironing board.

Expensive

Carriages Guest House ★★   Tucked away on 15 hectares (37 acres), a kilometer off the main road, Carriages is a secluded retreat in the heart of Pokolbin. A two-suite cottage, the Gatehouse, is on a separate part of the grounds. In the main two-story house, a veranda circles downstairs rooms, which are furnished in antique country pine. Upstairs, the two lofty gable suites center on huge fireplaces. The Gatehouse suites offer incredible luxury; although relatively new, the stained-glass windows and rescued timber give them a rustic feel (these two Jacuzzi rooms share a lounge with a full kitchen and an open fire). There are open fires in six of the rooms. (The two standard doubles don't have them.) Breakfast is served in your room, and Robert's Restaurant is next door. The friendly owner, Ben Dawson, assures me he'll take Frommer's readers up to the top of a nearby hill where they can see plenty of wild kangaroos.

Halls Rd., Pokolbin, NSW 2321. ℭ **02/4998 7591.** Fax 02/4998 7839. www.thecarriages.com.au. 10 units. A$185 (US$148) double; A$240–A$265 (US$192–US$212) suite; A$285 (US$228) Jacuzzi suite. Rates include breakfast. 2-night minimum on weekends. Ask about 10%–20% discounts weekdays. AE, MC, V. **Amenities:** Large heated outdoor pool; outdoor lit tennis court; Jacuzzi; massage; babysitting; laundry service; nonsmoking rooms. *In room:* A/C, TV, kitchenette, fridge, coffeemaker, hair dryer, iron/ironing board.

Hermitage Lodge   If you want to be in the heart of vineyard country, stay at this property, which is surrounded by vineyards. Standard rooms are large, sunny, and nicely decorated; they come with a queen-size bed and a double sofa bed. The spa suites are larger, with queen-size beds and double sofas, cathedral ceilings, Jacuzzis, and separate showers. The more expensive suites have a separate bedroom and bathrobes. Breakfast is served in all rooms. **Il Cacciatore** restaurant is one of the best in the region.

At Gillards and McDonalds roads, Pokolbin, NSW 2320. ℭ **02/4998 7639.** Fax 02/4998 7818. www.ozemail.com. au/~hlodge. 10 units. Weekend A$220 (US$175) standard double; A$240 (US$192) spa suite. Weekday A$145 (US$116) standard double; A$165 (US$132) spa suites. Extra person A$15 (US$12). 2-night minimum on weekends.

Moments **Something Special: A Cattle Station in the Upper Hunter**

Just off the Golden Highway, 2½ hours west of Cessnock and 4 hours north-west of Sydney, **Runnymede,** Golden Highway, Runnymede, Cassilis, NSW 2329 (© 02/6376 1183; fax 02/6376 1187), is an 800-hectare (2,000-acre) sheep-and-cattle ranch where you can get a taste of Aussie ranch life. The ranch—called a "station" in Australia—offers farm-style lodgings in a 1930s California-style bungalow. Two rooms have private bathrooms with shower, and the third shares the hosts' bathroom down the hall. The homestead has an open fire in the living room (and a rarely used TV). There are plenty of native birds in the gardens, and kangaroos are common. May is the best time to see sheep shearing, and August is the best time to witness lambing and calving. Guests rave about hosts Libby and David Morrow. David offers 1-hour tours of the property for around A$30 (US$24) per "Toyota load," and other tours throughout the district.

Doubles go for A$80 to A$90 (US$64–US$72). Rates include breakfast, but dinner is A$20 (US$16) per person extra (BYO wine or beer). No credit cards.

Rates include continental breakfast. Ask about weekday packages. AE, MC, V. **Amenities:** Restaurant; bar; medium-size outdoor pool; golf course nearby; Jacuzzi; bike rental (free for Frommer's readers); limited room service; babysitting; free self-service laundry; nonsmoking rooms. *In room:* A/C, TV, fridge, coffeemaker, hair dryer, iron/ironing board.

Moderate

Vineyard Hill Country Motel ✦   "Motel" is a bit of a misnomer for this place; it's more aptly described as a "fully self-contained chalet." Units are modern, with a separate bedroom, a lounge and dining area, a full kitchen, and a balcony with views across a valley of vineyards to the Brokenback Ranges in the distance. It's all terrifically rural, with cows wandering about and kangaroos and possums creeping around at dusk. There's no restaurant, but there is a gourmet deli on the premises. In the garden are a large pool and a Jacuzzi.

Lovedale Rd., Pokolbin, NSW 2321. © 02/4990 4166. Fax 02/4991 4431. www.vineyardhill.com.au. 8 units. Weekend A$155 (US$124) 1-bedroom unit; A$218 (US$174) 2-bedroom unit for 4. Weekday A$107 (US$86) 1-bedroom unit; A$165 (US$132) 2-bedroom unit. Extra person A$20 (US$16). Ask about weekday and long-weekend packages. AE, MC, V. **Amenities:** Large heated outdoor pool; Jacuzzi; limited room service; massage; babysitting; free laundry service; nonsmoking rooms. *In room:* A/C, TV, kitchen, minibar, fridge, coffeemaker, hair dryer, iron/ironing board.

IN THE UPPER HUNTER

Barrington Guest House ✦   Barrington Guest House is in a valley just outside the Barrington Tops National Park, 1½ hours from the main Hunter wine region. It retains an old-world charm and serves bacon and eggs for breakfast, scones and cream, and vegetables boiled soft enough for your dentures. The place has lace tablecloths in the dining room, a log fire beneath a higgledy-piggledy brick chimney, mahogany walls, high ceilings, and personalized service—despite the communal mealtimes and the lack of a menu. Rooms come with or without private bathroom; they're basic (no TV) but comfortable enough, and can be noisy if a party's in full swing in the dining room. This place is very popular with older travelers during the week but appeals to a range of ages on weekends. The guesthouse grounds attract plenty of animals and act as a wildlife reserve for several rescued kangaroos. Activities include horseback riding, guided walks through the rainforest, "billy tea" tours, night spotting for quolls (native cats) and possums, bush dancing, tennis, film evenings, and skeet shooting. It can be a very social scene, too.

Salisbury (3½ hr. from Sydney), NSW 2420. © 02/4995 3212. Fax 02/4995 3248. www.barringtonguesthouse.com.au. 21 guesthouse units, 13 with bathroom. Weekend double without bathroom A$240 (US$192); A$345 (US$276) double with bathroom. Weekday A$190 (US$152) double without bathroom; A$280 (US$224) double with bathroom. Rates include meals and activities. 2-night minimum on weekends. Ask about packages and child rates. AE, DC, MC, V. Free pickup from Dungog railway station. **Amenities:** Restaurant; bar; 2 lit tennis courts; tour desk; massage; laundry service; nonsmoking rooms. *In room:* Cottages only: TV, kitchen, fridge, coffeemaker, hair dryer, iron/ironing board.

WHERE TO DINE
IN CESSNOCK

Amicos MEXICAN/ITALIAN/PIZZA   You can't mistake the Mexican influence in the decor—bunches of chile peppers, cow skulls, ponchos, masks, and frescoes—but the Mediterranean/Italian connection is more evident in the menu. Mexican dishes include the usual nachos, enchiladas, burritos, barbecued chicken, and the like, and there are a few pastas and Mediterranean dishes, such as crumbed lamb brains. The pizzas are pretty good, and one could just about serve four people. The restaurant will deliver, too.

138 Wollombi Rd., Cessnock. © 02/4991 1995. Fax 02/4990 9302. Reservations recommended. Main courses A$12–A$20 (US$9.60–US$16); pizzas A$14–A$18 (US$11–US$14). MC, V. Daily 6–10pm.

IN POKOLBIN

The three restaurants in the Hunter with the biggest reputations are **Robert's Restaurant,** in the Peppers Convent Hunter Valley guesthouse; **Chez Pok,** in Peppers Guest House; and **Casuarina Restaurant.** See "Where to Stay," above.

Blaxland's Restaurant ✦ MODERN INTERNATIONAL   This atmospheric restaurant revolves around a winery theme, with pictures of vineyards on the walls, one of the most comprehensive Hunter wine lists in the area, and the owner's homemade vintages on the menu. Parts of the building date from 1829, with wooden trusses holding up the ceiling and exposed sandstone block walls. Popular dishes include roast spatchcock (baby chicken) and steamed mussels. A large open fire brings a glow to the white tablecloths in winter.

Broke Rd., Pokolbin. © 02/4998 7550. Fax 02/4998 7802. www.blaxlandsrestaurant.com.au. Reservations recommended. Main courses A$20–A$26 (US$16–US$21). A$3 (US$2.40) per person surcharge weekends and public holidays. AE, DC, MC, V. Daily 11am–10pm.

Café Enzo MODERN AUSTRALIAN   This charming little cafe offers a nice ambience and good cuisine. Pastas, pizzettas, antipasti, and steaks dominate the menu. The pizzetta with chargrilled baby octopus, squid, king prawns, Kalamata olives, fresh chile, onion, and freshly shaved Parmesan is particularly nice. Cakes and cheese plates are a specialty.

At the corner of Broke and Ekerts roads (adjacent to Peppers Creek Antiques, near Peppers Guest House), Pokolbin. © 02/4998 7233. Main courses A$10–A$18 (US$8–US$14); Devonshire tea A$7.50 (US$6). AE, DC, MC, V. Wed–Fri and Sun 10am–5pm; Sat 10am–10pm.

Casuarina Restaurant ✦✦ MODERN AUSTRALIAN   This superb restaurant has taken a slew of awards for its cooking in recent years. The surroundings are elegant, with lots of antiques below the very high wooden ceilings. Flambés are the signature meal here, the most popular being a flambé of chile lobster and prawn (for two people). Other dishes to write home about are Thai-style chicken curry and Caesar salad.

In Casuarina Restaurant and Country Inn, Hermitage Rd., Pokolbin. ℂ **02/4998 7888.** Fax 02/4998 7692. www. casuarina.com. Reservations recommended. Main courses A$27–A$34 (US$22–US$27). AE, DC, MC, V. Daily 7–11pm.

Robert's Restaurant ★★ MODERN AUSTRALIAN   Chef and owner Robert Molines has become a legend in Hunter Valley gourmet circles for coming up with great dishes that perfectly complement the region's wines. His restaurant is known for its eclectic mix of antiques and his country-style dishes, such as rabbit with olives and vegetables, rack of lamb from the wood-fired oven, and twice-roasted duckling. The meat-free specialty is wild mushroom risotto.

In the Pepper Tree complex, Halls Rd., Pokolbin. ℂ **02/4998 7330.** Main courses A$29–A$34 (US$23–US$27). A$4 (US$3.20) per-person surcharge weekends and public holidays. AE, DC, MC, V. Daily noon–5pm and 7pm–midnight.

3 Port Stephens: Dolphin- & Whale-Watching ★★

209km (136 miles) N of Sydney

Port Stephens, just 2½ hours north of Sydney, should be at the top of any New South Wales itinerary. It's a perfect add-on to a trip to the Hunter Valley (p. 202). Though you can come up from Sydney for the day, I recommend staying in the general area for at least 1 night. The sheltered Port Stephens bay is more than twice the size of Sydney Harbour, and is as clean as a newly poured bath. The sea literally jumps with fish, and the creamy islands and surrounding Tomaree National Park boast more species of birds than even Kakadu National Park in the Northern Territory. Two pods of bottle-nosed dolphins, around 70 individuals in all, call the bay home, and you are almost certain to see some on a dolphin-watching cruise. Port Stephens is also a fabulous place to watch whales during their migration to the breeding grounds farther north (roughly from June to mid-Nov—though they are less frequently seen in Aug). There is also a large breeding colony of koalas in Lemon Tree Passage on the south side of the Tomaree Peninsula, which makes up the southern shoreline of the bay.

The main town, **Nelson Bay** (pop. 7,000), is on the northern side of the peninsula. The township of Shoal Bay, farther along the peninsula, has a spectacular beach edged with wildflowers. Another small resort town, **Anna Bay,** is the largest development on the southern side of the peninsula, and has excellent surf beaches. The Stockton Bight stretches some 32km (20 miles) from Anna Bay south to the large industrial town of Newcastle. The beach here is popular with ocean fishermen who have the awful habit of driving their four-wheel-drives along it. The first 500m (1,640 ft.) of the beach is for swimming and surfing only. The Stockton Sand Dunes, which run behind the beach, are the longest in the Southern Hemisphere.

Opposite the Tomaree Peninsula, across the bay, are the small tourist townships of Tea Gardens and Hawks Nest, both at the mouth of the Myall River.

ESSENTIALS

GETTING THERE   To get to Port Stephens, take the Sydney-Newcastle Freeway (F3) to its end, then follow the Pacific Highway signs to Hexham and Port Stephens. **Port Stephens Coaches** (ℂ **1800/045 949** in Sydney, or 02/4982 2940; www.pscoaches.com.au) travel between Port Stephens and Newcastle, and to Nelson Bay from Sydney daily at 2pm. Buses from Sydney leave from Eddy Avenue, near Central Station; the journey takes 3½ hours. Round-trip tickets cost A$48 (US$38) for adults and A$32 (US$26) for children. There's no train service to Port Stephens. You must book ahead.

VISITOR INFORMATION The **Port Stephens Visitor Information Centre,** Victoria Parade, Nelson Bay (© **1800/808 900** in Australia, or 02/4981 1579; fax 02/4984 1855; www.portstephens.org.au), is open Monday through Friday from 9am to 5pm and Saturday and Sunday from 9am to 4pm.

SEEING THE AREA

Several operators offer **dolphin- and whale-watching cruises.** Some of the best are aboard *Imagine* (© **02/4984 9000;** www.imaginecruises.com.au), a 15m (49-ft.) catamaran operated by Frank Future and Yves Papin, two real characters. They offer a daily Island Discovery trip that includes dolphin-watching and a trip around the off-shore islands. The 4-hour cruise departs from D'Albora Marina in Nelson Bay daily at 11am and costs A$49 (US$39) for adults, and A$25 (US$20) for children 4 to 14, including lunch.

Four-hour whale-watching tours cost the same and leave at 11am from June 1 to November 15. You are most likely to spot humpback whales, but there's also a chance to see minke and southern right whales.

A dolphin-watching cruise runs from 10:30am to 12:30pm daily during summer and costs A$20 (US$16) for adults, A$13 (US$10) for children, and A$53 (US$42) for families. If you happen to be around on the weekend nearest a full moon, ask about overnight Full Moon Tours.

The **Port Stephens Ferry Service** (© **02/4981 3798,** or 0419/417 689 mobile) operates a 2½-hour Early Bird Dolphin Watch, with a stop at Tea Gardens township, daily at 8:30am. A similar 3½-hour cruise departs at noon (you can eat lunch in Tea Gardens), and a 2-hour dolphin-watching cruise departs at 3:30pm. All cruises cost A$17 (US$14) for adults, A$9 (US$7.20) for children, and A$40 (US$32) for families.

WHERE TO STAY

Port Stephens is very popular with Sydneysiders, especially during the Christmas holidays, January, and Easter, so you'll need to book well in advance then.

Peppers Anchorage Port Stephens ★★ This low-rise resort, split into a main guesthouse and four separate lodges, is built onto a headland and runs almost directly into the bay—it's stopped from sliding in by a boardwalk and a picturesque marina. Rooms are light and luxurious; the suites each have a good-size Jacuzzi, perfect for two. Rooms on the top floor have a large balcony, from which uninterrupted views take in the bay and the islands; those below have private verandas. Two rooms are designed for wheelchairs. A nearby beach is the perfect spot for a sunset stroll.

Finds **Through the Dunes on Horseback**

You can ride a horse through the dunes with **Sahara Horse Trails** (© **02/4981 9077;** www.saharatrails.com). The barn is on Port Stephens Road, before you reach Nelson Bay. A 2-hour trip costs A$60 (US$48), and a half-day excursion is A$120 (US$96). Bookings required 1 day in advance.

Corlette Point Rd., Corlette, NSW 2315. ✆ **1800/809 142** in Australia, or 02/4984 2555. Fax 02/4984 0300. www. peppers.com.au. 80 units. Weekend A$345 (US$276) double; A$396 (US$317) suite. Weekday A$291 (US$233) double; A$337 (US$269) suite. Weekday rates include breakfast. Ask about packages. AE, DC, MC, V. **Amenities:** Restaurant; bar; good-size heated outdoor pool; exercise room; Jacuzzi; sauna; children's program (public holidays only); tour desk; 24-hr. room service; massage; babysitting; laundry service; nonsmoking rooms. *In room:* A/C, TV, fax, dataport, minibar, coffeemaker, hair dryer, iron/ironing board.

Port Stephens Motor Lodge   Surrounded by tall trees and gardens, this motor lodge a short stroll from the main township is a peaceful place to stay. The standard rooms are quite plain, with raw-brick walls, a comfy double bed (and an extra single bed in most rooms), a private balcony, and an attached shower with half-tub. Adjacent to the lodge is a self-contained family unit for four; it has two bedrooms, a laundry, and water views. There's a barbecue area on the grounds. Rates peak during the Christmas holiday period.

44 Mangus St., Nelson Bay, NSW 2315. ✆ **02/4981 3366.** Fax 02/4984 1655. psmlodge@aol.com. 17 units. A$60–A$120 (US$48–US$96) standard double; A$88 (US$70) family unit weekday, A$120 (US$96) family unit weekend. Extra adult A$10 (US$8); extra child under 15 A$5 (US$4). AE, DC, MC, V. **Amenities:** Heated outdoor pool; coin-op laundry; nonsmoking rooms. *In room:* A/C, TV, coffeemaker, hair dryer, iron/ironing board.

Salamander Shores ★   Salamander Shores looks like a beached, ramshackle paddle steamer—it's all white-painted bricks and rails and stairs, fixed to the bay by a jetty. Set in a well-tended, sloping garden, this five-story hotel retains a certain 1960s charm, despite undergoing selective modernization. Standard rooms are similar to most motel rooms, but you really should throw caution to the wind and get a sea-view room—you won't regret it. These rooms have Jacuzzis and large balconies with extensive views of the bay. When the sun rises over the water and the garden is full of lorikeets and corellas, it couldn't be more picture-perfect. Down below is a pub and shop selling alcohol.

147 Soldiers Point Rd., Soldiers Point, NSW 2317. ✆ **1800/655 029** in Australia, or 02/4982 7210. Fax 02/4982 7890. www.salamander-shores.com. 90 units. A$109 (US$87) standard double; A$142 (US$114) garden-view double; A$161 (US$129) sea-view double; A$229 (US$183) family suite; A$264 (US$211) penthouse. Extra person A$18 (US$14). Ask about packages. AE, DC, MC, V. **Amenities:** 2 restaurants; bar; small heated outdoor pool; sauna; tour desk; babysitting; laundry service; nonsmoking rooms. *In room:* A/C, TV, minibar, coffeemaker, hair dryer, iron/ironing board.

WHERE TO DINE

Most people head to **Nelson Bay** for their meals because of the great views. You'll find a host of cheap takeout joints here. **Incredible Edibles,** corner of Donaldson and Stockton streets, Nelson Bay (✆ **02/4981 4511**), is a deli that serves good sandwiches.

Rob's on the Boardwalk CAFE   You can pick up a hearty American breakfast at this busy cafe overlooking the bay, or a snack throughout the day. Caesar salad is popular, as are the half-dozen oysters for A$13 (US$10). One of the best main courses is mixed seafood bouillabaisse. Prime Scotch filet with sautéed forest mushrooms, Jerusalem artichokes, gratin potatoes, and red-wine sauce would tempt the most red-blooded carnivore.

D'Albora Marina. ✆ **02/4984 4444.** Main courses A$12–A$23 (US$9.60–US$18). AE, DC, MC, V. Daily 8am until the last customer leaves.

4 North of Sydney along the Pacific Highway: Australia's Holiday Coast

The Pacific Highway leads over the Sydney Harbour Bridge and merges into the Sydney-Newcastle Freeway. It continues to the industrial coast town of Newcastle, bypassing Tuggerah Lake and Lake Macquarie (neither of real interest compared to what follows). From here, the Pacific Highway stays close to the coast until it reaches Brisbane, some 1,000km (620 miles) from Sydney.

Though the road is gradually being upgraded, conditions vary, and distances are long. Travelers should be aware that the route is renowned for its accidents. Though you could make it to Brisbane in a couple of days, you could also easily spend more than a week stopping off at the attractions along the way. The farther north you travel, the more tropical the landscape gets. By the time visitors reach the coastal resort town of Coffs Harbour, temperatures have noticeably increased, and banana palms and sugar-cane plantations start to appear.

Along the coast, you'll find excellent fishing and some superb beaches, most of them virtually deserted. Inland, the Great Dividing Range, which separates the wetter eastern plains from the dry interior, throws up rainforests, extinct volcanoes, and hobby farms growing tropical fruit as you head farther north toward Queensland. Along the way are a series of national parks, most of them requiring detours of several kilometers. Those you shouldn't miss include the **Dorrigo** and **Mount Warning** national parks, both of which encompass some of the country's best and most accessible rainforests.

PORT MACQUARIE
423km (262 miles) N of Sydney

Port Macquarie (pop. 28,000), about halfway between Sydney and the Queensland border, boasts some fabulous beaches; Flynn's Beach in particular is a haven for surfers. Boating and fishing are other popular pastimes.

ESSENTIALS

GETTING THERE From Sydney, motorists follow the Pacific Highway and then the Sydney-Newcastle Freeway (F3). **Eastern Australia Airways** (© 02/9691 2333) flies between Sydney and Port Macquarie. The coach trip from Sydney takes about 7 hours.

VISITOR INFORMATION The **Port Macquarie Visitor Information Centre,** at the corner of Clarence and Hay streets, under the Civic Centre (© 1800/025 935 in Australia, or 02/6581 8000; www.portmacquarieinfo.com.au), is open Monday through Friday from 8:30am to 5pm and Saturday and Sunday from 9am to 4pm.

EXPLORING THE AREA

The Billabong Koala and Wildlife Park, 61 Billabong Dr., Port Macquarie (© 02/6585 1060), is a family-owned nature park where you can get up close to hand-raised koalas, kangaroos, emus, wombats, many types of birds, and fish. You can pat the koalas at 10:30am, 1:30pm, and 3:30pm. There are also barbecue facilities, picnic grounds, and a restaurant. Allow 2 hours to fully experience this recommended wildlife park. It's open daily from 9am to 5pm; admission is A$8 (US$6.40) for adults and A$5 (US$4) for children.

The 257-passenger vessel *Port Venture* (© 02/6583 3058) offers a 2-hour scenic cruise on the Hastings River. It leaves from the wharf at the end of Clarence Street

Tuesday and Thursday through Sunday at 10am and 2pm. Cruises cost A$20 (US$16) for adults, A$8 (US$6.40) for children 6 to 14, and A$49 (US$39) for families. Reservations are essential. The boat also travels up the river on a 5-hour Barbecue Cruise every Wednesday at 10am. It docks at a private bush park along the way, and passengers can tuck into a traditional Aussie barbecue of steaks, fish, and salad. You can then fish, take a bushwalk, swim, or take a 20-minute four-wheel-drive trip. The cruise costs A$37 (US$30) for adults, A$18 (US$14) for children, and A$94 (US$75) for families. A 4-hour cruise leaves on Monday at 10am. It costs A$35 (US$28) for adults, A$15 (US$10) for children, and A$88 (US$70) for families.

WHERE TO STAY

El Paso Motor Inn   Right on the waterfront, the El Paso offers standard motel-type rooms; the more expensive deluxe doubles are a little larger and have newer furniture and a fresher coat of paint after being refurbished in 1998. Two rooms have Jacuzzis, and some come with kitchenettes. The third-floor three-room suite has good ocean views and a kitchenette.

29 Clarence St., Port Macquarie, NSW 2444. (© **1800/027 965** in Australia, or 02/6583 1944. Fax 02/6584 1021. 55 units. A$87 (US$70) standard double; A$97 (US$78) deluxe double; A$130 (US$104) Jacuzzi room; A$150 (US$120) suite. Extra person A$10 (US$8). A$30 (US$24) surcharge per room per night Easter, Christmas, and some long weekends. DC, MC, V. **Amenities:** Restaurant; bar; good-size heated outdoor pool; Jacuzzi; sauna; game room; tour desk; babysitting; nonsmoking rooms. *In room:* A/C, TV, minibar, coffeemaker, hair dryer, iron/ironing board.

COFFS HARBOUR: BANANA CAPITAL OF AUSTRALIA ⚘
554km (344 miles) N of Sydney; 427km (265 miles) S of Brisbane

Rainforests, beaches, and sand surround the relaxed capital of Australia's Holiday Coast. The state's "banana republic" headquarters—the area produces more bananas than any other in Australia—is bordered by hillsides furrowed with rows of banana palms. Farther inland, the rolling hills plateau into Dorrigo National Park, one of the best examples of accessible rainforests anywhere. Also inland is the Nymboida River, known for its excellent white-water rafting.

Coffs Harbour is a rather disjointed place, with an old town-center retail area; the Jetty Strip (with restaurants and fishing boats) near the best swimming spot, Park Beach; and a new retail area called the Plaza. Wide sweeps of suburbia separate the three areas; it's a difficult town to negotiate if you don't have a car.

ESSENTIALS

GETTING THERE   It takes around 7 hours to drive from Sydney to Coffs Harbour without stops; from Brisbane it takes around 5 hours. The Pacific Highway in this region is notoriously dangerous; many serious accidents have involved drivers enduring long hours behind the wheel. Ongoing road-widening projects should improve things. **Qantas** (© **13 13 13** in Australia) flies nonstop to Coffs Harbour from Sydney. Several coach companies, including **Greyhound Australia** (© **13 14 99** in Australia, or 07/4690 9950; www.greyhound.com.au), make the trip from Sydney in about 9 hours. A **Countrylink** (© **13 22 32** in Australia) train from Sydney costs A$79 (US$63).

VISITOR INFORMATION   The **Coffs Harbour Visitors Information Centre** (© **1800/025 650** in Australia, or 02/6652 1522) is just off the Pacific Highway, at the corner of Rose Avenue and Marcia Street, 2 blocks north of the city center. It's open daily from 9am to 5pm. A good general website is www.holidaycoast.com.au.

GETTING AROUND   If you don't have a car, you can get around on **Coffs Harbour Coaches** (© 02/6652 2877), which runs day trips around the local area on weekdays (including a town tour on Mon, and a trip to the magnificent Dorrigo National Park on Wed). **Blue Tongue Transport** ☆ (© 1800/258 386 in Australia, or 02/6651 8566) offers smaller group tours. They include a daily trip to Dorrigo National Park costing A$50 (US$40) for adults and A$40 (US$32) for children; a morning city tour for A$11 (US$8.80); and an upmarket afternoon champagne tour of town for A$22 (US$18).

VISITING THE BIG BANANA & OTHER THINGS TO DO

You can't miss the 10m (33-ft.) reinforced-concrete banana alongside the highway at the **Big Banana Theme Park** (© 02/6652 4355), 3km (2 miles) north of town. The park has an air-conditioned, diesel-powered train that takes visitors on a 1-hour tour of the 18-hectare (44-acre) banana plantation, which contains some 18,000 banana trees. Along the route it passes various off-the-wall exhibits relating to farming, Aborigines, and local history. It stops at the property's hydroponic glasshouses and at a viewing platform and cafeteria, which serves all things banana—cakes, breads, splits, shakes, and so on. The park is open daily from 9am to 4:30pm (3pm in winter). Admission is free, but the train tour costs A$10 (US$8) for adults, A$6 (US$4.80) for children, and A$25 (US$20) for families. I had my doubts about this place before I visited, but I ended up charmed—even if it was simply by the wackiness of the place.

The **Coffs Harbour Zoo** (© 02/6656 1330), 10 minutes north of town on the Pacific Highway, has plenty of koalas, as well as wombats, kangaroos, dingoes, Tasmanian devils, water birds, and aviaries. The award-winning native gardens are full of wild birds expecting a feed. The zoo is open daily from 8:30am to 4pm. Admission is A$12 (US$9.60) for adults, A$6 (US$4.80) for children, and A$30 (US$24) for families.

A free natural attraction is **Mutton Bird Island,** which you can get to from the Coffs Harbour jetty. A steep path leads up the side of the island, but views from the top are worth it. Between September and April the island is home to thousands of shearwaters (mutton birds), which make their nests in burrows in the ground.

If you prefer fish, try diving with gray nurse sharks, manta rays, and moray eels with **Island Snorkel and Dive** (© 02/6654 2860) or **Dive Quest** (© 02/6654 1930). The *Pamela Star* (© 02/6658 4379) offers good-value deep-sea-fishing trips for A$60 (US$48), including tackle, bait, and lunch. The boat leaves Coffs Harbour jetty at 7:30am and returns at 1:30pm daily.

For a taste of gold fever, head to **George's Gold Mine,** 40km (25 miles) west of Coffs Harbour on Bushman's Range Road (© 02/6654 5355 or 02/6654 5273). You get to go into an old-time gold mine, see the "stamper battery" crushing the ore, and pan for gold yourself. The mine is open Wednesday through Sunday (daily during school and public holidays) from 10:30am to 4pm. Admission is A$9 (US$7.20) for adults, A$4.50 (US$3.60) for children, and A$26 (US$21) for families.

Kiwi Down Under Farm (© 02/6653 4449) is a fascinating organic farm growing kiwi fruit and macadamia nuts, among other things. No nasty sprays are used here. Free 30- to 45-minute guided tours of the property leave at 2, 3, and 4pm on weekends and school holidays. The teashop on the premises serves amazing scones and jam for A$4.50 (US$3.60) and excellent vegetarian lunches for A$8.50 (US$6.80). The farm is 14km (8½ miles) south of Coffs Harbour; turn off at Gleniffer Road, just south of Bonville, and follow signs for 4km (2½ miles).

SHOPPING FOR ARTS & CRAFTS

The area has several recognized "crafts drives," where tourists can go in search of quality souvenirs. Pick up a free copy of *Discover the Coffs Harbour Region* from the tourist information center for details on the dozens of crafts shops in the area. One of the best is the **Australian Wild Flower Gallery** (✆ **02/6651 5763**), just off West High Street and Bennetts Road in Coffs Harbour proper. Wolfgang Shultze carves intricate designs out of pewter, silver, and gold to make detailed animal- and plant-inspired jewelry, charms, and spoons. Pieces cost A$5 to A$36 (US$4–US$29). The gallery is open daily from 9am to 5pm.

On the way to or from the Dorrigo rainforest, stop off at the township of **Bellingen,** 20 minutes south of Coffs Harbour on Waterfall Way. It's a pleasant place with several crafts shops. Among the best is **The Old Church,** 8 Church St., just off the main road (✆ **02/6655 0438**), crammed full of wooden crafts items, cards, furniture, wacky mobiles, incense, hats, and knickknacks, and surrounded by gardens and fruit trees. It's open daily from 8:30am to 5:30pm.

EXPLORING THE RAINFORESTS & OTHER OUTDOOR ADVENTURES

Coffs Harbour's main advantage is its position as a good base for exploring the surrounding countryside. You must see the World Heritage–listed **Dorrigo National Park** ★★, 68km (42 miles) west of Coffs Harbour, via Bellingen. Perched on the Great Dividing Range that separates the lush eastern seaboard from the arid interior, the rainforest here is one of the best I've seen in Australia. (It's a pity that so much fell to the axes of early settlers.) Entry is free.

The **Dorrigo Rainforest Centre** (✆ **02/6657 2309**) is the gateway to the park and has extensive information on the rainforest. Just outside is the 21m-high (69-ft.) **Skywalk,** which offers a bird's-eye view of the forest canopy. Several walks leave from the Rainforest Centre, the Glade Picnic Area (about 1km/½ mile away), and the Never-Never Picnic Area (a 10km/6¼-mile drive along Dome Rd.). Most tracks are suitable for wheelchairs. Bring a raincoat or an umbrella; it is a rainforest, after all! The **Dorrigo Tourist Information** office (✆ **02/6657 2486**) is in the center of Dorrigo township.

One of the best tour operators in the area is the award-winning **Mountain Trails 4WD Tours** (✆ **02/6658 3333;** fax 02/6658 3299). Full-day tours that include visits to two rainforest areas and a good lunch cost A$80 (US$64) for adults and A$60 (US$48) for children under 16. Half-day tours of one rainforest cost A$56 (US$45) for adults and A$40 (US$32) for children.

For a bit more personal action, try horseback riding through the rainforest 23km (14 miles) southwest of Coffs Harbour with **Valery Trails** (✆ **02/6653 4301**). Two-hour rides leave at 10am and 2pm daily and cost A$35 (US$28) per person. Reservations are essential.

Looking for an adrenaline rush? Then head to the **Raleigh International Raceway** (✆ **02/6655 4017**), where you can zip around the track behind the wheel of your very own go-kart. It's 23km (14 miles) south of Coffs Harbour and 3km (2 miles) along Valery Road off the Pacific Highway north of Nambucca Heads. Eleven high-speed laps cost A$27 (US$22), and 16 cost A$38 (US$30). It's open daily from 9am to 5pm (to 6pm in summer).

WHERE TO STAY

Coffs Harbour is a popular beachside holiday spot, with plenty of motels along the Pacific Highway offering standard roadside rooms for A$35 to A$49 (US$28–US$39). Vacancy signs are common outside Australian school holiday periods and the Christmas and Easter periods (when Coffs really fills up). A few to try are the **Caribbean Motel,** 353 High St., Coffs Harbour, NSW 2450 (© **02/6652 1500;** fax 02/6651 4158), with doubles ranging from A$55 to A$120 (US$44–US$96), depending on the season and the view; and the **Coffs Harbour Motor Inn,** 22 Elizabeth St., Coffs Harbour, NSW 2450 (© **02/6652 6388;** fax 02/6652 6493), with doubles for A$72 to A$108 (US$57–US$86), depending on the season.

Pelican Beach Resort Australis ★ *Value* This Bali-style resort complex is 7km (4½ miles) north of Coffs Harbour beside a long stretch of creamy sand. (The beach is dangerous for swimming.) Terraced over six levels, the resort's rooms all have balconies, and many have ocean views. Standard rooms are light and modern, with either twin or queen-size beds. Family rooms have a kitchenette, a dining area, and one queen-size and two single beds divided by a half wall. Suites have a separate bedroom, kitchenette, lounge area, and Jacuzzi. Two rooms are equipped for travelers with disabilities. The highest rates apply from December 26 through January 18. Outside in the landscaped gardens are a minigolf course and a volleyball court.

Pacific Hwy., Coffs Harbour, NSW 2450. © **1300/650 464** in Australia, or 02/6653 7000. Fax 02/6653 7066. 112 units. www.australishotels.com. A$120–A$215 (US$96–US$172) double; A$184–A$330 (US$147–US$264) family room for up to 4; A$236–A$463 (US$153–US$300) suite. Extra person A$33 (US$26). Ask about packages and discounts. AE, DC, MC, V. **Amenities:** Restaurant; bar; large lagoon-style pool; 3 tennis courts; exercise room; 2 Jacuzzis; sauna; children's center (weekends); game room; concierge; tour desk; car-rental desk; 24-hr. room service; babysitting; massage; free self-service laundry; dry cleaning; nonsmoking rooms. *In room:* A/C, TV, dataport, minibar, hair dryer, iron/ironing board.

Sanctuary Motor Inn Resort If you like animals, you'll love this animal sanctuary and guesthouse complex 2km (1¼ miles) south of town. Wandering around the grounds are wallabies, kangaroos, peacocks, and several species of native birds. The rooms are comfortable; the more expensive units are larger and more recently renovated. The executive room comes with a Jacuzzi. Four units have kitchens.

Pacific Hwy., Coffs Harbour, NSW 2450. © **02/6652 2111.** Fax 02/6652 4725. phciscato@hotmail.com.au. 38 units. A$88 (US$70) standard double; A$94 (US$75) superior double; A$150 (US$120) executive double. Extra person A$15 (US$12). Holiday surcharge A$25 (US$20) per room per night. Ask about Aussie auto club discounts. AE, DC, MC, V. **Amenities:** Restaurant; bar; large heated outdoor pool; minigolf; lit tennis and squash courts; Jacuzzi; sauna; room service (7–9am and 6–8pm); coin-op laundry. *In room:* A/C, TV w/free satellite channels, fridge, coffeemaker, hair dryer.

WHERE TO DINE

Seafood Mama's ★ ITALIAN/SEAFOOD This charming, informal, award-winning restaurant packs a mean barbecue seafood dish of octopus, prawns, fish, calamari, and mussels. It's a rustic, bottles-hanging-from-the-ceiling Italian joint right on the ocean. Also on the menu are some well-regarded veal and steak dishes, and plenty of pastas. Seafood Mama's is near the Pelican Beach and the older Nautilus resorts, 7km (4½ miles) north of Coffs Harbour. The restaurant will do takeout and deliver to your hotel.

Pacific Hwy. © **02/6653 6733.** Reservations recommended. Main courses A$13–A$25 (US$10–US$20). AE, DC, MC, V. Tues–Sat 6–10pm.

BYRON BAY: A BEACH BOHEMIA ★

790km (490 miles) N of Sydney; 200km (124 miles) S of Brisbane; 78km (48 miles) SE of Murwillumbah

At the easternmost point on the Australian mainland, the sun's rays hit Byron before anywhere else. This geographical position is good for two things: You can spot whales as they migrate north in June and July, and it's attractive to the town's "alternative" community. Painters, craftspeople, glass blowers, and poets are so plentiful they almost fall from the macadamia trees. The place is loaded with float tanks, "pure body products," beauty therapists, and massage centers. Though it attracts squadrons of backpackers to its party scene and discos each summer, many of the locals simply stay at home, sipping their herbal tea and preparing for the healing light of the coming dawn. Families love Byron Bay for the beautiful beaches, and surfers flock here for some of the best waves in the world.

ESSENTIALS

GETTING THERE   If you're driving up the north coast, leave the Pacific Highway at Ballina and take the scenic coast road via Lennox Head. It's around 10 hours by car from Sydney, and 2 hours from Brisbane.

   Regional Express (© **13 17 13** in Australia; www.regionalexpress.com.au) flies from Sydney to Ballina, south of Byron Bay. The round-trip fare is around A$280 (US$224). **Virgin Blue** (www.virginblue.com.au) also flies to Ballina. **Byron Bus Transfers** (© **02/6681 3354**) meets all flights and transfers to Byron Bay for A$20 (US$16) single and A$35 (US$28) round-trip. **Coolangatta Airport** is 1 hour north of Byron Bay (112km/69 miles). **Countrylink** (© **13 22 32** in Australia) runs daily trains from Sydney to Byron Bay; the one-way fare is A$98 (US$78) for adults and A$47 (US$37) for children, and the trip takes 12¾ hours. **Greyhound Australia** (© **13 14 99** in Australia, or 07/4690 9950; www.greyhound.com.au) buses from Sydney take 13½ hours; the one-way coach fare is A$69 (US$55).

ORGANIZED TOURS FROM SYDNEY   An unusual way to get to Byron is on a 5-day surf safari from Sydney with **Surfaris** (© **1800/634 941** in Australia; www.surfaris.com). You can learn to surf along the way as you stop off at several beaches, camping overnight. Trips leave Sydney on Monday morning and Byron Bay on Sunday morning. The safari costs A$499 (US$399), all-inclusive—though you need to bring a sleeping bag.

   Another great trip is with **Ando's Outback Tours** (© **1800/228 828** in Australia; www.outbacktours.com.au), which operates from Sydney every Sunday. It heads inland deep into the Outback on a 5-day trip and returns to Byron Bay. Among the highlights are visits to Lightning Ridge and the wild Glengarry opal fields (see "Outback New South Wales," later in this chapter). The trip costs A$435 (US$348). A return trip to Sydney from Byron Bay costs A$35 (US$28).

VISITOR INFORMATION   The **Byron Visitors Centre,** 80 Jonson St., Byron Bay, NSW 2481 (© **02/6680 9271**), is open daily from 9am to 5pm. A half-hour farther south is the **Ballina Tourist Information Centre,** on the corner of Las Balsas Plaza and River Street, Ballina (© **02/6686 3484**), open daily from 9am to 5pm. Two good websites are **www.byronbay.net.au** and **www.byronbay-online.com**.

SPECIAL EVENTS   Byron really goes to town during 4 days over the Easter weekend with the **East Coast Blues & Roots Festival** (www.bluesfest.com.au). Up to 30,000 people camp out to listen to up to 80 acts, including the likes of Ben Harper,

Midnight Oil, and Joan Armatrading. Book tickets on the Web. On the first Sunday of every month, the extraordinary local **crafts market** brings hippies and funky performers out from the hinterland. Byron Bay is very popular over the Christmas period, so book well in advance.

HITTING THE SURF & SAND
Many accommodations in Byron Bay offer free surfboards for guests. If yours doesn't, head to the **Byron Bay Surf Shop,** Lawson Street at the corner of Fletcher Street (© 02/6685 7536), which rents boards for A$12 (US$9.60) for 4 hours and A$20 (US$16) for 24 hours. The shop can also arrange surf lessons for around A$25 (US$20) per hour.

Wategos Beach and an area off the tip of Cape Byron called **"The Pass"** are two particularly good surf spots—and since each of the beaches faces a different direction, you are bound to find the surf is up on at least one. **Main Beach,** which stretches along the front of the town (it's actually some 50km/31 miles long), is good for swimming. West of Main Beach is **Belongil Beach,** the unofficial nudist beach (when authorities aren't cracking down on covering up). **Clarke's Beach** curves away to the east of Main Beach toward Cape Byron.

The **Cape Byron Lighthouse** on Cape Byron is one of Australia's most powerful. It's eerie to come up here at night to watch the stars and see the light reach some 40km (25 miles) out to sea. A nice walk just south of town goes through the rainforest of the **Broken Heads Nature Reserve.**

The best place to dive around Byron Bay is at **Julian Rocks,** about 3km (2 miles) offshore. Cold currents from the south meet warmer ones from the north here, which makes it a good spot to find a large variety of marine sea life. **Byron Bay Dive Centre,** 111 Jonson St. (© 02/6685 7149), charges A$70 (US$56) for the first dive and A$35 (US$28) for each subsequent dive. **Sundive,** in the Byron Hostel complex on Middleton Street (© 02/6685 7755), has cheaper initial dives (A$60/US$48 each).

EXPLORING THE HILLS & RAINFORESTS
Behind Byron you'll find hills that could make the Irish weep, as well as rainforests, waterfalls, and small farms burgeoning with tropical fruits. A good operator taking trips inland is **Forgotten Country Ecotours** (© 02/6687 7843). **Byron Bay to Bush Tours** (© 02/6685 6889 or 04/1866 2684; bush@mullum.com.au) operates day trips to the hippie hangout of **Nimbin** ★—where during my last visit I was approached four times in 10 minutes by people selling marijuana—and up into the rainforest, where you visit a macadamia-nut farm and have a barbecue on the company's organic farm. The trip leaves at 11am Monday through Saturday and costs A$30 (US$24). This company also operates trips to the Sunday market at Channon the second Sunday of each month and to the market at Bangalow on the fourth Sunday. These trips cost A$15 (US$12).

WHERE TO STAY
Real-estate agents **Elders R Gordon & Sons** (© 02/6685 6222; eldersbb@omcs. com.au) can book rooms and cottages in Byron Bay and in the hinterland. The **Byron Bay Accommodation Booking Office** (© 02/6680 8666; www.byronbayaccom. net) is very helpful for booking places to stay before you arrive.

Arts Factory Lodge *Finds* This is a wacky kind of place. Once famous as a music club popular with American draft-dodgers during the Vietnam War, it's now big with young travelers seeking an alternative place to stay and older folk who cut their hair short years ago. Accommodations include tepees, tents, rooms made from bark strips, and funky indoor "cubes." The so-called Love Shack is more standard, and quite tropical in appearance. Workshops include didgeridoo making, massage, yoga, and even boxing! The entertainment lineup includes live music, fire shows, Aboriginal culture, and sports. A cafe serves vegetarian meals, and the property has a great outdoor pool and lush gardens.

Skinners Shoot Rd., Byron Bay, NSW 2481. © 02/6685 7709. Fax 02/6685 8534. www.artsfactory.com.au. A$25 (US$20) dorm; A$63 (US$52) cube; A$70 (US$56) Love Shack. 3-night minimum. Discounts for 5 nights. **Amenities:** Cafe; outdoor pool; free use of bikes; free minibus to town.

The Byron Bay Waves Motel (The Waves) ★
This exceptional motel is only 60m (197 ft.) from Main Beach and just around the corner from the town center. Each of the very nice rooms comes with a queen-size bed, a marble bathroom with shower, and a king-size tub. Four rooms on the ground floor have a courtyard, and one is suitable for travelers with disabilities. Toasters, in-house massage, and beauty treatments are also available. The suites each have a king-size bed and a large balcony. The penthouse is a very plush, fully self-contained one-bedroom apartment. The six family rooms each sleep three adults, or two adults and two children.

Corner of Lawson and Middleton sts. (P.O. Box 647), Byron Bay NSW 2481. © 02/6685 5966. Fax 02/6685 5977. www.byron-bay.com/waves. 19 units. A$150–A$320 (US$120–US$256) double; A$250–A$380 (US$220–US$304) suite; A$250–A$480 (US$200–US$384) penthouse. Extra person A$20 (US$16). AE, DC, MC, V. **Amenities:** Massage; babysitting; laundry service; nonsmoking rooms. *In room:* A/C, TV, fax, minibar, coffeemaker, hair dryer, iron/ironing board, safe.

Byron Central Apartments
If you don't want to eat out all the time, then this is the place for you. The self-contained apartments come with a queen-size bed and free in-house movies. First-floor units have balconies. There are also a few loft-style apartments with separate dining, lounge, and sleeping areas. Units for people with disabilities are available. The landscaped garden has a barbecue. The apartments are a 2-minute walk from the beach and town. Rates are at their highest in the Christmas and New Year period; low season is April through September.

Byron St., Byron Bay, NSW 2481. © 02/6685 8800. Fax 02/6685 8802. www.byronbay.com/bca. 26 units. A$120–A$260 (US$96–US$208) standard apt. Ask about long-term discounts. AE, DC, MC, V. **Amenities:** Medium-size saltwater pool; coin-op laundry; nonsmoking rooms. *In room:* TV, kitchen, fridge, coffeemaker, hair dryer.

Holiday Village Backpackers ★
Byron Bay's original hostel is still one of the best. It's in the center of town next door to Woolworth's supermarket and only a few minutes' walk from the bus and train stops, the main beach, and the town center. The National Roads and Motorists' Association gives this place a five-star backpackers' rating, which is as good as it gets. Dorm rooms are clean, and doubles in the hostel are above average. Doubles come with a double bed, a fan, and a wardrobe. For a couple of dollars more you can stay in a self-contained unit with a separate bedroom, lounge, and kitchen area. On the premises are a volleyball court; Jacuzzi and pool; TV and video lounge (with a library); barbecues; basketball hoop; Internet and e-mail; and free surfboards, body boards, and bikes.

116 Jonson St., Byron Bay, NSW 2481. © 02/6685 8888. Fax 02/6685 8777. 42 units, 13 with bathroom. A$55–A$65 (US$44–US$52) hostel double; A$70–A$85 (US$56–US$68) self-contained double; A$21–A$29 (US$17–US$23) dorm bed. MC, V. **Amenities:** Medium-size heated outdoor pool; Jacuzzi; bike rentals; tour desk; coin-op laundry; nonsmoking rooms. *In room:* Fridge.

Taylor's Guest House ⭐⭐ This beautiful guesthouse sits on 2 secluded hectares (5 acres) of gardens and rainforest. The guest rooms are lavishly decorated in country style and come with either a queen- or king-size bed. The huge cottage has wrap-around verandas and long French windows, and is done up in bright Santa Fe–style colors. The cottage also comes with a laundry and has the largest bed in Australia—a 2.4×2.1m (8×7-ft.) antique English "Emperor" bed. The guesthouse is renowned for its cooking. Prices drop when you stay for longer than 1 night.

160 McGettigan's Lane, Ewingsdale, Byron Bay, NSW 2481. © 02/6684 7436. Fax 02/6684 7526. www.taylors. net.au. 5 units, 1 cottage. A$220 (US$18) double; A$330 (US$264) cottage. Rates include breakfast, cakes, biscuits, and predinner champagne cocktails. Dinner A$60 (US$48) per person. Surcharge 20% for doubles and 50% for cottage Easter and Christmas. AE, DC, MC, V. Children not accepted. **Amenities:** Restaurant; lounge; large heated outdoor pool; nonsmoking rooms. *In room:* TV, hair dryer, iron/ironing board.

WHERE TO DINE

Byron Bay's **Jonson Street** is crammed with eateries, so you certainly won't starve.

Beach Hotel Barbecue PUB/BARBECUE The outdoor meals at this pub near the beach make it popular with visitors and locals. About the cheapest thing on the menu is the burger, and the most expensive is steak. The Beach Hotel Bistro is open from 10am to 9pm daily and serves coffee, cakes, and snacks throughout the day; a lunch menu is served from noon to 3pm and dinner from 6 to 9pm.

In the Beach Hotel, at Bay and Jonson sts. © 02/6685 6402. Main courses A$3.90–A$14 (US$3.15–US$11). No credit cards. Daily noon–3pm.

Earth 'n' Sea PIZZA/PASTA This popular spot has been around for years and offers a fairly extensive menu of pastas and pizzas, including some unusual combinations such as prawns, banana, and pineapple. Pizzas come in three sizes; the small is just enough to satisfy the average appetite.

11 Lawson St. © 02/6685 6029. Reservations recommended. Main courses A$9.50–A$24 (US$7.60–US$19). AE, MC, V. Daily 5:30–11pm.

The Pass Café ⭐ MEDITERRANEAN Though not as well positioned as Rae's Restaurant and Bar (see below), The Pass Café rivals Rae's for breakfasts and lunches. If you happen to be heading to or from the local rainforest on the Cape Byron Walking Track, you'll find this a great place to stop off. Breakfast items range from simple fresh fruit and muffins to gourmet chicken sausages. Lunch specials include Cajun chicken, octopus, and calamari salad, as well as fresh fish, meat dishes, and plenty of good vegetarian options.

At the end of Brooke Dr., on Cape Byron Walking Track, Palm Valley. © 02/6685 6074. Main courses A$10–A$25 (US$8–US$20). MC, V. Sun–Wed 8am–3pm; Thurs–Sat 8am–6pm.

Rae's Restaurant and Bar ⭐ MODERN AUSTRALIAN/SEAFOOD You can't beat Rae's for its location or its food. It's right on the beach, about a 2-minute drive from the town center, and has a secluded, privileged air about it—in the nicest of ways. Inside it's all Mediterranean blue and white, perfectly complementing the waves hitting the sand. The menu changes daily, but you may find the likes of grilled Atlantic salmon, red curry of roast beef filet, braised lamb shanks, and yellowfin tuna. If you have any special dietary requirements, tell the chef, and he will go out of his way to please you. Next door to the restaurant, but part of the same establishment, is **Rae's on Watago's,** an exclusive AAA-rated five-star guesthouse offering luxury accommodations. There are seven units; prices run from A$350 (US$280) for a double suite to A$990 (US$792) for the penthouse suite.

Watago's Beach, Byron Bay. © 02/6685 5366. Fax 02/6685 5695. www.raes.com.au. Reservations recommended. Main courses A$30–A$35 (US$24–US$28) lunch, A$35–A$50 (US$28–US$40) dinner. AE, DC, MC, V. Daily 7–10pm; Sat–Sun noon–3pm.

Raving Prawn ☆ SEAFOOD   Fish cover the walls at this excellent place, and there's more than that on the menu. You can tuck into veal, chicken, or vegetarian dishes if you want to, but I wouldn't miss out on the fabulous signature dish, jewfish (a kind of grouper) with herb-mustard crust. Forest-berry tart is the best dessert on the menu.

Feros Arcade (between Jonson and Lawson sts.). © 02/6685 6737. Reservations recommended. Main courses A$19–A$27 (US$15–US$22). AE, DC, MC, V. Tues–Sat 6–10pm (until around 9pm in winter); daily 6–10pm during school holidays.

MURWILLUMBAH
321km (199 miles) N of Coffs Harbour; 893km (554 miles) N of Sydney; 30km (19 miles) S of Queensland border

The main town of the Tweed Valley, Murwillumbah is a good base for touring the surrounding area, which includes **Mount Warning,** picturesque towns, and countryside dominated by sugar cane and banana.

ESSENTIALS
GETTING THERE   Murwillumbah is inland from the Pacific Highway. The nearest airport is at **Coolangatta,** 34km (21 miles) away, over the Queensland border. **Countrylink** trains (© 13 22 42 in Australia) link Murwillumbah with Sydney, taking around 13 hours. The one-way fare is A$110 (US$88) in standard class, A$149 (US$119) in first class. **Greyhound Australia** (© 13 14 99 in Australia, or 07/4690 9950; www.greyhound.com.au) runs from Sydney to Murwillumbah; the trip takes 14½ hours.

VISITOR INFORMATION   The **Murwillumbah Visitors Centre,** at the corner of the Pacific Highway and Alma Street, Murwillumbah, NSW 2484 (© 02/6672 1340), is worth visiting before heading out to see more of the Tweed Valley or the beaches to the east. Another option is the **Tweed Heads Visitors Centre,** at the corner of Bay and Wharf streets, Tweed Heads, NSW 2485 (© 07/5536 4244). Both are open Monday through Friday from 9am to 5pm, and Saturday from 9am to 1pm.

SEEING THE AREA
If you're looking for a Big Avocado to go with your Coffs Harbour Big Banana, head for **Tropical Fruit World,** on the Pacific Highway (© 02/6677 7222), 15km (9½ miles) north of Murwillumbah and 15km (9½ miles) south of Coolangatta. The Tweed Valley's top attraction grows some 400 varieties of tropical fruit, which you can discover on an interesting 1½-hour tractor-train tour of the 81-hectare (200-acre) plantation, as well as on four-wheel-drive rainforest drives and riverboat rides. It's open daily from 10am to 5pm. Also on the property are a kiosk, fruit market, and gift shop. Admission to food and shopping areas is free. Guided tours cost A$22 (US$18) for adults, A$12 (US$9.60) for children 4 to 12.

The 1,154m (3,785-ft.) **Mount Warning** is part of the rim of an extinct volcano formed some 20 to 23 million years ago. You can hike around the mountain and to the top on trails in the Mount Warning World Heritage Park.

WHERE TO STAY & DINE

Crystal Creek Rainforest Retreat ★★ Crystal Creek is tucked away in a little valley of rainforest just 25 minutes by car from the Pacific Highway. Self-contained cabins skirt the edge of the rainforest that borders the Border Ranges National Park, a World Heritage site. There are plenty of native birds, possums, echidnas, wallabies, and bandicoots around and about. Guests can swim in the cold natural pools and laze around on hammocks strung up in the bush. Cabins have two comfortable rooms, a balcony, a kitchen, a barbecue, and plenty of privacy. Two glass-terrace cabins overlook the rainforest and mountain. All rooms have a king-size bed and a double Jacuzzi—with no curtains in the bathroom, because the rainforest gives enough privacy. Several tours are offered, including four-wheel-drive rainforest tours and visits to local country markets and arts-and-crafts galleries, as well as walking tours around the property. Guests cook their own food (bring it with you) or eat at the casual restaurant.

Brookers Rd., Upper Crystal Creek, Murwillumbah, NSW 2484. ⓒ 02/6679 1591. Fax 02/6679 1596. www.crystal creekrainforestretreat.com.au. 7 cabins. A$240–A$260 (US$192–US$208) double. Ask about weekday specials. AE, DC, MC, V. Pickup service from the airport, bus, and train stations available. Children not accepted. **Amenities:** Restaurant; Jacuzzi; 24-hr. room service; massage; nonsmoking rooms. *In room:* TV, CD player, kitchen, fridge, coffeemaker, hair dryer, iron/ironing board.

THE TWEED VALLEY AFTER DARK

The clubs up here on the border of Queensland are huge and offer cheap bistro meals as well as pricier ones in more upscale restaurants, inexpensive drinks at the bar, entertainment, and hundreds of poker machines. The biggest in New South Wales is the **Twin Towns Services Club,** Wharf Street, Tweed Heads (ⓒ **07/5536 2277**). Another worth checking out is **Seagulls Rugby League Club,** Gollan Drive, Tweed Heads (ⓒ **07/5536 3433**). Major entertainers such as Tom Jones and Joe Cocker have played here over the last few years. It's open 24 hours. To gain admittance to these "private" clubs, you must sign the registration book just inside the door. Tweed Heads is 40km (25 miles), or about a 30-minute drive, from Murwillumbah.

5 South of Sydney along the Princes Highway

Two main roads lead south out of Sydney: the M5, which turns into the Hume Highway, and the Princes Highway. Both routes connect Sydney to Melbourne, but the M5/Hume Highway route is quicker. A favorite with truckers and anyone in a hurry, the M5/Hume Highway will get you to Melbourne in about 12 hours. The Princes Highway is a scenic coastal route that can get you to Melbourne in 2 days, though the many attractions along the route make it well worth taking longer.

KIAMA
119km (74 miles) S of Sydney

Kiama (pop. 10,300) is famous for its **blowhole.** In fact, there are two, a large one and a smaller one; both spurt seawater several meters into the air. The larger of the two can jet water up to 60m (197 ft.), but you need a large swell and strong southeasterly winds to force the sea through the rock fissure with enough force to achieve that height. The smaller of the two is more consistent but fares better with a good northeasterly wind.

Pick up a map from the **Kiama Visitors Centre** (see below) to guide you on a Heritage Walk through the historic district of this quaint village, where you can tour a row of National Trust workers' cottages built in 1896. There's little reason to stay the night—plenty of more scenic places await farther south.

ESSENTIALS

GETTING THERE   From Sydney, travel south on the Princes Highway via the steelworks city of Wollongong. There's also regular train service from Sydney, and **Greyhound Australia** (© **13 14 99** in Australia, or 07/4690 9950; www.greyhound. com.au) coach service. The trip by coach takes about 2 hours, the train trip a little less.

VISITOR INFORMATION   The **Kiama Visitors Centre,** Blowhole Point, Kiama (© **02/4232 3322;** fax 02/4226 3260; www.kiama.net/default.htm), is open daily from 9am to 5pm.

JERVIS BAY: AN OFF-THE-BEATEN-TRACK GEM ★★
182km (113 miles) S of Sydney

Booderee National Park, at Jervis Bay, is nothing short of spectacular. You should come here even if it means missing out on some of Sydney's treasures. How does this grab you—miles of deserted beaches, the whitest sand imaginable, kangaroos you can stroke, lorikeets that mob you for food during the day and possums that do the same at night, pods of dolphins, great walks through gorgeous bushland, and a real Aboriginal spirituality-of-place? I could go on, but see for yourself.

ESSENTIALS

GETTING THERE   It's best to reach Jervis Bay via Huskisson, 24km (15 miles) southeast of Nowra on the Princes Highway. Approximately 16km (10 miles) south of Nowra, turn left onto the Jervis Bay Road to Huskisson. The entrance to Booderee National Park—formally named Jervis Bay National Park—is just after Huskisson. It's about a 3-hour drive from Sydney. You'll probably need at least 2 days to get to know the area. Watch out for the black cockatoos.

    Australian Pacific Tours (© **02/9247 7222;** fax 02/9247 2052; www.aptours.com. au) runs a dolphin-watching cruise to Jervis Bay from Sydney every day between early October and mid-April, and Monday and Thursday in winter. The 12-hour trip—7 hours of which are on the coach—includes a visit to the Kiama blowhole, a 3-hour luncheon cruise looking for bottlenose dolphins, and a stop on the way back at Fitzroy Falls in the Southern Highlands. The trip costs A$117 (US$94) for adults and A$109 (US$87) for children.

    East Coast Adventure Tours (© **1800/666 000** in Australia; www.beachnbush. com.au) takes backpackers and adventurous oldies on a 2-night trip to Jervis Bay every Friday evening. You walk deep into the huge Morton National Park, go on a dolphin cruise, and spend the rest of the weekend in Jervis Bay. The trip costs A$219 (US$175) per person.

VISITOR INFORMATION   For information on the area, contact the **Shoalhaven Visitors Centre,** at the corner of Princes Highway and Pleasant Way, Nowra (© **1800/024 261** in Australia, or 02/4421 0778; www.shoalhaven.nsw.gov.au). Pick up maps and book camping sites at the **Booderee National Park** office (© **02/4443 0977;** www.booderee.np.gov.au), located just beyond Huskisson; it's open daily from 9am to 4pm. **Hyams Beach Store** (© **02/4443 0242**) has an accommodations guide listing 34 rental properties for A$100 (US$80) and up for a weekend.

SEEING THE AREA

If you want to see the best spots, you'll need to pay the park-entrance fee of A$10 (US$8) per day; a standard NSW National Parks Pass doesn't work here. Places to visit include **Hyams Beach** ⋆, reputed to have the whitest sand in the world. Notice how it squeaks when you walk on it. Wear sunscreen! The reflection off the beach can burn your skin in minutes even on a cloudy day. **Hole in the Wall Beach** has interesting rock formations and a lingering smell of natural sulfur. Secluded **Summer Cloud Bay** offers excellent fishing.

Dolphin Watch Cruises, 74 Owen St., Huskisson (© **1800/246 010** in Australia, or 02/4441 6311; www.dolphinwatch.com.au), runs a hardy vessel out of Huskisson on the lookout for the resident pod of bottlenose dolphins—you have "more than a 95% chance of seeing them," the company claims. A 2-hour coffee cruise runs at 10am on Saturday and Sunday, public holidays, and school holidays, and costs A$20 (US$16) for adults and A$10 (US$8) for children. A 2½-hour dolphin watch and bay cruise leaves at 1pm and costs A$25 (US$20) for adults and A$12 (US$9.60) for children. It's possible to see humpback and southern right whales in June and July and from mid-September to mid-November. A 3-hour whale-watch cruise costs A$40 (US$32) for adults and A$30 (US$24) for children.

WHERE TO STAY & DINE

If you have a tent and camping gear, all the better. **Caves Beach** is a quiet spot (except when the birds chorus at dawn) just a stroll away from a good beach; it's home to eastern gray kangaroos. A campsite here costs A$8.65 (US$6.90) per tent in winter and A$11 (US$8.60) in summer and on public holidays. It's about a 250m (about ⅒-mile) walk from the car park to the campground. **Greenpatch** is more dirt than grass, but you get your own area, and it's suitable for motor homes. It's infested with over-friendly possums around dusk. A camp spot here costs A$13 (US$10) in winter and A$16 (US$13) in summer.

For supplies, head to the area's main towns, **Huskisson** (pop. 930) and **Vincentia** (pop. 2,350). The **Huskisson RSL Club,** overlooking the wharf area on Owen Street (© **02/4441 5282**), has a good bistro and a bar. You'll have to sign in inside the main entrance. The Huskisson Hotel (also called the "Husskie Pub") is down the road and has a nice beer garden and cheapish meals at lunchtime.

Huskisson Beach Tourist Resort   This resort is the very pinnacle of cabin accommodations on this part of the east coast. Cabins vary in price depending on size, but even the smallest has room enough for a double bed, triple bunks, and a small kitchen with microwave. Larger cabins have two separate bedrooms. There's a game room and barbecue facilities. Weekend prices are huge, so best to stay weekdays. Rates also rise significantly over Christmas and Easter.

Beach St., Huskisson, Jervis Bay, NSW 2540. ©/fax **02/4441 5142.** www.huskissonbeachtouristresort.com.au. 38 cabins. Weekdays A$75–A$140 (US$60–US$112); weekends A$140–A$320 (US$112–US$256). DC, MC, V. **Amenities:** Small heated outdoor pool; lit tennis court; coin-op laundry; nonsmoking rooms. *In room:* TV, kitchen, fridge, coffeemaker, hair dryer, iron/ironing board.

Jervis Bay Guest House ⋆   This relatively new guesthouse has four distinctly different rooms (different color schemes, beds, and so on), each with a private bathroom. One room has a Jacuzzi, and two rooms face the water and have coffeemakers. Breakfast is a hearty affair that could include emu sausages and thick slabs of bacon followed by a tropical fruit platter.

Tips   A Safety Warning

Jervis Bay is notorious for its car break-ins, a situation the local police force has been unable to control. If you park your car anywhere in the national park, remove all valuables, including things in the trunk.

1 Beach St., Huskisson, NSW 2540. © 02/4441 7658. Fax 02/4441 7659. www.jervisbayguesthouse.com.au. 4 units. A$145–A$220 (US$116–US$176) double. Rates include breakfast. AE, DC, MC, V. After the Jervis Bay Hotel, take the 2nd road to the left (Nowra St.) and follow it to the end. Children under 16 not accepted. **Amenities:** Lounge and game room; tour desk; massage; nonsmoking rooms. *In room:* A/C, hair dryer, iron/ironing board.

ULLADULLA
220km (136 miles) south of Sydney

Very much a supply town as well as a fishing center, especially for tuna, Ulladulla is a pleasant stopover on your journey south. This is also a good place to stock up on supplies from local supermarkets. On the outskirts of town (just to the south) are a series of saltwater lakes with good fishing, though you'll have competition from the pelicans. Inland is the giant Morton National Park, marked by the peak of Pigeonhouse Mountain. The 3- to 4-hour walk to the top and back starts at a parking lot a 30-minute drive from Ulladulla. The going is steep at first, but the trail levels out as it crosses a sandstone plateau. Another upward climb and you're rewarded with a magnificent view of peaks and ocean.

Several side roads worth exploring spur off between Ulladulla and Batemans Bay (see below). These lead to the tiny villages of Bawley Point and Kioloa, where holiday cottages nestle between isolated beaches, gum forests, and green patches studded with gray kangaroos.

There are more kangaroos at pristine **Pebbly Beach** ★ in Murramarang National Park, a short hop—20 minutes south—of Ulladulla. The furry creatures actually wander around the beach and adjacent campsite, or gather on the grassy dunes to graze. It's a good area for birding, too.

ESSENTIALS
GETTING THERE   Ulladulla is about a 3-hour drive from Sydney Central Business District down the Pacific Highway.

VISITOR INFORMATION   Ulladulla Visitors Centre, Civic Center, Princes Highway (© 02/4455 1269; www.shoalhaven.nsw.gov.au), is open Monday through Friday from 10am to 5pm, Saturday and Sunday from 9am to 5pm.

WHERE TO STAY & DINE
Ulladulla is well known for its food (particularly seafood and beef) and wine (there are a few boutique wineries in the area). For some of the best fish in Australia, head to one of the fish and chips shops on Wason Street, close to the harbor. The best is **Tiger Fish and Chips** (no phone). On the same street is **Torys Takeaway** (© 02/4454 0888), where you can buy good fish and chips on the ground floor for about a third of the price at the very nice restaurant above (**Torys Seafood Restaurant;** open in the evenings; same number) and stroll down to the harbor to eat among the seagulls.

Ulladulla Guest House ★★★   This fabulous, award-winning property is one of the best places to stay in Australia. Run by the friendly Andrew and Elizabeth Nowosad—try and guess his accent—the Ulladulla Guest House is an impressive AAA-rated five-star establishment. It's surrounded by small but lovely tropical gardens—Andrew insists his coconut palms are the only ones this far south—and overlooks the harbor. Unusually, the house is also a registered art gallery, and the walls are festooned with paintings for sale. Past the cozy lounge are three types of rooms. Two self-contained units with private entrances to the garden are the lowest in price. The one-bedroom unit has a queen-size bed and a foldout sofa bed, and the two-bedroom unit has a double bed in one room, two singles in another, and a double foldout sofa bed in the lounge. Luxury rooms have a queen-size bed, custom-made furniture, and original artwork. Executive rooms come with a marble bathroom and a Jacuzzi. There are three masseurs on standby. In the rates listed below, peak periods are weekends, public holidays, Easter, and Christmas school holidays. The hotel prides itself on its food, too.

39 Burrill St., Ulladulla, NSW 2539. ✆ **02/4455 1796.** Fax 02/4454 4660. www.guesthouse.com.au. 10 units. Garden room A$188 (US$150); luxury room A$208 (US$166); family room or executive room A$248 (US$198). 2-night minimum on weekends. 3-course dinner A$50 (US$40). AE, DC, MC, V. **Amenities:** Restaurant; lagoon-style heated outdoor pool; golf course nearby; exercise room; Jacuzzi; watersports equipment rental; bike rental; room service (7am–10pm); in-room massage; babysitting; laundry service; dry cleaning; nonsmoking rooms. *In room:* A/C, TV, fax, dataport, fridge, coffeemaker, hair dryer, iron/ironing board.

BATEMANS BAY
275km (171 miles) S of Sydney

This laid-back holiday town offers good surfing beaches, arts-and-crafts galleries, boat trips up the Clyde River, good game fishing, and bushwalks in the Morton and Deua national parks.

ESSENTIALS
GETTING THERE   Batemans Bay is a 3- to 4-hour drive from Sydney, depending on the traffic. (Avoid leaving Sydney at rush hour, and prepare for long delays on holidays.) **Premier Motor Service** (✆ **1300/368 100** in Australia, or 02/4423 5233) runs coaches to Batemans Bay from Sydney's Central Station.

VISITOR INFORMATION   **Batemans Bay Visitor Information Centre,** at the corner of Princes Highway and Beach Road (✆ **1800/802 528** in Australia, or 02/4472 6800), is open daily from 9am to 5pm.

GAME FISHING & A RIVER CRUISE
If you fancy some serious fishing, contact **OB1 Charters,** Marina, Beach Road, Batemans Bay (✆ **1800/641 065** in Australia, 02/4471 2738, or 0416/241 586 mobile; www.southcoast.com.au/ob1). The company runs full-day game-fishing trips and morning snapper-fishing trips (afternoon snapper trips in summer, too). Expect to encounter black marlin, blue marlin, giant kingfish, mako sharks, albacore tuna, yellowfin tuna, and blue tuna from November through June. The trip includes all tackle, bait, and afternoon and morning tea, but you must provide your own lunch. It costs A$900 (US$720) to hire the six-person boat for the day; if there are just a couple of you, the charter company may be able to fill the rest of the boat if you make reservations far enough in advance. Trips to catch snapper (a nice-tasting fish, which is not the same as red snapper) include all gear, bait, and morning or afternoon tea for A$80 (US$64) per person; these last about 6 hours.

A river cruise on **MV *Merinda,*** Innes Boatshed, Orient Street, Batemans Bay (② **02/4472 4052;** fax 02/4472 4754), is a pleasant experience. The 3-hour cruise leaves at 11:30am daily and travels inland past townships, forests, and farmland. It costs A$22 (US$18) for adults, A$11 (US$8.80) for children, and A$50 (US$40) for families; a fish and chips lunch is A$6 (US$4.80) extra, and a seafood basket for two is A$12 (US$9.60).

A NICE PLACE TO STAY

The Bay Soldiers Esplanade Motor Inn ⭐ *Kids*   This AAA-rated four-star motel right on the Batemans Bay river estuary has fabulous views and is close to the town center. Rooms are light and well furnished, and all have balconies (some with water views). Some doubles and suites have Jacuzzis; they cost the same as non-Jacuzzi rooms, so specify if you want one when booking. Eat at the hotel's restaurant or at the Batemans Bay Soldiers' Club, just opposite, which has a restaurant, a bistro, cheap drinks, and a free evening kids' club.

23 Beach Rd. (P.O. Box 202), Batemans Bay, NSW 2536. ② **1800/659 884** in Australia, or 02/4472 0200. Fax 02/4472 0277. www.esplanade.com.au. 23 units. A$107–A$179 (US$85–US$143) double; A$156–A$330 (US$125–US$264) suite. Extra person A$12 (US$9.60). Children under 18 stay free in parent's room. AE, DC, MC, V. **Amenities:** Restaurant; coin-op laundry; nonsmoking rooms. *In room:* A/C, TV, kitchenette, fridge, coffeemaker, hair dryer, iron/ironing board.

NAROOMA ⭐
345km (214 miles) SW of Sydney

Narooma is a seaside town with beautiful deserted beaches, a golf course right on a headland, a natural rock formation in the shape of Australia (popular with camera-wielding tourists), and excellent fishing. However, its major attraction is **Montague Island** ⭐⭐, the breeding colony for thousands of shearwaters (or mutton birds, as they're also called) and a hangout for juvenile seals.

Just 18km (11 miles) farther south is **Central Tilba** ⭐, one of the prettiest towns in Australia and the headquarters of the boutique ABC Cheese Factory. You'll kick yourself if you miss this charming historical township (pop. 35; 1 million visitors annually).

ESSENTIALS

GETTING THERE   Narooma is a 7-hour drive from Sydney down the Princes Highway. **Premier Motor Service** (② **1300/368 100** in Australia, or 02/4423 5233) runs coaches to Narooma from Sydney's Central Station.

VISITOR INFORMATION   The **Narooma Visitors Centre,** Princes Highway, Narooma (② **02/4476 2881;** fax 02/4476 1690; www.naturecoast-tourism.com.au), is open daily from 9am to 5pm.

WHAT TO SEE & DO: WHALES, GOLF & MORE

A must if you're visiting the area is a boat tour with **Narooma Charters** (② **02/4476 2240;** www.naroomacharters.com.au). It offers spectacular tours of the coast on the lookout for dolphins, seal colonies, and little penguins, and also includes a tour of Montague Island. Morning and afternoon tours take 3½ hours and cost A$69 (US$55) for adults, A$50 (US$40) for children, and A$198 (US$158) for families. A 4½-hour tour includes some of the world's best whale-watching (between mid-Sept and early Dec) and costs A$89 (US$71) for adults, A$70 (US$56) for children, and A$299 (US$239) for families. The last time I went on this trip, we saw no fewer than eight humpback whales, some of them mothers with calves. An evening tour to see fairy penguins on Montague Island and a visit to the seal colony costs A$69 (US$55) for adults, A$50 (US$40) for children, and A$198 (US$158) for a family. The company also offers game fishing from February to the end of June and scuba diving in the seal colonies from August to the end of December. You may also see giant fish-eating gray nurse sharks, dolphins, and even orcas. Dives cost A$66 (US$53) for a double dive, plus approximately A$33 (US$26) for gear rental.

Narooma Golf Club, Narooma (© **02/4476 2522**), has one of the most interesting and challenging coastal courses in Australia. A round of golf will cost you A$25 (US$20).

While you're in the area, I recommend stopping off at the **Umbarra Aboriginal Cultural Centre** ✮, Wallaga Lake, off the Princes Highway on Bermagui Road (© **02/4473 7232;** umbarra@acr.net.au). It's 20km (12 miles) south of Narooma. The center offers activities such as boomerang throwing, spear throwing, and painting with natural ochers for A$6.25 (US$5) per person, or A$20 (US$16) per family. There are also discussions, Aboriginal archival displays, and a retail store. It's open Monday through Friday from 9am to 5pm, Saturday and Sunday from 9am to 4pm (closed Sun in winter). The center's guides also offer 2- to 4-hour four-wheel-drive/walking trips of nearby **Mount Dromedary** ✮ and **Mumbulla Mountain,** taking in sacred sites. The tours cost A$45 (US$36) per person. Reservations are essential.

If you want to attempt Mount Dromedary without a guide, ask for directions in Narooma. The hike to the top takes around 3 hours.

WHERE TO STAY

Whale Motor Inn ✮   This nice, quiet motor inn has the best panoramic ocean views on the south coast and the largest rooms in town. Standard rooms have a queen-size bed and a single-person sofa bed. Standard suites have a separate bedroom, two sofa beds, and a kitchenette. Spacious executive and Jacuzzi suites are better furnished, and have a kitchenette and a balcony or patio.

Princes Hwy., Narooma, NSW 2546. © **02/4476 2411.** Fax 02/4476 1995. www.whalemotorinn.com.au. 17 units. A$90–A$145 (US$72–US$116). Extra person A$10 (US$8). AE, DC, MC, V. **Amenities:** Restaurant; small unheated outdoor pool; nonsmoking rooms. *In room:* A/C, TV, fridge, coffeemaker, hair dryer, iron/ironing board.

MERIMBULA

480km (298 miles) S of Sydney; 580km (360 miles) NE of Melbourne

This seaside resort (pop. approximately 7,000) is the last place of interest before the Princes Highway crosses the border into Victoria. Merimbula is a good center from which to discover the surrounding **Ben Boyd National Park** and **Mimosa Rocks National Park;** both offer bushwalking. Another park, **Bournda National Park,** surrounds a lake and has good walking trails and a surf beach.

Golf is the game of choice in Merimbula, and the area's most popular venue is the **Pambula-Merimbula Golf Club** (© **02/6495 6154**). You can spot kangaroos grazing on the fairways of the 27-hole course. It costs A$14 (US$11) for 9 holes, or A$25 (US$20) for the day. Another favorite is **Tura Beach Country Club** (© **02/6495 9002**), which is known for its excellent coastal views. A round of 18 holes costs A$20 (US$16).

Eden, 20km (13 miles) south of Merimbula, was once a major whaling port. The rather gruesome **Eden Killer Whale Museum,** on Imlay Street in Eden (© **02/6496 2094**), is the only reason to stop here. It has a dubious array of relics, including boats, axes, and remnants of the last of the area's killer whales, called Old Tom. The museum is open Monday through Saturday from 9:15am to 3:45pm, Sunday from 11:15am to 3:45pm. In January it's open daily from 9:15am to 4:45pm. Admission is A$5.50

(US$4.40) for adults and A$1.50 (US$1.20) for children. You can still see a scattering of whales off the coast in October and November.

ESSENTIALS

GETTING THERE   The drive from either Sydney or Melbourne takes about 7 hours. The **Greyhound Australia** (© **13 14 99** in Australia, or 07/4690 9950; www. greyhound.com.au) bus trip from Sydney takes more than 8 hours.

VISITOR INFORMATION   The **Merimbula Tourist Information Centre,** Beach Street, Merimbula (© **1800/150 457** in Australia, or 02/6495 1129; fax 02/6495 1250), is open daily from 9am to 5pm (10am–4pm in winter).

SPECIAL EVENTS   Jazz fans should head for the **Merimbula Jazz Festival** held over the long Queens Birthday weekend, the second weekend in June. A country-music festival takes place the last weekend in October.

WHERE TO STAY

Ocean View Motor Inn   This pleasant motel has good water views from 12 of its rooms (the best are nos. 9, 10, and 11). The rooms are spacious and modern, with plain brick walls, patterned carpets, and one long balcony serving the top six rooms. Fourteen units have kitchenettes. All have showers. It's a friendly place. Breakfast is delivered to your room for A$7.70 (US$6.15) extra.

Merimbula Dr. and View St., Merimbula, NSW 2548. © **02/6495 2300.** Fax 02/6495 3443. www.oceanviewmotor inn.com.au. 20 units. A$66–A$120 (US$53–US$96) double. Extra person A$11 (US$8.80). MC, V. **Amenities:** Medium-size solar-heated outdoor pool; limited room service; babysitting; coin-op laundry; nonsmoking rooms. *In room:* A/C, TV, kitchenette, fridge, coffeemaker.

6 The Snowy Mountains: Australia's Ski Country ⊛

Thredbo: 519km (322 miles) SW of Sydney; 208km (129 miles) SW of Canberra; 543km (337 miles) NE of Melbourne

Made famous by Banjo Paterson's 1890 poem "The Man from Snowy River," the Snowy Mountains are most commonly used for what you'd least expect in Australia—skiing. It starts to snow around June and carries on until September. During this time hundreds of thousands of people flock here to ski at the major ski resorts—Thredbo and Perisher Blue, and, to a lesser extent, Charlotte Pass and Mount Selwyn. It's certainly different skiing here, with ghostly white gum trees as the obstacles instead of pine trees.

The whole region is part of the **Kosciuszko** (pronounced Ko-zi-*os*-co) **National Park,** the largest alpine area in Australia. During the summer months the park is a beautiful place for walking, and in spring the profusion of wildflowers is exquisite. A series of lakes in the area, including the one in the resort town of Jindabyne, are favorites with trout fishermen.

Visitors stay in **Jindabyne,** 62km (38 miles) south of Cooma, or **Thredbo Village,** 36km (22 miles) southwest of Jindabyne. Jindabyne is a bleak-looking resort town on the banks of the man-made Lake Jindabyne, which came into existence when the Snowy River was dammed to provide hydroelectric power.

Thredbo Village is set in a valley of Mount Crackenback and resembles European-style resorts. From here, the Crackenback Chairlift provides access to an easy-grade pathway that leads to the top of Mount Kosciuszko, which at 2,228m (7,308 ft.) is Australia's highest peak. The mountain has stunning views of the alpine region and some good walks.

SNOWY MOUNTAIN ESSENTIALS

GETTING THERE   From Sydney, take the Eastern Distributor road toward Sydney Airport and turn right just before the planes, following the signs to Wollongong, and then Canberra, on the M5 motorway and the Hume Highway. Follow the Hume Highway south to Goulburn, where you turn onto the Federal Highway toward Canberra. From there take the Monaro Highway to Cooma, then follow the Alpine Way through Jindabyne and on to Thredbo. Tire chains may be necessary on the slopes in winter and can be rented from local service stations. The trip takes around 6 hours from Sydney with short breaks.

Qantas (✆ **13 13 13** in Australia) has daily flights from Sydney to Cooma. A connecting bus to the ski fields takes about 1 hour and operates from June through October. It's run by **Snowy Mountain Hire Cars** (✆ **02/6456 2957**) and costs A$48 (US$38) one-way.

In winter only (around June 19–Oct 5), **Greyhound Australia** (✆ **13 14 99** in Australia, or 07/4690 9950; www.greyhound.com.au) operates daily buses between Sydney and Cooma, via Canberra. The journey takes around 7 hours from Sydney and 3 hours from Canberra. A one-way ticket costs around A$50 (US$40).

VISITOR INFORMATION   Pick up information about the ski fields and accommodations options at the **Cooma Visitors Centre,** 119 Sharp St., Cooma, NSW 2630 (✆ **02/6450 1740;** fax 02/6450 1798); or at the **Snowy Region Visitor Centre,** Kosciuszko Road, Jindabyne, NSW 2627 (✆ **02/6450 5600;** fax 02/6456 1249; srvc@npws.nsw.gov.au). A good website is www.perisherblue.com.au.

HITTING THE SLOPES & OTHER ADVENTURES

Obviously, skiing is the most popular activity here. More than 50 ski lifts serve the fields of Perisher Valley, Mount Blue Cow, Smiggins Holes, and Guthega. Perisher Valley offers the best overall slopes; Mount Blue Cow is generally very crowded; Smiggins Holes offer good slopes for beginners; and Guthega has nice light, powdery snow and is less crowded. Thredbo has some very challenging runs and the longest downhill runs, but I prefer Perisher for atmosphere. A day's ski pass costs around A$87 (US$69) for adults, A$48 (US$38) for children 6 to 14.

Tips **Ski Condition Updates**

For up-to-date ski field information, call the **Snowy Region Visitor Centre** (✆ **02/6450 5600**).

A ski-tube train midway between Jindabyne and Thredbo on the Alpine Way travels through the mountains to Perisher Valley and then to Blue Cow. (A "ski-tube train" is a train that goes through a mountain tunnel.) It costs A$34 (US$27) return for adult skiers and A$19 (US$15) for kids. Ski gear can be rented at numerous places in Jindabyne and Thredbo.

In summer, the region is popular for hiking, canoeing, fishing, and golf. Thredbo Village has tennis courts, a 9-hole golf course, and mountain-bike trails.

WHERE TO STAY

You'll have to book months ahead to find a place during the ski season (especially on weekends). And don't expect to find a lot of bargains. The **Kosciuszko Accommodation Centre,** Nuggets Crossing, Jindabyne, NSW 2627 (✆ **1800/026 354** in Australia, or 02/6456 2022; fax 02/6456 2945), can help you find and book accommodations in the area. Other private agents who can help find you a spot for the night include the **Snowy Mountains Reservation Centre** (☎ **02/6456 2633**) and the **Thredbo Resort Centre** (☎ **1800/020 622** in Australia).

IN THREDBO

Riverside Cabins
These self-contained studio and one-bedroom cabins sit above the Thredbo River and overlook the Crackenback Range. They're also a short walk from the Thredbo Alpine Hotel and local shops. Most rooms have balconies. Rates vary wildly from weekday to weekend and season to season.

Thredbo, NSW 2625. ☎ 02/6459 4196 in Australia, or 02/6459 4299. Fax 02/6459 4195. www.thredbo.com. 36 units. Winter A$160–A$516 (US$128–US$412) double; summer A$117–A$164 (US$94–US$131) double. Ask about weekly rates. AE, DC, MC, V. *In room:* TV, kitchen, coin-op laundry, fridge, coffeemaker, hair dryer, iron/ironing board.

Thredbo Alpine Apartments
These apartments are very similar to the Riverside Cabins (see above) and are managed by the same people. All have balconies with mountain views. Some have queen-size beds. There's limited daily maid service, and free in-room movies. Summer rates apply from July 30 through September 2.

Thredbo, NSW 2628. ☎ 1800/026 333 in Australia, or 02/6459 4299. Fax 02/6459 4195. 35 units. Winter weekends A$210–A$441 (US$168–US$353) 1-bedroom apt; A$289–A$628 (US$231–US$502) 2-bedroom apt; A$394–A$770 (US$315–US$616) 3-bedroom apt; weekday rates about 20% cheaper. Summer A$127–A$164 (US$101–US$131) 1-bedroom apt; A$159–A$190 (US$127–US$152) 2-bedroom apt; A$180–A$210 (US$144–US$168) 3-bedroom apt. Ask about weekly rates. AE, DC, MC, V. Covered parking. **Amenities:** Coin-op laundry. *In room:* TV, kitchen, fridge, coffeemaker, hair dryer, iron/ironing board.

Thredbo Alpine Hotel
After the skiing is finished for the day, the center of activity in Thredbo is this large resort-style lodge. Rooms vary; those on the top floor of the three-story hotel have a king-size bed instead of a standard queen-size. The rooms are all wood-paneled and have free in-house movies. Thredbo's only nightclub is here.

P.O. Box 80, Thredbo NSW 2625. ☎ 02/6459 4200. Fax 02/6459 4201. www.thredbo.com.au. 65 units. Winter A$198–A$498 (US$158–US$396) double; summer A$129–A$189 (US$103–US$151) double. Rates include breakfast. Ask about weekly rates and packages. AE, DC, MC, V. **Amenities:** 2 restaurants; bistro; 4 bars; heated outdoor pool; golf course nearby; 3 lit tennis courts; Jacuzzi; sauna; tour desk; massage; room service (winter only); coin-op laundry; nonsmoking rooms. *In room:* TV/VCR, minibar, coffeemaker, hair dryer.

⌒ *Moments* In the Footsteps of the Man from Snowy River

Horseback riding is a popular activity for those wanting to ride like the "Man from Snowy River." **Reynella Kosciusko Rides,** in Adamanaby, 44km (27 miles) northwest of Cooma (☎ **1800/029 909** in Australia, or 02/6454 2386; fax 02/6454 2530; www.reynellarides.com.au), offers multinight rides through the Kosciuszko National Park from October to the end of April. Three-day, 4-night rides cost around A$799 (US$639), and the 5-day, 6-night ride A$1,207 (US$965). Transfers from Cooma cost around A$35 (US$28) each way. The trips are all-inclusive and include camping and homestead accommodations. Shorter rides are offered by **Jindabyne Trail Rides** (☎ **02/6456 2421;** fax 02/6456 1254). Gentle, 1½-hour rides on the slopes above Jindabyne cost A$25 (US$20) per person.

7 Outback New South Wales

The Outback is a powerful Australian image. Hot, dusty, and prone to flies, it can also be a romantic place where wedge-tailed eagles float in the shimmering heat as you spin in a circle, tracing the unbroken horizon. If you drive out here, you have to be constantly on the lookout for emus, large flightless birds that dart across roads open-beaked and wide-eyed. When you turn off the car engine, it's so quiet you can hear the scales of a sleepy lizard, as long as your forearm, scraping the rumpled track as it turns to taste the air with its long, blue tongue.

The scenery is a huge canvas with a restricted palette: blood red for the dirt, straw yellow for the blotches of Mitchell grass, searing blue for the surreally large sky. There is room to be yourself in the Outback, and you'll soon find that personalities often tilt toward the eccentric. It's a hardworking place, too, where miners and sheep and cattle farmers try to eke out a living in Australia's hard center.

BROKEN HILL ★★
1,157km (717 miles) W of Sydney; 508km (315 miles) NE of Adelaide

At heart, Broken Hill—or "Silver City," as it's been nicknamed—is still very much a hardworking, hard-drinking mining town. Its beginnings date to 1883, when the trained eye of a boundary rider named Charles Rasp noticed something odd about the craggy rock outcrops at a place called the Broken Hill. He thought he saw deposits of tin, but they turned out to be silver and lead. Today, the city's main drag, Argent Street, bristles with finely crafted colonial mansions, heritage homes, hotels, and public buildings. Look deeper and you see the town's quirkiness. Around one corner you'll find the radio station, built to resemble a giant wireless set with round knobs for windows, and around another the headquarters of the Housewives Association, which ruled the town with an iron apron for generations. Then there's the Palace Hotel—made famous in the movie *The Adventures of Priscilla, Queen of the Desert*—with its high painted walls and a mural of Botticelli's *Birth of Venus* on the ceiling two flights up.

Traditionally a hard-drinking but religious town, Broken Hill has 23 pubs (down from 73 in its heyday) and plenty of churches, as well as a Catholic cathedral, a synagogue, and a mosque to serve its 21,000 inhabitants.

ESSENTIALS
GETTING THERE By car, take the Great Western Highway from Sydney to Dubbo, then the Mitchell Highway to the Barrier Highway, which will take you to Broken Hill. **Southern Australian Airlines** (book through Qantas, ℂ 13 13 13 in Australia) also connects Broken Hill to Adelaide, Melbourne, and Mildura.

The ***Indian Pacific*** train stops here on its way from Sydney to Perth twice a week. It takes nearly 16 hours, leaving Sydney at 2:55pm on Saturday and Wednesday and arrives in Broken Hill at 6:45am the next day. The fare from Sydney is A$430 (US$344) for adults and A$349 (US$279) for children in a first-class sleeper, A$340 (US$272) for adults and A$259 (US$207) for children in an economy sleeper, and A$163 (US$130) for adults and A$82 (US$66) for children in an economy seat. Contact **Great Southern Railways** (ℂ **08/8213 4530;** www.gsr.com.au) for timetables, fares, bookings, and more information.

Greyhound Australia (ℂ **13 14 99** in Australia, or 07/4690 9950; www.greyhound.com.au) runs buses from Adelaide for A$58 (US$46); the trip takes 7 hours. The 16-hour trip from Sydney costs from A$93 (US$74).

VISITOR INFORMATION   The **Broken Hill Visitors Information Centre,** Blende and Bromide streets, Broken Hill, NSW 2880 (© **08/8087 6077;** fax 08/8088 5209; www.murrayoutback.org.au), is open daily from 8:30am to 5pm. The **National Parks & Wildlife Service (NPWS)** office is at 183 Argent St. (© **08/8088 5933**); and the **Royal Automobile Association of South Australia,** which offers reciprocal services to other national and international auto-club members, is at 261 Argent St. (© **08/8088 4999**).

Note: The area code in Broken Hill is **08,** the same as the South Australia code, not 02, the New South Wales code.

GETTING AROUND   **Silver City Tours,** 380 Argent St. (© **08/8087 3144**), conducts tours of the city and surrounding Outback. City tours take around 4 hours and cost A$45 (US$36) for adults and A$20 (US$16) for children. The company also offers a range of other tours of the area.

Recommended small-group tour operator, **Goanna Safari** (© **08/8087 6057;** www.goanna-safari.com.au), offers a large range of personalized tours of the Outback from Broken Hill, and a range of regular camping (with good camp beds and cooking fires) or accommodated tours. It's really worth checking their website before you leave home. Among the offerings is a 3-day, 2-night trip to Mootwingee, White Cliffs, and Menidee Lakes, where giant dams on the Darling River bristle with the half-drowned skeletons of gum trees and flutter with numerous species of wading birds, pelicans, and ducks. This trip costs A$656 (US$525) camping and A$694 (US$555) accommodated. Also available is a 3-day trip to Minindee, the Kinchega National Park, and Lake Mungo, a dry lake famous for the 45,000-year-old skeletons and artifacts discovered in it and for huge sand dunes and shimmering white cliffs known as the Walls of China. This costs A$582 (US$465) camping and A$694 (US$555) with accommodations.

Hertz (© **08/8087 2719;** fax 08/8087 4838) rents four-wheel-drive vehicles suitable for exploring the area.

EXPLORING THE TOWN: GALLERIES, A MINE TOUR & THE WORLD'S LARGEST SCHOOLROOM

With the largest regional public gallery in New South Wales and 27 private **galleries,** Broken Hill has more places per capita to see art than anywhere else in Australia. The **Broken Hill Regional Art Gallery,** Chloride Street, between Blende and Beryl streets (© **08/8088 5491**), houses an extensive collection of Australian colonial and Impressionist works. Look for the *Silver Tree,* a sculpture created out of the pure silver mined beneath Broken Hill. This is also a good place to see works by the "Brushmen of the Bush," a well-known group of artists, including Pro Hart, Jack Absalom, Eric Minchin, and Hugh Schultz, who spend many days sitting around campfires in the bush trying to capture its essence in paint. The gallery is open Monday through Friday from 10am to 5pm, and Saturday and Sunday from 1 to 5pm. Admission is A$3 (US$2.40) for adults, A$2 (US$1.60) for children, and A$6 (US$4.80) for families.

Other galleries worth visiting around town include **Absalom's Gallery,** 638 Chapple St. (© **08/8087 5881**), and the **Pro Hart Gallery,** 108 Wyman St. (© **08/8087 2441**). Both are open daily. Pro Hart's gallery is really worth a look. Apart from his own works—including pieces based on incidents and scenes relating to Broken Hill—his gallery is crammed with everything from a bas-relief of Salvador Dalí to a landscape by Claude Monet.

To get a real taste of mining in Broken Hill, take an underground tour at **Delprat's Mine** (*© 08/8088 1604*). Visitors go 120m (394 ft.) below the surface. Children under 6 are not allowed. Tours run Monday through Friday at 10:30am and Saturday at 2pm. The 2-hour tour costs A$23 (US$18) for adults and A$18 (US$14) for children.

Be sure not to miss the School of the Air and the Royal Flying Doctor Service base, both of which help show the enormity of the Australian interior. The **School of the Air**—the largest schoolroom in the world, with students scattered over 800,000 sq. km (312,000 sq. miles)—conducts lessons via two-way radios. Visitors can listen in on part of the day's first teaching session Monday through Friday at 8:30am (except public holidays). Bookings are essential and must be made through the **Broken Hill Visitors Information Centre** (see "Visitor Information," above). Tours costs A$3.50 (US$2.80) for adults and A$2.50 (US$2) for kids. The **Royal Flying Doctor Service base** is at the Broken Hill Airport (*© 08/8080 1777*). The service maintains communication with more than 400 outback stations, ready to fly at once in case of an emergency. The base at Broken Hill covers 25% of New South Wales, as well as parts of Queensland and South Australia. Explanations of the role of the flying doctor service run continuously at the base Monday through Friday from 9am to 5pm. Admission is A$5.50 (US$4.40) for adults, and A$2.75 (US$2.20) for children.

OTHER THINGS TO SEE & DO NEARBY

VISITING A GHOST TOWN   At least 44 movies have been filmed in the Wild West town of **Silverton** ★ (pop. 50), 23km (14 miles) northwest of Broken Hill. It's the Wild West Australian-style, though, with camels instead of horses sometimes placed in front of the **Silverton Pub,** which is well worth a visit for its kitschy Australian appeal. Silverton once had a population of 3,000, following the discovery of silver here in 1882, but within 7 years almost everyone had left. There are some good art galleries here, as well as a restored jail and hotel.

DISCOVERING ABORIGINAL HANDPRINTS   **Mutawintji National Park** ★ (also known and pronounced by its old name, Mootwingee), 130km (81 miles) northeast of Broken Hill, was one of the most important spiritual meeting places for Aborigines on the continent. Groups came from all over to peck out abstract engravings on the rocks with sharpened quartz tools and to sign their handprints to show they belonged to the place. The ancient, weathered fireplaces are still here, laid out like a giant map to show where each visiting group came from. Hundreds of ocher outlines of hands and animal paws, some up to 30,000 years old, are stenciled on rock overhangs. The fabulous 2-hour Outback trip from Broken Hill to Mootwingee is along red-dirt tracks not really suitable for two-wheel-drives. It should not be attempted after a heavy rain.

Mootwingee Heritage Tours (*© 08/8088 7000*) organizes inspections of the historical sites every Wednesday and Saturday at 10:30am Broken Hill time (11am Mootwingee, or Eastern Standard, time). The tours may be canceled in very hot

---

Fun Fact **What Time Is It, Anyway?**

Broken Hill runs its clocks on Central Standard Time, to correspond with South Australia. The surrounding country, however, runs half an hour faster at Eastern Standard Time.

Finds A Fabulous Place to Enjoy the Sunset

Just outside Broken Hill in the **Living Desert Nature Park** is the best collection of sculptures this side of Stonehenge. Twelve sandstone obelisks, up to 3m (10 ft.) high and carved totemlike by artists from as far away as Georgia, Syria, Mexico, and the Tiwi Islands, make up the Sculpture Symposium. Surrounding them on all sides is brooding mulga scrub. It's fantastic at sunset.

---

weather. The **NPWS office** in Broken Hill (© **08/8088 5933**) also has details. You can camp at the **Homestead Creek** campground for A$11 (US$8.80) a night. It has its own water supply.

EXPLORING WHITE CLIFFS ★★ White Cliffs, 290km (180 miles) east of Broken Hill, is an opal-mining town that's bigger than it looks. To escape the summer heat, most houses are built underground in mine shafts, where the temperature is a constant 72°F (22°C). Unlike Lightning Ridge (below), which produces mainly black opals, White Cliffs is known for its less valuable white opals—as is Coober Pedy in South Australia (see chapter 11). Prospecting started in 1889, when kangaroo shooters found the colorful stones on the ground. A year later the rush was on, and by the turn of the 20th century about 4,000 people were digging and sifting in a lawless, waterless hell of a place. White Cliffs is smaller than Coober Pedy and less touristy—which is its great charm. You also have more freedom to wander around the old opal tailings here, which is discouraged in Coober Pedy. Given the choice between White Cliffs and Lightning Ridge, I'd opt for the latter—though if you have time, you should see both.

The countryside here looks like an inverted moonscape, pimpled with bone-white heaps of gritty clay dug from the 50,000 mine shafts that surround the town. These days, White Cliffs is renowned for its eccentricity. Take **Jock's Place,** for instance, an underground museum full to the beams with junk pulled from old mine shafts. Then there's a house made of beer flagons, and a 9-hole **dirt golf course** where locals play at night with fluorescent green balls.

If you fancy an after-hours round of golf in the dirt (and who doesn't?), contact the secretary of the **White Cliffs Golf Club,** John Painter (© **08/8091 6715** after hours). He'll be happy to supply you with a golf club or two and a couple of balls for A$2 (US$1.60). If you have your own clubs, put A$2 (US$1.60) in the black box at the first tee—but be warned, bush playing can damage your clubs, and crows often make off with the balls. Visitors can play day or night; if you want some company, come on Sunday, when club members shoot it out.

WHERE TO STAY: ABOVE & BELOW GROUND

One option is to rent a local cottage from **Broken Hill Historic Cottages** (© **08/8087 9966**) for A$80 (US$64) a night.

Broken Hill Overlander Motor Inn This is my favorite place to stay in Broken Hill, although admittedly that's not really saying much in this Outback town. It's set way back from the road, has nice green areas and barbecue facilities, and is very quiet. The more expensive AAA-rated four-star rooms are much nicer than the cheaper options, and considerably larger. Two family rooms sleep up to six in a combination of single and queen-size beds. You can order off several menus supplied by local restaurants; the hotel supplies plates and cutlery.

142 Iodide St., Broken Hill, NSW 2880. © **08/8088 2566**, or reserve through Best Western (© **800/780-7234** in the U.S. and Canada, 0800/39 3130 in the U.K., 0800/237 893 in New Zealand, 13 17 79 in Australia). Fax 08/8088 4377. www.bestwestern.com.au/overlander. 15 units. A$85–A$135 (US$68–US$108) double; A$135 (US$108) 2-bed unit. Extra person A$10 (US$8). AE, DC, MC, V. **Amenities:** Small heated outdoor pool; sauna; tour desk; laundry service; dry cleaning; nonsmoking rooms. *In room:* A/C, TV, dataport, coffeemaker, fridge, hair dryer, iron/ironing board.

Mario the Palace Hotel *(Value* With its high painted walls, a mural of Botticelli's *Birth of Venus* on the ceiling two flights up, and an office crammed with stuffed animal heads and crabs, the Palace Hotel is an intriguing sanctuary. The owners have put a lot of work into restoring the place. The more expensive doubles are larger and come with a small lounge area, but all are comfortable and cool. Ten double rooms come with an attached shower. The Priscilla Suite is famous because that's where the transvestites stayed in *The Adventures of Priscilla, Queen of the Desert.* Mario owned the place for "donkey's years," as he says; he's now retired, and his family runs the hotel.

227 Argent St., Broken Hill, NSW 2880. © **08/8088 1699**. Fax 08/8087 6240. mariospalace@bigpond.com. 51 units, 10 with bathroom. A$44 (US$35) double without bathroom; A$53–A$70 (US$42–US$56) double with bathroom. Priscilla suite A$90 (US$72) for 2. AE, MC, V. **Amenities:** Bar; dining room. *In room:* A/C, TV, fridge, coffeemaker, iron/ironing board.

Underground Motel ★★ I love this place; it's worth making the scenic trip out to White Cliffs just to stay here for the night. All but two of the rooms are underground; they're reached by a maze of spacious tunnels dug out of the rock and sealed with epoxy resin to keep out the damp and the dust. The temperature below ground is a constant 72°F (22°C), which is decidedly cooler than a summer day outside. Rooms are comfortable though basic, with shared toilets and showers. Turn the light off, and it's dark as a cave. Every night guests sit around large tables and dig into the roast of the day. (Vegetarians have options, too.) The three-course meal costs A$25 (US$20).

Smiths Hill, White Cliffs (P.O. Box 427), NSW 2836. © **1800/021 154** in Australia, or 08/8091 6677. Fax 08/8091 6654. 30 units, none with bathroom. A$83 (US$66) double. Extra person A$24 (US$19). MC, V. **Amenities:** Restaurant; bar; small heated outdoor pool; coin-op laundry; nonsmoking rooms.

WHERE TO DINE

The best place for a meal Aussie-style is a local club. You'll find one of the best bistros at the **Barrier Social & Democratic Club,** 218 Argent St. (© **08/8088 4477**). It serves breakfast, lunch, and dinner. There's also a host of Chinese restaurants around town. The **Oceania Chinese Restaurant,** Argent Street (© **08/8087 3695**), has a A$7 (US$5.60) lunch special.

LIGHTNING RIDGE: OPALS GALORE ★★
793 (492 miles) NW of Sydney; 737km (457 miles) SW of Brisbane

Lightning Ridge, or "The Ridge" as the locals call it, is perhaps the most fascinating place to visit in New South Wales. Essentially, it's a hardworking opal-mining town in the arid northern reaches of New South Wales—where summer temperatures hover around the 113°F (45°C) mark. Lightning Ridge thrives off the largest deposit of black opals in the world. Good-quality opals can fetch a miner around A$8,000 (US$6,400) per carat, and stones worth more than A$500,000 (US$400,000) each are not unheard of. Tourists come to get a taste of life in Australia's "Wild West." A popular activity in the opal fields is to pick over the old heaps of mine tailings. Stories (perhaps tall tales) abound of tourists finding overlooked opals worth thousands.

I strongly recommend you visit the **Grawin** and **Glengarry opal fields** ⭐⭐, both about an hour or so from Lightning Ridge on a dirt track suitable for two-wheel-drive cars in dry weather only. (Check with the Tourist Information Centre before you go.) Bristling with drills and hoists pulling out bucketloads of dirt, these frontier townships buzz with news of the latest opal rush. If you can convince a local to take you there, all the better—the tracks can be misleading. **Ando's Outback Tours** (see "Byron Bay: A Beach Bohemia," earlier in this chapter) takes in Glengarry and Lightning Ridge on its 5-day trip.

ESSENTIALS

GETTING THERE   From Sydney, it takes about 9 hours to drive to Lightning Ridge, via Bathurst, Dubbo, and the fascinating town of Walgett. **Airlink** (✆ 02/6884 2435) flies to Lightning Ridge from Sydney via Dubbo.

VISITOR INFORMATION   The **Lightning Ridge Tourist Information Centre,** Morilla Street (P.O. Box 1779), Lightning Ridge, NSW 2834 (✆ 02/6829 0565; fax 02/6829 0565), is open Monday through Friday from 8:30am to 4pm. On weekends, call ✆ 02/6829 0429 or e-mail lridge@walgettshire.com.

SPECIAL EVENTS   If you're in Australia around Easter, make sure you come to Lightning Ridge for the **Great Goat Race** and the rodeo. A decent website for information is www.lightningridge.net.au.

SEEING THE TOWN

Any visit to Lightning Ridge should start with an orientation trip with **Black Opal Tours** (✆ 02/6829 0368; fax 02/6829 1206; www.blackopaltours.com). The company offers both a 3-hour morning tour and an afternoon tour for A$25 (US$20) for adults and A$22 (US$18) for kids.

Among the points of interest is the 15m-tall (49-ft.) **Amigo's Castle,** which dominates the worked-out opal fields surrounding the modern township of Lightning Ridge. Complete with turrets, battlements, dungeons, and a wishing well, the castle has been rising out of these arid lands for the past 18 years, with every rock scavenged from the surrounding area and lugged in a wheelbarrow or in a rucksack on Amigo's back. The wonderful Amigo hasn't taken out insurance on the property, so there are no official tours, though if he feels like a bit of company he'll show you around.

The **Artesian Bore Baths,** 2km (1¼ miles) from the post office on Pandora Street, are free, open 24 hours a day, and said to have therapeutic value. The water temperature hovers between 104°F and 122°F (40°C–50°C). A visit at night when the stars are out is amazing.

The **Bevan's Black Opal & Cactus Nursery** (✆ 02/6829 0429) contains more than 2,000 species of cactus and succulent plants, including rare specimens. Betty Bevan cuts opals from the family's mine, and many are on display. Admission is A$5 (US$4) to the cactus nursery, free to see the opals.

Lightning Ridge has plenty of opal shops, galleries, walk-in opal mines, and other unique things to see. You might want to take a look at **Gemopal Pottery** (✆ 02/6829 0375), on the road to the Bore Baths. The resident potter makes some nice pots out of clay mine tailings and lives in one of his five old Sydney railway carriages.

WHERE TO STAY & DINE

An interesting addition to the Lightning Ridge lodging scene is the **Lightning Ridge Hotel/Motel** (✆ 02/6829 0304; www.lightning-ridge-hotel-motel.com), set on 4 hectares (10 acres) of bush, complete with a birdbath to attract the native parrots. There are 40 log cabins here, as well as a trailer park (for your own trailer or motor home) and camping sites. Cabins cost A$56 (US$45) without bathroom, A$58 (US$46) with a bathroom; motel rooms go for A$77 (US$62) double, A$87 (US$69) triple, A$145 (US$118) quad. If you want to stay at the Glengarry opal fields, your only option is the **Glengarry Hilton,** a rustic outback pub (not associated with the major hotel chain). Here you stay in mobile units sleeping 24. A night costs A$15 (US$12).

The Wallangulla Motel   My choice of the four motels in town, The Wallangulla offers two standards of rooms, the cheaper ones being in an older section of the property. Newer rooms are better furnished and generally nicer; they're worth the extra money. Two large family rooms each have two bedrooms and a living room; one has a Jacuzzi. Guests can use the barbecue facilities. The Lightning Ridge Bowling Club across the road has a restaurant with pretty good food and a very cheap bistro; motel guests can charge meals to their room bills.

Morilla St. (at Agate St.), Lightning Ridge, NSW 2834. © **02/6829 0542.** Fax 02/6829 0070. www.wj.com.au/ wallangulla. 43 units. A$60–A$100 (US$48–US$80) double; A$80–A$115 (US$64–US$92) triple; A$90–A$125 (US$72–US$100) family room with Jacuzzi. AE, DC, MC, V. **Amenities:** Coin-op laundry; nonsmoking rooms. *In room:* A/C, TV, coffeemaker.

6

Brisbane

by Lee Mylne

Queensland's capital is relaxed, laid-back, and subtropical. Set along the banks of the wide, brown Brisbane River, this is a city that has grown up in recent years, confident in its appeal. It's one of those places that people don't always appreciate until they spend time there, but where the welcome is as warm as the weather. The city is green and leafy: Moreton Bay fig trees give shade, and in summer, the purple haze of jacarandas competes with the scarlet blaze of poinciana trees. A mango tree in the backyard is practically de rigueur.

The theme parks are south of the city, on the Brisbane–Gold Coast corridor. Brisbane folk don't consider that a drawback. They'll urge you to discover the city, rich in history and character, and get to know the locals. That's easy—friendly locals will start chatting with just about anyone.

Brisbane (pronounced *Briz*-bun) is known for its timber "Queenslanders," cottages and houses set high on stumps to catch the breeze, with wide verandas to keep out the midday sun. In some suburbs, Queenslanders have been converted to trendy cafes, restaurants, and shops selling antiques, clothes, and housewares.

In the city center, gracious colonial sandstone buildings stand next to modern glass towers. Wander in the city botanic gardens, in-line skate or bike along the riverfront pathways, have a drink in a pub beer garden, or get out on the river on a CityCat ferry. Several bridges cross the river, the most famous and attractive being the Story Bridge, on the Town Reach of the river (see "Brisbane's Bridge Climb," later in this chapter). Getting around is cheap and easy, good food—including fantastic seafood—is abundant, and accommodations are affordable, especially in some of the city's comfortable, elegant B&Bs.

Brisbane is in the southeast corner of the state, flanked by the Sunshine Coast, about 2 hours to the north, and the Gold Coast, 1 hour to the south. The Brisbane River flows into Moreton Bay, dotted with beautiful islands you can explore.

1 Orientation

ARRIVING

BY PLANE   About 20 international airlines serve Brisbane from Europe, Asia, and New Zealand, including Qantas, Air New Zealand, Pacific Blue, Singapore Airlines, Thai International, Malaysia Airlines, and Cathay Pacific. From North America, you can fly direct from Los Angeles to Brisbane on Qantas, but from other places you will likely fly to Sydney and connect on Qantas, or fly direct from Auckland, New Zealand.

Qantas (② 13 13 13 in Australia; www.qantas.com.au) and its subsidiary **Qantaslink** (book through Qantas) operate daily flights from state capitals, Cairns, Townsville, and several other regional towns. No-frills **Virgin Blue** (② 13 67 89 in Australia; www.virginblue.com.au) offers cheaper fares and service from all capital cities as well as Cairns, Townsville, Proserpine in the Whitsundays, Mackay, Rockhampton, and the Gold Coast in Queensland; Coffs Harbour and Newcastle in New South Wales; and Hobart in Tasmania. **Jetstar** (② 13 15 38 in Australia; www.jetstar. com.au) has daily service from Proserpine, Hamilton Island, Melbourne's Avalon airport, and Hobart and Launceston in Tasmania.

Brisbane International Airport is 16km (10 miles) from the city, and the domestic terminal is 2km (1¼ miles) farther away. The arrivals floor, on Level 2, has an information desk to meet all flights, help with flight inquiries, dispense tourist information, and make hotel bookings, and a check-in counter for passengers transferring to domestic flights.

Travelex currency-exchange bureaus are on the departures and arrivals floors. **Avis** (② 07/3860 4200), **Budget** (② 07/3860 4466), **Europcar** (② 07/3874 8150), **Hertz** (② 07/3860 4522), and **Thrifty** (② 1300/367 227) have desks on Level 2; in the airport there is also a free callboard connecting you to smaller local car-rental companies that sometimes offer better rates. Free showers and baby-changing rooms are on levels 2, 3, and 4; Level 4 has an ATM.

The domestic terminal has a Travelex currency-exchange bureau, showers, and the big four car-rental desks. (Call the telephone numbers above.)

For security reasons, luggage lockers are not available at either terminal.

Coachtrans (② 07/3238 4700; www.coachtrans.com.au) runs a shuttle between the airport and Roma Street Transit Centre every 30 minutes from 5am to 11pm. The one-way cost is A$9 (US$7.20) or A$11 (US$8.80) for hotel drop-off. The round-trip fare is A$15 (US$12) or A$17 (US$14). Family tickets are A$24 (US$19) or A$29 (US$23) one-way. The trip takes about 40 minutes, and reservations are not needed. No public buses serve the airport. A **taxi** to the city costs around A$20 (US$16) from the international terminal and A$25 (US$20) from the domestic terminal, plus A$2 (US$1.60) for departing taxis.

Airtrain (② 07/3211 2855; www.airtrain.com.au), a rail link between the city and Brisbane's domestic and international airport terminals, runs every 15 minutes from 5am to 9pm daily. Fares from the airport to city stations are A$10 (US$8) for the first adult, A$5 (US$4) for the first child, with discounts for each additional person in your group (for example, five or more adults pay A$6/US$4.80 each). The trip takes about 20 minutes. Airtrain also links the airport with the Gold Coast.

The Airtrain fare between the international and domestic terminals is A$3 (US$2.40). A taxi between terminals costs about A$9 (US$7.20).

BY TRAIN   Queensland Rail (② 13 22 32 in Queensland; www.qr.com.au) operates several long-distance trains to Brisbane from Cairns. The fast new Tilt Train takes about 25 hours and costs A$295 (US$236) for business class. The slower *Sunlander* takes 32 hours and costs A$197 (US$158) for a sitting berth, A$253 (US$202) for an economy-class sleeper, A$398 (US$318) for a first-class sleeper, or A$725 (US$580) for the all-inclusive Queenslander class. **Countrylink** (② 13 22 32 in Australia; www.countrylink.nsw.gov.au) runs daily train service to Brisbane from Sydney. The 14-hour trip costs A$115 to A$162 (US$92–US$130) in a sitting berth, and A$243 (US$194) for a sleeper. Be sure to book the through (all-train) service; on some runs,

Greater Brisbane

0   1 mi
0   1 km
N

↑ To the Sunshine Coast

1

✈
Brisbane
Airport

20

20

1

22

① FERNY HILLS

Hamilton
Albion   Brett's
Wharf

River

BULIMBA
④

31

Lutwyche Road

Fortitude
Valley

Paddington   New
Farm

Milton

Brisbane   CITY
CENTER   Kangaroo Point

Sir Samuel Griffith Dr.

Toowong
Cemetery

Milton Rd.

Coronation Dr.

West   East Brisbane
End   South
Brisbane   Woolloongabba   22

Brisbane   ③
Botanic Gardens   ②
Mt. Coot-tha

Great
Western
Freeway

St. Lucia
(University of
Queensland)

32

Brisbane

South East

1

Freeway

⑤
FIG TREE
POCKET

Hwy.

Ipswich Road

Centenary

15

To the
Gold Coast
→

AUSTRALIA
Brisbane
Canberra
0   1000 Mi
0   1000 Km

Australian Woolshed **1**
Brisbane Botanic Gardens Mt. Coot-tha **3**
Sir Thomas Brisbane Planetarium
    & Cosmic Skydome **2**
Lone Pine Koala Sanctuary **5**
Newstead House **4**

passengers must transfer to a coach in Murwillumbah, south of the border, tacking 2 hours onto the trip. This train-coach service has no sleepers.

All intercity and interstate trains pull into the city center's **Brisbane Transit Centre at Roma Street,** often called the Roma Street Transit Centre. From here, most city and Spring Hill hotels are a few blocks' walk or a quick cab ride away. The station has food outlets, showers, tourist information, and lockers.

Queensland Rail CityTrain (© **13 12 30** in Queensland) provides daily train service from the Sunshine Coast and plentiful service from the Gold Coast.

BY BUS All intercity and interstate coaches pull into the Brisbane Transit Centre (see "By Train," above). **Greyhound Australia** (© **13 14 99** in Australia, or 07/4690 9950; www.greyhound.com.au) serves the city several times daily. A one-way Cairns-Brisbane ticket costs A$201 (US$161); the trip takes 29½ hours. The Sydney-Brisbane trip takes 16½ hours and costs A$100 (US$80) one-way. Coachtrans provides daily service from the Gold Coast. Call **Transinfo** (© **13 12 30**) for details.

BY CAR The Bruce Highway from Cairns enters the city from the north. The Pacific Highway enters Brisbane from the south.

VISITOR INFORMATION

Brisbane Marketing has an information booth (© **07/3006 6290**) in the Queen Street Mall at Albert Street. It's open Monday through Thursday from 9am to 5:30pm, Friday 9am to 7pm or later, Saturday 9am to 4pm, and Sunday 10am to 4pm. The Roma Street Transit Centre (see "By Train," above) is another source of info (© **07/3236 2020**).

CITY LAYOUT

The city center's office towers shimmer in the sun on the north bank of a curve of the Brisbane River. At the tip of the curve are the lush Brisbane City Gardens (sometimes called the City Botanic Gardens). The 30m (98-ft.) sandstone cliffs of Kangaroo Point rise on the eastern side of the south bank; to the west are the South Bank Parklands and the Queensland Cultural Centre, known as South Bank. The **Goodwill Bridge,** for pedestrians and bikes only, links South Bank with the City Gardens. To the west 5km (3 miles), Mount Coot-tha (pronounced *Coo*-tha) looms out of the flat plain.

MAIN ARTERIES & STREETS It's easy to find your way around central Brisbane once you know that the east-west streets are named after female British royalty, and the north-south streets are named after their male counterparts. The northernmost is Ann, followed by Adelaide, Queen, Elizabeth, Charlotte, Mary, Margaret, and Alice. From east to west, the streets are Edward, Albert, George, and William, which becomes North Quay, flanking the river's northeast bank.

Queen Street, the main thoroughfare, becomes a pedestrian mall between Edward and George streets. Roma Street exits the city diagonally to the northwest. Ann Street leads all the way east into Fortitude Valley. The main street in Fortitude Valley is Brunswick Street, which runs into New Farm.

STREET MAPS The **Brisbane Map,** free from Brisbane Marketing (see "Visitor Information," above) or your concierge, is a lightweight map that shows the river and outlying suburbs, as well as the city. It's great for drivers because it shows parking lots and one-way streets on the confusing city-center grid. Rental cars usually come with street directories. Newsdealers and some bookstores sell this map; the state auto club, the **RACQ,** in the General Post Office, 261 Queen St. (© **13 19 05**), is also a good source.

NEIGHBORHOODS IN BRIEF

City Center The vibrant city center is where residents eat, shop, and socialize. Queen Street Mall, in the heart of town, is popular with shoppers and moviegoers, especially on weekends and Friday night (when stores stay open until 9pm). The Eagle Street financial and legal precinct has great restaurants with river views and, on Sunday, markets by the Riverside Centre tower and the Pier. Much of Brisbane's colonial architecture is in the city center, too. Strollers, bike riders, and in-line skaters shake the summer heat in the green haven of the Brisbane City Gardens at the business district's southern end.

Fortitude Valley "The Valley," as locals call it, was once one of the sleazier parts of town. Today, it is a stamping ground for street-smart young folk who meet in restored pubs and eat in cool cafes. The lanterns, food stores, and shopping mall of Chinatown are here, too. Take Turbot Street to the Valley's Brunswick Street, or venture a little farther to trendy James Street.

New Farm Always an appealing suburb, New Farm is an in-spot for cafe-hopping. Merthyr Street is where the action is, especially on Friday and Saturday night. From the intersection of Wickham and Brunswick streets, follow Brunswick southeast for 13 blocks to Merthyr.

Paddington This hilltop suburb, a couple of miles northwest of the city, is one of Brisbane's most attractive. Brightly painted Queenslander cottages line the main street, Latrobe Terrace, as it winds west along a ridge top. Many of the houses have been turned into shops and cafes, where you can browse, enjoy coffee and cake, or just admire the charming architecture.

Milton & Rosalie Park Road in Milton might not quite be a little bit of Europe, but it tries hard—right down to a replica Eiffel Tower above the cafes and shops. Italian restaurants line the street, buzzing with white-collar office workers who down cappuccinos at alfresco restaurants, scout interior design stores for a new objet d'art to grace the living room, and stock up on European designer rags. A few minutes' drive away, Baroona Road and Nash Street, in Rosalie, are catching up.

West End This small inner-city enclave is alive with ethnic restaurants, cafes, and the odd, interesting housewares or fashion store. Most action centers on the intersection of Vulture and Boundary streets, where Asian grocers and delis abound.

Bulimba One of the emerging fashionable suburbs, Bulimba has a long connection with the river through the boat-building industry. One of the nicest ways to get there is by CityCat. Oxford Street is the main drag, lined with trendy cafes and shops.

2 Getting Around

BY PUBLIC TRANSPORTATION

TransLink operates a single network of buses, trains, and ferries. For timetables and route inquiries, call **TransInfo** (© **13 12 30;** www.translink.com.au; Mon–Fri 6am–9pm, Sat–Sun 7am–9pm). An integrated ticket system operates, and the easiest place to buy your tickets are on the buses or at the train stations. You can also buy tickets and pick up maps and timetables at the Queen Street bus station information

Brisbane Accommodations, Dining & Attractions

ACCOMMODATIONS

Eton **8**
Hotel George Williams
(YMCA) **10**
Hotel Ibis Brisbane **11**
Stamford Plaza
Brisbane **16**
Thornbury House
Bed & Breakfast **4**

DINING ◆

e'cco bistro **3**
Explorers Café **9**
Jo Jo's **14**
Pier Nine **15**
Plough Inn **21**
Story Bridge Hotel **17**
Tognini's
BistroCafeDeli **5**
Walt Moden Dining **2**

ATTRACTIONS

City Hall **13**
Museum of
  Brisbane **13**
Newstead House **1**
Queensland Cultural
  Center/Queensland
  Performing Arts
  Complex **20**
Queensland Art
  Gallery **18**
Queensland
  Museum **19**
Roma Street
  Parkland **7**
South Bank
  Parklands **22**
St. John's Anglican
  Cathedral **6**

Cross River ───────
CityCat ─ ─ ─ ─
CityFerry ─·─·─·─
Information ⓘ

center (in the Myer Centre, off Queen St. Mall) and the Brisbane City Council customer service center at 69 Ann St. Tickets are also sold at some inner city newsdealers.

A trip in a single sector or zone on the bus, train, or ferry costs A$2 (US$1.60). A single ticket is good for up to 2 hours on a one-way journey on any combination of bus, train, or ferry. When traveling with a parent, kids under 5 travel free and kids 5 to 15 and students pay half fare. If you plan on using public transport a lot, a 10-Trip ticket may be a good investment.

You will probably not need to travel farther than four zones on the transport system, which will get you as far as the Australian Woolshed at Ferny Grove. This will cost you the princely sum of A$3.20 (US$2.55) each way. A 1-day ticket for four zones will cost A$6.40 (US$5.10).

On weekends and public holidays, it's cheaper to buy an **Off-Peak ticket,** which lets you travel all day for A$4.80 (US$3.85) for adults. The Off-Peak ticket is also available on weekdays, but you must plan your sightseeing around the fact that it cannot be used before 9am or between 3:30 and 7pm.

The **Brisbane Mobility Map,** produced by the Brisbane City Council, outlines wheelchair access to buildings in the city center and includes a detailed guide to the Queen Street Mall and a map of the Brisbane Botanic Gardens Mount Coot-tha. The council's disability-services unit also has a range of publications, including a Braille Trail and an access guide to parks, available from council customer service centers (© 07/3403 8888).

BY BUS   Buses operate from around 5am to 11pm weekdays, with less service on weekends. On Sunday, many routes stop around 5pm. Most buses depart from City Hall at King George Square, from Adelaide or Ann street. The Downtown Loop is a free bus service that circles the city center. The Loop's distinctive red buses run on two routes, stopping at convenient places including Central Station, Queen Street Mall, City Botanic Gardens, Riverside Centre, and King George Square. Look for the red bus stops. They run every 10 minutes from 7am to 5:50pm Monday through Friday.

BY FERRY   The fast **CityCat** ferries run to many places of interest, including South Bank and the Queensland Cultural Centre; the restaurants and Sunday markets at the Riverside Centre; and New Farm Park, not far from the cafes of Merthyr Street. They run every half-hour between Queensland University, approximately 9km (5½ miles) to the south, and Brett's Wharf, about 9km (5½ miles) to the north. Slower but more frequent CityFerry service (**Inner City** and **Cross River** ferries) stops at a few more points, including the south end of South Bank Parklands, Kangaroo Point, and Edward Street right outside the Brisbane City Gardens. Ferries run from around 6am to 10:30pm daily. Two hours on the CityCat takes you the entire length of the run.

BY TRAIN   Brisbane's suburban rail network is fast, quiet, safe, and clean. Trains run from around 5am to midnight (until about 11pm on Sun). All trains leave Central Station, between Turbot and Ann streets at Edward Street.

BY CAR OR TAXI

Brisbane's grid of one-way streets can be confusing, so plan your route before you set off. Brisbane's biggest car park is at the Myer Centre (enter from Elizabeth St.) and is open 24 hours (© 07/3229 1699). Most hotels and motels have free parking for guests.

Avis (© **13 63 33** or 07/3221 2900), **Budget** (© **1300/362 848** in Australia, or 07/3220 0699), **Europcar** (© **07/3006 7440**), and **Hertz** (© **13 30 39** or 07/3221 6166) all have outlets in the city center. **Thrifty** (© **1300/367 227** in Australia, or 07/3006 3255) is on the edge of the city center at 49 Barry Parade, Fortitude Valley.

For a taxi, call **Yellow Cabs** (© **13 19 24** in Australia) or **Black and White Taxis** (© **13 10 08** in Australia). There are taxi stands at each end of Queen Street Mall, on Edward Street and on George Street (outside the Treasury Casino).

FAST FACTS: Brisbane

American Express The office at 131 Elizabeth St. (© **1300/139 060**) cashes traveler's checks, exchanges foreign currency, and replaces lost traveler's checks. It's open 9am to 5pm Monday to Friday and 9am to noon Saturday.

Business Hours Banks are open Monday through Thursday from 9:30am to 4pm, until 5pm on Friday. See "The Shopping Scene," later in this chapter, for store hours. Some restaurants close Monday night, Tuesday night, or both; bars are generally open from 10 or 11am until midnight.

Currency Exchange **Travelex,** Lennons Plaza, Queen Street Mall between Albert and George streets (© **07/3229 8610**; www.travelex.com.au), is open Monday through Friday from 9am to 6pm, Saturday from 9:30am to 5pm, and Sunday from 10:30am to 4:30pm. Locations at the airport are open whenever flights are arriving.

Dentist The **Adelaide and Albert Dental Centre**, 245 Albert St. at Adelaide Street, opposite City Hall (© **07/3229 4121**), is open Monday through Friday from 8am to 6pm.

Doctor The **Travellers' Medical and Vaccination Centre** (© **07/3221 9066**; www. tmvc.com.au) is on Level 5 of the Qantas building, 247 Adelaide St., between Creek and Edward streets. It is open Monday and Friday from 8am to 5pm, Tuesday 9am to 7pm, Wednesday 8am to 9pm, Thursday 8am to 2pm, and Saturday 8:30am to 2pm. For after-hours emergencies, call © **0408/199 166.**

Embassies & Consulates The United States, Canada, and New Zealand have no representation in Brisbane; see chapter 4, "Sydney," for those countries' nearest offices. The British Consulate-General is at Level 26, Waterfront Place, 1 Eagle St. (© **07/3223 3200**).

Emergencies Dial © **000** for fire, ambulance, or police help in an emergency. This is a free call from a private or public telephone.

Hospitals The nearest one is **Royal Brisbane Hospital,** about a 15-minute drive from the city at Herston Road, Herston (© **07/3636 8111**).

Hot Lines **Lifeline** (© **13 11 14**) is a 24-hour emotional crisis counseling service.

Internet Access The **South Bank Information Centre,** Stanley Street Plaza, South Bank Parklands, open from 9am to 5:30pm Saturday to Thursday and until 7:30pm Friday, charges A$2 (US$1.60) per 15 minutes. In Paddington, the **Computer Café,** 107 Latrobe Terrace (© **07/3369 9077**), above Woolworths, is open Monday, Tuesday, and Thursday from 10am to 9pm, and Wednesday, Friday, and Saturday from 10am to 6pm.

Luggage Storage & Lockers **The Brisbane Transit Centre** on Roma Street (© 1800/ 632 640) has baggage lockers.

Newspapers & Magazines The *Courier-Mail* (Mon–Sat) and the *Sunday Mail* are Brisbane's daily newspapers. The free weekly *Brisbane News* is a good guide to dining, entertainment, and shopping.

Pharmacies (Chemist Shops) **T & G Corner Day & Night Pharmacy**, 141 Queen St. Mall (© 07/3221 4585), is open Monday through Thursday from 7am to 9pm, Friday from 7am to 9:30pm, Saturday from 8am to 9pm, Sunday from 8:30am to 5:30pm, and public holidays from 9am to 7:30pm.

Police Dial © 000 in an emergency, or © 07/3364 6464 for police headquarters. Police are stationed 24 hours a day in the Pavilion Arcade, 130 Queen St. (in the Queen St. Mall), near Albert Street (© 07/3224 4444).

Safety Brisbane is relatively crime free, but as in any large city, be aware of your personal safety, especially when you're out at night. Stick to well-lit streets and busy precincts.

Time Zone The time in Brisbane is Greenwich Mean Time plus 10 hours. Brisbane does not observe daylight savings time, which means it's on the same time as Sydney and Melbourne in winter, and 1 hour behind those cities October through March. For the exact local time, call © 1194.

Weather Call © 1196 for the southeast Queensland weather forecast.

3 Where to Stay

IN THE CITY CENTER
VERY EXPENSIVE
Stamford Plaza Brisbane ★★★   The Stamford is one of Brisbane's most beautiful hotels; brocade chairs and sofas, enormous still-life oils, gilt mirrors, and palms dot the marble lobby. It's also one of the few city hotels with river views from every room—especially stunning from the southern rooms at night, when the Story Bridge lights up. The plush rooms are not enormous, but all fit a king-size bed or two twins. What must be the biggest bathrooms in Brisbane sport small TVs. A riverside boardwalk leads from the hotel to the Eagle Street Pier restaurants, and the Brisbane City Gardens abut the hotel. In a historic 19th-century sandstone building adjacent to the hotel is one of Brisbane's grandest fine-dining restaurants, **Siggi's,** which also boasts a wine and tapas bar where you can puff on cigars with your cognac.

Edward and Margaret sts. (adjacent to the Brisbane City Gardens), Brisbane, QLD 4000. © 1800/773 700 in Australia, or 07/3221 1999. Fax 07/3221 6895. www.stamford.com.au. 252 units. A$520 (US$416) double; A$690–A$3,500 (US$552–US$2,800) suite. Extra person A$40 (US$32). Children under 12 stay free in parent's room with existing bedding. Ask about packages. AE, DC, MC, V. Covered parking. Train: Central, then taxi or walk 6 blocks. Bus: Downtown Loop. Ferry: Riverside Centre, Eagle St. **Amenities:** 3 restaurants; 3 bars; small outdoor heated lap pool; health club; Jacuzzi; sauna; bike rental; concierge; tour desk; car-rental desk; business center; salon; 24-hr. room service; in-room massage; babysitting; dry cleaning; 24-hr. butler service (for a fee); nonsmoking rooms. *In room:* A/C, TV/VCR w/pay movies, dataport, minibar, coffeemaker, hair dryer, iron.

EXPENSIVE

Mercure Hotel Brisbane ★   Sweeping views of the Brisbane River enliven many rooms at this bright 14-story hotel (rated four stars by AAA) across the water from South Bank. An A$3-million (US$2.4-million) refurbishment of all rooms in late 2002 gave them a fresh, contemporary look in red and cream. The four suites have river views, and the standard rooms are comfortable and unassuming. Rooms without water vistas have nice city views. Roma Street Transit Centre, Treasury Casino, Queen Street Mall, South Bank Parklands, and the Queensland Cultural Centre are all a short walk away.

85–87 North Quay (between Ann and Turbot sts.), Brisbane, QLD 4000. © 1300/656 565 in Australia, 800/221-4542 in the U.S. and Canada, 020/8283 4500 in the U.K., 0800/44 4422 in New Zealand, or 07/3236 3300. Fax 07/3236 1035. www.mercurebrisbane.com.au. 194 units. A$169–A$406 (US$135–US$325) double or studio suite; A$269–A$457 (US$215–US$366) executive suite. Extra person A$36 (US$29). Children under 16 stay free in parent's room with existing bedding. Ask about packages. AE, DC, MC, V. Parking A$10 (US$8). Train: Roma St. Bus: Downtown Loop. Ferry: North Quay (CityCat or CityFerry). **Amenities:** Restaurant; bar; outdoor pool; access to nearby health club (A$10/US$8); sauna; concierge; car-rental desk; airport shuttle; 24-hr. room service; babysitting; coin-op laundry; laundry service; dry cleaning; nonsmoking rooms. *In room:* A/C, TV w/pay movies, dataport, minibar, coffeemaker, hair dryer, iron.

MODERATE

Hotel Ibis Brisbane   You get what you pay for at this three-star sister property to the Mercure, around the corner (see above). In this case, it is basically a room, with few amenities you might expect in a large hotel. But if you don't mind doing without river views, porters, a pool, or other small luxuries, this could be the place for you. The hotel has rooms furnished in contemporary style, with sizable work desks and small but smart bathrooms.

27–35 Turbot St. (between North Quay and George St.), Brisbane, QLD 4000. © 1300/656 565 in Australia, 800/221-4542 in the U.S. and Canada, 020/8283 4500 in the U.K., 0800/44 4422 in New Zealand, or 07/3237 2333. Fax 07/3237 2444. www.accorhotels.com.au. 218 units. A$119–A$145 (US$95–US$116) double. Extra person A$30 (US$24). Children under 16 stay free in parent's room with existing bedding. Ask about packages. AE, DC, MC, V. Parking A$10 (US$8) at Mercure Hotel Brisbane (see above). Train: Roma St. Bus: Downtown Loop. Ferry: North Quay (CityCat or CityFerry). **Amenities:** 2 restaurants; 2 bars; car-rental desk; airport shuttle; coin-op laundry; laundry service; dry cleaning; nonsmoking rooms. *In room:* A/C, TV w/pay movies, fridge, coffeemaker, hair dryer, iron.

INEXPENSIVE

Eton ★ *Finds*   This heritage-listed cottage, not far from the Brisbane Transit Centre, has five rooms and an attic suite that sleeps three, all with en-suite bathrooms. The attic suite is a self-contained apartment with its own entrance and kitchen. Room no. 1, at the front of the house, is my pick—it has a claw-foot bathtub and king-size bed. Out the back is a garden courtyard, where you can have breakfast among the palms, ferns, and frangipani trees. New owners Matthew and Yang Lo were just about to take over at press time, so you may find some changes when you visit. No children under 4. No smoking indoors.

436 Upper Roma St., Brisbane, QLD 4000. © 07/3236 0115. www.babs.com.au/eton. 6 units (5 with shower only). A$110–A$130 (US$88–US$104) double; A$490 (US$392) apt weekly. Rates include breakfast (except apt). AE, MC, V. Limited free parking. Train: Roma St. **Amenities:** Access to guest laundry and kitchen. *In room:* A/C, TV, coffeemaker, hair dryer, iron.

Explorers Inn Hotel ★ *Value*   You'll be astonished to find such spruce decor and terrific value in one place—and in the heart of the city! Each tiny room at this former YWCA was designed by its architect owners to contain just the necessities, including a narrow desk. The front desk lends hair dryers, and the friendly staff will help with booking tours. All rooms are nonsmoking, but there is a smokers' lounge. There's also an Internet kiosk. If you book on the Internet, you can get breakfast for an extra A$5 (US$4). Downstairs is the good-value **Explorers Cafe** (see "Where to Dine," below) restaurant and bar. South Bank, the casino, the Roma Street Transit Centre, and Queen Street Mall are all close by.

63 Turbot St. (near George St.), Brisbane, QLD 4000. © **1800/623 288** in Australia, or 07/3211 3488. Fax 07/3211 3499. www.explorers.com.au. 58 units (all with shower only). A$79–A$109 (US$63–US$87) double; A$104 (US$83) family unit for up to 4. AE, DC, MC, V. Train: Roma St. Bus: Downtown Loop. **Amenities:** Restaurant (see "Where to Dine," below); tour desk; car-rental desk; secretarial services; coin-op laundry; laundry service; dry cleaning; nonsmoking rooms. *In room:* A/C, TV, fridge, coffeemaker.

Hotel George Williams ★ *Value* This 7-year-old hotel is so smart it's hard to believe it's a YMCA. Accommodations have vivid bedcovers, chrome chairs, and artsy bedside lamps on chrome stands. Rooms are small but some can sleep up to four adults. Among the useful facilities are a 24-hour front desk, safe-deposit boxes, and a hip cybercafe. Hair dryers are available on request. Guests have free access to the City Y health club, the largest hotel gym in Australia, which offers aerobics classes, personal trainers, and massage (for an extra fee). Four rooms are designed for guests with disabilities, and there is also easy access to the gym.

317–325 George St. (between Turbot and Ann sts.), Brisbane, QLD 4000. © **1800/064 858** in Australia, or 07/3308 0700. Fax 07/3308 0733. www.hgw.com.au. 81 units (most with shower only). A$93–A$135 (US$74–US$108) double. Extra person A$22 (US$18). Children under 4 stay free in parent's room. Ask about packages. AE, DC, MC, V. Limited free parking. Train: Roma St. Bus: Downtown Loop. Ferry: North Quay (CityCat or CityFerry). **Amenities:** Cafe; bar; health club; tour desk; coin-op laundry w/iron and ironing board; laundry service; dry cleaning; nonsmoking rooms. *In room:* A/C, TV, fridge, coffeemaker.

Thornbury House Bed & Breakfast ★ *Finds* A 15-minute walk to Spring Hill from the city center brings you to this 1886 Queenslander cottage on a quiet street. Hosts Christine and Gerry Scanlan have decked out every room individually with Oriental rugs, comfortable beds, bathrobes, and lovely old furniture and knickknacks. Those without attached bathrooms have their own private bathrooms down the hall. The attic suite sleeps three and has two bedrooms, a sitting room, and a bathroom. Two of the rooms have direct access to the front veranda. Breakfast is served in the ferny courtyard (a cool and restful place on a humid day), where you can help yourself to tea, coffee, cookies, and the newspaper any time of day. Guests have access to the house's washer, dryer, iron, fridge, and microwave. The airport bus stops at the front door.

1 Thornbury St., Spring Hill, Brisbane, QLD 4000. © **07/3839 5334.** www.babs.com.au/thornbury. 6 units (5 with shower only). A$100–A$110 (US$80–US$88) double; A$140 (US$112) apt. Rates include breakfast. AE, MC, V. Limited free parking; metered street parking A$5 (US$4). Train: Central. **Amenities:** Access to nearby pools, golf club, and health club; play area and toys; dry cleaning; fax, computer, and dataport available; pay phone; nonsmoking rooms. *In room:* A/C, TV, hair dryer.

IN PADDINGTON

Waverley ★★ *Finds* On the main shopping and restaurant strip in Paddington, this lovely three-story 1888 residence retains most of its original features, such as bay windows, tongue-and-groove walls, soaring ceilings, and polished timber floors. The two air-conditioned front rooms are spacious and individually furnished with supportive mattresses, comfy sofas, and attractive bathrooms. Two apartments (with kitchens and fans) are downstairs. Your hostess, Annette Henry, also known as "the muffin queen," cooks a hearty breakfast in the homey yellow kitchen. A rear deck on both levels overlooks two old mango trees, busy with possums at night and visited regularly by day by a pair of native butcherbirds. There's also a lounge. No smoking indoors.

5 Latrobe Terrace (at Cochrane St.), Paddington, Brisbane, QLD 4064. ℂ 07/3369 8973, or 0419/741 282 mobile. Fax 07/3876 6655. www.babs.com.au/paddington. 4 units (all with shower only). A$120 (US$96) B&B double; A$490 (US$392) apt per week. B&B rates include full breakfast. AE, DC, MC, V. Free parking for 4 cars. Bus: 375 or 377; stop 20m (65 ft.) away. Pickup from Roma St. Transit Centre available on request. **Amenities:** Coin-op laundry; safe; non-smoking rooms. *In room:* A/C, TV, kitchenette (apt only), fridge, coffeemaker, hair dryer, iron.

4 Where to Dine

Visitors are often surprised to find that Brisbane has a sophisticated dining scene. Stylish bistros and cafes line Merthyr Street in New Farm; cute cafes are plentiful in Paddington; Asian eateries are a good choice around the intersection of Vulture Street and Boundary Street in West End; and in Fortitude Valley ("the Valley" for short), you'll find Chinatown. A street full of upscale but laid-back restaurants, many with a Mediterranean flavor, sits under the kitsch replica Eiffel Tower on Park Road in Milton, and in the city center you can find slick riverfront restaurants at Eagle Street Pier and Riverside. The intersection of Albert and Charlotte streets buzzes with inexpensive, good-quality cafes.

IN THE CITY CENTER
EXPENSIVE

e'cco bistro ★★★ MODERN AUSTRALIAN   "Here it is" is one translation of the Italian *e'cco,* and that's the philosophy behind the food at this award-winning bistro. It serves simple food, done exceptionally well and with passion. In a former tea warehouse on the city fringe, it's one of Australia's best. Dishes include such delights as chermoula spiced lamb with eggplant and tomato chutney and minted sour cream, or salmon poached in tomato, chilli, and lemon-grass broth with crab ravioli and mussels. The bistro is enormously popular, and bookings are essential. Large windows, bold colors, and modern furniture make it a pleasant setting in a small but popular restaurant enclave. The price structure is simple (each course's offerings are all the same price), and there's an extensive wine list—many by the glass. You can bring your own wine; the corkage fee is A$5.50 (US$4.40) per bottle.

100 Boundary St. (at Adelaide St.). ℂ 07/3831 8344. Fax 07/3831 8460. www.eccobistro.com. Reservations required. Starters A$20 (US$16); main courses A$33 (US$26); desserts A$14 (US$11). AE, DC, MC, V. Tues–Fri noon–2:30pm; Tues–Sat 6–10pm. Also Mon noon–2:30pm and 6–10pm mid-Nov to Dec 25. Closed 10 days Dec 25 to early Jan. Metered street parking.

Pier Nine ★★★ MODERN AUSTRALIAN/SEAFOOD   Ask the locals for the best seafood in town, and they'll send you to this light-filled contemporary restaurant overlooking the river and Story Bridge. The menu changes daily; specialties include oysters shucked to order and served several ways or au naturel for the purist, and fresh local Moreton Bay bugs (a kind of crustacean). Try them chargrilled with a rocket and beetroot-leaf salad, papaya salsa, and a sauce verte. Or the three-crab (sand, spanner, and mud) lasagna. It's always busy, so if you turn up without a reservation, prepare to cool your heels at the oyster bar (which serves an abbreviated version of the menu after hours).

Eagle St. Pier, 1 Eagle St. ℂ 07/3226 2100. www.piernine.com.au. Reservations recommended. Main courses A$20–A$40 (US$16–US$32). AE, DC, MC, V. Mon–Fri 11:30am–10pm; Sat 4–10pm; Sun 12:30–10pm. Oyster bar is open until midnight; supper menu 10pm–midnight. Closed public holidays. Ferry: Riverside (CityCat); Edward St. or Riverside (CityFerry); Eagle St. Pier (Cross River Ferry). Underground parking.

Watt Modern Dining ★★ MODERN AUSTRALIAN   Whether it's for a leisurely weekend breakfast, lunch, or dinner before a show at the Brisbane Power house, this is a bright spot to be. With a menu of modern fare with Asian, Middle Eastern, and European influences, and a terrific wine list, Watt is one of my favorite places to eat out in Brisbane—partly because of the riverside setting in New Farm Park, and partly because of the great food. Dishes include interesting things like duck breast with potato and shallot cake, bok choy and Chinese red braise sauce, or eggplant involtini with tellagio cheese, raisins, pine nuts, and red pepper. The Park Lounge is great for drinks and light meals before the theater.

Brisbane Powerhouse, 119 Lamington St, New Farm (near the river). © **07/3358 5464**. www.watt.net.au. Reservations recommended. Main courses A$22–A$34 (US$18–US$27). AE, DC, MC, V. Tues–Fri 10am–late; Sat–Sun 8am–late. Ample nearby parking.

MODERATE

Jo Jo's INTERNATIONAL/CAFE FARE   A spectacular timber, limestone, and glass bar dominates the center of this casual cafe-style eating spot, housing more than 1,000 bottles of wine. Four menus—chargrill, Thai, pizza, and Mediterranean—are available, and the locals have dropped in here for years for a shopping pit stop or a postcinema meal. The food is well priced and good. You order at the bar and meals are delivered to the table (try to get one on the balcony overlooking the Queen St. Mall). Among your options are steaks and seafood from the grill; curries and stir-fries from the Thai menu; Mediterranean pastas, antipasto, and designer sandwiches; and gourmet toppings on wood-fired-oven pizzas.

1st floor, Queen St. Mall at Albert St. © **07/3221 2113**. www.jojos.com.au. Main courses A$8–A$29 (US$6.40–US$23). AE, DC, MC, V. Daily 9:30am–midnight; happy hour daily 4:30–6pm. Train or bus: Central.

INEXPENSIVE

Explorers Cafe _Value_ CAFE FARE   Great value—nothing costs more than A$12 (US$9.60)—is the hallmark of this basement restaurant in the Explorers Inn (see listing p. 251). One of the best-value a la carte menus in town offers standard fares such as soups, pastas, seafood, steaks, and chicken dishes, with a choose-and-pay-at-the-counter format and table service. There are also a couple of vegetarian options on the menu, which is the same for lunch and dinner.

Under the Explorers Inn, 63 Turbot St. (near corner of George St.). © **07/3211 3488**. Fax 07/3211 3499. www. explorers.com.au. Reservations recommended at lunch. Main courses A$8–A$12 (US$6.40–US$9.60); breakfast A$4–A$11 (US$3.20–US$8.80). AE, DC, MC, V. Daily 7–9:30am and 6–8pm; Mon–Fri noon–2pm. Train: Roma St. Bus: Downtown Loop.

IN SPRING HILL
MODERATE

Tognini's BistroCafeDeli MODERN AUSTRALIAN   Owners Mark and Narelle Tognini run this relaxed modern bistro, incorporating an extensive deli and walk-in cheese room. Popular with inner-city dwellers and business folk, it serves gourmet delights to eat in or take out. Sit at one of the communal tables and try potato gnocchi with blue cheese sauce, or maybe sweet corn and chive risotto with grilled Atlantic salmon. Don't pass up cinnamon poached pears and vanilla panna cotta—it's divine. There's another Tognini's at Baroona Road, Milton, but this one is more convenient if you're staying in the city.

Turbot and Boundary sts., Spring Hill. © **07/3831 5300**. Fax 07/3831 5311. www.togninis.com. Reservations not accepted. Main courses A$15–A$23 (US$12–US$18). AE, DC, MC, V. Mon–Fri 7am–6pm; Sat–Sun 8am–4pm. Closed Easter and Dec 25.

IN MOUNT COOT-THA
EXPENSIVE
The Summit ★★ MODERN AUSTRALIAN   It would be hard to find a better view of Brisbane than from this spot. A teahouse of some kind has been on this mountaintop for more than a century. Part 19th-century Queenslander house and part modern extension, the restaurant has wraparound covered decks with a view of the city and Moreton Bay. A changing menu features local produce and dishes with Asian and Mediterranean influences, teamed with Australian wines. Try saltwater barramundi (fish) filet, or roasted kangaroo loin. The early-bird offer—half-price main courses if you finish by 7pm—is available starting at 5:30pm. And when you've finished dining, spend some time on the observation deck—at night the city lights provide a glittering panorama.

At the Mt. Coot-tha Lookout, Sir Samuel Griffith Dr., Mt. Coot-tha. ℂ 07/3369 9922. Fax 07/3369 8937. www.brisbane lookout.com. Reservations recommended Fri–Sat night. Main courses A$27–A$34 (US$22–US$27). AE, DC, MC, V. Daily 11:30am–midnight; Sun brunch 8–10:30am. Closed for lunch Jan 1, Good Friday, Dec 26; closed for dinner Dec 25. Bus: 471. From Roma St. Transit Centre, take Upper Roma St. and Milton Rd. 3.5km (2¼ miles) west to the Western Fwy. roundabout at Toowong Cemetery, veer right into Sir Samuel Griffith Dr., and go approximately 3km (2 miles). Free parking.

IN EAST BRISBANE
MODERATE
Green Papaya ★ Value NORTH VIETNAMESE   Clean, fresh, and simple are the key words to describe owner-chef Lien Yeoman's approach to her native cuisine. Two cheerful rooms—painted yellow and blue—are usually crowded with a faithful clientele. If you don't know your *bo xao cay ngot* (spicy beef) from your *nom du du* (green papaya salad), the staff willingly gives advice. On Fridays (bookings essential) Lien creates her special Hanoi-style bouillabaisse. The restaurant is licensed, but you can bring your own bottled wine (no beer or spirits) for a corkage charge of A$3 (US$2.40) per person. Cooking classes run from time to time; call for a schedule. The restaurant also does takeout.

898 Stanley St. E. (at Potts St.), 1 block from Woolloongabba Cricket Ground, East Brisbane. ℂ 07/3217 3599. www.greenpapaya.com.au. Reservations recommended. Main courses A$10–A$36 (US$8–US$29); banquet menus (for minimum of 4 people) A$40–A$60 (US$32–US$48). AE, DC, MC, V. Tues–Sat 6–10pm; Fri lunch by reservation only. Closed Good Friday, Dec 25 to early Jan. Train: Woolloongabba. Parking at rear of restaurant and on-street.

IN ALBION
MODERATE
Breakfast Creek Hotel ★ STEAK   An A$4.5-million (US$3.6-million) renovation and restoration in 2002 gave fresh life to this Brisbane treasure. Built in 1889 and listed by the National Trust, the French Renaissance–style pub is fondly known as the Brekky Creek—or simply "the Creek." The quintessentially Queensland establishment is famed for its gigantic steaks (choose your own), served with Idaho potato, bacon sauce, coleslaw, slices of tomato, and a roll, and for serving beer "off the wood" (from the keg). Also on the premises, the Spanish Garden restaurant and the beer garden are always popular, and an outdoor dining area overlooks Breakfast Creek. The Substation No. 41 bar, created in the shell of a derelict electricity substation next to the hotel, makes the most of its exposed brick walls and soaring ceilings. The 4.5m-long (15-ft.) wooden bar is just the place to sip the latest cocktail.

2 Kingsford Smith Dr. (at Breakfast Creek Rd.), Albion. ℂ 07/3262 5988. www.breakfastcreekhotel.com. Main courses A$17–A$25 (US$14–US$20). AE, DC, MC, V. Daily noon–2:30pm; Mon–Fri 5:30–9:30pm; Sat 5–9:30pm; Sun 5–8:30pm. Pub Sun–Thurs 10am–10pm; Fri–Sat 10am–11pm. Substation No. 41 Sun–Thurs 10am–11pm; Fri–Sat 10am–2am. Bus: 300 or 322. Wickham St. becomes Breakfast Creek Rd.; the hotel is just off the route to the airport.

5 Exploring Brisbane

CUDDLING A KOALA & OTHER TOP ATTRACTIONS

Australian Woolshed *Overrated* If you've never seen a sheep or visited a farm, this might be a novelty for you, but don't be surprised if your Aussie friends cringe when you mention your intention to visit it. That said, this is a popular attraction with overseas visitors and school groups—you may have to contend with busloads of them. The ram show features eight trained Australian rams that "answer" to their names and walk through the audience to take their place beside their named spots on the stage. There's also sheep shearing, spinning, and sheepdog demonstrations, and you can get your hands dirty classing wool, milking cows, feeding kangaroos, and cuddling koalas (a photo costs A$15/US$12). The gift shop has quality Australian-made souvenirs. A rustic restaurant serves Aussie specialties, including billy tea and damper.

On some Friday and Saturday nights—usually about once a month—the Woolshed hosts a traditional bush dance and dinner, featuring country dancing, spoon-playing, singalongs, a live band, and a two-course dinner. Tickets cost A$40 (US$32) per person. The fun starts at 7pm. Reservations are essential.

148 Samford Rd., Ferny Hills. ✆ 07/3872 1100. www.auswoolshed.com.au. Admission to ram show A$18 (US$14) adults, A$14 (US$11) seniors and students, A$13 (US$10) children 3–14, A$49 (US$39) family (2 adults, 3 children). Billy tea and damper A$7 (US$5.60) adults, A$4.50 (US$3.60) children 3–14. Water slide A$7 (US$5.60) for 1 hr.; A$11 (US$8.80) for 4 hr. Minigolf A$5.50 (US$4.40) for 9 holes. AE, MC, V. Daily 8:30am–4:30pm (ram show 9:30am, 11am, 1pm, and 2:30pm). Closed Dec 25 and until noon Apr 25 (Anzac Day). Train: Ferny Grove (station is 800m/2,624 ft. from the Woolshed). By car, Kelvin Grove Rd. from the city becomes Enoggera Rd., then Samford Rd.; the trip is 14km (8½ miles). Large off-street free parking lot.

Brisbane Botanic Gardens Mount Coot-tha These 52-hectare (128-acre) gardens at the base of Mount Coot-tha feature Aussie natives and exotics you probably won't see at home, including an arid zone, a Tropical Dome conservatory housing rainforest plants, a cactus house, a bonsai house, fragrant plants, a Japanese garden, African and American plants, wetlands, and a bamboo grove. There are lakes and trails, usually a horticultural show or arts-and-crafts display in the auditorium on weekends, and a cafe. Free 1-hour guided tours leave the kiosk at 11am and 1pm Monday through Saturday (except public holidays). The Sir Thomas Brisbane Planetarium & Cosmic Skydome (see below) is also in the botanic gardens.

Mt. Coot-tha Rd., Toowong, 7km (4 miles) from the city. ✆ 07/3403 8888. www.brisbane.qld.gov.au. Free admission to Botanic Gardens. Sept–Mar daily 8am–5:30pm; Apr–Aug daily 8am–5pm. Bus: 471. Free parking.

City Hall Once the tallest building in Brisbane, City Hall is now dwarfed by the office blocks that surround it. Nevertheless, a ride in the old elevator to the top of the sandstone clock tower gives you a different perspective on the city center. A cheery elevator operator will give you a history of the building on your short ride to the third floor before letting you out into the glassed-in observation floor in the bell tower. If you're there on the quarter-hour, you'll get a close-up experience of the chimes. Try not to be there at midday, when the clock chimes 12—it's deafening.

King George Sq. (Ann and Adelaide sts.). ✆ 07/3403 8888. Free admission to City Hall; clock tower admission A$2 (US$1.60). Clock tower Mon–Fri 10am–3pm; Sat 10am–2:30pm. Closed Sun and public holidays.

Lone Pine Koala Sanctuary ★★ *Kids* This is the best place in Australia to cuddle a koala—and one of the few places where koala cuddling is still allowed. Banned in New South Wales and Victoria, koala cuddling is allowed in Queensland under strict conditions that ensure each animal is handled for less than 30 minutes a day—and gets every third day off! When it opened in 1927, Lone Pine had only two koalas, Jack and Jill; it is now home to more than 130. You can cuddle them anytime and have a photo taken holding one for A$15 (US$12); once you've purchased a photograph, your companions can take as many photos of you as they like with their own cameras. Lone Pine isn't just koalas—you can also hand-feed kangaroos and wallabies and get up close with emus, parrots, wombats, Tasmanian devils, skinks, lace monitors, frogs, bats, turtles, possums, and other native wildlife. There is a currency exchange, a gift shop, and a restaurant and cafe. You can also take advantage of the picnic and barbecue facilities.

The nicest way to get to Lone Pine is a cruise down the Brisbane River aboard MV *Mirimar* (© **07/3221 0300**), which leaves North Quay at the Queen Street Mall, next to Victoria Bridge, at 10am. The 19km (12-mile) trip to Lone Pine takes 90 minutes and includes commentary. You have 2 hours to explore Lone Pine before returning, arriving in the city at 2:45pm. The fare is A$44 (US$35) for adults and A$25 (US$20) for children 3 to 13, including a map and hotel pickup. Cruises run daily except April 25 (Anzac Day) and December 25.

Jesmond Rd., Fig Tree Pocket. © 07/3378 1366. Fax 07/3878 1770. www.koala.net. Admission A$18 (US$14) adults; A$13 (US$10) children 3–13; A$45 (US$36) families of 5. AE, DC, MC, V. Daily 8:30am–5pm; 1:30–5pm Apr 25 (Anzac Day). By car (20 min. from the city center), take Milton Rd. to the roundabout at Toowong cemetery, then Western Fwy. toward Ipswich. Signs point to Fig Tree Pocket and Lone Pine. Bus: 430 from platform B3 at Myer Centre, Queen St. Mall; hourly 8:45am–3:45pm weekdays, 8:30am–4:30pm weekends and public holidays. Bus fare A$2.80 (US$2.25) adults, A$1.40 (US$1.10) children. Taxi from the city center about A$24 (US$19). Ample free parking.

Museum of Brisbane   This smallish museum in the historic City Hall is designed to capture the history and essence of Brisbane. There's a theater that shows a short film about the city and a shop that stocks "made in Brisbane" items. Changing exhibitions relate the stories, events, and ideas that have shaped the city, as well as giving practical information for visitors. It is a good starting point for your visit.

City Hall, King George Sq. © 07/3403 8888. Free admission. Daily 10am–5pm. Closed Dec 25 and until noon Apr 25 (Anzac Day).

Newstead House ★   Brisbane's oldest surviving home has been restored to its late Victorian splendor in a peaceful park overlooking the Brisbane River. Wander the rooms, admire the gracious exterior dating from 1846, and on Sunday between March and November, take Devonshire tea. The U.S. Army occupied the house during World War II, and the first American war memorial built in Australia stands on Newstead Point, on the grounds.

Newstead Park, Breakfast Creek Rd., Newstead. © 1800/061 846 or 07/3216 1846. www.newsteadhouse.com.au. A$4.40 (US$3.50) adults, A$3.30 (US$2.65) seniors and students, A$2.20 (US$1.75) children 6–16, A$11 (US$8.80) families. Mon–Fri 10am–4pm; Sun 2–5pm. Last admittance 30 min. before closing. Closed Sat, Good Friday, Apr 25 (Anzac Day), Dec 24–Jan 1, and other public holidays. Bus: 300 or 302. Limited parking.

Queensland Cultural Centre *Kids*   This modern complex stretching along the south bank of the Brisbane River houses many of the city's performing arts venues as well as the state art gallery, museum, and library. With plenty of open plazas and fountains, it is a pleasing place to wander or just sit and watch the river and the city skyline. It's a 7-minute walk from town.

The **Queensland Performing Arts Centre** (© **07/3840 7444** administration Mon–Fri 9am–5pm, or 13 62 46 for all bookings; www.qpac.com.au) houses the 2,000-seat Lyric Theatre for musicals, ballet, and opera; the 1,800-seat Concert Hall for orchestral performances; the 850-seat Optus Playhouse Theatre for plays; and the

315-seat Cremorne Theatre for theater in the round, cabaret, and experimental works. The complex has a restaurant and a cafe. Guided tours of the theaters and public and backstage areas leave from the box office at 11:30am on Friday and take about 90 minutes. Reservations are advisable during school holidays (🕐 **07/3840 7444**). The cost is A$7.50 (US$6) adults and A$5 (US$4) children.

The **Queensland Art Gallery** ⭐ (🕐 **07/3840 7303;** www.qag.qld.gov.au) is one of Australia's most attractive galleries, with vast light-filled spaces and interesting water features inside and out. It is a major player in the Australian art world, attracting blockbuster exhibitions of works by the likes of Renoir, Picasso, and van Gogh, and showcasing diverse modern Australian painters, sculptors, and other artists. It also has an impressive collection of Aboriginal art. Admission is free. Free guided tours run Monday through Friday at 11am, 1pm, and 2pm; Saturday and Sunday at 11:30am, 1pm, and 2:30pm. There is a gift shop and bistro. The gallery is open Monday through Friday 10am to 5pm, weekends 9am to 5pm; closed Good Friday, December 25, and until noon on April 25 (Anzac Day). In late 2006, a second gallery, the **Queensland Gallery of Modern Art,** will open, providing more space for the collections of modern and contemporary Australian, indigenous Australian, Asian, and Pacific art.

The **Queensland Museum** (🕐 **07/3840 7555;** www.qmuseum.qld.gov.au), on the corner of Grey and Melbourne streets, underwent a major revamp in 2003 and looks the better for it. The museum houses an eclectic collection ranging from natural history specimens and fossils to a World War I German tank. Children will like the blue whale model; the dinosaurs, which include Queensland's own Muttaburrasaurus; and the interactive Sciencentre. The museum has a cafe and gift shop. Admission is free, except to the Sciencentre and traveling exhibitions. It's open daily 9:30am to 5pm; closed Good Friday, December 25, and until noon on April 25 (Anzac Day).

Adjacent to South Bank Parklands, across Victoria Bridge at western end of Queen St. 🕐 **07/3840 7100.** Admission to Sciencentre A$9 (US$7.20); A$28 (US$22) family of 6; extra child 5–16, A$7 (US$5.60). Ferry: South Bank (CityCat) or Old South Bank (Inner City Ferry). Bus: Numerous routes from Adelaide St. (near Albert St.), including 100, 111, 115, and 120, stop outside. Plentiful underground parking.

Roma Street Parkland Thousands of plants, including natives and some of the world's most endangered, have been used to create lush subtropical gardens in an unused railway yard. The effect is stunning. Areas of the gardens are themed. Free guided walks run Thursday through Sunday and on public holidays twice a day (10am and 2pm Sept–May, 11am and 2pm June–Aug), and self-guided walking tours for each theme area are available. The "art walk" helps visitors discover the interesting public art on display. On the premises are barbecues, picnic areas, and a playground. From King George Square, the park is about a 500m (1,640-ft.) walk along Albert Street.

Roma St.; information booths in Spectacle Garden and at Activity Centre. 🕐 **07/3006 4545.** Free admission. Daily 24 hr.; Spectacle Garden daily dawn–dusk. Train: Roma St. Station. By car, enter from Roma St. or the Wickham Terrace/College Rd./Gregory Terrace intersection.

Sir Thomas Brisbane Planetarium & Cosmic Skydome *(Kids)* After a major upgrade in early 2004, the planetarium has new seating and new digital multimedia systems that present real-time digital star shows and computer-generated images in the Cosmic Skydome theater. The popular and fascinating 40-minute astronomical show includes a re-creation of the Brisbane night sky using a Ziess star projector. There are special shows designed for kids between 5 and 8 at 11:30am and 2pm on weekends; the planetarium is not recommended for younger children.

In Brisbane Botanic Gardens Mt. Coot-tha, Mt. Coot-tha Rd., Toowong. ✆ 07/3403 2578. www.brisbane.qld.gov.au/planetarium. A$12 (US$9.60) adults, A$9.50 (US$7.60) seniors and students, A$6.80 (US$5.45) children under 15, A$31 (US$25) family of 4; exhibit-only pass A$2 (US$1.60) adults, A$1 (US80¢) children, A$5 (US$4) families. Tues–Fri 2:30–4:30pm (from 10am in Queensland school vacations); Sat 11am–7:30pm; Sun 11am–4:30pm. Shows Tues–Fri 3:15pm; Sat 12:30, 3:15, 6, and 7:30pm; Sun 12:30 and 3:15pm. Reservations recommended.

South Bank Parklands *Kids*   Follow the locals' lead and spend some time at this delightful 16-hectare (40-acre) complex of parks, restaurants, shops, playgrounds, street theater, and weekend markets. There's a man-made beach, lined with palm trees, with real waves and sand, where you can swim, stroll, and cycle the meandering pathways. Or sit over a cafe latte in one of the cafes and enjoy the city views. From the parklands it's an easy stroll to the museum, art gallery, and other parts of the adjacent Queensland Cultural Centre (see above). The South Bank Parklands are a 7-minute walk from town.

South Bank. ✆ 07/3867 2051 for Visitor Information Centre. Free admission. Park daily 24 hr.; Visitor Information Centre Sat–Thurs 9am–6pm; Fri 9am–8pm. From the Queen St. Mall, cross the Victoria Bridge to South Bank or walk across Goodwill Bridge from Gardens Point Rd. entrance to Brisbane City Gardens. Train: South Brisbane. Ferry: South Bank (CityCat or Cross River Ferry). Bus: Numerous routes from Adelaide St. (near Albert St.), including 100, 111, 115, and 120, stop at the Queensland Cultural Centre; walk through the Centre to South Bank Parklands. Plentiful underground parking in Queensland Cultural Centre.

St. John's Anglican Cathedral ★★   Brisbane's stunning neo-Gothic Anglican cathedral is in the final stages of completion—a mere 100 years after it was begun. Don't be put off by the scaffolding, which will likely still be swaddling it when you visit—from a glassed-off area inside, you can watch the stonemasons use traditional medieval building techniques as they work on the western transept (fronting Ann St.), due to be completed in 2007. Friendly, knowledgeable volunteer guides run tours and will point out some of the details that make this cathedral uniquely Queensland—like the carved possums on the organ screen and the hand-stitched cushions.

373 Ann St. (between Wharf and Queen sts.). ✆ 07/3835 2248. www.stjohnscathedral.com.au. Daily 9:30am–4:30pm; free tours Mon–Sat 10am, daily 2pm. Closed to visitors, except for services Apr 25 (Anzac Day), and Dec 25.

TAKING A CITY STROLL

Because Brisbane is leafy, warm, and full of colonial-era Queenslander architecture, it is a great city for strolling. Pick up one of the free Heritage Trail Maps from the Brisbane Marketing information booth (see "Visitor Information," earlier in this chapter) and explore on your own. The map books include a history of the area and excellent detailed information of historic buildings and other sights along the way.

A new "floating" **River Walk** connects more than 20km (13 miles) of pathways, roads, bridges, and parks along the Brisbane River. You can stroll along River Walk on the north bank of the river between the University of Queensland at St. Lucia and Teneriffe, and on the south bank from the West End ferry terminal at Orleigh Park to Dockside at Kangaroo Point.

For information on organized walking tours, see below.

6 Organized Tours

RIVER CRUISES   The best way to cruise the river, in my view, is aboard the fast **CityCat ferries** ★★. Board at Riverside and head downstream under the Story Bridge to New Farm Park, past Newstead House to the restaurant row at Brett's Wharves; or cruise upriver past the city and South Bank to the University of Queensland's lovely campus. (Take a look at its impressive Great Court while you're there.) This trip in either direction will set you back a whole A$3.80 (US$3.05). Or you can stay on for the full trip, which takes about 2 hours. For more information, see "Getting Around," earlier in this chapter.

For those who'd like commentary and a meal as they cruise, the **Kookaburra River Queen** paddle-wheelers (© **07/3221 1300**) are a good option. You can choose from a lunch or dinner cruise, and from a three-course menu or a seafood platter. Lunch cruises cost A$42 (US$34) and A$60 (US$48) for seafood; dinner cruises are A$60 (US$48) and A$75 (US$60). Prices are A$5 (US$4) higher on Friday and Saturday nights and public holidays. The boat departs from South Bank and picks up at the Eagle Street Pier (parking is available under the City Rowers tavern on Eagle St.). A A$25 (US$20) Devonshire tea option is also available.

BUS TOURS   For a good introduction to Brisbane, look no further than a City Sights bus tour run by **Brisbane City Council** (© **13 12 30** in Australia). **City Sights** buses stop at 19 points of interest in a continuous loop around the city center, Spring Hill, Milton, South Bank, and Fortitude Valley, including Chinatown. They take in various historical buildings and places of interest. The driver of the blue-and-yellow bus narrates, and you can hop on and off at any stop you like. The tour is a good value—your ticket also gives unlimited access to buses, ferries, and CityCats for the day, as well as discounts to some attractions. The bus departs every 45 minutes from 9am to 3:45pm daily except Good Friday, April 25 (Anzac Day), and December 25. The whole trip, without stopping, takes 90 minutes. Tickets cost A$20 (US$16) for adults, A$15 (US$12) for children 5 to 15. Buy your ticket on board. You can join anywhere along the route, but the most central stop is City Hall, stop 2, on Adelaide Street at Albert Street.

WALKING TOURS   The Brisbane City Council has a wonderful program called **Gone Walking** (© **07/3403 8888**). About 70 free guided walks are run each week from somewhere in the city or suburbs, exploring all kinds of territory, from bushland to heritage buildings to riverscapes to cemeteries. The walks are aimed at locals, not tourists, so you get to explore Brisbane side by side with the townsfolk. Every walk has a flexible distance option and usually lasts about an hour. Most are easy, but some are more demanding. Most start and finish near public transport and end near a food outlet.

Prepare for shivers up your spine if you take one of Jack Sim's **Ghost Tours** (★) (© **07/3844 6606**), which relive Brisbane's gruesome past. Three regular tours are run, taking in the historic Toowong and South Brisbane cemeteries and the now-disused Boggo Road Gaol. Cemetery tours are on Saturday nights and cost A$30 or A$40 (US$24 or US$32) for adults. Gaol tours are held on Sunday nights and cost A$30 (US$24) adults. Reservations are essential; no children under 12.

Free guided walks of the Brisbane **City Gardens** (© **07/3403 8888**) at Alice Street leave from the rotunda at the Albert Street entrance Monday through Saturday at 11am and 1pm (except public holidays and the first Mon of each month).

7 Enjoying the Great Outdoors
OUTDOOR ACTIVITIES

ABSEILING   The Kangaroo Point cliffs just south of the Story Bridge are a breeze for first-time abseilers (rappellers)—or so they say. Adventure company **WorthWild** (© **07/3395 6450;** www.worthwild.com.au) runs abseiling for beginners on Saturdays

---

Moments **Brisbane's Bridge Climb**

Brisbane boasts nine bridges across its wide river. The most interesting is the Story Bridge, built in 1940. If you are over 130cm (just over 4 ft. 3 in.) tall, you can "climb" this overgrown Meccano set. The Story Bridge Adventure Climb peaks at a viewing platform on top of the bridge, 44m (143 ft.) above the roadway and 80m (262 ft.) above the Brisbane River. Launched in 2005, this is only the third "bridge climb" in the world (after Sydney's and Auckland's), so make the most of the chance. You'll be rewarded with magnificent 360-degree views of the city, river, and Moreton Bay and its islands. The cost is A$100 (US$80) and climbs will run during the day, at sunset, and in the evening. Schedules were not set at press time, but check **www.story bridgeadventureclimb.com.au** or ℰ **07/3514 6900** for more information.

---

from 8 to 11:30am, usually about twice a month. It costs A$75 (US$60) per person, and you can abseil down as many times as you like during the session—most people get 8 to 10 descents in.

BIKING Bike tracks, often shared with pedestrians and in-line skaters, stretch for 400km (248 miles) around Brisbane. One great scenic route, about 9km (5½ miles) long, starts just west of the Story Bridge, sweeps through the Brisbane City Gardens, and follows the river all the way to the University of Queensland campus at St. Lucia. **Brisbane Bicycle Sales and Hire,** 87 Albert St. (ℰ **07/3229 2433;** www.brizbike.com), will rent you a bike and furnish you with the Brisbane City Council's free detailed bike maps. Rentals start at A$12 (US$9.60) for 1 hour and go up to A$25 (US$20) for the day; overnight rentals (A$45/US$36) are available. The price includes helmets, which are compulsory in Australia. **Valet Cycle Hire** (ℰ **07/3630 2772,** or 0408 003 198 mobile) operates from the bicycle station in the City Botanic Gardens, near the Alice Street gate, from 9:30am to late afternoon. The cost is A$15 (US$12) for 1 hour or A$20 (US$16) for 2 hours. You can also have your bike "valet" delivered to all city area accommodations for A$30 (US$24) for 4 hours or A$40 (US$32) for the day. The Brisbane City Council at City Hall (ℰ **07/3403 8888**) and Brisbane Marketing's information booth (see "Visitor Information," earlier in this chapter) also give out bike maps.

BUSHWALKING **Brisbane Forest Park** ★★, a 28,500-hectare (71,395-acre) expanse of bushland, waterfalls, and rainforest a 20-minute drive north of the city, has hiking trails ranging from just a few hundred meters up to 8km (5 miles). Some tracks have themes—one highlights the native mammals that live in the park, for example, and another, the 1.8km (just over 1-mile) **Mount Coot-tha Aboriginal Art Trail,** showcases contemporary Aboriginal art, with tree carvings, rock paintings, etchings, and a dance pit. Because the park is so big, most walks depart from one of the seven regional centers, which are up to a 20-minute drive from headquarters—you will need a car. Make a day of it and pack a picnic. At Park Headquarters, 60 Mount Nebo Rd., The Gap (ℰ **07/3300 4855;** www.brisbaneforestpark.qld.gov.au), you will find a wildlife display, a restaurant, a crafts shop, and an information center.

IN-LINE SKATING In-line skaters can use the network of bike and pedestrian paths. See "Biking," above, for locations that distribute maps, or just head down to the Brisbane City Gardens at Alice Street and find your own way along the river. **SkateBiz,** 101 Albert St. (© 07/3220 0157), rents blades for A$13 (US$10) for 2 hours, or A$20 (US$16) for up to 24 hours. Protective gear is included. Take a photo ID. The store is open from 9am to 5:30pm Monday through Thursday, 9am to 9pm Friday, 9am to 4pm Saturday, and 10am to 4pm Sunday.

8 The Shopping Scene

Brisbane's best shopping centers on **Queen Street Mall,** which has around 500 stores. Fronting the mall at 171–209 Queen St., under the Hilton, is the three-level **Wintergarden** shopping complex (© 07/3229 9755), housing upscale jewelers and Aussie fashion designers. Farther up the mall at 91 Queen St. (at Albert St.) is the **Myer Centre** (© 07/3223 6900), which has Brisbane's biggest department store and five levels of moderately priced stores, mostly fashion. The **Brisbane Arcade,** 160 Queen St. Mall (© 07/3221 5977), abounds with the boutiques of local Queensland designers. Just down the mall from it is the **Broadway on the Mall** arcade (© 07/3229 5233), which stocks affordable fashion, gifts, and accessories on two levels. Across from the Edward Street end of the mall is a smart new fashion and lifestyle shopping precinct, **MacArthur Central** (© 07/3007 2300), right next door to the GPO on the block between Queen and Elizabeth streets. This is where you'll find top-name designer labels, Swiss watches, galleries, and accessory shops.

The trendy suburb of **Paddington,** just a couple of miles from the city by cab (or take the no. 144 bus to Bardon), is the place for antiques, books, art, crafts, one-of-a-kind clothing designs, and unusual gifts. The shops—colorfully painted Queenslander cottages—line the main street, Given Terrace, which becomes Latrobe Terrace. Don't miss the second wave of shops around the bend.

SHOPPING HOURS Brisbane shops are open Monday through Thursday from 8:30am to 5:30pm, Friday 8:30am to 9pm, Saturday 8:30am to 5pm, and Sunday 10:30am to 4pm. On Friday evening in the city, the Queen Street Mall is abuzz with cinema-goers and revelers; the late (until 9pm) shopping night in Paddington is Thursday.

MARKETS Authentic retro '50s and '60s fashion, offbeat stuff like old LPs, secondhand crafts, fashion by up-and-coming young designers, and all kinds of junk and treasure are for sale at Brisbane's only alternative market, **Valley Markets,** Brunswick

---

Finds **Fireworks for Your Wall**

If the Aboriginal art you see in the usual tourist outlets doesn't do it for you, what you'll see at Brisbane's **Fire-Works Gallery** will. Upstairs in an old printery at 11 Stratton St., Newstead (© 07/3216 1250; www.fireworksgallery.com.au), this renowned gallery shows art by established and emerging artists from all over Australia. You may pale at some of the prices, but the stockroom at the back of the gallery may have something in your range. The staff will get your new acquisition shipped home for you. Open Tuesday to Friday 11am to 5pm, Saturday 11am to 3pm, or by appointment.

Street and Chinatown malls, Fortitude Valley (© **07/3006 6200**). Hang around in one of the many coffee shops and listen to live music. It's open Saturday and Sunday from 8am to 4pm.

Friday night is a fun time to visit the **South Bank Art and Craft Markets,** Stanley Street Plaza, South Bank Parklands (© **0414 888 041** mobile phone), when fairy lights illuminate the buzzing outdoor handicrafts market. The market is open Friday from 5 to 10pm, Saturday from 11am to 5pm, and Sunday from 9am to 5pm.

Brisbane folk like trawling the **Riverside Markets** ✦ at the Riverside Centre, 123 Eagle St. (© **07/3870 2807**), and the adjacent Eagle Street Pier Craft and Deli Markets (© **0414 888 041** mobile phone) for attractive housewares, colorful pottery, wooden blanket chests, handmade toys, painted flowerpots, and other stylish wares. It's on Sunday from 8am to 4pm.

For an authentic taste of Queensland's best produce, the **Farmers Markets** ✦✦ (© **0439/999 009**) operate on the second and fourth Saturday of each month, from 7am to noon, in the grounds of the Brisbane Powerhouse, Lamington Street, New Farm. Here you'll find much to tempt your palate, brought into the city by farmers from around the southeast part of the state. There are about 100 stalls, selling everything from fresh fruit and vegetables to homemade chutneys, quail, fresh seafood, free-range eggs, and pâtés. Foodies will be in heaven.

9 Brisbane After Dark

You can find out about festivals, concerts, and events, and book tickets through **Ticketek** (© **13 28 49** in Queensland; www.ticketek.com). You can book in person at Ticketek agencies, the most convenient of which are on Level E at the Myer Centre, 91 Queen St. Mall, and in the Visitor Information Centre at South Bank Parklands. Or try **Ticketmaster** (© **13 61 00;** www.ticketmaster7.com).

QTIX (© **13 62 46** in Australia; www.qtix.com.au) is a major booking agent for performing arts and classical music, including all events at the Queensland Performing Arts Complex (QPAC). There is a A$2.75 (US$2.20) booking fee per ticket. You can also book in person at the box office at QPAC between 8:30am and 9pm Monday to Saturday, and at the South Bank Parklands Visitor Information Centre.

The free weekly newspaper *Brisbane News* lists performing arts, jazz and classical music performances, art exhibitions, rock concerts, and public events. The free weekly *TimeOff,* published on Wednesday and available in bars and cafes, is a good guide to live music, as is Thursday's *Courier-Mail* newspaper.

THE PERFORMING ARTS

Many of Brisbane's performing arts events are at the **Queensland Performing Arts Centre (QPAC)** in the Queensland Cultural Centre (see "Exploring Brisbane," earlier in this chapter). The city also has a lively independent theater scene, with smaller companies making an increasing impact. To find out what's playing and to book tickets, contact QTIX (see above).

Queensland Theatre Company (© **07/3010 7600** for information; www.qld theatreco.com.au), the state theater company, offers eight or nine productions a year, from the classics to new Australian works. It attracts some of the country's best actors and directors. Most performances are at the Optus Playhouse or Cremorne Theatre at the Queensland Performing Arts Centre (QPAC), South Bank. Tickets cost A$19 (if you are under 25) to A$55 (US$15–US$44).

La Boite Theatre ⭐ (℗ **07/3007 8600** administration; www.laboite.com.au) is a well-established innovative company that performs contemporary Australian plays in the round. La Boite performs in the new 400-seat Roundhouse Theater, 6 Musk Ave., Kelvin Grove. Take bus no. 390 from the city to Kelvin Grove Road and get off at stop 7. Tickets cost A$38 to A$50 (US$30–US$40), previews A$33 (US$26).

Brisbane Powerhouse–Centre for the Live Arts, 119 Lamington St., New Farm (℗ **07/3358 8600;** www.brisbanepowerhouse.com.au), is a venue for innovative (some might say fringe) contemporary works. A former electricity powerhouse, the massive brick factory is now a dynamic art space for exhibitions, contemporary performance, and live art. The building retains its unique character, an industrial mix of metal, glass, and stark surfaces etched with 20 years of graffiti. It's a short walk from the New Farm ferry terminal along the riverfront through New Farm Park.

The state opera company, **Opera Queensland** (℗ **07/3875 3035** administration; www.operaqueensland.com.au), performs a lively repertoire of traditional as well as modern works, musicals, and choral concerts. Free talks on the opera you are about to see start in the foyer 45 minutes before every performance. Free close-up tours of the set are held after every performance (except the final night); book ahead through QTIX (℗ **13 62 46;** www.qtix.com.au). Most performances take place at the Queensland Performing Arts Centre (QPAC). Tickets range from A$35 to A$129 (US$28–US$103), or A$40 (US$32) at some performances if you're age 30 or under.

The **Queensland Orchestra** (℗ **07/3377 5000** for administration) provides classical music lovers with a diverse mix of orchestral and chamber music, with the odd foray into fun material, such as movie themes, Cole Porter hits, and gospel music. It schedules about 30 concerts a year. Free talks in the foyer begin 1 hour before major performances. The orchestra plays at the Concert Hall in the Queensland Performing Arts Centre (QPAC) or City Hall; more intimate works sometimes play at the Conservatorium Theatre, South Bank. Occasional "Tea and Symphony" concerts at City Hall include tea and coffee. Tickets for the Maestro concert series cost A$43 to A$56 (US$34–US$45), A$32 (US$26) if you are a student or under 26.

NIGHTCLUBS & BARS

Friday's   This indoor/outdoor bar, restaurant, and nightclub complex overlooking the Brisbane River is a haunt for "the Zoolander generation" of 18- to 40-year-olds. Gather on the large outdoor terrace with its huge island bar, or head for the restaurant, supper club, or dance floor. Music spans acid jazz, urban groove, and dance anthems from resident DJs, with the latest R&B, soul, and funk by live bands. Wednesday through Saturday nights see some kind of happy-hour deal, cocktail club, or drinks special; the dance action starts pumping around 9pm on Friday and Saturday. Upstairs in Riverside Centre, 123 Eagle St. ℗ 07/3832 2122. Cover A$7–A$10 (US$5.60–US$8). Ferry: CityCat to Riverside.

Treasury Casino   This lovely heritage building—built in 1886 as, ironically enough, the state's Treasury offices—houses a modern casino. Three levels of 100 gaming tables offer roulette, blackjack, baccarat, craps, sic-bo, and traditional Aussie two-up. There are more than 1,000 slot machines, five restaurants, and seven bars. It's open 24 hours. Live bands appear nightly in the Livewire Bar, and there's stand-up comedy on Wednesday night in the Premier's Bar. Queen St. between George and William sts. ℗ 07/3306 8888. Must be 18 years old to enter; neat casual attire required (no beachwear or thongs). Closed Good Friday, Dec 25, and until 1pm Apr 25 (Anzac Day). Train: Central or South Brisbane, then walk across the Victoria Bridge.

Finds Brisbane's Historic Pubs

Brisbane's attractive historic pubs, many of them recently revitalized, have wide, shady verandas and beer gardens just perfect for whiling away a sunny afternoon or catching a quick meal at night.

The best known is undoubtedly the **Breakfast Creek Hotel,** 2 Kingsford Smith Dr., Breakfast Creek (© **07/3262 5988;** see "Where to Dine," earlier in this chapter). Built in 1889, the hotel is a Brisbane institution. For many people, a visit to the city isn't complete without a steak and beer "off the wood" at the Brekky Creek.

Another landmark is the **Regatta Hotel,** 543 Coronation Dr., Toowong (© **07/3871 9595**). This heritage hotel with three stories of iron lace balconies is the perfect spot for a cool drink overlooking the Brisbane River. After a multimillion-dollar renovation in 2002, the place now bursts at the seams on weekends. The new **Boat Shed restaurant** (© **07/3871 9533**) is popular but not inexpensive—tables around the hotel verandas are a better choice.

Not far from the Regatta is the **Royal Exchange Hotel,** High Street, Toowong (© **07/3371 2555**). Known simply as "the RE," it's popular with students, probably because of its proximity to the University of Queensland. It has a great garden bar at the back.

The **Story Bridge Hotel,** 200 Main St., Kangaroo Point (© **07/3391 2266**), is well known as the venue for some of Brisbane's most unusual events, such as the annual Australia Day (Jan 26) cockroach races. Built in 1886, the pub is also a great place to find live music. In 2003 it was refurbished to the tune of A$3.2 million (US$2.5 million), creating a new restaurant and bar literally built into the base of the bridge, and a new beer garden under the bridge.

Another of the city's oldest pubs is the **Plough Inn** (© **07/3844 7777**) at South Bank Parklands, which has stood its ground through major changes in the neighborhood since 1885. There's even a ghost, they say . . .

Zenbar   Minimalist Manhattan-style interiors with an 8m-high (26-ft.) glass wall overlooking a bamboo garden make this one of the hippest joints in town. It's a restaurant as well, but the bar is packed on Friday and Saturday night with office workers and beautiful people. There are about 40 wines by the glass, but in this kind of place you should be drinking a margarita or martini. The music ranges from '70s underground jazz and lounge to ultramodern funk house on Friday; on Saturday, the mood changes to easy background music. Park level, Post Office Sq., 215 Adelaide St. © 07/3211 2333. Train: Central.

COOL SPOTS FOR JAZZ & BLUES

Brisbane Jazz Club ⭐ _Finds_   On the riverfront under the Story Bridge, this is the only Australian jazz club still featuring big band dance music (every Sun night). Watch out for the slightly sloping dance floor—it was once a boat ramp! Traditional and mainstream jazz is featured on Saturday nights. It's open Saturday 7:30 to 11:30pm,

Sunday 7:30 to 10:30pm, and sometimes Friday; phone and check what's on before heading over. 1 Annie St., Kangaroo Point. ℂ 07/3391 2006. Cover usually A$12 (US$9.60), higher for some guest acts. Ferry: CityCat to Holman St. Free parking lot.

Holiday Inn Jazz-n-Blues Bar One of Brisbane's leading live jazz venues is in an unlikely setting: a busy hotel. A mixed crowd in their 20s to 40s turns up to hear local, Australian, and international acts. Get there early—the place seats just 30, and the rest is standing room only. Open Wednesday, Thursday, and Saturday 6pm to late, and Friday at 4pm. Ground floor of the hotel, next to Brisbane Transit Centre, Roma St. ℂ 07/3238 2222. Cover charge varies. Train: Roma St.

10 Brisbane's Moreton Bay & Islands

The Brisbane River runs into Moreton Bay, which is studded with hundreds of small islands—and a few large ones. Some of them can be reached only by private vessel. Others are national parks and are accessible by tour boat or public ferry.

NORTH STRADBROKE ISLAND ★★

Affectionately called "Straddie" by the locals, the island was once home to a large Aboriginal population and still retains much of their history. The town of Dunwich was used as a convict outstation, Catholic mission, quarantine station, and benevolent institution. The historical museum at Dunwich has a display of historic photographs, items salvaged from shipwrecks, and information about the early settlement of the island; it's open from 10am to 2pm Wednesday and Saturday. A self-guided historical walk begins at the information center, where you can pick up a free map. A "must" for all visitors is the North Gorge Headlands Walk, for breathtaking views and for spotting turtles, dolphins, and whales.

GETTING THERE & GETTING AROUND Stradbroke Ferries (ℂ 07/3286 2666) operates water-taxi service from Toondah Harbour, Middle Street, Cleveland, to Dunwich (about 30 min.); the round-trip adult fare is A$15 (US$12), A$10 (US$8) for children 5 to 14. The vehicle barge (ℂ 07/3488 9777) takes walk-on passengers for A$11 (US$8.80) round-trip; the trip takes about 45 minutes. A bus meets almost every water taxi or ferry at Dunwich and connects it with the other two main settlements, Amity and Point Lookout. The trip to either place takes about 30 minutes and costs A$9 (US$7.20) round-trip for adults.

To get to Cleveland by public transport from Brisbane, take the train from Central Station to Cleveland Station (A$4/US$3.20), then walk about 300m (½ mile) to Middle Street.

VISITOR INFORMATION The **Tourist Information Centre** (ℂ 07/3409 9555) is on Junner Street, Dunwich, about 200m (656 ft.) from the ferry terminal. It is open weekdays from 8:30am to 5pm and weekends 9am to 3pm.

SOUTH STRADBROKE ISLAND ★★

A turn-of-the-20th-century shipwreck (with a cargo of whiskey and explosives) weakened the link between this lovely island and North Stradbroke, and nature did the rest. South Stradbroke is less well known than its sister island, but that's changing. The island has four camping grounds and three resorts. South Stradbroke Island is accessible from Hope Harbour, about a 45-minute drive south of Brisbane.

GETTING THERE & GETTING AROUND From Brisbane, take the Pacific Highway exit after Dreamworld (exit 57), and follow signs to Hope Harbour and to the departure terminal for the island. The resorts run boats for guests only; the only other way to get there is by water taxi. **Gold Coast Water Taxi** (© **0418 759 789**) takes groups to the island for A$90 (US$72) per transfer (10 people with no luggage, or 6 people plus camping gear). **Couran Island Cove Resort** (© **1800/268 726** or 07/5509 3000; www.couran.com) runs day tours. Prices start at A$65 (US$52) per person, which includes return transfers from Hope Harbour, morning tea, a guided rainforest tour, lunch, and use of resort facilities. The Fastcat ferry leaves Hope Harbour at 10:30am, and you can return on the 3 or 5pm boat.

MORETON ISLAND ★★

At more than 200 sq. km (78 sq. miles), Moreton is the second-largest sand mass in the world (after Queensland's Fraser Island) and has the world's largest sand hill, Mount Tempest. It's home to three settlements and the Tangalooma Wild Dolphin Resort, where guests and visitors on an extended day cruise can take part in hand-feeding a pod of wild dolphins that comes to the jetty each evening. Moreton has other attractions: You can visit the 42-hectare (104-acre) "desert" and toboggan down the sand dunes, snorkel around the 12 wrecks just north of the resort, and visit historic points of interest, including the sandstone lighthouse at Cape Moreton, built in 1857. A four-wheel-drive vehicle is essential for getting around, but the resort runs tours. Permits for access (A$33/US$26 per vehicle) and camping (A$4/US$3.20 per person or A$16/US$13 for a family of six per night) are available from national park rangers and ferry operators.

GETTING THERE & GETTING AROUND   The high-speed catamarans *Tangalooma Flyer* and *Tangalooma Jet* (© **1300/652 250**) leave Brisbane's Pinkenba wharf at Eagle Farm for Tangalooma on Moreton Island three times daily, at 8am (6am on Mon) 10am, and 5pm (noon on Sat and Sun). The trip takes 75 minutes. For a A$5 (US$4) charge, coaches pick up passengers at the Roma Street Transit Centre to connect with the launch, and will pick up from city hotels on request. Return transfers leave Tangalooma at 9am and 4pm and after the evening dolphin feeding session every day. On weekends, they also leave at 2pm. The round-trip fare is A$56 (US$45) for adults and A$28 (US$22) for children 3 to 14. The *Combie Trader* vehicular and passenger ferry (© **07/3203 6399;** www.moreton-island.com) departs from Scarborough on the Redcliffe Peninsula for Bulwer Wednesday through Monday. The trip takes about 2 hours; round-trip fares for walk-on passengers are A$35 (US$28) adults, A$30 (US$24) students over 15, and A$20 (US$16) children 5 to 15. The cost to take a four-wheel-drive and up to five passengers is A$155 (US$92). Day trips operate on Saturday (11am–4pm) and cost A$20 (US$16) adults, A$12 (US$9.60) children, and A$85 (US$68) family of four. Combie Trader also runs four-wheel-drive trips to the island on Monday, Tuesday, Friday, and Sunday. The cost—A$85 (US$68) adults and A$60 (US$48) children under 14—includes the ferry crossing, full day tour, and lunch. Times are subject to change.

To reach Scarborough by public transit from Brisbane, take bus no. 315 (Redcliffe Express) from stop 57, on Queen Street opposite Post Office Square, to Scarborough North and walk about 500m (½ mile). The fare is A$4 (US$3.20) for adults, half price for children. The trip takes 60 to 90 minutes.

ST. HELENA ISLAND ★★

For 65 years, from 1867 to 1932, St. Helena was a prison island, known as "the hell hole of the Pacific" to the nearly 4,000 souls incarcerated there. Today, the prison ruins are a tourist attraction, with a small museum in the restored and reconstructed Deputy Superintendent's Cottage.

GETTING THERE & GETTING AROUND   Entry to the island is by guided tour only. Excellent tours, most involving a re-enactment of life on the island jail, are run by **AB Sea Cruises** (✆ **07/3893 1240;** 8:30am–4:30pm Mon–Sat) on the launch *Cat-o-Nine-Tails,* leaving from Manly Boat Harbour. The cost is A$69 (US$55) adults, A$59 (US$47) seniors and students, A$39 (US$31) children 4 to 14. The tour leaves at 9:15am weekdays, returning at 2:15pm; on weekends and public holidays, it leaves at 11am and returns at 4pm. The price includes a box lunch. **St. Helena By Night Ghost Tours** run from Manly Boat Harbour on some Friday and Saturday nights. They include dinner, a dramatized version of life in the prison, and a few spooky surprises. Night tours leave at 7pm and return at 11:15pm; they cost A$79 (US$63) adults, A$74 (US$59) seniors and students, and A$44 (US$35) children. Reservations are essential.

To reach Manly Boat Harbour from Brisbane, take the train from Central Station to Manly (A$3.20/US$2.55) and walk about 100m (328 ft.). The trip takes about 50 minutes.

WHERE TO STAY ON THE ISLANDS

Moreton and South Stradbroke islands have resorts, and North Stradbroke has plenty of low-key accommodations. The smaller islands offer a variety of motels, cabins, motor-home parks, and camping grounds.

Couran Cove Island Resort ★★★ *(Finds*   You'll be lucky to find a more peaceful resort than this one, which is an island idyll in a class of its own. South Stradbroke Island has no cars—everyone gets around on foot, bicycle, or silent electric shuttle. And whether you're a beach or bush person, you'll find it here. You can hang around the pools or lagoon, head to the spectacular surf beach about 2km (1¼ miles) from the main resort, or stroll through remnants of primeval rainforest. The resort is committed to environmentally friendly practices, and is unique for its range of more than 100 recreational and sporting activities, including a 9m (30-ft.) rock-climbing wall, three-lane sprint track, baseball and softball pitching cage, and High Ropes Challenge course. There's also beach volleyball, bocce and lawn bowls, shuffleboard, surfing, fishing, a stargazing observatory, an extensive day spa, and a resident artist who gives lessons. There are lots of accommodations choices. My favorite is a nature cabin in the bush, but for water views and closer access to the restaurants and spa, choose one of the colorful waterfront units. All have kitchens, and there's a general store and "pantry service" that delivers supplies to your room. Waterfront units are air-conditioned, and other accommodations have ceiling fans; marine resort rooms have minibars. Smoking is allowed only in designated outdoor areas and on balconies, and no tobacco products are sold at the resort.

South Stradbroke Island, Moreton Bay (P.O. Box 224, Runaway Bay), QLD 4216. ✆ **1800/268 726** or 07/5509 3000. Fax 07/5509 3001. www.couran.com 357 units. Nature cabin for 3–8 from A$243 (US$194) per night; 3-night minimum. Waterfront room from A$317 (US$254) double; no minimum. AE, DC, MC, V. **Amenities:** 4 restaurants; poolside cafe; 10-lane heated pool and children's pool; driving range; putting green; free transfers to mainland golf courses; 2 tennis courts; 2 fully equipped exercise rooms; spa; extensive watersports equipment rentals; bike rental; children's programs; .25-hectare (½-acre) adventure playground; game room; tour desk; massage; babysitting; laundry service; dry cleaning. *In room:* TV w/pay movies, VCR, fax, dataport, kitchen, hair dryer, safe.

Tangalooma Wild Dolphin Resort ⭐ *Kids*   Once the Southern Hemisphere's largest whaling station, Tangalooma is the only resort on Moreton Island. Its big attraction is the pod of wild dolphins that visits the jetty each evening. Guests are guaranteed one chance during their visit to hand-feed the dolphins, but you can't swim with or touch the dolphins. The feeding is regulated, and your turn is over in a few seconds. Day-trippers can also take part in dolphin feeding for a cost of A$85 (US$68) adults and A$45 (US$36) children 3 to 14, as part of a day cruise.

Tangalooma is a good base for exploring the island, and a variety of tours are available, among them seasonal (late June to Oct) whale-watching cruises for a rate of A$95 (US$76) adults, A$55 (US$44) children. A dolphin research center is also based here. In 2002, the resort gained 96 new hotel rooms; 56 modern two-story family villas are only a year or so older. Villas are pricier than regular rooms, and a little farther from the resort facilities. Each has a full kitchen. The new hotel rooms sleep up to four and have such amenities as air-conditioning, minibars, and hair dryers, which the other rooms do not. However, older rooms have kitchenettes. Units in the main resort area sleep four to five people, and each has a private balcony. A general store is on-site.

Moreton Island, off Brisbane (P.O. Box 1102, Eagle Farm), QLD 4009. © **1300/652 250** or 07/3268 6333. Fax 07/3268 6299. www.tangalooma.com. 288 units (all with shower only). A$250–A$280 (US$200–US$224) double; A$280–A$340 (US$224–US$272) double for 1-bedroom apt (sleeps 5); A$460–A$560 (US$368–US$448) villa for up to 8. Children 3–14 sharing with adults A$20 (US$16). Rates include dolphin feeding. AE, DC, MC, V. **Amenities:** 2 restaurants; cafe; 2 outdoor pools; driving range; putting green; archery; tennis and squash courts; Jacuzzi; watersports equipment rental; children's programs; playground; tour desk; 4WD rental; babysitting; coin-op laundry. *In room:* TV, minibar, fridge, coffeemaker.

7

Queensland & the Great Barrier Reef

by Lee Mylne

Three times the size of Texas, with a population that clings to the coast but embraces the Outback for its icons, Queensland is a sprawling amalgam of stunning scenery, fantastic yarns, and eccentric personalities. Its most famous attraction is the Great Barrier Reef—by no means the only thing worth seeing. Great beaches and tropical weather make it hard to decide where to go first, and for how long.

White sandy beaches grace almost the entire coastline, and a string of islands and coral atolls dangles just offshore. At the southern end, Gold Coast beaches and theme parks keep tourists happy. In the north, from Townsville to Cape York, the rainforest teems with flora and fauna.

Brisbane is the state capital, a former penal colony that today brims with style. While Brisbane boasts world-class theater, shopping, markets, art galleries, and restaurants, it retains the relaxed warmth of a country town. For more on this city, see chapter 6.

Less than an hour's drive south of Brisbane is the **Gold Coast** "glitter strip," with its 35km (22 miles) of rolling surf and sandy beaches. North of Brisbane lies the aptly named **Sunshine Coast**—more white sandy beaches, crystal-clear waters, and rolling mountains dotted with villages.

Don't miss the wild beauty of the largest sand island in the world, **Fraser Island.** Each year from August to October, humpback whales frolic in the sheltered waters between Fraser Island and Hervey Bay—if you're in the area at this time, you won't want to miss the opportunity to experience the whales firsthand.

As you travel north, you'll be tempted by one tropical island after another until you hit the cluster of 74 that makes up the **Whitsunday** and **Cumberland** groups.

Then you enter a land where islands, rainforest, mountains, and rivers unite. Green sugar-cane fields are everywhere— **Mackay** is the largest sugar-producing region in Australia. This attractive city has its own beach, and the harbor is a departure point for cruises to the Great Barrier Reef and the Whitsunday Islands. The Whitsundays are on the same latitude as Tahiti, and for my money are equally lovely. The idyllic island group is laced with coral reefs rising out of calm, blue waters teeming with colorful fish— warm enough for swimming year-round.

North of the Whitsundays are **Dunk Island** and the rainforest settlement of **Mission Beach**—a perfect illustration of the contrasts in Tropical North Queensland. The port city of **Townsville** boasts 320 days of sunshine a year and marks the start of the Great Green Way—an area of lush natural beauty on the way to Cairns.

Then you come to **Cairns,** with rainforest hills and villages to explore and a harbor full of boats waiting to take you to the Reef. Cairns is a good base, but savvy travelers head an hour north to the village of **Port Douglas.**

EXPLORING THE QUEENSLAND COAST

VISITOR INFORMATION   The **Queensland Travel Centre** is a great resource on traveling and touring the state, including the Great Barrier Reef. Visit the Destination Queensland website at www.destinationqueensland.com or call *©* **13 88 33** in Australia. Tourism Queensland, which runs the Queensland Travel Centre and Destination Queensland, has offices in the United States and the United Kingdom—see "Visitor Information" in chapter 2.

You will also find excellent information on the **Great Barrier Reef Visitors Bureau**'s website (www.great-barrier-reef.com). This is not an official tourist office but part of a private company, **Travel Online** (*©* **07/3876 4644;** fax 07/3876 4645), which offers itinerary planning and booking services for a wide range of accommodations and tours throughout north Queensland.

For information on B&Bs and farm stays in Cairns, Port Douglas, Mission Beach, and Townsville, contact the **Bed & Breakfast and Farmstay Association of Far North Queensland,** P.O. Box 595, Ravenshoe, QLD 4888 (*©* **07/4097 7022;** www. bnbnq.com.au).

WHEN TO GO   Winter (June–Aug) is high season in Queensland; the water can be chilly—at least to Australians—but its temperature rarely drops below 72°F (22°C). August through January is peak visibility time for divers. Summer is hot and sticky across the state. In North Queensland (Mission Beach, Cairns, and Port Douglas), the monsoonal Wet season is from November or December through March or April. It brings heavy rains, high temperatures, extreme humidity, and cyclones. It's no problem to visit then, but if the Wet turns you off, consider the beautiful Whitsundays, which are generally beyond the reach of the rains and the worst humidity (but not cyclones).

GETTING AROUND   By Car   The Bruce Highway travels along the coast from Brisbane to Cairns. It is mostly a narrow two-lane highway, and the scenery most of the way is eucalyptus bushland, but from Mackay north you pass through sugar-cane fields, adding some variety to the trip.

Tourism Queensland (see "Visitor Information," above) publishes regional motoring guides. All you are likely to need, however, is a state map from the **Royal Automobile Club of Queensland (RACQ),** 300 St. Pauls Terrace, Fortitude Valley, Brisbane, QLD 4006 (*©* **13 19 05** in Australia). In Brisbane, you can get maps and advice from the more centrally located RACQ office in the General Post Office (GPO) building, 261 Queen St. For recorded road condition reports, call *©* **1300/ 130 595.** The **Department of Natural Resources** (*©* **07/3896 3216**) publishes excellent Sunmaps that highlight tourist attractions, national parks, and so on, although they are of limited use as road maps. You can get them at newsdealers and gas stations throughout the state.

By Train   Queensland Rail's **Traveltrain** (*©* **13 22 32** in Australia; www.traveltrain. qr.com.au) operates two long-distance trains along the Brisbane-Cairns route, a 32-hour trip aboard the *Sunlander* or about 8 hours less on the new high-speed **Tilt**

Queensland

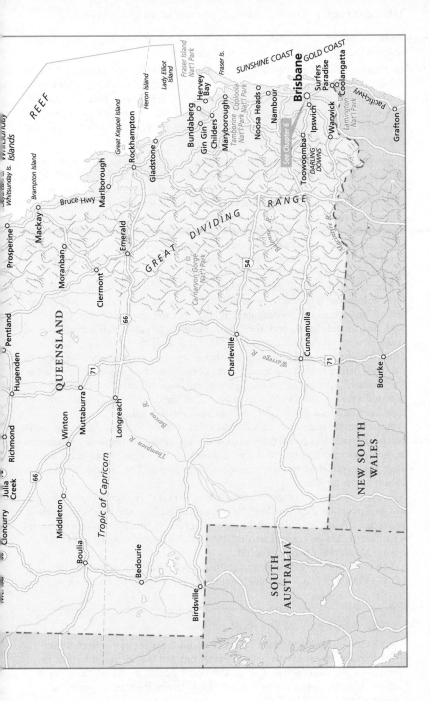

Train. Traveltrain also operates trains to Outback towns. See the "Getting Around Australia" section in chapter 2 for more details.

By Plane This is the fastest way to see a lot in such a big state. **Qantas** (② **13 13 13** in Australia; www.qantas.com.au) and its regional subsidiary **QantasLink** serve most coastal towns from Brisbane, and a few from Cairns. **Virgin Blue** (② **13 67 89** in Australia; www.virginblue.com.au) services Brisbane, Cairns, Townsville, Mackay, Proserpine on the Whitsunday coast, Rockhampton, Hervey Bay, the Gold Coast, and Maroochydore on the Sunshine Coast.

1 Exploring the Great Barrier Reef

It's the only living structure on Earth visible from the moon; at 348,700 sq. km (135,993 sq. miles), it's bigger than the United Kingdom; it's over 2,000km (1,240 miles) long, stretching from Lady Elliot Island off Bundaberg to just south of Papua New Guinea; it's home to 1,500 kinds of fish, 400 species of corals, 4,000 kinds of clams and snails, and who knows how many sponges, starfish, and sea urchins. The Great Barrier Reef is listed as a World Heritage site and is the biggest marine park in the world.

There are three kinds of reef on the Great Barrier Reef—fringing, ribbon, and platform. **Fringe reef** is the stuff you see just off the shore of islands and along the mainland. **Ribbon reefs** create "streamers" of long, thin reef along the outer edge of the Reef, and are only found north of Cairns. **Platform** or **patch reefs** are splotches of coral emerging off the continental shelf all the way along the Queensland coast. Platform reefs, the most common kind, are what most people think of when they refer to the Great Barrier Reef. Island resorts in the Great Barrier Reef Marine Park are either "continental," meaning part of the Australian landmass, or "cays," crushed dead coral and sand amassed over time by water action. Dazzling coral and marine life surround cays. On continental islands, the coral can be of varying quality.

Apart from the impressive fish life around the corals, the Reef is home to large numbers of green and loggerhead turtles, one of the biggest dugong (manatee) populations in the world, sharks, giant manta rays, and sea snakes. In winter (June–Aug), humpback whales gather in the warm waters around Hervey Bay and the Whitsunday Islands to give birth to calves.

To see the Reef, you can snorkel, dive, fish, or fly over it. For most people, the Great Barrier Reef means the Outer Reef, the network of platform and ribbon reefs that lie an average of 65km (40 miles) off the coast (about 60–90 min. by boat from the mainland). You should get out and see that, but there is plenty of fringing reef to explore around islands closer to the mainland.

Learning about the Reef before you get there will enhance your visit. **Reef Teach** ⭐⭐ (② **07/4031 7794**) is an evening multimedia presentation by Paddy Colwell, an

---

Tips **When to Visit the Reef**

April through November is the best time to visit the Great Barrier Reef. December through March can be uncomfortably hot and humid, particularly as far north as the Whitsundays, Cairns, and Port Douglas. In the winter months (June–Aug), the water can be a touch chilly (Aussies think so, anyway), but it rarely drops below 72°F (22°C).

The Great Barrier Reef

Torres Strait

Submerged Reefs

0   100 mi
0   100 km

Great Barrier Reef

AUSTRALIA

Sydney
Canberra

1000 Mi
1000 Km

Cape York

Weipa

PACIFIC OCEAN

Lizard Is.

Coral Sea

Cooktown

Daintree National Park

Green Is.

Port Douglas
Cairns

Fitzroy Is.

Mission Beach

Tully
Cardwell

Dunk Is.
Bedarra Is.

Orpheus Is.

1

1

Magnetic Is.

GREAT BARRIER REEF

MARINE PARK

Townsville

Charters Towers

Ayr

Airlie Beach
Proserpine

Whitsunday Islands

Flinders Hwy

78

GREAT DIVIDING RANGE

Mackay

Bruce Hwy.

Yeppoon

Great Keppel Is.

Tropic of Capricorn

Longreach

Landsborough

66

Hwy.

Rockhampton

Gladstone

Heron Is.

Lady Elliot Is.

QUEENSLAND

Bundaberg

Fraser Is.

Hervey Bay

Maryborough

Noosa
Sunshine Coast

Charleville

54

Caloundra

Dalby

Brisbane

71

Toowoomba

Ipswich

Gold Coast

Surfers Paradise

Lamington National Park

Coolangatta

> *Tips* **The Reef Tax**
>
> Every passenger over 4 years old must pay a A$4.50 (US$3.60) daily Environ-
> mental Management Charge (EMC), commonly called "reef tax," every time
> they visit the Great Barrier Reef. This money goes toward the management and
> conservation of the Reef. Your tour operator will collect it from you when you
> pay for your trip.

enthusiastic marine biologist and scuba diver. He tells you everything you need to
know about the Reef, from how it was formed and how coral grows, to what dangerous creatures to avoid and how to take successful underwater photos. The presentation takes place throughout the year at 14 Spence St., Cairns, Monday through
Saturday from 6:15 to 8:30pm, and costs A$13 (US$10) adults and A$6 (US$4.80)
children under 14.

Townsville is the headquarters of the Great Barrier Reef Marine Park Authority, and
a visit to its showcase, **Reef HQ** (p. 325), is a superb introduction. The star attraction
at the aquarium is a re-created living-reef ecosystem in a massive viewing tank. Find
out more about the Reef from the **Great Barrier Reef Marine Park Authority**
(© **07/4750 0700;** fax 07/4772 6093; www.gbrmpa.gov.au or www.reefhq.org.au).

DISCOVERING THE REEF

Snorkeling the Reef can be a wondrous experience. Green and purple clams, pink
sponges, red starfish, purple sea urchins, and fish from electric blue to neon yellow to
lime are truly magical sights. The rich colors of the coral only survive with lots of light,
so the nearer the surface, the brighter and richer the marine life. That means snorkelers are in a prime position to see it at its best.

If your Reef cruise offers a guided snorkel tour or "snorkel safari," take it. Some
include it as part of the price, but even if you pay an extra A$30 (US$24) or so, it is
worth it. Most safaris are suitable for both beginners and advanced snorkelers, and
are led by marine biologists who tell you about the fascinating sea creatures you are
seeing. Snorkeling is easy to master, and crews on cruise boats are always happy to
tutor you.

A day trip to the Reef also offers a great opportunity to go scuba diving—even if
you have never dived before. Every major cruise boat listed in "Day Trips to the Reef"
(below) and many dedicated dive boats listed in "Diving the Reef" (later in this chapter) offer introductory dives that allow you to dive without certification to a depth of
6m (20 ft.) in the company of an instructor. You will need to complete a medical ques-
tionnaire and undergo a 30-minute briefing on the boat. (Intro dives are also called
resort dives because many resorts offer something similar, giving you 1 or 2 hours'
instruction before taking you to a nearby reef to dive.)

CHOOSING A GATEWAY TO THE REEF

Cairns and **Port Douglas** are good places from which to visit the Reef—but the quality of the coral is just as good off any town along the coast between **Gladstone** and
Cairns. The Reef is pretty much equidistant from any point on the coast—about 90
minutes away by high-speed catamaran. An exception is **Townsville,** where the Reef
is about 2½ hours away. Think carefully about where to base yourself.

The main gateways, north to south, are **Port Douglas, Cairns, Mission Beach, Townsville, the Whitsunday Islands, Gladstone** (for Heron Island), and **Bundaberg.** The Whitsundays have the added attractions of dazzling islands to sail among; beautiful island resorts offering a wealth of watersports and other activities; and a large array of diving, fishing, and day cruises. Most important, you can snorkel every day off your island or join a sailing or cruise day trip to a number of magnificent inner reefs much nearer than the main Outer Reef. Many people stay in Cairns simply because of its easy international airport access.

If you are a nonswimmer, choose a Reef cruise that visits a coral cay, because a cay slopes gradually into shallow water and the surrounding coral. The **Low Isles** at Port Douglas; **Green Island, Michaelmas Cay,** or **Upolu Cay** off Cairns; **Beaver Cay** off Mission Beach; and **Heron Island** are all good locations.

DAY TRIPS TO THE REEF

The most common way to get to the Reef is on one of the motorized catamarans that carry up to 300 passengers each from Cairns, Port Douglas, Townsville, Mission Beach, and the Whitsunday mainland and islands. The boats are air-conditioned and have a bar, videos, and educational material, as well as a marine biologist who gives a talk on the Reef's ecology en route. The boats tie up at their own private permanent pontoons anchored to a platform reef. The pontoons have glass-bottom boats for passengers who don't want to get wet, dry underwater viewing platforms, usually a bar, sun decks, shaded seats, and often showers.

An alternative to traveling on a big tour boat is to go on one of the many smaller boats. These typically visit two or three Reef sites rather than just one. There are usually no more than 20 passengers, so you get more personal attention, and you get to know the other passengers. Another advantage is that you will have the coral pretty much all to yourself. The drawbacks of a small boat are that you have only the cramped deck to sit on when you get out of the water, and your traveling time to the Reef may be longer. If you're a nervous snorkeler, you may feel safer on a boat where you will be swimming with 300 other people.

Most day-trip fares include snorkel gear—fins, mask, and snorkel (plus wet suits in winter, although you rarely need them)—free use of the underwater viewing chambers and glass-bottom-boat rides, a plentiful buffet or barbecue lunch, and morning and

---

⌒ *Tips* Reef Health & Safety Warnings

Coral is very sharp, and coral cuts get infected quickly and badly. If you cut yourself, ask the staff on your cruise boat for antiseptic cream, and apply it to grazes as soon as you come out of the water.

The sun and reflected sunlight off the water can burn you fast. Remember to put sunscreen on your back and the back of your legs, especially around your knees and the back of your neck, and even behind your ears—all places that rarely get exposed to the sun but will be exposed as you swim facedown. Apply more when you leave the water.

Remember, the Great Barrier Reef is a marine park. Removing coral (living or dead), shells, or any other natural item is an offense. If everyone who has ever visited the Reef took a piece, it would not be worth coming to see what's left.

afternoon refreshments. Diving is an optional activity for which you pay extra. The big boats post snorkeling scouts to keep a lookout for anyone in trouble and to count heads periodically. If you wear glasses, ask whether your boat offers prescription masks—this could make a big difference to the quality of your experience! Don't forget, you can travel as a snorkel-only passenger on most dive boats, too.

The major launching points for day trips to the Reef are Port Douglas, Cairns, Mission Beach, Townsville, and the Whitsundays (see individual sections on these regions later in this chapter).

MAJOR REEF SITES

FROM CAIRNS   Approximately 20 reefs lie within a 1½-to-2-hour boat ride from Cairns. These are the reefs most commonly visited by snorkelers and divers on day trips, because they are so close and so pretty. Some reefs are small coral "bommies," or outcrops, that you can swim completely around in a matter of minutes, whereas others are miles wide. Some reefs have more than one good dive site; Norman Reef, for example, has at least four. Three of the most popular reefs with both snorkelers and divers are **Hastings, Saxon,** and **Norman** 🐠, which are all within a short boat ride of one another. Each has a wonderful array of coral, big colorful reef fish, schools of pretty rainbow-hued small reef fish, and the odd giant clam. Green sea turtles and white-tip reef sharks are common, especially at Saxon, though you will not necessarily spot one every day. Divers may see a moray eel and a grouper or two, barracuda, reef sharks, eagle and blue-spotted rays, and octopus. Norman is an especially lovely reef with several nice sites. South Norman has lovely sloping coral shelves. If you are an experienced diver and like swim-throughs, the Caves at Norman is a good spot; it has boulder and plate corals.

Some of the best diving anywhere on the Great Barrier Reef is on the **Ribbon Reefs** 🐠 on the outer Reef edge, which fringes the continental shelf off Cairns and Port Douglas. Glorious coral walls, abundant fish, and pinnacles make these a rich, colorful dive area with lots of variety. The currents can be stronger here, because the reefs are the last stop between the open sea, so drift dives are a possibility. The Ribbon Reefs are beyond the reach of day boats, but are commonly visited by live-aboard boats (see below). For divers, experts recommend **Steve's Bommie** and **Dynamite Pass.** Steve's Bommie is a coral outcrop in 30m (98 ft.) of water, topped with barracudas, and covered in colorful coral and small marine life. You can swim through a tunnel here amid crowds of fish. Dynamite Pass is a channel where barracuda, trevally, grouper, mackerel, and tuna gather to feed in the current. Black coral trees and sea whips grow on the walls, patrolled by eagle rays and reef sharks.

Cairns's most famous dive site is **Cod Hole** 🐠, where you can hand-feed giant potato cod as big as you are, or bigger. The site also has Maori wrasse, moray eels, and coral trout. Cod Hole is about 20km (13 miles) off Lizard Island, 240km (149 miles) north of Cairns, so it is not a day trip unless you are staying at exclusive Lizard Island (see "Where to Stay," later in this chapter). However, it is a popular stop with just about every live-aboard vessel, often combined in a trip to the Ribbon Reefs lasting about 4 days, or in a trip to the Coral Sea (see below) lasting between 4 and 7 days. Either itinerary makes an excellent dive vacation.

Keen divers looking for adventure in far-flung latitudes can visit the **Far Northern** region of the Great Barrier Reef, much farther north than most dive boats venture. Up in this large region you will find a wide choice of good sites, little explored by the average diver. Visibility is always clear. Graham McCallum, who has skippered dive boats

---

Moments **Overnighting on the Reef**

Down Under Dive (🕿 **1800/079 099** in Australia, or 07/4052 8300; fax 07/4031 1373; www.downunderdive.com.au) in Cairns offers a chance to "sleep on the Reef" aboard a 43m (141-ft.) 1890s-style brigantine, SV *Atlantic Clipper*. It's a sleek, romantic sailing ship with towering masts, a roomy Jacuzzi on the fore-deck, a cocktail bar, a comfortable dining room, and single, double, triple, or quad-share air-conditioned cabins. A motorized launch takes you from Cairns to the ship's reef mooring; from there you sail up to the four popular reef complexes of Norman, Hastings, and Saxon reefs, and Michaelmas Cay. The emphasis is on fun and relaxation, with lots of snorkeling and diving. Choose between a 2-day, 1-night stay in a three- or four-berth cabin for A$240 (US$192) for snorkelers or A$300 (US$240) for divers, and a 3-day, 2-night journey for A$380 (US$304) for snorkelers or A$480 (US$384) for divers. Add A$40 (US$32) per person per night for a twin or double cabin with shower. On a 2-day trip you will fit in up to 6 dives, and up to 10 on the 3-day trip. Prices include all dive and snorkel gear (including prescription masks), meals, and pickup from your Cairns accommodations. Transfers from the Northern Beaches and Port Douglas are extra.

---

on the Reef for many years, recommends the following sites: **Silvertip City** on Mantis Reef has sharks, pelagics, potato cod, and beautiful lion fish that patrol a wall up to 46m (150 ft.) deep. Another goodie is the **Magic Cave** swim-through adorned with lots of colorful fans, soft corals, and small reef fish. Sleeping turtles are often spotted in caves on the reefs off **Raine Island,** the world's biggest green turtle rookery. Visibility averages 24m (80 ft.) at Rainbow Wall, a colorful wall that makes a nice gentle drift dive with the incoming tide.

Some 100 to 200km (63–126 miles) east of Cairns, out in the **Coral Sea,** isolated mountains covered in reefs rise more than a kilometer (½ mile) from the ocean floor to make excellent diving. Although not within the Great Barrier Reef Marine Park, the Coral Sea is often combined into an extended live-aboard trip that also takes in Cod Hole and the Ribbon Reefs. The whole trip usually takes 4 to 7 days. In addition to showing you huge schools of pelagic and reef fish big and small, a wide range of corals, and excellent gorgonian fans, the area is a prime place to spot sharks. The most popular site is **Osprey Reef,** a 100-sq.-km (39-sq.-mile) reef with 1,000m (3,300-ft.) drop-offs, renowned for its fabulous year-round visibility of up to 70m (230 ft.). The highlight of most Osprey Reef itineraries is a **shark feeding** session. White-tip reef sharks are common, but the area is also home to gray reef shark, silvertips, and hammerheads. Green turtles, tuna, barracuda, potato cod, mantas, and grouper are also common.

Closer to shore, Cairns has several coral cays and reef-fringed islands within the **Great Barrier Reef Marine Park.** Less than an hour from the city wharf, **Green Island** is a 15-hectare (37-acre) coral cay with snorkeling equal to that on the Great Barrier Reef. It is also a popular diving spot. You can visit it in half a day if time is short.

The **Frankland Islands** are a pristine group of uninhabited rainforested isles edged with sandy beaches, reefs, and fish 45km (28 miles) south of Cairns. The islands are a rookery for **green sea turtles,** which snorkelers and divers often spot in the water. In February and March, you may even be lucky enough to see dozens of baby turtles hatching in the sand. **Michaelmas Cay** and **Upolu Cay** are two pretty coral sand blips in the ocean, 30km (19 miles) and 25km (16 miles) off Cairns, surrounded by reefs. Michaelmas is vegetated and is home to 27,000 sea birds; you may spot dugongs (manatees) off Upolu. Michaelmas and Upolu are great for snorkelers and introductory divers, but experienced divers are probably better off visiting the excellent sites at such reefs as Norman, Hastings, or Saxon.

FROM PORT DOUGLAS   The waters off Port Douglas boast just as many wonderful reefs and marine life forms as the waters around Cairns; the reefs are equally close to shore and equally colorful and varied. Some of the most visited reefs are **Tongue, Opal,** and **St. Crispin Reefs.** The **Agincourt** complex of reefs also has many excellent dive sites; experts recommend the double-figure-eight swim-through at the **Three Sisters,** where baby gray whaler sharks gather, and the wonderful coral walls of **Castle Rock,** where stingrays often hide in the sand. **Nursery Bommie** is a 24m (79-ft.) pinnacle that is a popular haunt with big fish like barracuda, rays, sharks, and moray eels; under the big plate corals of **Light Reef,** giant grouper hide out. Other popular sites are the staghorn coral garden (so named because the coral looks like a stag's antlers) at the **Playground;** one of the region's biggest swim-throughs at **The Maze,** where parrot fish and an enormous Maori wrasse hang out; the **Stepping Stones,** home of the exquisitely pretty clownfish (brightly colored little striped things); **Turtle Bommie,** where hawksbill turtles are frequently sighted; and **Harry's Bommie,** where divers see the occasional manta ray. Among the 15-plus dive sites visited by *Poseidon* (see below) are **Turtle Bay,** where you may meet "Killer," a friendly Maori wrasse; the **Cathedrals,** a collection of coral pinnacles and swim-throughs; and **Barracuda Pass,** home to coral gardens, giant clams, and schooling barracudas.

The closest Reef site off Port Douglas, the **Low Isles,** lies only 15km (9 miles) northeast. Coral sand and 22 hectares (55 acres) of coral surround these two tiny coral cays, which are covered in lush vegetation and are home to many seabirds. The coral is not quite as dazzling as the outer Reef's—head to the outer Reef if you have only 1 day to spend on the Great Barrier Reef—but the fish life here is rich, and you may spot sea turtles. Because you can wade out to the coral right from the beach, the Low Isles are a good choice for nervous snorkelers. A half-day or day trip to the Low Isles makes for a more relaxing day than a visit to outer Reef sites, because in addition to exploring the coral, you can walk or sunbathe on the sand or laze under palm-thatched beach umbrellas. *Note:* If you visit the Low Isles, wear old shoes, because the coral sand can be rough underfoot.

FROM MISSION BEACH   Mission Beach is the closest point on the mainland to the Reef, 1 hour by boat. The main site visited is **Beaver Cay,** a sandy coral cay

---

Fun Fact **The Floating P.O.**

Australia's only floating post office is on Agincourt Reef, about 72km (45 miles) off Port Douglas. The facility floats on the Quicksilver Connections pontoon, and your letter or postcard will be stamped with a special postmark from the Great Barrier Reef.

surrounded by marine life. The waters are shallow, making the cay ideal for both snorkelers eager to see the coral's vibrant colors and novice divers still getting a feel for the sport. It's a perfect spot for an introduction dive.

FROM TOWNSVILLE   Townsville's waters boast hundreds of large patch reefs, some miles long, and many almost never visited by humans. Here you can find excellent coral and fish life, including mantas, rays, turtles, and shark, and sometimes canyons and swim-throughs in generally good visibility. One of the best reef complexes is **Flinders Reef.** Actually located in the Coral Sea, beyond the Great Barrier Reef Marine Park boundaries, we mention it here because many dive trips incorporate it in Great Barrier Reef itineraries. At 240km (149 miles) offshore, it has 30m (100-ft.) visibility, plenty of coral, and big walls and pinnacles with big fish to match, like whaler shark and barracuda.

What draws most divers to Townsville, though, is one of Australia's best wreck dives, **SS *Yongala*** ⚓. Still largely intact, the sunken remains of this steamer lie 90km (56 miles) from Townsville, 16km (10 miles) off the coast, in 15 to 30m (50–98 ft.) of water with visibility of 9 to 18m (approx. 30–60 ft.). A cyclone sent the *Yongala* and its 49 passengers and 72-member crew to the bottom of the sea in 1911. Today it's surrounded by a mass of coral and marine life, including barracuda, enormous grouper, rays, sea snakes, turtles, moray eels, shark, cod, and reef fish. You can even enter the ship and swim its length, with care.

The *Yongala* is not for beginners—the boat is deep, and there is a strong current. Most dive companies require their customers to have advanced certification or to have logged a minimum of 15 dives with open-water certification. The boat is usually visited on a live-aboard trip of at least 2 days, but **Adrenalin Dive** (✆ **07/4724 0600**) runs day trips. Some companies run open-water certification dive courses that finish with a dive on the *Yongala,* but freshly certified scuba hounds might be wise to skip this advanced dive.

FROM THE WHITSUNDAYS   Visitors to the Whitsundays get to have their cake and eat it too; they can visit the outer Reef and enjoy some good dive and snorkel sites in and around the islands. Many islands have rarely visited fringing reefs, which you can explore in a rented dinghy. The reef here is just as good as off Cairns, with many drop-offs and drift dives, a dazzling range of corals, and a rich array of marine life, including whales, mantas, shark, reef fish, morays, turtles and pelagics. Visibility is usually around 15 to 23m (49–75 ft.).

The Stepping Stones on 800-hectare (1,976-acre) **Bait Reef** is one of the most popular sites on the outer Reef. It is made up of a series of pinnacles that abound with fish life and offer caverns, swim-throughs, and channels. A family of grouper often greets divers at Groupers Grotto on **Net Reef,** and a pod of dolphins hang around Net Reef's southeast wall. **Oublier Reef** has plate corals over 2m (7-ft.) wide in its lovely coral gardens.

Among the island sites, most folks' favorite is **Blue Pearl Bay** ⚓ off Hayman Island, whether they're snorkeling or diving. It has loads of corals and some gorgonian fans in its gullies, and heaps of reef fish, including Maori wrasse and sometimes even manta rays. It's a good place to make an introductory dive, walking right in off the beach. **Mantaray Bay** on Hook Island is renowned for its range of marine life, from small reef fish and nudibranchs to bigger pelagics farther out. Mantas hang around here in November. Another good snorkel and dive spot is **Black Reef** ⚓, commonly called **Bali Hai Island,** between Hayman and Hook islands. You'll see marvelous soft shelf and wall coral, tame Maori wrasse, octopus, turtles, reef shark, various kinds of rays including mantas, eagles and cow-tails, plus loads of fish. Divers may even see hammerhead shark.

FROM BUNDABERG   The southern reefs of the Great Barrier Reef are just as prolific, varied, and colorful as the reefs farther north off Cairns. However, because this part of the coast is less settled, fewer snorkel and dive boats visit them. Many are the virgin reefs in these parts that have never seen a diver.

The only reef visited by snorkelers and divers on a daily basis from Bundaberg is pretty **Lady Musgrave Island,** a vegetated 14-hectare (35-acre) national-park coral cay, 52 nautical miles off the coast. It is surrounded by a lagoon 8km (5 miles) in circumference, filled with hundreds of corals and some 1,200 of the 1,500 species of fish and other marine creatures found on the Great Barrier Reef.

Lady Musgrave Island is one of the **Bunker Group** of islands and reefs, which lie approximately 80km (50 miles) due north of Bundaberg. They are due east of Gladstone and closer to that town, but no boats visit them from there. Little explored by divers, these vividly colored reefs are some of the most pristine on the Great Barrier Reef. Farther south of Bunker Group is **Lady Elliot Island.** Although it lies outside the borders of the Great Barrier Reef Marine Park, Bundaberg's **Woongarra Marine Park** is a popular destination for divers visiting the Reef. This small park hugs the town's coastline in an area known as Bargara, and has loads of soft and hard corals, nudibranchs, wobbegongs, epaulette sharks, sea snakes, some 60 fish species, and frequent sightings of green and loggerhead turtles. Most of this is in water less than 9m (30 ft.) deep, and you can walk right into it off the beach.

Beyond Woongarra, 2.5 nautical miles (4.6km) offshore, is **Cochrane artificial reef,** where a few Mohawk and Beechcraft aircraft have been dumped to make a home for fish. Other sites off Bunbaberg in about 23m (75 ft.) of water include the **manta "cleaning station"** at Evan's Patch, a **World War II Beaufort bomber** with lots of marine life.

DIVING THE REEF ★

Divers have a big choice of dive boats that make 1-day runs to the Outer Reef and live-aboard dive boats making excursions that last up to a week. As a general rule, on a typical 5-hour day trip to the Reef, you will fit in about two dives. The companies listed in this section give you an idea of the kinds of trips available and how much they cost. This is by no means an exhaustive list—there are far too many to include here. "The Active Traveler" in chapter 2 has more tips for finding a dive operator. Prices quoted here include full gear rental; knock off about A$20 (US$16) if you have your own gear.

> **Tips** **Feeling Green?**
>
> If you are inclined to seasickness, come prepared with medication. Some boats sell a ginger-based anti-seasickness pill, but it doesn't always work!

FROM CAIRNS   **Tusa Dive Charters** (© **07/4040 6464;** www.tusadive.com) runs two 24m (72-ft.) dive boats daily to two dive sites from a choice of 21 locations on the Outer Reef. The day costs A$190 (US$152) for divers and A$130 (US$104) adult or A$80 (US$64) child ages 4 to 14 for snorkelers, with wet suits, guided snorkel tours, lunch, and transfers from your Cairns or northern beaches hotel. If you want to be shown the best spots under the water, you can take a guided dive for an extra A$20 (US$16). Day trips for introductory divers cost A$195 (US$156) for one dive or A$240 (US$192) for two. The groups are kept to a maximum of 28 people, so you get personal attention. The company is the Nitrox and Rebreather facility for north Queensland, and certified divers can take two introductory dives on Nitrox/Safe Air in 1 day for A$220 (US$176).

FROM PORT DOUGLAS The waters off Port Douglas are home to dramatic coral spires and swim-throughs at the Cathedrals; giant clams at Barracuda Pass; a village of parrot fish,

---

Tips **Pressed for Time?**

If you don't have time for a full day on the Reef, don't forget that you can dive the coral cay of Green Island, just 27km (16 miles) off Cairns, in half a day (see "Exploring the Islands" in the Cairns section, later in this chapter).

---

anemone fish, unicorn fish, and two moray eels at the soaring pinnacle of Nursery Bommie; fan corals at Split-Bommie; and many other wonderful sites.

Poseidon (© 07/4099 4772; www.poseidon-cruises.com.au) is a fast 24m (79-ft.) vessel that visits three Outer Reef sites. The day-trip price of A$145 (US$116) for adults, A$110 (US$88) for kids 3 to 12 includes snorkel gear, a marine biology talk, snorkel safaris, lunch, and pickups from Port Douglas hotels. Certified divers pay A$40 (US$32) extra for two dives or A$55 (US$44) extra for three, plus A$20 (US$16) gear rental. Guides will accompany you, free of charge, to show you great locations. Introductory divers pay A$50 (US$40) extra for one dive, and A$40 (US$32) each for the second and third. The vessel carries no more than 48 passengers, less than half its capacity, and gets you to the Reef in just over an hour, giving you 5 hours on the coral. The boat departs Marina Mirage daily at 8:30am. Transfers from Cairns and the Northern Beaches cost an extra A$15 (US$12) per adult and A$10 (US$8) per child.

FROM TOWNSVILLE Off Townsville, you can dive not only the Reef but also a wreck, the *Yongala* ★, which lies off the coast in 30m (98 ft.) of water with good visibility. **Diving Dreams** (© 07/4721 2500; fax 07/4721 2549; www.divingdreams.com) runs a day trip for around A$260 (US$208) and 2- or 3-day trips, which include dives at the *Yongala,* for around A$445 to A$545 (US$356–US$436).

FROM THE WHITSUNDAYS In and around the Whitsunday Islands, you can visit the Outer Reef and explore the many excellent Reef dive sites close to shore. One of the more established companies is **Reef Dive** (© 1800/075 120 in Australia, or 07/4946 6508; www.reefdive.com.au). Expect to pay about A$560 (US$448) per person for a 3-day, 3-night trip.

DIVE COURSES

Many dive companies in Queensland offer dive courses, from initial open-water certification all the way to dive master, rescue diver, and instructor level. To take a course, you will need to have a medical exam done by a Queensland doctor. (Your dive school will arrange it; it costs about A$50/US$40.) You will also need two passport photos for your certificate, and you must be able to swim! Courses usually begin every day or every week. Some courses take as little as 3 days, but 5 days is generally regarded as the best. Open-water certification usually requires 2 days of theory in a pool, followed by 2 or 3 days out on the Reef, where you make four to nine dives. Prices vary considerably, but are generally around A$600 (US$480) for a 5-day open-water certification course, or A$500 (US$400) for the same course over 4 nights.

Deep Sea Divers Den (© 07/4046 7333; fax 07/4031 1210; www.divers-den.com) has been in operation since 1974 and claims to have certified about 55,000 divers. The 5-day open-water course involves 2 days of theory in the pool in Cairns, and 3 days and 2 nights on a live-aboard boat. The course costs A$590 (US$472) per person, including all meals on the boat, nine dives (one a guided night dive), all your gear, a wet suit, and transfers from your city hotel. The same course over 4 nights, with 1 night on the boat and four dives, costs A$480 (US$384). New courses begin every day of the week.

> **Tips   Diving Reminders**
>
> Don't forget your "C" certification card. Bringing along your dive log is also a good idea. Remember not to fly for 24 hours after diving.

Virtually every Great Barrier Reef dive operator offers dive courses. Most island resorts offer them, too. You will find dive schools in Cairns, Port Douglas, Mission Beach, Townsville, and the Whitsunday Islands.

Companies offering dive courses appear under the relevant regional sections throughout this chapter.

2 Cairns

346km (215 miles) N of Townsville; 1,807km (1,120 miles) N of Brisbane

This part of Queensland is the only place in the world where two World Heritage–listed sites—the Great Barrier Reef and the Wet Tropics Rainforest—lie side by side. In parts of the far north, the rainforest touches the reef, reaching right down to sandy beaches from which you can snorkel the reef. Cairns is the gateway to these natural attractions, as well as man-made tourist destinations such as the Skyrail Rainforest Cableway. It's also a stepping-stone to islands of the Great Barrier Reef and the grasslands of the Gulf Savannah.

When international tourism to the Great Barrier Reef boomed a decade or two ago, the small sugar-farming town of Cairns boomed along with it. The town now boasts outstanding hotels, offshore island resorts, big Reef-cruise catamarans in the harbor, and too many souvenir shops. The only beach right in town is a man-made 4,000-sq.-m (43,000-sq.-ft.) saltwater lagoon and artificial beach on the Esplanade, which opened in early 2003 as part of a multimillion-dollar redevelopment of the city and port.

The 110-million-year-old rainforest, the Daintree, where plants that are fossils elsewhere in the world exist in living color, is just a couple of hours north of Cairns. The Daintree is part of the Wet Tropics, a World Heritage–listed area that stretches from north of Townsville to south of Cooktown, beyond Cairns, and houses half of Australia's animal and plant species.

If you are spending more than a day or two in the area, consider basing yourself on the city's pretty northern beaches, in Kuranda, or in Port Douglas (see "Port Douglas, Daintree & the Cape Tribulation Area," later in this chapter). Although prices will be higher in the peak season (Australian winter and early spring, July–Oct), affordable accommodations are available year-round.

ESSENTIALS
GETTING THERE   By Plane   Qantas (© **13 13 13** in Australia) has direct flights throughout the day to Cairns from Sydney and Brisbane, and at least one flight

Cairns

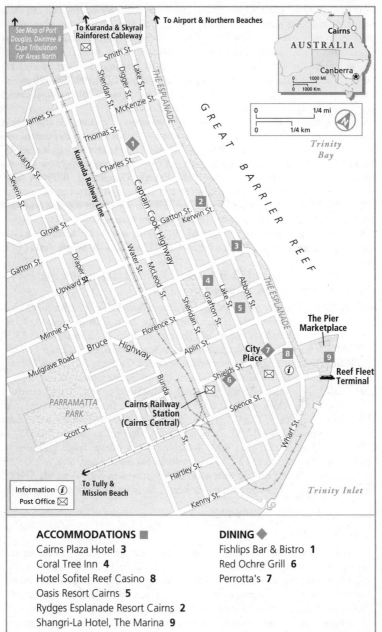

ACCOMMODATIONS ■
Cairns Plaza Hotel **3**
Coral Tree Inn **4**
Hotel Sofitel Reef Casino **8**
Oasis Resort Cairns **5**
Rydges Esplanade Resort Cairns **2**
Shangri-La Hotel, The Marina **9**

DINING ◆
Fishlips Bar & Bistro **1**
Red Ochre Grill **6**
Perrotta's **7**

a day from Darwin, Uluru (Ayers Rock), and Perth. From Melbourne you can sometimes fly direct, but most flights connect through Sydney or Brisbane. **QantasLink** also flies from Townsville, Hamilton Island in the Whitsundays, and Alice Springs. **Virgin Blue** (© 13 67 89 in Australia) flies to Cairns direct from Brisbane, Sydney, and Melbourne. **Jetstar** (© 13 15 38 in Australia) flies from Brisbane twice a day. New Qantas international subsidiary **Australian Airlines** (© 1300/799 798 in Australia) links Cairns with Sydney and the Gold Coast. Several international carriers serve Cairns from various Asian cities and New Zealand.

   Cairns Airport is 8km (5 miles) north of downtown. The domestic and international terminals are linked by a covered walkway—it takes about 5 minutes to walk between the two. The **Australia Coach** (© 07/4048 8355) shuttle, which costs A$7 (US$5.60) per person (children under 14 travel free), meets major flights at both terminals for transfers to city hotels. **Sun Palm Express Coaches** (© 07/4084 2626) provides transfers from the airport to the city and northern beaches. The one-way fare is A$13 (US$10) adults and A$7.50 (US$6) children 4 to 14 to the city, and A$15 (US$12) adults and A$7.50 (US$6) children to Palm Cove.

   A taxi from the airport costs around A$15 (US$12) to the city, A$30 (US$24) to Trinity Beach, and A$40 (US$32) to Palm Cove. Call **Black & White Taxis** (© 13 10 08 in Australia).

   Avis, Budget, Hertz, and **Thrifty** all have car-rental offices at the domestic and international terminals (see "Getting Around," below).

By Train   Long-distance trains operated by Queensland Rail's **Traveltrain** (© 13 22 32 in Queensland; www.traveltrain.qr.com.au) run from Brisbane several times a week. The new 160kmph (100mph) **Tilt Train** takes about 25 hours and costs A$295 (US$236) for business class. Northbound trains leave Brisbane at 6:25pm on Monday, Wednesday, and Friday; southbound runs depart Cairns at 8:15am on Wednesday, Friday, and Sunday. The train features luxury business-class seating, with an entertainment system for each seat, including multiple movie and audio channels.

   The *Sunlander,* which runs four times a week between Brisbane and Cairns, takes 32 hours and costs A$197 (US$158) for a sitting berth, A$253 (US$202) for an economy-class sleeper, A$398 (US$318) for a first-class sleeper, or A$725 (US$580) for all-inclusive Queenslander class (only available twice a week). Trains pull into the Cairns Central terminal (© 13 22 32 in Australia for reservations, or 07/4036 9250 for the terminal from 9am–5pm weekdays or 8:30am–noon Sat) on Bunda Street in the center of town. The station has no showers, lockers, or currency exchange booths,

---

Finds   **Staying Connected**

You can surf the Web and check your e-mail at the **Inbox Café,** 119 Abbot St. (© 07/4041 4677; fax 07/4041 4322), for A$1.50 (US$1.20) for 15 minutes, A$2.50 (US$2) for 30 minutes, or A$4 (US$3.20) an hour. It's open daily from 7am to midnight. The Inbox Café, which has seven computers, all with broadband, CD burners, and a live webcam, is Cairns's only licensed Internet cafe. The cafe food is by the **Red Ochre Grill** (see "Where to Dine," later in this chapter). It's fresh, tasty, and affordable, with breakfast available all day. There is a bar with lots of newspapers and magazines, and resident DJs play groovy tunes to set a relaxed mood, with an extra beat on weekend nights.

but you will find 24-hour ATMs outside the Cairns Central shopping mall, right above the terminal.

By Bus   Greyhound Australia (© **13 14 99**) buses pull into Trinity Wharf Centre on Wharf Street in the center of town. Buses travel from the south via all towns and cities on the Bruce Highway, and from the west from Alice Springs and Darwin via Tennant Creek on the Stuart Highway and the Outback mining town of Mount Isa to Townsville, where they join the Bruce Highway and head north. The 46-hour Sydney-Cairns trip costs A$301 (US$241); the 30-hour trip from Brisbane is A$201 (US$161); and from Darwin, the journey takes about 38 hours and costs A$441 (US$353).

By Car   From Brisbane and all major towns in the south, you'll enter Cairns on the Bruce Highway. To reach the northern beaches or Port Douglas from Cairns, take Sheridan Street in the city center, which becomes the Captain Cook Highway.

VISITOR INFORMATION   Tourism Tropical North Queensland's **Gateway Discovery Centre,** 51 The Esplanade, Cairns, QLD 4870 (© **07/4051 3588;** fax 07/4051 0127; www.tropicalaustralia.com), has information on Cairns and its environs, Mission Beach, Port Douglas, the Daintree Rain Forest, Cape York, and Outback Queensland. It's open daily from 8:30am to 5:30pm, and 10am to 2pm on public holidays. Closed December 25.

CITY LAYOUT   A major redevelopment of the Cairns Esplanade, completed in 2003, transformed the face of the city. The focal point is a 4,000-sq.-m (40,000-sq.-ft.) saltwater swimming lagoon with a wide sandy beach and surrounding parkland with public artworks and picnic areas. Suspended over the mud flats and providing a platform for birding, a timber boardwalk runs 600m (1,800 ft.) along the waterfront, and is lit for nighttime use. A walkway links the Esplanade to the Reef Fleet Terminal, the departure point for Great Barrier Reef boats.

Tips **Croc Alert!**

Dangerous crocodiles inhabit Cairns waterways. Do not swim in, or stand on the bank of, any river or stream.

Downtown Cairns is on a grid 5 blocks deep, bounded in the east by the Esplanade on the water and in the west by McLeod Street, where the train station and the Cairns Central shopping mall are. In between are shops, offices, and restaurants.

Heading 15 minutes north from the city along the Captain Cook Highway, you come to the **northern beaches:** Holloway's Beach, Yorkey's Knob, Trinity Beach, Kewarra Beach, Clifton Beach, Palm Cove, and Ellis Beach.

GETTING AROUND   **By Bus**   Sunbus (© **07/4057 7411**) buses depart City Place Mall at the intersection of Lake and Shields streets. Buy all tickets and passes on board, and try to have correct change. You can hail buses anywhere it's convenient for the driver to stop. Bus nos. 2 and 2A travel to Trinity Beach; nos. 1 and 1X (weekend express) travel to Palm Cove. The N route runs along the highway from the city to Palm Cove until 2:25am on Friday and Saturday nights, stopping at all beaches in between. Most other buses run from early morning until almost midnight.

By Car   Avis (© 07/4051 5911), **Budget** (© 07/4051 9222), **Hertz** (© 07/4051 6399), and **Thrifty** (© 07/4051 8099) have offices in Cairns city and at the airport.

One long-established local outfit, **Sugarland Car Rentals** (℃ 07/4052 1300), has reasonable rates. **Britz Campervan Rentals** (℃ 1800/331 454 in Australia, or 07/4032 2611), **Budget Campervan Rentals** (℃ 07/4032 2065), and **Maui Rentals** (℃ 1300/363 800 in Australia, or 07/4032 2065) rent motor homes. Britz and most major rental-car companies rent four-wheel-drive vehicles.

By Taxi Call **Black & White Taxis** (℃ 13 10 08).

DAY TRIPS TO THE REEF

Cairns passengers can board the most luxurious vessel visiting the Reef, the **Quicksilver Cruises** wave-piercer catamaran (℃ 07/4087 2100; www.quicksilver-cruises. com). It departs from the Reef Fleet Terminal at 8am and from Palm Cove Jetty on Cairns's northern beaches at 8:30am. It arrives at Port Douglas at 9:30am and leaves for the Reef at 10am. All of these trips run daily except on December 25. For the whole day from Cairns or Palm Cove, passengers pay A$190 (US$152) for adults, A$98 (US$78) for kids 4 to 14. The price includes hotel pickup.

If you prefer to visit the Reef straight from Cairns, large-scale operator **Great Adventures** (℃ 1800/079 080 in Australia, or 07/4044 9944; www.greatadventures. com.au) does daily cruises in fast, air-conditioned catamarans to a three-level pontoon on the Outer Reef. The pontoon has a children's swimming area, a semisubmersible, and an underwater observatory. You get at least 3 hours on the Reef. The cost for the day is A$162 (US$130) for adults, A$84 (US$67) for children 4 to 14, and A$414 (US$331) for families. Hotel transfers are available from Cairns, the northern beaches, and Port Douglas for an extra cost. The boat departs the Great Adventures terminal at the new Reef Fleet Terminal at 10:30am.

You can also depart Cairns with Great Adventures at 8:30am and spend 2 hours on Green Island en route. This gives you time to walk nature trails, rent snorkel gear and watersports equipment, or laze on the beach before continuing to the Outer Reef. This cruise costs an extra A$20 (US$16) per adult and A$10 (US$8) per child or A$50 (US$40) per family.

Sunlover Cruises (℃ 1800/810 512 in Australia, or 07/4050 1333; www.sunlover.com.au) has a choice of Outer Reef trips aboard its large, fast catamarans. One trip stops at Fitzroy Island briefly before heading to Moore Reef on the Outer Reef. The day costs A$187 (US$150) for adults, A$98 (US$78) for children 4 to 14, and A$480 (US$384) for a family of four, including transfers from city and

---

⸜Tips Diving Made Easy

Can't swim? Don't want to get your hair wet? Don't worry—you can still get underwater and see the wonders of the Reef. Several companies offer travelers the chance to don a dive helmet and "walk" underwater. Similar to old-style diving helmets, which allow you to breathe underwater, the helmet has air pumped into it by a hose. You walk into the water to a depth of about 4m (13 ft.), accompanied by instructors, and the reef is right before you. **Quicksilver Cruises** calls it "Ocean Walker"; with **Sunlover Cruises** and at **Green Island Resort** it's "Sea Walker." You must be at least 10 or 12 years old. The cost is about A$130 (US$104) for 20 minutes.

northern beaches hotels. This trip includes a glass-bottom boat ride and semisubmersible viewing.

Another Sunlover trip departs Cairns and picks up passengers at Palm Cove before heading to Arlington Reef. The price from Cairns is A$150 (US$120) for adults, A$79 (US$63) for kids, and A$387 (US$310) for a family, including hotel pick-ups. On both trips, you spend about 4 hours on the Reef. Introductory dives on either trip cost A$109 (US$87). Certified divers pay the same price, including all gear. Both cruises include lunch and transfers from Cairns and northern beaches hotels. Both boats depart from the Reef Fleet Terminal in Cairns at 10am daily.

Great Adventures, Quicksilver, and Sunlover all offer helicopter flights over the Reef from their pontoons—a truly spectacular experience. There are also fly-cruise trips.

An alternative to motoring to the Reef is to sail to it. **Ocean Spirit Cruises** (© **1800/644 227** in Australia, or 07/4031 2920; www.oceanspirit.com.au) operates two sailing cats that take no more than 150 passengers to Michaelmas Cay or Upolu Cay, lovely white-sand cays on the Outer Reef surrounded by rich reefs. This trip is a good value; it includes a pleasant 2-hour sail to either cay, a guided snorkeling safari, a guided beach walk, and a glass of bubbly and live music on the way home—in addition to the usual reef ecology talks, semisubmersible rides, lunch, and transfers from your Cairns or northern beaches hotel. Another plus is that you spend your out-of-water time on a beautiful beach, not on a pontoon or boat deck. You get about 4 hours on the Reef.

The day trip to Michaelmas Cay is A$169 (US$135) for adults, A$88 (US$70) for children 4 to 14, including transfers from Cairns (from Port Douglas they are A$39/US$31 per person extra). The day trip to Upolu Cay costs A$99 (US$79) for adults, A$76 (US$61) for kids. Transfers from Cairns and the northern beaches are A$12 (US$9.60) per person, and from Port Douglas they cost an extra A$39 (US$31) per person. Introductory dives cost A$95 (US$76), and certified divers pay A$65 (US$52) for one or A$110 (US$88) for two, all gear included, at Michaelmas Cay, less at Upolu. The boats depart Reef Fleet Terminal at 8:30am daily.

WHAT TO SEE & DO IN & AROUND CAIRNS

If you're staying in Cairns, also check out activities in and around Port Douglas (see section 3 of this chapter) and Mission Beach (see section 4 of this chapter). Many tour operators in Port Douglas, and a few in Mission Beach, offer transfers from Cairns.

LEARNING ABOUT ABORIGINAL CULTURE

Tjapukai Aboriginal Cultural Park ★★★ *Moments* Whether you choose the day or night experience, the Tjapukai (pronounced Jab-*oo*-guy) Aboriginal Cultural Park is one of the best chances you'll have to discover the history and culture of the Aborigines without going to Central Australia. American theater director Don Freeman and his French-Canadian dancer wife, Judy, founded the dance show in 1987, working with local Aborigines, including acclaimed dancer and songwriter David Hudson. Today it is a sophisticated, multiple-award-winning attraction with an international reputation. Don and Judy are still involved, but the park is 51% owned by the Aborigines who work there.

Housed in a striking modern building that incorporates Aboriginal themes and colors, the Tjapukai experience needs at least 2 to 3 hours. Start in the Creation Theatre, where performers use the latest in illusion, theatrics, and technology to tell the story of

> **Tips** Playing the Waiting Game
>
> Unless you are sure which tours you want to take, it often pays to wait until you get to Cairns to book them. Local travel agents, your hotel or B&B host, and other travelers in Cairns are often valuable sources of advice. Cairns has about 600 tour operators, so even in peak season, tours rarely book up more than 24 hours in advance.

the creation of the world according to the spiritual beliefs of Tjapukai people. Actors work with spectacular special effects and holographic images to illustrate the legends. The production is performed in the Tjapukai language, translated through headsets.

Move on through the Magic Space museum and gallery section of the complex to the History Theatre, where a 20-minute film relates the history of the Tjapukai people since the coming of white settlers 120 years ago.

Outside, a suspension bridge links the main building with a cultural village where you can try boomerang and spear throwing, attempt fire-making and didgeridoo playing, and learn about bush foods and medicines. In the open-sided Dance Theatre, Aboriginal men and women perform dances incorporating ancient and modern steps. Shows and demonstrations are planned so visitors can move from one to another easily, without missing anything. The complex also includes a restaurant and coffee shop. An arts and crafts gallery and shop stocks the work of Aboriginal artists and crafts workers.

Tjapukai by Night tours run daily from 7:30 to 10pm. They include interactive time in the Magic Space museum, a Creation Show performance, and an outdoor Serpent Circle—a new, interactive show featuring tap sticks for each guest to use, a join-in corroboree (an Aboriginal nighttime dance), and a ceremony involving fire and water. Following are a buffet dinner and dance show, and the chance to meet the Tjapukai dancers. The cost is A$96 (US$77) adults, A$48 (US$38) children, including transfers to and from Cairns.

Captain Cook Hwy. (beside the Skyrail terminal), Smithfield. © 07/4042 9900. Fax 07/4042 9990. www.tjapukai. com.au. Admission A$29 (US$23) adults, A$15 (US$12) children 4–14, A$73 (US$58) families. AE, DC, MC, V. Ask about packages that include transfers, lunch, and a guided Magic Space tour, or Skyrail and/or Scenic Rail travel to and from Kuranda. Daily 9am–5pm. Closed Jan 1 and Dec 25. Free parking. Bus: 1C or 1E. Book shuttle transfers from Cairns and northern beaches hotels (A$9.75/US$7.80 adults and A$4.90/US$3.90 children, one-way) through the park. Park is 15 min. north of Cairns and 15 min. south of Palm Cove.

MORE ATTRACTIONS
In Cairns

Cairns Rainforest Dome   For some visitors to Cairns, exploring the rainforest and its wildlife doesn't even involve leaving the hotel, thanks to the city's newest attraction. Here, 200 animals—including a huge saltwater crocodile called Goliath—are housed in a 20m-high (66-ft.) glass dome on the rooftop of the Hotel Sofitel Reef Casino (see "Where to Stay," later in this chapter). You can get up close with koalas, lizards, kookaburras, frogs, pademelons, turtles, and snakes. There are wildlife presentations and free guided tours throughout the day.

In the Hotel Sofitel Reef Casino, 35–41 Wharf St., Cairns, QLD 4870. © 07/4031 7250. Fax 07/4031 5265. www.cairnsdome.com.au. Admission A$22 (US$18) adults, A$11 (US$8.80) children, A$55 (US$44) for a family of 4. Daily 8am–6pm. Closed Dec 25.

Cairns Tropical Zoo *(Kids)*   Get a dose of your favorite Aussie wildlife here—some kind of talk or show takes place about every 15 or 30 minutes throughout the day, including koala cuddling (have your photo taken for an extra A$14/US$11), saltwater crocodile and lorikeet feedings, and cane toad racing. Lots of other animals are on show, too, like kangaroos (which you can hand-feed for A$1/US80¢ a bag), emus, cassowaries, dingoes, and native birds in a walk-through aviary. The park also runs a nocturnal tour, during which you can see many of the more elusive creatures on show. To take the park's 3-hour Cairns Night Zoo tour (www.cairnsnightzoo.com), book by 4pm on the same day (Mon–Thurs and Sat), earlier if you want transfers. The evening starts at 7pm and includes a wildlife spotlighting walk, during which you can pat a koala and a possum and feed kangaroos; a stargazing interlude; a barbecue dinner with beer and wine, billy tea, and damper; and dancing to an Aussie bush band.

Captain Cook Hwy. (22km/14 miles north of the city center), Palm Cove. *C* 07/4055 3669. Fax 07/4059 1160. www. cairnstropicalzoo.com. Admission A$26 (US$21) adults, A$13 (US$10) children 4–15. Cairns Night Zoo experience A$85 (US$68) adults, A$43 (US$34) children 4–15 (more if you want transfers from Cairns or Port Douglas). AE, DC, MC, V. Daily 8:30am–5pm. Closed Dec 25. Free parking. Bus: 1B. Transfers from Cairns through Down Under Tours (*C* 07/4035 5566) or from Port Douglas with Wildlife Discovery Tours (*C* 07/4099 6612).

Hartley's Crocodile Adventures ★★ *(Kids)*   Hartley's is the original Australian croc show, and after a move to a new location and a multimillion-dollar redevelopment in mid-2002, quite possibly the best. What makes it different from others is the fantastic natural setting—a 2-hectare (5-acre) lagoon surrounded by melaluca (Paperbark) and bloodwood trees and home to 23 estuarine crocs. The best time to visit is for the 3pm "croc attack" show, when you can witness the saltwater crocodile "death roll" during the 45-minute performance. At 11am you can see these monsters get hand-fed or hear an eye-opening talk on the less aggressive freshwater crocodiles. There are tours of the croc farm at 10am and 1:30pm; at 2pm there is a snake show; and 4:30pm is koala-feeding time. Cassowaries are fed at 9:30am and 4:15pm. This attraction makes a good stop en route to Port Douglas.

Capt. Cook Hwy. (40km/24 miles north of Cairns; 25km/16 miles south of Port Douglas). *C* 07/4055 3576. Fax 07/4059 1017. www.crocodileadventures.com. Admission (good for 3 days) A$26 (US$21) adults, A$13 (US$10) children 4–15, A$65 (US$52) families of 4. Daily 8:30am–5pm. Closed Dec 25. Free parking. Transfers from Cairns available through Down Under Tours (*C* 07/4035 5577) or from Cairns and Port Douglas through Wildlife Discovery Tours (*C* 07/4099 6612).

Royal Flying Doctor Visitors Centre   The Royal Flying Doctor Service (RFDS), the free aeromedical service that provides a "mantle of safety" for all Outback Australians, has a base in Cairns. Tours of the center start every 30 minutes from 9am to 4:30pm. You can also watch a film, attend a talk on how the service began, browse through memorabilia, and board a former RFDS plane. Allow about 45 minutes.

1 Junction St., Edge Hill. *C* 07/4053 5687. Admission A$5.50 (US$4.40) adults, A$2.75 (US$2.20) children, A$17 (US$14) families. Mon–Sat 8:30am–5pm. Closed Sun and public holidays. Bus: 6 or 6A.

EXPLORING THE ISLANDS

You don't have to go all the way to the Outer Reef to see coral. Less than an hour from the city wharf, Green Island has snorkeling equal to that on the Great Barrier Reef. Fitzroy Island has rainforest walks, coral accessible by dive and snorkel boat trips from the island, and watersports. See "Where to Stay," later in this section, for details about the resorts on both islands.

GREEN ISLAND   This 15-hectare (37-acre) coral cay, surrounded by dazzling coral and marine life, is just 27km (17 miles) east of Cairns. You can rent snorkel gear, windsurfers, and paddle-skis; take glass-bottom-boat trips; go parasailing; take an introductory or certified dive; walk vine-forest trails; or laze on the beach. The beach is coral sand, so it's a little rough underfoot. Day visitors have access to one of Green Island Resort's pools, its main bar, casual or upscale restaurants, and lockers and showers. Ask the beach staff to recommend the best snorkeling spots. If you don't snorkel, it's worth the admission charge to see the display of clown fish, potato cod, and anemones at the little underwater observatory, despite its cloudy old viewing windows. The island has a small attraction called **Marineland Melanesia** (℃ **07/4051 4032**), where you can see old nautical artifacts, primitive art, a turtle and reef aquarium, and live crocodiles. Admission is A$11 (US$8.80) adults, A$5 (US$4) kids; croc shows are at 10:30am and 1:45pm.

   Great Adventures (℃ **07/4044 9944;** www.greatadventures.com.au) and **Big Cat Green Island Reef Cruises** (℃ **07/4051 0444;** www.bigcat-cruises.com.au) run to Green Island from Cairns. A half-day trip with snorkel gear or a glass-bottom-boat cruise with Great Adventures costs A$58 (US$46), with full-day trips starting at A$98 (US$78) from Cairns. Big Cat makes a day trip for A$58 (US$46). Big Cat's boat is slower, but you still get more than 5 hours on the island. Great Adventures also has transfer-only rates of A$50 (US$40), which also gives access to the island's day facilities. Both companies pick up from hotels in Cairns, the northern beaches, and Port Douglas for an extra cost; Big Cat also runs to the island direct from Palm Cove.

FITZROY ISLAND   Scenic Fitzroy Island, a rainforested national park 45 minutes from Cairns, offers good diving. You can rent windsurfers, catamarans, and canoes; hike to the mountaintop lighthouse; view coral from a glass-bottom boat or take a short boat trip from the island to snorkel it; take a beginner's or certified dive; and swim in the pool. A day trip can cost as little as the round-trip ferry fare, A$36 (US$29) for adults and A$18 (US$14) for kids 4 to 14. Departures from Cairns are daily at 8:30 and 10:30am, and 4pm, returning at 9:30am, and 3 and 5pm. Make reservations through **Raging Thunder Adventures** (℃ **07/4030 7990;** www.raging thunder.com.au). Raging Thunder also runs full-day guided sea kayak expeditions to Fitzroy Island. Sea kayak trips include 3 hours of kayaking, snorkeling gear, lunch on a deserted beach, and a rainforest walk to the lighthouse; they cost A$135 (US$108) from Cairns, and participants must be over 12. You can also stay on the island for as little as A$31 (US$25) per person per night in bunkhouse accommodations (See "Where to Stay," below).

EXPLORING THE WET TROPICS RAINFOREST

The 110-million-year-old World Heritage–listed Daintree Rain Forest, 2 hours north of Cairns, gets most of the attention (see "Port Douglas, Daintree & the Cape Tribulation Area," later in this chapter), but tracts of rainforest closer to Cairns are just as pristine. These rainforests and the Daintree are part of the Wet Tropics, a World Heritage area that stretches from Cape Tribulation to Townsville. This dense, lush environment has remained unchanged by ice ages and other geological events, and the plants and animals retain primitive characteristics. In the tract's mangroves, eucalyptus woodlands, and tropical rainforest are 65% of Australia's bird species, 60% of its butterfly species, and many of its frogs, reptiles, bats, marsupials, and orchids.

Because so much rainforest wildlife is nocturnal and often difficult to spot, consider joining **Wait-a-While Rainforest Tours** (© 07/4098 2422; www.axioadventures. com.au) on a day-into-night tour into Daintree and Cape Tribulation national parks. The tours cost A$165 to A$265 (US$132–US$212), depending on your pickup point, and are designed to maximize your encounters with the wild things. They begin at 3pm and finish at about 11pm.

A SIDE TRIP TO KURANDA, A RAINFOREST VILLAGE ⭐

Few travelers visit Cairns without making at least a day trip to the mountain village of Kuranda, 34km (21 miles) northwest of Cairns near the Barron Gorge National Park. Although it's undeniably touristy, the cool mountain air and mist-wrapped rainforest refuse to be spoiled, no matter how many tourists clutter the streets. The shopping in Kuranda—for leather goods, Australian-wool sweaters, opals, crafts, and more—is more unusual than in Cairns, and the handful of cafes and restaurants are much more atmospheric. The town is easy to negotiate on foot; pick up a visitors' guide and map at the Skyrail gondola station or train station (see below) when you arrive.

GETTING THERE

Getting to Kuranda is part of the fun. Some people drive up the winding 25km (16-mile) mountain road, but the most popular approaches are to chuff up the mountainside in a scenic train, or to glide silently over the rainforest canopy in the world's longest gondola cableway, the Skyrail Rainforest Cableway.

The most popular round-trip is one-way on the Skyrail (mornings are best for photography) and the other way on the train.

BY SKYRAIL   The **Skyrail Rainforest Cableway** ⭐⭐⭐ (© 07/4038 1555; www. skyrail.com.au) is a magnificent feat of engineering and one of Australia's top tourism attractions. About 114 six-person gondolas leave every few seconds from the terminal in the northern Cairns suburb of Smithfield for the 7.5km (4½-mile) journey. The view of the coast as you ascend is so breathtaking that even those afraid of heights will find it worthwhile. As you rise over the foothills of the coastal range, watch the lush green of the rainforest take over beneath you. Looking back, you have spectacular views over Cairns and north towards Trinity Bay. On a clear day, you can see Green Island. There are two stops during the 90-minute trip, at Red Peak and Barron Falls. After about 10 minutes, you reach Red Peak. You are now 545m (1,788 ft.) above sea level, and massive kauri pines dominate the view. You must change gondolas at each station, so take the time to stroll around the boardwalks for the ground view of the rainforest. Guided walks start every 20 minutes.

On to Barron Falls station, built on the cleared site of an old construction camp for workers on the first hydroelectric power station on the Barron River in the 1930s. A rainforest information center has been established here, and there are boardwalks to the lookouts for wonderful views of the Barron Gorge and Falls. From Barron Falls station, the gondola travels over the thick rainforest of the range. It's easy to spot ferns and orchids and the brilliant blue butterflies of the region. As you reach the end of the trip, the gondola passes over the Barron River and across the Kuranda railway line into the station.

A one-way ticket is A$35 (US$28) for adults and A$18 (US$14) for children 4 to 14 or A$88 (US$70) for families of four; a round-trip ticket, including transfers from your Cairns or northern beaches hotel, is A$68 (US$54) for adults, A$34 (US$27) for children, A$170 (US$136) for families; from Port Douglas, it's A$82 (US$66) for adults, A$41 (US$33) for children, A$205 (US$164) for families. You must make a reservation to travel within a 15-minute time frame. Don't worry if it rains on the day you go—one of the best trips I've made on Skyrail was in a misty rain, which added a new dimension to the rainforest. The cableway operates daily except December 25 from 8:30am to 5:30pm, with the last boarding at the Cairns end at 4:15pm. The Skyrail terminal is on the Captain Cook Highway at Kamerunga Road, Caravonica Lakes, 15km (9½ miles) north of Cairns' city center.

BY SCENIC RAILWAY   The 34km (21-mile) **Kuranda Scenic Railway** (© 07/4036 9249; www.traveltrain.qr.com.au) is one of the most scenic rail journeys in the world. The train snakes through the magnificent vistas of the Barron Gorge National Park, past gorges and waterfalls on the 90-minute trip from Cairns to Kuranda. It rises 328m (1,076 ft.) and goes through 15 tunnels before emerging at the pretty Kuranda station, which is smothered in ferns. Built by hand over 5 years in the late 1880s, the railway track is today a monument to the 1,500 men who toiled to link the two towns, and the ride on the steam train adds to the atmosphere. The train departs Cairns Central at 8:30am daily and 9:30am Sunday through Friday (except Dec 25), and leaves Kuranda at 2pm Sunday through Friday and 3:30pm every day. The one-way fare is A$35 (US$28) for adults, A$18 (US$14) for children 4 to 16.

SKYRAIL/TRAIN COMBINATION TICKETS   In most cases, these packages represent convenience rather than savings. A package combining one-way travel on the Skyrail and a trip back on the Scenic Railway is A$70 (US$56) for adults and A$35 (US$28) for children; A$88 (US$70) for adults and A$44 (US$35) for kids with round-trip transfers from Cairns or the northern beaches. Skyrail runs a shuttle bus from most Cairns hotels. A package including the Skyrail, the Scenic Railway, and entry to the Tjapukai Aboriginal Cultural Park (see earlier in this chapter) is A$99 (US$79) for adults, A$50 (US$40) for kids, and A$248 (US$198) for a family of four, or A$117 (US$94) for adults, A$59 (US$47) for kids, and A$293 (US$234) for a family of four, including transfers from Cairns, the northern beaches, or Palm Cove. An option including the Skyrail, Scenic Railway, and Rainforestation (see below) is A$110 (US$88) for adults, A$55 (US$44) for kids. Book packages through Skyrail, Queensland Rail, or Tjapukai.

BY BUS   Whitecar Coaches (© 07/4091 1855) operates several daily buses to Kuranda from 46 Spence St., Cairns. The fare is A$4 (US$3.20) per person.

EXPLORING KURANDA

Kuranda is known for its markets that sell locally made arts and crafts, fresh produce, boomerangs, T-shirts, and jewelry. There are two markets—the small "original" markets at 7 Therwine St., behind Kuranda Market Arcade (open Wed–Fri and Sun 8am–3pm), which mainly sell cheap imports; and the 90-stall Heritage markets (open daily 9am–3pm), which offer better quality and a wider variety of goods. Try to visit Kuranda when both markets are open.

Even the Heritage markets have been invaded by commercial imported products, and in response, a group of about 50 local artisans sell their work in the **Kuranda Arts Co-Operative** ⭐, Shop 6, The Settlement, Rob Veivers Drive, next to the Butterfly Sanctuary (© 07/4093 9026). It's open from 10am to 4pm daily. You will find quality furniture crafted from recycled Australian hardwoods, jewelry, and handicrafts, among other items.

You can explore the rainforest, the river esplanade, or Barron Falls along a number of easy walking trails. If you want to learn about the rainforest, explore it with Brian Clarke of **Kuranda Riverboat Tours** (© 07/4093 7476 or 0412/159212), who runs informative 45-minute river cruises. The cruises depart hourly from 10:30am to 2:30pm from the riverside landing across the railway footbridge near the train station. Brian is a former crocodile hunter and has lived in the rainforest for more than 30 years. The cruise costs A$12 (US$9.60) for adults, A$6 (US$4.80) for children 5 to 15, and A$30 (US$24) for a family of four. Buy your tickets on board.

KURANDA'S NATURE PARKS

Of Kuranda's two walk-through aviaries, **Birdworld** (© 07/4093 9188), behind the Heritage markets off Rob Veivers Drive, is probably the most interesting; it has eye-catching macaws, a pair of cassowaries, and Australia's largest collection of free-flying birds. **The Aviary,** 8 Thongon St. (© 07/4093 7411), is good if you want to see a bigger range of Australian species. Birdworld is open daily from 9am to 4pm; admission is A$12 (US$9.60) for adults, A$5 (US$4) for children 4 to 14, A$29 (US$23) for families. The Aviary is open daily from 10am to 3:30pm; admission is A$12 (US$9.60) for adults, A$6 (US$4.80) for kids 4 to 16. Both aviaries are closed December 25.

Australian Butterfly Sanctuary ★ *Kids*   A rainbow-hued array of 1,500 tropical butterflies—including the electric-blue Ulysses and Australia's largest species, the Cairns bird wing—occupies a lush walk-through enclosure here. Take the free guided tour and learn about the butterfly's fascinating life cycle. The butterflies will land on you if you wear pink, red, and other bright colors, and don't be put off if it's raining—this attraction is good in any weather.

8 Rob Veivers Dr. © 07/4093 7575. Fax 07/4093 8923. www.australianbutterflies.com. Admission A$13 (US$10) adults, A$12 (US$9.60) seniors, A$6.50 (US$5.20) children 4–15, A$30 (US$24) families. AE, DC, MC, V. Daily 9:45am–4pm. Free guided tours every 15 min. 10am–3:15pm. Closed Dec 25. Street parking. Bus stop 7 min. from sanctuary.

Rainforestation Nature Park   At this 40-hectare (99-acre) nature and cultural complex, you can take a 45-minute ride into the rainforest in a World War II amphibious Army Duck. You'll hear commentary on orchids and other rainforest wildlife along the way. You can also see a performance by Aboriginal dancers; learn about Aboriginal legends and throw a boomerang on the Dreamtime Walk; or have your photo taken cuddling a koala in the wildlife park. You can do any of these activities separately, or do them all (except cuddle a koala) in a package that costs A$34 (US$27) for adults, A$17 (US$14) for kids 4 to 14, or A$85 (US$68) for a family of four. Koala photos are A$12 (US$9.60). The Army Duck runs on the hour beginning at 9am; the Aboriginal dancers perform at 10:30am, noon, and 2pm; and the 30-minute Dreamtime Walk leaves at 10, 11, and 11:30am, noon, and 12:30, 1:30, and 2:30pm.

Tips **Staying Warm in Kuranda**

If you visit Kuranda, don't forget to bring some warm clothing in winter. It can get nippy in the mountains, especially at night.

Kennedy Hwy., a 5-min. drive from the center of Kuranda. © **07/4085 5008.** Fax 07/4093 7578. www. rainforest.com.au. Shuttle from the Butterfly Sanctuary, Rob Veivers Dr., Kuranda, every 30 min. 10:45am–2:45pm for A$6 (US$4.80) adults, A$3 (US$2.40) children, A$15 (US$12) families, round-trip. AE, DC, MC, V. Daily 9am–4pm. Closed Dec 25. Ample free parking.

WHITE-WATER RAFTING & OTHER THRILLS

RnR Rafting ★ (© **07/4041 9444;** www.raft.com.au) and **Raging Thunder Adventures** (© **07/4030 7990;** www.ragingthunder.com.au) serve as one-stop booking shops for action pursuits in and around Cairns, including hot-air ballooning, skydiving, jet-boating, horseback riding, ATV (all-terrain vehicle) safaris, parasailing, and rafting. Ask about multipursuit packages.

BIKING **Dan's Mountain Biking** (© **07/4032 0666,** or 0419/930 128 mobile phone) runs a wide range of full- and half-day guided tours in small groups for A$75 to A$135 (US$60–US$108) per person.

BUNGEE JUMPING Contact **A. J. Hackett Bungy** (© **1800/622 888** in Australia, or 07/4057 7188). The cost is A$128 (US$102) per person including transport to the site, which is 20 minutes north of town on McGregor Road.

FISHING Cairns is the world's giant black marlin capital. Catches of more than 1,000 pounds hardly raise an eyebrow in this neck of the woods. The game-fishing season is September through December, with November the busiest. Book early—game boats are reserved months in advance. Game fishers can also battle Pacific sailfish, dogtooth and yellowfin tuna, Spanish mackerel, wahoo, dolphinfish, barracuda, and tiger shark. Reef anglers can expect to land coral trout, red emperor (sea perch), and sweetlip. Mangrove jack, barramundi, and tarpon lurk in the estuaries. Check out www.fishingcairns.com.au or contact **Destination Cairns Marketing,** 36 Aplin St. at Sheridan St. (© **1800/807 730** in Australia, or 07/4051 4066), to book a charter. Expect to pay around A$400 (US$320) per person or about A$1,900 (US$1,520) per day for a sole charter for heavy-tackle game fishing, A$350 (US$280) per person for light-tackle fishing, at least A$155 (US$124) for reef fishing, and A$135 (US$108) for a day or A$75 (US$60) for a half-day in the Cairns Inlet estuary.

WHITE-WATER RAFTING Several companies offer exciting white-water-rafting trips from Cairns on the Class III to IV **Tully River** ★★, 90 minutes south of Cairns near Mission Beach; the Class III Barron River in the hills behind the city; and the Class IV to V rapids of the inland Johnstone River. One of the best is **RnR Rafting** (© **07/4041 9444**).

One-day trips on the Tully are the most popular (see "Mission Beach: The Cassowary Coast," later in this chapter). The trip costs A$150 (US$120) from Cairns, or A$170 (US$136) from Port Douglas, including transfers.

Closer to Cairns, the gentler **Barron River** is a good choice for the timid. A halfday trip with RnR Rafting costs about A$88 (US$70) from Cairns or A$99 (US$79) from Port Douglas, including pickup from your accommodations and 2 hours of rafting. Prices do not include the A$6 (US$4.80) national park fee.

WHERE TO STAY

High season in Cairns includes 2 weeks at Easter, the period from early July to early October, and the Christmas holiday through January. Book ahead in those periods. In low season (Nov–June), many hotels offer discounts or are willing to negotiate.

Cairns has a good supply of affordable accommodations, both in the heart of the city and along the northern beaches. You can also stay in the peaceful village of Kuranda, or get away from it all at an island resort.

Don't think you have to stay in Cairns city if you don't have a car. Most tour and cruise operators will pick you up and drop you off in Cairns, on the northern beaches, or even in Port Douglas (see section 3, later in this chapter).

IN CAIRNS

Unless noted otherwise, all accommodations below are within walking distance of shops, restaurants, cinemas, the casino, the tourist office, bus terminals, the train station, and the departure terminals for Great Barrier Reef cruises.

Very Expensive

Hotel Sofitel Reef Casino ✦ Arguably the most stylish property in Cairns, this six-story hotel is 1 block from the water, with partial water views from some rooms, and nice city/hinterland outlooks from others. All the rooms have lots of natural light, high-quality amenities, Jacuzzis, bathrobes, and small balconies with smart timber furniture. The Cairns **casino** is attached to the hotel (see "Cairns After Dark," later in this chapter).

35–41 Wharf St., Cairns, QLD 4870. ✆ **1800/808 883** in Australia, 800/221-4542 in the U.S. and Canada, 020/8283 4500 in the U.K., 0800/44 4422 in New Zealand, or 07/4030 8888. Fax 07/4030 8777. www.accorhotels.com. 128 units. A$242–A$480 (US$194–US$384) double; A$710–A$2,000 (US$568–US$1,600) suite. Extra person A$33 (US$26). Children under 15 stay free in parent's room with existing bedding. AE, DC, MC, V. Free valet and self-parking. **Amenities:** 3 restaurants; bar; small rooftop pool; health club; Jacuzzi; sauna; concierge; tour desk; airport shuttle; business center; 24-hr. room service; babysitting; laundry service; dry cleaning. *In room:* A/C, TV/VCR, dataport, minibar, hair dryer, iron, safe.

Shangri-La Hotel, The Marina ✦ After a A$35-million-plus (US$28-million) renovation, this hotel became part of the swish Shangri-La group in mid-2004 and has a modern, sophisticated new look. Overlooking the marina, 36 new rooms are part of the exclusive Horizon Club. These units are contemporary in style and exceptionally spacious—more than 50 sq. m (538 sq. ft.), with 3.3m (11-ft.) ceilings. Bathrooms have ocean views, and the rooms have large terraces looking to the moored yachts and the mountains. The AAA-rated five-star hotel adjoins the Pier Shopping Centre and the new Esplanade lagoon, and is not far from the Reef Fleet Terminal.

Pierpoint Rd., Cairns, QLD 4870. ✆ **1800/222 448** in Australia, 0800/442 179 in New Zealand, 800/942 5050 in the U.S. and Canada, 020/8747 8485 in the U.K., or 07/4031 1411. Fax 07/4031 3226. www.shangri-la.com. 256 units. A$424–A$707 (US$339–US$566) double; A$621–A$784 (US$497–US$627) suite. Children under 18 stay free in parent's room with existing bedding. AE, DC, MC, V. Free outdoor and covered self-parking. **Amenities:** 2 restaurants; 2 bars; large outdoor pool and children's pool; nearby golf course; health club; Jacuzzi; sauna; video arcade; concierge; tour desk; car-rental desk; airport shuttle (on request); business center; shopping arcade; salon; 24-hr. room service; in-room massage; babysitting; coin-op laundry; dry cleaning; executive-level rooms. *In room:* A/C, TV/VCR w/pay movies, fax, dataport, kitchenette (suite and Horizon Club rooms only), minibar, coffeemaker, hair dryer, iron, safe.

Expensive

Oasis Resort Cairns (Value) The large pool, complete with swim-up bar and a little sandy beach, is the focus of this attractive six-story resort built in 1997. All the colorful, contemporary rooms have balconies with views over the tropical gardens, the mountains, or the pool. The suites, with a TV in the bedroom and a large Jacuzzi bathtub, could well be the best-value suites in town.

122 Lake St., Cairns, QLD 4870. ✆ **07/4080 1888.** Fax 07/4080 1889. www.oasis-cairns.com.au. 314 units. A$235–A$265 (US$188–US$212) double; A$405 (US$324) suite. Extra person A$44 (US$35). Children under 16 stay

free in parent's room with existing bedding. Free crib. Ask about packages. AE, DC, MC, V. Free valet and self-parking. **Amenities:** Restaurant; 2 bars; outdoor pool; health club; concierge; tour desk; airport shuttle; limited room service; babysitting; coin-op laundry; laundry service; dry cleaning. *In room:* A/C, TV w/pay movies, dataport, minibar, coffeemaker, hair dryer, iron, safe.

Rydges Esplanade Resort Cairns Despite its lack of obvious glitz, this 14-story hotel has been the choice of a number of movie stars—most famously Marlon Brando—while on location in Cairns. A 20-minute waterfront walk from downtown, the hotel offers a range of accommodations, from hotel rooms to four-bedroom penthouses (with private rooftop pool). The one- and two-bedroom apartments look out to the sea; hotel rooms have sea or mountain views. Some units have dataports; kitchenettes are in studios and apartments; and hotel rooms and apartments have minibars. The rooms are spacious, but the bathrooms are not, perhaps reflecting the hotel's Japanese market. Out back are cheaper studios and apartments, with upgraded furnishings; out front are a pool and sun deck.

The Esplanade (at Kerwin St.), Cairns, QLD 4870. © **1800/079 105** in Australia, or 07/4031 2211. Fax 07/4031 2704. www.matsonresort.com.au. 342 units. A$220–A$260 (US$176–US$208) double; A$160 (US$128) studio; A$165–A$360 (US$132–US$288) tower apt for up to 5; A$205 (US$164) 1-bedroom apt for up to 4; A$250 (US$200) 2-bedroom apt for up to 6; A$950 (US$760) 3-bedroom penthouse; A$1,200 (US$960) 4-bedroom penthouse. Extra person A$28 (US$22). Ask about packages. AE, DC, MC, V. Free covered parking. Bus stop about 100m (328 ft.) from the hotel. **Amenities:** 2 restaurants; 3 bars; 3 outdoor pools; golf course about 20 min. away; 2 lit tennis courts; health club w/aerobics classes; Jacuzzi; sauna; bike rental; concierge; tour desk; car-rental desk; airport transfers; shuttle service around city; salon; 24-hr. room service; in-room massage; babysitting; coin-op laundry; laundry service; dry cleaning; nonsmoking rooms. *In room:* A/C, TV w/pay movies, hair dryer, iron, safe.

Moderate

Cairns Plaza Hotel The harbor views at this seven-story complex are better than those at most of the more luxurious hotels in Cairns. Two blocks from town, the accommodations are a good size, with fresh, appealing furnishings and modern bathrooms. Suites and studios have kitchenettes. If your balcony does not have a water vista, you overlook a nice aspect of the city or mountains instead. Families can book a connecting suite and standard room to create more space and privacy.

145 The Esplanade (at Minnie St.), Cairns, QLD 4870. © **1800/117 787** in Australia, or 07/4051 4688. Fax 07/4051 8129. www.cairnsplaza.com.au. 60 units. A$145–A$155 (US$116–US$124) double; A$185 (US$148) suite; A$260 (US$208) connecting units. Extra person A$25 (US$20). AE, DC, MC, V. Limited free parking. **Amenities:** Restaurant; bar; small outdoor pool; golf course nearby; 4 lit tennis courts nearby; access to nearby health club; Jacuzzi; tour desk; car-rental desk; limited room service; massage; babysitting; coin-op laundry; dry cleaning. *In room:* A/C, TV w/free movies, dataport, minibar, coffeemaker, hair dryer, iron.

Inexpensive

Coral Tree Inn *Value* The focal point of this airy, modern resort-style motel a 5-minute walk from the city center is the friendly communal kitchen that overlooks the palm-lined saltwater pool and paved sun deck. It's a great spot to cook a steak or reef fish filet on the free barbecue and join other guests at the big shared tables. Local restaurants deliver, free fresh-roasted coffee is on the boil all day, and a vending machine sells wine and beer, so you don't even have to go down to the pub for supplies! The smallish, basic but neat motel rooms have painted brick walls, terra-cotta tile or carpeted floors, and new bathrooms with marble-look laminate countertops. In contrast, the eight suites, which have kitchenettes, are huge and stylish enough to do any corporate traveler proud. They are some of the best-value accommodations in town. All rooms have a private balcony or patio; some look out onto the commercial buildings next door, but most face the pool. Ask about packages that include cruises and other tours.

166–172 Grafton St., Cairns, QLD 4870. ℂ **07/4031 3744.** Fax 07/4031 3064. www.coraltreeinn.com.au. 58 units. A$118 (US$94) double; A$145 (US$116) suite. Extra person A$10 (US$8). AE, DC, MC, V. Limited free parking; ample street parking. **Amenities:** Bar; outdoor saltwater pool; access to nearby health club; bike rental; tour desk; car-rental desk; airport shuttle; babysitting; coin-op laundry; laundry service; dry cleaning; nonsmoking rooms; safe (at reception). *In room:* A/C, TV, dataport, fridge, coffeemaker, hair dryer, iron.

Lilybank Bed & Breakfast ⋆

This 1870s Queenslander homestead, originally a mayor's residence, is in a leafy suburb 6km (3¾ miles) from the airport and a 10-minute drive from the city. The large, attractive guest rooms, individually decorated with such features as wrought-iron beds and patchwork quilts, have good-size bathrooms. The largest room has French doors opening onto a "sleep-out" (an enclosed veranda with two extra beds). You can also stay in the gardener's cottage, with slate floors, stained-glass windows, a king-size bed, and a bar. The house is set in gardens with an attractive rock-lined saltwater pool. Breakfast is served in the garden room by the fishpond. Gregarious hosts Mike and Pat Woolford share their house with three poodles, an irrepressible galah, and a giant green tree frog. There's a guest TV lounge and kitchen, and phone, fax, and e-mail access. Many tours pick up at the door, and several good restaurants are a stroll away, so you don't need a car to stay here. A taxi from the airport costs approximately A$15 (US$12). No smoking indoors.

75 Kamerunga Rd., Stratford, Cairns, QLD 4870. ℂ **07/4055 1123.** Fax 07/4058 1990. www.lilybank.com.au. 6 units (4 with shower only). A$88–A$110 (US$70–US$88) double. Extra person A$33 (US$26). Rates include full breakfast. AE, MC, V. Free parking. Bus: 1E or 1G. Bus stop 120m (394 ft.) away. Children not accepted. **Amenities:** Outdoor pool; tour desk; massage (on request); coin-op laundry; nonsmoking rooms. *In room:* A/C, hair dryer, no phone.

ON THE NORTHERN BEACHES

A string of white sandy beaches starts 15 minutes north of the city center. Trinity Beach, 15 minutes from the airport, is secluded, elegant, and scenic. The most upscale is Palm Cove, 20 minutes from the airport. Here rainbow-hued shops and tasteful apartment blocks nestle among giant Paperbarks and palms fronting a postcard-perfect beach. It has several advantages over other beach suburbs: A 9-hole resort golf course and a gym are within walking distance, the Quicksilver Wavepiercer Great Barrier Reef cruise boat picks up passengers here daily, and it has the greatest choice of places to eat. Add 5 to 10 minutes to the traveling times above to reach the city.

Very Expensive

The Sebel Reef House & Spa Palm Cove ⋆⋆⋆

Picture yourself in a Somerset Maugham novel—substituting the Queensland tropics for Singapore—and you've almost got it. This is one of the most romantic hotels in Queensland, or all of Australia. The Reef House's guest list reads like an excerpt from Who's Who—the most recent addition being Bob Dylan and his band. But no matter who you are, you will not want to leave. The white walls are swathed in bougainvillea, and the beds with mosquito netting. Airy interiors feature rustic handmade artifacts and white wicker furniture. The Verandah Spa rooms, which have a Jacuzzi on the balcony, overlook the pool, waterfalls, and lush gardens. They have extra touches such as bathrobes and a CD player, as well as balconies within earshot of the ocean. The beachfront **restaurant,** on a large covered wooden deck beneath towering Paperbarks, is a favorite with locals and tourists alike for its unsurpassed ocean views, gentle breezes, and unpretentious food.

99 Williams Esplanade, Palm Cove, Cairns, QLD 4879. ℂ **1800/079 052** in Australia, or 07/4055 3633. Fax 07/4055 3305. www.reefhouse.com.au. 69 units (14 with shower only). A$385–A$545 (US$308–US$436) double; A$495–A$635 (US$396–US$508) suite. Extra person A$30 (US$24). Children under 14 stay free in parent's room with existing

> ### Tips   Safe Swimming
>
> All of the northern beaches have small, netted enclosures for safe swimming from October through May, when deadly stingers (box jellyfish) render all mainland beaches in north Queensland off-limits.

bedding. AE, DC, MC, V. Free limited covered parking; ample street parking. Bus: 1, 1B, 1X, 2X, or N. **Amenities:** Restaurant; bar; cafe; honor bar; 3 small heated outdoor pools; nearby golf course; spa; access to nearby health club; concierge; tour desk; airport shuttle; limited room service; massage; babysitting; coin-op laundry; laundry service; dry cleaning. *In room:* A/C, TV/VCR, kitchenette, minibar, coffeemaker, hair dryer, iron, safe.

Expensive

Outrigger Beach Club & Spa ⭐

A "resort within the resort," the Serenity Wing, with 42 suites and a private rainforest pool, is the final touch to this new complex on the beachfront. Opened in late 2002, the main hotel has rooms and apartments overlooking the water, with touches of Queensland colonial style. Hotel rooms are small but have Jacuzzis and timber outdoor furniture on the decks. Eight penthouses (three floors up) have private rooftop terraces and pools, but there's no elevator. A further 25 penthouses have Jacuzzis. The large lagoon-style pool has a sandy beach and swim-up bar. Coconut palms with white-painted trunks surround the lagoon, which is lit by flaming torches at night. Suites are more secluded, with kitchens, gas barbecues, washers and dryers, and state-of-the-art entertainment units, including DVDs and flatscreen televisions. Pampering awaits you at the Sanctum Spa, which has seven wet and dry treatment rooms and offers yoga classes as well as beauty and massage treatments for both men and women. If you are staying 5 nights or more and want to arrive in style, order the free limousine or Rolls-Royce transfers from Cairns Airport to Palm Cove. For guests staying 3 to 5 nights, the room rate includes coach transfers to the airport.

123 Williams Esplanade, Palm Cove, Cairns, QLD 4879. ✆ **800/688-7444** in the U.S., 1800/134 444 in Australia, or 07/4059 9200. Fax 07/4059 9222. www.outrigger.com. 220 units. A$281–A$374 (US$225–US$299) double with Jacuzzi; A$343–A$374 (US$275–US$299) double 1-bedroom suite; A$374–A$406 (US$299–US$325) double 1-bedroom suite with Jacuzzi; A$437–A$562 (US$350–US$450) 2-bedroom suite with Jacuzzi for up to 4; A$572–A$1,050 (US$458–US$840) 2-bedroom penthouse suite for up to 4. Extra person A$35 (US$28). 3-night minimum at Easter and Christmas to mid-January. AE, DC, MC, V. Secure parking. **Amenities:** 4 restaurants; 3 heated outdoor pools; golf course nearby; tennis court; gym; spa; concierge; tour desk; nonsmoking rooms. *In room:* A/C, TV w/pay movies, dataport, fridge, coffeemaker, hair dryer, iron, safe, Jacuzzi.

Moderate

Ellis Beach Oceanfront Bungalows ⭐ *Finds*

On arguably the loveliest of the northern beaches, about 30 minutes from Cairns, these bungalows and cabins sit under palm trees between the Coral Sea and a backdrop of mountainous rainforest. Lifeguards patrol the beach, and there are stinger nets in season as well as a shady pool and toddlers' wading pool. There's plenty of privacy, and the accommodations are basic but pleasant. You can sit on the veranda and gaze at the ocean. Keep an eye out for dolphins. Each bungalow and cabin sleeps four and has full kitchen facilities (with microwave, fridge, and freezer), but cabins have no en-suite bathroom (they use the communal facilities at the campground in the same complex). The property has coin-operated barbecues and phone and fax facilities.

Captain Cook Hwy., Ellis Beach, QLD 4879. ✆ **1800/637 036** in Australia, or 07/4055 3538. Fax 07/4055 3077. www.ellisbeachbungalows.com. 15 units (all with shower only). A$68–A$75 (US$54–US$60) double cabin; A$155–A$175 (US$124–US$140) double bungalow. Extra person A$15 (US$12) cabin, A$25 (US$20) bungalow.

3-night minimum June–Sept; 2-night minimum Oct–May. AE, MC, V. **Amenities:** Restaurant; 2 outdoor pools; golf course nearby; tour desk; car-rental desk; coin-op laundry. *In room:* A/C, ceiling fans, TV, kitchen, iron, no phone.

The Reef Retreat ★★   Tucked back one row of buildings from the beach is this little gem—a low-rise collection of contemporary studios and suites built around a swimming pool in a peaceful grove of palms and silver Paperbarks. All the rooms have cool tile floors and smart teak and cane furniture. The studios, renovated in 1996, are a terrific value and much larger than the average hotel room. In the oceanview suites, you can even lie in bed and see the sea. The extraprivate honeymoon suites (and some oceanview suites), built in 1997, have a Jacuzzi and a kitchenette outside on the balcony; a total of 20 units have Jacuzzis. There's a barbecue and a Jacuzzi on the grounds. There's no elevator. Units are cleaned twice weekly; one free cleaning for stays of 5 days or longer. Extra cleanings A$20 to A$30 (US$16–US$24).

10–14 Harpa St., Palm Cove, Cairns, QLD 4879. (*) **07/4059 1744.** Fax 07/4059 1745. www.reefretreat.com.au. 36 units (all with shower only). A$150 (US$120) studio double; A$160 (US$128) suite; A$170 (US$136) suite with Jacuzzi; A$180 (US$144) oceanview suite; A$270 (US$216) 2-bedroom apt for up to 4. Extra person A$25 (US$20). Children under 3 stay free in parent's room with existing bedding. Crib A$25 (US$20). AE, MC, V. Free parking. Bus: 1, 1B 1X, 2X, or N. **Amenities:** Outdoor saltwater pool; nearby golf course; nearby tennis courts; Jacuzzi; tour desk; car-rental desk; airport shuttle (A$15/US$12 per person one-way); coin-op laundry; laundry service; dry cleaning. *In room:* A/C, TV, dataport, kitchenette, fridge, coffeemaker, hair dryer, iron.

ISLAND RESORTS

Several island resorts are within the Great Barrier Reef Marine Park off Cairns. They afford safe swimming year-round, because the infestations of deadly marine stingers that plague this area from October through May don't make it to the islands. They also offer snorkeling and diving opportunities every day.

Very Expensive

Green Island Resort ★   Step off the beach at this Great Barrier Reef national park island, and you are surrounded by acres of coral. The resort is a high-class cluster of rooms tucked away in a dense vine forest. Each room is private, roomy, and elegantly outfitted, with polished wooden floors and a balcony looking into the forest. Windsurfing, surf-skiing, canoeing, diving and snorkeling (both on the island and on day trips to the outer Reef), glass-bottom-boat trips, guided rainforest walks, parasailing, and beach volleyball are among the activities available, or you can simply laze on the coarse white-coral sand or by the guests-only pool. Helicopter and seaplane flights and cruises are available. Room rates include many activities and equipment, such as nonmotorized sports, snorkel gear, and glass-bottom-boat trips; there's a charge for scuba diving and other activities using fuel. Both the resort and the island are small (you can walk around it in 45 min.), and it is a popular day-tripper destination. But after they leave at 4:30pm, the place is blissfully peaceful.

Green Island, 27km (17 miles) east of Cairns (P.O. Box 898, Cairns, QLD 4870). (*) **1800/673 366** in Australia, or 07/4031 3300. Fax 07/4052 1511. www.greenislandresort.com.au. 46 units. A$489–A$589 (US$391–US$471) double. Extra person A$93 (US$74). Rate includes launch transfers. Ask about packages. AE, DC, MC, V. Helicopter and seaplane transfers available. **Amenities:** 2 restaurants; 2 bars; 2 outdoor saltwater pools; spa; wide array of watersports equipment available; concierge; tour desk; laundry service; coin-op laundry. *In room:* A/C, TV, minibar, hair dryer, safe.

Lizard Island ★★★   Luxury lodges, huge potato cod so tame divers can pet them, snorkeling off the beach, and isolation—that's what lures the well-heeled to this small, exclusive resort. Lizard is a rugged 1,000-hectare (2,470-acre) national park island on the Great Barrier Reef, sparsely vegetated but stunningly beautiful, ringed by 24 white sandy beaches, with fringing reefs that support a multitude of marine life including giant clams. No day-trippers are allowed. Room rates include many activities: snorkeling and glass-bottom-boat trips, catamarans, paddle-skis, fishing tackle, tennis, and hiking trails, such as the muscle-straining 545m (.5-mile) climb to Cook's Look, where Captain Cook spied his way out of the treacherous reefs in 1770. You pay for fishing and diving trips to nearby Reef sites, including Cod Hole. Introductory dive lessons and night dives are available.

The 40 villas, elegant freestanding lodges tucked under palms along the beach or perched on cliff tops overlooking the bay, were renovated in 2000. They are built of timber and stone, in a casual tropical style, with earth and sea tone finishes. A guest lounge has Internet facilities, TV and video, bar facilities, and a book and games library. The recently expanded Azure Spa offers a Vichy shower, double-massage room and steam room, and a new range of therapies.

In mid-2003, the property added an even more exclusive accommodations option, **The Pavilion.** This villa offers complete privacy, sheer luxury, and spectacular panoramic views. It has private decks leading down to its own plunge pool, and comes with extras such as a laptop, binoculars, and Bollinger on arrival.

Lizard Island, 240km (149 miles) north of Cairns; 27km (17 miles) offshore (Voyages, G.P.O. Box 3589, Sydney, NSW 2001). © **1300/134 044** in Australia, or 02/8296 8010 (Sydney reservations office). Fax 02/9299 2477 (Sydney reservations office). www.voyages.com.au. 40 units (all with shower only). A$1,530 (US$1,224) double; A$1,820 (US$1,456) villa double; A$1,900 (US$1,520) suite double; A$3,300 (US$2,640) Pavilion double. Extra person A$460 (US$368). Rates include all meals and many activities. AE, DC, MC, V. Air transfers daily from Cairns (1 hr.; book through Qantas); round-trip advance-purchase fare about A$480 (US$384) per person. Aircraft luggage limit 15kg (33 lb.) per person. Air-charter transfers available. Children under 10 not accepted. **Amenities:** Restaurant; freshwater pool; lit tennis court; gym; spa; laundry service. *In room:* A/C, fans, dataport, minibar, coffeemaker, hair dryer, iron.

Moderate/Inexpensive

Fitzroy Island Resort This is probably the most affordable island resort on the Great Barrier Reef. It's targeted at a young crowd looking for action and ecofun in a pristine, beautiful location. It's no glamour-puss palace—a revamp a few years ago added a Hard Rock Cafe–style restaurant and spruced up the interiors. Fitzroy is a continental island offering little in the way of fringing coral and only a few narrow strips of coral sand. What it does have are catamarans, outrigger canoes, and surf skis; glass-bottom-boat rides; and hiking trails through dense national park forest to a lighthouse. Divers can make drift dives over the reefs dotted around the island to see manta rays, reef sharks, turtles, and coral. There is good snorkeling at two points around the island that you can reach twice a day on the dive boat, at an extra fee. You can also catch the Sunlover Cruises day trip to the outer Great Barrier Reef. The dive shop runs introductory and certified dives and certification courses. Each of the modestly comfortable beach cabins has a queen-size bed and two bunks in the back, as well as a TV, minifridge, coffeemaker, hair dryer, and iron. The rooms have ceiling fans and a large balcony with views through the trees to the sea. The bunkhouse accommodations are basic fan-cooled carpeted rooms with bunks, beds, or both. Bunkhouse guests can use the communal kitchen but must bring their own supplies from the mainland.

The restaurant is moderately priced, a kiosk sells takeout food, and the poolside grill and bar offers casual meals. The **Raging Thunder Beach Bar Restaurant** is open 6pm to 9pm during high season only.

Fitzroy Island, 35km (22 miles) southeast of Cairns (P.O. Box 1109, Cairns, QLD 4870). © **07/4051 9588.** Fax 07/4052 1335. www.fitzroyislandresort.com.au. 8 cabins (all with shower only); 32 bunkhouses, none with private bathroom. Cabins A$220 (US$176) double. Extra person A$35 (US$28). Bunkhouses A$31 (US$25) per person per bed (sharing with up to 3 other people); A$116 (US$93) double (sole use); A$250 (US$200) family bunkhouse for up to 4. Ask about packages. AE, DC, MC, V. Round-trip transfers 3 times daily from Cairns (approximately 45 min.) A$36 (US$29) adults, A$18 (US$14) children 4–14. **Amenities:** 2 restaurants; bar; outdoor pool; watersports equipment; tour desk; dive shop.

WHERE TO DINE
IN CAIRNS

For cheap eats, head to the Esplanade along the seafront; it's lined with cafes, pizzerias, fish-and-chips places, food courts, and ice-cream parlors.

Expensive

Fishlips Bar & Bistro ★★ MODERN AUSTRALIAN/SEAFOOD   Ask locals where they go for seafood—as opposed to where they send tourists—and they direct you to this 1920s bluebird-blue shack. Chef Ian Candy is renowned for his flair and innovation with seafood. All dishes come in small or large servings, and the local barramundi, or "barra," shows up in several incarnations—maybe beer-battered with rough-cut chips (fries) and fresh tartar sauce, simply grilled, or served with eggplant pickle and rocket pesto on chargrilled zucchini and onion with charred polenta. There are plenty of nonseafood options. Be daring—try the crocodile, pan-fried with pine nuts, coriander, and cumin. For dessert, don't go past the homemade ice cream with flavors that change each week. How nice to see that almost every choice on the wine list comes by the glass. Dine inside (air-conditioned for those humid nights) or on the front deck, with its bright blue pots and palm trees.

228 Sheridan St. (between Charles and McKenzie sts.) © 07/4041 1700. www.fishlips.com.au. Reservations recommended. Main courses A$12–A$19 (US$9.60–US$15) small sizes; A$20–A$41 (US$16–US$33) large sizes. AE, DC, MC, V. Fri noon–2:30pm; daily 6pm–late.

Red Ochre Grill ★ (Kids) GOURMET BUSH TUCKER   You could accuse this restaurant/bar of using weird and wonderful Aussie ingredients as a gimmick to pull in crowds, but the diners who have flocked here for the past 10 years know good food when they taste it. Daily specials are big on fresh local seafood, and the regular menu—which changes often—lets you devour the Aussie coat of arms in several different ways. Try salt-and-native-pepper crocodile and prawns with Vietnamese pickles and lemon aspen sambal, or kangaroo sirloin cooked over a mallee wood-fired grill, with a quandong chile glaze, sweet potato fritter, and bok choy. A renovation in 2004 gave the restaurant a fresh look, so it's slick enough for a big night out but still informal enough for a casual meal. It's independent, not part of the chain that has a branch in Alice Springs. There's also a kids' menu.

43 Shields St. © 07/4051 0100. www.redochregrill.com.au. Reservations recommended. Main courses A$9–A$28 (US$7.20–US$22) at lunch, A$19–A$32 (US$15–US$26) at dinner. Australian game platter A$45 (US$36) per person; seafood platter A$60 (US$48) per person. Tastes of Australia 4-course set menu A$60 (US$48) per person (minimum 2 people). AE, DC, MC, V. Daily noon–midnight; public holidays 6pm–midnight. Closed Dec 25.

Moderate

Perrotta's MODERN AUSTRALIAN   The locals flock here for brunch and lunch, particularly on weekends, and you can team it with a visit to the Cairns Regional Art Gallery (the cafe is just outside). Breakfast differs from the usual bacon and eggs or pancakes, offering delights such as smoked salmon and sweet-potato hash browns with sour cream, and avocado. Sweet tooths may go for French toast with cinnamon, caramelized apples, and honey mascarpone. For lunch there's a choice of bruschettas, focaccia, or panini, pasta dishes, or more individual dishes such as barbecued Cajun Spanish mackerel with tomato and basil salad. At dinner, try wild barramundi, braised duck leg, or lamb shanks. Remember to check out the specials board.

Abbott and Shields sts. ℃ 074031 5899. Reservations recommended. Breakfast A$2.50–A$8 (US$2–US$6.40); lunch A$6.50–A$12 (US$5.20–US$9.60); main courses at dinner A$13–A$24 (US$10–US$19). MC, V. Daily 8:30am–late.

ON THE NORTHERN BEACHES

Colonies MODERN AUSTRALIAN   It may not have the ocean frontage of the grander restaurants along Williams Esplanade, but the veranda of this cheery little aerie upstairs behind a seafront building is still within earshot of the waves. The atmosphere is simple, and the menu includes loads of inexpensive choices, such as pastas, soups, green chicken curry, and seafood. Licensed and BYO.

Upstairs in Paradise Village shopping center, Williams Esplanade, Palm Cove. ℃ 07/4055 3058. Fax 07/4059 1559. www.palmcoveonline.com/colonies. Reservations recommended. Main courses A$16–A$29 (US$13–US$23). AE, DC, MC, V. Daily 10am–10:30pm. Closed mid-Jan to mid-Mar. Bus: 1, 1B, 1X, 2X, or N.

Far Horizons MODERN AUSTRALIAN   You can't quite sink your toes into the sand, but you are just yards from the beach at this pleasant restaurant in the Angsana Resort. The laid-back fine-dining fare includes plenty of fresh seafood—the catch of the day comes with chunky homemade fries and tartar sauce, and there are interesting choices like Vietnamese salad with chargrilled reef fish. The restaurant sometimes sets up tables on the lawn among the palm trees beside the beach. The service is relaxed and friendly, and the crowd is a mix of guests from this and other nearby resorts. On Friday and Saturday night, a guitarist plays in the cocktail bar.

In the Angsana Resort, 1 Veivers Rd. (southern end of Williams Esplanade), Palm Cove. ℃ 07/4055 3000. Reservations recommended. Main courses A$24–A$29 (US$19–US$23). AE, DC, MC, V. Daily 6:30pm–midnight (last orders at 9:30pm). Bus: 1, 1B, 1X, 2X, or N.

CAIRNS AFTER DARK

Pick up a copy of the free entertainment newspaper *Barfly*, published on Thursday, for a guide to the week's after-hours action in Cairns. Top spots recommended by the locals include **Met Bar,** upstairs at 15 Spence St. (℃ 07/4041 0258), which is popular with the 25-to-45 market and features a sophisticated chocolate decor and a cigar lounge. Younger people and backpackers flock to **Gilligan's Bar,** 57–89 Grafton St. (℃ 07/4041 6566), where the 1000-person beer hall doubles as a nightclub with dance floor, DJs, live bands, and sport and music on the giant video screens. The **Hotel Sofitel Reef Casino,** 35–41 Wharf St. (℃ 07/4030 8888), has two levels of blackjack, baccarat, reef routine, roulette, sic-bo, money wheel, paradise pontoon, keno, and slot machines. It's open Monday through Thursday 10am to 4am, and straight through from 10am Friday until 4am Monday. It's closed Good Friday, April 25 (Anzac Day), and December 25. No entry for children under 18.

If you're over 18 but under 35 or so, and it's Saturday night, you may want to take the boat to the DJs or live bands at the **Raging Thunder Beach Bar** on Fitzroy Island (see Fitzroy Island Resort listing above). The Fitzroy Flyer leaves Cairns' Reef Fleet terminal at 4pm and 7pm, and returns at 1am on Sunday for A$15 (US$12). You must book ahead, through **Raging Thunder Adventures** (℃ 07/4030 7907).

3 Port Douglas ✸✸, Daintree & the Cape Tribulation Area

Port Douglas: 67km (42 miles) N of Cairns; Mossman: 19km (12 miles) N of Port Douglas; Daintree: 49km (30 miles) N of Port Douglas; Cape Tribulation: 34km (21 miles) N of Daintree

The tiny fishing village of Port Douglas is where the rainforest meets the reef. Just over an hour's drive from Cairns, through rainforest and along the sea, Port Douglas may be a one-horse town, but stylish shops and seriously trendy restaurants line the main

Port Douglas, Daintree & Cape Tribulation

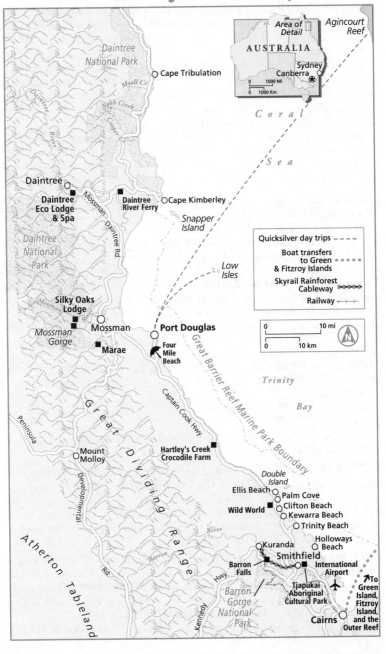

Daintree National Park

Myall Cr.

Cape Tribulation

Noah Creek

Cooper Creek

Daintree River

Coral

Sea

Agincourt Reef

Area of Detail

AUSTRALIA

Sydney
Canberra

0   1000 Mi
0   1000 Km

Daintree

Daintree Eco Lodge & Spa

Daintree River Ferry

Cape Kimberley

Snapper Island

Mossman Rd.

Daintree Rd.

Daintree National Park

Low Isles

Mossman River

Silky Oaks Lodge

Mossman

Mossman Gorge

Marae

Port Douglas

Four Mile Beach

Great Barrier Reef Marine Park Boundary

Trinity

Bay

Quicksilver day trips　－　－　－

Boat transfers
to Green　● ● ● ●
& Fitzroy Islands

Skyrail Rainforest
Cableway

Railway　┼─┼─┼

0   10 mi
0   10 km

Captain Cook Hwy.

Peninsula

Mount Molloy

Hartley's Creek Crocodile Farm

Double Island

Ellis Beach
Palm Cove
Clifton Beach
Wild World
Kewarra Beach
Trinity Beach

River

Barron

Kuranda

Holloways Beach

Smithfield

Barron Falls

International Airport

Tjapukai Aboriginal Cultural Park

Barron Gorge National Park

Kennedy Hwy.

Developmental

Atherton Tableland

Great Dividing Range

Cairns

↗ To Green Island, Fitzroy Island, and the Outer Reef

305

street, and beautiful Four Mile Beach is not to be missed. This is a favorite spot with celebrities big and small—you may find yourself dining next to anyone from Bill Clinton to Kylie Minogue, Sean Penn to the Australian rock band Midnight Oil to a minor soap star.

Travelers often base themselves in "Port," as the locals call it, rather than in Cairns, because they like the rural surroundings, the uncrowded beach, and the absence of tacky development (so far, anyway). Don't think you will be isolated—many reef and rainforest tours originate in Port Douglas, and many of the tours discussed in the Cairns section above pick up from Port Douglas.

Daintree National Park lies just north of Port Douglas; just north of that is Cape Tribulation National Park, another wild tract of rainforest and hilly headlands sweeping down to the sea. Exploring these two national parks is easy on a four-wheel-drive day safari from Port Douglas.

ESSENTIALS

GETTING THERE   Port Douglas is a scenic 65-minute drive from Cairns, in part along a narrow winding road that skirts the coast. Take Sheridan Street north out of the city as it becomes the Captain Cook Highway; follow the signs to Mossman and Mareeba until you reach the Port Douglas turnoff on your right.

One of the most pleasant ways to get to Port Douglas is to take one of the giant **Quicksilver Wavepiercer** ✯ (© 07/4087 2100) catamarans along the coast. They depart Reef Fleet Terminal in Cairns at 8am and Palm Cove jetty at 8:30am, and arrive in Port Douglas at 9:30am. You can also stay onboard and go straight to the Great Barrier Reef for the day for an extra charge (see "Discovering the Great Barrier Reef," below). The cost of the trip from Cairns is A$26 (US $21) one-way, A$39 (US$31) round-trip, half price for kids 4 to 14.

A one-way ticket aboard **Sun Palm Express Coaches** (© 07/4084 2626) to Port Douglas hotels is A$25 (US$20) from the Cairns airport. Fares for children 3 to 14 are half price.

A **taxi** from Cairns runs around A$100 (US$80); call **Black & White Taxis** (© 13 10 08 in Cairns).

There is no train to Port Douglas, and no scheduled air service. A small airport handles light aircraft and helicopter charters.

VISITOR INFORMATION   Contact the **Port Douglas Daintree Tourism Association,** P.O. Box 511, Port Douglas, QLD 4877 (© 07/4099 4588; www.pddt.com.au). The association has no visitor information office in Port Douglas. Instead, visitors should stop into a private tour information and booking center in town. One of the biggest and most centrally located is the **Port Douglas Tourist Information Centre,** 23 Macrossan St. (© 07/4099 5599), open from 7:30am to 6pm daily.

GETTING AROUND   Of the major rental companies, **Avis** (© 07/4099 4331) and **Thrifty** (© 07/4099 5555) have offices in Port Douglas. Check out the local companies, including **Port Douglas Car Rental** (© 07/4099 4988). All rent regular vehicles as well as four-wheel-drives, which you need if you plan to drive to Cape Tribulation. For a taxi, call **Port Douglas Taxis** (© 07/4084 2600).

A good way to get around the town's flat streets is by bike. **Bike 'n' Hike,** 40 Macrossan St. (© 07/4099 4000; www.bikenhike.com.au), is open daily from 8am to 6pm or later and rents a large range of good mountain bikes; prices start at A$11 (US$8.80) for a half-day, A$17 (US$14) for a full day. **Port Douglas Bike Hire,** at the corner of Warner and Wharf streets (© **07/4099 5799**), rents bikes for A$10 (US $8) for a half-day, A$14 (US$11) for a full day. It's open 9am to 5pm daily.

EXPLORING THE REEF & THE RAINFOREST

DISCOVERING THE GREAT BARRIER REEF   Without a doubt, the most glamorous large vessels visiting the Outer Reef are the **Quicksilver Wavepiercers** (© **07/4087 2100**) based in Port Douglas. These ultrasleek, high-speed, air-conditioned 37m (121-ft.) and 46m (151-ft.) catamarans carry 300 or 440 passengers to Agincourt Reef, a ribbon reef 39 nautical miles (72km/45 miles) from shore on the outer edge of the Reef. After the 90-minute trip to the Reef, you tie up at a two-story pontoon, where you spend 3½ hours.

Quicksilver departs Marina Mirage at 10am daily except December 25. The cost for the day is A$180 (US$144) for adults and A$93 (US$74) for kids 4 to 14. Guided snorkel safaris cost A$55 (US$44) per person, and introductory dives cost A$125 (US$100) per person. Qualified divers take a dive-tender boat to make one dive for A$87 (US$70) or two dives for A$129 (US$103) per person, all gear included. Because Quicksilver carries so many passengers, booking snorkel safaris and dives in advance is a good idea.

The dive boat *Poseidon* (see "Diving the Reef," earlier in this chapter) welcomes snorkelers. It presents a Reef ecology talk en route and takes you on a guided snorkel safari. The price of A$145 (US$116) for adults and A$110 (US$88) for children 3 to 12 includes lunch and transfers from Port Douglas hotels.

Snorkeling specialist boat *Wavelength* (© **07/4099 5031;** www.wavelength.com.au) does a full-day trip to the Outer Reef for A$155 (US$124) for adults, A$105 (US$84) for children 2 to 12, A$465 (US$372) for a family of four. The trip visits three different snorkel sites each day and incorporates a guided snorkel tour and a reef presentation by a marine biologist. It carries up to 30 passengers and includes snorkel gear, sunsuits, lunch, and transfers from your hotel. Both beginners and experienced snorkelers will like this trip. It departs daily at 8:15am from the Wavelength jetty, Wharf Street.

Another way to spend a pleasant day on the Great Barrier Reef, closer to shore, is to visit the **Low Isles,** 15km (9½ miles) northeast of Port Douglas. The isles are 1.5-hectare (3¾-acre) coral-cay specks of lush vegetation surrounded by white sand and 22 hectares (54 acres) of coral—which is what makes them so appealing. The coral is not quite as good as the outer Reef's, but the fish life is rich, and the proximity makes for a relaxing day.

The trip aboard the 30m (98-ft.) luxury sailing catamaran *Wavedancer* (© **07/4087 2100**), operated by Quicksilver, is A$124 (US$99) for adults, A$65 (US$52) for kids 4 to 14, and A$313 (US$250) for families. You have the option of making an introductory scuba dive for an extra A$106 (US$85) per person. The Wavepiercer departs Reef Fleet Terminal in Cairns at 8am and Palm Cove Jetty on the northern beaches at 8:30am to connect with Wavedancer departures from Port Douglas at 10am. Prices include hotel pickup.

EXPLORING DAINTREE NATIONAL PARK & CAPE TRIBULATION   The World Heritage–listed Daintree Rain Forest has remained largely unchanged over the past 110 million years. It is now home to rare plants that provide key links in the evolution story. In the 56,000-hectare (138,320-acre) **Daintree National Park,** you will find cycads, dinosaur trees, fan palms, giant strangler figs, and epiphytes like the basket fern, staghorn, and elkhorn. Nighttime croc-spotting tours on the Daintree River vie for popularity with early-morning cruises to see the rich bird life. Pythons, lizards, frogs, and electric-blue Ulysses butterflies attract photographers, and sport fishermen come here to do battle with big barramundi.

Just about everyone who visits Port Douglas takes a guided four-wheel-drive day trip into the beautiful Daintree and Cape Tribulation rainforests. Although they are two separate national parks, the forests merge into one.

You can rent a four-wheel-drive and explore on your own, but you won't understand much about what you are seeing unless you have a guide to explain it. Most companies basically cover the same territory and sights, including a 1-hour Daintree River cruise to spot crocs, a visit to the lovely Marrdja Botanical Walk, a stroll along an isolated beach, lunch at a pretty spot somewhere in the forest, and a visit to Mossman Gorge. Some tours also go to the picturesque Bloomfield Falls in Cape Tribulation National Park. Expect to pay about A$130 (US$104) per adult and about A$90 (US$72) per child. Trips that include Bloomfield Falls cost more. A company that provides an excellent, gently adventurous alternative is Pete Baxendell's **Heritage & Interpretive Tours** (© **07/4098 7897**; www.nqhit.com.au). On a daylong bushwalk into a tract of privately owned rainforest with Pete, a naturalist and professional tour guide, you taste green ants (be brave—it's quite an experience) and other native "bush tucker," discover how to rustle up a toothbrush from a shrub if you forgot to pack yours, learn about bush medicine and the wildlife around you, and clamber up a stream to a waterfall. He takes a maximum of six people at a time. Lunch and Port Douglas pickups are included in the price of A$110 (US$88) for adults and A$85 (US$68) for children. Walks run Tuesday and Saturday, leaving Port at 8:30am.

You can **charter** Pete and his 4WD on other days for day bushwalks for A$175 (US$140) per person (minimum of two) or for a "go anywhere" adventure for A$590 (US$472) per day. Pickups from the northern beaches cost A$45 (US$36) extra for bushwalks, but are included in the price for "go anywhere" charters. The charter prices compare favorably to a regular Daintree four-wheel-drive tour if there are three or more of you—and you get a tailored itinerary, Pete's knowledge, and the vehicle all to yourself. He often takes charter customers inland to Outback gold mining ghost towns, or north to tiny Cooktown, which boasts an excellent museum devoted to Australia's "discoverer," Capt. James Cook. If you have 2 days, he can take you farther west to see Aboriginal rock art and stay at an upscale tented camp, or to the amazing Undara Lava Tubes.

Other established operators are **Trek North Safaris** (© **07/4051 4328**) and **BTS Tours** (© **07/4099 5665**). As is the case in most tourist hot spots, some tour operators battle fiercely to pay tour desks the highest commission to recommend their tours, even though those tours may not necessarily be the best for your needs. Take tour desks' recommendations with a grain of salt, and ask other travelers for their recommendations. You may not see too much wildlife—rainforest animals are shy, camouflaged, nocturnal, or all three! Most four-wheel-drive tours will pick you up in Port Douglas at no charge; there is usually a small fee from Cairns and the northern beaches. Floods and swollen creeks can quash your plans to explore the Daintree in the Wet season (Dec–Mar or Apr), so keep your plans flexible.

If your chosen safari does not visit **Mossman Gorge,** 21km (13 miles) northwest of Port Douglas near the sugar town of Mossman, try to get there under your own steam. The gushing river tumbling over boulders, and the short forest walks are magical. (Don't climb on the rocks or enter the river, because strong currents are extremely dangerous and have claimed at least one life in recent years.)

Most four-wheel-drive Daintree tours include a 1-hour cruise on the **Daintree River** ⚓, but if yours does not, or you want to spend more time on the river, cruises are available on a variety of boats, ranging from open-sided "river trains" to small fishing boats. One of the best is with **Dan Irby's Mangrove Adventures** ⚓ (© **07/4090 7017;** www.mangroveadventures.com.au), whose small open boat can get up side creeks the bigger boats can't. Originally from Oklahoma, Dan has been in Australia for 30 years and is extremely knowledgeable about the wildlife and habitat. He takes no more than 10 people at a time on 2-, 3-, and 4-hour cruises. It is very important to make advance reservations with Dan (at least 24 hr. ahead, if possible) to ensure seats and to determine departure times. Chances are you will spot lots of fascinating wildlife on his 2-hour night cruise, but even if you don't, it's worth it just to see the stars! A 2-hour trip costs A$45 (US$36). Night trips depart from Daintree Eco Lodge, 20 Mossman Daintree Rd., 4km (2½ miles) south of Daintree village; day trips leave from the public jetty next to the Daintree River ferry crossing. You can combine both, taking an afternoon tour, followed by a 45-minute break for a snack at Daintree Eco Lodge, then the night tour. Take the Captain Cook Highway north to Mossman, where it becomes the Mossman Daintree Road, and follow it for 24km (15 miles) to the signposted turnoff for the ferry on your right. The ferry is 5km (3 miles) from the turnoff. You'll need a car to get there.

Birders love the Wet Tropics rainforests of which the Daintree and Cape Tribulation national parks are part. More than half of Australia's bird species have been recorded within 200km (120 miles) of this area. **Fine Feather Tours** (© **07/4094 1199;** www.finefeathertours.com.au) has a full-day bird-watching safari through the Wet Tropics to the edge of the Outback for A$205 (US$164), an afternoon cruise on the Daintree River for A$145 (US$116), and other tours.

Rainforest Habitat wildlife sanctuary (© **07/4099 3235;** www.rainforesthabitat. com.au) is a great place to see the animals that are too shy to be spotted in the wild. Here, 180 animal species from the Wet Tropics are in one place for you to see up close. You can see saltwater and freshwater crocodiles, hand-feed kangaroos, and have your photo taken beside (but not holding) a koala (10–11am and 3–4pm for the cost of a donation). The highlight is the walk-through aviary, which houses more than 100 Wet Tropics bird species, including cassowaries. You'll get the most out of your visit if you take one of the excellent free guided tours that leave every half-hour from 9am to 3pm. Rainforest Habitat is on Port Douglas Road at the turnoff from the Captain Cook Highway. Open daily (except Dec 25) from 8am to 5:30pm (last entry at 4:30pm). Admission is A$28 (US$22) for adults, A$14 (US$11) for kids 4 to 14. Between 8am and 11am, the park serves a champagne buffet breakfast for A$39 (US$31) for adults and A$20 (US$16) for kids, including admission. From July to October, you can experience Habitat After Dark, an evening tour that includes dinner and entertainment. It costs A$49 (US$39) adults and A$29 (US$23) kids. Allow at least 2 hours here.

Tips **Drat Those Aussie Mozzies!**

"Mozzies," as Aussies call mosquitoes, love the rainforest as much as people do, so throw some insect repellent in your day pack when touring the Daintree and Cape Tribulation. *Another tip:* Wear light-colored clothing, because mosquitoes are attracted to dark clothing.

DISCOVERING ABORIGINAL CULTURE   Members of the native KuKu-Yalanji tribe will teach you about bush medicines and food, Dreamtime legends, and the sacred sites their families have called home for tens of thousands of years. **KuKu-Yalanji Dreamtime Walks** ⚜ (© 07/4098 2595; www.yalanji.com.au) offers a guided walk through the rainforest to see cave paintings and visit "special sites"; the tour is followed by a Dreamtime story over billy tea and damper in a bark warun (shelter). You can buy artifacts from the tribe's information center, gift shop, and art gallery. Walks run for either 30 or 90 minutes. The 90-minute tours depart Monday through Friday at 10am, noon, and 2pm from the Kuku-Yalanji community, on the road to Mossman Gorge (1km/½ mile before you reach the Gorge parking lot). Short walks leave at 9am, 11am, 1pm and 3pm daily. Tours cost A$20 (US$16) for adults and A$13 (US$10) for children for 90 minutes; A$11 (US$8.80) adults and A$7 (US$5.60) children for 30 minutes.

Hazel Douglas of **Native Guide Safari Tours** ⚜ (© 07/4098 2206; www.nativeguidesafaritours.com.au) runs four-wheel-drive tours of the rainforest from an Aboriginal perspective. Hazel is a full-blooded Aboriginal who had a tribal upbringing in the Daintree. She imparts her traditional knowledge of plants, animals, Dreamtime myths, and Aboriginal history on a full-day tour departing at 9:15am from your Port Douglas hotel. Passengers from Cairns transfer on the Quicksilver catamaran and return either by coach (northern beaches) or catamaran (Cairns). The trip costs A$130 (US$104) for adults and A$80 (US$64) for children 3 to 14 from Port Douglas, and A$10 (US$8) extra from Cairns or the northern beaches. Charter and half-day tours are available.

MORE TO SEE & DO

Some companies in Cairns that offer outdoor activities will pick up from Port Douglas hotels. See "White-Water Rafting & Other Thrills," in the Cairns section earlier in this chapter for details.

The best outdoor activity in Port Douglas, however, is to do absolutely nothing on spectacular **Four Mile Beach** ⚜⚜. From May through September, the water is stinger-free. From October through April, swim in the stinger safety net. **Extra Action Water Sports** (© 07/4099 3175) offers parasailing, jet-skiing, and tube rides on Four Mile Beach. A half-hour on a jet ski or parafly is A$70 (US$56) solo or A$90 (US$72) tandem. The booking office is at the end of the jetty on the Port Douglas slipway.

Visitor greens fees at the championship **Sheraton Mirage** golf course on Port Douglas Road are A$145 (US$116) for 18 holes or A$85 (US$68) for 9 holes, including a cart. Club rental costs A$38 to A$60 (US$30–US$48). Whacking a ball on the hotel's aquatic driving range costs A$6.50 (US$5.20) for a bucket of 25 balls, A$13 (US$10) for 50 balls, plus A$2.15 (US$1.70) for club rental. Contact the **Pro Shop** (© 07/4099 5537).

Mowbray Valley Trail Rides (© 07/4099 3268), located 13km (8 miles) inland from Port Douglas, offers 2-hour horseback rides for A$88 (US$70). Half-day rides through rainforest and sugar-cane fields to Collards Falls, or to a swimming hole in the Hidden Valley, cost A$95 (US$76), including a barbecue lunch. It also runs full-day trips along the mountainous Bump Track (weather permitting), followed by a dip in a rainforest pool and barbecue lunch at Mowbray Falls for A$130 (US$104). Prices include transfers from your Port Douglas accommodations. Transfers from Cairns are A$25 (US$20) per person. **Wonga Beach Equestrian Centre** (© 07/4098 7583) does 3-hour rides through the rainforest and along Wonga Beach, 35 minutes north of Port Douglas, for A$89 (US$71) adults and A$79 (US$63) children, plus A$9 (US$7.20) per person for insurance. Transfers from Port Douglas are included. Rides start at 8:30am and 3pm.

Bike 'n' Hike (© **07/4099 4000;** www.bikenhike.com.au) takes small groups biking, hiking, and swimming in natural lagoons in the Mowbray Valley in the rainforest near Port Douglas. You don't need to be a strong cyclist to take

> ### The Secret of the Seasons
>
> High season in Port Douglas is roughly June 1 through October 31.

part, but you must be over 11. A half-day tour costs A$88 (US$70), including pickup from your Port Douglas hotel, a 27-speed mountain bike, helmet, gloves, backpack, snack, and drinks.

Every Sunday from 7:30am to 1pm, a colorful handicrafts and fresh food market sets up on the lawns under the mango trees beside Dickson Inlet at the end of Macrossan Street. Stalls offer everything from foot massages to fresh coconut milk. While you're here, take a peek, or attend a nondenominational service inside the pretty timber St. Mary's by the Sea church.

WHERE TO STAY

Port Douglas Accommodation Holiday Rentals (© **1800/645 566** in Australia, or 07/4099 4488; www.portdouglasaccom.com.au) has a wide range of apartments and homes for rent.

VERY EXPENSIVE

Sheraton Mirage Port Douglas ★★★   One of Australia's most luxurious properties, this low-rise Sheraton has 2 hectares (5 acres) of saltwater pools and a championship Peter Thomson–designed 18-hole golf course. It is a bit too far from Port's main street by foot, but a free shuttle runs from 9am to 6pm to the golf course's country club and health center, to Marina Mirage shopping center, and into town. All the rooms are large and light-filled, and the resort has undergone extensive refurbishment in the past year, with new color schemes, furniture, and artwork, and extras like ministereo systems. All rooms have minibars, PlayStations, and Internet access. You might fancy upgrading to a Mirage room with a corner Jacuzzi and king-size beds, but I thought the standard rooms just fine. The Sheraton handles rental of the 101 privately owned two-, three-, and four-bedroom luxury villas with golf course, garden, or sea views; the decor varies, but each has a kitchenette, a Jacuzzi, and two bathrooms.

Davidson St. (off Port Douglas Rd.), Port Douglas, QLD 4877. © **1800/073 535** in Australia; 800/325-3535 in the U.S. and Canada; 00800/325 353535 in the U.K., Ireland, and New Zealand; or 07/4099 5888. Fax 07/4099 4424, or Starwood Hotels reservation fax 07/4099 5398. www.sheraton-mirage.com.au. 394 units (including 101 villas). A$619–A$830 (US$495–US$664) double; A$2,895 (US$2,316) 1- or 2-bedroom suite; A$950–A$1,250 (US$760–US$1,000) 2-, 3-, or 4-bedroom villa. Extra person A$70 (US$56). Children under 17 stay free in parent's room with existing bedding. Discounts available. AE, DC, MC, V. Free valet and self-parking. Helicopter transfers available. **Amenities:** 3 restaurants; 2 bars; 25m (82-ft.) outdoor lap pool; 18-hole championship golf course w/country club and pro shop, aquatic driving range (w/targets in a lake), putting green, and golf clinics; 9 lit tennis courts; health club; spa; Jacuzzi; bike rental; daily day care for kids under 5 and kids' club for children 5–15 during school vacations (fee); concierge; tour desk; car-rental desk; business center (fee for Internet access); salon; 24-hr. room service; massage; babysitting; dry cleaning; nonsmoking rooms. *In room:* A/C, TV, dataport, coffeemaker, hair dryer, iron, safe.

EXPENSIVE

Port Douglas Peninsula Boutique Hotel ★★   Built in 1999 over three levels, this intimate studio apartment hotel fronting Four Mile Beach is one of the nicest places to stay in town. Every apartment features an open-plan living room/bedroom, a contemporary kitchenette (with microwave and dishwasher), and a groovy bathroom boasting a giant double tub (or Jacuzzi, in some units). Corner apartments are a little bigger. The decor is a stylish mélange of terra cotta, mosaic tiles, granite, and wicker, with classy extra touches like a CD player and boxed Twining's teas. Most units have great beach views from the roomy balcony or patio; a few look onto the green and mauve complex of petite Art Deco-ish pools, waterfalls, hot and cold Jacuzzis, and sun deck rising and falling on several levels. A 2-minute walk brings you to the main street.

9–13 The Esplanade, Port Douglas, QLD 4877. ℂ **1800/676 674** in Australia, or 07/4099 9100. Fax 07/4099 5440. www.peninsulahotel.com.au. 34 units. A$340–A$460 (US$272–US$368) double. Rates include full breakfast and round-trip transfers from Cairns airport. Ask about packages. AE, DC, MC, V. Free covered parking. Children under 15 not accepted. **Amenities:** Restaurant; small bar; large outdoor pool; hot and cold Jacuzzis; bike rental; tour desk; free guest laundry; laundry service; dry cleaning. *In room:* A/C, TV/VCR, dataport, kitchenette, coffeemaker, hair dryer, iron, safe.

MODERATE

Archipelago Studio Apartments ⭐
You won't find a friendlier or more convenient place to stay in Port Douglas than these apartments, 10 seconds from the beach and less than 10 minutes' walk from town. Hosts Wolfgang Klein and Christel Bader are eager to help with tour bookings and to give advice—and they also speak fluent German, conversational French, and some Spanish. The apartments are on the small side (most suit only three people, at the most), but all are well cared for and were refurbished in 2001. You can opt for a tiny Garden apartment with a patio; Balcony and Seaview apartments are a bit larger and have private balconies. Seaview apartments are quite roomy, and have side views of Four Mile Beach. Towels are changed daily and linen weekly, but general housekeeping service will cost A$20 (US$16) extra. There's no elevator and no porter, so be prepared to carry your luggage upstairs.

72 Macrossan St., Port Douglas, QLD 4877. ℂ **07/4099 5387.** Fax 07/4099 4847. www.archipelago.com.au. 21 units (all with shower only). High season (June–Oct) A$120–A$205 (US$96–A$164) double; low season A$105–A$175 (US$84–US$140) double. Additional person A$20 (US$16). 3-night minimum. MC, V. Free covered parking. Children under 6 not accepted. **Amenities:** Outdoor saltwater pool; nearby golf course; 6 nearby lit tennis courts; access to nearby health club; Jacuzzi; tour desk; coin-op laundry; laundry service; nonsmoking rooms. *In room:* A/C, TV, kitchenette, fridge, coffeemaker, hair dryer.

Port Douglas Retreat
This well-kept two-story studio apartment complex on a quiet street, featuring the white-battened balconies of the Queenslander architectural style, is a good value. Even some of the ritzier places in town can't boast its lagoonlike saltwater pool, surrounded by dense jungle and wrapped by an ample shady sun deck that cries out to be lounged on with a good book and a cool drink. The apartments are not enormous, but they're fashionably furnished with terra-cotta tile floors, wrought-iron beds, cane seating, and colorful bedcovers. All have large furnished balconies or patios looking into tropical gardens; some on the ground floor open onto the common-area boardwalk, so you might want to ask for a first-floor (second-story) unit. The town and beach are 5 minutes walk away. No smoking indoors.

The newer **Cayman Villas** (www.caymanvillas.com.au) next door are under the same management but are more expensive.

31–33 Mowbray St. (at Mudlo St.), Port Douglas, QLD 4877. ℂ **07/4099 5053.** Fax 07/4099 5033. www.portdouglas retreat.com.au. 36 units (all with shower only). High season (June–Oct) A$149 (US$119) double; low season (Nov–May) A$110 (US$88) double. Crib A$5.50 (US$4.40) per night. Minimum 3-night stay. AE, MC, V. Secure covered parking. **Amenities:** Outdoor saltwater pool; tour desk; car-rental desk; coin-op laundry; nonsmoking rooms. *In room:* A/C, TV w/free movies, kitchenette, iron.

INEXPENSIVE

Port O'Call Lodge   There's a nice communal feeling to this modest motel on a sub-urban street a 10-minute walk from town. Backpackers, families, and travelers on a budget seem to treat it like a second home, swapping stories as they cook a meal in the communal kitchen and dining room. The rooms are light, cool, and fresh with tile floors, loads of luggage and bench space, and small patios. The compact bathrooms are efficiently laid out with old but neat fixtures (bring your own hair dryer). Double rooms have a TV, clock radio, self-serve tea and coffee facilities, and minifridge. The hostel rooms have private bathrooms and no more than five beds or bunks in each. A 24-bed bunkhouse has facilities for travelers with disabilities. New double and quad rooms were added in 2004. At night the lively poolside Port O'Call Bistro is the place to be. Other features include free board games, a pay phone, Internet access, and a kiosk selling refreshments.

Port St. at Craven Close, Port Douglas, QLD 4877. © **1800/892 800** in Australia, or 07/4099 5422. Fax 07/4099 5495. www.portocall.com.au. 28 units (all with shower only). High season (Easter, May–Oct, Dec 25) A$59–A$109 (US$47–US$87) double; low season A$59–A$89 (US$47–US$71) double. Extra person A$15 (US$12). Hostel quad rooms A$27 (US$22) YHA/Hostelling International members, or A$28 (US$22) nonmembers; bunkhouse A$22 (US$18) YHA/Hostelling International members, A$23 (US$18) nonmembers. Children under 3 stay free in parent's room. MC, V. Free once-daily shuttle to and from Cairns and the airport Mon–Sat. Free parking. Bus: 1X (stop at front door). **Amenities:** Restaurant (see "Where to Dine in Port Douglas," below); outdoor pool; 3 golf courses nearby; access to nearby health club; bike rental; tour desk; coin-op laundry; nonsmoking rooms. *In room:* A/C, TV, safe.

A LUXURY B&B HIDEAWAY IN THE COUNTRY

Marae ★★   John and Pam Burden's architecturally stunning timber home, on a rural hillside 15km (9½ miles) north of Port Douglas, is a glamorous and restful retreat. The rustic-meets-sleek contemporary bedrooms have white mosquito nets and smart linens on king-size beds, and elegant bathrooms. The garden room opens onto a plunge pool overlooking the valley, and there is also a lap pool. Wallabies and bandi-coots (small marsupials) feed in the garden, kingfishers and honeyeaters use the pools, and butterflies are everywhere. A delicious tropical breakfast is served on the west deck in the company of a flock of red-browed finches and peaceful doves. Afterward you can wander the rainforest trails of Mossman Gorge, just a few miles away.

Lot 1, Chook's Ridge, Shannonvale (P.O. Box 133, Port Douglas, QLD 4877). © 07/4098 4900. Fax 07/4098 4099. www.marae.com.au. 3 units (2 with shower only). A$150 (US$120) double. 2-night minimum. Rates include full breakfast. MC, V. Covered parking. From Port Douglas, take Captain Cook Hwy. toward Mossman for 10km (6¼ miles), go left onto Mt. Molloy turnoff for 1km (½ mile), then right onto Ponzo Rd. for 2km (1¼ miles); Chook's Ridge is on your left. Children under 13 not accepted. **Amenities:** Outdoor plunge pool; nearby golf courses; tour desk; laundry service; nonsmoking rooms. *In room:* A/C, TV, hair dryer.

RAINFOREST HIDEAWAYS

Silky Oaks Lodge & Healing Waters Spa ★★   Relax in the hammock on your veranda and listen to the waters of the Mossman River gushing through the rainfor-est. Stroll down for a swim—no crocs here. Despite its popularity, this luxury resort tucked away at the edge of cane fields exudes a restful feeling. Treehouses are scattered through the rainforest and gardens, each tucked into its own private part of the gar-dens and rainforest; the five Riverhouses overlook the river frontage, and all have Jacuzzis. Each unit has timber floors, attractive furnishings, a king-size bed, bathrobes, a CD player—but no TV—and a double hammock to string up. The resort's most recent renovation, completed in 2001, included the addition of the Healing Waters Day Spa, where I had the best facial of my life. Last year, the spa tripled in size (no doubt word of how good it is has got out), and the central lodge and **Treehouse Restaurant** were given a fresh, contemporary new look. Rates include guided nature walks, mountain bikes, and nature slide shows, and there is a daily activities program. To reach Mossman Gorge's lovely walking trails, across the river, you'll need a car.

Finlayvale Rd., Mossman, 7km (4½ miles) west of Mossman township; 27km (17 miles) from Port Douglas (c/o Voyages, G.P.O. Box 3589, Sydney, NSW 2001). © **1300/134 044** in Australia, or 02/8296 8010 (Sydney reservations office). Fax 02/9299 2477 (Sydney reservations office) or 07/4098 1983 (lodge). www.voyages.com. 50 units. A$700–A$880 (US$560–US$704) double. Extra person A$150 (US$120). Rates include continental breakfast, 4-course dinner, morning and afternoon shuttle from Port Douglas. Ask about packages. AE, DC, MC, V. Town-car transfers A$140 (US$112) per car one-way from Cairns city or airport; stretch limousine transfers A$185 (US$148). Take Captain Cook Hwy. to Mossman, where it becomes the Mossman-Daintree Rd.; follow approximately 3.5km (2¼ miles) past Mossman and turn left onto Finlayvale Rd. at the small white-on-blue SILKY OAKS sign. Children under 10 not accepted. **Amenities:** Restaurant; bar; outdoor pool; lit tennis court; spa; tour desk; coin-op laundry; laundry service. *In room:* A/C, ceiling fans, minibar, coffeemaker, hair dryer, iron.

Thala Beach Lodge ★★ "Where are the walls?" may be your first question on arriving at this Balinese-style luxury hideaway in the rainforest outside Port Douglas. The reception area and lobby are open, to stunning effect. From the elevated restaurant, the impact is even greater, with sweeping views from the Daintree to Cape Grafton, south of Cairns. Thala (pronounced *Ta*-la) Beach is on a 59-hectare (146-acre) private peninsula, bordered on three sides by private beaches and coves. Owners Rob and Oonagh Prettejohn also own the well-established Kewarra Beach Resort on Cairns's northern beaches. Thala Beach opened in 1998, taking its inspiration from the flora and fauna of the World Heritage area that surrounds it. The secluded bungalows are spacious and comfortable, with timber-paneled walls and your choice of king-size or twin beds. All are built on high poles in the trees, where dazzling lorikeets and small red-faced flying foxes feed on blossoms and hang contentedly from the branches. The 16 Coral Sea bungalows overlook the ocean; the rest have forest and mountain views. Some of the bungalows are a bit of a hike from the public areas, but I thought it was a small price to pay for the privacy and the rainforest setting.

16km (10 miles) south of Port Douglas (P.O. Box 199, Smithfield, Cairns, QLD 4878). © **1800/251 958** in Australia (Small Luxury Hotels of the World), or 07/4098 5700 (lodge). Fax 07/4098 5837. www.slh.com/thala. 85 units. A$336–A$533 (US$269–US$426) double. AE, DC, MC, V. Free valet parking. Transfers from Cairns A$26 (US$21) per person. **Amenities:** Restaurant; bar; 2 outdoor pools; nearby golf course; tour desk. *In room:* A/C, ceiling fans, TV, minibar, coffeemaker, hair dryer, iron, safe.

A SPA IN THE RAINFOREST

Daintree Eco Lodge & Spa ★ Check in and head straight for the Daintree Spa. Here you can relax and soak up all kinds of pampering treatments, including the 90-minute, A$195 (US$156) Walbul-Walbul body treatment, in which you are wrapped in mud as you recline on a magnificent carved timber "wet bed," and the Yiri Jalaymba rain therapy treatment. It's bliss.

A multiple award winner for "green tourism," this lodge in the primeval forest books only a small number of guests. Don't think "eco" means sacrificing creature comforts: The large rooms, refurbished in 2000, boast marble floors, timber and bamboo furniture, and tiled bathrooms with robes. Five have Jacuzzis on their screened balconies.

You can join a yoga or Ki (based on Japanese aikido) session, laze by the small solar-heated pool, walk rainforest trails, join members of the local Aboriginal Kuku tribe on a bush tucker and native medicine stroll, or take a four-wheel-drive day trip to modern-day Aboriginal communities. The **Bilngkumu Restaurant** overlooks a lily pond and serves food with a gourmet bush-tucker slant. The lodge is 98km (61 miles) north of Cairns and 40km (25 miles) north of Port Douglas.

20 Daintree Rd. (4km/2½ miles south of Daintree village), Daintree, QLD 4873. © 1800/808 010 in Australia, or 07/4098 6100. Fax 07/4098 6200. www.daintree-ecolodge.com.au. 15 units (10 with shower only). A$530–A$580 (US$424–US$464) double. Extra person A$55 (US$44). Rates include full breakfast. Ask about packages. AE, DC, MC, V. Once-a-day scheduled minibus service to or from Mossman A$20 (US$16), to or from Port Douglas hotels A$55 (US$40), to or from Cairns hotels or Cairns airport A$75 (US$60) per person, one-way. On-call transfers by car A$40 (US$32) per person from Mossman, A$143 (US$114) per car from Port Douglas, A$165 (US$132) per car from Cairns, one-way. Stretch limousine transfers A$255 (US$204) per car one-way. Take Captain Cook Hwy. north to Mossman, where it becomes the Mossman-Daintree Rd.; follow to lodge. The road is paved all the way. No children under 7. Amenities: Restaurant; pool; spa; tour desk; laundry service. In room: A/C, TV, minibar, coffeemaker, hair dryer.

WHERE TO DINE IN PORT DOUGLAS

Nautilus ★★ TROPICAL/SEAFOOD   Bill and Hillary Clinton dined here during a visit Down Under, and by all accounts loved it. So did I. The restaurant, which has been keeping the locals happy since 1953, is set under the palm trees and stars, with a clever seating plan and unusual high-backed chairs that create a wonderfully intimate atmosphere. Local produce and seafood are the mainstays of the menu, which features such delights as deep-fried whole coral trout served with green papaya and bean-sprout salad; and Gulf mud crab, wok-steamed in Tom Yum coconut sauce with vanilla and coconut jasmine rice. Or you may prefer oven roasted Peking style duck, slow-roasted lamb rack, or one of the many other nonseafood choices.

17 Murphy St. (entry also from Macrossan St.), Port Douglas. © 07/4099 5330. www.nautilus-restaurant.com.au. Reservations recommended. Main courses A$38–A$45 (US$30–US$36). AE, DC, MC, V. Daily 5:30–10:30pm or until the last diners leave. Closed Feb. Children under 8 not accepted.

Port O'Call Bistro *Kids* CAFE/BISTRO   Locals patronize this poolside bistro and bar at the Port O'Call Lodge (p. 313) almost as often as guests do, because it offers good, honest food like lamb shanks and steaks in hearty portions at painless prices. The atmosphere is fun and friendly. There are pasta, curry and roast nights, and every night you can try one of the chef's blackboard surprises, including local beef and seafood. There are kids' meals as well as burgers, nachos, and pastas to appeal to everyone.

In the Port O'Call Lodge, Port St. at Craven Close. © 07/4099 5422. Main courses A$12–A$20 (US$9.60–US$16). MC, V. Daily 6pm–midnight.

Salsa Bar & Grill ★★ *Kids* MODERN/TROPICAL   This trendy restaurant, in a lovely timber Queenslander with wraparound verandas, has terrific food, great prices, and lively, fun service. Here you can choose simple fare such as gnocchi, Caesar salad, or fantastic spring rolls, or such mouthwatering delights as whitebait and crab fritters with wasabi aioli, wakame and beet salad; or pan-fried barramundi with tagliatelle, tomato vinaigrette, corn, and prosciutto salsa. Even if you usually resist dessert, don't. The buttermilk-and-almond-nougat panna cotta is to die for, and the chocolate Cointreau soufflé is a must. On Sunday, a salsa band plays and the place really gets jumping.

26 Wharf St. (at Warner St.). © 07/4099 4922. www.salsa-port-douglas.com.au. Reservations required. Main courses A$20–A$25 (US$16–US$20). AE, DC, MC, V. Mon–Sat 10am–midnight; Sun 8am–midnight.

4 The North Coast: Mission Beach ★★, Townsville & the Islands

For years the lovely town of **Mission Beach** was a well-kept secret. Farmers retired here; then those who liked to drop out and chill out discovered it; today, it's a small, prosperous, stunningly pretty rainforest town. The beach here is one of the most beautiful in Australia, a long white strip fringed with dense tangled vine forests, the only surviving lowlands rainforest in the Australian tropics. It is also one of the least crowded and least spoiled, so clever has Mission Beach been at staying out of sight, out of mind, and off the tourist trail.

The nearby **Tully River** is white-water-rafting heaven for thrill-seekers. You can also bungee jump and tandem sky dive when you're not rushing down the rapids, flanked by lush rainforest.

From Mission Beach it's a short ferry ride to **Dunk Island,** a large resort island that welcomes day-trippers. You can even sea kayak here from the mainland. Mission Beach is closer to the Great Barrier Reef than any other point along the coast—just an hour—and cruise boats depart daily from the jetty, stopping en route at Dunk Island.

A few hours' drive south brings you to the city of **Townsville,** also a gateway to the Great Barrier Reef, but more important to visitors as a gateway to Magnetic Island, a picturesque, laid-back haven for hikers and watersports enthusiasts.

MISSION BEACH: THE CASSOWARY COAST
140km (87 miles) S of Cairns; 240km (149 miles) N of Townsville

Tucked away off the Bruce Highway, the township of Mission Beach has managed to duck the tourist hordes. It's actually a conglomeration of four beachfront towns: South Mission Beach, Wongaling Beach, Mission Beach proper, and Bingil Bay. Most commercial activity centers on the small nucleus of shops and businesses at Mission Beach proper. It's so isolated that signs on the way into town warn you to watch out for ultrashy cassowaries emerging from the jungle to cross the road. Dense rainforest hides the town from view until you round the corner to Mission Beach proper and discover appealing hotels, neat shops, and smart little restaurants. Just through the trees is the fabulous beach. A mile or so north of the main settlement of Mission Beach is Clump Point Jetty.

ESSENTIALS
GETTING THERE   From Cairns, follow the Bruce Highway south. The Mission Beach turnoff is at the tiny town of El Arish, about 15km (9½ miles) north of Tully. Mission Beach is 25km (16 miles) off the highway. It's a 90-minute trip from Cairns. If you're coming from Townsville, a turnoff just north of Tully leads 18km (11 miles) to South Mission Beach.

Mission Beach Connections (© 07/4059 2709) operates door-to-door shuttles three times a day from Cairns and Cairns Airport for A$32 (US$26) or A$38 (US$30) adults and A$16/A$19 (US$13/US$15) children, and from the northern beaches for A$43 (US$34) adults and A$22 (US$18) children.

Greyhound Australia (© 13 14 99 in Australia) coaches stop in Mission Beach proper (not South Mission Beach) several times daily on the Cairns-Brisbane-Cairns runs. The fare is A$25 (US$20) from Cairns, A$195 (US$156) for the 26-hour-plus trip from Brisbane.

Five **trains** a week on the Cairns-Brisbane-Cairns route serve the nearest station, Tully, about 20km (13 miles) away. One-way travel from Cairns on the Tilt Train costs A$43 (US$34) for the 2-hour, 50-minute journey. From Brisbane, fares range from A$183 (US$146) in an economy seat to A$345 (US$276) for a first-class sleeper on the *Sunlander.* For more information, call Queensland Rail's long-distance division, **Traveltrain** (© 13 22 32 in Australia, or 07/3235 1122; www.traveltrain.qr.com.au). A taxi from Tully to Mission Beach with **Supreme Taxis** (© 07/4068 3937) is about A$40 (US$32).

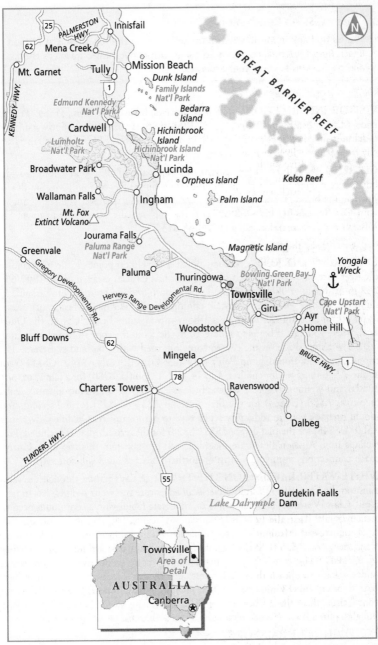

25
PALMERSTON HWY.
Innisfail
62
Mena Creek
Mt. Garnet
Tully
KENNEDY HWY.
Mission Beach
Dunk Island
Family Islands Nat'l Park
Edmund Kennedy Nat'l Park
Bedarra Island
Cardwell
Hichinbrook Island
Lumholtz Nat'l Park
Hichinbrook Island Nat'l Park
Broadwater Park
Lucinda
Orpheus Island
Wallaman Falls
Ingham
Palm Island
Mt. Fox Extinct Volcano
Jourama Falls
Paluma Range Nat'l Park
Magnetic Island
Greenvale
Gregory Developmental Rd.
Paluma
Thuringowa
Herveys Range Developmental Rd.
Bowling Green Bay Nat'l Park
Yongala Wreck
Townsville
Giru
Cape Upstart Nat'l Park
Woodstock
Ayr
Home Hill
Bluff Downs
62
Mingela
BRUCE HWY.
1
78
Charters Towers
Ravenswood
Dalbeg
FLINDERS HWY.
55
Burdekin Faalls Dam
Lake Dalrymple

GREAT BARRIER REEF
Kelso Reef

Townsville
Area of Detail
AUSTRALIA
Canberra

Tips **Mission Beach Money Matters**

There's no bank in Mission Beach; the only ATM in the township is at Mission Beach Resort, Wongaling Beach, so come with enough cash, traveler's checks, and credit cards to cover your expenses.

VISITOR INFORMATION   The **Mission Beach Visitor Centre,** Porters Promenade, Mission Beach, QLD 4852 (© 07/4068 7099; fax 07/4068 7066; www.mission beachtourism.com), is at the northern end of town. It's open Monday through Saturday from 9am to 5pm, and Sunday from 9am to 4pm.

GETTING AROUND   **Trans North Bus & Coach** (© 07/4068 7400) provides bus service linking the beach communities from Bingal Bay to South Mission Beach. Just flag the bus down outside your accommodations or wherever you see it. **Sugarland Car Rentals** (© 07/4068 8272) is the only rental-car company in town. For Mission Beach taxi service, call © 07/4068 8155.

WHAT TO SEE & DO

EXPLORING THE REEF   Mission Beach is the closest point on the mainland to the Reef, just 1 hour by the high-speed **Quick Cat Cruises** catamaran (© **1800/654 242** in Australia, or 07/4068 7289). The trip starts with an hour at Dunk Island, 20 minutes offshore, where you can walk rainforest trails, play on the beach, or parasail or jet ski for an extra fee. Then it's a 1-hour trip to sandy Beaver Cay on the Outer Reef, where you have 3 hours to snorkel or to check out the coral from a glass-bottom boat. There's no shade on the cay, so come prepared with a hat and sunscreen. The trip departs daily from Clump Point Jetty at 9:30am. It costs A$140 (US$112) for adults, A$70 (US$56) for children 4 to 14, and A$350 (US$280) for a family of four. Sunday and Wednesday specials cost as little as A$88 (US$70). An introductory scuba dive costs A$80 (US$64) for the first dive and A$35 (US$28) for the second. You should prebook your introductory scuba dive to ensure a place. Qualified divers pay A$60 (US$48) for the first dive, A$35 (US$28) for the second, all gear included. Free pickups from Mission Beach are included. You can also join this trip from Cairns; coach connections from your Cairns or northern beaches hotel will cost extra.

WHITE-WATER RAFTING ON THE TULLY   A day's rafting through the rainforest on the Class III to IV Tully River is an adventure you won't soon forget. In raftspeak, Class IV means "exciting rafting on moderate rapids with a continuous need to maneuver rafts." On the Tully, that translates to regular hair-raising but manageable rapids punctuated by calming stretches that let you float downstream. You don't need experience, just a decent level of agility and an enthusiastic attitude. **RnR Rafting** (© 07/4041 9444) runs a daily trip that includes 5 hours on the river with fun, expert guides, a barbecue lunch in the rainforest, and a video screening of your adventure. With transfers, the day costs A$140 (US$112) from Mission Beach; A$150 (US$120) from Cairns, the northern beaches, or Palm Cove; and A$170 (US$136) from Port Douglas, plus a A$10 (US$8) national park fee. You must be age 13 or over.

EXPLORING THE RAINFOREST & COAST   Walking, wildlife spotting, canoeing in the forest, and kayaking along the pristine coast are all worth doing. Hiking trails abound through national parks, in rainforests, through fan palm groves, and along the beach. The 8km (5-mile) **Licuala Fan Palm** track starts at the parking lot on the Mission Beach–Tully Road about 1.5km (1 mile) west of the turnoff to South Mission Beach. The track leads through dense forest and over creeks, and comes out on the El Arish–Mission Beach Road about 7km (4½ miles) north of the post office. When you come out, you can cross the road and keep going on the 1km (less than a mile) Lacey Creek loop in the Tam O'Shanter State Forest. A shorter Rainforest Circuit option leads from the parking lot at the start of the Licuala Fan Palm track and makes a 1km (less than a mile) loop incorporating a fan palm boardwalk. There's also a 10-minute "follow the cassowary footprints to the nest" children's walk leading from the parking lot.

If you would rather see the sea, take the 7km (4½-mile) Edmund Kennedy track, which starts below the Horizon resort at the southern end of the Kennedy Esplanade in South Mission Beach. You get views of the ocean and the rainforest on this trail. The Mission Beach Visitor Centre has free trail maps.

Ingrid Marker of **Sunbird Adventures** (© **07/4068 8229;** sunbird.adventures@ bigpond.com) offers a range of sea-kayaking and trekking expeditions that interpret the rich environment around you. No more than eight people are allowed on each trip, so you get personal attention and time to ask questions. The half-day sea-kayak expedition (A$55/US$44 per person) journeys around Bingil Bay. Night walks (A$30/US$24 per person), starting at 7pm and returning around 9:30pm, are held on Bicton Hill. These are great for kids because they spot glow-in-the-dark fungi, and frogs and shrimps in the streams. Ingrid also runs 3-day sea kayak camping trips, and a 3-day Misty Mountain Trails hike in the Tully River Gorge. They can be combined to make a 6-day trip, and prices for both can be worked out with Ingrid according to your needs. All trips include pickup from your accommodations, and all food is locally grown organic produce. Not all tours depart every day, so check with her first.

HITTING THE BEACH   Relaxing on the uncrowded beach is why everyone comes to Mission Beach. From June through September, you can swim anywhere, and the water is warm; October through May, stick to areas with stinger nets at Mission Beach proper (behind Castaways resort) and South Mission Beach.

A DAY TRIP TO DUNK ISLAND   If you're a beachcomber at heart, Dunk will fulfill your dreams. Just 5km (3 miles) offshore from Mission Beach, Dunk was the inspiration for writer E. J. Banfield's book *Confessions of a Beachcomber.* Banfield moved to Dunk at the turn of the 20th century to live out what he thought would be

---

⌒Tips   Wildlife Safety Tips

The endangered cassowary (a spectacular ostrichlike bird with a blue bony crown on its head) can kill with its enormous claws, so never approach one. If you disturb one, back off slowly and hide behind a tree.

Dangerous crocodiles inhabit the local waterways. Do not swim in, or stand on the bank of, any river or stream.

You will spend plenty of time lazing and strolling the area's 14km (8¾ miles) of beaches, but be careful about where you swim. Deadly marine stingers inhabit the sea from October through May; during these months, swim only in the stinger nets erected at Mission Beach and South Mission Beach.

a short life. He lived another 23 years, which must say something about the restorative powers of a piece of paradise. Ed and Bertha Banfield's graves are alongside the track to Mount Kootaloo.

Thick bushland and rainforest cover much of the island's 12 sq. km (4¾ sq. miles), most of which is a national park. The island is renowned for its myriad birds and electric-blue Ulysses butterflies.

You can stay at the upscale Dunk Island resort (see below) or pop over for the day to snorkel, hike in the forest, or do all sorts of watersports. **Dunk Island Ferry & Cruises** (© **07/4068 7211**) runs day trips for A$69 (US$55) for adults, A$25 (US$20) for kids 4 to 14, free for kids under 4. The cruise includes lunch, boom-netting (something like water-skiing, but partially submerged in a net pulled by a speedboat), a swing around Bedarra Island, and free snorkeling gear (with a A$20/US$16 refundable deposit). Daily departures are from Clump Point Jetty at 8:45 and 10:30am. You can also get to Dunk by **water taxi** (© **07/4068 8310**), which runs five times a day from Wongaling Beach. The round-trip fare is A$29 (US$23) for adults and A$15 (US$12) for kids 4 to 14. Ask at your hotel about transfers between Clump Point and South Mission Beach.

Once on Dunk, you pay as you go for activities and equipment rental. Everything from water-skiing to catamaran sailing is available, and Dunk has lovely beaches and half a dozen rainforest walking trails, ranging in duration from 15 minutes to 4 hours. On Monday and Thursday mornings, you can visit an artist's gallery reached on a 40-minute trail through the rainforest; admission is A$4 (US$3.20).

Ingrid Marker of Sunbird Adventures (see above) runs full-day guided **sea-kayak expeditions** ⭑ to Dunk Island. Ingrid says if you can pedal a bike for an hour, you can sea kayak for the hour it takes to get to the island. You glide over reefs, looking for sea turtles; spend the morning snorkeling in Coconut Bay; have a picnic lunch of oysters, mussels, and fresh produce (all organic) in Hidden Palm Valley; then hike the rainforest. At morning and afternoon tea you get a choice of nine organic teas and coffees. The trip costs A$95 (US$76) per person.

WHERE TO STAY IN MISSION BEACH

The Horizon ⭑   With its beguiling views across the pool to Dunk Island, its rainforest setting, and its impressive rooms, this resort perched on a steep hillside is one of the most comfortable and beautiful you will find. Even the least expensive rooms are spacious and have luxurious bathrooms. All but a handful of rooms have some kind of sea view; a half dozen retain the older-style bathrooms from a previous resort development, but the sea views from these rooms are the best. It's just a minute or two down the rainforest track to the beach.

Explorer Dr., South Mission Beach, QLD 4852. © **1800/079 090** in Australia, or 07/4068 8154. Fax 07/4068 8596. www.thehorizon.com.au. 55 units. A$220–A$420 (US$176–US$336) double. Child A$20 (US$16) extra. Ask about packages and specials. Rates higher Dec 22–Jan 2. AE, DC, MC, V. **Amenities:** 3 restaurants; bar; large saltwater pool; lit tennis courts; tour desk. *In room:* A/C, TV, minibar, coffeemaker, hair dryer, iron.

Mackays ⭓**Value**   This delightfully well-kept motel is one of the best deals in town. It's just 80m (262 ft.) from the beach and 400m (¼ mile) from the heart of Mission Beach. The friendly Mackay family repaints the rooms annually, so the place always looks brand new. All the rooms are pleasant and spacious, with white-tiled floors, cane sofas, colorful bedcovers, and very clean bathrooms. Those in the newer section are air-conditioned, and some have views of the attractive granite-lined pool and gardens. Rooms in the older painted-brick wing have garden views from a communal patio and no air-conditioning. Apartments don't have air-conditioning, either, but do have kitchenettes. Ask about special packages; they can be extremely good deals and may include extras like rafting on the Tully River and day trips to the Reef and Dunk Island.

7 Porter Promenade, Mission Beach, QLD 4852. © **07/4068 7212.** Fax 07/4068 7095. www.mackaysmission beach.com. 22 units, 12 with bathroom (10 with shower only). A$85–A$105 (US$68–US$84) double; A$120 (US$96) 1- and 2-bedroom apt. Higher rates apply at Easter. Extra adult A$20 (US$16); extra child under 14 A$10 (US$8). Crib A$10 (US$8). Ask about packages. AE, DC, MC, V. Free covered parking. **Amenities:** Outdoor pool; access to nearby tennis courts; access to bike rental; tour desk; car-rental desk; room service at breakfast; in-room massage; babysitting; coin-op laundry; nonsmoking rooms. *In room:* TV, fax, fridge, safe.

WHERE TO STAY ON DUNK ISLAND

Dunk Island ★ *Kids*   Families love Dunk Island because there's so much to do, but it's just as appealing for honeymooners or retired couples. For those who are more inclined to relaxation, Dunk has beautiful beaches and gentle pastimes like champagne sunset cruises. Just 5km (3 miles) offshore from Mission Beach, Dunk is a thickly rainforested 12 sq. km (7½-sq.-mile) island that attracts everyone. The island is renowned for bird life and neon-blue Ulysses butterflies, which you will see everywhere.

Among the free activities are windsurfing, catamaran sailing, paddle skiing, tennis and squash courts, fitness classes and aqua-aerobics, beach and pool volleyball, badminton, bocce, and archery, to name a few. You pay for a range of other activities, including guided jet-ski tours, parasailing, water-skiing, tube rides, tandem sky diving, game-fishing trips, motorboats, sunset wine-and-cheese cruises, and horse riding. The 18-hole golf course is Australia's only island resort course. A yacht calls to make trips around nearby islands, and a game-fishing boat picks up here regularly. The kids will love the playground and a visit to Coonanglebah (the island farm), as well as the kids' club. A private artists' colony in the rainforest sells works Monday and Thursday, from 10am to 1pm.

All four kinds of low-rise (two-story) accommodations were refurbished and restyled in 2003. The top-of-the-range units are the bright, spacious Bayview suites, which have virtually uninterrupted views over Brammo Bay and direct access to the beach. Set in small groups of four units (two units upstairs, two downstairs), suites have king-size beds, luxurious bathrooms, large L-shaped balconies, and extras such as CD players, bathrobes, and stocked minibars. Beachfront rooms are just that, with views over Brammo Bay from most units. Upstairs rooms have balconies, downstairs rooms have patios and open onto the gardens and the beach, and some have family configurations with one king-size and two single beds. Connecting rooms are available. A short stroll from the central complex, resort facilities, and beach are the comfortable Garden Cabanas as well as the Banfield rooms, which are great for families. To truly relax, visit the **Spa of Peace and Plenty,** two large tropical-style buildings connected by a floating boardwalk on a man-made lake, for a facial, massage, body wrap, or other pampering.

Off Mission Beach (c/o Voyages, G.P.O. Box 3589, Sydney, NSW 2001). © **1300/134 044** in Australia, or 02/8296 8010 (Sydney reservations office); resort 07/4068 8199. Fax 02/9299 2477 (Sydney reservations office). www. voyages.com.au 146 units (72 with shower only). A$500–A$810 (US$400–US$648) double. Rates include full breakfast and dinner. Extra adult A$150 (US$120), extra child 3–14 A$90 (US$72). Ask about packages. AE, DC, MC, V. Daily 45-min. flights operate from Cairns (book through Qantas or the resort). Aircraft luggage limit 16kg (35 lb.) per person. Dunk Island Ferry & Cruises (© **07/4068 7211**) makes round-trip ferry transfers from Mission Beach for A$32 (US$26) adults. Including the ferry fare, the company does daily door-to-door coach connections from Port Douglas for A$144 (US$115), Cairns for A$100 (US$80), and Cairns northern beaches for A$120 (US$96) adult. Fares for children 4–14 are half price. Disembarkation from the ferry is sometimes into shallow water—be prepared to get your feet wet! Airport pickups must be booked. Transfers also available by air charter and Quick Cat cruise boat (see "Exploring the Reef," above). **Amenities:** 3 restaurants; bar; 2 large outdoor pools; 18-hole golf course; 3 lit tennis courts (1 indoor); exercise room; spa; extensive watersports equipment rental; bike rental; daily kids' club for ages 3–14 (fee); babysitting; coin-op laundry. *In room:* A/C, ceiling fans, TV, minibar (beachfront units and suites only), fridge, coffeemaker, hair dryer, iron.

BEDARRA ISLAND: THE ULTIMATE LUXURY GETAWAY

Only a mile long, Bedarra is home to an exclusive 15-room resort favored by the rich, the famous, and anyone who treasures privacy. The staff is discreet, and day-trippers are banned. Rainforested and fringed by beaches, Bedarra is a few miles south of Dunk Island.

Bedarra Island ★★★ Bedarra is one of those rare and fabulous places that throws not just meals but vintage French champagne, fine cognac and wine, and other potable treats into the price, shocking though that price may be. If you feel like Louis Roederer Champagne at 3am, help yourself. The new-look Bedarra was injected with some contemporary style in 2001. The private villas have large verandas, and there's a sense of light and space in the public areas. The lobby, restaurant, and 24-hour bar are open, with ironbark and recycled timber beams, and feature panels of volcanic stone. Each villa, tucked into the rainforest, has a balcony and sea views. All come with generous living areas, king-size beds, CD players, bathrobes, and the important things in life, like double hammocks on the veranda, big double bathtubs, and aromatherapy oil-burners. Bathrooms offer divine pampering treats including signature Bedarra aromatherapy oils.

Four exclusive villas sit away from the main resort, perched on cliff tops overlooking Wedgerock Bay. The Pavilions at Bedarra and The Point offer superior facilities, including separate living and sleeping areas, large decks, and an outdoor area with a private plunge pool.

The emphasis here is on relaxation. Walk along rainforest trails, fish off the beach, snorkel. Take a catamaran, paddle-ski, or windsurf out on the water. These activities are free; chartering a yacht or game-fishing boat costs extra. To visit the Great Barrier Reef, you will need to transfer to Dunk Island to join the Quick Cat catamaran (see "Exploring the Reef," above). The Beachclub offers watersports facilities and a gym and massage therapy room as well as a lounge area with Internet access. Many guests do nothing more strenuous than have the chef pack a gourmet picnic with a bottle of bubbly and set off in search of a deserted beach. Dress at night is smart casual.

Off Mission Beach (c/o Voyages, G.P.O. Box 3589, Sydney, NSW 2001). *©* **1300/134 044** in Australia, or 02/8296 8010 (Sydney reservations office); fax 02/9299 2477 (Sydney reservations office). www.voyages.com.au 16 villas. A$2,100–A$3,300 (US$1,680–US$2,640) double. Rates include all meals, 24-hr. open bar, transfers from Dunk Island. Ask about packages. AE, DC, MC, V. Air or coach/ferry transfer to Dunk Island from Cairns (see above), then 15-min. boat transfer. Water transfers from Mission Beach available. Children under 16 not accepted. **Amenities:** Restaurant; bar; secluded outdoor pool w/private Jacuzzi area; lit tennis court; gym; watersports; massage; laundry service. *In room:* A/C, ceiling fan, TV/VCR, minibar, hair dryer, iron.

WHERE TO DINE IN MISSION BEACH

Friends MEDITERRANEAN/SEAFOOD The cozy interior and a hearty menu favoring local seafood make this place a long-standing favorite with locals. Appetizers include mussels Normandy, oysters done three ways, and garlic prawns. Main courses feature lamb shanks; steak with mushrooms or green peppercorn sauce; and chicken hot pot. Settle in with a homemade dessert and liqueur coffee after dinner. Licensed.

Porters Promenade (opposite Campbell St.), Mission Beach. *©* **07/4068 7107.** Reservations recommended. Main courses A$15–A$25 (US$12–US$20). AE, MC, V. Tues–Sat and Sun on long weekends 6:30–10:30pm or until the last diners leave. Closed 1 month during Feb–Mar.

TOWNSVILLE & MAGNETIC ISLAND
346km (215 miles) S of Cairns; 1,371km (850 miles) N of Brisbane

With a population of 140,000, Townsville claims to be Australia's largest tropical city. Because of its size, and an economy based on mining, manufacturing, education, and tourism, it is sometimes overlooked as a holiday destination. Unjustly so, I think. The people are friendly, the city is pleasant, and there's plenty to do. The town nestles by the sea below the pink face of Castle Rock, which looms 300m (about 1,000 ft.) directly above. The beachfront had a A$29-million (US$23-million) revamp a couple of years ago.

Townsville's major attraction is the world-class **Museum of Tropical Queensland,** where a full-size replica of HMS *Pandora* is the stunning centerpiece. The museum is next door to one of the city's most enduring attractions, the Reef HQ aquarium.

Remnants of bygone times are apparent in some of the surrounding towns, particularly **Charters Towers** and **Ravenswood,** which retain splendid examples of colonial architecture, historic hotels, museums, and displays of old gold mining machinery and cottages.

Cruises depart from the harbor for the Great Barrier Reef, about 2½ hours away. Just 8km (5 miles) offshore is Magnetic Island—"Maggie" to the locals—a popular place for watersports, hiking, and spotting koalas in the wild.

Although Townsville can be hot and humid in the summer—and sometimes in the path of cyclones—it is generally spared the worst of the Wet-season rains.

ESSENTIALS
GETTING THERE   Townsville is on the Bruce Highway, a 3-hour drive north of Airlie Beach and 4½ hours south of Cairns. The Bruce Highway breaks temporarily in the city. From the south, take Bruce Highway Alt. 1 route into the city. From the north, the highway leads into the city. The drive from Cairns to Townsville through sugar-cane fields, cloud-topped hills, and lush bushland is a pretty one—one of the most picturesque stretches in Queensland.

Qantas (*©* **13 13 13** in Australia; www.qantas.com.au) flies direct from Brisbane. **QantasLink** flies from Cairns, Sydney, Hamilton Island in the Whitsundays, and Mackay. **Virgin Blue** (*©* **13 67 89** in Australia) flies direct to Townsville from Brisbane and Sydney daily, and charter airline **Alliance Airlines** (*©* **1300/130 092** in Australia, or 07/3212 1297; www.allianceairlines.com.au) also has scheduled flights between Brisbane and Townsville twice a week.

Abacus Charters & Tours (*©* **07/4775 5544**) runs a door-to-door airport shuttle. It meets all flights from Brisbane, and from Cairns or elsewhere if you book in advance. A trip into town is A$7 (US$5.60) one-way or A$11 (US$8.80) round-trip. A **taxi** from the airport to most central hotels costs about A$12 (US$9.60).

Seven **Queensland Rail** (*©* **13 22 32** in Queensland, or 07/3235 1122; www.qr.com. au) long-distance trains stop at Townsville each week. The 19-hour Tilt Train journey from Brisbane costs A$256 (US$205). The 24-hour *Sunlander* journey costs A$171 (US$137) for an economy seat, A$398 (US$318) for a first-class sleeper.

Greyhound Australia (*©* **13 14 99** in Australia) coaches stop at Townsville many times a day on their Cairns-Brisbane-Cairns routes. The fare from Cairns is A$53 (US$42); trip time is 6 hours. The fare from Brisbane is A$172 (US$138); trip time is 23 hours.

VISITOR INFORMATION For an information packet, contact **Townsville Enterprise Limited,** P.O. Box 1043, Townsville, QLD 4810 (© **07/4726 2728;** www.townsvilleonline.com.au). It has two Information Centres. One is in the heart of town on Flinders Mall (© **1800/801 902** in Australia, or 07/4721 3660); it's open Monday through Friday from 9am to 5pm, and weekends from 9am to 1pm. The other is on the Bruce Highway 10km (6¼ miles) south of the city (© **07/4778 3555**); it's open daily from 9am to 5pm. For information on Magnetic Island, also check www.magnetic-island.com.au or www.magneticislandinfo.com.

GETTING AROUND Local **Sunbus** (© **07/4725 8482**) buses depart Flinders Mall. Car-rental chains include **Avis** (© **07/4721 2688**), **Budget** (© **07/4725 2344**), **Hertz** (© **07/4775 5950**), and **Thrifty** (© **07/4725 4600**).

Detours Coaches (© **07/4728 5311**) runs tours to most attractions in and around Townsville. For a taxi, call © **13 10 08.**

DAY TRIPS TO THE REEF

Most boats visiting the Reef from Townsville are live-aboard vessels that make trips of 2 or more days, designed for serious divers. **Barrier Reef Dive, Cruise & Travel** (© **1800/636 778** in Australia, or 07/4772 5800; www.divecruisetravel.com) runs day trips to Keeper Reef and John Brewer Reef. It takes only 1½ hours to reach John Brewer Reef, where you can make introductory dives for A$70 (US$56) for the first and A$35 (US$28) for the second, and certified divers can make two dives for A$70 (US$56); all gear is included. The cruise costs A$139 (US$111) for adults, A$109 (US$87) for seniors, A$74 (US$59) for children 5 to 15, and A$352 (US$282) for a family of four. The price includes lunch and morning and afternoon tea. There are freshwater showers on board. Cruises depart Townsville at 8:30am, with a pickup at Magnetic Island en route, and returns by about 5pm. Several other operators, including **Adrenalin Dive** (© **07/4724 0600**), have trips to the *Yongala* wreck, the Coral Sea, and the Reef.

THE TOP ATTRACTIONS

Museum of Tropical Queensland ★★ A stunning 2002 addition to Townsville's skyline is this A$22-million (US$17.6-million) museum, with its curved roof reminiscent of a ship in full sail. In pride of place is the amazing exhibition of relics salvaged from the wreck of HMS *Pandora,* which lies 33m (108 ft.) underwater on the edge of the Great Barrier Reef, 120km (74 miles) east of Cape York. The *Pandora* exhibit includes a full-scale replica of a section of the ship's bow and its 17m-high (56-ft.) foremast. Standing three stories high, the replica and its copper-clad keel were crafted by local shipwrights for the museum. *Pandora* sank in 1791, and the wreck was discovered in 1977. The exhibition traces the ship's voyage and the retrieval of the sunken treasure. The museum has six galleries, including a hands-on science center, and a natural history display that looks at life in tropical Queensland—above and below the water. Another is dedicated to north Queensland's indigenous heritage, with items from Torres Strait and the South Sea Islands as well as stories from people of different cultures about the settlement and labor of north Queensland. Touring exhibitions change every 3 months. Allow 2 to 3 hours.

70–102 Flinders St. (next to Reef HQ). © **07/4726 0600**, or 07/4726 0606 info line. www.mtq.qld.gov.au. Admission A$9 (US$7.20) adults, A$6.50 (US$5.20) seniors and students, A$5 (US$4) children 4–16, A$24 (US$19) family of 5. MC, V. Daily 9:30am–5pm. Closed Good Friday, Dec 25, and until 1pm Apr 25 (Anzac Day).

Reef HQ ★ Kids   Reef HQ is the education center for the Great Barrier Reef Marine Park Authority's headquarters and is the largest living coral reef aquarium in the world. It underwent a A$6.4-million (US$5.1-million) upgrade in 2002, but the highlight is still walking through a 20m-long (66-ft.) transparent acrylic tunnel, gazing right into a giant predator tank where sharks swim silently. The wreck of SS *Yongala* provides an eerie backdrop for blacktip and whitetip reef sharks, leopard sharks, and nurse sharks, sharing their 750,000-liter (195,000-gal.) home with stingrays, giant trevally, and a green turtle. Watching them feed is quite a spectacle. The tunnel also reveals the 2.5-million-liter (650,000-gal.) coral reef exhibit, with its hard and soft corals providing a home for thousands of colorful fish, giant clams, sea cucumbers, sea stars, and other creatures. During the scuba dive show, the divers speak to you over an intercom while they swim with the sharks and feed the fish. Other highlights include a marine creature touch tank, a wild sea-turtle rehabilitation center, plus great interactive activities for children. Reef HQ is an easy walk from the city center.

2–68 Flinders St. ⓒ 07/4750 0800. www.reefHQ.org.au. Admission A$22 (US$18) adults, A$17 (US$14) seniors and students, A$11 (US$8.80) children 4–16, A$54 (US$43) family of 5. AE, DC, MC, V. Daily 9am–5pm. Closed Dec 25. Public parking lot opposite Reef HQ. Bus: 1, 1A, or 1B (stop 3-min. walk away).

MORE THINGS TO SEE & DO

The Strand is a 2.5km (1½-mile) strip with safe swimming beaches, a fitness circuit, a great water park for the kids, and plenty of covered picnic areas and free gas barbecues. Stroll along the promenade or relax at one of the many cafes, restaurants, and bars while you gaze across the Coral Sea to Magnetic Island. For the more active, there are areas to in-line skate, cycle, walk, or fish, and a basketball half-court. Four rocky headlands and a picturesque jetty adjacent to Strand Park provide good fishing spots, and there are two surf lifesaving clubs to service the three swimming areas along The Strand. With 300 days of sunshine each year, Townsville is a place where you'll enjoy cooling off—in the Olympic-size Tobruk Pool, the seawater Rockpool, or at the beach itself. During summer (Nov–Mar), three swimming enclosures operate to keep swimmers safe from marine stingers. If watersports are on your agenda, try a jet ski, hire a canoe, or take to the latest in pedal skis. A state-of-the-art water park has waterfalls, hydrants, water slides, and water cannons, plus a huge bucket of water that continually fills until it overturns and drenches laughing children.

Don't miss the views of Cleveland Bay and Magnetic Island from **Castle Hill;** it's a 2.5km (1½-mile) drive or a shorter, steep walk up from town. To drive to the top, follow Stanley Street west from Flinders Mall to Castle Hill Drive; the walking trails up are posted en route.

At the **Billabong Sanctuary** (ⓒ **07/4778 8344;** www.billabongsanctuary.com.au) on the Bruce Highway 17km (11 miles) south of town, you can see Aussie wildlife in a natural setting; hold a koala, a (baby) crocodile, a python, or a wombat; and hand-feed kangaroos. Bring your own camera. Talks and shows run continuously starting at 8:30am; one of the most popular is the saltwater-crocodile feeding at 12:15 and 2:30pm. There are also gas barbecues, a food kiosk, and a pool. Admission is A$24 (US$19) for adults, A$22 (US$18) for students, A$13 (US$10) for kids 4 to 16, and A$67 (US$54) for a family of five. The sanctuary is open every day except December 25 from 8am to 5pm.

WHERE TO STAY

Holiday Inn Townsville   The "Sugar Shaker" (you'll know why when you see it) has been Townsville's favorite hotel for years, especially with the corporate set. Right on Flinders Mall, it's a stroll from Reef HQ, Museum of Tropical Queensland, and Magnetic Island ferries. The rooms are fitted out in sleek blond wood, and because the 20-story building is circular, every one faces the city, the bay, or Castle Hill. Suites have kitchenettes. The star attractions are the rooftop pool and sun deck with barbecues.

334 Flinders Mall, Townsville, QLD 4810. (C) **1800/079 903** in Australia, 800/835-7742 in the U.S. and Canada, 0345/581 666 in the U.K. or 020/8335 1304 in London, 0800/801 111 in New Zealand, or 07/4729 2000. Fax 07/4721 1263. www.sixcontinentshotels.com. 197 units. A$280–A$315 (US$224–US$252) double; A$375–A$450 (US$300–US$360) suite. Extra person A$33 (US$26). Children under 20 stay free in parent's room with existing bedding. Free crib. Ask about weekend rates, advance-purchase rates, and packages. AE, DC, MC, V. Free covered valet parking. **Amenities:** Restaurant; 2 bars; rooftop pool; free access to nearby gym; bike rental; secretarial services; 24-hr. room service; massage; babysitting; coin-op laundry; laundry service; dry cleaning. *In room:* A/C, TV w/pay movies, dataport, minibar, coffeemaker, hair dryer, iron.

The Rocks ⭐ *Finds* If you have a weakness for Victoriana, you will sigh with delight when you enter this exquisitely renovated old Queenslander home. The owners have fitted it with 19th-century antiques, from the crimson velvet settee to the grandfather clock in the drawing room. Even the meals are served on collectible dinnerware. Every room is decorated with lovely linens and old trunks; a few even have original washbasins tastefully wrapped in muslin "gowns." Four have bathrooms; the others share a historically decorated bathroom with a cast-iron claw-foot bath. Complimentary sherry is served at 6pm on the wide veranda, which has lovely views of Magnetic Island and Cleveland Bay. Despite the old-world ambience, the house has telephone, fax, Internet, and e-mail access for guests (although not in the guest rooms). Free tea and coffee are available. There's also an outdoor Jacuzzi, a billiards table (antique, of course), and a guest laundry. The Strand is a minute's stroll away, and you are a 5-minute walk from town and the Magnetic Island ferries.

20 Cleveland Terrace, Townsville, QLD 4810. (C) **07/4771 5700**, or 0416/044 409 mobile. Fax 07/4771 5711. www.therocksguesthouse.com. 7 units, 4 with private bathroom (shower only). A$105–A$119 (US$84–US$95) double; extra person A$25 (US$20). Rates include continental breakfast. AE, DC, MC, V. Limited free street parking. **Amenities:** Outdoor Jacuzzi; tour desk; airport shuttle; business center; laundry service. *In room:* A/C.

Seagulls Resort This popular low-key resort, a 5-minute drive from the city, is built around an inviting free-form saltwater pool in 1.2 hectares (3 acres) of dense tropical gardens. Despite the Esplanade location, the motel-style rooms do not boast waterfront views, but they are comfortable and a good size. The larger deluxe rooms have painted brick walls, a sofa, dining furniture, and a kitchen sink. Reef rooms and suites have kitchenettes; executive suites have Jacuzzis. Apartments have a main bedroom and a bunk bedroom, a kitchenette, dining furniture, and a roomy balcony. The rooms were last refurbished in late 1997, and the modest fittings are in good condition. The foyer was refurbished in late 2000, and the whole resort is wheelchair friendly, with bathroom facilities for people with disabilities. The accommodations wings surround the pool and its pretty open-sided restaurant, which is popular with locals. It's a 10-minute walk to The Strand; the resort makes free transfers to the city and Magnetic Island ferry terminals, and most tour companies pick up at the door.

74 The Esplanade, Belgian Gardens, QLD 4810. (C) **1800/079 929** in Australia, or 07/4721 3111. Fax 07/4721 3133. www.seagulls.com.au. 70 units (all with shower only). A$103–A$114 (US$82–US$91) double; A$139 (US$111) 2-bedroom apt; A$150 (US$120) executive suite. Extra adult A$15 (US$12); extra child under 14 A$9 (US$7.20). Crib A$9 (US$7.20). AE, DC, MC, V. Free parking. Bus: 7. **Amenities:** Restaurant; bar; 2 large outdoor saltwater pools, children's wading pool; access to nearby golf course; small tennis court; access to nearby health club; playground; tour desk; airport shuttle (A$3/US$2.40 one-way); business center; room service (dinner); coin-op laundry; laundry service (Mon–Fri); dry cleaning. *In room:* A/C, TV w/free movies, dataport, fridge, coffeemaker, hair dryer, iron.

WHERE TO DINE

Apart from the suggestions below, you will find more restaurants and cafes on **Palmer Street,** an easy stroll across the river from Flinders Mall, Flinders Street East, and The Strand.

Michel's Cafe and Bar MODERN AUSTRALIAN   This big contemporary space is popular with Townsville's in crowd. Choose a table on the sidewalk, or opt for air-conditioning inside. Owner-chef Michel Flores works in the open kitchen where he can keep an eye on the excellent servers. You might choose Louisiana blackened rib filet, kangaroo, or something more casual, like the stylish pizzas, pastas, seafood, or warm salads.

7 Palmer St. © 07/4724 1460. Reservations recommended. Main courses A$11–A$23 (US$8.80–US$18). AE, DC, MC, V. Tues–Fri 11:30am–3pm; Tues–Sun 5:30–10pm.

Zouí Alto ★★ MODERN AUSTRALIAN   This is not just one of the best restaurants in Townsville, it's one of the best in the country. Chef Mark Edwards, who has cooked for the king of Norway, turns out terrific food. His effusive wife, Eleni, runs the front of the house, which is idiosyncratically decked out in primary splashes and Greek urns. Main courses include ravioli with choice of filling—pumpkin and blue-vein cheese, sweet potato and ginger, or sun-dried tomato and goat's cheese. Arrive before sunset, to make the most of the spectacular 14th-floor views of Castle Hill on one side and the bay on the other.

At Aquarius on the Beach, 75 The Strand. © 07/4721 4700. Reservations recommended. Main courses A$18–A$22 (US$14–US$18). AE, MC, V. Tues–Sat 6:30–9:30pm. Bus: 1B.

A SIDE TRIP TO MAGNETIC ISLAND

8km (5 miles) E of Townsville

"Maggie" is a delightful 51-sq.-km (20-sq.-mile) national park island 20 minutes from Townsville by ferry. About 2,500 people live here, and it's popular with Aussies, who love its holiday atmosphere. It is a busy little place where visitors and locals zip about between the small settlements that dot the coast; in fact, the island has a good range of restaurants, laid-back cafes, and takeout joints. But peace-seeking visitors will find plenty of unspoiled nature to restore their souls. Most people come for the 20 or so pristine (and amazingly uncrowded) bays and white beaches, but hikers, botanists, and birders may want to explore the eucalyptus woods, patches of gully rainforest, and granite tors. (The island got its name when Captain Cook thought the "magnetic" rocks were interfering with his compass readings.) The place is famous for wild koalas that are easily spotted up in the gum trees by the side of the road; ask a local to point you to the nearest colony. Rock wallabies are often spotted in the early morning. Maggie, by and large off the tourist trail, is definitely a flip-flops kind of place.

VISITOR INFORMATION   The Magnetic Island Information Shop (© **1800/ 005 654** in Australia, or 07/4758 1862; www.magneticislandinfo.com) is at the Nelly Bay ferry terminal.

GETTING THERE & GETTING AROUND   Sunferries (© **1800/447 333** in Australia, or 07/4771 3855) runs 15 round-trips a day from the 168–192 Flinders Street East terminal and the Breakwater terminal on Sir Leslie Thiess Drive. Round-trip tickets are A$23 (US$18) for adults, A$12 (US$9.60) for children 5 to 15, and A$46 (US$37) for a family of five. The trip takes about 25 minutes.

Magnetic Island

You can take your car on the ferry, but most people get around by renting an open-sided minimoke (similar to a golf cart) from the many rental outfits on the island. Minimokes are unlikely to go much over 60kmph (36 mph). **Moke Magnetic (② 07/4778 5377)** rents them for around A$65 (US$52) a day. The **Magnetic Island Bus Service (② 07/4778 5130)** runs a 3-hour guided tour of the island for A$35 (US$28) for adults, A$15 (US$12) for kids 5 to 15.

Out & About on the Island

There is no end to the things you can do on Maggie—snorkeling, swimming in one of a dozen or more bays, catamaran sailing, water-skiing, paraflying, horseback riding on the beach, biking, tennis or golf, scuba diving, sea kayaking, sailing or cruising around the island, taking a Harley-Davidson tour, fishing, and more. Equipment for all these activities is for rent on the island.

Most activities spread out around Nelly Bay (where the ferry pulls in); the island's other two settlements, Arcadia and Horseshoe Bay; and Picnic Bay.

The island is not on the Great Barrier Reef, but surrounding waters are part of the Great Barrier Reef Marine Park. There is good reef snorkeling at Florence Bay on the southern edge, Arthur Bay on the northern edge, and Geoffrey Bay, where you can even reef-walk at low tide. (Wear sturdy shoes and do not walk directly on coral to avoid damaging it.) First-time snorkelers will have an easy time of it in Maggie's weak

Tips **Magnetic Island Travel Tips**

If you're going to Magnetic Island for the day, pick up a copy of the free *Magnetic Island Guide* from any tourist information center or hotel lobby or at the ferry terminal in Townsville before you go. Because there are so many activities and tours, it will help if you plan your day before you arrive. Also, there is no bank on the island, so carry cash (not every business will cash traveler's checks) and a credit card.

Be warned: Deadly marine stingers make swimming and snorkeling a bad idea October through May, except at the safe swimming enclosures at Picnic Bay and Horseshoe Bay. Lifesavers sweep and patrol Alma Bay, so it is usually safe. You can still do watersports on top of the water if your rental outlet provides a protective Lycra stinger suit, but you won't want to wear one of those in the sticky summer heat from November through March.

currents and softly sloping beaches. Outside stinger season, there is good swimming at any number of secluded bays all around the island. Reef-free Alma Bay, with its shady lawns and playground, is a good choice for families; Rocky Bay is a small, secluded cove.

One of the best, and therefore most popular, of the island's 20km (13 miles) of hiking trails is the Nelly Bay–Arcadia trail, a one-way journey of 5km (3 miles) that takes 2½ hours. The first 45 minutes, starting in rainforest and climbing to a saddle between Nelly Bay and Horseshoe, are the most interesting. Another excellent walk is the 2km (1.25-mile) trail to the Forts, remnants of World War II defenses, which, not surprisingly, have great 360-degree sea views. The best koala spotting is on the track up to the Forts off Horseshoe Bay Road. Carry water when walking—some bays and hiking trails are not near shops.

If you feel like splurging, consider a jet-ski circumnavigation of the island with **Adrenalin Jet Ski Tours & Hire** (© **07/4778 5533**). The half-day tour on two-seat jet skis costs A$135 (US$108) per person, which includes your wet suit, life jacket, and stinger suits in season. Tours depart from Horseshoe Bay morning and afternoon. Keep your eyes peeled for dolphins, dugongs (manatees), and sea turtles.

ORPHEUS ISLAND
80km (50 miles) N of Townsville; 190km (118 miles) S of Cairns

In the 1930s, actress Vivien Leigh and novelist Zane Grey were among the stars who sought seclusion on this beautiful island. More recently, rock star Elton John vacationed here. One of the Great Barrier Reef's most exclusive retreats, Orpheus Island Resort is a popular getaway for executives, politicians, and any savvy traveler eager for peace and beauty. The surrounding waters are home to 340 of the 350 or so coral species found on the Great Barrier Reef, 1,100 species of fish, green and loggerhead turtles, dolphins, manta rays, and, from June through September, humpback whales. With a maximum of 42 guests and no day-trippers, the only other people you will see are the attentive but unobtrusive resort staff and the occasional scientist from the James Cook University marine research station in the next bay.

Transfers are by eight-seat Cessna seaplane from Townsville daily or from Cairns twice a week. Fares are A$450 (US$360) from Townsville, A$780 (US$624) from

Cairns, or A$640 (US$512) originating in one place and returning to the other, per person round-trip. Book through the resort. Luggage limit is 15 kilograms (55 lb.) per person.

Orpheus Island Resort ⚓ If seclusion and tranquillity are what you are looking for, this is the place to find them. The resort is a cluster of rooms lining one of the prettiest turquoise bays you'll find anywhere. Most guests spend their time snorkeling over coral reefs, chilling with a good book or magazine in the Quiet Lounge, or lazing in a hammock. Free activities include tennis, snorkeling, catamaran sailing, canoeing, paddle-skiing, fishing, and taking a motorized dinghy around the shore to explore some of the island's 1,300 national park hectares (3,211 acres). You can pay to go game fishing, charter a boat or seaplane to the outer Reef, or do a dive course. A seven-course degustation-style menu is served nightly in the restaurant.

All the rooms and suites on Orpheus are beachfront. Most of the 17 Orpheus Retreats are in blocks of three, and each has a personal patio and a Jacuzzi. Four Nautilus Suites are more spacious, with separate lounge and bedroom areas, large private patios, and large Jacuzzis. Two have enclosed garden courtyards.

Orpheus Island, Great Barrier Reef (P.M.B. 15, Townsville, QLD 4810). ⓒ **07/4777 7377.** Fax 07/4777 7533. www. orpheus.com.au. 21 units. A$1,450 (US$1,160) Orpheus Retreat double; A$1,700 (US$1,360) Nautilus Suite double. Rates include all meals but not drinks. Ask about packages. AE, DC, MC, V. Children under 15 not accepted. **Amenities:** Restaurant; bar; 2 small outdoor pools, 1 w/swim-up bar; lit tennis court; exercise room; Jacuzzi; watersports rentals; concierge; business center with 24-hr. Internet access. *In room:* A/C, CD player, minibar, coffeemaker, hair dryer, iron, no phone.

5 The Whitsunday Coast & Islands

A day's drive or a 1-hour flight south of Cairns brings you to the dazzling collection of 74 islands known as the Whitsundays. No more than 3 nautical miles (3.4km) separate most of the islands, and altogether they represent countless bays, beaches, dazzling coral reefs, and fishing spots that make up one fabulous Great Barrier Reef playground. Sharing the same latitude as Rio de Janeiro and Hawaii, the water is at least 72°F (22°C) year-round, the sun shines most of the year, and in winter you'll require only a light jacket at night.

All the islands consist of densely rainforested national park land, mostly uninhabited. The surrounding waters belong to the Great Barrier Reef Marine Park. Don't expect palm trees and coconuts—these islands are covered with dry-looking pine and eucalyptus forests full of dense undergrowth, and rocky coral coves far outnumber the few sandy beaches. More than half a dozen islands have resorts that offer just about all the activities you could ever want—snorkeling, scuba diving, sailing, reef fishing, water-skiing, jet-skiing, parasailing, sea kayaking, hiking, rides over the coral in semi-submersibles, fish feeding, putt-putting around in dinghies to secluded beaches, playing tennis or squash, and aqua-aerobics classes. Accommodations range from small, low-key wilderness retreats to mid-range family havens to Australia's most luxurious resort, Hayman.

The village of Airlie Beach is the center of the action on the mainland. The Whitsundays are just as good a stepping-stone to the outer Great Barrier Reef as Cairns, and some people consider them better, because you don't have to make the 90-minute trip to the Reef before you hit coral. Just about any Whitsunday island has fringing reef around its shores, and there are good snorkeling reefs between the islands, a quick boat ride away from your island or mainland accommodations.

The Whitsunday Region

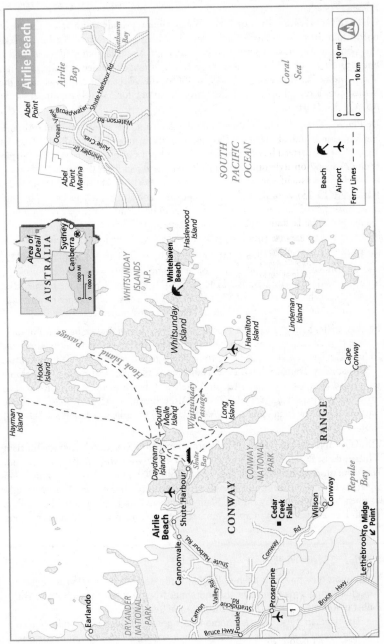

ESSENTIALS

GETTING THERE **By Car** The Bruce Highway leads south from Cairns or north from Brisbane to Proserpine, 26km (16 miles) inland from Airlie Beach. Take the Whitsunday turnoff to reach Airlie Beach and Shute Harbour. Allow a good 8 hours to drive from Cairns. There are several car-storage facilities at Shute Harbour. **Whitsunday Car Security** (© 07/4946 9666) will collect your car anywhere in the Whitsunday area and store it in locked covered parking for A$8 (US$6.40) per day or A$14 (US$11) overnight.

By Plane There are two air routes into the Whitsundays: Hamilton Island Airport, and Whitsunday Coast Airport at Proserpine on the mainland. **QantasLink** (© 13 13 13 in Australia) flies direct to Hamilton Island from Cairns, and Townsville. **Virgin Blue** (© 13 67 89 in Australia) flies to Proserpine direct from Brisbane, Melbourne, and Sydney, and with connections from Canberra, Adelaide, Hobart, and Launceston. **Jetstar** (© 13 15 38 in Australia) flies from Brisbane and Sydney to Proserpine and from Brisbane, Melbourne, and Sydney to Hamilton Island. If you stay on an island, the resort may book your launch transfers automatically. These may appear on your airline ticket, in which case your luggage will be checked through to the island.

By Train Several **Queensland Rail** (© 13 22 32 in Queensland, or 07/3235 1122; www.qr.com.au) long-distance trains stop at Proserpine every week. The one-way fare from Cairns on the Tilt Train is A$134 (US$107). Brisbane fares range from A$228 (US$182) on the Tilt Train to A$327 (US$262) for a first-class sleeper on the *Sunlander* or A$606 (US$485) for the all-inclusive Queenslander Class service.

By Bus **Greyhound Australia** (© 13 14 99 in Australia) operates plentiful daily services to Airlie Beach from Brisbane (trip time: around 19 hr.) and Cairns (trip time: 10 hr.). The fare is A$149 (US$119) from Brisbane and A$93 (US$74) from Cairns.

Whitsunday Transit (© 07/4946 1800) meets all flights and trains at Proserpine and provides door-to-door transfers to Airlie Beach hotels or to Shute Harbour. The fare from the airport is A$30 (US$24) to Airlie Beach, or A$32 (US$26) to Shute Harbour. From the train station, it is A$15 (US$12) to Airlie Beach or A$18 (US$14) to Shute Harbour.

VISITOR INFORMATION For information before you travel, contact **Tourism Whitsundays,** P.O. Box 83, Whitsunday, QLD 4802 (www.whitsundaytourism.com). The **Whitsundays Information Center** (© 1800/801 252 in Australia, or 07/4945 3711; fax 07/4945 3182) is in Proserpine, on the Bruce Highway in the town's south. It's open Monday to Friday from 8:30am to 5pm and weekends and public holidays (except Dec 25) from 9am to 3pm. Another useful website is www.whitsunday.net.au.

(*Tips* Safety Tips

Although they have not been sighted at Airlie Beach for several years, deadly marine stingers may frequent the shorelines from October through April. The best place to swim is in the beachfront Airlie Beach lagoon.

The rivers in these parts are home to dangerous saltwater crocodiles (which mostly live in fresh water, contrary to their name), so don't swim in streams, rivers, and water holes.

If you're staying in Airlie Beach, it's easier to pick up information from the private booking agents lining the main street. All stock a vast range of cruise, tour, and hotel information, and make bookings free of charge. They all have pretty much the same stuff, but because some represent certain boats exclusively, and because prices can vary a little from one to the next, shop around.

GETTING AROUND   Island ferries and Great Barrier Reef cruises leave from Shute Harbour, a 10-minute drive south of Airlie Beach on Shute Harbour Road. Most other tour-boat operators and bareboat charters anchor at Abel Point Marina, a 15-minute walk west from Airlie Beach.

Avis (© 07/4946 6318), **Hertz** (© 07/4946 4687), and **Thrifty** (© 07/4946 7727) have outlets in Airlie Beach and Proserpine Airport (telephone numbers serve both locations). Budget has no Whitsundays office.

Whitsunday Transit (© 07/4946 1800) runs half-hourly buses between Airlie Beach and Shute Harbour to meet all ferries. The fare is A$4.55 (US$3.65). An **Explorer Pass,** good for unlimited travel between Shute Harbour, Airlie Beach, Cannonvale, and Proserpine from 6am to 10:30pm on the date of issue, costs A$8 (US$6.40) for adults and A$4 (US$3.20) for children.

Most tour-boat operators pick up guests free from Airlie Beach hotels and pick up at some or all island resorts.

Fantasea Cruises' Blue Ferries (© 1800/650 851 in Australia, or 07/4946 5111) makes ferry transfers from Shute Harbour to the islands and between the islands. One-way transfers from the mainland cost A$19 (US$15) to South Molle, Long, and Daydream islands; A$30 (US$24) to Hamilton Island. Children 4 to 14 pay A$12 (US$9.60) and A$15 (US$12). Reservations are not necessary, but do book your arrival and departure ferry so that you don't miss your connections. Most islands receive a boat only every 2 to 4 hours, so it's a long wait if you miss your boat.

CHOOSING A WHITSUNDAY BASE

The advantages of staying on the mainland are cheaper accommodations, a choice of restaurants, and the freedom to visit a different island each day. The mainland has jet-skiing, kayaking, parasailing, catamaran rental, and windsurfing.

The main advantage of staying on an island is that swimming, snorkeling, bush-walking, and a huge range of watersports, many of them free, are right outside your door. The deadly stingers that can infest Airlie's shores do not make it to the islands, so swimming in the islands is safe year-round. You won't be isolated if you stay on an island, because most Great Barrier Reef cruise boats, "sail and snorkel" yacht excursions, Whitehaven Beach cruises, dive boats, fishing tour vessels, and so on stop at the island resorts every day or on a frequent basis. Be warned, however, that once you're "captive" on an island, you may be slugged with high food and drink prices. Bear in mind, too, that although most island resorts offer nonmotorized watersports, such as Windsurfers and catamarans, free of charge, you will pay for activities that use fuel, such as parasailing, water-skiing, and dinghy rental.

In some places in the Whitsundays, extreme low tides may reveal rocky mud flats below the sand line. Watersports can be limited at low tide because of the low water level.

EXPLORING THE ISLANDS & THE REEF

REEF CRUISES   **Fantasea Cruises** (© 07/4946 5111; www.fantasea.com.au) makes a daily trip to Hardy Reef from Shute Harbour, near Airlie Beach, in a high-speed,

Moments   Come Sail with Me

If "bareboating" is a mystery to you, take heart. You're not alone—it simply means you are sailing the boat yourself. And if that seems daunting, rest assured that thousands of people do it safely every year. Most of the many yacht-charter companies in the islands will want one person on the boat to have a little experience at the helm of a vessel, but don't worry if you don't know one end of a boat from another. You do not need a license, and sailing is surprisingly easy in these uncrowded waters, where the channels are deep and hazard-free and the seas are protected from big swells by the Great Barrier Reef. The 74 islands are so close to each other that one is always in sight, and safe anchorages are everywhere.

If you have no boating experience, the company may require you to take a skipper along for the first day at an extra cost of around A$200 (US$160) a day or A$250 (US$200) overnight. And if you think you know what you're doing but just want extra reassurance, you can take a skipper along for the first couple of hours for A$60 (US$48) to help you get the hang of things. Most companies mail you a preparation kit before you leave home. Before departure they give you a thorough 2- to 3-hour briefing and easy-to-read maps marking channels, anchorage points, and the very few dangerous reefs. Your charter company will radio in once or twice a day to check that you're still afloat, and you can contact the staff anytime for advice.

Most yachts are fitted for two to eight passengers. Try to get a boat with two berths more than you need if your budget will bear it, because space is always tight. The boats usually have a galley kitchen, a barbecue mounted to the stern, hot showers, a toilet, linens, a radio or stereo (or both), a motorized dinghy, and snorkeling equipment. Sleeping quarters are usually not all that luxurious and include a mix of single galley berths and one or two very compact private cabins. You can buy your own provisions or have the charter company stock the boat at an extra cost of about A$35 (US$28) per person per day. Most operators will load a Windsurfer, fishing tackle, and scuba-diving equipment on request for an extra fee, if they are not standard.

air-conditioned catamaran. The boat has a bar, and a biologist gives a marine ecology talk en route. You anchor at the massive Fantasea Reefworld pontoon, which holds up to 600 people, and spend up to 3½ hours on the Reef. The day trip costs A$161 (US$129) for adults, A$138 (US$110) for seniors and students, A$87 (US$70) for children 4 to 14, and A$379 (US$303) for a family of four. Guided snorkel safaris cost A$20 (US$16) extra. Cruise-dive packages are available for A$82 (US$66) extra for both introductory and certified dives. Cruises depart at 8am and pick up passengers at South Molle, Daydream, and Hamilton island resorts. Passengers from Long and Lindeman islands connect by water taxi.

A fun alternative is Fantasea's 2-day, 1-night **ReefSleep,** during which you spend the night on the pontoon. This gives you a fabulous chance to snorkel at night when the coral is luminescent in the moonlight and nocturnal sea creatures get busy. The

In peak season you may have to charter the boat for a week. At other times, most companies impose a minimum of 5 days, but many will rent for 3 nights if you ask, rather than let a vessel sit idle in the marina. Five nights is a good length; it allows you to get familiar enough with the boat to relax and enjoy yourself.

In peak season, expect to pay A$490 to A$680 (US$392–US$544) per night for a four- to six-berth yacht. Rates in the off season, and even in the Whitsundays' busiest time, June through August, will be anywhere from A$90 to A$120 (US$72–US$96) less. If you are prepared to book within 14 days of when you want to sail, the deals can be even better; you should be able to find a boat that late in the off season. You will be asked to post a credit card bond of around A$1,500 (US$1,200). Mooring fees apply if you want to stop at one of the island resorts overnight. A number of bareboat-charter companies offer "sail 'n' stay" packages that combine a few days of sailing with a few days at an island resort.

Most bareboat-charter companies will make complete holiday arrangements for you in the islands, including accommodations, transfers, tours, and sporting activities. Most companies operate out of Airlie Beach, Hamilton Island, or both. Two of the largest companies, **Australian Bareboat Charters** and **Whitsunday Rent-A-Yacht,** operate under the banner of Trinity Marine (© **1800/075 000** in Australia, or 07/4946 9232; www.rentayacht.com.au). Other well-known operators include **Queensland Yacht Charters** (© **1800/075 013** in Australia, or 07/4946 7400; fax 07/4946 7698; www.yachtcharters.com.au); **Sail Whitsunday** (© **1800/075 045** in Australia, or 07/4946 7070; fax 07/4946 7044); and **The Moorings** (© **888/952-8420** in the U.S., 1800/553 720 in Australia, or 07/4946 8044; www.moorings.com). Tourism Whitsundays (see "Visitor Information," above) can furnish you with a complete list of operators.

If you don't want to sail yourself, countless skippered sailing trips go through the islands (see "Sailing & Snorkeling Trips," below).

trip includes a marine biologist's slide presentation, two scuba dives, plenty of night snorkeling, two buffet lunches, dinner under the stars with wine, and breakfast and more snorkeling on the second day. You can stay in a clean, comfortable bunkroom for four for A$343 (US$274) per person, or in the double cabin, which has a king-size bed, for A$404 (US$323) per person. With so few guests per night, you have the Reef all to yourself.

SAILING & SNORKELING TRIPS ⭐ A cheaper alternative to skippering your own yacht—also called "bareboating"—around the Whitsundays (see the box "Come Sail with Me," above) is a journey on one of the numerous yachts offering 3-day, 2-night sailing adventures around the islands. You can get involved with sailing the boat as much or as little as you want, snorkel to your heart's content over one dazzling reef after another, beach comb, explore national park trails, learn to sail, stop at secluded

---

⌐ Tips The Secret of the Seasons

High season in the Whitsundays coincides with school vacations, which occur in January, in mid-April, from late June to early July, from late September to early October, and in late December. The Aussie winter, June through August, is popular, too. You have to book months ahead to secure high-season accommodations, but at any other time you can get some very good deals indeed. Specials on accommodations, sailing trips, day cruises, and diving excursions fairly leap off the blackboards outside the tour-booking agents in Airlie Beach.

---

bays, swim, sunbathe, and generally have a laid-back good time. A few companies offer introductory and qualified scuba diving for an extra cost per dive. Most boats carry a maximum of 12 passengers, so the atmosphere is always friendly and fun. The food is generally good, the showers are usually hot, and you sleep in comfortable but small berths off the galley. Some have small private twin or double cabins.

In peak season, expect to pay around A$600 (US$480) per person. Prices usually include all meals, Marine Park entrance fees, snorkel gear, and transfers to the departure point (Abel Point Marina or Shute Harbour). In the off season, the boats compete fiercely for passengers; you'll see signboards on the main street in Airlie Beach advertising standby deals.

Among the better-known operators are *Ragamuffin* (© 07/4946 7777), a 17m (56-ft.) oceangoing yacht; and **Prosail** (© 1800/810 116 in Australia, or 07/4946 5433; www.prosail.com.au), which runs trips on a fleet of 19 yachts. Prosail also offers 3-hour "day sails" on America's Cup yachts *Australia* and *Steak 'N Kidney,* giving you the chance to "race" in a mock challenge between the two boats. You can get involved in the racing, calling tactics, grinding, and even protesting an offending yacht, or just sit back and watch the action. Day sails start at 9am and 1pm, and cost A$79 (US$63) for adults, A$75 (US$60) for students and YHA members, and A$59 (US$47) for children 10 to 15 (not recommended for children under 10), including pickup from your accommodations. Prosail's 3-day, 2-night guided sailing trips through the Marine and Great Barrier Reef Marine parks cost around A$450 (US$360). All trips include sailing, snorkeling, scuba diving, and bushwalking, and you can sail on maxi-yachts such as *Matador, Condor, Broomstick,* and *Hammer.* The company also offers 6-day packages. Contact **Tourism Whitsundays** (see "Visitor Information," above) for details on other charters.

ISLAND HOPPING Day-trippers to Hamilton, Daydream, South Molle, Club Crocodile Long Island, and Hook Island resorts can rent the hotels' watersports equipment, laze by the beaches and pools, scuba dive, join the resorts' activities programs, hike their trails, and eat at some or all of their restaurants. See "The Whitsunday Island Resorts," below, for details on where to stay. Club Crocodile Long Island is a rather noisy, unpretentious resort that has plentiful watersports, picturesque hiking trails, wild wallabies, and a large beach-cum-tidal flat where you can relax on sun lounges.

You can get to the islands on your own by ferry (see "Getting Around," above), or take an organized day trip that visits one, two, or even three islands in a day. **Fantasea Cruises** (© 1800/650 851 in Australia, or 07/4946 5111; www.fantasea.com.au) and **Whitsunday Island Adventure Cruises** (© 07/4946 5255 for the booking agent) all offer them, as do several yachts.

SCENIC FLIGHTS   Expect to pay around A$200 (US$160) for a 30-minute flight over the Whitsundays (a spectacular sight from the air), about A$295 (US$236) for a seaplane flight to a private Reef pontoon to snorkel for a couple of hours, and up to A$290 (US$232) for a helicopter to drop you on an island with a champagne picnic and snorkel gear. **Hamilton Island Aviation** (© 07/4946 8249) and **Air Whitsunday** (© 07/4946 9111) offer a range of tours.

FISHING   Reef fishing is superb throughout the islands; red emperor, coral trout, sweetlip, and snapper are common catches. One of the most popular charter vessels is the 16m (52-ft.) timber cruiser *Moruya* (© 07/4946 7127, or 0415/185 653 mobile; www.fishingwhitsunday.com.au). Day trips depart Shute Harbour daily at 9:30am and return at 5:30pm. They include lunch, bait, and fishing rods. The crew will even clean your catch for you. Adults pay A$120 (US$96), seniors A$110 (US$88), children 4 to 14 A$75 (US$60), and a family of four A$315 (US$252).

The 12m (39-ft.) *Marlin Blue* (© 07/4946 5044, or 0427/009 575 mobile) takes reef and game anglers out from Abel Point Marina and South Molle Island Resort for A$245 (US$196) per person for a full day on a shared charter. That includes lunch, bait, and tackle; drinks are extra. The boat departs the mainland at 7am and returns around 5:30pm.

If you want to undertake your own fishing expedition, **Harbourside Boat Hire**, in Shute Harbour (© 07/4946 9330), rents motorized dinghies for A$60 (US$48) for a half-day or A$90 (US$72) for a full day. Half-cabin cruisers cost A$90 (US$72) for a half-day, A$150 (US$120) for a full day. They also rent fishing rods and sell tackle, bait, ice, and all your fishing needs.

ECOTOURS   Visitors to the Whitsundays can get up close and personal with crocodiles in their natural habitat with **Proserpine River Eco Tours** (book through Fantasea Cruises, © 07/4946 5111), which combines an open-air wagon ride through the pristine Goorganga wetlands and a boat trip on the river to learn more about one of Queensland's major crocodile-breeding grounds. This is the only place to see crocs in safety in the wild south of the Daintree. Bus pickups operate from Airlie Beach, Cannonvale, and Proserpine for the tours, which run about 4 hours, depending on tides, and cost A$85 (US$68) for adults, A$55 (US$44) for kids 4 to 14, and A$219 (US$175) for a family of four. Back on land, you'll enjoy billy tea, the best damper I've ever tasted (and they'll even give you the recipe), and a talk on native wildlife over a barbecue lunch.

GOLF   Serious golfers should not miss a round on arguably Australia's best resort course, the championship **Turtle Point golf course** ✿ at Laguna Whitsundays Resort, Kunapipi Springs Road, Midge Point (© 07/4947 7777), a 45-minute drive south of

---

⸢Finds⸥ Hitting the Sand at Whitehaven Beach

The 6km (3¾-mile) stretch of pure-white silica sand on **Whitehaven Beach** ★★ will leave you in rapture. The beach, on uninhabited Whitsunday Island, does not boast a lot of coral, but the swimming is good, and the forested shore is beautiful. Take a book and chill out. Some sailboat day trips visit it, as do several motorized vessel operators, including **Fantasea Cruises** (© 07/4946 5111). Expect to pay around A$80 (US$64) per person for the day, with lunch.

Moments Whale-Watching in the Whitsundays

Humpback whales migrate to the Whitsundays July through September to give birth. These fearless giants of the deep come right up to the boat. **Fantasea Cruises** (© **07/4946 5111**; www.fantasea.com.au) runs whale-watching cruises in season; trips feature an onboard talk and videos. The cost is about A$100 (US$80) per adult. If you don't see whales, you can go free another day, or choose another of Fantasea's cruises as an alternative.

Airlie Beach. An 18-hole round dodging wallabies, goannas, and kookaburras on the difficult fairways will set you back around A$70 (US$56) midweek, A$80 (US$64) weekends, plus A$35 (US$28) for clubs and cart.

SEA KAYAKING ★ If you have strong arms, sea kayaking is a wonderful way to enjoy the islands. Daydream Island and the beaches and bays of the North, Mid, and South Molle group of islands are all within paddling distance of the mainland. It's common to see dolphins, turtles, and sharks along the way. One long-established operator is **Salty Dog Sea Kayaking** (© **07/4946 1388;** www.saltydog.com.au), which takes escorted trips through the islands. Half-day trips run on Tuesday, Wednesday, and Saturday, and full-day trips on Monday, Thursday, and Friday, departing Airlie Beach at 8:30am. A half-day trip is A$58 (US$46) per person, and a day trip is A$115 (US$92). Three- and 6-day trips, during which you camp out, are A$395 (US$316) and A$1,190 (US$952). All rates include snorkel gear, meals, hotel pickup, and, on overnight trips, camping gear. The company also delivers sea kayaks anywhere in the Whitsundays. The price of a full day's rental starts at A$50 (US$40) for a single kayak, A$60 (US$48) for a double, including delivery and pickup and all safety equipment. A security deposit of A$200 (US$160) is required for rentals.

AIRLIE BEACH
640km (397 miles) S of Cairns; 1,146km (711 miles) N of Brisbane

The little town of Airlie Beach is the focal point of activity on the Whitsunday mainland. The town is only a few blocks long, but you will find an adequate choice of decent accommodations, a small selection of good restaurants and bars, a nice boutique or two, and facilities such as banks and a supermarket. Cruises and yachts depart from Shute Harbour, a 10-minute drive south on Shute Harbour Road, and Abel Point Marina, a 10-minute walk west along the foreshore or a quick drive over the hill on Shute Harbour Road.

Airlie Beach has a massive beachfront artificial lagoon, with sandy beaches and landscaped parkland, which solves the problem of where to swim in stinger season. The lagoon is the size of about six full-size Olympic swimming pools, set in 4 hectares (10 acres) of botanic gardens, with a children's pool, plenty of shade, barbecues, picnic shelters, toilets, showers, and parking.

Perched on the edge of the Coral Sea, with views across Pioneer Bay and the Whitsunday Passage, Airlie Beach has a village atmosphere; life revolves around the beach and marina by day, and the bars and restaurants by night.

The spit of land between Airlie Bay and Boathaven Bay is home to the Airlie Beach Sailing Club. Shute Harbour, 11km (7¾ miles) from Airlie Beach, is one of Queensland's busiest ports, filled with yachts, cruisers, water taxis, ferries, and fishermen. For a bird's-eye view, head to the Lions Lookout.

WHERE TO STAY

Coral Sea Resort ★   In Airlie Beach's best location, on the edge of Paradise Point, with 280-degree views of the ocean, this 6-year-old resort is one of the best places to stay on the Whitsunday mainland. The wide range of great accommodations styles suits everyone from honeymooners to families, and although it's relatively sprawling, the design is such that you can easily feel you're alone. All the rooms have a nautical feel. The Coral Sea suites are divine, complete with a Jacuzzi and double hammock on the balcony. There are four styles of suites, apartments, and family units. Bayview suites have a Jacuzzi inside. It's a 3-minute walk along the waterfront to Airlie Beach village.

25 Oceanview Ave., Airlie Beach, QLD 4802. ℂ **1800/075 061** in Australia, or 07/4946 6458. Fax 07/4946 6516. www.coralsearesort.com.au 78 units. A$210–A$265 (US$168–US$212) double; A$285–A$345 (US$228–US$276) double suite; A$295 (US$236) double 1-bedroom apt; A$310–A$340 (US$248–US$272) double 2-bedroom apt; A$310 (US$248) family unit for up to 5; A$340 (US$272) 1-bedroom penthouse; A$440 (US$352) double 2-bedroom penthouse; A$610 (US$488) double 3-bedroom penthouse. Extra person A$30 (US$24). Crib A$12 (US$9.60). 3-night minimum at Easter and Dec 26–Jan 5. Ask about packages. AE, DC, MC, V. Free parking. **Amenities:** Restaurant; bar; 25m (82-ft.) outdoor pool; exercise room; game room; tour desk; car-rental desk; 24-hr. room service; massage; babysitting; coin-op laundry; dry cleaning. *In room:* A/C, ceiling fans, TV w/satellite and free movies, kitchenette, minibar, coffeemaker, hair dryer, iron.

Martinique Whitsunday Resort ★   Apartments in this French Caribbean–style complex high on the hill above Airlie Beach have views that make the short but very steep walk from the town well worthwhile. The one-, two-, and three-bedroom apartments are roomy and light, and each has a big balcony. The wet-edge lap pool also overlooks the Coral Sea, and is surrounded by tropical gardens and waterfalls. There's a barbecue area, and you can also order kitchen supplies to be ready when you arrive. Apartments are serviced weekly, and each has a washing machine and dryer.

⌐Tips Great Whitsunday Walking

The Whitsundays Great Walk—one of six **Great Walks of Queensland**—covers 36km (22 miles) in Conway State Forest and Conway National Park, behind Airlie Beach. The trail starts in the parking lot at the end of Brandy Creek Road, a short drive from Cannonvale, and winds in three stages from Brandy Creek to Airlie Beach, with two campsites at 12km (7½-mile) intervals. The hills here are rich in giant strangler figs, ferns, and palms, and if you're lucky, you'll spot a giant blue Ulysses butterfly. Walkers should carry drinking water, because the water in natural systems is not good for drinking.

The Queensland Parks and Wildlife Service information center, Shute Harbour Road at Mandalay Road (ℂ **07/4946 7022**) 2.5km (1½ miles) northeast of Airlie Beach, has more information on this and other, shorter walks. It's open Monday through Friday from 8:30am to 5pm and most, but not all, Saturdays from 9am to 1pm.

Other Great Walks are on Fraser Island (p. 353), the Wet Tropics near Cairns, the Sunshine Coast hinterland, Gold Coast hinterland, and near Mackay. For more details on all walks, log onto www.epa.qld.gov.au.

18 Golden Orchid Dr. (off Shute Harbour Rd.), Airlie Beach, QLD 4802. © **07/4948 0401.** Fax 07/4948 0402. www.martiniquewhitsunday.com.au. A$180 (US$144) double 1-bedroom apt; A$210 (US$168) double 2-bedroom apt; A$330 (US$264) 3-bedroom apt for up to 6. Extra person A$25 (US$20). AE, DC, MC, V. Free covered parking. **Amenities:** Outdoor lap pool; exercise room; 2 Jacuzzis; tour desk. *In room:* A/C, ceiling fans, TV, kitchen, minibar, hair dryer, iron.

WHERE TO DINE

Mangrove Jack's Café Bar PIZZA/CAFE FARE   Bareboat sailors, local sugar farmers, Sydney yuppies, and European backpackers all flock to this big, open-fronted sports bar and restaurant. The mood is upbeat and pleasantly casual, the surrounds are spick-and-span, and the food passes muster. Wood-fired pizza with trendy toppings is the specialty. There is no table service; place your order at the bar and collect your food when your number is called. More than 50 wines come by the glass.

In the Airlie Beach Hotel, 16 The Esplanade (enter from Shute Harbour Rd.). © **07/4946 6233.** Reservations recommended. Main courses A$7.90–A$20 (US$6.30–US$16). AE, DC, MC, V. Daily 10am–midnight.

THE WHITSUNDAY ISLAND RESORTS

There are about 10 resorts of varying degrees of splendor; accommodations range from positively plush to comfortably midrange to downright old-fashioned.

VERY EXPENSIVE

Hayman ★★★   This is the most luxurious, glitzy, and glamorous resort in Australia. And an A$50-million (US$40-million) redevelopment in 2003 made it even more so. Check-in is done over a glass of bubbly aboard the resort's sleek launch, which meets you at Hamilton Island Airport. On arrival, you won't take long to find your way through the open-air sandstone lanais, cascading ponds, and tropical foliage to the fabulous hexagonal complex of swimming pools by the sea. Despite the luxury, Hayman is relaxed. Dress is beachwear by day, smart casual at night (pack something elegant for dinner, if you wish). An impressive lineup of activities is available, and it's probably fair to say the staff at Hayman can organize almost anything you desire.

While Hayman is renowned for the antiques, artworks, and fine objets d'art gracing its public areas, the accommodations are welcoming. Every room, suite, villa, and penthouse has a balcony or terrace, bathrobes, and valet service (and butler service in the penthouses). Pool Wing rooms with marble floors and bathrooms and tropically elegant furnishings have views over the pool, and to the sea from the third and fourth floors. Lagoon Wing rooms overlook a lagoon and have sea views from the third floor. The resort has new Lagoon rooms, suites and penthouses, 16 Retreat Rooms (each with private veranda, open patios, and outdoor rinse showers), a Jacuzzi, and a contemporary beachfront restaurant. For even greater privacy, the **Beach Villa,** opened in late 2002, has a private Balinese-style courtyard, walled gardens, a private infinity plunge pool, and personalized concierge service.

Hayman Island (33km/20 miles from Shute Harbour), Great Barrier Reef, QLD 4801. © **1800/075 175** in Australia, 800/745-8883 in the U.S. and Canada, 0800/1010-1111 in the U.K. and Ireland, 0800/44 1016 in New Zealand (Leading Hotels of the World), 02/9268 1888 (Sydney sales office), or 07/4940 1234 (the island). Fax 02/9268 1899 (Sydney sales office) or 07/4940 1567 (the island). www.hayman.com.au. 244 units. A$620–A$1,150 (US$496–US$920) double; A$2,100 (US$1,680) suite; A$2,800–A$4,500 (US$2,240–US$3,600) penthouse; A$3,500 (US$2,800) Beach Villa. 2-night minimum and 10% surcharge Dec 24–Jan 7. Children under 13 stay free in parent's room; A$140 (US$112) child over 12 sharing parent's room; 50% of room rate for child under 13 in adjoining room. Dining for children 5–12 half price. Ask about packages. AE, DC, MC, V. Resort launch meets all flights at Hamilton Island Airport for the 55-min. transfer. Helicopter and seaplane transfers available. **Amenities:** 4 restaurants; 2 bars; 3 pools (1 saltwater, 2 heated freshwater); beachside 9-hole golf putting green; 5 lit tennis courts (w/ball machine and coaching); extensive health club w/massage and sauna; outdoor Jacuzzi; watersports (including parasailing; water-skiing; windsurfing; catamarans; dive center offering dive day trips, courses, and gear rental); daily kids' club (ages 5–14), day care for younger kids; game room; concierge; tour desk; business center; shopping arcade; salon; 24-hr. room service; babysitting; laundry service; dry cleaning. *In room:* A/C, TV w/free and pay movies, fax, minibar, fridge, coffeemaker, hair dryer, iron, safe.

Peppers Palm Bay ⭐

A A\$7-million (US\$5.6-million) upgrade in 2001 transformed this Long Island hideaway, giving its beachfront bures (a kind of hut common in Polynesia) a glamorous Balinese style, with new decks and furnishings. The dining and bar area overlooks the gorgeous pool area, which is surrounded by timber decking, and a full day spa is now one of the attractions. This is a private and romantic spot, with no phone, radio, television, or air-conditioning in the rooms, but each veranda has a hammock. The large Club Crocodile Long Island resort is a 20-minute walk across the hill on the other side of the island, completely hidden from Palm Bay, but guests at Palm Bay Hideaway can use Club Crocodile's watersports facilities. Nonmotorized watersports such as kayaks are available at Palm Bay.

Palm Bay, Long Island (16km/10 miles southeast of Shute Harbour), Whitsunday Islands (P.M.B. 28, Mackay, QLD 4741). ℂ **1800/095 025** in Australia, or 07/4946 9233. Fax 07/4946 9309. www.peppers.com.au. 21 units. A\$380 (US\$304) double cabin; A\$580 (US\$464) double bure; A\$684 (US\$547) 2-bedroom bungalow. Rates include breakfast. Ask about packages. AE, DC, MC, V. Fantasea Cruises (ℂ **1800/650 851** in Australia, or 07/4946 5111) launch transfers from Hamilton Island Airport; water taxi transfers available from Shute Harbour. **Amenities:** Restaurant and bar; outdoor pool; lit tennis court; Jacuzzi; watersports; tour desk; massage; coin-op laundry; laundry service; dry cleaning. *In room:* Ceiling fan, minibar, coffeemaker, hair dryer, iron, no phone.

South Long Island Nature Lodge ⭐⭐

This lodge was designed to show off the Whitsundays' natural beauty. Tucked in a cove under towering hoop pines and palms, it is an environmentally sensitive establishment on a national park island. It appeals to people who want to explore the wilderness in basic comfort, without the crowds, noisy watersports, or artificial atmosphere of a resort. It's also a great place to meet other travelers. A maximum of 10 guests stay in simple but smart cabins facing the sea, each with a double and single bed, modern bathroom, and private deck facing the sea. Solar power rules, so there is no air-conditioning or TVs, hair dryers, irons, or other appliances. There is one public phone. Social life centers on an open-sided gazebo by the beach, equipped with a natural-history library and CDs, where everyone dines together at slab tables under the Milky Way on fabulous buffet-style campfire meals. Access is only by a short but stunning helicopter flight from Hamilton Island.

Daily excursions include sailing away on the lodge's gleaming 10m (33-ft.) catamaran, a helicopter flight to the Outer Reef and Whitehaven Beach, sea kayaking the mangroves to spot giant green sea turtles (which are common around the lodge), snorkeling the fringing reef on uninhabited islands, or bushwalking to a magical milkwood grove no one else knows about. Or you may prefer to just laze in a hammock or head off with a free sea kayak and snorkel gear. The beach is more tidal flat than sand, but clean and firm enough to sunbathe on. Wildlife abounds, including Myrtle, the lodge's pet kangaroo. Those who stay on this 1,215-hectare (3,001-acre) island consider it a plus that no ferries or cruise boats stop here and that the lodge is inaccessible to day-trippers.

Paradise Bay, Long Island (16km/10 miles southeast of Shute Harbour), Whitsunday Islands (P.O. Box 842, Airlie Beach, QLD 4802). ℂ **07/4946 9777.** Fax 07/4946 9777. www.southlongisland.com. 5 units (all with shower only). A\$3,439 (US\$2,751) per person for a minimum 5–night stay. A\$460 (US\$368) per person extra nights. No single supplement. Rates include all meals, helicopter transfers from Hamilton Island Airport, daily excursions, and equipment. MC, V. Children under 14 not accepted. *In room:* Fridge, coffeemaker, no phone.

EXPENSIVE

Daydream Island Resort ★★ *Kids*   After an A$40-million (US$32-million) refurbishment, one of the Whitsundays' oldest resorts is now one of Australia's most extensive and modern spa resorts. Since reopening, the resort has found a new clientele while retaining many of the features—such as the outdoor cinema and kids' club—that have always made it popular with families. The 16 therapy rooms at the Rejuvenation Spa have some of the most sophisticated equipment in the country. The state-of-the-art spa has an in-house naturopath and a range of computerized health analyses using equipment and tests usually found only in clinics in Europe and the United States, such as iridology and measurement of vitamin and mineral imbalances and antioxidant levels. Rooms are large, smart, and comfortable, with uninterrupted ocean views. The "village" at the southern end of the island, a short stroll along the boardwalk from the resort, has shops, cafes, a pool and bar, a water-activities center, and a tavern serving bistro-style meals. A rainforest walk stretches almost the entire length of the kilometer-long (just over half a mile) island; other activities include snorkeling, sailboarding, jet-skiing, parasailing, coral viewing, reef fishing, diving and dive school, tennis, volleyball, and minigolf.

Daydream Island (40km/25 miles northeast of Shute Harbour), Whitsunday Islands (P.M.B. 22, Mackay, QLD 4741.) ℂ **07/4948 8488.** Fax 07/4948 8499. www.daydreamisland.com. 296 units. A$330–A$450 (US$264–US$360) double; A$495–A$701 (US$396–US$561) suite; A$592–A$675 (US$474–US$540) family suite. Children under 15 stay free with existing bedding. Ask about packages. AE, MC, V. Fantasea Cruises (ℂ **1800/650 851** in Australia, or 07/4946 5111) provides launch transfers from Shute Harbour (15 min.) and from Long Island, South Molle, and Hamilton Island. **Amenities:** 3 restaurants; 3 bars; 3 freshwater outdoor pools (1 heated); 2 lit tennis courts; 3 Jacuzzis; watersports equipment; tour desk; coin-op laundry. *In room:* A/C, TV w/pay movies and PlayStation, dataport, minibar, coffeemaker, hair dryer, iron.

Hamilton Island ★★ *Kids*   More a vacation village than a single resort, Hamilton has the widest range of activities, accommodations styles, and restaurants of any Great Barrier Reef island resort. Thanks to an A$56-million (US$45-million) refurbishment over the past 5 years, the place is looking fresh. Accommodations choices are extralarge rooms and suites in the high-rise hotel; high-rise one-bedroom apartments; Polynesian-style bungalows in tropical gardens (ask for one away from the road for real privacy); and glamorous rooms in the two-story, adults-only Beach Club (with minimalist decor, a personal "host" to cater to every whim, and private restaurant, lounge, and pool for exclusive use of Beach Club guests); as well as one-, two-, three-, and four-bedroom apartments and villas. The best sea views are from the second-floor Beach Club rooms, from floors 5 to 18 of the Reef View Hotel, and from most apartments and villas. The hotel and Beach Club have concierge service. In-room amenities vary depending on your accommodations choice (for example, apartments have kitchens), so check when booking.

On one side of the island is a marina village with cafes, restaurants, shops, and a yacht club. On the other are the accommodations, a large and inviting free-form pool and swim-up bar, and the wide curve of Cat's Eye Beach. Hamilton offers a huge range of watersports, fishing trips, cruises, speedboat rides, Go-Karts, a "wire flyer" flying-fox hang glider, a pistol/clay target/rifle range, minigolf, an aquatic driving range, beach barbecue safaris in an army truck, hiking trails, an Aussie wildlife sanctuary where you can cuddle a koala or hold a baby crocodile, and an extensive daily activities program. Because a steep hill splits the resort, you need to get around by the free shuttle (which runs half-hourly during the day, and every 15 min. 5–10pm), by golf buggy (A$35/US$28 per hour or A$75/US$60 for 24 hr.), or on foot. Despite the price, everyone seems to go for the buggies, so the pace of the place can feel like rush hour. To get away, hit the beach or the hiking trails—most of the 750-hectare (1,853-acre) island is virgin bushland. The biggest drawback is that just about every activity costs extra (and it's usually not cheap), so you are constantly adding to your holiday bill.

Hamilton Island (16km/10 miles southeast of Shute Harbour), Whitsunday Islands, QLD 4803. (© **1800/075 110** in Australia, or 02/8353 8444 (Sydney reservations office), or 07/4946 9999 (the island). Fax 02/8353 8498 (Sydney reservations office), or 07/4946 8888 (the island). www.hamiltonisland.com.au. 820 units (some with shower only). A$260–A$306 (US$208–US$245) bungalow or Palm Terrace; A$340–A$410 (US$272–US$328) hotel double; A$565 (US$452) Beach Club double; A$509–A$996 (US$407–US$797) suite. Standard villas (3-night minimum): A$470 (US$376) 1-bedroom; A$550 (US$440) 2-bedroom; A$630 (US$504) 3-bedroom. Deluxe villas (3-night minimum): A$710 (US$568) 2-bedroom; A$790 (US$632) 3-bedroom; A$890 (US$712) 4-bedroom. Children under 14 stay free in parent's room with existing bedding and eat free from kids' menu at 4 restaurants. Rates include airport transfers. Ask about packages. AE, DC, MC, V. Airlines fly into Hamilton Island Airport. Fantasea Cruises (© **1800/650 851** in Australia, or 07/4946 5111) provides launch transfers from Shute Harbour and most other islands. No children in Beach Club. **Amenities:** 10 restaurants; 7 bars; 6 outdoor pools; minigolf and driving range; lit tennis courts; health club and spa; extensive range of watersports and activities; bike rental; child-care center for kids from 6 weeks to 14 years (in 3 groups); tour desk; business center; shopping arcade; salon; limited room service; massage; babysitting; coin-op laundry; laundry service (hotel only). *In room:* A/C, TV, fax, minibar, coffeemaker, hair dryer, iron, safe.

MODERATE

Hook Island Wilderness Resort This humble collection of cabins and campsites on a white sandy beach is one of the few really affordable island resorts on the Great Barrier Reef. That makes it popular with backpackers and anybody who just wants to dive, rent canoes, play beach volleyball, visit the underwater observatory, hike, fish in the four-person flat-bottom boat, laze in the pool and Jacuzzi, or chill out. Good snorkeling is footsteps from shore, and the resort's dive center conducts first-time and regular dives off the beach. Hook is a national park and the second-largest Whitsunday island. The cabins are very basic, with beds or bunks sleeping six or eight. All come with fresh bed linens; bring your own bath towels. A store sells essentials for campers, but the camp kitchen is not available to guests staying in cabins or bunkhouses.

Hook Island (40km/25 miles northeast of Shute Harbour), Whitsunday Islands (P.M.B. 23, Mackay, QLD 4741.) (© **07/4946 9380.** Fax 07/4946 9470. www.hookislandresort.com. 20 tent sites; 2 10-bed dormitories; 10 cabins, 4 with bathroom (shower only). A$89 (US$71) cabin without bathroom double; extra adult A$35 (US$28), extra child 4–14 A$22 (US$18). A$130 (US$104) cabin with bathroom double; extra person A$40 (US$32), extra child A$30 (US$24). Dorm bed A$35 (US$28) adult, A$20 (US$16) child 4–14. Tent site A$25 (US$20) adult, A$15 (US$12) child 4–14. Ask about packages. MC, V. Transfers from mainland A$36 (US$29) per person, round-trip. Boat leaves Shute Harbour 9am, Hook Island 3pm (trip time: 1 hr). Book through resort. **Amenities:** Restaurant; bar; outdoor pool; Jacuzzi; watersports equipment (snorkel gear, canoes, sea kayaks); tour desk. *In room:* A/C, minifridge, coffeemaker.

6 The Capricorn Coast & the Southern Reef Islands

South of the Whitsundays, the Bruce Highway travels through rural country until it hits the beaches of the Sunshine Coast just north of Brisbane. It may not be the tourism heartland of the state, but there's still plenty to discover. The most spectacular of the Great Barrier Reef islands, Heron Island, is off the coast from Gladstone. Heron's reefs are a source of enchantment for divers and snorkelers; its waters boast 21 fabulous dive sites. In summer giant turtles nest on its beaches, and in winter humpback whales cruise by.

North of Gladstone is Rockhampton and the Capricorn Coast, named after the Tropic of Capricorn that runs through it. Rockhampton is also a stepping-stone to the resort island of Great Keppel. The reefs and islands off Rockhampton are not a commonly visited part of the Great Barrier Reef, yet they offer some good dive sites, most of them not far out to sea. To the south, off the small town of Bundaberg, lies another tiny coral cay, Lady Elliot Island, which is a nesting site for tens of thousands of seabirds and has a first-rate fringing reef. Two little-known attractions in Bundaberg are its good shore scuba diving and a loggerhead turtle rookery that operates in summer on the beach. Farther south lies the world's largest sand island, the World Heritage–listed Fraser Island, which can be negotiated only on foot or by four-wheel-drive (see section 7 in this chapter).

ROCKHAMPTON: THE BEEF CAPITAL
1,055km (654 miles) S of Cairns; 638km (396 miles) N of Brisbane

You may hear Queenslanders talk dryly about "Rockvegas." Don't be fooled. "Rocky" is the unofficial capital of the sprawling beef-cattle country inland, and the gateway to Great Keppel Island, which boasts some of the few inexpensive island retreats in Queensland, but it bears no resemblance to Las Vegas. Heritage buildings line the Fitzroy River, where barramundi await keen fishermen. Every Friday night at the Great Western Hotel, bull-riding cowboys take to the rodeo ring to test their skills against local Brahman bulls.

ESSENTIALS
GETTING THERE   Rockhampton is on the Bruce Highway, a 3½-hour drive south of Mackay, and about 90 minutes north of Gladstone.

QantasLink (© **13 13 13** in Australia) has flights from Brisbane, Mackay, and Gladstone. **Virgin Blue** (© **13 67 89** in Australia) flies direct from Brisbane. **Jetstar** (© **13 15 38** in Australia) flies from Sydney.

Queensland Rail (© **13 22 32** in Queensland, or 07/3235 1122; www.qr.com.au) trains stop at Rockhampton daily. The trip from Brisbane takes just 7 hours on the high-speed Tilt Train; the fare is A$98 (US$78) in economy class and A$147 (US$118) in business class.

Greyhound Australia (© **13 14 99** in Australia) serves Rockhampton on its many daily runs between Brisbane and Cairns. The fare is A$91 (US$73) from Brisbane (trip time: 11½ hr.) and A$140 (US$112) from Cairns (trip time: 18 hr.).

VISITOR INFORMATION   Drop by the **Capricorn Tourism** information center, at the city's southern entrance on Gladstone Road at the Capricorn Spire (© **1800/ 676 701** in Australia, or 07/4927 2055; www.capricorntourism.com.au). It's open daily from 9am to 5pm.

GETTING AROUND   **Avis** (© **07/4927 3344**), **Budget** (© **07/4922 8064**), **Hertz** (© **07/4922 2721** airport, or 07/4927 8700 city), and **Thrifty** (© **07/4927 8755**) have offices in Rockhampton. The local bus is **Sunbus** (© **07/4936 2133**).

EXPLORING THE AREA: CAVERNS, ABORIGINAL CULTURE & MORE
The **Capricorn Caves** ✦ (© **07/4934 2883**; wwwcapricorncaves.com.au), 23km (14 miles) north of Rockhampton at Olsen's Caves Road, off the Bruce Highway, have been a popular attraction in this part of the world ever since Norwegian pioneer John Olsen stumbled upon them in 1882. The limestone caves originated in an ancient coral reef (380 million years old) and today are a maze of small tunnels and larger

Cannonvale
Airlie Beach
Prosperine
Whitsunday Island
Conway National Park
Bloomsbury
Seaforth
Brampton Island
Eungella National Park
Bucasia
Mackay
Hay Point
Sarina Beach
Sarina
■ *Cape Palmerstown National Park*

Dipperu National Park

St. Lawrence

SOUTH PACIFIC OCEAN

Yeppoon
Great Keppel Island
Rockhampton
Keppel Sands
Keppel Bay
• *Wilson Island*
Heron Island
Mount Morgan
Port Alma
BRUCE HWY.
Gladstone
Lady Musgrave Island
Tannum Sands
DAWSON HWY.
Calliope
Agnes Waters
' *Lady Elliot Island*
Biloela
BURNETT HWY.
Bundaberg
Bargara

Area of detail
AUSTRALIA

chambers. The 1-hour tour, which winds through large caverns with stalactite and sta-
lagmite formations before entering the 20m-high (66-ft.) Cathedral Cave, is A$16
(US$13) for adults, A$8 (US$6.40) for children 5 to 15. It departs daily (except Dec
25) on the hour from 9am to 4pm (closing time is 5pm). Spelunkers over age 16 can
squeeze through tunnels and chimneys and rock climb on a 3-hour adventure tour
that costs A$60 (US$48); book 24 hours ahead for this. From December 1 to January 10, you can catch the Summer Solstice light cave on a tour departing every morning at 11am. On the longest day of the year, the sun moves slowly over the Tropic of
Capricorn, and a ray of pure light pours through a hole in the limestone caves. It's
known as the Summer Solstice phenomenon and takes place at the only time of year
when the sun is directly over the Tropic of Capricorn. The caves are also home to
thousands of small insectivorous bats, which leave the cave at sunset to feed. Plan
enough time here to walk the 30-minute dry rainforest trail, watch the video on bats
in the interpretive center, and feed the wild kangaroos. If you like it so much you want
to stay, a motor-home park and campground are attached. Bus tours operate from
Rockhampton; contact the Caves for details.

The **Dreamtime Cultural Centre** (© **07/4936 1655;** www.dreamtimecentre.com.
au), on the Bruce Highway opposite the Yeppoon turnoff, 6km (3¾ miles) north of town,
showcases Aboriginal culture. There's a sandstone cave replica, a display on the dugong

(manatee) culture of the Torres Strait Islanders, and an Aboriginal crafts shop. The center is open Monday to Friday from 10am to 3:30pm. Admission, including a tour, is A$13 (US$10) for adults, A$9 (US$7.20) for seniors, A$6 (US$4.80) for students and backpackers, and A$11 (US$8.80) for kids. Regular tours of burial sites and rock art, with didgeridoo demonstrations and boomerang-throwing classes, start at 10:30am.

Rockhampton has two free public botanic gardens, both nice for a stroll and a barbecue picnic. The **Kershaw Gardens,** which display Aussie rainforest, wetland, and fragrant plants from north of the 30th parallel, also have a monorail and a pioneer-style slab hut where Devonshire teas are served. Enter off Charles Street. The **Rockhampton Botanic Gardens** (© 07/4922 1654), established in 1869, are quite lovely. Admission is free to the small zoo inside the grounds, which features 'roos, koalas, lorikeets, cassowaries, and a range of other creatures, including—rather bizarrely—two chimpanzees. The gardens are open 6am to 6pm daily, the zoo daily from 8am to 5pm. Enter off Ann Street or Spencer Street.

WHERE TO STAY

Rydges Capricorn Resort ★   The 20km (13 miles) of unbroken beach that fronts this resort—and the fact that it is the only resort of any size or style in this region—are reasons enough to visit. The resort is about 9km (5½ miles) from the pretty seaside town of Yeppoon, about 45km (28 miles) north of Rockhampton Airport. Open since 1986, the resort was built and is owned by Japanese businessman Yohachiro Iwasaki, and you will still hear the locals refer to it as "the Iwasaki Resort" despite its several changes of name over the years. Now showing its age a little, the resort is nevertheless cheerful and pleasant, and the rooms are spacious.

The best of the three accommodations blocks is The Palms, with views over the beach and out to Great Keppel Island. The main resort block is dominated by one of the largest freshwater swimming pools in the Southern Hemisphere, popular with visiting local families, especially on weekends. Accommodations vary: Some suites and all apartments have kitchenettes, hotel rooms have minibars, and two-bedroom apartments and Capricorn suites with kitchens have a washing machine and dryer. Set in 8,910 hectares (22,000 acres) of bushland, the resort also has extensive wetlands teeming with bird life. Wetlands tours are available for a fee, as are horseback riding, land yachting, fishing, canoeing, clay-pigeon shooting, WaveRunners, and rifle shooting. This is not the place for a quiet getaway—it is very popular with large and sometimes noisy conference groups—but there are lots of activities, and it may be just the place to break up your coastal trek.

Farnborough Rd. (P.O. Box 350), Yeppoon, QLD 4703. © **1800/075 902** in Australia, or 07/4925 2525. Fax 07/4925 2526. www.rydges.com. 279 units. A$270 (US$216) double; A$320 (US$256) junior suite; A$345 (US$276) junior suite with kitchenette; A$395 (US$316) Capricorn suite; A$425 (US$340) Capricorn suite with kitchenette; A$340 (US$272) 1-bedroom apt; A$415 (US$332) 2-bedroom apt. Free crib. Packages, including golf packages, available year-round. Rates include transfers from airport, bus, or train station; watersports; other activities. AE, DC, MC, V. Free covered parking. **Amenities:** 4 restaurants; 2 bars; outdoor freshwater pool w/adjoining heated beach-style pool; 2 18-hole golf courses; 4 lit tennis courts; exercise room; outdoor Jacuzzi; sauna; extensive watersports and other activities; bike rental; free daytime kids' club (fee for evening sessions); game room for children over 14; playground; concierge; tour desk; car-rental desk; business center; salon; limited room service; in-room and poolside massage; babysitting; laundry service; coin-op laundry; dry cleaning. *In room:* A/C, TV w/pay movies, coffeemaker, hair dryer, iron.

GREAT KEPPEL ISLAND

15km (9½ miles) E of Rockhampton

This 1,454-hectare (3,591-acre) island is home to one major resort, for the 18-to-35s, and a couple of smaller, family-oriented resorts. You can stay at one of the resorts or take a day trip from the mainland and pay to use many of the facilities, including watersports equipment, pools, and food outlets. Seventeen beaches on the island are accessible by walking trails or dinghy (which you can rent). The shallow waters and fringing reef make the island a good choice for beginner divers; experienced divers will see corals, sea snakes, turtles, and rays. If you stay overnight, you will most likely be rewarded with one of the spectacular sunsets for which the island is famous.

GETTING THERE   **Keppel Tourist Services** (℗ **07/4933 6744**) and **Freedom Fast Cats** (℗ **07/4933 6244**) operate launches that make the 30-minute crossing from Rosslyn Bay Harbour, about 55km (34 miles) east of Rockhampton, three or four times daily. The round-trip costs about A$31 (US$25) for adults, A$16 (US$13) for children 5 to 15, and A$78 (US$62) for a family of four.

From Rockhampton, take the Capricorn Coast scenic drive Route 10 to Emu Park and follow the signs to Rosslyn Bay Harbour. If you're coming to Rockhampton from the north, the scenic drive turnoff is just north of the city, and from there it's 46km (29 miles) to the harbor. You can leave your car in covered storage at **Great Keppel Island Security Car Park,** 422 Scenic Hwy., near the harbor (℗ **07/4933 6670**), for A$6.50 to A$8 (US$5.20–US$6.40) per day.

Rothery's Coaches (℗ **07/4922 4320**) runs from Kern Arcade on Bolsover Street in Rockhampton to Rosslyn Bay Harbour, and back, three times a day. You can request pickup from the airport, train station, or your hotel. Round-trip fares from town are A$17 (US$14) for adults; A$14 (US$11) for seniors, students, and children; A$42 (US$34) for a family of four. The round-trip airport fare is A$30 (US$24) for adults, A$25 (US$20) for seniors and students, A$14 (US$11) for children, and A$75 (US$60) for families.

Guests at Mercure Resort Great Keppel Island can fly from Rockhampton on a light plane, which takes about 15 minutes and costs A$138 (US$110) round-trip. Book through the resort (see below).

VISITOR INFORMATION   The **Great Keppel Island Information Centre,** at the ferry terminal at Rosslyn Bay Harbour (℗ **1800/774 488** in Australia), dispenses information about activities and accommodations.

WHERE TO STAY & DINE

Keppel Haven *(Value)*   Not far from the ferry drop-off point at the beach is this campground-style enclave of humble but pretty cabins and tents. It's a good choice for families. Each cabin has terra cotta–look floors, a bright kitchenette, a small double bedroom, four bunks (for the kids) in the living-dining area, fans, and a little porch. The permanent tents come with twin or double beds, four bunks separated by a canvas partition, and electricity. There are also two houses, each sleeping six, with full facilities. Bunkhouses have two rooms, each with four beds. Catamarans, Windsurfers, fishing tackle, snorkel gear, and dinghies are available on a pay-as-you-go basis. There's a general store selling basic groceries, and three communal kitchens and barbecues. If you're not staying in a cabin, bring your own towels or rent them.

Great Keppel Island, off Rockhampton, QLD 4700. ℗ 1800/35 6744 in Australia, or 07/4933 6744. Fax 07/4933 6429. www.keppelhaven.com.au. 40 permanent tents, none with bathroom; 12 cabins, all with bathroom (shower only). 12 bunkhouses (with 1 bathroom per 2 rooms). Tent A$18 (US$14) per person triple or quad share, A$20 (US$16) per person twin/double, A$28 (US$22) single. Cabins A$120 (US$96) twin or double; additional person A$20 (US$16) extra. Bunkhouses A$80 (US$64) double/twin; A$220 (US$176) houses (sleep 6). Linens in tents A$5 (US$4) per person per stay. Ask about 3-day, 2-night packages with Keppel Tourist Services that include ferry transfers and a half-day snorkeling or boom-netting cruise. MC, V. **Amenities:** Restaurant; watersports rentals; hair dryers at front desk. *In room:* Kitchenettes in cabins.

Mercure Resort Great Keppel Island   After several years catering almost exclusively to the 18-to-35s market, this popular resort has returned to what it has always done best: family holidays. Great Keppel made its name in Australia in the '70s, and has undergone many incarnations since then. In 2005, it was completely refurbished and some new family-friendly features introduced, such as a kids' club for 5- to 12-year-olds. It offers about 60 water- and land-based activities, and about 40 of them, including catamarans, paddle-skis, and Windsurfers, are free. Activities that cost extra include scuba diving, tandem sky diving, parasailing, guided snorkeling safaris, jet-skiing, sunset champagne sails, and reef-fishing trips, to name only a few. There are three types of accommodations: Hillside Villas with sea or bush views, garden rooms, and beachfront units—my pick because of their location.

Great Keppel Island, QLD 4700. © **1800/245 658** in Australia, or 07/4939 5044. Fax 07/4939 1775. www.great keppelresort.com.au 181 units. A$142 (US$114) double Garden View and Beachfront rooms; A$195 (US$156) double hillside villas. Ask about packages. AE, DC, MC, V. **Amenities:** 3 restaurants; 5 bars; 5 outdoor freshwater pools; 9-hole golf course; 3 lit tennis courts; gym; 2 Jacuzzis; kids' club (A$10–A$20/US$8–US$16 per 2- or 4-hour session); extensive watersports equipment and rental; concierge; tour desk; game room; salon; massage; coin-op laundry; laundry service; dry cleaning; nonsmoking rooms. *In room:* A/C, TV, fridge, coffeemaker, hair dryer, iron.

GLADSTONE: GATEWAY TO HERON ISLAND

550km (341 miles) N of Brisbane; 1,162 (720 miles) S of Cairns

The industrial port town of Gladstone is the departure point for breathtakingly beautiful Heron Island. It is also home to the delectable mud crab, best savored over a glass of wine at the award-winning Flinders Seafood Restaurant. About 25km (16 miles) south of the town (but off the Bruce Hwy.) are the twin beach towns of Boyne Island and Tannum Sands, which are worth the detour.

ESSENTIALS

GETTING THERE & GETTING AROUND   Gladstone is on the coast 21km (13 miles) off the Bruce Highway. **QantasLink** (book through Qantas) has many flights a day from Brisbane (trip time: 75 min.) and two direct flights a day from Rockhampton and Bundaberg.

Queensland Rail (© **13 22 32** in Queensland, or 07/3235 1122; www.qr.com.au) operates trains to Gladstone from Brisbane and Cairns most days. The fare from Brisbane (trip time: 6 hr. on the high-speed Tilt Train) is A$88 (US$70); fares from Cairns (trip time: 20 hr.) range from A$151 (US$121) for a seat to A$298 (US$238) for a first-class sleeper on the *Sunlander.*

Greyhound Australia (© **13 14 99** in Australia) operates daily coaches to Gladstone on the Brisbane-Cairns run. The fare is A$83 (US$66) from Brisbane (trip time: 10 hr.), A$155 (US$124) from Cairns (trip time: 20 hr.).

Avis (© 07/4978 2633), **Budget** (© 07/4972 8488), **Hertz** (© 07/4978 6899), and **Thrifty** (© 07/4972 5999) have offices in Gladstone.

VISITOR INFORMATION   The **Gladstone Information Centre** is in the ferry terminal at Gladstone Marina, Bryan Jordan Dr., Gladstone, QLD 4680 (© **07/4972 9000;** www.gladstoneregion.org.au). It's open from 8:30am to 5pm Monday through Friday, and from 9am to 5pm Saturday and Sunday.

WHERE TO STAY

Country Plaza International   This four-level hotel in the center of town runs a free shuttle to the wharf for guests bound for Heron Island. Gladstone's largest and best hotel, it caters primarily to business travelers, so it has ample facilities—spacious rooms with balconies, modern bathrooms, an upscale seafood restaurant, and a pool and sun deck. Most rooms have views over the port or the city. There are six three-bedroom apartments and one two-bedroom apartment.

100 Goondoon St., Gladstone, QLD 4680. © **07/4972 4499.** Fax 07/4972 4921. www.plazahotels.com.au/gladstone.htm. 80 units. A$115–A$125 (US$92–US$100) double; A$140–A$150 (US$112–US$120) apt. Rates include transfers from airport, coach terminal, marina, and train station. AE, DC, MC, V. Free covered parking. **Amenities:** Restaurant; bar; outdoor pool; business center; 24-hr. room service; laundry service; dry cleaning. *In room:* A/C, TV w/free movies, fax, dataport, minibar, coffeemaker, hair dryer, iron.

HERON ISLAND: JEWEL OF THE REEF ★★★

72km (45 miles) NE of Gladstone

The difference between Heron and other islands is that once there, you have no need to travel farther to the Reef. Step off the beach and you enter magnificent fields of coral that seem to stretch for miles. And the myriad life forms that abound here are accessible to everyone through diving, snorkeling, or reef walks at low tide, or aboard a semisubmersible vessel that allows you to view the ocean floor without getting wet. When geologist Joseph Bette Jukes named this piece of paradise in 1843, he overlooked the turtles for which it is now famous in favor of the reef herons that abounded. There has been a resort on Heron since 1932, and in 1943 the island became a national park. It is a haven for wildlife and people, and an experience of a lifetime is almost guaranteed at any time of year. Heron is a rookery for giant green and loggerhead turtles. Resort guests gather on the beach from late November to February to watch the female turtles lay eggs, and from February to mid-April to see the hatched babies scuttle down the sand to the water. Humpback whales pass through from June through September.

Three days on Heron gives you plenty of time to see everything. The island is so small that you can walk around it at a leisurely pace in about half an hour. One of the first things to do is to take advantage of the organized activities that operate several times a day and are designed so guests can plan their own days. Snorkeling and reef walking are major occupations for visitors—if they're not diving, that is. The island is home to 21 of the world's most stunning dive sites.

Guided walks provide another way to explore the island. Walks include a visit to the island's research station. As for the reef walk, just borrow a pair of sand shoes, a balance pole, and a viewing bucket, and head off with a guide at low tide. The walk can take up to 90 minutes, but there's no compulsion to stay; if it gets too hot, you can head to the sanctuary of your room or the shady bar area.

A fishing trip should also be on the agenda, even for the most inexperienced. The reef fish seem to just jump onto the hook, and the resort chef is happy to cook them for you for dinner!

GETTING THERE   A courtesy coach meets flights from Brisbane (with connections from other cities) at Gladstone airport at 10:30am to take guests to Gladstone Marina for the launch transfer to the island (trip time: 1 hr., 40 min.); it departs 11am daily (except Dec 25). Round-trip transfers aboard the sleek new 130-seater catamaran *Heron Spirit* cost A$186 (US$149) for adults, half price for kids 3 to 14. Helicopter transfers can be arranged for A$291 (US$233) per person one-way.

Moments   Up Close & Personal with a Turtle

The egg in my hand is warm, soft, and about the size of a Ping-Pong ball. At our feet, a giant green turtle sighs deeply as she lays a clutch of about 120 eggs in a pear-shaped chamber dug from the sand. A large tear rolls from her eye. In the distance, the wedge-tailed shearwaters call eerily to each other, backed by the sound of the ocean.

The egg-laying ritual of the turtles is central to a trip to **Heron Island** in the summer months. At night and in the early morning, small groups of people gather on the beaches to witness the turtles lumber up the beach, dig holes in the sand, and lay their eggs. (The turtles are not easily disturbed, and you can get very close.) Every night during the season, volunteer guides from the University of Queensland research station based on the island are on hand; you can watch and ask questions as the researchers tag and measure the turtles before they return to the water. The laying season runs December through February, and only one in 5,000 hatchlings will live to return in about 50 years to lay their own eggs.

Another good place to watch the turtles nesting is Mon Repos Beach, outside Bundaberg. **Mon Repos Conservation Park** is one of the two largest loggerhead-turtle rookeries in the South Pacific. The visitor center by the beach has a great display on the turtle life cycle and shows films at approximately 7:30pm daily in summer. Last year, the park introduced a new booking system for turtle-watching tours, to help cope with the crowds. Access to the beach is by ticket only, and you must book your visit to Mon Repos during the turtle season. Tickets are sold through the Coral Coast Visitor Information Centre (© **07/4153 8888**). Tours start at 7pm and you will be given a time for your tour—it's a better system, which saves waiting around in a long queue of people. Nesting happens around high tide; hatching usually occurs between 8pm and midnight. Take a flashlight if you can, and a sweater, as it can get quite cool.

The **Mon Repos Turtle Rookery** ★ (© **07/4159 1652** for the visitor center) is 14km (8¾ miles) east of Bundaberg's town center. Follow Bourbong Street out of town toward Burnett Heads as it becomes Bundaberg-Bargara Road. Take the Port Road to the left and look for the Mon Repos signs to the right. Admission to the visitor center is free from April through November (Mon–Fri 9am–4pm), but when the turtles start nesting, you pay A$5.50 (US$4.40) for adults, A$3 (US$2.40) for children ages 5 to 15. From November through March, the center is open daily from 7pm until midnight.

WHERE TO STAY ON HERON ISLAND

Heron Island Resort ★★★ *Kids*   This lovely, low-key resort has been transformed over the past few years, and changes to the accommodations mix and cosmetics continue. The latest additions are the chic Wistari Suites, each with a private garden and veranda. But new accommodations, a revamped central complex, and a stylish, contemporary new look have not changed the focus on the outdoors. The brilliant colors of the island's surrounding water and Reef are reflected in the interiors, and everything is light-filled and breezy. Heron's central complex is equal parts grand Queenslander home and sophisticated beach house, with smart bar and lounge areas open to ocean views and sunsets. Duplex-style Turtle rooms are designed for couples or families, with a casual living area and a veranda, or you can go for greater luxury in the suites or the private beach house.

The property has a lounge with a TV, public phones (only the four Point suites and the Beach House have private phones), and Internet access. The **Aqua Soul Spa** offers double treatment rooms, therapies designed for two, and the usual spa treatments and pampering. The spa complex is in a secluded spot on the edge of the island's pisonia forests, removed from the main resort.

Heron Island, off Gladstone, QLD 4680 (Voyages, G.P.O. Box 3589, Sydney, NSW 2001). © **1300/134 044** in Australia, or 02/8296 8010 (Sydney reservations office). Fax 02/9299 2477 (Sydney reservations office). www.voyages. com.au. 109 units (some with shower only). A$500 (US$400) Turtle room double; A$570 (US$456) Reef suite double; A$720 (US$576) Heron Beachside suite double; A$960 (US$768) Point suite, Wistari suite, or Beach House double. Extra adult A$160 (US$128), extra child 3–14 A$100 (US$80). Free crib. Rates include all meals and many activities. Ask about special packages. AE, DC, MC, V. No children allowed in Point suites or Beach House. **Amenities:** Restaurant; bar; outdoor pool; 2 lit tennis courts; spa; Jacuzzi; limited watersports equipment rental; Heron Kids Junior Rangers program (ages 7–12) during Australian school vacations; game room; activities desk; babysitting; coin-op laundry. *In room:* Ceiling fan, fridge, coffeemaker, hair dryer, iron.

BUNDABERG: GATEWAY TO LADY ELLIOT ISLAND

384km (238 miles) N of Brisbane; 1,439km (892 miles) S of Cairns

The small sugar town of Bundaberg is the closest to the southernmost point of the Great Barrier Reef. If you visit the area between November and March, allow an evening to visit the Mon Repos Turtle Rookery. Divers may want to take in some of Australia's best shore diving right off Bundaberg's beaches.

GETTING THERE & GETTING AROUND Bundaberg is on the Isis Highway, about 50km (31 miles) off the Bruce Highway from Gin Gin in the north and 53km (33 miles) off the Bruce Highway from just north of Childers in the south.

QantasLink (© **13 13 13** in Australia) flies from Brisbane daily and from Gladstone three times a week.

Queensland Rail (© **13 22 32** in Queensland, or 07/3235 1122; www.qr.com.au) trains stop in Bundaberg every day en route between Brisbane and Cairns. The fare is A$63 (US$50) from Brisbane in economy class or A$92 (US$74) business class on the Tilt Train; fares range from A$163 (US$130) for a seat to A$316 (US$253) for a first-class berth on the *Sunlander* from Cairns. The trip takes 4½ hours from Brisbane and 8¼ hours from Cairns on the Tilt Train; the *Sunlander* takes 6¾ hours from Brisbane and 25 hours from Cairns.

Greyhound Australia (© **13 14 99** in Australia) stops here many times a day on runs between Brisbane and Cairns. The 6½-hour trip from Brisbane costs A$64 (US$51). From Cairns it is a 22-hour trip, and the fare is A$172 (US$138).

Avis (© 07/4152 1877), **Budget** (© 07/4151 1355), **Hertz** (© 07/4151 2099), and **Thrifty** (© 07/4151 6222) all have offices in Bundaberg.

VISITOR INFORMATION There are two **Bundaberg Region Visitor Centres,** at 271 Bourbong St. (at Mulgrave St.) and at 186 Bourbong St., Bundaberg, QLD 4670 (© **1800/308 888** in Australia, or 07/4153 8888; www.bundabergregion.info). They are open daily from 9am to 5pm.

WHAT TO SEE & DO

The best shore diving in Queensland is in Bundaberg's **Woongarra Marine Park.** It has soft and hard corals, urchins, rays, sea snakes, and 60 fish species, plus a World War II Beaufort bomber wreck. There are several scuba operators. **Salty's Dive Centre** (℃ **1800/625 476** in Australia, or 07/4151 6244; www.saltys.net) rents dive gear for A$45 (US$36). It also runs day trips for A$100 (US$80), including all equipment. Five-day open-water and 4-day shore courses are A$580 (US$464) and A$169 (US$135), respectively. A 3-day, 3-night southern Great Barrier Reef dive cruise costs A$495 (US$396), plus A$65 (US$52) for all equipment rental. Night dives are free, but you pay A$10 (US$8) for chemical sticks and light.

WHERE TO STAY

Sun City Motel *Value*   This basic but neat and tidy motel is a short stroll across the river from the town center. The rooms are clean and well kept, and have a ceiling fan, toaster, and tea- and coffeemaking facilities. Three family rooms have a double bed and twin bunks. Home-cooked meals can be delivered to your room or you can use the guest barbecue and outdoor dining area. Hosts Sue and Steve will pick you up from the bus, train, or airport.

11a Hinkler Ave., North Bundaberg, QLD 4670. ℃ 1800/308 888 in Australia, or 07/4152 1099. Fax 07/4153 1510. www.suncitymotel.com.au. 12 units (all with shower only). A$60–A$65 (US$48–US$52) double. Extra adult A$12 (US$9.60), extra child under 8 A$8 (US$6.40). AE, DC, MC, V. Free covered parking. **Amenities:** Outdoor saltwater pool; nearby golf course; access to nearby health club; tour desk; limited room service; coin-op laundry; dry cleaning; nonsmoking rooms. *In room:* A/C, TV, fridge, coffeemaker, hair dryer, iron.

LADY ELLIOT ISLAND ⭑

80km (50 miles) NE of Bundaberg

The southernmost Great Barrier Reef island, Lady Elliot is a 42-hectare (104-acre) coral cay ringed by a wide, shallow lagoon filled with dazzling coral life. Reef walking, snorkeling, and diving are the main reasons people come to this coral cay, which is so small you can walk across it in 15 minutes. You may snorkel and reef walk during only the 2 to 3 hours before and after high tide, so plan your schedule accordingly. You will see dazzling corals and brilliantly colored fish, clams, sponges, urchins, and anemones. Divers will see a good range of marine life, including green and loggerhead turtles (which nest on the beach Nov–Mar). Whales pass by from June through September.

Lady Elliot is a sparse, grassy island rookery, not a lush tropical paradise, so don't expect white sand and palm trees. Some people will find it too spartan; others will relish chilling out in a beautiful, peaceful location with reef all around. Just be prepared for the smell and constant noise of those birds.

GETTING THERE   You reach the island by a 30-minute flight from Bundaberg or Hervey Bay. Book your air travel with your accommodations. Round-trip fares are

---

Tips **Look Out Below!**

When you land on the grass airstrip at Lady Elliot Island, you'll think you're on the set of Hitchcock's *The Birds*. The air is thick with tens of thousands of swirling noddy terns and bridled terns that nest in every available branch and leave their mark on every available surface—including you—so bring a big, cheap straw hat for "protection."

A$175 (US$140) for adults and A$88 (US$70) for children 3 to 12. There is a 10-kilogram (22-lb.) luggage limit. **Seair Pacific** (© **07/5599 4509;** www.seairpacific.com.au) operates day tours from Brisbane and the Gold Coast for A$599 (US$479) or from the Sunshine Coast for A$449 (US$359); prices include flights, snorkel gear, glass-bottom-boat ride, lunch, and guided activities.

WHERE TO STAY

Lady Elliot Island Resort ⭐ Accommodations here are fairly basic, but visitors come for the reef, not the room. Because of the relatively low number of guests, you pretty much get the reef to yourself. Top of the range are Island suites, which have one or two separate bedrooms, and great sea views from the deck. Most Reef rooms have a double bed and two bunks, and a deck with views through the trees to the sea. Shearwater bunk rooms sleep up to six. All room types have modern private bathrooms. The cool, spacious tent cabins have four bunks, electric lighting, and timber floors, but share the public toilets and showers used by day guests. The limited facilities include a boutique, a dive shop, and an education center. The resort has no air-conditioning, no keys (secure storage is at the front desk), no TVs, no radio, and one public telephone. The food is basic. A low-key program of mostly free activities includes glass-bottom boat rides, badminton, guided walks, and beach volleyball.

Great Barrier Reef, off Bundaberg (P.O. Box 206, Torquay, QLD 4655). © **1800/072 200** in Australia, or 07/5536 3644. Fax 07/5536 7285. www.ladyelliot.com.au. 40 units, 20 with bathroom (shower only). A$290 (US$232) tent cabin double; A$330 (US$264) Shearwater bunk room double; A$390 (US$312) Reef double; A$450 (US$360) 1-bedroom Island suite double; A$480 (US$384) 2-bedroom Island suite double; A$820 (US$656) 2-bedroom Island suite for 4. Extra child 3–12 A$75 (US$60). 3-night minimum Dec 24–Jan 5. Ask about 2-, 4-, 5-, and 7-night packages, and dive packages. Rates include breakfast and dinner. AE, DC, MC, V. **Amenities:** Cafe/bistro; dining room; saltwater pool; children's program (ages 3–12) during Queensland school holidays. *In room:* Ceiling or wall fans, no phone.

7 Fraser Island: Ecoadventures & Four-Wheel-Drive Fun

1,547km (959 miles) S of Cairns; 260km (161 miles) N of Brisbane; 15km (9½ miles) E of Hervey Bay

The biggest sand island in the world, this 162,000-hectare (400,140-acre) World Heritage–listed island off the central Queensland coast attracts a mix of ecotourists and Aussie fishermen. Fraser is a pristine vista of eucalyptus woodlands, dunes, clear creeks, ancient rainforest, blue lakes, ocher-colored sand cliffs, and a stunning 121km-long (75-mile) beach. For four-wheel-drive fans, Fraser's beauty lies in its complete absence of paved roads. On weekends when the fish are running, it's nothing to see 100 four-wheel-drives lining 75-Mile Beach, which is an authorized road. Pedestrians, beware!

You'll need more than a day here to see everything and to truly appreciate how stunning this place is. Allow at least 3 days to soak it all up, and to allow for the slow pace dictated by the sandy trails that pass for roads.

ESSENTIALS

GETTING THERE Hervey (pronounced *Har*-vey) Bay is the main gateway to the island. Take the Bruce Highway to Maryborough, then the 34km (21-mile) road to Hervey Bay. From the north, turn off the highway at Torbanlea, north of Maryborough, and cut across to Hervey Bay. Allow 3 hours from the Sunshine Coast, a good 5 hours from Brisbane.

Virgin Blue (© **13 67 89** in Australia) flies direct from Sydney to Hervey Bay four times a week, with connections from Adelaide and Melbourne.

   Greyhound Australia (© **13 14 99** in Australia) coaches stop in Hervey Bay on the Brisbane-Cairns-Brisbane routes. The 5-hour trip from Brisbane costs A$48 (US$38). From Cairns, the fare is A$183 (US$146) and the trip is almost 24 hours.

   The nearest **train** station is in **Maryborough West,** 34km (20 miles) from Hervey Bay. Passengers on the high-speed **Tilt Train** (Sun–Fri) can book connecting bus service to Pialba (a suburb of Hervey Bay) through **Queensland Rail** (© **13 22 32** in Queensland, or 07/3235 1122; www.qr.com.au). The fare from Brisbane for the 3½-hour Tilt Train trip is A$64 (US$51) in economy class and A$92 (US$74) in business class, including the bus fare. Fares are A$175 (US$140) in a seat and A$334 (US$267) in a first-class sleeper from Cairns (trip time: just under 27 hr.). Train passengers from the north must take a courtesy shuttle from Maryborough West to Maryborough Central, then take the next available local bus to Pialba.

   Guests at Kingfisher Bay Resort (p. 356) can get to the resort aboard the **Kingfisher Bay Fastcat,** which departs Urangan Boat Harbour at Hervey Bay at 8:45am, noon, 4, 6:30 (7pm Fri–Sat), and 10pm. Round-trip fare for the 40-minute crossing is A$44 (US$35) adults and A$22 (US$18) kids 4 to 14. The resort runs a courtesy shuttle from Hervey Bay's airport and coach terminal to the harbor. You can park free at the Fastcat terminal. Drive to the terminal first to unload your luggage at the Kingfisher Bay reception desk, then return to the parking lot and walk back (only 100m/328 ft.). **Fraser Coast Secure Vehicle Storage,** 629 The Esplanade (© **07/4125 2783**), a 5-minute walk from the terminal, has covered parking for less than A$10 (US$8) per 24 hours.

GETTING THERE & GETTING AROUND BY FOUR-WHEEL-DRIVE ⭐

Four-wheel-drives are the only vehicle transportation on the island. Many four-wheel-drive-rental outfits are based in Hervey Bay. You must be 21 or over to rent a 4WD. You'll pay about A$110 to A$230 (US$88–US$184) a day, plus around A$20 to A$35 (US$16–US$28) per day to reduce the deductible (usually A$4,000/US$3,200), plus a bond (typically A$500/US$400). You must also buy a government Vehicle Access Permit, which costs A$33 (US$26) from your rental-car company, Urangan Boat Harbour, or the River Heads boat ramp; or A$40 (US$32) from a Queensland Parks and Wildlife Service office on the island.

   Both **Bay 4WD Centre** (© **1800/687 178** in Australia, or 07/4128 2981; www.bay4wd.com.au) and **Ausbay 4WD Rentals** (© **1800/679 479** in Australia, or 07/4124 6177) rent four-wheel-drives; offer four-wheel-drive packages that include camping or accommodations; rent camping gear; organize Vehicle Access Permits, barge bookings, camping permits, and secure storage for your car; and pick you up from the airport, the coach terminal, or your hotel. **Kingfisher Bay 4WD Hire** (© **1800/249 330** in Australia, or 07/4120 3366; www.kingfisher-bay-4wdhire.com.au), at Kingfisher Bay Resort (see below), rents four-wheel-drives for A$230 (US$184) a day, plus a A$33 (US$26) Fraser Island driving permit and a A$2,000 (US$1,600) security deposit (by credit card) held until return of the vehicle in the original condition. The company allows half-day and 1-day rentals. Rates are cheaper if you book for a week. Book well in advance.

   Four-wheel-drives reach the island on the **Fraser Venture** barge (© **07/4125 4444**), which runs three times a day (four times on Sat) from River Heads, 17km (11 miles) south of Urangan Boat Harbour. Kingfisher Bay Resort (see below) also runs a barge from River Heads. The round-trip fare for a vehicle with up to four occupants

---

Tips **Four-Wheel-Drive Fundamentals**

Driving a four-wheel-drive vehicle is great fun and not hard to learn, but if you've never driven one before, get a good briefing from your rental company before you head out. Fraser's loose sand tracks can be tricky, and getting "bogged" (stuck) is common. The beach can be dangerous for the novice—if you travel too high up on the beach, you can get trapped in soft sand; if you travel too low, a surprise wave can bog your vehicle in treacherously soft sand under the water (and rust your car). Rental companies don't like that, and the attendants can smell salt on an axle a mile away! Stick to the firmest tracks, know the tides, and don't be afraid to ask for advice. You'll have to drive a lot slower on a four-wheel-drive trail than you would on a conventional road; take that into account when you plan your day. For example, it takes a full day to get to Indian Head and back, and then only when the tide is favorable. Look out for light planes landing on the beach (which is a runway as well as a road).

---

is A$115 (US$92), plus A$5.50 (US$4.40) per extra passenger. It is a good idea to book a place for the 45-minute crossing.

The **Rainbow Venture** and **Fraser Explorer** barges (© **07/5486 3154**) provide access to Rainbow Beach and operate continuously between Inskip Point and Hook Point between 6am and 5:30pm daily. The cost is A$65 (US$52) return for a vehicle and four passengers.

Fraser Island Taxi Service (© **07/4127 9188**) is another option for getting around. There is only one taxi on the island (a 4WD, of course), so it's important to book ahead. They will pick you up anywhere on the island, and will give you a quote on price before you set off. The taxi seats five, and there's also room for your luggage and fishing rods.

VISITOR INFORMATION   Contact the **Hervey Bay Tourism Bureau,** Urraween Road at Maryborough–Hervey Bay Road, Pialba (P.O. Box 8, Hervey Bay, QLD 4655; © **1800/811 728** in Australia, or 07/4125 9855; www.herveybaytourism.com.au). A better online source is www.hervey.com.au. The **Marina Kiosk** (© **07/4128 9800**) at Urangan Boat Harbour is a one-stop booking and information agency for all Fraser-related travel. Several Queensland Parks and Wildlife Service information offices are on the island.

There are no towns and very few facilities, food stores, or services on the island, so if you're camping, take all supplies with you.

ECOEXPLORING THE ISLAND

Fraser's turquoise lakes and tea-colored "perched" lakes in the dunes are among the island's biggest attractions. Brilliant blue **Lake McKenzie** is absolutely beautiful; a swim here may be the highlight of your visit. Lake Birrabeen is another popular swimming spot. Don't miss a refreshing swim in the fast-flowing clear shallows of **Eli Creek.** Wade up the creek for a mile or two and let the current carry you back down. You should also take the boardwalk through a verdant forest of palms and ferns along the banks of Wanggoolba Creek.

Don't swim at **75-Mile Beach,** which hugs the eastern edge of the island—it has dangerously strong currents and a healthy shark population. Instead, swim in the

Champagne Pools (also called the Aquarium)—pockets of soft sand protected from the worst of the waves by rocks. The bubbling seawater turns the pools into miniature spas. The pools are just north of **Indian Head,** a 60m (197-ft.) rocky outcrop at the northern end of the beach.

View the island's famous colored sand in its natural setting—the 70m (230-ft.) cliffs called **the Cathedrals,** which stretch for miles north of the settlement of Happy Valley on the eastern side of the island.

Some of Queensland's best fishing is on Fraser Island. Anglers can throw a line in the surf gutters off the beach. (Freshwater fishing is not allowed.) Bream, whiting, flathead, and swallowtail are the beach catches. Indian Head is good for rock species and tailor; the waters east off **Waddy Point** yield northern and southern reef fish. **Kingfisher Bay Resort** (see below) offers free fish clinics, rents tackle, and organizes half-day fishing jaunts.

From August through October, tour boats crowd the straits to see humpback whales returning to Antarctica with calves in tow. Kingfisher Bay Resort runs a whale-watching cruise from Urangan Harbour.

WHERE TO STAY

Fraser Island Retreat ★ *Finds*   This is the wild side of Fraser Island, just minutes from 75-Mile Beach. Don't come expecting a luxury resort—this one has comfortable timber cottages and all the amenities you need. There's a small pool, surrounded by a deck and deck chairs, and each cottage has a small veranda. The rooms all have fans, limited cooking facilities, and a VCR. (You can rent videos.) The bar-bistro is open for all meals, but be warned that day-tour buses stop here for lunch, so it can be crowded at that time. If you want to cook for yourself, there's a general store selling food and liquor. The store also has fuel, ice, and gas for campers. You can also hire a four-wheel-drive from the resort. There's a public phone. The only access is by plane (**Air Fraser Island,** © **1800/247 992** in Australia, or 07/4125 3600) or bus. **Fraser Island Tours** (© **07/4125 3933**) will transfer guests to the resort from Hervey Bay; it also runs day tours of the island for A$137 (US$110) adults and A$94 (US$75) children under 14.

Happy Valley, Fraser Island, QLD 4650. © **07/4127 9144.** Fax 07/4127 9131. www.fraserislandco.com.au. 9 units (all with shower only). A$125–A$160 (US$100–US$128) 1-bedroom lodge for up to 3; A$160–A$200 (US$128–US$160) family lodge for up to 5. Ask about packages. AE, MC, V. **Amenities:** Restaurant; bar; outdoor pool; tour desk; car-rental desk; babysitting; coin-op laundry. *In room:* TV/VCR, kitchenette, small fridge, no phone.

Kingfisher Bay Resort ★★ *Kids*   This sleek, environment-friendly ecoresort lies low along Fraser's west coast. Hotel rooms are smart and contemporary, with air-conditioning and a Japanese-style screen opening onto a balcony looking into the bush,

---

Tips **Please Don't Feed the Dingoes**

The dingoes that roam the island are emboldened by visitors who have—sometimes deliberately, sometimes unwittingly—fed them over the years. These dangerous wild animals have been responsible for one death and several serious attacks in recent years. Do not feed them, and keep your distance. Feeding or interacting with dingoes on Fraser Island can incur fines of up to A$3,000 (US$2,400). And be warned: The laws are strictly enforced by the rangers.

Moments **Another Great Walk**

The stunning Fraser Island World Heritage Area is the location for one of Queensland's six Great Walks (p. 339). The **Fraser Island Great Walk** (© **07/5459 6114;** www.epa.qld.gov.au) follows a continuous winding track from Dilli Village to Lake Garawongera. The main trail is 85km (53 miles) long and takes 6 to 8 days to complete, but offshoots provide short, full-day, overnight, and 2- to 3-day walks. The walk takes you to many of the island's popular landmarks, such as Lake McKenzie, Central Station, Wangoolba Creek, Valley of the Giants, and Lake Wabby.

---

but my pick is the two- and three-bedroom villas just a short walk from the main resort area and pools. The hillside villas, which have Jacuzzis on their balconies, are fairly luxurious, but guests must contend with that long haul up the hill. Each villa has a kitchen, washing machine, and dryer. An impressive lineup of ecoeducational activities includes daily four-wheel-drive tours with a ranger to points of interest around the island, free guided walks daily, and an excellent free Junior Eco-Ranger program on weekends and during school vacations. You can also join bird-watching tours, guided canoe trips, sunset champagne sails, and dolphin and dugong (manatee) spotting cruises. Wildlife videos play continuously in the lobby, and the on-site ranger office lists the animals and plants you are most likely to spot.

Fraser Island (P.M.B. 1, Urangan, QLD 4655). © **1800/072 555** in Australia, or 07/4120 3333. Fax 07/4120 3326. www.kingfisherbay.com. 262 units. A$270 (US$216) hotel double. A$816–A$1,080 (US$653–US$864) 3 nights in 2-bedroom villa for up to 5; A$969–A$1,260 (US$775–US$1,008) 3 nights in 3-bedroom villa for up to 6. 3-night minimum in villas. Extra person A$22 (US$18). Free crib. Ask about packages. AE, DC, MC, V. **Amenities:** 3 restaurants; 4 bars; 4 outdoor saltwater pools (1 w/water slide); lit tennis courts; Jacuzzi; watersports equipment rental and fishing tackle rental; kids' club; game room; tour desk; babysitting. *In room:* TV, fridge, coffeemaker, hair dryer, iron.

8 The Sunshine Coast

Warm weather, miles of pleasant beaches, trendy restaurants, and a relaxed lifestyle attract Aussies to the Sunshine Coast in droves. Despite some rather unsightly commercial development in recent years, the Sunshine Coast is still a great spot if you like lazing on sandy beaches and enjoying a good meal.

The Sunshine Coast starts at **Caloundra,** 83km (51 miles) north of Brisbane, and runs all the way to **Rainbow Beach,** 40km (25 miles) north of **Noosa Heads** ★, where the fashionable crowd goes. There's a wide range of accommodations, from inexpensive motels and holiday apartments to AAA-rated five-star hotels and resorts.

Most of Noosa's sunbathing, dining, shopping, and socializing takes place on trendy Hastings Street, in Noosa Heads, and on adjacent Main Beach. The commercial strip of Noosa Junction is a 1-minute drive away; a 3-minute drive west along the river takes you to the low-key town of Noosaville, where Australian families rent holiday apartments. Giving Noosa a run for its money in recent years is newly spruced-up Mooloolaba, about 30km (19 miles) south, which has a better beach and about 90 great restaurants.

A short drive away, in the hinterland, mountain towns like **Maleny, Montville,** and **Mapleton** lead to the stunning beauty of the **Glass House Mountains,** a dramatic series of 16 volcanic plugs.

SUNSHINE COAST ESSENTIALS

GETTING THERE   If you're **driving** from Brisbane, take the Bruce Highway north to the Aussie World theme park at Palmview, then exit onto the Sunshine Motorway to Mooloolaba, Maroochydore, or Noosa Heads. The trip takes about 2 hours.

Virgin Blue (𝒸 **13 67 89** in Australia) and **Jetstar** (𝒸 **13 15 38** in Australia) fly direct from Melbourne and Sydney. **Henry's Airport Bus Service** (𝒸 **07/5474 0199;** www.henrys.com.au) meets all flights; door-to-door transfers to Noosa Heads are A$18 (US$14) for adults, A$10 (US$8) for kids 4 to 14, or A$42 (US$34) for a family of four, one-way. Bookings are essential, and should be made 24 hours ahead if possible.

The nearest **train** station to Noosa Heads is in **Cooroy,** 25km (16 miles) away. **Queensland Rail** (𝒸 **13 22 32** in Queensland, or 07/3235 1122; www.qr.com.au) serves Cooroy once daily from Brisbane on its **CityTrain** (𝒸 **07/3235 5555**) network. The trip takes about 2½ hours, and the fare is A$16 (US$13). Other trains will take you there via Nambour or Caboolutre, but you will still have to then get a bus connection to get to Noosa Heads. Queensland Rail's long-distance trains from Brisbane pick up but do not drop off passengers in Cooroy, with the exception of the high-speed **Tilt Train** (which runs Sun–Fri). The fare is A$28 (US$22). The *Sunlander* makes several trips from Cairns each week; the fare is A$183 (US$146) for a seat, A$345 (US$276) for a first-class sleeper. Local bus company **Sunbus** (𝒸 **13 12 30** in Australia or 07/5450 7888) meets most trains at Cooroy station and travels to Noosa Heads; take bus no. 12.

Several **coach** companies have service to Noosa Heads from Brisbane, including **Suncoast Pacific** (𝒸 **07/5443 1011** on the Sunshine Coast, or 07/3236 1901 in Brisbane). **Greyhound Australia** (𝒸 **13 14 99** in Australia) has many daily services from all major towns along the Bruce Highway between Brisbane and Cairns. Trip time to Noosa Heads is 2 hours and 35 minutes from Brisbane, and just over 27 hours from Cairns. The fare is A$25 (US$20) from Brisbane and A$196 (US$157) from Cairns.

VISITOR INFORMATION   Contact **Tourism Sunshine Coast Ltd,** P.O. Box 264, Mooloolaba, QLD 4557 (𝒸 **07/5477 7311;** fax 07/5477 7322; www.sunshine coast.org). In Noosa, drop into the **Noosa Information Centre,** at the eastern roundabout on Hastings Street where it intersects Noosa Drive (𝒸 **07/5447 4988;** fax 07/5474 9494). It's open daily from 9am to 5pm. Other tourist information centers are: **Maroochy Tourism,** Sunshine Coast Airport (𝒸 **07/5448 9088**), and Sixth Avenue and Melrose Parade, Maroochydore (𝒸 **07/5479 1566**); and **Caloundra Visitor Information Centre,** 7 Caloundra Rd., Caloundra (𝒸 **07/5491 9233**).

GETTING AROUND   Major car-rental companies on the Sunshine Coast are **Avis** (𝒸 **07/5443 5055** Sunshine Coast Airport, or 07/5447 4933 Noosa Heads), **Budget** (𝒸 **07/5448 7455** airport, or 07/5474 2820 Noosa Heads), **Hertz** (𝒸 **07/5448 9731** airport, or 07/5447 2253 Noosa Heads), and **Thrifty** (𝒸 **07/5451 8426** airport, or 07/5447 2299 Noosa Heads). Many local companies rent cars and four-wheel-drives, including **Trusty** (𝒸 **07/5491 2444**).

The local bus company is **Sunbus** (𝒸 **07/5450 7888,** or 13 12 30 in Australia).

EXPLORING THE AREA

HITTING THE BEACH & OTHER OUTDOOR FUN   Main Beach, Noosa Heads, is the place to swim, surf, and sunbathe. If the bikini-clad supermodel look-alikes are too much for you, head to Sunshine Beach, just behind Noosa Junction off

The Sunshine Coast

Australia Zoo **5**
Big Pineapple **2**
Eumundi Markets **1**
Mary Cairncross Park **4**
Underwater World **3**

Information *i*
Lighthouse

AUSTRALIA
Area of Detail
Sydney
Canberra

0   1000 Mi
0   1000 Km

Rainbow Beach

Tin Can Bay

Great Sandy National Park

Forty Mile Beach

Teewah Coloured Sands

Wolvi

4WD

Kinaba Information Centre *i*

Lake Cootharaba

Noosa River

Laguna Bay

Noosa Heads

Noosa National Park

Tewantin

Noosaville

Sunshine Beach

Cooroy

Eumundi **1**

Coolum

Yandina

Mapleton Falls National Park

Nambour *i*

Sunshine Coast Airport

Mudjimba

Mapleton

Blackall Ranges Tourist Drive 23

Maroochydore *i*

Flaxton

Woombye **2**

Mooloolaba **3**

Conondale National Park

Montville

Buderim

Kondalilla Falls National Park

Blackall Ranges Tourist Drive 23

Maleny **4**

Landsborough

i

Caloundra

Glass House Mountains

Beerwah **5**

Bribie Island

0   10 mi
0   10 km

Mary River

Bruce Highway

BLACKALL RANGE

JIMNA RANGE

CONONDALE RANGE

Obi Obi Creek

Sunshine Coast Motorway

the David Low Way, about 2km (1¼ miles) from Noosa Heads. It's just as beautiful. Both beaches are patrolled 365 days a year.

Learn to surf with two-time Australian and World Pro-Am champion **Merrick Davis** (© **0418/787 577** mobile; www.learntosurf.com.au), who's lived here for about 10 years. Merrick and his team run 2-hour lessons on Main Beach daily for A$45 (US$36), 3-day certificate courses for A$125 (US$100), and 5-day courses for A$170 (US$136). They will pick you up and drop you off at your accommodations. They also rent surfboards, body boards, and sea kayaks.

If you want to rent a Windsurfer, canoe, kayak, surf ski, catamaran, jet ski, or fishing boat that you can play with on the Noosa River or take upriver into Great Sandy National Park (see below), check out the dozens of outfits along Gympie Terrace between James Street and Robert Street in Noosaville.

The **Aussie Sea Kayak Company** (© **07/5477 5335;** www.ausseakayak.com.au), at The Wharf, Mooloolaba, runs a 2-hour sunset paddle on the Maroochy River every day for A$45 (US$36)—including a glass of champagne on your return as a reward for all the hard work! Half-day tours run every day for 3 to 4 hours at Mooloolaba (A$65/US$52), day tours for 6 hours on Tuesday, Friday, and Saturday at Noosa (A$135/US$108). The company also runs overnight adventures to Moreton and North Stradbroke Islands, and to Fraser Island and the Whitsundays for up to 6 days.

EXPLORING NOOSA NATIONAL PARK   A 10-minute stroll northeast from Hastings Street brings you to the 432-hectare (1,067-acre) **Noosa National Park.** Anywhere you see a crowd looking upward, you're sure to spot a koala. They're often seen in the unlikely setting of the parking lot at the entrance to the park. A network of well-signposted walking trails leads through the bush. The most scenic is the 2.7km (1.5-mile) coastal trail. The shortest trail is the 1km (just over .5-mile) Palm Grove circuit; the longest is the 4.8km (3-mile) Tanglewood trail inland to Hell's Gates— definitely worth the effort.

GREAT SANDY NATIONAL PARK   Stretching north of Noosa along the coast is the 56,000-hectare (138,320-acre) Great Sandy National Park (often called Cooloola National Park). It's home to forests, beach, and freshwater lakes, including the state's largest, Lake Cootharaba. A popular activity is to cruise the Everglades formed by the Noosa River and tributary creeks. The park's information office, the **Kinaba Information Centre** (© **07/5449 7364;** daily 9am–3pm), is on the western shore of Lake Cootharaba, about 30km (19 miles) from Noosaville. It has a display on the area's geography and a mangrove boardwalk to explore; it's accessible only by boat, which you can easily rent from the numerous outfits in Noosaville. There are several half-day cruises into the Everglades, and guided kayak tours that explore the park's lower reaches.

The other option is to take a four-wheel-drive along Forty-Mile Beach, a designated highway with traffic laws, for a close-up view of the Teewah colored sand cliffs. This is a great place to get away from the crowds and enjoy nature's wonders. Lifeguards do not patrol the beach, so do not swim alone, and take care. Tours are available, or you can rent a four-wheel-drive and explore on your own. To reach the beach, cross the Noosa River on the ferry at Tewantin, then take Maximilian Drive for 4km (2½ miles) to the beach. Stock up on water, food, and gas in Tewantin. The ferry (© **07/5447 1321**) costs A$10 (US$8) per vehicle round-trip; it operates from 5:30am to 10:15pm Sunday through Thursday, and 5:30am to midnight Friday and Saturday.

WILDLIFE PARKS & THEME PARKS Small theme parks seem to thrive on the Sunshine Coast. Don't expect thrill rides, but you might find some of them a pleasant way to spend a few hours.

A transparent tunnel with an 80m (262-ft.) moving walkway that takes you through a tank filled with sharks, stingrays, groupers, eels, and coral is the highlight at **Underwater World** (© 07/5444 8488; www.underwaterworld.com.au), at The Wharf, Mooloolaba. Kids can pick up starfish and sea cucumbers in the touch pool, and there are displays on whales and sharks, shark breeding, freshwater crocodile talks, an otter enclosure, and a 30-minute seal show. You can swim with the seals (A$100/US$80) or dive with the sharks (A$95/US$76 for certified divers, including gear, or A$145/US$116 for nondivers). It's open daily (except Dec 25) from 9am to 6pm (last entry at 5pm). Admission is A$24 (US$19) for adults, A$17 (US$14) for seniors and students, A$14 (US$11) for children 3 to 15, and A$65 (US$52) for a family of five. Allow 2 hours to see everything, more if you want to attend all the talks.

At the **Big Pineapple** (© 07/5442 1333; www.bigpineapple.com.au), 6km (3¾ miles) south of Nambour on the Nambour Connection Road in Woombye—don't worry, you can't miss the 16m-tall (52-ft.) monument—you can take a train ride through a working pineapple plantation, ride through a rainforest and a macadamia farm in a macadamia nut–shaped carriage, and take a boat ride through a hydroponics greenhouse. The park also has a baby animal farm, kangaroos, koalas, a rainforest walk, a small but excellent nocturnal house called "Creatures of the Night," and a gift shop. It's open daily from 9am to 5pm; it opens later on April 25 (Anzac Day) and December 25 (call for exact time). Entry is free; each tour is priced separately so you can do all or just one, but the best option is to buy a family pass to all tours, which costs A$75 (US$60) for two adults and up to four children 4 to 14. Allow half a day if you do everything.

Farther south on Glass House Mountains Tourist Drive 24 at Beerwah, off the Bruce Highway, is crocodile-hunter Steve Irwin's amazing **Australia Zoo** ✯ (© 07/5436 2000; www.crocodilehunter.com). Steve and his wife, Terri, stars of the *Crocodile Hunter* television shows, have spent A$40 million (US$32 million) in recent years turning their zoo into a world-class attraction covering 100 hectares (251 acres). The highlight is the "crocoseum," a 5,000-seat stadium in which the daily croc feedings are held at noon. Other demonstrations and feedings are held regularly throughout the day, and you can also hand-feed 'roos, pat a koala, check out foxes and camels, and watch (even hold!) venomous snakes and pythons. You can also tour the Koala and Wildlife Hospital next door to see how sick and injured animals are cared for. Admission is A$34 (US$27) for adults, A$29 (US$23) for seniors and students, A$24 (US$19) for kids 3 to 14, and A$109 (US$87) for a family of five. The park is open daily from 9am to 4:30pm. Closed December 25. Courtesy buses will pick you up and return you to Beerwah railway stations or Noosa, Maroochydore, Alexandra Headlands, Mooloolaba, and Caloundra.

A SCENIC MOUNTAINTOP DRIVE THROUGH THE SUNSHINE COAST HINTERLAND

A leisurely drive along the lush green ridge top of the **Blackall Ranges** ✯ behind Noosa is a popular half- or full-day excursion. Mountain villages, full of crafts shops and cafes, and terrific views of the coast, are the main attractions. Macadamia nuts, peaches, and other homegrown produce are often for sale by the road at dirt-cheap prices.

On Saturday from 6:30am to 2pm, start at the colorful outdoor **Eumundi Markets** ★★ in the historical village of Eumundi, 13km (8 miles) west of Noosa along the Eumundi Road. Locals and visitors wander under the huge shady trees among dozens of stalls selling locally grown organic lemonade, fruit, groovy hats, teddy bears, antique linen, homemade soaps, handcrafted hardwood furniture—even live emu chicks! Get your face painted, your palm read, or your feet massaged. Listen to some didgeridoo music or bush poetry. When shopping's done, everyone pops into the cafes on Eumundi's main street.

From Eumundi, take the Bruce Highway to Nambour and turn right onto the **Nambour-Mapleton Road.** (The turnoff is just before you enter Nambour; if you hit the town, you've gone too far.) A winding 12km (7½-mile) climb up the range between rolling farmland and forest brings you to Mapleton. Stop at the pub for some spectacular views from the veranda. From here, detour almost 4km (2½ miles) to see the 120m (394-ft.) Mapleton Falls. A 200m (656-ft.) bushwalk departs from the picnic grounds and ends with great views over the Obi Obi Valley. There is also a 1.3km (¾-mile) circuit.

Back on the main **Mapleton-Maleny Road,** head south 3.5km (2 miles) through lush forest and farms to Flaxton Gardens. Perched on the cliff with breathtaking coast views is a wine cellar offering tastings and sales, plus a pottery, cafe, and gift shop. A bit farther south, you can detour right and walk the 4.6km (2.75-mile) round-trip trail to the base of 80m (262-ft.) Kondalilla Falls. You can swim here, too. It's a slippery downhill walk, and the climb back up can be tough.

Take the main road south for 5.5km (3½ miles) to **Montville.** This English-style village has become such a popular stop that it has lost some of its character, and lots of people decry its touristy facade. But everyone still ends up strolling the tree-lined streets and browsing the gift shops and galleries.

About 13km (8 miles) down the road is **Maleny,** more modern and less commercialized than Montville. Be sure to follow the signs to **Mary Cairncross Park** for spectacular views of the **Glass House Mountains** ★★, 16 volcanic plugs protruding out of the plains. The park has a food kiosk, a playground, free wood barbecues, and a rainforest information center; a 1.7km (1-mile) walking trail loops through the rainforest past some giant strangler figs.

You can either return to Noosa the way you came or, if you're in a hurry, drive down to Landsborough and rejoin the Bruce Highway.

WHERE TO STAY
EXPENSIVE

Hyatt Regency Coolum ★★   A couple of hours under the expert care of the therapists at the Sun Spa, and you'll feel years younger! This is one of the reasons the well-heeled flock to this sprawling bushland resort. The other is its 18-hole Robert Trent Jones, Jr.–designed golf course. The Sun Spa (which charges entrance fees of around A$13/US$10 a day as well as the cost of treatments) does everything from aromatherapy baths to triglyceride checks—130 treatments in all—and has massage rooms, aqua-aerobics, yoga, a 25m (82-ft.) lap pool, and much more. An almost-6-hour body detox costs A$400 (US$320), but you can get a minifacial or a half-hour massage for A$60 (US$48). *Australian Golf Digest* rated the golf course one of Australia's top five resort courses in 2000. Golf widows and widowers can play tennis; do decoupage in the Creative Arts Center; take the twice-daily free shuttle into Noosa to shop; and surf at the resort's private beach. A nightly shuttle runs to Noosa Heads restaurants for A$15 (US$12) per person, round-trip.

So spread out are the low-rise accommodations that guests rent a bike to get around, wait 15 minutes for the two free resort shuttles (frustrating sometimes!), or get into the healthy swing of things and walk. Accommodations all have contemporary decor and come as "suites" (one room divided into living and sleeping quarters); two-bedroom President's Villas with a kitchenette; villas in the Ambassador Club, which has its own concierge, pool, tennis court, and lounge; and two-story, three-bedroom Ambassador Club residences boasting rooftop terraces with a Jacuzzi. All the rooms were refurbished in 2004–05.

The Village Square is just that: an attractive cluster of shops, restaurants, bars, and takeout joints that makes up the heart of the resort.

Warran Rd., off David Low Way (approximately 2km/1¼ miles south of town), Coolum Beach, QLD 4573. Ⓒ 13 12 34 in Australia, 800/633-7313 in the U.S. and Canada, 0845/758 1666 in the U.K. or 020/8335 1220 in London, 0800/44 1234 in New Zealand, or 07/5446 1234. Fax 07/5446 2957. www.coolum.regency.hyatt.com. 323 units. A$220–A$395 (US$176–US$316) double; A$320–A$1,400 (US$256–US$1,120) villa; A$1,030–A$2,200 (US$824–US$1,760) Ambassadors' Club units. Rates include continental breakfast. Extra person A$45 (US$36). Children under 13 stay free in parent's room with existing bedding. Ask about golf, spa, and other packages. AE, MC, V. Valet parking A$18 (US$14). Free self-parking. Resort shuttle (A$18/US$14 per person, one-way) meets all flights at Sunshine Coast Airport. Town-car transfers from Brisbane Airport A$79 (US$63) per person, one-way. Limousine transfers available. **Amenities:** 4 restaurants; 3 bars; 9 outdoor pools (2 heated); golf course; 9 night/day tennis courts; health club and spa; watersports equipment rental; bike rental; children's programs daily for kids ages 6 weeks to 12 years (fee); concierge; tour desk; car-rental desk; business center; shopping arcade; limited room service; massage; babysitting; dry cleaning; nonsmoking rooms; executive rooms. *In room:* A/C, TV w/pay movies, fax, dataport, kitchenette, minibar, coffeemaker, hair dryer, iron, safe.

Sheraton Noosa Resort & Spa ★★★

A great place to enjoy a day spa by the sea is Noosa's first AAA-rated five-star resort. Right in the heart of Hastings Street, the Sheraton has a prime spot among the chic boutiques and restaurants. There are several styles of rooms, but the best in my book are those with views away from the beach looking right down the Noosa River to the mountains. Sit on the balcony at sunset and drink it in. All the rooms are extralarge, and all have Jacuzzis. You'll pay more for two-level poolside villas, which have private access to the pool area but no view. Some rooms have ocean (but not beach) views. The Aqua Day Spa has a Roman-bathhouse feel and offers a wide range of treatments. The restaurant, **Cato's**—named for the late Australian novelist Nancy Cato, who lived in Noosa—fronts Hastings Street and is a great place to watch the world go by.

Hastings St., Noosa Heads, QLD 4567. Ⓒ 1800/073 535 in Australia, 888/625-5144 in the U.S., or 07/5449 4888. Fax 07/5449 2230. www.sheraton.com. 169 units. A$550–A$1,000 (US$440–US$800) double high season (Dec 26–Jan 2); A$300–A$600 (US$240–US$480) double low season. AE, DC, MC, V. Free covered parking, valet parking. **Amenities:** Restaurant; 2 bars; outdoor heated pool; health club and sauna; spa; Jacuzzi; concierge; tour desk; 24-hr. room service; poolside and in-room massage; babysitting; use of free guest laundry; laundry service; dry cleaning. *In room:* A/C, TV w/free and pay movies, kitchenette w/microwave, minibar, fridge, coffeemaker, hair dryer, iron, safe.

MODERATE

Noosa Village Motel (Value)

All the letters from satisfied guests pinned up on the wall here are a testament to owners John and Mary Skelton's hard work in continually sprucing up this bright little motel in the heart of Hastings Street. The pleasant rooms are spacious and freshly painted, with a cheerful atmosphere, and all have ceiling fans. And at these rates, it's one of Hastings Street's best values.

10 Hastings St., Noosa Heads, QLD 4567. © 07/5447 5800. Fax 07/5474 9282. noosavillage@bigpond.com.au. 11 units (all with shower only). High season (Dec 24–Jan 14) A$195 (US$156) double, A$260 (US$208) family suite; low season A$115–A$125 (US$92–US$100) double, A$165 (US$132) family suite. Extra person A$10–A$15 (US$8–US$12). Ask about May–June specials. MC, V. Free parking. **Amenities:** Bike rental; tour desk; car-rental desk; room service (breakfast); babysitting; coin-op laundry; nonsmoking rooms. *In room:* TV, kitchenette, fridge, hair dryer.

IN THE HINTERLAND

Avocado Grove Bed & Breakfast Joy and Brian Baxter's modern, red-cedar Queenslander home is in a peaceful rural setting in the middle of an avocado grove just off the ridge-top road. The cozy, comfortable rooms have country-style furniture, full-length windows opening onto private verandas, and oil heaters for cool mountain nights. The big suite downstairs has a TV and kitchen facilities. Colorful parrots and other birds are a common sight. Guests are welcome to picnic on the peaceful sloping lawns, which have wonderful views west to Obi Obi Gorge in the Connondale Ranges.

10 Carramar Ct., Flaxton via Montville, QLD 4560. ©/fax 07/5445 7585. www.avocadogrove.com.au. 4 units, 3 with bathroom (shower only), 1 with private adjacent bathroom. A$130 (US$104) double; A$150 (US$120) suite. Rates include full breakfast. Ask about weekend and midweek packages. MC, V. Turn right off ridge-top road onto Ensbey Rd.; Carramar Ct. is the 1st left. **Amenities:** Tour desk; in-room massage; nonsmoking rooms. *In room:* Ceiling fan, coffeemaker, hair dryer.

WHERE TO DINE

Noosa's **Hastings Street** comes alive at night with vacationers wining and dining at restaurants as sophisticated as those in Sydney and Melbourne. Just stroll along and see what appeals to you—but be prepared to make a reservation in high season. For a great breakfast, try **Café Le Monde** at the southern end of Hastings Street (opposite the back of the Surf Club), or **Bistro C,** one of the few restaurants offering beachfront dining. Noosa Junction is a less attractive place to eat, but the prices are cheaper. There are about 90 restaurants at Mooloolaba.

Ricky Ricardo's ⭐ MODERN AUSTRALIAN Owners Leonie Palmer and Steven "Stef" Fisher, stalwarts of the Noosa restaurant scene, named their latest not for a Latin TV idol but for Stef's great-uncle Ricky, a "gentleman scallywag" whose zest for life this place reflects. I'd choose it for lunch over dinner simply because of the fantastic setting; the food is sensational at any time. You can sit over a long meal drinking in the view across the Noosa River while nibbling from an innovative tapas menu or something more substantial. The menu is Mediterranean style, with fresh seafood and regional produce used throughout, and changes seasonally.

2/2 Quamby Place (inside the shopping center), Noosa Sound. © 07/5447 2455. Reservations recommended. Main courses A$17–A$35 (US$14–US$28). AE, DC, MC, V. Daily noon–midnight.

Season ⭐ MODERN AUSTRALIAN With one of the few beachfront restaurant locations, this is one of Noosa's most popular restaurants. Former Sydney chef Gary

---

> ⌒ *Tips* **The Seasons of the Sunshine Coast**
>
> Room rates on the Sunshine Coast are mostly moderate, but they jump sharply in the Christmas period from December 26 to January 26, during school holidays, and in the week following Easter. Book well ahead at these times. Weekends are often busy, too.

Skelton has maintained his following, with vacationers from southern states rediscovering Season, and even if the locals balk at the A$10 (US$8) corkage fee for BYO wine, there's no question the food remains superb. Breakfast dishes can be as simple as muffins, or you can indulge yourself with buttermilk-and-banana pancakes (with palm sugar butter and maple syrup). For dinner? How about the pan-fried reef fish filet with broad beans, mash and sauce antiboise, or even simpler, crispfried fish and chips with tartar sauce and fresh lemon? Smoking is not permitted.

25 Hastings St., Noosa Heads. ⓒ 07/5447 3747. Reservations essential for dinner; accepted same day only. Main courses A$17–A$31 (US$14–US$25); breakfast items A$4–A$12 (US$3.20–US$9.60). AE, DC, MC, V. Daily 8am–10pm.

9 The Gold Coast

Love it or hate it, the Gold Coast is one of Australia's icons. Bronzed lifeguards, bikini-clad meter maids, tanned tourists draped with gold jewelry, high-rise apartment towers that cast long shadows over parts of the beach . . . but the glitz, the glitter, and the overdevelopment pale as soon as you hit the beach. The white sands stretch uninterrupted for 70km (43 miles), making up for the long strips of neon-lit motels and cheap souvenir shops. Since the '50s, Australians have flocked to this strip of coastline, and that hasn't changed. Today, they're lining up with tourists from around the world to get into the theme parks, but everyone can still find a quiet spot on the beach.

The Gold Coast's theme parks are not as large or as sophisticated as Disneyland, but they're exciting enough. Apart from the three major parks—Dreamworld, Warner Bros. Movie World, and Sea World—there are of plenty of smaller ones. If theme parks aren't your thing, there are also 40 golf courses, dinner cruises, and loads of adrenaline-fueled outdoor activities, from bungee jumping to jet-skiing. The best activity on the Gold Coast, though, is the natural kind, and it doesn't cost a cent—hitting the surf and lazing on the beach.

GOLD COAST ESSENTIALS

GETTING THERE   By Car   Access to the Gold Coast Highway, which runs the length of the Coast, is off the Pacific Highway from Sydney or Brisbane. The drive takes about 80 minutes from Brisbane. From Sydney it's an 11-hour trip, sometimes longer, on the crowded, run-down Pacific Highway.

By Plane   Domestic **flights** land at Gold Coast Airport, Coolangatta, 25km (16 miles) south of Surfers Paradise. **Qantas** (ⓒ **13 13 13**) operates direct flights from Sydney and Adelaide. **QantasLink** flies from Brisbane and Newcastle. **Virgin Blue** (ⓒ **13 67 89**) flies direct from Sydney, Melbourne, Canberra, and Adelaide. **Jetstar** (ⓒ **13 15 38** in Australia) flies from Melbourne. Qantas international subsidiary **Australian Airlines** (ⓒ **1300/799 798** in Australia) links the Gold Coast and Cairns. The **Gold Coast Tourist Shuttle** (ⓒ **13 12 30**) meets every flight and will transfer you to your accommodations; the fare is A$15 (US$12) one-way and A$26 (US$21) round-trip for adults, A$8 (US$6.40) or A$13 (US$10) round-trip for kids ages 4 to 13, A$38 (US$30) one-way or A$65 (US$52) round-trip for families of four. A **taxi** from the airport to Surfers Paradise is about A$30 (US$24) but may be higher if traffic is heavy.

The nearest international gateway is **Brisbane International Airport** (see chapter 6). The **Coachtrans Airporter** bus meets most flights and makes about 20 trips a day from the domestic and international terminals at Brisbane Airport to Gold Coast accommodations for A$35 (US$28) adults, A$18 (US$14) children 4 to 14. The trip takes about 90 minutes to Surfers Paradise. You do not need to book in advance unless you are on an evening flight; if you are, call © **13 12 30** in Queensland, or 07/3238 4700.

AirtrainConnect links Brisbane Airport and the Gold Coast by train and bus for A$39 (US$31) adults, A$20 (US$16) children 5 to 14, or A$100 (US$80) for a group of five. Take Airtrain to the Gold Coast, then an air-conditioned coach shuttle to any accommodations between Southport Spit at the northern end of the Gold Coast and Burleigh Heads to the south. Airtrain's SmartPass, for A$99 (US$79) per adult, A$53 (US$42) per child, or A$222 (US$178) for a family of four for 3 days, covers AirtrainConnect transfers, as well as unlimited door-to-door theme park transfers on the Gold Coast Tourist Shuttle and use of the local Surfside bus network, 24 hours a day. Passes are also available for 5 and 7 days.

By Bus **Coachtrans** (© **13 12 30** in Queensland, or 07/3238 4700) runs between Brisbane and Gold Coast hotels. The fare is A$35 (US$28) adults one-way, A$18 (US$14) for kids, or A$89 (US$71) for a family.

Greyhound Australia (© **13 14 99**) makes daily stops at Surfers Paradise from Sydney and Brisbane. The trip from Sydney takes 14 to 15 hours, and the fare is A$96 (US$77). Trip time from Brisbane is 90 minutes, and the fare is A$20 (US$16).

By Train Suburban trains (call **Queensland Rail Citytrain;** © **07/3235 5555**) depart Brisbane Central and Roma Street stations every 30 minutes for the 72-minute trip to the Gold Coast suburb of Robina. The fare is A$10 (US$8) adults, A$5 (US$4) children 5 to 14. Numerous local buses meet the trains to take passengers to Surfers Paradise.

If you come by train to Surfers Paradise from Sydney or other southern cities, service is on **Countrylink** (© **13 22 32** in Australia; www.countrylink.nsw.gov.au), and you will need to transfer to a connecting coach in Casino or Murwillumbah, just south of the Queensland border. The trip from Sydney takes 14 to 15 hours and the fare is A$110 (US$88) for a sitting berth and A$230 (US$184) for a sleeper.

VISITOR INFORMATION The **Gold Coast Tourism Bureau** (© **07/5538 4419;** www.goldcoasttourism.com.au) has an information kiosk on Cavill Avenue in Surfers Paradise. It is stacked with brochures on things to see and do, and the staff will book tours and arrange accommodations. The kiosk is open Monday through Friday from 8:30am to 5:30pm, Saturday and public holidays from 9am to 5:30pm, and Sunday from 9am to 3:30pm. A second information booth is at the corner of Griffith and Warner streets in Coolangatta. It is open from 8am to 4pm weekdays, from 8am to 3pm Saturdays, from 8am to 1pm public holidays.

To obtain material in advance, e-mail info@gctb.com.au or write to the bureau at P.O. Box 7091, Gold Coast Mail Centre, QLD 9726.

ORIENTATION The heart of the Gold Coast is **Surfers Paradise**—"Surfers" to the locals—a high-rise forest of apartment towers, shops, cheap eateries, taverns, and amusement parlors. The pedestrian-only Cavill Mall in the center of town connects the Gold Coast Highway to The Esplanade, which runs along the beach.

The Gold Coast Highway is the main artery that connects the endless beachside suburbs lining the coast. Just north of Surfers is **Main Beach** 🌟🌟, where Tedder Avenue abounds with shops, restaurants, and cafes. Heading south from Surfers, the

The Gold Coast

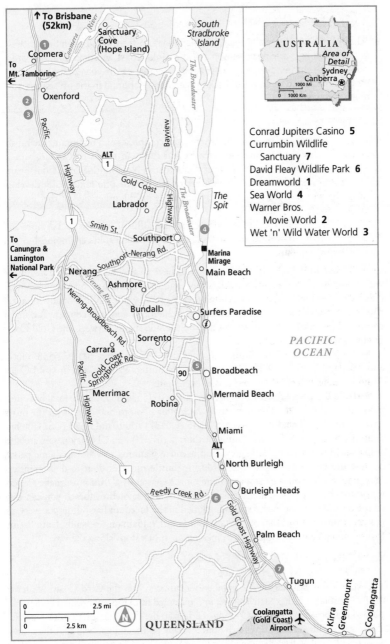

↑ **To Brisbane (52km)**

Sanctuary Cove (Hope Island)

South Stradbroke Island

● 1 Coomera

To Mt. Tamborine ←

○ Oxenford

2
3

Pacific

Bayview

The Broadwater

Coomera River

AUSTRALIA

Area of Detail

Sydney

Canberra ✪

0   1000 Mi
0   1000 Km

Conrad Jupiters Casino **5**
Currumbin Wildlife
   Sanctuary **7**
David Fleay Wildlife Park **6**
Dreamworld **1**
Sea World **4**
Warner Bros.
   Movie World **2**
Wet 'n' Wild Water World **3**

ALT 1

Gold Coast

Highway

Labrador ○

The Spit

1

Smith St.

Southport ○

To Canungra & Lamington National Park ←

Southport-Nerang Rd.

Nerang ○

Ashmore ○

Nerang River

4

■ Marina Mirage

● Main Beach

Bundall ○

● Surfers Paradise
ℹ

Nerang-Broadbeach Rd.

Sorrento ○

Carrara ○

PACIFIC OCEAN

Gold Coast Springbrook Rd.

Pacific Highway

90   5 ● Broadbeach

Merrimac ○

● Mermaid Beach

Robina ○

● Miami

ALT 1

1

● North Burleigh

Reedy Creek Rd.

6 ● Burleigh Heads

Gold Coast Highway

● Palm Beach

7 ● Tugun

0   2.5 mi
0   2.5 km

QUEENSLAND

Coolangatta (Gold Coast) ✈ Airport

Kirra ○

Greenmount

Coolangatta ○

367

Tips **The Secret of the Gold Coast Seasons**

School holidays, especially the Christmas vacation from mid-December to the end of January, are peak season on the Gold Coast. Accommodations are booked months in advance at these times. The rest of the year, occupancy levels plummet—and so do rates! Packages and deals abound in the off season, so make sure you ask.

---

main beach centers are **Broadbeach,** where retail complexes and restaurants are mushrooming; family-oriented **Burleigh Heads;** and the twin towns of **Coolangatta** in Queensland and **Tweed Heads** just over the border in New South Wales. Coolangatta still has a sleepy small-town feel that's ideal for families, despite some major development in the past few years. Gold Coast Airport is on the other side of the highway from Coolangatta township.

West of Surfers Paradise and Broadbeach are the affluent suburbs of **Ashmore** and **Nerang,** where luxury residential estates and many of the region's championship golf courses have sprung up.

GETTING AROUND   It's not necessary to have a car. The hotels listed below are within walking distance of the beach, shops, and restaurants, and many tour companies pick up at hotels. You can reach the theme parks by bus. A car is handy for a day trip to the hinterland, and to get around to restaurants and golf courses. Parking is cheap and plentiful in numerous lots and on the side streets between the Gold Coast Highway and The Esplanade.

Avis (© 07/5539 9388), **Budget** (© 07/5538 1344), **Hertz** (© 07/5538 5366), and **Thrifty** (© 07/5570 9999) have outlets in Surfers Paradise and at Gold Coast Airport. Endless local outfits rent cars at cheap rates.

Surfside Buslines (© **13 12 30** in Australia or 07/5571 6555) is the local bus company. Its best deal is the Freedom Pass, which allows you to hop on and off the buses anytime you like. The 3-day pass costs A$46 (US$37) adults and A$23 (US$18) children or A$115 (US$92) for a family of four; 5-, 7-, 10-, and 14-day passes are also available. This is a particularly good deal if you're planning to visit the theme parks, because the company's Gold Coast Tourist Shuttle operates door-to-door transfers four times every morning from anywhere on the coastal strip. You must make a reservation for this, but if you are staying in Surfers Paradise or Broadbeach you can hop on the Surfside Theme Park Express (included in the Freedom Pass). It leaves every 15 minutes from 8:25 to 11am on weekdays and until 9:45am on weekends, from Pacific Fair shopping center at Broadbeach, picking up at bus stops along the way.

WHAT TO SEE & DO ON THE COAST
HITTING THE BEACHES

The white sandy beaches are the number-one attraction on the Gold Coast. No fewer than 35 patrolled beaches stretch almost uninterrupted from the Spit north of Surfers Paradise to Rainbow Bay, south of Coolangatta. In fact, the Gold Coast is just one long fabulous beach—all you need do is step onto it at any point, and you will spot the nearest set of red and yellow flags that signal safe swimming. The most popular beaches are **Main Beach** ★★, **Surfers North, Elkhorn Avenue, Surfers Paradise, Mermaid Beach, Burleigh Heads, Coolangatta,** and **Greenmount.** All are patrolled 365 days a year.

DOING THE THEME PARKS

The big three are Dreamworld, Sea World, and Warner Bros. Movie World. Right next door to Movie World is Wet 'n' Wild Water World.

Sea World is the only major theme park in the center of town. The others are in northern bushland on the Pacific Highway, about 15 to 20 minutes away from Surfers Paradise. You can ride to the theme parks on the Gold Coast Tourist Shuttle (see above) or on **Surfside Buslines** (© **13 12 30** in Queensland) buses. Take bus no. 1A to Dreamworld and Wet 'n' Wild; bus no. 1A or X to Movie World; and bus no. 2 or 9 to Sea World.

If you are driving, take the M1 Pacific Motorway for about 15 to 20 minutes north of the Gold Coast or 40 minutes south of Brisbane for Wet 'n' Wild, Warner Bros. Movie World, and Dreamworld. Exits are all well signposted. All the theme parks have huge free parking lots.

Trains (© **13 12 30**) run to Coomera and Helensvale on the Brisbane–Gold Coast line. Queensland Rail Citytrain sells tickets to the theme parks at attended stations, including Brisbane Central, which saves the time of standing in line to get in, rather than any money.

Coachtrans (© **13 12 30** in Australia or 07/5506 9777) does daily transfers to the big three parks, as well as Wet 'n' Wild and Currumbin Sanctuary. Round-trip fare is A$16 (US$13) for adults, A$8 (US$6.40) for kids, and A$40 (US$32) for families. Book a day ahead if you can, especially in peak season.

Dreamworld 🌟 Kids   Adrenaline-crazed thrill-seekers will love the action rides, such as the aptly named Giant Drop, in which you free-fall 39 stories in 5 seconds, and the Tower of Terror, which propels you forward and upward at 4.5Gs before you fall backward 38 stories in 7 seconds. They'll also get a kick out of the hair-raising Cyclone roller coaster, with its 360-degree loop, and the Wipeout, which spins, twists, and tumbles you upside down in a random sequence (but only exerts a sissy 2.5Gs units of pressure). These high-octane offerings make the park's other attractions look tame. Dreamworld is a family fun park, Disney-style—except that here giant koalas called Kenny and Belinda roam the streets instead of Mickey Mouse. Kids will love Nick Central, the only Nickelodeon cartoon attraction outside the U.S.

Other activities include an IMAX theater, a native wildlife park where you can cuddle a koala and hand-feed kangaroos, river cruises livened up by a bushranger shootout, and a carousel and other rides for young kids. A big highlight is to watch trainers swim, wrestle, and play with Bengal tigers on Tiger Island. Souvenir stores, restaurants,

---

⟨Value⟩ Money-Saving Theme Park Passes

Sea World, Warner Bros. Movie World, and Wet 'n' Wild sell a **3 Park Super Pass** that includes a full day at each park plus a free return visit to the one you like best. It costs A$158 (US$126) for adults and A$100 (US$80) for kids 4 to 13. You can buy it at any of the parks, online, from a travel agency, or at most Gold Coast hotels, apartments, and tour desks. Sea World and Warner Bros. Movie World also sell a second-day return pass for A$30 (US$24) extra adult or A$19 (US$15) children, but you must buy it before leaving on your first day. Wet 'n' Wild's second-day pass is A$19 (US$15) adults and A$12 (US$9.60) children. **Dreamworld** has a second-day return pass for an extra A$15 (US$12).

cafes, and ice-cream shops abound, and there's a water-slide park, so bring your swimsuit.

Pacific Hwy. (25km/16 miles north of Surfers Paradise), Coomera. ℂ **1800/073 300** in Australia, 07/5588 1111, or 07/5588 1122 (24-hr. info line). www.dreamworld.com.au. Admission (all-inclusive except skill games, souvenir photos, and helicopter rides) A$60 (US$48) adults, A$38 (US$30) children 4–13. Daily 10am–5pm; Main St., Plaza Restaurant, and Koala Country open at 9am. Closed Dec 25 and until 1:30pm Apr 25 (Anzac Day). Extended hours during Easter and Dec–Jan. Free parking for 1,600 cars.

Sea World ★★ *Kids*   Four polar bears—Lia and Lutik, and Canadian orphan cubs Hudson and Nelson—are the star attractions at this marine park, and crowds flock to see them frolic, dive, and hunt for fish in a large pool. The cubs are usually out in the morning, and the bigger bears on show in the afternoon, but you'll probably make a day of it, so you'll get to see them all. A behind-the-scenes tour of their habitat costs A$50 (US$40) for adults, A$25 (US$20) for children 4 to 13 (Mon–Fri only). Sea World may not be as sophisticated as similar parks in the United States, but it has its own charm, plus all the things you'd expect to see—performing dolphins and sea lions, ski shows, an aquarium, shark feeding, and an array of rides. The newest attraction is Shark Bay, a A$13-million (US$10-million) exhibit where you can see some of the larger and more dangerous species, such as tiger sharks. You can also snorkel with the sharks for A$55 (US$44) per person (if you are 10 or over).

A monorail gets you around the park, and there's a free water-slide playground. Watersports are available for an extra fee. Adults (14 and over) can snorkel with seals or dolphins for A$105 or A$135 (US$84–US$108), including a souvenir photo. An hour-long Dolphin Dive Encounter uses "ocean-walker" technology to allow guests without dive qualifications to have a divelike encounter with dolphins. It costs A$170 (US$136) per person (you must be over 13). Younger kids can attend a 30-minute dolphin talk, pat one, and have their photo taken with one for A$70 (US$56).

Sea World Dr. (3km/1¾ miles north of Surfers Paradise), The Spit, Main Beach. ℂ **07/5588 2222**, or 07/5588 2205 (24-hr. info line). Fax 07/5591 1056. www.seaworld.com.au. Admission (all-inclusive except animal experiences, helicopter rides, and powered watersports) A$60 (US$48) adults, A$38 (US$30) children 4–13. AE, DC, MC, V. Daily 10am–5pm; 1:30–6:30pm Apr 25 (Anzac Day). Closed Dec 25. Free parking.

Warner Bros. Movie World ★ *Kids*   Australia's answer to Universal Studios just about matches its U.S. counterpart for thrills and spills. The park is based around working studios where *Scooby Doo,* starring Sarah Michelle Gellar and Freddie Prinze, Jr.; *The Phantom,* starring Billy Zane; *20,000 Leagues Under the Sea,* with Michael Caine; and *Streetfighter,* with Jean-Claude Van Damme, were filmed. If you already know how Superman flies across skyscrapers and you've heard a Foley sound studio in action, the train ride around the sets might not interest you, but it's a great introduction to cinema tricks for first-timers. The newest attraction is a walk-through *Matrix* exhibit. Hair-raising, tummy-turning rides include the indoor Scooby-Doo Spooky Coaster roller coaster, the Lethal Weapon roller coaster, and the simulated high-speed chase of Batman—The Ride. Don't miss the hilarious Police Academy Stunt Show. Young kids can take rides and see stage shows by Yosemite Sam and Porky Pig in the Looney Tunes Village, and there's a Looney Tunes Parade through the streets each day. Most parades and shows take place between 11am and 4pm.

Pacific Hwy. (21km/13 miles north of Surfers Paradise), Oxenford. ℂ **07/5573 3999**, or 07/5573 8485 (recorded info). www.movieworld.com.au. Admission (all-inclusive) A$60 (US$48) adults, A$38 (US$30) children 4–13. AE, DC, MC, V. Daily 9:30am–5:30pm; rides and attractions operate 10am–5pm. Closed Dec 25 and until 1:30pm Apr 25 (Anzac Day). Free parking.

Wet 'n' Wild Water World *Kids*   Hurtling down a seven-story piece of fiberglass at 70kmph (43 mph) is just one of many water-slide options at this aquatic fun park. The rides have names like Double Screamer, Mammoth Falls, the Twister, Terror Canyon, and White Water Mountain. That just about says it all. Scaredy-cats can stick to the four regular white-water flumes, float gently past palm-studded "islands" at Calypso Beach, swim in the artificial breakers in the Wave Pool or in the regular pool, or soak in a spa at Whirlpool Springs. There's also a water playground for young kids. Every night in January, and Saturday night September through April, is Dive-In Movie night, during which film fans can recline on a rubber tube in the pool while watching the flick on a giant screen. The park is very popular and very crowded, and to get a tube or a seat you have to get there early. The water is heated to 79°F (26°C) April to September, there are lifeguards on duty, you can rent towels and lockers, and you can use the hot showers. An "afternoon rate" of A$19 (US$15) adults and A$12 (US$9.60) children applies after 3pm, or after 4:30pm on dive-in movie nights.

Pacific Hwy. (next to Warner Bros. Movie World), Oxenford. ℂ **07/5556 1610** (administration), or 07/5573 2255 (24-hr. recorded info). www.wetnwild.com.au. Admission A$38 (US$30) adults, A$24 (US$19) children 4–13. AE, DC, MC, V. Jan daily 10am–9pm; Feb and Oct–Dec daily 10am–5pm; Mar–Apr and Sept daily 10am–4:30pm; May–Aug daily 10am–4pm. Closes at 9pm on Dive-In Movie nights. Closed Dec 25 and until 1:30pm Apr 25 (Anzac Day). Free parking.

EXPLORING THE WILDLIFE PARKS

Currumbin Wildlife Sanctuary *Kids*   Currumbin began life as a bird sanctuary, and it is almost synonymous with the wild rainbow lorikeets that flock here by the hundreds twice a day for feeding. It's quite an experience—flocks of chattering birds descend onto visitors holding trays of food for them. Photographers go crazy, and tourists love it. The amazingly beautiful birds have a vivid green back, blue head, and red-and-yellow chest. Lorikeet feeding is at 8am and 4pm. Don't miss it.

You can also have your photo taken cuddling a koala, hand-feed kangaroos, take a free miniature steam-train ride through the park, and attend animal talks and feeding demonstrations. An Aboriginal song-and-dance show takes place daily. The park's 27 hectares (67 acres) are home to 1,400 native birds and animals, including two enormous saltwater crocodiles, and the wetlands on the grounds attract lots of native birds. Allow several hours to see everything. A highlight is the free-flight birds show at 11am and 2pm. Nighttime Wildlight tours are run daily at 7:15pm, and last for around 2½ hours. They cost A$49 (US$39) adults and A$27 (US$22) children 4 to 13.

28 Tomewin St., Currumbin (18km/11 miles south of Surfers Paradise). ℂ **07/5534 1266**. www.currumbin-sanctuary. org.au. Admission A$25 (US$20) adults, A$17 (US$14) children 4–13. AE, DC, MC, V. Daily 8am–5pm. Closed Dec 25 and until 1pm Apr 25 (Anzac Day). Ample free parking. Bus: 1 or 1A (stop 15m/49 ft. from entrance).

David Fleay Wildlife Park *Value*   Established in 1952 by Australian naturalist David Fleay, this is one of Australia's premier wildlife parks. You'll see a platypus, saltwater and freshwater crocodiles, wallabies, kangaroos, glider possums, dingoes, wombats, the rare Lumholtz's tree kangaroo, and a big range of Australian birds, including emus, cassowaries, wedge-tailed eagles, black swans, and lorikeets. You walk on a series of raised boardwalks through picturesque mangrove, rainforest, and eucalyptus habitats, where most of the animals roam free. The nocturnal house, open from 11am to 5pm daily, is where you'll see many of the most elusive animals, including Australia's answer to the Easter bunny, the bilby.

Talks and feeding demonstrations throughout the day include a reptile show and saltwater-croc feeding—usually only October through April, when the crocs are hungry. Aboriginal rangers give talks about weaponry, bush medicine, and their links with this region. Volunteers also give free guided tours throughout the day. The Queensland National Parks and Wildlife Service (QNPWS) has run the park since 1983; David Fleay continued to live here until his death in 1993. Because the QNPWS frowns on handling animals, you can't cuddle a koala or hand-feed kangaroos here. There's a cafe, gift shop, and picnic tables.

West Burleigh Rd. (17km/11 miles south of Surfers Paradise), West Burleigh. © 07/5576 2411. Admission A$13 (US$10) adults, A$8.50 (US$6.80) seniors and students, A$6.50 (US$5.20) children 4–17, A$33 (US$26) family of 6. MC, V. Daily 9am–5pm. Closed Dec 25. Ample free parking.

WHERE TO STAY
VERY EXPENSIVE

Palazzo Versace ⚐   You almost have to see this to believe it. In the unlikely location of the Australian Gold Coast, fashion designer Donatella Versace has created a tribute to her late brother, Gianni, in the form of an extravagantly opulent resort, furnished exclusively with Versace gear. You'll either love it or hate it—there's no in-between.

Everything was imported from Italy, from the river stones that pave the porte-cochere to the massive antique chandelier that dominates the vast, marbled lobby. Vaulted ceilings are hand-detailed in gold, and huge marble columns dominate. The rooms are decorated in four colors (red, blue, gold, and orange), and are less confronting than the public areas. Everything in them—furniture, cutlery, crockery, toiletries, the lot—is Versace (either from the home wares collection or specially created for the hotel). Many of the rooms overlook the huge pool, the Broadwater (a stretch of ocean), and the marina. As you'd expect, everything is beautifully appointed, and you'll enjoy strolling the corridors lined with Gianni's artwork and designs. There's an extensive spa and health club in the basement. You can choose from eight room types (Donatella stays in the A$3,000/US$2,400 Imperial Suite) or from a pool of two- and three-bedroom condominiums. All rooms and suites have Jacuzzis; condos have kitchens. And of course, should you get the urge to shop, there's a Versace boutique.

94 Sea World Dr., Main Beach, QLD 4217. © **1800/098 000** in Australia, or 07/5509 8000. Fax 07/5509 8888. www.palazzoversace.com. 205 units, 72 condos. A$405 (US$324) double superior room; A$455 (US$364) double superior suite; A$475 (US$380) double superior lagoon view room; A$605 (US$484) deluxe suite; A$755 (US$604) Broadwater suite; A$1,200–A$1,600 (US$960–US$1,280) condominium. AE, DC, MC, V. **Amenities:** 3 restaurants; 2 bars; saltwater heated lagoon pool and 27 other pools (some exclusive to condos); health club and spa; wet and dry sauna; concierge; tour desk; business center; salon; 24-hr. room service; massage; laundry service; dry cleaning; non-smoking rooms. *In room:* A/C, TV w/pay movies, dataport, PlayStation, minibar, fridge, coffeemaker, hair dryer, iron, safe, Jacuzzi.

MODERATE

Mercure Resort Surfers Paradise ⚐ *Kids*   Parents, if your idea of a holiday is to not even see your kids for most of the day, this place is for you. The resort has a licensed child-care center for little ones as young as 6 weeks and up to 5 years old. For 5- to 12-year-olds, there's the Gecko Club, complete with pedal minicars, the Leonardo painting room, and an underwater-themed pirate adventure world. You can laze around the leafy pool area and watch the kids play on the water slide. The child-care center charges moderate fees, and the Gecko Club is free; both operate daily year-round. The low-rise building is comfortable, and rooms have views of the pool or the gardens. All rooms were refurbished in November 2000. Family quarters sleep up to five in two separate rooms, and some (the family studios) have kitchenettes.

The resort rents a wide range of kiddy stuff such as prams (strollers), bottle warmers, car seats, and PlayStations, and it has a mini-market and takeout meal service. The

Tips **Book Ahead for Indy & Easter Madness!**

Most accommodations require a 1-week minimum stay during school holiday periods and a 4-day minimum stay at Easter. When the Gold Coast Indy car race takes over the town for 4 days in October, hotel rates skyrocket and most hostelries demand a minimum stay of 3 or 4 nights. Don't leave accommodations bookings to the last minute! Contact the **Gold Coast Tourism Bureau** (© **07/5536 7765**; www.goldcoasttourism.com.au) to find out the exact dates.

big range of activities makes this a great value for families, and the center of Surfers Paradise and the patrolled beach are a few blocks across the highway. Some rooms are near the highway, so ask for a quiet spot.

122 Ferny Ave., Surfers Paradise, QLD 4217. © **1800/074 111** in Australia, 800/221-4542 in the U.S. and Canada, 0181/283 4500 in the U.K., 0800/44 4422 in New Zealand, or 07/5579 4444. Fax 07/5579 4496. www. mercuresurfers.com.au. 405 units. A$210 (US$168) resort room for up to 4; A$250 (US$200) deluxe room for up to 4; A$290 (US$232) resort family room for up to 5. Ask about special packages. AE, DC, MC, V. Free covered parking. Bus: 1 or 1A (stop outside the resort). **Amenities:** 2 restaurants; cafe/sandwich bar; bar; 4 outdoor pools; 2 tennis courts; exercise room; Jacuzzi; sauna; child-care center and kids' club; game room/video arcade; concierge; tour desk; shuttle bus; business center; babysitting; coin-op laundry; dry cleaning. *In room:* A/C, TV/VCR w/free and pay-per-view movies, kitchenette, fridge, coffeemaker, hair dryer, iron, safe.

GOOD-VALUE VACATION APARTMENTS

Apartments make good sense for families and for any traveler who wants to self-cater to save money. Because the Gold Coast has a dramatic oversupply of apartments that stand empty except during school vacations, you can get a spacious modern unit with ocean views for the cost of a midrange hotel. Apartment-block developers got in quick to snag the best beachfront spots when the Gold Coast boomed in the 1970s, so apartment buildings, not hotels, have the best ocean views. The **Gold Coast Booking Centre** (© **1300/737 111;** www.gcbc.com.au) is a centralized booking service that offers great deals at more than 1,200 apartments in Surfers Paradise and Broadbeach.

Enderley Gardens   Just a block from the beach, and centered on a large lagoon-style pool, this older-style apartment block is a short walk from Cavill Mall. Units are spacious, and all have balconies. They are simply but neatly furnished, with a large kitchen and laundry facilities. Like many apartments on the Gold Coast, these are not air-conditioned, but they have ceiling fans and the sea breeze is a good substitute. There are two barbecue areas, and the low-rise (four-story) block makes this a good choice for families or older people

32 Enderley Ave., Surfers Paradise, QLD 4217. © **1300/553 800** in Australia, or 07/5570 1511. Fax 07/5592 3878. www.enderleygardens.com.au. 86 units. High season A$239 (US$191) double 1-bedroom apt, A$458 (US$366) double 2-bedroom apt; low season A$165 (US$132) 1-bedroom apt, A$278 (US$222) 2-bedroom apt. Extra person A$30 (US$24). 4-night minimum during Indy, 5-night minimum at Christmas. AE, DC, MC, V. Free secure covered parking. **Amenities:** Large outdoor pool (heated in winter); wading pool; half-court tennis; Jacuzzi; sauna; playground; tour desk; babysitting. *In room:* TV, kitchen, iron.

Equinox Resort *Value* *Kids*   This well-maintained older-style apartment block is just across the road from the beach and a short walk from Cavill Mall and the restaurants and cafes of Main Beach. You can choose between a studio with a balcony and basic tea- and coffeemaking facilities, or forego the balcony for a full kitchen in a suite. Or you can connect a studio and suite to make a two-bedroom apartment that has it all.

Some of the studios have air-conditioning, and they are ideal for up to three people. There are two barbecue areas, and a roof-top sun deck. It's good value for location, price, and comfort.

3458 Main Beach Parade, Surfers Paradise, QLD 4217. ℂ 1300/553 800 in Australia, or 07/5538 3288. Fax 07/5538 6862. www.equinoxresort.com.au. 90 units. High season A$239 (US$191) studio, A$292 (US$234) suite, A$465 (US$372) 2-bedroom apt; low season A$165 (US$132) studio, A$177 (US$142) suite, A$282 (US$226) 2-bedroom apt. Extra person A$30 (US$24). 4-night minimum during Indy, 5-night minimum at Christmas. MC, V. Free underground secure parking. **Amenities:** Outdoor pool (heated in winter); 2 tennis half-courts; squash court; gym; Jacuzzi; sauna; game room; tour desk; babysitting. *In room:* TV, kitchen, fridge, hair dryer, iron.

WHERE TO DINE

The Gold Coast is full to the rafters with good restaurants. Many stylish new restaurants and cafes, most reasonably priced, are springing up around **Surf Parade** and **Victoria Avenue** in Broadbeach, as well as in the nearby **Oasis shopping mall.** Other trendy spots are the stylish **Marina Mirage** shopping center, opposite the Sheraton on Sea World Drive in Main Beach, and the hip **Tedder Avenue** cafes in Main Beach.

THE GOLD COAST AFTER DARK

There's a genuine Rolls Royce parked in the corner at **Rolls** nightclub, at the Sheraton Mirage, Sea World Drive, Main Beach (ℂ 07/5591 1488). You can reserve it as your booth for the night. A mixed-age crowd of sophisticated locals rubs shoulders with hotel guests. There is a A$5 (US$4) cover; the club opens Friday and Saturday night. At 10:30pm they push back the tables at **Saks,** Marina Mirage, Sea World Drive, Main Beach (ℂ 07/5591 2755) and the elegant cafe and wine bar turns into a dance floor for fashionable 20- and 30-somethings. Friday, Saturday, and Sunday are the coolest nights to turn up, and there's a live band Sundays; no cover.

It's not as big as some Vegas casinos, but **Conrad Jupiters Casino,** Gold Coast Highway, Broadbeach (ℂ 07/5592 8282), has plenty to keep the gambler amused—70 gaming tables and 1,300-plus slot machines with roulette, blackjack, Caribbean stud poker, baccarat and minibaccarat, craps, Pai Gow, and sic-bo. The 1,100-seat Jupiter's Theatre stages floor shows and concerts; and there are three bars, including an English-style pub. Of the five restaurants, the good-value **Food Fantasy** buffet is outrageously popular, so be prepared to wait. The casino is open 24 hours. You must be 18 to enter, and smart, casual dress is required.

10 The Gold Coast Hinterland: Back to Nature

The cool, green Gold Coast hinterland is only a half-hour drive from the coast, but it is a world away from the neon lights, theme parks, and crowds. Up here, at an altitude of 500 to 1,000m (1,640–3,280 ft.), the tree ferns drip moisture, the air is crisp, and the pace is slow.

Mount Tamborine shelters several villages known for their crafts shops, galleries, cafes, and B&Bs. Easy walking trails wander from the streets through rainforest and eucalyptus woodland, and as you drive you will discover magnificent views.

The impressive 20,200-hectare (49,895-acre) **Lamington National Park** lies south of Mount Tamborine. The park, at around 1,000m (3,328 ft.) above sea level, is a eucalyptus and rainforest wilderness crisscrossed with walking trails. It's famous for its colorful bird life, wallabies, possums, and other wildlife. The road to the park is full of twists and turns, and as you wind higher and higher, tangled vines and dense eucalyptus and ferns make a canopy across the road—it's so dark you need headlights. The park is about 90 minutes from the coast, but once you're ensconced in your mountain retreat, the world will seem remote.

The hinterland is close enough to the Gold Coast and Brisbane to make a pleasant day trip, but you will almost certainly want to stay overnight, or longer, once you breathe that restorative mountain air.

MOUNT TAMBORINE

40km (25 miles) NW of Surfers Paradise; 70km (43 miles) S of Brisbane

Crafts shops, teahouses, and idyllic vistas are Mount Tamborine's attractions. The mountaintop is more a plateau than a peak, and it's home to a string of villages, all a mile or two apart—Eagle Heights, North Tamborine, and Mount Tamborine proper. Many shops and cafes are open only Thursday through Sunday.

ESSENTIALS

GETTING THERE & GETTING AROUND   From the Gold Coast, head to Nerang and follow signs to Beaudesert. The Mount Tamborine turnoff is off this road. Alternatively, take the Pacific Highway north to Oxenford and take the Mount Tamborine turnoff, the first exit after Warner Bros. Movie World. Many tour operators run minibus and four-wheel-drive day trips from the Gold Coast, and some run tours from Brisbane. An alternative to the tours is to pay A$25 (US$20) for the day to ride the **Tamborine Trolley Co.** buses (© **07/5545 2782**), modeled on early-20th-century trams, which run on a 25km (16-mile) circuit linking four wineries, a distillery, a pub, cafes, restaurants, antiques shops, markets, galleries, hang-gliding lookouts, and rainforest walks. The circuit takes an hour, and you can hop on and off as you like. Owner-operator Sue Netherway will organize transport to Mount Tamborine on request. She also runs an hour-long "discovery" tour for A$10 (US$8) per person and a full-day food and wine tour every Thursday and Friday for A$70 (US$56), or A$95 (US$76) with pickup from the Gold Coast.

VISITOR INFORMATION   Head to the **Gold Coast Tourism Bureau** (see "Visitor Information" under "The Gold Coast," earlier in this chapter) to stock up on information and tourist maps before you set off. Brisbane Marketing (see "Visitor Information" in chapter 6) also has information. The **Tamborine Mountain Information Centre** is in Dougherty Park, where Geissmann Drive joins Main Western Road in North Tamborine (© **07/5545 3200**; www.tamborinemtncc.org.au). It's open daily from 10:30am to 3:30pm.

EXPLORING THE MOUNTAIN

With a map at hand, you are well equipped to drive around Mount Tamborine's roads, admire the wonderful views over the valleys, and poke around the shops. New Age candles, homemade soaps, maple-pecan fudge, framed tropical watercolors, German cuckoo clocks, and Aussie antiques are some of the things you can buy in the many stores. The best place to shop is the quaint strip of galleries, cafes, and shops known as **Gallery Walk** on Long Road, between North Tamborine and Eagle Heights. Eagle Heights has few shops but great views back toward the coast. North Tamborine is mainly a commercial center with the odd nice gallery or two. Mount Tamborine itself is mainly residential.

Allow time to walk some of the trails that wind through forest throughout the villages. Most are reasonably short and easy. The Mount Tamborine Information Centre has maps marking them.

WHERE TO STAY

Tamborine Mountain Bed & Breakfast ⭐   Ideally situated close to rainforest walks, arts and craft shops, wineries, and restaurants, Tony and Pam Lambert's restful timber home has stunning 180-degree views to the ocean from the breakfast balcony. Laze by the open fire in the timber-lined living room, or on the lovely veranda where rainbow lorikeets, kookaburras, and crimson rosellas flit about over the bird feeders. The ferny gardens have four purpose-built rustic timber rooms, each individually decorated in cottage style and linked to the house by covered walkways. Rooms are heated in winter. No smoking indoors.

19–23 Witherby Crescent, Eagle Heights, QLD 4721. (C) 07/5545 3595. Fax 07/5545 3322. www.tmbb.com.au. 4 units (all with shower only). A$130 (US$104) double midweek; A$160 (US$128) double weekend. Rates include continental breakfast Mon–Fri, full breakfast weekends. MC, V. Free parking. Children under 12 not accepted. **Amenities:** Nonsmoking rooms. *In room:* A/C, TV/VCR, small fridge, coffeemaker, iron.

LAMINGTON NATIONAL PARK ★★
70km (43 miles) W of Gold Coast; 115km (71 miles) S of Brisbane

Subtropical rainforest, 2,000-year-old moss-covered Antarctic beech trees, giant strangler figs, and misty mountain air characterize Lamington's high, narrow ridges and plunging valleys. Its great stretches of dense rainforest make it one of the most important subtropical parks in southeast Queensland, and one of the loveliest. The park has 160km (99 miles) of walking trails that track through thick forest, past ferny waterfalls, and along mountain ridges with soaring views across green valleys. The trails vary in difficulty and length, from 1km (.5-mile) strolls to 23km (14-mile) treks.

The park is a haven for bird lovers, who come to see and photograph the rosellas, bowerbirds, rare lyrebirds, and other species that live here, but that's not the only wildlife you will see. Groups of small wallabies, called pademelons, graze outside your room. In summer you may see giant carpet pythons curled up in a tree or large goannas sunning themselves on rock ledges. Near streams you may be stopped by a hissing Lamington spiny crayfish, an aggressive little monster 6 inches long, patterned in royal blue and white. The park comes alive with owls, possums, and sugar-gliders at night.

Most visitors are fascinated by the park's Antarctic beech trees, which begin to appear above the 1,000m (3,280-ft.) line. Like something from a medieval fairy tale, these mossy monarchs of the forest stand 20m (66 ft.) tall and measure up to 8m (26 ft.) in girth. They are survivors of a time when Australia and Antarctica belonged to the supercontinent Gondwana, when it was covered by wet, tropical rainforest. The species survived the last Ice Age, and the trees at Lamington are about 2,000 years old, suckered off root systems about 8,000 years old. The trees are a 2½-hour walk from O'Reilly's Rainforest Guesthouse (see below).

EXPLORING LAMINGTON NATIONAL PARK
The easiest way to explore the park is to base yourself at **O'Reilly's Rainforest Guesthouse** in the Green Mountains section of the park, or at **Binna Burra Mountain Lodge** in the Binna Burra section (see "Where to Stay & Dine," below). Most of the trails lead from one or the other of these resorts, and a 23km (14-mile) **Border Trail** connects them; it follows the New South Wales–Queensland border for much of the way, and most reasonably fit folk can walk it in a day. Guided walks and activities at both resorts are for guests only; however, both properties welcome day visitors who just want to walk the trails (which is free). Both have inexpensive cafes for day-trippers.

It is a good idea to bring a torch (flashlight) and maybe binoculars for wildlife spotting. The temperature is often 10° to 20°F (4°–5°C) cooler than on the Gold Coast, so bring a sweater in summer and bundle up in winter when nights get close to freezing. September through October is orchid season, and the frogs come out in noisy abundance in February and March.

GETTING THERE   By Car   O'Reilly's is 37km (23 miles) from the town of Canungra. The road is twisty and winding, so take it slow. Allow an hour from Canungra to reach O'Reilly's, and plan to arrive before dark. Binna Burra is 35km (22 miles) from Nerang via Beechmont, or 26km (16 miles) from Canungra, on a winding mountain road. From the Gold Coast go west to Nerang, where you can turn off to Binna Burra via Beechmont, or go on to Canungra, where you will see the O'Reilly's and Binna Burra turnoffs. From Brisbane, follow the Pacific Highway south and take the Beenleigh/Mount Tamborine exit to Mount Tamborine. From there, follow signs to Canungra. Allow a good 2½ hours to get to either resort from Brisbane, and 90 minutes from the Gold Coast. Binna Burra sells unleaded fuel; O'Reilly's has emergency supplies only.

By Coach   The **Mountain Coach Company** (© **07/5524 4249**) does daily transfers to O'Reilly's and Binna Burra from the Gold Coast, leaving the airport at 8am, picking up at hotels along the way, and arriving at O'Reilly's at around noon. The return trip leaves O'Reilly's at 2:30pm, arriving at the airport by 5:30pm. **Allstate Scenic Tours** (© **07/3003 0700**) makes a daily coach run from outside the Roma Street Transit Centre in Brisbane at 8:30am, arriving at O'Reilly's at 12:30pm. The return trip leaves O'Reilly's at 2pm and gets to Brisbane at 6pm.

The Binna Burra resort runs a shuttle from Gold Coast Airport at 1:30pm daily and from Nerang railway station at 2pm, arriving at Binna Burra at 3pm. Reserve a spot when booking accommodations.

VISITOR INFORMATION   The best sources of information on hiking are O'Reilly's Rainforest Guesthouse and Binna Burra Mountain Lodge (see "Where to Stay & Dine," below); ask them to send you copies of their walking maps. There is a national parks information office at both properties. For detailed information on hiking and camping in the park, contact the ranger at Lamington National Park, Green Mountains section (at O'Reilly's), Canungra, QLD 4211 (© **07/5544 0634**).

WHERE TO STAY & DINE

Both of these mountaintop retreats have long and interesting histories. Both offer walking trails of a similar type and distance; guided walks, including nighttime wildlife-spotting trips; hearty food; and a restful, enjoyable experience. They offer similar experiences; the differences are perhaps in style, with O'Reilly's having become a more sophisticated and modern operation in recent years. Look into the special-interest workshops both properties run throughout the year, which can be anything from gourmet weekends to mountain-jogging programs.

Binna Burra Mountain Lodge ★★ *(Kids)*   Binna Burra is a postcard-perfect mountain lodge. The original cabins, built in 1935, are still in use; they've been outfitted with modern comforts but not with contemporary "inconveniences," such as telephones, televisions, radios, and clocks. All the accommodations have pine-paneled walls, floral bedcovers, heaters, and electric blankets. The most attractive and spacious are the mud-brick and weatherboard Acacia cabins, which have private bathrooms and the best views over the Numinbah Valley. The two kinds of Casuarina cabins are less expensive—the nicest are the small and cozy huts with a pitched ceiling, a washbasin, and a nice aspect into the forest and over the valley. Less atmospheric are the bunkroom-style units that sleep four to six people—good for families and groups of friends. Guests in Casuarina cabins share bathroom facilities, which include a Jacuzzi.

Meals are served in the stone-and-timber dining room. Seating is communal, so you get to meet other travelers. Free tea and coffee are on the boil all day. Also here are a crafts shop, a natural history library, and conference rooms.

Beechmont via Canungra, QLD 4211. ℂ **1800/074 260** in Australia, or 07/5533 3622. Fax 07/5533 3747. www.BinnaBurraLodge.com.au. 41 cabins, 22 with bathroom (shower only). A$154–A$312 (US$123–US$250) B&B-only double; A$234–A$504 (US$187–US$403) double with all-inclusive meals and activities. A$40 (US$32) B&B or A$65 (US$52) all-inclusive for child 5–14. Ask about packages. 2-night minimum weekends, 3-night minimum public holiday weekends, 4-night minimum at Easter, 5–night minimum at Christmas. AE, DC, MC, V. **Amenities:** Restaurant; bar; free kids' club (ages 5–14) Sat and school vacations; babysitting; coin-op laundry. In room: Minibar, fridge, coffeemaker, no phone.

O'Reilly's Rainforest Guesthouse ✶✶ *Kids* Highlights of your stay will be the chance to hand-feed brilliantly colored rainforest birds every morning and the fact that the staff will remember you by name. Nestled high on a cleared plateau, the buildings are closed in on three sides by dense tangled rainforest and open to picturesque mountain views to the west. The timber resort complex is inviting, with upmarket new suites and a major refurbishment of older rooms adding a touch of luxury. The comfortable guest lounge has an open fire, old-fashioned sofas and chairs, and an upright piano. The six rooms in the Toolona block, built in the 1930s, have communal bathrooms and basic furniture. The six refurbished motel-style Garden View rooms have handcrafted maple furniture. The seven Bithongabel rooms are singles. Mountain View rooms look out to the McPherson Ranges and have balconies; the six family rooms in this block have bunks for kids, and two rooms have wheelchair access. Three large Canopy Suites have a king-size four-poster bed, fireplace, Jacuzzi, library, stereo/CD player, minibar, and bar. One of the former O'Reilly family homes has been transformed into two new guest units, called "Vince" and "Lona" after the second-generation couple who raised their 10 children in the house. Each unit has two bedrooms (one with a king-size four-poster), two bathrooms, a separate living room, and a two-way fireplace. The large decks have a Jacuzzi, from which you can look out to magical sunsets. Polished timber floors, cedar shutters, handcrafted maple furniture, a minibar, and a stereo add the final touches.

At mealtime, the maitre d' assigns you to a table in the dining room, so you get to meet other guests. If you do not buy a meal package, buffet breakfasts and lunches cost A$26 (US$21) each, and a three-course dinner is A$48 (US$38). Before dinner, head to the hexagonal timber bar, perched up high for great sunset views, for half-price cocktails (5–6:30pm). Among other facilities are a cafe and gift shop, a basketball court, and free tea, coffee, and cookies all day.

Via Canungra, Lamington National Park Rd., Lamington National Park, QLD 4275. ℂ **1800/688 722** in Australia, or 07/5502 4911. www.oreillys.com.au. 72 units. A$200–A$325 (US$160–US$260) double; A$480 (US$384) canopy suite; A$750 (US$600) 2-bedroom suite. Free crib. Rates include all meals and activities. Children under 18 stay free with existing bedding. 2-night minimum weekends, 3-night minimum long weekends, 4-night minimum New Year's, Easter, Christmas. Ask about 2-night and longer packages. Meal plan A$84 (US$67) adults, A$42 (US$34) children 11–15, A$26 (US$21) children 4–10 for 3 meals per day; 2-meal packages available. AE, DC, MC, V. **Amenities:** Restaurant; bar; heated outdoor plunge pool; lit tennis court; Jacuzzi; sauna; kids' club (age 6 and up) on weekends and school vacations; game room; massage; babysitting; coin-op laundry. In room: Fridge, coffeemaker.

8

The Red Centre

by Marc Llewellyn

The Red Centre is the landscape many of us conjure up when we think of the Outback—vast horizons, red sand as far as the eye can see, mysterious monoliths, cloudless blue sky, harsh sunlight, and the rhythmic twang of the didgeridoo. It's home to sprawling cattle ranches, ancient mountain ranges, "living fossil" palm trees that survived the Ice Age, cockatoos and kangaroos, red gorges, pretty water holes, and Ayers Rock, now officially called by its Aboriginal name, Uluru.

Aboriginal people have lived here for thousands of years, since long before the Pyramids were a twinkle in a pharaoh's eye, but the Centre is still largely unexplored by non-Aboriginal Australians. One highway cuts from Adelaide in the south to Darwin in the north, and a few roads and four-wheel-drive tracks make a lonely spider web across it; in many areas, non-Aborigines have never set foot.

Alice Springs is the only big town in central Australia. So let's get one thing straight—Alice Springs and Uluru are *not* side by side. Uluru is 462km (286 miles) away. You can see it in a day from Alice Springs, but it's an effort.

The Red Centre is more than just the Rock. Give yourself a few days to experience all there is—visiting the impressive Olgas (or Kata Tjuta, its Aboriginal name) near Uluru (Ayers Rock), walking the rim of Kings Canyon, riding a camel down a dry riverbed, poking around Aboriginal rock carvings, swimming in water holes, or staying at an Outback homestead. Alice Springs gives you a better flavor for the Outback than Uluru. If you base yourself there, it's easy to radiate out to less crowded but still beautiful attractions like Palm Valley, Ormiston Gorge, and Trephina Gorge Nature Park, each an easy day trip. Too many visitors jet in, snap a photo of the Rock, and head home, only to miss the essence of the desert.

1 Exploring the Red Centre

VISITOR INFORMATION The **Central Australian Tourism Industry Association** (see "Visitor Information" under "Alice Springs," below) can send you a brochure pack. It is your best one-stop source of information.

Most of the Red Centre lies within the Northern Territory. The **Northern Territory Tourist Commission,** Tourism House, 43 Mitchell St., Darwin, NT 0800 (© **13 61 10** in Australia, or 08/8999 3900; www.ntholidays.com), maintains a site for adventurous independent travelers at **www.ozoutback.com.au.** The commission publishes a helpful annual guide to central Australia that details hotels, tour operators, car-rental companies, and attractions, and operates a division that offers package deals on complete trips.

WHEN TO GO April, May, September, and October have sunny days (coolish in May, hot in Oct). Winter (June–Aug) means mild temperatures with cold nights. Summer (Nov–Mar) is ferociously hot and best avoided. In summer, limit exertions to early morning and late afternoon, and choose air-conditioned accommodations. Rain is rare but can come at any time of year.

DRIVING TIPS The **Automobile Association of the Northern Territory,** 79–81 Smith St., Darwin, NT 0800 (ℂ **08/8981 3837**), offers emergency breakdown service to members of affiliated overseas automobile associations and dispenses maps and advice. It has no office in the Red Centre. For a recorded report of **road conditions,** call ℂ **1800/246 199** in Australia.

Only a handful of highways and arterial roads in the Northern Territory are sealed (paved) roads. A conventional two-wheel-drive car will get you to 95% of what you want to see, but consider renting a four-wheel-drive for complete freedom. All the big car-rental chains have them. Some attractions are on unpaved roads good enough for a two-wheel-drive car, but your car-rental company will not insure a two-wheel-drive for driving on them.

Outside settled areas, the territory has no speed limit, but before you hit the gas, consider the risk of hitting the wildlife: camels, kangaroos, and other protected native species. Locals stick to a comfortable 120kmph (75 mph) or less. Avoid driving at night, early morning, and late afternoon, when 'roos feed; beware of cattle lying down on the warm bitumen at night. A white road sign bearing a black circle outline crossed by a diagonal black line indicates the point when speed restrictions no longer apply. Make sure you have a full tank of gas before setting out.

Road trains (trucks hauling more than one container) and fatigue caused by driving long distances are two other major threats. For details on safe driving, review the tips in the "By Car" section of "Getting Around Australia" in chapter 2.

If you plan to "go bush" in remote regions not covered by this guide, you may need a permit from the relevant Aboriginal lands council to cross Aboriginal land. This can be a drawn-out bureaucratic affair that takes weeks, so plan ahead. The Northern Territory Tourist Commission (see "Visitor Information," above) can put you in touch with the appropriate council. All good road maps mark Aboriginal lands clearly.

OTHER TRAVEL TIPS **Always carry drinking water.** When hiking, carry 4 liters (about a gal.) per person per day in winter, and a liter (¼ gal.) per person per hour in summer. Wear a broad-brimmed hat, high-factor sunscreen, and insect repellent.

Bring warm clothing for chilly evenings in winter.

TOUR OPERATORS Numerous coach, minicoach, and four-wheel-drive tour operators run tours that take in Alice Springs, Kings Canyon, and Uluru. They depart from Alice Springs or Uluru, offering accommodations ranging from spiffy resorts, comfortable motels, and basic cabins to shared bunkhouses, tents, or swags (sleeping

---

⟮*Tips* **Buzz Off!**

Uluru is notorious for plagues of flies in summer. Don't be embarrassed to cover your head with the fly nets sold in souvenir stores—you'll look like the Dreamtime Beekeeper from Outer Space, but there will be "no flies on you, mate," an Aussie way of saying you are doing the right thing.

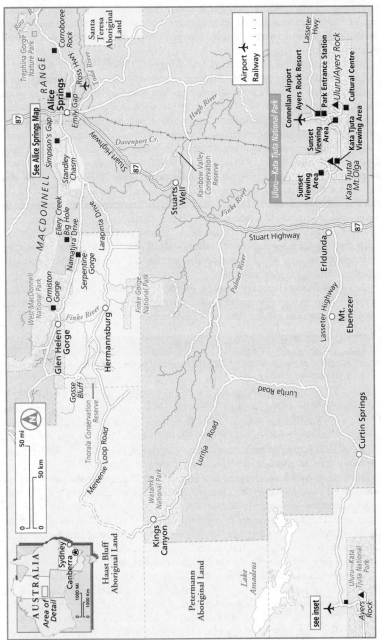

The Red Centre

Airport ✈
Railway ▭

See Alice Springs Map

Ras
Trephina Gorge Nature Park
Corroboree Rock
Ross River
Santa Teresa Aboriginal Land
RANGE
Ross HWY.
Todd River
Alice Springs
Emily Gap
Simpson's Gap
87
Standley Chasm
MACDONNELL
Ellery Creek Big Hole
Namatjira Drive
Serpentine Gorge
Larapinta Drive
Davenport Cr.
Hugh River
Stuart Highway
Rainbow Valley Conservation Reserve
Finke River
Stuarts Well
West MacDonnell National Park
Ormiston Gorge
Glen Helen Gorge
Finke River
Hermannsburg
Finke Gorge National Park
Palmer River
Stuart Highway
Erldunda
87
Lasseter Highway
Mt. Ebenezer
Gosse Bluff
Tnorala Conservation Reserve
Mereenie Loop Road
Luritja Road
Luritja Road
Curtin Springs
Haast Bluff Aboriginal Land
Watarrka National Park
Kings Canyon
Petermann Aboriginal Land
Lake Amadeus
Uluru–Kata Tjuta National Park
see inset
Ayers Rock

Uluru–Kata Tjuta National Park

Lasseter Hwy.
Connellan Airport
Ayers Rock Resort
Park Entrance Station
Uluru/Ayers Rock
Cultural Centre
Sunset Viewing Area
Kata Tjuta Viewing Area
Sunset Viewing Area
Kata Tjuta/ Mt. Olga

50 mi
50 km
0

AUSTRALIA
Area of Detail
Sydney
Canberra
1000 Mi
1000 Km
0

bags) under the stars. Most pack the highlights into a 2- or 3-day trip, though leisurely trips of 6 days or more are available. Many offer one-way itineraries between Alice and the Rock (via Kings Canyon if you like), or vice versa, which will allow you to avoid backtracking.

Among the reputable companies are **AAT Kings** (© **1800/334 009** in Australia, or 03/9274 7422 for the Melbourne central reservations office; www.aatkings.com), which specializes in coach tours but also has four-wheel-drive camping itineraries; **Alice Springs Holidays** (© **08/8953 1411;** www.alicespringsholidays.com.au), which does upscale soft-adventure tours for groups; **Sahara Outback Tours** (© **08/ 8953 0881;** www.saharatours.com.au), which conducts camping safaris in small groups for all ages; and **Discovery Ecotours,** formerly Uluru Experience and Alice Experience (© **1800/803 174** in Australia, or 08/8956 2563; www.ecotours.com.au), which specializes in ecotours for groups. **Tailormade Tours** (© **08/8952 1731**) and **VIP Travel Australia** (© **1800/806 412** in Australia, or 08/8956 2388; www.vip australia.com.au) customize luxury tours in limos, minicoaches, and four-wheel-drives, and offer treats like desert barbecues and champagne tailgate dinners overlooking the Rock or the Olgas. You can book Sahara Outback Tours and Tailormade Tours through **Alice Springs Tour Professionals** (© **08/8953 0666;** www.alicetour professionals.com.au), a one-stop shop that represents a number of Alice Springs–based tour and sightseeing companies.

Aboriginal Desert Discovery Tours (© **08/8952 3408;** www.aboriginalart.com.au), owned by Alice Springs Aboriginal people, teams up its Aboriginal guides with Alice-based tour companies to offer tours with an Aboriginal slant.

2 Alice Springs

462km (286 miles) NE of Uluru (Ayers Rock); 1,491km (924 miles) S of Darwin; 1,544km (957 miles) N of Adelaide; 2,954km (1,831 miles) NW of Sydney

"The Alice," as Australians fondly dub it, is the unofficial capital of Outback Australia. In the early 1870s, a handful of telegraph-station workers struggled nearly 1,600km (992 miles) north from Adelaide through the desert to settle by a small spring in what must have seemed like the ends of the earth. Alice Springs, as the place was called, was just a few huts around a repeater station on the ambitious telegraph line that was to link Adelaide with Darwin and the rest of the world.

Today Alice, as it's also known, is a city of 27,000 people, with supermarkets, banks, and the odd nightclub. It's a friendly, rambling, unsophisticated place. No matter what direction you come from, you will soar for hours over a vast, flat landscape to get here. That's why folks are so surprised when they reach Alice Springs and see low but dramatic mountain ranges, rippling red in the sunshine. Many people excitedly mistake them for Uluru, but that baby is about 462km (286 miles) down the road. The craggy hills close by are the **MacDonnell Ranges.**

Many tourists visit Alice only to get to Uluru, but Alice has charms all its own, albeit mostly of a small-town kind. The red folds of the MacDonnell Ranges hide lovely gorges with shady picnic grounds. A planned 250km (155-mile) hiking trail is partly ready for your boots now. The area has an old gold-rush town to poke around in, quirky little museums, wildlife parks, a couple of cattle stations (ranches) that welcome visitors, a couple of nice day trips, and one of the world's top 10 desert golf courses. You could easily fill 2 or 3 days.

Alice Springs

ACCOMMODATIONS ■
Alice on Todd **4**
Alice Springs Resort **4**
Aurora Alice Springs **11**
Best Western Elkira
    Motel **17**
Desert Palms Resort **7**
Rydges Plaza Resort
    Alice Springs **8**

DINING ◆
Bar Doppio **12**
Bojangles Saloon and
    Restaurant **13**
Casa Nostra **3**
Malathi's Restaurant
    & Sean's Irish Bar **16**
Overlanders
    Steakhouse **15**

Palms Restaurant **4**
Red Ochre Grill **11**

ATTRACTIONS ●
Aboriginal Art
    & Culture Centre **14**
Alice Springs Cultural
    Precinct **5**
Alice Springs Desert
    Park **6**
Alice Springs Reptile
    Centre **18**
Alice Springs Telegraph
    Station Historical
    Reserve **2**
National Pioneer Women's
    Hall of Fame **10**
Royal Flying Doctor
    Service **10**
School of the Air **1**

Northern
Territory

0   250 Mi
0   250 Km

Alice Springs
○

see inset below

Railway
Station

Ross
Park

Billy
Goat
Hill

Olive Pink
Flora Reserve

Power Station

The Fairway

Newland
Park

Traeger
Park

**Alice Springs
Golf Club**

DOWNTOWN AREA

Larapinta
Park

Todd River (normally dry)

To Airport

0   1/4 mi
0   1/4 km

**Lasseter's
Casino**

Information ⓘ
Post Office ✉
Cemetery

Panorama Guth

**Bus
Station**

Billy
Goat
Hill

This is the heart of the Aboriginal Arrernte people's country, and Alice is a rich source of tours, shops, and galleries for those interested in Aboriginal culture, art, or souvenirs. There is a sad side to this story. Not every Aborigine succeeds in splicing his or her ancient civilization with the 21st century, and the result is dislocated communities living in the riverbed with only alcohol for company.

ESSENTIALS

GETTING THERE **By Plane** Qantas (© 13 13 13 in Australia) flies direct from Sydney, Adelaide, Darwin, Cairns, Broome, and Uluru (Ayers Rock). Flights from most other cities connect via Sydney or Adelaide. **Virgin Blue** (© 13 67 80 in Australia; www.virginblue.com.au) flies to Alice Springs direct from Sydney, with connections from Adelaide, Brisbane, the Gold Coast, and Melbourne. The company offers heavily discounted prices if you book online well in advance. Prices start at around A$199 (US$145) one-way. **Airnorth** (© 1800/627 474 in Australia, or 08/8945 2866) does a "Centre Run" from Darwin via Katherine and Tennant Creek Monday through Saturday.

The **Alice Springs Airport Shuttle** (© 1800/621 188 in the Northern Territory, or 08/8953 0310) meets all major flights, but not always those from small towns like Tennant Creek. It transfers you to your Alice hotel door for A$10 (US$8) one-way or A$18 (US$14) round-trip. A taxi from the airport to town, a distance of 15km (9⅓ miles), is around A$25 (US$20).

By Train The *Ghan* train, named after Afghan camel-train drivers who carried supplies in the Red Centre during the 19th century, makes the trip from Adelaide to Alice every week, continuing to Darwin. The twice-weekly Adelaide-Alice service (leaving Adelaide on Wed and Fri) takes roughly 24 hours. The route is often treeless and empty, if fascinatingly so; don't be concerned that you'll miss it by overnighting on the train. The train has sleeper berths. For fares and schedules, contact **Great Southern Railway** (© 13 21 47 in Australia, or 08/8213 4592; www.gsr.com.au) or see "Getting Around Australia," in chapter 2, for its booking agencies abroad.

By Bus **Greyhound** (13 14 99 in Australia, or 07/4690 9950; www.greyhound. com.au) runs from Adelaide and Darwin. It's a 21-hour trip from Adelaide, and the fare is around A$180 (US$144). The 21-hour trip from Darwin costs about A$195 (US$156). The 36-hour trip from Cairns costs A$360 (US$288). A daily 5¾-hour run connects with Uluru (Ayers Rock); the fare is around A$75 (US$60).

By Car Alice Springs is on the Stuart Highway linking Adelaide and Darwin. Allow a very long 2 days or a more comfortable 3 days to drive from Adelaide, the same from Darwin. From Sydney, connect to the Stuart Highway via Broken Hill and Port Augusta north of Adelaide; from Cairns, head south to Townsville, then west via the town of Mount Isa to join the Stuart Highway at Tennant Creek. Both routes are long and dull. From Perth it is an even longer, duller drive across the Nullarbor Plain to connect with the Stuart Highway at Port Augusta. If you fancy a driving holiday of the area, with rental car and accommodations included, then check out www.ntholidays.com. An example is a 6-day trip from Alice to Uluru/Ayers Rock, The Olgas, Kings Canyon and then back to Alice Springs for A$952 (US$761).

VISITOR INFORMATION The **Central Australian Tourism Industry Association (CATIA) Visitor Information Centre,** 60 Gregory Terrace, Alice Springs, NT 0870 (© **08/8952 5800;** www.centralaustraliantourism.com), is the official one-stop shop for bookings and touring information for the Red Centre, including Alice Springs, Kings Canyon, and Uluru–Kata Tjuta National Park (Ayers Rock). It also acts as the visitor center for the Parks & Wildlife Commission of the Northern Territory. It's open Monday through Friday from 8:30am to 5:30pm and weekends and public holidays from 9am to 4pm. It also has a desk at the airport.

SPECIAL EVENTS   The town hosts a couple of bizarre events. The **Camel Cup** camel race takes place on the second Saturday in July. In late September, folks from hundreds of miles around

---

Tips   Safety in the Centre

Alice is a safe place, but steer clear of dark streets and the riverbed at night, when some teenagers can make a nuisance of themselves.

---

come out to cheer the **Henley-on-Todd Regatta** ⭐, during which gaudily decorated, homemade bottomless "boats" race down the dry Todd River bed. Well, what else do you do on a river that flows only 3 days a year? See "Australia Calendar of Events" in chapter 2 for more details on this event.

GETTING AROUND   Virtually all tours pick you up at your hotel.

If your itinerary traverses unpaved roads, as it may in outlying areas, you will need to rent a four-wheel-drive vehicle, because regular cars will not be insured on an unpaved surface. However, a regular car will get you to most attractions. **Avis** (© 08/8953 5533), **Budget** (© 08/8952 8899), **EuropCar** (© 08/8955 5994), **Hertz** (© 08/8952 2644), local company **Outback Auto Rentals** (© 1800/652 133 in Australia, or 08/8953 5333), and **Thrifty** (© 08/8952 9999) all rent conventional and four-wheel-drive vehicles. You may get a better deal on car rental by going through the **Outback Travel Shop** (© 08/8955 5288; www.outbacktravelshop.com.au) in Alice Springs, a booking agent that negotiates bulk rates with most Alice car-rental companies.

Hertz, Thrifty, and Outback Auto Rentals rent **camping kits** holding everything you need, including a tent, sleeping bags, and a gas stove. A kit usually costs aroundA$385 (US$308) for two people for five days. Book them in advance. carrying camping gear, as well as your luggage, probably means you have to hire a larger car too!

Many rental outfits for motor homes (camper vans) have Alice offices. They include **Britz Campervan Rentals** (© 08/8952 8814), **Hertz Campervans** (© 08/8953 5333), **Kea Camper (Australia)** (© 1800/252 555), and **Maui Rentals** (© 08/8952 8049). As an example of price, another outfitter, **Apollo Campers** (© 1800/777 779 in Australia; www.apollocamper.com), rents two- to three-berth vans for around A$100 (US$80) a day, with pickup and drop-off at several major centers. A four-wheel-drive version costs A$165 to A$220 (US$132–US$175) a day. This can work out to be significantly cheaper than staying in hotels and going on tours.

The best way to get around town without your own transport is aboard the **Alice Wanderer** bus (see "Organized Tours," below). Taxi fares are exorbitant, presumably because there's only one main outfit in town, **Alice Springs Taxis** (© **13 10 08**).

CITY LAYOUT   **Todd Mall** is the heart of town. Most shops, businesses, and restaurants are here or within a few blocks' walk. Most hotels, the casino, the golf course, and many of the town's attractions are a few kilometers outside of town. The dry Todd River "flows" through the city east of Todd Mall.

SEEING THE SIGHTS IN ALICE

Aboriginal Art & Culture Centre   Set up by the Southern Arrernte Aboriginal people, this center houses a small, intriguing museum with exhibits on Aboriginal life. It displays a timeline of the Aboriginal view of history since "contact" (the arrival of Europeans). It's worth a visit if you're interested in indigenous cultures. It sells artifacts and art. Allow 15 to 60 minutes.

86 Todd St. ⓒ 08/8952 3408. Free admission. Daily 8am–5pm.

Alice Springs Cultural Precinct   At least one or two of the attractions here will probably pique your interest. All of them are within walking distance of each other. The **Museum of Central Australia** mostly shows local fossils, natural history displays, and meteorites. Some impressive Aboriginal and contemporary Aussie art is on display at the **Araluen Centre** (box office ⓒ 08/8951 1122), the town's performing arts hub; check out the "Honey Ant Dreaming" stained-glass window in its foyer. Aviation nuts may want to browse the old radios, aircraft, and wreckage in the **Aviation Museum,** which preserves the territory's aerial history. You can buy stylish crafts, and sometimes catch artists at work, in the **Territory Craft** gallery. You may want to amble among the outdoor sculptures, including the 15m (49-ft.) *Yeperenye Dreamtime Caterpillar,* or among the gravestones in the cemetery, where "Afghani" camel herders (from what is now Pakistan) are buried facing Mecca. To reach the precinct, take a cab, Alice Wanderer bus, or Desert Park Transfers (see "Organized Tours," below). There is a picnic area, but save your meal for the Alice Springs Telegraph Station Historical Reserve (below).

Larapinta Dr. at Memorial Ave., 2km (1¼ miles) south of town. ⓒ 08/8951 1120. Admission (includes Museum of Central Australia, Araluen Centre, Central Australian Aviation Museum, Territory Craft, and Memorial Cemetery) A$8 (US$6.40) adults; A$5 (US$4) seniors, students, and children 5–16; A$20 (US$16) families. Daily 10am–5pm. Closed Good Friday and Dec 25.

Alice Springs Desert Park ★   By means of an easy 1.6km (1-mile) trail through three reconstructed natural habitats, this impressive wildlife and flora park shows you 120 or so of the animal species that live in the desert around Alice but that you won't spot too easily in the wild (including kangaroos you can walk among). Most of the creatures are small mammals (like the big-eared bilby), reptiles (cute thorny devil lizards), and birds. Don't miss the excellent **Birds of Prey** ★★ show. There's a cafe here, too. The **Alice Wanderer** bus (ⓒ 1800/722 111 in Australia, or 08/8952 2111; www.alicewanderer.com.au) includes a visit to the park with its town tour (see Alice Wanderer below). The 2-day pass costs A$68 (US$54) for adults and A$54 (US$43) for children, and includes park entry fee. Allow 2 to 3 hours.

Larapinta Dr., 6km (3¾ miles) west of town. ⓒ 08/8951 8788. Admission A$18 (US$14) adults, A$9 (US$5.85) students and children 5–16, A$40 (US$26) families. Daily 7:30am–6pm (last suggested entry 4pm; 'roo and emu exhibit closes 4:30pm). Closed Dec 25.

Alice Springs Reptile Centre *Kids*   Kids can walk around with pythons or bearded dragons (lizards) on their shoulders, all day if they want, at this Aussie reptile park. The easygoing proprietor lifts up the cages' glass fronts for better photos, and lets kids hand-feed bugs to the animals at feeding time. Some 30 species are on display, including the world's deadliest snake—Australia's inland taipan—and big goannas. Allow an hour.

9 Stuart Terrace (opposite the Royal Flying Doctor Service). ⓒ 08/8952 8900. Admission A$7 (US$5.60) adults, A$4 (US$3.20) children under 17, A$20 (US$16) families. Daily 9am–5pm. Closed Jan 1 and Dec 25.

Alice Springs Telegraph Station Historical Reserve ⭐ (Finds) Alice Springs began life in 1871 as this charming telegraph repeater station, set by a pretty water hole amid red bouldery hills, sprawling gums full of parrots, and mercifully green lawns. An oasis in the harsh Alice landscape, it's a place tourists often overlook. Arm yourself with the free map or join a free 45-minute tour. You can wander around the old stationmaster's residence; the telegraph office, with its Morse code machine tap-tapping away; the shoeing yard packed with blacksmith's equipment; and the stables, housing vintage buggies and saddlery. From the on-site computer, you can "telegraph" e-mails to your friends. May through October, "kitchen maids" in period dress serve scones (biscuits) and damper (campfire bread) from the original wood-fired ovens. The park has pet camels, and sometimes orphaned kangaroo joeys. Allow a good hour, more to walk one of the several hiking trails leading from the extensive grounds. This is a lovely picnic spot. There is a gift shop and coffee and snacks for sale, too. To get there, take a cab or Alice Wanderer bus (see "Organized Tours," below) or the 4km (2.5-mile) riverside pedestrian/bike track that starts near the corner of Wills Terrace and Undoolya Road.

Stuart Hwy., 4km (2½ miles) north of town (beyond the School of the Air turnoff). ℂ 08/8952 3993. Free admission to picnic grounds and trails; station A$6.50 (US$5.20) adults, A$3.50 (US$2.80) children 5–15. Daily 8am–5pm (picnic grounds and trails until 9pm). Station closed Dec 25.

Royal Flying Doctor Service Alice is a major base for this airborne medical serv-ice that treats people living and traveling in the vast Outback. An interesting 20-minute tour runs every half-hour, featuring a video and a talk in the communications room; allow another 30 minutes or so to browse the small museum. Some of the recorded conversations between doctors and patients are intriguing. There is a nice garden cafe and a gift shop.

8–10 Stuart Terrace (at end of Hartley St.). ℂ 08/8952 1129. www.flyingdoctor.net. Admission A$6 (US$4.80) adults, A$2.50 (US$2) children 6–15. Mon–Sat 9am–5pm (last tour 4pm); Sun and public holidays 1–5pm. Closed Jan 1 and Dec 25.

School of the Air Sitting in on school lessons may not be your idea of a vacation, but this school is different—it broadcasts by radio to a 1.3-million-sq.-km (507,000-sq.-mile) "schoolroom" of 140 children on Outback stations. That's as big as Ger-many, Great Britain, Ireland, New Zealand, and Japan combined—or twice the size of Texas. Visitors watch and listen in when classes are in session; outside class hours, you may hear taped classes. You can browse the kids' artwork, photos, video, and many other displays in the well-organized visitor gallery. Free 30-minute tours run throughout the day.

80 Head St. (2.5km/1½ miles from town). ℂ 08/8951 6834. Admission A$3.50 (US$2.80) adults, A$2.50 (US$2) chil-dren 5–16, A$12 (US$9.60) families. Mon–Sat and public holidays 8:30am–4:30pm; Sun 1:30–4:30pm. Closed Jan 1 and Dec 25–26. Bus: 3 or Alice Wanderer (see "Organized Tours," below).

ORGANIZED TOURS

AROUND TOWN & OUT IN THE DESERT The **Alice Wanderer** bus (ℂ **1800/722 111** in Australia, or 08/8952 2111; www.alicewanderer.com.au) does a running loop of town attractions every 70 minutes starting at 9am, with the last departure at 4pm. Hop on and off as you please, and enjoy the commentary from the driver. The bus departs daily from the south end of Todd Mall. Tickets are sold on board and cost A$38 (US$30) for adults, and A$30 (US$24) for kids 4 to 14. Call for free pickup from your hotel. The company also runs full-day tours to outlying areas, including to the West McDonnel Ranges (daily apart from Tues), costing A$110 (US$88) for adults and A$88 (US$70) for kids; to Bond Springs Cattle Station, Monday to Friday, costing A$105 (US$84) for adults and A$88 (US$70) for kids; and to Santa Teresa Aboriginal Community, on Mondays, Wednesdays, and Thursdays. Here you can meet local Aborigines, and view and purchase their artwork. This tour costs A$130 (US$104) for adults and A$104 (US$83) for kids.

The bus calls at most of the attractions above, plus the **Old Ghan Museum & Road Transport Hall of Fame,** housing the original Ghan train that plied the Adelaide–Alice Springs line from 1929 to 1980; and **Panorama Guth,** an art gallery housing a 360-degree painting of central Australian landscapes by artist Henk Guth.

The company also runs other tours around the area, including a trip out to the rocky West MacDonnell Ranges. It's well worth checking out the Alice Wanderer website to help you plan your time before you visit.

Many Alice-based companies offer minicoach or four-wheel-drive day trips and extended tours of Alice and of outlying areas including the East and West Macs, Hermannsburg, and Finke Gorge National Park. Among the well-regarded ones are: **Discovery Ecotours** (*C* **08/8956 2563;** www.ecotours.com.au); **Alice Springs Holidays** (*C* **1800/801 401** in Australia, or 08/8953 1411; www.alicespringsholidays.com.au); and **Alice Springs Tour Professionals** (*C* **1800/673 391** in Australia, or 08/8953 0666; www.alicetourprofessionals.com.au), which books a number of reliable tour operators and adventure outfitters. See "Exploring the Red Centre," earlier in this chapter, for more information.

Several companies run tours by motorcycle or four-wheel-drive ATV (all-terrain vehicle). One option is **Central Oz Tours** (*C* **08/8953 4755;** http://centraloz.biz).

ABORIGINAL TOURS I recommend a visit to the **Aboriginal Art & Culture Centre** (6 Todd St., Alice Springs; www.aboriginalart.com.au). The **half-day tour** *✿* features an explanation of the Dreamtime creation era; a gentle bush tucker walk; a chance to throw a boomerang and spear; talks about tools and weapons over billy tea and damper; and a dance performance at which you can have a go yourself, and have your photo taken with the dancers. You may have seen the dancers performing in the opening ceremony of the Sydney 2000 Olympic Games. Threaded through all this is an ongoing discussion of Aboriginal culture, beliefs, family relationships, and a view of history both ancient and modern through Aboriginal eyes. You have a chance to buy art. The experience wraps up with a didgeridoo lesson at 1pm. The tour departs daily at 8am and costs A$83 (US$66) for adults and A$44 (US$35) for children under

---

Moments Billy Tea & Damper

Any tour in the Outback isn't complete without the traditional bushman's meal of billy tea and damper. Billy tea is made from tea leaves, and sometimes eucalyptus leaves, put into water (traditionally from a water hole or river) and boiled in an open-topped canister on an open fire. You don't have to stir it; the trick is to pick up the canister by the wire handle and swing the whole thing around, sometimes over your head—centrifugal force keeps the liquid in (don't try this at home, though). Damper is simply flour, water, and salt mixed into dough and thrown in the ashes of the fire to cook into bread. Yummy.

12, including hotel pickup. The center also organizes an Aboriginal Cultural Performance, with lots of dancing, atmosphere, and twinkling stars. Dinner includes kangaroo and barramundi fish. The performance, with dinner and wine, costs A$79 (US$63) for adults and A$30 (US$24) for kids.

An interesting activity at the center is learning to play the didgeridoo at the "Didgeridoo University." A 1-hour session costs A$12 (US$9.20) for adults and A$5.50 (US$4.40) for kids.

CAMEL SAFARIS   You might not associate camels with Australia, but the camel's ability to get by without water was key to opening the arid inland parts of the country to European settlement in the 1800s. With the advent of cars, they were released into the wild, and today more than 200,000 roam central Australia. Australia even exports them to the Middle East! **Frontier Camel Tours** (© **1800/806 499** in Australia, or 08/8953 0444; www.cameltours.com.au) runs short camel rides daily costing A$10 (US$8) for adults and A$6 (US$4.80) for kids. A 1-hour sunset tour with dinner at the company's camel farm, where you can browse its camel museum and shop, costs A$105 (US$84) for adults and A$75 (US$60) for kids 5 to 12, including hotel transfers. It departs daily at 4pm April through October, and at 5pm November through March, and gets back around 5½ hours later. Kids under 6 can join the ride if the cameleer on duty agrees. A breakfast ride, leaving at 6:30am and returning at 9:30am, costs A$80 (US$64) for adults and A$45 (US$36) for children. The company also runs camel tours near Uluru (Ayers Rock).

HOT-AIR BALLOON FLIGHTS   Dawn balloon flights above the desert are popular in central Australia. You have to get up 90 minutes before dawn, though. Several companies offer flights. **Outback Ballooning** (© **1800/809 790** in Australia, or 08/8952 8723; www.outbackballooning.com.au) is one of the most upscale. A 1-hour flight followed by champagne breakfast in the bush costs A$300 (US$240), with a 20% discount for kids under 17. A 30-minute breakfast flight costs A$200 (US$160). Kids under 6 are discouraged from participating because they cannot see over the basket. Don't make any other morning plans—you probably won't get back to your hotel until close to noon.

ACTIVE PURSUITS

BIKING   A gently undulating 17km (11-mile) **bike trail** weaves from John Flynn's Grave on Larapinta Drive, 7km (4⅓ miles) west of town, through the bushland and desert foothills of the MacDonnell Ranges to Simpson's Gap (p. 395). **Centre Cycles,** Lindsay Avenue at Undoolya Road (© **08/8953 2966**), rents bikes for around A$10 (US$8) for 4 hours (plus a A$50/US$40 refundable deposit). *Note:* Carry water, because the two taps en route are a long way apart. Bike in cooler months only.

BUSHWALKING   The 250km (155-mile) **Larapinta Trail** winds west from Alice through the sparse red ranges, picturesque semidesert scenery, and rich bird life of the West MacDonnell National Park (p. 395). Sections range from easy to hard. The shortest is 8km (5 miles), ranging up to several 23-to-29km (14–18-mile) stretches. The **Parks & Wildlife Commission of the Northern Territory** office in Alice Springs (© **08/8951 8211**) and the **CATIA Visitor Information Centre** (see "Visitor Information," earlier in this chapter) dispense trail maps and information. Camp facilities are simple at best on popular routes, nonexistent on less-traveled sections. *Warning:* Always carry drinking water. The trail may close in extremely hot summer periods.

Alice Wanderer Centre Sightseeing Tours (© **1800/66 9111** in Australia, or 08/8952 2111) runs to road access points along the trail, where you can mostly pick up a choice of 1-, 2-, or 3-day hikes. Several outfitters run guided, supported hikes along trail sections.

GOLF The **Alice Springs Golf Club** ⚐, 1km (just over ½ mile) from town on Cromwell Drive (© **08/8952 5440**), boasts a Thomson-Wolveridge course rated among the world's top desert courses by touring pros. The course is open from sunup to sundown. Nine holes cost A$20 (US$16); 18 holes, A$30 (US$24). Club rental costs A$25 (US$20), and a cart, which many locals don't bother with, goes for A$30 (US$24). It's best to book a tee time.

SHOPPING AT THE SOURCE FOR ABORIGINAL ART

Alice Springs is the best place in Australia to buy **Aboriginal art and crafts** ⚐. You will find no shortage of stuff: linen and canvas paintings, didgeridoos, spears, clapping sticks, *coolamons* (a dish used by women to carry anything from water to babies), animal carvings, baskets, and jewelry, as well as books, CDs, and all kinds of non-Aboriginal merchandise printed with Aboriginal designs. Prices can soar into the thousands for large canvases by world-renowned painters, but you will find plenty of small works for under A$250 (US$200). Major artworks sell unmounted for ease of shipment, which most galleries arrange. Store hours can vary with the seasons and the crowds, so it pays to check ahead.

See artists at work when you drop by **Jukurrpa Artists,** Stott Terrace between Gap Road and Leichhardt Terrace (© **08/8953 1052**). This Aboriginal women's cooperative studio and gallery sells the "pattern and dot" paintings of the Western Desert style, plus crafts such as carvings and jewelry, weapons, and tools.

Aboriginal-owned **Warumpi Arts,** 105 Gregory Terrace (© **08/8952 9066**), sells wooden artifacts, seed necklaces, and canvas and linen paintings in the earth-hued designs of the Papunya people, who live 250km (155 miles) west of Alice. Another Aboriginal-owned gallery, **Papunya Tula Artists,** 78 Todd St. (© **08/8952 4731**), sells paintings on canvas and linen from Papunya and other artists living in the desert as far as 700km (434 miles) west of Alice Springs.

Several stores on Todd Mall sell affordable Aboriginal art and souvenirs. The biggest, the **Original Dreamtime Gallery,** 63 Todd Mall (© **08/8952 8861**), stocks a huge selection, and packs, mails (anywhere in the world), and insures your purchases free of charge. It also shows visiting exhibitions of Aboriginal art.

Arunta Art Gallery & Bookshop, 70 Todd St. (© **08/8952 1544**), stocks a great range of books on Aboriginal art, language, and archaeology, as well as Australian history, geology, wildlife, and biographies.

If you're interested in investing in serious artwork, speak to Roslyn Premont, proprietor of **Gallery Gondwana,** 43 Todd Mall (© **08/8953 1577**). She has written a book on desert art, and her gallery sells only top-notch works.

A big range of art, didgeridoos, artifacts, music, and books is on sale at the **Aboriginal Art & Culture Centre,** 86 Todd St. (© **08/8952 3408**).

Today's Aboriginal bands mix ancient and hip new rhythms to create some wonderful sounds. For the country's biggest range of indigenous music, head to the **CAAMA (Central Australian Aboriginal Media Association)** ⚐ store at 101 Todd St. (© **08/8952 9207**). It also stocks books on Aboriginal art and issues; videos in PAL and NTSC format (on everything from how to fix your broken-down Ford the bushman's way, to Aboriginal people's memories of their first contact with "white man"); children's books with Aboriginal story lines; a line of Aboriginal-print fabrics, clothes, diaries, stationery, and greeting cards; Aboriginal artifacts and jewelry; and cute Yamba the Honey Ant dolls, modeled after a kids' character on the local Aboriginal television station, Imparja.

WHERE TO STAY

Alice's hotel stock is not grand. Many properties have dated rooms and modest facilities; they're no match for the gleaming standard of **Ayers Rock Resort** (described later in this chapter). You may pay lower rates than those listed in the summer off season (Dec–Mar), and even as late as June. Peak season typically runs from July through October or November. Besides the more upmarket properties below, there are several backpacker resorts offering dorm rooms and doubles. One of the best is **Annie's Place,** 4 Traegar Ave., Alice Springs, NT 0870 (© **1800/359 089** in Australia, or 08/8952 1545; www.anniesplace.com.au). Doubles cost between A$50 (US$28) for a room with shared bathroom and A$60 (US$48) for one with your own.

EXPENSIVE

Alice Springs Resort ✦ This friendly, well-run, low-rise property is a 3-minute walk from town over the Todd River. Ask for one of the standard rooms renovated in 2002 (the unrenovated ones are airy and comfortable, but those bright green carpets and dated peach floral curtains are hard on the eye!), or go for the big deluxe rooms built in 1999. In summer, it's nice to repair to the pool under a couple of desert palms after a hot day's sightseeing. A fire glows in the **Gumtree Lounge** bar on winter evenings.

34 Stott Terrace, Alice Springs, NT 0870. © **800/225-9849** in U.S., © 1300/134 044 in Australia, or 08/8951 4545. Fax 08/8953 0995. www.alicespringsresort.com.au. 144 units (108 with shower only). A$200–A$234 (US$160–US$187) double. Extra person A$25 (US$20). Children under 12 stay free in parent's room with existing bedding. Ask about packages with Ayers Rock Resort and Kings Canyon Resort. AE, DC, MC, V. Free parking. **Amenities:** Restaurant; 2 bars; solar-heated outdoor pool; bike rental; concierge; tour desk; airport shuttle; secretarial services; limited room service; in-room massage; babysitting; laundry service; dry cleaning. *In room:* A/C, TV w/pay movies, minibar, hair dryer, iron.

Bond Springs Outback Retreat ✦ *Finds* This working 1,515-sq.-km (585-sq.-mile) cattle ranch is a great place to get a taste of Outback life with a real Aussie family. A reader said it reminded her of the kind of place you'd see in *The Thorn Birds.* Janice Heaslip welcomes guests to her homestead, inviting them to join country dinners with the family and accommodating them in simple but appealing rooms and cottages. Cottages have coffeemakers. A TV is in the guest lounge. The Heaslips run a good range of day trips, overnight bush camps, and tours throughout the Red Centre, making this a good base for exploring. Ask about 3- and 5-day packages, some of which include tours and accommodations at Kings Canyon Resort and Ayers Rock Resort. No smoking indoors.

Note: All but the last 6km (3¾ miles) of the road to the ranch is paved. Car-rental companies do not allow driving on unpaved roads, but they may permit it here; check with your company.

25km (16 miles) north of Alice Springs (P.O. Box 4, Alice Springs, NT 0870). © **08/8952 9888.** Fax 08/8953 0963. www.outbackretreat.com.au. 5 units, 3 with bathroom. A$231–A$277 (US$185–US$221) double. Rates include full breakfast. Extra adult A$58 (US$46); extra child 6–15 A$47 (US$38). Dinner A$55 (US$44) per person. MC, V. Closed Dec 25–Jan. Transfers from Alice Springs A$40 (US$32) from town, A$80 (US$64) from airport, one-way, per vehicle. **Amenities:** Unheated outdoor pool; outdoor tennis court; laundry service. *In room:* A/C, fridge, hair dryer, no phone.

MODERATE

Alice on Todd ★ *Kids*   A new addition to the Alice accommodations scene, Alice on Todd has nice one- and two-bedroom apartments. It's a very good option, particularly if you have kids (if they're under 4 they stay free). The hotel overlooks the Todd River and is just a short stroll from town. The two luxury two-bedroom apartments each have an extra sofa bed.

Strehlow St. and South Terrace (P.O. Box 8454), Alice Springs, NT 0870. ✆ 08/8953 8033. www.aliceontodd.com. 34 units. AE, MC, V. A$98 (US$78) studio apt; A$120 (US$96) 1-bedroom apt; A$150 (US$120) 2-bedroom apt; A$160 (US$128) luxury 2-bedroom apt. **Amenities:** Outdoor pool; game room. *In room:* A/C, TV, kitchenette, fridge, coffeemaker, iron, washing machine.

Aurora Alice Springs   This pleasant hotel (formerly the Territory Inn) is smack in the center of town. Rooms in the newer wing are standard motel-style lodgings, all large and decorated nicely. Those in the original wing are small and a little dark; they have a pretty heritage theme, with floral bedcovers and lace curtains. One suite has a Jacuzzi. The courtyard has a barbecue, and the front desk loans hair dryers. The tiny pool and Jacuzzi are tucked away in a utilitarian corner, so this is not the place for chilling out poolside; stay here to be within walking distance of shops and restaurants.

Leichhardt Terrace (backing onto Todd Mall), Alice Springs, NT 0870. ✆ 1800/089 644 in Australia, or 08/8950 6666. Fax 08/8952 7829. www.aurora-resorts.com.au. 108 units (all with shower only). A$150–A$170 (US$120–US$136) double. Extra person A$20 (US$16). Children under 14 stay free in parent's room with existing bedding. AE, DC, MC, V. Free parking. Hotel provides transfers from airport (A$11/US$8.80) per person one-way; also picks up from train. **Amenities:** Restaurant (Red Ochre Grill; see "Where to Dine," below); small heated outdoor pool; Jacuzzi; tour desk; airport shuttle; limited room service; babysitting; laundry service; dry cleaning. *In room:* A/C, TV w/pay movies, minibar, fridge, iron.

Rydges Plaza Resort Alice Springs ★ *Value*   Next to the golf club and near Lasseter's Casino, this is one of Alice's fanciest resorts. Three stories of rooms wrap around the pool and an ample sun deck. All rooms are spacious. Each has a balcony—some look onto the pool, some toward town, some over the red ranges. Barbecues take place around the pool at lunch and dinner from September through March.

Barrett Dr. (1.5km/1 mile from town center), Alice Springs, NT 0870. ✆ 1800/226 466 in Australia, or 0800/446 187 in New Zealand (Rydges Resorts); resort direct 1800/675 212 in Australia, or 08/8950 8000. Fax 08/8953 0475. www.rydges.com. 235 units. A$160–A$215 (US$128–US$172) double; A$350–A$500 (US$280–US$400) suite. Extra person A$25 (US$20). Children under 13 stay free in parent's room with existing bedding. Free cribs. Ask about packages. AE, DC, MC, V. Free parking. **Amenities:** Restaurant; bar; heated outdoor pool; 2 lit tennis courts; exercise room w/plunge pool; Jacuzzi; sauna; bike rental; tour desk; airport shuttle; secretarial services; 24-hr. room service; babysitting; laundry service; dry cleaning. *In room:* A/C, TV w/pay movies, dataport, minibar, hair dryer, iron.

INEXPENSIVE

Best Western Elkira Motel   The cheapest rooms in the heart of town—decent ones, that is—are at this unpretentious motel. Standard rooms are dated, with lots of wood and tile floors, and a fridge and shower. Two standard family rooms come with a double bed and three singles. The 42 deluxe rooms have a little more space; nine have microwaves, and some have queen-size beds. Nine family rooms are nicer still, and come with a kitchenette. They cost the same as normal deluxe rooms and are well worth asking for even if you're traveling as a couple. All deluxe family rooms and a few deluxe doubles have bathrooms. The seven budget rooms are a little dated, and though small, they are comfortable and quiet. They come with a double bed, TV, shower, fridge, and hair dryer. Two units have Jacuzzis. Ask for a room away from the road, because the traffic is noisy during the day. Look out for the friendly Doberman called Charlie.

65 Bath St. (opposite Kmart), Alice Springs, NT 0870. © 1800/809 252 in Australia, or 08/8952 1222. Fax 08/8953 1370. www.elkira.com.au. 58 units (some with shower only). A$110–A$140 (US$88–US$112) double or family room. Extra adult A$15 (US$12); extra child under 3 A$5 (US$4). AE, DC, MC, V. Free parking. **Amenities:** 2 restaurants; unheated outdoor pool; nearby golf course; Jacuzzi; tour desk; car-rental desk; airport shuttle; limited room service; laundry service; dry cleaning; nonsmoking rooms. *In room:* A/C, TV, fax, dataport, fridge, coffeemaker, hair dryer, iron, safe.

Desert Palms Resort ⭐ *Value*   Next to Lasseter's Casino (where the food can be awful) and the Alice Springs Golf Club (where guests have honorary membership), these cheery cabins behind manicured palms and pink bougainvillea are one of the nicest places to stay in Alice. Don't be deterred by their poky prefab appearance; inside they are surprisingly large, well kept, and inviting, with a pine-pitched ceiling, a minikitchen, a sliver of bathroom sporting white tiles and fittings, and a pert furnished front deck. Four rooms are suitable for travelers with disabilities. A sun deck and pool with its own little island is out front. The pleasant staff at the front desk loans hair dryers, processes film, does laundry, sells basic grocery and liquor supplies, and books tours.

74 Barrett Dr. (1km/½ mile from town), Alice Springs, NT 0870. © 1800/678 037 in Australia, or 08/8952 5977. Fax 08/8953 4176. www.desertpalms.com.au. 80 units (all with shower only). A$115 (US$92) double; A$130 (US$104) triple; A$140 (US$112) quad. Extra person A$10 (US$8). AE, DC, MC, V. **Amenities:** Large unheated outdoor pool; golf course nearby; half-size tennis court; access to nearby health club; tour desk; car-rental desk; free coach station/ train station/airport shuttle twice daily; free resort-to-town shuttle 4 times daily; massage; laundry service; dry cleaning; nonsmoking rooms. *In room:* A/C, TV, dataport, kitchenette, fridge, coffeemaker.

WHERE TO DINE
EXPENSIVE

Overlanders Steakhouse ⭐ STEAK/AUSSIE TUCKER   This landmark on the Alice dining scene is famous for its "Drover's Blowout" menu, which assaults the megahungry with soup and damper, then a platter of crocodile *vol-au-vents,* camel and kangaroo filet, and emu medallions—these are just the *appetizers*—followed by Scotch filet, or barramundi (freshwater fish), and dessert. There's a regular menu with a 700-gram (1-lb., 10-oz.) steak, plus lots of lighter fare like oysters and spinach crepes. The barnlike interior is Outback all through, from the rustic bar to the saddlebags hanging from the roof beams. An "Overlanders' Table" seats solo diners together.

72 Hartley St. © 08/8952 2159. Reservations required in peak season. Main courses A$23–A$35 (US$18–US$28); Drover's Blowout A$44 (US$35). AE, DC, MC, V. Daily 6–10pm.

Palms Restaurant ⭐⭐ MODERN AUSTRALIAN   Ask the locals for the best chow in town, and this is where they'll send you. It serves sophisticated fare, like catch of the day in carrot and blood orange beurre blanc. Bush tucker creeps onto the menu, in dishes such as peppered kangaroo filet with sweet potato mash. A lighter menu is served at lunch. The wine list is split between easy drinkers at reasonable prices and a premium list with some wonderful Australian labels, even Henschke's Hill of Grace, which some say is Australia's best red. Live piano music plays nightly. No smoking inside until 9pm.

At the Alice Springs Resort, 34 Stott Terrace. © 08/8951 4545. Reservations recommended at dinner. Main courses A$25–A$28 (US$20–US$22). AE, DC, MC, V. Daily 6am–9:30pm.

MODERATE

Malathi's Restaurant & Sean's Irish Bar ASIAN/WESTERN   In an unprepossessing building a couple of blocks from Todd Mall, Malathi's serves an eclectic assortment of Asian dishes plus a few Aussie choices, such as grain-fed steak. The Asian food is outstanding. I can recommend lamb korma, a kind of mild curry. You might want to try Lakshmi king prawns cooked in Indian flavors, or Thai coconut curry. Vegetarians have some good choices. Takeout is available, too. The bar serves cheap Irish stews, live bands play (sometimes), and Guinness is always available. The restaurant has a wine list, and you can bring your own wine, subject to a A$5 (US$4) corkage fee per bottle.

51 Bath St. (opposite Kmart). © **08/8952 1858**. Reservations recommended. Main courses A$15–A$28 (US$12–US$23); many dishes under A$21 (US$17). AE, DC, MC, V. Restaurant Mon–Sat 5:30–10pm or later; bar daily 3:30–9:30pm.

Red Ochre Grill ✿ GOURMET BUSH TUCKER   If you've never tried wallaby mignons on a bed of native pasta and polenta cake with native berry and red-wine cream sauce, or barramundi (fish) baked in Paperbark with wild lime and coriander butter, here's your chance. The chef at this upscale chain fuses native Aussie ingredients with dishes from around the world. Although it might seem a touristy formula, the food is mouthwatering. Dine in the contemporary interior fronting Todd Mall, or outside in the attractive courtyard.

Todd Mall. © **08/8950 6666**. Reservations recommended at dinner. Main courses A$9–A$21 (US$7.20–US$17) lunch, A$15–A$23 (US$12–US$19) dinner; A$13–A$16 (US$11–US$13) buffet breakfast. AE, DC, MC, V. Daily 6:30am–10pm.

INEXPENSIVE

Bar Doppio ✿ EAST/WEST CAFE FARE   If you're in need of a dose of cool—style, as well as air-conditioning—this arcade cafe is the place to chill over good coffee and feast on cheap, wholesome food. Sacks of coffee beans are stacked all over, gypsy music plays, no tables and chairs match, and the staff doesn't care if you sit here all day. It's largely vegetarian, but fish and meat figure on the blackboard menu. Try lamb chermoula cutlets on Gabriella potatoes with rocket, red onion, and tomato salad; chickpea curry; warm Turkish flatbread with dips; or spuds with hot toppings. Hot and cold breakfast choices stay on the menu until 11am. Takeout is available. It's BYOB.

2 and 3 Fan Arcade (off the southern end of Todd Mall). © **08/8952 6525**. Main courses A$7–A$16 (US$5.60–US$13); sandwiches average A$6 (US$4.80). No credit cards. Mon–Fri 7:30am–5:30pm; Sat 7:30am–4:30pm; Sun 10am–4:30pm; Fri–Sat 6–9pm. Closed holidays and Dec 25–Jan 1.

Bojangles Saloon and Restaurant ✿ BURGERS/STEAKS/MODERN AUSTRALIAN   Swing open the saloon doors and enter a world of cowhide seats, thick wooden tables, Western-style knickknacks, original American Civil War guns, and so on. The front bar is friendly and serves good beers by the bottle or schooner, and food such as burgers, nachos, salads, and fish and chips. The restaurant out back has more gourmet offerings, but either way it's a great atmosphere. Aussie-style country and folk singers strum away in the evenings, and the bar staff is terrific.

80 Todd St. © **08/8952 2873**. Main courses A$7–A$18 (US$5.60–US$15) front bar, A$12–A$25 (US$9.60–US$20) restaurant. AE, DC, MC, V. Daily noon–3pm and 6–10pm.

Casa Nostra ✿✿ (Value) ITALIAN   The only difference between this cheery home-spun family eatery and every other Italian restaurant in the world is that this one has autographed photos of Tom Selleck pinned to the wall. Judging by his scrawled praise, Tom loved eating here (when on location in Alice filming *Quigley Down Under*) as much as the locals do. You've seen the red-checked tablecloths and the basket-clad Chianti bottles before, but the food is surprisingly good. A long list of pastas (including masterful carbonara), pizzas, and chicken and veal dishes are the main offerings. All meals are available to take out. BYO.

Corner of Undoolya Rd. and Sturt Terrace. (C) **08/8952 0549**. Reservations recommended. Main courses A$11–A$18 (US$8.80–US$15). MC, V. Mon–Sat 5–10pm. Closed Dec 25–Jan.

3 Road Trips from Alice Springs

The key attraction of a day trip to the MacDonnell Ranges is unspoiled natural scenery and few crowds. Many companies run coach or four-wheel-drive tours—half- or full-day, sometimes overnight—to the West and East Macs. Some options appear in "Organized Tours" in the "Alice Springs" section, earlier in this chapter. Expect to pay about A$100 (US$80) for a full-day trip. Families and backpackers alike love getting around with **Wayward Bus** ✪ (C) **08/8410 8833**; www.waywardbus.com.au). The company runs buses across the desert from Alice Springs on a 3-night camping trip stopping off at Kings Canyon and Uluru. You can sleep in a tent or a "swag"—a heavy waterproof sleeping bag (you can see the stars as you drop off). Tours cost A$330 (US$264), plus A$25 (US$20) park entry fee, for adults and A$235 (US$188) for kids up to 15.

THE WEST MACDONNELL RANGES ✪

WEST MACDONNELL NATIONAL PARK   The 300km (186-mile) round-trip drive west from Alice Springs into West MacDonnell National Park is a stark but picturesque trip to a series of red gorges, semidesert country, and the occasional peaceful swimming hole.

From Alice, take Larapinta Drive west for 18km (11 miles) to the 8km (5-mile) turnoff to **Simpson's Gap**, a water hole lined with ghost gums. Black-footed rock wallabies hop out on the cliffs in the late afternoon (so you may want to time a visit here on your way back to Alice). There are a couple of short trails, including a .5km (.33-mile) Ghost Gum circuit, and a 17km (11-mile) round-trip trail to Bond Gap. Swimming is not permitted. The place has an information center/ranger station and free barbecues.

Twenty-three kilometers (14 miles) farther down Larapinta Road, 9km (5½ miles) down a turnoff, is **Standley Chasm** (C) **08/8956 7440**). This rock cleft is only a few meters wide but 80m (262 ft.) high, reached by a 10-minute creek-side trail. Aim to be here at midday, when the walls glow orange in the overhead sun. A kiosk sells snacks and drinks. Admission is A$6 (US$4.80) for adults and A$4.50 (US$3.60) for seniors and children 5 to 14. The chasm is open daily from 8am to 6pm (last entry at 5pm; closed Dec 25).

Six kilometers (3¾ miles) past Standley Chasm, you can branch right onto Namatjira Drive or continue to Hermannsburg Historical Precinct (see below). If you take Namatjira Drive, you'll go 42km (26 miles) to picturesque **Ellery Creek Big Hole.** The spring-fed water is so chilly that the tourism authority warns swimmers to take a flotation device in case of cramping. A 3km (2-mile) walking trail explains the area's geological history.

Eleven kilometers (7 miles) farther along Namatjira Drive is **Serpentine Gorge,** where a trail leads up to a lookout for a lovely view of the ranges through the gorge walls. Another 12km (7½ miles) on are **ocher pits,** which Aboriginal people quarried for body paint and for decorating objects used in ceremonial performances. Twenty-six kilometers (16 miles) farther west, 8km (5 miles) from the main road, is **Ormiston**

Tips **Road Trips to the East & West Macs**

Facilities are scarce outside Alice, so bring food (perhaps a picnic, or meat to barbecue), drinking water, and a full gas tank. Leaded, unleaded, and diesel fuel are for sale at Glen Helen Resort and Hermannsburg. Wear walking shoes.

Many of the water holes dry up too much to be good for swimming—those at Ellery Creek, Ormiston Gorge, and Glen Helen are the most permanent. Being spring-fed, they can be intensely cold, so take only short dips to avoid cramping and hypothermia, don't swim alone, and be careful of underwater snags. Don't wear sunscreen, because it pollutes drinking water for native animals.

Two-wheel-drive rental cars will not be insured on unsealed (unpaved) roads—that means the last few miles into Trephina Gorge Nature Park, and the 11km (7-mile) road into N'Dhala Gorge Nature Park, both in the East Macs. If you are prepared to risk it, you will probably get into Trephina in a two-wheel-drive car, but you will need a four-wheel-drive for N'Dhala and Arltunga. The West MacDonnell road is paved to Glen Helen Gorge; a few points of interest may require driving for short lengths on unpaved road. Before setting off, drop into the CATIA Visitor Information Centre (see "Visitor Information," earlier in this chapter) for tips on road conditions and for details on the free ranger talks, walks, and slide shows that take place in the West and East Macs from April through October. Entry to all sights, parks, and reserves (except Standley Chasm) is free.

Gorge and Pound (✆ **08/8956 7799** for the ranger station/visitor center). This is a good spot to picnic, swim in the wide deep pool below red cliffs, and walk a choice of trails, such as the 30-minute Ghost Gum Lookout trail or the easy 7km (4-mile) scenic loop (allow 3–4 hr.). The water is warm enough for swimming in the summer. You can camp here for A$6.60 (US$5.30) per adult, and A$3.30 (US$2.60) per child 5 to 15. The campground has no powered sites but does have hot showers, toilets, and free barbecues.

A bit farther on is **Glen Helen Gorge,** where the Finke River cuts through the ranges, with more gorge swimming, a walking trail, guided hikes, and helicopter flights. Modest **Glen Helen Resort** (✆ **1800/896 110** in Australia, or 08/8956 7489; www.glenhelen.com.au) has 25 motel rooms (A$143/US$114 double); bunkhouses for four (A$19/US$15 per person); and campgrounds (A$9/US$7.20 per person for a tent site, A$22/US$18 double for a powered campsite). Also here are a restaurant serving three meals a day; a bar; and barbecues for which the resort sells meat packs. The resort offers 2-day trips of the area.

GETTING THERE You can arrange to be dropped off by **The Alice Wanderer** (✆ **08/8952 2111;** www.alicewanderer.com.au) at several stops in the Ranges. It costs A$75 (US$60) for two people for the return trip to Simpsons Gap; A$95 (US$76) to Standley Chasm; A$170 (US$136) to Serpentine Gorge; and A$200 (US$160) to Ormiston Gorge. If you plan to camp out, call ✆ **1300 650 730** to register your intentions (it's voluntary but worth it if you get lost—a rescue team will try to find you). You must pay a A$50 (US$40) refundable deposit by credit card. Take plenty of water. The Alice Wanderer also does group tours to the area.

HERMANNSBURG HISTORICAL PRECINCT   An alternative to visiting the West Mac gorges is to stay on Larapinta Drive all 128km (79 miles) from Alice Springs to the old **Lutheran Mission** at the **Hermannsburg Historical Precinct** (© 08/8956 7402). Some maps show this route as an unpaved road, but it is paved. Settled by German missionaries in the 1870s, this is a cluster of restored farmhouse-style mission buildings. There are a museum, a gallery housing landscapes by Aussie artist Albert Namatjira, and tearooms serving apple strudel from an old German recipe. The mission is open daily from 9am to 4pm (10am–4pm Nov–Mar). Admission to the precinct with tea or coffee is A$4.50 (US$3.60) for adults, A$3 (US$2.40) for school-age kids, or A$12 (US$9.60) for a family, plus A$3.50 (US$2.80) per adult or A$2.50 (US$2) per child for a guided gallery tour, which departs every hour. The precinct is closed from December 24 to January 2 or 3, and on Good Friday.

FINKE GORGE NATIONAL PARK   Just west of Hermannsburg is the turnoff to the 46,000-hectare (113,620-acre) **Finke Gorge National Park,** 16km (10 miles) to the south on an unpaved road (or about a 2-hr. drive west of Alice Springs. Turn south off Larapinta Dr. just west of Hermannsburg. Access along the last 16km/10 miles of road, which follows the sandy bed of the Finke River, is limited to 4WD vehicles only. Heavy rains may cause this section of the road to be impassable). The park is most famous for **Palm Valley,** where groves of rare *Livistona mariae* cabbage palms have survived since central Australia was a jungle millions of years ago. You will need a four-wheel-drive to explore this park. Four walking trails between 1.5km (1 mile) and 5km (3 miles) take you among the palms or up to a lookout over cliffs; one is a signposted trail exploring Aboriginal culture. There is a campsite about 4km (2½ miles) from the palms; it has showers, toilets, and free barbecues. Collect your firewood outside the park. Camping is A$6.60 (US$5.30) for adults, A$3.30 (US$2.60) for kids 5 to 15. For information, call the CATIA Visitor Information Centre in Alice Springs before you leave, because there is no visitor center in the park. The ranger station (© 08/8956 7401) is for emergencies only.

THE EAST MACDONNELL RANGES

Not as many tourists tread the path on the Ross Highway into the East Macs, but if you do, you'll be rewarded with lush walking trails, fewer crowds, and traces of Aboriginal history. I even spotted wild camels on my visit.

The first points of interest are **Emily Gap,** 10km (6 miles) from Alice, and **Jessie Gap,** an additional 7km (4½ miles), a pretty picnic spot. You can cool off in the Emily Gap swimming hole if there is any water. Don't miss the "Caterpillar Dreaming" Aboriginal art on the wall, on your right as you walk through.

At **Corroboree Rock,** 37km (23 miles) farther, you can make a short climb up the outcrop, which was important to local Aborigines. The polished rock "seat" high up in the hole means Aboriginal people must have used this rock for eons.

Twenty-two kilometers (14 miles) farther is the turnoff to **Trephina Gorge Nature Park,** an 18-sq.-km (7-sq.-mile) beauty spot with peaceful walking trails ranging from 45 minutes to 4½ hours. The last 5km (3 miles) of the 9km (5½-mile) road into the park are unpaved, but you can make it in a two-wheel-drive car.

N'Dhala Gorge Nature Park, 10km (6 miles) past Trephina Gorge Nature Park, houses an "open-air art gallery" of rock carvings, or petroglyphs, left by the Eastern Arrernte Aboriginal people. An interesting 1.5km (1-mile) signposted trail explains the Dreamtime meanings of a few of the 6,000 rock carvings, hundreds or thousands of years old, that are thought to be in this eerily quiet gorge. A four-wheel-drive vehicle is a must to traverse the 11km (7-mile) access road.

The Ross Highway is paved all the way to Ross River Resort, 86km (53 miles) from Alice Springs.

4 Kings Canyon ★

Anyone who saw the movie *The Adventures of Priscilla, Queen of the Desert* will remember the stony plateau the transvestites climb to gaze over the plain below. You can stand on that same spot (wearing sequined underpants is optional) at **Kings Canyon** ★ in **Watarrka National Park** (© 08/8956 7460 for park headquarters). As the crow flies, it is 320km (198 miles) southwest of Alice Springs. The sandstone walls of the canyon drop about 100m (330 ft.) to rock pools and centuries-old gum trees. There is little to do except walk the dramatic canyon rim for a sense of the peaceful emptiness of the Australian Outback.

GETTING THERE The best way is to drive. No regular flights operate, but **Ayers Rock Scenic Flights** (© 08/8956 2345; www.phs.com.au/ayresroc) does an aerial day trip from Ayers Rock Resort that incorporates a guided canyon walk; it costs A$595 (US$340) per person.

Numerous **four-wheel-drive** tour outfits head to Kings Canyon from Alice Springs or Uluru (Ayers Rock), with time allowed for the rim walk. See "Exploring the Red Centre," earlier in this chapter, for recommended companies.

With a four-wheel-drive, you can get to Kings Canyon from Alice Springs on the unpaved Mereenie Loop Road. The regular route is the 480km (349-mile) trip from Alice Springs south on the Stuart Highway, then west onto the Lasseter Highway, then north and west on the Luritja Road. All three roads are paved. Uluru (Ayers Rock) is 306km (190 miles) to the south on a paved road; from Yulara, take the Lasseter Highway east for 125km (78 miles), then turn left onto Luritja Road and go 168km (104 miles) to Kings Canyon Resort. The resort sells leaded and unleaded petrol and diesel.

GETTING AROUND **AAT Kings** (© 1800/334 009 in Australia, 08/8952 1700 in Alice Springs, or 08/8956 2171 in Uluru/Ayers Rock; www.aatkings.com) provides a 1-day tour to Kings canyon from the Ayers Rock Resort for A$103 (US$82) per person. You can book through AAT Kings or the resort.

EXPLORING THE PARK

The way to explore the canyon is on the 6km (3.75-mile) **walk** up the side (short but steep!) and around the rim. Even if you're in good shape, it's a strenuous 3- to 4-hour hike. It leads through a maze of rounded sandstone formations called the Lost City, across a bridge to a fern-fringed pocket of water holes called the Garden of Eden, and back along the other side through more sandstone rocks. There are lookout points en route. If you visit after the odd rainfall, the walls teem with waterfalls. In winter, don't set off too early, because sunlight doesn't light up the canyon walls to good effect until midmorning.

If you're not up to making the rim walk, take the shady 2.6km (1.5-mile) round-trip trail along the mostly dry **Kings Creek bed** on the canyon floor. It takes about an hour. Wear sturdy boots, because the ground can be rocky. This walk is all right for young kids and travelers in wheelchairs for the first kilometer (.5 mile).

Both walks are signposted. Avoid the rim walk in the middle of the day between September and May, when it's too hot.

You can also explore the park from an Aboriginal viewpoint with **Lilla Aboriginal Tours** (book through Kings Canyon Resort). Aboriginal guides take you on an easy 1km (.5-mile) walk to sacred caves and rock-painting sites. You learn about the art-works, hear the Dreamtime events that created the land around you, discover plant medicines and food, and have a go at throwing a spear and a boomerang. The tour lasts 1½ to 2 hours and departs at 9am and 4pm daily (closed mid-Dec to mid-Jan) from the Lilla community, 14km (8¾ miles) from Kings Canyon Resort. The resort offers transfers for A$20 (US$16) per person, round-trip, or A$30 (US$24) for two of you. The tour costs A$39 (US$31) for adults, A$33 (US$26) for seniors and students, and A$27 (US$22) for kids 5 to 16.

Professional Helicopter Services (© 08/8956 7873; www.phs.com.au) makes 15-minute flights over the canyon for A$90 (US$72) per person.

WHERE TO STAY & DINE

Apart from campgrounds, the only place to stay in Watarrka National Park is at Kings Canyon Resort.

Kings Canyon Resort ⚐ This attractive, low-slung complex 7km (4⅓ miles) from Kings Canyon blends into its surroundings. All but four of the larger deluxe rooms were built in 1999 and have desert views from glass-enclosed Jacuzzis. The remaining rooms are typical hotel accommodations, comfortable enough, with restful range views from the balcony. Thirty-two units have Jacuzzis. The double/twin, shared quad, and family lodge rooms are adequate low-budget choices, with a communal kitchen and bathroom facilities. Children are not permitted in lodge rooms unless you book the entire room. The resort has a well-stocked minimart where you can buy meat for the barbecues. Live entertainment plays some nights, and a ranger gives a slide show several nights a week. Internet access is available.

Luritja Rd., Watarrka National Park, NT 0872. © **1800/817 622** in Australia, or 08/8956 7442. Fax 08/8956 7426. www.voyages.com.au. 164 units, 128 with bathroom; 72 powered campsites and tent sites. July–Nov A$330–A$397 (US$264–US$317) hotel double; Dec–June A$277–A$343 (US$221–US$275) hotel double. Extra adult A$27 (US$22). Children under 16 stay free in parent's room with existing bedding. July–Nov A$100 (US$80) lodge double; A$168 (US$135) quad; A$185 (US$148) family unit for up to 5. Dec–June A$98 (US$78) lodge double; A$163 (US$130) quad; A$178 (US$142) family. Tent site A$28 (US$22) double; powered site A$32 (US$26) double. Extra adult A$11 (US$8.80); extra child 6–15 A$5 (US$4) in powered campsite. Children under 16 dine free at restaurant breakfast and dinner buffets with an adult. Ask about packages with Ayers Rock Resort and Alice Springs Resort. AE, DC, MC, V. **Amenities:** Restaurant; cafe; 2 bars; 2 outdoor unheated pools; outdoor lit tennis court; volleyball court; bike rental (from nearby gas station); tour desk; limited room service; coin-op laundry. *In room:* A/C, TV, fridge. Hotel only: TV w/pay movies, minibar, hair dryer, iron.

5 Uluru–Kata Tjuta National Park (Ayers Rock/The Olgas) ⚐

462km (286 miles) SW of Alice Springs; 1,934km (1,199 miles) S of Darwin; 1,571km (974 miles) N of Adelaide; 2,841km (1,761 miles) NW of Sydney

Uluru (Ayers Rock) is the Australia tourism industry's pinup icon, a glamorous red stone that has probably been splashed on more posters than Cindy Crawford has been on magazine covers. Just why people trek from all over the world to gawk at it is a bit of a mystery. For its size? Hardly—nearby Mount Conner is three times as big. For its shape? Probably not—most folks agree the neighboring Kata Tjuta (the Olgas) is more picturesque. You can put its popularity down to the faint shiver up the spine and the indescribable sense of place it evokes in anyone who looks at it. Even Aussie bushmen reckon it's "got somethin' spiritual about it."

In 1985 the **Uluru–Kata Tjuta National Park** ⚶ was returned to its Aboriginal owners, the Pitjantjatjara and Yankunytjatjara people, known as the Anangu, who manage the property jointly with the Australian government. People used to speculate that the Rock was a meteorite, but we now know it was formed by sediments laid down 600 million to 700 million years ago in an inland sea and thrust up above ground 348m (1,141 ft.) by geological forces. With a circumference of 9.4km (6 miles), the Rock is no pebble, especially because two-thirds of it is thought to be underground. On photos it looks like a big smooth blob. In the flesh, it's more interesting—dappled with holes and overhangs, with curtains of stone draping its sides, creating little coves hiding water holes and Aboriginal rock art. It also changes color from pink to a deep wine red depending on the slant of the sun.

Don't think a visit to Uluru is just about snapping a few photos and going home. You can walk around the Rock, climb it (although the local Aborigines prefer you don't), fly over it, ride a camel to it, circle it on a Harley-Davidson, trek through the Olgas, eat in an outdoor restaurant, tour the night sky, and join Aboriginal people on guided walks.

Give yourself at least a day in the Uluru area; you could easily stay two or three.

Isolation (and a lack of competition) makes things like accommodations, meals, and transfers expensive. A coach tour or four-wheel-drive camping safari is often the cheapest way to see the place. See "Exploring the Red Centre," at the beginning of this chapter, for recommended tour companies.

ESSENTIALS

GETTING THERE **By Plane** **Qantas** (© **13 13 13** in Australia) flies to Ayers Rock (Connellan) Airport direct from Sydney, Alice Springs, Perth, and Cairns. Flights from other ports go via Alice Springs. The airport is 6km (3¾ miles) from

---

⎛Tips **The Rock in a Day?**

It's a loooong day to visit Uluru in a day from Alice by road. Many organized coach tours pack a lot—perhaps a Rock base walk or climb, Kata Tjuta (the Olgas), the Uluru–Kata Tjuta Cultural Centre, and a champagne sunset at the Rock—into a busy trip that leaves Alice around 5:30 or 6am and gets you back late at night. **Murray Cosson's Australian Outback Flights** (© **08/8952 4625;** www.australianoutbackflights.com.au) offers an aerial day trip from Alice Springs that includes flights over Kings Canyon, Gosse Bluff meteorite crater, and Lake Amadeus; a rental car at Uluru (Ayers Rock); national park entry fee; and lunch. It costs A$660 (US$528) per person (minimum two passengers). There are more tour options too.

You should consider a day trip only between May and September. At other times, it's too hot to do much from early morning to late afternoon.

Ayers Rock Resort. Expect to pay around A$320 (US$256) one-way. A free shuttle ferries all resort guests, including campers, to their door.

By Car   Take the Stuart Highway south from Alice Springs 199km (123 miles), turn right onto the Lasseter Highway, and go 244km (151 miles) to Ayers Rock Resort. The Rock is 18km (11 miles) farther on. (Everyone mistakes the flat-topped mesa they see en route for Uluru; it's Mount Conner.)

Only Avis, Hertz, and Thrifty have Uluru depots: Thrifty charges around A$110 (US$88) a day for bookings under 3 days; Hertz charges A$137 (US$109) a day for bookings under 7 days; and Avis charges A$137 (US$109) a day for bookings of 2 days or less. If you want to rent a car in Alice Springs and drop it at Uluru, brace yourself for a one-way penalty.

VISITOR INFORMATION   For information before you leave, contact the **Central Australian Tourism Industry Association (CATIA),** 60 Gregory Terrace, Alice Springs (✆ **08/8952 5800;** www.centralaustraliantourism.com), or drop into its **Visitor Information Centre** in Alice Springs. One of the best online sources is Ayers Rock Resort's site (www.voyages.com.au).

The **Ayers Rock Resort Visitor Centre,** next to the Desert Gardens Hotel (✆ **08/8957 7377**), has displays on the area's geology, wildlife, and Aboriginal heritage, plus a souvenir store. It's open daily from 8:30am to 7:30pm. You can book tours at the **tour desk** in every hotel at Ayers Rock Resort, or visit the **Ayers Rock Resort Tour & Information Centre** (✆ **08/8957 7324**) at the shopping center in the resort complex. It dispenses information on and books tours as far afield as Kings Canyon and Alice Springs. It's open daily from 7:30am to 8:30pm.

One kilometer (½ mile) from the base of the Rock is the **Uluru–Kata Tjuta Cultural Centre** ✵ (✆ **08/8956 3138**), owned and run by the Anangu, the Aboriginal owners of Uluru. It uses eye-catching wall displays, frescoes, interactive recordings, and videos to tell about Aboriginal Dreamtime myths and laws. It's worth spending some time here to understand a little about Aboriginal culture. A National Park desk has information on ranger-guided activities and animal, plant, and bird-watching checklists. The center also has a cafe, a souvenir shop, and two Aboriginal arts and crafts galleries. It's open daily from early in the morning to after sundown; exact hours vary from month to month.

PARK ENTRANCE FEES   Entry to the Uluru–Kata Tjuta National Park is A$25 (US$20) per adult, free for children under 16, valid for 3 days. The cost of many organized tours includes the entry fee.

ETIQUETTE   The Anangu ask you not to photograph sacred sites or Aboriginal people without permission, and to approach quietly and respectfully.

GETTING AROUND

Getting around the park is expensive. Ayers Rock Resort runs a **free shuttle** every 15 minutes or so around the resort complex from 10:30am to after midnight, but to get to the Rock or Kata Tjuta (the Olgas), you will need to take transfers, join a tour, or have your own wheels. The shuttle also meets all flights.

BY SHUTTLE   Uluru Express (✆ **08/8956 2152;** www.uluruexpress.com.au) provides a minibus shuttle from Ayers Rock Resort to and from the Rock about every 50 minutes from before sunrise to sundown, and several times a day to the Olgas. The basic shuttle costs A$35 (US$28) for adults and A$20 (US$16) for kids (including to

---

> **Tips** Water, Water . . .
>
> Water taps are scarce and kiosks nonexistent in Uluru–Kata Tjuta National Park. Always carry your own drinking water when sightseeing.

---

see the sunset); a sunrise trip costs A$40 (US$32) for adults and A$20 (US$16) for kids. To the Olgas, it costs A$50 (US$40) for adults and A$25 (US$20) for children. A 3-day pass covering as many trips as you like to both sites costs A$140 (US$112) for adults and A$60 (US$48) for kids. A combined Uluru and Olgas trip costs A$55 (US$44) for adults and A$30 (US$24) for kids. All fares are round-trip.

BY CAR   If there are two of you, the easiest and cheapest way to get around is likely to be a rental car. All roads in the area are paved, so a four-wheel-drive is unnecessary. Expect to pay around A$70 to A$95 (US$56–US$76) per day for a medium-size car. Rates drop a little in low season. Most car-rental companies give you the first 100km (63 miles) free and charge A30¢ (US25¢) per kilometer after that. Take this into account, because the round-trip from the resort to the Olgas is just over 100km (63 miles), and that's without driving about 20km (13 miles) to the Rock and back. **Avis** (*©* **08/8956 2266**), **Hertz** (*©* **08/8956 2244**), and **Thrifty** (*©* **08/8956 2030**) book four-wheel-drives through their Darwin offices. All rent regular cars and four-wheel-drives.

The **Outback Travel Shop** *©* (*©* **08/8955 5288;** www.outbacktravelshop.com.au), a booking agent in Alice Springs, often has better deals on car-rental rates than you'll get by booking direct.

BY ORGANIZED TOUR   Several tour companies run a big range of daily sunrise and sunset viewings, circumnavigations of the Rock by coach or on foot, guided walks at the Rock or the Olgas, camel rides, observatory evenings, visits to the Uluru–Kata Tjuta Cultural Centre, and innumerable permutations and combinations of all of these. Some offer "passes" containing the most popular activities. Virtually every company picks you up at your hotel. Among the most reputable are **Discovery Ecotours** (formerly Uluru Experience and Alice Experience), **AAT Kings, Tailormade Tours,** and **VIP Travel Australia** (see "Exploring the Red Centre" at the start of this chapter for details).

ABORIGINAL TOURS   Because **Anangu Tours** *©©* (*©* **08/8956 2123;** www.anangutours.com.au) is owned and run by the Rock's Aboriginal owners, its tours give you firsthand insight into Aboriginal culture. Tours are in the Anangu language and translated by an interpreter. They are not cheap, but if you are going to spend money on just one tour, this group is a good choice.

The company does a **Kuniya** walk during which you visit the Uluru–Kata Tjuta Cultural Centre and the Mutitjulu water hole at the base of the Rock, learn about bush foods, and see rock paintings, before watching the sunset. It departs daily at 2:30pm March through October, 3:30pm November through February. With hotel pickup, the tour costs A$85 (US$68) for adults and A$60 (US$48) for children. If you drive to the Cultural Center yourself, it costs A$55 (US$44) for adults and A$27 (US$21) for kids. There's also a 4½-hour breakfast tour costing A$108 (US$86) for adults and A$74 (US$59) for children. It includes a base tour and demonstrations of bush skills and spear-throwing.

For an Aboriginal insight into the Rock without paying for a tour, join the free **Mala Walk** ⭐ (see "Walking, Driving, or Busing Around It," below); it discusses Aboriginal culture and is often led by an Aboriginal park ranger.

DISCOVERING ULURU (AYERS ROCK)

AT SUNRISE & SUNSET   The peak time to catch the Rock's beauty is sunset, when oranges, peaches, pinks, reds, and then indigo and deep violet creep across its face as if it were a giant opal. Some days it's fiery, other days the colors are muted. A sunset-viewing car park is on the Rock's western side. Plenty of sunset and sunrise tours operate from the resort. A typical sunset tour is that offered by **AAT Kings** (✆ 08/8956 2171; www.aatkings.com): It departs 90 minutes before sunset, includes a free glass of wine with which to watch the "show," and returns 20 minutes after sundown; the cost is A$38 (US$30) for adults, A$26 (US$21) for children 4 to 14. AAT Kings offers several other tours around the area, so if large-group touring is your thing then I really suggest you check out their website before leaving home.

At sunrise the colors are less dramatic, but many folks enjoy the spectacle of the Rock unveiled by the dawn to birdsong. You'll need an early start—most tours leave about 75 minutes before sunup.

CLIMBING IT   Aborigines refer to tourists as *minga*—little ants—because that's what we look like crawling up Uluru. Climbing this thing is no picnic—there's sometimes a ferociously strong wind that can blow you right off, the walls are almost vertical in places

---

Moments **Dinner in the Desert**

Why sit in a restaurant when you can eat outside in the dust? Because you came to the Outback to be outside, that's why. Ayers Rock Resort's **Sounds of Silence dinner** ⭐ makes outside eating a fascinating event. In an outdoor clearing, you sip champagne and nibble canapés as the sun sets over the Rock to the strains of a didgeridoo played by a white man (the excuse is that didgeridoos don't come from this part of the world but from Arnhemland—though there seem to be plenty of local Aboriginals who play). We hope you've zeroed in on people you want to sit with by now, because you head to communal white-clothed, candlelit tables and a serve-yourself meal of kangaroo and barramundi (a large freshwater fish). Last time I was here, they served pretty poor pumpkin soup to begin, the main courses varied from bland to nice, and the Aussie wines were bad examples. However, after dinner, the lanterns fade, and you are left with stillness (apart from an occasional dingo looking for scraps). It is the first time some city folk have ever heard silence. Next, an astronomer points out the constellations of the Southern Hemisphere, and you have a chance to see the stars through telescopes. Sounds of Silence is held nightly, weather permitting, and costs A$120 (US$96) for adults and A$60 (US$48) for children under 15, including transfers from Ayers Rock Resort. It's mighty popular, so book 3 months ahead in peak season. Book through the Ayers Rock Resort office in Sydney (✆ **1300/139 889** in Australia or 02/9339 1040).

(you have to hold onto a chain), and it can be freezing cold or insanely hot. Quite a few people have died climbing the rock from heart attacks, heat stress, or simply falling off. If you're not in good shape; have breathing difficulties, heart trouble, or high or low blood pressure; or are just plain scared of heights, don't do it. The Rock is closed to climbers during bad weather; when temperatures exceed 97°F (36°C), which they often do from November to March; and when wind speed exceeds 25 knots, so climb in the stillness of early morning. *Warning:* Wherever you go at Uluru and Kata Tjuta (the Olgas), bring lots of drinking water with you from the resort.

If that doesn't put you off, you'll be rewarded with views of the plain, Kata Tjuta (the Olgas), and Mount Conner. The surface is rutted with ravines about 2.5m (8¼ ft.) deep, which demand scrambling. The climb takes at least 1 hour up for the fit, and 1 hour down. The less sure-footed should allow 3 to 4 hours all told.

Note: The Anangu do not like people climbing Uluru, because the climb follows the trail their ancestral Dreamtime Mala men took when they first came to Uluru. They allow people to climb but strongly prefer that they don't.

WALKING, DRIVING, OR BUSING AROUND IT A paved road runs around the Rock. The easy 9.4km (6-mile) **Base Walk** circumnavigating Uluru takes about 2 hours, but allow time to linger around the water holes, caves, folds, and overhangs that make up its walls. A shorter walk is the easy 1km (.5-mile) round-trip trail from the **Mutitjulu** parking lot to the pretty water hole near the Rock's base, where there is some rock art. The **Liru Track** is another easy trail; it runs 2km (1.25 miles) from the Cultural Centre to Uluru, where it links with the Base Walk.

Make time for the free daily 2km (1¼-mile) **Mala Walk** ✦, where the ranger, who is often an Aborigine, explains the Dreamtime myths behind Uluru, talks about Aboriginal lifestyles and hunting techniques in days past, and explains the significance of the rock art and other sites you see along the way. The 90-minute trip leaves the Mala Walk sign at the base of the Uluru climb at 10am May through September, and at a cooler 8am October through April.

Before setting off on any walk, it's a good idea to arm yourself with the self-guided walking notes available for A$1.10 (US90¢) from the Cultural Centre (see "Visitor Information," above).

Most companies offer base tours. As an example, **Discovery Ecotours** (© 1800/ 803 174; www.discoveryecotours.com.au) conducts a 5-hour guided base tour that gives you insight into natural history, rock art, and Dreamtime beliefs. It's scheduled to coincide with sunrise. The tour costs A$110 (US$88) for adults and A$85 (US$68) for children 6 to 15, but it's not suitable for kids under 10. The company also runs a 4-hour sunset trip to the Olgas for A$80 (US$64) for adults and A$60 (US$48) for kids.

FLYING OVER IT Several companies do scenic flights by light aircraft or helicopter over Uluru, Kata Tjuta (the Olgas), nearby Mount Conner, the vast white saltpan of Lake Amadeus, and as far as Kings Canyon. Helicopters don't land on top of the Rock, however. As a guide to the flights available, **Professional Helicopter Services** (© 08/8956 2003; www.phs.com.au) does a 12- to 15-minute flight over Uluru for A$105 (US$84) per adult, and a 25- to 30-minute flight, which includes the Olgas, for A$205 (US$164). Kids under 13 usually pay half-price (depending more on their weight than on their age). You can drive to the helicopter site on a Harley-Davidson for A$50 (US$40) one-way and A$75 (US$60) round-trip.

Tips **Travel Tip**

Most tourists visit Uluru in the mornings and Kata Tjuta (the Olgas) in the afternoon. Reverse the order (do the Valley of the Winds walk in the morning and Uluru in the afternoon) and you'll find both spots a little more silent and spiritual.

MOTORCYCLING AROUND IT   Harley-Davidson tours are available as sunrise or sunset rides, laps of the Rock, and various other Rock and Kata Tjuta (Olgas) tours with time for the Olgas walks. A blast out to the Rock at sunset with **Uluru Motorcycle Tours** (© **08/8956 2019**) will set you back A$145 (US$116), which includes a glass of champagne. The guide drives the bike; you sit behind and hang on. Self-ride tours are available, too, at a hefty price. You can rent a Harley for a half-day for A$365 (US$292).

VIEWING IT ON CAMELBACK   Legend has it that a soul travels at the same pace as a camel; it's certainly a peaceful way to see the Rock. **Frontier Camel Tours** (© **1800/806 499** in Australia, or 08/8956 2444; www.cameltours.com.au) makes daily forays aboard "ships of the desert" to view Uluru. Amble through red-sand dunes with great views of the Rock, dismount to watch the sun rise or sink over it, and ride back to the depot for billy tea and beer bread in the morning, or champagne in the evening. The 1-hour rides depart Ayers Rock Resort 1 hour before sunrise or 1½ hours before sunset, and cost A$95 (US$76) per person, including transfers from your hotel. For A$60 (US$48) per person you can ride out into the desert to view Uluru and the Olgas from a distance. The tour leaves daily at midday and takes around 1 and a half hours. Each day between 10:30am and midday, you can visit the camels free of charge and take a short ride for A$10 (US$8) for adults, A$5 (US$4) for kids 6 to 12, or A$25 (US$20) for a family. All tours leave from the Camel Depot at the Ayers Rock Resort.

EXPLORING THE OLGAS

Although not everyone has heard of massive **Mount Olga** ⭐ (or "the Olgas"), a sister monolith an easy 50km (31-mile) drive west of Uluru, many folks who have say it's lovelier and more mysterious, and I agree. Known to the Aborigines as Kata Tjuta, or "many heads," the Olgas' 36 momentous red domes bulge out of the earth like turned clay on a potter's wheel. The tallest dome is 200m (656 ft.) higher than Uluru. The Olgas are more important in Aboriginal Dreamtime legend than Uluru.

Two walking trails take you in among the domes: the 7.4km (4.5-mile) **Valley of the Winds** ⭐ walk, which is fairly challenging and takes 3 to 5 hours, and the easy 2.6km (1.5-mile) **Gorge** walk, which takes about an hour. The Valley of the Winds trail is the more rewarding in terms of scenery. Both have lookout points and shady stretches. The Valley of the Winds trail closes when temperatures rise above 97°F (36°C).

WHERE TO STAY & DINE

Ayers Rock Resort not only is in the township of Yulara—it is the township. Located about 30km (19 miles) from the Rock, outside the national park boundary, it is the only place to stay. It is an impressive, contemporary complex, built to a high standard, very efficiently run, and attractive—all things you can end up paying an arm and a leg for. Because everyone either is a tourist or lives and works here, it has a village atmosphere—with a supermarket; a bank; a post office; a news agency; babysitting services; a medical center; a beauty salon; several gift, clothing, and souvenir shops; a place to buy beer; and a gas station.

You have a choice of seven places to stay within the complex, from hotel rooms and apartments to luxury and basic campsites. In keeping with this village feel, no matter where you stay, even in the campground, you are free to use all the pools, restaurants, and other facilities of every hostelry, except the rather glamorous Sails in the Desert pool, which is reserved for Sails guests.

Voyages Hotels & Resorts manages Ayers Rock Resort, Alice Springs Resort, and Kings Canyon Resort. You can book accommodations for all three properties through the central reservations office in Sydney (℃ **1300/139 889** in Australia, or 02/9339 1040; fax 02/9332 4555; www.voyages.com.au). Ask about packages that include one, two, or all three resorts. *Warning:* Shop around for prices on the Internet and with travel agencies. My experience is that people staying here have paid a whole range of prices.

High season is July through November. Book well ahead.

A tour desk, same-day dry-cleaning and laundry service, and babysitting are all available at each hostelry and campground.

In addition to the dining options below, the resort's small shopping center has the pleasant **Gecko's Café,** which offers wood-fired pizzas, pastas, and sandwiches; a bakery; an ice creamery; and takeout. Sails in the Desert, Desert Gardens, and the Outback Pioneer Hotel & Lodge can provide picnic hampers and breakfast backpacks. Kids under 15 dine free at any of the hotels' buffets in the company of an adult. It's a good idea to bring some wine with you, because the place really has things sewn up, including prices.

VERY EXPENSIVE

Longitude 131 ★★★   You can find this African-style luxury safari camp, with perfect views of Uluru, in the sand dunes a mile or two from the main complex. The camp was finished in June 2002, mostly burned down in 2003, and reopened in July 2004. It offers 15 top-class air-conditioned tents, each with a private bathroom and a balcony overlooking the rock. The resort is promoting them as "six star." (How long until we have a seven star, rather than the usual five?) Whatever—A$9 million (US$7.2 million) on 15 tents makes them pretty expensive. A central facility, **Dune House,** holds a restaurant (with superb food), bar, library, and shop.

Yulara Dr., Yulara, NT 0872. ℃ **08/8957 7888.** Fax 08/8957 7474. 15 units. A$1,625 (US$1,300) tent for 2. Rates include walking and bus tours around the area, meals, selected drinks. 2-night minimum. AE, DC, MC, V. **Amenities:** Restaurant; bar; unheated outdoor pool; free airport shuttle. *In room:* No phone.

Sails in the Desert ★★   This top-of-the-range hotel offers expensive, contemporary-style rooms, many overlooking the pool and six with Jacuzzis (though watch your head on the glass doors leading to the private balcony, if you have one—I had a bruise for days). You can't see the Rock from your room, but most guests are too busy sipping cocktails by the pool to care. The pool area is shaded by white "sails" and surrounded by sun lounges. The lobby art gallery has artists in residence. The **Kuniya** restaurant serves elegant a la carte fine-dining fare with bush tucker ingredients; **Winkiku** is a smart a la carte and buffet venue; and the lively **Rockpool** (open seasonally) serves Thai fare poolside.

Yulara Dr., Yulara, NT 0872. © **08/8957 7888.** Fax 08/8957 7474. 232 units. High season A$507–A$595 (US$405–US$476) double, A$894 (US$715) suite; low season A$466–A$544 (US$373–US$435) double, A$830 (US$664) suite. Extra person A$36 (US$30). AE, DC, MC, V. **Amenities:** 3 restaurants; bar; large unheated outdoor pool; 2 outdoor lit tennis courts; free airport shuttle; limited room service. *In room:* A/C, TV w/pay movies, dataport, minibar, hair dryer, iron.

EXPENSIVE

Desert Gardens Hotel ✦ This is the only hotel with views of the Rock (albeit rather distant ones), from some of the 84 deluxe rooms. The accommodations are not as lavish as Sails in the Desert, but they're equally comfortable and have elegant furnishings. In 2002, 34 new rooms were built, and in 2001 the existing 100 standard rooms were refurbished with new bathrooms, bedding, and carpets. The **White Gums** restaurant serves a la carte flame grill and buffet meals.

Yulara Dr., Yulara, NT 0872. © **08/8957 7888.** Fax 08/8957 7716. 218 units (100 with shower only). High season A$426–A$494 (US$341–US$396) double; low season A$395–A$460 (US$316–US$368) double. Extra person A$27 (US$22). AE, DC, MC, V. **Amenities:** 2 restaurants; bar; unheated outdoor pool; free airport shuttle; limited room service. *In room:* A/C, TV w/pay movies, minibar, hair dryer, iron.

Emu Walk Apartments ✦ These bright, contemporary apartments have full kitchens, separate bedrooms, and roomy living areas. They have daily maid service. There's no restaurant or pool, but Gecko's Café and the market are close, and you can cool off in the Desert Gardens Hotel pool next door.

Yulara Dr., Yulara, NT 0872. © **08/8957 7888.** Fax 08/8957 7742. 59 apts (all with shower only). High season A$426 (US$341) 1-bedroom apt, A$512 (US$409) 2-bedroom apt for 4; low season A$395 (US$316) 1-bedroom apt, A$472 (US$377) 2-bedroom apt for 4. Extra person A$36 (US$29). AE, DC, MC, V. **Amenities:** Free airport shuttle; limited room service. *In room:* A/C, TV w/pay movies, kitchen, minibar, hair dryer, iron.

The Lost Camel ✦ This AAA-rated 3½-star hotel opened its doors in late 2002 on the site of the resort's demolished Spinifex Lodge, which once offered the best budget deals outside the campgrounds. It's aimed at young urbanites and is as bright, crisp, and modern as something you might find in Sydney's Darlinghurst. (Don't you just love that urban feel in the red dirt? You could forget you are in the Outback altogether.) The Red Camel offers lush courtyards and a generous swimming pool. Bang goes that budget, though.

Yulara Dr., Yulara, NT 0872. © **08/8957 7888.** Fax 08/8957 7474. 99 units. High season A$385 (US$308) double; low season A$350 (US$280) double. AE, DC, MC, V. **Amenities:** Bar; unheated outdoor pool; free airport shuttle. *In room:* A/C, minibar, hair dryer, iron, safe.

Moments **When You See the Southern Cross for the First Time . . .**

Light pollution is extremely low in the Red Centre, so the night sky is a dazzler. At the Ayers Rock Observatory, you can check out your zodiac constellation and take a 1-hour tour of the Southern Hemisphere heavens (they're different from the Northern Hemisphere stars).

To visit the observatory, you must join a tour with **Discovery Ecotours** (© **1800/803 174** in Australia, or 08/8956 2563; www.discoveryecotours. com.au), which provides hotel pickup and a tour. Tours depart twice a night; times vary. They cost A$32 (US$25) for adults, A$24 (US$14) for children 6 to 15. Family rates are available on request.

Outback Pioneer Hotel and Lodge   A happy all-ages crowd congregates at this midrange collection of hotel rooms, budget rooms, shared bunkrooms, and dorms. Thirty new rooms were added in 2002, offering clean, simple accommodations with private bathrooms; these are cheaper than the standard hotel rooms but more expensive than the existing budget rooms. Standard rooms come with a queen-size bed and a single; these have TVs with pay movies, a fridge, a minibar, and a phone. Some budget rooms have a TV and a fridge; 24 of the budget rooms come with two bunk beds and have private bathrooms. A dozen budget rooms have a double bed and a bunk; these share bathrooms. Each quad bunkroom holds two sets of bunk beds; these are coed and share bathrooms. Children under 16 aren't allowed in bunkrooms unless you book the entire room. Plenty of lounge chairs sit by the pool, and there's also an Internet lounge. The Bough House Restaurant offers buffets, and a dirt-cheap kiosk sells burger-style fare. What seems like the entire resort gathers nightly at the great-value **Outback Pioneer Barbeque** ★★. This barn with big tables, lots of beer, and live music is the place to join the throngs throwing a kangaroo steak or emu sausage on the communal cook-it-yourself barbie.

Yulara Dr., Yulara, NT 0872. ℂ 08/8957 7888. Fax 08/8957 7615. 125 units, all with private bathroom; 12 budget rooms without bathroom; 30 budget rooms with bathroom; 32 quad bunkrooms; 20-bed male-only dorm without bathroom, 20-bed female-only dorm without bathroom. High season A$383 (US$306) double, A$184 (US$147) budget room with bathroom, A$162 (US$129) budget room without bathroom; low season A$350 (US$280) double, A$172 (US$138) budget room with bathroom, A$152 (US$121) budget room without bathroom. Bunkroom bed A$40 (US$32), dorm bed A$32 (US$26) year-round. AE, DC, MC, V. **Amenities:** 2 restaurants; bar; unheated outdoor pool; free airport shuttle. *In room:* A/C.

INEXPENSIVE

Moderately priced cabins and inexpensive bunkhouse and dorm beds are available at the Outback Pioneer Hotel and Lodge, above.

Ayers Rock Campground   Instead of red dust you get green lawns at this campground, which has barbecues, a playground, Internet access, a small general store, and clean communal bathrooms and kitchen. If you don't want to camp but want to travel cheap, consider the modern cabins. They're a great value; each has air-conditioning, a TV, a kitchenette with a fridge, dining furniture, a double bed, and four bunks. They book up quickly in winter.

   Thrifty (ℂ **08/8956 2030**) at Uluru rents its customers a complete camping kit with sleeping bags, tents, cooking equipment, and so on for A$401 (US$320) for five days out of Ayres Rock. You must hire as part of a car deal (a medium-size car with camping gear for five days, plus good insurance will cost around A$1,070/US$856). You need to book hire cars in Uluru at least two weeks ahead. Contact **Hertz** (ℂ **08/8956 2244**) for a similar deal.

Yulara Dr., Yulara, NT 0872. ℂ 08/8956 2055. Fax 08/8956 2260. 220 tent sites, 198 powered sites, 14 cabins, none with bathroom. A$150 (US$120) cabin for up to 6; A$25 (US$20) double tent site; A$30 (US$24) powered motor-home site; A$25 (US$20) unpowered site. AE, DC, MC, V. **Amenities:** Unheated outdoor pool; playground; free airport shuttle; coin-op laundry. *In room:* No phone.

9

The Top End

by Lee Mylne

The "Top End" is a last frontier, a vast sweep of barely inhabited country from Broome on the west coast to Arnhemland in the Northern Territory and eastern Queensland. Most of it is in the Northern Territory, and the term also differentiates the northern part of the Territory from the Red Centre. It is a place of wild, rugged beauty and, sometimes, hardship.

The Northern Territory's capital, Darwin, is a small city, rich, modern, and tropical. Katherine is famous for its river gorge. Visit an Aboriginal community, canoe along lonely rivers, and soak in thermal pools. To the east of Darwin is Kakadu National Park, home to wetlands teeming with crocs and birds; one-third of the country's bird species are here. Farther east is Arnhemland, a stretch of rocky escarpments and rivers owned by Aborigines and seen by few others.

Life in the Top End is different than life elsewhere in Australia. Its slightly lawless image is one the locals enjoy. Isolation, the summer Wet season, monsoons, predatory crocodiles, and other dangers make 'em tough up here.

1 Exploring the Top End

Read "Exploring the Red Centre," in chapter 8; it contains information on traveling the entire Northern Territory.

VISITOR INFORMATION The **Northern Territory Tourist Commission,** Tourism House, 43 Mitchell St., Darwin, NT 0800 (© **13 30 68** in Australia, or 08/8951 3900; www.travelnt.com), can supply information on Darwin, Litchfield National Park, Kakadu National Park, Katherine, and other destinations in the territory. The commission has websites tailored for international travelers (**www. australiasoutback.com**) and for the self-drive market (**www.ntexplore.com**). It also publishes a helpful annual guide to the Top End that details many hotels, tour operators, rental-car companies, and attractions, and a separate fishing guide. The Commission's Territory Discoveries division offers package deals.

The **Tourism Top End** information center in Darwin and **Katherine Visitor Information Centre** (listed in the "Darwin" and "Katherine" sections of this chapter) can supply information about the Top End in addition to their local regions.

WHEN TO GO Most folks visit the Top End in the winter **Dry season** ("the Dry"). It's more than likely that not a cloud will grace the sky, and temperatures will be comfortable, even hot in the middle of the day. The Dry runs from **late April to late October/early November.** It is high season, so book every hotel or tour in advance.

The **Wet season** ("the Wet") runs from **November through March or April,** sometimes starting as early as October and sometimes lasting a few weeks longer in the

---

> ⌐**Tips** **Croc Alert!**
>
> **Saltwater crocodiles** are a threat in the sea, estuaries, lakes, wetlands, pools, and rivers of the Top End—even well inland. They live in fresh water, too. *Never* jump in the water or stand on the bank unless you are willing to risk becoming a croc's lunch!

Kimberley. While rain does not fall 24 hours a day, it still comes down in buckets for an hour or two each day, mainly in the late afternoon or at night. The land floods as far as the eye can see, the humidity is murderous, and the temperatures hit nearly 104°F (40°C). The floods cut off many attractions, sometimes suddenly, and some tour companies shut up shop for the season. Cyclones may hit the coast during the Wet, with the same savagery and frequency as hurricanes hit Florida. Many people find the "buildup" to the Wet, in October and November, when clouds gather but do not break, to be the toughest time.

Despite that, many people love traveling in the Wet. Waterfalls become massive torrents, lightning storms crackle across the afternoon sky, the land turns green, cloud cover keeps the worst of the sun off you, crowds vanish, and there is an eerie beauty to it all. Keep your plans flexible to account for floods, take it slowly in the heat, and carry lots of drinking water. Even if you normally camp, sleep in air-conditioned accommodations now. Book tours ahead, because most operate on a reduced schedule. See the tips about traveling in the Wet, below.

GETTING AROUND   The **Automobile Association of the Northern Territory (AANT)**, 79–81 Smith St., Darwin, NT 0800 (*©* **08/8981 3837;** www.aant.com.au), is a good source of maps and road advice. See also the Northern Territory Tourist Commission's site (www.ntexplore.com), which is designed specifically for those setting out on a driving holiday.

The Northern Territory has no open-road speed limit, but drivers should be careful to keep to a reasonable speed and leave enough distance to stop safely.

Most Aboriginal land is open to visitors, but in some cases you must obtain a permit first. If you are taking a tour, this will be taken care of, but independent travelers should apply to the relevant Aboriginal Land Council for permission.

Always carry 4 liters (1 gal.) of **drinking water** per person a day when walking (increase to 1 liter/¼ gal. per person per hour in summer). Wear a broad-brimmed hat, high-factor sunscreen, and insect repellent containing DEET (such as Aerogard and RID brands) to protect against the dangerous Ross River Fever virus carried by mosquitoes in these parts.

Deadly **marine stingers** (see "Bugs, Bites & Other Wildlife Concerns" in chapter 2) put a stop to ocean swimming in the Top End from roughly October to April or May.

TRAVELING IN THE WET   Some roads will be underwater throughout the Wet, while others can flood unexpectedly, leaving you cut off for hours, days, or even months. Flash floods pose dangers to unwary motorists. Don't cross a flooded road unless you know the water is shallow, the current gentle, and the road intact. Never wade into the water, because crocodiles may be present. If you're cut off, the only thing to do is wait, so it's smart to travel with food and drinking water in remote parts. Check road conditions every day by calling the **Northern Territory Department of**

The Northern Territory

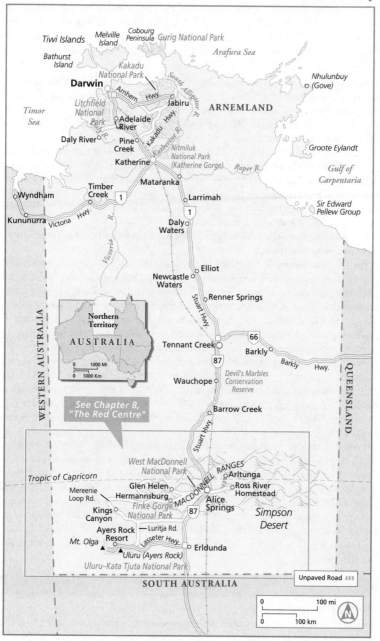

Tiwi Islands

Melville Island

Cobourg Peninsula

Gurig National Park

Arafura Sea

Bathurst Island

Kakadu National Park

Nhulunbuy (Gove)

Darwin

Arnhem Hwy.

South Alligator R.

Jabiru

ARNEMLAND

Timor Sea

Litchfield National Park

Adelaide River

Kakadu Hwy.

Daly River

Pine Creek

Katherine R.

Groote Eylandt

Katherine

Nitmiluk National Park (Katherine Gorge)

Roper R.

Gulf of Carpentaria

Mataranka

Wyndham

Timber Creek

1

Larrimah

1

Sir Edward Pellew Group

Kununurra

Victoria Hwy.

Victoria R.

Daly Waters

Northern Territory

AUSTRALIA

0   1000 Mi
0   1000 Km

Elliot

Newcastle Waters

Renner Springs

Stuart Hwy.

WESTERN AUSTRALIA

66

Tennant Creek

Barkly

Barkly   Hwy.

See Chapter 8, "The Red Centre"

87

Wauchope

Devil's Marbles Conservation Reserve

QUEENSLAND

Barrow Creek

Stuart Hwy.

West MacDonnell National Park

MACDONNELL RANGES

Arltunga

Tropic of Capricorn

Glen Helen

Hermannsburg

Ross River Homestead

Mereenie Loop Rd.

Finke Gorge National Park

Alice Springs

87

Simpson Desert

Kings Canyon

Ayers Rock Resort

Luritja Rd.

Lasseter Hwy.

Mt. Olga

Erldunda

Uluru (Ayers Rock)

Uluru–Kata Tjuta National Park

SOUTH AUSTRALIA

Unpaved Road ▮▮▮

0   100 mi
0   100 km

N

Infrastructure, Planning & Environment's 24-hour recorded report on road conditions (© **1800/246 199** in Australia); dropping into or calling the AANT (see "Getting Around," above) in Darwin during office hours; or tuning in to local radio stations as you drive. Local tour companies, tourist bureaus, and police stations should also be able to help.

TOUR OPERATORS   Organized tours can bust the hassles posed by distance, isolation, and Wet floods in the Top End, and the guides will show and tell you things you almost certainly would not discover on your own. A loop through Darwin, Litchfield National Park, Kakadu National Park, and Katherine is a popular route that shows you a lot in a short time.

Reputable companies include **AAT Kings** (© **08/8941 3844;** www.aatkings.com); **Odyssey Safaris** (© **1300/134 044** in Australia or 02/9299 2103; www.odysaf.com.au); **Sahara Outback Tours** (© **1800/806 240** in Australia, or 08/8953 0881; www.sahara tours.com.au); **Adventure Tours** (© **1300/654 604** in Australia, or 08/8309 2277; www.adventuretours.com.au); and **Billy Can Tours** (© **1800/813 484** in Australia, or 08/8947 1877; www.billycan.com.au).

VIP Touring Australia (© **08/8956 2388;** www.vipaustralia.com.au) offers luxury organized and tailor-made tours.

Far Out Adventures ⭑ (© **02/6557 6076,** or 0427/152 288 mobile; www.farout. com.au) does tailor-made four-wheel-drive safaris into Kakadu, Darwin, Arnhemland, Litchfield National Park, Katherine, the Kimberley, and more Top End regions. Proprietor-guide Mike Keighley will create a private adventure to suit your interests, budget, and time restrictions. Accommodations can range from luxury hotels to "under the stars" in Aussie bush swags. Touring with Mike can involve hiking, fishing, meeting or camping with his Aboriginal mates, canoeing, exploring seldom-seen Aboriginal rock art, taking extras like scenic flights, and swimming under (croc-free) waterfalls. Mike is one of a select group of operators with Australia's Advanced Eco Tour Accreditation and Savannah Guide status, and has a tremendous knowledge of the Top End's geography, Aboriginal culture, and ecology. Fun and personal, his trips are accompanied by good wine (sometimes in locations like a bird-filled lagoon at sunset) and "bush gourmet" meals.

Lord's Kakadu & Arnhemland Safaris (© **08/8948 2200;** www.lords-safaris.com) is based in Jabiru and operates charter tours throughout Kakadu and Arnhemland. Owner Sab Lord was born on a buffalo station in Kakadu before it was a national park, and has a strong rapport with local Aborigines. His small-group 4WD tours, which can be tailor-made, visit the Injalak Hill rock-art sites in Arnhemland and the arts center at Oenpelli and have exclusive access to the Minkinj Valley. Day tours to Arnhemland cost A$180 (US$144) for adults and A$130 (US$104) for children under 14. They operate May to November. The company also runs tours to Jim Jim and Twin Falls.

2 Darwin

1,489km (923 miles) N of Alice Springs

Australia's proximity to Asia is never more apparent than when you are in Darwin. The northernmost capital, named after Charles Darwin, is an exotic blend of frontier town, Asian village, and modern life. With a population of about 90,000, Darwin has had a turbulent history—and it shows. This city has battled just about everything that

Darwin

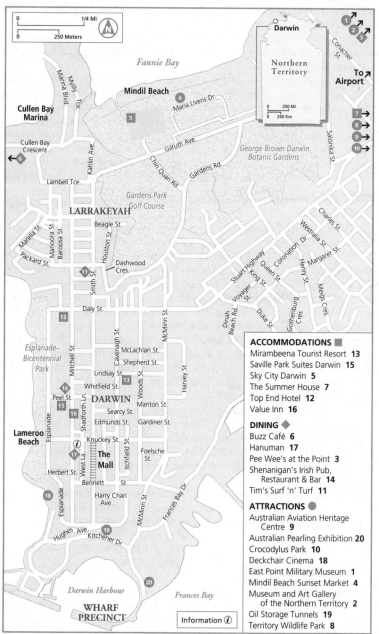

0 / 1/4 Mi
0 / 250 Meters

Fannie Bay

Mindil Beach ④

Maria Liveris Dr.

Cullen Bay Marina

Cullen Bay Crescent

⑥

Lambell Tce.

Kahlin Ave.

Marina Blvd.

Myilly Tce.

Gilruth Ave.

Chin Quan Rd.

Gardens Rd.

Gardens Park Golf Course

LARRAKEYAH

Beagle St.

Marella St.

Manoora St.

Baroosa St.

Packard St.

Houston St.

Dashwood Cres.

Smith St.

⑪

Daly St.

⑫

Esplanade–Bicentennial Park

Cavenagh St.

McLachlan St.

Shepherd St.

Lindsay St.

Whitfield St.

Mitchell St.

Woods St.

McMinn St.

Harvey St.

⑬

DARWIN

⑭

Peel St.

⑮

⑯

Searcy St.

Edmunds St.

Gardiner St.

Manton St.

Shadforth Ln.

Lameroo Beach

Esplanade

ⓘ

Knuckey St.

⑰

The Mall

West La.

Litchfield St.

Foelsche St.

Herbert St.

Bennett St.

⑱

Esplanade

Harry Chan Ave.

McMinn St.

Frances Bay Dr.

Hughes Ave.

Kitchener Dr.

⑲

⑳

Darwin Harbour

WHARF PRECINCT

Frances Bay

Darwin

Northern Territory

0 / 250 Mi
0 / 250 Km

Conacher St.

To Airport

Salonika St.

George Brown Darwin Botanic Gardens

Charles St.

Westralia St.

Coronation Dr.

Henry St.

Margaret St.

Meigs Cres.

Stuart Highway

Queen St.

King St.

Voyager St.

Duke St.

Gothenburg Cres.

Dinah Beach Rd.

① ② ③

⑦ → ⑧ → ⑨ → ⑩ →

ACCOMMODATIONS ■
Mirambeena Tourist Resort **13**
Saville Park Suites Darwin **15**
Sky City Darwin **5**
The Summer House **7**
Top End Hotel **12**
Value Inn **16**

DINING ◆
Buzz Café **6**
Hanuman **17**
Pee Wee's at the Point **3**
Shenanigan's Irish Pub, Restaurant & Bar **14**
Tim's Surf 'n' Turf **11**

ATTRACTIONS ●
Australian Aviation Heritage Centre **9**
Australian Pearling Exhibition **20**
Crocodylus Park **10**
Deckchair Cinema **18**
East Point Military Museum **1**
Mindil Beach Sunset Market **4**
Museum and Art Gallery of the Northern Territory **2**
Oil Storage Tunnels **19**
Territory Wildlife Park **8**

Information ⓘ

man and nature could throw at it. Most of its buildings date from the mid-1970s; Cyclone Tracy wiped out the city on Christmas Eve 1974. Don't bother bringing a jacket and tie here. Shorts and sandals will get you most places—even the swankiest official state invitations stipulate "Territory Rig" dress, meaning long pants and a short-sleeved open-neck shirt for men.

Darwin is most commonly used as a gateway to Kakadu National Park, Katherine Gorge, and the Kimberley, and many Australians have never bothered to visit it—or at least not for long. And that's a real shame, because it is an attractive and interesting place. Give yourself a day or two to wander the pleasant streets and parklands, visit the wildlife attractions, and discover some of the city's rich history. Then take time for some wetlands fishing in outlying regions, or shop for Aboriginal art and the Top End's South Sea pearls. An easy day trip is **Litchfield National Park** ★★, one of the Territory's best-kept secrets, boasting the kind of beautiful waterfalls to swim under that you only see on holiday brochures.

ESSENTIALS

GETTING THERE   Qantas (© **13 13 13** in Australia; www.qantas.com) serves Darwin daily from most state capitals; flights either are direct or connect in Alice Springs. Qantas also flies direct from Cairns. **Virgin Blue** (© **13 67 89** in Australia; www.virginblue.com) flies direct to Darwin from Brisbane, Sydney, and Melbourne, with connections from Cairns, Canberra, the Gold Coast, Adelaide, and Perth. **Airnorth** (© **08/8920 4001;** www.airnorth.com.au) flies from Broome and Kununurra in Western Australia. There are also direct flights to Darwin from Asia.

Darwin Airport Shuttle Services (© **1800/358 945** in the Northern Territory, or 08/8981 5066) meets every flight and delivers to any hotel between the airport and city for A$8.50 (US$6.80) one-way or A$15 (US$12) round-trip. Children 6 to 13 pay A$4.50 (US$3.60), or A$8 (US$6.40) round-trip. Bookings aren't essential. A cab to the city is around A$25 (US$20). **Avis, Budget, Hertz,** and **Thrifty** have airport desks (see "Getting Around," below, for phone numbers).

Greyhound Australia (© **13 14 99** in Australia; www.greyhound.com.au) makes a daily coach run from Alice Springs. The trip takes around 20 hours, and the fare is A$237 (US$190). Greyhound also has a daily service from Broome via Kununurra and Katherine; this trip takes around 24 hours and costs A$302 (US$242). They also run from Cairns via Townsville and Tennant Creek, a 40-hour trip costing A$441 (US$353).

With the opening of the long-awaited Alice Springs–Darwin railway line in 2004, the Top End now has its first rail link. Great Southern Railway's *Ghan* (© **13 21 47** in Australia; www.trainways.com.au) runs a weekly round-trip between the two cities, leaving Alice Springs on Monday at 4pm and arriving in Darwin about 24 hours later. The return trip leaves Darwin on Wednesday at 10am. The adult one-way fare is A$240 (US$192) for a "day-nighter" seat, A$880 (US$704) for a sleeper, or A$1,150 (US$920) for a first-class sleeper.

Darwin is at the end of the Stuart Highway. Allow at least 2 long days, 3 to be comfortable, to drive from Alice. The nearest road from the east is the long and dull Barkly Highway, which connects with the Stuart Highway at Tennant Creek, 922km (572 miles) south. The nearest road from the west is Victoria Highway, which joins the Stuart Highway at Katherine, 314km (195 miles) to the south.

VISITOR INFORMATION   Tourism Top End runs the official visitor center, Knuckey Street at Mitchell Street, Darwin, NT 0800 (© **08/8936 2499;** www.tourism

topend.com.au). It is the place to go for maps, bookings, national park notes, and information on Darwin and other regions throughout the Northern Territory, including Arnhemland, Katherine, and Kakadu and Litchfield national parks. It's open Monday to Friday from 8:30am to 5:45pm, Saturday from 9am to 2:45pm, and Sunday and public holidays from 10am to 1:45pm.

CITY LAYOUT   The city heart is the **Smith Street pedestrian mall.** One street over is the **Mitchell Street Tourist Precinct,** with backpacker lodges, cheap eateries, and souvenir stores. Two streets away is the harborfront **Esplanade.** In the old **Wharf Precinct,** a walk from town, are a couple of tourist attractions, a jetty popular with fishermen, and a working dock. **Cullen Bay Marina** is a hub for restaurants, cafes, and expensive boats; it's about a 25-minute walk northwest of town. Northwest of town is **Fannie Bay,** where you'll find the Botanic Gardens, sailing club, golf course, museum and art gallery, and casino.

GETTING AROUND   For car and four-wheel-drive rentals, call **Avis** (℡ 08/8981 9922), **Budget** (℡ 08/8981 9800), **EuropCar** (℡ 08/8941 0300), **Hertz** (℡ 08/8941 0944), or **Thrifty** (℡ 08/8924 0000).

Darwinbus (℡ **08/8924 7666**) is the local bus company. Its 1-day Tourcard allows unlimited travel on the network until midnight for A$5 (US$4) adults, A$2.50 (US$2) kids 5 to 14. The city terminus is on Harry Chan Place (off Smith St., near State Sq.). Get timetables there, or from the Tourism Top End visitor center (see "Visitor Information," above).

The **Tour Tub bus** (℡ **08/8985 6322**) does a loop of most city attractions and major hotels between 9am and 4pm daily. Hop on and off as you like all day for A$25 (US$20) for adults, A$15 (US$12) for children 4 to 12. It departs the Knuckey Street end of Smith Street Mall, opposite Woolworths, every hour.

Darwin Day Tours (℡ **1300/721 365** in Australia or 08/8923 6523) has a range of sightseeing tours.

Darwin Radio Taxis (℡ **13 10 08**) is the main cab company. Taxi stands are at the Knuckey Street and Bennett Street ends of Smith Street Mall.

EXPLORING DARWIN

Darwin's parks, harbor, and tropical clime make it lovely for strolling during the Dry. The tourist office distributes a free map showing a Historical Stroll of 17 points of interest around town. The **Esplanade** makes a pleasantly short and shady saunter, and the 42-hectare (104-acre) **George Brown Darwin Botanic Gardens** (℡ **08/8981 1958**), on Gardens Road 2km (1¼ miles) from town, has paths through palms, orchids, every species of baobab in the world, and mangroves. Entry is free. Take bus no. 4 or 6; the buses drop you at the Gardens Road entrance, but you might want to walk straight to the visitor center (open 8:30am–4pm daily) near the Geranium Street entrance (open 24 hr.) to pick up self-guiding maps to the Aboriginal plant-use trails.

The pleasant 5km (3-mile) trail along **Fannie Bay** from the Skycity Darwin hotel and casino to the East Point Military Museum is also worth doing. Keep a lookout for some of the 2,000 wild wallabies on the east side of the road near the museum.

Darwin has two wildlife parks that are worth visiting. At the **Territory Wildlife Park** (℡ **08/8988 7200;** www.territorywildlifepark.com.au), 61km (38 miles) south of Darwin at Berry Springs, you can take a free shuttle or walk 6km (3.75 miles) of bush trails to see native Northern Territory wildlife in wonderfully re-created natural habitats, including monsoon rainforest boardwalks, lagoons with hides (shelters for watching birds), a walk-through aviary, a walk-through aquarium housing sting rays and sawfish, and a nocturnal house with marsupials such as the bilby. Bats, birds, spiders, crocs, frill-neck lizards, kangaroos, and other creatures also make their homes here (but not koalas, because they don't live in the Territory). A program of animal talks runs throughout the day. The best is the birds of prey show, at 10am and 3pm. Go first thing to see the animals at their liveliest, and allow 4 hours to see everything, plus 45 minutes' traveling time. Open daily from 8:30am to 6pm (last entry at 4pm), and closed December 25. Admission is A$18 (US$14) for adults, A$9 (US$7.20) for students and children 5 to 16, and A$40 (US$32) for a family of six. Take the Stuart Highway for 50km (31 miles) and turn right onto the Cox Peninsula Road for another 11km (7 miles).

In addition to housing a small crocodile museum, **Crocodylus Park** (© 08/8922 4500), a 15-minute drive from town at 815 McMillan's Rd., Berrimah (opposite the police station), holds croc-feeding sessions and free hour-long guided tours at 10am, noon, and 2pm. It doubles as Darwin's zoo, with exotic species including lions, Bengal tigers, leopards, and monkeys on display. It's open daily from 9am to 5pm (closed Dec 25). Admission is A$25 (US$20) for adults, A$20 (US$16) for seniors, A$13 (US$10) for children 3 to 15, and A$65 (US$52) for a family group. Bus no. 5 (Mon–Fri only) from Darwin will drop you about a 5-minute walk from the park entrance.

The **Museum and Art Gallery of the Northern Territory,** Conacher Street, Bullocky Point (© 08/8999 8201), also holds an attraction for crocodile fans—the preserved body of **Sweetheart,** a 5m (16-ft.) man-eating saltwater croc captured in Kakadu National Park. The museum and gallery is a great place to learn about Darwin's place in Australia's modern history. It has sections on Aboriginal, Southeast Asian, and Pacific art and culture, and a maritime gallery with a pearling lugger and other boats that have sailed into Darwin from Indonesia and other northern parts. A highlight is the Cyclone Tracy gallery, where you can stand in a small, dark room as the sound of the cyclone rages around you. The gallery and museum are open from 9am to 5pm Monday through Friday, and 10am to 5pm weekends and public holidays; closed January 1, Good Friday, and December 25 and 26. The cafe has lovely bay views. Admission is free to the permanent exhibits. Take bus no. 4 or 6.

Darwin was bombed 64 times during World War II, and 12 ships were sunk in the harbor. It was an Allied supply base, and many American airmen were based here. The **East Point Military Museum,** East Point Road, East Point (© 08/8981 9702; www. epmm.com.au), housed in a World War II gun command post, plays a video of the 1942 and 1943 Japanese bombings. It has small but fine displays of photos, memorabilia, artillery, armored vehicles, weaponry old and new, and gun emplacements outside. Open daily from 9:30am to 5pm (closed Good Friday and Dec 25). Admission is A$10 (US$8) adults, A$9 (US$7.20) seniors, A$5 (US$4) children, and A$28 (US$22) families.

Even if you are not a military or aircraft buff, you may enjoy the excellent **Australian Aviation Heritage Centre** ✪, 557 Stuart Hwy., Winnellie (© 08/8947 2145). A B-52 bomber on loan from the United States is the prized exhibit, but the center also boasts a B-25 Mitchell bomber, Mirage and Sabre jet fighters, rare Japanese Zero fighter wreckage, and funny, sad, and heart-warming (and heart-wrenching) displays on World War II and Vietnam. Hours are daily from 9am to 5pm (closed Good Friday, Dec 25). Admission is A$11 (US$8.80) for adults, A$8 (US$6.40) for seniors and students, A$6 (US$4.80) for children 6 to 12, and A$28 (US$22) for families. Guided tours are at 10am, 2pm, and 4pm. The Heritage Centre is 10 minutes from town; take the no. 5 or 8 bus.

Empty **World War II oil storage tunnels** (© 08/8985 6333), on Kitchener Drive in the Wharf Precinct, house a collection of black-and-white photographs of the war in Darwin, each lit up in the dark. The simple but haunting attraction is worth a visit. Admission is A$4.50 (US$3.60) per person. The tunnels are closed in February. They open from 9am to 4pm daily May through September; October through April, hours are Tuesday through Friday from 10am to 2pm, weekends and holidays from 10am to 4pm.

On the Esplanade stands a monument to the destroyer **USS *Robert E. Peary,*** which went down in Darwin Harbour, with a loss of 88 lives.

Despite all this destruction, some of Darwin's historic buildings—or at least parts of them—have survived, and you can see them around the city center.

For an insight into Darwin's pearling industry, visit the **Australian Pearling Exhibition** (© 08/8999 6573), on Kitchener Drive near the Wharf Precinct. It has displays following the industry from the days of the lugger and hard-hat diving to modern farming and culture techniques. It's open from 10am to 5pm daily, except January 1, Good Friday, and December 25 and 26. Tickets cost A$6.60 (US$5.30) for adults, A$3.30 (US$2.65) for children, and A$17 (US$14) for a family of five.

If you have an evening free, get out on the harbor. **Australian Harbour Cruises** (© 08/8941 4000; www.australianharbourcruises.com.au) offers 3-hour sunset cruises aboard the restored lugger *Anniki.* They leave Cullen Bay Marina daily at 5pm and cost A$50 (US$40) for adults and A$30 (US$24) for kids 3 to 15. The price includes a glass of bubbly and some nibbles, and you can buy more drinks. **Darwin Cruises and Charters** (© 08/8942 3131; www.darwinharbourcruises.com.au) operates a sunset champagne cruise aboard the sailing schooner *Tumlaren,* which costs A$50 (US$40) per adult and A$30 (US$24) for children 4 to 14. A sit-down three-course dinner cruise aboard the *Alfred Nobel* costs A$80 (US$64) adults and A$53 (US$42) children. Both cruises leave Cullen Bay Marina at 5pm.

The Top End's wetlands and warm oceans are **fishing** ⚲ heaven. The big prey is barramundi, or "barra." Loads of charter boats conduct jaunts of up to 10 days in the river and wetland systems around Darwin, Kakadu National Park, and into remote Arnhemland.

The same company that runs Darwin's Tour Tub bus runs the **Northern Territory Fishing Office** (© 08/8985 6333; www.ntfishingoffice.com.au), a booking agent for a number of fishing charter boats offering barramundi day trips and extended wetland safaris, reef fishing, light tackle sportfishing, fly fishing, and estuary fishing. A day's barra fishing on wetlands near Darwin will cost around A$250 (US$200) per person; for an extended barra safari, budget about A$420 (US$336) per person per day. If you simply want to cast a line in Darwin Harbour for trevally, queenfish, and barra, the company will take you out for A$75 (US$60) per person for a half-day, or A$135 (US$108) per person for a full day. It also rents skipper-yourself fishing boats and tackle. Check out **www.fishingtheterritory.com** for detailed information on fishing tours, guides, and everything you need to know to make your arms ache from reeling 'em in!

THE DARWIN SHOPPING SCENE
Darwin's best buys are Aboriginal art and crafts, pearls, opals, and diamonds.

For a good range of authentic Aboriginal artworks and artifacts at reasonable prices, check out **Raintree Aboriginal Fine Arts Gallery,** Shop 5, 20 Knuckey St.

(✆ **08/8941 2732**). To make a heavyweight investment in works by internationally sought-after artists, visit the Aboriginal-owned **Aboriginal Fine Arts Gallery,** on the second floor at the corner of Knuckey and Mitchell streets (✆ **08/8981 1315;** www.aaia.com.au). Its website is a useful guide to art and artists.

The world's best South Sea pearls are farmed in the Top End seas. Buy, or just drool in the window, at **Paspaley Pearls,** off Smith Street Mall on Bennett Street (✆ **08/8982 5515**). **The World of Opal,** 44 Smith St. Mall (✆ **08/8981 8981**), has a re-creation of an opal mine in the showroom. If you fancy a pink diamond (the world's rarest) from the Argyle Diamond Mine in Kununurra (see "Kununurra" in chapter 10), you can get them at **Creative Jewellers,** 27 Smith St. Mall (✆ **08/8941 1233**), an Argyle-appointed supplier that buys direct from the mine. It also stocks the champagne diamonds for which Argyle is renowned and other Argyle diamond colors, as well as South Sea pearls and opals. The jewelers try to fashion pieces for overseas visitors in a short time to match your traveling schedule.

Jokes about "snapping handbags" abound in croc country. For your own croc-skin fashion statement, head to **di Croco,** in the Paspaley Pearls building in Smith Street Mall (✆ **08/8941 4470**). You'll find bags, purses, wallets, card holders, belts, pens, and other accessories, all made from saltwater croc skins farmed locally.

WHERE TO STAY

April through October is the peak Dry season; hotels usually drop their rates from November through March (the Wet).

VERY EXPENSIVE

Skycity Darwin ⭐ *Value*   After a A$10-million (US$8-million) refurbishment of the whole resort, and the addition of 10 new AAA-rated five-star Superior Rooms (completed in mid-2005), this upscale hotel has a whole new look. Attached to Darwin's casino on Fannie Bay, the hotel has been taken over in the past year by the Skycity Entertainment Group. The complex resembles a tropical palace, with white blocky architecture and 7 hectares (18 acres) of gardens on Mindil Beach, next to the Botanic Gardens. The rooms are a cocktail of European-style, contemporary Spanish furniture, and tropical elegance. All have balconies. It's worth paying a little extra for an ocean-facing room in the Dry season so you can watch Darwin's great sunsets. The new Superior Rooms feature cool marble in the bathrooms with the added luxury of spa baths; full-length glass windows provide views of the lush tropical gardens and beachfront; and private balconies. A longish beachside stroll brings you to the Museum and Art Gallery, and the Mindil Beach Sunset Markets take place right outside on Thursday and Sunday nights in the Dry season. A free shuttle runs four times a day to and from the city. There are also 10 rooms for families and travelers with disabilities.

Gilruth Ave., Mindil Beach, Darwin, NT 0800. ✆ **1800/891 118** in Australia, or 08/8943 8888. Fax 08/8943 8999. www.skycitydarwin.com.au. 109 units. A$300 (US$224) double; A$510 (US$344) suite. Extra person A$46 (US$37). Children under 14 stay free in parent's room with existing bedding. AE, DC, MC, V. Free valet and self-parking. Bus: 4 or 6. **Amenities:** 3 restaurants; 3 bars; nightclub; outdoor pool; children's pool; free access to nearby 9-hole golf course and 20 tennis courts; exercise room; Jacuzzi; sauna; concierge; tour desk; car-rental desk; business center; 24-hr. room service; massage; babysitting; free guest laundry; laundry service; dry cleaning; VIP suites. *In room:* A/C, TV/VCR w/pay movies, dataport, minibar, coffeemaker, hair dryer, iron.

EXPENSIVE

Saville Park Suites Darwin ⭐⭐   This eight-floor apartment hotel, a block from Smith Street Mall and overlooking the Esplanade, is one of Darwin's most comfortable, elegant lodgings. Rich, dark cane lobby armchairs and sofas are welcoming and rooms feature sleek contemporary-style spacious studios and one- and two-bedroom apartments that boast their own private balcony with great views. Premium Harbour View apartments have an eclectic blend of Asian-style teak, mahogany, and wicker furniture. The kitchens feature new modern granite bench tops and stainless steel appliances and the two penthouses include 104cm (40 in.) plasma screens with digital surround sound. An extensive upgrade to the whole hotel, completed in early 2005, includes a smart new color scheme throughout the guest rooms and a warm inviting new lobby, befitting the hotel's tropical surrounds. All rooms and apartments have views of Darwin Harbour or the city skyline. A pantry-stocking service does grocery shopping. Premium apartments have CD players and all apartments have separate dataports. Some rooms don't have balconies but are a generous size.

88 The Esplanade (at Peel St.), Darwin, NT 0800. ℂ 1300/881 686 in Australia, or 08/8943 4333. Fax 08/8943 4388. www.savillesuites.com.au. 204 units. A$255 (US$204) double; A$255 (US$204) studio apt; A$280–A$355 (US$224–US$284) 1-bedroom apt; A$485–A$1,190 (US$388–US$952) 2-bedroom apt. Children under 15 stay free in parent's room with existing bedding. AE, DC, MC, V. Parking A$5.50 (US$4.40). **Amenities:** Restaurant; bar; outdoor pool; access to nearby golf course and health club; Jacuzzi; bike rental; concierge; tour desk; car-rental desk; business center; salon; limited room service (5:30am–10pm); massage; babysitting; laundry service; dry cleaning (Mon–Sat); nonsmoking rooms; executive-level rooms. In room: A/C, TV w/pay movies, minibar, coffeemaker, hair dryer, iron.

MODERATE

Mirambeena Tourist Resort You're just a stone's throw from the city center at this modern hotel complex, where the tempting swimming pools, the Jacuzzis, and the treetop restaurant, all shaded by the leaves of a sprawling strangler fig, have a castaway-island feel. Each room is a decent size and has a garden or pool view. Management will supply a minibar on request. Town houses with kitchenettes are good for families, if you can handle sharing the compact bathroom with your kids.

64 Cavenagh St., Darwin, NT 0800. ℂ 1800/891 100 in Australia, or 08/8946 0111. Fax 08/8981 5116. www.mirambeena.com.au. 225 units (all with shower only). A$157–A$217 (US$126–US$174) double; A$246 (US$197) town house for up to 4. Extra person A$27 (US$22). Children under 3 stay free in parent's room. AE, DC, MC, V. Free limited parking; street parking. Bus: 4, 5, 6, 8, or 10. **Amenities:** Restaurant; poolside cafe; 2 bars; 2 outdoor pools; children's pool; exercise room; 2 Jacuzzis; bike rental; game room; tour desk; secretarial services; limited room service; babysitting; coin-op laundry; laundry service; dry cleaning. In room: A/C, TV w/free movies, fridge, hair dryer, iron, safe.

The Summer House ★★ (Finds) A groovy, stylish tropical hideaway is a rare thing in the rough-and-ready Territory, but that's what Jill Farrand has created in her home in a converted apartment block. The place is in a leafy suburb 3km (2 miles) from town, on the local bus route. Two roomy suites sport white walls, trendy polished concrete floors, and wrought-iron furniture (one has giant Balinese armchairs and 3m-high/10-ft.

⌐ **Tips** **Where Can I Swim?**

Crocodiles and stingers render Darwin's lovely beaches a no-swim zone year-round. Locals sunbathe on Casuarina Beach and swim within view of the sea in **Lake Alexander** in East Point Reserve. About an hour's drive from the city, on the way to the Territory Wildlife Park, **Berry Springs Nature Park** has swimming holes along Berry Creek, with steps for easy access, and small waterfalls that create natural whirlpool action. They may be closed in the Wet season.

exotic flower arrangements), while a third has a retro look. All suites have louvered windows to encourage a breeze, hip mosaic bathrooms, one or two bedrooms, a living area, and a kitchenette. The two-bedroom unit has a TV. Jill delivers a nice continental breakfast. A Jacuzzi in the jungly garden is great for cooling off on hot nights. It's a gay-friendly place. Children are also welcome. No smoking indoors.

3 Quarry Crescent, Stuart Park (P.O. Box 104, Parap, NT 0820). ℂ **08/8981 9992.** www.interbed.com.au/summer house.htm. 3 units (all with shower only). A$120 (US$96) double; A$160 (US$128) 2-bedroom apt for up to 4. Rates include continental breakfast. AE, MC, V. Free parking. Bus: 5, 6, 8, or 10. From the airport, take the Stuart Hwy. 5km (3 miles) to Stuart Park; turn left onto Woolner Rd., right onto Iliffe St., right onto Armidale St., and left onto Quarry Crescent. **Amenities:** Jacuzzi; coin-op laundry. In room: A/C, kitchenette, hair dryer, iron, no phone.

INEXPENSIVE

Top End Hotel   This two-story hotel has a quiet ambience, despite the trendy complex of bars, restaurant, sports-betting outlets, and a liquor store on one side. Most of the rooms face a rectangular saltwater swimming pool surrounded by an inviting lawn, sun lounges, and tall palms rather than the bar complex. The front desk sells breakfast and dinner meat packs for you to cook on the barbie. The good-size rooms were renovated in 2000; each has quality fittings and a furnished patio or balcony. You're just across the road from the Esplanade (where fish come into shore at high tide to be hand-fed by visitors), close to restaurants, and a 1km (½-mile) stroll from Smith Street Mall.

Mitchell St. (at Daly St.), Darwin, NT 0801. ℂ **1800/626 151** in Australia, or 08/8981 6511. Fax 08/8941 1253. www. bestwestern.com.au/topend. 40 units (all with shower only). A$136 (US$109) double. AE, DC, MC, V. Free parking. Bus: 4, 5, 6, 8, or 10. **Amenities:** Restaurant; 3 bars; outdoor saltwater pool; tour desk; room service; babysitting; coin-op laundry; laundry service; dry cleaning. In room: A/C, TV w/free movies, fridge, coffeemaker.

Value Inn _Value_   The cheerful rooms at this neat little hotel in the Mitchell Street Tourist Precinct are extremely compact but tidy, with colorful modern fittings. Each room is just big enough to hold both a queen-size and a single bed, and a small writing table. The views aren't much, but you'll probably spend your time in the nearby cafes. Smith Street Mall and the Esplanade walking path are 2 blocks away. There is a public pay phone, cold drink and coffee vending machines, an iron on each floor, microwave ovens on the first and second floors, and a very small garden swimming pool off the parking lot.

50 Mitchell St., Darwin, NT 0800. ℂ **08/8981 4733.** Fax 08/8981 4730. www.valueinn.com.au. 93 units (all with shower only). A$59–A$99 (US$47–US$79) double. AE, MC, V. Limited free parking. **Amenities:** Outdoor pool; tennis courts; access to nearby golf course and gym; bike rental; tour desk; car-rental desk; coin-op laundry; dry cleaning. In room: A/C, TV, fridge, no phone.

WHERE TO DINE

Cullen Bay Marina, a 25-minute walk or a short cab ride from town, is packed with trendy restaurants and cafes. If it's Thursday, don't even think about eating anywhere other than the **Mindil Beach Sunset Market** ★★. And on Saturday, head to the suburban Parap markets for Asian goodies (see the box, "Cheap Eats & More!" below). The cool crowd hangs at **Roma Bar Cafe,** 9 Cavenagh St. (ℂ **08/8981 6729**), for good coffee and a cheap nosh; it's open from 7am to 5pm Monday through Friday, from 8am to 2pm Saturday and Sunday.

EXPENSIVE

Buzz Café ★★ MODERN AUSTRALIAN   This smart, busy waterfront cafe is as well known for its "loo with a view" as it is for its terrific food and relaxed atmosphere.

> ⸢*Value*⸥ **Cheap Eats & More!**
>
> If it's Thursday, join the entire city at the **Mindil Beach Sunset Market** 🍴🍴
> to feast at the 60 terrific (and cheap—most dishes are A$4–A$6/US$3.20–
> US$4.80 a serving!) Asian, Greek, Italian, and Aussie food stalls; listen to live
> music; wander among almost 200 arts-and-crafts stalls; and mix and mingle
> with masseurs, tarot card readers, and street performers as the sun sets into
> the sea. The action runs from 5 to 10pm in the Dry (approximately
> May–Oct). A smaller market of about 50 stalls runs Sunday between about
> mid-May and late September from 4 to 9pm. The markets' season changes
> from year to year, so if you're visiting Darwin on the seasonal cusp, in April
> or September, check whether they are on by calling the organizers
> (© **08/8981 3454**). The beach is about a A$7.50 (US$6) cab ride from town,
> or take bus no. 4. The Tour Tub's last run of the day, at 4pm (see "Getting
> Around," earlier in this chapter), goes by the markets.
>
> On Saturdays (7:30am–1:30pm), head to suburban **Parap Markets** 🍴,
> which transform a small street into a corner of Asia. The focus is on food,
> with a sprinkling of arts and crafts, and it's a favorite place for locals to have
> breakfast or brunch, choosing from the Southeast Asian soups, noodle
> dishes, and satays, washed down with fresh-squeezed tropical fruit drinks.
> The market stalls cover only about a block, on Parap Road in Parap (© **0438/
> 882 373** mobile).

The men's bathroom just nudges out the women's for interest value. Ladies, get a man
to take you in there to see what I mean—everybody does! The food is flavorsome East-
meets-West fare like jungle curry of chicken with snake beans and green peppercorns,
and pan-fried barramundi on potato mash in lemon-butter sauce; the lamb shanks are
so huge almost no one can finish them. Wash it down with a cocktail.

The Slipway, Cullen Bay Marina. © **08/8941 1141.** Reservations recommended in the Dry (May–Oct). Main courses
A$17–A$30 (US$14–US$24). AE, DC, MC, V. Mon–Fri noon–2am; Sat–Sun 10:30am–2am (brunch until 11:30am).
Bus: 4 or 6.

Hanuman 🍴 CONTEMPORARY THAI/NONYA/TANDOORI   Elegant black
walls and a moody Eastern atmosphere make this city restaurant popular as a business
venue by day and as a rendezvous for couples, families, and more business folk by
night. You can rely on it for interesting dishes such as roasted duck in a red curry of
coconut, fresh pineapple, kaffir lime, and sweet basil, or fish baked whole in banana
leaves, Melaccan-style, with ground galangal, hot chile, lemon grass, and kaffir lime
leaves. There is also a separate tandoori menu. Service is prompt and friendly.

28 Mitchell St. © **08/8941 3500.** Reservations recommended. Main courses A$17–A$24 (US$14–US$19). AE, DC,
MC, V. Mon–Fri noon–2:30pm; daily 6:30–11pm.

Pee Wee's at The Point 🍴🍴 MODERN AUSTRALIAN   Surrounded on three
sides by forest, this modern steel-and-glass venue affords views of Fannie Bay from
just about every table, inside, out on the deck, or down on the lawn. The owners—
two chefs and a sommelier—offer an extensive wine list that includes some older and

hard-to-find Australian wines. The food emphasizes fresh local produce and employs some interesting tastes. Some of the dishes have an Asian twist, and local fare includes kangaroo filet, ocean-caught saltwater barramundi, and local shell scallops—try them sizzled in lime-zest chile butter, with a marinated green-papaw salad. Get there in time to watch the sun set.

Alec Fong Lim Dr., East Point Reserve (4km/2½ miles from town). ℂ **08/8981 6868.** Reservations recommended, especially in the Dry (May–Oct). Main courses A$21–A$43 (US$17–US$34). AE, DC, MC, V. Daily 6pm–late. Closed Dec 26. Free parking. Cab fare from the city about A$15 (US$12).

MODERATE

Shenanigan's Irish Pub, Restaurant & Bar ✦ IRISH PUB FARE   Hearty Irish stews and braised beef–and–Guinness pies (plus the odd pint of Guinness itself) get everyone in the mood for eating, talking, and dancing at this convivial bar and restaurant. A friendly mix of solo travelers, families, seniors, and backpackers eat and drink in atmospheric wooden booths, standing up at bar tables, or by the fire. Besides hearty meat dishes, there is lighter stuff like salmon salad and vegetarian brochettes, and nightly specials, such as chicken and chile pasta or poached barramundi in white-wine sauce with fries and salad. Live bands play on Wednesday, Friday, Saturday, and Sunday nights.

69 Mitchell St. (at Peel St.). ℂ **08/8981 2100.** Reservations recommended. Main courses A$12–A$24 (US$9.60–US$19); daily specials A$9.50–A$14 (US$7.60–US$11). AE, DC, MC, V. Mon–Fri 10am–2am; Sat–Sun 11am–late.

INEXPENSIVE

Tim's Surf 'n' Turf ✦ *Value* *Kids* STEAK/SEAFOOD   Locals fairly bash down the door to get into this unpretentious restaurant under a cheap motel on the city fringe. The surroundings are not the attraction, so what is? Hearty, no-nonsense food cooked well, and served in portions big enough to feed an army. No namby-pamby steaks

---

Moments Movie Stars under the Stars

Lie back in a canvas deck chair under the stars at the **Deckchair Cinema** (ℂ **08/8981 0700;** www.deckchaircinema.com) to watch Aussie hits, foreign films, and cult classics. A move in 2004 to a new setting on the edge of Darwin Harbour (opposite Parliament House on the Esplanade) gave a new lease on life to this Darwin institution, run by the Darwin Film Society. Take a picnic dinner and get there early to soak up the scene: the twinkling lights from boats anchored in the Arafura Sea, and the fabulous sunsets. A smart new kiosk sells wine, beer, soft drinks, and snacks. There are 250 deck chairs as well as about 100 straight-backed seats, and staffers can supply cushions and even insect repellent if you need it. Entry is by a walkway from the Esplanade, or by car off Kitchener Drive (there's a parking lot). The box office opens at 6:30pm and movies start at 7:30pm daily in the Dry (Apr–Nov), with double features on Friday and Saturday. Tickets are A$13 (US$10) adults, A$6 (US$4.80) children, and A$30 (US$24) for a family of four, or A$20 (US$16) adults, A$9 (US$7.20) children, and A$45 (US$36) family for double features. You can only pay with cash, and no bookings are taken. (In the Wet, the movies screen indoors so call for details of the current venue.)

here—Tim's are monsters, up to 700 grams (26 oz.), over an inch thick, and grain-fed (a boon in Australia, where the beef is mostly grass-fed and a little chewy). Garlic prawns, crocodile schnitzel, lasagna, oysters, quiche, and roast of the day are typical menu items. There are meals for kids, who eat free before 6:30pm (one kid for each adult in the party). You'll get a complimentary port after dinner and free ice cream for dessert.

In the Asti Motel, Smith St. at Packard Place. © **08/8981 9979**. Main courses A$7–A$21 (US$5.60–US$17); many dishes around A$12 (US$9.60); seafood platter for 2 A$35 (US$28); crocodile from A$13 (US$10). AE, DC, MC, V. Daily 7–9am, noon–2pm, and 5:30–9:30pm. Bus: 4 or 6; bus stop within 100m (328 ft.).

DARWIN AFTER DARK

The gaming tables at the **Skycity Darwin Casino,** Gilruth Avenue, Mindil Beach (© **08/8943 8888**), are in play from noon until 4am Sunday to Thursday, until 6am Friday and Saturday. Slot machines operate 24 hours. The dress code allows neat jeans, shorts, and sneakers, but men's shirts must have a collar.

A good spot to catch Darwin's Technicolor sunsets is the supercasual **Darwin Sailing Club,** Atkins Drive on Fannie Bay (© **08/8981 1700**). Ask the manager to sign you in. Dine on affordable meals outdoors while a family of goannas (monitor lizards) swirls around your feet looking for meaty scraps. The bar is open from 10am until midnight Sunday through Thursday, and until 2am Friday and Saturday.

The cafes and restaurants of **Cullen Bay Marina** are a good place to be day or night, but especially for Dry season sunsets.

If it's Thursday, you are mad to be anywhere except the **Mindil Beach Sunset Market** ★★ (see "Cheap Eats & More!" above).

A SIDE TRIP TO LITCHFIELD PARK

120km (74 miles) S of Darwin

An easy 90-minute drive south of Darwin is a miniature Garden of Eden full of forests, waterfalls, rocky sandstone escarpments, glorious swimming holes, and prehistoric cycads that look as if they belong on the set of *Jurassic Park*. Litchfield National Park is much smaller (a mere 146,000 hectares/360,620 acres) and much less famous than its big sister, Kakadu, but it is no less stunning.

The park's main attractions are the spring-fed swimming holes, like the magical plunge pool at **Florence Falls** ★★★, 29km (18 miles) from the forest. It's a 15-minute hike down stairs to the water, so the easily accessible pool at **Wangi Falls** ★, 49km (30 miles) from the eastern entrance, gets more crowds. (It's a beautiful spot, surrounded by cliffs and forests with a lookout from the top.) More idyllic grottos are 4km (2½ miles) from Florence Falls at **Buley Rockhole,** a series of tiered rock pools and waterfalls. You can't swim at **Tolmer Falls,** but during the Wet when they're flowing, take the boardwalk about 400m (1,312 ft.) to the lookout and see the cascade against a backdrop of red cliffs.

There are a number of short **walking trails** through the park, such as the half-hour Shady Creek Circuit from Florence Falls up to the parking lot.

Parts of the park are also home to thousands of 2m-high (6½-ft.) **"magnetic" termite mounds,** so called because they run north-south to escape the fierce midday heat. (See a picture of the mounds in the color insert at the front of this book!) There are a display hut and a viewing point 17km (11 miles) from the park's eastern entrance.

Most of the park's swimming holes are regarded as crocodile-free; the same is *not* true of the Finniss and Reynolds rivers in the park, so no leaping into those!

To get there from Darwin, head south for 86km (53 miles) on the Stuart Highway and follow the park turnoff on the right through the town of Batchelor for 34km (21 miles). A number of minicoach and four-wheel-drive day trips run from Darwin. Katherine-based tour operator **Travel North** (© **1800/089 103** in Australia, or 08/8971 9999) runs a day tour to Litchfield that starts in Darwin and ends in Katherine, a convenient way to combine sightseeing and transport if you plan to visit both. It costs A$139 (US$111) adults and A$114 (US$91) children 5 to 15. Crowds of locals can shatter the peace in Litchfield on weekends, especially in the Dry season, but the park is worth visiting, crowds or no crowds.

The **Parks & Wildlife Commission** office in Batchelor, on the corner of Nurdina Street and Pinaroo Crescent (© **08/8987 8986**), has maps and information; most locations of interest have signboards. Entry to the park is free.

Roads to most swimming holes are paved, although a few are accessible only by four-wheel-drive. In the Wet season (approximately Nov–Apr), some roads—usually the four-wheel-drive ones—may be closed, and the Wangi water hole may be off-limits due to turbulence and strong currents. Check with the Parks & Wildlife Commission before you leave Darwin during this time.

A number of locations throughout the park have basic campsites. The camping fee per night is A$6.60 (US$5.30) for adults, A$3.30 (US$2.65) for kids under 16, or A$15 (US$12) for a family of two adults and four kids. A kiosk at Wangi Falls sells some supplies, but stock up on fuel and alcohol in Batchelor.

3 Kakadu National Park ⟨★

257km (159 miles) E of Darwin

Kakadu National Park, a World Heritage area, is Australia's largest national park, covering a massive 1.7 million hectares (4.3 million acres).

Cruising the lily-clad wetlands to spot crocodiles, plunging into exquisite natural swimming holes, hiking through spear grass and cycads, fishing for prized barramundi, soaring in a light aircraft over torrential waterfalls during the Wet season, photographing thousands of birds flying over the eerie red sandstone escarpment that juts 200m (650 ft.) above the flood plain, and admiring some of Australia's most superb Aboriginal rock-art sites—these are the activities that draw people to Kakadu. Some 275 species of birds and 75 species of reptiles inhabit the park, making it one of the richest wildlife habitats in the country.

Kakadu is an ecological jewel. But be aware that the vast distances between points of interest in the park, and the sameness that infects so much Australian landscape, can detract from Kakadu's appeal for some people. Wildlife here is not the breathtaking equivalent of an African game park, where herds roam the plains—which is why even Australians get so excited when they spot a kangaroo in the wild. It is best in the late Dry, around September and October, when crocs and birds gather around shrinking water holes. Wildlife viewing is not particularly good in the Wet season, when birds disperse widely and you may not see a single croc.

The name "Kakadu" comes from "Gagudju," the group of languages spoken by Aborigines in the northern part of the park, where they and their ancestors are believed to have lived for 50,000 years. Today, Aborigines manage the park as its owners with the Australian government. This is one of the few places in Australia where some Aborigines stick to a traditional lifestyle of hunting and living off the land. You won't see them, because they keep away from prying eyes, but their culture is on display at a cultural center and at rock-art sites. Kakadu and the vast wilds of Arnhemland to the east are the birthplace of the "X-ray" style of art for which Aboriginal artists are famous.

JUST THE FACTS

VISITOR INFORMATION   Both the park entrances—the northern station on the Arnhem Highway used by visitors from Darwin and the southern station on the Kakadu Highway for visitors from Katherine—hand out free visitor guides with maps. In the Dry they also issue a timetable of free ranger-guided bushwalks, art-site talks, and slide shows taking place that week. Entry to the park is free.

Park headquarters is at the **Bowali Visitor Centre** (📞 **08/8938 1120**), on the Kakadu Highway, 5km (3 miles) from Jabiru, 100km (62 miles) from the northern entry station, and 131km (81 miles) from the southern entry station. The attractive, environmentally friendly Outback-style center shows a program of 1-hour videos on the park's natural history and Aboriginal culture, stocks maps and park notes, has a library and displays, and has a gift shop and a cafe. Information officers are on hand to help you plan your visit (they provide tour times, costs, and telephone numbers, but do not make bookings). You may want to spend a good hour or so here, more to see a video. It is open daily from 8am to 5pm.

You can also book tours and get information at the **Jabiru Travel Centre,** Shop 6, Tasman Plaza, Jabiru, NT 0886 (📞 **08/8979 2548**).

Before you arrive, you can find information on Kakadu, and book tours to it, at the Tourism Top End visitor information center in Darwin. You can also contact the rangers at **Kakadu National Park** (📞 **08/8938 1120;** www.deh.gov.au/parks/kakadu).

WHEN TO GO   Kakadu has two distinct seasons: Wet and Dry. The Dry (May–Oct) is overwhelmingly the best time to go, with temperatures around 86°F (30°C) and sunny days. Many tours, hotels, and even campsites are booked a year in advance, so make sure you have reservations.

In the Wet season, November through April, floodwaters cover much of the park, some attractions are cut off, and the heat and humidity are extreme. Some tour companies do not operate during the Wet, and ranger talks, walks, and slide shows are not offered. The upside is that the crowds vanish, the brownish vegetation bursts into green, waterfalls swell from a trickle to a roar, and lightning storms are spectacular, especially in the hot "buildup" to the season in October and November. The landscape can change dramatically from one day to the next as floodwaters rise and fall, so be prepared for surprises—both nice ones (like giant flocks of geese) and unwelcome ones (like blocked roads). Although it can pour down all day, it's more common for the rain to fall in late-afternoon storms and at night. Take it easy in the humidity, and don't even think about camping in this heat—stay in air-conditioned accommodations.

GETTING THERE   Follow the Stuart Highway 34km (21 miles) south of Darwin, and turn left onto the Arnhem Highway to the park's northern entrance station. The trip takes 2½ to 3 hours. If you're coming from the south, turn off the Stuart Highway at Pine Creek onto the Kakadu Highway, and follow the Kakadu Highway for 79km (49 miles) to the park's southern entrance. **Greyhound Australia** (📞 **13 14 99** in Australia) travels daily (subject to seasonal and road conditions) from Darwin, stopping at Jabiru and Cooinda, for A$56 (US$45) round-trip.

A big range of coach, minibus, and four-wheel-drive tours and camping safaris, usually lasting 1, 2, or 3 days, depart from Darwin daily. These are a good idea, because many of Kakadu's geological, ecological, and Aboriginal attractions come to life only with a guide. The best water holes, lookouts, and wildlife-viewing spots change dramatically from month to month, even from day to day.

LOGISTICAL TIPS Kakadu is a big place—about 200km (124 miles) long by 100km (62 miles) wide—so plan to spend at least a night. Day trips are available from Darwin, but it's too far and too big to see much in a day.

Most major attractions are accessible in a two-wheel-drive vehicle on sealed (paved) roads, but a four-wheel-drive vehicle allows you to get to more falls, water holes, and campsites. Car-rental companies will not permit you to take two-wheel-drive vehicles on unpaved roads. **Thrifty** (© **08/8979 2552**) rents cars at the Gagadju Crocodile Holiday Inn, Flinders Street, Jabiru; otherwise, rent a car in Darwin. If you rent a four-wheel-drive in the Wet season (Nov–Apr), always check floodwater levels on all roads at the **Bowali Visitor Centre** (© **08/8938 1120**). The Bowali Visitor Centre, many attractions such as Nourlangie and Yellow Water Billabong, and the towns of Jabiru and Cooinda usually stay above the floodwaters year-round.

Facilities are limited. The only town of any size is **Jabiru** (pop. 1,455), a mining community where you can find banking facilities and a few shops. The only other real settlements are the park's four accommodations houses.

SEEING THE HIGHLIGHTS
EN ROUTE TO KAKADU

En route to the park, stop in at the **Fogg Dam Conservation Reserve** (© **08/8988 8009** is the ranger station), 25km (16 miles) down the Arnhem Highway and 7km (4⅓ miles) off the highway. You'll get a close-up look at geese, finches, ibis, brolgas, and other wetland birds from lookouts over ponds of giant lilies, or by walking through monsoon forests to viewing blinds. There are two lookouts on the road and three walks, two of 2.2km (1.5 miles) round-trip and one of 3.6km (2.25 miles) round-trip. Entry is free. Crocs live here, so don't swim, and keep well away from the water's edge. To take a ranger-guided walk, you must book by calling © **08/8999 4555.**

Four kilometers (2½ miles) down the Arnhem Highway at Beatrice Hill, you may want to stop at the **Window on the Wetlands Visitor Centre** (© **08/8988 8188**), a hilltop center with views across the Adelaide River flood plain and displays and touch-screen information on the wetlands' ecology. It's free and open daily from 7:30am to 7:30pm.

Just past Beatrice Hill on the highway at the Adelaide River Bridge (look out for the statue of a grinning croc), **Adelaide River Queen Cruises** (© **1800/888 542** in Australia, or 08/8988 8144) runs the original **jumping crocodiles cruise.** From the relative safety of a restored paddle steamer, you can watch wild crocodiles leap out of the water for hunks of meat dangled over the edge by the boat crew—but don't lean out too far! It's an unabashed tourist trap, with a souvenir shop that sells all things croc, including crocodile toilet seat covers. It may not be to my, or your, taste, but because crocs typically move fast only when they attack, it may be your only chance to witness their immense power and speed. The 90-minute cruise departs at 9 and 11am and 1 and 3pm May through August, and 9am, 11am, and 2:30pm September through April (closed Dec 24–25). The cruise costs A$36 (US$29) for adults, A$32 (US$26) for seniors, and A$20 (US$16) for children 5 to 15. If you need transport, **Darwin Day Tours** (© **08/8924 1111**) and **Goanna Eco Tours** (© **1800/003 880** in Australia) both run tours from Darwin that include the cruise.

Tips **Never Smile at a You-Know-What!**

The Aboriginal Gagudju people of the Top End have long worshipped a giant crocodile called Ginga, but the way white Australians go on about these reptilian relics of a primeval age, you'd think they worshipped them, too. There is scarcely a soul in the Northern Territory who will not regale you with his or her personal croc story, and each one will be more outrageous than the last.

Aussies may be good at pulling your leg with tall tales, but when they warn you not to swim in crocodile country, they're deadly serious. After all, crocodiles are good at pulling your leg, too—literally. Here are some tips:

1. There are two kinds of crocodile in Australia: the highly dangerous and enormously powerful saltwater or "estuarine" croc; and the "harmless" freshwater croc, which will attack only if threatened or accidentally stood on. Saltwater crocs can and do swim in the ocean, but they live in fresh water.

2. Don't swim in *any* waterway, swimming hole, or waterfall unless you have been specifically told it is safe. Take advice only from someone like a recognized tour operator or a park ranger. You can never be sure where crocodiles lurk from year to year, because during every Wet season crocs head upriver to breed, and they spread out over a wide flooded area. As the floodwaters subside, they are trapped in whatever water they happen to be in at the time—so what was a safe swimming hole last Dry season might not be croc-free this year.

3. Never stand on or walk along a riverbank, and stand well back when fishing. A 6m (20-ft.) croc can be 1 inch beneath the surface of that muddy water yet remain invisible. It moves fast, so you won't see it until you're in its jaws.

4. Plant your campsite and clean your fish at least 25m (82 ft.) back from the bank.

And if you do come face to face with a crocodile? There is little you can do. Just don't get into this situation in the first place!

TOP PARK ATTRACTIONS

WETLANDS CRUISES   One of Kakadu's biggest attractions is **Yellow Water Billabong,** a lake 50km (31 miles) south of the Bowali Visitor Centre at Cooinda (pop. about 20). It's rich with freshwater mangroves, Paperbarks, pandanus palms, water lilies, and masses of birds gathering to drink—sea eagles, honking magpie geese, kites, china-blue kingfishers, and jacanas, called "Jesus birds" because they seem to walk on water as they step across the lily pads. This is also one of the best places in the park to spot saltwater crocs. Cruises in canopied boats with running commentary depart near Gagudju Lodge Cooinda six times a day starting at 6:45am in the Dry (Apr–Nov) and four times a day starting at 8:30am in the Wet (Dec–Mar). A 90-minute cruise costs A\$40 (US\$32) for adults and A\$15 (US\$12) for children 2 to 14. A 2-hour cruise (available in the Dry only) costs A$45 (US$36) for adults and A$17 (US$14) for children. Book through **Gagudju Lodge Cooinda** (p. 431).

Fair warning: In the Wet, when the Billabong floods and joins up with Jim Jim Creek and the South Alligator River, the bird life spreads far and wide over the park and the crocs head upriver to breed, so don't expect wildlife viewing to be spectacular.

Another good cruise is the **Guluyambi East Alligator River Cruise** (✆ **1800/089 113** in Australia, or 08/8979 2411). The East Alligator River forms the border between Kakadu and isolated Arnhemland. Unlike the Yellow Water cruise, which focuses on crocs, birds, and plants, this excursion teaches you about Aboriginal myths, bush tucker, and hunting techniques. The cruise lasts 1 hour, starting at 9 and 11am, and 1 and 3pm daily May through October. A free shuttle will take you from the Border Store, at Manbiyarra just before the river, to the boat ramp. It costs A$30 (US$24) for adults and A$15 (US$12) for children 4 to 14.

ABORIGINAL ART & CULTURE   There are as many as 5,000 art sites throughout the park, though for cultural reasons the Aboriginal owners make only a few accessible to visitors. Dating the rock art is controversial, but some paintings may be 50,000 years old. The best are **Nourlangie Rock** and **Ubirr Rock.** Nourlangie, 31km (19 miles) southeast of the Bowali Visitor Centre, features "X-ray"-style paintings of animals; a vivid, energetic striped Dreamtime figure of **Namarrgon** ✦, the "Lightning Man"; and modern depictions of a white man in boots, a rifle, and a sailing ship. You'll also find rock paintings at **Nanguluwur,** on the other side of Nourlangie Rock, and a variety of excellent sites at Ubirr Rock, which is worth the steep 250m (820-ft.) climb for the additional art sites higher up the cliff, and for the views of the flood plain.

Ubirr Rock can be cut off in the Wet, but the views of afternoon lightning storms from the top at that time are breathtaking.

Moments   **A Side Trip to a Tiwi Island**

Separated from the northern mainland by a narrow strait are the Tiwi Islands, Bathurst and Melville. The Tiwi culture is distinct from that of the Aborigines, and one of the main reasons for visiting is to see firsthand their distinctive art style. **Tiwi Tours** (✆ **1800/811 633** in Australia, or 08/8922 2777) takes small groups on 1- and 2-day tours to Bathurst Island (Melville Island is closed to the public). They include visits to two art centers where you can watch artists at work and buy their paintings, carvings, silk-screen printing, and basketwork at "island prices"—usually up to a third cheaper than buying the same item in Darwin. You will learn the history of the islands, have morning tea with some Tiwi women and see them making baskets, and visit a mock burial site. The 2-day tour includes overnight camping. There are no commercial accommodations on the island, and the 1-day tour probably satisfies most people's curiosity. The 1-day tour costs A$325 (US$260) adults and A$275 (US$220) children; the 2-day tour is A$574 (US$459) adults and A$500 (US$400) children. Both include the round-trip light-plane airfare from Darwin (it's about a 30-min. flight) and meals. Tours operate Monday to Friday, except public holidays.

Unlike most sites in Kakadu, Ubirr is not open 24 hours—it opens at 8:30am April through November and at 2pm December through March, and closes at sunset year-round. There are a 1.5km (1-mile) signposted trail past Nourlangie's paintings (short trails to the art sites shoot off it), an easy 1.7km (1-mile) trail from the parking lot into Nanguluwur, and a 1km (.5-mile) circuit at Ubirr. Access to the sites is free.

Displays and videos about bush tucker, Dreamtime creation myths, and lifestyles of the local Bininj Aborigines are at the **Warradjan Aboriginal Cultural Centre** ⟨★⟩ (⟨𝒞⟩ **08/8979 0051**) at Cooinda. This building was built in the shape of a pig-nose turtle at the direction of the Aboriginal owners. It has a quality gift shop selling items like didgeridoos, bark paintings by local artists, and baskets woven from pandanus fronds. The center is open daily from 9am to 5pm, and admission is free. A 1km-long (.5-mile) trail connects it to Gagudju Lodge Cooinda and the Yellow Water Billabong.

SCENIC FLIGHTS   Scenic flights over the flood plains and the surprising rainforest-filled ravines of the escarpment are worth taking if the strain is not too great on your wallet. They're much more interesting in the Wet than in the Dry, because the flood plains spread and Jim Jim Falls and Twin Falls swell from their Dry season trickle to a roaring flood. Viewing it from the air is also the best way to appreciate the clever crocodile shape of the Gagudju Crocodile Holiday Inn. **North Australian Helicopters** (⟨𝒞⟩ **1800/898 977** in Australia, or 08/8972 2444) operates flights from Jabiru from A$80 (US$64), but to see Jim Jim and Twin Falls, you must take the flight costing A$420 (US$336) per person. **Kakadu Air Services** (⟨𝒞⟩ **1800/089 113** in Australia, or 08/8979 2411) runs 30-minute fixed-wing flights from Jabiru and Cooinda for A$86 (US$69) adult or A$58 (US$46) children 4 to 14.

SWIMMING, FISHING & BUSHWALKING IN THE PARK

In the eastern section of the park rises a massive red-sandstone escarpment that sets the stage for two waterfalls, **Jim Jim Falls** and **Twin Falls.** In the Dry, the volume of water may not be all that impressive, but the settings are magical. Both are accessible by four-wheel-drive only, and neither is open in the Wet. At Twin Falls, you must swim or float the last 500m (1,640 ft.) to the base of the falls—and be warned that saltwater crocodiles have been found in this area.

A campground near Jim Jim Falls and Twin Falls has sites for 200 people. **Garnamarr Campground** (named for the red-tailed black cockatoo commonly found in Kakadu) doesn't accept reservations, so check at the Bowali Visitor Centre (⟨𝒞⟩ **08/8938 1121**) before driving there, to see whether it is full. The campground manager collects the fee of A$5.40 (US$4.30) per adult per night (cash only). A gate at the campground controls access to Jim Jim and Twin Falls and is locked between 8:30pm and 6:30am.

WHERE CAN I SWIM?

Some people swim at spots that are generally regarded as croc-free, such as Jim Jim Falls and water holes such as Gubara (it's a long walk, but it can be lovely in the Wet), Maguk, and Koolpin Gorge. However, you do so at your own risk. Although rangers survey the swimming holes at the start of the season, and crocodiles are territorial creatures that stick to one spot, no one can guarantee that a saltwater crocodile has not moved into a swimming hole.

A good indication that a hole is croc-free is the presence of other people swimming. Crocs tend to eat whatever's moving pretty much immediately, so if people are swimming happily, the pool is almost certainly croc-free! Macabre it may be, but it's a tool

---

Moments A Swim in the Falls

Remember the idyllic pool that Paul Hogan and Linda Koslowski plunged into in *Crocodile Dundee?* That was **Gunlom Falls,** 170km (105 miles) south of the Bowali Visitor Centre. A climb to the top rewards you with great views of southern Kakadu. It is generally regarded as croc-free and safe for swimming. Access is by four-wheel-drive; it is cut off in the Wet.

---

many people use to gauge a pool's safety. Ask at the Bowali Visitor Centre which pools are croc-free that year (it can change from year to year) before setting off into the park. If you are unsure about a water hole's safety, the only place rangers recommend you swim is your hotel pool. Water hole depths change dramatically with the season. Check with the Bowali Visitor Centre for the swimming spots that are best at the time you visit.

A 1km (½-mile) walk over rocks and through rainforest leads to a **deep green plunge pool** ⚔ at Jim Jim Falls, 103km (64 miles) from the Bowali Visitor Centre. An almost perfectly circular 150m (492-ft.) cliff surrounds the water. Allow 2 hours to drive the final 60 unpaved kilometers (37 miles) off the highway. Due to floodwaters, Jim Jim Falls may not open until as late as June. At nearby Twin Falls, the waterfalls descend into a natural pool edged by a sandy beach, surrounded by bush and high cliffs.

Kakadu Gorge and Waterfall Tours ⚔ (book through Gagudju Lodge Cooinda; ✆ 08/8979 0145) runs an excellent small-group day trip for active people. You bushwalk into Jim Jim Falls for a swim and morning tea, four-wheel-drive through the bush, and then paddle in a canoe past a "friendly" freshwater crocodile (the kind that does not typically attack humans) to Twin Falls for swimming and lunch. Tours depart daily from Jabiru and Cooinda from May through November and cost A$135 (US$108) for adults, A$115 (US$92) for kids 4 to 14 (no kids under 4 allowed). Book in advance for July, the busiest month.

Kakadu's wetlands are brimful of barramundi, and Territorians like nothing more than to hop in a tin dinghy barely big enough to resist a croc attack and go looking for them. **Kakadu Fishing Tours** (book through Gagudju Lodge Cooinda; ✆ 08/8979 0145) takes you fishing in a 5m (17-ft.) sportfishing boat. Tours depart from Jabiru, 5km (3 miles) east of the Bowali Visitor Centre, and cost A$120 (US$96) per person for a half-day (A$190/US$152 if there is only one of you) and A$240 (US$192) per person for a full day. The company will pick you up from your Kakadu accommodations.

Wide-ranging **bush and wetlands walking trails,** including many short strolls and six half- to full-day treks, lead throughout the park. Typical trails include a .75km (less than .5-mile) amble through the Manngarre Monsoon Forest near Ubirr Rock; an easy 3.8km (2.5-mile) circular walk at the Iligadjar Wetlands near the Bowali Visitor Centre; and a tough 12km (7.5-mile) round-trip trek through rugged sandstone country at Nourlangie Rock.

One of the best wetlands walks is at **Mamukala wetlands,** 29km (18 miles) from Jabiru. Thousands of magpie geese feed here, especially in the late Dry season around October. An observation platform gives you a good view, and a sign explains the dramatic seasonal changes the wetlands undergo. Choose from a 1km (.5-mile) or 3km

(1.75-mile) round-trip meander. The Bowali Visitor Centre sells hiking-trail maps. There are also some challenging unmarked trails along creeks and gorges, for which you will need good navigational skills.

WHERE TO STAY & DINE

High season is usually from April 1 to late October or early November.

Gagudju Crocodile Holiday Inn ✦ Some people think this hotel is grossly kitsch; others declare it an architectural masterpiece. I liked it. It was built to the specifications of its owners, the Gagudju Aborigines, in the form of their spirit ancestor, a giant crocodile called Ginga. The building's entrance is the "jaws," the two floors of rooms are in the "belly," the circular parking lot clusters are "eggs," and so on. From the ground, it's hard to work out, but from the air the shape is quite distinct. Love it or hate it, it is the most luxurious place to stay in Kakadu, a stylish modern hotel with basic but comfortable rooms. Guests can use the town's 9-hole golf course, tennis courts, and Olympic-size swimming pool a few blocks away. The lobby doubles as an art gallery selling the works of local Aborigines, and a trail leads to the Bowali Visitor Centre.

1 Flinders St. (5km/3 miles east of Bowali Visitor Centre), Jabiru, NT 0886. ✆ **1300/666 747** in Australia, 800/465-4329 in the U.S. and Canada, 0800/405060 in the U.K., 1800/553 155 in Ireland, 0800/322 222 in New Zealand, or 08/8979 2800. Fax 08/8979 2707. www.gagudju-crocodile.holiday-inn.com. 110 units. A$205–A$250 (US$164–US$200) double. Discounts often available in the Wet. Children under 20 stay free in parent's room with existing bedding. Free crib. AE, DC, MC, V. **Amenities:** Restaurant; 2 bars; small outdoor pool; concierge; tour desk; car-rental desk; secretarial services; limited room service; babysitting; coin-op laundry; laundry service. *In room:* A/C, TV w/free movies, minibar, coffeemaker, hair dryer, iron.

Gagudju Lodge Cooinda These modest but pleasant accommodations are set among tropical gardens at the departure point for Yellow Water Billabong cruises. The simply furnished tile-floor bungalows are big and comfortable. They're air-conditioned, with ceiling fans, TVs, fridges, coffeemakers, and irons. You can request a hair dryer. Budget rooms are just bunk beds (four have double beds) in an air-conditioned corrugated iron demountable, or portable cabin, with shared bathrooms. They rent on a per-bed basis, so you may have to share with a stranger.

The lodge is something of a town center, with a general store, gift shop, currency exchange, post office, fuel, and other useful facilities. Cook up a 'roo steak at the nightly do-it-yourself barbecue in the rustic and ultracasual **Barra Bar & Bistro,** or go for the bush tucker a la carte meals at lunch or dinner in **Mimi's** ✦, which has a nice "bush sophisticated" ambience. The Barra Bistro serves a full buffet breakfast and an all-day snack menu, with live entertainment in the Dry season. Dining options can be limited between December and March, in the Wet. Scenic flights take off from the lodge's airstrip, and the Warradjan Aboriginal Cultural Centre is a 15-minute walk away.

Kakadu Hwy. (50km/31 miles south of Bowali Visitor Centre), Jim Jim, NT 0886. ✆ **1800/500 401** in Australia, 800/835-7742 in the U.S. and Canada, 0800/897 121 in the U.K., 1800/553 155 in Ireland, 0800/801 111 in New Zealand, or 08/8979 0145. Fax 08/8979 0148. www.gagudjulodgecooinda.com.au. 48 bungalows (all with shower only), 24 budget rooms (none with bathroom), 80 powered and 300 unpowered campsites. Lodge: A$198 (US$158) double. Extra person A$28 (US$22). Children under 14 stay free in parent's room. Free cots. Budget rooms: A$31 (US$25) per bed. Campsites: A$13 (US$10) per adult, powered; A$10 (US$8) per adult, unpowered. Children under 14 stay free in campsites. Bungalow and budget room discounts often available in Wet season. AE, DC, MC, V. **Amenities:** 2 restaurants; small outdoor pool; tour desk; babysitting; coin-op laundry.

4 Katherine

314km (195 miles) S of Darwin; 512km (317 miles) E of Kununurra; 1,177km (730 miles) N of Alice Springs

The key draw to the farming town of Katherine (pop. 11,000) is Katherine (Nitmiluk) Gorge. It's small by the standards of, say, the Grand Canyon, but its dramatic sheer orange walls dropping to a blue-green river make it an unexpected delight in the middle of the dry Arnhemland plateau that stretches to the horizon.

The gorge and its surrounding river ecosystem are in the 292,008-hectare (721,260-acre) **Nitmiluk National Park.** In the Dry, the gorge is a haven not just for cruisers but for canoeists, who must dodge the odd "friendly" freshwater crocodile as they paddle between the walls. In the Wet, the gorge can become a torrent at times, and jet boating is sometimes the only way to tackle it. Hikers will find trails any time of year throughout the park. Farther afield are hot springs, water holes, uncrowded rivers to canoe, and Aboriginal communities where visitors can make dot paintings and find bush tucker.

ESSENTIALS

GETTING THERE   **Greyhound Australia** (© **13 14 99** in Australia) buses stop in Katherine on their Darwin–Alice Springs routes. From Darwin, it's about a 4½-hour trip costing A$66 (US$53). From Alice, with departures once a day, it's about a 15-hour journey, for which the fare is A$192 (US$154). Greyhound also runs to Katherine daily from Broome via Kununurra, a journey of about 23 hours costing A$248 (US$198).

Visitors to Katherine can hop aboard the *Ghan* (see "Getting Around Australia" in chapter 2) in Adelaide or Alice Springs and hop off in Katherine. The train leaves Adelaide on Sunday at 5:15pm and Alice Springs on Monday at 4pm. The trip from Alice takes about 16 hours. One-way fares are A$240 (US$192) for a "day-nighter" seat or A$880 to A$1,150 (US$704–US$920) for a sleeper. Contact **Great Southern Railways** (© **13 21 47** in Australia; www.trainways.com.au) for details on connections from Sydney and Melbourne.

At press time, there were currently no airlines operating flights into Katherine.

Katherine is on the Stuart Highway, which links Darwin and Alice Springs. From Alice Springs, allow a good 2 days to make the drive. The Victoria Highway links Katherine with Kununurra to the west. There is no direct route from the east; from, say, Cairns, you need to go via Townsville, Mount Isa, and Tennant Creek, a long, dull journey.

VISITOR INFORMATION   The **Katherine Visitor Information Centre,** Lindsay Street at Katherine Terrace, Katherine, NT 0850 (© **1800/653 142** or 08/8972 2650; www.krta.com.au), has information on things to see—not only all around Katherine, but as far afield as Kakadu National Park and the Kimberley. It's open Monday through Friday from 8:30am to 6pm and weekends from 10am to 3pm in the Dry season; in the Wet it's open Monday through Friday from 9am to 5pm.

The **Nitmiluk Visitor Centre,** on the Gorge Road, 32km (20 miles) from town (© **08/8972 1886**), dispenses information on the Nitmiluk National Park and sells tickets for gorge cruises, which depart outside. The center has maps; displays on the park's plant life, birds, geology, and Aboriginal history; a gift shop; and a cafe. It's open daily from 7am to 7pm, sometimes closing a little earlier in the Wet. Entry to the park is free.

GETTING AROUND   Hertz (℡ 08/8971 1111), **Europcar** (℡ 08/8971 2777), and **Thrifty** (℡ 08/8972 3183) have outlets in Katherine.

Travel North (℡ 1800/089 103 in Australia, or 08/8971 9999) makes transfers from Katherine hotels to the cruise, canoe, and helicopter departure points at the Nitmiluk Visitor Centre three times a day. Round-trip fares are A$21 (US$17) for adults and A$11 (US$8.80) for children. Most Katherine activities and attractions can be booked through Travel North. The company runs many local tours and activities, such as horseback cattle musters, visits to an old homestead, half-day trips to Mataranka Thermal Pools (see below), and tours of up to 5 days taking in Katherine, Darwin, Litchfield and Kakadu national parks, and outlying Aboriginal communities.

For personalized tours both off the beaten path and around town, contact **Far Out Adventures** ✦ (℡ 0427 152288 mobile), described below.

EXPLORING KATHERINE GORGE (NITMILUK NATIONAL PARK)

Cruising the gorge in an **open-sided boat** is the most popular way to appreciate its beauty. Katherine Gorge is actually a series of 13 gorges, but most cruises ply only the first two, because the second gorge is the most photogenic.

Travel North (see "Getting Around," above) operates all cruises. Most people take the 2-hour cruise, which departs four times a day and costs A$40 (US$32) for adults and A$16 (US$13) for children 5 to 15. There is also a 4-hour cruise at least once daily, although you will probably be satisfied with 2 hours. An 8-hour cruise-hike safari to the fifth gorge is available from about May to mid-October only. Wear sturdy shoes; because each gorge is cut off from the next by rapids, all the cruises involve some walking along the bank.

In the height of the Wet season, the cruises may not operate when the floodwaters really start to swirl. Instead, Travel North runs a **jet boat** as far as the third gorge. This 45-minute adventure costs A$49 (US$39) for adults and A$35 (US$28) for kids 5 to 15. Departure times vary with the floodwater conditions.

Cruising is nice, but in a **canoe** ✦ you can discover sandy banks and waterfalls, and get up close to the gorge walls, the birds, and those crocs. (Don't worry—they're the freshwater kind and not typically regarded as dangerous to humans.) Rocks separate the gorges, so be prepared to carry your canoe quite often. You may even want to camp out on the banks overnight. A half-day canoe rental from Travel North is A$33 (US$26) for a single canoe and A$49 (US$39) for a double, with a A$20 (US$16) cash deposit. Canoeing the gorge is popular, so book canoes ahead, especially in the Dry season.

Guided paddles are a good idea, because you will learn and see more. The most knowledgeable company is **Gecko Canoeing** ✦ (℡ 1800/634 319 in Australia, or 08/8972 2224; www.geckocanoeing.com.au), whose tours are known for their ecotourism content. Gecko's guides have Australia's elite Savannah Guide status. They offer 3- to 7-day canoeing-camping safaris on the Katherine River, as well as a 1-day canoe safari at a cost of A$178 (US$142) per person. The company also runs canoeing and camping safaris (with any other activities you like, such as mountain biking, rock climbing, wildlife photography, hiking, or fishing) of up to 18 days in little-explored wildernesses and river systems across the Top End. Tours run only between April and November, with departures on request, and can be tailored to your needs.

Some 100km (62 miles) of **hiking trails** crisscross Nitmiluk National Park, ranging in duration from 1 hour to the lookout to 5 days to Edith Falls (see below).

Trails—through rocky terrain and forests, past water holes, and along the gorge—depart the Nitmiluk National Park ranger station, in the Nitmiluk Visitor Centre, where you can pick up trail maps. Overnight walks require a deposit of A$20 to A$50 (US$16–US$40) per person, and a A$3.30 (US$2.65) per-person camping permit, payable at the Nitmiluk Visitor Centre.

One of the nicest spots in the park is 42km (26 miles) north of Katherine, 20km (13 miles) off the Stuart Highway. **Edith Falls** ✸ is an Eden of natural (croc-free) swimming holes bordered by red cliffs, monsoonal forest, and pandanus palms. Among the bushwalks leading from Edith Falls is a 2.6km (1.5-mile) round-trip trail, which takes about 2 hours and incorporates a dip at the upper pool en route.

More than the gorge itself, the aerial views of the ravine-ridden Arnhem Plateau, which stretches uninhabited to the horizon, are arresting. **North Australian Helicopters** (✆ **1800/621 717** in Australia, or 08/8972 1666) offers daily flights of 3, 8, and all 13 gorges for A$60 to A$180 (US$48–US$144) per person, adult or child. Take at least an eight-gorge flight to get a sense of Australia's wild vastness. In the Wet, flights from Katherine take travelers to see Jim Jim Falls in Kakadu National Park.

ABORIGINAL CULTURE TOURS, HOT SPRINGS & MORE

On a 1-day visit to the **Manyallaluk Aboriginal community** ✸, a 90-minute drive southeast from Katherine, you chat with Aborigines about how they balance traditional ways with modern living; take a short bushwalk to look for native medicines and bush tucker like green ants (they're refreshing!); try lighting a fire with two sticks, weaving baskets, throwing spears, painting on bark, and playing a didgeridoo; and take a dip in a natural water hole. You can buy locally made Aboriginal art and artifacts at better prices than you may find elsewhere. Lunch is a barbecue featuring stuff like high-grade kangaroo filet, kangaroo tail, Scotch filet steak, or barramundi cooked on hot coals. Some visitors rush into these tours and expect the community to be a kind of Aboriginal theme park with a new attraction every 10 minutes, but that's not how it is. It's an unstructured experience (this is the community's home), so it's up to you to take part.

A 1-day tour from Katherine costs A$143 (US$114) for adults and A$79 (US$63) for children 5 to 15, or A$110 (US$88) adults and A$67 (US$54) for kids if you drive yourself. There are basic camping facilities, including tent sites and powered and unpowered sites. The last 35km (22 miles) of road is unsealed (unpaved), and rental cars will be insured only if they are four-wheel-drive. The tour runs Monday through Friday from April to September, and Monday, Wednesday, and Friday in October and November, but hours may be reduced, or the place may close, in the Wet. Call ahead before setting off no matter what the time of year, because sometimes the place closes for cultural reasons. Call Manyallaluk—The Dreaming Place (✆ **08/8975 4727**), or book through Travel North (see "Getting Around," above).

About 110km (68 miles) south of Katherine, you can soak your aches away at the **Mataranka Thermal Pools.** The man-made pools are fed by 93°F (34°C) spring water, which bubbles up from the earth naturally at a rate of 16,495 liters (4,124 gal.) per minute! It's a little paradise, surrounded by palms, pandanus, and a colony of flying foxes. The pools are open 24 hours, and admission is free. They are 7km (4⅓ miles) along Homestead Road, which is off the Stuart Highway 1.5km (1 mile) south of Mataranka township. They make a welcome stop on the very long drive from Alice Springs.

If you can't be bothered to drive to Mataranka, you can soak in the pleasantly warm **Katherine Hot Springs,** under shady trees 3km (2 miles) from town on Riverbank Drive. Entry is free.

At the **School of the Air,** Giles Street (ℭ **08/8972 1833**), you can sit in on an 800,000-sq.-km. (312,000-sq.-mile) "classroom" as children from the Outback do their lessons by radio. Forty-five-minute tours begin on the hour at 9am, 10am, 11am, 1pm, and 2pm. Tours also run during school holidays and public holidays, minus the on-air classes. The school is open Monday through Friday from 9am to 3pm, mid-March to mid-December. Admission is A$5 (US$4) for adults and A$2 (US$1.60) for school-age kids.

Mike Keighley of **Far Out Adventures** ⚘ (ℭ **0427/152 288**) runs upmarket tailor-made tours that include areas around Katherine such as the 5,000-sq.-km. (1,930-sq.-mile or 1.2-million-acre) Elsey Cattle Station, 140km (87 miles) southeast of Katherine, made famous as the setting of the Aussie book and film *We of the Never Never.* Meet children of the Mangarrayi Aborigines, sample bush tucker, learn a little bush medicine, and swim in a vine-clad natural "spa-pool" in the Roper River. Mike has been accepted as an honorary family member of the Mangarrayi people and is a mine of information about Aboriginal culture and the bush.

WHERE TO STAY

The Nitmiluk National Park ranger station in the Nitmiluk Visitor Centre has maps of available "bush campsites" throughout the park. These are very basic sites—no showers, no soaps or shampoos allowed (they pollute the river system), and simple pit toilets or none at all. Most are beside natural swimming holes. You must stop for a camping permit at the ranger station beforehand; the camping fee is A$3.30 (US$2.65) per person per night.

Travel North runs the **Nitmiluk Gorge Caravan Park** (ℭ **1800/089 103** in Australia, or 08/8972 1253; fax 08/8972 3989), next to the Nitmiluk Visitor Centre, where wallabies often hop into the grounds. Fees are A$9 (US$7.20) per adult, A$5.50 (US$4.40) per child for a tent site, and A$22 (US$18) double for a powered site (A$9/US$7.20 for each extra person).

Knotts Crossing Resort At this low-key resort, you have a choice of huge, well-furnished motel rooms, some with kitchenettes, minibars, and in-room dataports and fax machines; cabins with a kitchenette inside and a private bathroom just outside the door (but no phone); or campgrounds, all located amid the tropical landscaping. The "village" rooms are a good budget choice, built in 1998 and smartly furnished with a double bed and bunks, a kitchenette, and a joint veranda facing a small private pool with a barbecue. Locals meet at the casual bar beside the pool, and **Katie's Bistro** is one of the smartest places to eat in town.

Corner of Giles and Cameron sts., Katherine, NT 0850. ℭ **1800/222 511** in Australia, or 08/8972 2511. Fax 08/8972 2628. www.knottscrossing.com.au. 123 units (some with shower only), 75 powered and unpowered campsites. A$75 (US$60) double cabin; A$100 (US$80) double "village" room; A$125–A$150 (US$96–US$116) double motel room; A$145 (US$108) motel family room for 4. Extra adult A$10 (US$8); extra child under 13 A$5 (US$4). Unpowered site A$10 (US$8) per person per night. Powered site A$22 (US$18) per night single or double; extra adult A$10 (US$8); extra child A$5 (US$4). Rates include transfers from airport or bus stop. AE, DC, MC, V. **Amenities:** Restaurant; bar; 2 outdoor pools (1 large and attractive, 1 small); Jacuzzi; tour desk; car-rental desk; limited room service; coin-op laundry; laundry service; dry cleaning. *In room:* A/C, TV w/pay movies, fridge.

10

Perth & Western Australia

by Lee Mylne

Many international visitors—and for that matter, many east coast Australians—never make it to Western Australia. It's too far away, too expensive to fly to, and too big when you get there, they say. That's all true, especially about its size (2.5 million sq. km/975,000 sq. miles), but don't dismiss a trip out of hand. Domestic flights are getting cheaper all the time, and international travelers can use air coupons (see chapter 2). It's worth the trip for some of Australia's best snorkeling and diving, most historic towns, splendid natural scenery, and fantastic wine regions. Every spring (that's Sept–Nov Down Under), wild-flowers carpet much of the state. The capital, **Perth** ⭐, has great food, a fabulous outdoor life of biking and beaches, plenty of smallish museums well worth a look, and a beautiful historic port, Fremantle.

The **Southwest** ⭐⭐ "hook" of the state, below Perth, is the prettiest part of Western Australia, and the easiest region to visit outside of Perth. Massive stands of karri and jarrah trees stretch to the sky, the surf is world-class, and the coastline is rugged. The Southwest's Margaret River region turns out some of Australia's most acclaimed wines. En route to the Southwest is a special phenomenon—a visit by **wild dolphins** ⭐⭐ to the town of Bunbury. You can swim with them, if they are in the mood for socializing.

Head east 644km (400 miles) inland from Perth and you strike what, in the 1890s, was the richest square mile of gold-bearing earth the world has ever seen. The mining town of **Kalgoorlie** ⭐, still Australia's biggest gold producer (nearly 2,000 oz. a day), is a place of ornate 19th-century architecture. If Australia has an answer to the Wild West, Kalgoorlie is it.

Head north of Perth and you're in the Outback. Red sands, scrubby trees, and spinifex grass are all you see for hundreds of miles. About 850km (527 miles) north of Perth, wild dolphins make daily visits to the shores of Monkey Mia. Another 872km (541 miles) on is one of Australia's best-kept secrets, a 260km (161-mile) coral reef called **Ningaloo** ⭐⭐, along the isolated Outback shore. It's a second, largely undiscovered, Great Barrier Reef.

The rugged northwest portion of Western Australia is known as **the Kimberley,** where cattle farming, pearl farming, and tourism thrive in a rocky moonscape of red cliffs, waterfalls, rivers, sparse gums, and wetland lagoons. Here you can visit a million-acre cattle station (ranch) rich in Aboriginal rock-art sites, tour the world's largest diamond mine, cruise the lush Ord River to see hundreds of native birds, ride a camel on the beach, and shop for the world's biggest South Sea pearls.

Western Australia

EXPLORING THE STATE

VISITOR INFORMATION The **Western Australian Tourism Commission** is the official source of information on the state. Its website (www.westernaustralia.com) provides a good overview, and you may find the **Australian Tourist Commission**'s website (www.australia.com), or the Web pages of local tourism boards (see "Visitor Information" in each regional section of this chapter) useful. A private company, **Visit WA** (www.visitwa.com.au), offers an online tour-planning service.

Also contact the **Western Australia Visitor Centre** in Perth, which dispenses information about the state and makes bookings. See section 1 of this chapter for information. The Department of Conservation and Land Management website (www.calm.wa.gov.au) has information on national and marine parks.

WHEN TO GO Perth is blessed with long, dry summers and mild, wet winters. You'll want warm gear in the Southwest in winter, but temperatures rarely hit the freezing point. Far north of Perth, summer is hell; temperatures soar to between 104°F and 120°F (40°C–49°C). Avoid these parts from December to March; February is worst. Winter (June–Aug) in the mid-, northern, and inland reaches of the state is pleasantly cool—warm enough for ocean swimming—and sometimes even hot.

GETTING AROUND Before you plan a driving tour of this state, consider the distances (it's three times as big as Texas) and the mostly flat, monotonous countryside. The Southwest forests make pretty driving; elsewhere, you should fly, especially if time is a factor.

If you do hit the road, remember that Western Australia is largely devoid of people, gas stations (keep the gas tank full!), and emergency help. Road trains and wildlife pose more of a threat on the roads than in any other state. Avoid driving at night, dusk, and dawn—all prime animal-feeding times. Read "Road Conditions & Safety," in "Getting Around Australia" in chapter 2, before setting off.

The **Royal Automobile Club of Western Australia,** 228 Adelaide Terrace, Perth, WA 6000 (© **13 17 03;** www.rac.com.au), is a good source of maps and motoring advice. For a recorded road-condition report, call **Main Roads Western Australia** (© **1800/013 314** in Australia).

Skywest (© **1300/660 088** in Australia; www.skywest.com.au) is the state's major regional airline. **Qantas** (© **13 13 13** in Australia; www.qantas.com.au) also provides service to smaller centers.

Greyhound Australia (© **13 14 99** in Australia) is the only interstate coach company serving Western Australia. It travels from Adelaide to Perth, up the coast to Broome, and across to Darwin. The only train to Western Australia from outside the state is the *Indian Pacific* ⚘, from Sydney via Adelaide and Kalgoorlie to Perth (see "Getting Around Australia," in chapter 2). Inside the state, long-distance trains run only in the southern third. They are operated by the **Public Transport Authority (PTA),** also known as TransWA (© **1300/662 205** in Western Australia, or 08/9326 2600; www.transwa.wa.gov.au), from Perth to Bunbury, 2¼ hours south of Perth; to Northam, an hour or so east in the Avon Valley; and to Kalgoorlie. TransWA also runs coach services north to Kalbarri, Geraldton, and Meekatharra, to the southwest regions of Augusta and Pemberton, south to Albany and east to Esperance.

All major car- and motor-home-rental companies have offices in Perth.

TOUR OPERATORS Western Australia's two biggest coach tour companies, **Australian Pinnacle Tours** (© **1800/999 069** in Australia, or 08/9417 5555;

www.pinnacletours.com.au) and **Feature Tours** (© **1800/999 819** in Australia, or 08/9475 2900; www.ft.com.au) serve Perth, the Southwest, Monkey Mia, the North-west Cape, and attractions about a day's drive away, such as Wave Rock (a large, wave-shaped rock; see the box "Catching a Silent Wave," below) and the Pinnacles (weird limestone formations in the desert). Australian Pinnacle Tours also does four-wheel-drive tours. **Overland 4WD Safaris** (© **08/9524 7122**) runs four-wheel-drive safaris with an off-the-beaten-track bent from Perth throughout the state.

Aerial tours make sense in Western Australia. Look into the personalized or set tours offered by **Complete Aviation Services** (© **1800/632 221** in Australia, or 08/9478 2749; www.casair.com.au) or **Kookaburra Air** (© **08/9354 1158**; www.kookaburra.iinet.net.au). Tours from Perth can take you throughout Western Australia, including the Kimberley, the Top End, and the Red Centre.

Landscope Expeditions ★★ is an excellent tour program run by the state Conservation and Land Management Department, or CALM. The University of Western Australia handles bookings (© **08/6488 2433**; fax 08/6488 1066 for a free schedule; www.calm.wa.gov.au). You'll be helping CALM scientists on research projects, such as monitoring endangered loggerhead turtles on Dirk Hartog Island, studying Australia's sea lion colonies in the Abrolhos Islands near the edge of the continental shelf, or recording animal and plant species in Cape Arid National Park on the south coast, among others.

Moments   **Tiptoeing through the Wildflowers**

Every year from August to mid-November, the southern half of Western Australia is blessed with a carpet of 12,000 species of white, yellow, mauve, pink, red, and blue **wildflowers** ★★.

Wildflower shows and festivals in country towns throughout the state accompany the annual blossoming, and coach- and rail-tour companies ferry enthusiasts from all around Australia and the globe on wildflower tours. You can check out the wildflowers on day trips from Perth or on longer jaunts of up to 5 days or so. September and October are the peak months.

If time is short, you can go to Perth's Kings Park & Botanic Garden (p. 454), which conducts free guided walks through its 2,000 species during its 10-day Wildflower Festival every September.

Because Australian flora is adapted to desert conditions, it tends to sprout on dry, sunny days following a rain shower. The Western Australian Tourism Commission's Perth Visitor Centre (see "Visitor Information," below) can keep you up to speed on whatever spot is blooming brightest that week, and the staff can book you on one of the coach and rail wildflower tours. The commission produces a 40-page **Wildflower Holiday Planner** brochure that describes self-drive wildflower routes, accommodations and events en route, and wildflower tour operators. Download it from the commission's website (www.westernaustralia.com).

Interstate buses, trains, and hotels fill up fast in wildflower season, so book ahead.

> (*Moments* **Catching a Silent Wave**
>
> The incredible **Wave Rock** ★★, a 4-hour drive east of Perth, attracts thousands of visitors each year. Standing 15m (49 ft.) tall and running for 110m (361 ft.), the multicolored "wave" of granite has been shaped by wind and water over an estimated 500 million years. Stand at its base, and it feels as if a huge, silent surf wave will break right on top of you!
>
> Wave Rock is about 340km (210 miles) east of Perth, near the wheat-belt town of Hyden. See "Tour Operators" above for details on two companies that stop here.

1 Perth ★

4,405km (2,731 miles) W of Sydney; 2,389km (1,481 miles) S of Broome

Perth likes to boast that it gets more sunshine than any other city in Australia, some 300 days a year. That fact gives the city its youthful, energetic, outdoorsy vibrancy. Tall silver buildings glint in a blue sky, and the sparkling ocean and glorious white beaches are just a bus ride from downtown. There's so much to do here. Wander through the impressively restored historic warehouses, museums, and working docks of bustling **Fremantle;** stock up at the plentiful Aboriginal art and souvenir stores; visit great art galleries and museums; eat at some of the country's best restaurants; go snorkeling and sea kayaking with wild sea lions; bushwalk through a 400-hectare (1,000-acre) park in the middle of the city; and pedal your bike to a great snorkeling spot on **Rottnest Island** ★★, a miniature reef resort 19km (12 miles) offshore.

More than most other Aussie capitals, Perth gives you good choices of side trips: Drop in on the Benedictine monks in the Spanish Renaissance monastery town of **New Norcia** ★, nip out to the Swan Valley vineyards, or spend a few days in **Margaret River** ★★ country, one of Australia's top wine regions. The long, dry summer is the best time to visit; winter is rainy.

ORIENTATION

ARRIVING By Plane Qantas (© **13 13 13** in Australia; www.qantas.com.au) flies at least once a day from all mainland capitals as well as Broome and Cairns. **Qantaslink** flies direct from Alice Springs, Uluru (Ayers Rock), and several small towns in Western Australia. **Virgin Blue** (© **13 67 89** in Australia; www.virginblue.com.au) flies direct from Sydney, Melbourne, Adelaide, Brisbane, the Gold Coast, and Broome, with connections from other cities.

Perth Airport is 12km (7½ miles) northeast of the city. Allow 15 to 20 minutes to transfer between the international and domestic terminals. Both have ATMs, showers, baby-changing rooms, a mailbox (newsdealers sell stamps), and limited tourist information. Internet kiosks and currency-exchange bureaus are in the international and Qantas domestic terminals. The international terminal has cellphones for rent. At the international terminal, look out for Customer Service Officers in bright gold jackets. **Avis** (© 08/9277 1177 domestic terminal, 08/9477 1302 international terminal), **Budget** (© 08/9277 9277), **EuropCar** (© 08/9226 5033), **Hertz** (© 08/9479 4788), and **Thrifty** (© 13 12 86 in WA) have desks at both terminals.

Perth

ACCOMMODATIONS ■
Duxton Hotel Perth **12**
The Melbourne **5**
Mercure Hotel Perth **13**
Miss Maud Swedish Hotel **15**
River View on Mount Street **9**
The Sebel Perth **14**
Sullivans Hotel **10**
Sebel Residence, East Perth **18**

DINING ◆
Basil Leaves Cafe **21**
Fast Eddy's Café **4**
44 King Street **6**
Fraser's **7**
Miss Maud Swedish
  Restaurant **15**
Mount Street Café & Food Store **9**
Vultures Restaurant & Café **1**

ATTRACTIONS ●
Aquarium of Western Australia **20**
Art Gallery of Western Australia **3**
Cohunu Koala Park **17**
Holmes à Court Gallery **19**
Kings Park & Botanic Garden **8**
Perth Mint **16**
Perth Zoo **11**
Western Australian Museum **2**

The **Airport City Shuttle** (© **08/9277 7958**) meets all flights within 30 to 45 minutes of customs clearance or luggage collection for domestic flights. There is no need to book. City transfers from the international terminal cost A$13 (US$10) adults one-way; from the domestic terminal, A$11 (US$8.80) adults one-way. Transfers between the domestic and international terminals are A$9 (US$7.20). The **Fremantle Airport Shuttle** (© **1300/668 687** in Australia, or 08/9335 1614) operates regular service each day from the airport to hotels or anywhere else in Fremantle; you must book in advance. The fare is A$20 (US$16) per person and gets cheaper the bigger your group is—down to A$10 (US$8) per person for three or more people traveling together.

Public **bus** no. 37 runs to the city from the domestic terminal. No buses run from the international terminal. A **taxi** to the city is about A$28 (US$22) from the international terminal and A$21 (US$17) from the domestic terminal, including a A$2 (US$1.60) fee for picking up a taxi at the airport.

By Train   The 3-day journey to Perth from Sydney via Broken Hill, Adelaide, and Kalgoorlie aboard the *Indian Pacific* ✺, operated by Great Southern Railway (© **13 21 47** in Australia; www.trainways.com.au), is an experience. The train runs twice a week each direction. The one-way fare ranges from A$1,640 (US$1,312) in first class with meals and en-suite bathroom, to A$1,250 (US$1,000) in comfy second class (meals cost extra, and bathrooms are shared), down to A$513 (US$410) for sit-up-all-the-way coach class (not a good idea). Connections are available from Melbourne on the *Overland* train. See "Getting Around Australia" in chapter 2 for contact details in Australia and abroad. The **Prospector** train makes the 7¾-hour trip from Kalgoorlie daily; call the **Public Transport Authority** (**PTA;** © **1300/662 205** in Western Australia, or 08/9326 2600; www.transwa.wa.gov.au).

All long-distance trains pull into the East Perth Terminal, Summers Street off Lord Street, East Perth. A taxi to the city center costs about A$10 (US$8).

By Bus   **Greyhound Australia** (© **13 14 99** in Australia) runs daily from Sydney (trip time: 60 hr.) to Adelaide and once a week from Adelaide to Perth (about 36 hr.). It also has service daily from Darwin via Kununurra and Broome (about 59 hr.). Traveling from Alice Springs requires a connection in Adelaide and takes about 55 hours. The Sydney-Perth fare is A$428 (US$342), Adelaide-Perth is A$287 (US$230), Darwin-Perth is A$615 (US$492), and Alice Springs–Perth is A$499 (US$399).

By Car   There are only two interstate routes—the 2,389km (1,481-mile) route from Broome in the north, and the 2,708km (1,679-mile) odyssey from Adelaide, which includes hundreds of miles along some of the world's straightest roads on the treeless Nullarbor Plain. Arm yourself with an up-to-date road map before setting off. It's not a bad idea to contact the South Australian or Western Australian state auto clubs (listed under "Getting Around Australia," in chapter 2) for advice on crossing the lonely Nullarbor. Both routes are mostly featureless and semidesert, passing sheep ranches or wheat fields most of the way, with very few towns en route. For that reason, I don't recommend either!

VISITOR INFORMATION   The **Western Australian Visitor Centre,** Albert Facey House, 469 Wellington St. at Forrest Place, Perth (© **1300/361 351** in Australia, or 08/9483 1111; www.westernaustralia.com), is the official visitor information source for Perth and the state. It's open Monday through Thursday from 8:30am to 6pm (to 5:30pm in winter, May–July), Friday from 8:30am to 7pm (to 6pm in winter), and

Saturday from 8:30am to 12:30pm year-round. The City of Perth's **i-City Information Kiosk,** in the Murray Street Mall near Forrest Place, is open Monday to Thursday and Saturday 9:30am to 4:30pm, Friday 9:30am to 8pm, and Sunday noon to 4:30pm (closed public holidays). Volunteer staff members lead free 90-minute guided tours Monday to Friday at 11am and 2pm, Saturday at 11am, and Sunday at 2pm. There's no need to book. Another source of information and maps (plus a free booking service) is **Perth Tourist Lounge,** Level 2, Carillon Arcade off 207 Murray St. Mall (© **08/9481 4400;** www.perthtourist.com.au), open Monday through Saturday 9am to 5:30pm, Sunday noon to 5pm (closed public holidays).

For an untouristy lowdown on the city's restaurants, cultural life, shops, bars, nightlife, concerts, and the like, buy the excellent glossy quarterly magazine *Scoop* (A$9.95/US$7.95; www.scoop.com.au), available in bigger newsstands.

CITY LAYOUT   The city center is 19km (12 miles) upriver from the Indian Ocean, on the north bank of a broad reach of the Swan River. **Hay Street** and **Murray Street** are the two major thoroughfares, 1 block apart; pedestrian malls between William and Barrack streets bisect both. It helps to know that Adelaide Terrace becomes St. Georges Terrace at Victoria Avenue.

MAPS   Of the many free pocket guides to Perth available at tour desks and in hotel lobbies, *Your Guide to Perth & Fremantle* (Countrywide Publications) has the **best street map.** It shows one-way streets, public toilets and telephones, taxi stands, post offices, police stations, and street numbers, as well as most attractions and hotels. The **Royal Automobile Club of Western Australia** (see "Exploring the State," above) is a good source of maps to the state, as is **The Perth Map Centre,** 900 Hay St. (© **08/9322 5733**). You will find tourist maps at the Perth Visitor Centre and the Perth Tourist Lounge (see "Visitor Information," above).

NEIGHBORHOODS IN BRIEF

City Center   The central business district (called the CBD in Australia) is home to shops and department stores. A good introduction to Perth's charms is to take in the views from the pedestrian and bike path that skirts the river along Riverside Drive. Within walking distance is Kings Park & Botanic Garden.

Northbridge   Just about all of Perth's nightclubs, and a good many of its cool restaurants, bars, and cafes, are in this 5-block precinct north of the railway line. It's within easy walking distance of the city center, or take the free Blue CAT buses. The rough boundaries are James, Beaufort, Aberdeen, and Lake streets. What locals call the Cultural Centre—the Western Australian Museum, the Art Gallery of Western Australia, the State Library,

and the Perth Institute of Contemporary Arts—is here, too.

Subiaco   This well-heeled suburb is on the other side of Kings Park. Saturday morning wouldn't be the same for Perth's see-and-be-seen crowd without a stroll through "Subi's" villagelike concoction of cafes, markets, boutiques, antiques shops, and art galleries. Most of the action is near the intersection of Hay Street and Rokeby (pronounced *Rock*-er-bee) Road. Take the train to Subiaco station.

Fremantle   Not only is "Freo" a working port, it's also Perth's second city heart, and a favorite weekend spot to eat, shop, and sail. A 1980s restoration of Victorian warehouses turned Freo into a marvelous example of a 19th-century seaport—like San Francisco's

Fisherman's Wharf without the commercial taint. Fremantle is 19km (12 miles) downriver, at the mouth of the Swan.

Scarborough Beach This is one of Perth's prize beaches, 12km (7½ miles) north of the city center. The district is a little tatty, with an oversupply of cheap takeout food outlets, but if you like sun, sand, and surf, this is the place to be. You will find bars, restaurants, and surf-gear rental stores here. Allow 15 to 20 minutes to get here by car, 35 minutes on the bus.

GETTING AROUND

BY PUBLIC TRANSPORTATION **Transperth** (www.transperth.wa.gov.au) runs Perth's buses, trains, and ferries. For route, bus stop, and timetable information, call ℭ **13 62 13** in Western Australia or 08/9428 1900, or drop into the Transperth Info-Centres at the Plaza Arcade off Hay Street Mall, the Perth Railway Station, the Wellington Street bus station, or the City Bus Port on Mounts Bay Road. You can transfer from bus to ferry to train on one ticket within its expiration time of 2 or 3 hours. Travel costs A$2 (US$1.60) in one zone (to Subiaco, for instance), and A$3 (US$2.40) in two, which gets you most places, including Fremantle. Non–West Australian seniors and students don't qualify for discounted fares; kids ages 5 to 14 do.

By Bus The Wellington Street Bus Station (next to Perth Railway Station at Forrest Place) and the City Bus Port on Mounts Bay Road are the two main depots. The vast majority of buses travel along St. Georges Terrace. Drivers do not always stop unless

---

Tips **Take a Free Ride**

A welcome freebie in Perth is the **Free Transit Zone (FTZ)**. You can travel free on trains and buses within this zone any hour, day or night. It is bounded by Kings Park Road, Fraser Avenue, Thomas Street, and Loftus Street in the west; Newcastle Street in the north; and the river in the south and east. Basically, this means you can travel to Kings Park, Northbridge, east to major sporting grounds, and anywhere in the city center free. Signs mark the FTZ boundaries; just ask the driver if you're unsure. FTZ boundaries for trains are City West station on the Fremantle line and Claisebrook on the Midland and Armadale lines.

MultiRider passes give you 10 trips at a savings of 15%; they come in a range of prices good for various numbers of zones. A **DayRider** pass allows 1 day of unlimited travel after 9am on weekdays and all day on weekends and public holidays, and costs A$7.50 (US$6). A **FamilyRider** pass is valid for unlimited all-day travel to any destination and back, for a group of seven people with a maximum of two adults. FamilyRiders are aimed at Perth families and so are valid only on weekends and public holidays, after 9am weekdays during Western Australian school holidays, after 6pm year-round Monday through Thursday, and after 3pm Friday. They cost A$7.50 (US$6). Passes, collectively known as FastCards, are sold at newsdealers and at Transperth InfoCentres. To use the passes, validate them in the machines on the bus, train platform, or ferry wharf.

you hail the bus. Buy tickets from the driver. Buses run from about 5:30am until about 10:30 or 11:30pm, depending on the route.

The best way to get around town is on the free **CAT** (Central Area Transit) buses that run a continual loop of the city and Northbridge. The Red CAT runs east-west every 5 minutes, Monday through Friday from 6:50am to 6:20pm, and once every 25 minutes from 10am to 6:15pm weekends. The Blue CAT runs north-south as far north as Northbridge and south to Barrack Street Jetty every 7 minutes from 6:50am. The last Blue CAT service is at 6:20pm Monday through Thursday, and on Friday it continues every 15 minutes from 6:20pm until 1am Saturday. Saturday it runs from 8:30am to 1am the next day every 15 minutes, and Sunday every 15 minutes from 10am to 5pm. The Yellow CAT runs between East Perth and the city center every 10 minutes from 6am to 9am and every 15 minutes from 9am to 6:20pm weekdays, and every 35 minutes 10am to 6:15pm weekends. There is no CAT service on public holidays. Look for the silver CAT bus stops with the black cat on them. Transperth Info-Centres (see above) dispense free route maps.

Perth Tram Co. tours (see "Whale-Watching Cruises, Tram Trips & Other Tours," later in this chapter) are a good way to get around, too.

By Train   Trains are fast, clean, and safe. They start at about 5:30am and run every 15 minutes or more often during the day, and every half-hour at night until midnight. All trains leave from Perth Railway Station opposite Forrest Place on Wellington Street. Buy your ticket before you board, at the vending machines on the platform.

By Ferry   You will probably use ferries only to visit Perth Zoo. They run every half-hour or so, more often in peak hours, every day from 6:50am weekdays and 7:50am weekends and public holidays, until 7:15pm (or until 9:15pm Fri–Sat in summer, Sept–Apr) from the Barrack Street Jetty to Mends Street in South Perth. Buy tickets before you board from the vending machine on the wharf. The trip takes 7 minutes.

By Taxi   Perth's two biggest taxi companies are **Swan Taxis** (© 13 13 30) and **Black & White Taxis** (© 13 10 08). Ranks (stands) are at Perth Railway Station and at the Barrack Street end of Hay Street Mall.

By Car   Perth's signposting is notorious for telling you where you have been, not where you are going—for example, some interstate highways are announced with insignificant signs more suited to a side street.

The major car-rental companies are **Avis** (© 08/9325 7677), **Budget** (© 08/9480 3111), **EuropCar** (© 08/9277 9144), **Hertz** (© 08/9321 7777), and **Thrifty** (© 08/9464 7444). All except Hertz also have outlets in Fremantle.

FAST FACTS: Perth

American Express The office at 645 Hay St. Mall (© **08/9221 0777**) is open Monday through Friday from 9am to 5pm and Saturday from 9am to noon.

Business Hours Banks are open Monday through Thursday from 9:30am to 4pm and until 5pm Friday. Shopping hours are usually from 9am to 5:30pm Monday through Friday (until 9pm on Thurs in the suburbs and Fremantle, and until 9pm Fri in the city), and from 9am to 5pm on Saturday. On Sunday most (but not all) major stores open from noon to 4pm or later in the city, and from noon to 6pm in Fremantle.

Currency Exchange Go to the American Express office (see above) or **Interforex,** Shop 24, London Court, off Hay Street Mall (© **08/9325 7418;** Sat–Thurs 9am–6pm, Fri 9am–9pm). Interforex has a Fremantle bureau at the corner of William and Adelaide streets (© **08/9431 7022;** daily 8am–8pm).

Dentist **LifeCare Dental** (© **08/9221 2777,** or 08/9383 1620 after hours) is on the Upper Walkway Level, Forrest Chase shopping complex, 425 Wellington St., opposite Perth Railway Station. Open daily from 8am to 8pm.

Doctor **Central City Medical Centre** is on the Perth Railway Station concourse, 420 Wellington St. (© **08/9221 4747**). Open daily 8am to 7pm.

Embassies & Consulates The **United States Consulate-General** is at 16 St. Georges Terrace (© **08/9202 1224**). The **Canadian Consulate** is at 267 St. Georges Terrace (© **08/9322 7930**). The **British Consulate-General** is at 77 St. Georges Terrace (© **08/9224 4700**). The Irish **Consulate-General** is at 10 Lilika Rd., City Beach (© **08/9385 8247**).

Emergencies Dial © **000** for fire, ambulance, or police in an emergency. This is a free call; no coins are needed from a public phone.

Hospitals **Royal Perth Hospital** in the city center has a public emergency/casualty ward (© **08/9224 2244**). Enter from Victoria Square, which is off Murray Street.

Luggage Storage & Lockers The **Perth Tourist Lounge** (see "Visitor Information," above) stores luggage, and there are baggage lockers at the international and domestic terminals at the airport.

Pharmacies **Forrest Chase Pharmacy** (© **08/9221 1691**), on the upper level of the Forrest Chase shopping center, 425 Wellington St. (near the dentist's office listed above), is open Monday through Thursday from 8am to 7pm (and until 9pm Fri), Saturday from 8:30am to 6pm, and Sunday from 10am to 6pm. **Shenton Pharmacy,** 214 Nicholson Rd., Subiaco (© **08/9381 1358** business and after hours), will deliver across Perth.

Police Dial © **000** in an emergency. **Perth Police Station,** 60 Beaufort St. (© **08/9223 3715**), and **Fremantle Police Station,** 45 Henderson St. (© **08/9430 1222**), are open 24 hours. To be connected to the nearest station, dial © **13 14 44.**

Safety Perth is safe, but steer clear of the back streets of Northbridge—where groups of teenagers sometimes congregate at night—even if you are not alone.

Time Zone Western Australian time (WST) is Greenwich Mean Time plus 8 hours and does not change for daylight saving time. It is normally 2 hours behind Sydney, except October through March, when New South Wales goes to daylight saving. Call © **1194** for the exact local time.

Weather Call © **1196** for a recorded local weather forecast.

WHERE TO STAY

The city center has loads of hotels. That means competition can be high, especially Friday through Sunday when the business travelers go home, so ask about lower rates on weekends. You may strike a deal on a weeknight if business is slow. Many hotels throw breakfast or some other feature into midweek packages. Most hotels have rooms for travelers with disabilities.

IN THE CITY CENTER
Very Expensive

Duxton Hotel Perth ★★   The best uninterrupted views of the Swan River from a hotel room are from the south-side rooms at this chic 21st century–meets–Art Deco hotel. Only a few years old as a hotel, the place was created out of old tax office chambers. A sandstone portico fronts the bronze-paneled lobby with its Siena marble floor, and the rooms sport blond oak furniture with 1930s curves, elegant marquetry, and ample bathrooms. Superior rooms have extra-large bathrooms (some with Jacuzzis); executive-level rooms have TVs in the bathrooms, CD players, and faxes and printers; and suites have separate living rooms. Make time to see and be seen lazing around the petite swimming pool colonnaded like a Roman bath.

1 St. Georges Terrace (at Victoria Ave. next to Perth Concert Hall), Perth, WA 6000. ℂ 1800/681 118 in Australia, or 08/9261 8000. Fax 08/9261 8020. www.duxton.com.au. 306 units (several with shower only). A$400–A$520 (US$320–US$416) double; A$538–A$600 (US$430–US$480) suite. Extra person A$28 (US$22). Children under 16 stay free in parent's room with existing bedding. Ask about packages and upgrades. AE, DC, MC, V. Valet parking A$15 (US$12). Bus: Red CAT Stop 11 (Victoria Ave.). **Amenities:** Restaurant; bar; small heated pool; fitness center; Jacuzzi; sauna; concierge; airport shuttle; business center; 24-hr. room service; in-room massage; babysitting; coin-op laundry; laundry service; dry cleaning; executive-level rooms. *In room:* A/C, TV w/pay movies, dataport, minibar, coffeemaker, hair dryer, iron.

Expensive

The Melbourne Hotel ★ *Value*   This 1897 hotel in Perth's downtown West End, restored to its ornate gold rush–era originality in 1997 and updated again in 2003, is a great value, because its facilities and rooms match those of most AAA-rated five-star hotels. While the exterior retains its original appearance, the public areas, restaurant, and guest rooms have a stylish new look as well as some of their original trappings, like decorative pressed-metal ceilings and brass-trimmed fans. Suites are a single room with a sitting area. Go for the outside rooms (those on the second floor open onto the wide veranda), because inside rooms lack views. The atmospheric street-front **Melbourne Bar** has live music on Friday nights.

Corner of Hay and Milligan sts., Perth, WA 6000. ℂ 1800/685 671 in Australia, or 08/9320 3333. Fax 08/9320 3344. www.melbournehotel.com.au. 36 units (all with shower only). A$240 (US$192) double; A$280 (US$224) suite. Ask about packages. AE, DC, MC, V. Valet parking A$17 (US$14). Bus: Red CAT Stop 18 (QVI), over freeway footbridge from corner of St. Georges Terrace and Milligan St. Train: Perth Central. **Amenities:** Restaurant; cafe; bar; access to nearby health club, golf course, and tennis courts; concierge; tour desk; car-rental desk; airport shuttle; secretarial services; 24-hr. room service; babysitting; laundry service; dry cleaning (Mon–Sat). *In room:* A/C, TV w/free movies, fax, dataport, minibar, coffeemaker, hair dryer, iron.

Moderate

Miss Maud Swedish Hotel ★   Many of the rooms in this homey hotel in the heart of town have been gutted and totally rebuilt within the past 2 years. New furnishings include the Scandinavian colors of yellow and blue, while others have a crisp Nordic look of cream and pale blue. A private sun deck is tucked away among the rooftops. The real Miss Maud, Maud Edmiston, wants guests to feel they are in a European family hotel like those in her Swedish homeland, and she succeeds—in part due to the staff, which is more polite and on the ball than that in most AAA-rated five-star hotels. The breakfast included in the room rate is a fabulous buffet at **Miss Maud Swedish Restaurant** downstairs (p. 451).

97 Murray St. (at Pier St.), Perth, WA 6000. © **1800/998 022** in Australia, or 08/9325 3900. Fax 08/9221 3225. www.missmaud.com.au. 52 units (40 with shower only). A$88–A$150 (US$70–US$120) double. Extra adult A$30 (US$24), extra child 4–13 A$15 (US$12). Rates include smorgasbord breakfast. AE, DC, MC, V. Parking A$12 (US$9.60) 1 block away. Bus: Red CAT Stop 1 (Pier St.); Blue CAT Stop 5 (Murray St. Mall E.). **Amenities:** Restaurant/bar (see "Where to Dine," below); takeout pastry shop; access to nearby health club; tour desk; car-rental desk; airport shuttle; limited room service (7am–9pm); babysitting; coin-op laundry; laundry service; dry cleaning. *In room:* A/C, TV/VCR w/pay movies, dataport, minibar, coffeemaker, hair dryer.

The Sebel Residence East Perth ★★★ Perth's newest and most stylish place to stay opened in October 2003. A little out of the city center, but with views over the river, the spacious, modern apartment hotel lies steps from the new restaurant precinct of Cove Promenade. Decorated in cool white and gray, with tangerine and lime accents, it's good enough to move into permanently! Each unit has a small desk with dataport and bathrobes in the wardrobe. Some apartments have balconies overlooking the river, and some have Jacuzzis. Each one-bedroom apartment has a full kitchen with microwave, and a washer and dryer. You can combine a studio and a one-bedroom apartment to make a two-bedroom unit. If you'd rather eat out, a convenient arrangement allows you to add meals at some local restaurants to your hotel bill. Internet access is also available in the lobby, and the staff is friendly and helpful. This is a sister property to the **Sebel Perth,** 37 Pier St. (© **08/9325 7655**), which boasts the biggest standard hotel rooms in the city.

60 Royal St., East Perth, WA 6004. © **1800/999 004** (Mirvac in Australia), or 08/9223 2500. Fax 08/9218 8717. www.mirvachotels.com.au. 57 units. A$149 (US$119) studio; A$195 (US$156) 1-bedroom apt double; A$310 (US$248) 2-bedroom apt. Free cribs. Ask about weekend, overnight, honeymoon, and suite packages. AE, DC, MC, V. Free covered parking. Train: Claisebrook. Bus: Yellow CAT. **Amenities:** Heated outdoor lap pool; well-equipped gym; tour desk; car-rental desk; secretarial services; babysitting; laundry service; dry cleaning. *In room:* A/C, TV w/free movies, DVD, stereo, dataport, kitchen, minibar, coffeemaker, hair dryer, iron, safe.

Sullivans Hotel This family-owned hotel about 1.5km (1 mile) from town is popular with Europeans for its small-scale ambience. Despite being on the main road into the city, none of the rooms seem noisy. They're simply furnished with laminate fittings, not glamorous but roomy. Larger deluxe rooms come with desks, safes, and balconies with views over parkland and the freeway to the river. There are also two-bedroom apartments with kitchenettes. Out back is a pleasant little pool with a sun deck and barbecue. Bikes are free, the restaurant is affordable, and the front desk has free 24-hour Internet access for guests. Some rooms have dataports. The Swan River is a stroll away, the city is a 10-minute walk, and Kings Park is a short, steep climb up the hill.

166 Mounts Bay Rd., Perth, WA 6000. © **1800/999 294** in Australia, or 08/9321 8022. Fax 08/9481 6762. www. sullivans.com.au. 68 units (66 with shower only). A$120–A$140 (US$96–US$112) up to 4 people in room; A$150 (US$120) 1-bedroom apt; A$190 (US$152) 2-bedroom apt. Ask about packages. Weekly rates available. AE, DC, MC, V. Free parking. Bus: 71, 72, or 78 (hotel is within Free Transit Zone). **Amenities:** Restaurant/bar; small outdoor pool; free bikes; tour desk; airport shuttle; limited room service; babysitting; coin-op laundry; laundry service; dry cleaning; Internet access. *In room:* A/C, TV w/free movies, coffeemaker, hair dryer.

Inexpensive
Mercure Hotel Perth ★ *Value* This is a well-priced, comfortable, conveniently located hotel right in the heart of Perth. Helpful staff and basic accommodations make this an easy choice. There are 15 suites if you need more space than a standard hotel

room, and a heated pool on the rooftop. Mercure is part of the French Accor group, which also has the inexpensive **Hotel Ibis Perth** on Murray Street (© **08/9322 2844**) and the **Formule 1** hotel near Perth Airport (© **1300/884 400** in Australia).

10 Irwin St. (between Hay St. and St. George's Terrace), Perth, WA 6000. © **08/9326 7000**; Accor 1300/656 565 in Australia, 800/221-4542 in the U.S. and Canada, 0870/609 0961 in the U.K., or 0800/44 4422 in New Zealand. Fax 08/9221 3344. www.accorhotels.com. 233 units (all with shower only). A$135 (US$108) double. Extra person A$36 (US$29). Children under 16 stay free in parent's room with existing bedding. AE, DC, MC, V. Valet parking A$13 (US$10). Bus: Red CAT Stop 1 or 2. **Amenities:** Restaurant; cafe; 2 bars; heated rooftop pool; gym; Jacuzzi; sauna; concierge; tour desk; car-rental desk; airport shuttle; shopping arcade; 24-hr. room service; babysitting; coin-op laundry; dry cleaning (Mon–Sat). *In room:* A/C, TV w/movies, dataport, fridge, coffeemaker, iron.

River View on Mount Street 🏆 *Value*   On a quiet, leafy street a short walk from the city and Kings Park, these roomy studio apartments in a 1960s block were refurbished in 1999 with new kitchens and bathrooms, fresh carpets and curtains, and smart-looking fittings. The result is great style at a great price. Some have distant views of the river, a few blocks away, and some sleep three. Maid service is weekly. The helpful on-site managers loan hair dryers and irons. You can have breakfast at the **Mount Street Café** downstairs (p. 451), which also sells prepared curries and deli items. No smoking.

42 Mount St., Perth, WA 6000. © **08/9321 8963**. Fax 08/9322 5956. www.riverview.au.com (not "riverview.com.au"). 50 units (all with shower only). A$85–A$95 (US$68–US$76) apt. Weekly rates available. AE, MC, V. Limited free parking. Bus: Red CAT Stop 18 (QVI), over freeway footbridge from corner of St. Georges Terrace and Milligan St. **Amenities:** Cafe (see "Where to Dine," below); access to nearby golf course and health club; tour desk; car-rental desk; airport shuttle; coin-op laundry; laundry service; dry cleaning; nonsmoking rooms. *In room:* A/C, TV, dataport, kitchenette, fridge, coffeemaker, hair dryer, iron.

ON THE BEACH

Hotel Rendezvous Observation City Perth 🏆   One of the few beachside places in Perth is this 17-story complex right on the never-ending sands of Scarborough Beach. Its no-fuss ambience makes it popular with vacationers from around the world. Most of the rooms, refurbished in 2004, have private balconies with ocean views. Some rooms have dataports, and most suites have separate sleeping quarters. A Day Spa opened in mid-2005. Among the entertainment venues are a British-style pub popular with locals, a live music lounge, and a dance club.

The Esplanade, Scarborough Beach, WA 6019. © **1800/067 680** in Australia, or 08/9245 1000. Fax 08/9245 1345. www.rendezvoushotels.com. 333 units (150 with shower only). A$250–A$310 (US$200–US$248) double; from A$550 (US$440) suite. Extra person A$50 (US$40). Children under 18 stay free in parent's room with existing bedding. Ask about packages. AE, DC, MC, V. Valet parking A$20 (US$16); self-parking A$7 (US$5.60). Bus: 400. **Amenities:** 2 restaurants; cafe; 4 bars; heated outdoor pool; children's wading pool; 2 outdoor day/night tennis courts; health club; spa; Jacuzzi; sauna; limited watersports-equipment rentals; bike rental; concierge; tour desk; daily courtesy shuttle between hotel, Perth city, Burswood casino, Fremantle, local mall; business center (Mon–Fri); shopping arcade; salon; 24-hr. room service; in-room massage; babysitting; coin-op laundry; laundry service; dry cleaning; executive-level rooms. *In room:* A/C, TV w/pay movies, kitchenette, minibar, coffeemaker, hair dryer, iron.

IN FREMANTLE

There's a perpetual holiday atmosphere in this picturesque port city. Although you're 19km (12 miles) from Perth's city center, public transport is good, so you can happily explore all of Perth from here—and many top attractions are in Freo anyhow. There are good restaurants and a happening nightlife, too.

Esplanade Hotel Fremantle 🏆   Freo's best hotel is this low-rise 1897 colonial building wrapped by two verandas, centered on a buzzing four-story atrium lobby. A A$15-million (US$12-million) expansion in 2003 added 41 rooms to the hotel as well as a 1,000-seat convention center. The nicely maintained rooms have views of the street, the pool, or the distant harbor across a park. Some studio units have Jacuzzis. Eleven rooms are designed for wheelchair access and have showers for the disabled. The larger pool in the courtyard is a good place to chill out without getting buffeted by the pesky local sea breeze, the "Fremantle Doctor." It's in the heart of Freo's cafes, shops, and attractions. Internet bookings can save you up to around A$140 (US$112) per night.

Marine Terrace at Essex St., Fremantle, WA 6160. ℰ **1800/998 201** in Australia, or 08/9432 4000. Fax 08/9430 4539. www.esplanadehotelfremantle.com.au. 300 units (some with shower only). A$292–A$325 (US$234–US$260) double; A$338–A$419 (US$270–US$335) studio; A$445–A$619 (US$356–US$495) suite. Extra person A$38 (US$30). Children under 13 stay free in parent's room with existing bedding. Crib free. Ask about packages. AE, DC, MC, V. Valet parking A$19 (US$15); paid street parking nearby. Train: Fremantle. Fremantle Airport Shuttle (see "Arriving: By Plane," earlier in this chapter). **Amenities:** 2 restaurants; cafe; 2 bars (one poolside); 2 heated outdoor pools; gym; 3 outdoor Jacuzzis; sauna; bike rental; concierge; tour desk; business center; 24-hr. room service; in-room massage; babysitting; coin-op laundry; laundry service; dry cleaning (Mon–Sat). *In room:* A/C, TV w/pay movies, dataport, minibar, coffeemaker, hair dryer, iron.

WHERE TO DINE

An array of upscale choices, plus terrific, cheap ethnic spots make Perth's restaurant scene as sophisticated as Sydney's and Melbourne's—which is to say, great. You'll find many good choices in "restaurant city," Northbridge.

For inexpensive pasta, a Turkish bread sandwich, or excellent coffee and cake, you can't beat Perth's homegrown **DOME** chain of cafes. Look for the dark green logo at Trinity Arcade between Hay Street Mall and St. Georges Terrace (ℰ **08/9226 0210**); 149 James St., Northbridge (ℰ **08/9328 8094**); 13 S. Terrace, Fremantle (ℰ **08/9336 3040**); 19 Napoleon St., Cottesloe (ℰ **08/9383 1071**); 26 Rokeby Rd., Subiaco (ℰ **08/9381 5664**); and Henderson Street on Rottnest Island (ℰ **08/9292 5026**)—to name just a few.

Western Australian law bans smoking in enclosed public spaces, including restaurants.

IN THE CITY CENTER
Expensive

Fraser's ★★★ *Moments* MODERN AUSTRALIAN/SEAFOOD What a sensational view! The city skyscrapers and Swan River look so close you could almost reach out and touch them—and even better, the victuals match the vista. Executive chef Chris Taylor's sure hand with seafood, which composes about 70% of the long menu, has made this hilltop restaurant a finalist for national restaurant of the year awards more than once. Fresh tiger prawns with Vietnamese mint and tatsoi, with a black vinegar dressing is typical. To maximize the view, ask for a seat on the terrace.

Fraser Ave. (near the Information Kiosk), Kings Park. ℰ **08/9481 7100.** Reservations required. Main courses A$30–A$39 (US$24–US$31). AE, DC, MC, V. Daily 7:30am–late. Closed Good Friday. Ample free parking. Bus: 33 stops outside the Information Kiosk. Red CAT Stop 25 (Havelock St.) is 1 block north of the gates.

Moderate

44 King Street ★★ MODERN AUSTRALIAN Socialites and hip corporate types adorn this sophisticated hangout. The interior is a mix of industrial design and European cafe, with dark timber tables, exposed air ducts, and windows onto the street. The open kitchen produces a daily changing menu of weird and wonderful choices with exotic ingredients—such as fennel-roasted duck with paella of Valencia, the Javanese Mie-Goreng and peanut-crusted prawns, or Cajun pink snapper with sweet potato frites and avocado sour cream. Not only does the menu helpfully list wine suggestions for each dish, but it also offers taster-size glasses from around A$3 (US$2.40) to A$8.50 (US$6.80) from a 200-strong wine list. Lots of folks drop in just for coffee, roasted on-site, and the famous cakes. All meals are available to take out.

44 King St. © 08/9321 4476. Reservations not accepted. Tasting menu A$3.50–A$13 (US$2.80–US$10) breakfast, A$18–A$33 (US$14–US$26) lunch and dinner. AE, DC, MC, V. Daily 7am–midnight. Bus: Red CAT Stop 28 (King St.); Blue CAT Stop 1 (Cloisters).

Miss Maud Swedish Restaurant *Value* INTERNATIONAL   "Good food and plenty of it" is the motto at Miss Maud's homey establishment, and the crowds packing the place prove it works. Most diners skip the long a la carte menu and go straight for the smorgasbord. At breakfast, that means 50 dishes, including pancakes cooked before your eyes. At lunch and dinner you can tuck into soup, 10 salads, a big range of seafood (including oysters at dinner), cold meats, roasts, hot vegetables, pasta, cheeses, European-style breads, half a dozen tortes, fruit, and ice cream—65 dishes in all. Service is fast and polite.

Below the Miss Maud Swedish Hotel, 97 Murray St. (at Pier St.). © 08/9325 3900. Reservations recommended. Smorgasbord breakfast A$19 (US$15) Mon–Fri, A$20 (US$16) weekends and holidays; lunch A$28 (US$22) Mon–Sat, A$30 (US$24) Sun and holidays; dinner A$35 (US$28) Sun–Thurs, A$37 (US$30) Fri, and A$39 (US$31) Sat and holidays. Smorgasbord discounts for children 4–13. A la carte main courses, sandwiches, and light meals A$6–A$20 (US$4.80–US$16). AE, DC, MC, V. Daily 6:45–10am (11am on weekends and holidays), noon–2:30pm (3pm on weekends and holidays), 5:30–10pm (9.30pm Sat and holidays). Coffee and cake served all day. Bus: Red CAT Stop 1 (Pier St.); Blue CAT Stop 5 (Murray St. Mall E.).

Mount Street Café and Food Store ★★ MODERN AUSTRALIAN   Chef Toby Uhlrich turns out yummy dine-in and takeout fare at this charming alfresco cafe on the edge of the central business district. Come for lunches like risotto with asparagus, chicken, roasted almonds, and Parmesan, or your choice of light snacks from the deli cabinet. Breakfasts are equally fresh and delicious. Dine inside at a few tables, or out on the shaded stone terrace. Drop by anytime for cakes and good coffee, but be prepared to fight the regulars for a table. BYO (corkage fee A$2.50/US$2).

Under River View on Mount St. apts, 42 Mount St. © 08/9485 1411. Reservations recommended on weekends. Breakfast A$5.80–A$17 (US$4.65–US$14); main courses A$14–A$21 (US$11–US$17). AE, MC, V. Daily 7:30am–5pm. Bus: Red CAT Stop 18 (QVI), over freeway footbridge from corner of St. Georges Terrace and Milligan St.

Inexpensive

Basil Leaves Café *Finds* ASIAN   An extensive menu of predominantly Thai dishes is served up without fuss at this simple but popular restaurant in the rapidly developing East Brook Village in East Perth. There's the usual array of chicken, beef, lamb, and pork dishes, with several more expensive seafood dishes, and some tasty curries. The service is friendly and efficient.

Shop 37, 82 Royal St., East Perth (at Plain St.). © 08/9221 8999. Main courses A$12–A$20 (US$4–US$12). MC, V. Mon–Fri 11:30am until late; daily 5pm till late. BYO. Bus: Yellow CAT.

Fast Eddy's Café FAST FOOD   A hefty menu of steaks, burgers, sandwiches, soups, pancakes, sundaes, shakes, and full fry-up brekkies (breakfasts) are served all hours at this popular chain. The interior sports 1930s soap-powder posters and Coca-Cola advertisements. One side is table service; the same food minus the side orders will cost you about half the already-low prices at the Victorian-era-meets-1950s counter-service diner and takeout section on the other side.

454 Murray St. (at Milligan St.). © 08/9321 2552. Main courses A$5–A$15 (US$4–US$12). MC, V. Daily 24 hr. Red CAT Stop 27 (Milligan St.).

IN NORTHBRIDGE

Vulture's Restaurant & Café ⚜ ECLECTIC/MODERN AUSTRALIAN   This roomy, relaxed, and groovy restaurant has a knack for suiting all occasions and all folk, from couples sharing a romantic dinner in the street-side courtyard to teenage night-clubbers hanging out after a big night. The place is scattered with funky bric-a-brac, from Indian eagle totems to Balinese four-poster wedding beds—you can even sit inside them on cushions and eat at a low coffee table, instead of at the regular tables. The main courses are sophisticated and skillfully cooked—rack of spring lamb with rosemary and apricot crust, served with a layered sweet potato cake and sugar snap peas, or seared Atlantic salmon filet with wasabi mash and palm sugar dressing, for example. There is also plenty of light stuff, such as Thai green-chile mussels, nachos, or pastas.

Francis St. at William St., Northbridge. ℂ **08/9227 9087**. Reservations recommended for dinner Fri–Sat. Main courses A$18–A$30 (US$14–US$24); dine-in or takeout sandwiches at lunch A$7–A$9 (US$5.60–US$7.20). Kids' menu A$7 (US$5.60). AE, DC, MC, V. Sun–Thurs 11am–1am; Fri–Sat 11am–2am or later. Bus: Blue CAT Stop 9 (TAFE).

AT THE BEACH

The Blue Duck ⚜⚜ *Kids* INTERNATIONAL/PIZZA   For ocean views and a lively atmosphere, it's hard to beat this casual restaurant perched right over the sand. Although the interior lacks the balcony's panoramic position, it has an upbeat seaside ambience and is just as packed as the porch. The all-day menu (available starting at noon) has lots of light choices like crispy duck salad and Mediterranean and Asian tasting plates, as well as steaks, grilled fish, gourmet burgers, and wood-fired pizzas with creative toppings.

151 Marine Parade, North Cottesloe. ℂ **08/9385 2499**. Reservations recommended. Breakfast A$4–A$14 (US$3.20–US$11); main courses A$11–A$27 (US$8.80–US$22, with many meals under A$20/US$16). Buffet break-fast Sat–Sun and holidays A$15–A$25 (US$12–US$20). Kids' menu A$7–A$9 (US$5.60–US$9.60). AE, DC, MC, V. Mon–Fri 6am until late (from 6:30am in winter); weekends and public holidays 7am until late. Bus: 71, 72, 73, or 883.

Indiana Tea House ⚜ MODERN AUSTRALIAN   The colonial Asian trappings (bamboo bird cages, plaster lions, and palms) and cane chairs at this bathhouse-turned-restaurant on Cottesloe Beach will make you want to head straight for the tropical timber bar and order a cocktail. Try a Cottesloe Sunset. Actually, the tasteful stucco building with bay windows and wooden floors is new—it just looks old. The menu slants heavily toward seafood, including a mild Thai green seafood curry with a medley of seafood including prawns, calamari, fish and scallops, or a fresh whole fish, filled with a julienne of vegetables and coriander, oven-baked and served with lime butter. Other options include rib-eye filet steak, lamb, and chicken dishes. This place is just as popular with business folk cutting deals as it is with arty types browsing the papers over their cafe lattes. Go in the daytime to make the most of those ocean views, or at sunset.

99 Marine Parade (on Cottesloe Beach opposite Forrest St.), Cottesloe. ℂ **08/9385 5005**. Reservations recom-mended. Main courses A$26–A$48 (US$21–US$38). AE, DC, MC, V. Daily noon–4pm and 6pm–late. Bus: 71, 72, 73, or 883.

IN FREMANTLE

La Pizzeria WOOD-FIRED PIZZA/SEAFOOD   Freo has loads of restaurants, but this joint stands out for its upbeat, easy ambience. It has terrazzo tables, a concrete and timber floor, and a stainless steel bar. Pizzas come straight from the funky wood-fired oven at the rear, bearing toppings like grilled eggplant, roast capsicum, and mushrooms.

Tips   Java Joints

Don't leave Freo without a "short black" (that's an espresso) or a "flat white" (coffee with milk) at the port's "cappuccino strip" on South Terrace. On weekends the street bursts at the seams with locals flocking to alfresco Italian-style cafes that serve good java and excellent focaccia, pasta, and pizza. **DOME, Old Papa's,** and **Gino's** are three to look for.

La Pizzeria serves traditional pastas and seafood main courses, too. Licensed and BYO beer and wine.

95 Market St. ℭ **08/9430 6126.** Pizzas A$13–A$18 (US$10–US$14); main courses A$16–A$22 (US$13–US$18). AE, DC, MC, V. Mon–Thurs noon–10pm; Fri–Sun noon–10:30pm. Train: Fremantle.

WHAT TO SEE & DO IN PERTH

AQWA (Aquarium of Western Australia) *Kids*   You won't catch performing dolphins a la Sea World, but there's plenty to see here, including a moving walkway through an underwater tunnel with a view of sharks, rays, turtles, and fish; a touch pool that has a small shark; and lots of aquariums that showcase the marine life of the Western Australian coast, including pretty leafy sea dragons, coral reefs, jellyfish, cuttlefish, sea snakes, crocodiles, and deadly stonefish that look remarkably like stones. Keepers feed the sharks and the touch-pool creatures daily, and a program of talks and movies on marine creatures runs throughout the day. For A$99 (US$79) plus A$15 (US$12) for snorkel gear or A$30 (US$24) for dive gear, you can **swim with the sharks.** You may need to book this experience weeks in advance. Allow half a day here.

Sorrento Quay at Hillarys Boat Harbour, 91 Southside Dr., Hillarys. ℭ **08/9447 7500.** Admission A$23 (US$18) adults, A$18 (US$14) seniors and students, A$13 (US$10) children 4–15, free for children under 4, A$65 (US$52) family of 4. Daily 10am–5pm; sometimes later in Jan. Closed Dec 25. Train: Joondalup line to Warwick, transfer to bus 423. By car, take Mitchell Fwy. 23km (14 miles) north, turn left onto Hepburn Ave. and proceed to roundabout at entrance to Hillarys Boat Harbour; AQWA is at the western end of the harbor. Free parking.

Art Gallery of Western Australia   Most outstanding among this state gallery's international and Australian works is the Aboriginal art collection, regarded as the finest in Australia. Free 1-hour tours of a particular collection run Tuesday through Friday and Sunday; Friday tours are at 12:30pm, others at 1pm.

Roe St. and Beaufort St. (enter near the walkway opposite Perth Railway Station), Northbridge. ℭ **08/9492 6600** administration, or 08/9492 6622 recorded info line. Free admission. Entry fee may apply to special exhibitions. Daily 10am–5pm. Closed Good Friday, Dec 25, and until 1pm Apr 25 (Anzac Day). Train: Perth. Bus: Blue CAT Stop 7 (Museum).

Cohunu Koala Park *Kids*   Not all states in Australia permit **koala cuddling,** but Western Australia does, and this large park set in bushland is the only place in Western Australia where you can do it. You can also feed 100 kangaroos, wallabies, and emus wandering in natural enclosures, see wombats and dingoes, walk through an aviary housing Aussie native birds, and see wild water birds on the ponds. The Caversham Wildlife Park in the Swan Valley (see "Side Trips from Perth," later in the chapter) has a bigger and more intriguing range of native species, but it does not allow koala cuddling.

Off Mills Rd. E., Gosnells (in the suburb of Martin on some maps). ℭ **08/9390 6090.** Admission A$20 (US$16) adults, A$10 (US$8) children 5–14. Koala-cuddling photos A$38 (US$30), or A$20 (US$16) if you take the photo yourself. Daily 10am–5pm; koala photo sessions 10am–4pm. Closed Dec 25. Train: Armadale line to Gosnells, then cab (about A$15/US$12). Bus: 219. By car, take Riverside Dr. across Swan River onto Albany Hwy., follow for approximately 25km (16 miles) to Gosnells, turn left onto Tonkin Hwy. and right onto Mills Rd. E. (about 35-min. drive from city). A cab from the city is about A$40 (US$32).

Holmes à Court Gallery This small riverside gallery offers rotating exhibitions from one of the country's most outstanding private art collections, that of Janet Holmes à Court, Australia's richest woman. Many of the works are Aboriginal or by well-known Australian artists such as Sidney Nolan.

11 Brown St., East Perth. (© **08/9218 4540**. Free admission. Thurs–Sun noon–5pm. Closed public holidays. Train: Claisebrook.

Kings Park & Botanic Garden Smack against the city center and Swan River is this 400-hectare (988-acre) hilltop park of botanic gardens and bushland. You can inspect weird and wonderful Western Australian flora; experience the solitude of the bush; and bike, hike, or drive an extensive network of roads and trails. Visiting the spring **wildflower displays** (which peak Sept–Oct) is a highlight for many. During the wildflower festival and on some other special occasions such as Christmas and Anzac Day (Apr 25), the lemon-scented gums lining Fraser Avenue are illuminated. There are barbecue and picnic facilities, several extensive playgrounds, bikes for rent (behind the Visitor Information Centre), tearooms, and the incomparable **Fraser's** restaurant (p. 450).

Pick up self-guiding maps from the Visitor Information Centre, or join one of the free guided walks leaving from opposite the flower clock on Fraser Avenue. Walks depart daily at 10am and 2pm and take 1½ hours, or 2 or 3 hours for bushwalks (May–Oct only). The **Perth Tram Co.** (© **08/9322 2006**) runs 1-hour tours of the park and neighboring University of Western Australia in replica 1899 wooden trams. Tours depart from outside the Information Kiosk on Fraser Avenue daily at 11am, 12:15pm, 1:15pm, and 2:15pm. Tickets cost A$12 (US$9.60) for adults, A$10 (US$8) for seniors, A$6 (US$4.80) for children under 15, and A$30 (US$24) for families. Buy tickets on board. You can stop en route and rejoin a later tram if you like.

Fraser Ave. off Kings Park Rd. (© **08/9480 3659** information kiosk, or 08/9480 3600 administration. Free admission. Park daily 24 hr. Information Kiosk daily 9:30am–4:30pm (closed Dec 25). Hours are approximate and may vary. Bus: 33 stops outside the Information Kiosk and extends into the park on Sat afternoon, and much of the day Sun and public holidays. Red CAT Stop 25 (Havelock St.) is 1 block north of the gates.

Perth Mint This lovely historic building—built in the 1890s to mint currency from the Kalgoorlie gold rush—produced the victors' gold medals for the Sydney 2000 Olympic Games. Bullion is still traded here. The key event is a gold pour demonstration (on the hour starting at 10am weekdays, and 10am—noon on weekends and public holidays). You can also see samples of the 2000 Olympics medals, engrave a medallion with your own message, handle a 400-ounce gold bar, see gold coins being minted, and ogle the country's biggest collection of nuggets. A 30-minute

---

Moments **Picture Perfect**

For the only photo of Perth you'll need, snap the view over the city and river from the War Memorial in Kings Park—it's superb day or night.

free guided tour departs half an hour before every pour. A shop sells gold coins and nugget jewelry.

310 Hay St. (at Hill St.), East Perth. $\mathcal{C}$ **08/9421 7223**. Admission A$6.50 (US$5.20) adults, A$5.50 (US$4.40) seniors and students, A$3.30 (US$2.65) school-age children. Shop admission free. Mon–Fri 9am–4pm; Sat–Sun and holidays 9am–1pm. Closed Jan 1, Good Friday, Apr 25 (Anzac Day), and Dec 25. Red CAT Stop 10 (Perth Mint).

Perth Zoo *Kids*   This is a good place to see kangaroos, koalas, numbats, wombats, quokkas, emus, echidnas (the Aussie answer to the porcupine), dingoes, snakes, frogs, and just about every other kind of Aussie wildlife, mostly housed in natural habitats, or in a walk-through aviary. There are plenty of exotic animals, too, including orang-utans, Rothschild's giraffes, zebras, lions, rhinos, and elephants. Feeding demonstrations and talks run throughout the day. You can do a behind-the-scenes tour, and buy paintings by the zoo's elephants. Koala cuddling is not permitted; for that, head to Cohunu Koala Park (see above).

20 Labouchere Rd., South Perth. $\mathcal{C}$ **08/9474 3551** for recorded information, or 08/9474 0444 administration. Admission A$16 (US$13) adults, A$8 (US$6.40) children 4–15, A$43 (US$34) family of 4. Daily 9am–5pm. Ferry: Barrack St. Jetty to Mends St. Jetty, South Perth. Bus: 30 or 31. Ample free parking.

Western Australian Museum *Kids*   Kids will like the dinosaur gallery, the drawers full of insects, the blue whale skeleton on the well-stocked aquatic zoology floor, the "megamouth" shark preserved in a tank in the ground in the courtyard, and assorted other examples of Australia's weird natural creatures. The main attraction for grown-ups is one of the best collections of Aboriginal artifacts and rare photographs in the country. Allow 90 minutes to see most highlights.

Francis St. at Beaufort St. (or enter off James St. Mall), Northbridge. $\mathcal{C}$ **08/9427 2700**. Free admission; donation requested. Fee may apply for temporary exhibitions. Daily 9:30am–5pm; Closed Good Friday, Dec 25, and until 1pm Apr 25 (Anzac Day) and Dec 26. Train: Perth. Bus: Blue CAT Stop 8 (Museum).

HITTING THE BEACHES

Perth shares Sydney's good luck in having beaches in the metropolitan area—19 of them, in fact, laid end to end along the 35km (21-mile) Sunset Coast from Cottesloe in the south to Quinns Rocks in the north. Mornings are best, because a strong afternoon wind, known as the "Fremantle Doctor," can be unpleasant, especially in summer. Always swim between the red and yellow flags, which denote a safe swimming zone.

During summer (the last Sat in Sept to the last Sun in Apr), bus nos. 400 and 408 run to Scarborough Beach every 15 minutes each day. Bus no. 458 stops half-hourly on weekends and public holidays and hourly on weekdays at most beaches from Fremantle to Hillarys. It operates in both directions. You can take a surfboard under 1.2m (4 ft.) on these buses.

The three most popular beaches are Cottesloe, Scarborough, and Trigg.

COTTESLOE   This pretty crescent, graced by the Edwardian-style Indiana Tea House (see above), is Perth's most fashionable beach. It has safe swimming and a small surf break. A couple of good cafes are nearby. Train: Cottesloe, then walk several hundred meters. Bus: 102.

SCARBOROUGH   Scarborough's white sands stretch for miles from the base of the Hotel Rendezvous Observation City, Perth. Swimming is generally safe, and surfers are always guaranteed a wave, although inexperienced swimmers should take a rain check when the surf is rough. The busy shopping precinct across the road means there's always somewhere to buy lunch and drinks. Bus: 400.

TRIGG   Surfers like Trigg best for its consistent swells. Bus: 400 to Scarborough, then a 10-minute walk north.

A DAY OUT IN FREMANTLE ★★

The heritage port precinct of **Fremantle,** 19km (12 miles) from downtown Perth on the mouth of the Swan River, is probably best known outside Australia as the site of the 1987 America's Cup challenge. Before that event, the city embarked on a major restoration of its gracious but derelict warehouses and Victorian buildings. Today "Freo" is a bustling district of 150 National Trust buildings, alfresco cafes, museums, galleries, pubs, markets, and shops in a masterfully preserved historical atmosphere. It's still a working port, so you will see fishing boats unloading and yachts gliding in and out of the harbor. Perth's population makes a beeline for the place every weekend, resulting in a wonderful hubbub of buzzing shoppers, merchants, java drinkers, yachties, tourists, and fishermen. Allow a full day to take in even half the sights—and don't forget to knock back a beer or two on the veranda of one of the gorgeous old pubs.

ESSENTIALS

GETTING THERE   Parking is plentiful, but driving is frustrating in the maze of one-way traffic. Most attractions are within walking distance (or accessible on the free CAT bus), so take the train to Fremantle and explore on foot.

A nice way to get to Freo and see Perth's river suburbs is on the cruises that run once or twice a day from Barrack Street Jetty. See "Whale-Watching Cruises, Tram Trips & Other Tours," below, for cruise operators.

GETTING AROUND   The silver Fremantle CAT bus makes a running loop of local attractions every 10 minutes Monday through Friday from 7:30am to 6:30pm, and on weekends and holidays from 10am to 6:30pm, except Good Friday and December 25 and 26. It is free and departs from the train station.

VISITOR INFORMATION   The **Fremantle Tourist Bureau** is in Town Hall, Kings Square (at High St.), Fremantle, WA 6160 (© **08/9431 7878;** www. fremantlewa.com.au). It's open Monday through Friday from 9am to 5pm and Saturday 10am to 3pm. Closed Sundays. The best website is that of the Fremantle Council, www.fremantle.wa.gov.au.

SEEING THE SIGHTS IN FREMANTLE

You'll want to explore some of Freo's excellent museums and other attractions, but take time to stroll the streets and admire the 19th-century offices and warehouses, many painted in rich, historically accurate colors. When you arrive, wander down to the docks—either Victoria Quay, where sailing craft come and go, or Fishing Boat Harbour, off Mews Road, where the boats bring in their catches—to get a breath of salt air.

Fremantle Trams (© **08/9339 8719**)—an old tram carriage on wheels, not tram tracks—conducts various tours that last 45 or 90 minutes. I found the commentary uninteresting and hard to follow, but this is a fun way to see a lot in a short time if you don't want much real information about what you're seeing. The tours depart from Fremantle Town Hall 10 times a day starting at 10am, with the last tour at 4pm. Tickets cost A$10 and A$15 (US$8 and US$12) adults, A$9 and A$14 (US$7.20 and US$11) seniors, and are free for children under 16 traveling with two adults. The popular Friday-night Ghostly Tour includes a fish and chips dinner and admission to a range of attractions. It costs A$35 (US$28) adults and A$30 (US$24) children under 15. You must book for Friday nights but not for other tours, and your ticket will include discount entry to Fremantle Prison.

Freo's best **shopping** is for arts and crafts, from hand-blown glass to Aboriginal art to alpaca-wool clothing. Worth a look are the assorted art, crafts, and souvenir stores on **High Street** west of the mall; the **E Shed markets** on Victoria Quay (Fri–Sun and Mon holidays 9am–6pm); and **Bannister Street CraftWorks,** 8–12 Bannister St. (© **08/9336 2035**), an arts cooperative where you often spy the artists at work (Tues–Sun 11am–5:30pm, public holidays 1–5:30pm). The 170 stalls at the **Fremantle Markets,** 74 South Terrace at Henderson Street (© **08/9335 2515**), mostly sell cheap imported handicrafts, jewelry, housewares, and clothing, as well as inexpensive food. They're open Friday from 9am to 9pm, Saturday from 9am to 5pm, and Sunday and Monday holidays from 10am to 5pm.

The most popular watering holes are the **Sail & Anchor,** 64 S. Terrace (© **08/9335 8433**), which has its own brewery; the **Norfolk,** 47 S. Terrace at Norfolk Street (© **08/9335 5405**); and the beautifully restored front bar and garden courtyard at **Phillimore's Café & Bar** at His Majesty's Hotel, on Phillimore Street at Mouat Street (© **08/9335 9596**). The happening "cappuccino strip" on South Terrace is good for people-watching.

Fremantle Arts Centre   Housed in a striking neo-Gothic 1860s building built by convicts, this center contains one of Western Australia's best contemporary arts and crafts galleries, with a constantly changing array of works. A shop sells crafts from Western Australia, a bookstore stocks Australian art books and literature, and the courtyard cafe is the perfect place to hang out. Free concerts play on the lawn every Sunday and public holiday between September and May from 2 to 4pm. Also here is the Fremantle History Museum (see the next listing).

1 Finnerty St. at Ord St. © **08/9432 9555.** Free admission. Daily 10am–5pm. Closed Jan 1, Good Friday, and Dec 25–26.

Fremantle History Museum ✦   Housed in a convict-built former lunatic asylum next to the Fremantle Arts Centre, this small but densely packed museum uses lots of old photographs and personal possessions to paint a realistic picture of what life was like for Fremantle's first settlers, the Aborigines they displaced, and later generations up to the present day.

In the Fremantle Arts Centre (see above), 1 Finnerty St. at Ord St. © **08/9430 7966.** Free admission; donation requested. Sun–Fri 10:30am–4:30pm; Sat and public holidays 1–5pm. Closed Jan 1, Good Friday, and Dec 25–26.

Fremantle Prison ✦   Even jails boasted attractive architecture in the 1850s. This limestone jail, built to house 1,000 inmates by convicts who no doubt ended up inside it, was a maximum-security prison until 1991. Take the 75-minute main tour to see cells re-created in the style of past periods of the jail's history, bushranger (highwayman) Joe Moondyne's "escape-proof" cell, the gallows, the workshops, the chapel, the hospital, jailers' houses, and cell walls featuring some wonderful artwork by the former inmates. The ticket price includes an additional 45-minute tour (the precinct tour) that visits the other areas, including the women's prison and commissariat, hourly after the main tour. You must book ahead for the 90-minute **candlelight tours** ✦ on Wednesday and Friday only.

1 The Terrace. © **08/9336 9200.** www.fremantleprison.com. Free admission to prison precinct and visitor center. Tours A$15 (US$12) adults, A$12 (US$9.60) seniors and students, A$7.50 (US$6) children 4–15, A$40 (US$32) families of 5. Candlelight tour A$19 (US$15) adults, A$15 (US$12) seniors and students, A$10 (US$8) children, A$50

(US$40) families. Daily 10am–6pm. Main tours every 30 min. 10am–5pm. Precinct tours every hour 11:30am–4:30pm. Candlelight tours Wed and Fri 7pm winter, 7:30pm summer. Closed Good Friday and Dec 25.

The Roundhouse   This 12-sided jail is the oldest public building in the state (built in 1831). There are few displays, but it's worth a visit for history's sake, and for the sea views on the other side. The time cannon, just to its west, is a replica of a gun salvaged from an 1878 wreck. The cannon is fired and a **time ball** dropped at 1pm daily, just as it was in the 1800s, from a deck overlooking the ocean. You might be that day's honorary gunner chosen from the crowd! The Roundhouse is a short walk from the Fremantle train station. You can also walk through the Whalers Tunnel to Bathers Beach. Volunteer guides are on hand to explain it all.

10 Arthur Head (enter over the railway line from High St.). ℂ **08/9336 6897**. Admission by gold coin donation, A$1 or A$2 (US80¢ or US$1.60). Daily 10:30am–3:30pm. Closed Good Friday and Dec 25.

Shipwreck Galleries   The massive hulk of the Dutch ship *Batavia,* wrecked north of Perth in 1629, will stop you in your tracks as you enter one of the first displays in this fascinating museum. The *Batavia*'s story is of survival and betrayal; most of the survivors of the wreck were massacred by a handful of mutineers. You will love the tales of old wrecks and displays of pieces of eight, glassware, cannon, and other deep-sea treasure recovered off the Western Australian coast. The museum is renowned for its work in maritime archaeology. Displays date from the 1600s, when Dutch explorers became the first Europeans to encounter Australia.

Cliff St. ℂ **08/9431 8444**. Admission by donation. Daily 9:30am–5pm. Closed Good Friday, Dec 25, and until 1pm Apr 25 (Anzac Day) and Dec 26. Free tours daily 10am, 11am, 2pm, and 3pm (check at reception).

Western Australian Maritime Museum ★★   I could (and did) spend hours wandering in this fascinating museum, now in a new home at the western end of Victoria Quay. The museum looks at Fremantle's history and present-day operations as a port, signaling and piloting, navigation ancient and modern, current sailing technology, naval defense, sea trade, and Aboriginal maritime heritage. It also features historic and rare boats, including *Australia II* (the Aussie yacht that won the America's Cup). You can tour HMAS *Ovens,* an Oberon-class submarine, every half-hour starting at 10am. You can buy a joint ticket for the museum and sub, or just for the sub. Museum staffer Elaine Berry leads a 90-minute **Maritime Precinct Walk** for A$10 (US$8) for adults, A$7.50 (US$6) for seniors and groups of four or more, and A$3 (US$2.40) for school-age kids; book by calling the museum at ℂ **08/9431 8455**. Tours can be scheduled to suit your schedule.

Victoria Quay. ℂ **08/9431 8444**. Admission A$10 (US$8) adults, A$3 (US$2.40) children 5–15, A$5 (US$4) seniors and students, A$22 (US$18) for family of 6. Free admission 2nd Tues of each month. Admission to submarine only A$8 (US$6.40) adults, A$5 (US$4) seniors and students, A$3 (US$2.40) children 5–15, A$22 (US$18) family. Daily 9:30am–5pm. Closed Good Friday, Dec 25, and until 1pm Apr 25 (Anzac Day) and Dec 26.

WHALE-WATCHING CRUISES, TRAM TRIPS & OTHER TOURS

Boat Torque Cruises (ℂ 08/9421 5888), **Golden Sun Cruises** (ℂ 08/9325 9916), and **Oceanic Cruises** (ℂ 08/9325 1191) run an assortment of morning, afternoon, sunset, luncheon, dinner, half-, and full-day cruises on the Swan River. Some go as far as Fremantle, and to historic homes and vineyards in the Swan Valley. Oceanic Cruises offers a lunch cruise to see wild sea lions at Carnac Island, just off Fremantle. The cruise from Perth costs A$99 (US$79) adults, A$89 (US$71) children 13 to 17, A$59 (US$47) kids 4 to 12 (less from Fremantle). **Captain Cook Cruises** (ℂ 08/9325 3341) also runs cruises on the Perth-Fremantle route; it offers an Aboriginal cultural cruise that includes a guided bushland walk that costs A$37 (US$30) adults, A$33 (US$26) seniors and students, and A$20 (US$16) kids 4 to 14. Lunch costs A$18 (US$14) more.

From September through November, Perth's waters are alive with southern right and humpback **whales** returning from the north with their calves. To join a 2- or 3-hour jaunt to watch them, contact Boat Torque Cruises or Oceanic Cruises. Departure days and times vary from year to year with every cruise operator, so check ahead. Prices range from A$30 (US$24) to around A$50 (US$40), and about half price for kids.

The **Aquarium of Western Australia,** or **AQWA** (© 08/9447 7500) runs whale-watching tours on Wednesdays, weekends, and public holidays during the season (Oct to early Dec) at 9am and 11:30am. Tours, limited to 12 people, are on board an ocean rafter that gives "eye level" encounters with the magnificent mammals. The cost of A$90 (US$72) per person includes admission to AQWA. Bookings are essential.

The **Perth Tram Co.** (© 08/9322 2006) makes a daily loop of the city, the casino, and Kings Park in replica 1899 wooden trams; hop on and off as often as you wish. Tickets, which you buy on board, cost A$15 (US$12) for adults, A$13 (US$10) for seniors, A$7 (US$5.60) for children under 15, and A$37 (US$30) for families. City-casino, city–Kings Park, and casino–Kings Park single legs are also available. Join anywhere; the tram starts at 565 Hay St. at 9:40am and makes six narrated 90-minute loops a day.

Feature Tours (© 1800/999 819 in Australia, or 08/9475 2900; www.ft.com.au) runs half- and full-day coach tours to attractions in and around Perth.

ACTIVE PURSUITS

BIKING   Perth's superb bike-track network stretches for miles along the Swan River, through Kings Park, around Fremantle, and all the way down the beaches. A great 9.5km (6-mile) track around Perth Water, the broad expanse of river in front of the central business district, starts at the Swan River on Riverside Drive and goes over the Causeway bridge, back along the other bank and over the bridge at the Narrows back to the city. The state Department of Transport's cycling division, Bikewest, publishes a range of useful bike-route maps to the city. They are available in bike shops, from most newsdealers, and at the **Perth Map Centre,** 900 Hay St. (© 08/9322 5733).

Rental from **Koala Bike Hire,** in the car park behind Fraser's restaurant in Kings Park (© 08/9321 3061), is A$5 (US$4) for an hour, or A$16 (US$13) for the day, which includes a helmet (required by law in Australia), lock, and maps of Kings Park.

GOLF   Most convenient to the city is Burswood Park Golf Course, part of the **Burswood International Resort Casino,** across the river on the Great Eastern Highway, Burswood (© 08/9362 7576 pro shop). A 9-hole round is just A$17 (US$14) weekdays and A$20 (US$16) weekends. A cart for 9 holes is A$22 (US$18), and club rental is A$17 (US$14).

Even more scenic are the 27 championship fairways designed by Robert Trent Jones, Jr., at **Joondalup Resort,** Country Club Boulevard, Connolly, a 25km (16-mile) drive north of Perth (© 08/9400 8811 pro shop); and **The Vines** in the Swan Valley (© 08/9297 3000 resort, or 08/9297 0777 pro shop), which has two 18-hole bushland courses. Joondalup was ranked the number-one Resort Golf Course in Australia by *Golf Australia* magazine in 2005. Kangaroos often come onto both courses. You'll pay around A$40 (US$32) for 9 holes or A$99 (US$79) for 18 holes weekdays at Joondalup; or A$140 (US$112) on Saturdays, A$109 (US$87) on Sundays, including use of a buggy. At The Vines, fees are around A$35 to A$45 (US$28–US$36) for 9 holes and A$60 to A$70 (US$48–US$56) for 18 (or A$85–A$93/US$66–US$74 on weekends, depending on which course you choose). Add A$22 (US$18) per person for a cart.

SAILING   The tallest Tall Ship in Australia, the lovely three-masted barquentine **STS *Leeuwin II*** (© **08/9430 4105;** www.leeuwin.com), sails from B Shed at Victoria Quay, Fremantle, when it is not out on voyages around Australia. You may be one of up to 40 passengers, but you still get the chance to try your hand at sailing the way it used to be done. The ship takes 3- or 4-hour sails in the mornings and afternoons, and at sunset on weekends. The cost is A$66 (US$53) adults or A$33 (US$26) children 12 and under, or A$59 (US$47) for adults and A$33 (US$26) children for sunset sails. Offered less often, "full day" sails run from 10am to 3pm and cost A$99 (US$79) for adults and A$55 (US$44) for children.

Experienced sailors can sometimes find a spot in Thursdays' summer twilight events with members of the **Royal Perth Yacht Club,** Australia II Drive, Crawley (© **08/9389 1555;** ask for the sailing administrator), if there is a place available. It's not spinnaker sailing, so the action is at an easy pace. All-white dress standards apply.

SCUBA DIVING & SNORKELING   Just 19km (12 miles) off Perth, Rottnest Island's corals, reef fish, wrecks, and limestone caverns, in 18-to-35m (59–115-ft.) visibility, are a gift from heaven to Perth divers and snorkelers. Contact **Rottnest Malibu Diving** (© **08/9292 5111**) on Rottnest Island (see "Side Trips from Perth," below) to rent gear or join a dive trip.

SURFING   You will find good surfing at many city beaches, Scarborough and Trigg in particular. See the "Hitting the Beaches" section, earlier in this chapter. Rottnest Island (see "Side Trips from Perth," below) also has good breaks. **Murray Smith Surf Centre,** Shop 14, Luna Maxi Mart, Scarborough (© **08/9245 2988**), rents long boards for A$20 (US$16) for half a day or A$30 (US$24) for the day, plus a A$100 (US$80) refundable deposit. It also rents body boards. **Surfing WA** (© **08/9448 0004**) runs surfing classes for A$50 (US$40) per person per hour for groups of up to eight people. It gets cheaper the bigger your group is. Boards, wet suits, and sunscreen are provided.

THE SHOPPING SCENE

Most shops are downtown on the parallel **Hay Street** and **Murray Street malls,** 1 block apart, and in the network of arcades running off them, such as the Plaza, City, Carillon, and Tudor-style **London Court** arcades. Off Murray Street Mall on Forrest Place is the **Forrest Chase shopping complex,** housing the Myer department store and boutiques on two levels. Add to your collection of international designer brands on posh **King Street.**

If you want to avoid the chains, spend half a day in **Subiaco** ⚓ or "Subi," where Hay Street and Rokeby Road are lined with smart boutiques, art galleries, cafes, antiques shops, and markets. The Colonnade shopping center at 388 Hay St. showcases groovy young Aussie fashion designers in its Studio 388 section.

Fremantle's shopping is mostly limited to a good selection of crafts, markets, and Aboriginal souvenirs.

Shops are open until 9pm on Friday in the city, and until 9pm on Thursday in Subiaco and Fremantle.

Finds **Desert Designs**

Aboriginal artist **Jimmy Pike** grew up in Western Australia's Sandy Desert and was one of the first to start transferring his Dreamtime art and designs to fabrics, in 1981. He died in 2002, but his commercial work lives on in clothing and accessories—including children's gear—bearing his designs at the **Desert Designs** boutique, 114 High St. Mall, Fremantle (✆ **08/9430 4101**). For paintings and limited-edition prints by Jimmy Pike and many other Aboriginal artists, visit the **Japingka Gallery,** 47 High St., Fremantle (✆ **08/9335 8265**). It also stocks didgeridoos, artifacts, and stunning high-quality hand-tufted woolen floor rugs.

ABORIGINAL ARTS & CRAFTS   **Creative Native,** 32 King St. (✆ **08/9321 5470**), stocks Perth's widest range of Aboriginal arts and crafts. Upstairs is a gallery selling original works by some renowned Aboriginal artists. There's another branch at 65 High St., Fremantle (✆ **08/9335 7438**).

Indigenart, 115 Hay St., Subiaco (✆ **08/9388 2899**), and 82 High St., Fremantle (✆ **08/9335 2911**), stocks works on canvas, paper, and bark, as well as artifacts, textiles, pottery, didgeridoos, boomerangs, and sculpture, by world-famous and lesser-known Aboriginal artists from all over Australia.

JEWELRY   Western Australia is renowned for farming the world's best **South Sea pearls** off Broome, for Argyle **diamonds** mined in the Kimberley, and for being one of the world's biggest **gold** producers.

Artisans of the Sea, corner of Marine Terrace and Collie Street, Fremantle (✆ **08/ 9336 3633**), sells elegant South Sea pearls and gold jewelry.

Some of Perth's other leading jewelers, where you can buy opals, Argyle diamonds, and Broome pearls, are **Costello's,** Shop 5–6, London Court (✆ **08/9325 8588**), and **Linneys,** 37 Rokeby Rd., Subiaco (✆ **08/9382 4077**).

For opals to suit all budgets, head to the Perth outlet of **Quilpie Opals,** Shop 6, Piccadilly Arcade off Hay Street Mall (✆ **08/9321 8687**).

PERTH AFTER DARK

Scoop (see "Visitor Information," earlier in this chapter) is a good source of information on festivals and concerts, performing arts, classical music, exhibitions, and the like. Your best guide to dance clubs, rock concerts, gig listings, art-house cinemas, theater, and art galleries is the free weekly *X-press* magazine, available at pubs, cafes, and music venues every Thursday. The *West Australian* and *Sunday Times* newspapers publish a limited amount of entertainment information, including cinema guides.

Two ticket agencies handle most of the city's major performing arts, entertainment, and sporting events: the performing arts–oriented **BOCS** (✆ **1800/193 300** in Australia, or 08/9484 1133; www.bocsticketing.com.au) and the sports-and-family-entertainment-oriented **Ticketmaster 7** (✆ **13 61 00;** www.ticketmaster7.com). Book opera, ballet, the orchestra, and the Black Swan Theatre Company (see below) through BOCS.

THE PERFORMING ARTS   The **West Australian Opera** (✆ **08/9321 5869** administration) and **West Australian Ballet** (✆ **08/9481 0707** administration) usually perform at **His Majesty's Theatre,** 825 Hay St., a restored "grande dame" venue from the early 1900s. Perth's leading theatrical company, the **Black Swan Theatre Company** (℃ **08/6389 0311** administration), plays at theaters around town. The **West Australian Symphony Orchestra** (℃ **08/9326 0000**) usually performs at the **Perth Concert Hall,** 5 St. Georges Terrace, next to the Duxton Hotel. This hall has the best acoustics of any such venue in Australia; such acts as the London Philharmonic, comedian Billy Connolly, and legendary blues guitarist B. B. King have performed here.

Perth is an outdoors kinda place. In summer, look for outdoor concerts or jazz at **Perth Zoo** (℃ **08/9474 3551** for recorded information, or 08/9474 0444 administration); movies at Perth's several outdoor cinemas; and open-air concerts, plays, and movies in **Kings Park** (℃ **08/9480 3600**).

PUBS, BARS & NIGHTCLUBS   Northbridge houses most of the city's lively pubs and dance clubs. Don't forget that Freo has good pubs, too (see "A Day Out in Fremantle," earlier in this chapter).

For a trendy take on the traditional pub, head to the **Brass Monkey,** 209 William St. at James Street, Northbridge (℃ **08/9227 9596**). Downstairs are several bars, including a wine bar serving gourmet pizzas, and a beer garden. Wednesday to Saturday, head upstairs to the Glasshouse for live entertainment, including the Laugh Resort comedy club at 8pm Wednesday for a A$10 (US$8) cover.

In Subiaco, suits flock to the "Subi," also known as the **Subiaco Hotel,** 465 Hay St. at Rokeby Road (℃ **08/9381 3069**), a popular historic pub with a stylish cafe, great cocktails, and live jazz on Wednesday and Saturday nights.

If your "dancing till 6am" days are over but you still know how to hit the floor, check out **Margeaux's,** a nightclub popular with the over-30 crowd, in the Parmelia Hilton, 14 Mill St. (℃ **08/9215 2000**). It's open Saturday 9pm to 3:30am.

In Fremantle, the **Metropolis,** 58 S. Terrace (℃ **08/9336 1880**), is a complex of five dance floors and eight bars on several levels. It's open Friday 9pm to 5am, Saturday 9pm to 6am, and Sunday 9pm to 1am.

BURSWOOD CASINO   A 2,300-seat theater that features some major international stars is in the **Burswood International Resort Casino,** on the Great Eastern Highway just over the river from the city (℃ **08/9362 7777** for information; BOCS [see above] for bookings). Live bands, disco, cabaret performers, or karaoke play nightly, and there are nine restaurants and six bars, including a nightclub. The main gaming floor has 88 tables and 1,300 gaming machines. Some of the casino's most popular games include roulette, blackjack, and two-up. There's also a VIP players' room and a Keno Lounge. The 24-hour casino operates every day except Good Friday, April 25 (Anzac Day), and December 25, and is open to everyone over the age of 18. Dress code is "neat and tidy," with smarter standards after 7pm. It's about a A$16 (US$13) cab ride from the city, or take a train to Burswood station.

2 Side Trips from Perth

ROTTNEST ISLAND: GETTING FACE TO FACE WITH THE FISHES ★★
19km (12 miles) W of Perth

The delightful wildlife reserve of Rottnest Island, off the Perth coast, is like the city's own Great Barrier Reef in miniature. Its jewel-bright waters, warm currents, rocky coves, and many sheltered beaches harbor **coral reefs** and 360 kinds of fish that make for fabulous snorkeling. You may spot humpback whales September through December, and dolphins surfing the waves anytime. The island is also home to 10,000 **quokkas,** cute otterlike marsupials that reach up to your knees. A wonderful thing about Rottnest is that there are no cars. Everyone gets around by bike (or bus, if you tire of pedaling over the mostly moderate-grade hills). The island is 11km (7 miles) long and 4.5km (3 miles) across at its widest point.

ESSENTIALS

GETTING THERE   Boat Torque Cruises (© **08/9421 5888**) and **Oceanic Cruises** (© **08/9325 1191**) operate at least three times a day from Perth (trip time: about 1 hr., 45 min.), and four to seven times a day from Fremantle (trip time: about 25 min.). The **Rottnest Express ferry** (© **08/9335 6406**) runs four or five times a day from Fremantle only. Round-trip fares average about A$63 (US$50) from Perth, or about A$50 (US$40) from Fremantle. Boat Torque and Oceanic pick you up free from most Perth and Fremantle hotels. You pay about A$5 (US$4) more if you return on a later day. Most boat operators offer day-trip and accommodations packages.

   Rottnest Air Taxi (© **1800/500 006** in Western Australia, or 08/9292 5027; www.rottnest.de) provides aerial transfers in four or six-seater (including the pilot) aircraft. A same-day round-trip in a four-seater costs A$198 (US$158) for the whole plane. **Kookaburra Air** (© **08/9354 1158;** www.kookaburra.iinet.net.au) also operates a range of tours to Rottnest.

VISITOR INFORMATION   The **Rottnest Island Visitor & Information Centre** (© **08/9372 9752**) is right at the end of the jetty on the island. The center is run by the **Rottnest Island Authority** (© **08/9432 9111;** www.rottnest.wa.gov.au). The Perth Visitor Centre (see "Visitor Information" in the Perth section, earlier in this chapter) also has information.

GETTING AROUND   Ferries pull into the jetty in the main town, Thomson Bay Settlement (often just called Settlement). **Rottnest Bike Hire** (© **08/9292 5105**), next to the Rottnest Hotel near the jetty, rents 1,800 bikes of every size, speed, and type, as well as holders for everything from surfboards to babies. An 18-speed bike is A$20 (US$16) for a 24-hour day (plus a A$25/US$20 refundable deposit), including a helmet (compulsory in Australia) and lock. There is no need to reserve a bike.

   The yellow **Bayseeker** bus does half-hourly circumnavigations, calling at 16 stops, including all the best bays. An all-day ticket costs A$7 (US$5.60) for adults, A$3.50 (US$2.80) for children 4 to 12, and A$17 (US$14) for families of four (extra child A$1.65/US$1.30). Buy tickets on board.

   A free bus runs regularly between the airport and four of the five small communities around the island—Thomson Bay Settlement, Geordie, Fay's, and Longreach Bays. It does not run to the Basin, which is a 15-minute walk from Settlement.

ISLAND ORIENTATION TOURS

Many first-time visitors take the 2-hour **Island Coach Tour** because it is a good introduction to the bays and the island's cultural and natural history—and because it includes a stop to see the quokkas. It costs A$22 (US$18) for adults, A$11 (US$8.80) for kids 4 to 12, and A$50 (US$40) for families of four (extra child A$5/US$4). Departure times vary, but you can expect tours to run twice a day, usually around 10:30am and 1:30pm. Buy tickets from the Visitor Centre.

SNORKELING, DIVING, SURFING & FISHING

Most people come to Rottnest to snorkel, swim, surf, dive, or fish. As soon as you arrive, rent a bike and your preferred aquatic gear, and pedal around the coast until you come to a beach that suits you. (Don't forget to carry drinking water and food, because the only shops are at Settlement.) The Basin, Little Parakeet Bay, Little Salmon Bay, and Parker Point are good **snorkel** spots. The Visitor Centre sells maps to suggested snorkel trails. **Surfers** should try Cathedral Rocks or Strickland Bay. **Fishermen** will catch squid, salmon, and tailor, as well as all kinds of reef fish. The island's dive shop, **Rottnest Malibu Diving** (© **08/9292 5111**), near the jetty, rents snorkel gear, dive gear, wet suits, surfboards, body boards, aqua-bikes, and fishing tackle. The company conducts two daily trips to some of the 100-plus dive sites around Rottnest. Some feature limestone caverns and some of the island's 14 shipwrecks. A shore or boat dive with all gear included is A$60 (US$48). If you have never dived before, a 1- to 2-hour theory lesson followed by a boat dive is A$200 (US$160), including round-trip transport from Perth.

FOR HISTORY BUFFS

Rottnest has quite a bit to offer history buffs, who may want to walk (45-min.), cycle, or take a train (see below) to the Oliver Hill 1930s gun emplacements, which have intact 9¼-inch guns and battery tunnels housing an engine room, a plotting room, and observation posts. You can explore the 1.5km (1-mile) heritage trail on your own (maps are at the Visitor Centre), or take a guided 1-hour tour at 9:30am or on the hour from 11am to 2pm. The train, the *Captain Hussey*, was launched in late 2003. It departs from the station near the Visitor Centre hourly from 10:30am to 2:30pm. The fare is A$15 (US$12) for adults, A$7.70 (US$6.15) for children 4 to 12, and A$39 (US$31) for families of four (extra child A$3.85/US$3.10), including the tour (except the last trip, which starts after the last tour).

Volunteer guides run several free 1-hour walking tours. One is a historical tour of architectural points of interest around Thomson Bay, many of which were built in the 19th century, such as the governor's residence, the chapel, the octagonal prison, the small **museum** (© **08/9372 9752;** open daily 11am–4pm), and the former Boys' Reformatory. Another heritage trail takes you to the memorial marking de Vlamingh, the Dutch explorer who named the island Rott Enest (Rat Nest) in 1696 when he mistook quokkas for rats. There are also quokka walks, an Aboriginal historical walk, and a walk to Bathurst lighthouse.

WHERE TO STAY & DINE

Call the **Rottnest Island Authority's accommodations booking service** (© **08/ 9432 9111**) to book one of the island's 250-plus holiday homes, apartments, cabins, or historic cottages, or the campground. Don't expect anything new or upscale. Water and electricity restrictions mean no accommodations are air-conditioned. Book well in advance all through summer; accommodations during the peak Western Australian school vacation times are allotted through a lottery system, for which you must submit an application.

Apart from the very nice restaurants at the hotels listed below, the casual tearooms, and a couple of lackluster takeout joints, your only other dining option is the excellent **DOME Cafe** at the jetty.

Shoulder season is usually April through May, and September through November or December. The winter season is June through August.

Quokka Arms   Formerly the Rottnest Hotel, this 1864 building near the jetty began life as the state governor's summer residence, and underwent a major renovation in late 2004. Now, day-trippers gather in the sports bar or the large open-air beer garden to admire the ocean views over an ale or two. The building contains pleasant, motel-style rooms, some with a small patio and sea views. Apart from the Lakeside units at Rottnest Lodge (below), these are the best hotel rooms on the island. Guests have the use of a barbecue. No smoking indoors.

Bedford Ave, Rottnest Island, WA 6161. © **08/9292 5011.** Fax 08/9292 5188. www.axismgt.com.au/rottnesthotel. 18 units (all with shower only). Peak season (Dec–Jan) A$180–A$200 (US$144–US$160) double; shoulder season A$160–A$180 (US$128–US$144) double; low season A$150–A$170 (US$120–US$136) double. Extra person A$40 (US$32). Crib A$15 (US$12). Rates include continental breakfast. Ask about midweek packages. AE, DC, MC, V. **Amenities:** 2 restaurants; bar; beer garden; nonsmoking rooms. *In room:* TV, fridge, no phone.

Rottnest Lodge   The Premium Lakeside Rooms at this former colonial barracks and prison are Rottnest's most luxurious accommodations. They have king-size beds, flagstone floors, cream-painted brick walls, contemporary furnishings, and a living area with a wood fireplace. Some have salt-lake views, not always pretty when the water dries up. The remaining Lakeside, Deluxe, Standard, "Quod," and Family rooms, which sleep 2 to 10, are in the historic quarters and are mostly dark, viewless, and small. The two-bedroom family rooms have the advantage of a kitchen and laundry. The lodge is just a few minutes' stroll from the jetty and Visitor Centre.

Kitson St., Rottnest Island, WA 6161. © **08/9292 5161.** Fax 08/9292 5158. www.rottnestlodge.com.au. 80 units (all with shower only). A$185–A$250 (US$148–US$200) Deluxe double; A$155–A$210 (US$124–US$168) Standard double; A$140–A$175 (US$112–US$140) Quod twin room; A$190–A$235 (US$152–US$188) Quod quad; A$195–A$300 (US$156–US$240) Lakeside double; A$385–A$460 (US$308–US$368) Family apt. Extra person A$60 (US$48). Ask about packages. AE, DC, MC, V. **Amenities:** Restaurant; 2 bars; small lagoon-style pool. *In room:* TV w/free movies, fridge, coffeemaker, hair dryer.

IN PURSUIT OF THE GRAPE IN THE SWAN VALLEY ★
20km (13 miles) NE of Perth

Twenty minutes from the Perth city center is the Swan Valley, home to two of Australia's biggest wine labels. In the area are 30 or so wineries, along with a wildlife park, antiques shops, a few galleries, several good restaurants, and Australia's best golf resort. Some restaurants and wineries close Monday and Tuesday.

Lord Street from the Perth city center becomes Guildford Road and takes you to the historic Art Deco town of Guildford at the start of the Swan Valley. The **Swan Valley and Eastern Region Visitors Centre** is at the corner of Meadow and Swan streets, Guildford (© **08/9379 9400;** www.swanvalley.com.au). It's open daily except Christmas from 9am to 4pm. Several companies (see "Whale-Watching Cruises, Tram Trips & Other Tours," earlier in this chapter) run day tours or day cruises from Perth, and local companies run tours by black cab or Rolls Royce. The winery at **Sandalford Caversham Estate** (© **08/9374 0000**) runs its own upscale cruise from Perth that includes a 2-hour winery tour, three-course lunch matched to wines, wine tasting en route and at the winery, souvenir wine glass, and a wine-education kit. The cruise operates on Wednesdays and Sundays and costs A$129 (US$103) adults and A$65 (US$52) children under 17. It includes coach return to Perth.

TOURING THE WINERIES & OTHER THINGS TO DO
Most Swan wineries are small, family-run affairs. An exception is **Houghton Wines,** Dale Road, Middle Swan (© **08/9274 9540;** www.houghton-wines.com.au), Western Australia's oldest, biggest, and most venerable winery. The beamed timber cellar

holds old winemaking machinery, and there are lovely picnic grounds—in November, mauve jacaranda trees blossom gloriously—a cafe, and an art gallery selling works by locals. Open 10am to 5pm daily except Good Friday and December 25.

The other big-name winery is **Sandalford Caversham Estate,** 3210 W. Swan Rd., Caversham (© **08/9374 9374;** www.sandalford.com). You may want to take its 90-minute winery tour, which takes you along walkways over the high-tech production areas. The A$18 (US$14) fee includes a tasting of premium wine and a wine-education kit. It runs three times daily. The winery also has a good gift shop, a pretty vine-covered casual dining area, and a pleasant restaurant.

Both wineries' cellar doors are open daily for free tastings from 10am to 5pm.

The popular **Margaret River Chocolate Company** has an outlet at 5123 W. Swan Rd. (near the Reid Hwy.), West Swan (© **08/9250 1588**). It does sales and tasting, and you can watch chocolate making through the viewing window. Open daily from 10am to 5pm.

After a move in 2003 to Whiteman Park, West Swan, the **Caversham Wildlife Park & Zoo** (© **08/9248 1984**) has smart new homes for its collection of 200 species of mostly Western Australian wildlife. You can stroke koalas (but not hold them), feed kangaroos, pet farm animals, take a camel ride, and, sometimes, cuddle joeys and wombats. It's open daily from 8:30am to 5:30pm, closed December 25. Admission is A$14 (US$11) for adults, A$10 (US$8) for seniors and students, and A$6 (US$4.80) for children 2 to 14.

Antiques lovers should browse the strip of shops on James Street, Guildford (most shops are open daily), or visit **Woodbridge,** a beautifully restored 1883 manor house on Ford Street, West Midland (© **08/9274 2432**). The house is open Thursday through Tuesday from 1 to 4pm; closed Good Friday, all of July, and December 25. Admission is A$5 (US$4) for adults, A$3 (US$2.40) for seniors and children under 16, and A$10 (US$8) for a family of six. Its river-view tearooms serve lunch.

Drop into **Guildford Village Potters** © 08/9279 9859), 22 Meadow St. (next to the Visitors Centre), to check out work by about 20 local women. You may find it hard to resist the raku (open-fired) glazes—I did. Open 9:30am to 3pm weekdays, 9:30am to 4pm weekends and holidays.

One of Perth's best boutiques, the **Swan Valley Boutique** (© **08/9377 2070**) is in an unlikely location: off Johnson Street, Guildford. It serves coffee while you try on clothes by big-name Aussie fashion designers.

WHERE TO STAY

Hansons Swan Valley ★★   Sleek and sophisticated sums up this B&B. White walls and groovy furniture a la Philippe Starck are the hallmarks of this elegant abode, created by former advertising executives Jon and Selina Hanson as the kind of B&B they would like to stay in themselves. Most rooms have king-size beds; all have bathrobes and minibars stocked with cheese, chocolates, and other goodies. Each has its own tiny courtyard or access to the upstairs balcony. Six have Jacuzzis. Start the day with hearty fare in the sunny breakfast room, wander out to enjoy bucolic views of the 10-hectare (25-acre) farm, and end it in the stylish restaurant. No smoking indoors.

60 Forest Rd., Henley Brook, WA 6055. © 08/9296 3366. Fax 08/9296 3332. www.hansons.com.au. 10 units (all with shower only). A$200–A$290 (US$160–US$232) double. Rates include full breakfast. Ask about packages. Children under 15 not accepted. AE, DC, MC, V. Take West Swan Rd. to Henley Brook and turn right at Little River Winery onto Forest Rd.; Hansons is on the left at the end of the road. **Amenities:** Restaurant (see "Where to Dine," below); small outdoor pool; limited room service; in-room massage (with 2-hr. notice); laundry service; dry cleaning; non-smoking rooms. *In room:* A/C, TV/VCR, minibar, hair dryer, iron.

Novotel Vines Resort ⚸   This rural retreat has one of the best resort golf courses in Australia, and is the most upscale place in the Swan Valley. Most rooms or apartments in the low-rise accommodations have balconies looking onto the 36-hole golf course, where kangaroos often join the players, or over the pool or vineyard. The rooms are of a high standard, if a bit stiff and citified. A suite consists of a room with a living area and a Jacuzzi.

Verdelho Dr., Belhus (near Upper Swan), WA 6069. Accor © **1300/656 565** in Australia, 800/221 4542 in the U.S. and Canada, 0870/609 0961 in the U.K., 0800/44 4422 in New Zealand, or 08/9297 3000. Fax 08/9297 3333. www.vines.com.au. 156 units. A$232 (US$186) double; A$296 (US$237) suite; A$312 (US$250) 2-bedroom apt; A$387 (US$310) 3-bedroom apt. Children under 16 stay free in parent's room with existing bedding. Ask about packages. AE, DC, MC, V. Take West Swan Rd. to Upper Swan and turn left on to Millhouse Rd. The resort entrance is about 1.5km (1 mile) on the right. **Amenities:** 2 restaurants; 2 bars; large outdoor lap pool; children's pool; golf course (guest discounts available on application); 4 tennis courts (2 floodlit); 2 squash courts; exercise room; Jacuzzi; concierge; salon; room service (11am–10pm); laundry service; dry cleaning. *In room:* A/C, TV w/pay movies, dataport, minibar, coffeemaker, hair dryer, iron.

WHERE TO DINE

Hansons ⚸⚸ MODERN AUSTRALIAN   This slick restaurant attached to Hansons Swan Valley (see "Where to Stay," above) seats 80 inside and 120 outside. You can choose from a prix-fixe blackboard menu with a glass of wine (available noon–2pm and 6:30–8:30pm) or the a la carte menu, which includes hearty fare such as twice-cooked duck with sour cherry sauce and grilled milk-fed pork sausages. Desserts include a wickedly "adults only" hot fudge sundae and there's also a A$13 (US$10) kids' menu.

60 Forest Rd., Henley Brook. © **08/9296 3366.** www.hansons.com.au. Reservations recommended. Main courses A$24–A$33 (US$19–US$26). AE, DC, MC, V. Daily from noon for lunch, and from 6:30pm for dinner. Take W. Swan Rd. to Henley Brook and turn right at Little River Winery into Forest Rd. Hansons is on the left at the end of the road.

Lamont Winery Cellar Door MODERN AUSTRALIAN   The cellar door kitchen serves food all day Wednesdays to Sunday from a "grazing menu" which features casual fare like pizza or antipasto to eat outside at the farm tables. A gallery on the grounds shows Western Australian art and crafts.

85 Bisdee Rd. (off Moore Rd.), Millendon, near Upper Swan. © **08/9296 4485.** Reservations recommended. A$8.80–A$18 (US$7.05–US$14) main courses AE, DC, MC, V. Wed–Sun 10am–5pm. Closed Dec 25–Jan 1. Take the Great Northern Hwy. to Baskerville, near Upper Swan, take a right onto Haddrill Rd. for 1.6km (1 mile), turn right onto Moore Rd. for 1km (just over ½ mile), and make a right onto Bisdee Rd.

NEW NORCIA: A TOUCH OF EUROPE IN AUSTRALIA ⚸
132km (82 miles) N of Perth

It's the last thing you expect to see in the Australian bush—a Benedictine monastery town with elegant European architecture, a fine museum, and a collection of Renaissance art—but New Norcia is no mirage. Boasting a population of 70 (when everyone's at home), this pretty town and the surrounding 8,000-hectare (19,760-acre) farm were established in 1846 by Spanish Benedictine missionaries. Visitors can tour beautifully frescoed chapels, marvel at one of the finest religious art collections in Australia, stock up on famous New Norcia nut cake straight from the monastery's 120-year-old wood-fired ovens, and attend prayers with the 15 monks who live here.

In complete contrast, just 10km (6¼ miles) south of the monastery and town is the **New Norcia Deep Space Ground Station,** run by the European Space Agency. You can tour the ground station Saturday and Sunday from noon to 2:30pm (Easter–Oct) and watch a video on the Mars Express mission and New Norcia's role in collecting data from the mission. Buy your ticket (A$5/US$4 per person) from the Museum and Art Gallery in town.

New Norcia is an easy 2-hour drive from Perth. From downtown, take Lord Street, which becomes Guildford Road, to Midland, and follow the Great Northern Highway to New Norcia. The **Public Transport Authority** (**PTA**; ✆ **1300/662 205** in Western Australia, or 08/9326 2000; www.transwa.wa.gov.au) runs a coach from Perth on Sunday, Tuesday, Thursday, and Friday for A$16 (US$13) one-way. Day tours from Perth are available. There is no train service.

Conference groups can book the town solid, so reserve accommodations and tours in advance, especially in wildflower season from August through October.

You can get information at the **New Norcia Tourist Information Centre,** New Norcia, WA 6509 (✆ **08/9654 8056;** www.newnorcia.wa.edu.au), in the Museum and Art Gallery, off the highway behind St. Joseph's, beside the Trading Post and Roadhouse. It keeps the same hours as the museum (see below).

EXPLORING THE TOWN & MONASTERY

The New Norcia Tourist Information Centre's intriguing 2-hour **walking tours** are a must. Tickets cost A$13 (US$10) for adults and A$5.50 (US$4.40) for children 12 to 17, free for younger children. Tours depart daily except December 25 at 11am and 1:30pm, and they allow time for you to attend prayers with the monks if you wish. The guide leads you around some of the town's 27 National Trust–classified buildings and gives insight into the monks' lifestyle. You will also see the frescoes in the old monastery chapel and in St. Ildephonsus's and St. Gertrude's colleges. Much of the monastery is closed to visitors, but the tour does show you the fruit gardens and a glimpse of the men-only courtyard. Heritage walking-trail maps (A$3.30/US$2.65), available at the Tourist Information Centre, include more buildings not visited on the tour, such as the octagonal apiary.

The **Museum and Art Gallery** ✪ is full of relics from the monks' past—old mechanical and musical instruments, artifacts from the days when New Norcia was an Aboriginal mission, gifts to the monks from the queen of Spain, and an astounding collection of paintings by Spanish and Italian artists, dating from the 1400s. Give yourself at least an hour here. The museum and gallery are open daily August through October from 9:30am to 5pm, and November through July from 10am to 4:30pm (closed Dec 25). Admission is A$6.50 (US$5.20) for adults, A$5.50 (US$4.40) for seniors and students, and A$2 (US$1.60) for children 6 to 12. Don't leave the gift shop without some of the famous New Norcia nut cake, made at the monastery bakery.

Apart from joining the monks for 15-minute prayers in the monastery chapel five times a day (noon and 2:30pm are the most convenient for day visitors), you can join them for Mass in the Holy Trinity Abbey Church Monday through Saturday at 7:30am and on Sunday at 9am, or at 5:30pm for vespers.

WHERE TO STAY & DINE

St. Benedict's rules of hospitality are paramount in this unusual town. This means that part of the monastery is open to guests, usually those who are looking for a quiet, reflective place to stay and don't mind abiding by a few rules. The accommodations are spartan, and the cost is a donation (A$50/US$40 per person per day is suggested). Call the guesthouse (✆ **08/9654 8002**) to book. For others, the hotel (below) is the best bet.

New Norcia Hotel   When they thought a Spanish royal visit to New Norcia was imminent in 1926, the monks built this grandiose hotel fit for, well, a king. Sadly, the royals never materialized, and the building was used for parents visiting children boarding at the town's colleges. In 1955, it became a hotel. The grand central staircase, soaring pressed-metal ceilings, and imposing Iberian facade hint at its former splendor. The rooms are very simple but comfortable. About 5 years ago, they gained new carpets, curtains, and beds. Only one has a private bathroom, air-conditioning, and a TV. It's nice to eat a meal at the bar or the charmingly faded dining room, and to wander out of your room to sit on the massive veranda upstairs. Breakfast is available for A$11 (US$8.80) continental or A$18 (US$14) cooked; kids eat for half price. The bar gets jumping on Friday and Saturday nights when local farmers come to town. No smoking.

Great Northern Hwy., New Norcia, WA 6509. ℭ **08/9654 8034.** Fax 08/9654 8011. hotel@newnorcia.wa.edu.au 17 units, 1 with bathroom. A$77 (US$62) double without bathroom; A$90 (US$72) double with bathroom. Extra person A$15 (US$12). AE, MC, V. **Amenities:** Restaurant; bar; nonsmoking rooms. *In room:* Fridge, coffeemaker, iron, no phone.

3 Margaret River & the Southwest: Wine Tasting in the Forests ⟨★⟨★

Margaret River: 290km (180 miles) S of Perth

For most Australians, the words "Margaret River" are synonymous with great wine. The area's 42 wineries are scattered among statuesque forests of karri, the world's third-tallest tree species. The wineries produce only about 1% of Australia's wine output, yet they turn out around 10% of the country's top "premium" wines. But there's much more for even Aussies to discover about the Southwest—like the spectacular surf breaks on the 130km (81-mile) coast from Cape Naturaliste in the north to Cape Leeuwin on the southwest tip of Australia; the coastal cliffs, perfect for abseiling (rappelling) and rock climbing; and the honeycomb of limestone caves filled with stalagmites and stalactites. Whales pass by June through December, wildflowers line the roads August through October, and wild birds, kangaroos, and shingle-backed lizards are everywhere. If you like hiking, pack your boots, because there are plenty of trails, from a 15-minute stroll around Margaret River township to a 6-day Cape-to-Cape trek along the sea cliffs. The Southwest is one of Australia's last great wildernesses.

Like wine regions the world over, the Southwest has more than its fair share of cozy B&Bs, galleries, and some super restaurants. Plan to stay at least 2 days.

ESSENTIALS

GETTING THERE   It's a 3½-hour drive to Margaret River from Perth; take the inland South Western Highway (the quickest route) or the more scenic Old Coast Road to Bunbury, and pick up the Bussell Highway to Margaret River.

Air Australia (ℭ **08/9332 5011;** www.airaustralia.net) operates charter flights from Perth's Jandakot airport and a Busselton–Margaret River air taxi service twice a day on weekdays for about A$140 (US$112) per person one-way. **Leeuwin Estate** winery (ℭ **08/9430 4099;** www.leeuwinestate.com.au) arranges charter flights from Perth for A$280 (US$280) per person, including flight, tour and tastings, and lunch in the restaurant.

Southwest Coachlines (ℭ **08/9324 2333**) runs daily service, and two trips on weekends and public and Western Australian school holidays, to Margaret River from Perth for about A$31 (US$25). The **Public Transport Authority** (**PTA;** ℭ **1300/602 205** in Western Australia, or 08/9326 2600; www.transwa.wa.gov.au) runs coach service from Perth, twice daily Sunday through Friday. It takes about 5½ hours. You can also connect to this coach service in Bunbury by taking the twice-daily *Australind* train from Perth to Bunbury—it shaves travel time down to a bit over 4½ hours. Fares are A$31 (US$25) with either mode. Schedules can differ on a public holiday or during Western Australian school vacations. There is no train service.

VISITOR INFORMATION   You will pass many wineries before you get to Margaret River township, but it's worth heading first to the **Margaret River Visitor Centre** to pick up a winery guide. It's at 100 Bussell Hwy. (at Tunbridge St.), Margaret River, WA 6285 (© **08/9757 2911;** www.margaretriverwa.com). It is open daily from 9am to 5pm; closed December 25.

GETTING AROUND   Nine kilometers (5½ miles) past Busselton, which marks the start of the Southwest, the Bussell Highway makes a sharp left and heads south among the wineries through Vasse. It continues 25km (16 miles) on through the tiny village

---

Moments **Taking a Dip with Flipper**

The wild dolphins that come to Monkey Mia's shore (see "The Midwest & the Northwest: Where the Outback Meets the Sea," later in this chapter) are justly famous. But just 2½ hours' drive south of Perth, en route to Margaret River, is a place where you can *swim* ★★ with these creatures. And the tourist hordes that invade Monkey Mia are largely absent!

At the **Dolphin Discovery Centre,** Koombana Drive, Bunbury (© **08/9791 3088;** www.dolphindiscovery.com.au), bottlenose dolphins come into shore in Koombana Bay. You can "float" with them free in the "interaction zone" on the beach in front of the discovery center, under the watchful eye of volunteer guides. The water is only waist-deep, so you can stand if you like. You must not actively swim, chase, or touch them, but they are free to touch you. Reservations are not necessary.

From November to April, the center runs **2-hour boat tours** to swim with some of the bay's 100-plus dolphins in deeper water for A$115 (US$92); you must be over 8. **Naturaliste Charters** (© **1300/361 351** in Australia, or 08/9755 2276) runs excellent 90-minute **dolphin watch cruises** twice daily (except Dec 25 or in bad weather) from the center at 11am and 2pm; they cost A$33 (US$26) adults and A$22 (US$18) kids 4 to 12. The center has showers, a cafe, and a good little ecodisplay on the dolphin life cycle; admission to that is A$4 (US$3.20) adults; A$2 (US$1.60) seniors, students, and children; A$9 (US$7.20) families. The center is open daily from 8am to 5pm (Sept–May) and from 10am to 3pm (June–Aug); closed December 25.

Monkey Mia's fame as a dolphin spot means it draws crowds, so rangers control interaction with the dolphins. You are unlikely to get to touch or swim with dolphins here. So why go all the way to Monkey Mia? Because sightings are almost guaranteed every day. At Bunbury, dolphins don't show up about a third of the time (the best chance of seeing them is 8am–noon). *Note:* You can hand-feed wild dolphins at **Tangalooma Wild Dolphin Resort** near Brisbane (see chapter 6).

Tips **A Wine-Buying Tip**

Most wineries don't deliver internationally, so the place to buy wine if you want to take it out of Australia is the **Margaret River Regional Wine Centre,** 9 Bussell Hwy., Cowaramup (℃ **08/9755 5501;** www.mrwines.com). It stocks about every local wine; does daily tastings of select vintages; and sells maps, visitor guides, and winery guides. The expert staff will help you make your choices, and even tailor your day's foray. It is open Monday through Saturday from 10am to 8pm, and Sunday from noon to 6pm (closed Good Friday, Dec 25, and sometimes Jan 1). You can also order through the website.

---

of Cowaramup, 11km (7 miles) farther through Margaret River proper, and 43km (27 miles) on to windswept Cape Leeuwin and the tiny fishing port of Augusta, on Australia's south coast.

A car is close to essential. **Hertz** (℃ **13 30 39** in Australia, or 08/9758 8331) has an office in Margaret River, or call **Avis** (℃ **1800/679 880** in Australia for reservations in the Southwest). For a taxi, call **Margaret River Taxi Service** (℃ **13 10 08** or 08/9757 3444).

Several companies run sightseeing and winery tours from Margaret River or Perth.

TOURING THE WINERIES

Fans of premium wines will have a field day. Cabernet sauvignon and merlot are the star red varieties, while chardonnay, semillon, and sauvignon blanc are the pick of the bunch of whites. Most wineries offer free tastings from 10am to 4:30pm daily. Most cluster north of Margaret River, around Cowaramup.

The region's top winery is **Leeuwin Estate** ⭐, Stevens Road, Margaret River (℃ **08/9430 4099**). It has a towering reputation, especially for chardonnay; its Art Series label is among Australia's best. Winery tours run three times a day. A relative newcomer, **Voyager Estate,** Stevens Road, Margaret River (℃ **08/9757 6354**), has exquisite rose gardens and a South African Cape Dutch–style cellar. These wines are gaining a good reputation. Other labels to look for are Arlewood Estate, Cape Mentelle, Cullen Wines, Devil's Lair, Evans & Tate, Madfish (Howard Park Wines), Lenton Brae, Pierro, and Sandalford Wines. Vasse Felix winery makes two highly drinkable "quaffers"—Aussie slang for easy-drinking, inexpensive wines—called Theatre Red and Theatre White.

BEYOND THE WINERIES: CAVES, BUSH TUCKER & MORE

Six of the Southwest's 350 or so limestone caves are open to the public. Some contain elaborate stalactite formations. Before or after you visit, stop at **CaveWorks** eco-interpretive center, Lake Cave, Caves Road, 15km (9 miles) south of Margaret River's Wallcliffe Road (℃ **08/9757 7411**). It's open daily except December 25 from 9am to 5pm. Entry is free if you tour Lake, Jewel, or Mammoth cave, otherwise A$3 (US$2.40) for adults, A$2 (US$1.60) for children 4 to 15.

Lake Cave, right outside CaveWorks and 300 steps down an ancient sinkhole, contains a tranquil pond that reflects the exquisite stalactites. Four kilometers (2½ miles) north along Caves Road is **Mammoth Cave,** where you can see the fossilized jaw of a baby zygotaurus trilobus, an extinct giant wombat. **Jewel Cave,** 8km (5 miles) north of Augusta on Caves Road, is the prettiest. Tours of Lake and Jewel and self-guided tours (using a CD audio system) of Mammoth each cost A$17 (US$14) for adults, A$7.50 (US$6) for children 4 to 16, A$46 (US$37) for a family of four. A Grand Tour Pass to all three plus CaveWorks saves you a little money. Mammoth is open from 9am to 5pm (last tour at 4pm); tours of Lake and Jewel run hourly from 9:30am to 3:30pm. Sometimes extra tours are scheduled during school vacations. The caves are open every day except December 25. Book tours through CaveWorks.

Calgardup and Giants caves, run by the Department of Conservation and Land Management (CALM), are more challenging. The caves are not electrically lit, and there are no guides. Visitors receive helmets, lamps, and information, and may spend as long as they like exploring. **Calgardup Cave** goes to a depth of 27m (81ft.) and has boardwalks to help negotiate it. Calgardup is on Caves Road, about 12 minutes' drive south of Margaret River and 3 minutes north of the Conto's Road turnoff. It is open from 9am to 4:15pm daily. **Giants Cave,** 20 minutes south of Margaret River on Caves Road, is one of the largest and deepest caves on the Leeuwin-Naturaliste Ridge. It is 575m (1,725 ft.) long and about 86m (258 ft.) deep. It's open 9:30am to 3:30pm on school and public holidays, and some other times. Entry to Calgardup or Giants costs A$10 (US$8) adult, A$5 (US$4) child, including helmets and lamps. Buy tickets at the **National Park Information Centre** (© 08/9757 7422) at Calgardup Cave. The center also has walking maps and information on camping sites and activities in the Leeuwin-Naturaliste National Park.

Another "adventure cave" where you get down and dirty crawling on your hands and knees—in the protective clothing supplied—is **Ngilgi Cave,** Caves Road, Yallingup (© 08/9755 2152), for A$70 (US$56) for anyone over 15. A guided tour departs daily at 9:30am and takes about 3 hours. Book 24 hours ahead. Ngilgi's main chamber has translucent stalactite "shawls," which anyone can explore on a semiguided tour (guides are available to answer questions and explain points of interest but do not conduct visitors through the caves). This costs A$15 (US$12) for adults and A$6 (US$4.80) for children 5 to 17, or A$42 (US$34) for a family, and runs half-hourly from 9:30am to 3:30pm (4pm during school vacations, 5pm during Christmas school vacations). Flashlight tours cost A$18 (US$14) adults and A$12 (US$9.60) children (minimum A$140/US$112 group). The cave is open every day except December 25.

Food-based attractions are opening up in the area all the time. You can pick your own kiwi, raspberries, and other fruit at the **Berry Farm,** 222 Bessell Rd., outside Margaret River (© 08/9757 5054), or buy them ready-made as attractively packaged sparkling, dessert, and port wines; jams; and vinegars. At the **Margaret River Chocolate Company,** Harman's Mill Road (at Harman's Rd. S.), Metricup (© 08/9755

(*Moments* Under the Stars with the Stars

Every February or March, **Leeuwin Estate Winery** (© 08/9430 4099; www. leeuwinestate.com.au) stages an **outdoor concert** ⭐ starring some leading showbiz light (past performers have included include Sting, k. d. lang, Shirley Bassey, Julio Iglesias, and Diana Ross, among others) and usually a major orchestra, attended by 6,000 picnicking guests. Tickets are about A$110 (US$88). This is a big local event, so book months ahead.

> ### *Moments* Scenic Drives
>
> **Boranup Drive** ⭐ is a magical detour off Caves Road through towering karris (though keep in mind that your rental car is not insured on its unpaved surface). It leaves Caves Road 6km (3¾ miles) south of Mammoth Cave and rejoins it after a 14km (8¾-mile) meander. **Caves Road** is a 106km (66-mile) north-south drive through forest and farms, from Busselton to Augusta on Cape Leeuwin in the south.

6555), you can participate in free tastings, watch the candy-making through a window, and, of course, buy up the sweet stuff. Open daily 9am to 5pm.

Plenty of **hiking trails** are in this area, whether you want an easy stroll to a whale-watch lookout, an afternoon's ramble through the forest, or an overnight trek. The tourist information center in Margaret River (see "Visitor Information," above) sells trail maps, including maps to all the open sections of the Cape-to-Cape cliff-edge walk from Cape Naturaliste to Cape Leeuwin.

Try to make time for a tour offered by **"Bushtucker Woman" Helen Lee** ⭐ (© **08/9757 1084,** or 0419/911 971 mobile; www.bushtuckertours.com). On one tour, she has you canoeing up the river, exploring a cave, and eating smoked emu, grub pâté, and other Aboriginal delicacies on a river island. It runs daily from 9:45am to 2pm and costs A$50 (US$40) for adults and A$30 (US$24) for kids under 16. Her winery tour has an alternative bent incorporating short karri-forest walks, insights into organic winemaking, tastings of up to 40 wines at five or six wineries, a visit to Leeuwin Estate's herb garden, and a gourmet lunch at a local winery. She'll teach you things like how vaporized peppermint oil from the native trees condenses on the grapes to create the distinctive flavor of Margaret River whites. The 6-hour tour departs daily at 11am and costs A$60 (US$48) per person.

Surfing lessons ⭐ from four-time Western Australian professional surfing champion **Josh Palmateer** (© **08/9757 3850,** or 0418/958 264 mobile) are a must! Two-hour lessons in the gentle surf at Rivermouth Beach (they will pick you up and take you to the beach) run daily and cost A$100 (US$80) for a private lesson or A$40 (US$32) per person if you join a group, including use of wet suits and boards. Lessons run September through June. They also rent boards and wetsuits, if you are already a Master of the Surf Universe and want to try legendary Smiths Beach or the Three Bears (Mama, Papa, and Baby) break at Yallingup, the double-barreled North Point at Gracetown, or the plentiful breaks at Prevelly Park.

From June through December, **whales** play just offshore all along the coast. There is a whale lookout near the Cape Naturaliste lighthouse. Daily 3-hour whale-watching cruises with **Naturaliste Charters** ⭐ (© **08/9755 2276**) depart June through August from Augusta (where you'll also see fur seals and often dolphins). September through December, cruise departures switch to Dunsborough, where whales rest their calves. The boat is fitted with an underwater camera connected to a TV and a hydrophone, so you can see and hear the creatures. Cruises cost A$48 (US$38) for adults, A$42 (US$34) for seniors and students, and A$27 (US$22) for children 4 to 12, A$140 (US$112) for a family of four, free for children under 4.

WHERE TO STAY

Margaret River is the best place to stay in the Southwest because it has all the amenities, like banks, a supermarket, restaurants, and shops. The blink-and-you'll-miss-it hamlet of **Cowaramup,** 11km (6¾ miles) north of Margaret River township, is close to wineries and has a general store, a cafe, and one or two interesting crafts shops. **Vasse** is a tiny settlement at the northern edge of the Southwest, 36km (23 miles) north of Margaret River. Some places may require a minimum 2-night stay on weekends.

IN MARGARET RIVER

Basildene Manor ★   This lovely National Trust–classified farmhouse was built by the local lighthouse keeper in 1912 out of local stone. Following a supremely tasteful refurbishment in 1997 by the friendly proprietors, Garry Nielsen and Julie Whittingham, it's now a gentrified B&B with attractive guest rooms. Some lead off an impressive jarrah gallery overlooking the cozy "Main Hall" with its open fire, and there are guest lounges with books and videos to borrow. Suites are large rooms with sitting areas, and eight of them added in 1999 have Jacuzzi bathrooms. Breakfast is served in the pretty conservatory overlooking the 5.5-hectare (14-acre) grounds. In-house dining is provided by local restaurant **Vat 107** (see "Where to Dine," below). No smoking indoors.

Lot 100 Wallcliffe Rd. (2km/1¼ miles west of town), Margaret River, WA 6285. ℂ 08/9757 3140. Fax 08/9757 3383. www.basildene.com.au. 17 units (all with shower only). A$244–A$369 (US$195–US$295) double. 2-night stay required on weekends. Rates include full breakfast. AE, DC, MC, V. Free parking. Children under 15 not accepted. **Amenities:** Heated outdoor pool (Nov–Apr); tennis court; room service; in-room massage; free guest laundry; laundry service; dry cleaning; nonsmoking rooms; Internet access. *In room:* A/C, TV/VCR, minibar, coffeemaker, hair dryer, iron.

Heritage Trail Lodge ★   Although they're on the highway right "in" Margaret River (within walking distance of restaurants), this row of salmon-pink cabin-style

---

Tips **Galleries Galore**

The natural beauty of the Margaret River region has inspired many artists to make their homes here. You can meet them, watch them work, and perhaps buy a unique souvenir to take home by following the **Artisans Map,** available from tourist information centers, hotels, and galleries. The map shows around 30 studios and galleries.

Just outside Margaret River, stop off to see potters Rod Dilkes and Tova Hoffman creating their lustrous "phoenix" bowls with iridescent glazes. The **Dilkes-Hoffman Studio** is on Caves Road, 4km (2½ miles) north of Walcliffe Road (ℂ 08/9757 2998). Others in the "don't miss" category are **Gunyulgup Galleries,** Gunyulgup Valley Drive (off Caves Rd.) near Yallingup (ℂ 08/9755 2177), and **Yallingup Galleries** on Caves Road (ℂ 08/9755 2372), where you can see the work of many fine Australian artists, furniture makers, jewelers, and craftspeople. Serious lovers of glass art should head to **Fox Galleries,** Karridale, south of Margaret River (ℂ 08/9758 6712). Master glassmaker Alan Fox opens his studio only on Sunday from 10am to 5pm and weekdays by appointment. The going rate for one of his exquisite pieces is A$20,000 to A$30,000 (US$16,000–US$24,000), and if you've got the money, you're in good company—Queen Elizabeth has a piece in her private collection.

rooms, built in 1997, sit in a serene karri forest, out of sight of town. Each spacious unit (including the room for travelers with disabilities) has king double or king twin beds and a double Jacuzzi, from which you can see the forest. The rooms back onto a 35-minute bushwalk trail. Welcoming proprietors Hugh and Maxine Beckingham serve a delicious gourmet breakfast of local produce including cereals, yogurt, local jams, cheeses, and breads in the sunny pine dining room. They can help you plan your itinerary. No smoking indoors.

31 Bussell Hwy. (almost .5km/¼ mile north of town), Margaret River, WA 6285. ℃ **08/9757 9595.** Fax 08/9757 9596. www.heritage-trail-lodge.com.au. 10 units (all with shower only). A$210–A$259 (US$168–US$207) double. Extra person A$35 (US$28). Rates include gourmet continental breakfast. Ask about midweek packages. AE, DC, MC, V. Children under 16 not accepted. **Amenities:** Nonsmoking rooms. *In room:* A/C, TV, minibar, coffeemaker, hair dryer, iron.

IN COWARAMUP

The Noble Grape English cottage gardens surround this recently built colonial-style B&B. Each well-maintained room is motel-like but homey and welcoming, with a modern bathroom, a comfy sitting area, and a small rear patio opening onto bird-filled trees. One is suitable for travelers with disabilities, and a family unit with two bedrooms sleeps five. Although you're on the highway here, the rooms are quiet. Hair dryers are at reception. No smoking indoors.

Lot 18, Bussell Hwy., Cowaramup, WA 6284. ℃/fax **08/9755 5538.** www.noblegrape.com.au. 6 units (all with shower only). A$115–A$150 (US$92–US$120) double; A$15 (US$12) child under 12. Extra person A$25 (US$20). Rates include continental breakfast. Ask about packages. AE, DC, MC, V. **Amenities:** Coin-op laundry; nonsmoking rooms. *In room:* Ceiling fans, TV, fridge, coffeemaker, no phone.

WHERE TO DINE

Good restaurants are attached to a number of wineries, including Vasse Felix, Drift-wood Estate, and Brookland Valley Vineyard. **Leeuwin Estate's restaurant** ✫✫, Stevens Road, Margaret River (℃ **08/9430 4099**), has terrific food. It's cozy in winter, and in summer its deck overlooking lawns is just the spot for lunch.

Newtown House ✫✫ MODERN FRENCH/AUSTRALIAN The Southwest boasts some of the best restaurants in Australia, and this is one of 'em. Folks come from far and wide to savor chef Stephen Reagan's dishes, such as rare local venison with roast pears, beets, and red-wine glaze. Desserts are no letdown—caramel soufflé with lavender ice cream and hot caramel sauce is typical. Located in a historic homestead, the restaurant consists of two simple, intimate rooms with sisal matting and contemporary, boldly colored walls. Even better, it's BYO. You can also drop by for morning or afternoon tea.

737 Bussell Hwy. (9km/5½ miles past Busselton), Vasse. ℃ **08/9755 4485.** Reservations recommended, especially at dinner. Main courses A$20–A$25 (US$16–US$20) lunch, A$27–A$32 (US$22–US$26) dinner. AE, DC, MC, V. Tues–Sat 10am–10:30pm or later.

Vat 107 ✫ *Overrated* MODERN AUSTRALIAN Touted by many West Australians as "one of the best restaurants in Australia," Vat 107 serves undeniably very good food, but the service on my visit was not up to the same standard, which was disappointing after such rave reviews from the locals. Dishes included flame-grilled lamb on truffled polenta with balsamic and grilled mushroom, and grilled Margaret River marron (a crustacean) on tomato, basil, cucumber, mint, and buffalino cheese salad. You'll have room for dessert—perhaps sticky date walnut and fig pudding with toffee sauce and honeycomb.

Tips **If Wine Is Not Your Tipple**

If your tastes run more to beer than champagne, head for **Bootleg Brewery,** the "beer oasis" on Pusey Road, Wilyabrup (✆ **08/9755 6300**). You'll find a range of amber fluids, including traditional ales and European styles, all brewed on the premises. Complementing the great beers is a menu of tasty dishes such as beery beef potpie and venison burgers, as well as the usual soups, fish and chips, and other pub-style food. Main courses cost around A$18 to A$22 (US$14–US$18), and the riverside setting—complete with a playground—is a relaxing spot for lunch after a tough morning on the tourist trail. Open daily 10am to 4:30pm; lunch served noon to 3pm. Make a reservation on weekends and holidays.

---

107 Bussell Hwy., Margaret River. ✆ **08/9758 8877**. Reservations recommended. Main courses A$16–A$35 (US$13–US$28). AE, MC, V. Daily 11am–late.

Wino's ★★ *Finds* MODERN AUSTRALIAN   Tapas, tastes, and terrific atmosphere. This gets my vote for the best place to eat in Margaret River. You can sit in the buzzing bar or head to the quieter restaurant section. We went for the tapas plates and "bar grits"—sardines wrapped in prosciutto with caperberries and gremolata, duck-liver parfait with orange reduction, and octopus salad. Small pizzas came with toppings like sweet potato, pimento and feta; anchovy, olives and chiles; and salami, red onion, and rocket pesto. You order wine by the "taste," glass, or bottle. In the restaurant, there's heartier fare, such as confit of duck and venison *osso buco.* Contemporary art and sculpture enliven the atmosphere, and there's outdoor seating. The friendly staff completes the picture.

85 Bussell Hwy., Margaret River. ✆ **08/9758 7155**. Reservations recommended. Tapas and bar grits A$3.70–A$8.60 (US$2.95–US$6.90); bar pizzas A$12 (US$9.60); main courses A$12–A$29 (US$9.60–US$23). AE, MC, V. Daily 11am–late.

4 The Goldfields ★

595km (369 miles) E of Perth

After Paddy Hannan struck gold in 1893, the wheat-belt town of Kalgoorlie found itself sitting on the "Golden Mile," the richest square mile of gold-bearing earth in the world. Today **Kalgoorlie** ★ (pop. 32,000) is still an Outback gold-rush boomtown, a mixture of yesteryear charm and 21st-century corporate gold fever. The town perches on the edge of the Super Pit, the world's biggest open-cut gold mine, 4.5km (2¾ miles) long, 1.5km (1 mile) wide, and 290m (951 ft.) deep. It yields up to 850,000 ounces of the yellow stuff every year—over 2,000 ounces a day. An estimated 13 million ounces is still in the ground.

Walking down the wide streets fronted with wrought-iron lace verandas is like stumbling onto a Western movie set. Countless bars still enjoy the roaring trade they did in the 1890s—only now they serve suited-up gold-mining executives from Adelaide and Perth.

Life on the Golden Mile is not so lively for everyone, however. Just down the road 39km (24 miles) is **Coolgardie** (pop. 1,100), another 1890s boomtown whose gold ran out in 1963. The town's semiabandoned air is a sad foil to Kalgoorlie's energy.

Much of the lovely architecture remains, so you can wander the gracious streets and a few museums for a pleasant nostalgia buzz.

ESSENTIALS

GETTING THERE   Qantas (© **13 13 13** in Australia) flies to Kalgoorlie from Perth daily. **Skywest** (© **1300/660 088** in Australia; www.skywest.com.au) flies from Perth daily.

Greyhound Pioneer (© **13 20 30** in Australia) makes the 8-hour trip once a week from Perth for A$127 (US$102). Greyhound's service from Adelaide also runs once a week, takes around 27 hours, and costs A$284 (US$227). **Goldrush Tours** (© **1800/620 440** in Australia, or 08/9021 2954) runs 6¾-hour express coach service from Perth Sunday through Friday for A$55 (US$44) adults, A$39 (US$31) children under 15.

Kalgoorlie is a stop on the 3-day *Indian Pacific* ⚡ train service, which runs between Sydney and Perth through Adelaide twice a week in both directions. See section 15, "Getting Around Australia," in chapter 2, for contact details. The new *Prospector* train makes nine trips a week from Perth to Kalgoorlie for A$68 (US$54) adults, A$34 (US$27) kids 5 to 15. Contact the **Public Transport Authority** (© **1300/602 205** in Western Australia, or 08/9326 2600; www.transwa.wa.gov.au).

From Perth, take the Great Eastern Highway. If you want to make the extremely dull 2,182km (1,353-mile) journey on the Eyre Highway from Adelaide, which features the longest straight stretch of highway in the world on the empty Nullarbor Plain, contact the South Australian or Western Australian state auto clubs listed under "Getting Around Australia," in chapter 2, for advice. There are only a handful of small towns and gas stops en route.

VISITOR INFORMATION   The **Kalgoorlie Goldfields Visitor Centre,** 250 Hannan St., Kalgoorlie, WA 6430 (© **1800/00 GOLD** in Australia, or 08/9021 1966; www.kalgoorlie.com/tourism), dispenses information on Kalgoorlie, Coolgardie, and outlying ghost towns and regions. The center's inexpensive walking trail map to the town's architecture is worth buying. The center is open Monday through Friday from 8:30am to 5pm, and Saturday, Sunday, and public holidays from 9am to 5pm. The **Coolgardie Tourist Bureau,** 62 Bayley St., Coolgardie, WA 6429 (© **08/9026 6090**), is open daily from 9am to 5pm.

GETTING AROUND   Avis (© 08/9021 1722), **Budget** (© 08/9093 2300), **Europcar** (© 08/9022 4922), **Hertz** (© 08/9093 2211), and **Thrifty** (© 08/9021 4722) have offices in Kalgoorlie.

Local tour operators will take you prospecting in outlying regions. They also offer coach and four-wheel-drive bush tours of Kalgoorlie, Coolgardie, and outlying ghost towns. Tours range from half a day to several days.

⌐**Fun Fact** **Streets Paved with . . . Gold?**

In Kalgoorlie's early days, its streets were paved with a blackish spoil from the mining process called "tellurides." When someone realized tellurides contain up to 40% gold and 10% silver, those streets were ripped up in one big hurry. The city fathers had paved the streets with gold and didn't even know it!

WHAT TO SEE & DO

As you might guess, gold is a common thread running through many of the town's attractions. One of the best is the **Mining Hall of Fame** (© **08/9026 2700;** www.mininghall.com), Broad Arrow Road, 6km (3¾ miles) north of the Tourist Centre on the Goldfields Highway. Opened in late 2001, it has five interactive galleries focusing on modern high-tech mining. Find out how prospecting is done, learn how the business of mining is conducted, go underground in an old mine, pan for gold, watch a gold pour, see a video in a re-created miner's tent, and pore over an extensive collection of mining memorabilia, machinery, and huts in a miners' village. It's open daily from 9am to 4:30pm, except January 1 and December 25 and 26. Admission for aboveground activities only is A$15 (US$12) for adults, A$12 (US$9.60) for seniors and students, A$8 (US$6.40) for children, and A$35 (US$28) for families. If you want to join the underground tour, too, the prices are A$20 (US$16) adults, A$16 (US$13) seniors and students, A$12 (US$9.60) children, and A$50 (US$40) families. Underground tours and gold panning start four times a day, more often during school holidays. To get there, join a tour or jump in a taxi—walking and cycling are not advised. Allow half a day to see everything.

The **WA Museum Kalgoorlie-Boulder,** 17 Hannan St. (© **08/9021 8533**), is worth a look; you'll see the first 400-ounce gold bar minted in town, nuggets and jewelry, and historical displays. It is open daily from 10am to 4:30pm, closed Good Friday and December 25. Admission is free (donation requested). Tours are at 11am and 2:30pm. Allow an hour.

Don't leave town without ogling the **Super Pit** open-cut mine—it makes giant dump trucks look like ants. The lookout is at Outram Street in Boulder, off the Goldfields Highway. It's open daily from about 6am to about 7pm, but may be temporarily closed during the daily blast; check the time with the visitor center. Entry is free.

Another reminder of the days when miners spent their spare time trying for riches of another kind by indulging in two-up (a simple game involving betting on a penny landing heads or tails) can be found about 12km (7½ miles) north of Boulder on the Goldfields Highway. The original shanty that housed the **Bush Two-Up School** still stands, but the only place to try it yourself is Sheffields restaurant in the **Recreation Hotel,** Burt Street (at Lionel St.), Boulder (© **08/9093 3467**), which runs two-up games on Friday, Saturday, and Sunday at 4:30pm. You must be 18 or over to play.

The **Royal Flying Doctor Service** (© **08/9093 7500**) base at Kalgoorlie-Boulder Airport is open for visitors to browse memorabilia, see a video, and look over an aircraft (if one is in). It is open Monday through Friday from 10am to 3pm. Admission is by donation. Tours run on the hour, and take 45 minutes.

Full-blood Aborigine Geoffrey Stokes of **Yamatji Bitja Aboriginal Bush Tours** ★ (© **08/9021 5862,** or 0407/378 602 mobile) grew up the Aboriginal way in the bush. On his full-day four-wheel-drive tours, you'll forage for bush tucker, learn bushcraft, and do things like eat witchetty grubs, cook kangaroo over a fire, or track emus. Tours cost A$200 (US$160) for two people (the minimum party size), A$80 (US$64) for extra adults, half price for kids 4 to 12. Geoff also offers campfire evenings, and overnight or longer tours in the bush.

Kalgoorlie's—and maybe Australia's—most unusual attraction must be **Langtrees 181,** 181 Hay St. (© **08/9026 2181**), a working brothel styled into a sex industry museum in the heart of Kalgoorlie's (in)famous red-light district. For the most part housed in red and pink corrugated-iron sheds festooned with colored lights, this neck of town is a popular drive-by spot among the blue-rinse bus-tour set, who get a kick out of returning the cheery waves of the workers standing in their doorways. Ninety-minute tours, fun rather than sleazy, of some of the 12 themed rooms cost A$35 (US$28). Tours depart at 1, 3, and 6pm daily.

Wandering **Coolgardie's** quiet streets, which are graced with historic facades, is a stroll back in time. More than 100 signboards throughout the town, many with photos, detail what each site was like at the turn of the 20th century.

The **Goldfields Exhibition,** 62 Bayley St. (© **08/9021 1966**), tells the town's story in a lovely 1898 building once used as the mining warden's courthouse. (The Tourist Bureau is also here.) Admission is A$3.30 (US$2.65) for adults, A$2.75 (US$2.20) for seniors, A$1.10 (US90¢) for children under 16, and A$7.70 (US$6.15) for a family. It's open daily except December 25 from 9am to 5pm. Coolgardie also has a couple of small museums, including a neat little pharmaceutical museum, a railway museum, and a National Trust–owned 1895 house, now restored with period interiors, that's open for tours.

WHERE TO STAY

The **Kalgoorlie Goldfields Visitor Centre** offers a free accommodations booking service (© **08/9021 1966;** fax 08/9021 2180; kbtc@emerge.net.au).

All Seasons Plaza Hotel Kalgoorlie   Corporate travelers like the practical comforts, upscale restaurant, and location—within walking distance of the heart of Kalgoorlie's nightlife and main street—of this AAA-rated four-star property. The rooms are spacious and well appointed, with balcony views over the city and Golden Mile. The restaurant has an extensive wine list, and the cocktail bar buzzes in the evening.

45 Egan St., Kalgoorlie, WA 6430. © 1300/656 565 in Australia, 800/221-4542 in the U.S. and Canada, 0870/609 0961 in the U.K., 0800/44 4422 in New Zealand, or 08/9021 4544. Fax 08/9091 2195. www.accorhotels.com.au. 100 units (all with shower only). A$113–A$147 (US$90–US$118) double. Extra person A$36 (US$29). Ask about weekend packages. AE, DC, MC, V. Free parking. **Amenities:** Restaurant; bar; outdoor pool; tour desk; secretarial services; limited room service; coin-op laundry; laundry service (Mon–Fri); dry cleaning (Mon–Fri). *In room:* A/C, TV w/free movies, minibar, coffeemaker, hair dryer, iron.

WHERE TO DINE

Akudjura ⚡ MODERN AUSTRALIAN   The Italianate outdoor terrace under sailcloth, timber floors, curved silver bar, and blond-wood furniture make this Kalgoorlie's first groovy restaurant. The bright young waitstaff provides snappy service from a long and stylish menu featuring items like chicken Caesar salad, smoked salmon fettuccine, kangaroo steak, and seafood dishes (yep, even in the desert) like Tasmanian salmon in citrus and cilantro dressing. Lighter fare is available outside meal hours.

418 Hannan St. (next to Hannan's View Motel). © 08/9091 3311. Reservations recommended. Main courses A$13–A$32 (US$10–US$26); lunch averages A$13 (US$10). AE, DC, MC, V. Daily 7am to around 10pm.

5 The Midwest & the Northwest: Where the Outback Meets the Sea ⚡

The midwest and northwest coasts of Western Australia are treeless, riverless semi-desert, occupied by vast sheep stations and a handful of people. Temperatures soar to over 115°F (46°C) in summer, and the Outback sand burns orange in the blazing sun. But it's not the land you come here for—it's what's in the sea. Since the 1960s, a pod of **bottlenose dolphins** has been coming into shallow water at **Monkey Mia** ⚡, the World Heritage–listed Shark Bay Marine Park, to greet shore-bound humans. The dolphins' magical presence has generated worldwide publicity and drawn people from every corner of the globe.

Another 87km (54 miles) by road north on the Northwest Cape, adventure seekers from around the world come to **snorkel with awesome whale sharks** ⋆—measuring up to 18m (59 ft.) long—every fall (Mar to early June). The Cape's parched shore and green waters hide an even more dazzling secret, though—a barrier reef 260km (161 miles) long and 2km (1¼ miles) wide called **Ningaloo Marine Park** ⋆⋆. It protects 250 species of coral and 450 kinds of fish, dolphins, mantas, whales, turtles, and dugongs (manatees) in its 5,000 sq. km (1,950 sq. miles). Some people say Ningaloo is as good as, if not better than, the Great Barrier Reef. Even the Great Barrier Reef can't beat Ningaloo Reef's proximity to shore—just a step or two off the beach delivers you into a magical underwater garden. What is so amazing about the reef is not that it is here, but that so few people know about it—a mere 8,000 tourists a year visit. That means beaches you'll have pretty much to yourself, seas teeming with life because humans haven't scared it away, unspoiled scenery, and a genuine sense of the frontier.

The midwest and northwest are lonely, remote, and really too hot to visit between November and March. The best time to visit is April through October, when it is warm enough to swim, though snorkelers might want a wet suit June through August. Both regions are too far south to share the Top End's sticky Wet season, and humidity is always low. Facilities, gas, and fresh water are scarce, and distances are immense, so be prepared.

SHARK BAY (MONKEY MIA) ⋆
853km (529 miles) N of Perth; 1,867km (1,157 miles) SW of Broome

Monkey Mia's celebrity dolphins may not show on time—or at all—but they rarely pass up a visit. Apart from these delightful sea mammals, Shark Bay's waters heave with fish, turtles, the world's biggest population of dugongs (11,000 at last count), manta rays, sea snakes and, June through October, humpback whales. On the tip of the Peron Peninsula, which juts into the Shark Bay Marine Park, is **Francois Peron National Park.** The park is home to many endangered species, white beaches composed entirely of shells, and "living fossils"—rocklike structures on the shore (called stromatolites) that are Earth's first life. The bay's only municipality is the one-time pearling town of **Denham** (pop. 500), 129km (80 miles) from the main coastal highway. It has a hotel or two, a bakery, a newsdealer, and a few fishing-charter and tour operators. There is no community, only the pleasant but basic Monkey Mia Dolphin Resort (p. 483).

ESSENTIALS

GETTING THERE   Skippers Aviation (✆ **1300/729 924** in Australia; www.skippers. com.au) flies five times a week from Perth to Shark Bay Airport (also called Monkey Mia Airport), 18km (11 miles) from Monkey Mia Dolphin Resort. The fare is A$362 (US$290), cheaper for advance purchase tickets. The **Shark Bay Airport Bus** (✆ **08/ 9948 1358**) meets every flight and transfers you to Monkey Mia Dolphin Resort for A$8 (US$6.40) per person one-way.

There is no train to Shark Bay. **Greyhound Australia** (✆ **13 14 99** in Australia) travels daily from Perth and Broome. These services connect three times a week at the Overlander Roadhouse at the Shark Bay turnoff on the North West Coastal Highway. The trip from Perth costs A$98 (US$78) and takes about 12 hours. From Broome it costs A$218 (US$174) and takes about 26 hours through featureless landscape—not recommended.

> ⎛ *Tips* **Where Can I See the Dolphins?**
>
> The main advantage to making the trek to **Monkey Mia** to see dolphins is that sightings are virtually guaranteed every day. But it's crowded, and rangers strictly monitor behavior with the dolphins—not the interactive frolic you might have imagined. At **Bunbury** ★★, a 2½-hour drive south of Perth, you can *swim* with wild dolphins (see "Taking a Dip with Flipper," earlier in this chapter). Here the critters show up near shore only about two-thirds of the time. But the daily dolphin-watch cruise into deeper water has an almost 100% sighting success rate.

Beware of wildlife on the lonely, uninteresting 9- to 10-hour drive from Perth, and keep the gas tank full. From Perth, take the Brand Highway 424km (263 miles) north to Geraldton, then the North West Coastal Highway for 280km (174 miles) to the Overlander Roadhouse. Turn left onto the Denham-Hamelin Road and follow it for 152km (94 miles) to Monkey Mia, which is 27km (17 miles) past Denham. If you want to break the journey, the **All Seasons Inn Geraldton,** Brand Highway, Geraldton, WA 6530 (② **08/9921 2455**), has smart, clean motel rooms, with work desks and mini bars. Rates are A$105 (US$84) double; specials are available most nights. With miles of white sandy beaches and a variety of historical sites to visit, the hotel is a convenient base from which to enjoy "wildflower country." It also has a relaxed restaurant and bar, swimming pool, free in-house movies, and a children's playground.

Numerous coach, four-wheel-drive, and aerial tours run from Perth. **World Heritage Tours and Travel** (② **1800/645 022** in Australia, or 08/9581 5666; book through www.visitwa.com.au) offers a wide range.

VISITOR INFORMATION   Wide-ranging ecological information on Shark Bay Marine Park, Francois Peron National Park, and Hamelin Pool Marine Nature Reserve, as well as details on local tours, are available at the **Monkey Mia Dolphin Information Centre** (② **08/9948 1366**) in Monkey Mia Dolphin Resort (see "Where to Stay & Dine," below). Videos run throughout the day, and researchers (who are mostly from American universities) give free talks and slide shows most nights. The state Department of Conservation and Land Management (② **08/9948 1208**; www.calm.wa.gov.au) runs the center. The official information outlet is the **Shark Bay Tourist Bureau,** 71 Knight Terrace, Denham, WA 6537 (② **08/9948 1253**; www.sharkbay.asn.au), which is open daily from 8am to 5pm (until 6pm in winter), though you will probably find the Monkey Mia Visitor Centre just as helpful.

GETTING AROUND   **Shark Bay Car Hire** (② **08/9948 1247**) delivers cars and four-wheel-drives to the airport and the resort from its Denham office. Several companies run tours to all the main attractions.

FAST FACTS   Admission to the **Monkey Mia Reserve,** in which Monkey Mia Dolphin Resort is located, is A$6 (US$4.80) per adult, A$2 (US$1.60) per child under 16, and A$12 (US$9.60) per family. Resort guests as well as day-trippers pay this fee.

There are ATMs at the **Heritage Resort,** 73 Knight Terrace (at Durlacher St.), Denham (② **08/9948 1133**), and the local supermarket, but no banks. A banking agency is in the post office in Denham.

MEETING THE DOLPHINS

At 7am, guests at Monkey Mia Dolphin Resort are already gathering on the beach in quiet anticipation of the dolphins' arrival. By 8am three or more dolphins usually show, and they come and go until the early afternoon. Because of the crowds the dolphins attract (about 40 people a session in low season, coach loads in high season), a park ranger instructs everyone to line up knee-deep in the water as the playful swimmers cruise by your legs. You may not approach them or reach out to pat them, but they sometimes come up to touch people of their own accord. Feeding times are different each day so the dolphins won't become dependent on the food. Once the crowd disperses, savvy swimmers dive into the water just up the beach outside the no-swimmers-allowed Dolphin Interaction Area, because the dolphins may head there after the "show." Apart from the Monkey Mia Reserve entry fee, there is no charge to see the creatures.

A GREAT SEA-LIFE CRUISE, LIVING "FOSSILS" & MORE

Don't do what so many visitors do—see the dolphins, then shoot back to Perth. Stay to see Shark Bay's incredible marine life on the sailing catamaran *Shotover* ★ (© **1800/241 481** in Australia, or 08/9948 1481). During a 2½-hour dugong (manatee) cruise, you will see a huge range of creatures, possibly hammerhead sharks, a baby great white, sea snakes, turtles, dolphins, and, of course, dugongs. Every passenger is given polarized sunglasses, which help you spot underwater animals. Sometimes you see dozens of dugongs (though they leave the area from mid-May to Aug). The cruise departs from Monkey Mia Dolphin Resort at 1pm daily and costs A$59 (US$47). The *Shotover* also runs a fascinating 2-hour dolphin cruise every morning—worth doing even if you've already seen the dolphins on the shore. It costs A$54 (US$43) per person.

On your way in or out of Monkey Mia, stop by **the Hamelin Pool Historic Telegraph Station** (© **08/9942 5905**), 41km (26 miles) from the highway turnoff. A small museum houses old equipment, farming tools, and historical odds and sods from the 19th-century days when Monkey Mia was a repeater station on a telegraph line. The A$5.50 (US$4.40) admission fee to the museum includes an explanation of the **stromatolites,** rocky formations about a foot high that were created by the planet's first oxygen-breathing cells—in other words, Earth's first life. You might want to skip the museum, but do wander down to **Shell Beach** and have a look. The "sand" on the beach consists of millions of tiny white shells, which were quarried as bricks to build some of the local buildings. There is a cafe and gift store here, too.

You can explore the saltpans, dunes, coastal cliffs, short walking trails, and old homestead in the nearby 52,500-hectare (129,675-acre) **Francois Peron National**

Value **Save on Park Passes**

Entry to many national parks in Western Australia, including Cape Range and Francois Peron, costs A$9 (US$7.20) per car. If you are planning to visit a few during your stay, a Holiday Park Pass is worth the money. It costs A$23 (US$18) for a vehicle carrying up to eight people and is valid for 4 weeks. Obtain passes through the Department of Conservation and Land Management (www.calm.wa.gov.au). Holiday Park Passes are not valid for Monkey Mia Dolphin Reserve.

Park, either alone (you will need a four-wheel-drive) or on a half- or full-day tour—although not everyone will appreciate the park's harsh scenery. You should spot wallabies, birds, and emus, and you may see turtles, dolphins, rays, dugongs, and, in season, whales from the cliffs. Other activities include half- and full-day game and deep-sea-fishing trips from Denham, scuba diving, excursions to the deserted beaches and 180m (590-ft.) cliffs of nearby Dirk Hartog Island, and a couple of pearl-farm tours.

WHERE TO STAY & DINE

Monkey Mia Dolphin Resort   Set right on the beach the dolphins visit, this oasis of green lawns and palms doubles as a town settlement, and is the only place to stay at Monkey Mia (all other accommodations are 27km/17 miles away, in Denham). The beachside Dolphin Lodge and backpacker lodge opened in 2004. The 24 motel-style beachside units at the front of the Dolphin Lodge offer a more upmarket option than was previously available. Each has a king-size bed, private bathroom, and hair dryer. Ground-floor units open right onto the dolphin beach, and first-floor units have balconies. The backpacker lodge, with its own Monkey Bar and large communal kitchen, is behind the Dolphin Lodge. It holds four- and seven-bed dormitories as well as shared and family rooms with bathrooms. The new accommodations complement the existing villas (which sleep three to five people); air-conditioned demountable (portable cabin) "park homes" with cooking facilities; and trailer and camping sites. The pleasant open-sided all-day restaurant overlooks the sea; the resort has a minimarket, an Internet cafe, and a dive shop; and you can hire a kayak or boat. Most tours in the area depart from here. A 1.5km (1-mile) nature trail leads from the resort.

Monkey Mia Rd., Shark Bay (P.O. Box 119, Denham, WA 6537). © **1800/653 611** in Australia, or 08/9948 1320. Fax 08/9948 1034. www.monkeymia.com.au. 57 powered trailer sites; 20 tent sites; 13 park homes, 6 with bathroom; 60 villas; 24 motel units (all with shower only). A$9 (US$7.20) per person tent site; A$19 (US$15) per person in backpacker dorm; A$87–A$96 (US$70–US$77) park home for up to 6; A$156–A$173 (US$125–US$138) double or triple Garden Villa; A$198 (US$158) double or triple Beachfront Villa; A$173 (US$138) double Dolphin Lodge. Extra person A$11 (US$8.80). Linen A$11 (US$8.80) per person per stay in park homes and trailers. Weekly rates available. AE, DC, MC, V. Free parking. **Amenities:** Restaurant; 2 bars; takeout cafe; outdoor pool; 2 outdoor tennis courts; Jacuzzi (fed by naturally warm underground water); use of snorkel gear; tour desk; car-rental desk; massage; babysitting; coin-op laundry. *In room:* A/C, TV, small fridge, coffeemaker.

THE NORTHWEST CAPE

Exmouth: 1,272km (789 miles) N of Perth; 1,567km (972 miles) SW of Broome

Driving along the only road on the Northwest Cape is like driving on the moon. Hundreds of red anthills taller than you march away to the horizon, sheep and 'roos threaten to get under the wheels, and the sun beats down from a harsh blue sky. On the Cape's western shore is coral-filled **Coral Bay** (pop. 120), a tiny cluster of dive shops, backpacker lodges, a low-key resort, and charter boats nestled on sand so white, water so blue, and ocher dust so orange you'd think the townsfolk computer-enhanced the colors. North of town are deserted sandy beaches edged by coral. On the Cape's east coast is **Exmouth** (pop. 3,500), born in 1967 as a support town to the Harold E. Holt Naval Communications Station, a joint Australian–United States center.

Apart from whale shark diving, the reason you come here is to scuba dive and snorkel in Ningaloo Marine Park. You can also take four-wheel-drive trips over the Cape Range National Park, which covers much of the cape, and surrounding sheep stations. Ningaloo Marine Park stretches from Bundegi Beach on the Cape's east coast around its northern tip and down its western side.

Exmouth and Coral Bay are 150km (93 miles) apart. Coral Bay is several degrees cooler than Exmouth and has divine diving, swimming, and snorkeling; a restaurant, some takeout, and a bar or two; a small supermarket; and little else. It has no ATMs. Exmouth is hot and charmless, but it has more facilities, including a supermarket, an ATM, an outdoor cinema, rental cars, a swimming beach 1km (½ mile) away, and one or two smarter accommodations and dining options. Most tours not having to do with the reef, such as four-wheel-drive safaris, leave from Exmouth. Both towns have plenty of dive, snorkel, fishing, and whale-watch companies. Wherever you stay, it's best to book ahead in whale shark season (from Mar to early June). Carry drinking water everywhere you go.

ESSENTIALS

GETTING THERE **Skywest** (© **1300/660 088** in Australia; www.skywest.com.au) flies from Perth daily. A shuttle bus meets every flight and takes you to your Exmouth hotel for A$18 (US$14) one-way. It does not accept reservations. (Have the cash on you; there's no ATM at the airport.) **Coral Bay Adventures** (© **08/9942 5955**) makes transfers, on demand, from the airport to Coral Bay, approximately 120km (74 miles) away, for A$55 (US$44) adults, A$35 (US$28) children under 13, one-way.

Greyhound Australia (© **13 14 99**) operates three times a week from Perth (trip time: 19 hr.) to Exmouth and Coral Bay. The fare is A$187 (US$150). Another option, which takes about the same time and costs the same, is Greyhound's daily Perth-Broome service, which connects with a service to Exmouth at the turnoff on the highway at Giralia in the wee hours of the morning. There is no train service.

The 14-hour drive from Perth (plus rest stops) is through lonely country on a two-lane highway. Check that your contract allows you to drive your rental car this far north, and includes unlimited mileage. Wildlife will be thick on the ground, and gas stations thin. From Perth, take the Brand Highway north to Geraldton, 424km (263 miles) away, then the North West Coastal Highway for 623km (386 miles) to Minilya gas station; the Exmouth turnoff is 7km (4⅓ miles) north of Minilya. Exmouth is a further 225km (140 miles) along the cape from the turnoff. Overnight at the **Mercure Inn Geraldton,** Brand Highway, Geraldton, WA 6530 (© **08/9921 2455;** A$140/US$112 double), or in Carnarvon, the only town between Geraldton and Exmouth. Everything else that looks like a town on your map is just a gas station. But keep in mind that even the gas stations can be 200km (130 miles) apart. The longer, lonelier drive from Broome is even less recommended.

VISITOR INFORMATION The **Exmouth Visitor Centre,** Murat Road, Exmouth, WA 6707 (© **1800/287 328** in Western Australia, or 08/9949 1176; www.exmouth-australia.com), is open April through October daily from 8:30am to 5pm, and from 10am to 3pm on weekends November through March. The **Milyering Visitors Centre,** 52km (32 miles) northwest of Exmouth, is the Cape Range National Park's information center, run by the Department of Conservation and Land Management (CALM). It is open daily from 10am to 12:30pm and 1:15 to 4pm. You can pick up a hiking-trail map of the park from CALM's office on Nimitz Street, Exmouth. **Coral Bay Adventures** runs a tour information and booking center on Robinson Street, Coral Bay, WA 6701 (© **08/9942 5955;** www.users.bigpond.com/coralbay).

There is only one ATM on the Cape, in Exmouth.

GETTING AROUND Tours and dive operators pick up from either Exmouth or Coral Bay accommodations, but not usually from both. The roads to Exmouth and

Coral Bay are paved, and so is the only road around the Cape's coast. **Avis** (© **08/9949 2942**), **Budget** (© **08/9949 1534**), and local operator **Allens Car Hire** (© **08/9949 2403**) have offices in Exmouth; there is no car rental in Coral Bay.

Ningaloo Reef Bus (© **08/9949 1776**) runs from Exmouth hotels to various beaches around the cape, stopping at the Milyering Visitors Centre en route. It runs Monday, Tuesday, Friday, and Saturday April through October, and daily November through March. The round-trip fare to the snorkel beauty spot of Turquoise Bay is A$20 (US$16) adults, A$10 (US$8) children, and A$55 (US$44) families. You can even hire a snorkel (but not fins) on the bus for A$5 (US$4).

DIVING WITH WHALE SHARKS ★★

Diving is not the correct term for this activity, because it's by snorkeling that you get close to these leviathans of the deep. Whale sharks are sharks, not whales, and are the world's biggest fish, reaching an alarming 12 to 18m (39–58 ft.) in length. Terrified? Don't be. Their gigantic size belies their gentle nature and swimming speed; despite having mouths big enough to swallow a boatload of snorkelers, they eat plankton. Several boat operators take people out to swim alongside the fish when they appear from late March to mid-June. A day trip with one of the longest established whale-shark companies, **Exmouth Diving Centre** (© **08/9949 1201;** www.exmouthdiving. com.au) or its Coral Bay sister company, **Ningaloo Reef Diving Centre** (© **08/9942 5824;** www.ningalooreefdive.com), costs A$320 (US$256) for snorkeling or A$360 (US$288) including a scuba dive, including all gear.

DIVING, SNORKELING, FISHING & 4WD TOURS

Scuba dive ★ the Cape's unspoiled waters, and you will see marvelous reef formations, grouper, manta rays, octopus, morays, potato cod (which you can hand-feed), and other marvels at a dozen or more sites. Divers often spot humpback and false killer whales and large sharks, while snorkelers may see dolphins, dugongs, and turtles. Loads of dive companies in Exmouth and Coral Bay (including the two listed in "Diving with Whale Sharks," above) rent gear and run daily dive trips and learn-to-dive courses. A two-dive day trip costs A$170 (US$136) with all gear supplied.

Three great snorkeling spots are: right off the shore at Coral Bay; Bundegi Beach, 14km (nearly 9 miles) north of Exmouth; and **Turquoise Bay** ★, a 60km (37-mile) drive from Exmouth. In deeper waters off Coral Bay, you can snorkel with **manta rays** ★ with a "wingspan" of up to 7m (23 ft.). Companies in both towns run manta and reef-snorkel trips, and rent snorkel gear. The Cape has loads of swimming beaches; for safety's sake, never swim alone.

Reef fish, tuna, and Spanish mackerel are common catches in these waters, and black, blue, and striped marlin run outside the reef September through January. Up to a dozen boats operate reef and **game-fishing day trips** ★ out of Exmouth and Coral Bay, and tackle and tin fishing dinghies are easy to rent in either town.

Green and loggerhead **turtles** ★ lay eggs at night from November through February or March on the Cape's beaches. Take a flashlight and go looking for them, or join one of several turtle-watch tours from either town. August through October, boats run cruises from either town to spot **humpback whales.**

Because the Cape has few roads, and even fewer sights along the way, take an off-road 240km (149-mile) four-wheel-drive escapade with **Neil McLeod's Ningaloo Safari Tours** ★ (© **08/9949 1550;** www.ningaloosafari.com). You will explore the arid limestone ridges of 50,581-hectare (124,935-acre) Cape Range National Park, snorkel Turquoise Bay, climb a lighthouse, and cruise orange-walled Yardie Creek Gorge to spot rock wallabies—snacking on Neil's mum's fruitcake along the way. This full-day trip departs your Exmouth hotel at 7:30am and returns at 6pm. It costs A$155 (US$124) for adults and A$115 (US$92) for children under 13. A 5-hour afternoon tour costs A$65 (US$52) adults and A$50 (US$40) children. In turtle-breeding season (Nov–Mar), Neil runs evening tours for A$45 (US$36) adults and A$35 (US$28) children.

WHERE TO STAY & DINE
IN EXMOUTH
Potshot Hotel Resort The grounds are hot and dusty, but the building is in a modern complex. The brick motel rooms are cool and spacious; the homestead rooms are smaller, older, and more basic (they don't have phones). There are two-bedroom apartments, and across the road are newer three-bedroom apartments, some with Jacuzzis. The cocktail bar around the pool is the only shady place in town to enjoy a drink, which explains its popularity with locals. The restaurant is scant on atmosphere but has a long menu, good food, and a nice wine list. Prices are between A$15 and A$30 (US$12–US$24). There's a seafood buffet on Friday and Saturday nights.

Murat Rd., Exmouth, WA 6707. (C) **08/9949 1200.** Fax 08/9949 1486. www.potshotresort.com. 97 units (all with shower only). A$90 (US$72) double homestead room; A$124–A$135 (US$99–US$108) resort studio room for up to 4; A$160 (US$128) 1-bed king spa room; A$145–A$240 (US$116–US$192) 2-bedroom apt; A$205–A$290 (US$164–US$232) 3-bedroom apt. Extra person A$12 (US$9.60). Maid service in apt A$22–A$33 (US$18–US$26) per day. AE, DC, MC, V. **Amenities:** 3 restaurants; 4 bars; 3 small outdoor pools; coin-op laundry; hair dryer; iron. *In room:* A/C, TV, fridge, coffeemaker.

IN CORAL BAY
Ningaloo Reef Resort This low-rise complex of motel rooms, studios, and apartments stands out as the best place to stay among Coral Bay's profusion of backpacker hostels. Located on a blissfully green lawn with a swimming pool overlooking the bay, the rooms are nothing fancy or new, but they're clean, with views toward the bay and the pool. Some have kitchens. The place has a nice communal air, thanks to the bar doubling as the local pub.

At the end of Robinson St., Coral Bay, WA 6701. (C) **08/9942 5934.** Fax 08/9942 5953. www.ningaloo reefresort.com.au. 34 units, all with bathroom (shower only). A$143–A$148 (US$114–US$118) double; A$180–A$290 (US$144–US$232) apt. Extra person A$11 (US$8.80). Weekly rates available. MC, V. **Amenities:** Restaurant; bar; outdoor pool; coin-op laundry; hair dryer; iron. *In room:* A/C, TV, no phone.

6 The Kimberley: A Far-Flung Wilderness ⭐

Most Aussies would be hard put to name a single settlement, river, or mountain in the Kimberley, so rarely visited and sparsely inhabited is this wilderness. It is an ancient land of red, rocky plateaus stretching for thousands of miles, jungly ravines, endless bush, crocodile-infested wetlands, surreal-looking boab trees with trunks shaped like bottles, lily-filled rock pools, lonely island-strewn coastline, droughts in winter, and floods in summer. The dry, spreading scenery might call to mind Africa or India. In the Dry season (the Dry), the area's biggest river, the Fitzroy, is empty, but in the Wet season (the Wet), its swollen banks are second only to the Amazon in the volume of water that surges to the sea.

Aqua and scarlet are two colors that will hit you in the eye in the Kimberley—a luminous aqua for the sea and the fiery scarlet of the fine soil called "pindan." The area is famous for Wandjina-style Aboriginal rock art depicting people with circular

The Kimberley Region

hairdos that look more than a little like beings from outer space. It is also known for another kind of rock art known as "Bradshaw figures," sticklike representations of human forms, which may be the oldest art on earth. A mere 25,000 people live in the Kimberley's 420,000 sq. km (1.6 million sq. miles). That's three times the size of England.

The unofficial capital of the East Kimberley is **Kununurra.** The small agricultural town serves as the gateway to wildlife river cruises; the **Bungle Bungles** ⟡, a massive labyrinth of beehive-shaped rock formations; and **El Questro** ⟡⟡, a million-acre cattle ranch where you can hike, fish, and cruise palm-filled gorges by day and sleep in comfy permanent safari tents or glamorous homestead rooms by night (it's open from Apr to early Nov). The main town in the West Kimberley is the Outback port of **Broome** ⟡ whose waters give up the world's biggest and best South Sea pearls. Linking Kununurra and Derby, not far (relatively) from Broome, is the Gibb River Road, an isolated four-wheel-drive track through cattle-station country that is becoming popular with adventure travelers.

Off the West Kimberley coast lies a jigsaw puzzle of 10,000 or more barely inhabited islands, the **Bonaparte** ⟡ and **Buccaneer Archipelagos** ⟡, the latter named in honor of the pirate's pirate, William Dampier, who sailed here in 1688. In fact, much of the appeal of this coastline lies in the knowledge that few Westerners have laid eyes on it since the first explorers of the 17th century.

ESSENTIALS

VISITOR INFORMATION The **Kimberley Tourism Association,** P.O. Box 554, Broome, WA 6725 (ⓒ **08/9193 6660;** www.kimberleytourism.com), supplies information on the entire region. The **Kununurra Visitor Centre** (p. 490) and the **Broome Visitor Centre** (p. 495) also handle inquiries about things to see and do across the entire Kimberley, and you can drop into their information offices once you arrive.

Best of the Kimberley (ⓒ **1800/450 850** in Australia, or 08/9192 6070; www.kimberleytravel.net) is a Broome-based agency marketing a large range of tours and experiences, including four-wheel-drive safaris, aerial tours, bushwalking and horseback riding, and cruising. It sells accommodations and tour packages as well as a huge range of day trips, tours, and activities, and specializes in personalized vacations. Visits to the remote Dampier Peninsula to fish and go mud-crabbing with an Aboriginal family, and self-fly packages around this vast region for private pilots (aircraft rental included) are among the agency's more unusual offerings.

GETTING AROUND Enormous distances, high gasoline costs (often A$1 per liter or more, equivalent to US$3.20 per gal.), Wet season floods, and very limited roads and facilities can make traveling the Kimberley expensive and time-consuming. The place has lots of attractions so remote they can only be reached by aerial tours or charter boats. Many more are accessible only on unpaved roads, for which your two-wheel-drive rental car is not insured and which it probably can't handle. If you don't want to rely on tours, rent a four-wheel-drive (available in Broome and Kununurra). Allow for an average speed of 60kmph (37 mph) on the area's rough unsealed roads, and never exceed 80kmph (50 mph), because unexpected dips and smooth patches can take you by surprise. Most outfits will allow one-way rentals between Broome and Kununurra, or vice versa, at a surcharge of approximately A$350 to A$550 (US$280–US$440). Review "Road Conditions & Safety," "What If Your Vehicle Breaks Down?," and

"Tips for Four-Wheel Drivers," in the "Getting Around Australia" section of chapter 2 before setting off.

Kimberley Camping & Outback Supplies, 65 Frederick St., Broome (© **08/ 9193 5909**), sells and rents every piece of camping equipment you need, from tents and "mozzie" (mosquito) nets to cooking utensils, plus outdoor clothing.

Taking a guided four-wheel-drive camping or accommodated safari is a neat way to sidestep the challenges of Kimberley travel. Safaris depart Broome, Kununurra, or Darwin, and last between 2 days and 2 weeks. A popular route is the cross-Kimberley journey between Broome and Kununurra. If you opt for this route, look for tours that traverse the Gibb River Road, rather than the scenically dull highway via Halls Creek and Fitzroy Crossing. The Gibb River Road is an adventurous unpaved "back road" between Kununurra and Broome that offers access to gorges, low red ranges, swimming holes (ask directions to croc-free ones), walking trails, barramundi fishing, and campsites or basic homestead accommodations on vast cattle stations (ranches).

Most safaris run only in the Dry season, April or May through October or November. Respected operators include **East Kimberley Tours** (© **08/9168 2213;** www. eastkimberleytours.com.au); **APT Kimberley Wilderness Adventures** (© **1800/ 675 222** in Australia; www.kimberleywilderness.com.au); **Adventure Tours** (© **1300/ 654 604** in Australia; www.adventuretours.com.au); and **Australian Pinnacle Tours** (© **1800/999 069** in Australia, or 08/9417 5555; www.pinnacletours.com.au).

Broome Aviation (© **1300/136 629** in Australia, or 08/9192 1369; www.broome aviation.com) and **King Leopold Air** (© **08/9193 7155;** www.kingleopold air.com.au), based in Broome, and **Alligator Airways** (© **1800 632 533** in Australia, or 08/9168 1333; www.alligatorairways.com.au) and **Slingair Heliwork** (© **1800/ 095 500** in Australia, or 08/9169 1300; www.slingair.com.au), based in Kununurra, run a range of flight-seeing tours all over the Kimberley, lasting from a couple of hours to several days. Some involve sightseeing on the ground, hiking, four-wheel-drive trips, overnights at fishing camps, or stops at cattle stations.

KUNUNURRA
827km (513 miles) SW of Darwin; 1,032km (640 miles) E of Broome

Given the arid conditions in the Kimberley, it's quite a surprise to swoop over a field of sugar cane as you come in to land at Kununurra. This rather ramshackle little town (pop. 5,000) is an agricultural center created by the damming of the mighty Ord River to form **Lake Argyle.**

Kununurra itself (the name is Aboriginal for "meeting of big waters") has little to spark your interest, but it is the gateway to several outstanding attractions. A cruise or canoe trip down the **Ord River** to see wild birds, dramatic cliffs, and crocs is a must. So is a flight over, or a hike into, the **Bungle Bungles,** monumental orange domes of rock that look like giant beehives. The world's biggest diamond mine is not in South Africa but out in the rugged Kimberley wilds near Kununurra, and it can be visited by air every day. The town is also a gateway to **El Questro Wilderness Park** ★★, a million-acre cattle station (ranch) where you can hike magnificent gorges, fish, cruise rivers, ride horses, and see some of Australia's most breathtaking Aboriginal art. It is open from April to early November, closed during the summer Wet season.

ESSENTIALS
GETTING THERE   Air North (© **1800 627 474** in Australia, or 08/8920 4001; www.airnorth.com.au) flies from Broome and Darwin daily. There is no train to

Kununurra. **Greyhound Australia** (© **13 14 99** in Australia) serves the town daily from Perth via Broome and daily from Darwin via Katherine. From Perth the trip takes about 49 hours, from Broome about 15 hours. The one-way fare from Perth is A$494 (US$395). From Darwin, the trip time is around 10 hours, and the fare is A$161 (US$129).

Kununurra is 512km (323 miles) west of Katherine on the Victoria Highway. The Great Northern Highway from Broome connects with the Victoria Highway 45km (28 miles) west of Kununurra. The Gibb River Road is a four-wheel-drive scenic route from Derby, east of Broome; it connects with the Great Northern Highway 53km (33 miles) west of Kununurra.

VISITOR INFORMATION   The **Kununurra Visitor Centre** is at Coolibah Drive, Kununurra, WA 6743 (© **08/9168 1177;** www.eastkimberley.com). Hours change with the season, but it's usually open daily from 9am to 5pm from April to September, and from 9am to 5pm weekdays and 9am to noon Saturdays between October and March (closed Sun and public holidays during this time).

GETTING AROUND   **Avis** (© 08/9169 1258), **Budget** (© 08/9168 2033), **Europcar** (© 08/91682133), **Hertz** (© 08/9169 1424), and **Thrifty** (© 08/9169 1911) all rent four-wheel-drive vehicles. Hertz also rents camping gear.

WHAT TO SEE & DO

ON THE ORD RIVER   Several cruise outfits offer trips on the Ord River or Lake Argyle, a man-made blue inland sea ringed by red cliffs and bigger than 19 Sydney Harbours. Go for the Ord. The Ord River is one of the most picturesque waterways in Australia, lined by red cliffs in parts, and teeming with all kinds of wetland birds and freshwater crocodiles. Jeff Haley of **Triple J. Tours** ✦ (© **08/9168 2682;** www.triplejtours.net.au) runs excellent cruises. The company has three boats and several itineraries, which vary from Dry season to Wet. The most popular starts with a 70km (43-mile) narrated coach ride to Lake Argyle, continues with a wander through a historic homestead, and ends with a 55km (34-mile) cruise down the Ord back to Kununurra. The boat travels fast, and Jeff pulls in at numerous tranquil spots. This costs A$110 (US$88) for adults and A$70 (US$56) for children 4 to 15, including pickup from your hotel for an 11:30am start, and afternoon tea. You get back by around sunset.

Big Waters Kimberley Canoe Safaris (© **1800/641 998** in Australia, or 08/9169 1998; www.adventure.kimberley.net.au) offers a popular 3-day self-guided canoeing and camping safari down the Class I (that means "gentle") Ord River in two-person Canadian canoes. It costs A$145 (US$116) per person. During the Wet you can do a 1-day tour for A$45 (US$36) per person.

A day on the river to fish for barramundi with Greg Harman's **Ultimate Adventures** (© **08/9168 2310;** www.wn.com.au/ultimateadvent) costs around A$250 (US$200) per person, more if there is only one of you. Greg also offers trips of up to 10 days to remote fishing camps.

DIAMONDS IN THE ROUGH   Turning out an impressive 38 million carats a year—that's more than 8 tons of pure diamond—is the world's biggest diamond mine, the **Argyle Diamond Mine,** 176km (109 miles) from Kununurra. It is the only mine in the world that produces pink diamonds in commercial quantities; champagne, cognac, yellow, green, and white rocks also come from this mine. During a 3½- to 4-hour visit, you will see rough and polished gems, watch gems get extracted from the open-cut mine (as long as safety conditions permit), and, if you like, buy diamonds. For security reasons, you must join an aerial tour with **Belray Diamond Mine Tours** (© **08/9168 1014**), which you can also book through **Alligator Airways** (© **08/ 9168 1333;** www.alligatorairways.com.au). Opt for a flight that covers the nearby Purnululu (Bungle Bungles) National Park and Lake Argyle as well; this option costs A$385 (US$308). Belray Diamond Tours runs a coach trip Thursdays only, June through September. It costs A$245 (US$196) per person, and it's a 2½-hour drive each way. Kids under 12 are not permitted on mine tours.

SPENDING THE DAY AT EL QUESTRO WILDERNESS PARK ★★   You do not have to stay at El Questro (see "Where to Stay," below) to enjoy the wonderful facilities. After aristocratic Englishman Will Burrell bought the million-acre cattle ranch in 1991, he turned it into a kind of Outback holiday camp where anyone from international celebrities to humble four-wheel-drive enthusiasts could revel in its rugged beauty. It's a working cattle station, and visitors can get involved in the cattle operation, which includes 7,000 head of Brahman cattle in the far north of the wilderness park. The all-inclusive overnight **Mount Cockburn Safari** costs A$900 (US$720) per adult and A$450 (US$360) for children under 12. The safari is an option for guests staying at El Questro Homestead, Emma Gorge Resort, or the Station Township Bungalows, with overnight accommodations during the safari at the luxury new Mt. Cockburn Lodge, opened in mid-2005 on 30km (19 miles) of rugged, isolated coastline. Your group of no more than 12 guests will stay in six funky "Goondis" (Aboriginal for "shelter"), complete with goose-feather pillows, luxurious showers, and slate floors. The safari includes a lunch on the mud flats (with French champagne), an overland adventure, and over-water expedition. You will effectively circumnavigate the entire Cockburn Range on the safari, a mammoth feat.

But if that's not for you, there are many other options. Go barramundi fishing and heli-fishing in pristine wetlands and rivers; soak under palm trees in the thermal waters of Zebedee Springs (open until noon daily); hike gorges, some of which hide pockets of rainforest; take half-day four-wheel-drive fishing safaris; cruise tranquil Chamberlain Gorge; horseback ride across stony plains; photograph red rocky ranges; join rangers on bird-watching or "bush tucker" tours; or explore a rich lode of Aboriginal rock paintings. It's an unspoiled, primeval place.

El Questro is open from late March to early November (it closes in the Wet, Nov–Mar). It is 100km (62 miles) west of Kununurra by road (58km/36 miles on the sealed Great Northern Hwy. toward Wyndham, then the graded gravel Gibb River Rd.). To enter, visitors must purchase a 7-day **Wilderness Park Permit,** which costs A$15 (US$12) per person; children under 12 enter free. Buy permits from El Questro's Kununurra office, in Tourism House on Coolibah Drive, where the staff will give you a map and point out all there is to see and do, or at Station Township. The Township is a settlement where El Questro's main facilities (bungalows, restaurant, airstrip, camping areas, stables, and so forth) are. It acts as a kind of headquarters—most tours and activities depart here, and it's where you can buy road and other supplies and fuel, and rent four-wheel-drives and camping gear. Consider renting a four-wheel-drive in Kununurra or at Station Township. Transfers from the Homestead and Emma Gorge, both within the wilderness park, cost A$60 (US$48) per person to join tours and activities departing Station Township, so while it is not crucial to have your own four-wheel-drive, it is less costly. Having your own vehicle also means you can explore independently. El Questro Reservations rents them for A$130 to A$176 (US$104–US$141) per day, plus around

A30¢ (US25¢) per kilometer after the first 100km (62 miles). It's best to book them ahead because the fleet size is limited.

If you're short on time, the station's 12-hour ranger-guided **day trips** from Kununurra are a good idea. They include the highlights of a Chamberlain Gorge cruise to see Aboriginal Wandjina rock art and a soak in Zebedee Springs, plus a gorge walk, lunch at Station Township's Steakhouse restaurant, and four-wheel-drive transfers, for A$165 (US$132) per person. Ask the staff to identify which swimming spots are croc-free, and don't swim anywhere else!

You pay for most activities—from A$65 (US$52) for a 2-hour horse ride to A$595 (US$476) for a half-day's saltwater heli-fishing. Typical prices are A$44 (US$35) for a gorge cruise, A$75 (US$60) for a 4-hour four-wheel-drive trip to watch the sun set over the Cockburn Range, or A$185 (US$148) for a half-day barramundi-fishing trip. The rangers are friendly and knowledgeable. The tour desk also arranges such off-station activities as day trips on the Ord River or around Kununurra, trips to the Argyle diamond mine and the Bungle Bungles, and extended tours throughout the Kimberley as far afield as Mitchell Falls.

Four-wheel-drive transfers for guests operate from Kununurra; a ranger drives and gives a commentary en route. The cost is A$150 (US$120) per adult round-trip to Emma Gorge, or A$180 (US$144) to Station Township; children under 12 are half price. If you are driving yourself, take the Great Northern Highway 58km (36 miles) from Kununurra toward Wyndham, then the (unsealed) Gibb River Road 25km (16 miles) to Emma Gorge Resort (which is 2km/1¼ miles along an access road), or a farther 27km (17 miles) to the station store. You can take a flight from Kununura to El Questro for A$470 (US$376). A private VIP jet service, **Oasis OzVacations** (℃ 02/ 9238 6209; www.oasisozvacations.com), flies from Sydney and Melbourne to Kununurra airport.

WHERE TO STAY
At El Questro

All of the accommodations accept American Express, MasterCard, and Visa. All have public pay phones, but no in-room phones or TVs.

El Questro Homestead ★★★   Perched over the Chamberlain River on the edge of a gorge, this homestead is one of the world's most luxurious yet simple getaways. Visitors (make that *wealthy* visitors) come for the sense of seclusion and the wilderness experience. You stay in airy rooms furnished in a blend of Aussie country style and Indonesian antiques, with a view of the gardens and the river from your veranda. The premier suite even has a bathtub on the veranda! Guests relax outside or in the inviting TV lounge. You can choose to dine at the big communal table at breakfast and lunch, or alone on your private balcony. At dinner you dine at tables for two set up wherever you like—halfway down the gorge cliff face overhanging the river, out by the pool, and so on. The homestead is 119km (74 miles), or about 1¾ hours, from Kununurra. Station Township is 9km (5½ miles) away.

Gibb River Rd., approximately 100km (62 miles) southwest of Kununurra (P.O. Box 909, Kununurra, WA 6743). Accor ℃ **1300/656 565** in Australia, 800/221-4542 in the U.S. and Canada, 020/8283 4500 in the U.K., 0800/44 4422 in New Zealand, or ℃ 08/9169 1777. Fax 08/9169 1383. www.elquestro.com.au. 6 units (all with shower only). A$850–A$950 (US$680–US$760) per person per night double or twin. Rates include all meals, open bar, laundry service, and all activities except helicopter flights. AE, MC, V. 2-night minimum. Children under 16 not accepted. 4WD transfers from Kununurra A$85 (US$68) per person (scheduled) or A$165 (US$132) per person (private). Air transfers from Kununurra, Broome, Darwin, Alice Springs, and Uluru (Ayers Rock) on request; baggage limit can be as little as

5kg (11 lb.) on flights from Kununurra or Darwin. **Amenities:** Small outdoor pool; tennis court; Jacuzzi; tour bookings; laundry service. *In room:* A/C, hair dryer, no phone.

Emma Gorge Resort ★★

Ten new "tented cabins" have been added in 2005 to the neatly kept oasis of permanent tents mounted on lush lawns under pandanus palms at the foot of the soaring red Cockburn Range at Emma Gorge Resort. This is a great way to experience the wilderness without sacrificing comfort. The "tents" are very comfortable, with polished wooden floors, electric lights, fans, insect screens, nice firm beds with goose-feather pillows, Indian cotton sheets and quilts, and flashlights for getting around at night. Those without bathrooms share clean and modern facilities. The reception desk stocks items like sunscreen and souvenirs, and lends hair dryers. The rustic restaurant serves gourmet bush-tucker meals that would put many big-city restaurants to shame, and has a retractable roof for stargazing. There is also a new viewing platform for the best views of the spectacular Saddleback Ridge, overlooking El Questro Valley. Free to guests is access to a 1.6km (1-mile) trail along lush Emma Gorge to the natural swimming hole and trickling waterfall enclosed by 46m (150-ft.) cliffs. Emma Gorge is 85km (53 miles), an hour's drive, from Kununurra. Station Township is 27km (17 miles) away.

See contact details for El Questro Homestead, above. 55 tented cabins, 37 with bathroom (shower only). A$135–A$185 (US$108–US$148) double; A$220 (US$176) deluxe tented cabins for up to 4. AE, MC, V. Transfers A$55 (US$44) per person each way; children under 12 half price. **Amenities:** Restaurant; bar; outdoor pool; tour desk; coin-op laundry. *In room:* No phone.

Station Township Bungalows

These basic but comfortable bungalow-style rooms in the heart of Station Township are good for anyone without their own transportation—tours depart from right outside. The nicest units are the eight newish ones with balconies directly overhanging the Pentecost River. Two of the four original stone bungalows sleep six but rent for the same price. The front desk lends hair dryers. The **Steakhouse** restaurant and bar serves three meals a day of the steak and barramundi kind, and there is often live music and outback entertainment at the Swinging Arm Bar. A swimming hole is nearby. The bungalows are 110km (68 miles), about 90 minutes, from Kununurra.

See contact details for El Questro Homestead, above. 12 bungalows (with shower only). A$270 (US$216) bungalow for up to 4. Transfers A$70 (US$56). AE, MC, V. **Amenities:** Restaurant; bar; tour desk; 4-wheel-drive rental desk; coin-op laundry. *In room:* A/C, fridge, coffeemaker, no phone.

Station Township Riverside Camping

In addition to the other El Questro options, there are two camping areas. **Black Cockatoo Riverside Camping** has 45 campsites near the station store, and 28 more secluded riverside campsites lie within a 6km (3¾-mile) drive. All campsites are the same price, A$15 (US$12) per person per night; free for children under 12. Campers share shower facilities and a laundry, and use the bungalows' restaurant. No bookings are taken for campsites. *Note:* The Wilderness Park Permit fee is not included in the campground fee.

In Kununurra

Country Club Hotel

Just down the road from the tourist bureau, this low-rise hotel is your best bet among Kununurra's modest choice of accommodations. Set in tropical gardens, it has a lovely shaded pool with sun lounges and a bar, and a couple of simple dining and bar venues. The rooms are nothing flashy, but they're neat and clean, with plenty of space. The front desk lends hair dryers.

47 Coolibah Dr., Kununurra, WA 6743. ⓒ **1800/808 999** in Australia, or 08/9168 1024. Fax 08/9168 1189. www. countryclubhotel.com.au. 88 units (80 with shower only). Dry season (Apr–Oct) A$168 (US$134) double, A$222 (US$178) 2-bedroom apt; Wet season (Nov–Mar) A$148 (US$118) double, A$191 (US$153) 2-bedroom apt. Extra person A$24 (US$19). AE, DC, MC, V. **Amenities:** 2 restaurants; 3 bars; outdoor pool; tour desk; coin-op laundry. *In room:* A/C, TV, fridge, hair dryer.

PURNULULU (BUNGLE BUNGLES) NATIONAL PARK ✦
250km (156 miles) S of Kununurra

Rising out of the landscape 250km (155 miles) south of Kununurra are thousands of enormous sandstone domes 200 to 300m (656–984 ft.) high called the Bungle Bungles. They are thought to have been named after either "bundle bundle" grass or the bungle beetle. The Bungle Bungles get their distinctive orange-and-gray stripes from algae found in the permeable layers and mineral graining in nonpermeable layers. The formations are 360 million years old.

The domes look spectacular from the air—that's the way most people see them, and it's the only way to see them in the Wet, because the park is closed to ground traffic January 1 to March 31, sometimes later. As the waters subside, the soaring gorges and forested creeks at the base of the Bungle Bungles are accessible to hikers. Highlights are the beehive-shaped walls of Cathedral Gorge, the rock pool at Frog Hole Gorge, and palm-filled Echidna Chasm. Keep an eye peeled for rainbow bee-eaters, flocks of budgerigars, rare nail-tailed wallabies, and euros, a kind of kangaroo. It's a lonely, quiet, contemplative, and dramatic place.

VISITOR INFORMATION   For information, call the **Department of Conservation and Land Management** (ⓒ 08/9168 4200) in Kununurra. There's also a **visitor center/ranger station** (ⓒ 08/9168 7300) in the park.

GETTING THERE & GETTING AROUND   Most folks take a scenic flight over the park in a light aircraft from Kununurra with **Slingair Heliwork** (ⓒ **1800/095 500** in Australia, or 08/9169 1300) or **Alligator Airways** (ⓒ **1800/632 533** in Australia, or 08/9168 1333). The flight takes about 2 hours, incorporates a flight over Lake Argyle and the impressive Argyle Diamond Mine, and costs A$220 (US$176) for adults and A$140 (US$112) for children 3 to 12. Both companies also do day trips that combine the flight with hiking, though they're pricey, starting at A$485 (US$388) for adults and A$390 (US$312) for kids. **East Kimberley Tours** (see "Getting Around," in the Kimberley section) runs an array of four-wheel-drive and fly-drive camping and hiking safaris into the park, including some 1-day "express" versions.

BROOME ✦
2,389km (1,481 miles) N of Perth; 1,859km (1,152 miles) SW of Darwin

Part rough Outback town, part glam seaside resort, the pearling port of **Broome** (pop. 11,000) is a hybrid of Australia and Asia you won't see anywhere else. Chinese and Japanese pearl divers worked the pearling luggers in this isolated little town in the old days, and as the Chinese settled here, they affixed their distinctive architecture to typical Australian buildings. The result is a main street so cute it could be a movie set, with neat rows of Australian corrugated iron stores wrapped by verandas and trimmed with Chinese peaked roofs.

The people are unique, too, because Anglo-Saxon and Irish Aussies and Chinese, Filipino, and Malayan pearl workers often married Aboriginal women. The Japanese tended to return home, but not all of them made it—cyclones, the "bends," sharks, and crocodiles all took their toll. The Japanese legacy in the town is a divers' cemetery with Asian inscriptions on 900 rough-hewn headstones.

For such a small and remote place, Broome is surprisingly sophisticated. Walk the streets of Chinatown and you'll rub shoulders with Aussie tourists, itinerant workers, Asian food-store proprietors, tough-as-nails cattle hands, and well-heeled visitors from Europe and America who down good coffee at a couple of trendy cafes. Broome's South Sea pearls are still its bread and butter, but the timber pearling luggers have been replaced with gleaming high-tech vessels equipped with helipads and stainless steel security doors.

To be honest, it's kind of hard to explain Broome's appeal. There is not much to do, but it's a nice place to be. You can shop for pearls, and it's a good base for exploring the Kimberley. But most people simply come to laze by the jade-green Indian Ocean on Cable Beach, ride camels along the sand as the sun plops into the sea, fish the unplundered seas, mosey around the art galleries and jewelry stores, and soak up the gorgeous reds, blues, and greens of the Kimberley coast.

ESSENTIALS

GETTING THERE   **Qantas** flies direct from Sydney, Melbourne, and Perth. **Qantaslink** (© 13 13 13 in Australia) flies from Alice Springs. **Virgin Blue** (© 13 67 89 in Australia) flies direct to Broome from Perth and Adelaide, with connections from other cities. **Skywest** (© 1300/660 088 in Australia; www.skywest.com.au) flies from Perth daily.

Greyhound Australia (© 13 14 99 in Australia) has daily service from Perth. It takes around 34 hours. The fare is A$313 (US$250). Greyhound's daily service from Darwin via Katherine and Kununurra takes around 24 hours; the one-way fare is A$302 (US$242). There is no train service.

Broome is 34km (21 miles) off the Great Northern Highway, which leads from Perth in the south and Kununurra to the east. Many companies (including those listed under "Essentials" in the "Kimberley" section, earlier in this chapter) run four-wheel-drive camping safaris to Broome on the Gibb River Road, an unpaved Outback scenic route from Kununurra.

VISITOR INFORMATION   The **Broome Visitor Centre** is on the Great Northern Highway (locals call it the Broome Hwy.) at Bagot Street, Broome, WA 6725 (© 1800/883 777 in Australia, or 08/9192 2222; www.broomevisitorcentre.com.au). It's open Monday through Friday from 8am to 5pm. On Saturday, Sunday, and public holidays, it's open from 9am to 4pm in the Dry (Apr–Sept), and from 9am to 1pm in the Wet (Oct–Mar).

Book hotels and tours well in advance of the peak June-through-August season.

GETTING AROUND   **Avis** (© 08/9193 5980), **Budget** (© 08/9193 5355), **Europcar** (© 08/9193 7788), **Hertz** (© 08/9192 1428), and **Thrifty** (© 08/9192 2210) all rent conventional cars and four-wheel-drives. Hertz also rents camping-gear kits and car-top tents that affix to the larger four-wheel-drives. Among the motorhome companies are **Apollo Motorhome Holidays** (© 08/9192 3087) and **Britz** (© 1800/331 454 in Australia, or 08/9192 2647).

The **Pearl Town Bus Service** (© 08/9193 6585) does an hourly loop of most attractions from 7:10am to 6:15pm daily. From May to October, it also runs every half-hour from 9am to 3pm. A single adult fare is A$2.70 (US$2.15), or A$6 (US$4.80) for a family of four. A five-trip adult ticket is A$12 (US$9.60).

Broome Taxis (℃ **08/9192 1133**) operates the airport shuttle; book ahead if you want a transfer to your hotel door. For a cab, call **Roebuck Taxis** (℃ **1800/880 330**).

Several coach and four-wheel-drive companies run a variety of day tours of the town, plus trips of a day or several days to natural attractions farther afield, like Windjana and Geikie Gorges, Tunnel Creek, and the Dampier Peninsula (described in "Beyond Broome," below).

WHAT TO SEE & DO

When you arrive, head to **Chinatown,** in the town center on Carnarvon Street and Dampier Terrace, to get a feel for the town. It's not all that Chinese anymore, but most shops, cafes, and galleries are here.

Probably the most popular Dry season pastime is lazing on the 22km (14 miles) of glorious, white sandy **Cable Beach** ✿. The beach is 6km (3¾ miles) out of town; the bus runs there regularly. A beach hut near Cable Beach Club Resort Broome (see "Where to Stay & Dine," below) rents beach and watersports equipment in the Dry. In the Wet, about November through April, the water is off-limits due to marine stingers—it's incredibly frustrating! Crocodiles, on the other hand, do not like surf, so you should be safe swimming here. Go to the beach for at least one of the magnificent sunsets in the Dry, when the sun sinks into the sea behind the romantic outlines of pearling luggers.

A novel way to experience the beach is on a **camel ride.** Several outfits offer rides; the most popular time is at sunset as the sun drops over the ocean. A 1-hour sunset ride with **Red Sun Camels** (℃ **08/9193 7423**) costs A$40 (US$32) adults, A$25 (US$20) kids 6 to 16. Kids under 6 pay A$10 (US$8), but they must ride with an adult.

Four-time state surf champ **Josh Palmateer** ✿ (℃ **0418/958 264** mobile) gives 2-hour surf lessons on the beach in July and August for A$100 (US$80) per person, or A$55 (US$44) per person for two (cheaper if you join a group). He supplies the boards and the wet suits, and the lessons are great fun.

Don't miss the **Pearl Luggers** ✿✿, 31 Dampier Terrace (℃ **08/9192 2059**). A 75-minute session includes a look over two restored Broome pearling luggers, a browse through a small pearling museum, and a riveting and hilarious talk about pearl diving by former pearl divers. Admission is A$19 (US$15) adults, A$17 (US$14) seniors and students, A$9 (US$7.20) kids over 9. The attraction is open daily from 9am to 5pm April through October, and from 10am to 3:30pm November through March. Tours

---

Moments **Staircase to the Moon**

You've heard of a stairway to heaven? Well, Broome has a **staircase to the moon** ✿. On the happy coincidence of a full moon and a 10m (33-ft.) tide (which happens on about 3 consecutive nights a month Mar–Oct), nature treats the town to a show. The light of the rising moon falls on the rippled sand and mudflats in Roebuck Bay, looking like a "staircase to the moon." The best places to see it are from the cliff-top restaurant at the **Mangrove Resort Hotel** (see "Where to Stay & Dine," below), and from the food and crafts markets at Town Beach. Live music plays at the Mangrove most staircase nights, including a didgeridoo player to accompany the rising moon.

depart at 9am, 11am, 2pm and 4pm in the Dry, and 11am and 2pm in the Wet (11am only on weekends). Closed December 25.

A **dinosaur footprint** 120 million years old is on show at very low tide on the cliff at Gantheaume Point, 6km (3¾ miles) from town. The town authorities have set a plaster cast of it higher up on the rocks, so you can see it anytime. Bring your camera to snap the point's breathtaking palette of glowing scarlet cliffs, white beach, and jade-turquoise water.

You should also take a peek at the haunting **Japanese pearl divers' cemetery** on Port Drive. Entry is free.

During a tour of the **Willie Creek Pearl Farm** (© 08/9192 6000), 38km (24 miles) north of town, you will see the delicate process of an oyster getting "seeded" with a nucleus to form a pearl, learn about pearl farming, and learn what to look for when buying a pearl. You can also buy them in the showroom. The tour costs A$25 (US$20) adults, A$12 (US$9.60) children, and A$65 (US$52) for a family of four. You must book the tour ahead whether you drive yourself or not. Tides can cut off the four-wheel-drive-only road to the farm; it is wise to take a coach tour, which costs A$59 (US$47) adults, A$30 (US$24) children 6 to 16, including the price of the pearl-farm tour. Tours run daily April to September and every day except Tuesday and Saturday from October to March.

If you have not seen any crocs in the wild during your travels, you can take a 1-hour tour at the **Broome Crocodile Park,** next to Cable Beach Club Resort Broome, Cable Beach Road (© 08/9193 7824). Admission is A$15 (US$12) for adults, A$12 (US$9.60) for seniors and students, A$8 (US$6.40) for kids 5 to 15, and A$38 (US$30) for families. Tours run once or twice daily, but hours vary with the seasons, so call ahead. The park is owned by adventurer, naturalist, and filmmaker Malcolm Douglas, and you might also care to visit the **Malcolm Douglas Wildlife Wilderness Park,** on the highway about 16km (10 miles) out of town, which is devoted to Australia's rare and endangered animals. For information, contact the crocodile park.

Several art galleries sell vivid oil and watercolor Kimberley landscapes and a small range of Aboriginal art. A historic pearling master's house, **Matso's,** 60 Hamersley St. (© 08/9193 5811), stocks the biggest range of European and Aboriginal paintings, sculpture, pottery, carvings, and books in its Monsoon Gallery. It has a lovely veranda cafe and a boutique brewery that turns out unusual recipes like alcoholic ginger beer. The gallery is open daily from 10am to 5pm; the cafe is open daily from 8am until late.

On Saturday from 8am to 1pm, browse the **markets** in the gardens of the colonial Courthouse at the corner of Frederick and Hamersley streets. It used to be the official station for the cable from Broome to Java. Don't bet the ranch on this tale being gospel, but locals like to tell you that when the British authorities packed up the building materials for the courthouse in Britain and addressed it to "The Kimberley," they meant them to end up in the Kimberley, South Africa. Instead, the stuff arrived in the Kimberley, Australia. The town kept the building and so can proudly lay claim to having Australia's only Zulu-proof courthouse.

A number of boats run **sunset cruises** on Roebuck Bay or off Cable Beach. **Fishing** ✤ for trevally, barracuda, barramundi, queenfish, tuna, shark, sailfish, marlin, salmon (in the May–Aug run), and reef fish is excellent around Broome; fly- and sportfishing are also worth a go. Rent tackle and try your luck from the deep-water jetty near Town Beach 2km (1¼ miles) south of town, or join one of several charter boats, such as **FAD Game Fishing Charters** (© **0410/649 135;** www.fadcharters. com.au), for a day trip. **Pearl Sea Coastal Cruises** (see "Boating the Kimberley Coast," below) runs live-aboard fishing trips up the coast. Cyclones, rain, high winds, and strong tides can restrict fishing December through March.

More than one-third of Australia's bird species live in the Kimberley. The blue, green, yellow, and violet Gouldian finch; Nankeen night heron; tawny frogmouth; and hundreds more species get "twitchers" excited. **The Broome Bird Observatory** research station (© **08/9193 5600**), 25km (16 miles) out of town on Roebuck Bay, monitors the thousands of migratory wetlands birds that gather here from Siberia. Entry is A$5 (US$4) per person, and it also offers a range of tours. A 2½-hour tour from Broome costs A$73 (US$58) adults (or A$48/US$38 self-drive). There are basic accommodations and camping facilities at the observatory.

Australia's first family of pearling, the Paspaleys, sell their wonderfully elegant jewelry at **Paspaley Pearls,** Carnarvon Street at Short Street (© **08/9192 2203**). **Linneys** (© **08/9192 2430**) is another reputable jeweler nearby.

Don't leave without taking in a movie at the **Sun Pictures** outdoor cinema, Carnarvon Street near Short Street (© **08/9192 1077**). Built in 1916, these are the oldest "picture gardens" in the world. The audience sits in canvas deck chairs. Tickets are A$12 (US$9.60). Open nightly except December 25—even through the Wet.

WHERE TO STAY & DINE

Cable Beach Club Resort Broome ★★★

For some Aussies, a visit to Broome is just an excuse to stay at this chic Asia-meets-Outback resort, which blends Australian frontier architecture and decor—corrugated-iron walls inside as well as out, verandas, Aboriginal art—with Chinese elements like red-and-green latticework, pagoda roofs, silky red bathrobes, and Asian cotton bedcovers. A A$10-million (US$8-million) refurbishment completed in early 2005 smartened up the whole resort, including the addition of a day spa. The huge standard rooms are gorgeous and have a decent-size living area and balcony. Bungalows (which sleep five or six) have central bedrooms wrapped on three sides by a veranda, and kitchens. The luxury private villas and Pool Terrace studios have direct access to the adults-only pool. For glamour, it's tough to match the colonial-pearling-master suites, lavishly decked out with eye-popping Asiatic antiques and valuable Australian art. These are truly to die for, so ask about suite packages, which offer remarkably good value. A dune blocks full sea views, because the authorities won't allow buildings visible from the sand. The resort also has a guest-activities program and an art gallery and pearl boutique. It is a 5-minute drive or a 6km (3¾-mile) bus ride into town.

Cable Beach Rd., Broome, WA 6725. © **1800/099 199** in Australia, or 08/9192 0400. Fax 08/9192 2249. www.cable beachclub.com. 263 units (some with shower only). May–Oct A$337–A$437 (US$270–US$350) double; A$475–A$527 (US$380–US$422) bungalow; A$759–A$941 (US$607–US$753) villa; A$941–A$1,520 (US$753–US$1,216) suite. Extra person A$40 (US$32). Children under 12 stay free in parent's room with existing bedding. Apr discounts A$70–A$90 (US$56–US$72), much more for suites. Significant discounts mid-Oct to Mar. Ask about packages. AE, DC, MC, V. Town bus. **Amenities:** 3 restaurants (2 seasonal); cafe; bar; 2 outdoor pools (family pool and adults-only saltwater pool, both chilled in Wet season and heated in winter); 2 floodlit tennis courts; gymnasium; golf course nearby; spa; kids' club (ages 2–12 for A$12/US$9.60 per hour, A$30/US$24 half-day, A$50/US$40 full day); concierge; tour desk; airport shuttle; business center; limited room service; in-room massage; babysitting; laundry service; dry cleaning. *In room:* A/C, TV w/free movies, minibar, coffeemaker, hair dryer, iron.

Mangrove Resort Hotel ★

The best views in Broome are across Roebuck Bay from this recently refurbished modest but appealing cliff-top hotel, a 5-minute walk from town. There's no faulting the well-kept, roomy deluxe rooms with sea views. Sixteen extra-large executive rooms were added in 2002, and there are also four suites with kitchenettes, separate bedrooms, and Jacuzzis. The swimming pools and Jacuzzis are set in the lawns overlooking the bay. It's worth hightailing it back from sightseeing just to watch dusk fall over the bay from **The Tides** ✿, a lovely outdoor restaurant serving fresh, affordable food. The restaurant's tables and chairs sit out on the lawns under the palms and along the cliff edge. Inside, **Charters** restaurant is one of Broome's best. The town bus stops across the road.

47 Carnarvon St., Broome, WA 6725. ℭ **1800/094 818** in Australia, or 08/9192 1303. Fax 08/9193 5169. www.mangrovehotel.com.au. 70 units (66 with shower only). Apr–Sept A$170–A$205 (US$136–US$164) double, A$265–A$295 (US$212–US$236) suite; Oct–Mar A$145–A$178 (US$116–US$142) double, A$235–A$275 (US$188–US$220) suite. Extra person A$35 (US$28). Children under 3 stay free in parent's room. Ask about Wet-season packages. AE, DC, MC, V. Amenities: 2 restaurants; 2 bars; 2 outdoor pools; 2 Jacuzzis; tour desk; spa; courtesy car from airport; limited room service; coin-op laundry; laundry service; dry cleaning. *In room:* A/C, TV w/free movies, fridge, coffeemaker, hair dryer, iron.

BEYOND BROOME

North of Broome, the Kimberley gets wild. It's a place with almost no human settlement, best suited to those who love nature at its most raw and isolated. Swimming in the ocean and rivers is off-limits, except in croc-free rock pools.

Stretching 220km (136 miles) north of Broome, the **Dampier Peninsula** is home to several Aboriginal communities that sell artworks, and a wonderful pearl-shell church built by missionaries.

The 350-million-year-old walls of **Windjana Gorge,** 240km (149 miles) east of Broome, reveal fossilized marine creatures laid down in the Devonian period. A trail leads you past the walls, which rise as high as 100m (328 ft.) above the desert floor. The 30m-high (98-ft.) walls of **Geikie Gorge** (pronounced *Geek*-ee), 418km (259 miles) east of Broome, are part of the same ancient coral-reef system as Windjana; you explore Geikie Gorge on walking trails or on a short cruise run by rangers. Either gorge can be explored on a long day trip from Broome.

Much farther north are the tidal whirlpools, gorges, and rainforested waterfalls of **Walcott Inlet;** the utter isolation of the gorges, rock plateaus, and river of the 600,000-hectare (1.5-million-acre) **Prince Regent Nature Reserve;** and the four tiers of picturesque **Mitchell Falls.**

There are no roads to most of these places (except four-wheel-drive tracks to the Dampier Peninsula and Mitchell Falls), so you need to explore by scenic flight from Broome or Kununurra or by boat. From July through September or later, plane and boat passengers often spot humpback whales along this coast.

BOATING THE KIMBERLEY COAST

Boating this vast, unspoiled Kimberley coastline is a true adventure. Here you can fish in rivers without names, hike through spectacular gorges, laze on isolated beaches, gaze at Aboriginal rock art, eat oysters fresh off the rocks, spot giant marine turtles, shower under waterfalls, swim in the odd croc-free rainforest pool, and feel the wilderness is yours. But extremely strong tidal currents of up to 11m (36 ft.), high cliffs, sharks, and saltwater crocodiles all pose dangers, so you should be reasonably fit and independent to travel by boat. This is a big region; you will need to take an extended charter trip lasting anywhere from 5 to 14 days.

Several boat operators run fishing and adventure trips from Broome, Derby (221km/137 miles northeast), or Darwin. Some incorporate short inland expeditions on foot, by light aircraft, or by four-wheel-drive. North Star Cruises (below) even travels with its own helicopter for flight-seeing and heli-fishing. Some boats take scuba divers to Rowley Shoals, a marvelous outcrop of coral reef and giant clams 260km (161 miles) west off Broome. Find a vessel that suits you—some offer comfortable private cabins, while others are camp-on-the-beach jobs. Some of the most established operators are **North Star Cruises** (© **08/9192 1829;** www.northstarcruises.com.au) and **Pearl Sea Coastal Cruises** (© **08/9193 6131;** www.pearlseacruises.com), both operating from Broome; and **Buccaneer Sea Safaris** (© **08/9191 1991;** www.west net.com.au/buccaneer), operating out of Derby. Contact the Broome Tourist Bureau for an up-to-date list of the boats plying the coast, because some boats come and go from year to year.

The 35m (115-ft.) motorized catamaran *Coral Princess* and her sister vessel *Oceanic Princess* make 10-day Broome-Darwin and Darwin-Broome voyages from April through September. Accommodations are in standard and deluxe staterooms or in budget cabins (all with private bathrooms). Facilities include a Jacuzzi, sun deck, cocktail bar, and dining room. The voyages depart about 10 times a year. You can go ashore at least once a day to swim (in croc-free pools only), fish, hike in spectacular scenery, croc-spot on river cruises, barbecue on an island beach, take optional scenic helicopter flights over Mitchell Falls, or see Aboriginal art. Fares range from A$5,800 to A$7,350 (US$4,640–US$5,880) per person, twin-share. Contact **Coral Princess Cruises** (© **07/4040 9999;** www.coralprincesscruises.com); in the U.S., contact S. H. Enterprises, 245-M, Mt. Hermon Rd. #B, Scotts Valley, CA 05066 (© **800/ 441-6880** or 831/335-4954; Coralpss@aol.com).

11

Adelaide & South Australia

by Marc Llewellyn

Adelaide (pop. 1 million) has a major advantage over the other state capitals in that it has Outback, vineyards, wetlands, animal sanctuaries, a major river, and mountain ranges virtually on its doorstep. Meals and lodgings are cheaper in Adelaide than in Sydney or Melbourne. If you plan to travel outside the city, a trip to one of the wine-growing areas has to be on your itinerary. Of all the wine areas, the **Barossa Valley** is the most interesting. Centered on Tanunda, the Barossa is known for its German architecture as well as its dozens of pretty hamlets, fine restaurants, and vineyards offering cellar-door tastings.

If you want to see animals instead of, or in addition to, grapes, you're in luck. You're likely to come across the odd kangaroo or wallaby near the main settlements, especially at dusk, or you could visit one of the area's wildlife reserves. Otherwise, head into the Outback or over to **Kangaroo Island,** without a doubt the best place in Australia to see concentrated numbers of native animals in the wild.

Another place well worth visiting is the craggy **Flinders Ranges,** some 460km (285 miles) north of Adelaide. Though the scenery along the way is mostly unattractive grazing properties devoid of trees, the Flinders Ranges offer an incredible landscape of multicolored rocks, rough-and-ready characters, and even camel treks in the semidesert. On the other side of the mountains, the real Outback starts.

The **South Australian Outback** is serenely beautiful, with giant skies, red earth, little water, and wildflowers after the rains. Out here you'll find bizarre opal-mining towns, such as **Coober Pedy,** where summer temperatures can reach 122°F (50°C) and where most people live underground to escape the heat.

If you prefer your landscape with more moisture, head to the **Coorong,** a waterbird sanctuary rivaled only by Kakadu National Park in the Northern Territory (see chapter 9).

EXPLORING THE STATE

VISITOR INFORMATION   The **South Australian Visitor & Travel Centre,** 18 King William St. (© **1300/655 276** in Australia, or 08/8303 2033; fax 08/8303 2249; www.southaustralia.com), is the best place to find information on Adelaide and South Australia. It's open weekdays from 8:30am to 5pm and weekends from 9am to 2pm. There's also an information booth at the King William Street end of Rundle Mall.

For general information about South Australia's national parks, contact the **Department of Environment and Natural Resources Information Centre,** Australis House, 77 Grenfell St., Adelaide, SA 5000 (© **08/8204 1910**). It's open Monday through Friday from 9am to 5pm.

GETTING AROUND   South Australia, at four times the size of the United Kingdom, has a lot of empty space between places of interest. The best way to see it is by car. Limited rail service connects Adelaide with some areas. The Stuart Highway bisects the state from south to north; it runs from Adelaide through the industrial center of Port Augusta (gateway to the Flinders Ranges), and through Coober Pedy to Alice Springs in the Red Centre. The Eyre Highway travels westward along the coastline and into Western Australia, and the Barrier Highway enters New South Wales just before the mining city of Broken Hill (see chapter 5). The Princes Highway takes you east to Melbourne. If you plan to drive into the Outback regions, contact the **Royal Automobile Association of South Australia (RAA),** 41 Hindmarsh Sq., Adelaide, SA 5000 (© **13 11 11** in South Australia, or 08/8202 4500; www.raa.net). The RAA provides route maps and emergency breakdown service.

Greyhound Australia (© **13 14 99** in Australia, or 07/4690 9950; www.greyhound. com.au) operates bus service to and around South Australia. Within the state, the largest operator is **Premier Stateliner** (© **08/8415 5500;** www.premierstateliner. com.au). It runs a half-day city sights tour of Adelaide costing A$42 for adults and A$21 for kids; a day trip to the Barossa Valley costing A$69 for adults and A$35 for kids; a 2-day trip to the Barossa Valley with accommodations for A$195 for adults and A$150 for kids; a half-day trip to Hahndorf for A$42 for adults; and a day trip to the River Murray, including a boat cruise, costing A$99 (US$79) for adults and A$45 (US$36) for kids.

1 Adelaide

Adelaide has a reputation as a quieter place than some of the other state capitals and relishes the peace of its parklands and surrounding vineyards. In many ways it's something of a throwback to the comfortable lifestyle of 1950s Australia—a lifestyle that the more progressive state capitals have left behind.

Numerous parks and gardens, wide tree-lined streets, the River Torrens running through its center, sidewalk cafes, colonial architecture, and, of course, the churches help make the "city of churches" a pleasant, open city, perfect for strolling or bicycling.

Though the immigrant population has added a cosmopolitan flair to the restaurant scene, Adelaide still has a feeling of old England about it. That's not surprising when you learn that Adelaide was the only capital settled by English free settlers rather than by convicts, and that it attracted more after World War II, when Brits flocked here to work in the city's car and appliance factories.

But it was earlier immigrants, from Germany, who gave Adelaide and the surrounding area a romantic twist. Arriving as refugees fleeing religious strife in their country in the 1830s, German immigrants brought winemaking skills and established wineries. Today, more than one-third of all Australian wine—including some of the world's best—comes from areas within about an hour's drive from Adelaide. As a result, Adelaidians of all socioeconomic groups are more versed in wine than even the French and regularly compare vintages, wine-growing regions, and winemaking trends.

Any season is a good time to visit Adelaide, though May through August can be chilly and January and February hot.

ESSENTIALS
GETTING THERE   By Plane   Qantas (© **13 13 13** in Australia) flies to Adelaide from the other major state capitals. The discount carrier **Virgin Blue** (© **13 67 89** in

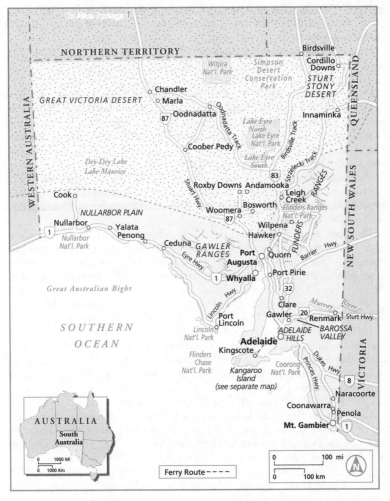

Australia; www.virginblue.com.au) flies direct from Melbourne, with connections from other state capitals and some major towns. Check the website for cheap deals. Adelaide International Airport is 5km (3 miles) west of the city center. Major car-rental companies (Avis, Budget, Hertz, and Thrifty) have desks in both the international and domestic terminals.

The **Skylink** (© **08/8332 0528;** www.coachaust.com.au) connects the airport with major hotels and the rail and bus stations. On weekdays, buses leave the terminals at 30-minute intervals from 5:30am to 9:30pm, and on weekends and public holidays hourly (on the half-hour). Adult tickets are A$7.50 (US$6) one-way, A$13 (US$10) round-trip. Children's tickets cost A$2.50 (US$2) each way.

By Taxi A taxi to the city from the airport will cost around A$19 (US$15).

By Train The **Keswick Interstate Rail Passenger Terminal,** 2km (1¼ miles) west of the city center, is Adelaide's main railway station. The terminal has a small snack bar and a cafe.

Contact **Great Southern Railways** (© **13 21 47** in Australia, or 08/8213 4530; www.gsr.com.au) for information, timetables, fares, and bookings for all trains described below.

One of the great trains of Australia, the *Indian Pacific* ✦ transports passengers from Sydney to Adelaide (trip time: 28 hr.) and from Perth to Adelaide (trip time: 36 hr.) twice a week, on Monday and Thursday. One-way tickets from Sydney to Adelaide are A$590 (US$472) for adults and A$465 (US$372) for children in first class; A$450 (US$360) for adults and A$325 (US$260) for children in an economy sleeper; and A$225 (US$180) for adults and A$109 (US$87) for children in coach. From Perth to Adelaide the one-way fare is A$1,250 (US$1,000) for adults and A$850 (US$680) for children in first class; A$960 (US$768) for adults and A$576 (US$460) for children in an economy sleeper; and A$309 (US$247) for adults and A$155 (US$124) for children in coach.

The other legendary Australian train is the *Ghan,* which runs from Adelaide to Alice Springs and onto Darwin weekly November through April, twice a week May through October, and has three weekly return services from Adelaide to Alice Springs in the peak season of May, June and July. Trip time from Alice Springs to Adelaide is 20 hours. From Alice Springs to Adelaide and vice versa, the one-way fare is A$890 (US$712) for adults and A$605 (US$484) for children in first class; A$680 (US$544) for adults and A$408 (US$326) for children in an economy sleeper; and A$215 (US$172) for adults and A$97 (US$78) for children for an economy seat. From Adelaide to Darwin it costs A$1,830 (US$1,464) for adults and A$1,244 (US$995) for kids in first class; A$1,390 (US$1,112) for adults and A$834 (US$667) for kids in an economy sleeper, and A$440 (US$352) for adults and A$198 (US$158) for kids in an economy seat. It's a hard trip in an economy sleeper though, and all those old socks (it's custom for people to take off their shoes) make it smelly.

The round-trip fare for the *Indian Pacific* and *Ghan* works out to twice the one-way fare or just a few dollars cheaper. Full-time students with a recognized student card from any institution may travel for child prices, or just a little more, on all trains. Backpackers and students should consider the Great Southern Railway Pass, which allows unlimited travel on the *Ghan, Indian Pacific,* and *Overland* (see below) for 6 months. It costs A$450 (US$360). Those without a student card can still travel in the same conditions for A$590 (US$472).

The *Overland* operates four weekly round-trips. It offers daylight service from Adelaide to Melbourne and overnight service from Melbourne to Adelaide (trip time: 12 hr.). From Melbourne to Adelaide, one-way ticket prices are A$175 (US$140) for adults and A$139 (US$111) for children in first class, and A$59 (US$47) for adults and A$42 (US$33) for children in an economy seat. It's a little cheaper from Adelaide to Melbourne, and there are good round-trip discounts.

By Bus Intercity coaches serve the central bus station, 101 Franklin St. (© **08/8415 5533**), near Morphett Street in the city center. **Greyhound Australia** (© **13 14 99** in Australia, or 07/4690 9950; www.greyhound.com.au) runs buses between Adelaide and all other major cities. The trip from Melbourne takes 11 hours and costs A$60 (US$48); from Sydney, 25 hours and A$130 (US$104); and from Alice Springs, 21 hours and A$180 (US$144).

Adelaide

Church	✝
Information	ⓘ
Post Office	✉
Railway	+++

AUSTRALIA

Adelaide

ACCOMMODATIONS
City Park Motel **29**
Hilton Adelaide **26**
Hyatt Regency Adelaide **11**
Moore's Brecknock Hotel **28**
North Adelaide Heritage Group **3**
Novotel Adelaide on Hindley **18**
Old Lion Apartments **7**
Princes Lodge Motel **6**
Rockford Adelaide **17**
Saville Park Suites Adelaide **16**

DINING
Amalfi **23**
Austral Hotel **22**
The Grange **26**
Jasmin Indian Restaurant **21**
Jolleys Boathouse Restaurant **9**
The Manse **4**
Matsuri **27**
Mekong Thai **19**
The Oxford **5**
Rigoni's Bistro **20**

ATTRACTIONS
Adelaide Casino **10**
Adelaide Zoo **8**
Art Gallery of South Australia **14**
Botanic Gardens **15**
National Railway Museum **2**
National Wine Centre of Australia **25**
South Australian Maritime Museum **1**
South Australian Museum **13**
Tandanya Aboriginal Cultural Institute **24**
The Migration Museum **12**

Adventurous types should consider traveling to Adelaide from Melbourne (or vice versa) on the **Wayward Bus,** operated by the Wayward Bus Touring Company, P.O. Box 7076, Adelaide, SA 5000 (© **1800/882 823** in Australia, or 08/8232 6646; www.waywardbus.com.au). The fare is A$310 (US$248) with backpacker's accommodations and around A$440 (US$352) with motel accommodations. You spend about 3 hours a day on the bus, and the driver acts as your guide. The fare includes a picnic or cafe lunch each day and entry to national parks. You can leave the trip and rejoin another later. Reservations are essential. The 21-seat buses also makes the trip in 4-day trip from Alice Springs to Adelaide, via Coober Pedy and the Flinders National Park (and vice versa), leaving twice weekly. This includes 2 nights camping and 2 nights in a bunkhouse. The trip costs A$395 (US$316) from Adelaide to Coober Pedy, and A$770 (US$616) from Adelaide to Alice Springs.

Wayward Bus also runs 8-day overland trips traveling between Adelaide and Alice (or vice versa), via Uluru, Katatjuta (Olgas), Kings Canyon, Coober Pedy, Lake Eyre, William Creek, Wilpena Pound, the Flinders Ranges, and the Clare Valley wineries. It's a mix of camping, swags (thick sleeping bags), dugout cave, and hostel accommodations. It costs A$790 (US$632). Check the website for more tours.

Another bus company, the **Nullarbor Traveller** (P.O. Box 72, Glensside, SA 5065; © **08/8364 0407;** www.the-traveller.com.au), takes adventurous travelers from Adelaide to Perth in 9 days across the Nullarbor Plain. The tour includes a mixture of camping and pub accommodations and most meals. It costs A$995 (US$796). A good area website is **www.nullarbornet.com.au**.

By Car To drive from Sydney to Adelaide on the Hume and Sturt highways takes roughly 20 hours; from Melbourne it takes around 10 hours on the Great Ocean Road and Princes Highway; from Perth it takes 32 hours on the Great Eastern and Princes highways; and from Alice Springs it takes 15 hours on the remote Stuart Highway. For more information on driving distances, consult www.auinfo.com/distancecalc_process.asp.

VISITOR INFORMATION Go to the **South Australia Visitor & Travel Centre,** 18 King William St. (© **1300/655 276** in Australia, or 08/8303 2033; fax 08/8303 2249),

---

Tips The Adelaide & WOMADelaide Festivals

Adelaide is home to Australia's largest performing arts festival, the **Adelaide Festival,** which takes place over 3 weeks in March in even-numbered years. The next festival will be held March 3 to March 19, 2006. (The lineup will be available online in late 2005.) The festival includes literary and visual arts as well as dance, opera, classical music, jazz, cabaret, and comedy. The festival includes a Writers' Week and the **Adelaide Fringe Festival.**

In February or March, the 3-day **WOMADelaide Festival** of world music takes place. Crowds of 60,000 or more turn up to watch Australian and international artists. The next festival will be held March 10 to March 12, 2006.

For more information, visit www.adelaidefestival.org.au, www.adelaide fringe.com.au, and www.womadelaide.com.au.

Value **A Money-Saving Transit Pass**

If you plan to get around the city on public transportation, it's a good idea to purchase a **Daytrip ticket,** which covers unlimited travel on buses, trams, and city trains within the metropolitan area for 1 day. The pass costs A$6.40 (US$5.10) for adults and A$3.20 (US$2.55) for children 5 to 15 and is available at most train stations, newsstands, and the **Passenger Transport Board Information Centre (℃ 08/8210 1000).**

---

for maps, travel advice, and hotel and tour bookings. It's open weekdays from 8:30am to 5pm, weekends from 9am to 2pm. The info booth on Rundle Mall (℃ **08/8203 7611)** is open daily from 10am to 5pm.

CITY LAYOUT Adelaide is easy to navigate because of its gridlike pattern, planned down to each wide street and airy square by Colonel William Light in 1836. The city's official center is **Victoria Square,** where you'll find the Town Hall. Bisecting the city from south to north is the main thoroughfare, **King William Street.** Streets running perpendicular to King William Street change their names on either side; Franklin Street, for example, changes into Flinders Street. Of these cross streets, the most interesting are the restaurant strips of **Gouger Street** and **Rundle Street,** the latter running into the pedestrian-only shopping precinct of Rundle Mall. Another is **Hindley Street,** with inexpensive restaurants and nightlife. On the banks of the River Torrens just north of the city center, you'll find the Riverbank Precinct, the home of the Festival Centre, the Convention Centre, and the Skycity Adelaide Casino. Bordering the city center on the north and south are **North Terrace,** which is lined with galleries and museums and leads to the Botanic Gardens, and **South Terrace.**

Follow King William Street south and you'll be chasing the tram to the beachside suburb of **Glenelg;** follow it north, and it crosses the River Torrens and flows into sophisticated **North Adelaide,** an area crammed with Victorian and Edwardian architecture. The main avenues in North Adelaide, **O'Connell** and **Melbourne streets,** are lined with restaurants, cafes, and bistros that offer the tastes of a multicultural city.

Northwest of the city center is **Port Adelaide,** a seaport and the historic maritime heart of South Australia. It's home to some of the finest colonial buildings in the state, as well as good pubs and restaurants.

GETTING AROUND **By Bus** Adelaide's public bus network covers three zones, and fares are calculated according to the number of zones traveled. The city center is in Zone 1. The fare in Zone 1 is A$1.80 (US$1.45) from 9am to 3pm on weekdays and A$3 (US$2.40) at most other times. You can buy tickets on board or at kiosks around the city. You can get timetable and destination information over the phone or in person from the **Passenger Transport Board Information Centre (℃ 08/8210 1000),** on the corner of Currie and King William streets. It's open Monday through Saturday from 8am to 6pm and Sunday from 10:30am to 5:30pm.

The free **CityLoop bus** (no. 99C) operates every 15 minutes (Mon–Thurs 8:30am–6pm; Fri 8:30am–9pm; Sat 8:30am–5pm) around the city center, along North Terrace, East Terrace, Grenfell Street, Pulteney Street, Wakefield Street, Grote Street, Morphett Street, Light Square, Hindley Street, and West Terrace. Another free bus, the **Bee Line** (no. 99B), runs along North Terrace, down King William Street to Victoria Square. Routes are well signposted. All free city buses are wheelchair accessible.

Bus nos. 181 and 182 run from the city to North Adelaide.

The **Adelaide Explorer bus** (© **08/8231 7172;** www.adelaideexplorer.com.au) stops at 26 sights around town, including Glenelg, and costs A$30 (US$24) for adults, A$19 (US$15) for children, and A$70 (US$56) for families of four. Buy tickets on the bus. The loop takes a leisurely 3 hours, with commentary, and you can get on and off when you want. The first bus departs from 38 King William St., on the corner of Rundle Mall (next to Haigh's Chocolates) at 9am. The company will pick you up from your hotel between 8 and 8:30am if you call ahead, and will drop you off at the airport (with your luggage) as part of the fare. Call or e-mail ahead. The last loop starts at 1:30pm, ending at 4:30pm.

By Tram   The **Glenelg Tram** runs between Victoria Square and the beachside suburb of Glenelg. Tickets cost A$3.60 (US$2.90) for adults and A$1.60 (US$1.30) for children 5 to 14 from 9am to 3pm. The journey takes 29 minutes.

By Taxi & Car   The major cab companies are **Yellow Cabs** (© **13 22 27** in South Australia), **Suburban** (© **08/8211 8888**), and **Amalgamated** (© **08/8223 3333**). **Access Cabs** (© **1300/360 940** in South Australia) offers wheelchair taxis.

Major car-rental companies are **Avis,** 136 N. Terrace (© **08/8410 5727**); **Budget,** 274 N. Terrace (© **08/8223 1400**); **Hertz,** 233 Morphett St. (© **08/8231 2856**); and **Thrifty,** 296 Hindley St. (© **08/8211 8788**).

The **Royal Automobile Association of South Australia (RAA),** 41 Hindmarsh Sq. (© **13 11 11** in South Australia, or 08/8202 4500; www.raa.net), has route maps and provides emergency breakdown services.

FAST FACTS: Adelaide

American Express   The office, Shop 32, Rundle Mall (© **1300/139 060**), is open Monday to Friday 9am to 5pm, and Saturday 9am to noon.

Business Hours   Generally, banks are open Monday through Thursday from 9:30am to 4pm and Friday from 9:30am to 5pm. Stores are generally open Monday through Thursday from 9am to 5:30pm, Friday from 9am to 9pm, Saturday from 9am to 5pm, and Sunday from 11am to 5pm.

Currency Exchange   Banks and hotels, the casino, and the Myer department store in Rundle Mall cash traveler's checks. The **Thomas Cook** office is at Shop 4, Rundle Mall (© **08/8231 6977**). It's open Monday to Friday 9am to 5pm, and Saturday from 10am to 4pm.

Dentist   Contact the **Australian Dental Association Emergency Information Service** (© **08/8272 8111**), open weeknights from 5 to 9pm, and Saturday and Sunday from 9am to 9pm. It will put you in touch with a dentist. You can also contact the office of **Dr. Brook,** 231 North Terrace (© **08/8223 6988**), during normal business hours.

Doctor   Contact the **Royal Adelaide Hospital,** North Terrace (© **08/8222 4000**). **The Travellers' Medical & Vaccination Centre,** 29 Gilbert Place (© **08/8212 7522**), offers vaccinations and travel-related medicines.

Emergencies   Dial © **000** to call an ambulance, the fire department, or the police in an emergency.

Hospitals The **Royal Adelaide Hospital,** North Terrace (© **08/8222 4000**), is in the city center.

Hot Lines The **Crisis Care Centre** (© 13 16 11 in Australia); the **Royal Automobile Association of South Australia,** or RAA (© 08/8202 4500); the **Disability Information and Resource Centre** (© 08/8223 7522).

Internet Access The **Ngapartji Multimedia Centre,** 211 Rundle St. (© **08/8232 0839**), offers e-mail and Internet access Monday through Thursday from 8:30am to 9pm, Friday and Saturday from 9am to 10pm, and Sunday from noon to 7pm. Other access points are on Hindley Street: **Talking Cents,** 53 Hindley St. (© **08/8212 1266**), and **Café Boulevard,** 13 Hindley St. (© **08/8231 5734**).

Lost Property If you've lost something on the street, contact the nearest police station. For items left on public transport, contact the **Lost Property Office,** on the main concourse of the Adelaide Railway Station on North Terrace (© **08/ 8218 2552**); it's open Monday through Friday from 9am to 5pm.

Luggage Storage & Lockers There are luggage lockers at Adelaide Airport in the domestic terminal. At the **Central Bus Station** on Franklin Street (© **08/8415 5533**), luggage lockers cost A$2 (US$1.60) for 24 hours.

Pharmacies (Chemist Shops) **Burden Chemists,** Shop 11, Southern Cross Arcade, King William Street (© **08/8231 4701**), is open Monday through Thursday from 8am to 6pm, Friday from 8am to 8pm, and Saturday from 9am to 1pm.

Post Office The **General Post Office (GPO),** 141 King William St., Adelaide, SA 5000 (© **08/8216 2222**), is open Monday through Friday from 8am to 6pm and Saturday from 8:30am to noon. General delivery mail (poste restante) can be collected Monday through Friday from 8am to 5pm and Saturday 8:30am to noon.

Restrooms Public restrooms are at the Central Market Arcade, between Grote and Gouger streets, in both Hindmarsh and Victoria squares, and at James Place (off Rundle Mall).

Safety Adelaide is a safe city, though it's wise to avoid walking along the River Torrens and through side streets near Hindley Street after dark.

WHERE TO STAY

The **South Australia Visitor & Travel Centre** (see "Visitor Information," above) can supply information on B&Bs and homestays around the state. Satellite or cable TV is rare in South Australian hotels, though some provide pay-per-view movies.

IN THE CITY CENTER
Very Expensive

Hilton Adelaide ★★   The Hilton is a luxurious establishment just around the corner from a host of restaurants on Gouger Street. The lobby is polished marble with a cascading fountain and piano music tinkling throughout. Guest rooms are pleasant, with all you might expect from a classy establishment. There are 11 rooms equipped for travelers with disabilities. The Hilton has fabulous deals—A$210 (US$170) for standard and A$235 (US$190) for executive rooms—"subject to availability" (which means when it's not full). Each business room has a modem port and fax. I was surprised to find **Charlie's Bar**—full of photos of famous Charlies—virtually empty even on a Saturday night. In a pinch I'd probably choose the Hyatt (see below) for the extensive views, but there's not much difference between them.

233 Victoria Sq., Adelaide, SA 5000. © **1800/222 255** in Australia, or 08/8217 2000. Fax 08/8217 2001. www.hilton. com. 380 units. A$325–A$335 (US$260–US$270) double; A$440 (US$352) executive floor; A$650 (US$520) suite. Extra person A$45 (US$36). Children under 12 stay free in parent's room. AE, DC, MC, V. Parking A$16 (US$13). Tram stops in front of hotel. Bus: Bee Line to Victoria Sq. **Amenities:** 2 restaurants; bar; heated outdoor pool; tennis court; health club; Jacuzzi; sauna; concierge; salon; 24-hr. room service; massage; babysitting; laundry service; dry cleaning; nonsmoking rooms. *In room:* A/C, TV w/pay movies, dataport, minibar, coffeemaker, hair dryer, iron, safe.

Hyatt Regency Adelaide ★★ The 20-story Hyatt Regency is in the heart of the city and part of the complex that includes the Adelaide Festival Centre, the Casino, the Exhibition Hall, and the Convention Centre. The property overlooks the River Torrens and nearby parklands, and there are some wonderful views from the higher floors. The Hyatt doesn't scrimp, which shows in the attention to detail in the rooms. Guests staying in club-level Regency rooms get a good complimentary breakfast and free evening drinks and canapés. **Waves,** a cabaret-nightclub, offers a lively combination of video, disco, and live music; it's free for guests, though it can be dull and the drinks are expensive. Afternoon tea is served in the Atrium Lounge, which gets surprisingly full as the night wears on.

North Terrace, Adelaide, SA 5000. © **13 12 34** in Australia, 800/233-1234 in the U.S. and Canada, or 08/8231 1234. Fax 08/8231 1120. www.hyatt.com. 367 units. A$250–A$300 (US$200–US$240) double; A$300–A$340 (US$240–US$272) Regency Club City View; A$320–A$360 (US$256–US$288) Club River Park View; A$390 (US$312) executive suite; A$840 (US$672) deluxe suite. Extra person A$50 (US$40). Children under 13 stay free in parent's room. Regency Club City View and Club River Park View rates include breakfast. Ask about packages and weekend discounts. AE, DC, MC, V. Parking A$18 (US$14). Bus: CityLoop. **Amenities:** 3 restaurants; lounge; bar; nightclub; heated outdoor pool; health club and Jacuzzi; concierge; business center; 24-hr. room service; massage; babysitting; laundry service; dry cleaning. *In room:* A/C, TV w/pay movies, high-speed Internet access, minibar, hair dryer, iron.

Expensive

Novotel Adelaide on Hindley Only a short stroll from the center of town, the Novotel is a good value, especially if you visit on the weekend, when the rates go down. Otherwise, it's not as classy as the Hyatt and the Hilton. What you get for your money is a good, recently renovated, bright room. Ask at the reception desk for a robe—they aren't provided in standard rooms.

65 Hindley St., Adelaide, SA 5000. © **08/8231 5552.** Fax 08/8237 3800. www.accorhotel.com. 217 units. Weekday A$202 (US$161) double, A$245 (US$196) suite; weekend A$150 (US$120) double, A$193 (US$156) suite. Children under 15 stay free in parent's room. Ask about package deals. AE, DC, MC, V. Parking A$17 (US$14). Bus: CityLoop. **Amenities:** Brasserie; bar; heated outdoor pool; health club; concierge; business center; 24-hr. room service. *In room:* A/C, TV w/pay movies, modem, fax, minibar, hair dryer, iron.

Moderate

Rockford Adelaide (The Townhouse) *Value* Totally refurbished in 2001, Adelaide's newest boutique hotel changed hands in 2004. It's a 10- to 15-minute walk

---

Tips **Plan Ahead**

If you plan to be in town during the Adelaide Festival, make sure you book accommodations *well* in advance. The town can be packed during Christmas and New Year's, so it's wise to book well in advance then, too.

from the center of town, 5 minutes from the casino, and near the nightclub and red-light district. Rooms are spacious, comfortable, and modern. The refurbishment did not result in a massive hike in prices, which makes this place a good value option.

164 Hindley St., Adelaide, SA 5000. © **1800/606 562** in Australia, or 08/8211 8255. Fax 08/8231 1179. www. rockfordhotels.com.au. 68 units. A$135 (US$108) standard double; A$172 (US$137) business double; A$182 (US$145) executive double. Children under 12 stay free in parent's room. Off-season and weekend discounts available. Check for Internet specials. Ask about package deals. AE, DC, MC, V. Free parking. **Amenities:** Restaurant; bar; heated outdoor pool; golf course nearby; access to nearby health club; sauna; concierge; limited room service; laundry service; dry cleaning; nonsmoking rooms. *In room:* A/C, TV/DVD w/free movies, dataport, minibar, hair dryer, iron.

Saville Park Suites Adelaide ⋆ You can't miss this conglomerate of russet-red bricks on the outskirts of the city center (about a 10-min. walk). Rooms are nice and spacious, if a bit formal, which is not surprising because the place is popular with business travelers. On the premises is the **Zipp Restaurant and Wine Bar,** where Tommy Chang serves an innovative menu.

255 Hindley St., Adelaide, SA 5000. © **1800/882 601** in Australia, or 08/8217 2500. Fax 08/8217 2519. www. savillesuites.com. 142 units. A$146 (US$117) studio for 2; A$167 (US$133) 2-bedroom suite for up to 4. AE, DC, MC, V. Parking A$5 (US$4). **Amenities:** Restaurant; free access to nearby City Gym; outdoor Jacuzzi; concierge; tour desk; car-rental desk; limited room service; babysitting; coin-op laundry; dry cleaning; nonsmoking rooms; rooms for those w/limited mobility. *In room:* A/C, TV w/pay movies, VCR (on request), dataport, kitchen, minibar, fridge, coffeemaker, hair dryer, iron.

Inexpensive

Adelaide City Park Motel ⋆ The spacious rooms in this high-end boutique motel have modern furnishings and nice bathrooms with showers. Some rooms have private balconies overlooking parkland. Family rooms sleep from four to six people: the largest has a double bed and two sets of bunks. The best double room is number 45, which has two double beds and a large balcony.

471 Pulteney St., Adelaide, SA 5000. © 08/8223 1444 or 1800 231 444 in Australia. Fax 08/8223 1133. www.city park.com.au. 18 units (nonsmoking rooms). A$88 (US$70) double without bathroom; A$99 (US$80) double with bathroom; A$130 (US$104) double with balcony; A$110–A$130 (US$88–US$104) triple; A$120–A$180 (US$96–US$144) family. Extra person A$15 (US$12). AE, DC, MC, V. Limited parking by arrangement. The tram to Glenelg is five minutes walk away; 4 streets up is a bus stop for the free City Loop Bus. **Amenities:** Restaurant; bar; tour desk; car-rental desk; dry cleaning service. *In room:* A/C, TV, fridge, coffeemaker, iron, microwave.

Moore's Brecknock Hotel Adelaide's original Irish pub, built in 1851, still attracts a lot of Irish patrons who come here for the great selection of beer and reasonably priced home-style cooking—it reputedly serves Adelaide's best hamburgers. It's also very popular with American guests who use the hotel accommodations upstairs as a base from which to discover Kangaroo Island and other parts of the state. The Brecknock, about 4 blocks from Victoria Square, is run by Kerry Moore and his Canadian wife, Tricia. Live bands play downstairs on Friday, Saturday, and Sunday, but the music finishes at 1am on Friday and Saturday and at 10pm on Sunday, so you shouldn't have too much trouble sleeping. Rooms are large, if a little spartan, and decorated in your granny's old-world style. Some rooms have a single bed as well as a double. Each has a sink, with the bathrooms down the hall.

Next door is **Nomads Backpackers** (© **08/8211 8985;** www.nomads-backpackers. com), which is associated with the hotel.

401 King William St., Adelaide, SA 5000. © 08/8231 5467. Fax 08/8410 1968. www.brecknockhotel.com.au. 10 units, none with bathroom. A$70 (US$56) double; A$90 (US$72) triple. Rates include continental breakfast. AE, DC, MC, V. Free parking. Tram: Glenelg route. **Amenities:** Restaurant; 3 bars; bike rental; tour desk; car-rental desk; coin-op laundry; dry cleaning; nonsmoking rooms. *In room:* A/C, fax, fridge, coffeemaker, iron, safe.

IN NORTH ADELAIDE

This suburb across the river is an interesting place with nice architecture and good restaurants. It's about a 10-minute bus ride from the city center.

Expensive

North Adelaide Heritage Group ★★★ *(Finds)*   It's worth coming all the way to Adelaide just for the experience of staying in one of these out-of-this-world apartments, cottages, or suites. Each of the 21 properties in North Adelaide and Eastwood are fabulous. I recommend particularly the former Friendly Meeting Chapel Hall, which was once the headquarters of the mouthwatering "Albert Lodge No. 6 of the Independent Order of Oddfellows, Manchester Unity Friendly Society, and the Court Huntsman's Pride No. 2478 of the Ancient Order of Foresters Friendly Society." The structure, a small, simple gabled hall of bluestone rubble trimmed with brick, resembles a small church. Built in 1878, it's stocked with period pieces and antiques and rounded off with a modern, fully stocked kitchen; a huge Jacuzzi; a queen-size bed; and a CD player and TV.

Another standout place is the George Lowe Esquire unit. The huge 19th-century apartment is decorated with antiques and has a huge four-poster bed, a lounge, and a full kitchen. Guests also have use of nice gardens. Owners Rodney and Regina Twiss have added little touches that make you feel at home, from magazines liberally piled everywhere to bacon and eggs in the fridge. The company also offers three apartments in the old North Adelaide Fire Station; the ground-floor apartment comes with a full-size, bright red, very old fire engine. All properties are within easy walking distance of the main attractions in the area, as well as tennis courts (around A$20/US$13 an hour) and Adelaide Golf Links (*©* **08/8267 2171;** A$18/US$12 weekdays, A$21/US$14 weekends).

Office: 109 Glen Osmond Rd., Eastwood, SA 5063. *©* **08/8272 1355.** Fax 08/8272 1355. www.adelaideheritage. com. 21 units. A$145–A$330 (US$116–US$264) double. Extra person A$60–A$85 (US$48–US$68). Child under 12 A$30 (US$24). AE, DC, MC, V. Free parking. **Amenities:** Golf course nearby; tennis courts nearby; Jacuzzi; concierge; car-rental desk; free bus to city center; limited room service; massage; dry cleaning. *In room:* A/C, TV, kitchenette, fridge, coffeemaker, hair dryer, iron.

Old Lion Apartments ★   These pleasant apartments are in a renovated brewery. The complex is about a 15-minute walk from the city center and is on a direct bus route. Rooms are spacious, with high ceilings, and come with a kitchenette, a living room, French doors separating bedrooms from living quarters, a shower and bathtub, and a good-size balcony. All apartments also have use of a washing machine and dryer. VCRs and videos are available for rent at the front desk. Continental breakfast costs A$8.50 (US$6.80) extra.

9 Jerningham St., North Adelaide, SA 5006. *©* **08/8223 0500.** Fax 08/8223 0588. www.majapts.com.au. 57 units. A$182 (US$145) studio apt; A$193 (US$154) 1-bedroom apt; A$221 (US$177) 2-bedroom apt; A$262 (US$209) 3-bedroom apt. Extra adult A$17 (US$14); extra child 3–12 A$5.50 (US$4.40). AE, DC, MC, V. Free parking. Bus: 184, 224, 226, 228, or 229. **Amenities:** Concierge; tour desk; car-rental desk; limited room service; dry cleaning. *In room:* A/C, TV (VCRs and videos on request), kitchenette, fridge, coffeemaker, hair dryer, iron.

Princes Lodge Motel   One of the best motels in Adelaide, the Princes Lodge looks more like a large private home than a simple brick roadside structure. Rooms are nicely decorated and generally come with a double and a single bed. There are three family rooms; one has a double and three singles, and another has six beds in one room. The motel is within walking distance of the restaurant strip on O'Connell

Street, on a bus route that follows King William Street, and a A$6 (US$4.80) taxi ride from the city center.

73 Lefevre Terrace, North Adelaide, SA 5006. ⓒ **08/8267 5566**. Fax 08/8239 0787. www.princeslodge.com.au. 21 units. A$60 (US$48) double with separate bathroom; A$70 (US$56) double with attached bathroom. Rates include continental breakfast. AE, DC, MC, V. Bus: 222 from Victoria Sq. **Amenities:** Golf course nearby; tour desk; car-rental desk; coin-op laundry. In room: A/C, TV, dataport, fridge, coffeemaker, hair dryer, iron.

IN GLENELG

I'd recommend, without hesitation, staying in Glenelg rather than in the city center. The journey to the city center by car or tram takes less than 30 minutes, and the airport is less than 10 minutes away. Add to this the sea, the lovely beach, the fun fair (amusement park), the great shops, the good pub, and the nice accommodations, and you have a perfect place to relax on your holiday.

Atlantic Tower Motor Inn   If you're looking for relatively inexpensive accommodations near the beach, this is your place. You can't miss the tubular building, with its slowly revolving restaurant on the 12th floor. Rooms are simple but bright, and have nice park views through large windows. Each has a double and a single bed. Deluxe rooms are a bit nicer and come with bathrooms rather than just showers. Suites have two rooms and excellent views; the most expensive have Jacuzzis. The gently turning **Rock Lobster Cafe** upstairs is open for lunch on Thursday, Friday, and Sunday, and dinner every evening.

760 Anzac Hwy., Glenelg, SA 5045. ⓒ **08/8294 1011**. Fax 08/8376 0964. www.atlantictower.citysearch.com.au. 27 units (20 with shower only). A$96 (US$77) double; A$115 (US$92) deluxe double; A$165 (US$132) suite. Extra person A$12 (US$9.60). Children under 15 stay free in parent's room. AE, DC, MC, V. Free parking. Tram: Glenelg route to stop 20. **Amenities:** Restaurant; tour desk; car-rental desk; room service; laundry service; dry cleaning; nonsmoking rooms. In room: A/C, TV, fax, minibar, hair dryer, iron.

Stamford Grand Adelaide ★★   A classic Adelaide photo is of trams awaiting passengers in front of the Stamford Grand. Located right on the beach, this classy hotel offers nice rooms with modern furnishings; many overlook the beach, the ocean, and the pier. **The Pier and Pines** is a popular bar bursting with youngish crowds most nights; for a mellower scene, there's Horizons piano bar, which offers quality live music, particularly on weekends.

Moseley Sq. (P.O. Box 600), Glenelg, SA 5045. ⓒ **1800/882 777** in Australia, or 08/8376 1222. Fax 08/8376 1111. 240 units. A$322 (US$257) double; A$349–A$546 (US$279–US$437) suite. Children under 12 stay free in parent's room. AE, DC, MC, V. Parking A$10 (US$8). Tram: Glenelg route. **Amenities:** 2 restaurants; 2 bars; indoor pool; health club and Jacuzzi; concierge; business center; 24-hr. room service. In room: A/C, TV w/pay movies, minibar, hair dryer, iron.

WHERE TO DINE

With more than 600 restaurants, pubs, and cafes, Adelaide boasts more dining spots per capita than anywhere else in Australia. Many cluster in areas such as Rundle Street, Gouger Street, and North Adelaide—where you'll find almost every style of cuisine you can imagine. For cheap noodles, laksas, sushi, and cakes, head to Adelaide's popular **Central Markets** (ⓒ **08/8203 7494**), behind the Hilton Adelaide between Gouger and Grote streets.

Because of South Australia's healthy wine industry, you'll find that many of the more expensive restaurants have extensive wine lists—though with spicier foods, it's probably wiser to stick with beer or a fruity white in a pinch. Many Adelaide restaurants allow diners to bring their own wine (BYO), but most charge a steep corkage fee to open your bottle—A$6 (US$4.80) or so is not uncommon.

Finds Something Different: Dining Tours

Adelaide's Top Food And Wine Tours (© 08/8263 0265; www.topfoodandwine tours.com.au) offers a range of food-based tours including both dawn and mid-morning tours of the Central Market. Tours cost A$48 (US$38) for adults and A$25 (US$20) for kids.

IN THE CITY CENTER
Very Expensive

The Grange ★★ MODERN AUSTRALIAN   The Grange is an open-plan restaurant specializing in contemporary food by Adelaide's most influential chef, Cheong Liew. Liew offers an innovative fusion of Western and Asian ingredients, rounded off with an extensive wine list. The menu begins with a choice of two starters, one of them Liew's signature dish, "the four dances of the sea"—an antipasto of fish, octopus in garlic sauce, prawn sushi, raw cuttlefish, and black noodles. For the next course you could choose baby abalone, lobster baked with bourbon and lime, or Japanese quail with chestnuts and Chinese mushrooms.

In the Hilton Adelaide, 233 Victoria Sq. © 08/8217 2000. Reservations required. 3-course dinner A$81 (US$65); 4-course dinner A$97 (US$78). AE, DC, MC, V. Tues–Sat 7–10:30pm.

Moderate

Amalfi ITALIAN   Come here for good cooking at reasonable prices in a lively atmosphere. The pizzas are the best in Adelaide—though a little expensive—and good veal and pasta dishes are always on the menu. Be sure to check out the daily specials, where you can pick a very good fish dish or two.

29 Frome St. (just off Rundle St.). © 08/8223 1948. Reservations recommended. Main courses A$14–A$17 (US$11–US$14). AE, DC, MC, V. Mon–Thurs 11:30am–3pm and 5:30–11pm (until midnight Fri); Sat 5:30pm–midnight.

Austral Hotel *Value* MODERN AUSTRALIAN   This large pub, with its dark timber and forest-colored wallpaper, is a pleasant place for a well-priced pub meal. You can eat at the bar, outside on the street, or in the dining room. The bistro serves burgers, fish and chips, pastas, laksas, and Thai curries. The restaurant is a bit more upscale and offers risotto, handmade crab ravioli, beef filets, chicken dishes, venison, paella, and baby octopus.

205 Rundle St. © 08/8223 4660. www.theaustral.com. Reservations recommended. Main courses A$6.50–A$14 (US$5.20–US$11) in bistro, A$15–A$22 (US$12–US$18) in restaurant. AE, MC, V. Mon–Sat 11am–late. Bus station nearby.

Jasmin Indian Restaurant NORTH INDIAN   Prices have crept up as this place has gotten more popular, but this family-run Adelaide institution a block south of Rundle Mall is still a good value. It won the Restaurant Association's award for best Indian restaurant in 2000. Indian artifacts and signed cricket bats from visiting Indian teams decorate the walls. The atmosphere is comfortable yet busy, and the service is professional. The house special is very hot beef vindaloo, but all the old favorites, such as tandoori chicken, butter chicken (a big seller), lamb korma, and malabari beef with coconut cream, ginger, and garlic are here, too. Mop it all up with nan bread, and cool your palate with a side dish of raita. The *suji halwa* (semolina pudding with nuts) is the best I've tasted. Smoking is not permitted.

31 Hindmarsh Sq. ℂ **08/8223 7837.** Reservations recommended. Main courses A$19–A$20 (US$15–US$16); lunch banquet A$27 (US$22); dinner banquet A$35 (US$28). AE, DC, MC, V. Tues–Fri noon–2:30pm; Tues–Sat 5:30–10:30pm.

Jolleys Boathouse Restaurant ⚜ MODERN AUSTRALIAN   Jolleys is on the banks of the River Torrens, with views of boats, ducks, and black swans. Business-people and ladies who lunch rush for the three outside tables, but if you miss out, the bright and airy interior, with its cream-colored tablecloths and directors' chairs, isn't too much of a letdown. You might start with goat's curd ravioli with red pesto and chives. Moving on, you could tuck into roasted duck with hazelnut risotto. (Ignore the peaceful quacking out on the river if you can.) Banana and cardamom soufflé for dessert is wicked.

Jolleys Lane. ℂ **08/8223 2891.** Reservations recommended. Main courses A$21–A$27 (US$17–US$22). AE, DC, MC, V. Daily noon–2:30pm; Mon–Sat 6:30–9:30pm.

Matsuri ⚜ JAPANESE   I like the atmosphere in this very good restaurant on the popular Gouger Street restaurant strip. Takaomi Kitamura, world-famous ice sculptor and sushi master, prepares the sushi and sashimi dishes, some of the best in Australia. Monday night is "sushi festival night," when sushi is half price. During happy hour Wednesday through Sunday, sushi is 30% off if you place your order before 7pm. (You can preorder over the phone and eat later.) Promised, too, is a 10% discount if you show this Frommer's guide. Other popular dishes include vegetarian and seafood tempura, *yose nobe* (a hot pot of vegetables, seafood, and chicken), and *chawan mushi* (a steamed custard dish). The service is friendly and considerate. The corkage fee is a steep A$4.50 (US$3.60) a bottle.

167 Gouger St. ℂ **08/8231 3494.** Reservations recommended. Main courses A$8.60–A$28 (US$6.90–US$22). AE, DC, MC, V. Fri noon–2pm; Wed–Mon 5:30–10pm.

Mekong Thai THAI/MALAYSIAN/HALAL *(Value)*   Though this place is not much to look at—with simple tables and chairs, some outside in a portico—it has a fiery reputation for good food among in-the-know locals. The food is spicy and authentic, and the portions are filling. It's also a vegetarian's paradise, with at least 16 meat-free mains on the ethnically varied menu. It's Adelaide's only fully halal (suitable for Muslims) restaurant.

68 Hindley St. ℂ **08/8231 2914.** Main courses A$11–A$13 (US$8.80–US$10). AE, DC, MC, V. Daily 5:15–10:30pm or later.

Rigoni's Bistro ITALIAN   On a narrow lane west of King William Street, this traditional Italian trattoria is often packed at lunch and less frantic in the evening. It's big and bright, with high ceilings and russet quarry tiles. A long bar runs through the middle of the dining room; brass plates mark the stools of regular diners. The food is very traditional and quite good. The chalkboard menu often changes, but you are likely to find lasagna, veal in white wine, marinated fish, and various pasta dishes. There's also an extensive salad bar with a variety of antipasto, and an outside dining area.

27 Leigh St. ℂ **08/8231 5160.** Reservations recommended. Main courses A$15–A$22 (US$12–US$18); antipasto bar (lunch only) A$12–A$14 (US$9.60–US$11). AE, DC, MC, V. Mon–Fri noon–2:30pm; Mon–Sat 6:30–10pm.

IN NORTH ADELAIDE

The Manse ⚜⚜ SEAFOOD   Swiss chef Bernhard Oehrli has a fine touch when it comes to seafood, and I recommend this place wholeheartedly. The cozy restaurant spreads out into several rooms, with log fires to keep you warm in winter and room to dine outside on sunnier days. As for the food, the scallops are almost fresh enough to waddle off the warmed cucumber base and head for sea, and rare tuna in Japanese-style tempura is so delicate it literally melts in your mouth. If you want something other than seafood, you can't go wrong with a signature dish of venison with black pepper and spiced beet glaze. For dessert, try warm chocolate gâteau or rhubarb gratin with ice cream.

142 Tynte St., North Adelaide. © **08/8267 4636.** Reservations recommended. Main courses A$27–A$33 (US$22–US$26). AE, DC, MC, V. Fri noon–3pm (set menu); Mon–Sat 6:30–10pm. Bus: 182, 224, 226, 228, or 229.

SEEING THE SIGHTS

Adelaide is a laid-back city. It's not jam-packed with tourist-oriented attractions like some of the larger state capitals, though The Migration Museum (see below) is easily one of the best museums in Australia. The best way to enjoy this pleasant city is to take things nice and easy. Walk beside the River Torrens, ride the tram to the beach-side suburb of Glenelg, and spend the evenings sipping wine and sampling some of the country's best alfresco dining.

THE TOP ATTRACTIONS

Art Gallery of South Australia ★ Adelaide's premier public art gallery has a good range of local and overseas works and a fine Asian ceramics collection. Of particular interest are Charles Hall's *Proclamation of South Australia 1836,* Nicholas Chevalier's painting of the departure of explorers Burke and Wills from Melbourne; several works by Australian painters Sidney Nolan, Albert Tucker, and Arthur Boyd; and some excellent contemporary art. For an introduction, take a free guided tour. The bookshop has an extensive collection of art publications. Allow 1 to 2 hours.

North Terrace. © **08/8207 7000.** Free admission. Daily 10am–5pm. Guided tours Mon–Fri 11am and 2pm; Sat–Sun 11am and 3pm. Closed Dec 25. Bus: City Loop.

The Migration Museum ★ *(Finds)* This tiny museum, dedicated to immigration and multiculturalism, is one of the most important and fascinating in Australia. With touching personal displays, it tells the story of the waves of immigrants who have helped shape this multicultural society, from the boatloads of convicts who came here in 1788 to the ethnic groups who have trickled in over the past 2 centuries. Allow 1 hour.

82 Kintore Ave. © **08/8207 7580.** Admission by donation. Mon–Fri 10am–5pm; Sat–Sun and public holidays 1–5pm. Closed Good Friday and Dec 25. Bus: Any to North Terrace.

The National Wine Centre of Australia ★ This architectural masterpiece concentrates on Australia's 53 wine regions. Interactive exhibits and displays allow you to blend your own virtual wine. The Tasting Gallery displays an extensive range of Australian wines, and wine-tasting packages allow you to sample some of the rarest vintages. A restaurant and bar overlook the Wine Centre, which has its own vineyard. You can fit in a trip here with a visit to the nearby Botanic Gardens.

Hackney Rd. (eastern end of N. Terrace). © **08/8222 9288.** www.wineaustralia.com.au. Admission A$11 (US$8.80) adults, A$6 (US$4.80) children under 18 accompanied by an adult, A$29 (US$23) families. Wine-tasting packages A$5–A$20 (US$4–US$16). Mon–Fri 9am–5:30pm. Closed Good Friday and Dec 25. Limited parking. Bus: CityLoop to Botanic Gardens.

South Australian Maritime Museum This Port Adelaide museum commemorates over 150 years of maritime history. Most of the exhibits are in the 1850s Bond

Store, but the museum also incorporates an 1863 lighthouse and three vessels moored alongside Wharf No. 1, a short walk away. The fully rigged replica of the 16m (54-ft.) ketch *Active II* is very impressive. Allow 1½ hours. Port Adelaide is approximately 30 minutes from the city center by bus.

126 Lipson St., Port Adelaide. © **08/8207 6255**. Admission A$8.50 (US$6.80) adults, A$3.50 (US$2.80) children, A$22 (US$18) families. Daily 10am–5pm. Closed Dec 25. Bus: 151 or 153 from North Terrace opposite Parliament House to stop 40 (Port Adelaide). Train: Port Adelaide.

South Australian Museum ⋆   The star attraction of this interesting museum is the Australian Aboriginal Cultures Gallery. On display is an extensive collection of utensils, spears, tools, bush medicine, food samples, photographs, and the like. Also in the museum is a sorry-looking collection of stuffed native animals (sadly including a few extinct marsupials, such as the Tasmanian tiger); a good collection of Papua New Guinea artifacts; and excellent mineral and butterfly collections.

If you're interested in learning more about the exhibits, take a Behind-the-Scenes Tour. The tours take place after museum hours and cost A$12 (US$9.60) for adults. Allow 2 hours to see the museum.

North Terrace, between State Library and Art Gallery of South Australia. © **08/8207 7500**. Free admission. Daily 10am–5pm. Closed Good Friday and Dec 25.

Tandanya Aboriginal Cultural Institute ⋆⋆   This place offers a great opportunity to experience Aboriginal life through Aboriginal eyes. Exhibits change regularly, but all give insight into Aboriginal art and cultural activities. At noon every day there's a didgeridoo performance. A shop sells Aboriginal art and books on Aboriginal culture, and a cafe on the premises serves several bush tucker (native food) items. Allow 1 hour.

253 Grenfell St. © **08/8224 3200**. Admission A$4 (US$3.20) adults, A$3 (US$2.40) children under 14, A$10 (US$8) families. Daily 10am–5pm. Bus: City Loop.

THE FLORA & THE FAUNA

Adelaide Zoo *Kids*   To be honest, if you've experienced the wonderful Melbourne Zoo, or even Taronga Zoo in Sydney, the Adelaide Zoo is probably not worth your while. But if this is your only chance to see a kangaroo in captivity, then plan a visit. Of course, other Australian animals live at the zoo, and the nicely landscaped gardens and lack of crowds make it a pleasant place for an entertaining stroll. The zoo houses the only pygmy blue-tongue lizard in captivity in Australia; the species was thought to be extinct since the 1940s, until a live specimen was discovered inside the belly of a dead snake. Allow 1 hour.

Frome Rd. © **08/8267 3255**. Admission A$15 (US$12) adults, A$8 (US$6.40) children. Daily 9:30am–5pm. Bus: 272 or 273 from Currie St. to stop 2 (5 min.).

Botanic Gardens   You'll feel as though you're at the heart of the city when you stroll through the huddles of office workers having picnic lunches on the lawns. Highlights include a broad avenue of Moreton Bay figs, duck ponds, giant water lilies, an Italianate garden, a palm house, and the Bicentennial Conservatory—a glass dome full of rainforest species. You might want to have lunch surrounded by bird song and lush vegetation in the **Botanic Gardens Restaurant** (© **08/8223 3526**), in the center of the park; it's open daily from 10am to 5pm.

North Terrace. © **08/8222 9311**. Free admission. Mon–Fri 8am–sundown; Sat–Sun 9am–sundown.

FOR TRAIN BUFFS

National Railway Museum This former Port Adelaide railway yard houses Australia's largest and finest collection of locomotive engines and rolling stock. The 104 or so items on display include some 30 engines. Among the most impressive trains are the gigantic "Mountain" class engines, and "Tea and Sugar" trains that once ran between railway camps in remote parts of the desert. Entrance includes a train ride. Allow 1½ hours.

Lipton St., North Adelaide. (ⓒ **08/8341 1690**. Admission A$9 (US$7.20) adults, A$3.50 (US$2.80) children, A$20 (US$16) families. Daily 10am–5pm. Bus: 151 or 153 from North Terrace, opposite Parliament House, to stop 40 (approx. 30 min.).

ORGANIZED TOURS

Grayline Day Tours (ⓒ **1300/858 687** in Australia; www.grayline.com) operates a city sightseeing tour for A$39 (US$31) for adults and A$20 (US$16) for children. It operates from 9:30am to noon Monday through Saturday. The bus can pick you up at your hotel. Other Grayline tours take in central Adelaide, with either Hahndorf or Cleland Wildlife Park included; the Flinders Ranges; and Kangaroo Island.

ENJOYING THE GREAT OUTDOORS

BIKING Adelaide's parks and riverbanks are very popular with cyclists. Rent your bicycle from **Linear Park Bikes,** Elder Park, King William Road (ⓒ **08/8223-6271**). The rate is A$15 to A$20 (US$12–US$16) for 24 hours, including helmet, lock, and baby seat (if needed). **Recreation SA** (ⓒ **08/8226 7301**) publishes a brochure showing Adelaide's bike routes. Pick one up at the **South Australia Visitor & Travel Centre** (see "Visitor Information," earlier in this chapter). **The Map Shop,** 6 Peel St. (ⓒ **08/8231 2033**), is also a good source for maps.

HIKING & JOGGING The banks of the River Torrens are a good place for a jog. The fit and adventurous might want to tackle the **Heysen Trail,** a spectacular 1,600km (992-mile) walk through bush, farmland, and rugged hill country that starts 80km (50 miles) south of Adelaide and goes to the Flinders Ranges by way of the Adelaide Hills and the Barossa Valley. For more information on the trail, visit the **South Australia Visitor & Travel Centre** (see "Visitor Information," earlier in this chapter).

GOLF The **City of Adelaide Golf Course** (ⓒ **08/8267 2171**) is close to town and has two short 18-hole courses and a full-size championship course. Greens fees are A$14 to A$17 (US$11–US$14) weekdays and A$17 to A$19 (US$14–US$15) weekends, depending on the course. Club rental is available. Ask about cheaper prices after 4pm.

SPECTATOR SPORTS

CRICKET The **Adelaide Oval** (ⓒ **08/8300 3800**), on the corner of War Memorial Drive and King William Street, is the venue for international matches during the summer season. The Institute Building, part of the State Library of S.A., displays the **Don Bradman Collection** ⓒ **08/8207 7595.** The cricket legend died in Adelaide in 2001.

FOOTBALL Unlike New South Wales, where Rugby League is the most popular winter sport, in Adelaide you'll find plenty of Australian Rules fanatics. Games are usually played on Saturday at the **Adelaide Oval** (see above) or at **Football Park** (ⓒ **08/8268 2088**), Turner Drive, West Lakes. The home teams are the Adelaide Crows and the Port Adelaide Power. Games are played February through October, with the finals in September and October. Tickets must be purchased well in advance from **BASS** (ⓒ **13 12 46** in South Australia, or 08/8400 2205).

<Finds **Shopping for Opals**

South Australia is home to the world's largest sources of white opals. (The more expensive black opals generally come from Lightning Ridge in New South Wales.) There are plenty of places to buy around town, but **Opal Field Gems,** 33 King William St. (© 08/8212 5300), is one of the best. As a rule, you're not going to find any bargains, so just buy what you like (and can afford—good opals cost many thousands of dollars).

THE SHOPPING SCENE

Rundle Mall (between King William and Pulteney sts.) is Adelaide's main shopping street. This pedestrian-only thoroughfare is home to the big names in fashion.

Adelaide's Central Markets (© 08/8203 7494), behind the Adelaide Hilton Hotel between Gouger and Grote streets, make up the largest produce market in the Southern Hemisphere. They're a good place to shop for vegetables, fruit, meat, fish, and the like, although the markets are worth popping into even if you're not looking for picnic fixings. The markets, held in a warehouselike structure, are open Tuesday from 7am to 5:30pm, Thursday from 9am to 5:30pm, Friday from 7am to 9pm, and Saturday from 7am to 3pm.

The six-story **Myer Centre,** next door to the Myer department store, 22–38 Rundle Mall, has a Body Shop (on the ground floor), for beauty products; an Australian Geographic shop (on level 3), for top-quality Australiana; and Exotica (level 2), where you can find unusual futuristic gifts.

Just off Rundle Mall, at Shop no. 6 in the City Cross Arcade, is **L'Unique** (© 08/8231 0030), a good crafts shop selling South Australian pottery, jewelry, woodcraft, hand-blown glass, and original paintings.

Elsewhere, the renowned **Jam Factory Craft and Design Centre,** in the Lions Art Centre, 19 Morphett St. (© 08/8410 0727), sells an excellent range of locally made ceramics, glass, furniture, and metal items. You can also watch the craftspeople at work here.

Head to the **R.M. Williams** shop on Gawler Place (© 08/8232 3611) for the best simple boots you're likely to find, as well as other Aussie fashion icons, including Akubra hats, moleskin pants, and Driza-bone coats.

ADELAIDE AFTER DARK

The *Adelaide Advertiser* lists all performances and exhibitions in its entertainment pages. The free tourist guide *Today in Adelaide,* available in most hotels, also has information. Tickets for theater and other entertainment events in Adelaide can be purchased from **BASS ticket outlets** (© 13 12 46 in South Australia, or 08/8400 2205) at the following locations: Festival Theatre, Adelaide Festival Centre, King William Road; Centre Pharmacy, 19 Central Market Arcade; Verandah Music, 182 Rundle St.; and on the fifth floor of the Myer department store, Rundle Mall.

THE PERFORMING ARTS

The major concert hall is the **Adelaide Festival Centre,** King William Road (© 08/8216 8600 for general inquiries, or 08/8400 2205 for box office). The Festival Centre encompasses three auditoriums: the 1,978-seat Festival Theatre, the 612-seat Playhouse, and the 350-seat Space Centre. This is the place in Adelaide to see opera, ballet, drama, orchestral concerts, the Adelaide Symphony Orchestra, plays, and experimental drama.

The complex also includes an outdoor amphitheater used for jazz, rock 'n' roll, and country-music concerts; an art gallery; a bistro; a piano bar; and the Silver Jubilee Organ, the world's largest transportable concert-hall organ (built in Austria to commemorate Queen Elizabeth II's Silver Jubilee).

The Adelaide Repertory Festival presents five productions a year, ranging from drama to comedy, at the **Arts Theatre,** 53 Angus St. (© **08/8221 5644**). Playwrights Alan Ayckbourne and Terrence Rattigan are among the many who have had plays performed here. The theater, which is a short walk from many hotels and restaurants, is also the home of the Metropolitan Musical Theatre Company, which presents two musical comedy productions a year. Tickets cost around A$16 (US$13) for adults and A$11 (US$8.80) for children.

Her Majesty's Theatre, 58 Grote St. (© **08/8216 8600**), is a 1,000-seat venue opposite Central Markets that presents drama, comedy, musicals, dance, opera, and recitals. Tickets generally cost A$30 to A$55 (US$24–US$44).

THE BAR & CLUB SCENE

Adelaide's nightlife ranges from twiddling your thumbs to nude lap dancers. For adult entertainment (clubs with the word *strip* in the name) head to **Hindley Street**—there are a few pubs there, but I wouldn't recommend them. For information on gay and lesbian options, pick up the *Adelaide Gay Times.*

The popular **Universal Wine Bar,** 285 Rundle St. (© **08/8232 5000**), is the perfect place to start an evening, with great atmosphere and good wines by the glass.

Most pubs are open from 11am to midnight. For all-age pubs, locals will point you toward **The Austral,** 205 Rundle St. (© **08/8223 4660**); **The Exeter,** 246 Rundle St. (© **08/8223 2623**); **The Lion,** at the corner of Melbourne and Jerningham streets (© **08/8367 0222**); and the **British Hotel,** 58 Finniss St. (© **08/8267 2188**), in North Adelaide, where you can cook your own steak on the courtyard barbecue. Also popular with visitors and locals alike is the **Earl of Aberdeen,** 316 Pulteney St., at Carrington Street (© **08/8223 6433**), a colonial-style pub popular for after-work drinks. **The Port Dock,** 10 Todd St., Port Adelaide (© **08/8240 0187**), was licensed as a pub in 1864; it brews four of its own beers and pumps them directly to its three bars with old English beer engines.

TRYING YOUR LUCK AT THE CASINO

Right next to the Adelaide Hyatt, and dwarfed by the old railway station containing it, is the **Adelaide Casino** (now officially called "SkyCity" to make it sound trendier), North Terrace (© **1800/888 711** in Australia, or 08/8212 2811). The casino has two floors of gaming tables and slot machines, as well as four bars and several dining options, including a fast-food station and the excellent Pullman buffet restaurant. The casino is open Sunday through Thursday from 10am to 4am and Friday and Saturday from 10am to 6am.

2 Side Trips from Adelaide

THE BAROSSA: ON THE TRAIL OF THE GRAPE ★

More than a quarter of Australia's wines, and a disproportionate number of top labels, originate in the Barossa and Eden valleys—collectively known as the **Barossa.** Beginning just 45km (28 miles) northeast of Adelaide and easily accessible, the area has had an

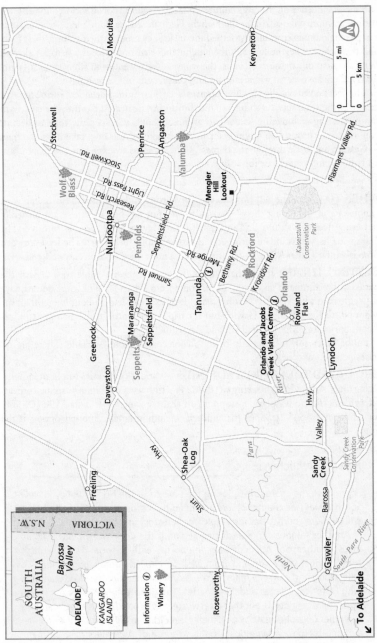

enormous influence on the city's culture. In fact, Adelaidians of all socioeconomic levels partake in more wine talk than the French. German settlers from Silesia, who came to escape religious persecution, first settled the area. They brought their culture, their food, and their vines. They built the Lutheran churches that dominate the Barossa's skyline. With the help of English aristocrats, the wine industry went from strength to strength. Today, there are over 50 wineries in an area that retains its German flavor.

The focal points of the area are **Angaston,** farthest from Adelaide; **Nuriootpa,** the center of the rural services industry; and **Tanunda,** the nearest town to the city. Each has interesting architecture, crafts and antiques shops, and specialty food outlets. If you are adventurous, you might want to rent a bike in Adelaide, take it on the train to **Gawler,** and cycle through the Barossa. Other options are exploring the area by hot-air balloon, motorcycle, or limousine.

ESSENTIALS

WHEN TO GO   The best times to visit the Barossa and other South Australian wine regions are in the spring (Sept–Oct), when it's not too hot and there are plenty of flowering trees and shrubs, and in the fall (Apr–May), when the leaves turn red. The main wine harvest is in late summer and early autumn (Feb–Apr). The least crowded time is winter (June–Aug). Hotel prices can be more expensive on the weekend.

GETTING THERE   If you have a car (by far the most flexible way to visit the Barossa), I recommend taking the scenic route from Adelaide. (The route doesn't have a specific name, but it's obvious on a map.) It takes about half an hour longer than the Main North Road through Gawler, but the trip is well worth it. Follow signs to Birdwood, Springton, Mount Pleasant, and Angaston.

Public buses run infrequently to the major centers from Adelaide. There are no buses between wineries.

ORGANIZED TOURS FROM ADELAIDE   Various companies run limited sightseeing tours. **Adelaide Sightseeing** (© 08/8231 4144; www.adelaidesightseeing.com.au) offers a day trip from Adelaide, stopping off at three wineries. It costs A$90 (US$72) for adults and A$45 (US$36) for children, including lunch. Another option is the

---

Tips So Much Wine, So Little Time

If you have the choice of exploring the Barossa or the Hunter Valley in New South Wales (see chapter 5), I recommend the **Barossa,** which despite being a little more touristy has more to offer in history and architecture.

Another famous wine-producing region is the **Coonawarra,** 381km (236 miles) southeast of Adelaide near the border with Victoria; it's particularly convenient if you're driving from Melbourne. The area is only 12km (7½ miles) long and 2km (1¼ miles) wide, but the scenic countryside is crammed with historical villages and 16 wineries. The **Clare Valley,** 135km (84 miles) north of Adelaide, is another pretty area; it produces some outstanding examples of cool-climate wine. Finally, the **McLaren Vale,** south of Adelaide, is home to some 42 vineries producing some of Australia's best aromatic white wines as well as shiraz.

Barossa Wine Train (✆ **08/8212 7888**), which departs from Adelaide Railway Station on Thursday, Saturday, and Sunday. A variety of day-tour and overnight packages are available. Another option is a vintage car from the **Mirror Image Vintage Touring Co.** (✆ **08/8621 1400;** www.mirror-image.com.au). Chevrolets, stretch limos, or Caravelles rent for 1 hour to 2 days with a chauffeur-guide.

VISITOR INFORMATION   The **Barossa Wine and Visitor Information Centre,** 66–68 Murray St., Tanunda, SA 5352 (✆ **08/8563 0600;** www.barossa-region.org), is open Monday through Friday from 9am to 5pm, and Saturday and Sunday from 10am to 4pm. It's worth popping into the center's audiovisual display for an introduction to the world of wine; entry is A$2.75 (US$2.20) for adults, free for children. You'll need an hour or so to look around.

Wines are often cheaper at the **Tanunda Cellars** bottle shop, or retail outlet, at 14 Murray St., Tanunda (✆ **08/8563 3544;** www.tanundacellars.com.au), than at the winery door. The historic 1858 stone shop also houses one of Australia's finest collections of vintage wines.

TOURING THE WINERIES

With some 50 wineries offering free cellar-door tastings, daily tours charting the winemaking process, or both, you won't be stuck for places to visit. All wineries are well signposted. Below are just a few of my favorite places, but don't be shy about stopping whenever you come across a winery that takes your fancy. *A tip:* Try a sparkling red. Noses may turn up elsewhere, and it takes some getting used to, but bear in mind that the world's wine industry now hangs on Australia's every offering; it may well be the great tipple of the future.

Orlando and Jacobs Creek Visitor Centre   This large winery was established in 1847 and is the home of many award-winning brands. Its big seller is the Jacobs Creek brand, now sold worldwide. Premium wines include the Lawson Shiraz and the Jacaranda Ridge Cabernet; new vintages of either will set you back at least A$45 (US$36) a bottle. There's a cafe and a picnic area with barbecues. The Visitor Centre opened in May 2002.

Barossa Hwy., Rowland Flat. ✆ 08/8521 3000. Daily 10am–5pm.

Penfolds   Australia's biggest wine producer churns out some 23 million liters (5.8 million gal.) from this winery every year. Penfolds also owns other wineries all over the country. It all started when Dr. Christopher Rawson planted a few vines in 1844 to make wine for his patients. The winery now houses the largest oak barrel maturation cellars in the Southern Hemisphere.

Nuriootpa. ✆ 08/8568 9408. Mon–Fri 10am–5pm; Sat–Sun 11am–5pm.

Rockford   Most of the buildings here were constructed in 1984 out of recycled local materials, but you'd never know it. The wine is pressed between mid-March and the end of April, in the traditional way with machinery from the turn of the 20th century. It's a fascinating sight. Demand for Rockford wines, especially Basket Pressed Shiraz, far exceeds supply.

Krondorf Rd., Tanunda. ✆ 08/8568 9408. Mon–Sat 11am–5pm.

Seppelts ⭐   This National Trust–listed property was founded in 1857 by Joseph Seppelt, an immigrant from Silesia. The wine tour around the gardens and bluestone buildings is considered one of the best in the world. On a nearby slope, check out the family's Romanesque mausoleum, skirted by planted roadside palms, built during the 1930s recession to keep winery workers employed.

Seppeltsfield. (*C* **08/8568 6200**. Adults A$7 (US$5.60), children 5–16 A$2 (US$1.60). Mon–Fri 10am–5pm; Sat–Sun 11am–5pm. Tours hourly Mon–Fri 11am–3pm; Sat–Sun 11:30am, 1:30pm, and 2:30pm.

Wolf Blass   This winery's Germanic-style black-label vintages have an excellent international reputation, while its cheaper yellow-label vintages are the toast of many a Sydney dinner party. The Wolf Blass **museum** is worth a peek.

Sturt Hwy., Nuriootpa. (*C* **08/8568 7300**. Mon–Fri 9am–5pm; Sat–Sun 10am–5pm.

Yalumba   This winery was built in 1849, making it the oldest family-owned wine-making business in Australia. It's also huge. Keep an eye out for the sad-looking Himalayan bear in the corner of the large tasting room; its sad look can be attributed to a run-in with a hunting rifle, it's been Yalumba's advertising symbol ever since. The winery's **Signature Red Cabernet-Shiraz** ✦ is among the best you'll ever taste.

Eden Valley Rd., Angaston. (*C* **08/8561 3200**. www.yalumba.com.au. Mon–Fri 8:30am–5pm; Sat 10am–5pm; Sun noon–5pm.

WHERE TO STAY

There are plenty of standard motels and lots of interesting B&Bs throughout the Barossa, some with rooms for as little as A$60 (US$48). Weekends often find lodgings sold out and prices higher than on weekdays. The **Barossa Wine and Visitor Information Centre** (see "Visitor Information," above) can provide information on additional accommodations choices and off-season deals.

Barossa Valley (SA) Tourist Park   This peaceful place is back from the road and abuts a nature lake and wildlife reserve. The cabins are simple but come with just about everything you need for a pleasant stay. Cabins have a combination of doubles, singles, and bunk beds. If you don't have your own linen, you'll pay A$5 (US$4) per single bed and A$10 (US$8) per double.

Penrice Rd., Nuriootpa SA 5355. (*C* **08/8562 1404**. Fax 08/85622 615. www.barossa-tourist-park.com.au. 27 cabins, 19 with bathroom. A$36 (US$29) double without bathroom; A$45–A$60 (US$36–US$48) double with bathroom; family unit A$65 (US$52). Extra adult A$5 (US$4); extra child 3–15 A$3 (US$2.40). AE, DC, MC, V. **Amenities:** Outdoor pool nearby; 2 tennis courts; coin-op laundry. *In room:* A/C, TV, kitchenette, coffeemaker, iron.

Collingrove Homestead ✦✦✦ *Finds*   In my opinion, Collingrove is the best country-house experience not just in the Barossa but, dare I say it, in Australia. Built in 1856, it was originally the home of John Howard Angas, one of those involved in the initial settlement of South Australia. Additions were made as Angas's sheep business prospered. The hallway is festooned with spears, artillery shells, rifles, oil portraits, and the mounted heads of stags and tigers. English oak paneling and creaky floorboards add a certain nuance, and the cedar kitchen, library, glorious dining room, and various other places burst with antiques and knickknacks. What the quaint, individually decorated guest rooms lack in modern amenities (phones and TVs) they make up for in charm. One unit, room no. 5, does have a TV (with pay movies), as well as a mini-bar. The modern communal Jacuzzi is in the old stables, with flagstone floors and old horse harnesses; there's also a flagstone-floored tennis court.

Even if you don't stay here, you can indulge in Devonshire tea on the terrace daily for A$5 (US$4) and can tour the property Monday through Friday from 1 to 4:30pm and Saturday and Sunday from 11am to 4:30pm. The tour costs A$4 (US$3.20) for adults and A$1.50 (US$1.20) for children. Dinner by prior arrangement costs A$95 (US$76) per person. Tea, the popular Sunday brunch, and dinner are open to the public.

Eden Valley Rd., Angaston, SA 5353. (℘) **08/8564 2061**. Fax 08/8564 3600. www.collinggrovehomestead.com.au. 6 units, 4 with bathroom. A$210 (US$168) luxury double; A$250 (US$200) deluxe double. Rates include full breakfast. AE, DC, MC, V. **Amenities:** Restaurant; tennis court; Jacuzzi; in-room massage; babysitting; nonsmoking rooms. *In room:* Hair dryer.

The Hermitage of Marananga ★ This is far and away the best of the area's
motels. The rooms are awkwardly shaped but have been renovated. Each has a small balcony. The main building is old-fashioned and bursting with character. It's also cool in the heat of summer. Outside there are fantastic views over the valley and to the ranges beyond. Good walks lead around the property, and at dusk you'll see plenty of kangaroos in the surrounding fields. The apartment has a private balcony overlooking the vineyards, a separate bedroom, and a double sleeper sofa in the living room.

Corner of Seppeltsfield and Stonewell roads, Marananga, SA 5351. (℘) **08/8562 2722**. Fax 08/8562 3133. www. hermitageofmarananga.com.au. 11 units, including 1 apt. Sun–Fri A$230 (US$184) double, A$330 (US$264) Jacuzzi room or apt; Sat A$330 (US$264) double, A$430 (US$344) Jacuzzi room or apt. Rates include breakfast. AE, DC, MC, V. Free parking. **Amenities:** Restaurant; heated outdoor pool; tour desk; massage; dry cleaning. *In room:* A/C, TV/DVD, minibar, coffeemaker, hair dryer, iron.

Marble Lodge ★★ Wake up and smell the roses—there are plenty in the beauti-
ful gardens surrounding this romantic historic property (as well as a tennis court, and several deer and kangaroos). Away from the main house is a lodge made of local marble that holds two suites. The larger has two rooms and an open fireplace. The second is a large bed/sitting room, with an open fireplace. Both have access to the shared Jacuzzi and are tastefully furnished in antiques. There's always fresh fruit, homemade biscuits, and chocolates in the room, and it's a 5-minute walk to three local restaurants. A double room in the homestead, with shared bathroom, is sometimes available.

21 Dean St., Angaston, SA 5351. (℘) **08/8564 2478**. Fax 08/8564 2941. www.marblelodge.com.au. 2 units. A$170 (US$136) double. Rates include breakfast, bottle of champagne, and minibar drinks. MC, V. **Amenities:** Tennis court; Jacuzzi; room service until 8pm; nonsmoking rooms; e-mail and fax facilities. *In room:* A/C, TV w/pay movies, fax, mini-bar, fridge, coffeemaker, hair dryer, iron.

WHERE TO DINE

The Barossa prides itself on its cuisine as well as its wine, so you'll find plenty of places of note to eat, many of them serving traditional German food. A hot spot for lunch or dinner is **Vintner's Bar & Grill,** Nuriootpa Road, Angaston (℘ **08/8564 2488**); the wine list is six pages long! Try bay-leaf risotto with prawns or roast veal rack with crisp polenta. Main courses cost A$22 to A$27 (US$18–US$22). It's open for lunch daily and Monday through Saturday for dinner. Another choice is **Salters,** Satram Winery, Nuriootpa Road, Angaston (℘ **08/8564 3344**); local produce is the specialty, with main courses such as slow-roasted baby pork, milk-fed lamb, and crisp-based pizzas. Main courses are A$20 to A$26 (US$16–US$21). It's open daily for lunch and from 6pm Wednesday to Saturday for dinner. Perhaps the best German-style bakery in the valley is the **Lyndoch Bakery,** on the Barossa Highway, Lyndoch (℘ **08/8524 4422**). In Angaston, you must stop off at **The Seasons of the Valley,** 6 Washington St. (℘ **08/8564 3688**). The restored 1840 homestead house has cottage gardens and a sunny veranda as well as delicious meals for A$15 to A$18 (US$12–US$14). It's open daily 10am to 5pm.

THE ADELAIDE HILLS

A 25-minute drive from Adelaide and visible even from the main shopping street, you'll find the tree-lined slopes and pretty valleys, orchards, vineyards, winding roads, and historic townships of the **Adelaide Hills.** You might want to walk part of the Heysen Trail (see "Enjoying the Great Outdoors" in the Adelaide section, earlier in this chapter), browse through the shops in Hahndorf, stop in Melba's Chocolate Factory in Woodside, or visit Cleland Wildlife Park or Warrawong Sanctuary. Otherwise, it's a nice outing just to hit the road and drive. Should you decide to stay overnight, the area offers lots of cozy B&Bs.

ESSENTIALS

GETTING THERE   The Adelaide Hills are 25 minutes from Adelaide by car on Greenhill and Glen Osmond roads. **Adelaide Sightseeing** (© **08/8231 4144;** www. adelaidesightseeing.com.au) runs outings to the gorgeous town of Hahndorf (see below). An afternoon excursion to Hahndorf costs A$49 (US$39) for adults and A$23 (US$24) for children. The company also offers trips to Kangaroo Island, costing A$181 (US$145) for adults and A$116 (US$93) for kids; the Flinders ranges, costing A$248 (US$198) for adults and A$261 (US$209) for kids; the Coorong, costing A$95 (US$76) for adults and A$50 (US$40) for kids; and the Great Ocean Road, costing A$235 (US$188) for adults and A$165 (US$132) for kids.

VISITOR INFORMATION   Visitor information and bookings are available through the **Adelaide Hills Tourist Information Centre,** 41 Main St., Hahndorf (© **08/8388 1185**). It's open Monday through Friday from 9am to 4pm. Maps are also available at the **South Australia Travel Centre** in Adelaide.

WOODSIDE: CHOCOLATE LOVERS UNITE!

Visitors come here for **Melba's Chocolate Factory,** Henry Street (© **08/8389 7868**), where chocoholics will find a huge range of handmade chocolates. Melba's is part of Heritage Park, a complex that includes a wood turner, a cheese maker, a ceramics studio, a leather maker, and a crafts shop. It's open Monday through Friday from 10am to 4pm, and Saturday, Sunday, and holidays from noon to 5pm.

MYLOR: GETTING BACK TO NATURE

Mylor is 25km (16 miles) southeast of Adelaide, and 10km (6 miles) south of Mount Lofty via the town of Crafters. Here you'll find the **Warrawong Sanctuary,** Stock Road, Mylor (P.O. Box 1135), Stirling, SA 5152 (© **08/8370 9197;** fax 08/8370 8332; www.efl.com.au). Unlike the inhabitants of many other wildlife parks, the animals here are not kept in enclosed runs. Instead, park founder Dr. John Wamsley took a 14-hectare (35-acre) tract of farmland, replanted it with natural bush, fenced it off, and went around shooting the introduced rabbits, cats, dogs, and foxes that plague much of Australia. Then the good doctor reintroduced native animals such as kangaroos, various types of wallabies, bandicoots, beetongs, platypuses, possums, frogs, birds, and reptiles. They are all thriving, not only because he eliminated their unnatural predators but also because he re-created waterways, rainforests, and blackwater ponds. The animals roam free while you're guided through on a 1½-hour dawn or sunset walk (A$18/US$14 adults, A$12/US$9.60 children). There's a restaurant on the premises, and you can even stay overnight in large cabins with bathrooms, wall-to-wall carpeting, and air-conditioning. The cabins cost A$125 (US$100) per person with both dawn and dusk tours, a two-course dinner, and breakfast.

Compared to Cleland Wildlife Park (see below), the Warrawong Sanctuary has fewer species—you won't find any koalas, for example—but it's more educational and you get the feeling that you're in the wild rather than in a zoo.

HAHNDORF: GERMAN HERITAGE, CRAFTS & MORE ✦

This historic German-style village is one of South Australia's most popular tourist destinations. Lutherans fleeing religious persecution in eastern Prussia founded the town, which is 29km (18 miles) southeast of Adelaide, in 1839. They brought their wine-making skills, foods, and architectural inheritance, and put it all together here. Hahndorf still resembles a small German town in appearance and atmosphere, and is included on the World Heritage List as a Historical German Settlement. Walking around, you'll see **St. Paul's Lutheran Church,** erected in 1890. **The Wool Factory, L'Unique Fine Arts & Craft,** and **Bamfurlong Fine Crafts** are worth checking out and are within walking distance of Main Street.

WHERE TO STAY

The Hahndorf Resort ✦   This large resort has a variety of accommodations as well as approximately 80 trailer and tent sites. Lodgings include air-conditioned cabins, and motel-style rooms with queen-size beds (some have an extra single) and a shower. The chalets look as if they're straight out of Bavaria; each can accommodate two to five people in one or two bedrooms. Each has a full kitchen and an attached bathroom with shower. Some of them overlook a small lake. The larger spa chalets come with Jacuzzis. An on-site animal sanctuary has a few emus, kangaroos, and horses.

145A Main St., Hahndorf, SA 5245. (© **08/8388 7921.** Fax 08/8388 7282. www.hahndorfresort.com.au. 60 units. A$68 (US$46) cabin; A$99 (US$80) motel room; A$125–A$159 (US$100–US$127) chalet. Extra adult A$12 (US$9.20); extra child A$5.50 (US$4.40). AE, DC, MC, V. **Amenities:** Restaurant; heated outdoor pool; 2 putting greens; half-size tennis court; small gym; bike rental; limited room service; coin-op laundry. *In room:* A/C, TV, kitchenette, minibar, coffeemaker, iron.

WHERE TO DINE

If you want a treat, head to the **Bridgewater Mill,** Mt. Barker Road, Bridgewater (© **08/8339 3422**). In an impressive 1860s stone building with a terrace near a waterwheel, this place serves some of the best-regarded food in the country. Try duck with braised cherries. Main courses cost A$31 (US$25); a three-course menu, served Sunday only, is A$68 (US$54). It's open for lunch Thursday to Monday.

OAKBANK: A DAY AT THE RACES

The **Easter Oakbank Racing Carnival** is part of the Australia-wide "picnic races" that take place in small towns throughout the nation. The Oakbank horse races attract crowds in excess of 110,000 a day over the long Easter weekend (and smaller crowds at other times). General admission is A$10 (US$8), plus another A$5 (US$4) for admission to the grandstand. The **Oakbank Racing Club** (© **08/8212 6279**) is just off the main road; you can't miss it.

WHERE TO STAY

Adelaide Hills Country Cottages ★★ These cottages have won several tourism awards. They are 1km (½ mile) apart and surrounded by 60 hectares (150 acres) of scenic countryside. The Apple Tree cottage, from around 1860, sleeps up to five, has a Jacuzzi and antiques, and overlooks an orchard and a lake; the Gum Tree Cottage sleeps four and has wonderful country views; and the Lavender Fields Cottage sleeps up to four and overlooks a lily-fringed duck pond. All of the cottages have open fireplaces and full kitchens. This is a great place to relax and a good base for exploring the area. You'll get a couple of free drinks and a fruit basket upon arrival. Oakbank is 30 minutes from Adelaide, 7 minutes from Hahndorf, and less than 1 hour from the Barossa Valley.

P.O. Box 100, Oakbank, SA 5243. (© **08/8388 4193.** Fax 08/8388 4733. www.ahcc.com.au. 5 cottages. A$235–A$290 (US$188–US$232) cottage; A$205–A$260 (US$164–US$208) cottage for more than 1 night. Extra person A$70 (US$56). Rates include provisions for breakfast. Weekly discounts available. AE, DC, MC, V. **Amenities:** Jacuzzi; tour desk; coin-op laundry; nonsmoking rooms. *In room:* A/C, TV/VCR, kitchen, coffeemaker, hair dryer, iron.

MOUNT LOFTY: VIEWS & 'ROOS

Visitors make the pilgrimage to the top of 690m (2,263-ft.) **Mount Lofty,** 16km (10 miles) southeast of Adelaide, for the panoramic views over Adelaide, the Adelaide plains, and the Mount Lofty Ranges. There are several nice bushwalks from the top.

Almost at the top of Mount Lofty, off Summit Road, is the **Cleland Wildlife Park** (© **08/8339 2444;** www.environment.sa.gov.au/parks/cleland). Here you'll find all the usual Australian animals, including the largest male red kangaroo I've ever seen. Though the park is not as good as similar wildlife parks elsewhere in Australia, it does have a very good wetlands aviary. One of the drawbacks of Cleland is that it has some unimaginative enclosures, notably the one for the Tasmanian devils. The park is open daily from 9:30am to 4:30pm. Visitors can meet at the Tasmanian devil enclosure at

2pm and join the animal feed run by following a tractor around the park as it drops off food.

Admission to Cleland is A$13 (US$10) for adults, A$8 (US$6.40) for children 3 to 14, and A$35 (US$28) for families. Koala holding is allowed during photo sessions from 2 to 4pm daily (but not on very hot summer days); on Sunday and public holidays there's an additional session from 10am to noon. The privilege will cost you A$12 (US$9.60) per photo. A kiosk and restaurant are on the premises.

Public transport to either place is a bit of a hassle. To get to the Mount Lofty Lookout, take bus no. 163 Monday through Friday, or no. 165 Saturday and Sunday, from Currie Street in the city. Ask the driver to drop you off at Crafters. The trip takes 30 minutes. From there you'll need to take a short taxi ride to the top; prearrange pickup with **Tony's Taxi's** (✆ **08/8388 5988**).

To get to Cleland, take bus no. 822 from Currie Street to stop 19b. There are only two runs daily, at 10am and noon, Monday through Friday. Take the 10am bus and ask the bus driver for the exact return time. The trip to Cleland takes 40 minutes.

WHERE TO DINE

While you're atop Mount Lofty, have lunch at **The Summit** restaurant (✆ **08/8339 2600**). Look out for the kangaroo filet with chile, lemon grass, and coconut sauce, and venison on rosemary polenta. Main courses cost A$22 to A$26 (US$18–US$21). It's open for lunch Monday and Tuesday, and for dinner Wednesday to Sunday. The **Summit Café** here also sells good sandwiches and cakes, and Devonshire tea for A$8 (US$6.40).

3 Kangaroo Island ⓕⓕⓕ

110km (68 miles) S of Adelaide

There is nowhere better than Kangaroo Island to see Australian marsupials in the wild. Spend a few days here with the right guide and you can walk along a beach past a colony of sea lions; spot hundreds of New Zealand fur seals playing; creep through the bush on the trail of wallabies or kangaroos; spot sea eagles, black swans, sacred ibis, pelicans, little penguins, the rare glossy black cockatoo, and other birds; come across goannas; pick out bunches of koalas hanging sleepily in the trees above your head; and, if you're lucky, see platypus, echidna, bandicoots, and reclusive pygmy possums—the list goes on.

The secrets to Kangaroo Island's success are its perfect conditions, the most important of which is the fact that there are no introduced foxes or rabbits to prey on the native inhabitants or their environment. The island was also never colonized by the dingo—Australia's "native" dog—which is believed to have been introduced from Asia some 4,000 years ago. About one-third of the island is unspoiled national park, and there are plenty of wildlife corridors to give the animals a chance to move about the island, lessening the problems of inbreeding.

While the animals are what most people come to see, no one goes away without also being impressed by the scenery. Kangaroo Island has low mallee scrubland, dense eucalyptus forests, rugged coastal scenery, gorgeous beaches, caves, lagoons, and blackwater swamps. The effect of 150 years of European colonization has taken its toll, though. In South Australia as a whole, some 27 mammal, 5 bird, 1 reptile, and 30 plant species have become extinct since the English seafarer Matthew Flinders arrived in 1802.

Kangaroo Island

The island's history is a harsh one. Aborigines inhabited the island as early as 10,000 years ago but abandoned it for unexplained reasons. In the 19th century, pirates, mutineers, deserters from English, French, and American ships, and escaped convicts from the eastern colonies settled here. Sealers also arrived and devastated the seal and sea lion population—in just 1 year, 1803 to 1804, they killed more than 20,000 animals. Between 1802 and 1836, Aboriginal women from both the mainland and Tasmania were kidnapped, brought to Kangaroo Island, and forced to work catching and skinning seals, kangaroos, and wallabies, and lugging salt from the salt mines.

In 1836, Kangaroo Island became the first place in South Australia to be officially settled. The state's capital was Kingscote (which was abandoned a couple of years later in favor of Adelaide). In spite of its early settlement, Kangaroo Island had very few residents until after World War II, when returned soldiers set up farms here. Today, more than a million sheep are raised on the island. The island also acts as an official bee sanctuary to protect the genetic purity of the Ligurian bee, introduced in 1881, and it is believed to be the only place in the world where this strain of bee survives.

ISLAND ESSENTIALS

WHEN TO GO   The best time to visit Kangaroo Island is between November and March (though you'll have difficulty finding accommodations over the Christmas

Cape Gantheaume

school-holiday period). July and August tend to be rainy, and winter can be cold (though often milder than on the mainland around Adelaide). Many companies offer 1-day trips to Kangaroo Island from Adelaide, but I would advise you to tailor your holiday to spend at least 2 days here. Three or even 5 days would be better. There really is a lot to see, and you won't regret spending the extra time.

GETTING THERE **Emu Airways** (© **08/8234 3711**), with up to six daily departures, and **Regional Express** (© **13 17 13** in Australia; www.regionalexpress.com.au) serve Kangaroo Island from Adelaide. Flights leave from the General Aviation Terminal, Kel Barclay Avenue, Adelaide. The General Aviation Terminal is about a 20-minute walk (or shorter taxi ride!) from the main airport terminal. The flight from Adelaide to Kangaroo Island usually takes about 25 minutes.

If you prefer to go by sea, **Kangaroo Island SeaLink** (© **13 13 01** in Australia, or 08/8202 8688; www.sealink.com.au) operates two vehicle and passenger ferries four times daily (up to 10 times in peak periods) from Cape Jervis on the tip of the Fleurieu Peninsula on the mainland to Penneshaw on Kangaroo Island. The trip takes 40 minutes and costs A$64 (US$51) round-trip for adults, A$32 (US$26) for children 3 to 14, and A$138 (US$110) for cars. Connecting bus service from Adelaide to Cape Jervis costs an extra A$36 (US$29) for adults, and A$18 (US$14) for children round-trip.

Value **An Island Bargain**

I'd advise buying an **NP&WSA Island Pass** if you'll be exploring the island on your own for 3 days or more and visiting the national park and attractions more than once. It costs A$42 (US$34) for adults, A$30 (US$24) for children, and A$110 (US$88) for families, and includes guided tours of Seal Bay, Kelly Hill Caves, Cape Borda, and Cape Willoughby. The pass also includes access to Flinders Chase National Park. The pass doesn't cover penguin tours or camping fees. It's available at Tourism Kangaroo Island in Penneshaw and at the national parks office in Kingscote (see "Visitor Information," below).

Off-peak prices may be cheaper; check when booking. Count on 3 hours for the whole trip from Adelaide if you take the connecting bus. Bookings are essential.

SeaLink also runs a range of island tours, including the 2-day, 1-night "K.I. coast to coast," which costs from A$289 (US$231) per person sharing a double room. SeaLink also offers a wide range of accommodations, day tours, and adventure activities and offers Adelaide hotel pickups for selected tours.

VISITOR INFORMATION   **Tourism Kangaroo Island,** Gateway Information Centre, Howard Drive (P.O. Box 336), Penneshaw, Kangaroo Island, SA 5222 (© **08/8553 1185;** fax 08/8553 1255; www.tourkangarooisland.com.au), has plenty of maps and information and can assist visitors with accommodations and tour information. For more information on the island's national parks, contact **National Parks and Wildlife South Australia,** known as NP&WSA, 39 Dauncey St. (P.O. Box 39), Kingscote, SA 5223 (© **08/8553 2381;** fax 08/8553 2531), open Monday through Friday from 9am to 5pm.

In addition, hotel and motel staff members generally can provide tourist brochures and sightseeing advice.

ISLAND LAYOUT   Kangaroo Island is Australia's third-largest island, 156km (97 miles) long and 57km (35 miles) wide at its widest point. The distance across the narrowest point is only 2km (1¼ miles). Approximately 3,900 people live on the island. More than half live on the northeast coast in the three main towns: Kingscote (pop. 1,800), Penneshaw (pop. 250), and American River (pop. 200). The island's major attractions are farther from the mainland: Flinders Chase National Park is in the far west, Lathami Conservation Park is on the north coast, and Seal Bay and Kelly's Caves are on the south coast.

GETTING AROUND   Apart from twice-daily SeaLink bus service, which connects Kingscote, Penneshaw, and American River, there is no public transport on the island. **Airport Shuttle Service** (© **1800/750 850**) meets all flights to Kangaroo Island and will take passengers to Kingscote, Emu Bay, and American River. The one-way trip to Kingscote costs A$10 (US$8) for adults and A$5 (US$4) for children; to Emu Bay, A$17 (US$14) for adults and A$8 (US$6.40) for children; to American River A$33 (US$26) for adults and A$15 (US$12) for children. Book the return trip from your accommodations to the airport in advance.

Major roads between Penneshaw, American River, Kingscote, and Parndana are paved, as are the road to Seal Bay and all major roads within Flinders Chase National Park. Most other roads are made of ironstone gravel, and can be very slippery if the driver approaches corners too quickly. All roads are accessible by two-wheel-drive vehicles; if you're in a rental car from the mainland, make sure your policy allows you to drive on Kangaroo Island's roads. Avoid driving at night—animals rarely fare best in a car collision.

Car-rental agencies on the island include **Budget** (© 08/8553 3133 or 08/8553 1034; fax 08/8553 2888), **Hertz & Kangaroo Island Rental Cars** (© 1800/088 296 in Australia, or 08/8553 2390; fax 08/8553 2878), and **Wheels over Kangaroo Island** (© 1800/750 850 in Australia, or 08/8553 3030; woki@ozemail.com.au). You can pick up cars at the airport or ferry terminals.

ORGANIZED TOURS If you want to keep expenses down, you can't go wrong with one of the tours organized by **Kangaroo Island Ferry Connections** (© 08/8553 1233; www.ki-ferryconnections.com). The most popular includes afternoon pickup from the main bus station in Adelaide, coach and ferry to the island, a penguin tour that evening, and dorm accommodations (you can pay a little extra to upgrade to a double room, or for more expensive hotels). The next day involves 10 hours of touring, taking in most of the main attractions. That evening you return to Adelaide. The tour costs A$220 (US$176).

If you make your own way to the island you can join one of several day tours, departing Penneshaw or American River Thursday, Saturday, Sunday, Monday and Wednesday, also stopping off at many of the main attractions. The tour costs A$99 (US$80) for adults and A$74 (US$59) for children 3 to 14 years old.

More expensive options include **Kangaroo Island Wilderness Tours** (© 08/8559 5033; www.wildernesstours.com.au), which operates from the island with several small four-wheel-drive vehicles (maximum six people). Three different 1-day trips cost A$270 to A$290 (US$216–US$232) per person, including transfers, an excellent lunch with wine, and park entry fees. Two-, 3-, and 4-day trips, including all meals and accommodations, cost A$710 (US$568), A$1,150 (US$920), and A$1,590 (US$1,272) per person, respectively.

Another excellent operator on the island is **Adventure Charters of Kangaroo Island,** Playford Highway, Cygnet River, SA 5223 (© 08/8553 9119; www.adventure charters.com.au), with the knowledgeable and gregarious Craig Wickham at the helm. Day trips cost A$272 (US$218) a day with a big lunch, or A$501 (US$400) for a 1-day safari including flights from and to Adelaide.

Another option is **Wayward Bus** (© 08/8410 8833; www.waywardbus.com.au) from Adelaide. Two-day trips depart Monday, Wednesday, and Saturday and cost A$365 (US$292) in hostel accommodations (you can pay extra for an upgrade).

EXPLORING THE ISLAND

The island is bigger than you might think, and you can spend a fair bit of time getting from one place of interest to the next. Of the many places to see on the island, **Flinders Chase National Park** is one of the most important. Your first stop should be the Flinders Chase Visitors Centre, where you can purchase park entry, view the interpretive display, dine at the licensed cafe, purchase souvenirs, and obtain parks information. After 30 years of lobbying, reluctant politicians finally agreed to preserve this region of the island in 1919. Today, it makes up around 17% of the island and is home to true wilderness, some beautiful coastal scenery, two old lighthouses, and plenty of animals. Birders have recorded at least 243 species here. Koalas are so common that they're almost falling out of the trees. Platypuses have been seen, but you'll probably need to make a special effort and sit next to a stream in the dark for a few hours for any chance of spotting one. The Platypus Waterholes walk is a 2-hour walk that's great for all ages. It begins at the Flinders Chase Visitors Centre and has a shorter option that's suitable for wheelchairs. This walk offers the best opportunity to see the elusive platypus. Kangaroos, wallabies, and brush-tailed possums, on the other hand, are so tame and numerous that the authorities were forced to erect a barrier around the Rocky River Campground to stop them from carrying away picnickers' sandwiches!

The most impressive coastal scenery is at **Cape du Couedic,** at the southern tip of the park. Millions of years of crashing ocean have created curious structures, like the hollowed-out limestone promontory called Admiral's Arch and the aptly named Remarkable Rocks, where you'll see huge boulders balancing on top of a massive granite dome. Admiral's Arch is home to a colony of some 4,000 New Zealand fur seals that play in the rock pools and rest on the rocks. During rough weather this place can be spectacular. A paved road leads from Rocky River Park Headquarters to Admiral's Arch and Remarkable Rocks, where there are a parking lot and a loop trail. There's a road, parking lot, and trail system around the Cape du Couedic heritage lighthouse district.

You shouldn't miss out on the unforgettable experience of walking through a colony of Australian sea lions at Seal Bay. The **Seal Bay Conservation Park (© 08/8559 4207)** was created in 1972, and some 100,000 people visit it each year. Boardwalks through the dunes to the beach reduce the impact of so many feet. The colony consists of about 500 animals, but at any one time you might see up to 100 basking with their pups. The rangers who supervise the area lead guided trips throughout the day, every 15 to 30 minutes from 9am to 4:15pm. If you come here without a coach group, you must join a tour. Tours cost A$11 (US$8.80) for adults and A$7.50 (US$6) for children.

Lathami Conservation Park, just east of Stokes Bay, is a wonderful place to see wallabies in the wild. Just dip under the low canopy of casuarina pines and walk silently, keeping your eyes peeled. You're almost certain to spot them. If you're fortunate, you may even come across a rare glossy cockatoo—it's big and black and feeds mainly on casuarina nuts.

Another interesting spot, especially for birders, is **Murray Lagoon,** on the northern edge of Cape Gantheaume Conservation Park. It's the largest lagoon on the island and a habitat for thousands of water birds. Contact the NP&WSA (see "Visitor Information," above) for information on a ranger-guided Wetland Wade.

If you want to see little **penguins**—tiny animals that stand just 33 centimeters (13 in.) tall—forget the touristy show at Phillip Island near Melbourne. On Kangaroo Island, you can see them in a natural environment at both Kingscote and Penneshaw. The **NP&WSA (© 08/8553 2381)** conducts the tours. Call ahead to confirm times, which are subject to change. Nightly tours in Kingscote depart from the reception desk at the Ozone Seafront Hotel and cost A$7.50 (US$6) for adults, A$6 (US$4.80) for children. The Penneshaw Penguin Centre, adjacent to the beach and Lloyd Collins Reserve, has the largest penguin colony on the island. Tours depart twice per evening

---

Tips **Don't Feed the Animals, Please**

Don't feed *any* native animals. Kangaroos and wallabies might beg, but they are lactose intolerant and can go blind or fall ill from being fed human food.

Culling Koalas—A National Dilemma

Koalas are cute. They're fluffy, they're sleepy, and they're awesomely cuddly. They also eat an awful lot. In the early 1920s, 18 koalas were introduced to Kangaroo Island. Over the years, without predators and disease, and with an abundant supply of eucalyptus trees, they have prospered. By 1996, there were an estimated 4,000 koalas, and their favorite trees were looking ragged. Some of the koalas were already suffering; some people even claimed the animals were starving to death.

The state government decided that the only option was to shoot Australia's ambassador to the world. The public outcry was enormous; Japan even threatened to advise its citizens to boycott Down Under. But what could be done? Some scientists maintained that the koalas could not be relocated to the mainland because there were few places left to put them. Conservationists blamed Kangaroo Island's farmers for depleting the island of more than 50% of its vegetation. The koala is endangered; the smaller northern variety is threatened with extinction in New South Wales; the larger subspecies in Victoria, which includes the Kangaroo Island koalas, is also under threat. A compromise was reached: The koalas are to be trapped and neutered, a few thousand per year, until their numbers stabilize. A few conscientious farmers will plant more trees. Other farmers will, no doubt, continue to see the koalas as pests.

and cost A$6 (US$4.80) for adults, A$4.50 (US$3.60) for kids, free for children under 12.

For fabulous, though pricey, **fishing** for everything from King George whiting, trevally, and snapper to mullet and mackerel, contact **Kangaroo Island Fishing Charters** (© 08/8553 1328; www.kifishchart.com.au). Prices for a day out start at A$125 (US$100), including lunch; a half-day trip costs A$90 (US$72), and you keep what you catch. **American River Fishing Charters** (© 0417/869 346 mobile) also runs trips.

Finally, Kangaroo Island is renowned for its fresh food, and across the island you'll see signs beckoning to you to have a taste of cheese, honey, wine, or the like. One place worth a stop is **Clifford's Honey Farm** (© 08/8553 8295), which is open daily from 9am to 5pm. The farm is the home of the protected Ligurian honeybee, found nowhere else on earth but on the island. **Island Pure Sheep Dairy** (© 08/8553 9110) is another worthwhile stop. Tours and tastings are conducted at milking time (1–5pm). It's a great chance to sample delicious sheep's milk, yogurts, and mouthwatering haloumi cheese. Ask at the tourist office for directions to both.

WHERE TO STAY

The island has a wide variety of places to choose from, from B&Bs to campgrounds. If you feel like sleeping in one of 40 cottages or coastal lodgings, contact **Kangaroo Island Remote and Coastal Farm Accommodation** (© 08/8553 1233; fax 08/8553 1190; www.ki-ferryconnections.com). Prices range from A$65 to A$100 (US$52–US$80).

The staff can also arrange lodgings in local farms, homes, and B&Bs for A$60 to A$110 (US$48–US$88) for a double with breakfast.

The NP&WSA (see "Visitor Information," above) also rents basic but comfortable lodgings, including relatively isolated **lighthouse cottages** ★★ at Cape Willoughby, Cape Borda, and Cape du Couedic. The price is A$21 to A$37 (US$17–US$30) per adult per night, and the minimum charge per stay is A$49 to A$110 (US$39–US$88) per cottage.

If you're on a supertight budget, head to the **Penneshaw Youth Hostel,** 43 North Terrace, Penneshaw, Kangaroo Island, SA 5222 (© **08/8553 1284;** fax 08/8553 1295), with dorm beds for A$22 (US$18) and doubles for A$72 (US$57). It costs a few dollars less for YHA members.

Camping is allowed at designated sites around the island and in national parks for a minimal fee. There are many beach, river, and bush camping spots, including the Rocky River site in the Flinders Chase National Park.

IN & NEAR KINGSCOTE

Ozone Seafront Hotel   The best-known of Kangaroo Island's lodgings, the Ozone gets its name from the aroma of the sea—which virtually laps at its door. It's a nice, centrally located choice offering comfortable rooms with plenty of space; the majority of the more expensive ones have views of Nepean Bay. Family rooms have a double bed and two single beds. Prices are highest on Saturday night.

The Foreshore (P.O. Box 145), Kingscote, SA 5223. © 08/8553 2011. Fax 08/8553 2249. www.ozonehotel.com. 37 units. A$220–A$286 (US$176–US$228) double; A$242–A$308 (US$193–US$246) Victorian double; A$297–A$374 (US$237–US$299) suite. Extra person A$13 (US$10). AE, DC, MC, V. **Amenities:** 2 restaurants; 3 bars; heated outdoor pool; golf course nearby; Jacuzzi; sauna; tour desk; limited room service; babysitting; laundry service. *In room:* A/C, TV, fridge, coffeemaker, hair dryer, iron.

Wisteria Lodge ★   All rooms at the modern and definitely unglamorous-looking Wisteria Lodge are standard motel-type accommodations, with exposed brick walls and gray carpets. They have views over Nepean Bay. Deluxe rooms offer a Jacuzzi and queen-size beds. Packages include transport to the island, transfers, meals, and day tours. Reservations are essential for the restaurant.

7 Cygnet Rd., Kingscote, SA 5223. © 08/8553 2707. Reservations: Flag Inns (© 800/624-3524 in the U.S. and Canada, 0800/892 407 in the U.K., 0800/803 524 in New Zealand, or 13 24 00 in Australia). Fax 08/8553 2200. www.wisterialodgeki.com. 20 units. A$140 (US$112) double; A$160 (US$128) triple; A$178 (US$142) double Jacuzzi room; A$200 (US$160) triple Jacuzzi room. Extra adult A$20–A$22 (US$16–US$18); extra child 3–12 A$15–A$19 (US$12–US$15). Ask about packages. AE, DC, MC, V. **Amenities:** Restaurant; heated outdoor pool; half-size tennis court; Jacuzzi; children's center; tour desk; car-rental desk; business center; limited room service; laundry service; dry cleaning; nonsmoking rooms. *In room:* A/C, TV, minibar, fridge, coffeemaker, hair dryer.

IN AMERICAN RIVER

Popular with fishermen, American River is 37km (23 miles) from Kingscote. It lacks a beach but offers black swans on Pelican Lagoon. Wild wallabies abound, and egrets, magpies, and cockatoos offer early wake-up calls.

Casuarina Coastal Units   These simple, country-style accommodations are not flashy, but they offer a cozy budget option. Each comes with a double bed, two singles, and an attached shower. The property has a playground and fish-cleaning facilities.

9 Ryberg Rd., American River, SA 5221. ©/fax 08/8553 7020. www.casuarinaonki.com. 6 units. A$85 (US$68) double; A$75 (US$60) double for more than 1 night. MC, V. **Amenities:** Coin-op laundry. *In room:* TV.

Kangaroo Island Lodge ⭑ Though Kangaroo Island Lodge was built in 1801, it has been so overhauled that you would be hard pressed to find anything rustic remaining. It's a nicely appointed property with pleasant, quiet motel-style rooms, a good pool, Jacuzzi, sauna and a restaurant and bar (entrees average A$20/US$16). Some units contain kitchens. The lodge looks over Pelican Lagoon (famous for its, well, pelicans), but it's a little too far away from it to make the water-view rooms worth the extra cost.

Scenic Rd., American River, SA 5221. ℂ **08/8553 7053**. Fax 08/8553 7030. www.kilodge.com.au. 38 units. A$165 (US$132) water-view double; A$135 (US$108) poolside double. Extra person A$24 (US$19). AE, DC, MC, V. **Amenities:** Restaurant; heated outdoor pool; tennis court; game room; tour desk; car-rental desk; limited room service; coin-op laundry; nonsmoking rooms. *In room:* A/C, TV, fridge, hair dryer, iron.

Wanderers Rest This pleasant guesthouse sits on a hillside with panoramic views across the sea to the mainland. It has large, comfortably furnished rooms with balconies. All rooms come with king-size beds that convert to twins, and showers (no tubs). Breakfasts are hearty, packed lunches are available, and dinnertime can be a hoot, with guests sipping beer and wine around the dining-room table and tucking into King George whiting caught that day. Other meals include steak, lamb chops, local oysters, and a vegetarian stir-fry.

Bayview Rd. (P.O. Box 34), American River, SA 5221. ℂ **08/8553 7140**. Fax 08/8553 7282. www.wanderersrest. com.au. 9 units. A$189 (US$151) double; A$244 (US$195) triple. Rates include full breakfast. Ask about packages and ferry transport deals. AE, DC, MC, V. Limited parking. Children under 12 not accepted. **Amenities:** Restaurant; heated outdoor pool; game room; tour desk; car-rental desk. *In room:* A/C, TV, minibar, coffeemaker, hair dryer.

IN PARNDANA

Developed by soldier settlers after World War II, Parndana today is a rural service center 25 minutes by car from Seal Bay and Stokes Bay. It's just around the corner from Parndana Wildlife Park, which has more than 50 aviaries with collections of native and other birds, some of them rare and protected.

The Open House ⭑ The best thing about The Open House is mealtime, when guests sit around a communal table and dive into delicious home-cooked meals. The rooms—two with queen-size beds, one with two singles, and a family room sleeping up to four—are comfortable and homey. Each has a ceiling fan and a private bathroom with shower. The owners are friendly and can offer good advice on what to do around the island.

70 Smith St., Parndana, SA 5221. ℂ **08/8559 6113**. Fax 08/8559 6088. www.theopenhouse.com.au. 4 units. A$150 (US$120) per person with dinner and breakfast; A$115 (US$92) per person with breakfast only; A$100 (US$80) per child under 12 with dinner and breakfast; A$70 (US$56) per child with breakfast only. MC, V. **Amenities:** Restaurant; nonsmoking rooms. *In room:* Hair dryer.

ON THE SOUTHWEST COAST

Hanson Bay Cabins ⭑ *Finds* On the southwest coast of the island on the South Coast Road, this property is a row of comfortable log cabins perched above a fabulous beach. Each cabin has a large picture window facing the ocean, a full kitchen, a bathroom, two bedrooms (including a double bed and three singles in all), and a wood stove. Bring your own food and supplies from Kingscote, American River, or Penneshaw. The ocean can get wild and dramatic around here, with strong offshore winds whipping up the sand and spray. The cottages are near most of the major attractions, so they make a good base. Salmon are often caught off the beach.

Hanson Bay Company, P.O. Box 614, Kingscote, SA 5225. ☎ **08/8853 2603**. Fax 08/8853 2673. www.esl.com.au/hansonbay. 6 cabins. A$170 (US$136) double; A$132 (US$106) double for more than 1 night. Extra adult A$30 (US$24); extra child A$20 (US$16). AE, DC, MC, V. **Amenities:** Bike rental; coin-op laundry; nonsmoking rooms. *In room:* Kitchen, fridge, coffeemaker, hair dryer, iron (on request).

WHERE TO DINE

Most accommodations on Kangaroo Island provide meals for guests (usually at an additional cost). In addition, most day tours around the island include lunch. You'll find a few cheap takeout booths scattered around the island at the most popular tourist spots. For lunch, you can get sandwiches at Roger's Deli on Dauncey Street, behind the Ozone Hotel, in Kingscote.

IN PENNESHAW

Dolphin Rock Café FAST FOOD   Here you'll find plastic tables and chairs and budget meals. The meals, including individual pizzas, and french fries and gravy, are popular with backpackers. Also on offer are fish and chips, hamburgers, and chicken. Across the road, the fairy penguins come in at dusk.

43 N. Terrace (next to the YHA). ☎ **08/8553 1284**. Main courses A$4–A$12 (US$3.20–US$9.60). AE, MC, V. Summer daily 7am–8:30pm; winter Wed–Mon 7:30am–7:30pm.

ELSEWHERE

Cape Willoughby Café ★★ LOCAL PRODUCE   This fabulous restaurant perches on a cliff top on the far eastern tip of the island, right next to Cape Willoughby Lighthouse (an attraction in itself) and about 30km (19 miles) from Penneshaw. One wall is all glass, and the veranda affords terrific ocean views. King George whiting is a specialty, as are desserts (the sticky date pudding is mouthwatering). Outside of lunch hours (12:30–2:30pm), the cafe serves coffee and cakes. Forty-five-minute tours of the lighthouse leave from the lighthouse office at 10 and 11am, and 12:30 and 2pm daily. They cost A$6 (US$4.80) for adults, A$4.50 (US$3.60) for children, and A$17 (US$14) for families.

Cape Willoughby. ☎ **08/8553 1333**. Reservations required for lunch. Main courses A$20–A$27 (US$16–US$22). MC, V. Daily 10am–4pm for coffee and cakes; 12:30–2:30pm for lunch.

4 Outback South Australia

South Australia is the driest state in Australia. This becomes quite apparent once you leave behind the parklands of Adelaide and head into the interior. The Outback is as harsh as it is beautiful. Much of it consists of stony desert, saltpans, and sand hills, roamed by kangaroos and wild goats. After spring rains, though, the area can burst alive with wildflowers.

It was always difficult to travel through these parts, and even today only four main routes traverse it. One of them, the **Birdsville Track,** is famed in Outback history as the trail along which stockmen once drove their herds of cattle south from Queensland. Another, the **Strzelecki Track,** runs through remote sand-dune country to Innamincka and on to Coopers Creek. Both of these tracks cut through the "dog fence"—a 5,600km-long (3,472-mile) barrier designed to keep dingoes out of the pastoral lands to the south.

If you follow the **Stuart Highway** or the **Oodnadatta Track,** you'll pass the mining towns of Coober Pedy, Andamooka, and Mintabie, where people from all over the world have been turned loose in the maddening search for opal. Out here, too, are national parks, such as the daunting Simpson Desert Conservation Park, with its seemingly endless blood-red sand dunes and spinifex plains; and Lake Eyre National Park, with its dried-up saltpan that, during rare floods, is a temporary home to thousands of water birds.

THE FLINDERS RANGES NATIONAL PARK ★
460km (285 miles) N of Adelaide

The dramatic craggy peaks and ridges that make up the Flinders Ranges rise out of the South Australian desert. The colors of the rock vary from deep red to orange, with sedimentary lines visible as they run down the sides of cliffs. Much of the greenery around here is stunted arid-land vegetation. Growing shoots and saplings, which for decades were nibbled away before they grew up, have started to turn what was once bare land back into bush. This is the result of a devastating rabbit virus introduced in 1996, and the continued culling of hundreds of thousands of wild goats. The most remarkable attraction is **Wilpena Pound,** a natural circle of cliff faces that form a gigantic depression on top of a mountainous ledge. The wind whipping over the cliff edges can produce exhilarating white-knuckle turbulence if you fly over it in a light aircraft. Kangaroos and emus can sometimes be seen wandering around the park, but outside the park, kangaroos are heavily culled.

ESSENTIALS
GETTING THERE   By car, take Highway 1 out of Adelaide to Port Augusta (3½ hr.), then head east on Route 47 via Quorn and Hawker (45 min.). It's another hour to Wilpena Pound, next to the tiny settlement of Wilpena. Alternatively, take the scenic route, which doesn't have a specific name, through the Clare Valley (around 5 hr.): From Adelaide, head to Gawler and then through the Clare Valley; follow signs to Gladstone, Melrose, Wilmington, and Quorn.

Premier Stateliner (© **08/8415 5500;** www.premierstateliner.com.au) runs five buses every day from Adelaide to Port Augusta for A$35 (US$28) one-way. The company also runs buses to Wilpena Pound via Hawker and Quorn, leaving Adelaide at 8:30am Wednesday and 11am Friday. Fares each way are A$44 (US$35) to Quorn, A$58 (US$46) to Hawker, and A$63 (US$50) to Wilpena Pound. Buses return to Adelaide from Wilpena Pound at 11am on Thursday, 7:15pm on Friday (arriving in Adelaide at 5am), and 3:05pm on Sunday.

Heading Bush Adventures (© **08/8356 5501;** www.headingbush.com) has great trips, including a 10-day tour to the Flinders Ranges, the Oodnadatta Track, Coober Pedy, the Simpson Desert, Uluru (Ayers Rock), the Olgas, Kings Canyon, and Aboriginal communities. This remarkable trip, which focuses on Aboriginal culture, costs A$1,200 (US$1,000)—or A$995 (US$797) with a YHA card—and includes meals and bush camping.

Tips An Outback Travel Warning

If you intend to drive through the Outback, take care. Distances between points of interest can be vast; water, gas, food, and accommodations are far apart. Always travel with a good map and plenty of advice. If you plan to travel off-road, a four-wheel-drive vehicle is a must.

Another good operator is **Banksia Adventures** (© **08/8236 9141;** www.banksia-adventures.com.au), which has 1- to 4-day trips to the Flinders, either in hotels or camping. The 1-day trip, including a hotel, costs A$225 (US$180), the 2-day trip A$585 (US$468), the 3-day trip A$925 (US$740), and the 4-day trip A$1,335 (US$1,068). Camping is about 25% cheaper. This company also offers camping trips to salty Lake Eyre when it floods (it flooded in 2000 and was due to flood again at the time of writing), as well as the Great Aussie Pub Crawl. On this trip you fly by light plane from Adelaide and visit remote Outback pubs. You stay overnight at good hotels, including the Prairie Hotel in the Flinders and underground at Coober Pedy. The trip costs A$3,795 (US$3,036) and is all-inclusive, with as much beer as you can drink.

Covering a huge slice of the Outback from Adelaide is another great operator, **South Australian Scenic Tours** (© **08/8289 3970;** www.oztourism.com.au/sascenic tours), which hits the dirt roads for 10-day trips up the Birdsville Track to remote townships and historic sites. You continue along the Strezelecki Track to Innamincka (where the explorers Burke and Wills came to a tragic end), cruise on Cooper Creek, and take in the Sturt Stony Desert and the Flinders Ranges. Expect to see plenty of wildlife, including kangaroos, emus, and possibly even the very rare yellow-footed rock wallaby. The trip costs A$2,167 (US$1,733). A 3-day Flinders Ranges trip with this company costs A$682 (US$545), and a 4-day Kangaroo Island tour is A$946 (US$757).

Most operators will also make up personalized tours on request.

VISITOR INFORMATION   Before setting off, contact the **Flinders Ranges and Outback of South Australia Regional Tourism Association (FROSATA),** P.O. Box 2083, Port Augusta, SA 5700 (© **1800/633 060** in Australia), for advice on roads and conditions. I strongly recommend a visit to the **Wadlata Outback Centre,** 41 Flinders Terrace, Port Augusta, SA 5700 (© **08/8642 4511**), an award-winning interactive museum and information center. The museum costs A$7 (US$5.60) for adults and A$4.50 (US$3.60) for children and is open Monday through Friday from 9am to 5:30pm, Saturday and Sunday from 10am to 4pm.

In Hawker, both the Mobil service station and the post office also act as information outlets.

GETTING AROUND   By Car   If you decide to explore on your own using a rental car, I recommend renting one in Adelaide.

WHERE TO STAY

Andu Lodge ★   This fabulous backpackers' lodge is one of the best in Australia. In Quorn, in the central Flinders Ranges (42km/26 miles from Port Augusta), the upscale former hotel is air-conditioned in summer and heated in winter. It has nice clean rooms (dorms sleep six). There's also a nice TV room, a laundry, a computer for e-mailing, and a kitchen area. The hostel runs a range of trips with an emphasis on Aboriginal culture and ecotourism. Guests can also rent mountain bikes. Quorn (pop. 1,300) is where the old *Ghan* railway started and finished, and where part of the movie *Gallipoli* was filmed. The town has four friendly pubs, all serving meals for A$6.50 to A$7.50 (US$5.20–US$6). The lodge also offers 1-, 2-, and 3-day tours of the Flinders Ranges.

12 First St., Quorn, SA 5043. © **08/8648 6020** or 1300 730 701 in Australia; Fax 08/8648 6030. steveandpaula andulodge@bigpond.com. 64 units. A$60 (US$48) double; A$87 (US$70) family room for up to 6; A$20 (US$16) dorm

bed. Breakfast included. MC, V. Free parking. **Amenities:** Shared lounge w/VCR; bike rental; tour desk; coin-op laundry; nonsmoking rooms. *In room:* No phone; TV in family rooms.

Prairie Hotel ★★ *(Finds)*   If you are going to stay anywhere near the Flinders Ranges, stay here. The tiny, tin-roofed, stonewalled pub offers a memorable experience and is well worth the dusty 89km (55-mile) drive north alongside the Ranges from Hawker on the A83. A new addition to the pub contains nice rooms, each with a queen-size bed and a shower. The older-style rooms are smaller and quaint. Three units have Jacuzzis. The bar out front is a great place to meet the locals and other travelers (who all shake their heads in wonder that this magnificent place is still so undiscovered). Meals, prepared in a style the hotel likes to call "Flinders Feral Food," are very nearly the best I've had in Australia. Among the specialties are kangaroo tail soup to start and a mixed grill of emu sausages, camel steak, and kangaroo as a main course. The owner's brother runs remarkable scenic flights over Wilpena Pound and out to the salt lakes. From here you could head to the township of William Creek for a side trip to see the giant salt lake, Lake Eyre, and then onward west to Coober Pedy.

Corner of High St. and West Terrace, Parachilna, SA 5730. © 08/8648 4844. Fax 08/8648 4606. www.prairie hotel.com.au. 12 units. A$125–A$170 (US$100–US$136) double; A$225 (US$180) double with Jacuzzi. Extra person A$35–A$45 (US$28–US$36). Rates include light breakfast. AE, DC, MC, V. **Amenities:** Restaurant; bar. *In room:* A/C, minibar, coffeemaker.

Wilpena Pound Resort   The nearest place to the Wilpena Pound, this partly refurbished resort almost monopolizes the overnight tourist market around here. Standard rooms are adequate and offer respite from the summer heat. The self-contained units are rooms with a queen-size and a single bed, a stovetop, a microwave, a basin, and cooking utensils. The resort also operates a campground. You can borrow a hair dryer at the reception desk. There are some good walks around the area. Half-hour scenic flights over the Ranges cost A$95 (US$76) per person for two people, or A$80 (US$64) per person for 20 minutes. The resort also offers four-wheel-drive tours of the area.

Wilpena Pound, SA 5434. © 1800/805 802 in Australia, or 08/8648 0004. Fax 08/8648 0028. www.wilpena pound.com.au. 60 units. A$115–A$145 (US$92–US$116) motel double; A$160–A$170 (US$128–US$136) self-contained unit. Extra adult A$22 (US$18); extra child 2–14 A$6.50 (US$5.20). Campsite A$22 (US$18); tent site A$16 (US$13). AE, DC, MC, V. **Amenities:** Restaurant; bar; bistro; general store; outdoor pool; game room; tour desk; laundry service; nonsmoking rooms. *In room:* A/C, TV, fridge, coffeemaker.

WHERE TO DINE

The **Old Ghan Restaurant,** Leigh Creek Road, Hawker (© **08/8648 4176**), is open for lunch and dinner Wednesday through Sunday; the restaurant used to be a railway station on the Ghan railway line to Alice Springs before the line was shifted sideways due to flooding. The food is unexciting, but the homemade pies have a following. If you find yourself in Port Augusta, the area's main town, head to the **Standpipe Motor Inn** (© **08/8642 4033**) for excellent Indian food. The quiet rooms are nice enough; a double goes for A$80 (US$64).

COOBER PEDY ★

854km (529 miles) NW of Adelaide; 689km (427 miles) S of Alice Springs

Tourists come to this Outback opal-mining town for one thing: the people. More than 3,500 people, from 44 nations, work mainly underground here. The majority suffer from opal fever, which keeps you digging on the trail of the elusive shimmering rocks.

Though some residents are secretive and keep to themselves, many others are colorful characters ready to stop for a chat and spin a few yarns.

Historically, Coober Pedy was a rough place, and it still has a certain Wild West air about it. The first opal was found here in 1915, but it wasn't until 1917, when the Trans Continental Railway was completed, that people began seriously digging for opals. Since then, they have mainly lived underground—not surprising when you encounter the heat, the dust, and the flies for yourself.

The town got its name from the Aboriginal words *kupa piti*, commonly thought to mean "white man's burrow." Remnants of the holes left by early miners are everywhere, mostly in the form of bleached-white hills of waste called "mullock heaps." It's rather discouraged for tourists to wander around the tailing sites, because locals get fed up when visitors fall down the mineshafts.

As for the town, there isn't much to look at, except a couple of underground churches, some casual restaurants, a handful of opal stores, and the necessary service businesses. In the center of town you'll find lots of outdoor buildings; the hotels and youth hostel have aboveground entrances but rooms below ground. All are within stumbling distance of each other on the main street.

ESSENTIALS

GETTING THERE   **Regional Express** (© **13 17 13** in Australia; www.regional express.com.au) flies to Coober Pedy from Adelaide. The round-trip fare is about A$340 (US$272). Check the website for discounted fares and specials. **Greyhound Australia** (© **13 14 99** in Australia, or 07/4690 9950; www.greyhound.com.au) runs buses from Adelaide to Coober Pedy for A$76 (US$61) for adults and A$61 (US$49) for children one-way. The trip takes about 12 hours. The bus from Alice Springs to Coober Pedy costs A$75 (US$60) for adults and A$60 (US$48) for children. Passengers bound for Uluru (Ayers Rock) transfer at Erldunda.

If you drive from Adelaide, it will take you about 9 hours to reach Coober Pedy along the Stuart Highway. It takes 7 hours to drive the 700km (434 miles) to Alice Springs.

VISITOR INFORMATION   The **Coober Pedy Tourist Information Centre,** Hutchison Street, Coober Pedy (© **1800/637 076** in Australia, or 08/8672 5298), is open Monday through Friday from 8:30am to 5pm (closed holidays). A good website, www.opalcapitaloftheworld.com.au, gives a rundown of adventure operators in the area.

SEEING THE TOWN

Radeka's Downunder Motel (see "Where to Stay," below) runs half-day tours of the opal fields, including a visit to an underground mine. It costs A$30 (US$24) for adults and A$15 (US$12) for kids.

If you want to see parts of Australia that most Australians never see, join an honest-to-goodness **Mail Run** ✮ for a 12-hour journey out into the bush. Tours leave Monday and Thursday from Coober Pedy's **Underground Books** (© **08/8672 5558**)—yep, it's a bookshop underground—and travel along 600km (372 miles) of dirt roads to Oodnadatta and William Creek cattle station, stopping at five stations along the route. It can get pretty hot and dusty outside (think endless horizons of flat lands), but it's relatively comfortable inside the air-conditioned four-wheel-drive, and you'll have the chance to see such wildlife as eagles, emus, and the ever-present kangaroos. Bring your own lunch or buy it along the way. Tours cost around A$120

Moments A Fabulous Four-Wheel-Drive Adventure

With a rented vehicle from Adelaide, the **Prairie Hotel** (p. 541) is a day's drive north through the Clare Valley wine region. Stop off along the way for a traditional Aussie lunch at **Bluey Blundstone's Café** in Melrose (© **08/8666 2173**). The next day it's a 3- to 4-hour drive to William Creek, an Outback town with a takeout restaurant, pub and hotel, satellite phone box, campground, and general store. **Explore the Outback Camel Safaris** (© **08/8672 3968**; www.austcamel.com.au/explore) offers 4-day camel safaris across the desert from here (check the website for alternate ways to get to William Creek). Just 20km (12 miles) before you reach town is a turnoff to **Lake Eyre,** a giant salt lake that flooded in 2000 and 2001, and should hold water for a couple of years. **Wrightsair** (© **0418/336 748** mobile) offers 1-hour flights over Lake Eyre for A$110 (US$88) per person. Camping beside the lake is a magical experience. The next day it's a 166km (103-mile) drive to Coober Pedy, and then a 9-hour drive back to Adelaide.

(US$96) for adults and A$75 (US$60) for children under 12, though kids might find the long trip difficult. This up-close-and-personal look at life in the bush could easily be one of the most memorable experiences you have in Australia.

WHERE TO STAY

The Backpacker's Inn at Radeka's Downunder Motel ✦ The other "underground" rooms in Coober Pedy are built into the side of a hill, but the centrally located hostel here is actually underground—some 6.5m (21 ft.) directly below the topside building. This makes for nice temperatures year-round. Odd-looking dorms have no doors and are scooped out of the rock. Most contain just four beds; two large dorms sleep up to 20 people. The twin rooms are simply furnished but pleasant. The motel rooms are quite comfortable and come with TVs, coffeemakers, and attached bathrooms with shower. Some have a kitchenette. Room no. 9 is huge, with a double and two sets of bunk beds. All motel rooms are dug out of the side of a hill. Radeka's also runs a good opal tour.

1 Oliver St., Coober Pedy, SA 5723. © 08/8672 5223. Fax 08/86725821. 150 units, 10 motel rooms. A$22 (US$18) dorm bed; A$52 (US$42) dorm double; A$90 (US$72) motel double; A$110 (US$88) motel family suite. Extra person A$15 (US$12). AE, MC, V. Free parking. **Amenities:** Bar; kitchen/dining room; tour desk; coin-operated laundry; TV and video room; pool table.

The Desert Cave Hotel Though it's not the only underground hotel in the world (there's a wonderful one in White Cliffs, New South Wales), this is the only one with a pool and Jacuzzi. Nineteen units are underground. Personally, I find the place a little soul-less. The bar's "pokie" (gambling) machines are noisy, and you can hear your neighbors in the next room. (Heaven help you if the TV is turned up loud.) The hotel can arrange transfers from the airport (A$6.50/US$5.20).

Hutchison St. (P.O. Box 223), Coober Pedy, SA 5723. © 1800/088 521 in Australia, or 08/8672 5688. Fax 08/8672 5198. www.desertcave.com.au. 50 units. A$175 (US$140) double; A$195 (US$156) family room for 5. Extra person A$20 (US$16). Ask about packages. AE, DC, MC, V. Free parking. **Amenities:** Restaurant; bar; outdoor pool; golf nearby; health club w/Jacuzzi; sauna; tour desk; car-rental desk; limited room service; laundry service; dry cleaning; nonsmoking rooms. *In room:* TV, minibar, coffeemaker, hair dryer, iron.

WHERE TO DINE

The **Opal Inn** (© 08/8672 5054) offers good-value counter meals of the typical pub-grub variety. Head to **Traces** (© 08/8672 5147), the township's favorite Greek restaurant, for something a bit different.

5 The Coorong

Few places in the world attract as much wildfowl as the **Coorong,** one of Australia's most precious sanctuaries. The Coorong area includes the mouth of the Murray River, huge Lake Alexandrina, smaller Lake Albert, and a long, thin sand spit called the Younghusband Peninsula. The **Coorong National Park** encompasses a small, but by far the most scenic, part of this area. The area is under environmental threat due to pollutants coming south in the Murray River from farmlands to the north. It still supports large colonies of native and visiting birds, such as the Australian pelican, black swan, royal spoonbill, greenshank, and extremely rare hooded plover.

If it were possible to count all the birds here, you'd probably run out of steam after some 45,000 ducks, 5,000 black swans, 2,000 Cape Barren geese, and 122,000 waders. This last figure is even more significant when you consider the total South Australian population of waders (200,000), and the overall Australian population (some 403,000).

Add to these figures the thousands of pelicans—with around 3,000 birds nesting here, it's the largest permanent breeding colony in Australia—and gulls, terns, and cormorants, and you'll realize why the Coorong and Lower Murray Lakes form one of the most important water-bird habitats in Australia.

The national park, which stands out starkly against the degraded farmland surrounding it, is also home to several species of marsupials, including wombats.

The best time to visit the Coorong is in December and January, when the lakes are full of migratory birds from overseas. However, plenty of birds can be spotted year-round. *Note:* Binoculars and patience are highly recommended.

ESSENTIALS

GETTING THERE   The best way to visit the Coorong is by car. I highly recommend a guided tour of the area once you arrive at the main settlement of Goolwa, on the western fringe of the waterways, or at Meningie, on the eastern boundary. From Adelaide, follow the Princes Highway along the coast.

VISITOR INFORMATION   The **Goolwa Tourist Information Centre,** BF Lawrie Lane, Goolwa (© 08/8555 1144; www.alexandrina.sa.gov), has information on the area and can book accommodations. It's open from 9am to 5pm daily.

GETTING AROUND   The best operator in the area is **Coorong Nature Tours** (© 08/8574 0037, or 0428/714 793 mobile; www.coorongnaturesours.com), based in Narrung. David Dadd, a delightful, unassuming Cockney who fell in love with the Coorong when he arrived at the age of 11, runs the tours. He offers memorable 1-, 2-, and 3-day tours of the area, with pickup in Meningie or Adelaide. Full-day tours cost A$132 (US$105) per person from Meningie or A$185 (US$148) per person from Adelaide. Reservations are essential.

WHERE TO STAY

Goolwa has plenty of hotels, B&Bs, campgrounds, and trailer parks, as does the main road that runs parallel to the national park. One of the ones I prefer is the **Goolwa**

Camping and Tourist Park, 40 Castle Rd., Goolwa, SA 5214 (© **08/8555 2144**). It has 70 trailer sites and a large area for tents. A two-berth van costs A$25 (US$20) a night, and a six-berth van costs A$35 (US$28) for the first two people; it's A$5 (US$4) for an extra adult or A$3 (US$2.40) for an extra child. Bring your own bedding.

Grahams Castle Resort This former conference center is a AAA-rated three-star backpackers' accommodations. Rooms are very basic, with two single beds, heating, and a shower shared between two rooms. It's very popular with budget groups, so it can get noisy.

Corner of Castle and Bradford sts., Goolwa, SA 5214. © **1800/243 303** in Australia, or 08/8555 3300. Fax 08/8555 3828. 22 units. A$15 (US$12) per person. AE, DC, MC, V. **Amenities:** Restaurant; bar; heated outdoor pool; tennis court; tour desk. *In room:* No phone.

Poltalloch ★★ Smack in the middle of nowhere on the eastern edge of the Coorong, Poltalloch is a working farm property—with plenty of cows, ducks, chickens, and dogs wandering about—that seems more like a village. The whole place is classified as a heritage building by the National Trust of South Australia, and history is evident everywhere, from the cottages once used by farmhands to the giant wooden shearing shed and other outbuildings crammed with relics from the past.

You have a choice of five cottages on the property. The Shearer's Hut is a stone cottage that sleeps up to nine people; the Overseer's stone cottage sleeps up to eight people; the Boundary Rider's Cottage is built of timber, iron, and stone, and sleeps five; and the Station Hand's Cottage sleeps four. The Shearer's Quarters is mainly for large groups and sleeps 12. All of the units are modern and comfortable inside and have their own kitchen facilities and barbecues. I stayed in the Station Hand's Cottage, once the home of Aboriginal workers. I loved the mix of rural feeling and modern conveniences.

There's a private beach if you want to swim in the lake, and guests have the use of a dinghy, a canoe, and a Ping-Pong table. Breakfast provisions are available for A$15 (US$12) per person. Coorong Nature Tours will pick you up from here for no extra charge. There's plenty of bird life all around.

Poltalloch. P.M.B. 3, Narrung via Tailem Bend, SA 5260. © **08/8574 0043**. Fax 08/8574 0065. www.poltalloch.com.au. 5 units. A$110–A$160 (US$88–US$128) per cottage. Extra person A$35 (US$28). MC, V. **Amenities:** Tennis court; use of watersports equipment; nonsmoking rooms. *In room:* A/C, TV, kitchen, fridge, coffeemaker, iron.

12

Melbourne

by Marc Llewellyn

Melbourne (pronounced *Mel*-bun), the capital of Victoria and Australia's second-largest city, is a cultural melting pot. For a start, more people of Greek descent live here than in any other city except Athens. Chinese, Italian, Vietnamese,and Lebanese immigrants have all left their mark. Almost one-third of Melbournians were born overseas or have parents who were born overseas. With such a diverse population, and with trams rattling through the streets and stately European architecture surrounding you, you could forget you're in Australia.

Melbourne, which has a population of well over three million, enjoys a reputation for being at the head of the pack when it comes to shopping, restaurants, fashion, music, nightlife, and cafe culture. It frequently beats out other state capitals in bids for major international concerts,

plays, exhibitions, and sporting events, such as the Formula One Grand Prix.

The city also revels in a healthy rivalry with its northern neighbor, Sydney, but it's interesting to note that almost all Melbournians adore their city—often described as the "most livable" in the world—whereas Sydneysiders are mostly half-hearted in their praise for their home.

Melbourne's roots go back to the 1850s, when gold was found in the surrounding hills. British settlers took up residence and prided themselves on coming freely to their city, rather than having been forced here in convict chains. The city grew wealthy and remained largely a conservative bastion until World War II, when another wave of immigration, this time mainly from southern Europe, made it a more relaxed place.

1 Orientation

ARRIVING

BY PLANE   **Qantas** (© **13 13 13** in Australia; www.qantas.com.au) and discount airline **Virgin Blue** (© **13 67 89** in Australia; www.virginblue.com.au) both fly to Melbourne from all state capitals. Qantas's new discount arm, **Jetstar** (© **13 15 38** in Australia, or 03/8341 4901; www.jetstar.com.au) flies to and from Sydney, Hobart, and Launceston. Check websites above for huge discount offers: for example, A$89 (US$71) return from Sydney to Melbourne. Jetstar flies in and out of **Avalon Airport,** about a 50-minute-drive to Melbourne city center. **Sunbus** (© **03/9689 6880**) meets all flights and runs back to the airport from 167 Franklin Street and the Spencer Street Transit Centre. One-way tickets cost A$17 (US$14) for adults and A$26 (US$21) for a two-way journey. Kids cost A$8 (US$6.40) each way.

Melbourne's main international and domestic airport is **Tullamarine Airport,** 22km (14 miles) northwest of the city center. If you're traveling from Sydney, the flight will take you around 1 hour, 20 minutes. It's a 5-minute walk between the international and domestic terminals. Travelers' information desks, on both levels of the international terminal, are open from 6am until the last flight. The international terminal has snack bars, a restaurant, currency-exchange facilities, duty-free shops, and mailboxes. There's also a post office, open daily from 9am to 5pm; stamps are available from vending machines after hours. ATMs are available at both terminals. Showers are on the first floor of the international area. Baggage carts are free in the international baggage claim hall but cost A$3 (US$2.40) in the parking lot, departure lounge, or domestic terminal. Baggage lockers cost A$4 to A$8 (US$3.20–US$6.40) per day, depending on size. The **Hilton Melbourne Airport** (© **03/9338 2322**) is within walking distance of the terminals.

Thrifty (© **1800/652 008** in Australia, or 03/9330 1522), **Budget** (© **13 27 27** in Australia), **Avis** (© **1800/225 533** in Australia, or 03/9338 1800), **Hertz** (© **13 30 39** in Australia, or 03/9379 9955), and **Delta Europcar** (© **1300/131 390** in Australia, or 03/9417 2311) have airport rental desks. The Tullamarine freeway to and from the airport joins with the CityLink, an electronic tollway system. Drivers need a CityLink pass. A 24-hour pass costs $9.10 (US$7.30). Check with your car-rental company.

Skybus (© **03/9670 7992**; www.skybus.com.au) picks up passengers in front of the baggage claim area every 15 minutes from 7am to 6:30pm; half-hourly from 7pm until 12:30am; and hourly from 1 to 5am.

The trip into the center takes around 35 minutes and costs A$13 (US$10) one-way for adults and A$6 (US$4.80) for children under 17. The service travels direct to

Spencer Street Railway Station, where free shuttle buses transfer you to city hotels. When you want to return to the airport, book the Skybus service a few hours in advance and allow at least 40 minutes for traveling time. Buy from Skybus desks outside the baggage claim areas or at the Travellers Information Desk in the international terminal.

A **taxi** to the city center takes about 30 minutes and costs around A$45 (US$36).

BY TRAIN   Interstate trains arrive at **Spencer Street Railway Station,** Spencer and Little Collins streets (5 blocks from Swanston St. in the city center). Taxis and buses connect with the city.

The **Sydney-Melbourne *XPT*** travels between Australia's two largest cities daily; trip time is 10½ hours. The full fare for economy class is A$110 (US$88) on the day of travel; A$66 (US$83) 1 week in advance; and A$55 (US$44) 2 weeks in advance. First-class fares are A$154 (US$123), A$92 (US$74), and A$77 (US$62), respectively. A first-class sleeper costs $231 (US$185), A$169 (US$135), and A$154 (US$123), respectively. Students presenting an ISIC international student card pay the 2 weeks in advance price in all categories, even if booked on the day of travel. For more information, contact **Countrylink** (© **13 22 32** in Australia; www.countrylink.info).

The ***Overland*** provides daily service to and from Melbourne and Adelaide (trip time: 12 hr.). From Melbourne to Adelaide it's an overnight trip, costing A$175 (US$140) in first class and A$59 (US$47) in a sleeper chair. The day trip from Adelaide to Melbourne costs A$149 (US$119) in first class and A$59 (US$47) in second class. Round-trips cost A$245 (US$196) in first class and A$118 (US$94) in a sleeper chair. For more information, contact **Great Southern Railways** (© **13 21 47** in Australia; www.gsr.com.au).

Daylink services also connect Melbourne with Adelaide. This trip is by train from Melbourne to Bendigo, and by bus from Bendigo to Adelaide. Total trip time is 11 hours, and the fare is A$62 (US$49) for adults and A$31 (US$25) for children. The **Canberra Link** connects Melbourne with the nation's capital; it's a train journey from Melbourne to Wadonga, and bus from there to Canberra. The journey takes around 11 hours and costs A$59 (US$47) for adults, and A$37 (US$30) for kids. First-class fares are around A$20 (US$16) more expensive. For information and reservations, contact **V/Line** (© **13 61 96** in Australia; www.vlinepassenger.com.au).

BY BUS   Several bus companies connect Melbourne with other capitals and regional areas of Victoria. Among the biggest are **Greyhound Australia** (© **13 14 99** in Australia, or 07/4690 9950; www.greyhound.com.au). Coaches serve Melbourne's **Transit Centre,** 58 Franklin St., 2 blocks north of the Spencer Street Railway Station. Trams and taxis serve the station; **V/Line buses** (© **13 61 96** in Australia; www.vlinepassenger.com.au), which travel all over Victoria, depart from the Spencer Street Bus Terminal.

BY CAR   You can drive from Sydney to Melbourne along the Hume Highway (a straight trip of about 9½ hr.), via Goulburn in NSW (good for supplies), and Wangaratta in Victoria (where you can detour into the Victorian Alps if you wish). Another route is along the coastal Princes Highway, for which you will need a minimum of 2 days, with stops. For information on all aspects of road travel in Victoria, contact the **Royal Automotive Club of Victoria** (© **03/9607 2222;** www.racv.com.au).

VISITOR INFORMATION

The first stop on any visitor's itinerary should be the **Melbourne Visitor Centre,** Federation Square, Swanston and Flinders streets (② **03/9658 9658;** www.thats melbourne.com.au). The center serves as a one-stop shop for tourism information, accommodations and tour bookings, event ticketing, public transport information, and ticket sales. Also here are an ATM, Internet terminals, and interactive multimedia providing information on Melbourne and Victoria. The center is open daily from 9am to 6pm. The Melbourne Greeter Service also operates from the Melbourne Visitor Centre. This service is available in 20 languages and connects visitors to enthusiastic local volunteers who offer free one-on-one, half-day orientation tours of the city. Book at least 3 days in advance (② **03/9658 9658;** greeter@melbourne.vic.gov.au). The Melbourne Visitor Centre also operates staffed information booths in Bourke Street Mall.

You'll find some information services at **Information Victoria,** 356 Collins St. (② **1300/366 356** in Australia). In the central city area, also look for **Melbourne's City Ambassadors**—people, usually volunteers, who give tourist information and directions.

Good websites about the city include CitySearch Melbourne, http://melbourne.city search.com.au; as well as the official City of Melbourne site, www.melbourne.vic. gov.au; and the official tourism site for the city, www.visitmelbourne.com, and a locally run site, www.onlymelbourne.com.au.

CITY LAYOUT

Melbourne is on the Yarra River and stretches inland from Port Philip Bay, which lies to its south. On a map, you'll see a distinct central oblong area surrounded by Flinders Street to the south, Latrobe Street to the north, Spring Street to the east, and Spencer Street to the west. Cutting north-to-south through its center are the two main shopping thoroughfares, Swanston Street and Elizabeth Street. Cross streets between these major thoroughfares include Bourke Street Mall, a pedestrian-only shopping promenade. If you continue south along Swanston Street and over the river, it turns into St. Kilda Road, which runs to the coast. Melbourne's various urban "villages," including South Yarra, Richmond, Carlton, and Fitzroy, surround the city center. The seaside suburb of St. Kilda is known for its diverse restaurants. If you've visited Sydney, you'll find Melbourne's city center smaller and far less congested with people and cars.

NEIGHBORHOODS IN BRIEF

Melbourne is huge. At more than 6,110 sq. km (2,383 sq. miles), it's one of the biggest cities in the world. Below are the areas of most interest to visitors.

City Center Made up of a grid of streets north of the Yarra River, the city center is bordered by Flinders, Latrobe, Spring, and Spencer streets. There's some good shopping and charming cafes, and in recent years an active nightlife has sprung up with the opening of a swath of funky bars and restaurants playing live and recorded music to suit all ages. The gateway to the city is the brown Flinders Street Station, with its dome and clock tower, flanked by the stunning new Federation Square precinct.

Chinatown This colorful section centers on Little Bourke Street between Swanston and Exhibition streets. The area marks Australia's oldest permanent Chinese settlement, dating from the 1850s, when a few boardinghouses catered to Chinese prospectors lured by gold rushes. Plenty of cheap restaurants crowd its alleyways. Tram: Any to the city.

Carlton North of the city center, Carlton is a rambling suburb famous for the Italian restaurants along Lygon Street with outdoor seating—though the quality of the food varies. It's the home of the University of Melbourne, so there's a healthy student scene. From Bourke Street Mall, count on a 15-minute walk to the restaurant strip. Tram: 1 or 22 from Swanston Street.

Fitzroy A ruggedly bohemian place, 2km (1¼ miles) north of the city center, Fitzroy is raw and funky, filled with students and artists and popular for people-watching. Fitzroy revolves around Brunswick Street, with its cheap restaurants, busy cafes, late-night bookshops, art galleries, and pubs. Around the corner, on Johnston Street, is a growing Spanish quarter with tapas bars, flamenco restaurants, and Spanish clubs. Tram: 11 from Collins Street.

Richmond One of Melbourne's earliest settlements is a multicultural quarter noted for its historic streets and back lanes. Victoria Street is reminiscent of Ho Chi Minh City, with Vietnamese sights, sounds, aromas, and restaurants everywhere. Bridge Road is a discount-fashion precinct. Tram: 48 or 75 from Flinders Street to Bridge Road; 70 from Batmans Avenue at Princes Bridge to Swan Street; 109 from Bourke Street to Victoria Street.

Southgate & Southbank This flashy entertainment district on the banks of the Yarra River opposite Flinders Street Station (linked by pedestrian bridges) is home to the Crown Casino, Australia's largest gaming venue. Southbank has a myriad of themed restaurants, bars, cafes, nightclubs, cinemas, and designer shops. On the city

side of the river is the Melbourne Aquarium. All are a 10-minute stroll from Flinders Street Station. Tram: 8 from Swanston Street.

Docklands Near the city center, at the rear of the Spencer Street station, this industrial area has become the biggest development in Melbourne. NewQuay on the waterfront has a diverse range of restaurants, shops, and cinemas. To celebrate the dominance of the Australian Rules Football, Melbournians recently constructed a 52,000-seat stadium, the Telstra Dome, to house their favorite game. Docklands is accessible by the free city circle tram or by river cruise boats.

St. Kilda Hip and bohemian in a shabby-chic sort of way, this bayside suburb (6km/3¾ miles south of the city center) has Melbourne's highest concentration of restaurants, ranging from glitzy to cheap, as well as some superb cake shops and delis. Historically it was Melbourne's red-light district. The Esplanade hugs a pleasant "beach" (with brown water) and is the scene of a lively arts and crafts market on Sundays. Acland Street houses many restaurants. Check out Luna Park, one of the world's oldest fun parks, built in 1912, and ride the historic wooden roller coaster. Tram: 10 or 12 from Collins Street; 15 or 16 from Swanston Street; 96 from Bourke Street.

South Yarra/Prahan This posh part of town abounds with boutiques, cinemas, nightclubs, and galleries. Chapel Street is famous for its upscale eateries and designer-fashion houses, while Commercial Road is popular with the gay and lesbian community. Off Chapel Street in Prahan is Greville Street, a bohemian enclave of retro boutiques and music outlets. Every Sunday from noon to 5pm the Greville Street Market offers arts, crafts, old clothes, and jewelry. Tram: 8 or 72 from Swanston Street.

South Melbourne One of the city's oldest working-class districts, South Melbourne is known for its historic buildings, old-fashioned pubs and hotels, and markets. Tram: 12 from Collins Street; 1 from Swanston Street.

The River District The muddy-looking Yarra River runs southeast past the fabulous Royal Botanic Gardens and near other attractions such as the Victorian Arts Centre, the National Gallery of Victoria, the Sidney Myer Music Bowl, and the Melbourne Cricket Ground, all described later in this chapter. Birrarung Marr is the first new major parkland in Melbourne in over 100 years.

Williamstown A lack of extensive development has left this outer waterfront suburb with a rich architectural heritage. It centers on Ferguson Street and Nelson Place—both reminiscent of old England. On the Strand overlooking the sea is a line of bistros and restaurants, and a World War II warship museum. Ferry: from Southgate, the World Trade Center, or St. Kilda Pier.

2 Getting Around

BY PUBLIC TRANSPORTATION

Trams, trains, and buses are operated by several private companies, including the National Bus Company, Yarra Trams, and Connex, to name a few. Generally, both tourists and locals travel around the city and inner suburbs by tram.

BY TRAM 🚋 Melbourne has the oldest tram network in the world. Trams are an essential part of the city, and a major cultural icon. Several hundred trams run over 325km (202 miles) of track. Instead of phasing out this non-smoggy method of transport, Melbourne is busily expanding the network.

Tram travel within the city and to all suburbs mentioned in this chapter costs A\$2.20 (US\$1.80) for adults, A\$1.20 (US95¢) for children for a single journey. Or you can buy a **2-Hour Metcard,** good for unlimited transport on buses or trams for up to 2 hours, for A\$3.10 (US\$2.50) for adults and A\$1.80 (US\$1.45) for children. If you plan to pack in the sightseeing, try the **Zone 1 Metcard Daily ticket,** which allows travel on all transport (trams and trains) within the city and close surrounding suburbs mentioned in this chapter from 5:30am to midnight (when transportation stops). It costs A\$5.90 (US\$4.70) for adults and A\$3.10 (US\$2.15) for children.

Buy single-trip and 2-hour tram tickets at ticket machines on trams, special ticket offices (such as at the tram terminal on Elizabeth St., near the corner of Flinders St.), at most newsdealers, and at Metcard vending machines at many railway stations. A Metcard needs to be validated by the Metcard Validator machine on the tram, on the station platform, or on the bus before each journey; the only exception to this is the 2-Hour Metcard purchased from a vending machine on a tram, which is automatically validated for that journey only. Vending machines on trams only accept coins—but give change—whereas larger vending machines at train stations accept coins and paper money and give change up to A\$10 (US\$8).

You can pick up a free route map from the Melbourne Visitor Centre, Federation Square, or the **Met Information Centre,** 103 Elizabeth St., at the corner of Collins Street (© **13 16 38** in Australia; www.metlinkmelbourne.com.au), which is open Monday through Friday from 8:30am to 4:30pm, and Saturday from 9am to 1pm.

The **City Circle Tram** is the best way to get around the center of Melbourne—and it's free. The burgundy-and-cream trams travel a circular route between all the major central attractions, and past shopping malls and arcades. The trams run, in both directions, every 10 minutes between 10am and 6pm, except Good Friday and December 25. The trams run along all the major thoroughfares including Flinders and Spencer streets. Burgundy signs mark City Circle Tram stops.

Normal trams stop at numbered green-and-gold tram-stop signs, sometimes in the middle of the road (so beware of oncoming traffic!). To get off the tram, press the red button near handrails or pull the cord above your head.

BY EXPLORER BUS

Melbourne Explorer Gray Line (© 1300/858 687 in Australia) operates buses that pick up and drop off at 21 stops around the city, including the Melbourne Aquarium, Crown Casino, Queen Victoria Market, Captain Cook's Cottage, Chinatown, Melbourne Zoo, and the Botanic Gardens, among others. The full circuit takes an hour. There's full commentary on board. You can hop on and off during the day. A bus returns to each stop half-hourly. The first bus leaves Town Hall on Swanston Street at 9:30am and the last at 3pm. Tickets cost A$36 (US$29) for adults, A$18 (US$14) for children under 14. Buy from the driver or at the little tour booth outside Melbourne Town Hall.

BY BOAT

Melbourne River Cruises (© 03/9614 1215; www.melbcruises.com.au) offer a range of boat trips up and down the Yarra River, including to Williamstoen and Docklands. It's a really interesting way to get a feel for the city and the tours include commentaries. One-way tours cost from A$17 (US$13) (return fare A$29/US$23) for adults and A$9.80 (US$7.80) (return A$15/US$12) for kids. Family fares are also available. Call ahead to confirm cruise departure times, as they change, and pick up tickets from the Blue Melbourne River cruises kiosks at Federation Square Riverfront (opposite Flinders St. Station).

BY TAXI

Cabs are plentiful in the city, but it may be difficult to hail one in the city center late on Friday and Saturday night. Taxi companies include **Silver Top** (© 13 10 08 in Australia, or 03/9345 3455), **Embassy** (© 13 17 55 in Australia, or 03/9277 3444), and **Black Cabs Combined** (© 13 22 27 in Australia). A large, illuminated rooftop light indicates that a cab is free.

BY CAR

Driving in Melbourne is not always fun. Roads can be confusing, there are trams and aggressive drivers everywhere, and there is a strange rule about turning right from the left lane at major intersections in the downtown center (which leaves the left-hand lane free for oncoming trams and through traffic). Here, you must wait for the lights to turn amber before turning. Also, you must always stop behind a tram if it stops, because passengers usually step directly into the road. Add to this the general lack of parking and expensive hotel valet parking, and you'll know why it's better to get on a tram instead. For road rules, pick up a copy of the Victorian Road Traffic handbook from bookshops or from a **Vic Roads** office (© 13 11 71 in Australia for the nearest office).

Major car-rental companies, all with offices at Tullamarine Airport, include **Avis,** 400 Elizabeth St. (℃ 03/9663 6366); **Budget,** 398 Elizabeth St. (℃ 03/9203 4844); **Hertz,** 97 Franklin St. (℃ 03/9698 2555); **Thrifty,** 390 Elizabeth St. (℃ 03/9663 5200); and **National,** 110 A'beckett St. (℃ 13 10 45 in Australia). Expect to pay at least A$40 (US$32) a day for a small car.

FAST FACTS: Melbourne

American Express The main office is at 235 Collins St. (℃ **03/9633 6333**). It's open Monday through Friday from 9am to 5:30pm, and Saturday from 9am to noon.

Business Hours In general, stores are open Monday through Wednesday and Saturday from 9am to 5:30pm, Thursday from 9am to 6pm, Friday from 9am to 9pm, and Sunday from 10am to 5pm. The larger department stores stay open on Thursday till 6pm and Friday until 9pm. Banks are open Monday through Thursday from 9:30am to 4pm, and Friday from 9:30am to 5pm.

Camera Repair **Vintech Camera Repairs,** 5th Floor, 358 Lonsdale St. (℃ **03/9602 1820,** or 0418-515 662 mobile), is well regarded.

Consulates The following English-speaking countries have consulates in Melbourne: United States, Level 6, 553 St. Kilda Rd. (℃ **03/9526 5900**); United Kingdom, Level 17, 90 Collins St. (℃ **03/9650 4155**); and Canada, 1st Floor, 123 Camberwell Rd., Hawthorn (℃ **03/9811 9999**).

Dentist Call the **Dental Emergency Service** (℃ **03/9341 0222**) for emergency referral to a local dentist.

Doctor The "casualty" department at the **Royal Melbourne Hospital,** Grattan Street, Parkville (℃ **03/9342 7000**), responds to emergencies. The **Traveller's Medical & Vaccination Centre,** 2nd Floor, 393 Little Bourke St. (℃ **03/9602 5788**), offers full vaccination and travel medical services.

Emergencies In an emergency, call ℃ **000** for police, ambulance, or the fire department.

Internet Access There are numerous Internet cafes along Elizabeth Street, between Flinders and Latrobe streets, and also around Flinders Lane, and Little Bourke Street in the Chinatown area. Most are open from early until well into the night.

Lost Property Contact the nearest police station or visit the Melbourne Town Hall, Swanston Street (℃ **03/9658 9774**).

Pharmacies (Chemist Shops) The **McGibbony & Beaumont Pharmacy** is in the Grand Hyatt hotel complex, 123 Collins St. (℃ **03/9650 1823**). It's open Monday through Thursday from 8am to 6:30pm, Friday from 8am to 7pm, Saturday from 9:30am to 2:30pm, and Sunday from 9:30am to noon.

Post Office The well-known General Post Office (GPO) at the corner of Bourke Street Mall and Elizabeth Street has closed. The post office at 230 Elizabeth St. (℃ **13 13 18** in Australia) is open Monday through Friday 8:30am to 5:30pm, Saturday 9am to 4pm, and Sunday 10am to 4pm.

Safety St. Kilda might be coming up in the world, but walking there alone at night still isn't wise. Parks and gardens can also be risky at night, as can the area around the King Street nightclubs.

Taxes Sales tax, where it exists, is included in the price, as is the 10% Goods and Services Tax (GST). There is no hotel tax in Melbourne.

Telephones For directory assistance, call © **1223**; for international directory assistance, call © **1225**.

Weather Call © **1196** for recorded weather information.

3 Where to Stay

Getting a room is generally easy enough on weekends, when business travelers are back home. You need to book well in advance, however, during the city's hallmark events (say, the weekend before the Melbourne Cup, and during the Grand Prix and the Ford Australia Open). Hostels in the St. Kilda area tend to fill up quickly in December and January.

Once considered dead after offices closed for the day, the city center has been rejuvenated in recent years, and you'll feel right in the heart of the action if you stay there. Otherwise, the suburbs are all exciting satellites, with good street life, restaurants, and pubs—and just a quick tram ride from the city center. Transportation from the airport to the suburbs is a little more expensive and complicated than to the city center, however.

If you arrive without booked accommodations, contact either of the **travelers' information desks** (© **03/9297 1814**), on both floors of the international terminal and open daily from 6am to the last flight. Or try the **Best of Victoria Booking Service,** Melbourne Visitor Centre, Federation Square (© **03/9650 3663**), open weekdays from 9am to 6pm and weekends from 9am to 5pm.

IN THE CITY CENTER
VERY EXPENSIVE

Crown Towers ★★ One of Melbourne's finest hotels, Crown Towers is part of the Crown Casino complex, on the banks of the Yarra River. The hotel is grand and impressive. People often gasp as they enter the glittering lobby paved in black marble. The complex has an enormous collection of gambling machines (called "pokies" in Australia), as well as gaming tables. Upstairs in the hotel, standard guest rooms are cozy. Superior guest rooms occupy floors 5 to 15, and those above the 10th floor have spectacular city views. Deluxe rooms, which run up to the 28th floor, are similar, and all have great views. The hotel is a 10-minute walk from the main shopping streets; trams stop right outside.

Crown Casino offers 24-hour gambling. The 900-seat Showroom features live entertainment nightly, and a 14-screen cinema complex and three cabaret theaters provide additional activities. There are plenty of eateries and designer shops around here, too.

8 Whiteman St., Southbank, Melbourne, VIC 3006. © **1800/811 653** in Australia, or 03/9292 6868. Fax 03/9292 6600. www.crownltd.com.au. 500 units. A$720 (US$576) double; A$1,150–A$1,250 (US$920–US$1,000) suite. Extra person A$55 (US$44). Children under 12 stay free in parent's room. AE, DC, MC, V. Parking A$25 (US$20). **Amenities:**

Where to Stay in Central Melbourne

Adelphi **11**
Albert Heights Executive Apartments **3**
Crown Towers **15**
Georgian Court Guest House **8**
Grand Hotel **14**
Grand Hyatt Melbourne **10**
Hotel Lindrum **9**
Hotel Sofitel **7**
Ibis Melbourne **1**
Kingsgate Hotel **13**
The Nunnery **4**
Oakford/Somerset Executive Apartments **5**
Ramada Melbourne **12**
Toad Hall **2**
The Windsor **6**

Victoria
Melbourne

3 restaurants; Olympic-size indoor pool; health club; concierge; tour desk; car-rental desk; business center; 24-hr. room service; massage; babysitting; laundry service; dry cleaning; nonsmoking rooms; executive rooms. *In room:* A/C, TV w/pay movies, dataport, minibar, coffeemaker, hair dryer, iron.

Grand Hyatt Melbourne ★★

The Grand Hyatt is a glitzy, glamorous affair, situated in the best part of town, just a short walk from Swanston Street, Elizabeth Street, Chinatown, and public transport. Rooms are large and luxurious, and come with a nice-size marble bathroom and all the details you'd expect from a five-star establishment. Prices vary with the view over the city, which can be almost Hong Kong–like from the top floors. Regency Club guests get breakfast, snacks all day, and sushi and drinks in the evening. **Monsoon's** is a popular late-night disco in the hotel.

123 Collins St., Melbourne, VIC 3000. (C) **13 12 34** in Australia, 800/233-1234 in the U.S. and Canada, or 03/8843 1300. Fax 03/9650 3491. www.melbourne.grand.hyatt.com. 547 units. A$450 (US$360) Hyatt Guest double; A$570 (US$456) deluxe double; A$600 (US$480) Regency Club double; A$840–A$3,300 (US$672–US$2,640) suite. Extra person A$55 (US$44). Children under 18 stay free in parent's room. Ask about weekend rates and packages. AE, DC, MC, V. Parking A$4 (US$3.20). **Amenities:** 2 restaurants; large indoor pool; 2 outdoor lit tennis courts; health club; concierge; tour desk; car-rental desk; business center; 24-hr. room service; in-room massage; babysitting; laundry service; dry cleaning; nonsmoking rooms; executive-level rooms. *In room:* A/C, TV w/pay movies, dataport, minibar, coffeemaker, hair dryer.

Hotel Lindrum ★★ *(Finds)*

If you like your hotels stylish and contemporary, then the Hotel Lindrum is for you. It's quite typical of the new wave of modern hotels that emphasize trendy interior design. Standard rooms, if you can call them that, have a queen-size bed or two singles, lots of hardwood, soft lighting, and forest greens—and even a CD player. Superior rooms have king-size beds and lovely polished wood floorboards, and deluxe rooms have wonderful views across to the Botanic Gardens through large bay windows. The hotel boasts a smart restaurant and a cigar bar with an open fire.

26 Flinders St., Melbourne, VIC 3000. (C) **03/9668 1111.** www.hotellindrum.com.au. 59 units. A$355 (US$172) standard double; A$395 (US$316) superior room; A$405 (US$324) deluxe room. AE, DC, MC, V. Parking A$15 (US$12) off-site. **Amenities:** Restaurant; cigar bar; billiard room; laundry service; nonsmoking rooms; rooms for guests w/limited mobility. *In room:* A/C, TV w/free movies, dataport, coffeemaker, iron.

Sofitel Melbourne ★★

I guarantee you'll like this beautiful luxury hotel, located in the best area of Collins Street, just a short walk from the major shopping and business district. The hotel features a glass-topped atrium that allows natural light to flood in and a great bar with wonderful city views on the 35th floor. Breakfasts in **Café La** are fabulous, and also come with views. Rooms are quite large and very pleasant and were renovated in late 2004 and throughout 2005 (hence the massive room-rate rise since the last edition of *Frommer's Australia*). They come with a flatscreen TV, all the latest high-tech gizmos, and the most comfortable king-size bed I've ever slept in. The service is impressive, and the only fault I could find is that there seem to be far too few elevators, which can get annoying after a couple of days.

25 Collins St., Melbourne, VIC 3000. (C) **03/9653 0000.** Fax 03/9650 4261. www.sofitelmelbourne.com. 363 units. A$450 (US$368) double; A$600 (US$480) suite. Extra person A$50 (US$40). 1 child under 12 stays free in parent's room. Ask about weekend rates and packages. AE, DC, MC, V. Parking A$26 (US$21). **Amenities:** 2 restaurants; bar; exercise room; Jacuzzi; concierge; tour desk; car-rental desk; business center; shopping arcade; 24-hr. room service; massage studio; babysitting; laundry service; dry cleaning; nonsmoking rooms. *In room:* A/C, TV/VCR, dataport, minibar, coffeemaker, hair dryer, iron.

The Windsor ★★

The Windsor is Australia's only surviving authentic "grand" hotel. It opened in 1883 (as "The Grand") and was restored to its original condition by Oberoi Hotels International. This charmingly upper-crust establishment oozes sophistication and has hosted such notable guests as Lauren Bacall, Muhammad Ali, and Omar Sharif. The lobby is luxuriously carpeted, and the staff friendly and efficient. Standard rooms are comfortable, with high ceilings and tasteful furnishings. Each has a good-size bathroom. Deluxe rooms are twice as big, and many have striking views of Parliament House and the Melbourne Cathedral across the way. Suites are huge and furnished with antiques. Guests can choose from 10 types of pillows, including an aromatherapy version filled with rose petals and herbs. The Windsor is a member of both Leading Hotels of the World and Small Luxury Hotels of the World.

The Grand Ballroom, with ornate ceilings, leather furniture, gorgeous carpets, and plenty of gold leaf, is a most impressive place to eat; it's open to nonguests for buffet lunch Friday at noon.

103 Spring St., Melbourne, VIC 3000. 🕐 **1800/033 100** in Australia, or 03/9633 6000. Fax 03/9633 6001. www.thewindsor.com.au. 180 units. A$500 (US$400) superior double; A$580 (US$464) deluxe double; A$650–A$2,400 (US$520–US$1,920) suite. AE, DC, MC, V. Parking A$20 (US$16). **Amenities:** Restaurant; 2 bars; health club; concierge; business center; 24-hr. room service; babysitting; laundry service; dry cleaning. *In room:* A/C, TV w/pay movies, minibar, coffeemaker, hair dryer, iron.

EXPENSIVE

Adelphi Hotel It may be worth staying in this designer boutique hotel, a minute's walk from the city center, just for the experience of taking a dip in its top-floor 25m (82-ft.) lap pool, which juts out from the end of the building and overhangs the streets below. The pool has a glass bottom, so you can watch pedestrians below as you float. The rooms are similarly modern, with colorful leather seating and lots of burnished metal. Deluxe rooms differ from the so-called "Premier King" rooms in that they come with a bathtub. Executive rooms come with a separate lounge. Within the hotel is **Ezard**, a well-regarded restaurant offering Modern Australian fare. You might find some of the staff members quite self-important—just smile and humor them. At least one Frommer's *Australia* reader has complained that the place needs work on its service—taking away used food trays from outside doors and laundry carts loaded with dirty linens sooner.

187 Flinders Lane, Melbourne, VIC 3000. 🕐 **1800/800 177** in Australia, or 03/9650 7555. Fax 03/9650 2710. www.adelphi.com.au. 34 units (most with shower only). A$325 (US$260) Premier King Room; A$375 (US$300) deluxe double; A$625 (US$500) executive suite. Rates include breakfast. Extra person A$65 (US$52). AE, DC, MC, V. Parking A$14 (US$11). **Amenities:** Restaurant; cafe/bar; heated outdoor pool; exercise room; sauna; bike rental; concierge; tour desk; business center; babysitting; dry cleaning; nonsmoking rooms; executive rooms. *In room:* A/C, TV, DVD/CD, dataport, minibar, coffeemaker, hair dryer, iron.

Grand Hotel 🏨🏨 This majestic former railway department headquarters is striking for its remarkable scale and imposing Italianate facade. Building started on the six-story site in 1887, and additions were still being made in 1958. It became a hotel in 1997 and is now managed by Sofitel. Suites have plush red Pullman carpets, a full kitchen with a dishwasher, a CD player, a second TV in the bedroom, and great views over the railway tracks and onto the new Docklands area beyond—though rooms are whisper quiet. All rooms are similar but vary in size; some have balconies. Many of the suites are split level, with bedrooms on the second floor.

33 Spencer St., Melbourne, VIC 3000. 🕐 **1300/361 455** in Australia, or 03/9611 4567. Fax 03/9611 4655. www.accorhotel.com. 118 units. A$209–A$435 (US$167–US$348) studio suite; A$229–A$475 (US$183–US$380) 1-bedroom suite; A$364–A$590 (US$291–US$472) 2-bedroom suite; A$800 (US$640) 3-bedroom suite. Extra person A$44 (US$35). Children under 14 stay free in parent's room. Ask about weekend and seasonal packages. AE, DC, MC,

V. Parking A$13 (US$10). Tram: 48 or 75 from Flinders St. **Amenities:** Restaurant; bar; golf course nearby; exercise room; Jacuzzi; sauna; concierge; tour desk; car-rental desk; 24-hr. room service; in-room massage; babysitting; laundry service; dry cleaning; nonsmoking rooms. *In room:* A/C, TV w/pay movies, dataport, kitchen, minibar, fridge, coffeemaker, hair dryer, iron.

Ramada Melbourne ★ *Finds*   Opened in 2003, this compact four-star hotel opposite Flinders Street Railway Station offers light and comfortable rooms. It's quiet and welcoming and is a short walk to the main shopping streets. It's a stroll away from Federation Square, the Crown Casino Entertainment Complex, and the Southbank district. You can get some wonderful packages, including a weekend special for A$145 (US$116) per night with breakfast.

270 Flinders St., Melbourne, VIC 3000. ℂ **1300/726 232** in Australia, or 03/9654 6888. Fax 03/9654 0368. www.ramadamelbourne.com.au. 179 units. A$340 (US$272) standard room; A$350 (US$280) with water views. Extra person A$45 (US$36). Ask about packages. AE, DC, MC, V. Parking A$20 (US$16). **Amenities:** Restaurant; bar; business center; 24-hr. room service; nonsmoking rooms. *In room:* A/C, TV w/pay movies, high-speed Internet, minibar, coffeemaker, hair dryer, iron, safe.

MODERATE

Ibis Melbourne ★ *Value*   A good deal, the Ibis is next door to the bus station and a short walk from the central shopping areas. Rooms in the AAA-rated four-star hotel are spacious, immaculate, and bright, and have attached showers. Apartments have kitchenettes and tubs. Guests can use of the swimming pool, sauna, and Jacuzzi up the road at the historic Melbourne City Baths.

15–21 Therry St., Melbourne, VIC 3000. ℂ **1300/656 565** in Australia, 800/221-4542 in the U.S. and Canada, 0800/44 44 22 in New Zealand, or 03/9639 2399. Fax 03/9662 9263. www.ibishotel.com. 250 units (some with shower only). A$109–A$119 (US$87–US$95) double; A$149 (US$119) 1-bedroom apt. Extra person A$30 (US$24). Children under 12 stay free in parent's room. Ask about packages. AE, DC, MC, V. Parking A$11 (US$8.80). **Amenities:** Free use of nearby pool, sauna, and Jacuzzi. *In room:* A/C, TV, minibar, coffeemaker, iron.

Oakford/Somerset Executive Apartments ★★   These apartments, in an 1884 National Trust–listed building, are some of the best I've seen. They are a good alternative for travelers who like to cook their own food. The spacious apartments come with full kitchens, including a dishwasher, and maid service; three-bedroom units are all split-level. Those in the south block are older in style but have contemporary furnishings. Those in the north block are new and a little more upscale; they're farther back from the road, too. More than half the units have a tub, but specify when booking if you want to make sure you get one.

Another option to consider is the well-placed **Oakford on Lygon** ★★, 2–9 Finlay St., Carlton, VIC 3053 (ℂ **03/8341 4777**), about a 10-minute walk from the city center. The rooms here have no kitchen but offer great value, and I highly recommend them. The room rates below are the prices you can get booked over the Oakford website, the cheapest option.

24 Little Bourke St., Melbourne, VIC 3000. ℂ **1800/818 237** in Australia, or 03/9663 2888. Fax 03/9639 1537. www.oakford.com. 82 apts. A$108 studio (US$86); A$110 (US$88) 1-bedroom apt; A$148 (US$118) 2-bedroom apt; A$178 (US$142) 3-bedroom apt. Extra person A$22 (US$18). Ask about weekend packages, corporate rates, and long-term discounts. AE, DC, MC, V. Parking A$10–A$20 (US$8–US$16). **Amenities:** Restaurant; small heated outdoor pool; exercise room; Jacuzzi; sauna; business center; limited room service; dry cleaning; nonsmoking rooms. *In room:* A/C, TV w/pay movies, dataport, kitchen, minibar, fridge, coffeemaker, hair dryer, iron.

INEXPENSIVE

Kingsgate Hotel   A 10-minute walk from the city, this interesting hotel feels like a basic B&B, though a total refurbishment—"to attract airline staff"—recently gave it a better look. From the outside, it resembles a terrace building, but inside it's a maze of corridors and rooms. The staff is very friendly. The least expensive economy rooms are for backpackers only. They have two single beds and a hand basin; there's barely enough room to swing a backpack. Pricier executive rooms are light and spacious, with double beds or two twins as well as en-suite bathrooms. The 15 or so deluxe quad rooms have double beds and two singles. A cooked breakfast costs A$7 (US$5.60) extra. Check the hotel's website for really good deals.

131 King St., Melbourne, VIC 3000. ✆ **1300/734 171** in Australia, or 03/9629 4171. Fax 03/9629 7110. www.kings gatehotel.com.au. 225 units, 104 with bathroom. A$99–A$129 (US$80–US$103) double; A$119–A$149 (US$95–US$119) triple; A$169 (US$135) deluxe quad. AE, DC, MC, V. Parking A$7 (US$5.60) at Crown Casino, a 5-min. walk away. **Amenities:** Tour desk; executive-level rooms. *In room:* TV.

Toad Hall ⋆ *Value* "It's one of the best in Australia," one well-traveled guest said of Toad Hall. I have to agree; this 1858 mansion offers excellent value. It's just down the road from Queen Victoria Market, Melbourne Central train/tram station, and only a few minutes' walk to the main shopping areas. Dorms are segregated by sex, with four to six bunk beds in each. Doubles and twins are small but, like the dorms, clean and quite comfortable, with springy beds. I really liked the large communal kitchen, dining room, and courtyard.

441 Elizabeth St., Melbourne, VIC 3000. ✆ **03/9600 9010.** Fax 03/9600 9013. www.Toadhall-hotel.com.au. 85 dorm beds in 16 rooms; 8 doubles, 4 with bathroom; 12 twin rooms, 2 with bathroom. A$70 (US$56) double/twin without bathroom; A$90 (US$72) double/twin with bathroom; A$25 (US$20) dorm bed. MC, V. Parking A$6 (US$4.80). **Amenities:** Tour desk; coin-op laundry; nonsmoking rooms; 3 TV lounges. *In room:* Fridge, coffeemaker.

IN CARLTON

Albert Heights Executive Apartments ⋆ For good, moderately priced accommodations with cooking facilities (so you can cut down on meal costs), you can't go wrong with the Albert Heights, a favorite of American travelers. It's in a nice area of Melbourne, about a 10-minute walk from the city center. There are parks at each end of the street. Each self-contained unit in the brick building is large and attractive. If you want your own space or are traveling with your family, you can use the sofa bed in the living room. Standard apartments come with a double bed; deluxe one-bedroom apartments with a queen-size bed; and deluxe two-bedroom apartments with a queen-size and two large singles. Each unit comes with a full kitchen with a microwave (no conventional oven), dining area, and large bathroom. Check the website for major discounts.

83 Albert St., East Melbourne, VIC 3002. ✆ **1800/800 117** in Australia, or 03/9419 0955. Fax 03/9419 9517. www.albertheights.com.au. 34 units. A$170 (US$136) standard apt; A$215 (US$172) deluxe 1-bed apt; A$235 (US$188); deluxe 2-bed apt. Extra adult A$20 (US$16); extra child A$15 (US$12). Ask about special deals. AE, DC, MC, V. Free parking. Tram: 42 or 109. **Amenities:** Jacuzzi; tour desk; car-rental desk; babysitting; laundry service; dry cleaning; nonsmoking rooms. *In room:* A/C, TV, dataport, kitchen, fridge, coffeemaker, hair dryer, iron, safe.

Georgian Court Guest House The comfortable Georgian Court's appearance hasn't changed much since it was built in 1910—and it still fits like a favorite shirt. The sitting and dining rooms have high ceilings and offer old-world atmosphere. The guest rooms, furnished with little more than pine furniture and a double bed, still have charm. The Georgian Court is behind the Hilton, a 15-minute walk from the city center. One room comes with a queen-size bed and a Jacuzzi.

21 George St., East Melbourne, VIC 3002. ✆ **03/9419 6353.** Fax 03/9416 0895. www.georgiancourt.com.au 31 units, 21 with bathroom. A$109 (US$87) double without bathroom; A$129 (US$103) double with bathroom; A$139 (US$111) queen spa room. A$10–A$20 (US$8–US$16) surcharge during busy periods. Extra adult A$20 (US$16),

extra child under 15 A$12 (US$9.60). Rates include buffet breakfast. AE, DC, MC, V. Free parking. Tram: 75 from Flinders St., or 48 from Spencer St. **Amenities:** Access to nearby health club; tour desk; car-rental desk; coin-op laundry; dry cleaning; nonsmoking rooms. *In room:* A/C, TV, fridge, coffeemaker, hair dryer, iron, safe.

IN FITZROY

The Nunnery Guesthouse ★★ *Value* This former convent offers pleasant accommodations just a short tram ride from the city center. On the city's edge, the Nunnery is perfectly situated near the restaurant and nightlife scenes of Brunswick and Lygon streets, in nearby Carlton. This informal, friendly place is well suited to couples and families. The Nunnery is split into three separate buildings, the Guesthouse, the Townhouse and the Nunnery Budget Accommodation. Built in the 1860s, the Guesthouse has high ceilings, handmade light-fittings, polished floorboards, marble fireplaces and a hand-turned staircase. The Townhouse was built in the early 1900s, and is comfy, stylish and decorated with tasteful furnishings and artwork. Rooms in both buildings have wooden floors, rugs, leafy views, and are quite lovely. All rooms share bathrooms. There are no elevators. The Budget Accommodation is in the former home of the Daughters of Charity, built in the 1880s. It features a grand staircase, stained glass windows and religious artwork. The rooms are simple (some come with a TV) but pleasant, and there's dorm accommodation too. All rooms are nonsmoking.

116 Nicholson St., Fitzroy, Melbourne, VIC 3065. © **1800/032 635** in Australia, or 03/9419 8637. Fax 03/9417 7736. www.nunnery.com.au. 30 units, none with bathroom. Guesthouse A$100 (US$80) double; A$120 (US$) family. Breakfast included. Townhouse A$110–$125 double. /Backpackers' section A$23–$27 (US$18–US$22) bunk rooms; A$85 (US$56) double; A$95 triple. Guesthouse rates include breakfast. MC, V. Free parking (reservation required). Tram: 96 to stop 13 (East Brunswick). **Amenities:** Tour desk; car-rental desk; kitchen; lounge; coin-op laundry. *In room:* TV.

IN ST. KILDA

Fountain Terrace ★★ *Finds* Built in 1880, Fountain Terrace has been lovingly restored to its former glory by Penny and Heikki Minkkinen. This boutique guesthouse has real character and is a wonderful alternative to traditional city hotels. It's on a tree-lined street just a few minutes' walk from the sea and to the many restaurants on Fitzroy and Acland streets. It's very classy inside with comfortable communal areas, including a sunny drawing room where breakfast is served at an antique refectory table. The rooms, which are named after famous Australian writers, artists, and pioneers, have all those classic old-fashioned hallmarks of a historical house, including nice prints on the walls and old fireplaces. Each one is a real individual, so it's well worth while checking out the pictures on their website.

28 Mary St. (parallel to Fitzroy St.), St. Kilda West, Melbourne, VIC 3182. © **03/9593 8123.** Fax 03/9593 8696. www.fountainterrace.com.au. 7 units. A$165–$235 (US$132–US$188) double. Rates include breakfast. AE, DC, MC, V. Free parking. Tram: 96, 16, 112, or St. Kilda. **Amenities:** Nonsmoking rooms. *In room:* TV, coffeemaker, hair dryer.

Hotel Tolarno ★ The quirky Hotel Tolarno is right in the middle of St. Kilda's cafe and restaurant strip, and a long stone's throw away from the beach. Rich red carpets bedeck the corridors throughout the 1950s and 1960s retro-style building. Rooms vary, but all are modern and nice. The most popular, the deluxe doubles, are in the front of the building and have balconies overlooking the main street. Thy are larger than the standard rooms. Superior doubles come with a microwave and two have Japanese baths. Suites come with a separate kitchen and lounge. Suites don't have balconies, though some have Jacuzzis.

42 Fitzroy St., St. Kilda, Melbourne, VIC 3182. © **1800/620 363** in Australia, or 03/9537 0200. Fax 03/9534 7800. www.hoteltolarno.com.au. 31 units. A$115 (US$92) standard double; A$125 (US$100) deluxe double; A$145

(US$116) superior double; A$180–A$200 (US$144–US$160) suite for up to 4. Extra person A$20 (US$16). AE, DC, MC, V. Free on-street parking. Tram: 16 from Swanston St. or 96 from Flinders St. **Amenities:** Restaurant; bar; 4 lit tennis courts; bike rental; concierge; tour desk; car-rental desk; room service; massage; babysitting; nonsmoking rooms. *In room:* A/C, TV, dataport, kitchenette, fridge, coffeemaker, hair dryer, iron.

Olembia Private Hotel   This sprawling Edwardian house, built in 1922, is set back from a busy street behind a leafy courtyard. It's popular with tourists, business travelers, and young families; everyone gets together for frequent video nights, wine and cheese parties, and barbecues. The rooms are simply furnished, with little more than a double bed or two singles, a desk, a hand basin, and a wardrobe. Dorm rooms have between three and six beds. Guests share six bathrooms. There's a comfortable sitting room. The Olembia is near St. Kilda beach and the restaurants lining Acland Street.

96 Barkly St., St. Kilda, Melbourne, VIC 3182. © **03/9537 1412**. Fax 03/9537 1600. www.olembia.com.au. 23 units, none with bathroom. A$75 (US$60) double; A$24 (US$19) dorm room. AE, MC, V. Free parking. Tram: 96 from Bourke St. to stop 138. **Amenities:** Bike rental; coin-op laundry; nonsmoking rooms. *In room:* No phone.

IN SOUTH YARRA

Hotel Claremont   The high ceilings and the mosaic tiles in the lobby welcome visitors into this old-world hotel. It's an attractive place, though sparsely furnished. The AAA-rated three-star rooms are comfortable enough; each comes with either a double or a single bed. There is no elevator in this three-story building with 72 stairs, so it could be a bad choice for travelers with disabilities. Internet access is available.

189 Toorak Rd., South Yarra, Melbourne, VIC 3141. © **1300/301 630** in Australia, or 03/9826 8000. Fax 03/9827 8652. www.hotelclaremont.com. 80 units, none with bathroom. A$78 (US$62) double; A$30 (US$24) dorm (6 bed). Extra person A$20 (US$16). Children stay free in parent's room. Rates include continental breakfast. AE, DC, MC, V. Free on-street parking. **Amenities:** Coin-op laundry; nonsmoking rooms. *In room:* TV.

The Hotel Como ★★★   Winner of many tourism awards, The Hotel Como deservedly basks in its reputation for excellent service and terrific accommodations, which include studio rooms (some with shower only), one-room suites (some with kitchen or kitchenette), one- or two-bedroom suites (all with kitchen, some with an office), and luxurious (and pricey) penthouse and executive suites. Some units have a private Japanese garden. The hotel is especially adept at accommodating business travelers: All rooms have video-conferencing capability, and three complimentary limousines carry guests to the city center each weekday morning. Weekend packages represent very good value. In my opinion it's the best major hotel in Melbourne.

630 Chapel St., South Yarra, VIC 3141. © **1800/033 400** in Australia, 800/552-6844 in the U.S. and Canada, 0800/389 7791 in the U.K., 0800/446 110 in New Zealand, or 03/9825 2222. Fax 03/9824 1263. www.mirvac hotels.com.au. 107 units. A$600 (US$480) studio; A$680 (US$544) 1-bedroom suite; A$800 (US$640) 2-bedroom suite; A$930 (US$744) penthouse; A$1,300 (US$1,040) Como/executive suite. Ask about weekend packages. AE, DC, MC, V. Parking A$15 (US$12). **Amenities:** 2 restaurants; bar; indoor pool; health club; Jacuzzi; sauna; bike rental; game room; concierge; tour desk; car-rental desk; business center; salon; 24-hr. room service; massage; babysitting; laundry service; dry cleaning; nonsmoking rooms; currency exchange. *In room:* A/C, TV w/pay movies, CD stereos, dataport, kitchen, minibar, coffeemaker, hair dryer, iron, safe.

4 Where to Dine

Melbourne's ethnically diverse population ensures a healthy selection of international cuisines. Chinatown, in the city center, is a fabulous hunting ground for Chinese, Malaysian, Thai, Indonesian, Japanese, and Vietnamese fare, often at bargain prices. Carlton has plenty of Italian cuisine, but the outdoor restaurants on Lygon Street aim at unsuspecting tourists and can be overpriced and disappointing; avoid them. Richmond is crammed with Greek and Vietnamese restaurants, and Fitzroy has cheap Asian, Turkish, Mediterranean, and vegetarian food. To see and be seen, head to Chapel Street or Toorak Road in South Yarra, or to St. Kilda, where you can join the throng of Melbournians dining out along Fitzroy and Acland streets. Most of the cheaper places in Melbourne are strictly BYO (bring your own wine or beer). Smoking is not allowed in cafes and restaurants, so please think twice before offending both staff and fellow patrons.

IN THE CITY CENTER
EXPENSIVE
Flower Drum ★★★ CANTONESE   Praise pours in from all quarters for this upscale restaurant just off Little Bourke Street, Chinatown's main drag. Take a slow elevator up to the restaurant, which has widely spaced tables (perfect for politicians and businesspeople to clinch their deals). Take note of the specials—the chefs are extremely creative and utilize the best ingredients they find in the markets each day. The signature dish is Peking duck; buttered garfish is my favorite. King crab dumplings in soup is a great starter. One or 2 days in advance, you can order a banquet for two or more diners that includes more unusual dishes, such as abalone.

17 Market Lane. ✆ 03/9662 3655. Reservations required. Main courses A$30–A$45 (US$24–US$36). AE, DC, MC, V. Mon–Sat noon–2:30pm and 6–10pm; Sun 6–10:30pm.

Koko ★★ JAPANESE   Though you'll find plenty of Japanese sushi and noodle bars around Chinatown, there's nothing quite like raw fish with a bit of panache. A visit to Crown Casino Entertainment Complex can be a memorable experience in itself, but stop off here and you'll wish you could remember these tastes forever. The restaurant has contemporary-traditional decor, with a goldfish pond in the center of the main dining room and wonderful views over the city. There are separate teppanyaki grills and screened tatami rooms where you sit on the matted floor. If you can manage boiled eel with rice, go for it. Otherwise, yaki udon, or cooked "sushi" of roast chicken, duck, prawns, and rare beef, is popular. A selection of 10 different sakes helps digestion.

Level 3, Crown Towers, Southbank. ✆ 03/9292 6886. Reservations required. Main courses A$27–A$32 (US$22–US$26). AE, DC, MC, V. Daily noon–2:30pm and 6–10:30pm.

MODERATE
Bamboo House ★ NORTHERN REGIONAL CHINESE/CANTONESE   If Flower Drum (see above) is full or breaks your budget, try this place, esteemed by both the Chinese community and local business big shots. The service is a pleasure, and the food—especially chicken with shallot sauce—is worth writing home about. The waiters will help you construct a feast from the myriad Cantonese and northern Chinese dishes. (Don't leave without a taste of the duck in plum sauce!) Other popular dishes include pan-fried dumplings, spring onion pancakes, and the signature dish, Szechuan smoked duck.

47 Little Bourke St. ✆ 03/9662 1565. Reservations recommended. Main courses A$20–A$28 (US$16–US$22). AE, DC, MC, V. Mon–Fri noon–3pm; Mon–Sat 5:30–11pm; Sun 5:30–10pm.

Becco ★ MODERN ITALIAN   Tucked away in a lane, this favorite of Melbournians has not disappointed in 7 years of winning awards and accolades. Here you find

Babka Bakery **6**
Bamboo House **7**
Becco **8**
Brunetti **1**
Café Segovia **18**
Chocolate
  Buddha **20**
Flower Drum **11**
Grossi Florentino **10**
Hopetoun
  Tearooms **17**
Il Bacaro **13**
Il Primo **3**
Il Solito Posto **15**
Irish Times **19**
Koko **21**
Le Restaurant **14**
Mario's **5**
Nudel Bar **9**
Shakahari **4**
Sheni's Curries **16**
Supper Inn **12**
Vue du Monde **2**

stylish service and stylish customers, all without pretension. The cuisine mixes Italian favors with Australian flair in such offerings as crumbed prawns with radicchio and chile aioli, and delicate panettone pudding with cinnamon. On the upstairs level is the ultracool late-night bar, **Bella Vista Social Club** (p. 581).

11–25 Crossley St., near Bourke St. ℭ **03/9663 3000.** Main courses A$22–A$31 (US$18–US$25). AE, DC, MC, V. Mon–Sat noon–3pm and 6–11pm; Sun 5:30–10pm.

Grossi Florentino ★ ITALIAN   Under the management of the Grossi family, this restaurant is probably the best Italian restaurant in Melbourne. It has a casual bistro downstairs, next to the Cellar Bar (where you can pick up a bowl of pasta for around A$13/US$10); upstairs is the fine-dining restaurant, with its chandeliers and murals reflecting the Florentine way of life. The food is traditional Italian, including the signature wet-roasted suckling lamb and suckling pig. On the menu, too, are risotto, seafood, and steak dishes. The chocolate soufflé is special.

80 Bourke St. ℭ **03/9662 1811.** Fax 03/9662 2518. www.grossiflorentino.com. Reservations recommended. Main courses A$38–A$42 (US$30–US$34). AE, DC, MC, V. Mon–Fri noon–3pm; Mon–Sat 6–11pm.

Il Bacaro ★ ITALIAN   Walk into Il Bacaro and you'll feel as if you've been transported to Venice. Dominated by a horseshoe-shaped bar, it's jam-packed with small tables and weaving waiters carrying dishes like carpaccio of tuna or semolina gnocchetti with duck ragout. The pasta dishes and the risotto of the day always go down well, as do the salad side dishes. It's often crowded at lunch with local businesspeople digging deep into the excellent wine list.

168–170 Little Collins St. ℭ **03/9654 6778.** Reservations recommended. Main courses A$20–A$32 (US$16–US$26). AE, DC, MC, V. Mon–Fri noon–4pm; Mon–Sat 6pm–midnight.

Il Solito Posto NORTHERN ITALIAN   This below-ground restaurant consists of two parts. The casual bistro has a blackboard menu offering good pastas, soups, and salads. Then there's the sharper and more upmarket trattoria, with its a la carte menu offering the likes of steak, fish, and veal dishes. The coffee is excellent, too.

113 Collins St., basement (enter through George Parade). ℭ **03/9654 4466.** Reservations recommended. Main courses A$15–A$17 (US$12–US$14) in bistro, A$25–A$33 (US$20–US$26) in trattoria. AE, DC, MC, V. Mon–Fri 7:30am–1am; Sat 9am–1am. Closed late Dec to early Jan.

Irish Times IRISH/MODERN AUSTRALIAN   An Irish bar more authentic than most, the character-filled Irish Times serves up generous portions and Guinness on tap. Popular dishes include warm chicken salad, mussels in creamy broth, Caesar salad, and Irish dishes such as "boxty"—patties of mashed potato, leek, and onion with tomato relish. A live band plays Thursday and Friday at 9:30pm and Saturday at 10:30pm.

427 Little Collins St. ℭ **03/9642 1699.** Reservations recommended. Main courses A$10–A$25 (US$8–US$20). AE, DC, MC, V. Mon–Fri 5pm–midnight; Sat 5pm–3am.

Nudel Bar NOODLES   A favorite with city slickers, the Nudel Bar serves a variety of noodle dishes to diners at the crowded tables and bar. Examples include cold, spicy green-tea noodles and *mee goring* (a noodle dish with peanuts and, here, often chicken). Sticky rice pudding is a favorite for dessert.

76 Bourke St. ℭ **03/9662 9100.** Reservations recommended Fri–Sat night. Main courses A$13–A$18 (US$10–US$14). AE, DC, MC, V. Mon–Fri 11am–10:30pm; Sat 11am–11pm; Sun 4–10:30pm.

INEXPENSIVE

Café Segovia ★★ *Finds* CAFE   Café Segovia is one of the most atmospheric cafes in Australia, with a smoky, sensual interior reminiscent of Spain. Seating is also available outside in the arcade, but you'll have to come early at lunchtime to nab a chair. It serves typical cafe food, such as focaccias, cakes, and light meals. There's live music Thursday and Friday.

33 Block Arcade. © 03/9650 2373. Main courses A$8–A$13 (US$6.40–US$10). AE, DC, MC, V. Mon–Fri 7:30am–11pm; Sat 8am–6pm; Sun 9am–5pm.

Chocolate Buddha *Finds* NOODLES   This place offers mostly organic produce, including some organic wines. Based generally on Japanese-inspired noodle, ramen, and soba dishes to which the kitchen adds meat, chicken, or seafood, it's casual yet particularly satisfying dining. The food is creative, and the view across the square to the Yarra River and Southbank is a delight at dusk.

Federation Sq., corner of Flinders and Swanson sts. © 03/9654 5688. Main courses A$13–A$17 (US$10–US$14). AE, MC, V. Daily noon–10:30pm.

Hopetoun Tearooms ★ CAFE   The first cup of coffee served in this Melbourne institution left the pot in 1892. It's very civilized, with green-and-white Regency wallpaper and marble tables. The cakes are very good. Scones, croissants, and grilled food are also available. A minimum charge of A$5 (US$4) per person applies from noon to 2pm.

Shops 1 and 2, Block Arcade, 280–282 Collins St. ©/fax 03/9650 2777. Main courses A$4.50–A$8.50 (US$3.60–US$6.80); sandwiches A$4.50–A$6.50 (US$3.60–US$5.20); focaccias A$7–A$8.50 (US$5.60–US$6.80). AE, DC, MC, V. Mon–Thurs 8:30am–5pm; Fri 8:30am–6pm; Sat 10am–3:30pm.

Sheni's Curries SRI LANKAN   This tiny (it seats 30), basic, very busy place offers a range of excellent-value, authentic Sri Lankan curries. You can dine here or take your lunch special to go. Choose from three vegetable dishes and a selection of meat and seafood options. All meals come with rice, three types of chutney, and a papadum. You can also buy extra items such as samosas and roti.

Shop 16, 161 Collins St. (corner of Flinders Lane and Russell St., opposite the entrance to the Grand Hyatt). © 03/9654 3535. Lunch specials A$5.50–A$12 (US$4.40–US$9.60). No credit cards. Mon–Fri 11am–4pm.

Supper Inn CANTONESE   Head here if you get the Chinese-food munchies late at night. It's a friendly place with a mixed crowd of locals and tourists chowing down on such dishes as steaming bowls of *congee* (rice-based porridge), barbecued suckling pig, mud crab, or stuffed scallops. Everything here is the "real thing!"

15 Celestial Ave. ©/fax 03/9663 4759. Reservations recommended. Main courses A$10–A$15 (US$8–US$12). AE, DC, MC, V. Daily 5:30pm–2:30am.

CARLTON

Brunetti ★ TRATTORIA/PASTICCERIA   For a real Italian experience, come here to sample excellent cakes, gelato, and coffee while gazing at the *trompe l'oeil* paintings and frescoes on the walls. The authentic lunch dishes are also worth sampling. The best thing this side of Rome.

198–204 Faraday St., Carlton. © 03/9347 2801. Main courses A$12–A$25 (US$9.60–US$20). Cafe dishes A$3–A$8 (US$2.40–US$6.40). AE, DC, MC, V. Mon–Fri 7am–10:30pm; Sat 8am–10:30pm. Tram: 1, 15, 21, or 22 traveling north on Swanston St.

> *Tips* **The Staff of Life**
>
> The enticing aroma of fresh bread attracts you to **Babka Bakery,** a Russian-style cafe-bakery run by a delightful gaggle of girls. Come for breakfast or a light lunch of eggs on fresh sourdough, quiches, tarts, and brioches. Or perhaps try the homemade borscht. It's at 358 Brunswick St. in Fitzroy (② **03/9416 0091**).

Il Primo ⭐ SOUTHERN EUROPEAN   This restaurant is tucked away in a pair of historic houses in the Italian sector of Carlton. The three cozy dining areas have antique bricks, wood-beamed ceilings, and tiled floors. It feels as though you're dining in a wine cellar, and indeed, there's a great wine list, including a range of unlabeled local wines at rock-bottom prices. The menu changes regularly, but you'll often see veal parmigiana, warm kangaroo salad, fish, garlic prawns, risotto, and pasta dishes. Live jazz brings in the customers every night from 10 or 11pm to closing time.

242 Lygon St., Carlton. ② **03/9663 6100.** Reservations recommended. Main courses A$17–A$28 (US$14–US$22). AE, DC, MC, V. Sun–Tues 6:30am–1am; Wed–Sat 6:30am–3am. Tram: 1, 15, 21, or 22 traveling north on Swanston St. (stop 12).

Shakahari VEGETARIAN   Good vegetarian food isn't just a meal without meat; it's a creation in its own right. Shakahari assures you of a creative meal that's not at all bland. The large restaurant is quite low-key, but the service can be a bit inconsistent. Sate Samsara (skewered, lightly fried vegetables and tofu pieces with peanut dip) is a winner, as is couscous, served in a vast earthenware pot. Also available are curries, croquettes, tempura avocado, and veggie burgers (on a plate with salad, not in a bun).

201–203 Faraday St., Carlton. ② **03/9347 3848.** Main courses A$15 (US$12). AE, DC, MC, V. Mon–Sat noon–3:30pm; Sun–Thurs 6–9:30pm; Fri–Sat 6–10:30pm. Tram: 1, 15, 21, or 22 traveling north along Swanston St.

Vue du Monde MODERN FRENCH   Striving for a refined experience similar to that of a European Michelin-starred restaurant, this small but oh-so-stylish establishment produces mostly exceptional food. If pig's trotter stuffed with caramelized sweetbreads or assiette of mushrooms and truffle is what you desire, then you will not be disappointed. Vue du Monde also has an excellent wine list.

295 Drummond St., Carlton. ② **03/9347 0199.** Main courses A$36 (US$29); 2-course dinner A$50 (US$40). AE, DC, MC, V. Tues–Fri noon–2:30pm; Tues–Sat 6:30–11pm. Tram: 1, 15, 21, or 22 traveling north on Swanston St.

FITZROY

Mario's ITALIAN   This place has ambience, groovy '60s decor, great coffee, and impeccable professional service. Offerings include a varied range of pastas and cakes. Breakfast is served all day. The art on the wall, all by local artists, is always interesting and for sale, too.

303 Brunswick St., Fitzroy. ② **03/9417 3343.** Main courses A$12–A$18 (US$9.60–US$14). AE, DC, MC, V. Mon–Fri 7am–10:30pm; Sat 8am–10:30pm.

SEASIDE DINING IN ST. KILDA

Chinta Blues MALAYSIAN   Head to this very popular eatery if you're looking for simple, satisfying food with a healthy touch of spice. The big sellers are laksa, mei goreng, chicken curry, sambal spinach, and a chicken dish called ayam blues. Lots of noodles, too. It's very busy, especially at lunch.

ACCOMMODATIONS ■
Fountain Terrace **1**
Hotel Tolarno **2**
Olembia Private Hotel **3**

DINING ◆
Chinta Blues **6**
Donovans **5**
La Porchetta Pizza Restaurant **4**

6 Acland St., St. Kilda. ℂ **03/9534 9233**. Reservations recommended. Main courses A$10–A$19 (US$8–US$15). AE, MC, V. Mon–Sat noon–2:30pm; Mon–Wed 6–10pm; Thurs–Sat 6–10:45pm; Sun noon–9:45pm. Tram: 16 from Swanston St. or 96 from Bourke St.

Donovans 👌👌 MODERN MEDITERRANEAN   Donovans is so near the sea you expect the fish to jump through the door and onto the plate—and it does serve extremely fresh seafood. The restaurant is all higgledy-piggledy and charming, with lots of cushions, a log fire, and the sound of jazz and breakers on the beach. The menu includes a mind-boggling array of dishes, many big enough for two. Chef Robert Castellani's trademarks include steamed mussels, linguine with seafood, and stuffed squid. The bar is perfect for watching the sun go down.

40 Jacka Blvd., St. Kilda. ℂ **03/9534 8221**. Reservations recommended. Main courses A$23–A$36 (US$18–US$29). AE, DC, MC, V. Daily noon–10:30pm. Tram: 12 from Collins St., 16 from Swanston St., or 94 or 96 from Bourke St.

La Porchetta Pizza Restaurant *(Value* PIZZA   This busy, large, very noisy pizza joint is a good deal. It offers some 22 different pizzas, with the largest just large enough to fill two. A range of pasta dishes, chicken, seafood, veal, and steaks are also on the menu. The pace here means it's not for the faint-hearted.

80 Acland St., St. Kilda. ℂ **03/9534 1888**. Main courses A$5–A$14 (US$4–US$11); pizzas A$6–A$7.80 (US$4.80–US$6.25); pastas A$6–A$9 (US$4.80–US$7.20). No credit cards. Sun–Thurs 11am–midnight; Fri–Sat 11am–2am. Tram: 16 from Swanston St. or 96 from Bourke St.

MORE ETHNIC EATS IN SOUTH YARRA

Kanpai JAPANESE   You have to make reservations well in advance to get a seat at this popular restaurant on the Chapel Street restaurant strip. The sushi and sashimi dishes are very fresh, and the miso soup is well worth plundering with your chopsticks. There's also a good vegetarian selection.

569 Chapel St., South Yarra. ⓒ 03/9827 4379. Reservations recommended. Main courses A$12–A$34 (US$9.60–US$27). AE, DC, MC, V. Daily noon–11pm. Tram: 6, 8, or 72 from Swanston St.

Tandoor Indian Restaurant ⭑ INDIAN   This basic Indian restaurant was far less crowded than many of the others on the Chapel Street strip when I last visited, and all I can say is that the "in" crowd didn't know what they were missing. The curries here are rich and spicy, and the vegetarian paneer–butter masala and cheese kofta are some of the best I've tasted in Australia. Some dishes, such as crab masala curry, are truly inspirational. The main courses are quite large, so you'll probably not need a first course, but I highly recommend side dishes of nan bread (one per person) and cucumber raita to cool the palate.

517 Chapel St., South Yarra. ⓒ 03/9827 8247. Reservations recommended Fri–Sat night. Main courses A$11–A$22 (US$8.80–US$18). AE, DC, MC, V. Tues–Fri and Sun noon–2:30pm; daily 6–11pm. Tram: 6, 8, or 72 from Swanston St.

DOCKLANDS

Meccabah ⭑⭑ *Finds Kids*   Overlooking the Yarra River in the up-and-coming water-side precinct of Docklands, and a short trip from the city center, is this excellent Middle Eastern restaurant. You could go for a main course, such as lamb with preserved lemon, green olives and harissa, but I recommend tucking into the meze plates—little dishes of gorgeous delicacies. Expect the likes of pastry filled with Middle Eastern cheeses or Moroccan chicken, sweet potato falafels with tahini sauce, spicy Turkish kofte with yogurt—whatever you choose (and I've tried all of them), you'll be really impressed. There's also an interesting range of Turkish pizzas here too, such as one with roast pumpkin, chile, pomegranate jam and feta cheese, or sardine, caramelized onion, roast tomato, and olives. The wine list is really good and not that pricey either. Highly recommended. You could cruise up the river to get here with Melbourne River Cruises (see "Getting Around," earlier in this chapter).

55 Newquay Promenade, Docklands. ⓒ 03/9642 1300. www.meccabah.com. Reservations recommended. Main courses A$16–A$20 (US$13-US$16); meze plates A$11 (US$8.80). AE, DC, MC, V. Daily 11am–11pm. Tram: 30 or 48 from Latrobe or Swanston sts.

5 Seeing the Sights

Melbourne's attractions may not have quite the fame as some of Sydney's, but visitors come here to experience the contrasts of old-world architecture and the exciting feel of a truly multicultural city.

THE TOP ATTRACTIONS

Federation Square ⭑⭑   Touted as "Melbourne's civic and cultural hub for the 21st century," Federation Square is a conglomerate of attractions centered on wacky architecture and a large open piazza-type area cobbled with misshapen paving. Here you'll find the **National Gallery of Victoria: The Ian Potter Centre–Australian Art** (p. 571), the **Australian Centre for the Moving Image (ACMI),** and a one-stop Visitor Centre (see "Visitor Information," earlier in this chapter). The huge three-level National Gallery of Victoria building contains the largest collection of Australian art

Birrarung Marr **18**
Cook's Cottage **9**
Federation Square **13**
Fitzroy Gardens **8**
Gold Treasury
  Museum **11**
IMAX Theatre **4**
Latrobe's Cottage **22**
Melbourne Aquarium **16**
Melbourne Museum **5**
Melbourne Observation
  Deck **15**
Melbourne Zoo **2**
National Gallery
  of Victoria:
  the Ian Potter Centre
  —Australian Art **12**
National Gallery
  of Victoria,
  International **19**
Old Melbourne Gaol **3**
Queen Victoria Markets **1**
Shrine of
  Remembrance **20**
St. Patrick's Cathedral **7**
St. Paul's Cathedral **14**
State Houses
  of Parliament **6**
Treasury Gardens **10**
Victorian Arts Centre **17**

Church
Information
Post Office
Tram Line

in the country, including many works by Sidney Nolan, Russell Drysdale, and Tom Roberts, as well as Aboriginal and Torres Strait Islanders. The Gallery is a major focus for art festivals and special events. Numerous cafes and coffee shops operate throughout the precinct. The ACMI center includes two state-of-the-art cinemas and large areas where visitors can view movies, videos, and digital media. It's worth visiting the square just to see the extraordinary architecture, made up of strangely reflective geometrical designs, and the impressive glassed Atrium. Lots of events happen in the square's 450-seat amphitheater, including theatrical performances and free concerts. Other events take place on the plaza and along the banks of the Yarra River.

Flinders St. to the Yarra River (running north-south; to the left, facing Flinders St. Railway Station). www.federation square.com.au. Outdoor spaces open 24 hr. Free admission; charges for some special events and exhibitions. Tram: City Circle.

Gold Treasury Museum   Designed by the architect J. J. Clarke (when he was only 19) and built in 1857, the Old Treasury Building is an imposing neoclassical sandstone structure that once housed precious metal from the Ballarat and Bendigo gold rushes. The gold was stored in eight thick-walled vaults underground and protected by iron bars. The "Built on Gold" Exhibition in the vaults is a high-tech multimedia show featuring videos and displays showing how the gold was dug up, sold, transported, and housed. In the basement are the restored quarters of a caretaker who lived there from 1916 to 1928. The ground floor holds the "Melbourne: A City Built on Gold" display, which shows how Melbourne was built using the profits from the gold rushes. A temporary exhibition gallery on the premises features anything from prints to gold-thread embroidery. Allow about 1 hour.

Old Treasury Building, Spring St. (top of Collins St.). ✆ **03/9651 2233**. Admission A$7 (US$5.60) adults, A$3.50 (US$2.80) children, A$18 (US$14) families. Mon–Fri 9am–5pm; weekends and public holidays 10am–4pm. Bus: City Explorer.

IMAX Theatre *Kids*   This eight-story movie screen rivals the world's largest screen, at Sydney's Darling Harbour. Recent subjects have been outer space, the African Serengeti, and the deep oceans.

Melbourne Museum Complex, Rathdowne St., Carlton. ✆ **03/9663 5454**. Admission from A$14 (US$11) adults, A$9.95 (US$8) children. Daily 10am–10pm. Tram: 1 or 22 from Swanston St.

Melbourne Aquarium *Overrated*   Opened in early 2000, the Melbourne Aquarium stretches over three levels and features a Barrier Reef–type exhibit, some interesting jellyfish displays, and an enormous walk-through tank with larger fish, sharks, and rays. However, it's pretty disappointing compared to the ones in Sydney and doesn't live up to the hype. Allow 30 minutes.

Tips **Sorting Out Your Sightseeing**

Much of Melbourne's appeal comes from soaking up the atmosphere on a walk around the city. If you have time to see only one major attraction, by all means make it the **Melbourne Zoo.** Other top-of-the-list sights include **Federation Square,** the **National Gallery of Victoria,** and the **Royal Botanic Gardens.** If you have time, head to **Phillip Island** to see the fairy penguins.

Corner of Queens Wharf Rd. and Kings St., opposite Crown Casino. (C) **03/9620 0999**. www.melbourneaquarium. com.au. Admission A$21 (US$17) adults, A$11 (US$8.80) children under 16, A$49 (US$39) families. Daily 9:30am–6pm. Tram: City Circle.

Melbourne Museum ★★ *Kids* This museum opposite the 19th-century Royal Exhibition Buildings is Australia's largest and in my mind one of the most interesting. Some of the highlights include a real blue whale skeleton (you can't miss it), an indoor rainforest, and a truly brilliant insect and butterfly collection with lots of real-life exhibits, including cockroaches, ant colonies, and huge spiders. Apart from that there's interactive exhibits and science displays; Bunjikata, the award-winning Aboriginal and Torres Strait Islander Centre; and bits and pieces of social history, including a stuffed race horse called Phar Lap. Check out the brightly colored Children's Museum, which will bring hours of enjoyment to the little ones. A big thumbs up! Allow 2 hours.

Melbourne Museum, 11 Nicholson St., Carlton. (C) **13 11 02** in Australia. Admission A$6 (US$4.80) adults, free for children under 16. Daily 10am–5pm. Tram: 86 or 96 to the Museum and Royal Exhibition Building tram stop at the corner of Nicholson and Gertrude sts., or the free City Circle Tram to Carlton Gardens.

Melbourne Observation Desk From the 55th floor, near the top of the tallest building in the Southern Hemisphere, you get 360-degree views of the whole of Melbourne and beyond. See if you can spot the Melbourne Cricket Ground (MCG) and the Crown Casino. A 20-minute film shows you what you're looking at, but you might as well just take a map up and figure it out for yourself. Of interest are the displays telling about life in Melbourne, past and present. There's a cafe here, too. Allow 1 hour.

Rialto Building, Collins St. (between William and King sts.). (C) **03/9629 8222**. Admission A$12 (US$9.60) adults, A$7 (US$5.60) children, A$32 (US$26) families. Daily 10am–11pm. Parking underneath. Tram: Any tram on Collins St.

Melbourne Zoo ★★ *Kids* This place is a must-see. Built in 1862, it's the oldest zoo in the world, and among the best. There are some 3,000 animals here, including the ever-popular kangaroos, wallabies, echidnas, koalas, wombats, and platypuses. Rather than being locked in cages, most animals are in almost natural surroundings or well-tended gardens. Don't miss the butterfly house, with its thousands of colorful occupants flying around; the free-flight aviary; the lowland gorilla exhibit; and the tree-top monkey displays. Allow at least 1 hour if you just want to see the Australian natives, and around 2½ hours for the whole zoo.

Elliott Ave., Parkville. (C) **03/9285 9300**. www.zoo.org.au. Admission A$20 (US$16) adults, A$9.50 (US$7.60) children under 14, A$50 (US$40) families. Daily 9am–5pm. Free guided tours daily; go to the Friends of the Zoo Office to arrange tours. Free parking. Tram: 55 going north on William St. to stop 25; 19 from Elizabeth St. to stop 16 (then a short walk to your left, following signposts). Train: Royal Park Station.

National Gallery of Victoria, International Opened to critical acclaim in late 2003, the NGV International is a showcase for Australia's finest collections of international art. There are four Gainsboroughs and four Constables here, as well as paintings by the likes of Bonnard, Delacroix, Van Dyck, El Greco, Monet, Manet, Magritte, and Rembrandt. Architecturally, the building is a masterpiece, with high ceilings, fabulous lighting, and great open spaces.

180 St. Kilda Rd. (C) **03/8620 2222**. www.ngv.vic.gov.au. Free admission to general collection; fees for some temporary exhibitions. Daily 10am–5pm. Tram: 1, 3, 5, 6, 8, 16, 22, 25, 64, 67, or 72 from Swanston St. to Victorian Arts Centre stop (ask driver).

National Gallery of Victoria: The Ian Potter Centre–Australian Art ★ This fascinating gallery, featuring 20 rooms dedicated to Australian art, opened in 2002 in the heart of Federation Square. Some 20,000 objects are stored here, but only about 800 are on display at any one time. Aboriginal art and colonial art collections are the centerpieces of the gallery, but you will find modern paintings here, too. Temporary exhibitions include anything from ceramics to shoes. There are also a couple of cafes.

Federation Sq. (runs north-south from Flinders St. to the Yarra River). ℂ **03/8662 1555**. www.ngv.vic.gov.au. Free admission. Mon–Thurs 10am–5pm; Fri 10am–9pm; Sat–Sun 10am–6pm. Bus: City Explorer.

Old Melbourne Gaol ★★ (Finds)
I love this cramped former prison, with its tiny cells and spooky collection of death masks and artifacts of 19th-century prison life. Some 135 hangings took place here, including that of notorious bandit (and Australian hero) Ned Kelly, in 1880. The scaffold where he was hanged is still in place, and his gun, as well as a suit of armor used by a member of his gang, is on display. The jail closed in 1929. Profiles of former prisoners give a fabulous perspective of what it was like to be locked up here. Chilling night tours run every Sunday and Wednesday (call ahead to check the schedule). They cost A$19 (US$15) for adults, A$11 (US$8.80) for children, and A$46 (US$37) for a family; the tour is not recommended for children under 12. Allow 1 hour or more.

Russell St. ℂ **03/9663 7228**. Admission A$13 (US$10) adults, A$7.50 (US$6) children, A$34 (US$27) families. Daily 9:30am–4:30pm. Tram: City Circle tram to corner of Russell and Latrobe sts.

Queen Victoria Market ★
This Melbourne institution covers several blocks. There are hundreds of indoor and outdoor stalls, where you can find anything from live rabbits to bargain clothes. The markets can get cramped, and there's a lot of junk to sort through, but you'll get a real taste of Melbourne and its ethnic mix. Look out for the interesting delicatessen section and cheap eateries. Allow at least an hour.

The 2-hour **Foodies Dream Tour** of the market explores its food and heritage. It departs Tuesday, Thursday, Friday, and Saturday at 10am and costs A$22 (US$18) for adults and A$15 (US$12) for children under 15, including sampling. Well-known chefs give cooking classes, costing A$65 (US$52) per session. Call ℂ **03/9320 5835** for reservations.

Between Peel, Victoria, Elizabeth, and Therry sts. on the northern edge of the city center. ℂ **03/9269 5835**. www.qvm.com.au. Tues–Thurs 6am–2pm; Fri 6am–6pm; Sat 6am–3pm; Sun 9am–4pm. Food stalls closed Sun. Tram: Any tram traveling north along William St. or Elizabeth St.

Rippon Lea House Museum & Historic Garden
This grand Victorian house, 8km (5 miles) from the city center, is worth a visit to get a feel for old-money Melbourne. Socialite Sir Frederick Thomas Sargood built Rippon Lea House, which has dozens of rooms, between 1868 and 1903; a pool and ballroom were added in the 1930s. Though the Romanesque architecture is interesting (note the stained glass and polychrome brickwork), the real attraction is the surrounding 5.3 hectares (13 acres) of landscaped gardens, which include a conservatory, a lake, a lookout tower, an orchard, and extensive flower beds and shrubbery. If you're here on a weekend, on a public holiday, or during school vacations, you might like to drop into the tearoom, which is open from 11am to 4pm. Allow 2 hours.

192 Hotham St., Elsternwick. ℂ **03/9523 6095**. Admission A$9 (US$7.20) adults, A$5 (US$4) children 5–16, A$20 (US$15) families. Daily 10am–5pm (house closes at 4:45pm). Daily guided tours of house every half-hour 10:30am–4pm; tour of estate 2pm. Closed Good Friday and Dec 25. Tram: 67 to stop 40, then walk up Hotham St. Bus: 216/219 from Bourke and Queen sts. in the city to stop 4. Train: Sandringham Line from Flinders St. Station to Rippon Lea Station.

St. Patrick's Cathedral Though lacking the intricacy of design of St. Paul's (see below), Roman Catholic St. Patrick's is another interesting Gothic Revival construction with exceptional stained-glass windows. Built between 1858 and 1940 (consecrated in 1897), St. Patrick's was closely associated with immigrants from Ireland escaping the mid-19th-century potato famine. In the courtyard out front is a statue of the Irish patriot Daniel O'Connell. Allow 15 minutes.

Cathedral Place. ✆ **03/9662 2233**. Mon–Fri 6:30am–6pm; Sat–Sun 7:15am–7:30pm.

St. Paul's Cathedral Built from 1880 to 1892 from the designs of William Butterfield, a famous English Gothic Revival architect, Anglican St. Paul's Cathedral is noteworthy for its highly decorative interior and the English organ built by T. S. Lewis. Step inside to see gold mosaics on walls, Victorian tessellated tiles on the floors, intricate woodcarvings, and stained-glass windows. The cathedral sports the second-highest spire (98m/321 ft.) in the Anglican Communion. A boys' choir sings at 5:10pm Monday through Friday during school times, and on Sunday at 10:30am and 6pm. Outside is a statue of Matthew Flinders, the first sailor to navigate the Australian mainland between 1801 and 1803. Allow 15 minutes.

Flinders and Swanston sts. ✆ **03/9650 3791**. Daily 7:30am–6pm. Services Sun 8, 9, and 10:30am; Eucharist 6pm. Choral evensong Mon–Fri 7:45am, 12:15pm, 5:10pm. Cathedral shop daily 10am–4pm.

State Houses of Parliament Now the home of the Victorian Parliament, this imposing monument to Victorian (as in Queen Victoria) architecture at the top of a run of sandstone steps was built in 1856. During the Australian Federation (1900–27), it was used as the National Parliament; it's also known as Parliament House. When the State Government is in session—generally on Tuesday afternoon and all day Wednesday and Thursday between March and July, and again between August and November (there's a break between sessions)—you can view the proceedings from the public gallery. However, you should ring ahead and check, as sitting times do vary. During nonsitting times, both the extremely opulent Upper House and the less ornate Lower House chambers are open to the public. Allow 30 minutes.

Spring St. ✆ **03/9651 8568** or 03/9651 8569. www.parliament.vic.gov.au. Mon–Fri 9am–5pm. Free guided tours Mon–Fri 10 and 11am, noon, and 2, 3, and 3:45pm when Parliament is not in session. Reservations recommended.

PARKS & GARDENS

Birrarung Marr, along the Yarra River east of Federation Square on Batman Avenue (✆ **03/9658 9658;** www.melbourne.vic.gov.au/parks), is Melbourne's first new major parkland in more than 100 years. *Birrarung* means "river of mists" in the Woiwurrung language of the Wurundjeri people who originally inhabited the area; *marr* equates with the side of the river. Wide open spaces and large, sculptured terraces were designed to host some of Melbourne's best events and festivals throughout the year, and the terraces give way to spectacular views of the city, Southbank, King's Domain, and the Yarra River.

The **Royal Botanic Gardens** ★★, 2km (1¼ miles) south of the city on Birdwood Avenue, off St. Kilda Road (✆ **03/9252 2300**), are the best gardens in Australia and well worth a few hours of wandering. More than 40 hectares (99 acres) are lush and blooming with more than 12,000 plant species from all over the world. Don't miss a visit to the oldest part of the garden, the Tennyson Lawn, with its 120-year-old English elm trees. Other special corners include a fern gully, camellia gardens, an herb garden, rainforests packed with fruit bats, and ponds full of ducks and black swans. You can wander at your own pace or take one of the free guided walks that leave the

National Herbarium Building, F Gate, Sunday through Friday at 11am and noon. Bring snacks and your picnic blanket to Shakespeare in the Park, a popular summer event. Performances are in January and February, and tickets cost around A$30 (US$24). Call ✆ **03/9252 2300** for details. The gardens are open November through March daily from 7:30am to 8:30pm; April, September, and October daily from 7:30am to 6pm; and May through August daily from 7:30am to 5:30pm. Admission is free. To get there, catch the tram on Route 8, traveling south, and get off at stop 21. Allow 2 to 4 hours.

Nearby, in King's Domain, take a look at Victoria's first Government House, **Latrobe's Cottage** (✆ **03/9654 5528**). It was built in England and transported to Australia brick by brick in 1836. Admission is A$2 (US$1.60). The cottage is open from 11am to 4pm Monday, Wednesday, Saturday, and Sunday. On the other side of Birdwood Avenue is the **Shrine of Remembrance,** a memorial to the servicemen lost in Australia's wars. It's designed so that at 11am on Remembrance Day (Nov 11), a beam of sunlight hits the Stone of Remembrance in the Inner Shrine. Note the eternal flame in the forecourt. King's Domain is stop 12 on the Route 15 tram traveling south along St. Kilda Road.

In Fitzroy Gardens, off Wellington Parade, is **Cooks' Cottage** (✆ **03/9419 4677**), which was moved to Melbourne from Great Ayton, in Yorkshire, England, in 1934 to mark Victoria's centenary. The cottage was built by the parents of Captain Cook, and today it provides the opportunity to learn about his voyages of discovery around the world. Inside, it's spartan and cramped, not unlike a ship's cabin. Admission is A$3.70 (US$3) for adults, A$1.80 (US$1.40) for children 5 to 15, and A$8.80 (US$7) for a family. It's open daily from 9am to 5pm (until 5:30pm in summer). Also east of the central business district are the **Treasury Gardens.** Look for the memorial to John F. Kennedy near the lake. To reach Treasury Gardens and Fitzroy Gardens, take tram no. 75 traveling east along Flinders Street. Get off at stop 14 for Treasury Gardens, stop 14A for Fitzroy Gardens.

6 Enjoying the Great Outdoors or Catching an Aussie Rules Football Match

OUTDOOR ACTIVITIES

BALLOONING   **Melbourne by Balloon,** Balloon Sunrise Office, 41 Dover St., Richmond (✆ **03/9427 7596;** fax 03/9427 7597), offers flights over the city plus a champagne breakfast once you hit the ground. Dawn flights cost A$310 (US$248) for adults, and A$220 (US$176) for children under 12—but if they're under 1.2m (4 ft.) tall, they won't be able to see over the basket. Reservations are essential.

BIKING   Extensive bicycle paths wind through the city and suburbs. For details on the 20 most popular routes, pick up a copy of *Melbourne Bike Tours,* published by **Bicycle Victoria** (✆ **03/9328 3000;** fax 03/9328 2288; www.bv.com.au), available at most bookshops. Bicycle Victoria also runs several major cycling tours throughout the state every year.

You can rent a bike from **Hire a Bike** at St. Kilda Pier (✆ **03/9531 7403**); non-Australians must show their passports.

GOLF   One of the best public golf courses in Australia is **Yarra Bend,** Yarra Bend Road, Fairfield (✆ **03/9481 3729**). Greens fees A$21 (US$17) Monday to Friday, A$22 (US$18) Saturday and Sunday; children pay A$10 (US$8). Club rental is an extra A$25 (US$20) for a full set and A$12 (US$9.60) for a half-set.

Tips   A Lot in Common(wealth)

The Melbourne 2006 Commonwealth Games will be held from March 15 to March 26, 2006. It's billed as the largest event Melbourne has seen since the Olympics were held here in 1956. Some 4,500 athletes from 71 nations, which make up the British Commonwealth, are due to compete. Fourteen of the 16 sports will be held within a 3km (4-mile) radius of the city center with the redeveloped MCG holding both the opening and closing ceremonies and all the track and field events.

Hotels will be booked solid, so if you are planning on visiting Melbourne, avoid this time, unless of course you are coming to the games, or book early enough.

For general information on the Games check out the official website, **www.melbourne2006.com.au**, or call ℰ **03/9613 2006.**

The exclusive **Royal Melbourne Golf Club,** in the suburb of Black Rock, 24km (15 miles) from the city center, is rated as one of the world's 10 best golf courses. It's open to members only, but if you belong to a top-notch golf club at home, you might be able to wheedle your way in.

For more information on golf in Victoria, contact the **Victorian Golf Association,** 15 Bardolph St., Burwood (ℰ **03/9889 6731**).

IN-LINE SKATING   The promenade in St. Kilda is the most popular place to strap on skates. You can rent all you need at **Rock'n 'n' Roll'n,** 11a Fitzroy St., St. Kilda (ℰ **03/ 9525 3434**). The first hour costs A$10 (US$8). Successive hours are less expensive.

TENNIS   The venue for the Australian Open, the **Melbourne Park National Tennis Centre,** on Batman Avenue (ℰ **03/9286 1244**), is a great place to play. When tournaments are not scheduled, its 22 outdoor courts (including the show courts) and four indoor courts are open to the public. You can rent courts Monday through Friday from 7am to 11pm, Saturday and Sunday from 9am to 6pm. Charges range from A$14 to A$30 (US$11–US$24) per hour, depending on the court and time of day (outdoor courts are cheapest). Show courts 1, 2, and 3 are for rent at the same prices. Racquets are available for A$3 (US$2.40).

SPECTATOR SPORTS

CAR RACING   The annual **Australian Formula One Grand Prix** takes place in early March at Albert Park, about 3km (2 miles) from central Melbourne. Call Ticketmaster (ℰ **13 61 22** in Australia) or the Grand Prix Hotline (ℰ **13 16 41** in Australia, or 03/9258 7100) for information on tickets, accommodations, and airfares. Also check out the Grand Prix's website at www.grandprix.com.au.

CRICKET   From October through March, cricket's the name of the game in Melbourne. The **Melbourne Cricket Ground (MCG),** Brunton Avenue, Yarra Park, Jolimont (ℰ **03/9657 8879**), is perhaps Australia's most hallowed cricket field. The facility (the main stadium for the 1956 Melbourne Olympic Games) can accommodate 97,500 people. For the uninitiated, "one-day" games are the ones to look out for; "Test" games take several days to complete. Buy tickets at the gate or in advance from **Ticketmaster** (ℰ **13 61 00** in Australia; www.ticketmaster.com).

Tours of the MCG and its museum start every half-hour daily from 10am to 3pm. Tours cost A$10 (US$8) for adults, A$6 (US$4.80) for children, and A$25 (US$20) for a family. The tour price includes admission to the Australian Gallery of Sport and the Olympic Museum, which are also at the MCG. They're open daily from 9:30am to 4:30pm. The Olympic Museum traces the development of the modern Olympics with individual display sections for each city. Also in the complex is a coffee shop that serves snacks and lunch.

FOOTBALL   Melbourne's number-one sport is **Australian Rules Football**—or simply "the footy"—a skillful, often violent game the likes of which you've never seen (unless you have ESPN). Melbourne is home to 10 of the 16 Australian Football League (AFL) teams, with the others coming from Adelaide, Perth, Sydney, and Brisbane. The season starts on the third weekend in March and ends with the Grand Final on the last Saturday in September. The most accessible fields are at the Melbourne Cricket Ground (take tram no. 75 along Wellington Parade) and the Optus Oval at Carlton (take tram no. 19 from Elizabeth St.). Tickets cost around A$16 (US$13) per person, or A$30 (US$24) for a family. For game information, call **AFL Headquarters** (© **03/9643 1999**). Buy tickets through **Ticketmaster** (© **13 61 00** in Australia; www.ticketmaster7.com).

HORSE RACING   The **Melbourne Cup,** on the first Tuesday in November, has been contested by the best of Australia's thoroughbreds (and a few from overseas) since 1861. Melbourne society puts on a show, dressing up for the occasion, and the entire nation stops in its tracks to at least tune in on TV.

The city has four race tracks: **Flemington** (which holds the Melbourne Cup), Epson Road, Flemington (© **03/9371 7171**); **Moonee Valley,** McPherson Street, Mooney Ponds (© **03/9373 2222**); **Caulfield,** Station Street, Caulfield (© **03/9257 7200**); and **Sandown,** Racecourse Drive, Springvale (© **03/9518 1300**). If you're staying in the city center, Flemington and Moonee Valley are the easiest to get to. Take tram no. 57 from Flinders Street to reach the Flemington racetrack, and catch tram no. 59 from Elizabeth Street to Moonee Valley.

TENNIS   The **Australian Open** ⚲, one of the four Grand Slam events, is played during the last 2 weeks of January every year at the Melbourne Park National Tennis Center, Batman Avenue (© **03/9286 1244**). Tickets go on sale in mid-October and are available through **Ticketek** (© **03/9299 9079**) and on the Open's website, www.ausopen.org. To get there, take a train from the Flinders Street Station at the bottom of Swanston Street to Richmond Station and catch the special Tennis Center tram from there.

7 Shopping

Ask almost any Melbournian to help you plan your time in the city, and he or she will advise you to shop till you drop. All Australia regards Melbourne as a shopping capital—it has everything from fashion houses to major department stores and unusual souvenir shops. If you're coming from Sydney, I say save your money until you get to Melbourne, and then indulge!

Start at the magnificent city arcades, such as the **Block Arcade** (between Collins and Little Collins sts.), which has more than 30 shops, including the historic Hopetoun Tearooms (p. 565), and the **Royal Arcade** (stretching from Little Collins St. to the Bourke St. Mall). Then hit the courts and lanes around **Swanston Street** and the huge **Melbourne Central shopping complex** between Latrobe and Lonsdale streets.

Next, fan out across the city, taking in **Chapel Street** in South Yarra, for its Australian fashions, and **The Jam Factory,** 500 Chapel St., South Yarra (℃ **03/9826 0537**), which is a series of buildings with a range of shops and food outlets, including a branch of U.S.-based Borders, as well as 16 cinema screens. Get there on tram no. 8 or 72 from Swanston Street.

There's also **Toorak Road** in Toorak, for Gucci and other high-priced, high-fashion names; **Bridge Road** in Richmond, for budget fashions; **Lygon Street** in Carlton, for Italian fashion, footwear, and accessories; and **Brunswick Street** in Fitzroy, for a more alternative scene.

Serious shoppers might like to contact **Shopping Spree Tours** (℃ **03/9596 6600**), a company that takes you to exclusive and alternative shopping venues, manufacturers, and importers you wouldn't be likely to find by yourself. Tours depart Monday through Saturday at 8:30am and cost A$60 (US$48) per person, including lunch and a visit to the Melbourne Observation Deck.

MELBOURNE SHOPPING FROM A TO Z

ABORIGINAL CRAFTS

The Aboriginal Gallery of the Dreaming   This place stocks an extensive range of acrylic dot paintings and represents more than 120 artists. Boomerangs, didgeridoos, pottery, jewelry, bark paintings, prints, books, and music are also available. 73–77 Bourke St. Mall. ℃ **03/9650 3277.**

Original & Authentic Aboriginal Art   Stop here for original artworks, traditional bark paintings, and informative presentations. 90 Bourke St. ℃ **03/9663 5133.** www.auth aboriginalart.com.au.

CRAFTS

An interesting arts-and-crafts market takes place on the Esplanade in St. Kilda on Sunday from 9am to 4pm. Take tram no. 16 from Swanston Street or no. 96 from Bourke Street.

The Australian Geographic Shop   Head here for high-quality Australiana, including crafts, books, and various gadgets. Shop 130, Melbourne Central, 300 Lonsdale St. ℃ **03/9639 2478;** and Galleria Shopping Plaza, Little Collins St. ℃ **03/9670 5813.**

DEPARTMENT STORES

David Jones   Like Myer (see below), its direct competition, David Jones—or DJ's, as it's affectionately known—spans 2 blocks, separated into men's and women's stores, and offers similar goods. The men's fashions in particular leave a lot to be desired. 310 Bourke St. Mall. ℃ **03/9643 2222.**

Myer   The grande dame of Melbourne's department stores has 12 floors of household goods, perfume, jewelry, and fashions stretching over 2 blocks. It's one of the largest stores in the world. The food section on the ground floor includes, among other things, good sushi. The clothes are better here than at David Jones. 314 Bourke St. Mall. ℃ **03/9661 1111.**

FASHION

High-fashion boutiques line the eastern stretch of **Collins Street,** between the Grand Hyatt and the Hotel Sofitel, and **Chapel Street** in South Yarra. In addition, many thousands of retail shops and factory outlets are around the city, many of them concentrated on **Bridge Road** near Punt Road and **Swan Street** near Church Street in Richmond. You'll find designer clothes, many just last season's fashions, at a fraction of the original price.

Collins Street features most international labels as well as shoe heaven **Miss Louise,** 123 Collins St. (© **03/9654 7730**). Nearby Flinders Lane has earned style status with the likes of **Alice Euphemia,** 241 Flinders Lane (© **03/9650 4300**), which stocks upcoming Australian and New Zealand designers. Stop at **Aesop,** 238 Flinders Lane (© **03/9654 1331**), for its aromatherapy creams and lotions; down the road is **Christine,** 181 Flinders Lane (© **03/9654 2011**), where women have been known to faint over the accessories. **Little Collins Street** is another fashion-rat run. At 150 Little Collins St., look for local labels **Bettina Liano** (© **03/9654 1912**), **Scanlan & Theodore** (© **03/9650 6195**), and **Verve** (© **03/9639 5886**).

Country Road Country Road is one of Australia's best-known names for men's and women's fashion. The cool, classic looks don't come cheap, but the quality is worth it. County Road also sells designer cooking equipment and housewares. 252 Toorak Rd. and other locations, including Chapel St., South Yarra. © **1800/801 911** in Australia, or 03/9824 0133.

R.M. Williams Head here for genuine Australian gear: boots, Driza-bone coats, and Akubra hats. In the Melbourne Central complex, between Latrobe and Lonsdale sts. © **03/9663 7126.**

Saba Australian designer Joseph Saba has several in-vogue, very expensive boutiques for men and women in Melbourne, including one for each sex on Chapel Street (nos. 538 and 548) in South Yarra. This store caters to both men and women. 264 Collins St. © **03/9654 3524.**

Sam Bear Sam Bear is a good bet for Outback-style fashions: Driza-bone coats, Akubra bush hats, R.M. Williams boots and clothing, and my favorite, Blundstone boots. It also sells a solid range of camping equipment. 225 Russell St. © **03/9663 2191.**

Surf, Dive 'N Ski Australia In addition to surfboards, boogie boards, and sunglasses, this store stocks a wide range of hip and happening beachwear at reasonable

---

Fun Fact Death by Chocolate

If you love chocolate, sign up now for a chocolate walk (© **03/9815 1228** or 04/1215 8017; www.chocoholictours.com.au). The **Chocolate Indulgence Walk** takes you on a tasting tour of Cadbury's, Myer, New Zealand Natural Ice Creamery, Chocolate Box, and Darrell Lea, and finishes with chocolate cake at a cafe. The 2-hour tour leaves Saturday at 12:30pm. The **Chocolates & Other Desserts Walk** includes tasting plenty of ice creams and chocolates around town as you tour kitchens and talk to chefs. The tour finishes with afternoon tea at the Grand Hyatt. This tour leaves Saturday at 2:30pm. The **Chocolate Brunch Walk,** during which you try coffee and pastries at some of Melbourne's grooviest cafes. Each tour costs A$28 (US$22), free for children under 6. Reservations are essential. You can find out more information about each tour and reserve at the phone number/web site listed above.

prices. All the big names in Australian surf wear are here, including Ripcurl, Quicksilver, and Billabong. The Jam Factory, Chapel St., South Yarra. © 03/9826 4071.

Vegan Wares   Instead of leather, Vegan Wares uses microfiber to create tough, stylish shoes, bags, and belts. It's not just for vegetarians; carnivores enjoy it, too! 78 Smith St., Collingwood. © 03/9417 0230.

FOOD

Haigh's Chocolates   Indulge in some 50 types of Australia's best chocolate, from milk to dark to fruit flavored. I recommend the Sparkling Shiraz truffle if you need a serious treat. 26 Collins St. © 03/9650 2114; and Shop 27, Block Arcade, 282 Collins St. © 03/9654 7673.

Melbourne Candy Kitchen   If you have a sweet tooth, you're likely to spend a fortune at this traditional little candy shop that makes its goodies before your eyes. Rock candy is a specialty, and you can get your name (or the name of someone back home) spelled out in its center. Shop 20, Royal Arcade. © 03/9663 5654.

JEWELRY

Altman & Cherny   Even if you're not in the market to buy, it's worth coming here to check out "Olympic Australia," the largest precious-gem opal in the world. It was found in Coober Pedy in South Australia in 1956 and is valued at A$2.5 million (US$2 million). The store offers tax-free shopping for tourists armed with both a passport and an international airline ticket. 128 Exhibition St., near Little Collins St. © 03/9650 9685.

Dinosaur Designs   Dinosaur Designs is taking the jewelry design world by storm with its range of artistic pieces made out of resin. The shop has modern housewares as well. None of it's cheap, but the odd item won't break the bank. 562 Chapel St., South Yarra. © 03/9827 2600.

e.g.etal   Shop here for fresh, innovative jewelry by 50 or so of Australia's leading and emerging designers. 185 Little Collins St. © 03/9663 4334.

8 Melbourne After Dark

Melbourne can be an exciting place once the sun has set. The pubs and bars are far better than those in Sydney. Friday and Saturday nights will see most pubs (of both the trendy and the down-to-earth variety) packed to the rafters, and at lunchtime those that serve food are popular, too. To find out what's happening, check the Friday entertainment guide in the *Age,* Melbourne's daily broadsheet.

THE PERFORMING ARTS

Melbourne is the most dynamic performing-arts city in Australia. Its theaters offer the whole gamut, from offbeat independent productions to large-scale Broadway-style musicals. The city is also the home of the most prestigious festivals, with the annual **Melbourne Fringe Festival** (the first 3 weeks in Oct) and the annual **Melbourne International Comedy Festival** (from the end of Mar to roughly the end of Apr), attracting the best of Australian and international talent.

Venues all over the city participate in the Melbourne International Comedy, and the Fringe Festival sees the streets, pubs, theaters, and restaurants playing host to everyone from jugglers and fire-eaters to musicians and independent productions covering all art forms. Try to get tickets if you're in town during either festival, but keep

---

Value   Half-Price Tickets

Buy tickets for entertainment events, including opera, dance, and drama, on the day of the performance from the **Half-Tix Desk** in the Melbourne Town Hall on Swanston Street (📞 **03/9650 9420**). The booth is open Monday from 10am to 2pm, Tuesday through Thursday 11am to 6pm, Friday 11am to 6:30pm, and Saturday 10am to 2pm. Tickets must be purchased in cash. Available shows are displayed on the booth door; note that you can't get show information over the phone.

---

in mind that hotels fill up fast at these times. For more information, visit www.melbournefringe.org.au or www.comedyfestival.com.au.

Another good time to plan your visit is during the annual **Melbourne International Film Festival** (mid-July through the 1st week in Aug), when new releases, shorts, and avant-garde movies play at venues around the city. For details and schedules, check www.melbournefilmfestival.com.au.

For information on upcoming theater productions and reviews, check out www.stageleft.com.au. The official government entertainment information site, www.melbourne.vic.gov.au/events, shows "What's On" in the theater world for up to 2 months in advance, as well as what's happening in dance, film, comedy, music, exhibitions, sports, and tours.

The best place to buy tickets for everything from theater to major sporting events, and to obtain details on schedules, is **Ticketmaster** (📞 **1800/062 849** in Australia, 13 61 00, or 03/9299 9079; www.ticketmaster7.com).

THE HEART OF MELBOURNE'S CULTURAL LIFE

Victorian Arts Centre ★★   The spire atop the Theatres Building of the Victorian Arts Center, on the banks of the Yarra River, crowns the city's leading performing arts complex. Beneath it, the State Theatre, the Playhouse, and the Fairfax present performances that are the focal point of culture in Melbourne.

The **State Theatre,** seating 2,079 on three levels, can accommodate elaborate stagings of opera, ballet, musicals, and more. The **Playhouse** is a smaller venue that often books the Melbourne Theatre Company. The **Fairfax** is more intimate still, and is often used for experimental theater or cabaret.

Adjacent to the Theatres Building is the **Melbourne Concert Hall,** home of the Melbourne Symphony Orchestra and the State Orchestra of Victoria, and often host to visiting orchestras. Many international stars have graced this stage, which is known for its excellent acoustics.

100 St. Kilda Rd. 📞 **1300/136 166** for tickets, or 03/9281 8000. Fax 03/9281 8282. www.vicartscentre.com.au. Tickets A$20–A$140 (US$16–US$112).

ADDITIONAL VENUES & THEATERS

Check the *Age* to see what productions are scheduled during your visit. Odds are that the leading shows will take place in one of the following venues:

The Comedy Club   The Comedy Club is a Melbourne institution. Come here to see local and international comedy acts, musicals, and special shows. It offers a dinner and show Friday and Saturday for A$40 to A$45 (US$32–US$36), depending on the performer; show only Thursday through Saturday approximately A$20 (US$16). Level 1, 380 Lygon St., Carlton. ☎ 03/9348 1622.

Comedy Theatre The Comedy Theatre, with its ornate Spanish Rococo interior, feels intimate even though it seats more than 1,000 people. Plays and musicals usually fill the bill, but dance companies and comedians also appear. 240 Exhibition St. ☎ 03/9299 9886 or Ticketek (☎ 13 28 49).

The Forum Theatre The Forum books well-known bands and international comedians. Tables and chairs are in cabaret-style booths, from which you can order drinks and meals. 154 Flinders St. ☎ 03/9299 9886.

Her Majesty's Theatre A fire destroyed the original theater here, but the current structure retains the original facade and the Art Deco interior added during a 1936 renovation. Musicals, such as the Australian premier of *Chicago,* frequent the boards. 219 Exhibition St. ☎ 03/9663 3211.

The Princess Theatre This huge facility hosts extravaganza productions. The theater opened its doors in 1886, and it still has a dramatic marble staircase and ornate plaster ceilings. 163 Spring St. ☎ 03/9663 3300.

The Regent Theatre Built in 1929, The Regent fell into disrepair, and its stage was dark for 25 years. Now, after a A$35-million (US$28-million) renovation, it's been restored to its former glory. Tickets are available in the U.S. through ATS Tours (☎ 800/423-2880). The theater offers a range of dining packages. 191 Collins St. ☎ 03/9299 9800.

Sidney Myer Music Bowl This huge outdoor entertainment center, run under the auspices of the Victorian Arts Center Trust, schedules opera, jazz, and ballet in the warmer months (and ice skating in the winter). King's Domain, Alexandra Ave. ☎ 03/9281 8360.

CINEMAS

Most of the city cinemas are within 2 blocks of the intersection of Bourke and Russell streets. Tickets cost A$9 to A$14 (US$7.20–US$11). Among the independent cinemas, the one that stands out is the **Astor,** 3 Chapel St., at the corner of Chapel and Dandenong roads, East St. Kilda (☎ 03 9510 1414). Housed in a superb Art Nouveau building, the Astor shows classic movies.

THE CLUB & MUSIC SCENE

Melbourne's nightclub scene used to center on King Street, and while that area is still popular with large disco-style venues, the city is now awash in unique, hidden bars and clubs. It's best just to follow the crowds—or in some cases that couple slipping down a side lane and disappearing into a dimly lit entrance. Otherwise, the following options are more enduring in their appeal.

Bella Vista Social Club Owned by the team at Becco (see "Where to Dine," earlier in this chapter), BVSC is upstairs from the popular restaurant. Ultramodern in a microsuede way, this place jumps with a late-night crowd of many splendid hues—arty young things mingling with the suits, all watching the goings-on in the laneway below on a large-screen hookup. 11–25 Crossley St. ☎ 03/9663 3000.

Bennetts Lane Jazz Club ★ Often exceptional and always varied, this venue is simply the best in Melbourne for jazz. The back-lane location may be a little hard to find, but inside it's everything you've always imagined a jazz club to be. The best international players seek it out. 25 Bennetts Lane. ☎ 03/9663 2856. www.bennettslane.com. Cover A$10 (US$8).

Cicciolina Back Bar　This softly lit, alluring hideaway offers plush leather booths and a fine range of cocktails. Add a particularly attentive staff, and you've got one of the best little bars in the greater St. Kilda region. 130 Acland St. (enter from arcade), St Kilda. © 03/9525 3333.

Double Happiness　This tiny but hugely atmospheric bar is detail at its best. The retro-Asian theme would make Chairman Mao proud. Mix with the hip crowd from the CBD (Central Business District), and try the "Gang of Four" cocktail (mango, vodka, Cointreau, and lemon). 21 Liverpool St (off Bourke St). © 03/9650 4488. www.double-happiness.org.

Hi-Fi Bar & Ballroom　Featuring lots of live music—mostly of the hard rock and contemporary persuasion—and patronized by the younger set, this cavernous underground venue features many visiting acts. 125 Swanson St. © 03/9654 7617. www.the hifi.com.au. Cover Sat A$20 (US$16).

Honky Tonks　Head down a dark lane into a nondescript warehouse and up a flight of wooden stairs to discover this bar's happy revelers enjoying live laid-back jazz or a DJ weaving his magic on the turntables. The cocktail bar is buzzing and the view from the deep lounges across the Yarra River to the Botanic Gardens is surreal. Duckboard Place. © 03/9662 4555.

KingPin　Why not combine your two favorite pastimes? Ten-pin bowling and drinking! Experience the purple lounge, which really mixes it up, with cool DJs and great cocktails. In the Crown Casino complex, this venue is open 24/7, so happy days really are here again. 8 Whiteman St., Southbank. © 03/9292 7009. Cover varies. Bowling around A$20 (US$16).

Melbourne Supper Club　Upstairs from an ever-popular European cafe-restaurant, the Melbourne Supper Club is a perfect post-theater venue. Deep leather lounges and a giant circular window that looks onto the beautifully lit Parliament House buildings make this bar a place to idle, smoke a cigar, or dwell over a bottle of your favorite wine. 161 Spring St. © 03/9654 6300.

Misty　Funk meets Barbarella in this ultrahip and arty venue, one of the quintessential Melbourne bars. Here, down a cobbled lane, smooth cocktails mix with live combos or soulful DJs. 3–5 Hosier Lane. © 03/9663 9202.

Revolver　This venue usually pumps with techno music, although bands play on weekends with dancing later. 229 Chapel St., Prahan. © 03/9521 5985. Cover weekends A$10 (US$8).

Tony Starrs Kitten Club　Don't be put off by the name—this is one great place. A restaurant-bar on the lower level serves an array of excellent tapas and more exotic fare. But the action is at the upstairs Galaxy Lounge, where most nights you'll find entertainment—ranging from the peculiar to the animated to just plain bizarre. Don't forget to visit the Love Lounge, with its floor-to-ceiling red fabric, heart-shaped lounges, and secluded booths. The club is open for lunch and dinner until 1am. 267 Little Collins St. © 03/9650 2448. Cover Sat A$5 (US$4).

WHERE TO SHARE A PINT

Pubs generally stay open from midmorning until at least midnight most nights. Many remain open until 2 or 3am on Friday and Saturday night, and you can always find a few open 24 hours.

Finds **Pick a Card . . . for a Unique Pub Crawl**

All the rage in Melbourne just now is a pack of 52 playing cards called **Bar Secrets Melbourne** (www.bar-secrets.com). The cards have pictures of and information (including maps) on the hippest and most unusual pubs and cocktail bars in town. Locals pick out a few at random, and the night's planned. The cards cost A$9.95 (US$8) at bookshops and newsdealers in town. They are well worth seeking out. Last time I visited Melbourne I found myself weaving up dark alleyways, climbing into lofts and down into basements, and always found myself somewhere unique.

Belgian Beer Café Bluestone   Belgian beer culture in all its forms. Pretend that you're in Brussels in this extremely atmospheric cafe. Full-bodied Belgian brews dominate. While downing your pint, try the traditional streamed mussels. In warmer weather, sitting in the parklike garden is a delight. 557 St. Kilda Rd. ✆ **03/9529 2899.**

Bridie O'Reillys   Bridie O'Reillys is one of Melbourne's best Irish pubs, complete with traditional dark-wood decor and good beer. The two-level pub has 19 different beers on tap (seven of them Irish). There is live Irish music every night starting around 9pm. The place gets quite crowded on weekends. 62 Little Collins St. (just off Exhibition St.). ✆ **03/9650 0840.**

Chaise Lounge   Any semblance of barroom normality breaks down at this chic boudoir-style place featuring lipstick-colored walls, a bust of a Roman god, diamante-strung curtains, lay-down sofas, and glitter balls. Basement, 105 Queen St. ✆ **03/9670 6120.**

Cookie   The latest hot place to hang out is an unlikely combination of good-value Thai eatery, beer hall, and smart cocktail bar, complete with plastic doilies and murals. It's only open from noon to 11pm daily. 252 Swanston Street. ✆ **03/9663 7660.**

The Cricketers Club Bar   Locals come to this popular English-style pub to lift a glass surrounded by the relics of Australia's summer passion. Glass cases are packed full of cricket bats, pads, and stumps, and the plush green carpets and solid mahogany woodwork give the place a touch of class. In The Windsor Hotel, 103 Spring St. ✆ **03/9653 0653.**

The Croft Institute   This laneway (at the end of an alley)bar is a small, lurid, bottle-green establishment, which is notably famous for its powerful cocktails, and the city's largest private collection of laboratory apparatus. For the young only. 21–25 Croft Alley. ✆ **03/9671 4399.**

Jimmy Watson's Wine Bar   While probably not the best spot for a pint, Jimmy's is somewhat of an institution. One of Melbourne's oldest wine bars, it's a cozy affair where all types of people chat while sampling a vast range of wines. In the attached dining area, excellent food is expertly teamed with the perfect wine. Come to talk or simply read the paper. 333 Lygon St., Carlton. ✆ **03/9347 3985.**

The Prince St. Kilda   This pub is a legend among the locals. Though refurbished, it retains its original rough-at-the-edges appearance. Bands, some of them big names, play most nights. 2 Acland St., St Kilda. ✆ **03/9536 1100.**

Windsor Castle   Up Chapel Street and through Prahan are Windsor and its best-kept secret, the Windsor Castle Hotel, home of the local stylemeisters. This is a perfect weekend meeting place for good pub food, which you can enjoy in the sunny court-yard or in the plush interior. You'll find DJs and barbecue on weekends. Look for the giant pink elephants outside. At the corner of Albert and Upton sts., Windsor. (℃ **03/9525 0239.**

The Young and Jacksons Hotel After a major renovation, Melbourne's oldest (and arguably most famous) pub is a newfound pleasure, whether for a drink or a meal in the stylish upstairs restaurant or bistro areas. Head upstairs to see the naked *Chloe,* a famous painting brought to Melbourne for the Great Exhibition in 1880. The pub, which was built in 1853 and started selling beer in 1861, has a few years on *Chloe,* which was painted in Paris in 1875. The painting has a special place in the hearts of customers. At the corner of Flinders and Swanston sts. (℃ **03/9650 3884.**

THE CASINO

Crown Casino Australia's largest casino is a plush affair that's open 24 hours. You'll find all the usual roulette and blackjack tables and so on, as well as an array of gam-ing machines. Believe me, you can lose big here. There are some 25 restaurants and 40 bars on the premises. A good choice for lunch is the **Red Emperor.** Its Cantonese *yum cha* is superb, as is the service. There's a great view of the Yarra River. It's open Monday through Saturday from noon to 3pm, Sunday 11am to 4pm. Casino: Clarendon St., Southbank. (℃ **03/9292 6868.** Red Emperor: 3 Southgate Ave., upper level Southgate. (℃ **03/9699 4170.** Yum cha items A$3.85–A$8.80 (US$3–US$7). AE, DC, MC. V.

9 Side Trips from Melbourne

DANDENONG RANGES

40km (25 miles) E of Melbourne

Melbournians traditionally do a "day in the Dandenongs" from time to time, topping off their getaway with Devonshire tea, scones, and jam at one of the many cafes en route. Up in the cool, high country you'll find native bush, famous gardens, the Dan-denong Ranges National Park, historic attractions such as the Puffing Billy—a vintage steam train—and plenty of restaurants and cozy B&Bs. The Dandenong Ranges National Park is one of the state's oldest, set aside in 1882 to protect its mountain ash forests and lush tree-fern gullies.

GETTING THERE To get to the area, take the Burwood Highway from Mel-bourne, then the Mount Dandenong Tourist Road, which starts at Upper Ferntree Gully and winds through the villages of Sassafras, Olinda, Mount Dandenong, and Kalorama to Montrose. If you take a turnoff to Sherbrook, or extend your journey into a loop taking in Seville, Woori Yallock, Emerald, and Belgrave, you'll see a fair slice of the local scenery. A really good tour operator is **A Tour With A Difference** ((℃ **03/9754 1699;** www.atwad.com.au). They pick up from Melbourne hotels in a 10-person bus and do lots of great things in the Dandenongs, including a ride on the Puffing Billy. The tour costs just A$125 (US$100) and includes morning tea, lunch, and all entry fees.

VISITOR INFORMATION The **Dandenong Ranges & Knox Visitor Informa-tion Centre,** 1211 Burwood Hwy., Upper Ferntree Gully, VIC 3156 ((℃ **1800/645 505** in Australia, or 03/9758 7522; fax 03/9758 7533), is open daily from 9am to 5pm.

NATURE WALKS

Most people come here to get out of the city for a pleasant bushwalk, and in that way it's the equivalent of Sydney's Blue Mountains. Some of the better walks include the

Warragul Hwy.

Drouin

Korumburra

180

181

10 mi

10 km

0

0

Warburton

YARRA VALLEY

Healesville

DANDENONG RANGES NATL-PARK

Hwy.

153

Yarra Glen

Maroondah

Lilydale

Mt. Dandenong

Olinda

Belgrave

Emerald

Princes

Kooweerup

Gippsland

RANGES

DANDENONG

Upper Ferntree Gully

South

180

FRENCH ISLAND

Newhaven

Melbourne

ALT 1

Nepean

Hwy.

Stony Pt.

Cowes

Phillip Island

Dromana

Balnarring

Penguin Parade

31

Port Phillip Bay

MORNINGTON PENINSULA

79

Rosebud

Rye

B a s s   S t r a i t

Queenscliff

Portsea

Sorrento

BELLARINE PENINSULA

Melton

Werribee

8

1

Bacchus Marsh

Bellarine Hwy.

Geelong

100

Princes

Great Ocean Rd.

1

250 Mi

250 Km

0

Victoria

Melbourne

Ferry ----
i Information
   Wineries

585

easy 2.5km (1.5-mile) stroll from the **Sherbrook Picnic Ground** through the forest, and the **Thousand Steps** and the **Kokoda Track Memorial Walk,** a challenging rain-forest track from the Fern Tree Gully Picnic Ground up to One Tree Hill. Along the way are plaques commemorating Australian troops who fought and died in Papua New Guinea in World War II.

FOR GARDENING BUFFS

Bonsai Farm If you don't like to crane your neck when it comes to looking at trees, then visit this large display of petite bonsais. Some of them are many decades old and cost a pretty penny.

Mt. Dandenong Tourist Rd., Mt. Dandenong. ℂ **03/9751 1150.** Free admission. Wed–Sun 11am–5pm. Train to Croydon, then bus no. 688.

National Rhododendron Gardens From September through November, thousands of rhododendrons and azaleas burst into bloom in these magnificent gardens. There are 42 lovely hectares (104 acres) in all, with a 3km (1.75-mile) walking path leading past flowering exotics and native trees as well as great vistas over the Yarra Valley. A tearoom is open every day in the spring and on weekends at other times. Visitors flock here in summer for the glorious walks, and again in autumn when the leaves are turning.

The Georgian Rd., Olinda. ℂ **03/9751 1980.** Admission Sept–Nov A$6.70 (US$5.30) adults, A$2.20 (US$1.70) children 10–16, A$14 (US$11) families; Dec–Aug A$5.60 (US$4.50) adults, A$2.20 (US$1.70) children, A$14 (US$11) families. Daily 10am–4:30pm. Closed Dec 25. Train to Croydon, then bus no. 688 to the gardens, or train to Belgrave and bus no. 694.

Tesselaar's Bulbs and Flowers Tens of thousands of flowers are on display here, putting on a flamboyantly colorful show in the spring (Sept–Oct). Expect to see a dazzling variety of tulips, daffodils, rhododendrons, azaleas, fuchsias, and ranunculuses. Bulbs are on sale at discount prices at other times.

357 Monbulk Rd., Silvan. ℂ **03/9737 9811.** Admission during tulip festival (around Sept 12–Oct 11) A$14 (US$11) adults, free for children under 16 accompanied by an adult; free for everyone rest of the year. During tulip festival daily 10am–5pm; rest of year Mon–Fri 8am–4:30pm, Sat–Sun 1–5pm. Train to Lilydale, then bus no. 679.

William Ricketts Sanctuary *Moments* This wonderful garden, in a forest of mountain ash, features clay figures representing the Aboriginal Dreamtime. The sculptures were created over the lifetime of sculptor William Ricketts, who died in 1993 at the age of 94. The garden encompasses fern gullies and waterfalls spread out over 13 hectares (32 acres), with the sculptures occupying .8 hectare (2 acres).

Mt. Dandenong Tourist Rd., Mt. Dandenong. ℂ **03/9751 1300.** www.parkweb.vic.gov.au. Admission A$5.20 (US$4.20) adults, A$4.20 (US$3.40) students, A$2 (US$1.60) children 10–16, A$13 (US$10) families. Daily 10am–4:30pm. Closed Dec 25 and days of total fire ban. Train to Croydon, then bus no. 688.

FOR TRAIN BUFFS

Puffing Billy Railway *Kids* For almost a century, Puffing Billy steam railway has chugged over a 13km (8-mile) track from Belgrave to Emerald Lake. Passengers ride on open carriages and enjoy lovely views as the train passes through forests and fern gullies and over a National Trust–classified wooden trestle bridge. Trips take around an hour each way. A further stretch of track to Gembrook opened in 1998. Daily trips to Gembrook take an extra 45 minutes and cost A$26 (US$21) for adults, A$13 (US$10) for children. Night trains also run on occasional Saturdays.

Belgrave Station, Belgrave. ℂ **03/9754 6800** (recorded information). www.puffingbilly.com.au. Admission A$18 (US$9.60) adults, A$10 (US$8) children 4–16, A$51 (US$41) families. Mon–Fri 10:30 and 11:15am, noon, 2:30pm;

Sat–Sun 10:30 and 11:45am, 1:30, and 3:15pm. Closed Dec 25. Train from Flinders St. Station in Melbourne to Belgrave; Puffing Billy station is a short walk away.

WHERE TO DINE

Churinga Café CAFE   This is a nice place for a quick lunch or morning or afternoon tea. It has pleasant gardens and is just across from the William Ricketts Sanctuary. You can get everything from curries to traditional British fare. Devonshire tea costs A$6 (US$4.80).

1381 Mt. Dandenong Tourist Rd., Mt. Dandenong. ℂ 03/9751 1242. Main courses A$13–A$14 (US$10–US$11). AE, DC, MC, V. Sat–Wed 10:30am–4:30pm.

Wild Oak Café MODERN AUSTRALIAN   For good home cooking, you can't beat this cozy cafe. The food includes the likes of chargrilled steak, smoked Atlantic salmon risotto, linguine with prawns, and Cajun chicken. The restaurant has a few vegetarian selections and a roaring log fire in winter.

232 Ridge Rd., Mt. Dandenong. ℂ 03/9751 2033. Main courses A$16–A$19 (US$13–US$15). DC, MC, V. Daily 10am–10pm.

YARRA VALLEY ✶
61km (40 miles) E of Melbourne

The Yarra Valley is a wine-growing region east of Melbourne. It's dotted with villages, historic houses, gardens, crafts shops, antiques centers, and restaurants, as well as dozens of wineries. There are some good bushwalks, and the Healesville Sanctuary is one of the best places in Australia to see native animals.

ESSENTIALS

GETTING THERE   McKenzie's Bus Lines (ℂ 03/9853 6264) operates bus service from Lilydale Railway Station to Healesville. (Catch a train from Melbourne's Spencer St. Station to Lilydale; the trip takes about an hour.) Buses connect with trains roughly 12 times a day; call for exact connection times.

If you're driving, pick up a map of the area from the Royal Automotive Club of Victoria (ℂ 03/9790 3333) in Melbourne. Maps are free if you're a member of an auto club in your home country, but remember to bring your membership card. Alternatively, you can pick up a map at the tourist office. Take the Maroondah Highway from Melbourne to Lilydale and on to Healesville. The trip takes around 1 hour and 15 minutes.

VISITOR INFORMATION   Pick up details on attractions and lodging at the **Yarra Valley Visitor Information Centre,** Old Court House, Harker Street, Healesville (ℂ 03/5962 2600; fax 03/5962 2040). It's open daily from 9am to 5pm.

EXPLORING THE VALLEY

There are three principal roads in the valley: Melba Highway, Maroondah Highway, and Myers Creek Road, which form a triangle. Within the triangle are three smaller roads, Healesville–Yarra Glen Road, Old Healesville Road, and Chum Creek Road, which all lead to wineries. Most people start their tour of the Yarra Valley from Lilydale and take in several cellar-door tastings at vineyards along the route.

Balloon Aloft (ℂ 1800/028 568 in Australia) offers dawn balloon rides over the wineries for A$255 (US$204) for adults and A$170 (US$136) for children over 8. The flight includes a champagne breakfast.

Healesville Sanctuary ⭐ (Finds) Forget about seeing animals in cages—this preserve is a great place to spot native animals in almost-natural surroundings. You can see wedge-tailed eagles, dingos, koalas, wombats, reptiles, and more, all while strolling through the peppermint-scented gum forest, which rings with the chiming of bellbirds. Sir Colin McKenzie started the sanctuary in 1921 as a center to preserve endangered species and educate the public. There's a gift shop, a cafe serving light meals, and picnic grounds.

Badger Creek Rd., Healesville. ⓒ **03/5957 2800.** Fax 03/5957 2870. www.zoo.org.au. Admission A$19 (US$15) adults, A$9.50 (US$7.60) children, A$48 (US$38) families. Daily 9am–5pm. Train from Flinders St. Station to Lilydale, then bus no. 685.

WHERE TO STAY & DINE

Melba Lodge ⭐ These stylish, modern accommodations are in Yarra Glen, in the heart of the Yarra Valley wine region. Of the luxurious guest rooms, four have queen-size beds, and two have king-size beds and a Jacuzzi; all have private bathrooms. There's a comfortable lounge with an open fire, and a billiard room. The lodge is only a few minutes' walk from historic Yarra Glen, which has antiques shops and a crafts market. There are plenty of restaurants and wineries around, too. It's a short drive to the Healesville Sanctuary.

939 Melba Hwy., Yarra Glen, VIC 3775. ⓒ **03/9730 1511.** Fax 03/9730 1566. www.melbalodge.com.au. 8 units. A$130 (US$104) queen room; A$190 (US$152) king room. Rates include cooked breakfast. AE, DC, MC, V. **Amenities:** Bar; Jacuzzi; business center; massage; nonsmoking rooms. *In room:* A/C, TV.

Sanctuary House Motel Healesville This place is very handy for visiting the sanctuary and even better if you want to relax and sample some good Yarra Valley wine. Just 400m (1,312 ft.) from the Healesville Sanctuary, Sanctuary House sits in some 4 hectares (10 acres) of beautiful bushland. The rooms are typical motel-style. Also available are two units with kitchens and amenities to assist travelers with disabilities. These go for A$140 (US$112) on weekends, A$130 (US$104) weekdays. A five-bedroom farmhouse nearby sits on 8 hectares (20 acres) featuring a pool and log fireplace; to rent it, go through the motel.

Badger Creek Rd. (P.O. Box 162, Healesville, VIC 3777). ⓒ **03/5962 5148.** Fax 03/5962 5392. www.sanctuary house.com.au. 12 units (all with shower). A$80–A$90 (US$64–US$72) double. MC, V. Train from Flinders St. Station to Lilydale, then bus no. 685. **Amenities:** Restaurant; small outdoor heated pool; Jacuzzi; sauna; children's play area; game room; massage; babysitting; laundry service; nonsmoking rooms. *In room:* A/C, TV, fridge, hair dryer, iron.

PHILLIP ISLAND: PENGUINS ON PARADE ⭐
139km (86 miles) S of Melbourne

Phillip Island's **penguin parade,** which happens every evening at dusk, is one of Australia's most popular animal attractions. There are other, less crowded places in Australia where watching homecoming penguins feels less staged (Kangaroo Island in South Australia comes to mind) but at least guides and boardwalks protect the little ones and their nesting holes from the throngs. Nevertheless, the commercialism of the Penguin Parade puts a lot of people off—busloads of tourists squashed into a sort of amphitheater hardly feels like being one with nature. Phillip Island also offers nice beaches, good bushwalking, fishing, and Seal Rocks. If you have the time, you could spend at least 2 days here.

ESSENTIALS
GETTING THERE Most visitors come to Phillip Island on a day trip from Melbourne and arrive in time for the Penguin Parade and dinner. Several tour companies

run day trips. Among them are **Gray Line** (© 03/9663 4455), which operates penguin trips daily departing Melbourne at 1:30pm and returning at around 11:30pm. Tours cost A$80 (US$64) for adults and A$40 (US$32) for children. Gray Line also offers full-day trips including the Dandenong Ranges and a ride on the Puffing Billy steam train.

An excellent budget option is a half-day trip with **Melbourne Sightseeing** (© 03/9663 3388). Tours depart Melbourne daily at 1:30pm and include visits to a cattle farm where you can hand-feed kangaroos, the Koala Conservation Centre, and a seal colony, as well as the Penguin Parade. The coach returns to Melbourne at 10:30pm. The trip costs A$75 (US$60) for adults (A$49/US$39 with a YHA card) and A$38 (US$30) for children. For the same price, an express bus leaves Melbourne at 5:30pm (returning at 11pm) and travels directly to the Penguin Parade.

If you're driving on your own, Phillip Island is an easy 2-hour trip from Melbourne along the South Gippsland Highway and then the Bass Highway. A bridge connects the highway to the mainland.

V/Line trains (© 13 22 32 in Australia, or 03/9619 5000; www.vlinepassenger. com.au) run in summer from Flinders Street Station to Phillip Island via Dandenong. The trip takes 2¼ hours and costs A$13 (US$10) one-way.

VISITOR INFORMATION The **Phillip Island Information Centre,** Phillip Island Tourist Road, Newhaven (© 1300/366 422 in Australia, or 03/5956 7447; www.phillipisland.net.au), is an attraction in itself, with interactive computer displays, dioramas giving visitors a glimpse into the penguins' world, and a small theater. It's open daily from 9am to 5pm (to 6pm in summer).

EXPLORING THE AREA

Visitors approach the island from the east, passing through the town of **Newhaven.** Just a little past Newhaven is the Phillip Island Information Centre.

The main town on the island, **Cowes** (pop. 2,400), is on the north coast. A stroll along its Esplanade is worthwhile. The Penguin Parade is on the far southwest coast.

The trip to the west coast of Phillip Island's Summerland Peninsula ends in an interesting rock formation called **The Nobbies.** This strange-looking outcropping can be reached at low tide by a basalt causeway. You'll get some spectacular views of the coastline and two offshore islands from here. On the farthest of these islands is a population of up to **12,000 Australian fur seals,** the largest colony in Australia (bring your binoculars). This area is also home to thousands of nesting silver gulls.

On the north coast of the island, you can explore **Rhyll Inlet,** an intertidal mangrove wetland, where you can see wading birds such as spoonbills, oystercatchers, herons, egrets, cormorants, and the rare bar-tailed godwit and whimbrel.

Birders will also love **Swan Lake,** another breeding habitat for wetland birds.

Elsewhere, walking trails lead through heath and pink granite to **Cape Woolamai,** the island's highest point, where there are fabulous coastal views. From September through April, the cape is home to thousands of short-tailed shearwaters (also known as mutton birds).

If you really want to see a bit of the island (instead of just seeing the parade and dashing off), consider taking one of the 15 different tours offered by Mike Cleeland's **Island Nature Tours,** RMB 6080, Cowes, Phillip Island, VIC 3922 (© 03/5956 7883).

PHILLIP ISLAND ATTRACTIONS

Koala Conservation Centre ⭐ Koalas were introduced to Phillip Island in the 1880s, and at first they thrived in the predator-free environment. However, overpopulation, the introduction of foxes and dogs, and the clearing of land for farmland and roads have taken their toll. Though you can still see a few koalas in the wild, the best place to find them is at this sanctuary, set up for research and breeding purposes. Visitors can get quite close to them, especially on the elevated boardwalk, which lets you peek into their treetop homes. For the best viewing, come around 4pm, when the ordinarily sleepy koalas are on the move.

Fiveways, Phillip Island Tourist Rd., Cowes ✆ **03/5952 1307**. A$5.60 (US$4.50) adults, A$2.60 (US$2) children under 16, A$14 (US$11) families. Daily 10am–5pm.

Phillip Island Penguin Reserve ✿ *Kids* The Penguin Parade takes place every night at dusk, when hundreds of little penguins appear at the water's edge, gather in the shallows, and waddle up the beach toward their burrows in the dunes. They're the smallest of the world's 17 species of penguins, standing just 33 centimeters (13 in.) high, and they're the only penguins that breed on the Australian mainland. Fences and viewing stands were erected in the 1960s to protect the nesting areas. Flash photography is banned because it scares the little guys. Wear a sweater or jacket, because it gets chilly after the sun goes down. A kiosk selling food opens an hour before the penguins turn up. Reservations for the Penguin Parade are essential on weekends and public holidays and in summer.

If you get to Phillip Island on your own and don't have a car, the **Penguin Parade Bus** (✆ **03/5952 1042** or 04/1736 0370) will pick you up from your hotel. The round-trip price is A$19 (US$15) for adults and A$11 (US$8.80) for children and includes a ticket for the Penguin Parade.

Summerland Beach, Phillip Island Tourist Rd., Cowes. ✆ **1300/366 422** in Australia, or 03/5951 2800. www. penguins.org.au. Admission A$14 (US$11) adults, A$7 (US$3.20) children 4–13, A$35 (US$28) families. Visitor center summer daily 9am–6pm, winter daily 9am–5pm; penguins arrive at sunset.

WHERE TO STAY
Penguin Hill Country House B&B This private home with views over sheep paddocks to Bass Strait is within walking distance of the Penguin Parade. Each room has good views and is stocked with antiques (as is much of the house) and queen-size beds. Two have an attached bathroom with shower, and the third has a private bathroom across the hall. There's a TV and a phone in the cozy lounge. The hosts can pick you up from Cowes.

Backbeach and Ventnor roads (RMB 1093), Cowes, Phillip Island, VIC 3922. ✆/fax **03/5956 8777**. 3 units. A$130 (US$104) double. Rates include cooked breakfast. AE, MC, V. Children not accepted. **Amenities:** TV lounge; tour desk; business center; limited room service; coin-op laundry; nonsmoking rooms. *In room:* TV, fax, hair dryer, iron.

Rothsaye on Lovers Walk ✿✿ The penguins are just down the road and the beach is right on the doorstep—who could ask for anything more? The suites here are adjacent to the owner's home, and the one-bedroom cottage is set slightly apart. All rooms come with antiques and king-size beds. You also get a fruit basket, free fishing gear, beach chairs and umbrellas, magazines, and fresh flowers. Lovers Walk, a romantic floodlit path, leads from the doorstep to the center of Cowes. The owners also have a new beachside property nearby called Abaleigh on Lovers Walk. The two gorgeous suites here come with kitchens, barbecues, and good water views. They cost A$215 (US$172) a night.

2 Roy Ct., Cowes 3922. ✆/fax **03/5952 2691**. www.rothsaye.com.au 4 suites, 1 cottage. A$140–A$190 (US$112–US$152) suite; A$140–A$190 (US$112–US$152) cottage. Rates include breakfast. MC, V. Children not accepted. **Amenities:** Golf course nearby; tour desk; laundry service; nonsmoking rooms. *In room:* A/C, TV/VCR, kitchen, coffeemaker, hair dryer, iron.

AROUND PORT PHILLIP BAY

West of Melbourne, the Princes Highway (or Hwy. 1) heads toward Geelong via Werribee. South of Melbourne, the Nepean Highway travels along the coast to the Mornington Peninsula as far as Portsea. If you have time to stay the night, you can combine the two options, heading first down to the Mornington Peninsula (see below) and then taking the car and passenger ferry from Sorrento to Queenscliff (see below).

WERRIBEE

This small country town is 32km (20 miles) southwest of Melbourne, a 30-minute drive along the Princes Freeway. Trains run from Melbourne to Werribee station; a taxi from the station to the zoo costs around A$5 (US$4).

The Mansion at Werribee Park ✦ Known as "the palace in the paddock," this 60-room Italianate mansion was built in 1877. It was quite the extravagant project in its day. In addition to touring the house, which has wonderful antique furniture, you may stroll around the grounds—132 hectares (326 acres) of formal gardens and bushland fronting the Werribee River—and have a picnic. You can also make advance arrangements to take one of the popular carriage rides that make their way through the property. Allow 1 to 2 hours. The mansion offers a great afternoon tea.

K Rd., Werribee. Ⓒ **13 19 63** in Australia, or 03/9741 2444. www.visitvictoria.com/mansions. Free admission to park and picnic grounds; admission to mansion A$12 (US$9.20) adults, A$6 (US$4.80) children 5–15, A$29 (US$23) families. Nov–Mar daily 10am–5pm; Apr–Oct daily 10am–4pm. Closed Dec 25.

Victoria's Open Range Zoo at Werribee From inside your zebra-striped safari bus, you can almost touch the mainly African animals that wander almost freely over the plains—no depressing cages here. This high-caliber open-air zoo is closely associated with the Melbourne Zoo. There is also a walk-through section featuring African cats, including cheetahs, and monkeys. The safari-bus tour takes 50 minutes.

K Rd., Werribee. Ⓒ **03/9731 9600.** www.zoo.org.au. Admission A$19 (US$15) adults, A$9.50 (US$7.60) children, A$48 (US$38) families. Daily 9am–5pm (entrance gate closes at 3:30pm). Safari tours hourly 10am–3pm.

THE MORNINGTON PENINSULA

The Mornington Peninsula, a scenic 40km (25-mile) stretch of windswept coastline and hinterland 80km (50 miles) south of Melbourne, is one of Melbourne's favorite day-trip and weekend-getaway destinations. The coast is lined with good beaches and thick bush consisting almost entirely of tea trees. (Early colonists used it as a tea substitute.) The **Cape Shanck Coastal Park** stretches along the peninsula's Bass Strait foreshore from Portsea to Cape Shanck. It's home to gray kangaroos, southern brown bandicoots, echidnas, native rats, mice, reptiles, bats, and many forest and ocean birds. The park has numerous interconnecting walking tracks providing access to some remote beaches.

The Mornington Peninsula has become a popular wine-producing region. The peninsula's fertile soil, temperate climate, and rolling hills produce excellent wine, particularly pinot noir, shiraz, and chardonnay. Many wineries offer cellar-door tastings, others have excellent restaurants.

Along the route to the south you could stop at the **Morning Peninsula Regional Gallery,** 4 Vancouver St., Mornington (Ⓒ **03/5975 4395**), to check out the work of famous Australian artists (open Tues–Sun 10am–5pm), or visit Arthurs Seat State Park to take a short hike or ride a chairlift to a 300m (984-ft.) summit offering glorious views over the surrounding bush. At Sorrento, take time out to spot pelicans on the jetty, or visit the town's many galleries.

Also on the Mornington Peninsula is Australia's oldest and most famous maze, **Ashcombe Maze & Water Gardens,** Red Hill Road, Shoreham (© **03/5989 8387**), which also has extensive water and woodland gardens. There is even a rose maze made out of 1,300 rose bushes, which is spectacular when in full bloom over the spring and summer months. There's also a pleasant cafe with indoor and outdoor dining. The park is open daily from 10am to 5pm; admission is A$7 (US$5.60) for adults, and A$4 (US$3.20) for children.

GETTING THERE   From Melbourne, take the Mornington Peninsula Freeway to Rosebud, and then the Point Nepean Road. If you want to cross Port Phillip Bay from Sorrento to Queenscliff, take the **Queenscliff Sea Road Ferry** (© **03/5258 3255;** fax 03/5258 1877), which operates daily every hour on the hour between 8am and 6pm (there's an 8pm ferry Fri–Sat from mid-Sept to mid-Dec and daily from mid-Dec until Easter Thursday). Ferries from Queenscliff operate from 7am to 5pm (plus a 7pm ferry on days listed above). The fare is around A$48 (U$27) for cars, but changes slightly depending on season. Foot-passenger fares are A$9 (US$7.20) for adults, A$7 (US$5.60) for children 5 to 15, and A$1 (US80¢) for children under 5. The crossing takes 35 to 40 minutes.

VISITOR INFORMATION   The **Peninsula Visitor Information Centre,** Point Nepean Road, Dromana (© **1800/804 009** in Australia, or 03/5987 3078), has plenty of maps and information on the area and can also help book accommodations. It's open daily from 9am to 5pm. You can get more information on this and all the other Victorian National Parks by calling © **13 19 63** or visiting www.parks.vic.gov.au.

Where to Stay & Dine

The Portsea Hotel   The rooms in this typical Australian motel on the seafront are done up with country-style furnishings. The standard twin rooms are basic; all share bathrooms. Doubles have double beds and attached bathrooms with showers. Units with bathrooms also have TVs and refrigerators. The outdoor beer garden is pleasant on a sunny day.

3746 Point Nepean Rd., Portsea, VIC 3944. © **03/5984 2213.** Fax 03/5984 4066. www.portseahotel.com.au. 25 units, 6 with bathroom. A$110–A$130 (US$93–US$74) double without bathroom; A$130–A$160 (US$114–US$128) double with bathroom; A$170–A$195 (US$136–US$156) bay-view suite. More expensive prices are for weekends. Winter discounts (around 20%) available. AE, DC, MC. V. **Amenities:** Restaurant; 3 bars; golf course nearby; tour desk; laundry service. *In room:* A/C, coffeemaker.

13

Victoria

by Marc Llewellyn

Australia's southernmost mainland state is astoundingly diverse. Within its boundaries are 35 national parks, encompassing every possible terrain, from rainforest and mountain ranges to sun-baked Outback desert and a coast where waves crash dramatically onto rugged sandstone outcroppings.

Melbourne (see chapter 12) may be this rugged state's heart, but the mighty Murray River, which separates Victoria from New South Wales, is its lifeblood, providing irrigation for vast tracts of semidesert land.

Most visitors to Victoria start out exploring Melbourne's cosmopolitan streets and then visit a few local wineries before heading for the gold fields around the historic city of Ballarat. Lots of them only experience a fraction of Victoria, but this wonderful and not overly touristed region is worth a closer look.

Visitors with more time might head inland to the mountains (perhaps for skiing or bushwalking at Mount Hotham or Falls Creek), or seek out the wilderness of Snowy River National Park. Others head to the outback, to the Grampians National Park, and to Mildura through open deserts and past pink lakes and red sand dunes.

Lots of options await, and because many of them are rural, you'll find prices for accommodations very affordable. Whatever itinerary you choose, you're sure to find adventure and dramatic scenery.

See "Side Trips from Melbourne," in chapter 12, for information on the Dandenong Ranges, Yarra Valley, Phillip Island, and the Mornington Peninsula.

EXPLORING THE STATE

VISITOR INFORMATION Pick up brochures and maps at the Victoria Visitor Information Centre (at the Melbourne Town Hall, Corner Swanston Street & Little Collins Street in Melbourne; ℂ 13 28 42 in Australia; www.visitvictoria.comor call the **Victoria Tourism Information Service** (ℂ 13 28 42) from anywhere in Australia to talk to a consultant about your plans. The service, open daily from 8am to 6pm, will also send you brochures. If you need information along the way, look for blue road signs with a rectangular white or yellow information symbol.

GETTING THERE **V/Line** (ℂ 13 61 96 in Victoria, or 13 22 32 in New South Wales) runs a limited network of trains to various places in Victoria, and continuing trips to most major centers with connecting buses. Several bus companies connect Melbourne with regional areas of Victoria; the biggest is **Greyhound Australia** (ℂ 13 14 99 in Australia, or 07/4690 9950; www.greyhound.com.au).

1 Ballarat: Gold-Rush City ★★

113km (70 miles) W of Melbourne

Ballarat, Victoria's largest inland city (pop. 90,000), is all about gold. In 1851, two prospectors found gold nuggets scattered on the ground at a place known as, ironically, Poverty Point. Within a year, 20,000 people had drifted into the area, and Australia's El Dorado gold rush had begun.

In 1858, the second-largest chunk of gold discovered in Australia (the Welcome Nugget) was found, but by the early 1860s, most of the easily obtainable yellow metal was gone. Larger operators continued digging until 1918, and by then Ballarat had developed enough industry to survive without mining. Today, you can still see the gold rush's effects in the impressive buildings, built from the miners' fortunes, lining Ballarat's streets.

ESSENTIALS

GETTING THERE From Melbourne, Ballarat is a 1½-hour drive on the Great Western Highway. **V/Line** (© **13 61 96** in Victoria, or 13 22 32 in New South Wales) runs trains between the cities every day; the trip takes less than 2 hours. The return fare is approximately A$34 (US$27) for adults and A$12 (US$9.60) for children. Ask about family-saver fares. A public bus connects the Ballarat train station with the town center.

Several companies offer day trips from Melbourne. They include **AAT Kings** (© **1300/556 100** in Australia, or 02/9252 2788; www.aatkings.com.au). A full-day tour costs A$108 (US$86) for adults and A$54 (US$43) for children.

VISITOR INFORMATION The **Ballarat Visitor Information Centre,** 39 Sturt St. (at the corner of Albert St.), Ballarat, VIC 3350 (© **1800/648 450** in Australia, or 03/5320 5741; www.ballarat.com), is open daily from 9am to 5pm.

SEEING THE SIGHTS

Ballarat contains many reminders of the gold-rush era, but it all really comes to life in the colonial-era re-creation on Sovereign Hill.

Ballarat Fine Art Gallery After you've learned the story of the Eureka Uprising (see the next listing), you may find it moving to come here and see the original Eureka flag. This provincial gallery also houses a collection of Australian art, including works by Sydney Nolan, Fred Williams, and Russell Drysdale. Look out for Tom Roberts's *Charcoal Burners* and Phillip Fox's *Love Story.*

40 Lydiard St. N. © **03/5320 5858**. Admission A$5 (US$4) adults, A$2.50 (US$2) students, free for children under 16. Daily 9am–5pm. Closed Good Friday and Dec 25.

(*Value* **Ballarat Combination Passes**

The **Ballarat Eureka Pass** includes unlimited 3-day entry to the Eureka Stockade Centre, Sovereign Hill, The Gold Museum, and Ballarat Fine Art Gallery. It costs A$36 (US$28) for adults, A$17 (US$13) for children 5 to 15, and A$92 (US$74) for families. A **Gold Pass** includes entry to The Gold Museum and Sovereign Hill, as well as a mine tour. It costs A$30 (US$24) for adults, A$15 (US$11) for children, and A$78 (US$62) for families.

Victoria

Blood on the Southern Cross ★ (Moments) This 80-minute early-evening presentation re-creates the Eureka Uprising, one of the most important events in Australia's history, in a breathtaking sound-and-light show that covers Sovereign Hill's 25 hectares (62 acres). Bring something warm to wear, because it can get chilly at night.

After gold was discovered, the government devised a system of gold licenses, charging miners a monthly fee even if they came up empty-handed. The miners had to buy a license every month, and corrupt gold-field police (many of whom were former convicts) instituted a vicious campaign to extract the money.

When license checks intensified in 1854, even though most of the surface gold was gone, resentment flared. Prospectors began demanding political reforms, such as the right to vote, parliamentary elections, and secret ballots.

The situation exploded when the Eureka Hotel's owner murdered a miner but was set free by the government. The hotel was burned down in revenge, and more than 20,000 prospectors joined together, burned their licenses in a huge bonfire, and built a stockade over which they raised a flag.

Troops arrived at the "Eureka Stockade" the following month, but by then only 150 miners remained behind its walls. The stockade was attacked at dawn, and in the 15-minute skirmish, 24 miners were killed and 30 wounded. The civil uprising forced the government to act: The licenses were replaced with "miners rights" and cheaper fees, and the vote was introduced to Victoria.

Sovereign Hill, Bradshaw St. © **03/5333 5777**. www.sovereignhill.com.au. Reservations required. Admission A$37 (US$30) adults, A$20 (US$16) children 5–15, A$100 (US$80) families. Package with daytime entry to Sovereign Hill (see below) A$62 (US$50) adults, A$31 (US$25) children, A$162 (US$129) families. Package with buffet dinner and stay at Sovereign Hill Lodge (see below) A$152 (US$122) adults, A$65 (US$52) children, A$405 (US$324) families. Call ahead for information about other packages. 2 shows nightly Mon–Sat (times vary seasonally). Closed early Aug.

Eureka Stockade Centre You can't miss this building, with its huge sail, signifying the flag of the Southern Cross, above the original miners' stockade. Relive the action of the battle through multimedia displays. The Contemplation Room, where you are asked to think about Australian history while listening to a trickling water soundscape, is a bit too hokey for me.

Eureka St. © **03/5333 1854**. www.eurekaballarat.com. Admission A$8 (US$6.40) adults, A$4 (US$3.20) children, A$22 (US$18) families. Tues–Sun and Mon holidays 9am–5pm. Closed Dec 25.

The Gold Museum This interesting museum houses a large collection of gold nuggets found at Ballarat, as well as alluvial deposits, gold ornaments, and coins. It also holds gallery displays relating to the history of gold mining in the area. One hour should be enough to take in the museum.

Bradshaw St. (opposite Sovereign Hill). © **03/5337 1107**. Admission A$7.30 (US$5.80) adults, A$3.50 (US$2.80) children. See Gold Pass above. Daily 10am–5:30pm.

Sovereign Hill ★★ (Kids) Australia's best outdoor museum transports you back to the 1850s and the heady days of the gold rush. More than 40 stone-and-wood reproduction buildings, including shops and businesses on Main Street, sit on the 25-hectare (62-acre) former gold-mining site. There are also tent camps around the diggings on the lowest part of the site, which would have been the outskirts of town. There is a lot to see and do, so expect to spend at least 4 hours.

The township bustles with actors in period costumes going about their daily business. In addition to seeing how miners and their families lived, visitors can pan for real gold, watch lessons in Victorian classrooms, ride in horse-drawn carriages, and watch potters, blacksmiths, and tanners make their wares.

On top of Sovereign Hill are the mineshafts and pithead equipment. The fascinating tour of a typical underground gold mine takes around 45 minutes. The **Voyage to Discovery** museum has artifacts from the gold rush, dioramas of mining scenes, and interactive computer displays. A restaurant, several cafes, coffee shops, and souvenir stores are around the site.

Bradshaw St. Ⓒ **03/5331 1944.** www.sovereignhill.com.au. Admission (including mine tour and Gold Museum) A$30 (US$24) adults, A$15 (US$12) children 5–15, A$78 (US$60) families. Daily 10am–5pm. Closed Dec 25. Bus: 9 from Curtis St.

WHERE TO STAY

The Ansonia ✪   This boutique hotel in a restored Victorian building sports a glass atrium that runs the length of the property and is filled with plants and wicker chairs. Studio rooms are simply but comfortably furnished and have nice polished floorboards. The executive doubles are larger and a little plusher, and apartments have a separate lounge room. The two family rooms can sleep four people in two bedrooms. There is a comfortable library and sitting room with an open fire and tea- and coffeemaking facilities, and plenty of flowers and art everywhere. Smoking is not allowed on the property.

32 Lydiard St. S., Ballarat, VIC 3350. Ⓒ **03/5332 4678.** Fax 03/5332 4698. www.ballarat.com/ansonia.htm. 20 units. A$142 (US$114) studio; A$158 (US$126) executive double; A$175 (US$140) suite; A$225 (US$180) apt; A$225 (US$180) family room. Packages available. AE, DC, MC, V. Free parking. **Amenities:** Restaurant; tour desk; babysitting; laundry service; dry cleaning; nonsmoking rooms. *In room:* TV, dataport, hair dryer, iron.

Ballarat Heritage Homestay ✪ *Finds*   If you'd enjoy staying in a historic cottage, you might want to try Ballarat Heritage Homestay. Some of these Victorian and Edwardian cottages date from gold rush days. All of them are very different, but all have a historic feel. Two cottages have claw-foot tubs, and one has a Jacuzzi. Generally there's a queen-size and a double, and sometimes two singles in each cottage. All the cottages have two or three bedrooms, open fires, and gas heating. The B&B room has a queen-size bed and sole use of a lounge.

185 Victoria St. (P.O. Box 1360, Ballarat Mail Centre, VIC 3354). Ⓒ **1800/813 369** in Australia, or 03/5332 8296. Fax 03/5331 3358. www.heritagehomestay.com. 5 cottages, 1 B&B unit. All rates for 2 people: Cottages A$200 (US$160) 1-night weekend stay (available for some cottages only); A$330–A$420 (US$264–US$336) 2-night weekend stay; A$160–A$180 (US$128–US$144) 1-night weekday stay. B&B A$150 (US$120) weekend; A$135 (US$108) weeknight. Rates include breakfast. Extra adult A$30 (US$20); extra child under 18 A$15 (US$12). AE, DC, MC, V. **Amenities:** TV lounge. *In room:* Kitchen, hair dryer, iron.

The Sovereign Hill Lodge   The colonial-style wooden buildings adjacent to Sovereign Hill were built to resemble an 1850s government camp that was used to control (and tax) the mine fields. The residence building has rooms with queen-size beds and a set of single bunks, and the Offices building has heritage rooms with four-poster beds and Baltic pine furnishings, some with Jacuzzis. There are eight double rooms in the Superintendent's house; the Barracks houses dorm rooms that sleep up to eight people (A$55/US$44 double). There's a bar, 24-hour reception, and a game room. Guests get a 10% discount off entry to Sovereign Hill.

Magpie St., Ballarat, VIC 3350. Ⓒ **03/5333 3409.** Fax 03/5333 5861. www.sovereignhill.com.au. 37 units. A$126 (US$101) double; A$138 (US$110) heritage room. Extra person A$14 (US$11). Ask about their many packages. AE, DC, MC, V. Free parking. **Amenities:** Restaurant; bar; babysitting; laundry service; nonsmoking rooms. *In room:* A/C, TV, iron.

WHERE TO DINE

Robin Hood Family Bistro BISTRO The Robin Hood is in a big old pub—not exactly a place where you'd expect to find a bistro catering to healthy eating. The bistro, though, is a past winner of the Real Meal Award, handed out by the Australian Hoteliers Association and aimed at promoting healthier pub food. Everything here is made with low-fat and low-cholesterol ingredients. On the menu you'll find steak-and-kidney pie, beef curry, and several types of steak. Not healthy so far, perhaps, but there's an extensive salad bar, and all main courses come with a healthy portion of vegetables.

33 Peel St. N. ⓒ 03/5331 3348. Reservations recommended Fri–Sat. Main courses A$8–A$20 (US$6.40–US$16). AE, DC, MC, V. Daily 11:30am–2pm and 5:30–8pm.

2 The Great Ocean Road: One of the World's Most Scenic Drives ⟨★⟨★

Geelong: 75km (47 miles) SW of Melbourne; Torquay: 94km (58 miles) SW of Melbourne; Port Campbell National Park: 285km (177 miles) SW of Melbourne; Peterborough: 200km (124 miles) SW of Melbourne; Warrnambool: 263km (163 miles) SW of Melbourne

The Great Ocean Road—which hugs the coast from Torquay through Anglesea, Lorne, Apollo Bay, Port Campbell, and Peterborough, until it ends at Warrnambool—is one of Australia's most spectacular drives. The scenery along the 106km (66-mile) route includes huge cliffs, ocean vistas, beaches, rainforests, and some incredible rock formations. The most spectacular section is the 27km (17-mile) stretch between Princeton (the start of Port Campbell National Park) and Peterborough. The settlements along the highway are small, but they offer a number of accommodations choices.

The best way to travel along the Great Ocean Road is to drive yourself at a leisurely pace, stopping wherever your fancy takes you. The main attractions are in the coastal Port Campbell National Park, so don't be surprised if you're not overly impressed until you get there. If you are traveling on to Adelaide, you could stop off for 1 night along the Great Ocean Road and spend another night in the Coorong in South Australia (see section 5, "The Coorong," in chapter 11).

ESSENTIALS

ORGANIZED TOURS **Let's Go Bush Tours** (ⓒ 03/9640 0826) offers a 2-day excursion that departs Melbourne on Wednesday and Saturday. The trip is less rushed than others, and you get to stay in the company's house on the highest point of the Great Ocean Road. The expedition costs A$99 (US$79), including dinner, breakfast, and accommodations.

The large coach operator **AAT Kings** (ⓒ 1300/556 100 in Australia; www.aat kings.com.au) runs daily trips along the Great Ocean Road—a journey I wouldn't like to attempt in a day. Tours cost A$116 (US$93) for adults, and A$58 (US$46) for children. **Gray Line Sightseeing Tours** (ⓒ 1300/858 687 in Australia or 03/9663 4455; www.grayline.com) also has daily trips for a similar price; you can pay online in U.S. dollars.

Wild-Life Tours (ⓒ 1300/650 288 in Australia or 03/9747 1882; www.wildlife tours.com.au) offers several well-priced multiday backpacker-style tours that take in the Great Ocean Road tour from Melbourne. A 1-day tour costs A$65 (US$52). The company also offers trips from Melbourne to see the Penguins on Parade on Phillip Island, and also trips between Melbourne and Sydney, and Melbourne and Adelaide. Prices do not include accommodations or food. Inquire about discounts.

Autopia Tours (© **03/9419 8878;** www.autopiatours.com.au) offers a 1-day tour from Melbourne taking in all the sights and including a bushwalk in the fabulous Otway Rainforest. It costs A$75 (US$60). The company also does a more relaxed 3-day tour for A$165 (US$132) without accommodations, though it can arrange rooms for you in hostels or hotels.

V/Line (© **13 61 96** in Victoria, or 03/9619 5000) runs combined train-coach Coast Link service to Warrnambool, via Geelong, Lorne, Apollo Bay, and Port Campbell. The train leaves Melbourne daily at 8:50am, 12:40pm, and 6:08pm—but check before turning up. You transfer to a bus at Geelong. The bus tours the Great Ocean Road, stopping at lookout points (and for lunch) and continues to Warrnambool. The round-trip cost is A$80 (US$64) for adults and A$39 (US$31) for children. Ask about family-saver fares.

VISITOR INFORMATION   Most places along the route have their own information centers. If you're coming from Melbourne, stop at the **Geelong & Great Ocean Road Visitors Centre,** Stead Park, Princess Highway, Geelong, VIC 3220 (©/fax **03/5275 5797;** www.greatoceanrd.org.au). You can book accommodations here, which you should do in advance, especially in summer. The really good website gives you plenty of tour options. There's also a visitor center at the **National Wool Museum,** 26 Moorabool St., Geelong (© **1800/620 888** in Australia, or 03/5222 2900).

Along the route, the **Port Campbell Visitor Information Centre,** Port Campbell National Park, Morris Street, Port Campbell (© **03/5598 6382**), is a good place to pick up brochures. It has some interesting displays and an audiovisual show of the area, and also acts as a hotel-booking service for the area. It's open from 9am to 5pm daily.

If you're approaching from the north, visit the **Camperdown Visitor Information Centre,** Court House, Manifold Street, Princes Highway, Camperdown (© **03/5593 3390**). It's open Monday through Friday from 9:30am to 5pm, Saturday from 9:30am to 4pm, and Sunday from 11am to 4pm.

EXPLORING THE COASTAL ROAD

Along the route you might want to stop off at **Torquay,** a township dedicated to surfing. The main surf beach is much nicer than the one farther down the coast in Lorne. Check out **Surfworld Museum,** Surfcity Plaza, Beach Road, West Torquay (© **03/5261 4606**), which has interactive exhibits dealing with surfboard design and surfing history, and video of the world's best surfers. Admission is A$6.50 (US$5.20) for adults, A$4.50 (US$3.60) for children, and A$18 (US$14) for families. **Bells Beach,** just down the road, is world-famous in surfing circles for its perfect waves.

Lorne has some nice boutiques and is a good place to stop for lunch or stay the night. The stretch from Lorne to Apollo Bay is one of the most spectacular sections of the route; the road narrows and twists and turns along a cliff edge with the ocean on the other side. **Apollo Bay** is a pleasant town that was once a whaling station. It has good sandy beaches and is more low-key than Lorne.

Next you come to the **Angahook-Lorne State Park,** which protects most of the coastal section of the Otway Ranges from Aireys Inlet, south of Anglesea, to Kennett River. It has many well-marked rainforest walks and picnic areas at Shelly Beach, Elliot River, and Blanket Bay. There's plenty of wildlife around.

About 13km (8 miles) past Apollo Bay, just off the main road, you can stroll on the **Maits Rest Rainforest Boardwalk.** A little farther along the main road, an unpaved road leads north past Hopetoun Falls and Beauchamp Falls to the settlement of **Beech Forest.** Seven kilometers (4⅓ miles) farther along the main road, another unpaved road heads south for 15km (9⅓ miles) to a windswept headland and the **Cape Otway Lighthouse,** one of several along the coast. Built by convicts in 1848, the 100m-tall (328-ft.) lighthouse is open to tourists. Admission is A$6.50 (US$5.20) for adults and A$3.50 (US$2.80) for children. It's open daily from 9am to 5pm. Ask about guided tours.

Back on the main road, your route heads inland through an area known as **Horden Vale** before running to the sea at Glenaire—there's good surfing and camping at **Johanna,** 6km (3¾ miles) north of here. Then the Great Ocean Road heads north again to **Lavers Hill,** a former timber town. Five kilometers (3 miles) southwest of Lavers Hill is small **Melba Gully State Park,** where you can spot glowworms at night and walk along routes of rainforest ferns. Keep an eye out for one of the last giant gum trees that escaped the loggers—it's some 27m (88 ft.) in circumference and is estimated to be more than 300 years old.

The next place of note is Moonlight Head, which marks the start of the **Shipwreck Coast**—a 120km (74-mile) stretch running to Port Fairy that claimed more than 80 ships in only 40 years at the end of the 19th century and the beginning of the 20th.

Just past Princetown starts the biggest attraction of the trip, **Port Campbell National Park** 🏵🏵. With its sheer cliffs and coastal rock sculptures, it's one of the most immediately recognizable images of natural Australia. You can't miss the **Twelve Apostles,** a series of rock pillars standing in the foam just offshore. Other attractions are the **Blowhole,** which throws up huge sprays of water; the **Grotto,** a rock formation intricately carved by the waves; **London Bridge,** which looked quite like the real thing until the center crashed into the sea in 1990 (leaving a bunch of tourists stranded on the wrong end); and the **Loch Ard Gorge. Port Fairy,** a lovely fishing town once called Belfast by Irish immigrants who settled here to escape the potato famine, is also on the Shipwreck Coast.

Not far past the town of Peterborough, the Great Ocean Road heads inland to Warrnambool. It eventually joins the Princes Highway heading toward Adelaide.

WHERE TO STAY ALONG THE WAY

The **Great Ocean Road Accommodation Centre,** 136 Mountjoy Parade, Lorne, VIC 3232 (✆ **03/5289 1800**), rents cottages and units along the route.

IN LORNE

Lorne is a good option for a night's rest. Though the beach is nothing special, it's a great place to learn to surf. There are plenty of restaurants, and lots of boutiques.

Cumberland Lorne Conference & Leisure Resort 🏵 *Value*   This sporty resort, totally renovated in 2003, stands out like a sore thumb between the sea and the foothills of the Otway Ranges. Still, I highly recommend it—it's a good deal, and quite luxurious. Every apartment has a queen-size bed and a sofa bed, a kitchen, a laundry, a Jacuzzi, a balcony, and free in-house movies. All units have large bathrooms with tub/shower combinations. More than half of the rooms have panoramic ocean views; the rest overlook gardens. Two-bedroom apartments have two extra single beds, and split-level penthouses have two Jacuzzis and two balconies.

150–178 Mountjoy Parade, Lorne, VIC 3232. (✆ **1800/037 010** in Australia, or 03/5289 2400. Fax 03/5289 2256. www.cumberland.com.au. 99 units. Summer A$285–A$325 (US$228–US$340) 1-bedroom apt, A$345–A$385 (US$276–US$308) 2-bedroom apt, A$385–A$425 (US$308–US$340) penthouse; off season A$230–A$270

(US$184–US$216) 1-bedroom apt, A$290–A$330 (US$232–US$264) 2-bedroom apt, A$330–A$370 (US$264–US$296) penthouse. Ask about packages. AE, DC, MC, V. **Amenities:** Restaurant; small indoor pool; 2 lit tennis courts; exercise room; Jacuzzi; sauna; watersports rental; children's center; concierge; tour desk; business center; 24-hr. room service; in-room massage; babysitting; dry cleaning; nonsmoking rooms. *In room:* A/C, TV w/pay movies, kitchenette, fridge, coffeemaker, hair dryer, iron.

Great Ocean Road Cottages *(Kids)*   This complex has it all, although with so many people (and quite a few children) around, it can be a little noisy in summer. The self-contained cottages, set away from each other in a quiet patch of bushland, lie about a 5-minute walk from the town center. Each cottage is a two-story wooden hut with a double bed, two twin beds, and a pullout mattress. There's also a bathroom and a full kitchen. Just down the road is Waverley House, a historic mansion that holds seven apartments. All of them are air-conditioned; they vary enormously in size and furnishings.

Also on the property is **Great Ocean Road Backpackers** (www.yha.org.au), which offers dorm-style accommodations. It has 53 dorm beds, seven double rooms, and four family rooms (each with a queen-size bed and two singles).

Great Ocean Rd. Cottages: 10 Erskine Ave. (P.O. Box 60), Lorne, VIC 3232. © **03/5289 1070.** Fax 03/5289 2508. www.greatoceanroadcottages.com. Waverley House: Waverley Ave. and Great Ocean Rd. (P.O. Box 60), Lorne, VIC 3232. © **03/5289 2044.** www.waverleyhouse.com. 10 cottages, 7 apts. A$170 (US$136) cottage weekend, A$150 (US$120) cottage weeknight. Weekly stays only in high season (Dec 26–Jan 26); A$145 (US$116) 1-bed apt weekday, A$165 (US$132) weekend (A$180/US$144 daily high season); A$255 (US$204) 2-bed apt weekday, A$295 (US$236) weekend (A$330/US$264 daily high season). Dorms: A$20 (US$16) for YHA members and A$23 (US$18) for nonmembers; doubles A$25 (US$20) and A$30 (US$24); family rooms A$75 (US$60) and A$90 (US$72). 2-night minimum for cottages on weekends. AE, DC, MC, V. **Amenities:** Jacuzzi; free use of bikes; free laundry; nonsmoking rooms. *In room:* TV/VCR, kitchenette, fridge, coffeemaker, hair dryer.

IN APOLLO BAY

Bayside Gardens   Opposite the beach, with good ocean views from the front rooms, Bayside Gardens is a pleasant place to stay—and you can save money on meals by cooking in your own kitchen. Each unit has a separate bedroom with a double bed, a lounge area, kitchen, and attached bathroom with shower. Rooms at the front can be noisy if you're not used to living beside an ocean. There are wood fires in some of the units, and all rooms have central heating. Fry your fish on barbecues scattered around the grounds. It's a 10-minute walk to town.

219 Great Ocean Rd., Apollo Bay, VIC 3233. ©/fax **03/5237 6248.** www.baysidegardens.com.au. 10 units. Feb–Dec A$70–A$110 (US$56–US$88) 1- and 2-bedroom apts. 1-week minimum Jan; A$980 (US$784) per week. Higher rates apply Jan, Easter, Christmas, and public holidays. MC, V. **Amenities:** Coin-op laundry; nonsmoking rooms. *In room:* TV, kitchen, fridge.

IN PORT CAMPBELL

Macka's Farm *(Finds) (Kids)*   This working farm is inland from the Twelve Apostles. The units all have kitchens, so you can cook your own feast. Otherwise, you can order meals by prior arrangement outside peak season, or visit one of the nearby restaurants. Rooms sleep between six and eight in a mixture of singles and doubles. There's no TV—but who needs it when there are lots of pigs, cows, ducks, and chickens running around? Overall, it's a great farm experience.

RSD 2305 Princetown Rd., Princetown, VIC 3269. © **03/5598 8261.** Fax 03/5598 8201. www.mackasfarm.com.au. 3 units. A$130–A$165 (US$104–US$132) double, depending on season (but check the website because there are dozens of different price categories). Extra person A$28 (US$22). MC, V. From the Twelve Apostles, go 2km (1¼ miles), turn at the sign for Macka's Farm, and go 4km (2½ miles) inland. *In room:* Kitchen, fridge, hair dryer.

WHERE TO DINE IN LORNE

Marks of Lorne ✦ INTERNATIONAL Lorne's best restaurant is a classy joint with simple wooden chairs and tables set in an elegant fashion in a cool, yellow-walled interior. Dishes include fried calamari salad, spicy octopus, risotto, and oven-baked vine-wrapped goat cheese and macadamia nut parcel on eggplant pâté with red capsicum purée. The bar is open for coffee and drinks all day.

Mount Joy Parade. ℂ **03/5289 2787.** Main courses A$12–A$23 (US$9.60–US$18). AE, MC, V. Daily noon–2:30pm and 6–9pm. Closed May and weekday lunch in winter.

Ozone Milk Bar *Value* AUSTRALIAN MILK BAR An Aussie icon, a milk bar is a kind of downmarket cafe that sells everything from shakes and pies to newspapers. This one sells good pies and quiche, a veggie burger I wouldn't recommend, chicken-filet sandwiches, cookies, ice cream, and small homemade cakes. The milk shakes are particularly good. You can sit inside or around three tables outside. There's a Thai place next door, but it's very unwelcoming.

Mount Joy Parade. ℂ **03/5289 1780.** Menu items A$1.80–A$4 (US$1.40–US$3.20). No credit cards. Daily 7am–6pm (until 11pm Dec 25–Jan).

3 The Murray River ✦

Mildura: 544km (337 miles) NW of Melbourne; Albury-Wodonga: 305km (189 miles) NE of Melbourne; Echuca: 210km (130 miles) N of Melbourne

The Murray is Australia's version of the Mississippi River. Though it's a rushing torrent of white water at its source in the Snowy Mountains, it becomes slow and muddy brown by the time it forms the meandering border between Victoria and New South Wales. The Darling River, which starts in Queensland, feeds the Murray; together they make Australia's longest river.

Aborigines once used the Murray as a source of food and transportation, and later the water carried paddle steamers, laden with wool and crops from the land it helped irrigate. In 1842, the Murray was "discovered" by explorers Hamilton Hume and William Howell on the first overland trek from Sydney to Port Phillip, near Melbourne. As Hume later wrote, on their trek the explorers "suddenly arrived at the bank of a very fine river—at least 60m wide, apparently deep, the bank being 2.4m or 2.7m above the level, which is overflowed at the time of flood . . . In the solid wood of a healthy tree I carved my name." You can still see the carved initials on a tree standing by the riverbank in Albury, on the border between the two states.

ESSENTIALS

GETTING THERE Most visitors cross the river during an overland drive between cities. There are two ways to the Murray from Melbourne: the 2½-hour route down the Midland Highway to Echuca, and the Calder Highway to Mildura, a 6-hour drive. Traveling from Melbourne to Mildura is practical only if you're continuing to Broken Hill, which is 297km (184 miles) north of Mildura. Those in a hurry to get to and from Sydney can travel via the river-straddling twin towns of Albury-Wodonga on the Hume Highway (about a 12-hr. trip with short stops).

V/Line (ℂ **13 61 96** in Victoria, or 03/9619 5000) runs regular train service to Mildura, Echuca, and Albury-Wodonga.

VISITOR INFORMATION The **Echuca and Moama and District Visitor Information Centre,** 2 Heygarth St., Echuca, VIC 3564 (ℂ **1800/804 446** in Australia or 03/5480 7555; fax 03/5482 6413; www.echucamoama.com), has plenty of maps and information about accommodations and river cruises. It's open daily from 9am to 5pm. The **Mildura Visitor Information & Booking Centre,** 180–190 Deakin Ave., Mildura, VIC 3502 (© **1800/039 043** in Australia or 03/5021 4424; fax 03/5021 1836; www.visitmildura.com.au), offers similar services. It's open Monday through Friday from 9am to 5:30pm and weekends from 9am to 5pm. If you're passing through Albury-Wodonga, contact the **Gateway Visitors Information Centre,** Gateway Village, Lincoln Causeway, Wodonga, VIC 3690 (© **1800/800 743** in Australia or 02/6041 3875; fax 02/6021 0322). It's open daily from 9am to 5pm.

RIVER CRUISES & OTHER FUN STUFF

IN MILDURA   Mildura is one of Australia's most important fruit-growing areas. There was a time, however, when this was semiarid red-dust country. The area bloomed because of a little ingenuity and, of course, the Murray. The original irrigation system consisted of two English water pumps and the manual labor of hundreds of immigrants, who were put to work clearing scrub and digging channels through the new fields. Today, the hungry land soaks up water.

Several paddle steamers leave from Mildura wharf. One of the nicest boats is **PS *Melbourne*** (© **03/5023 2200;** fax 03/5021 3017; www.murrayriver.com.au), which was built in 1912 and is still powered by steam. It offers 2-hour trips leaving at 10:50am and 1:50pm daily (but check times in advance because they do change). The fare is A$19 (US$15) for adults and A$7.50 (US$6) for children, free for children under 5.

PS *Melbourne*'s sister ship, the ***Rothbury,*** was built in 1881; a conventional engine has replaced its steam engine. It offers a winery cruise every Thursday from 10:30am to 3:30pm, stopping at a winery for tastings and a barbecue lunch. The trip costs A$42 (US$34) for adults and A$20 (US$16) for children. The *Rothbury* has evening dinner cruises Thursday from 7 to 10pm for A$40 (US$32) for adults and A$18 (US$14) for children. You can also take the paddleboat to the Golden River Zoo (see below) during school holiday periods; it leaves Mildura Wharf at 9:50am on Wednesday, returning at 3pm. The trip costs A$32 (US$25) for adults and A$16 (US$13) for children 5 to 14, including zoo entry.

On dry land, the **Golden River Zoo,** Flora Avenue, Mildura (© **03/5023 5540**), is a pleasant place to see native animals. The zoo fronts the river 4km (2½ miles) from the city center down 11th Street. The animals virtually follow you around (on the lookout for food) as you walk through their large enclosures. Admission is A$12 (US$9.60) for adults and A$6 (US$4.80) for children, including a barbecue lunch at noon, a tractor-train ride down to the river at 1:30pm, and an animal show. The zoo is open daily from 10am to 5pm; closed December 25.

IN ECHUCA   The paddle steamer *Emmylou* (© **03/5480 2237;** fax 03/5480 2927) operates out of Echuca. A 2-day, 2-night cruise leaves Wednesday at 6pm and returns at noon on Friday (check sailings beforehand). The cruise includes (depending on river levels) a visit to the Barmah, an area famous for its wetlands and the largest red gum trees in the world, or a stop at Perricoota Station. The trip costs A$415 to A$435 (US$332–US$348) per person. Children 4 to 14 receive a 25% discount. An overnight trip leaves on Saturday at 6pm and returns at 10am on Sunday. It costs A$195 to A$210 (US$156–US$168) per person, including breakfast; dinner is extra. The *Emmylou* also offers day trips costing A$15 (US$12) for adults and A$7.50

Moments Ned Kelly Country

The Australian legend Ned Kelly, the eldest of eight children, was born to Irish parents in Victoria in 1854. At the age of 12 his ex-convict father died and his family settled near relatives at Greta, 240km (150 miles) northeast of Melbourne.

Like many other poor families, the Kellys took up the government's offer of cheap land. As part of the deal, they had to clear the bushland, build a house, and plant crops. More often than not, the land parcels were too small and the soil too poor for them to make a living. The only recourse for many was to steal horses and cows from wealthy landowners, who owned huge tracts of the best land.

At 16, Ned Kelly was convicted of horse-rustling and sentenced to 3 years in Jail. A few years later, his mother was imprisoned for allegedly attacking a police officer named Fitzpatrick, who was accused of attacking Ned's sister first. During the scuffle, Ned shot Fitzpatrick through the wrist. Ned escaped—with a bounty on his head.

On the 26 October 1878, together with friends Joe Byrne and Steve Hart, Ned and his brother came across police camped at Stringy Bark Creek. Ned believed the police intended to kill him and his brother, so he called on them to surrender. Three officers resisted, and in the fight that followed Kelly shot them dead.

In the years that followed Ned and his gang avoided capture with the help of locals, who sympathized with their situation. During this time, the Kelly Gang robbed two banks, and during each robbery Ned gave one of his hostages a letter, explaining to the government how he'd been persecuted by police.

Then, in June 1880, Ned made his last stand. Police surrounded the Kelly Gang at the Glenrowan Hotel. Prepared for the fight, the four bushrangers put on suits of armor made from steel. It was no use. Twenty-eight bullets penetrated Ned's body. But, unlike the others in the gang, he survived. He was hanged in Melbourne Gaol on November 11, 1880. He was 25 years old.

(US$6) for kids for 1 hour, and A$18 (US$14) for adults and A$9 (US$7.20) for kids for 1½ hours.

The **Port of Echuca** (© **03/5482 4248;** www.portofechuca.org.au) is definitely worth a look. The three-level red-gum wharf was built in 1865 and is still in use by paddle steamers. The Port owns PS *Adelaide,* the oldest operating wooden-hulled paddle steamer in the world (1866), PS *Pevensey* (1911), and PS *Alexander Arbuthnot* (1923). One-hour cruises on the latter two, including a port tour, run daily at 10:15 and 11:30am, and 1, 2:15, and 3:30pm (though ring ahead to check, as they do change). They cost A$24 (US$19) for adults, A$13 (US$10) for children, and A$60 (US$48) for a family. You can look around the wharf on a guided tour, priced at A$12

If you're driving down from Sydney to Melbourne, I suggest you spend a few days exploring the region before making a side trip to the High Country. If you're driving down from Sydney you might want to stay the night in a two-bedroom cabin at the **Gundagai Tourist Park** (© **02/6944 1620**), in Gundagai (about 4 hr. from Sydney). Cabins cost from A$72 (US$55) a night. Another option is a night at the wonderful **King River Stables** ★★ (© **03/5721 8195**) in Wangaratta (about 6½ hr. from Sydney). This set of beautifully converted former horse stables are set amongst fields full of cows and horses. The lounge room stares out across an enormous billabong with a resident pelican. It costs A$125 (US$100) double, including breakfast.

Use Wangaratta as a base to discover Ned Kelly Country. A short hop from Wangaratta is Milawa, where there are quite a few wineries offering cellar-door tastings along the **Milawa Gourmet Trail** (www.milawagourmet.com), as well as the interesting **Milawa Cheese Company** (Factory Rd., Milawa; © **03/5727 3588**). Pick up some local cheeses, chutneys, and meats for a picnic lunch here, or eat in the nice cafe.

Close by is historic Beechworth, one of Victoria's best-preserved gold rush towns. There are over 30 buildings listed by the National Trust here, from pubs, churches, and government offices to miners' cottages and the jail where Ned Kelly was imprisoned. The delightful Beechworth Bakery, on the main road, offers a nice selection of cakes, pies, and pastries.

You can also visit Glenrowan, a quiet little town surrounded by more wineries and orchards. Here you'll find a 6m-high (18 ft.) outdoor statue of Ned Kelly clad in his homemade armor and helmet, with rifle in hand. Worth a look is **Kate's Cottage Museum** (© **03/5766 2448**), which contains a vast collection of Kelly memorabilia and an authentic replica of the Kelly homestead complete with furnishings. Meanwhile, **Kellyland** (© **03/5766 2367**) is an animated theatrical portrayal of the Kelly Gang's final stand, which uses original props including a handgun once owned by Ned Kelly. The show lasts about 40 minutes and begins every half-hour from 9:30am to 4:30pm daily.

You could combine Milawa, Beechworth, and Glenrowan in a packed day trip before heading back to Wangaratta or onward to Bright.

(US$9.20) for adults and A$7.50 (US$6) for children, and A$33 (US$26) for a family. Outside the Port, the Echuca Port Precinct offers various things to do, including carriage rides and old penny arcade machines in Sharpes Magic Movies, in an old riverboat warehouse.

A TRIP INTO THE OUTBACK   **Mungo National Park** ★ is a unique, arid region 110km (68 miles) northeast of Mildura, off the Sturt Highway. The park is famous for its red sand dunes and shifting sands, and I highly recommend you see it. You can get there on your own, but it's best to have a four-wheel-drive vehicle. People come here to see the Walls of China, a moonscape of intricately weathered red sand. The walls edge Lake Mungo, once a huge freshwater lake during the last Ice Age, now dry.

A 60km (37-mile) driving tour starting at the visitor center at the park's entrance takes you across the lakebed to the Walls of China. Several short walks begin at the camp-sites at the park entrance. Call the **National Parks & Wildlife Service NSW** (© **1300/361 967** in Australia) for more information on Mungo. Just outside the park, the **Mungo Lodge** (© **03/5029 7297;** www.mungolodge.com.au) offers afford-able motel accommodations and a casual restaurant.

An interesting option, if you have the money, is a 5-night tour of the Outback with **Discover Australia** (© **1800 73 2001** in Australia, or 08/9486 7880; www.discover australia.com.au). The tour leaves Broken Hill in NSW and costs A$1,660 (US$1,328) twin share including accommodations, meals, fees, and air-conditioned four-wheel-drive transport. Otherwise there's a long 2-day trip, also from Broken Hill, with **Goanna Safari** (© **08/8087 6057;** www.goanna-safari.com.au). The trip costs A$389 (US$311) camping, or A$433 (US$346) in basic accommodations. Meals are included.

WHERE TO STAY
IN MILDURA
Mildura Grand Hotel ★★★   This 19th-century hotel is right in the center of Mil-dura, overlooking the Murray River. Double rooms are comfortable, and many have been refurbished. Suites are bigger, and some have balconies and garden views. State suites are plush and come with a king-size bed. The Presidential suite (the most expen-sive) is Art Deco inspired, with a large marble bathroom and Jacuzzi. This place is famous for **Stefano's** ★ one of several dining spots run by celeb chef Stefano di Pietri's Voted best restaurant in Victoria in 2002-03, Stefano's offers a set menu of five to six courses for A$66 (US$53), featuring the best local produce.

Seventh St., Mildura, VIC 3500. © **1800/034 228** in Australia, or 03/5023 0511. Fax 03/5022 1801. www.mildura grandhotel.com. 102 units. A$110–A$143 (US$88–US$115) double; A$176–A$462 (US$141–US$369) suite. Rates include breakfast. Extra person A$22 (US$18). Ask about packages. AE, DC, MC, V. **Amenities:** 3 restaurants; 4 bars; large heated outdoor pool; golf course nearby; access to nearby health club, Jacuzzi, and sauna; 24-hr. concierge; shopping arcade; 24-hr. room service; in-room massage; laundry service; dry cleaning; nonsmoking rooms; executive rooms. In room: A/C, TV w/pay movies, minibar, coffeemaker, hair dryer, iron.

IN ECHUCA
Echuca Gardens B&B and YHA   This popular two-story log-cabin B&B offers evening gatherings around the piano, as well as a Jacuzzi in the front yard surrounded by murals and landscaped water gardens. Rooms are decorated in native flower themes, and all have balconies. It's a short stroll from the B&B to either the river or a state forest. The YHA next door has a basic twin room and two dorm rooms, each with four beds. Beds go for A$20 (US$14) for YHA members and A$24 (US$19) for nonmembers.

103 Mitchell St., Echuca, VIC 3564. © **03/5480 6522,** or 0419 881 054 mobile. Fax 03/5482 6951. www.echuca gardens.com. 3 B&B units, 3 hostel units. B&B room A$150 (US$120) weekends, A$130 (US$104) weekdays. Rates include breakfast. MC, V. **Amenities:** Jacuzzi; sauna; bike rental; tour desk; massage; coin-operated laundry; non-smoking rooms. In room: A/C, TV, hair dryer.

BRIGHT
310km (193 miles) NE of Melbourne; 700km (435 miles) SW of Sydney; 74km (46 miles) E of Wangaratta

Set in a valley and surrounded by pine forests, Bright offers good access to the sur-rounding High Country and ski fields. The town is famous for the colors of its Euro-pean trees in fall. There are nice walks around here, especially along the pretty Ovens River, while another option is to hire bicycles and take off through the countryside down a former railway track. Cycling at least part of the **Rail Trail** ✬ (www.rail trail.com.au) will give you a nice feel for the area, with its surrounding mountains, farms, and river. The track stretches 94km (58 miles) from Bright to Wangaratta, but you can turn back whenever you want, of course. Rent bikes (and skis if you're off to the snowfields) in Bright.

VISITOR INFORMATION

Stop by the **Bright Visitors Centre,** 119 Gavan St., Bright (✆ **03/5755 2275**), open 8:30am to 5pm daily.

GETTING THERE

V/Line trains (www.vline.com.au) run between Melbourne and Bright, via Wangaratta, daily. Return fares cost A$95 (US$76), though if you travel in off-peak times it costs A$48 (US$38) return. However, it's difficult to get around the area without your own transport.

WHERE TO STAY & DINE

The website **www.alpinelink.com.au** offers a comprehensive list of places to stay in Bright, including the Alinga Longa Lodge (see below). The best place to eat in town in **Simone's of Bright** (98 Gavan St.; ✆ **03/5755 2266**). It serves great Italian food in a refined atmosphere, with main courses around A$18 to A$25 (US$14–US$20). Otherwise, Bright has plenty of family-friendly cafes, restaurants, and pizza joints.

Alinga Longa Lodge   The large two-bedroom units here are in need of an update but they are comfortable enough for a couple of days, especially if you're traveling with kids. The full kitchen means you never have to eat out!

12 Gavan St. (Great Alpine Rd.), Bright 3741. ✆ 03/5755 1073. 6 units. A$90–A$120 (US$72–US$96) double. AE, DC, MC, V. **Amenities:** Small outdoor pool; playground; tour desk; free bikes and toboggans; laundry service. *In room:* TV, kitchen.

4 The High Country

Victoria's High Country consists of the hills and mountains of the Great Dividing Range, which runs from Queensland, through New South Wales, to just before Ballarat, where it drops away and reappears in the mountains of the Grampians, in the western part of Victoria. The range separates inland Australia from the greener coastal belt. The highest peak in the Victoria segment of the range is Mount Bogong which, at just 1,988m (6,521 ft.), is minuscule by world mountain standards.

The main attractions of the High Country are its natural features, which include moorland and typical mountainous alpine scenery. It's also popular for outdoor activities, including hiking, canoeing, white-water rafting, mountain-bike riding, and rock climbing. The High Country is also the home of the Victorian ski fields, based around Mount Buller, Mount Stirling, Falls Creek, Mount Buffalo, and Mount Hotham. If you plan to go walking here, make sure you have plenty of water and sunscreen, as well as a tent and a good-quality sleeping bag. As in any alpine region, temperatures can plummet dramatically. In summer, days can be very hot and nights very cold.

SNOWY RIVER NATIONAL PARK ✬

390km (242 miles) NE of Melbourne

The Snowy River National Park, with its lovely river scenery and magnificent gorges, protects Victoria's largest forest wilderness areas. The Snowy River was once a torrent worthy of Banjo Paterson's famous poem, but since Snowy Mountain Hydro-Electric erected a series of dams, it's become a mere trickle of its former self.

GETTING THERE & GETTING AROUND There is no public transit in this area. The two main access roads are the Gelantipy Road from Buchan and the Bonang Freeway from the logging township of Orbost. MacKillop's Road (also known as Deddick River Rd.) runs across the park's northern border from Bonang to a little south of Wulgulmerang. The area around MacKillop's Bridge, along MacKillop's Road, has spectacular scenery and the park's best campgrounds, set beside some nice swimming holes and sandy river beaches. The Barry Way leads through the main township of Buchan, where you'll find some of Australia's best caves.

VISITOR INFORMATION The main place to get information on the Snowy River National Park and Alpine National Park is the **Buchan Caves Information Centre,** in the Buchan Caves complex. It's open daily from 9am to 4pm (closed Dec 25). Or call **Parks Victoria** (© **13 19 63** in Victoria, or 03/5155 9264).

EXPLORING THE BUCHAN CAVES

The **Buchan Caves** ★ (© **03/5155 9264**) are in a scenic valley that is particularly beautiful in autumn, when all the European trees are losing their leaves. Tourists can visit the Royal and Fairy caves (which are quite similar), with their fabulous stalactites and stalagmites. There are several tours daily: April to September at 11am, 1pm, and 3pm; October to March at 10 and 11:15am, 1, 2:15, and 3:30pm. Entry to one cave costs A$10 (US$8) for adults, A$5 (US$4) for children 5 to 16, and A$25 (US$20) for families of five.

To reach the caves from the Princes Highway, turn off at Nowa Nowa (it's well signposted). If you're coming south from Jindabyne in New South Wales (see chapter 5), follow the Barry Way, which runs alongside the Snowy River.

ALPINE NATIONAL PARK ★★
333km (206 miles) NE of Melbourne; 670km (415 miles) SW of Sydney

Victoria's largest national park, at 646,000 hectares (1.6 million acres), the Alpine National Park connects the High Country areas of New South Wales and the Australian Capital Territory. The park's scenery is spectacular, encompassing most of the state's highest mountains, wild rivers, impressive escarpments, forests, and high plains. Much of the park was devastated by horrific bushfires in December 2002, and it is slowly recovering. It's green, but evidence of the fire lingers; you'll still see blackened tree trunks. The flora is diverse; in all, some 1,100 plant species have been recorded within the park's boundaries, including 12 not found anywhere else. Walking here is particularly good in spring and summer, when a carpet of wildflowers covers the Bogong High Plains. Other impressive walking trails include the 5.7km (3.5-mile) route through Bryce Gorge to The Bluff, a 200m-high (356-ft.) rocky escarpment with panoramic views. Of the numerous other walking trails in the park, the best known is the Alpine Walking Track, which bisects the park for 400km (248 miles) from Walhalla to the township of Tom Groggin, on the New South Wales border. There are plenty of access roads into the park, some of which close in winter.

If you're a keen walker, you could strap on your boots and see the area by foot. **Ecotrek** (© **08/8383 7198;** www.ecotrek.com.au) offers an 8-day Bogong Alpine Traverse trek, including 4 nights camping and 3 nights in ski lodges. You carry your own pack, but the pain is worth it for the incredible panoramic views of peaks, plains, and forested valleys. The trek costs A$1,420 (US$1,136), including round-trip transport to Melbourne.

Horseback-riding treks are another option for seeing the area. **Stoney's High Country** ★★ (© **03/5775 2212;** www.stoneys.com.au) acts as a one-stop shop for local tour operators offering trail rides. A 2-hour ride in the foothills costs A$50 (US$40); a day ride to higher elevations, A$180 (US$144); a weekend ride, around A$380 (US$304); and a 7-day ride, A$1,610 (US$1,288). Longer rides generally take place on specific dates—check the website. Stoney's can also help you organize a custom ride, on dates of your choice. Longer tours generally include camping, food, and just about everything else, though you should check whether you'll need a sleeping bag.

GETTING THERE Routes from Melbourne include the Great Alpine Road (B500), the Kiewa Valley Highway (C531), and the Lincoln Road from Heyfield. The Bluff is accessible from Mansfield along the Maroodah Highway.

HITTING THE SLOPES: THE HIGH COUNTRY SKI RESORTS

Most of **Victoria's ski areas** ★ are in, or on the edge of, the Alpine National Park (see above). The ski season in the Victorian High Country is June through October, with July and August the most popular months.

MOUNT HOTHAM
373km (231 miles) NE of Melbourne

Mount Hotham (1,750m/5,740 ft.) is an intimate ski resort significantly smaller than those at Falls Creek (see below). There are eight lifts serving runs from beginner to advanced. The resort also offers some good off-piste (off-trail) cross-country skiing, including a route across the Bogong High Plains to Falls Creek. Some of the lifts are quite far apart, although there's a free "zoo cart" and bus transport system in winter along the main road. Resort entry costs A$20 (US$16) per car for a day, payable at the entry gates or at the Mount Hotham Resort Management office (see "Visitor Information," below). Ski tickets are available from **Mount Hotham Skiing Company** (© **03/5759 4444**). Full-day lift tickets cost A$82 (US$66) for adults and A$43 (US$34) for children.

GETTING THERE From Melbourne, take the Hume Highway via Harrietville, or the Princes Highway via Omeo. The trip takes around 5½ hours (the Hume Hwy. is slightly quicker). **Qantas** (© **13 13 13** in Australia) flies to Mount Hotham Airport from Melbourne and Sydney. Car entry to the resort costs A$27 (US$22) a day.

Trekset Mount Hotham Snow Service (© **03/9370 9055**) runs buses to Mount Hotham daily during the ski season. They depart Melbourne's Spencer Street Coach Terminal at 9am. The trip takes 6 hours and costs A$125 (US$100) for adults and A$60 (US$48) for children under 15 for a round-trip. There are also coaches from Wangaratta and Bright to Mount Hotham. You need to book in advance.

VISITOR INFORMATION **Mount Hotham Resort Management,** Great Alpine Road, Mount Hotham (© **03/5759 3550**), is as close as you'll come to an information office. It has plenty of brochures. It's open daily from 8am to 5pm during ski season, and Monday through Friday from 9am to 5pm at other times. The general Mount Hotham website is **www.mthotham.com.au**.

WHERE TO STAY The **Mt. Hotham Accommodation Service** (© **1800/032 061;** www.mthothamaccommodation.com.au) can book rooms and advise you on special deals, including flights. Another option is **Falls Creek Reservations Centre** (© **1800/453 525** in Australia). During the ski season, most places will want you to book for a week. Prices are significantly lower in the non-ski season.

FALLS CREEK ⭑
375km (233 miles) NE of Melbourne

One of Victoria's best ski resorts, and my favorite, Falls Creek is on the edge of the Bogong High Plains overlooking the Kiewa Valley. This compact alpine village is the only one in Australia where you can ski from your lodge to the lifts and back again from the ski slopes. The nightlife is also very good in the ski season, with plenty of party options as well as a range of walk-in lodge restaurants.

The ski fields are in two parts, the Village Bowl and Sun Valley, with 17 lifts covering more than 90 trails. There are plenty of intermediate and advanced runs, as well as a sprinkling for beginners. You'll also find some of Australia's best cross-country skiing; Australia's major cross-country skiing event, the Kangaroo Hoppet, takes place here on the last Saturday in August every year. Entry to the resort costs A$13 (US$10) for a day pass and A$25 (US$20) if you intend to stay put for a while. Full-day lift tickets cost A$82 (US$66) for adults and A$43 (US$34) for children. Combined lift and ski-rental tickets are also available (roughly twice as expensive). Call the **Falls Creek Ski Lifts** (© **03/5758 3280**) for details. The ski lifts can also arrange accommodations.

Falls Creek is a pleasant place to visit in summer, when you can go bushwalking, horseback riding, and trout fishing. **Angling Expeditions** (©/fax **03/5754 1466**) is the best option for fly-fishing for trout in the alpine area during spring, summer, and fall. Trips last from 3 hours to all day and are suitable for everyone from beginners to experts. Overnight trips are also available. Horseback-riding operators include **Falls Creek Trail Rides** (© **03/5758 3655**) and **Bogong Horseback Adventures** (© **03/5754 4849**).

GETTING THERE Pyles Coaches (© **03/5754 4024;** www.pyles.com.au) runs buses to the ski resort from Melbourne every day during the ski season (end of June to end of Sept), departing Melbourne at 9am and Falls Creek at 5pm. The round-trip fare is A$130 (US$104) for adults and A$98 (US$72) for children under 16 and includes the resort entrance fee. The company also runs shuttle buses to and from Albury (A$72/US$58 round-trip for adults and A$62/US$50 for kids), just over the border in New South Wales and accessible by train or air from Sydney; and between Mount Beauty and Falls Creek. Reservations are essential.

If you're driving from Melbourne, take the Hume Highway to Wangaratta, and then through Myrtleford and Mount Beauty to Falls Creek. The trip takes around 4½ hours. From Sydney, take the Hume Highway to Albury-Wodonga and follow the signs to Mount Beauty and the snowfields. If you arrive in the ski season, a resort worker will direct you to a car park and bring you back in a little buggy to the resort entrance, from where you can take a caterpillar-tracked Oversnow taxi to your hotel. It costs A$14 (US$11) one-way and A$25 (US$20) return for adults and A$9.30 (US$7.50) one-way and A$17 (US$14) return for children 5 to 15. Or you could attempt the short but (probably) slippery walk yourself.

VISITOR INFORMATION The **Falls Creek Information Centre,** 1 Bogong High Plains Rd., Falls Creek (© **03/5758 3490;** www.fallscreek.com.au), is open daily from 8am to 5pm. Buy lift tickets in the booth next door between mid-June and October. The website has good general information and lists ski ticket prices.

Where to Stay & Dine

Falls Creek is a year-round resort with a good range of accommodations. It tends to fill up fast during the ski season. As you might expect, room rates are much higher during the ski season. The **Falls Creek Reservation Centre** (✆ **1800/453 525** in Australia, or 03/5758 3100; fax 03/5758 3337; www.fallscreek.net) can tell you what deals are available and can book rooms.

If you fancy a self-contained apartment or free-standing chalet, try the **Frueauf Village** complex (✆ **03/9593 6125;** www.fvfalls.com.au). These 28 properties were built in 2001 and 2002. The smallest unit, basically a nice studio, costs A$413 (US$330) per couple for a 2-night stay in the earliest and latest part of the ski season and jumps to a whopping A$990 (US$792) for 2 nights in the peak period. From there the sky's almost the limit.

Feathertop Alpine Lodge ⭐ *Finds*   I really like this pleasant old-fashioned winter ski lodge nestled among the gum trees. Hosts Pip and Mark Whittaker have made it into one of the friendliest getaways in the mountains, and its relatively small size makes it easy for you to get to know other guests. Rooms are functional yet cozy, and sleep two to four people. Standard rooms have a double or twin singles, and no TV, and "classic" rooms have either a king- or queen-size bed and a TV. All have showers attached. The lounge room is large and comfortable, with good views, a well-stocked bar, and a library.

Parallel St. (P.O. Box 259), Falls Creek, VIC 3699. ✆ 03/5758 3232. Fax 03/5758 3514. www.ski.com.au/feathertop. 10 units. Winter A$180–A$260 (US$144–US$208) standard double; A$200–A$290 (US$160–US$232) "classic" double. Rates include dinner and breakfast. AE, MC, V. Amenities: Restaurant; golf course nearby; 4 tennis courts (summer); health club nearby; children's center; tour and activities desk; business center; babysitting; coin-op laundry; nonsmoking rooms.

Summit Ridge Alpine Lodge ⭐   Summit Ridge is an AAA-rated 4½-star property made from local rock and timber. All rooms are quite nice, if a little stark. Standard units come with a set of bunk beds and a couple of useless little desks. Queen units have a queen-size bed and a couch, plus beautiful mountain views. The mezzanine suites are split-level with the bedroom upstairs; they have king-size beds and an attached bathroom with tub. There's a lounge and dining room on the ground floor and a library on the second. If the mist holds off, there are some fine valley views. The hosts pay a lot of attention to detail, and the homemade bread is worth waking early for. The **restaurant** excels in fine dining. The owner can take you on early-morning ski runs. The most expensive rates in the ranges below apply in August.

Schuss St., Falls Creek, VIC 3699. ✆ 03/5758 3800. Fax 03/5758 3833. www.summitridge.com.au. A$220–A$400 (US$176–US$320) standard double; A$260–A$460 (US$208–US$368) queen double; A$300–A$480 (US$240–US$384) mezzanine suite. Children 5–14 25% off adult rate. Rates include breakfast and dinner. AE, DC, MC, V. Closed Oct to mid-June. Children under 5 not accepted. Amenities: Restaurant; bar; exercise room; Jacuzzi; sauna; in-room massage; babysitting; coin-op laundry. In room: TV, minibar, coffeemaker, hair dryer.

MOUNT BUFFALO NATIONAL PARK ⭐⭐
350km (217 miles) NE of Melbourne

Based around Mount Buffalo, this is the oldest (1898) national park in the Victorian High Country. The scenery is spectacular, with huge granite outcrops and plenty of waterfalls. As you ascend the mountain you pass through dramatic vegetation changes, from tall snow gum forests to subalpine grasslands. In summer, carpets of silver snow daisies, royal bluebells, and yellow Billy Button flowers bloom on the plateau. Animals and birds include wallabies, wombats, cockatoos, lyrebirds, and mobs of crimson rosellas, which congregate around the campsite at Lake Catani (popular for swimming and canoeing). Other favorite sports include advanced hang gliding and serious rock climbing. There are also more than 90km (56 miles) of walking trails. The area is regenerating after bushfires in late 2002.

Mount Buffalo is also home to Victoria's smallest ski resort, with just five lifts and a vertical drop of 157m (515 ft.). There are also 11km (6¾ miles) of marked cross-country ski trails. There's also a good toboggan slope for kids opposite the ski lifts.

ENTRY FEES & LIFT TICKETS A day pass for entry into Mount Buffalo ski resort is A$14 (US$11) per car in ski season, A$9.50 (US$7.90) otherwise. Two-day and 3-day passes are also available. Full-day lift tickets cost around A$57 (US$46) for adults, A$34 (US$27) for children under 14. A family ticket costs A$154 (US$123). Combination lift and ski-lesson packages are available. Buy lift tickets at the park offices (© **13 19 63** in Victoria, or 03/5756 2328) from 9am to 3pm.

GETTING THERE From Melbourne or Sydney take the Hume Highway to Wangaratta, then follow the Great Alpine Road to Porepunkah, just before Bright. From there follow the Mount Buffalo Tourist Road up the hill (about 1 hr.).

VISITOR INFORMATION The nearest center is the **Bright Visitor Information Centre,** 119 Gavan St., Bright (© **03/5755 2275**).

WHERE TO STAY

Mt. Buffalo Chalet ★★ *(Finds* This rambling mountain guesthouse was built in 1910 and retains a wonderful old-world feel. Standard rooms are small with a comfortable bed and share a bathroom. Classic rooms are small but have their own bathrooms. Heritage rooms are larger, with a nice old-time feel; some have good views (ask for a View Heritage room). Tower rooms have excellent park views and are popular with honeymooners. Treetop rooms, which also have great views, are set apart from the main building. These also have a kitchenette and separate lounge, which makes them good for small families. The property has a large lounge room and a billiards room, both with open fireplaces. Rates are highest from Christmas to mid-January and over Easter weekend; lower rates apply in summer. Meals are available for both guests and visitors.

Mount Buffalo National Park, VIC 3740. © **1800/037 038** in Australia, or 03/5755 1500. Fax 03/5755 1892. www.mtbuffalochalet.com.au. 97 units, 72 with bathroom (some with shower only). A$100–A$150 (US$80–US$120) standard room without bathroom; A$140–A$200 (US$112–US$160) classic room with bathroom; A$190–A$300 (US$152–US$240) Heritage view room with bathroom; A$210–A$320 (US$168–US$256) Tower; A$240–A$350 (US$192–US$280) Treetops with balcony. Rates include park entry. Children's rates 50% less. AE, DC, MC, V. **Amenities:** Restaurant; bar; 2 grass tennis courts; exercise room; Jacuzzi; sauna; canoe rental; bike rental; kids' club (weekends and school holidays); activities desk; massage; babysitting; coin-op laundry; nonsmoking rooms. *In room:* Fridge, coffeemaker.

5 The Northwest: Grampians National Park

260km (161 miles) NW of Melbourne

One of Victoria's most popular attractions, the rugged **Grampians National Park** rises some 1,000m (3,280 ft.) from the plains, appearing from the distance like some kind of monumental island. The park, which is an ecological meeting place of Victoria's western volcanic plains and the forested Great Dividing Range, contains one-third of all the wildflowers native to Victoria and most of the surviving Aboriginal rock art in southeastern Australia. Almost 200 species of birds, 35 species of mammals, 28 species of reptiles, 11 species of amphibians, and 6 species of freshwater fish have been discovered here. Kangaroos, koalas, emus, gliders, and echidnas are easy to spot.

The main town in the Grampians is Halls Gap, which is in a valley between the southern tip of the Mount Difficult Range and the northern tip of the Mount William Range. It's a good place to stock up on supplies. The Wonderland Range, with its stunning scenery, is close to Halls Gap, too. There are plenty of short strolls, and longer bushwalks are available.

A must-do stop is the **Brambuk Aboriginal Living Cultural Centre** ⍟ (© **03/5356 4452**), adjacent to the park visitor center (see below). It offers an excellent introduction to the area's Aboriginal history and accessible rock-art sites. A 15-minute movie highlighting local Aboriginal history costs A$4.40 (US$3.50) for adults and A$2.50 (US$2) for children. Otherwise, entrance to the center is free. The center is open daily from 10am to 5pm.

ESSENTIALS

GETTING THERE   By car, the park is accessible from the Western Highway at Ararat, Stawell (pronounced *Storl*), and Horsham. Alternatively, you can reach the southern entrance from the Glenelg Highway at Dunkeld. The western areas of the park are off the Henty Highway (A200).

V/Line (© **13 61 96** in Victoria, or 03/9619 5000) has daily train and bus service to Halls Gap from Melbourne. (The train goes to Stawell, and a bus continues to Halls Gap.) The trip takes around 4 hours.

GETTING AROUND   Paved roads include the **Grampians Tourist Road,** which cuts through the park from Dunkeld to Halls Gap; the **Mount Victory Road,** from Halls Gap to Wartook, and the **Roses Gap Road,** which runs from Wartook across to Dadswells Bridge on the Western Highway. Many other roads in the park are unpaved, but most are passable with a two-wheel-drive car.

Autopia Tours (© **03/9419 8878;** www.autopiatours.com.au) offers all-day tours of the park and surrounds from Melbourne, leaving every Monday, Wednesday, and Saturday (call ahead to check departure times and pickup points). The tour stops at Aboriginal rock-art sites, waterfalls, and lookouts. There's not much walking involved, but you certainly get the chance to spot native animals and ferret around among the native flora. The tour includes lunch and morning and afternoon tea, and costs A$70 (US$56).

VISITOR INFORMATION   The **Grampians National Park Visitor Centre** (© **03/5356 4379**), 2.5km (1½ miles) south of Halls Gap, is open daily from 9am to 5pm. It has plenty of maps and brochures, and the rangers can advise you on walking trails and camping spots. Check out **www.visitgrampians.com.au**.

WHERE TO STAY

You can rent a caravan (trailer) or a cabin for the night at **Halls Gap Lakeside Caravan Park** (© **03/5356 4281**), 5km (3 miles) from town on the shores of Lake Bellfield. Cabins cost A$52 to A$125 (US$42–US$100).

The Mountain Grand Guesthouse   This old-fashioned guesthouse maintains a comfortable AAA-rated 3½-star standard. These days it's promoting itself as a business retreat, and tourists get all the benefits of the corporate extras, such as exceptional service. Some rooms are quite small, with country-style furniture and double beds. There are also larger rooms, some of which have Jacuzzis. The **Balconies Restaurant** overlooks the garden and valley. The owner is a keen musician, and on Saturday night professional musicians provide music to dine by. Later, they move downstairs to the **Limelight Cafe/Bar** and play till late.

Main Rd., town center, Halls Gap, Grampians. © 03/5356 4232. Fax 03/5356 4254. www.mountaingrand.com.au. 13 units. A$130 (US$104) double with breakfast; A$196 (US$157) double including breakfast, lunch, and dinner. 2-night minimum on weekends. AE, DC, MC, V. Children not accepted. **Amenities:** 2 restaurants; 2 bars; free laundry. *In room:* A/C, fridge, coffeemaker, iron.

Canberra

by Marc Llewellyn

If you mention you're heading to Canberra (pronounced *Can*-bra, with very open vowels), most Australians will raise an eyebrow and say, "Why bother?" Even many Canberrans will admit that it's a great place to live but they wouldn't want to visit.

So what is it about Canberra (pop. 310,000) that draws so much lackluster comment? Simply put, Australians aren't used to having things so nice and ordered. In many ways, Canberra is like Washington, D.C., or any other town that was a planned community from the start. Some see its virtues as bland: The roads are wide and in good order, the buildings are modern, and the suburbs are pleasant and leafy. Canberra is also the seat of government and the home of thousands of civil servants—enough to make almost any freethinking, individualist Aussie shudder.

But to me, Canberra's differences are the very things that make it special. The streets aren't clogged with traffic, and there are plenty of opportunities for safe biking—try that in almost any other city center and you'll be dusting the sides of cars and pushed onto the sidewalks in no time. Canberra has plenty of open spaces, parklands, and monuments, and an awful lot to see

and do—from museum and gallery hopping to ballooning with a champagne glass in your hand or boating on Lake Burley Griffin. You can pack a lot into a few days.

Canberra was born after the Commonwealth of Australia was created in 1901. Melbourne and Sydney, even then jockeying for preeminence, each bid to become the federal capital. In the end, Australian leaders decided to follow the example of their U.S. counterparts by creating a federal district; in 1908 they chose an undeveloped area between the two cities.

Designing the new capital fell to Chicago landscape architect Walter Burley Griffin, a contemporary of Frank Lloyd Wright. The city he mapped out was christened Canberra (a local Aboriginal word meaning "meeting place"), and by 1927, the first meeting of parliament took place.

Originally the land that became Canberra was predominantly grass plains. Over the years, millions of trees have been planted in and around the city, earning it the nickname "the bush capital." Unfortunately, massive bushfires in January 2003 destroyed much of the surrounding forest and more than 500 homes in the suburbs.

1 Orientation

ARRIVING

BY PLANE   **Qantas** (© **13 13 13** in Australia) runs frequent daily service to Canberra from all state capitals.

The Canberra Airport is about 10 minutes from the city center. It has car-rental desks, a currency exchange, a bar, a bistro, and a mailbox for cards and letters (but no post office). The newsdealer sells stamps. There are no lockers or showers.

The **Airliner Bus** (© **02/6299 3722;** www.deanesbusline.com.au) operates a 20-minute shuttle between the central business district and the airport Monday to Friday, leaving hourly. The one-way fare is A$5 (US$4).

BY TRAIN   Countrylink (© **13 22 32** in Australia; www.countrylink.nsw.gov.au) runs three Canberra Xplorer trains daily between Sydney and Canberra. The 5-hour trip costs around A$70 (US$56) in first class and A$50 (US$40) in economy; children pay half price, and a round-trip costs double. Many people book Countrylink transport-hotel packages (call **Countrylink Holidays,** © **13 28 29**), which can save you quite a bit. Depending on the accommodations in Canberra, prices range from A$90 to A$190 (US$72–US$152) a night for a couple, and if you book in advance (the company recommends 2 weeks), you can save up to 40% on the fare through a Rail Escape package. Countrylink has an office at Wynyard CityRail station in Sydney.

From Melbourne, the **Canberra Link,** run by **V/Line** (© **13 61 96** in Australia), involves a 5-hour bus trip and a 3½-hour train trip. It costs A$55 (US$44) for adults and A$34 (US$27) for children and students.

Canberra Railway Station (© **02/6239 6707**) is on Wentworth Avenue, Kingston, about 5km (3 miles) southeast of the city center. Coaches connect the railway station to the center.

BY BUS   Greyhound (© **13 14 99** in Australia, or 07/4690 9950; www.greyhound.com.au) does six runs a day from Sydney to Canberra; the trip takes 4 to 4½ hours. Tickets cost around A$35 (US$28) for adults, A$32 (US$26) for students with an ISAC (International Student Activity Card), and A$28 (US$22) for children 3 to 14.

From Melbourne, tickets to Canberra cost A$60 (US$48) for adults, A$50 (US$40) for students, and A$45 (US$36) for children. Advance-purchase fares can be as much as 35% lower.

Murrays Australia (© **13 22 51** in Australia; www.murrays.com.au) runs from Sydney to Canberra three times a day for A$35 (US$28) for adults and A$19 (US$15) for children. Ask for YHA member discounts. Book over the Internet for further discounts. Several sightseeing companies in Sydney, including **AAT King's** and **Australia Pacific Tours,** offer day trips to Canberra.

Interstate buses arrive at **Jolimont Tourist Centre,** at the corner of Northbourne Avenue and Alinga Street, Canberra City.

BY CAR   The ACT (Australian Capital Territory) is surrounded by New South Wales. Sydney is 306km (190 miles) northeast, and Melbourne is 651km (404 miles) southwest of Canberra. From Sydney, you can use an extension to the M5 motorway that links with the Eastern Distributor highway near Sydney Airport. Turn left before you reach the airport and follow signs to Wollongong, then the M5. The drive takes between 3 and 3½ hours. From Melbourne, take the Hume Highway to Yass and switch to the Barton Highway; the trip will take about 8 hours.

VISITOR INFORMATION

The **Canberra Visitors' Centre,** 330 Northbourne Ave., Dickson (© **1300/554 114** in Australia, or 02/6205 0044), dispenses information and books accommodations. The office is open Monday through Friday from 9am to 5:30pm, and Saturday and Sunday from 9am to 4pm. The official government website (www.visitcanberra.com.au) is worth checking out.

SPECIAL EVENTS   A host of free events—from concerts to competitions—is part of the annual **Canberra National Multicultural Festival** the first 3 weeks of March.

Canberra

Black Mountain ▲ 1

AUSTRALIAN NATIONAL BOTANIC GARDENS 2

General Post Office ✉

BRADDON

Bunda St.

Mount Ainslie

Childers St.
Alinga St.

6

CIVIC

Petrie St. 8

7

9 ℹ

10

Northbourne Avenue

Ballumbir St.

Ainslie Ave.

Coranderrk St.

Euree St.

REID

13

Limestone Ave.

ACTON

Vernon Circle

Australian National University 5

London Circuit

Akuna St.

11 Binara St.

12

Constitution Ave.

Anzac Parade

COMMONWEALTH PARK

14

RUSSELL

Parkes Way

Lake Burley Griffin

4

Commonwealth Ave. Bridge

■ **National Library of Australia**

KINGS PARK

STIRLING PARK

Commonwealth Avenue

15

16

17

18

GREVILLEA PARK

King George Terrace 19

PARKES

United States Embassy

Kings Avenue

Kings Ave. Bridge

CAPITAL HILL

YARRALUMLA

28

Adelaide Ave.

Capital Circle 20

State Circle

Brisbane Ave.

21

TELOPEA PARK

Wentworth

22

23

AUSTRALIA

Sydney

Canberra ✳

0   1000 Mi
0   1000 Km

Melbourne Ave.

National Circuit 27

Dominion Circuit

Empire Circuit

MANUKA PARK

Giles St.

KINGSTON

24

FORREST

COLLINS PARK

26

GRIFFITH

Canberra Ave.

25 **Canberra Railway Station**

ACCOMMODATIONS ■
The Brassey of Canberra **21**
City Walk Hotel **8**
Crowne Plaza Canberra **11**
Forest Inn and Apartments **27**
Hyatt Hotel Canberra **15**
Kingston Court Apartments **22**
University House **5**
Victor Lodge **24**

DINING ◆
The Boat House by the Lake **23**
Caffe Della Piazza **6**
Chairman and Yip **10**
Little Saigon **7**
The Palette Cafe **28**
Portia's Place **25**
Tosolini's **9**
The Tryst **26**

ATTRACTIONS ●
Australian Institute of Sport **3**
Australian National Botanic Gardens **2**
Australian War Memorial **13**
Casino Canberra **12**
High Court of Australia **17**
National Capital Exhibition **14**
National Gallery of Australia **18**
National Museum of Australia **4**
Old Parliment House **19**
Parliament House **20**
Questacon–The National Science and Technology Centre **16**
Telstra Tower **1**

Information ℹ
Post Office ✉
Mountain ▲

0   1/4 mi
0   1/4 km
Ⓝ

The fun includes Canberra Day (a local public holiday, the third Mon in Mar), a hot-air balloon fiesta, fireworks displays, food and wine promotions, plenty of music, and a large range of other activities that draw on Australia's ethnic mix. Visitors may find it a little more difficult to book accommodations during this time, but you should always be able to find something. There are many other major events, including the flower show **Floriade,** the **Subaru Rally of Canberra,** the **Canberra 400 V8 Super-cars** meeting, and the **National Folk Festival.** Check dates at www.visitcanberra.com.au.

CITY LAYOUT

The first thing that strikes a visitor to Canberra is its parklike feel (amazing, because there was barely a tree on the original site). Half a dozen avenues radiate from **Capital Hill,** where Parliament House stands. Each of these broad, tree-shaded streets leads to a traffic circle, from which more streets emanate. Around each hub, the streets form a pattern of concentric circles—not the easiest layout for visitors trying to find their way.

Another of Canberra's most notable features is **Lake Burley Griffin,** created by damming the Molonglo River. The centerpiece of the lake is the **Captain Cook Memorial Jet,** a spire of water that reaches 147m (482 ft.) into the air. Wedged between Commonwealth Avenue and Kings Avenue is the suburb of **Parkes,** also known as the National Triangle. Here you'll find many of the city's most impressive attractions, such as the National Gallery of Australia, the High Court of Australia, and Questacon—the National Science and Technology Centre. (For information on these sites, visit www.nationaltriangle.com.au/tri.) Many embassies and consulates are in the suburb of **Yarralumla,** east of Capital Hill; most of the other suburbs are filled with pleasant homes and small retail areas.

Canberra's main shopping district is on the other side of the lake, centered on Northbourne Avenue, one of the city's main thoroughfares. Officially Canberra City, this area is more commonly known as **"Civic."** Northeast of Civic is **Mount Ainslie,** with the Australian War Memorial at its foot; from its summit there are spectacular views of the city and beyond. Another good lookout point is the top of the **Telstra Tower** on Black Mountain, west of Civic and reached by Black Mountain Drive.

2 Getting Around

BY CAR **Advantage Car Rentals,** 74 Northbourne Ave. (corner of Barry Dr.; ℂ 1800/504 460 in Australia, or 02/6257 6888), has cars from A$35 (US$28) per day, including 200km (124 miles) per day. **Budget** (ℂ 02/6257 1305), **Hertz** (ℂ 02/6249 6211), **Thrifty** (ℂ 1300/367 227), **Avis** (ℂ 02/6249 6088), and **Delta Europcar** (ℂ 13 13 90) have desks at the airport.

If you rent your own wheels, you might follow one or more of the six tourist drives marked with signs; pick up details from the Canberra Visitors' Centre.

BY TAXI Canberra's only taxi company is **Canberra Cabs** (ℂ 13 22 27 in Australia).

BY BUS **ACTION** (ℂ 13 17 10 in Australia, or 02/6207 7611; www.action.act. gov.au) coordinates Canberra's bus system. The central bus terminal is on Alinga Street, in Civic. Single tickets cost A$2.40 (US$1.90) for adults and A$1.30 (US$1) for children 5 to 15. Weekly tickets cost A$24 (US$19), and 10-ride tickets cost A$21 (US$17). Children travel for around half price. Purchase all tickets on the bus or from most newsdealers and ACTION interchanges (transfer points).

For schedules, call ACTION Monday through Saturday from 7am to 9pm, and Sunday from 8am to 6pm. Pick up bus route maps at bus interchanges, newsdealers, and the Canberra Visitors' Centre.

Canberra Day Tours (✆ **02/6298 3344;** www.canberradaytours.com.au) offers a day tour by bus including visits to Old Parliament House, the Australian War Memorial, Parliament House, the Embassy region, Telstra Tower, and a cruise on Lake Burley Griffin. It costs A$69 (US$55) for adults and A$49 (US$39) for kids under 14.

BY BICYCLE   Canberra is unique in Australia for its extensive system of cycle tracks—some 120km (74 miles) of them—which makes sightseeing on two wheels a pleasurable experience. See "Outdoor Pursuits," later in this chapter, for details on bike rental.

FAST FACTS: Canberra

American Express   The office at **Centerpoint,** Shop 1, 185 City Walk (at the corner of Petrie Plaza), Civic (✆ **02/6247 2333**), is open Monday through Friday from 9am to 5pm, and Saturday from 9am to noon.

Business Hours   Banks are generally open Monday through Thursday from 9:30am to 4pm and Friday from 9:30am to 5pm. Stores and offices are open Monday through Friday from 9am to 5:30pm. Many shops, particularly in the large malls, open on weekends and until 9pm Fridays.

Climate   The best time to visit Canberra is in spring (Sept–Nov) or autumn (Mar–May). Summers are hot and winters are cool and crisp.

Currency Exchange   Cash traveler's checks at banks; at **American Express** (above); or at **Thomas Cook,** at the Petrie Plaza entrance of the Canberra Centre (✆ **02/6257 2222**), open Monday through Friday from 9am to 5pm and Saturday from 9:30am to 12:30pm.

Dentist   Canberra lacks a dental emergency referral service. A reputable dentist is **Lachland B. Lewis,** Level 3, 40 Allara St., Civic (✆ **02/6257 2777,** or for emergency calls only 02/6295 9495 on weekends).

Doctor   The **Capital Medical Centre,** 2 Mort St., Civic (✆ **02/6257 3766**), is open Monday through Friday from 8:30am to 4:30pm. A standard consultation costs A$30 (US$24). The **Travellers' Medical & Vaccination Centre,** Level 5, 8–10 Hobart Place, Civic (✆ **02/6257 7154**), offers vaccinations and travel medicines. Standard consultations cost A$40 (US$32) and up.

Embassies & Consulates   The **British High Commission** (consular section) is on the 10th floor of the SAP Building, corner of Bunda and Akuna streets, Canberra City (✆ **02/6270 6666**); the **Canadian High Commission** is at Commonwealth Avenue, Yarralumla (✆ **02/6270 4000**); the **U.S. Embassy** is at Moonah Place, Yarralumla (✆ **02/6214 5600**); and the **New Zealand High Commission** is at Commonwealth Avenue, Yarralumla (✆ **02/6270 4211**).

Emergencies   Call ✆ **000** for an ambulance, the police, or the fire department.

Eyeglasses   For repairs, glasses, and contact lenses, try **OPSM Express,** Shop 5, Lower Ground Floor, Canberra Centre, Civic (✆ **02/6249 7344**). It's open 9am to 5:30pm Monday through Thursday, 9am to 9pm Friday, and 9am to 4pm Saturday.

Hospitals For medical attention, go to the **Canberra Hospital,** Yamba Drive, Garran (© **02/6244 2222**), or call the **Accident & Emergency Department** (© **02/ 6244 2324**).

Hot Lines **Rape Crisis Centre** (© 02/6247 2525); **Drug/Alcohol Crisis Line** (© 02/ 6205 4545, 24 hr.); **Lifeline Crisis Councelling** (© 13 11 14); **Salvation Army Councelling Service** (© 02/9331 6000); **Poison Information Centre** (© 02/6285 2852); **National Roads & Motorists Association** (© 13 21 32).

Internet Access The **National Library,** Parkes Place, Parkes (© **02/6262 1111**), has e-mail facilities available Monday through Thursday 9am to 5pm. Internet access is readily available around town at other libraries and in Internet cafes. The Canberra Visitors' Centre can provide you with a full list.

Pharmacies (Chemist Shops) The **Canberra Centre Pharmacy,** Civic (© **02/6249 8074**), is open during general shopping hours. A number of after-hours pharmacies are listed in the Canberra Yellow Pages.

Photographic Needs **Fletchers Fotographics,** Shop 2, 38 Akuna St., Civic (© **02/ 6247 8460**), is the best place to buy camera gear and film. It also repairs cameras and sells secondhand equipment.

Post Office The **Canberra GPO,** 53–73 Alinga St., Civic (© **02/6209 1680**), is open Monday through Friday from 8:30am to 5:30pm. The general delivery (poste restante) address is c/o Canberra GPO, ACT 2601.

Restrooms Found near the city bus exchange, City Hall, and London Circuit.

3 Where to Stay

Canberra has a good scattering of places to stay, and generally accommodations are much cheaper than in most other state capitals. Many people travel to Canberra during the week, so many hotels offer cheaper weekend rates. You should always ask about special deals. The rates given below are rack rates, or what the hotels hope they'll get on a good day—you can often get a room for less. The Canberra Visitors' Centre (© **1300/554 114**) can provide information about accommodations options.

VERY EXPENSIVE

Hyatt Hotel Canberra ★★   Visiting heads of state and pop stars make this their residence of choice in Canberra, and it's not hard to see why. It has a great location, only a 2-minute drive from the city center, in the shadow of Parliament House, and between Lake Burley Griffin and the Parliamentary Triangle. Originally the Hotel Canberra, it opened in 1924 and was based on the low-slung "prairie" design of the now-destroyed Imperial Hotel in Tokyo. For many years the Hyatt was an important part of Canberra's social and political life, with key decisions affecting all Australians being made over drinks in the bar. All staff members wear 1920s costumes to add to the atmosphere.

Some 39 rooms are in the original two-story section. The rooms have more historic appeal, but they are darker than their modern counterparts, which were added in the 1980s. Standard rooms have a king-size bed and marble bathrooms. They all come with the little luxuries you'd expect from a hotel of this class.

Commonwealth Ave., Yarralumla, ACT 2600. ℂ **13 12 34** in Australia, 800/233-1234 in the U.S. and Canada, 0181/335 1220 in London, 0845/758 1666 elsewhere in the U.K., 0800/441 234 in New Zealand, or 02/6270 1234. Fax 02/6281 5998. www.hyatt.com.au. 249 units. A$380 (US$304) standard double; A$605 (US$484) executive suite; A$1,200 (US$960) diplomatic suite. Extra person A$28 (US$22). Children under 18 stay free in parent's room. Ask about weekend packages and special rates. AE, DC, MC, V. Free parking. **Amenities:** Restaurant; cafe; indoor pool; lit tennis court; extensive health club and spa; bike rental; concierge; business center; 24-hr. room service; laundry service. *In room:* A/C, TV w/pay movies, minibar, hair dryer, iron, safe.

EXPENSIVE

Crowne Plaza Canberra ⭐⭐   This hotel is next door to the National Convention Centre and Casino Canberra. Its car-oriented approach makes it a little inconvenient for pedestrians, but the gardens (Glebe Park) at the back are good for early-morning strolls. Rooms face onto internal balconies that look down to the restaurants below. Standard rooms are user-friendly and comfortable; most come with one queen-size bed or two doubles. Park-view doubles overlook the gardens. Weekend rates drop dramatically. For example, standard rooms drop from A$300 (US$240) to A$190 (US$152), with breakfast included.

1 Binara St., Canberra, ACT 2601. ℂ **1300/363 300** in Australia. Fax 02/6257 4903. www.crowneplaza.com. 295 units. A$300 (US$240) standard double; A$315 (US$252) park-view double; A$425–A$500 (US$340–US$400) suite. Extra person A$35 (US$28). Weekend discounts available. Children under 15 stay free in parent's room. AE, DC, MC, V. Free parking. **Amenities:** Restaurant; bar; medium-size indoor pool; health club; concierge; business center; 24-hr. room service; laundry service. *In room:* A/C, TV, minibar, hair dryer, iron, safe.

MODERATE

The Brassey of Canberra ⭐   Rooms in this 1927 heritage-listed building, formerly a boardinghouse for visiting government officials, are large, quiet, and somewhat plush. The garden bar and piano lounge are popular. Other good points include its proximity to Parliament House and other major attractions, and the hearty breakfasts. The hotel underwent extensive renovations a few years ago, which included the remodeling of many of the doubles into larger heritage rooms.

Belmore Gardens, Barton, ACT 2600. ℂ **1800/659 191** in Australia, or 02/6273 3766. Fax 02/6273 2791. www.brassey.net.au. 81 units. A$132 (US$105) double; A$165 (US$132) double family room; A$141 (US$113) heritage double; A$187 (US$150) heritage family room. Rates include full breakfast. Check for specials. AE, DC, MC, V. Free parking. Bus: 36 to National Press Club. **Amenities:** Restaurant; bar; coin-op laundry; dry cleaning. *In room:* A/C, TV, dataport, minibar, coffeemaker, hair dryer, iron.

Forrest Inn and Apartments *(Kids*   The Forrest Inn is far from fancy, but it's close to the Manuka shops and restaurants and Parliament House. The outside of this 1960s property looks tacky, but the interior has been refurbished. The motel-style rooms are small and colorless; the apartments are nicer and have full-size kitchens, so I recommend that you spend a little more money and go for these. Two-bedroom apartments are perfect for families, and even the one-bedroom apartments have a single bed in the living room.

30 National Circuit, Forrest, ACT 2603. ℂ **1800/676 372** in Australia, or 02/6295 3433. Fax 02/6295 2119. www.forrestinn.com.au. 102 units. A$110 (US$88) motel room; A$150 (US$120) 1-bedroom apt; A$175 (US$140) 2-bedroom apt. AE, DC, MC, V. Free parking. Bus: 39 to Rydges Canberra Hotel. **Amenities:** Restaurant; limited room service (motel only); coin-op laundry. *In room:* A/C, TV, minibar, hair dryer, iron.

Kingston Court Apartments ⭐   Situated about 1km (½ mile) from the Parliamentary Triangle and 6km (3¾ miles) from Civic, this apartment complex is a good option if you're looking for the comforts of home. The apartments are modern and spacious and come with a full kitchen, washer and dryer, and a balcony or a private courtyard.

4 Tench St., Kingston, ACT 2604. ℂ **1800/655 754** in Australia, or 02/6295 2244. Fax 02/6295 5300. www.kingston terrace.com.au. 36 units. A$160 (US$128) apt for 2. Extra adult A$20 (US$16); extra child A$10 (US$8). AE, DC, MC, V. Free parking. Bus: 38. **Amenities:** Small outdoor heated pool; half-size tennis court. *In room:* A/C, TV/VCR, dataport, kitchen, minibar, fridge, hair dryer, iron.

University House ★ University House, less than 2km (1¼ miles) from the city center, offers a pleasant alternative to run-of-the-mill hotels in a similar price bracket. Large twin rooms come with two single beds; suites have a sitting room and a queen-size bed; one-bedroom apartments have a bedroom with a queen-size bed, a sitting room, and a kitchenette; and two-bedroom apartments are huge, with two large bedrooms, a dining room, a lounge, and a full kitchen. All units have bathrooms with showers and tubs.

Australian National University, Balmain Crescent, Acton (G.P.O. Box 1535, Canberra, ACT 2601). ℂ **1800/814 864** in Australia, or 02/6249 5211. Fax 02/6249 5252. www.anu.edu.au/unihouse. 104 units. A$124 (US$99) twin; A$126–A$149 (US$100–US$119) suite; A$136 (US$109) 1-bedroom apt; A$190 (US$152) 2-bedroom apt. Ask about packages, especially during low season. AE, DC, MC, V. Free secured parking. Bus: 34. **Amenities:** Restaurant; cafe; tennis court; access to nearby health club; bike rentals; car-rental desk; babysitting; coin-op laundry; laundry service; dry cleaning; nonsmoking rooms. *In room:* TV, fridge, hair dryer.

INEXPENSIVE

City Walk Hotel You can hardly get closer to the city center than at this former YWCA turned budget hotel. Being right near the Jolimont Tourist Centre bus interchange, it picks up a lot of business from backpackers and budget travelers arriving by bus. The rooms are pretty basic, but clean. The hostel was completely refurbished in 2003. It has five double rooms with shared bathrooms, three of which have two extra single beds. One room (no. 204) has air-conditioning. Family rooms sleep up to 10 people, all in one room. The communal facilities include a kitchen, telephone, tea- and coffeemakers, and a lounge area with TV and VCR.

2 Mort St., Civic, ACT 2601. ℂ **1800/600 124** in Australia, or 02/6257 0124. Fax 02/6257 0116. www.citywalk hotel.com.au. 55 units, 18 with bathroom (shower only). A$60 (US$48) double without bathroom; A$70 (US$56) double with bathroom; A$95–A$125 (US$76–US$100) family room; A$22–A$24 (US$18–US$19) dorm bed. Extra adult A$12 (US$9.60). MC, V. **Amenities:** Coin-op laundry; Internet cafe. *In room:* TV, fridge, coffeemaker, no phone.

Victor Lodge *(Value)* Backpackers, parliamentary staff, and budget travelers frequent this friendly place, next to Kingston's shops and about a 15-minute drive from the city center. Rooms vary, from dorms with three, four, or five beds to modern, simple doubles. Each has a wash basin. There are communal showers and toilets and a courtyard. The staff picks up guests from the train and bus stations daily and drops off guests in town every morning. It's a nice place, but you'll have to decide whether you want to put up with the short trek into the city.

The owners also own the reasonable **Best Western** motel next door at 27 Dawes St. (ℂ **02/6295 2111;** http://motelmonaro.bestwestern.com.au). It charges A$95 (US$76) for a double. Apparently, long-suffering parents often park their teenage kids at the lodge and live it up at the motel.

29 Dawes St., Kingston, ACT 2604. ℂ **02/6295 7777.** Fax 02/6295 2466. www.victorlodge.com.au. 29 units, none with bathroom. A$59 (US$47) double; A$23 (US$19) dorm bed. Rates include continental breakfast. MC, V. Free parking. Bus: 38, 39, or 50. **Amenities:** Bike rental; tour desk; coin-op laundry; nonsmoking rooms; Internet facilities; TV room. *In room:* A/C, TV, iron.

4 Where to Dine

EXPENSIVE

The Boat House by the Lake ⭐⭐ MODERN AUSTRALIAN   On the shores of Lake Burley Griffin, The Boat House is a pleasant dining retreat with uninterrupted water views. The large dining room's floor-to-ceiling windows capture the view, and the outside terrace is nice for a pre- or postdinner retreat. To start, try Coffin Bay oysters, either natural with lemon, or topped with litchi, avocado, and chile salsa. Then go for Japanese peppered beef filet on garlic mashed potatoes with braised mushrooms, asparagus tempura, and wasabi hollandaise sauce. The wine list features local vintages. The Boat House was named the best restaurant in the ACT in 2001, and was a finalist in the American Express Best Restaurant awards the same year.

Grevillea Park, Menindee Dr., Barton, ACT. ⓒ 02/6273 5500. Reservations required. Main courses A$16–A$22 (US$13–US$18). AE, DC, MC, V. Mon–Fri noon–3pm; Mon–Sat 6–10:30pm.

Chairman and Yip ⭐⭐ ASIAN AUSTRALIAN   This is, without doubt, one of Canberra's best restaurants. Upbeat and popular with political bigwigs, it really is the place to see and be seen. The fish specials are good and spicy, with combinations of chile, cilantro, lemon grass, and galangal perking up your taste buds. I always go for prawns with homemade chile jam, served on vermicelli noodles with mango salsa. Abalone and lobster also find their way onto the menu. Panna cotta is the signature dessert.

108 Bunda St., Civic. ⓒ 02/6248 7109. Reservations required. Main courses A$16–A$22 (US$13–US$18). AE, DC, MC, V. Sun–Fri noon–3pm; daily 6–11pm.

MODERATE

The Palette Café ⭐ CAFE/MODERN AUSTRALIAN   This is a great choice for lunch, especially because it's in the same building as Canberra's largest private art gallery. You can eat inside, surrounded by artwork, or claim a table outside in the sunny courtyard. Standout dishes include grilled asparagus spears with Japanese scallops and almond hollandaise, and chile-salted baby octopus. Caesar salads are particularly good, as are mushrooms with a sauce of soy, Japanese rice wine, honey, and coriander. The etchings, paintings, and sculptures on display are of high quality and are well priced.

Beaver Gallery, 81 Denison St., Deakin. ⓒ 02/6282 8416. Main courses A$12–A$18 (US$9.60–US$14). AE, MC, V. Daily 10am–5pm.

Tosolini's ⭐ CAFE/MODERN AUSTRALIAN   Because it's right next to the busy central bus terminal and close to the major shopping areas, Tosolini's really pulls in the passing crowd. You can sit out on the sidewalk terrace and watch the world go by. Eggs Benedict (A$7.50/US$6), served at breakfast, may be the best you've ever eaten. Lunchtime and dinner fare is almost as good. Battered flathead and pan-fried broadbill (both are local fish) are tasty, but Tosolini's really made its name with its pastas and focaccias.

Corner of London Circuit at East Row, Civic. ⓒ 02/6247 4317. Main courses A$15–A$18 (US$12–US$14). AE, DC, MC, V. Sun–Mon 7:30am–5pm; Tues–Sat 7:30am–10:30pm.

The Tryst ⭐⭐ *Finds* MODERN AUSTRALIAN   The personal touches and service shine here, and the food is consistently delicious. The restaurant is tastefully decorated in upscale cafe style, with the kitchen staff on show as they rustle up some of the capital's best tucker. It's relaxed, feeling more communal than intimate on busy nights. My favorite dish is Atlantic salmon served with beurre blanc sauce and potatoes; other popular choices include eye filet steak and pumpkin risotto. If you have room left for dessert, don't miss out on sticky date pudding served with hot butterscotch sauce, pralines, and ice cream—it's as good as it sounds. The long list of daily specials that complement the extensive menu could keep you busy for weeks.

Bougainville St., Manuka. ⓒ **02/6239 4422.** Reservations recommended. Main courses A$15–A$23 (US$12–US$18). AE, DC, MC, V. Daily noon–2:30pm; Mon–Sat 6–10pm.

INEXPENSIVE

Caffe Della Piazza ✶ ITALIAN/CAFE
Good eating isn't hard to find in Canberra, and this place is up there with the best. It has won several awards for its Italian-inspired cooking, including the catering industries' award for the best restaurant in the state. The restaurant offers both indoor and outdoor dining in pleasant surroundings, and is a good place to pop in for a light meal and a coffee or for something more substantial. Pastas cost around A$11 (US$8.80), and the best seller is chicken breast strips in machiato sauce. You need to book early for Friday or Saturday evening.

19 Garema Place, Civic. ⓒ **02/6248 9711.** Reservations recommended. Main courses A$6.50–A$18 (US$5.20–US$14). AE, DC, MC, V. Daily 10:30am–midnight.

Little Saigon *Value* VIETNAMESE
This spacious restaurant has minimalist decor and floor-to-ceiling windows offering views of the city center. Tables are on either side of an indoor pond, and there's a bar in the back of the restaurant. The menu is vast, with lots of noodle dishes as well as spicy seafood, duck, chicken, pork, beef, and lamb. The top seller is lemon-grass and chile chicken.

Alinga St. and Northbourne Ave., Civic. ⓒ **02/6230 5003.** Main courses A$12–A$15 (US$9.60–US$12). AE, DC, MC, V. Daily 10am–3pm and 5–10:30pm.

Portia's Place CANTONESE/MALAYSIAN/PEKING
A small restaurant serving excellent traditional cookery, Portia's Place often fills up early and does a roaring lunchtime trade. The best things on the menu are lamb ribs in shang tung sauce, King Island filet steak in pepper sauce, flaming pork (brought to your table wrapped in foil and, yes, flaming), and Queensland trout stir-fried with snow peas.

11 Kennedy St., Kingston. ⓒ **02/6239 7970.** Main courses A$9.80–A$19 (US$7.80–US$15). AE, DC, MC, V. Daily noon–2:30pm; Sun–Wed 5–10pm; Thurs–Sat 5–10:30pm.

5 Seeing the Sights

Australian Institute of Sport
This institution provides first-class training and facilities for Australia's elite athletes. Tours, led by one of the institute's athletes, include visits to the gymnasium, basketball courts, and Olympic swimming pool to see training in progress. There is also a fascinating interactive display where visitors can test their sporting skills.

Leverrier Crescent, Bruce. ⓒ **02/6214 1444.** Admission A$12 (US$9.60) adults, A$6 (US$4.80) children, A$33 (US$26) families. Tours leave the AIS shop Mon–Fri 11:30am and 2:30pm; Sat–Sun 10, 10:20, and 11:30am, and 1 and 2:30pm. Bus: 80 from city center.

Australian War Memorial ✶✶
This monument to Australian troops who gave their lives for their country is truly moving and well worth a visit. Artifacts and displays tell the story of Australia's conflicts abroad. You won't soon forget the exhibition on Gallipoli, the bloody World War I battle in which so many Anzac (Australian and

Moments Up, Up & Away . . .

Balloon Aloft (© **02/4938 1955**; www.balloonaloft.com.au) offers fabulous 45-minute sunrise flights over Canberra Monday through Friday for A$210 (US$168) for adults and A$140 (US$112) for children 6 to 12, including a champagne breakfast on touchdown. On weekends a 1-hour trip costs A$250 (US$200) for adults and A$160 (US$128) for children; breakfast costs A$25 (US$20) for adults and A$10 (US$8) for kids.

Dawn Drifters (© **02/6285 4450**; fax 02/6281 5315; www.dawndrifters. com.au) will also send you soaring. One-hour champagne flights are A$195 (US$156) for adults Monday through Friday, A$230 (US$184) on weekends and holidays. Children go for 40% of the adult price. Breakfast is A$20 (US$16) extra.

New Zealand Army Corps) servicemen were slaughtered. The Hall of Memory is the focus of the memorial, where the body of the Unknown Soldier lies entombed. (His remains were brought back from a World War I battlefield in 1993.) The memorial also holds one of the largest collections of Australian art in the world, including works by Tom Roberts, Arthur Streeton, and Grace Cossington-Smith. Recently added exhibits include a film showing the surrender of Singapore, projected onto the actual table on which the surrender was signed, and a simulated ride aboard an original Lancaster bomber. ANZAC Hall and Bradbury Aircraft Hall house significant aircraft and large pieces of war memorabilia.

At the head of Anzac Parade on Limestone Ave. © 02/6243 4211. Free admission. Daily 10am–5pm (when the Last Post is played). Closed Dec 25. Guided tours at 10, 10:30, and 11am, and 1:30 and 2pm. Bus: 33 or 40.

Canberra Deep Space Communication Complex ✫   This information center, which stands beside huge tracking dishes, is a must for anyone interested in space. There are plenty of models, audiovisual recordings, and displays, including a space suit, space food, and archival film footage of the Apollo moon landings. The complex is still active, tracking and recording results from the Mars Pathfinder, *Voyager 1* and *2,* and the Cassini, Soho, Galileo, and Ulysses space exploration projects, as well as providing a link with NASA spacecraft. This is a great stop on the way back from the Tidbinbilla Nature Reserve (p. 628). There's no public bus service, but several tour companies offer programs that include the complex.

Tidbinbilla, 39km (24 miles) southwest of Civic. © 02/6201 7880. www.cdscc.nasa.gov. Free admission. Summer daily 9am–8pm; rest of year daily 9am–5pm.

High Court of Australia   The High Court, an impressive concrete-and-glass building that overlooks Lake Burley Griffin and stands next to the National Gallery of Australia, was opened by Elizabeth II in 1980. It is home to the highest court in Australia's judicial system and contains three courtrooms, a video display, and a huge seven-story-high public hall. When the court is in session, visitors can observe the proceedings from the public gallery. Check ahead for session details.

Overlooking Lake Burley Griffin, Parkes Place. © 02/6270 6811. www.hcourt.gov.au. Free admission. Mon–Fri 9:45am–4:30pm. Closed public holidays. Bus: 34.

National Capital Exhibition   If you want to find out more about Canberra's beginnings—and get a memorable view of Lake Burley Griffin, the Captain Cook Memorial Water Jet, and the Carillon in the bargain—then head here. The displays are well done, and a film provides an overview of the city's design.

On the lakeshore at Regatta Point in Commonwealth Park. (C) **02/6257 1068**. Free admission. Daily 9am–6pm (until 5pm in winter).

National Gallery of Australia   Linked to the High Court by a pedestrian bridge, the National Gallery showcases both Australian and international art. The permanent collection and traveling exhibitions are on display in 11 separate galleries. You'll find paintings by big names such as Claude Monet and Jackson Pollock, and Australian painters Arthur Boyd, Sidney Nolan, Arthur Streeton, Charles Condor, Tom Roberts, and Albert Tucker. The exhibition of Tiwi islander burial poles in the foyer is also interesting (the Tiwi Islands include Melville and Bathurst islands off Darwin), and there's a large collection of Aboriginal bark paintings from central Australia. Free guided tours start daily at 11am and 2pm. On Sunday and Thursday at 11am, a free tour focuses on Aboriginal art. A sculpture garden surrounding the gallery has 24 sculptures and is always open to the public.

Parkes Place. (C) **02/6240 6502**. www.nga.gov.au. Free admission (except for major touring exhibitions). Daily 10am–5pm. Closed Dec 25. Bus: 36 or 39 from Old Parliament House, or 34 from Parkes Place in front of the High Court.

National Museum of Australia ⭐   The first official all-encompassing museum dedicated to the nation of Australia opened in 2001 to rave reviews. Using state-of-the-art technology and hands-on exhibits, the museum concentrates on three main themes: Australian society and its history since 1788; the interaction of people with the Australian environment; and Aboriginal and Torres Strait Islander cultures and histories. It relies more on images and sound than on historic objects to tell the stories of Australia. Allow a couple of hours if it grabs you, and 30 minutes to rush around baffled if it doesn't.

Boat & Ghost Tours in Canberra

If you want to cruise Lake Burley Griffin then team up with **Lake Cruises** ((C) **0419 418 846** mobile; www.lakesidecruises.com.au). Cruises take place on weekends only on a cute replica of an Edwardian launch, licensed to carry 10 passengers. One-hour cruises cost A$10 (US$8) for adults and A$5 (US$4) for kids 10 to 17. Kids under 10 travel free. Book ahead.

If you like ghosts and the paranormal, head out across the city with Australia's resident cryptonaturalist, **Tim the Yowie Man** (he officially changed his name to this). The **Weird Canberra Ghost and History Tour** takes place on the last Friday and Saturday of the month (except Dec). Tours last 90 minutes and leave from outside the Griffin Centre (opposite Gus' Café on Bunda St., Civic) at 7pm, 9pm and 11pm. They cost A$49 (US$39) for adults (children might get a bit scared). Call (C) **0414 232 244** (mobile) for details or visit www.paranormalaustralia.com.

Acton Peninsula (about 5km/3 miles from the city center). ℂ **1800/026 132** or 02/6208 5000. www.nma.gov.au. Free admission (fees for special exhibitions). Daily 9am–5pm.

Old Parliament House

The seat of government from 1927 to 1988, the Old Parliament House is now home to exhibitions from the National Museum and the Australian Archives. The National Portrait Gallery is also here, and outside on the lawn is the Aboriginal Tent Embassy, which was set up in 1972 in a bid to persuade the authorities to recognize the land ownership claims of Aboriginal and Torres Strait Islander people. The red, black, and yellow Aboriginal flag first came to prominence here. Interestingly, the Australian Heritage Commission now recognizes the campsite as a place of special cultural significance.

On King George Terrace, midway between the new Parliament House (see below) and the lake. ℂ **02/6270 8222.** www.oldparliamenthouse.gov.au. Admission A$2 (US$1.60) adults, A$1 (US80¢) children, A$5 (US$4) families. Daily 9am–5pm. Bus: 39.

Parliament House

Conceived by American architect Walter Burley Griffin in 1912, but not built until 1988, Canberra's focal point was designed to blend organically into its setting at the top of Capital Hill; only a national flag supported by a giant four-footed flagpole rises above the peak of the hill. In good weather, picnickers crowd the grass that covers the roof, where the view is spectacular. Inside are more than 3,000 works of Australian arts and crafts, and extensive areas of the building are open to the general public. Just inside the main entrance, look for a mosaic by Michael Tjakamarra Nelson, *Meeting Place,* which represents a gathering of Aboriginal tribes. There's also a 20m-long (66-ft.) tapestry by Arthur Boyd in the Great Hall on the first floor and one of the four known versions of the Magna Carta in the Great Hall beneath the flagpole. Free 50-minute guided tours run throughout the day.

Parliament is usually in session Monday through Thursday between mid-February and late June and from mid-August to mid-December. Both the Lower House—the House of Representatives (where the prime minister sits)—and the Upper House (the Senate) have public viewing galleries. The best time to see the action is during Question Time, which starts at 2pm in the Lower House. If you turn up early, you might get a seat; otherwise, make reservations for gallery tickets through the **sergeant-at-arms** (ℂ **02/6277 4889**) at least a day in advance. Free 45-minute tours of the building start every 30 minutes beginning at 9am.

Capital Hill. ℂ **02/6277 5399.** Free admission. Daily 9am–5pm. Closed Dec 25. Bus: 39.

Questacon—The National Science and Technology Centre (Kids)

Questacon offers some 200 hands-on exhibits that can keep you and your inner child occupied for hours. Exhibits cluster in six galleries, each representing a different aspect of science. The artificial earthquake is a big attraction. The center is great for kids, but skip it if you've already visited the Powerhouse Museum (p. 159) in Sydney.

King Edward Terrace, Parkes. ℂ **02/6270 2800.** Admission A$10 (US$8) adults, A$5 (US$4) children, A$6.50 (US$5.20) students, A$28 (US$22) families. Daily 10am–5pm. Closed Dec 25. Bus: 34.

Telstra Tower

The tower, which rises 195m (640 ft.) above the summit of Black Mountain, has both open-air and enclosed viewing galleries that provide magnificent 360-degree views over Canberra and the surrounding countryside. Those who dine in the pricey, revolving **Tower Restaurant** (ℂ **02/6248 7096**) receive a refund of their admission charge. There's no bus service to the tower.

Black Mountain Dr. ℂ **02/6248 1911.** Admission A$3.30 (US$2.65) adults, A$1.10 (US90¢) children. Daily 9am–10pm.

Tidbinbilla Nature Reserve *(Moments)*   A huge bushfire in January 2003 destroyed much of this once-glorious nature reserve and killed all but one of its resident koalas. Things recover quickly in Australia, though, and many of the animals are back. Expect to see kangaroos and wallabies in their natural environment. In the new wetlands section, visitors "walk on water" on elevated boardwalks and viewing platforms, which afford looks at pelicans, blue-billed ducks, and other water fowl. Bushbird feeding time is 2:30pm daily. For the more adventurous, trails run to the mountaintops. Unlike other wildlife parks around the country, this one has plenty of space, so sometimes you'll have to look hard to spot the animals. A printed guide is available from the visitor center. Call the visitor center for information on free, ever-changing weekend talks and walks.

There's no public bus service, but several tour companies offer programs that include the reserve. **Go Bush Tours** (© **02/6231 3023;** www.gobushtours.com.au) runs tours to the reserve as well as the neighboring Canberra Deep Space Communication Complex for A$66 (US$53), including morning tea and lunch.

Tidbinbilla. Paddys River Rd., RMB 141 via Tharwa, ACT 2620. © **02/6205 1233.** Fax 02/6205 1232. www.environment. act.gov.au. Admission A$9 (US$7.20) per vehicle. Daily 9am–6pm (8pm in summer). Visitor center Mon–Fri 9am–4:30pm; Sat–Sun 9am–5:30pm. Take Tourist Rte. 5 (following large brown signs with orange number) from central Canberra.

BOTANIC GARDENS & A NEARBY NATIONAL PARK

The **Australian National Botanic Gardens** *(Moments)*, Clunies Ross Street, Black Mountain, Acton (© **02/6250 9540**), are home to the best collection of Australian native plants anywhere. The gardens, on 51 hectares (126 acres) on the lower slopes of Black Mountain, feature a Eucalyptus Lawn containing more than 600 species of eucalyptus, a rainforest area, a Tasmanian alpine garden, and self-guided walking trails. Free guided tours depart from the visitor center at 11am on weekdays and 11am and 2pm on weekends. The gardens are open daily from 9am to 5pm (to 8pm in summer). The visitor center is open daily from 9:30am to 4:30pm. There's no bus service to the gardens.

The **Namadgi National Park** *(Moments)* covers almost half of the Australian Capital Territory. Parts of the park, which has rolling plateaus, good trout-fishing streams, and dense forest, are just 30km (19 miles) from Canberra. Marked hiking trails run throughout the park. Spring is the best time to visit for the prolific display of bush flowers. In the past, sections of the park were cleared for sheep grazing, but these days the pastures are popular with hundreds of gray kangaroos. (They're easiest to spot in the early morning and late afternoon.) At Yankee Hat, off the Nass/Boboyan Road, is an Aboriginal rock-art site. The **Namadgi Visitors Centre** (© **02/6207 2900**), on the Nass/Boboyan Road, 3km (1¾ miles) south of the township of Tharwa, has maps and information on walking trails. The January 2003 fires burned much of the park, but the forests regenerate rapidly, and the animals are back in abundance.

6 Outdoor Pursuits

BIKING   With 120km (74 miles) of bike paths, Canberra is made for exploring on two wheels. Rent a bike from **Mr. Spoke's Bike Hire,** Barrine Drive, near the ferry terminal, Acton (© **02/6257 1188**). Bikes for adults cost A$12 (US$9.60) for an hour; A$20 (US$16) for a half-day, and A$30 (US$24) for a full day.

BOATING   **Burley Griffin Boat Hire,** Barrine Drive, near the ferry terminal, Acton (© **02/6249 6861**), rents paddle boats for A$20 (US$16) per hour and canoes for A$14 (US$11) per hour. It's open daily. **Row 'n' Ride,** near the MacDermott Place Boat Ramp, Belconnen (© **02/6254 7838**), is open on weekends and school and public holidays and offers canoes from A$9 (US$7.20) per hour, kayaks for A$10 (US$8) per hour, and mountain bikes for A$9 (US$7.20) per hour.

GLIDING The **Canberra Gliding Club** (© **02/6257 1494** or 02/6452 3994) offers joy flights and trial instructional flights on weekends and public holidays from the Bunyan Airfield. Flights cost A$60 (US$48).

SWIMMING The indoor heated pool at the **Australian Institute of Sport** (© **02/ 6214 1281**), Leverrier Crescent, Bruce, a short drive northwest of Civic, is open to the public at certain times during the day (call ahead to check schedules). Adults pay A$4 (US$3.20) to swim, and children pay A$2 (US$1.60). You must wear swimming caps, which you can buy there for A$2.50 (US$2). It costs A$6 (US$4.80) to use the pool, Jacuzzi, and sauna.

TENNIS The **National Tennis and Squash Centre,** Federal Highway, Lyneham (© **02/6247 0929**), has squash courts available for A$12 to A$16 (US$9.60–US$13) per hour, depending on when you want to play. Tennis courts can be booked for A$9.50 to A$15 (US$7.60–US$12). The Australian Institute of Sport (p. 625) also rents courts.

7 Canberra After Dark

The **"Times Out"** section in Thursday's *Canberra Times* has entertainment listings.

Of the pubs in town, the best in the city center are the British-style **Wig & Pen,** on the corner of Limestone and Alinga streets (© **02/6248 0171**); the popular **Moosehead's Pub,** 105 London Circuit, in the south of the city (© **02/6257 6496**); the **Phoenix,** 21 E. Row (© **02/6247 1606**), which has live music upstairs (cover charge); and **P. J. O'Reileys** (© **02/6230 4752**), on the corner of West Row and Alinga Street, an authentic-style Irish pub. **King O'Malleys** (© **02/6257 0111**), Mort Street, is another popular Irish pub in the city.

A good nightclub for the young at heart is the American-style **Bobby McGee's Entertainment Lounge** in the Rydges Canberra Hotel, London Circuit (© **02/6257 7999**). It's open Monday, Thursday, Friday, and Saturday nights. Entry runs A$3 to A$7 (US$2.40–US$5.60).

If you're looking to roll some dice, the **Casino Canberra,** in Glebe Park, 21 Binara St., Civic (© **1800/806 833** in Australia, or 02/6257 7074), is a small, older-style casino offering all the usual casino games daily from noon to 6am. Dress regulations prohibit leisurewear, running shoes, and denim, but overall it's a casual place to lose some money.

Tasmania

by Marc Llewellyn

The name "Tasmania" suggests an unspoiled place, with vast stretches of wilderness roamed by strange creatures like the Tasmanian devil. Many mainland residents still half-jokingly refer to their "country cousins" on the island as rednecks. In truth, most Tasmanians are hospitable and friendly people, lacking the harsh edge that big cities can foster. Most also care passionately for the environment, decrying the belief that anything that moves deserves a bullet and anything that stands still needs chopping down.

Visitors to Tasmania are surprised by its size, though compared to the scale of the rest of Australia, the distances are certainly more manageable. Dense rainforests, mountain peaks, alpine meadows, great lakes, eucalyptus stands, and fertile farmland are all easily accessible, but you should be prepared for several hours of concentrated driving between the main attractions. Among Tasmania's chief attractions is its natural environment. More than 20% of the island has been declared a World Heritage area, and nearly a third of the island is protected within 14 national parks.

Tasmania's other main draw is its history. Remains of the Aboriginal people who lived here for tens of thousands of years are evident in isolated rock paintings, engraving, stories, and the aura of spirituality that still holds tight in places where modern civilization has not yet reached.

Europeans arrived in Tasmania (or Van Diemen's Land, as it was once known) in 1642, when the seafarer Abel Tasman set anchor off its southwest coast. It wasn't identified as an island until 1798. Tasmania made its mark as a dumping ground for convicts, who were more often than not transported for petty crimes in their homeland. The brutal system of control, still evident in the ruins at Port Arthur and elsewhere, spilled over into persecution of the native population. The last full-blooded Tasmanian Aborigine died in 1876, 15 years after the last convict transportation. Most had already died of disease and maltreatment at the hands of the settlers.

1 Exploring Tasmania

VISITOR INFORMATION The **Tasmanian Travel and Information Centre** (© **1300/655 145** in Australia; www.discovertasmania.com.au) operates visitor centers in more than 30 towns throughout the state. It can arrange travel passes, ferry and bus tickets, car rentals, cruises, and accommodations.

Pick up a copy of *Travelways,* Tourism Tasmania's tourist tabloid, for details on transportation, accommodations, restaurants, and attractions around Tasmania.

WHEN TO GO The best time to visit Tasmania is between October and April, when the weather is at its best. By May, nights are getting cold, days are getting

Tasmania

0	20 mi	
0	20 km	

Ferry Route – – –

Bonorong Park Wildlife Centre **3**
Cataract Gorge **1**
Freycinet National Park **2**
Royal Tasmanian Botanical Gardens **4**
Tasmanian Devil Park Wildlife
   Rescue Centre **5**

shorter, and the deciduous trees are starting to turn golden. Winters (June–Aug), especially in the high country, can be quite harsh—though that's the best time to curl up in front of a blazing fire. The east coast is generally milder than the west coast, which is buffeted by the "Roaring 40s"—the winds that blow across the ocean and the 40-degree meridian, from as far away as Argentina.

The busy season for tourism runs December through February, as well as during public holiday and school holiday periods. Unlike the rest of Australia, Tasmanian schools have three terms. Term dates are from the second week in February to the last week in May; the third week in June to the first week in September; and the fourth week in September to the first week in December.

GETTING THERE   The quickest way to get to Tasmania is by air. **Qantas** (© **13 13 13** in Australia; www.qantas.com) flies from the mainland to Hobart and Launceston. **Virgin Blue** (© **13 67 89** in Australia; www.virginblue.com.au) offers discounted trips from Melbourne to Hobart and Launceston, with connections from other capitals, if you book early from the website. **Jetstar,** a Qantas offshoot (© **13 15 38** in Australia; www.jetstar.com.au), also flies to Hobart and Launceston. Two-way fares cost from around A$100 (US$80) if booked on the Net. **Regional Express** (© **13 17 13** in Australia; www.regionalexpress.com.au) flies from Melbourne to Devonport and Burnie in the state's north.

Two high-speed ferry services connect Melbourne and Tasmania. The *Spirit of Tasmania I* and *II* can each carry 1,400 passengers as well as cars. They make the crossing from Melbourne's Station Pier to Tasmania's Devonport (on the north coast) in around 10 hours. The ferries leave both Melbourne and Devonport at 9pm and arrive at around 7am. From roughly December 20 to April 27, there's also day service on weekends, leaving both ports at 9am and arriving at 7pm. Prices are based on "shoulder" and "peak" times: The shoulder seasons run from roughly August 31 to December 6, and from January 27 to April 27. A one-way seat costs A$81 to A$183 (US$79–US$146) for adults depending on season, and A$82 to A$101 (US$66–US$81) for children. Three- to four-berth cabins cost from A$112 to A$244 (US$90–US$195) for adults and A$97 to A$185 (US$78–US$150) for kids depending on the season and if you have a porthole. Twin cabins cost A$126 to A$273 (US$101–US$218) for adults and A$107 to A$205 (US$86–US$164) for children. Deluxe cabins cost A$295 to A$387 (US$236–US$310) for adults and A$177 to A$383 (US$142–US$307) for kids. Transporting a standard-size car costs A$55 (US$44) from December 6 to January 25, free the rest of the year.

In early 2004, the *Spirit of Tasmania III* commenced sailing between Sydney and Devonport. At press time, the vessel was experiencing increased competition from airlines

---

Tips **Tasmania's Tricky Roads**

Driving in Tasmania can be dangerous; there are more accidents involving tourists on Tasmania's roads than anywhere else in Australia. Many roads are narrow, and bends can be tight, especially in the mountainous inland regions, where you may also come across black ice early in the morning or at anytime in winter. Marsupials are also common around dusk, and swerving to avoid them has caused countless crashes.

Value National Park Entry Fees

A **Tassie Holiday Pass** costs A$33 (US$26) and allows entry for a car and passengers to Tasmania's national parks for 2 months. Pedestrians, cyclists, motorcyclists, and coach passengers pay A$14 (US$11) for 2 months. Occasional users
can buy a 24-hour pass for A$10 (US$8) per car; walkers, cyclists, motorcyclists,
and coach passengers pay A$3.50 (US$2.80) per day. Passes are available at all
major parks and Tasmanian Visitor Information Centres. For more information,
contact the **Parks and Wildlife Service** (© 03/6233 8203). The Tasmanian Parks
and Wildlife Service's website (www.parks.tas.gov.au) provides information on
the island's national parks.

and was discounting heavily. However, by the time you read this it might be scrapped, so
definitely check when you are planning your trip. The 650-passenger car ferry departs
Sydney at 3pm on Tuesday, Friday, and Sunday, and Devonport at 3pm on Monday,
Thursday, and Saturday. There are only two sailings per week in winter (roughly May
31–Aug 29). The trip takes 20 hours. One-way fares start at A$160 (US$128) for passage in a hostel-type dorm; A$230 (US$184) in a three- to four-berth cabin; and A$270
(US$216) in a double cabin. Cars travel free. Prices vary with the seasons and may be
adjusted, so check the website.

Make reservations for any of the ferries through **TT-Line** (© **1800/634 906** in
Australia, or 03/9206 6211; www.spiritoftasmania.com.au). Special offers are regularly available. **Tasmanian Redline Coaches** (© **03/6336 1446**) connect with each
ferry and transfer passengers to Launceston and Hobart.

GETTING AROUND   The regional airline **Tasair** (© **03/6248 5088;** www.tasair.
com.au) flies to some settlements in Tasmania. **Par Avion** (© **03/6248 5390;**
www.paravion.com.au) concentrates on the southwest World Heritage areas of the
state and also operates wonderful sightseeing tours. A 2½-hour southwest wilderness
flight, for example, costs A$176 (US$141).

Tasmanian Redline Coaches (© **03/6336 1446;** www.redlinecoaches.com.au)
and **Tassielink** (© **1300/300 520** in Australia, or 03/6272 6611; www.tigerline.
com.au) operate coach service statewide. Associated with Tassielink are **Tigerline
Coaches** (same phone and website), which offers a series of coach tours to major
places of interest. **Hobart Coaches** (© **1800/030 620** in Australia, or 03/6234 4077)
runs trips around the Hobart area.

The cheapest way to get around by coach is to buy a travel pass. The **Tassielink
Explorer Pass,** which covers all Tassielink routes, comes in four categories: A 7-day
pass good for travel within 15 days is A$172 (US$138); a 10-day pass for travel in 15
days is A$205 (US$164); a 14-day pass for travel in 20 days is A$237 (US$190); a
21-day pass for travel in 30 days is A$280 (US$224).

Driving a car from Devonport on the north coast to Hobart on the south coast
takes less than 4 hours. From Hobart to Strahan on the west coast also takes around
4 hours, while the journey from Launceston to Hobart takes about 2 hours. The
Royal Automobile Club of Tasmania, Murray and Patrick streets, Hobart (© **13 27
22** in Australia), can supply maps.

TOUR OPERATORS Dozens of operators run organized hiking, horse trekking, sailing, caving, fishing, bushwalking, diving, cycling, rafting, climbing, kayaking, and canoeing trips. For a full listing, see the "Outdoor Adventure" section of *Travelways*, the Tasmanian tourist board's publication (see "Visitor Information," above).

One of the best operators is **Tasmania Adventure Tours** (© **1300/654 604** in Australia, or 038/8309 2277; www.adventuretours.com.au). It offers a 3-day East Coast Explorer tour from Devonport, taking in Launceston, Freycinet National Park, and Port Arthur, before finishing in Hobart. The tour costs A$375 to A$495 (US$300–US$396) depending on accommodations. A 6-day Taste of Tasmania Tour starts in Devonport, takes in Mount Field National Park, Lake St. Clair, Strahan, Cradle Mountain, Freycinet, and Port Arthur, and ends up in Hobart. This tour costs A$720 to A$950 (US$576–US$760). Other tours are available. Call for departure days.

Peregrine Adventures (© **03/9662 2800;** www.peregrine.net.au) runs rafting tours of the Franklin River, which carves its way through some of the most beautiful, rugged, and inaccessible wilderness in the world. Another good operator is the **Roaring 40's Ocean Kayaking Company** (© **1800/653 712** in Australia; www.roaring 40skayaking.com.au); both companies offer paddling expeditions lasting from 1 to 11 days. **Tasmanian Expeditions,** based in Launceston (© **1800/030 230** in Australia, or 03/6267 5000; www.tasmanianexpeditions.com.au), runs a whole range of cycling, trekking, and rafting trips around the country, some starting or finishing in Hobart.

SUGGESTED ITINERARIES Planning my first trip to Tasmania, I'd pack my walking boots, raincoat, and shorts, and head first to either **Launceston** or **Hobart,** the island's two main cities. I'd take in **Freycinet National Park** for its wonderful scenery and abundant wildlife, stop at **Port Arthur** for its beautiful setting and disturbing convict past, and head to the central highlands for a stomp around **Cradle Mountain.** If I had more time, I'd drive to **Strahan** on the far west coast to discover the southwest wilderness, take some time to go trout fishing in the central lakes, and head to the quaint coastal towns of the north.

2 Hobart

198km (123 miles) S of Launceston

Tasmania's capital (pop. 126,000), second in age only to Sydney, is an appealing place worth visiting for a couple of days. Hobart's main features are its wonderful harbor and the colonial cottages that line the narrow lanes of Battery Point. As in Sydney, Hobart's harbor is the city's focal point, attracting yachts from all over the world. Down by the waterfront, picturesque Salamanca Place bursts with galleries, pubs, cafes, and an excellent market on Saturdays. Europeans settled in Hobart in 1804, a year after Tasmania's first colony was set up at Risdon (10km/6¼ miles up the Derwent River). Hobart, the southernmost Australian state capital, is closer to the Antarctic coast than it is to Perth in Western Australia; navigators, whalers, and explorers have long regarded it as the gateway to the south.

ESSENTIALS

GETTING THERE Qantas (© **13 13 13** in Australia), **Virgin Blue** (© **13 67 89** in Australia), and **Jetstar** (© **13 15 38** in Australia) carry passengers from the mainland. The trip from the airport to the city center takes about 20 minutes and costs about A$25 (US$20) by taxi. The **Airporter Bus** (© **0419/382 240** mobile) meets

Hobart

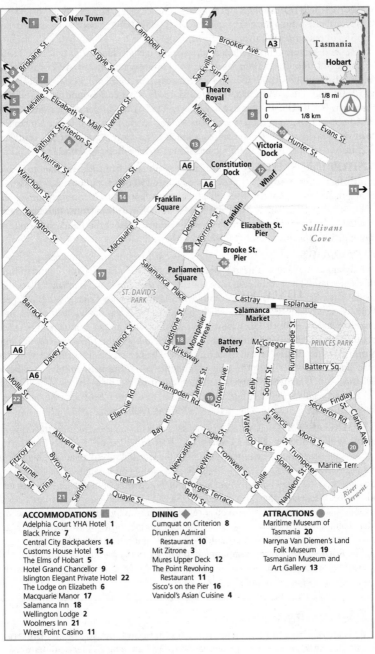

To New Town

Tasmania

Hobart

Brisbane St.

Argyle St.

Campbell St.

Brooker Ave.

A3

Sackville St.

Sun St.

Melville St.

Elizabeth St. Mall

Liverpool St.

Market Pl.

Theatre Royal

9

Evans St.

Hunter St.

10

Victoria Dock

Bathurst St.

Criterion St.

Murray St.

Collins St.

A6

Constitution Dock

A6

12

Wharf

11

Watchorn St.

Harrington St.

Macquarie St.

14

Franklin Square

Despard St.

Morrison St.

Franklin

Elizabeth St. Pier

Sullivans Cove

15

Brooke St. Pier

16

Barrack St.

17

Salamanca Place

Parliament Square

ST. DAVID'S PARK

Castray

Esplanade

Salamanca Market

PRINCES PARK

A6

Davey St.

Wilmot St.

Gladstone St.

Montpelier Retreat

18

Kirksway

Battery Point

McGregor St.

Runnymede St.

Battery Sq.

Molle St.

A6

22

Ellerslie Rd.

Hampden Rd.

Bay Rd.

James St.

Stowell Ave.

19

Kelly St.

South St.

Francis St.

Secheron Rd.

Findlay St.

Clarke Ave.

Albuera St.

Newcastle St.

Logan St.

DeWitt St.

Cromwell St.

Waterloo Cres.

Sloane St.

Trumpeter St.

Mona St.

Marine Terr.

20

Fitzroy Pl.

Turner St.

Byron St.

Erina

Star St.

21

Sandy

Crelin St.

Quayle St.

St. Georges Terrace

Bath St.

Colville

Napoleon St.

River Derwent

ACCOMMODATIONS
Adelphia Court YHA Hotel **1**
Black Prince **7**
Central City Backpackers **14**
Customs House Hotel **15**
The Elms of Hobart **5**
Hotel Grand Chancellor **9**
Islington Elegant Private Hotel **22**
The Lodge on Elizabeth **6**
Macquarie Manor **17**
Salamanca Inn **18**
Wellington Lodge **2**
Woolmers Inn **21**
Wrest Point Casino **11**

DINING
Cumquat on Criterion **8**
Drunken Admiral Restaurant **10**
Mit Zitrone **3**
Mures Upper Deck **12**
The Point Revolving Restaurant **11**
Sisco's on the Pier **16**
Vanidol's Asian Cuisine **4**

ATTRACTIONS
Maritime Museum of Tasmania **20**
Narryna Van Diemen's Land Folk Museum **19**
Tasmanian Museum and Art Gallery **13**

planes and delivers passengers to hotels in the city and farther afield for A$9.20 (US$7.40) one-way to the city center for adults (A$16/US$13 both ways) and A$4.60 (US$3.70) one-way for kids.

Car- and camper-rental offices at the airport include **Hertz** (© 03/6237 1155), **Advance** (© 1800/030 118 in Australia; www.advancecars.com.au), **Avis** (© 03/6248 5424), **Budget** (© 1300/362 848 in Australia, or 03/6248 5333), and **Thrifty** (© 1800/030 730 in Australia, or 03/6234 1341). Cars cost around A$55 (US$44) for 1 day, A$50 (US$40) per day for 2 days, A$45 (US$36) per day for 4 days, and A$40 (US$32) per day for a week or more. You might find even better bargains in town with lower-priced rental companies such as **Lo-Cost Auto Rent** (© 1800/030 023 in Australia, or 03/6231 0550) and **Range Rent-a-Bug** (© 03/6231 0300).

VISITOR INFORMATION Information is available from the **Tasmanian Travel and Information Centre,** 20 Davey St. (© **03/6230 8233;** tasbookings@tasvisinfo. com.au). It's open Monday through Friday from 8:30am to 5:15pm, Saturday and public holidays from 9am to 4pm, and Sunday from 9am to 1pm (9am–4pm Dec–Apr). You can pick up information on the state's national parks at the **Lands Information Bureau,** 134 Macquarie St. (© **03/6233 8011**).

CITY LAYOUT Hobart straddles the Derwent River on the south coast of Tasmania. **Salamanca Place** and nearby **Battery Point** abut Sullivan's Cove, home to hundreds of yachts. The row of sandstone warehouses that dominate Salamanca Place date to the city's heyday as a whaling base in the 1830s. Behind Princes Wharf, Battery Point is the city's historic district, which in colonial times was the home of sailors, fishermen, whalers, coopers, merchants, shipwrights, and master mariners. The open ocean is about 50km (31 miles) down the river, though the Derwent empties into Storm Bay, just 20km (12 miles) downstream. The central business district is on the west side of the water, with the main thoroughfares—**Campbell, Argyle, Elizabeth, Murray,** and **Harrington streets**—sloping down to the busy harbor. The Tasman Bridge and regular passenger ferries cross the Derwent River. Set back from and overlooking the city is 1,270m-tall (4,166-ft.) **Mount Wellington.**

GETTING AROUND Central Hobart is very small, and most of the attractions are in easy walking distance. **Metro Tasmania** (© **03/6233 4232** or 13 22 01; www.metro tas.com.au) operates public buses throughout the city and suburban areas. Single tickets cost A$1.60 to A$3.70 (US$1.30–US$3) depending on how far you're going. **Day Rover** tickets are good between 9am and 4:30pm and after 6pm during the week and all day on weekends; they cost A$4.20 (US$3.40). A family day ticket costs A$12 (US$9.50). Purchase tickets from bus drivers. If you plan on busing about, stop at the Metro Shop, in the General Post Office building on the corner of Elizabeth and Macquarie streets, and pick up a timetable, brochures, and sightseeing information.

The **Roche-O'May ferry company** (© **03/6223 1914;** www.ontas.com.au/cartela) operates morning and afternoon tea cruises, and lunch and dinner cruises on the

---

Tips **Staying Connected**

It's relatively hard to find public Web access in Hobart, but you can try **Drifters Internet Café,** in Salamanca Galleria, Shop 9/33 Salamanca Place (© **03/6224 3244**). The cafe charges A$5 (US$4) per half-hour.

Cartela, a wooden-hulled, former steam-powered ferry built in Hobart in 1912. One-hour afternoon cruises cost A$12 (US$9.60), 2-hour afternoon cruises cost A$16 (US$13), and lunch and dinner cruises are A$24 (US$19). Call for departure times. The company also runs ferry service on the *Wanderer,* with coffee, tea, and full commentary. It stops at the Wrest Point Casino, the Royal Tasmanian Botanical Gardens, Sullivan's Cove, and the old suburb of Belle Reeve. These ferries leave Brooke Street Pier on Franklin Wharf at 10:30am, noon, 1:30pm, and 3pm. The 1½-hour cruise costs A$10 (US$8) for adults, A$5 (US$4) for children, and A$25 (US$20) for a family.

Tasmanian Tours & Travel Tigerline (© **1300/653 633** in Australia, or 03/6272 6611) offers a range of sightseeing tours of Hobart and its surroundings.

SPECIAL EVENTS The **Sydney-to-Hobart Yacht Race,** starting in Sydney on December 26, fills the Constitution Dock Marina and harbor area close to overflowing with spectators and partygoers when the ships turn up in Tasmania. The race takes anywhere from 2 to 4 days, and the sailors and fans stay on to celebrate New Year's Eve. Food and wine lovers indulge themselves after the race during the 2-month-long **Hobart Summer Festival,** which starts on December 28.

EXPLORING THE CITY & ENVIRONS

Simply strolling around the harbor and popping into the shops at Salamanca Place can keep you nicely occupied.

Also take a look around Battery Point, an area chock-full of colonial stone cottages. The area got its name from a battery of guns set up on the promontory in 1818 to defend the town against potential invaders (particularly the French). Today, there are plenty of tearooms, antiques shops, cozy restaurants, and atmospheric pubs interspersed between grand dwellings. One of the houses worth looking into is **Narryna Van Diemen's Land Folk Museum,** 103 Hampden Rd. (© **03/6234 2791**), which depicts the life of upper-class pioneers. It's open Tuesday through Friday from 10:30am to 5pm and Saturday and Sunday from 2 to 5pm (closed July). Admission is A$5 (US$4) for adults and A$2 (US$1.60) for children. Also in this area is the **Maritime Museum of Tasmania** ⒜, 16 Argyle St. (© **03/6234 1427**), one of the best museums of its type in Australia. It's open daily from 10am to 5pm, and admission is A$7 (US$5.60) for adults, A$4 (US$3.20) for children 4 to 16, and A$16 (US$13) for a family.

The National Trust (© **03/6223 7570**) offers a 3-hour **Battery Point Heritage Walk** at 9:30am every Saturday from the wishing well in Franklin Square. It costs A$11 (US$8.80) for adults and A$3 (US$2.40) for children 6 to 16 and includes morning tea.

For magnificent views over Hobart and across a fair-size chunk of Tasmania, drive to the **Pinnacle** on top of Mount Wellington, about 40 minutes from the city center. Take a warm coat; the wind in this alpine area can bite. An extensive network of walking trails offers good hiking. Pick up a copy of *Mt. Wellington Day Walk Map and Notes* from the **Department of Environment Tasmap Centre,** at the Lands Building, 134 Macquarie St. (© **03/6233 3382**).

THE TOP ATTRACTIONS

Bonorong Park Wildlife Centre ⒦ⁱᵈˢ   I don't think I've ever seen so many wallabies in one place—they were hopping all over. There are lots of other native animals around here, too, including snakes, koalas, Tasmanian devils, and wombats. The Bush Tucker shed serves lunch, billy teas (basically tea brewed in a metal pot with a gum leaf thrown in), and damper (Australian-style campfire bread). Koala cuddling isn't allowed in Tasmania, but if you're around at feeding time, it's possible to stroke one—they're not as shy as you might think. Feeding times are 12:30 and 3pm daily. The park is on the side of a steep hill, so travelers in wheelchairs are likely to fare badly. Allow 1 hour.

Briggs Rd., Brighton. ℰ **03/6268 1184**. Admission A$11 (US$8.80) adults, A$6 (US$4.80) children under 15. Daily 9am–5pm. Closed Dec 25. Bus to Glenorchy from the central bus terminal in Hobart (about 10 min.), then take bus 125 or 126 to the park. Drive north on Rte. 1 to Brighton; it's about 25 min. north of Hobart and is well signposted.

Cadbury Chocolate Factory 🛧
Eat chocolates until they make you sick on this Willy Wonka–type trip. Book well ahead, because chocolate tours are very popular. Keep in mind you'll need to climb lots of stairs inside the factory, where you'll see chocolate being made. You can visit the factory on a ferry tour (details below), or go through Tasmanian Tours & Travel Tigerline (ℰ **1300/653 633** in Australia or 03/6272 6611), which runs half-day coach tours out of Hobart Monday through Friday from 9:30am. These cost A$35 (US$28) for adults, A$12 (US$9.60) for children, A$99 (US$79) for a family.

Claremont, 16km (10 miles) north of Hobart. ℰ **1800/627 367** in Australia, or 03/6249 0333. Tours A$13 (US$10) adults, A$6.50 (US$5.20) children, A$32 (US$26) families. Tours Mon–Fri 9, 9:30, 10, 10:30, and 11am, noon, 1, and 1:30pm.

Cascade Brewery Tours
Cascade Premium is one of the best beers in the country, in my opinion. To see how this heady amber nectar is produced, head to Australia's oldest brewery and tag along on a fascinating 2-hour tour, which includes a stroll through the grand old Woodstock Gardens behind the factory. The tour involves lots of stairs.

Cascade Rd., South Hobart. ℰ **03/6221 8300**. Tours (which include tastings) A$13 (US$10) adults, A$6.50 (US$5.20) children 5–12, A$32 (US$26) families. Tours Mon–Fri 9, 9:30, 10, 10:30, and 11am, noon, 1, and 1:30pm. Closed public holidays. Reservations required. Bus: 44, 46, or 49 (stop 18).

Female Factory Historic Site and Island Produce Fudge Factory 🛧 *Finds*
This is an interesting stopover if you're visiting the Cascade Brewery or Mount Wellington. You get not only a trip around the successful fudge-making factory, but a guided tour around the remains of the women's prison next door. The tales told here will make the hairs on your neck stand on end—like the fact that 17 out of every 20 children born within the walls of the institution died soon after birth, and that women who died were tossed into an unmarked mass grave. All the proceeds of the tour go toward preserving the prison. Allow 1½ hours.

16 Degraves St., South Hobart. ℰ **03/6223 1559**. Fax 03/6223 1556. www.femalefactory.com.au. Tours A$9 (US$7.20) adults, A$7 (US$5.60) students, A$4.50 (US$3.60) children, A$25 (US$20) family. MC, V. Tours Easter Tuesday to Dec 24 Mon–Fri 9:30am (closed weekends and public holidays); Dec 26 to Easter Monday daily 9:30am, Mon–Fri 2pm. Bus: 43, 44, 46, or 49 from GPO to South Hobart and Cascade Rd. (stop 14).

Royal Tasmanian Botanical Gardens 🛧
Established in 1818, these gardens are known for English-style plant and tree layouts—including a great conifer collection—a superb Japanese garden (better than some I've seen in Kyoto, Japan), and colorful seasonal blooming plants. A busy road nearby somewhat disturbs the peaceful atmosphere. A restaurant provides lunch and teas. To walk here from the city center, partly along a pleasant country lane known as Soldier's Walk, takes around 40 minutes—but it's badly signposted. (When you come to a shelter and plaque with a missing YOU-ARE-HERE marker, turn right—the gardens are walled and there's an obvious entrance gate.)

On the Queens Domain near Government House. ℰ **03/6234 6299**. Free admission to Botanical Shop and Botanical Discovery Center; conservatory A$2 (US$1.60). Daily 8am–6:30pm (until 5pm in winter). Bus: 17.

Tasmanian Museum and Art Gallery ⚘ Come here to find out more about Tasmania's Aboriginal heritage, its history since settlement, and the island's wildlife. Traveling art exhibitions are mounted from time to time, but always on display are the paintings of the colonial era. The art gallery has a particularly impressive collection of paintings by Tom Roberts and by several convict artists. The pride of the collection is *The Conciliation* by Benjamin Duttereau, the second-most historically significant painting in Australia, after Tom Roberts' *Shearing of the Rams,* which you can see in the National Gallery of Victoria in Melbourne. Allow 1 to 2 hours.

40 Macquarie St. ℂ 03/6211 4177. Free admission. Daily 10am–5pm.

ORGANIZED TOURS

You'll get a good introduction to the city on the daily **Hobart Historic Walk** (ℂ **03/6225 4806**), a 2-hour leisurely stroll through historic Sullivan's Cove and Battery Point. Tours start at 10am daily from September through May and on request from June through August. They cost A$17 (US$14) for adults, free for children under 12. The tour requires a minimum of six people; group discounts are available.

Several companies run boat tours of the harbor. **Captain Fells Ferries** (ℂ **03/6223 5893**) offers morning tea, lunch, afternoon, and dinner cruises. An afternoon cruise onboard a little historic ferry costs, for example, costs A$11 (US$8.80) for adults, A$6 (US$4.80) for children, and A$28 (US$22.40) for a family.

The company also runs Cadbury Factory Tours, which include coach transfers, a tour of the factory, a harbor cruise, and a two-course lunch for A$35 (US$28) for adults and A$20 (US$16) for children; these leave at 9:45am Monday through Thursday. Cruises depart from Franklin Wharf behind the wooden cruise-sales booths beside Elizabeth Street Wharf at the bottom of Elizabeth Street.

The **Cruise Company** (ℂ **03/6234 9294**) operates river trips along the Derwent to the Cadbury Chocolate Factory. Cruises depart at 10am Monday through Friday, returning at 2:30pm, and cost A$37 (US$29) for adults and A$18 (US$14) for children 5 to 15. The price includes entry and a guided tour of the factory. The boat leaves from Brooke Street Pier. Also of interest is the company's 2-hour Ironpot Cruise (to the lighthouse of that name at the mouth of the Derwent). The scenic tour of the river leaves Brooke Street Pier at 2pm every Saturday in summer and costs A$22 (US$18) for adults and A$5 (US$4) for children.

THE SHOPPING SCENE

If you are in Hobart on a Saturday, don't miss the **Salamanca Market** ★★, in Salamanca Place—it's one of the best markets in Australia. Some 200 stalls offer everything from fruit and vegetables to crafts made from pottery, glass, and native woods. The market is open from 8:30am to 3pm.

Salamanca Place itself has plenty of crafts and souvenir shops that are worth exploring, though the prices reflect the fashionable area. The best bookshop in town is a beauty; it sells a large range of new and secondhand books, many relating to Tasmania. Find the **Hobart Bookshop** at 22 Salamanca Sq. (ℂ **03/6223 1803**). For great chocolate and the best licorice, head to **Darrell Lea,** shop 36 in the Cat & Fiddle Arcade, between Collins and Liverpool streets. There are plenty of other interesting shops here, too.

Store hours are Monday through Thursday from 9am to 6pm, Friday from 9am to 9pm, and Saturday from 9am to noon (though some open all day).

Value Booking Accommodations Online

Asia Travel (http://asiatravel.com/australia.html) offers substantial savings on some of the properties recommended in this chapter if you book online. At press time, these included the Hotel Grand Chancellor in Hobart, the Colonial Motor Inn in Launceston, Freycinet Lodge, and Cradle Mountain Lodge.

WHERE TO STAY

Hobart has some of the best hotels, guesthouses, and B&Bs in Australia. For something different, you can stay with a Tasmanian family either in town or at a farm in the country, or arrange accommodations in one of the many boutique B&Bs throughout Tasmania. Contact **Heritage Tasmania Pty Ltd.,** P.O. Box 780, Sandy Bay, TAS 7005 (© **03/6233 5511;** fax 03/6233 5510). Nightly B&B rates range from about A$60 (US$48) to around A$160 (US$128) for a double. There are 20 **YHA youth hostels** in Tasmania; locations include Devonport (© **03/6424 5696**), Bicheno (© **03/6375 1293**), Coles Bay (© **03/6257 0115**), Mount Field National Park (© **03/6288 1369**), Stanley (© **03/6458 1266**), and Strahan (© **03/6471 7255**). Most have dorms as well as inexpensive double rooms. The state YHA office is at 28 Critereon St., Hobart (© **03/6234 9617**).

VERY EXPENSIVE

Hotel Grand Chancellor ✦   If you prefer standard hotel accommodations to a stately old homestead, book a room at this imposing property overlooking the yachts and fishing boats in Victoria Dock. Standard rooms are large and comfortable, with large polished granite bathrooms. More than 50% of the rooms have water views. Eight rooms are equipped for travelers with disabilities. The lobby is an impressive marble-and-granite construction complete with a large curved window to catch the action on the docks. There's also a first-class restaurant specializing in innovative Tasmanian cuisine.

1 Davey St., Hobart, TAS 7000. © **03/6235 4535.** Fax 03/6223 8175. www.hgchobart.com.au. 234 units. A$260 (US$208) double; A$365 (US$292) executive suite. Extra person A$30 (US$24). Check the website for good deals. Children under 15 stay free in parent's room. AE, DC, MC, V. Free parking. **Amenities:** Restaurant; lounge w/good views; heated indoor pool; health club; concierge; business center; salon; 24-hr. room service; massage; babysitting; laundry service; rooms for those w/limited mobility. *In room:* A/C, TV w/pay movies, dataport, minibar, hair dryer, iron.

Wrest Point Casino ✦✦   A pricey face-lift in 1998 transformed this Hobart icon, built in 1973, and launched Australia's annual A$2-billion (US$1.7-billion) casino industry. Beside the Derwent River, 3km (almost 2 miles) from the city center, the complex looks out across the harbor and the city and up to Mount Wellington. All rooms feature Tasmanian oak furniture and plush carpets, and more expensive units have exceptional views. While it may not be as convenient to the city center as the Hotel Grand Chancellor (though it's certainly walkable), the views make it a class above. Adjacent to the casino is the 61-room **Wrest Point Motor Inn,** which has nice rooms costing between A$120 and A$131 (US$96–US$104). Taxis from Wrest Point to the city cost around A$7 (US$5.60), and the bus operates to and from the city every 15 minutes.

410 Sandy Bay Rd., Sandy Bay, TAS 7005. © **03/6225 0112.** Fax 03/6225 3744. www.wrestpoint.com.au. 197 units. A$242–A$264 (US$193–US$211) double; A$330 (US$264) suite with Jacuzzi. Extra adult A$33 (US$26). AE, DC, MC,

V. Free parking. Bus: Busy Bee route 54 or 55 from Franklin Sq., Macquarie St., to stop 15. **Amenities:** 3 restaurants; 3 bars; nightclub; large indoor pool; 9-hole putting course; 2 lit tennis courts; health club; playground; concierge; business center; 24-hr. room service; massage; babysitting; laundry service; harbor boardwalk w/indoor and outdoor entertainment; boutique casino. *In room:* A/C, TV w/pay movies, dataport, minibar, hair dryer, iron, safe.

EXPENSIVE

The Elms of Hobart   This lovely National Trust–classified mansion is too far from the city (2km/1¼ miles) to walk to, and I think both the Islington and Macquarie Manor are nicer. However, it's just .5km (⅓ mile) from a wide range of restaurants along the popular North Hobart food strip. Each room has heritage appeal and is furnished with antiques. The property has a "grog" room, where guests can help themselves to beer and wine on an honor system, and a quaint front living room. Two outstanding features are the Tasmanian oak staircase and paneling. Rooms at the front face the road and can be noisy. Smoking is not permitted.

452 Elizabeth St., North Hobart, TAS 7000. (℅ **03/6231 3277.** Fax 03/6231 3276. www.theelmsofhobart.com. 6 units. A$145–A$220 (US$116–US$176) double. Rates include full breakfast. AE, DC, MC, V. Free parking. Bus: Any up Elizabeth St. from the city. Children under 11 not accepted. **Amenities:** Lounge; tour desk; nonsmoking rooms. *In room:* TV, dataport, coffeemaker, hair dryer.

Islington Elegant Private Hotel   This 1845 private home is popular with American travelers. Rooms are large and simple, each with a queen-size bed. "Grand" units are slightly roomier. Antiques, cedar woodwork, and elegant furnishings contribute to an air of gentility. French doors open onto a garden and a pool. The breakfast room is small and sunny, and the chessboard, piano, and open fire add charm to the front parlor. The last time I visited, the guests had found the place so relaxing they'd all retired for their afternoon snooze. Smoking is not permitted. The Islington is 1.5km (1 mile) from the city on the way to Mount Wellington.

321 Davey St., Hobart, TAS 7004. (℅ **03/6223 3900.** Fax 03/6224 3167. www.historichouses.com.au. 8 units. A$170 (US$136) standard double; A$180 (US$144) grand double. Rates include continental breakfast. AE, DC, MC, V. Free parking. Take the A6 Hwy. from the airport to Davey St.; stay in the right lane and go straight ahead when the road turns left. Bus: 44, 46, 48, or 49 from the city. Children not accepted. **Amenities:** Heated outdoor pool. *In room:* TV, coffeemaker.

The Lodge on Elizabeth ★   The Lodge on Elizabeth is in the second-oldest building in Tasmania, some parts of which date to 1810. Originally a gentleman's residence, it later became the first private boys' school in Tasmania. It's well situated just a 12-minute walk from Salamanca Place and is surrounded by restaurants. All rooms are decorated with antiques; many are quite romantic, with four-poster beds. Standard rooms have just a shower, whereas deluxe rooms come with more antiques and a large granite bathroom with a Jacuzzi. Complimentary drinks are served in the communal living room in the evening, and a good continental breakfast buffet goes for A$12 (US$9.60).

249 Elizabeth St., Hobart, TAS 7000. (℅ **03/6231 3830.** Fax 03/6234 2566. www.thelodge.com.au. 13 units. A$110 (US$88) small double with bathroom; A$140 (US$112) large double with bathroom; A$160 (US$128) double with spa. Extra person A$30 (US$24). AE, DC, MC, V. **Amenities:** Tour desk; car-rental desk; coin-op laundry; dry cleaning; nonsmoking rooms. *In room:* TV, dataport, fridge, coffeemaker, hair dryer, iron.

Macquarie Manor ★★   As soon as you walk into this classic colonial-style manor you'll know you want to stay. Macquarie Manor was built in 1875 as a doctor's surgery and residence. Extra rooms were added in 1950. Thick carpets and double-glazed windows keep the place very quiet, even though it's on the main road, 2 blocks from the central bus terminal. Rooms, which vary enormously, are comfortable and elegantly furnished. One room is suitable for people with disabilities. The staff is very friendly and will be happy to escort you around the premises in search of your favorite room. Check out the delightful dining room, and the drawing room complete with old couches and a grand piano. Parking is just to the left down the side of the main building. Smoking is not permitted.

172 Macquarie St., Hobart, TAS 7000. © 1800/243 044 in Australia, or 03/6224 4999. Fax 03/6224 4333. www.mac manor.com.au. 18 units (most with shower only). A$160 (US$128) double; A$190 (US$152) Heritage suite; A$210 (US$168) Macquarie suite. Extra adult A$33 (US$26); extra child A$17 (US$14). Rates include full breakfast. AE, DC, MC, V. Free parking. **Amenities:** Tour desk; dry cleaning; nonsmoking rooms. *In room:* TV, minibar, coffeemaker, hair dryer, iron.

Salamanca Inn Conveniently located on the edge of the central business district and toward the waterfront near Battery Point, Salamanca Inn features modern and pleasant apartments. The whole place was refurbished in 2000 and features queen-size beds, leather couches, Tasmanian oak furniture, galley-style kitchens, and spacious living areas. The more expensive suites are a bit plusher.

10 Gladstone St., Hobart, TAS 7000. © 1800/030 944 in Australia, or 03/6223 3300. Fax 03/6223 7167. www. salamancainn.com.au. 68 units. A$198 (US$158) 1-bedroom apt; A$220 (US$176) 2-bedroom suite; A$260 (US$208) 2-bedroom deluxe suite. Extra adult A$25 (US$20), extra child 3–14 A$15 (US$12). Ask about weekend and long-stay packages. AE, DC, MC, V. Free parking. Bus: 54B. **Amenities:** Restaurant; bar; indoor pool; Jacuzzi; tour desk; business center; room service; babysitting; laundry service; dry cleaning. *In room:* TV, free in-house movies, dataport, kitchenette, minibar, fridge, coffeemaker, hair dryer, iron.

MODERATE

Black Prince If you're looking for someplace centrally located and unfussy, then try the Black Prince, an American-influenced pub with a 1950s bent. All rooms come with a shower and a bathtub. Room no. 8 is the landlord's favorite, because "it's nearer to the stairs so you don't have to walk too far" (presumably beneficial when you've had a few beers). Downstairs, the American-style bar, Joe's Garage, is popular, especially on weekends. The American-influenced restaurant serves budget-priced steaks and chicken dishes. Lunch is offered Monday through Friday, and dinner Monday through Saturday.

145 Elizabeth St., Hobart, TAS 7000. © 03/6234 3501. Fax 03/6234 3502. 10 units. A$70 (US$56) double. Rates include breakfast. AE, DC, MC, V. **Amenities:** Restaurant; bar. *In room:* TV, coffeemaker.

Wellington Lodge ⭐ This charming Victorian-style town house (ca. 1885) is just a 10-minute walk (through Hobart's Rose Garden) from the main shopping area and Salamanca Place. Expect wooden floorboards, a country feel, and period antiques. Complimentary port is served every evening in the guest lounge. The airport bus will drop you off here. Smoking is not permitted.

7 Scott St., Hobart, TAS 7000. © 03/6231 0614. Fax 03/6234 1551. www.wwt.com.au/wellingtonlodge. 4 units. A$110–A$130 (US$88–US$104) double. Extra person A$30 (US$26). Rates include full breakfast. MC, V. Free parking. Bus: Any route to the Aquatic Center. Children under 11 not accepted. **Amenities:** Nonsmoking rooms. *In room:* TV, fridge, hair dryer.

Woolmers Inn Situated 2km (1¼ miles) south of the city, Woolmers Inn offers cozy one- or two-bedroom units with fully equipped kitchens. One unit is suitable for travelers with disabilities. Sandy Bay is Hobart's main suburb; it's halfway between the casino and the city (within walking distance of Salamanca Place) and features a "golden mile" of boutique shopping.

123–127 Sandy Bay Rd., Hobart, TAS 7000. © **1800/030 780** in Australia, or 03/6223 7355. Fax 03/6223 1981. woolmersinn@bigpond.com.au. 36 units. A$121 (US$97) 1-bedroom apt; A$149 (US$119) 2-bedroom apt. Rates 10% higher from mid-Dec to end of Jan, and cheaper in winter. AE, DC, MC, V. Free parking. Bus: Sandy Bay route (no number) from Elizabeth St. Mall on Elizabeth St. **Amenities:** Tour desk; babysitting; coin-op laundry; dry cleaning. *In room:* TV/VCR, kitchen, fridge, coffeemaker, hair dryer, iron.

INEXPENSIVE

Adelphi Court YHA Hostel   The Adelphi is a typical clean and friendly Australian youth hostel. All dorm rooms sleep four people. There is a communal kitchen, a dining room serving breakfast, and a barbecue area. It's 3km (1¾ miles) from the city center.

17 Stoke St., New Town (YHA Tasmania, G.P.O. Box 174, Hobart, TAS 7001). © **03/6228 4829.** Fax 03/6278 2047. www.yha.com.au. 9 dorms; 16 doubles, 2 with bathroom. A$56 (US$45) per person twin/double without bathroom; A$65 (US$52) double with bathroom; A$20 (US$16) dorm bed. Non-YHA members pay A$3.50 (US$2.80) per person per night extra. MC, V. Free parking. Bus: 15 or 16 from Argyle St. to stop 8A, or any bus from Stop E at Elizabeth St. Mall to bus stop 13. **Amenities:** Game and TV room; tour-booking desk; coin-op laundry; nonsmoking rooms. *In room:* No phone.

Central City Backpackers   This place is typical of backpacker-type accommodations—cheap and cheerful, a little frayed around the edges, but right in the heart of things. The central shopping district is outside the door; it's only a short walk to the harbor, and a 2-minute walk to the central bus terminal.

138 Collins St., Hobart, TAS 7000. © **1800/811 507** in Australia, or 03/6224 2404. Fax 03/6224 2316. www. centralbackpackers.com.au. 80 units. A$22 (US$18) twin per person; A$44 (US$35) double; A$18 (US$14) dorm bed. No credit cards. **Amenities:** Bar (summer only); tour desk; coin-op laundry; Internet access; pool table; kitchen; dining room. *In room:* No phone.

Customs House Hotel *(Value)*   You won't find a better value than the rooms above this historic sandstone pub overlooking the waterfront. Built in 1846, the property offers simple, colonial-style rooms, without luxuries such as TVs and telephones. Four have water views overlooking the old sailing ship the *May Queen,* which used to carry wood up the Derwent River. Other rooms look across Parliament House. Guests make the best of a shared TV room. Downstairs, a friendly public bar overlooks the water, and at the back of the building is a popular seafood restaurant known for its scallops.

1 Murray St., Hobart, TAS 7000. © **03/6234 6645.** Fax 03/6223 8750. www.customshousehotel.com. 13 units, 2 with bathroom. A$75 (US$60) double without bathroom; A$80 (US$64) double with bathroom. Rates include continental breakfast. AE, DC, MC, V. **Amenities:** Restaurant; 2 bars; dry cleaning; kitchenette w/fridge. *In room:* No phone.

WHERE TO DINE

Tasmania is known for its fresh seafood, including oysters, crab, crayfish, salmon, and trout. Once cheap, in recent years prices have crept up to match or even surpass those on the mainland. Generally, the food is of good quality.

EXPENSIVE

Mures Upper Deck *✹* SEAFOOD   This large and bustling waterfront restaurant offers great views of bobbing yachts as well as very fine seafood caught on the owner's own fishing boats. I recommend starting with a bowl of potato soup, or the signature Mures Oysters topped with smoked salmon, sour cream, and salmon caviar. The most popular main courses are blue-eye filet Martinique—a Creole-inspired sweet fish curry with coconut cream and banana sauce—and the giant seafood platter for two. The best summer dessert is the restaurant's famous summer pudding, which almost bursts with berries. In winter, Granny Leatherwood Pudding—made of apples and Australian leatherwood honey and served with cinnamon ice cream—is worth the trip. The complex also includes **Lower Deck,** a popular self-service family restaurant where you can dine well for under A$15 (US$12).

Between Victoria and Constitution Docks, Hobart. ⓒ **03/6231 2121.** Reservations recommended. Main courses A$20–A$25 (US$16–US$20). AE, DC, MC, V. Daily noon–10pm.

The Point Revolving Restaurant TASMANIAN/AUSTRALIAN This revolving restaurant on the 17th floor of the Wrest Point Hotel Casino is known for its spectacular harbor and mountain views. Criticism of its consistency has led to a complete review of its cuisine over the last couple of years, but fortunately its specialties— prawns flambé in curry sauce and Caesar salad—have remained through regular menu upgrades. The crêpes suzette are wonderful. The service is friendly and relaxed. This place is packed on weekends.

In the Wrest Point Hotel Casino, 410 Sandy Bay Rd. ⓒ **03/6225 0112.** Reservations recommended. Main courses from A$12 (US$9.60) lunch, from A$17 (US$14) dinner. Fixed-price 3-course menu A$26 (US$21) lunch, A$43 (US$34) dinner Fri–Sat, A$34 (US$27) dinner Sun–Thurs. AE, DC, MC, V. Daily noon–2pm and 6:30–9:30pm.

MODERATE

Drunken Admiral Restaurant ⭐ SEAFOOD The Drunken Admiral, opposite the Hotel Grand Chancellor on the waterfront, is an extremely popular spot with tourists, and can get raucous on busy evenings. The main attraction is its famous seafood chowder, swimming with anything that was on sale at the docks that morning. The large Yachties seafood grill is a full plate of squid, scallops, fish, mussels, and prawns, but there are plenty of simpler fish dishes on the menu, too. Otherwise splash out on Sperm Whale Sally's Shellfish Platter or perhaps Captain Nimrod's Depth Charge Platter. The salad bar spreads over a sailing dingy and can be raided as often as you want, but it's rather uninteresting, so you'll probably be content with just one dip.

17–19 Hunter St. ⓒ **03/6234 1903.** Reservations required. Main courses A$14–A$23 (US$11–US$18). AE, DC, MC, V. Daily 6–10:30pm.

Mit Zitrone ⭐⭐ MODERN AUSTRALIAN Chef and owner Chris Jackman has earned quite a reputation in Tasmania. His twice-cooked eggs with chile-palm sugar are a huge seller. Hot smoked blue-eye cod with ginger and wok-fried greens, and chicken and mushroom sausages with wide noodles, spinach, and anchovy sauce are sensational. The informal restaurant, which is basically an old shop, has bright yellow citrus walls and wooden floors and furniture. You can also drop in for coffee and cake.

333 Elizabeth St., North Hobart. ⓒ **03/6234 8113.** Reservations recommended. Main courses A$17 (US$14). AE, DC, MC, V. Mon–Sat 10am–2pm; Tues–Sat 6–10pm.

Sisco's on the Pier SPANISH/MEDITERRANEAN/INTERNATIONAL Sisco's has undergone a transformation in recent years from a typical Spanish eatery with roving guitar players to a more upmarket international affair. Today it's known for its paella, Moreton Bay bugs (a kind of small crayfish) with chocolate, garlic prawns with squid-ink spaghetti, and chargrilled octopus. The restaurant is light and bright, with a large outdoor balcony.

Upper Level, Murray St. Pier. ⓒ **03/6223 2059.** Reservations recommended. Main courses A$17–A$18 (US$14–US$15). AE, DC, MC, V. Mon–Fri noon–3pm; Mon–Sat 6pm–midnight.

Vanidol's Asian Cuisine ASIAN Very popular with both locals and tourists, Vanidol's serves a variety of Thai, Indonesian, and Indian dishes. Beef salad with basil, chile, and mint is very good, as are barbecue prawns served with sweet tamarind sauce.

Fish cooked in a light-red curry sauce is another specialty. Smoking is not permitted between 6 and 9pm.

353 Elizabeth St., North Hobart. © **03/6234 9307**. Reservations recommended. Main courses A$13–A$18 (US$10–US$14). AE, MC, V. Tues–Sun 6 to around 11pm.

INEXPENSIVE

Cumquat on Criterion ⭐ *Value* ASIAN/AUSTRALIAN   This cafe is an excellent breakfast venue, offering everything from egg on toast to traditional porridge with brown sugar. On the menu for lunch and dinner you could find Thai beef curry, laksa, a daily risotto, and chermoula-marinated fish. The desserts can be great. Vegetarians, vegans, and those on a gluten-free diet are very well catered for, as are carnivores.

10 Criterion St. © **03/6234 5858**. Reservations recommended. Main courses A$7.50–A$15 (US$6–US$12). No credit cards. Mon–Fri 8am–6pm.

HOBART AFTER DARK

Built in 1837, the 747-seat **Theatre Royal,** 29 Campbell St. (© **03/6233 2299**), is the oldest live theater in the country. It's known for its excellent acoustics and its classical Victorian decor. Ticket prices vary depending on the performance, but A$25 (US$20) is average.

If theater's not your thing, you may be interested in the **Hobart Historic Pub Tour** (© **03/6225 4806**), which traces the city's development through hotel watering holes—an important part of life in Hobart early in the 19th century. The 2-hour tour takes in four pubs; visitors enjoy a drink in each as guides give an account of the building's place in Hobart's drinking history. Tours depart Sunday through Thursday at 5pm, and cost A$35 (US$28), including a drink at each pub.

Opened in 1829 as a tavern and a brothel frequented by whalers, **Knopwood's Retreat,** 39 Salamanca Place (© **03/6223 5808**), is still a raucous place to be on Friday and Saturday evenings, when crowds cram the historic interior and spill out onto the streets. Light lunches are popular throughout the week, and occasionally you'll find jazz or blues on the menu.

My favorite drinking hole in Hobart is **Irish Murphy's,** 21 Salamanca Place (© **03/6223 1119**), an atmospheric pub with stone walls and lots of dark wood. Local bands play Friday and Saturday evenings.

If you want to tempt Lady Luck, head to the **Wrest Point Casino,** in the Wrest Point Hotel, 410 Sandy Bay Rd. (© **03/6225 0112**), Australia's first legal gambling club. Smart, casual attire required (collared shirts for men).

A SIDE TRIP TO MOUNT FIELD NATIONAL PARK ⭐

80km (50 miles) NW of Hobart

Mount Field National Park is one of the prettiest in Tasmania. It was proclaimed a national park in 1916 to protect a plateau dominated by dolerite-capped mountains and dramatic glaciated valleys. Mount Field West is the highest point at 1,417m (4,647 ft.), and in the central and western regions of the park in particular, there are examples of lakes and tarns formed in the Ice Age of 30,000 years ago. The most mountainous regions support alpine moorlands of cushion plants, pineapple and sword grass, waratahs, and giant pandani. You can get a good look at these changing environments on a 16km (10-mile) drive from the park entrance to Lake Dobson along an unpaved and often badly rutted road, which is not suitable for conventional vehicles in winter or after heavy rain.

Bennett's and rufous wallabies are common, as are wombats, barred bandicoots, Tasmanian devils, and quolls. Platypuses inhabit the lakes. Birds common to the park include black cockatoos, olive whistlers, green rosellas, honeyeaters, currawongs, wedge-tailed eagles, and lyrebirds, which were introduced from Victoria in the 1930s. Also here are rare native hens, yellow wattlebirds, and dusky robins.

There are many walking trails in the park, including one to Tasmania's most photographed waterfalls, the spectacular 45m (148-ft.) **Russell Falls,** near the park's entrance. The walk to the falls along a paved, wheelchair-accessible track takes 15 minutes and passes ferns and forests, with some of Tasmania's tallest trees, mighty swamp gums up to 85m (279 ft.) high.

GETTING THERE **Tassielink** (© **1300/300 520** in Australia, or 03/6272 6611; www.tigerline.com.au) offers daily service from December through March for A$35 (US$28) one-way. A day tour with the same company, leaving Monday, Wednesday, and Saturday, costs A$110 (US$88) for adults and A$75 (US$60) for kids. All fares are from Hobart. By car, take the Lyall Highway from Hobart to the Gordon River and follow the signs after the township of Westerway.

WHERE TO STAY

National Park Hotel Located 300m (984 ft.) inside the park, this typical one-story Aussie hotel has basic rooms, some with a sink. There's a TV in the lounge bar. The hotel can book horseback-riding expeditions within the park.

2366 Gordon River Rd., National Park, TAS 7140. © **03/6288 1103.** 7 units, none with bathroom. A$60 (US$48) double. Rates include full breakfast. MC, V. **Amenities:** Bar; lounge; golf course nearby. *In room:* No phone.

Russell Falls Holiday Cottages These cottages are right at the entrance to the park, in a rural setting with rolling fields. Each is spacious and comfortable, with gas heat and an attached toilet and shower, as well as a lounge and dining room.

Lake Dobson Rd., National Park, TAS 7140. © **03/6288 1198.** 4 units. A$77 (US$61) for 2 people. Extra adult A$13 (US$10), extra child under 16 A$8 (US$6.40). MC, V. *In room:* TV, kitchen, fridge, iron.

3 Port Arthur: Discovering Tasmania's Convict Heritage ⟨★⟩

102km (63 miles) SE of Hobart

Port Arthur, on the Tasman Peninsula, is one of Australia's prettiest harbors. It houses the extensive remains of Tasmania's largest penal colony—essentially Australia's version of Devil's Island. It's the state's number-one tourist destination, and you really should plan to spend at least a whole day in this incredibly picturesque, yet haunting, place.

From 1830 to 1877, Port Arthur was one of the harshest institutions of its type anywhere in the world. It was built to house the settlement's most notorious prisoners, many of whom had escaped into the bush from lesser institutions. Nearly 13,000 convicts found their way here, and nearly 2,000 died while incarcerated. A strip of land called Eaglehawk Neck connects Port Arthur to the rest of Tasmania. Guards and dogs kept watch over this narrow path, while the authorities circulated rumors that the waters around the peninsula were shark-infested. Only a few convicts ever managed to escape, and most of them either perished in the bush or were tracked down and hanged. Look out for the blowhole and other coastal formations, including Tasman's Arch, Devil's Kitchen, and the Tessellated Pavement, as you pass through Eaglehawk Neck.

ESSENTIALS

GETTING THERE   Port Arthur is a 1½-hour drive from Hobart on the Lyell and Arthur highways. **Tasmanian Tours & Travel Tigerline** (© **1300/653 633** in Australia, or 03/6272 6611; www.tigerline.com.au) runs trips from Hobart to the former penal settlement on Tuesday, Wednesday (in summer only), Thursday, Friday, and Sunday. Tours cost A$60 (US$48) for adults and A$38 (US$30) for children 4 to 16. Another option also takes in Bushmills Pioneer Settlement, a sawmill near Port Arthur with old buildings and a narrow-gauge steam railway. This tour costs A$70 (US$56) for adults and A$60 (US$48) for children 4 to 16. Tours depart from 199 Collins St. at 9am and return around 5:30pm. Both trips include a guided tour of the Port Arthur site.

EXPLORING THE SITE

The **Port Arthur Historic Site** ★★ (© **03/6251 2310;** www.portarthur.org.au) is large and scattered, with some 30 19th-century buildings. (Most of the main ones were damaged during bushfires in 1877, shortly after the property ceased to be a penal institution.) You can tour the remains of the church, guard tower, model prison, and several other buildings. It's best to tour the area with a guide, who can describe what the buildings were originally used for. Don't miss the fascinating museum in the old lunatic asylum, which has a scale model of the prison complex, as well as leg irons and chains.

The site is open daily from 9am to 5pm; admission is A$24 (US$19) for adults, A$11 (US$8.80) for children 4 to 12, and A$52 (US$42) for a family. The admission price is good for 2 consecutive days and includes a walking tour and a boat cruise around the harbor, which leaves eight times daily in summer. There is also a separate cruise to the **Isle of the Dead** off the coast of Port Arthur twice a day; some 1,769 convicts and 180 free settlers were buried here, mostly in mass graves with no headstones. The cruise costs an extra A$10 (US$8) for adults, A$6.50 (US$5.20) for kids, and A$29 (US$23) for a family.

The main feature of the visitor center is a fabulous **Interpretive Gallery,** which takes visitors through the process of sentencing in England to transportation to Van Diemen's Land. The gallery contains a courtroom, a section of a transport ship's hull, a blacksmith's shop, a lunatic asylum, and more. Allow between 3 and 4 hours to explore the site and the gallery.

EN ROUTE TO PORT ARTHUR

On the way to Port Arthur you might want to stop off at the historic village of Richmond and at the Tasmanian Devil Park Wildlife Rescue Centre.

Richmond is just 26km (16 miles) northeast of Hobart and is the site of the country's oldest bridge (1823), the best-preserved convict jail in Australia (1825), and several old churches, including St. John's Church (1836), the oldest Catholic church in the country. Richmond also has plenty of tearooms, crafts shops, galleries, and antiques stores.

(*Finds* **Something Spooky**

Lantern-lit **Ghost Tours of Port Arthur** ★ leave nightly at 6:30, 8:30, and 9:30pm (only 8:30pm during winter months) and cost A$16 (US$12) for adults and A$9.50 (US$7.60) for children. A family ticket (two adults and up to six children) costs A$40 (US$32). Reservations are essential; call © **1800/659 101** in Australia.

Eighty kilometers (50 miles) from Hobart is the **Tasmanian Devil Park Wildlife Rescue Centre,** Port Arthur Highway, Taranna (© **03/6250 3230;** fax 03/6230 3406), which houses orphaned or injured native animals, including Tasmanian devils, quolls, kangaroos, eagles, and owls. The park is open daily from 9am to 5pm. Admission is A$12 (US$9.60) for adults, A$6 (US$4.80) for children, and A$30 (US$24) for a family. Tasmanian devils are fed daily at 10am, 11am, and 5pm. The adjoining World Tiger Snake Centre, a unique medical research project, contains some 1,500 highly venomous snakes.

WHERE TO STAY & DINE

Port Arthur Motor Inn If you decide to stop over rather than drive all the way back to Hobart (remember, marsupials get killed all the time on the roads at night—and they can do a lot of damage to a rental car), this AAA-rated 3½-star motor inn is a good choice. The attractive rooms overlook the historic site. A range of packages are available, including a room with dinner, breakfast, and the ghost tour; or a room, 2 days' entrance to the Port Arthur site, the ghost tour, and breakfast, which both run A$109 (US$87) per person.

Port Arthur Historic Site, Arthur Hwy., Port Arthur, TAS 7182. © **1800/030 747** in Australia, or 03/6250 2101. Fax 03/6250 2417. www.portarthur-inn.com.au. 35 units. A$99 (US$79) double. Extra person A$15 (US$12). Children under 12 stay free in parent's room. AE, DC, MC, V. Free parking. Bus: Hobart Coaches (© **1800/030 620** in Australia, or 03/6234 4077) from Hobart (weekdays). **Amenities:** Restaurant; playground; coin-op laundry. *In room:* TV, coffeemaker, iron.

4 Freycinet National Park ★★

206km (128miles) NE of Hobart; 214km (133 miles) SW of Launceston

If you only have time to visit one place in Tasmania, make sure it's **Freycinet National Park.** The Freycinet Peninsula hangs down off the eastern coast of Tasmania. It's a place of craggy pink-granite peaks, spectacular white beaches, wetlands, heathland, coastal dunes, and dry eucalyptus forests. This is the place to come to spot sea eagles, wallabies, seals, pods of dolphins, and humpback and southern right whales during their migration to and from the warmer waters of northern New South Wales from May through August. The township of **Coles Bay** is the main staging post, and there are many **bushwalks** in the area. The **Moulting Lagoon Game Reserve**—an important breeding ground for black swans and wild ducks—is signposted along the highway into Coles Bay from Bicheno. Some 10,000 black swans inhabit the lake, so it's unusual not to see them. Six kilometers (3¾ miles) outside town and inside the national park is the **Cape Tourville Lighthouse,** which allows extensive views north and south along the coast and across several of the small islands in the Tasman Ocean.

Spectacular **Wineglass Bay** ★★, named one of the world's top 10 beaches by *Outside* magazine, is a lovely spot for a walk.

ESSENTIALS

GETTING THERE There are no direct public buses from Hobart. **Tasmanian Redline Coaches** (© **03/6336 1446**) run from 112 George St., Launceston, to Bicheno at 2pm Monday through Thursday, and at 3:45pm on Friday, and take less than 3 hours. **Tassielink** (© **1300/300 520** in Australia, or 03/6272 6611; www.tigerline.com.au) runs buses from Launceston to Bicheno on Monday, Wednesday, Friday, and Sunday at 8:30am. From Bicheno, catch a local bus run by **Bicheno**

Coach Services (© 03/6257 0293, or 0419 570 293 mobile) for the 35-minute trip to the park. Buses leave at 9am daily and 3pm Sunday through Friday. Buses also meet every coach from Launceston, but you need to book in advance. **Tasmanian Tours & Travel Tigerline** (© 1300/653 633 in Australia, or 03/6272 6611; www.tigerline. com.au) offers a day trip to Freycinet with an optional walking trip to Wineglass Bay (see below) from Hobart on Friday and Sunday in summer only. It costs A$59 (US$47) for adults and A$40 (US$32) for children.

From Hobart it's about a 3-hour drive to the park.

VISITOR INFORMATION The **Visitor Information Centre** (© 03/6375 1333; fax 03/6375 1533) on the Tasman Highway at Bicheno can arrange tour bookings. Otherwise, the **Tasmanian Travel and Information Centre** in Hobart (© 03/6230 8383) can supply you with maps and details. Daily entry to the park costs A$10 (US$8) per vehicle.

EXPLORING THE PARK

If you have time to do only one walk, head out from Freycinet Lodge on a 30-minute uphill hike past spectacularly beautiful pink-granite outcrops to **Wineglass Bay Lookout** for breathtaking views. You can then head down to Wineglass Bay itself and back up again. The walk takes around 2½ hours. A longer route takes you along the length of **Hazards Beach,** where you'll find plenty of shell middens—seashell refuge heaps—left behind by the Aborigines who once lived here. This walk takes 6 hours.

Tasmanian Expeditions (© 1800/030 230 in Australia, or 03/6334 3477; fax 03/6334 3463; www.tas-ex.com) offers a 3-day trip from Launceston and back that includes 2 nights in cabins at Coles Bay. The trip includes guided walks to Wineglass Bay and Mount Amor. It costs A$620 (US$496) and departs year-round on Wednesday. The company also offers 6- and 12-night walking, rafting, and cycling trips.

Not to be missed is a trip aboard Freycinet Sea Charter's vessel *Kahala* (© 03/6257 0355; fax 03/6375 1461), which offers whale-watching between June and September; bay and game fishing, dolphin-watching, diving, scenic and marine wildlife cruises, and sunset cruises. Half-day cruises cost A$60 (US$48) per person with a minimum of four adults onboard. Full-day cruises cost A$100 (US$80) per person.

WHERE TO STAY & DINE

Camping is available in the park for A$10 (US$8) per tent, though water is scarce. For inquiries, call the **Parks and Wildlife Service** (© 03/6257 0107).

Freycinet Lodge ★★ I can't praise this ecofriendly lodge enough. Comfortable one- and two-room cabins spread unobtrusively through the bush, connected by raised walking tracks. Each has a balcony, and the more expensive ones have a huge Jacuzzi. (The deluxe cabins are recently refurbished, and some have water views.) Twenty cabins have their own kitchens. The main part of the lodge houses a lounge room and an excellent restaurant that sweeps out onto a veranda overlooking the limpid green waters of Great Oyster Bay. The lodge is right next to the white sands of Hazards Beach, and from here it's an easy stroll to the start of the Wineglass Bay walk.

Freycinet National Park, Coles Bay, TAS 7215. © 03/6257 0101. Fax 03/6257 0278. www.freycinetlodge.com.au. 60 units. A$190 (US$152) standard cabin; A$225 (US$180) cabin with Jacuzzi; A$255 (US$204) deluxe cabin with Jacuzzi. Check the website for good-deal packages. AE, DC, MC, V. **Amenities:** 2 restaurants; bar; outdoor tennis court; bike rental; activities desk; coin-op laundry; Internet kiosk; nonsmoking rooms. *In room:* Fridge, coffeemaker, hair dryer.

HOBART TO LAUNCESTON: THE "HERITAGE HIGHWAY"

By the 1820s several garrison towns had been built between Launceston and Hobart, and by the middle of the 19th century convict labor had produced what was considered to be the finest highway of its time in Australia. Today, many of the towns along the route harbor magnificent examples of Georgian and Victorian architecture. It takes about 2 hours to drive between Launceston and Hobart on the "Heritage Highway" (officially known as the A1, or the Midland Hwy.), but you need 2 days to fully explore.

ROSS ★

121km (75 miles) N of Hobart; 78km (48 miles) S of Launceston

One of Tasmania's best-preserved historic villages, picturesque Ross was established as a garrison town in 1812 on a strategically important crossing point on the Macquarie River. **Ross Bridge,** the third oldest in Australia, was built in 1836 to replace an earlier span made of logs. The bridge is decorated with Celtic symbols, animals, and faces of notable people of the time. It is lit up at night, and there are good views of it from a dirt track that runs along the river's north bank.

The town's **main crossroads** is the site of four historic buildings, humorously known as "temptation" (represented by the Man-o'-Ross Hotel), "salvation" (the Catholic church), "recreation" (the town hall), and "damnation" (the old jail). The **Ross Female Factory,** built in the early 1840s, consists of ruins, a few interpretive signs, and a model of the original site and buildings inside the original Overseer's Cottage. Entry is free. Women convicts were imprisoned here from 1847 to 1854.

The **Tasmanian Wool Centre** and tourist information center, on Church Street (© 03/6381 5466), holds an exhibition detailing the growth of the region and the wool industry since settlement. It's open daily from 9am to 5pm (until 6pm Jan–Mar). Entry costs A$4 (US$3.20) for adults, A$2 (US$1.60) for children, and A$10 (US$8) for a family.

Where to Stay & Dine

Colonial Cottages of Ross ★ These delightful historic cottages sit on the edge of the village in a rural setting complete with a small apple orchard. Apple Dumpling Cottage (ca. 1880) is a two-bedroom wooden structure, sleeping four, with impressive sandstone fireplaces. The spacious Church Mouse Cottage (ca. 1840), set in an old Sunday school, sleeps just two. Captain Samuel's Cottage (ca. 1830), accommodates six people in three bedrooms, with two double and two single beds. Finally, Hudson Cottage (ca. 1850) sleeps four. All cottages have modern bathrooms and kitchen facilities.

12 Church St., Ross, TAS 7209. © 03/6381 5354. Fax 03/6381 5408. mjohnson@southcom.com.au. 4 units. A$138–A$156 (US$110–US$125) for 2. Extra person A$25–A$33 (US$20–US$27). MC, V. *In room:* TV, kitchen.

The Ross Village Bakery and Inn This coaching inn, built in 1832, offers homey rooms done in old English style. One room has a double bed, another a double and two singles. The third is a double, which opens onto a fourth room that has two singles (suitable as a family room). A separate lounge has a TV and free tea, coffee, sherry, and cakes. The bakery on the premises, an excellent place for lunch, serves filled baked potatoes and some of the best pies in Australia, baked in a wood-fired oven dating from 1860.

15 Church St., Ross, TAS 7209. © 03/6381 5246. Fax 03/6381 5360. 4 units. www.rossbakery.com.au. A$110 (US$88) per room. AE, MC, V. **Amenities:** Bakery; TV lounge. *In room:* Hair dryer.

5 Launceston ⓐ

198km (123 miles) N of Hobart

Tasmania's second-largest city is Australia's third oldest, after Sydney and Hobart. Situated at the head of the Tamar River, 50km (31 miles) inland from the state's north coast, and surrounded by delightful undulating farmland, Launceston is a pleasant city crammed with elegant Victorian and Georgian architecture and plenty of remnants of convict days. Unfortunately, shortsighted local and state governments are gradually overseeing the chipping away of its great architectural heritage in favor of the usual parking garages and ugly concrete monoliths. However, Launceston (pop. 104,000) is still one of Australia's most beautiful cities and has plenty of delightful parks and churches. It's also the gateway to the wineries of the Tamar Valley, the highlands and alpine lakes of the north, and the stunning beaches to the east.

ESSENTIALS

GETTING THERE   Qantas (ⓒ **13 13 13** in Australia), **Virgin Blue** (ⓒ **13 67 89** in Australia), and **Jetstar** (ⓒ **13 15 38** in Australia) carry passengers from Sydney and Melbourne to Launceston. The **Airport Shuttle** (ⓒ **0500/512 009** mobile in Australia) provides transportation between city hotels and the airport from 8:45am to 5pm daily for A$10 (US$8) each way.

Tasmanian Redline Coaches depart Hobart for Launceston several times daily (trip time: around 2 hr., 40 min.). The one-way fare is A$25 (US$20). Launceston is 1½ hours from Devonport if you plan to take a ferry from Melbourne across Bass Strait to Devonport. The bus ride from Devonport to Launceston costs around A$17 (US$14).

The drive from Hobart to Launceston takes just over 2 hours on Highway 1.

VISITOR INFORMATION   The **Gateway Tasmania Travel Centre,** at the corner of St. John and Paterson streets (ⓒ **03/6336 3133;** fax 03/6336 3118; gateway.tas@ microtech.com.au), is open Monday through Friday from 9am to 5pm, Saturday from 9am to 3pm, and Sunday and holidays from 9am to noon.

CITY LAYOUT   The main pedestrian shopping mall, Brisbane Street, along with St. John and Charles streets on either side, forms the heart of the central area. The Victorian-Italianate Town Hall is 2 blocks north on Civic Square, and opposite the red-brick Post Office building dating from 1889. The Tamar River slips quietly past the city's northern edge and is crossed at two points by Charles Bridge and Tamar Street. City Park, to the northeast of the central business district, is a nice place for a stroll.

EXPLORING THE CITY & ENVIRONS

Launceston is easy to explore on foot. A must for any visitor is a stroll with **Launceston Historic Walks** ⓐ (ⓒ **03/6331 3679;** harris.m@bigpond.com), which leave from the Gateway Tasmania Travel Centre Monday through Friday at 9:45am. (Weekend walks can also be arranged.) The 1-hour walk gives a fascinating insight into Launceston's history and costs A$10 (US$8). **City Sights** (ⓒ **03/6336 3122**), on the corner of St. John and Paterson streets, runs city tours daily by replica tram. Tours cost A$23 (US$18) for adults and A$16 (US$13) for children under 16. **Tasmanian Tours & Travel Tigerline** (ⓒ **1300/653 633** in Australia or 03/6272 6611) operates a half-day coach tour of the city, plus a boat cruise, on Monday, Wednesday, and Friday at 9:30am. It costs A$39 (US$31) for adults and A$23 (US$18) for children.

A must-see is **Cataract Gorge** ✮, the result of violent earthquakes that rattled Tasmania some 40 million years ago. It's a wonderfully scenic area just 10 minutes from Launceston. The South Esk River flows through the gorge and collects in a small lake traversed by a striking yellow suspension bridge and the longest single-span chairlift in the world. The chairlift (ⓒ **03/6331 5915**) is open daily from 9am to 4:30pm (except June 23–Aug 11, when it operates Sat–Sun only), and costs A$5 (US$4) for adults and A$3 (US$2.40) for children under 16. Outdoor concerts sometimes take place on the lake bank. The hike to the Duck Reach Power Station takes about 45 minutes. Take good footwear and a raincoat. Other walks in the area are shorter and easier. The **Gorge Restaurant** (ⓒ **03/6331 3330**) and the kiosk next door serve meals with glorious views from the outdoor tables.

Tamar River Cruises (ⓒ **03/6334 9900**) offers lunch, afternoon, and evening buffet dinner cruises up the Tamar River from Home Point Wharf in Launceston.

Mountain biking is popular in this area. Contact **Tasmanian Expeditions** (ⓒ **1800/030 230** in Australia, or 03/6334 3477) for information on its 4- to 7-day trips along the east coast in summer. You can rent bicycles from the youth hostel at 36 Thistle St. (ⓒ **03/6344 9779**) for A$11 (US$8.80) per day for a touring bike or A$18 (US$14) per day for a mountain bike. (You can also rent bushwalking equipment, including boots, tents, sleeping bags, and stoves.)

The **Trevallyn State Recreation Area,** on the outskirts of Launceston off Reatta Road, is a man-made lake surrounded by a beautiful wildlife reserve with several walking tracks. There are barbecue facilities, picnic areas, and a beach.

OTHER ATTRACTIONS

Aquarius Roman Baths   Adorned with gold, Italian marble, and works of art, this remarkable Romanesque structure is worth visiting just for the architectural experience. Indulge in warm-, hot-, and cold-water baths; visit the steam room; or get a massage or a beauty makeover.

127 George St. ⓒ **03/6331 2255**. www.romanbath.co.au. 30-min. massage and entry to Roman baths A$65 (US$52). Other packages available. Mon–Fri 8:30am–9pm; Sat–Sun 9am–6pm.

The Old Umbrella Shop   Built in the 1860s, this unique shop is the last genuine period store in Tasmania and has been operated by the same family since the turn of the 20th century. Umbrellas spanning the last 100 years are on display, and modern "brollies" and souvenirs are for sale. Allow 15 minutes.

60 George St. ⓒ **03/6331 9248**. Free admission. Mon–Fri 9am–5pm; Sat 9am–noon.

The Penny Royal World & Gunpowder Mill   This amusement park, with its sailboat, barges, trams, and historic gunpowder mills, is large enough to occupy an entire day. Admission includes a tram ride and a trip up Cataract Gorge and the Tamar River on the paddle steamer MV *Lady Stelfox.*

Off Bridge Rd. ⓒ **03/6331 6699**. Admission A$16 (US$13) adults, A$6.50 (US$5.20) children, A$35 (US$28) family of 2 adults and up to 6 children. Daily 9am–4:30pm. Closed Dec 25.

The Queen Victoria Museum & Art Gallery   Opened in honor of Queen Victoria's Golden Jubilee in 1891, this museum houses a large collection of stuffed wildlife, including the extinct Tasmanian tiger, or thylacine. There are also temporary exhibits and historical items on display. Allow 1 hour.

2 Wellington St. ⓒ **03/6323 3777**. Free admission. Daily 10am–5pm. Closed Dec 25.

WHERE TO STAY
VERY EXPENSIVE

Peppers Seaport Hotel ★★   One of Australia's most respected boutique-hotel operators, Peppers Retreats & Resorts, opened this hotel on the Tamar riverfront in April 2004. The hotel is part of a major redevelopment of the Seaport Dock area—just 5 minutes by car from downtown—which also includes new restaurants, entertainment venues, and shopping facilities. The hotel is built on the site of an old dry dock and has been designed in the shape of a ship. The decor is luxurious and contemporary nautical in style, using soft, light colors, natural timbers, and chromes. Rooms are quite spacious and most have balconies either looking out over the river, or over the town center to the mountains beyond. Each has a good kitchenette and an extra foldout sofa bed.

28 Seaport Blvd., Launceston, TAS 7250. (©) **03 6345 3333**. Fax 03/6345 3300. www.peppers.com.au. 60 units. A$150 (US$120) river-view double; A$240 (US$192) city-view double; A$303–A$448 (US$242–US$358) suite. AE, DC, MC, V. Car: From the Mall on Brisbane St., turn right onto St. John St., turn right onto York St. Proceed 3 blocks and turn right onto Bathurst St. Proceed 1.5km (1 mile) and on the left is the Seaport Precinct. **Amenities:** Restaurant; bar; tour desk. *In room:* A/C, TV, kitchenette, minibar, coffeemaker, hair dryer, iron, in-room laundry.

EXPENSIVE

Alice's Cottages & Spa Hideaways ★★★   I highly recommend these delightful cottages: **Alice's Place,** which sleeps two, was made entirely from bits and pieces of razed historic buildings; **Ivy Cottage** is a restored Georgian house (ca. 1831). Both places are furnished with antiques and fascinating period bric-a-brac. Kitchens are fully equipped, and both units have large Jacuzzis; they share a garden. Guests come and go as they please, and stay here on their own. (Check in at the reception area, 129 Balfour St.) Also available are **Alice's Hideaways,** five other cottages in a colonial Australian theme, some of which sleep four; and four cute cottages collectively known as **The Shambles.** A recent addition is **Aphrodites Delux Spa,** a large, regal setup with a formal dining room.

129 Balfour St., Launceston, TAS 7250. (©) **03/6334 2231**. Fax 03/6334 2696. www.cottagesofthecolony.com.au. 11 units. Alice's Place A$197 (US$157) for 2; Ivy Cottage A$197 (US$157) for 2. Alice's Hideaways: Bonnie Doon, Captain Stirlings, Camelot, and French Boudoir A$197 (US$157). Shambles cottages A$160 (US$128). Aphrodites A$230 (US$184); 2-night minimum. Extra person A$55 (US$44). Rates include breakfast ingredients left in your fridge. AE, DC, MC, V. Free parking. *In room:* A/C, TV, kitchen.

Hotel Grand Chancellor Launceston ★★   This centrally located European-influenced "grand" hotel is only a short stroll from the main shopping precinct, public gardens, and other city features. The rooms are large and elegant and the restaurant is good, too. Standard rooms have two double beds or a king-size bed. There's a piano bar and a brasserie, too. Smoking is not permitted.

29 Cameron St., Launceston, TAS 7250. (©) **1800/555 811** in Australia, or 03/6334 3434. Fax 03/6331 7347. 158 units. A$220 (US$176) double; A$245 (US$196) room with Jacuzzi; A$290–A$500 (US$232–US$400) suite. Children stay free in parent's room. Ask about packages. AE, DC, MC, V. Free parking. **Amenities:** Restaurant; bar; concierge; car-rental desk; business center; 24-hr. room service; massage by arrangement; babysitting; coin-op laundry; laundry service; nonsmoking rooms. *In room:* A/C, TV, dataport, minibar, coffeemaker, hair dryer, iron.

York Mansions ★★★   If you feel that where you stay is as important to your visit as what you see, then you must stay here. Within the walls of the National Trust–classified York Mansions, built in 1840, are five spacious apartments, each with a distinct character. The Duke of York apartment is fashioned after a gentleman's drawing room, complete with rich leather sofa, antiques, and an extensive collection of historic books.

The light and airy Duchess of York unit has two bedrooms, hand-painted silk panels, and a Jacuzzi. Each apartment has its own kitchen, dining room, living room, bedrooms, bathroom, and laundry. A CD player and large-screen TV add modern touches. The ingredients for a hearty breakfast can be found in the refrigerator. There's also a delightful cottage garden.

9–11 York St., Launceston, TAS 7250. ℭ **03/6334 2933.** Fax 03/6334 2870. www.yorkmansions.com.au. 5 units. A$198–A$224 (US$158–US$179). Extra person A$55 (US$44). Rates include breakfast provisions. AE, DC, MC, V. Free parking. **Amenities:** Tour desk; laundry service; nonsmoking rooms. *In room:* TV/VCR, dataport, kitchen, minibar, coffeemaker, hair dryer, iron.

MODERATE

Innkeepers Colonial Motor Inn ⭐ Those who desire tried-and-true above-standard motel lodging will feel at home at the recently refurbished Colonial, a place that combines old-world ambience with modern facilities. The large rooms have attractive furnishings. They're fairly standard and attract a large corporate clientele. The complex incorporates the Old Grammar School next door, with the **Quill and Cane Restaurant** operating in a onetime schoolroom, and **Three Steps On George,** Launceston's liveliest nightspot, making use of the former boys' gym.

31 Elizabeth St., Launceston, TAS 7250. ℭ **03/6331 6588.** Fax 03/6334 2765. www.colonialinn.com.au. 63 units. A$148 (US$118) double; A$165–A$245 (US$132–US$196) suite. Extra person A$15 (US$12). Lower weekend rates. Children under 3 stay free in parent's room. AE, DC, MC, V. Free parking. **Amenities:** Restaurant; lounge; tour desk; limited room service; laundry service. *In room:* A/C, TV, minibar, coffeemaker, hair dryer, iron.

Waratah on York ⭐⭐ The Waratah on York is a carefully renovated Victorian mansion, built in 1862 for Alexander Webster, an ironmonger by trade and mayor of Launceston in the 1860s and 1870s. The current owners have spent considerable time and energy restoring the property to its former glory. Some of the original features—pressed brass ceiling roses and a staircase with a cast-iron balustrade—remain, while others have been faithfully re-created. Six rooms come with a Jacuzzi, one with a balcony, and another with a sunroom. All have high ceilings and ornate (but nonfunctional) fireplaces. The executive rooms have four-poster beds and sweeping views of the Tamar River.

12 York St., Launceston, TAS 7250. ℭ **03/6331 2081.** Fax 03/6331 9200. www.waratahonyork.com.au. 9 units. A$172 (US$137) standard double; A$196 (US$159) double with Jacuzzi; A$230 (US$184) executive suite with Jacuzzi. Rates include continental breakfast. AE, DC, MC, V. Free parking. **Amenities:** Bar; lounge w/fireplace; tour desk; business facilities; massage; laundry service; same-day dry cleaning; nonsmoking rooms. *In room:* TV, minibar, coffeemaker, hair dryer, iron.

INEXPENSIVE

Hillview House The rooms at this restored farmhouse are nothing fancy, but are quite comfortable. Each comes with a double bed and a shower. The family room has an extra single bed; it's the nicest unit and has the best views. The hotel overlooks the city, and the large veranda and colonial dining room have extensive views over the city and the Tamar River.

193 George St., Launceston, TAS 7250. ℭ **03/6331 7388.** Fax 03/6331 7388. 9 units. A$90 (US$72) double; A$105 (US$84) family room for 3. Rates include full breakfast. MC, V. Free parking. **Amenities:** Laundry service. *In room:* TV.

Hotel Tasmania In the heart of town, this budget hotel offers simple rooms with modern furnishings and attached showers. Downstairs there's a saloon-style bar with a cowboy theme, which schedules live music Wednesday, Friday, and Saturday. The popular **Saloon nightclub** also kicks off late on Wednesday, and it's free for students before 11pm.

191 Charles St., Launceston, TAS 7250. ℂ 03/6331 7355. Fax 03/6331 2414. www.saloon.com.au. 25 units. A$75 (US$60) double. Extra person A$19 (US$15). Rates include continental breakfast. AE, MC, V. Free street parking. **Amenities:** Restaurant; bar. *In room:* TV, fridge, coffeemaker.

WHERE TO DINE

Most places to eat in Launceston don't have a fixed closing time; rather, they close when the last customer has eaten.

EXPENSIVE

Fee & Me Restaurant ★★ MODERN AUSTRALIAN   Perhaps the best restaurant in Launceston, Fee & Me is in a grand old mansion. The menu is structured so that diners choose a selection from five categories, each one moving from light to rich. An extensive wine list complements selections for each course. A five-course meal could go something like this: Tasmanian smoked salmon with salad, capers, and a soft poached egg; followed by chile oysters with coconut sauce and vermicelli noodles; then ricotta and goat cheese gnocchi with creamed tomato and red capsicum; followed by Asian-style duck on bok choy with citrus sauce; topped off with coffee and chicory soufflé. The dishes change frequently, so you never know what you might find.

Corner of Charles and Frederick sts. ℂ 03/6331 3195. Reservations recommended. A$42 (US$34) for 3 courses; A$48 (US$38) for 4 courses; A$50 (US$40) for 5 courses. AE, DC, MC, V. Mon–Sat 7–10:30pm.

MODERATE

O'Keefe's Hotel ASIAN/TASMANIAN   This pub-based eatery earns high praise for its variety of well-prepared dishes. You can choose such delicacies as Thai curry and laksa; seafood dishes such as scallops, prawns, and sushi; and plenty of pastas and grills. There's also a range of good salads.

124 George St. ℂ 03/6331 4015. Reservations recommended. Main courses A$11–A$25 (US$8.80–US$20). AE, MC, V. Daily 11am–2am.

Shrimps ★ SEAFOOD   Come here for the best selection of seafood in Launceston. Built in 1824 by convict labor, it has a classic Georgian exterior. Tables are small and well spaced. The best meals are off the blackboard menu, which generally includes at least eight fish dishes. Usually available are wonderful Tasmanian mussels, whitebait, Thai-style fish cakes, and freshly split oysters. Everything is very fresh and seasonal.

72 George St. (at the corner of Paterson St.). ℂ 03/6334 0584. Reservations recommended. Main courses A$14–A$19 (US$11–US$15). AE, DC, MC, V. Mon–Sat noon–2pm and 6:30–10pm.

Star Bar Cafe ★ MEDITERRANEAN   Many consider this Tasmania's best bistro. It offers a range of dishes, such as mee goreng, beets, and quail risotto; grilled octopus, steaks, and chicken livers; and pizzas and breads cooked in the wood-fired oven. In winter, guests congregate around a large open fire.

113 Charles St. ℂ 03/6331 9659. Reservations recommended. Main courses A$12–A$20 (US$9.60–US$16). AE, MC, V. Mon–Wed 11am–11pm; Thurs–Sat 11am–midnight; Sun noon–10pm.

INEXPENSIVE

Konditorei Cafe Manfred PATISSERIE   This German patisserie had to move to larger premises to keep up with demand for its sensational cakes and breads. It also added an a la carte restaurant serving up the likes of pastas and steaks. Light meals include croissants, salads, and cakes. You can eat inside or outside.

106 George St. ℭ **03/6334 2490**. Light meals A$4–A$5 (US$3.20–US$4); main courses A$9–A$18 (US$7.20–US$14). AE, DC, MC, V. Mon–Fri 9am–5:30pm; Sat 8:30am–4pm.

A CAFE

Croplines Coffee Bar ⭐ *(Finds* CAFE   If you crave good coffee, bypass every other place in Launceston and head here. It's a bit hard to find, and you may have to ask for directions, but basically it's behind the old Brisbane Arcade. The owners are dedicated to coffee, grinding their beans on the premises daily. If coffee's not your cup of tea, then try the hot chocolate—it's the best I've tasted.

Brisbane Court, off Brisbane St. ℭ **03/6331 4023**. Coffees and teas A$1.80–A$2.60 (US$1.45–US$2.10). Cakes under A$3 (US$2.40). AE, MC, V. Daily 8am–5:30pm.

6 Cradle Mountain & Lake St. Clair National Park ⭐⭐

85km (53 miles) S of Devonport; 175km (109 miles) NW of Hobart

The national park and World Heritage area that encompasses both Cradle Mountain and Lake St. Clair is one of the most spectacular regions in Australia and, after Hobart and Port Arthur, the most visited place in Tasmania. The 1,545m (5,068-ft.) mountain dominates the north part of the island, and the long, deep lake is to its south. Between them lie steep slopes, button grass plains, majestic alpine forests, dozens of lakes filled with trout, and several rivers. **Mount Ossa,** in the center of the park, is Tasmania's highest point at 1,617m (5,304 ft.). The **Overland Track** (see "Hiking the Overland Track," below), links Cradle Mountain with Lake St. Clair and is the best known of Australia's walking trails. Another option in the area is a visit to the **Walls of Jerusalem National Park,** a high alpine area with spectacular granite walls, small lakes, and old-growth forest.

ESSENTIALS

GETTING THERE   Tassielink (ℭ **1300/300 520** in Australia, or 03/6272 6611; www.tigerline.com.au) runs buses to Cradle Mountain from Hobart, Launceston, Devonport, and Strahan. Its special summer Overland Track service drops off passengers at the beginning of the walk (Lake St. Clair) and picks them up at Cradle Mountain. From Launceston this service costs A$99 (US$79) one-way for adults and A$89 (US$71) for students. From Hobart it costs A$90 (US$72) one-way for adults and A$81 (US$65) for students. Another option is to be picked up in Launceston and dropped off in Lake St. Clair, then picked up in Cradle Mountain and driven to Hobart, for A$70 (US$56) for adults and A$63 (US$50) for students. Check the website for departure times, which change. The company also runs a day tour from Launceston, including short walks, for A$89 (US$71) for adults and A$55 (US$44) for children.

Maxwells Cradle Mountain–Lake St. Clair Charter Bus and Taxi Service (ℭ/fax **03/6492 1431**) runs buses from Devonport and Launceston to Cradle Mountain. The fare starts at A$35 (US$28). The buses also travel to other areas nearby, such as the Walls of Jerusalem, as well as Lake St. Clair. Buses also run from the Cradle Mountain campground to the start of the Overland Track.

Motorists enter the park off the Lyall Highway from Hobart, via Deloraine or Poatina from Launceston, and via Sheffield or Wilmot from Devonport. Both Cradle Mountain and Lake St. Clair are well signposted.

VISITOR INFORMATION   The park headquarters, **Cradle Mountain Visitor Centre** (ℭ **03/6492 1133;** fax 03/6492 1120; www.parks.tas.gov.au), on the northern edge of the park outside Cradle Mountain Lodge, offers the best information on walks and treks. It's open daily 8am to 5pm (6pm in summer).

EXPLORING THE PARK

Cradle Mountain Lodge (see "Where to Stay & Dine," below) runs a daily program of guided walks, abseiling (rappelling), rock-climbing, and trout-fishing excursions for lodge guests. The park has plenty of trails that can be attempted by people equipped with directions from the staff at the park headquarters (see "Visitor Information," above). Be warned, though, that the weather changes quickly in the high country; so go prepared with wet-weather gear and always tell someone where you are headed. Of the shorter walks, the stroll to Pencil Pines and the 5km (3-mile) walk to Dove Lake are the most pleasant. Between June and October it's sometimes possible to cross-country ski in the park.

WHERE TO STAY & DINE

Cradle Mountain Lodge ★★ If you like luxury with your rainforests, then this award-winning lodge is the place for you. Cradle Mountain Lodge is marvelous. Just minutes from your bed are giant buttresses of 1,500-year-old trees, moss forests, mountain ridges, limpid pools and lakes, and hordes of scampering marsupials. The cabins are comfortable, the food excellent, the staff friendly, and the open fireplaces well worth cuddling up in front of for a couple of days. Each modern wood cabin has a potbellied stove as well as an electric heater for chilly evenings, a shower, and a small kitchen. There are no telephones or TVs in the rooms—but who needs them? Spa cabins come with carpets, a Jacuzzi, and a balcony offering a variety of views. Some have a separate bedroom. Two cabins have limited facilities for travelers with disabilities. Guests have the use of the casual, comfortable main lodge where almost every room has a log fire.

G.P.O. Box 478, Sydney, NSW 2001. 📞 **13 24 69** in Australia, or 03/6492 1303. P&O Resorts: 📞 **800/225-9849** in the U.S. and Canada, 020/7805-3875 in the U.K., 1800/737 678 in Australia, or 02/9364 8900. Fax 02/9299 2477. www.cradlemountainlodge.com.au. 96 units. A$230 (US$184) Pencil Pine cabin double; A$290 (US$232) spa cabin double; A$360 (US$288) spa suite. Extra person A$58 (US$46). Children under 3 stay free in parent's room. Ask about winter packages. AE, DC, MC, V. Free parking. **Amenities:** Cafe; 2 bars; laundry service. *In room:* Kitchenette, no phone.

Waldheim Cabins For a real wilderness experience, head to these cabins run by the Parks and Wildlife Service, located 5km (3 miles) from Cradle Mountain Lodge. Nestled between button grass plains and temperate rainforest, they are simple and affordable and offer good access to plenty of walking tracks. Each heated cabin has single bunk beds, basic cooking utensils, crockery, cutlery, and a gas stove. Each accommodates four or eight people; if your party is smaller, you won't have to share with strangers. Two outbuildings with sanitary facilities (composting toilets and showers) serve all the cabins. Generated power is provided for lighting between 6 and 11pm only. Stores and fuel can be bought at Cradle Mountain Lodge. Bring your own bed linen and toiletries. Guests can pick up keys from the National Park Visitor Centre, just inside the national park, daily between 8am and 5:30pm.

Cradle Mountain Visitor Centre, P.O. Box 20, Sheffield, TAS 7306. 📞 **03/6492 1110.** Fax 03/6492 1120. Cradle@dpiwe.tas.gov.au. 8 cabins. Cabin A$70 (US$56) for 2 adults; A$25 (US$20) for each additional adult; A$9.90 (US$7.90) for each additional child 6–16; children under 6 stay free in parent's room. Linen A$5.50 (US$4.40) per person. MC, V. *In room:* No phone.

LAKE ST. CLAIR ★

Australia's deepest natural freshwater lake is a narrow, 15km-long (9⅓-mile) waterway, enclosed within the Cradle Mountain–Lake St. Clair National Park. On the lake's

Finds Hiking the Overland Track

The best-known hiking trail in Australia is the **Overland Track** 🌟🌟, an 85km (53-mile) route between Cradle Mountain and Lake St. Clair. The trek takes 5 to 10 days and goes through high alpine plateaus, button grass plains, heathland, and rainforests, and passes glacial lakes, ice-carved crags, and waterfalls. The trek gives you a good look at the beauty of Tasmania's pristine wilderness, and although the first day is quite tough, you soon get into the rhythm. After climbing to Pelion Gap, the track gradually descends southward toward the towering myrtle forests on the shores of Lake St. Clair. There are many rewarding side trips, including the 1-day ascent of Mount Ossa (1,617m/5,304 ft.), Tasmania's highest peak.

Several companies offer guided walks of the Overland Track October through April. For those who wish to do it solo, simple public huts (on a first-come, first-served basis) and camping areas are available. Every summer up to 200 people a day start the trek. Most trekking companies employ at least two guides who carry tents and cooking gear, while you carry your sleeping bag, lunch, and personal belongings. Wet-weather gear is essential, because heavy downpours can be frequent. Make sure your boots are well broken in, to avoid blisters.

Tasmanian Expeditions (© 1800/030 230 in Australia, or 03/6334 3477; www.tas.ex.com) offers 3-day walking tours around Cradle Mountain, staying at Waldheim Cabins. The tours depart from Launceston and cost A$620 (US$496), all-inclusive. Trips leave every Sunday and Wednesday between October and May, with extra trips from Christmas to the end of January. The company also offers a full 8-day trek on the Overland Track from Launceston. The price is A$1,490 (US$1,192), all-inclusive; renting wet-weather gear costs A$55 (US$44) extra. These trips depart every Saturday between November and April, with extra trips from late December to the end of January. Another trip, a 6-day Cradle Mountain and Walls of Jerusalem National Park trip, includes 3 nights of wilderness camping and 3 nights in a cabin. It costs A$1,240 (US$992) and leaves every Sunday between October and mid-May. Many people have reported that this trek was the highlight of their trip to Australia.

I also recommend **Cradle Mountain Huts,** P.O. Box 1879, Launceston, TAS 7250 (© 03/6331 2006; fax 03/6331 5525; www.cradlehuts.com.au). Six-day walks cost A$1,995 (US$1,596); rates are all-inclusive and include transfers to and from Launceston. Children under 12 are not permitted. The huts are fully equipped, heated, and quite comfortable, with showers, a main living area, and a full kitchen. You get a good three-course meal every night. The treks leave daily between Christmas and early February, and around five times a week between November and April.

southern edge is **Cynthia Bay,** site of an informative ranger station where you must register if you're attempting the Overland Track from this end, as well as a restaurant, cabin accommodations, and a backpackers' hostel operated by **Lakeside St. Clair** (© **03/6289 1137**). National park rangers run several tours between Boxing Day and the end of February, including spotlighting tours and guided walks around the area. Call © **03/6289 1172** for details.

7 The West Coast

296km (184 miles) NW of Hobart; 245km (152 miles) SW of Devonport

Tasmania's west coast is wild and mountainous, with a scattering of mining and logging towns and plenty of wilderness. The pristine Franklin and Gordon rivers tumble through World Heritage areas once contested by loggers, politicians, and environmentalists, whereas the bare, poisoned hills that make up the eerily beautiful "moonscape" of Queenstown show the results of mining and industrial activity. **Strahan** ☆ (pronounced *Strawn*), the only town of any size in the area, is the starting point for cruises up the Gordon River and into the rainforest.

ESSENTIALS

GETTING THERE   **Tassielink** (© **1300/300 520** in Australia, or 03/6272 6611; www.tigerline.com.au) runs coaches between Strahan and Launceston, Devonport, and Cradle Mountain every Tuesday, Thursday, and Saturday; it serves Hobart on Friday and Sunday. Operating days tend to change, so check the website. The trip from Launceston takes over 8 hours. The drive from Hobart to Strahan takes about 4½ hours without stops. From Devonport, allow 3½ hours. Although the roads are good, they twist and turn and are particularly hazardous at night, when marsupial animals come out to feed. The cheapest way to travel between these places is by bus with a **Tassielink Explorer Pass.**

VISITOR INFORMATION   **Strahan Visitors Centre,** on The Esplanade (© **03/6471 7622;** fax 03/6471 7533), is open daily from 10am to 6pm in autumn and winter and to 8pm in spring and summer. It has good information on local activities. A good website for the area is www.westcoasttourism.com.au.

CRUISING THE RIVERS & OTHER ADVENTURES

Gordon River Cruises (© **03/6471 7187**) offers a half-day trip daily at 9am, an afternoon cruise at 2pm in the first 3 weeks of January, and a full-day trip from October to the end of May. Cruises take passengers across Macquarie Harbour and up the Gordon River past historic **Sarah Island,** where convicts—working in horrendous conditions—once logged valuable Huon pine. During a stop at **Heritage Landing,** you can get a taste of the rainforest on a half-hour walk. The full-day cruise in the high season (Oct–May) includes lunch and a guided tour through the convict ruins on Sarah Island. Cruises depart from the Main Wharf on The Esplanade, in the town center. The full-day cruises, including a meal, cost A$80 (US$64) for an internal seat, A$105 (US$84) for a window recliner, and A$175 (US$140) for a seat upstairs with the captain.

   World Heritage Cruises (© **03/6471 7174;** www.worldheritagecruises.com.au) offers daily "Heritage Cruises" year-round, leaving Strahan Wharf at 9am and returning at 3pm, or 2pm returning at 8pm. The company's MV *Wanderer III* stops at Sarah Island, Heritage Landing, and the salmon and trout farm at Liberty Point. Meals and drinks are available on board. The cruises cost A$65 (US$52) for adults, A$25

(US$20) for children 5 to 14 (free for children under 5), and A$165 (US$132) for a family of five. It also offers a Morning Express cruise starting at 9am and returning at 1.30pm. (It doesn't stop at Sarah Island.) This cruise costs A$60 (US$48) for adults, A$22 (US$18) for children, and A$145 (US$116) for a family.

West Coast Yacht Charters (C 03/6471 7422) runs 2-day, 2-night sailing cruises for A$390 (US$312) for adults and A$185 (US$148) for children, all-inclusive. The company also offers other cruises.

Although cruises are the main attraction in the area, you can also enjoy jet-boat rides, sightseeing in a seaplane that lands on the Gordon River, helicopter flights, and four-wheel-drive tours.

WHERE TO STAY & DINE

Franklin Manor ⭐ Built in 1886 as the home of the harbormaster, this superior B&B offers standard rooms with queen-size beds, deluxe rooms with king-size ones, and a very plush executive deluxe room. Also on the premises are four delightful cottages, which allow you to really get away from it all. The main lounge is comfortable and warmed by a log fire; the simple Huon-pine bar in the foyer and the wine cellar operate on the honor system. The specialties at the manor's restaurant include salmon, duck, seafood, beef, and venison.

The Esplanade, Strahan, TAS 7468. C 03/6471 7311. Fax 03/6471 7267. www.franklinmanor.com.au. 18 units, including 4 cottages. A$176 (US$141) standard double; A$210 (US$168) deluxe double or cottage; A$245 (US$196) executive deluxe. Rates include breakfast. AE, DC, MC, V. Ask about winter discounts. Free parking. **Amenities:** Bar; tour desk; car-rental desk; business center; limited room service; massage; babysitting; laundry service. *In room:* TV, coffeemaker, iron.

Gordon Gateway Chalets These modern self-contained units are on a hill with good views of the harbor and Strahan township. Each has cooking facilities, so you can save on meal costs. The two-bedroom suites have bathtubs, the studios just showers. Breakfast is provided on request. Guests have the use of a barbecue area. One unit has facilities for travelers with disabilities.

Grining St., Strahan, TAS 7468. C 03/6471 7165. Fax 03/6471 7588. www.gordongateway.com.au. 19 units. A$130 (US$104) studio; A$260 (US$208) suite. Winter discounts available. MC, V. **Amenities:** Playground; tour desk; massage; babysitting; coin-op laundry; nonsmoking rooms. *In room:* TV, kitchenette, fridge, coffeemaker, hair dryer, iron, safe.

Ormiston House ⭐⭐ Ormiston House is a gem. Built in 1899 for the family that gave it its name, under the present owners it has become a sort of shrine to their predecessors. Each room is styled to represent one of the original family members. Each is intricately furnished and wallpapered in busy designs and comes with a good-size bathroom. There's a pleasant morning room and a restaurant serving good food. The owners are very friendly and have plenty of time for their guests. Smoking is not permitted.

⌒Moments Dune Buggy Rides

What's more fun than scooting across the sand in a dune buggy? **Four-Wheelers** (C 03/6471 7622, or 0419/508 175 mobile) offers 40-minute rides across the **Henty Sand Dunes** ⭐, about 10 minutes north of Strahan. Trips cost A$40 (US$32). Longer trips are offered outside the summer months.

Tasmanian Devil Disaster

Made famous as the angry, spinning creature in the Warner Brothers cartoons, the Tazzie devil is in real trouble. Back in 1996 mysterious red, fleshy lumps appeared on the faces of the animals in northern Tasmania. This cancer, possibly caused by a virus, makes it hard for them to eat, and can even suffocate them as it spreads to the throat. Most quickly weaken and die of starvation within a few weeks. In some areas the population of adult devils has been reduced by 90%, and the disease is spreading rapidly across the state. It's estimated that around half the state's 150,000 Tasmanian devils have been killed by the disease, and some scientists believe it may wipe out the wild population entirely. Healthy specimens are being captured and relocated to try and preserve the species from extinction.

The Esplanade, Strahan, TAS 7468. ✆ **03/6471 7077.** Fax 03/6471 7007. www.ormistonhouse.com.au. 5 units. A$200–A$260 (US$160–US$208) double. Extra person A$62 (US$49). Rates include breakfast. AE, DC, MC, V. **Amenities:** Bar; lounge; concierge; tour desk; laundry service; nonsmoking rooms. *In room:* A/C, TV, coffeemaker, hair dryer, iron.

STANLEY

140km (87 miles) W of Devonport; 430km (267 miles) NW of Hobart

Among the least-known areas of Tasmania, the coastline east of Devonport can throw up some surprises. Not least of them is "The Nut," a kind of miniature Ayers Rock rising from the sea and towering above the township of Stanley. The Nut is the remains of a volcanic plug that forced its way through a crack in the earth's crust some 12 million years ago. You can walk to the top or, if you're brave, take a chairlift for A$8 (US$6.40) for adults, A$5 (US$4) for children. A warning, though: Don't attempt to ride the chairlift back down if you're afraid of heights—the descent is incredibly steep, and there's no getting off! A small buggy on top will take you on a tour of The Nut for A$8 (US$6.40), free for children under 10.

WHERE TO STAY

The Old Cable Station ★   Darryl Stafford, an ex-logger, and his wife, Heather, have turned the former exchange building for the telephone line from the mainland into a cozy B&B. The rooms are comfortable; two have TVs, but you'll probably spend all your time in the lounge chatting around the fire anyway. Darryl is as Aussie as you can get and will keep you entranced for hours with his stories. Seal cruises are wildlife-viewing packages are offered. The restaurant serves home-cooked dinners daily.

West Beach Rd., Stanley, TAS 7331. ✆ **03/6458 1312.** Fax. 03/6458 2009. www.users.bigpond.com/staffordseals. 4 units. A$95 (US$76) double; A$125–A$135 (US$100–US$108) suite with Jacuzzi. Rates include continental breakfast. MC, V. **Amenities:** Restaurant; lounge; tour desk; laundry service. *In room:* Kitchen, fridge, coffeemaker, hair dryer.

WHERE TO DINE

Hursey Seafoods SEAFOOD   Plenty of people rate this little place as having the best seafood in Australia. Downstairs is a casual cafe, where you choose what you want from fish tanks; upstairs is a more formal restaurant. An unusual specialty is mutton bird (shearwater), an oily seabird that you either like seeing flying around or like seeing on your plate. You can't have it both ways.

2 Alexander Terrace, Stanley. ✆ **03/6458 1103.** Main courses A$10 (US$8) in cafe, A$18 (US$14) in restaurant. MC, V. Takeout/cafe daily 9am–6pm; restaurant daily 6–10pm.

Appendix A:
Australia in Depth

by Marc Llewellyn

The land Down Under is a modern nation coming to terms with its identity. The umbilical cord with Mother England has been cut, and the nation is still trying to find its position within Asia.

One thing Australia realized early on was the importance of tourism to its economy. Millions flock here every year. You'll find Australians to be helpful and friendly, and services, tours, and food and drink to rival any in the world. Factor in the landscape, the native Australian culture, the sunshine, the animals, and some of the world's best cities, and you've got a fascinating, accessible destination full of amazing diversity and variety.

1 Australia's Natural World

THE LAND OF THE NEVER-NEVER

People who have never visited Australia wonder why such a huge country has a population of just 19 million people. The truth is, Australia can barely support that many. About 90% of those 19 million people live on only 2.6% of the continent. Climatic and physical land conditions ensure that the only relatively decent rainfall occurs along a thin strip of land around Australia's coast. The vast majority of Australia is harsh Outback, characterized by saltbush plains, arid brown crags, shifting sand deserts, and salt lake country. People survive where they can in this great arid land because of one thing—the Great Artesian Basin. This saucer-shaped geological formation comprises about one-fifth of Australia's landmass, stretching over much of inland New South Wales, Queensland, South Australia, and the Northern Territory. Beneath it are massive underground water supplies stored during Jurassic and Cretaceous times (some 66 million–208 million years ago), when the area was much like the Amazon basin is today.

Bore holes bring water to the surface and allow sheep, cattle, and humans a respite from the dryness.

The Queensland coast is blessed with one of the greatest natural attractions in the world. The **Great Barrier Reef** stretches some 2,000km (1,240 miles) from off Gladstone in Queensland, to the Gulf of Papua, near New Guinea. It's relatively new, not more than 8,000 years old, although many fear that rising seawater, caused by global warming, will cause its demise. As it is, the non-native Crown of Thorns starfish and a bleaching process believed to be the result of excessive nutrients flowing into the sea from Australia's farming land, is already causing significant damage. The Reef is covered in chapter 7.

AUSTRALIA'S FAUNA

NATIVE ANIMALS Australia's isolation from the rest of the world over millions of years has led to the evolution of forms of life found nowhere else. Probably the strangest of all is the **platypus.** This monotreme, or egg-laying marsupial, has webbed feet, a ducklike bill, and a tail like a beaver's. It lays eggs, and the young suckle from their mother. When a specimen was first brought back to Europe, skeptical scientists insisted it was a fake—a concoction of several different animals sewn together. You will probably never see this shy, nocturnal creature in the wild, although there are a few at Sydney's Taronga Zoo.

Another strange one is the **koala.** This fluffy marsupial eats virtually indigestible gum (eucalyptus) leaves and sleeps about 20 hours a day. There's just one koala species, although those found in Victoria are substantially larger than their brethren in more northern climes. Australia is also famous for **kangaroos.** There are 45 different kinds of kangaroos and wallabies, ranging in scale from small rat-size kangaroos to the man-size red kangaroos.

The animal you're most likely to come across in your trip is the **possum,** named by Capt. James Cook after the North American "opossum," which he thought they resembled. (In fact they are from an entirely different family of the animal kingdom.) The brush-tailed possum is commonly found in suburban gardens, including those in Sydney. Then there's the **wombat.** There are four species of this bulky burrower in Australia, but the common wombat is most frequently found. You might come across the smaller hairy-nosed wombat in South Australia and Western Australia.

The **dingo,** thought by many to be a native of Australia, was in fact introduced—probably by Aborigines. They vary in color from yellow to a russet red, and are heavily persecuted by farmers. Commonly seen **birds** include the fairy penguin along the coast, black swans, parrots and cockatoos, and honeyeaters. **Tasmanian devils** can be found in (you guessed it) the island/state of Tasmania, though a virulent disease has swept through the animals and decimated the wild population.

DANGEROUS NATIVES **Snakes** are common throughout Australia, but you will rarely see one. The most dangerous land snake is the taipan, which hides in the grasslands in northern Australia—one bite contains enough venom to kill up to 200 sheep. If by the remotest chance you are bitten, you must immediately demobilize the limb, wrapping it quite tightly (but not tight enough to restrict the blood flow) with a cloth or bandage, and head to the nearest hospital where antivenin should be available.

There are two types of **crocodile** in Australia: the harmless freshwater croc, which grows to 3m (10 ft.); and the dangerous estuarine (or saltwater) crocodile, which reaches 5 to 7m (16–23 ft.). Freshwater crocs eat fish; estuarine crocs aren't so picky. *Never* swim in, or stand on the bank of, any river, swamp, or pool in northern Australia unless you know *for certain* it's croc-free.

Spiders are common all over Australia, with the funnel web spider and the redback spider being the most aggressive. Funnel webs live in holes in the ground (they spin their webs around a hole's entrance) and stand on their back legs when they're about to attack. Red-backs have a habit of resting under toilet seats and in car trunks, generally outside the main cities. Caution is a good policy.

If you go bushwalking, check your body carefully. **Ticks** are common, especially in eastern Australia, and can cause severe itching and fever. If you find one on you, dab it with methylated spirits or another noxious chemical. Wait awhile and pull it out gently with tweezers, taking care not to leave the head behind.

Fish to avoid are stingrays, porcupine fish, stonefish, lionfish, and puffer fish. Never touch an **octopus** if it has blue rings on it, or a cone shell, and be wary of the painful and sometimes deadly tentacles of the box **jellyfish** along the northern Queensland coast in summer. If you happen to brush past one of these creatures, pour vinegar over the affected site immediately—local authorities leave bottles of vinegar on the beach for this purpose. Vinegar deactivates the stinging cells that haven't already affected you, but doesn't affect the ones that already have.

In Sydney, you might come across "stingers" or "blue bottles" as they are also called. These long-tentacled blue jellyfish can inflict a very nasty stinging burn that can last for hours. Sometimes you'll see warning signs on patrolled beaches. The best remedy if you are severely stung is to wash the affected area with freshwater and have a very hot bath or shower.

2 The People Down Under

It's generally considered that more races of people live in Australia at the present time than anywhere else in the world, including North America. Heavy immigration has led to people from some 165 nations making the country their home. In general, relations between the different ethnic groups have been peaceful. Today Australia is an example of a multicultural society, despite an increasingly vocal minority that believes that Australia has come too far in welcoming people from races other than their own.

THE ABORIGINES   When Capt. James Cook landed at Botany Bay in 1770 determined to claim the land for the British Empire, at least 300,000 Aborigines were already on the continent. Whether you believe a version of history that suggests the Aboriginal people were descendants of migrants from Indonesia to the north, or the Aboriginal belief that they have occupied Australia since the beginning of time, there is scientific evidence that people were walking the continent at least 120,000 years ago.

At the time of the white "invasion" of their lands, there were at least 600 different, largely nomadic tribal communities, each linked to their ancestral land by **"sacred sites"** (certain features of the land, such as hills or rock formations). They were hunter-gatherers, spending about 20 hours a week harvesting the resources of the land, rivers, and the ocean. The rest of the time was taken up by a complex social and belief system, as well as by life's practicalities, such as making utensils, weapons, and musical instruments such as didgeridoos and clapsticks.

The basis of Aboriginal spirituality rests in the **Dreamtime** stories, in which spirits created everything—land, stars, mountains, the moon, the sun, the oceans, water holes, animals, and humans. Much Aboriginal art is related to their land and the sacred sites that are home to the Dreamtime spirits. Some Aboriginal groups believe these spirits came in giant human form, while others believed they were animals or huge snakes. According to Aboriginal custom, individuals can draw on the power of the Dreamtime spirits by reenacting various stories and practicing certain ceremonies.

Aboriginal groups had encountered people from other lands before the British arrived. Dutch records from 1451 show that the Macassans, from islands now belonging to Indonesia, had a long relationship trading Dutch glass, smoking pipes, and alcohol for edible sea slugs, from Australia's northern coastal waters, which they sold to the Chinese in the Canton markets. Dutch, Portuguese, French, and Chinese vessels also encountered Australia—in fact, the Dutch fashion for pointy beards caught on through northern Australia long before the 1770 invasion.

When the British came, bringing their **diseases** with them, coastal communities were virtually wiped out by smallpox. Even as late as the 1950s, large numbers of Aborigines in remote regions of South Australia and the Northern Territory succumbed to deadly outbreaks of influenza and measles.

Although relationships between the settlers and local Aborigines were initially peaceful, conflicts over land and food soon led to skirmishes in which Aborigines were massacred and settlers and convicts attacked—Governor Phillip was speared in the back by an Aborigine in 1790.

Within a few years, some 10,000 Aborigines and 1,000 Europeans had been killed in Queensland alone, while in Tasmania, a campaign to rid the island entirely of local Aborigines was ultimately successful, with the last full-blooded Tasmanian Aborigine dying in 1876. By the start of the 20th century, the Aboriginal people were considered a dying race. Most of those who remained lived in government-owned reserves or Church-controlled missions.

Massacres of Aborigines continued to go largely or wholly unpunished into the 1920s, by which time it became official government policy to remove light-skinned Aboriginal children from their families and to sterilize young Aboriginal women. Many children of the "stolen generation" were brought up in white foster homes or church refuges and never reunited with their biological families—many children with living parents were told that their parents were dead.

Today, there are some 283,000 Aborigines living in Australia, and in general a great divide still exists between them and the rest of the population. Aboriginal life expectancy is 20 years lower than that of other Australians, with overall death rates between two and four times higher. Aborigines make up the highest percentage of the country's prison population, and many Aborigines die while incarcerated.

A landmark in Aboriginal affairs occurred in 1992 when the High Court determined that Australia was not an empty land *(terra nullius)* as it had been seen officially since the British invasion. The **"Mabo" decision** resulted in the **1993 Native Title Act,** which allowed Aboriginal groups, and the ethnically distinct people living in the Torres Strait islands off northern Queensland, to claim government-owned land if they could prove continual association with it since 1788. The later **"Wik" decision** determined that Aborigines could make claims on government land leased to agriculturists. The federal government, led by the right-leaning Prime Minister John Howard, curtailed these rights following pressure from farming and mining interests.

Issues currently facing the Aboriginal population include harsh mandatory sentencing laws (enacted in Western Australia and the Northern Territory state governments in 1996 and 1997, respectively), which came to international attention in 2000. The Aboriginal community believes such laws specifically target them. When a 15-year-old Aboriginal boy allegedly committed suicide less than a week before he was due to be released from a Northern Territory prison in early 2000, and a 21-year-old Aboriginal youth was imprisoned for a year for stealing A$23 (US$15) worth of fruit cordial and cookies, Aboriginal people protested, activists of all colors demonstrated, and even the United Nations weighed in with criticism.

Added to this was the simmering issue of the federal government's decision not to apologize to the Aboriginal people for the "stolen generation." In March 2000, a government-sponsored report stated there was never a "stolen generation," while independent researchers believed the report underestimated how many people were personally affected.

Before the Sydney 2000 Olympic Games, a popular movement involving people of all colors and classes called for reconciliation and an apology to the Aboriginal people. In Sydney, an estimated 250,000 people marched across the Sydney Harbour Bridge. The Liberal (read "conservative") Government refused to bow to public pressure. Despite threats of boycotts and rallies during the Olympics, the Games passed without major disturbance, and a worldwide audience watched as Aboriginal runner Cathy Freeman lit the Olympic cauldron.

THE REST OF AUSTRALIA

"White" Australia was always used to distinguish the Anglo-Saxon population from that of the Aboriginal population.

These days, though, a walk through any of the major cities would show that things have changed dramatically. About 100,000 people emigrate to Australia each year. Of these, approximately 12% were born in the U.K. or Ireland and 11% in New Zealand. More than 21% hail from China, Hong Kong, Vietnam, or the Philippines. Waves of immigration have brought in millions of people since the end of World War II. At the last census in 1996, more than a quarter of a million Australian residents were born in Italy; some 186,000 in the former Yugoslavia, 144,000 in Greece, 118,000 in Germany, and 103,000 in China. So what's the typical Australian like? Well, he's hardly Crocodile Dundee.

3 Australian History 101

IN THE BEGINNING In the beginning there was the **Dreamtime**—at least according to the Aborigines of Australia. Between then and now, perhaps, the supercontinent referred to as **Pangaea** split into two huge continents called **Laurasia** and **Gondwanaland.** Over millions of years, continental drift carried the landmasses apart. Laurasia broke up and formed North America, Europe, and most of Asia. Meanwhile, Gondwanaland divided into South America, Africa,

India, Australia and New Guinea, and Antarctica. **Giant marsupials** evolved to roam the continent of Australia: Among them were a plant-eating animal that looked like a wombat the size of a rhinoceros; a giant squashed-face kangaroo standing 3m (10 ft.) high; and a flightless bird the same size as an emu, but four times heavier. The last of these giant marsupials are believed to have died out some 40,000 years ago, possibly helped towards extinction by Aborigines.

Dateline

- 120,000 B.C. Evidence suggests Aborigines living in Australia.
- 60,000 B.C. Aborigines living in Arnhemland in the far north fashion stone tools.
- 24,500 B.C. The world's oldest known ritual cremation takes place at Lake Mungo.
- A.D. 1606 Dutch explorer Willem Jansz lands on far

north coast of Van Diemen's Land (Tasmania).
- 1622 First English ship to reach Australia wrecks on the west coast.
- 1642 Abel Tasman charts the Tasmanian coast.
- 1770 Capt. James Cook lands at Botany Bay.
- 1787 Capt. Arthur Phillip's First Fleet leaves England with convicts aboard.

- 1788 Captain Phillip raises British flag at Port Jackson (Sydney Harbour).
- 1788–1868 Convicts are transported from England to the colony of Australia.
- 1793 The first free settlers arrive.
- 1830 Governor Arthur lines up 5,000 settlers across Van Diemen's Land to walk the length of the island to capture and rid it of all Aborigines.

EARLY EXPLORERS   The existence of Australia had been in the minds of Europeans since the Greek astronomer Ptolemy drew a map of the world in about A.D. 150 showing a large landmass in the south, which he believed had to be there to balance out the land in the Northern Hemisphere. He called it *Terra Australis Incognita*—the unknown southland.

Evidence suggests Portuguese ships reached Australia as early as 1536 and even charted part of its coastline. In 1606 William Jansz was sent by the Dutch East India Company to open up a new route to the Spice Islands, and to find New Guinea, which was supposed to be rich in gold. He landed on the north coast of Queensland and fought with local Aborigines. Between 1616 and 1640, many more Dutch ships made contact with Australia as they hugged the west coast of what they called "New Holland," after sailing with the *westerlies* (west winds) from the Cape of Good Hope.

In 1642, the Dutch East India Company, through the governor general of the Indies, Anthony Van Diemen, sent Abel Tasman to search out and map the great south land. During two voyages, he charted the northern Australian coastline and discovered Tasmania, which he named Van Diemen's Land.

THE ARRIVAL OF THE BRITISH
In 1697, English pirate William Dampier published a book about his adventures. The text mentions Shark Beach on the northwest coast of Australia as the place his pirate ship made its repairs after robbing ships on the Pacific Ocean. Sent to further explore by England's King William III, Dampier returned and found little to recommend.

Capt. James Cook turned up in 1770 and charted the east coast in his ship HMS *Endeavor*. He claimed the land for Britain and named it New South Wales, probably as a favor to Thomas Pennant, a Welsh patriot and botanist who was a friend of the *Endeavour*'s botanist, Joseph Banks. On April 29, Cook landed at Botany Bay, which he named after the discovery of scores of plants hitherto unknown to science. Turning northward, Cook passed an entrance to a possible harbor, which appeared to offer safe anchorage, and named it Port Jackson after the secretary to the admiralty, George Jackson. Back in Britain, King George III viewed Australia as a potential colony and repository of Britain's overflowing prison population, which could no longer be transported to the United States of America following the War of Independence.

The First Fleet left England in May 1787, made up of 11 store and transport

- **1850** Gold discovered in Bathurst, New South Wales.
- **1852** Gold rush begins in Ballarat, Victoria.
- **1853** The last convict arrives in Van Diemen's Land and to celebrate, the colony is renamed Tasmania after Abel Tasman.
- **1860** The white population of Australia reaches more than one million.
- **1875** Silver found at Broken Hill, New South Wales.
- **1889** Australian troops fight in the Boer War in South Africa.
- **1895** Banjo Paterson's "The Man from Snowy River" published.
- **1901** The six states join together to become the Commonwealth of Australia.
- **1902** Women gain the right to vote.
- **1911** Australian (non-Aboriginal) population reaches 4.4 million.
- **1915** Australian and New Zealand troops massacred at Gallipoli.
- **1927** The federal capital is moved from Melbourne to Canberra.
- **1931** The first airmail letters are delivered to England by

continues

ships (none of them were bigger than the passenger ferries that ply modern-day Sydney Harbour from Circular Quay to Manly) led by Arthur Phillip. Aboard were 1,480 people, including 759 convicts. Phillip's flagship, *The Supply,* reached Botany Bay in January 1788, but Phillip decided the soil was poor and the surroundings too swampy. On January 26, now celebrated as Australia Day, he settled for Port Jackson (Sydney Harbour) instead.

SETTLING DOWN The convicts were immediately put to work clearing land, planting crops, and constructing buildings. The early food harvests were failures, and by early 1790, the fledgling colony was facing starvation.

Phillip decided to give some convicts pardons for good behavior and service, and even grant small land parcels to those who were really industrious. In 1795, coal was discovered; in 1810 Governor Macquarie began extensive city building projects; and in 1813 the explorers Blaxland, Wentworth, and Lawson forged a passage over the Blue Mountains to the fertile plains beyond.

When gold was discovered in Victoria in 1852, and in Western Australia 12 years later, hundreds of thousands of immigrants from Europe, America, and China flooded into the country in search

of their fortunes. By 1860, more than a million non-Aboriginal people were living in Australia.

The last 10,000 convicts were transported to Western Australia between 1850 and 1868, bringing the total shipped to Australia to 168,000.

FEDERATION & THE GREAT WARS

On January 1, 1901, the six states that made up Australia proclaimed themselves to be part of one nation, and the Commonwealth of Australia was formed. In the same ceremony, the first governor general was sworn in as the representative of the queen, who remained head of state. In 1914, Australia joined the Mother Country in war. In April the following year, the Australian and New Zealand Army Corps (ANZAC) formed a beachhead on the peninsula of Gallipoli in Turkey. The Turkish troops had been warned, and 8 months of fighting ended with 8,587 Australian dead and more than 19,000 wounded.

Australians fought in World War II in North Africa, Greece, and the Middle East. In March 1942, Japanese aircraft bombed Broome in Western Australia and Darwin in the Northern Territory. In May 1942, Japanese midget submarines entered Sydney Harbour and torpedoed a ferry before being destroyed. Later that year, Australian volunteers fought an

---

Charles Kingsford Smith and Charles Ulm.

- **1931** The Arnhemland Aboriginal Reserve is proclaimed.
- **1932** Sydney Harbour Bridge opens.
- **1942** Darwin bombed; Japanese minisubmarines found in Sydney Harbour.
- **1953** British nuclear tests at Emu in South Australia lead to a radioactive cloud that kills and injures many Aborigines.

- **1956** Olympics held in Melbourne.
- **1957** British atomic tests conducted at Maralinga, South Australia. Aborigines again affected by radiation.
- **1962** Commonwealth government gives Aborigines the right to vote.
- **1967** Aborigines granted Australian citizenship and are counted in census.

- **1968** Australia's population passes 12 million following heavy immigration.
- **1971** The black, red, and yellow Aboriginal flag flown for the first time.
- **1973** Sydney Opera House completed.
- **1976** The Aboriginal Land Rights (Northern Territory) Act gives some land back to native people.

incredibly brave retreat through the jungles of Papua New Guinea on the Kokoda Trail against superior Japanese forces. Australian troops fought alongside Americans in subsequent wars in Korea and Vietnam and sent military support to the Persian Gulf conflicts.

RECENT TIMES Following World War II, mass immigration to Australia, primarily from Europe, boosted the population. In 1974 the left-of-center Whitlam government put an end to the White Australia policy that had largely restricted black and Asian immigration since 1901. In 1986 the official umbilical cord to Britain was cut when the Australian Constitution was separated from that of its motherland. Australia had begun the march to complete independence.

In 1992 the High Court handed down the "Mabo" decision that ruled that Aborigines had a right to claim government-owned land if they could prove a continued connection with it. The following year, huge crowds filled Sydney's Circular Quay to hear that the city had won the 2000 Olympic Games.

New venues were built for the Olympics; some of these were temporary, while others are now used as arenas for professional and amateur sports. A new expressway and train link were built to connect the spruced-up airport to the city center, and Sydney welcomed thousands of international visitors to the 2-week extravaganza starting in September 2000. The Games put medal-winning Australian athletes Cathy Freeman and swimmer Ian Thorpe in the spotlight, and spurred a new wave of interest and tourism in the land Down Under.

4 Aussie Eats & Drinks

THE EATS

It took a long time for the average Australian to realize that there is more to food than English-style sausage and mashed potatoes, "meat and three veg," and a Sunday roast. It wasn't long ago that spaghetti was something foreigners ate, and zucchini and eggplant considered exotic. Then came mass immigration and all sorts of foods that people had only read about in *National Geographic*.

The first big wave of Italian immigrants in the 1950s caused a national scandal. The great Aussie dream was to have a quarter-acre block of land with a Hills Hoist (a circular revolving clothesline) in the backyard. When Italians started hanging their freshly made pasta

- **1983** Ayers Rock given back to local Aborigines, who rename it Uluru.
- **1983** Australia wins the Americas Cup, ending 112 years of American domination of the event.
- **1986** Queen Elizabeth II severs the Australian Constitution from Great Britain's.
- **1988** Aborigines demonstrate as Australia celebrates its Bicentennial with a reen-

actment of the First Fleet's entry into Sydney Harbour.
- **1991** Australia's population reaches 17 million.
- **1994** High Court "Mabo" decision overturns the principle of *terra nullius*, which suggested Australia was unoccupied at time of white settlement.
- **1996** High Court hands down *Wik* decision, which allows Aborigines the right to

claim some Commonwealth land.
- **2003** Bushfires ravage much of NSW and Victoria. Hundreds of homes are burned to the ground in the capital city, Canberra. The country faces a severe drought.
- **2004** Tasmania celebrates its Bicentennial.
- **2005** Australia increases the number of troops serving in Iraq.

Fun Fact **Witchetty Grubs, Lilli-Pillies & Other Good Eats**

In the past decade or so, many Australian chefs have woken up to the variety and tastes of "bush tucker," as native Aussie food is tagged. Now it's all the rage in the most fashionable restaurants where wattle seed, lemon myrtle, or some other native taste has a place in one or two dishes on the menu. Below is a list of those foods you may encounter in trendy restaurants:

Bush Tucker	Explanation
Bunya nut	Crunchy nut of the bunya pine, about the size of macadamias.
Bush tomato	Dry, small darkish fruit more like raisins in look and taste.
Cranberry (native)	Small berry that tastes a bit like an apple.
Illawarra plums	Dark berry with a rich, strong, tangy taste.
Kangaroo	A red meat with a strong gamey flavor. Tender when correctly prepared, tough when not. Excellent smoked.
Kakadu plum	Wonderfully sharp tangy green fruit that boasts the highest recorded vitamin C level of any food.
Lemon aspen	Citrusy, light yellow fruit with a sharp tangy flavor.
Lemon myrtle	Gum leaves with a fresh lemony tang; often used to flavor white meat.
Lilli-pillies	Delicious juicy, sweet pink berry; also called a riberry.
Macadamia nut	Sweet white nut. Macadamias come from Australia, not Hawaii as most of us think.
Quandong	A tart, tangy native peach.
Rosella	Spiky red petals of a flower with a rich berry flavor; traditionally used by Europeans to make rosella jam.
Wattle seed	Roasted ground acacia seeds that taste a little like bitter coffee; commonly used by Europeans in pasta or desserts.
Wild lime	Smaller and more sour than regular lime; good in salads.

One ingredient you will *not* see on menus is **witchetty grubs;** most people are too squeamish to eat these fat, slimy white critters. They live in the soil or in dead tree trunks and are a common protein source for Aboriginals. You eat them alive, not cooked. If you are offered one in the Outback, either freak out (as most locals would do) or enjoy its pleasantly nutty taste as a reward for your bravery!

out to dry on this Aussie icon, it caused an uproar, and some clamored for the new arrivals to be shipped back. As Australia matured, southern European cuisine became increasingly popular until olive oil was sizzling in frying pans the way only lard had previously done.

In the 1980s, waves of Asian immigrants hit Australia's shores. Suddenly, everyone was cooking with woks. These days, this fusion of flavors and styles has melded into what's now commonly referred to as "Modern Australian"—a distinctive cuisine blending the spices of the east with the flavors of the west.

THE DRINKS

THE AMBER NECTAR   The great Aussie drink is a "tinnie" (a can) of beer. Barbecues would not be the same without a case of tinnies, or "stubbies" (small bottles). In the hotter climes, you may be offered a polystyrene container or "stubby holder" in which to place your beer to keep it cool.

Australian beers vary considerably in quality, but of course there's no accounting for tastes. Among the most popular are Victoria Bitter (known as "VB"), XXXX (pronounced "four ex"), Fosters, and various brews produced by the Tooheys company. All are popular in cans, bottles, or on tap (draft). My favorite beer is Cascade, a German-style beer that you'll usually find only in a bottle. It's light in color, strong in taste, and made from Tasmanian water straight off a mountain. If you want to get plastered, try Coopers—it's rather cloudy in looks, very strong, and usually ends up causing a terrific hangover. Most Australian beers range from 4.8% to 5.2% alcohol.

In New South Wales, bars serve beer by the glass in a "schooner" or a smaller "midi"—though in a few places it's also served in British measurements, by pints and half pints. In Victoria you should ask for a "pot," or the less copious "glass." In South Australia a schooner is the size of a NSW midi, and in Western Australia a midi is the same size as a New South Wales midi, but a glass about half its size is called a "pony." Confused? My advice is to gesture with your hands like a local to show whether you want a small glass or a larger one.

By the way, you have to be 18 to buy alcohol.

THE VINO   Australian winemaking has come a long way since the first grape vines were brought to Australia on the First Fleet in 1788. These days, more than 550 major companies and small winemakers produce wine commercially in Australia. Vintages from Down Under consistently beat competitors from other wine-producing nations in major international shows. The demand for Australian wine overseas has increased so dramatically in the past few years that domestic prices have risen, and new vineyards are being planted at a frantic pace.

The best recent vintages are 1998 and 2002. The 2003 vintage was good but not up to the standard of 1998 and 2000, when low rainfall meant smaller and more intensely flavored grapes.

Appendix B:
Useful Toll-Free Numbers & Websites

AIRLINES

Air New Zealand
☎ 800/262-1234 or 800/262-2468 in the U.S.
☎ 800/663-5494 in Canada
☎ 0800/737-767 in New Zealand
www.airnewzealand.com

British Airways
☎ 800/247-9297 in the U.S.
☎ 0345/222-111 or 0845/77-333-77 in the U.K.
☎ 1300/767 177 in Australia
www.british-airways.com

Cathay Pacific
☎ 020/8834 8888 in the U.K.
☎ 13 17 47 in Australia
www.cathaypacific.com/uk

Malaysia Airlines
☎ 0870/607 9090 in the U.K. and Ireland
☎ 13 26 27 in Australia
www.malaysiaairlines.com.my
www.malaysiaairlineseurope.com

Qantas
☎ 800/227-4500 in the U.S. and Canada
☎ 0845/774 7767 in the U.K.
☎ 13 13 13 in Australia
www.qantas.com.au

Singapore Airlines
☎ 0870/608 8886 in the U.K.
☎ 13 10 11 in Australia
www.singaporeair.com/uk

Thai Airways International
☎ 0870/6060 911 in the U.K.
☎ 1300/651 960 in Australia
www.thaiair.com

United Airlines
☎ 800/241-6522 in the U.S.
www.united.com

CAR-RENTAL AGENCIES

Avis
☎ 800/331-1212 in the U.S.
☎ 800/TRY-AVIS in Canada
☎ 0870/6060-100 in the U.K. and Ireland
☎ 0800/655 111 in New Zealand
www.avis.com

Budget
☎ 800/527-0700 in the U.S.
☎ 1300/362 848 in Australia
☎ 800/268-8900 in Canada
☎ 01344/484-100 in the U.K.
☎ 0800/652 227 in New Zealand
www.budget.com

Europcar
☎ 877/940-6900 in the U.S. and Canada
☎ 1300/13 13 90 in Australia
☎ 0870/607-5000 in the U.K.
☎ 1/614-2800 in Ireland
☎ 0800/800 409 in New Zealand
www.deltaeuropcar.com.au

Hertz
☎ 800/654-3131 in the U.S., or 800-654-3001 for international reservations
☎ 13 30 39 in Australia
  ☎ 020/7026-0077 in the U.K.
  ☎ 1/676-7476 in Ireland
  ☎ 0800/654 321 in New Zealand
www.hertz.com

Red Spot Car Rentals
☎ 1300/668 810 in Australia
☎ 02/9317 5771
www.redspotrentals.com.au

Thrifty
ⓒ 800/367-2277 in the U.S.
ⓒ 1300/367 227 in Australia
ⓒ 1800/51-5800 in Ireland
ⓒ 0800/783-0405 in the U.K.
ⓒ 0800/73 7070 in New Zealand
www.thrifty.com

MAJOR HOTEL & MOTEL CHAINS

Accor/Mercure/Sofitel
ⓒ 800/221-4542
www.accorhotels.com

Best Western International
ⓒ 800/528-1234
www.bestwestern.com

Hilton Hotels
ⓒ 800/HILTONS
www.hilton.com

Hyatt Hotels & Resorts
ⓒ 800/228-9000
www.hyatt.com

Inter-Continental Hotels & Resorts
ⓒ 888/567-8725
www.interconti.com

ITT Sheraton
ⓒ 800/325-3535
www.starwood.com

Marriott Hotels
ⓒ 800/228-9290
www.marriott.com

Sheraton Hotels & Resorts
ⓒ 800/325-3535
www.sheraton.com

Westin Hotels & Resorts
ⓒ 800/937-8461
www.westin.com

Index

See also Accommodations and Restaurant indexes, below.

Abbreviations, 5
**Aboriginal & Tribal Art Centre
(Sydney), 177**
Aboriginal art and culture
Alice Springs, 5, 384, 386,
388–389, 390–391
best places to learn about,
15–16
Brambuk Aboriginal Living
Cultural Centre, 613
Darwin, 417–418
Dreamtime Cultural Centre
(near Rockhampton),
345–346
Kakadu National Park,
17, 428–429
Kalgoorlie, 478
Kings Canyon, 399
Manyallaluk Aboriginal
community, 15, 434
Melbourne, 577
Mount Coot-tha Aboriginal
Art Trail, 261
Mutawintji National Park,
236–237
N'Dhala Gorge Nature Park,
398
Perth, 461
Port Douglas area, 310
Sydney, 177–178
Uluru–Kata Tjuta National
Park (Ayers Rock/The
Olgas), 402–403
Umbarra Aboriginal Cultural
Centre, 230
**Aboriginal Art & Culture
Centre (Alice Springs),
15, 386, 388–389**
Abseiling (rappelling), 8, 65
Brisbane, 260–261
Accommodations, 51. *See also*
Accommodations Index
best, 18–22
tips on, 80–84
Active vacations, 63–68

Adelaide, 501–520
accommodations, 509–513
American Express, 508
business hours, 508
currency exchange, 508
doctors and dentists, 508
emergencies, 508
Internet access, 509
layout of, 507
lost property, 509
nightlife, 519–520
organized tours, 518
outdoor activities, 518
pharmacies (chemist shops),
509
post offices, 509
restaurants, 513–516
restrooms, 509
shopping, 519
side trips from, 520–529
sights and attractions,
516–518
transportation, 507–508
traveling to, 502–504, 506
visitor information, 506–507
Adelaide Festival, 506
**Adelaide Festival Centre,
519–520**
The Adelaide Hills, 526–529
Adelaide Zoo, 517
**Aerial tours (scenic flights),
70–71**
Kakadu National Park, 429
Kings Canyon, 399
Nitmiluk National Park, 434
Uluru–Kata Tjuta National
Park (Ayers Rock/The
Olgas), 400, 404
Western Australia, 439
the Whitsundays, 337
Airfares, 49–51, 57, 69
Airlie Beach, 338–340
Airlines, 1, 55–56, 69
bankrupt, 58
Air passes, 69–70
Airport security, 56–57

Air travel, 69–71
film and video and, 60
jet lag, 59
shipping your luggage, 57
staying comfortable in long-
haul flights, 58–60
Alexander, Lake, 419
Alice Springs, 97, 379, 382–395
accommodations, 391–393
layout of, 385
organized tours, 387–389
outdoor activities, 389–390
road trips from, 395–398
shopping, 390–391
sights and attractions,
386–387
special events, 385
transportation, 385
traveling to, 384
visitor information, 384–385
**Alice Springs Cultural Precinct,
386**
Alice Springs Desert Park, 386
**Alice Springs Reptile Centre,
386**
**Alice Springs Telegraph Station
Historical Reserve, 17, 387**
Alpine National Park, 608–609
American Express, 85
Adelaide, 508
Brisbane, 249
Canberra, 619
Melbourne, 553
Perth, 445
Sydney, 116
**Amigo's Castle (Lightning
Ridge), 239**
**Anangu Tours (Ayers Rock),
15, 96, 402**
Angahook-Lorne State Park, 599
Angaston, 522, 524, 525
Anna Bay, 211
Anzac Memorial (Sydney), 168
Apollo Bay, 599
**The Aquarium (Champagne
Pools; Fraser Island), 356**

Aquariums and marine-life parks
Melbourne, 570–571
Perth, 453, 459
Sea World (Main Beach, Gold Coast), 369, 370
Sydney, 160
Aquarius Roman Baths (Launceston), 652
AQWA (Aquarium of Western Australia; Perth), 453, 459
Araluen Centre (Alice Springs), 386
Archibald Fountain (Sydney), 168
Argyle, Lake, 489
Argyle Diamond Mine, 490–491
Artesian Bore Baths (Lightning Ridge), 239
Art galleries
Broken Hill, 235
Broome, 497
Darwin, 417–418
Margaret River region, 474
Sydney, 178
Art Gallery of New South Wales (Sydney), 165, 168
Art Gallery of South Australia (Adelaide), 516
Art Gallery of Western Australia (Perth), 453
Arts and crafts. See also Aboriginal art and culture
Byron Bay, 220
Coffs Harbour, 217
Kuranda, 294
Melbourne, 577
Sydney, 179
Arts Theatre (Adelaide), 520
Ashcombe Maze & Water Gardens (Shoreham), 592
ATMs (automated teller machines), 35–36
Australia Day, 39
Australian Aviation Heritage Centre (Darwin), 17, 416
Australian Ballet, 184
Australian Butterfly Sanctuary (Kuranda), 10, 295
Australian Capital Territory (ACT), 29
Australian Chamber Orchestra, 184
Australian Craftworks (Sydney), 179
Australian Formula One Grand Prix (Melbourne), 40, 575
Australian Geographic (Sydney) Ikonstore, 181

Australian Institute of Sport (Canberra), 624
Australian Museum (Sydney), 165–166
Australian National Botanic Gardens (Canberra), 628
Australian National Maritime Museum (Sydney), 17, 159
Australian Open (Melbourne), 576
Australian Pearling Exhibition (Darwin), 417
Australian Reptile Park (Sydney), 161–162
Australian Surf Life Saving Championships, 40
Australian War Memorial (Canberra), 18, 624–625
Australian Wine Centre (Sydney), 183
Australian Woolshed (Brisbane), 256
Australia Zoo (Beerwah), 361
Auswalk, 68
The Aviary (Kuranda), 295
Aviation Museum (Alice Springs), 386
Ayers Rock Campground, 408
Ayers Rock Observatory, 407
Ayers Rock (Uluru), 403–405

Bait Reef, 281
Ballarat, 594–598
Ballarat Fine Art Gallery, 594
Ballooning
Alice Springs, 389
Canberra, 625
the Hunter Valley, 206
Melbourne, 574
Yarra Valley, 587
Balmoral, 165
The Barossa, 520–525
The Barossa Valley, 8, 501
Barossa Wine and Visitor Information Centre (Tanunda), 523
Batemans Bay, 228–229
Bathurst Island, 428
Battery Point Heritage Walk (Hobart), 637
Beaches. See also specific beaches
best, 12–13
the Gold Coast, 368
Perth, 455–456
Sydney, 163–165
Beaver Cay, 280–281
Bed & breakfasts (B&Bs), 81

Bedarra Island, 322
Beech Forest, 600
Bellingen, 217
Bells Beach, 599
Belongil Beach, 220
Belvoir Street Theatre (Sydney), 184
Ben Boyd National Park, 230
Berry Farm (near Margaret River), 472
Berry Springs Nature Park, 419
Bevan's Black Opal & Cactus Nursery (Lightning Ridge), 239
Bicentennial Park (Sydney), 168
Big Banana Theme Park (Coffs Harbour), 216
Big Pineapple (Woombye), 361
Biking and mountain biking, 65–66
Adelaide, 518
Alice Springs, 389
Bright, 607
Brisbane, 261
Cairns, 296
Canberra, 619, 628
the Hunter Valley, 206
Launceston, 652
Melbourne, 574
Perth, 459
Port Douglas, 306–307, 311
Rottnest Island, 463
Sydney, 173–174
The Billabong Koala and Wildlife Park (Port Macquarie), 214–215
Billabong Sanctuary (Townsville), 325
Bird-watching, 66. See also Penguins
The Coorong, 544
Fogg Dam Conservation Reserve, 426
the Kimberley, 498
Lamington National Park, 376
Birdworld (Kuranda), 295
Birrarung Marr (Melbourne), 573
The Blackall Ranges, 361
Blackheath, 200–201
Black Reef (Bali Hai Island), 281–282
Blood on the Southern Cross (Ballarat), 596
Blowholes
Kiama, 224, 225
Port Campbell National Park, 600

The Blue Mountains,
   8, 14, 192–202
   bushwalking and other active
      endeavors, 194–195
   guided tours from Sydney,
      192–194
   Katoomba, 195–199
   in suggested itineraries,
      94, 97, 98, 99
   visitor information, 192
Blue Mountains National Park,
   169
Blue Pearl Bay, 281
Boating. *See* **Canoeing;**
   Kayaking; Sailing; White-
   water rafting
Boat tours and cruises. *See*
   also **Great Barrier Reef**
   Batemans Bay, 229
   near Beatrice Hill, 426
   Brisbane, 259–260
   Broome, 497
   Canberra, 626
   Daintree River, 309
   Darwin, 417
   day trips to Great Barrier
      Reef, 278–282
   Echuca, 603–605
   Great Sandy National Park, 360
   Hobart, 639
   Kakadu National Park,
      427–428
   Katherine Gorge (Nitmiluk
      National Park), 433–434
   the Kimberley, 499–500
   Kuranda, 295
   Launceston, 652
   Magnetic Island, 329
   Mildura, 603
   Ord River, 490
   Perth, 458–459
   Port Arthur, 647
   Port Macquarie, 214
   Shark Bay, 482
   Sydney, 156, 171–173
   Tasmania's west coast,
      659–660
Bonaparte Archipelago, 488
Bondi Beach, 97, 164
Bondi Icebergs Club (Sydney),
   175
Bonorong Park Wildlife Centre
   (Hobart), 637–638
Bonsai Farm (Mt. Dandenong),
   586
Booderee National Park, 225
Books, recommended, 84–85
Bootleg Brewery (Wilyabrup),
   476

Boranup Drive, 473
Botanic Gardens (Adelaide), 517
Bournda National Park, 230
Bowali Visitor Centre, 425, 426
Brambuk Aboriginal Living
   Cultural Centre, 613
Bright, 606–607
Brisbane, 2, 241–269
   accommodations, 250–253
   arriving in, 241–244
   currency exchange, 249
   doctors and dentists, 249
   exploring, 256–259
   Internet access, 249
   layout of, 244
   main arteries and streets, 244
   Moreton Bay and Islands,
      266–269
   neighborhoods in brief, 245
   nightlife, 263–266
   organized tours, 259–260
   outdoor activities, 260–262
   pubs, 265
   restaurants, 253–255
   shopping, 262–263
   street maps, 244
   time zone, 250
   transportation, 245–249
   visitor information, 244
Brisbane Botanic Gardens
   Mount Coot-tha, 256
Brisbane Forest Park, 261
Brisbane Jazz Club, 265–266
Brisbane Powerhouse–Centre
   for the Live Arts, 264
Broken Hill, 11, 16, 100, 234–238
Broken Hill Regional Art
   Gallery, 235
Bronte Beach, 164
Broome, 16, 488, 494–499
The Broome Bird Observatory,
   498
Broome Crocodile Park, 497
Buccaneer Archipelago, 488
Buchan Caves, 608
Buley Rockhole, 423
Bunbury, 10, 481
Bundaberg, 351–352
   day trips to Great Barrier Reef
      from, 282
Bundeena, 170
Bungee jumping, Cairns, 296
Bungle Bungles (Purnululu)
   National Park, 488, 494
Bunker Group, 282
Burley Griffin, Lake, 618
   tours, 626
Burswood International Resort
   Casino (Perth), 462

Bushwalking (hiking),
   14–15, 65
   Adelaide, 518
   Alice Springs, 389–390
   Alpine National Park, 608–609
   the Blue Mountains, 194–195,
      200
   Brisbane, 261
   Dandenong Ranges, 584, 586
   Fraser Island, 357
   Freycinet National Park, 648
   Kakadu National Park,
      429, 430
   Katherine Gorge (Nitmiluk
      National Park), 433–434
   Lamington National Park,
      376–377
   Litchfield National Park, 423
   Margaret River, 473
   Noosa National Park, 360
   the Overland Track, 658
   Port Douglas, 311
   Sydney, 169, 173
   Uluru–Kata Tjuta National
      Park (Ayers Rock/The
      Olgas), 404, 405
   West MacDonnell National
      Park, 395
Business hours, 85
Bus travel, 72–73
Byron Bay, 219–223

Cable Beach, 12, 496
Cadbury Chocolate Factory
   (near Hobart), 638
Cairns, 13, 284–304
   accommodations, 296–303
   day trips to Great Barrier Reef
      from, 278–280, 288–289
   diving the Great Barrier Reef
      from, 282–283
   exploring islands near,
      291–292
   exploring the wet tropics rain-
      forest near, 292–296
   Internet access, 286
   layout of, 287
   nightlife, 304
   outdoor activities, 296
   restaurants, 303–304
   side trip to Kuranda, 293–296
   sights and attractions,
      289–291
   in suggested itineraries, 94–96
   transportation, 287–288
   traveling to, 284, 286–287
   visitor information, 287
Cairns Rainforest Dome, 290

Cairns Tropical Zoo, 291
Calendar of events, 39–41
Calgardup Cave, 472
Caloundra, 357
Camel rides, safaris, and tours, 66
    Alice Springs, 389
    Broome, 496
    Uluru–Kata Tjuta National Park (Ayers Rock/The Olgas), 405
Cameras, digital, 60, 61
Camping, Station Township Riverside Camping (El Questro), 493
Canberra, 615–629
    accommodations, 620–622
    American Express, 619
    arriving in, 615–616
    business hours, 619
    currency exchange, 619
    doctors and dentists, 619
    embassies and consulates, 619
    hospitals, 620
    Internet access, 620
    layout of, 618
    nightlife, 629
    outdoor activities, 628–629
    post office, 620
    restaurants, 623–624
    sights and attractions, 624–628
    special events, 616, 618
    tours, 626
    transportation, 618–619
    visitor information, 616
Canberra Deep Space Communication Complex, 625
Canoeing, 9, 66–67
    Canberra, 628–629
    Katherine Gorge (Nitmiluk National Park), 433
    the Kimberley, 490
Canowindra, 100
Cape Byron Lighthouse, 220
Cape du Couedic, 534
Cape Otway Lighthouse, 600
Cape Shanck Coastal Park, 591
Cape-to-Cape, 15, 469, 473
Cape Tourville Lighthouse, 648
Cape Tribulation National Park, 308
Cape Woolamai, 589
Capital Theatre (Sydney), 185
Capricorn Caves, 344–345
The Capricorn Coast, 343–353
Captain Cook Memorial Jet (Canberra), 618

Caravan (trailer) parks, the Hunter Valley, 207
Car racing, Melbourne, 575
Car rentals, 51, 74–75
Car travel, 73–80. See also Four-wheel-driving
    auto clubs, 77–78
    breakdowns and emergency assistance, 79
    driving rules, 76–77
    insurance, 75
    maps, 77
    petrol (gasoline), 76
    road conditions and safety, 78–79
    road signs, 77
    sample driving distances and times, 74–75
Cascade Brewery Tours (Hobart), 638
Casinos
    Adelaide, 520
    Cairns, 304
    Canberra, 629
    Hobart, 645
    Melbourne, 584
    Perth, 462
Castle Hill (Townsville), 325
Cataract Gorge (Launceston), 652
The Cathedrals, 356
Caversham Wildlife Park & Zoo, 466
Caves (caving), 67
    Capricorn Caves, 344–345
    Jenolan Caves, 94, 201–202
    near Margaret River, 471–472
Caves Beach, 226
Caves Road, 471, 472, 473
CaveWorks (near Margaret River), 471
Cellphones, 53–55
Centennial Park (Sydney), 168
Central Tilba, 16, 229
Cessnock, 206–207
Champagne Pools (the Aquarium; Fraser Island), 356
Charters Towers, 323
Children, families with
    information and resources, 47–48
    suggested itineraries for, 97–99
    Sydney attractions, 171
Chinatown (Broome), 496
Chinatown (Melbourne), 549–550
Chinese Garden (Sydney), 159

Chocolate, Melbourne, 578, 579
City Hall (Brisbane), 256
The Clare Valley, 522
Clarke's Beach, 220
Cleland Wildlife Park (Mount Lofty), 528–529
Clifford's Honey Farm (Kangaroo Island), 535
Clovelly Beach, 164
Cobblers Beach, 164
Cochrane artificial reef, 282
Cod Hole, 278
Coffs Harbour, 215–218
Coffs Harbour Zoo, 216
Cohunu Koala Park (Perth), 453–454
Coles Bay, 648
Commonwealth Games, Melbourne 2006, 39, 575
Consulates, 85–86
Coober Pedy, 12, 17, 501, 541–544
Coo-ee Aboriginal Art Gallery and Shop (Sydney), 177
Coogee, 164
Cook and Phillip Park (Sydney), 175
Cooks' Cottage (Melbourne), 574
Coolgardie, 476, 477, 479
The Coonawarra, 522
The Coorong, 501, 544–545
Coral Bay, 483–486
Coral Sea, 13, 279
Corroboree Rock, 397
Cottesloe, 455
Cottesloe Beach, 12–13
Cowaramup, 475
Cowes, 589
Cradle Mountain, 15, 634, 656–658
Credit cards, 37
Cricket
    Adelaide, 518
    Melbourne, 575–576
    Sydney, 176
Crocodiles, 43–44
    Australia Zoo (Beerwah), 361
    Broome area, 497
    Darwin area, 416, 418, 426
    jumping crocodiles cruise (near Beatrice Hill), 426
    Kakadu National Park, 427–428
Crocodylus Park (Darwin), 416
Cruises. See Boat tours and cruises

Currency and currency
exchange, 34–35
Currumbin Wildlife Sanctuary,
10, 371
Customs House (Sydney), 166
Customs regulations, 32–34
Cynthia Bay, 659

Daintree, The, 95, 284
Daintree National Park,
307–309
Daintree Rain Forest, 292–293
Daintree River, 309
Dampier Peninsula, 499
Dandenong Ranges,
584, 586–587
Darwin, 412–424
accommodations, 418–420
exploring, 415–417
layout of, 415
nightlife, 423
restaurants, 420–423
shopping, 417–418
side trip to Litchfield Park,
423–424
transportation, 415
traveling to, 414
visitor information, 414–415
Darwin Sailing Club, 423
David Fleay Wildlife Park (West
Burleigh), 371–372
Deckchair Cinema (Darwin),
422
Deep vein thrombosis, 44, 59
Delprat's Mine (Broken Hill),
236
Denham, 480
Department stores
Melbourne, 577
Sydney, 179
Didj Beat Didjeridoo's
(Sydney), 177
Digital cameras, 60, 61
Dingoes, Fraser Island, 356
Dinosaur footprint (near
Broome), 497
Disabilities, travelers with,
45–46
Dolphins and dolphin-watching,
436
Dolphin Discovery Centre
(Bunbury), 470
Jervis Bay, 226
Monkey Mia (Shark Bay),
479–482
Narooma, 229
Port Stephens, 212
swimming with dolphins, 10

Done Sydney Observatory, 166
Dorrigo National Park, 217
Drayton Family Wines, 205
Dreamtime Cultural Centre
(near Rockhampton),
345–346
Dreamworld (Coomera),
369–370
Dromedary, Mount, 230
Dubbo, 100
Dunk Island, 316, 319–320,
321–322
Duty-free shops, Sydney, 180
Dynamite Pass, 278

Eagle Heights, 375, 376
East Coast Blues & Roots
Festival (Byron Bay),
219–220
Easter Oakbank Racing
Carnival, 528
The East Macdonnell Ranges,
397–398
East Point Military Museum
(Darwin), 416
Echo Point Road, 196
Echuca, 603–605
Economy-class syndrome, 44, 59
Ecotours (ecoexploring)
Fraser Island, 355–356
the Whitsundays, 337
Eden, 230
Eden Killer Whale Museum,
230–231
Edith Falls, 434
Edmund Kennedy track, 319
Electricity, 85
Eli Creek, 355
Elizabeth Bay House (Sydney),
166
Ellery Creek Big Hole, 395
El Questro, 488
El Questro Wilderness Park,
489, 491–492
Embassies and consulates,
85–86
Emergencies, 86
Emily Gap, 397
Entry requirements, 30–32
Escorted tours, 62–63
Eumundi Markets, 362
Eureka Stockade Centre
(Ballarat), 596
Exmouth, 483–486

Falls Creek, 610–611
Falls Reserve, 199

Families with children
information and resources,
47–48
suggested itineraries for,
97–99
Sydney attractions, 171
Fannie Bay, 415
Farm stays, 82
Far Northern region of the
Great Barrier Reef, 278–279
Far Out Adventures,
15, 412, 433, 435
Fashions (clothing)
Melbourne, 577–579
Sydney, 180–181
Featherdale Wildlife Park
(Sydney), 162, 171
Federation Square
(Melbourne), 568, 570
Female Factory Historic Site
and Island Produce Fudge
Factory (Hobart), 638
Ferries, Sydney, 114, 170, 171
Festivals and special events,
39–41
Film, flying with, 60
Films, recommended, 84–85
Finke Gorge National Park, 397
Fire-Works Gallery (Brisbane),
262
Fishing, 8–9, 67
Batemans Bay, 228
Broome, 497–498
Cairns, 296
Darwin, 417
Falls Creek, 610
Kakadu National Park,
429, 430
Kangaroo Island, 535
the Northwest Cape, 485
Rottnest Island, 464
Fitzroy Island, 288, 292
Flinders Chase National Park,
533–534
Flinders Ranges, 501
Flinders Ranges National Park,
539–541
Flinders Reef, 281
Florence Falls, 423
Floriade (Canberra), 40–41
Fogg Dam Conservation
Reserve, 426
Football (rugby league)
Adelaide, 518
Melbourne, 576
Sydney, 176
Fort Denison (Sydney),
156, 169
Forty-Mile Beach, 360

Four Mile Beach, 12, 310
Four-wheel-driving and tours, 217
Coober Pedy area, 543
the Daintree, 308–309
Forty-Mile Beach, 360
Fraser Island, 8, 354–355
Kings Canyon, 398
Narooma area, 230
the Northwest Cape, 485–486
tips for, 79–80
Francois Peron National Park, 480, 482–483
The Frankland Islands, 279–280
Fraser Island, 8, 353–357
Fraser Island Great Walk, 357
Fremantle, 440, 443–444
accommodations, 449–450
restaurant, 452–453
shopping, 457
sights and attractions, 456–458
Fremantle Arts Centre, 457
Fremantle History Museum, 457
Fremantle Prison, 457–458
Fremantle Trams, 456–457
Freycinet National Park, 15, 648–650
Friday's (Brisbane), 264
Frommers.com, 50
Fur seals, 473, 529, 534, 589

Gantheaume Point, 497
Gavala Aboriginal Art & Cultural Education Centre (Sydney), 178
Gawler, 522
Gay and lesbian travelers
information and resources, 46–47
Sydney, 39
clubs, 186–187
Gay & Lesbian Mardi Gras, 186
Geikie Gorge, 499
Gemopal Pottery (Lightning Ridge), 239
George Brown Darwin Botanic Gardens, 415
George's Gold Mine, 216
The Ghan, 71–72
Giants Cave, 472
Gladstone, 348–349
Glass House Mountains, 357, 362
Glengarry opal fields (Lightning Ridge), 239
Glen Helen Gorge, 396

Glenrowan, 605
The Gold Coast, 365–374
accommodations, 372–374
hinterland, 374–378
nightlife, 374
restaurants, 374
seasons, 368
Golden River Zoo (Mildura), 603
The Goldfields, 476–479
Goldfields Exhibition (Kalgoorlie), 479
The Gold Museum (Ballarat), 596
Gold Treasury Museum (Melbourne), 570
Golf, 67
Adelaide, 518
Alice Springs, 390
Melbourne, 574–575
Merimbula, 230
Narooma, 230
Perth, 459–460
Port Douglas, 310
Sydney, 174
White Cliffs, 237
the Whitsundays, 337–338
Goodwill Bridge (Brisbane), 244
Goolwa Camping and Tourist Park, 544
GORP (Great Outdoor Recreation Pages), 68
Government House (Sydney), 168
Grampians National Park, 612–614
Grawin opal fields (Lightning Ridge), 239
Great Barrier Reef, 5, 274–284
choosing a gateway to, 276–277
day trips to, 277–282
Cairns, 288–289
Port Douglas, 280, 307
Townsville, 323, 324
health and safety warnings, 277
overnighting on, 279
scuba diving, 282–284
in suggested itineraries, 95, 98–99
Great Barrier Reef Marine Park, 279
Great Keppel Island, 346–348
Great Ocean Road, 8, 598–602
Great Sandy National Park, 360
Great Walks of Queensland, 339

Green Island, 279, 283, 288, 291, 292, 301
Grenfell, Mount, 100
The Grotto, 600
Guildford, 465
Gunlom Falls, 430

Hahndorf, 17, 527–528
Halls Gap Lakeside Caravan Park, 613
The Hamelin Pool Historic Telegraph Station, 482
Harbor cruises. See Boat tours and cruises
Hartley's Crocodile Adventures (near Cairns), 291
Hazards Beach, 649
Healesville Sanctuary, 588
Health concerns, 43–45
Health insurance, 41–42, 44
Henley-on-Todd Regatta, 40, 385
"Heritage Highway" (A1, or Midland Hwy.), 650
Her Majesty's Theatre (Adelaide), 520
Her Majesty's Theatre (Sydney), 185
Hermannsburg Historical Precinct, 397
Heron Island, 10, 13, 343, 349–351
Hervey Bay, 9
The High Country (Victoria), 607–612
High Court of Australia (Canberra), 625
High season, 38
Hiking (bushwalking), 14–15, 65
Adelaide, 518
Alice Springs, 389–390
Alpine National Park, 608–609
the Blue Mountains, 194–195, 200
Brisbane, 261
Dandenong Ranges, 584, 586
Fraser Island, 357
Freycinet National Park, 648
Kakadu National Park, 429, 430
Katherine Gorge (Nitmiluk National Park), 433–434
Lamington National Park, 376–377
Litchfield National Park, 423
Margaret River, 473

Hiking *(cont.)*
  Noosa National Park, 360
  the Overland Track, 658
  Port Douglas, 311
  Sydney, 169, 173
  Uluru–Kata Tjuta National
    Park (Ayers Rock/The
    Olgas), 404, 405
  West MacDonnell National
    Park, 395
Hobart, 634–646
  accommodations, 640–643
  exploring, 637–639
  layout of, 636
  nightlife, 645
  organized tours, 639
  restaurants, 643–645
  shopping, 639
  special events, 637
  transportation, 636–637
  traveling to, 634, 636
  visitor information, 636
Hole in the Wall Beach, 226
**Holiday Inn Jazz-n-Blues Bar
  (Brisbane), 266**
Holidays, 38–39
**Holmes à Court Gallery (Perth),
  454**
**Hong Kong, Magnetic Island,
  329**
Horden Vale, 600
**Horseback riding and trekking,
  8, 67**
  Alpine National Park, 609
  the Blue Mountains, 201
  Coffs Harbour, 217
  Port Douglas area, 310–311
  Port Stephens, 212–213
  Snowy Mountains, 233
Horse racing
  Melbourne, 576
  Sydney, 176
Hot-air ballooning
  Alice Springs, 389
  Canberra, 625
  the Hunter Valley, 206
  Melbourne, 574
  Yarra Valley, 587
**Houghton Wines (Middle
  Swan), 465–466**
House swaps, 81–82
Hunter Estate Winery, 205
The Hunter Valley, 202–211
Huskisson, 226
Hyams Beach, 12, 226
Hyde Park (Sydney), 168
**Hyde Park Barracks Museum
  (Sydney), 160**
**Hyundai Hopman Cup
  (Perth), 39**

I MAX Theatre
  Melbourne, 570
  Sydney, 159
Indian Head, 356
Indian Pacific train, 4, 71, 72,
  234, 438, 442, 477, 504
In-line skating
  Brisbane, 262
  Melbourne, 575
  Sydney, 174
Insurance, 41–42
Internet access, 51–53, 86
**Interpretive Gallery
  (Port Arthur), 647**
**Island Pure Sheep Dairy
  (Kangaroo Island), 535**
Isle of the Dead, 647
Itineraries, suggested, 91–102
  Australia in 1 week, 91–95
  Australia in 2 weeks, 96–97
  driving from Sydney to
    Melbourne, 99–100
  for families with children,
    97–99
  Margaret River region,
    101–102

J apanese pearl divers'
  cemetery (Broome), 497
Jenolan Caves, 94, 201–202
Jervis Bay, 9, 225–227
Jessie Gap, 397
Jewel Cave, 471–472
Jim Jim Falls, 429, 430
Jindabyne, 231
Jock's Place (White Cliffs), 237
Jogging
  Adelaide, 518
  Sydney, 174
Johanna, 600
Julian Rocks, 220

K akadu National Park, 10,
  14–15, 424–431
  Aboriginal art and culture,
    428–429
  accommodations and
    restaurants, 431
  attractions, 427–428
  bushwalking, 429
  en route to, 426
  logistical tips, 426
  scenic flights, 429
  seasons, 425
  swimming, 429–430
  traveling to, 425–426
  visitor information, 425

**Kalgoorlie, 16–17, 476, 477,
  478, 479**
Kangaroo Island, 11, 529–538
Kangaroos, as road hazard, 78
Kata Tjuta (the Olgas), 5
**Kate's Cottage Museum
  (Glenrowan), 605**
Katherine, 432–435
Katherine Hot Springs, 435
Katoomba, 195–199
Kayaking, 8, 66–67
  Canberra, 629
  Fitzroy Island, 292
  Maroochy River, 360
  Mission Beach, 319
  the Whitsundays, 338
Kelly, Ned, 604–605
Kellyland, 605
**Kershaw Gardens
  (Rockhampton), 346**
Kiama, 224–225
The Kimberley, 5, 436, 486–500
  transportation, 488–489
  visitor information, 488
**Kings Canyon, 11, 96–97,
  398–399**
Kingscote, 530, 532, 536
**Kings Park & Botanic Garden
  (Perth), 454**
**Kiwi Down Under Farm (near
  Coffs Harbour), 216**
Koala Park (Sydney), 162
Koalas, 28
  Cohunu Koala Park (Perth),
    453–454
  culling, 535
  Kangaroo Island, 533
  Sydney, 162
Kosciuszko National Park, 231
Kununurra, 488, 489–494
Kuranda, 95, 293–297
Kuranda Arts Co-Operative, 294
Kuranda Scenic Railway, 294
**Ku-ring-gai Chase National
  Park, 169–170**
**Ku-ring-gai Wildflower Garden
  (Sydney), 170**

L a Boite Theatre (Brisbane),
  264
**Lady Elliot Island, 13–14, 282,
  352–353**
Lady Jane Bay, 164
Lady Musgrave Island, 282
Lake Cave, 471
**Lake St. Clair National Park,
  15, 656–659**
**Lamington National Park,
  14, 374–375, 376–378**

Langtrees 181 (Kalgoorlie), 478–479
Larapinta Trail, 14, 389
Lathami Conservation Park, 534
Latrobe's Cottage (Melbourne), 574
Launceston, 17, 651–656
Lavers Hill, 600
Lee, "Bushtucker Woman" Helen, 473
Leeuwin Estate Winery (Margaret River), 471, 472
Leura, 199
Lexmark Indy 300 Carnival, 40
Licuala Fan Palm track, 319
Lightning Ridge, 11, 238–240
Lilla Aboriginal Tours, 399
Lindemans Hunter River Winery, 205
Liquor laws, 86
Litchfield National Park, 414, 423–424
Lizard Island, 13, 301–302
Loch Ard Gorge, 600
Lofty, Mount, 528
London Bridge, 600
Lone Pine Koala Sanctuary (Brisbane), 9, 256–257
Lorne, 599
accommodations, 600–601
restaurants, 602
Lost and found, 86
Lost-luggage insurance, 42
The Low Isles, 280, 307
Low season, 38
Luna Park (Sydney), 159

MacDonnell Ranges, The, 11, 382
Magic Cave, 279
Magnetic Island, 327–329
Main Beach (Byron Bay), 220
Main Beach (Gold Coast), 366
Main Beach (Noosa Heads), 358
Maits Rest Rainforest Boardwalk, 599–600
Mala Walk, 404
Malcolm Douglas Wildlife Wilderness Park (near Broome), 497
Maleny, 362
Mammoth Cave, 471
Mamukala wetlands, 430–431
Mangarrayi People, 15, 435
Manly to Spit Bridge Scenic Walkway (Sydney), 169
The Mansion at Werribee Park, 591

Mantaray Bay, 281
Manyallaluk: The Dreaming Place (Katherine), 15, 434
Mapleton-Maleny Road, 362
Margaret River, 469–476
in suggested itineraries, 101–102
Margaret River Chocolate Company (West Swan), 466, 472–473
Margaret River Regional Wine Centre (Cowaramup), 471
Marineland Melanesia (Green Island), 292
Maritime Museum of Tasmania (Hobart), 637
Markets
Adelaide, 519
Brisbane, 262–263
Broome, 497
Byron Bay, 220
Darwin, 421
Eumundi, 362
Fremantle, 457
Melbourne, 572
Sydney, 182
Mary Cairncross Park, 362
Mataranka Thermal Pools, 434
MAXVISION Cinema (Katoomba), 196
MCA (Museum of Contemporary Art; Sydney), 160
McGuigan Brothers Winery, 205
McKenzie, Lake, 355
The McLaren Vale, 522
McWilliams Mount Pleasant Winery, 205
Medical insurance, 41–42, 44
Medlow Bath, 200
Melba Gully State Park, 600
Melba's Chocolate Factory (Woodside), 526
Melbourne, 546–592
accommodations, 554–562
arriving in, 546–548
business hours, 553
consulates, 553
doctors and dentists, 553
Internet access, 553
layout of, 549
neighborhoods in brief, 549–551
nightlife, 579–584
parks and gardens, 573–574
post office, 553
restaurants, 562–568
shopping, 576–579
side trips from, 584–592

sights and attractions, 568–574
transportation, 551–553
visitor information, 549
Melbourne Aquarium, 570–571
Melbourne Concert Hall, 580
The Melbourne Cup, 40, 576
Melbourne International Film Festival, 580
Melbourne Museum, 571
Melbourne Observation Desk, 571
Melbourne Zoo, 571
Melville Island, 428
Merimbula, 230–231
Merimbula Jazz Festival, 231
Michaelmas Cay, 280
The Migration Museum (Adelaide), 18, 516
Milawa Cheese Company, 605
Milawa Gourmet Trail, 605
Mildura, 100
Mimosa Rocks National Park, 230
Mindil Beach Sunset Market (Darwin), 421
Mining Hall of Fame (Kalgoorlie), 478
Mission Beach, 12, 16, 270, 277, 315–322
day trips to Great Barrier Reef, 280–281
day trips to Great Barrier Reef from, 318
Mitchell Falls, 499
Money matters, 34–37
Monkey Mia Reserve (Shark Bay), 10, 479–483
Mon Repos Conservation Park (Bundaberg), 2, 350
Mon Repos Turtle Rookery, 350
Montague Island, 9, 229
Montville, 362
Moreton Island, 267, 269
Morning Peninsula Regional Gallery (Mornington), 591
The Mornington Peninsula, 591–592
Mossman Gorge, 308
Motorcycle tours
the Blue Mountains, 196
Sydney, 173
Uluru–Kata Tjuta National Park (Ayers Rock/The Olgas), 405
Motor home rentals (camper vans), 75–76
Moulting Lagoon Game Reserve, 648

Mountain biking. *See* Biking and mountain biking
Mount Buffalo National Park, 611–612
Mount Coot-tha Aboriginal Art Trail, 261
Mount Field National Park, 645–646
Mount Hotham, 609–610
Mount Tamborine, 375–376
Mount Tomah Botanic Gardens, 197
Mount View Estate, 205
Mrs. Macquarie's Chair (Sydney), 168
Mumbulla Mountain, 230
Mungo National Park, 605–606
Murray Lagoon, 534
Murray River, 602–607
Murray Valley, 100
Murwillumbah, 223–224
Museum and Art Gallery (New Norcia), 468
Museum and Art Gallery of the Northern Territory (Darwin), 416
Museum of Brisbane, 257
Museum of Central Australia (Alice Springs), 386
Museum of Contemporary Art (MCA; Sydney), 160
Museum of Sydney, 166–167
Museum of Tropical Queensland (Townsville), 323, 324
Museums, best, 17–18
Music stores, Sydney, 182–183
Mutawintji National Park, 236–237
Mutton Bird Island, 216
Mylor, 526–527

Namadgi National Park, 628
Namarrgon, 428
Nambour-Mapleton Road, 362
Nanguluwur, 428
Narooma, 229–230
Narryna Van Diemen's Land Folk Museum (Hobart), 637
National Capital Exhibition (Canberra), 626
National Gallery of Australia (Canberra), 626
National Gallery of Victoria, International (Melbourne), 571
National Gallery of Victoria: The Ian Potter Centre–Australian Art (Melbourne), 571–572

National Museum of Australia (Canberra), 18, 626–627
National Parks & Wildlife Centre (Sydney), 107
National Pass Walk, 199
National Railway Museum (North Adelaide), 518
National Rhododendron Gardens (Olinda), 586
The National Wine Centre of Australia (Adelaide), 516
N'Dhala Gorge Nature Park, 398
Ned Kelly Country, 604–605
Nelson Bay, 211
Newhaven, 589
New Norcia, 467–469
New Norcia Deep Space Ground Station, 467–468
New Norcia Museum & Art Gallery, 17–18
New South Wales, 25–26, 190–240
Outback, 234–240
what's new in, 1–2
Newstead House (Brisbane), 257
New Year's Eve, 41
Ngilgi Cave, 472
Nimbin, 220
Ningaloo, 436
Ningaloo Marine Park, 480
Ningaloo Reef, 14
Nitmiluk Gorge Caravan Park, 435
Nitmiluk National Park, 432
The Nobbies, 589
Noosa Heads, 357
Noosa National Park, 360
North Stradbroke Island, 266
North Sydney Olympic Pool, 175
The Northwest Cape, 10, 11, 439, 480, 483–485
Nourlangie Rock, 428
Nuriootpa, 522, 523, 524, 525
Nursery Bommie, 280

Oakbank, 528
Oceanworld Manly (Sydney), 162
Old Melbourne Gaol, 572
Old Parliament House (Canberra), 627
The Old Umbrella Shop (Launceston), 652
Olga, Mount (the Olgas), 405
Opals
Adelaide, 519
Lightning Ridge, 238–239
Sydney, 183

Opera Australia (Sydney), 184
Opera Queensland (Brisbane), 264
Ord River, 489, 490
Original & Authentic Aboriginal Art (Sydney), 178
Orlando and Jacobs Creek Visitor Centre (Rowland Flat), 523
Ormiston Gorge and Pound, 395–396
Orpheus Island, 329–330
Osprey Reef, 279
Ossa, Mount, 656
Otford, 170
The Outback, 8
best places to experience, 11–12
New South Wales, 234–240
South Australia, 501, 538–544
Victoria, 605–606
Outer Edge Expeditions, 68
Outfitters and operators, 68
Overland Track, 658

Package tours, 60–62
Palmateer, Josh, 473, 496
Palm Beach (Sydney), 12, 165, 174
Palm Valley, 397
Pandora, HMS (wreck), 324
Parap Markets, 421
Parasailing, Sydney, 174
Parliament House (Canberra), 627
Passports, 32, 87
Pearl Luggers (Broome), 496–497
Pearls, 418, 461, 488, 495, 498, 500
Broome area, 496–497
Pebbly Beach, 9
Penfolds (Nuriootpa), 523
Penguins
Kangaroo Island, 534–535
Montague Island, 229
Phillip Island, 588, 589, 590
The Penny Royal World & Gunpowder Mill (Launceston), 652
Perth, 436, 440–462
accommodations, 447–450
arriving in, 440, 442
beaches, 455–456
business hours, 445–446
consulates, 446
doctors and dentists, 446
emergencies, 446
layout of, 443

maps, 443
neighborhoods in brief, 443–444
nightlife, 461–462
outdoor activities, 459–460
pharmacies, 446
restaurants, 450–453
seasons, 438
shopping, 460–461
    Fremantle, 457
side trips from, 462–469
sights and attractions, 453–455
in suggested itineraries, 101, 102
time zone, 446
transportation, 444–445
visitor information, 442–443
weather forecasts, 446
Perth Mint, 454–455
Perth Tram Co., 454
Perth Zoo, 455
Peterson's Champagne House, 205
Peterson's Vineyard, 205
Phillip Island, 588–590
Phillip Island Penguin Reserve, 590
Pokolbin, 205–211
Port Arthur, 646–648
Port Arthur Historic Site, 647
Port Campbell National Park, 600
Port Douglas, 13, 16, 304–315
    day trips to Great Barrier Reef from, 280, 307
    diving the Great Barrier Reef from, 283
Port Fairy, 600
Port Macquarie, 214–215
Port of Echuca, 604
Port Phillip Bay, 591–592
Port Stephens, 211–213
Powerhouse Museum (Sydney), 159–160
Prince Regent Nature Reserve, 499
Princes Highway, 224–231
Puffing Billy Railway (Belgrave), 586–587
The Puppet Shop at the Rocks (Sydney), 179
Purnululu (Bungle Bungles) National Park, 494
Pylon Lookout (Sydney), 157

Quay Deli (Sydney), 140
Queensland, 2, 26, 270–378

Queensland Art Gallery (Brisbane), 258
Queensland Cultural Centre (Brisbane), 257
Queensland Gallery of Modern Art (Brisbane), 258
Queensland Museum (Brisbane), 258
Queensland Orchestra (Brisbane), 264
Queensland Performing Arts Centre (QPAC; Brisbane), 257–258, 263
Queensland Theatre Company (Brisbane), 263
Queen Victoria Building (QVB; Sydney), 177
Queen Victoria Market (Melbourne), 572
The Queen Victoria Museum & Art Gallery (Launceston), 652
Questacon—The National Science and Technology Centre (Canberra), 627

Rail passes, 72
Rainbow Beach, 357
Raine Island, 279
Rainforestation Nature Park (Kuranda), 295–296
Rainforest Habitat, 309
Rainforests
    Byron Bay, 220
    Cairns area, 290–296
    Coffs Harbour area, 217
    Daintree Rain Forest, 292–293
    Mission Beach area, 318–319
    in suggested itineraries, 98–99
Raleigh International Raceway (near Coffs Harbour), 217
Ravenswood, 323
The Red Centre, 26–27, 379–408
    exploring, 379–382
Reef HQ (Townsville), 325
Regions in brief, 25–29
Restaurants. See also Restaurant Index
    best, 22–24
Rhyll Inlet, 589
Ribbon Reefs, 278
Richmond, 647
Rippon Lea House Museum & Historic Garden (Melbourne), 572
River cruises. See Boat tours and cruises

River Walk (Brisbane), 259
Road trains, 78–79
Rockford (Tanunda), 523
Rockhampton, 344–346
Rockhampton Botanic Gardens, 346
Roma Street Parkland (Brisbane), 258
Ross, 650
Ross Bridge, 650
Ross Female Factory, 650
Rothbury Estate, 205
Rottnest Island, 14, 462–465
The Roundhouse (Perth), 458
Royal Botanic Gardens (Melbourne), 573–574
Royal Botanic Gardens (Sydney), 168
Royal Flying Doctor Service
    Alice Springs, 387
    Broken Hill, 236
    Kalgoorlie, 478
Royal Flying Doctor Visitors Centre (Cairns), 291
Royal National Park (Sydney), 170
Royal Tasmanian Botanical Gardens (Hobart), 638
Rugby league football
    Adelaide, 518
    Melbourne, 576
    Sydney, 176
Runnymede, 209
Russell Falls, 646

Safety, 45, 87
Sailing (yachting), 67
    Perth, 460
    Sydney, 176
    Whitsunday Islands, 5, 334–336
St. Clair, Lake, 657–659
St. Helena Island, 267–268
St. James Church (Sydney), 167
St. John's Anglican Cathedral (Brisbane), 259
St. Mary's Cathedral (Sydney), 167
St. Patrick's Cathedral (Melbourne), 573
St. Paul's Cathedral (Melbourne), 573
Salamanca Market (Hobart), 639
Sandalford Caversham Estate, 465, 466
Satellite phones, 55
Scarborough, 455

Scarborough Beach, 444
Scenic flights (aerial tours),
  70–71
    Kakadu National Park, 429
    Kings Canyon, 399
    Nitmiluk National Park, 434
    Uluru–Kata Tjuta National
      Park (Ayers Rock/The
      Olgas), 400, 404
    Western Australia, 439
    the Whitsundays, 337
Scenic Railway (the Blue
  Mountains), 196
School of the Air
    Alice Springs, 387
    Broken Hill, 236
    Katherine, 435
Scuba diving, 63–65. See also
  Sharks, diving/snorkeling
  with
    best sites for, 13–14
    Bundaberg, 352
    Byron Bay, 220
    courses, 283–284
    Great Barrier Reef, 282–284
    the Northwest Cape, 485
    Perth, 460
    Rottnest Island, 464
    Sydney, 174
Sea kayaking. See Kayaking
Seal Bay Conservation Park,
  534
Seal colonies, Narooma,
  229–230
Seasons, 37–38
Sea turtles, 278, 280, 341, 350
    the Northwest Cape, 485
Sea World (Main Beach, Gold
  Coast), 369, 370
Senior travelers, 47
Seppelts (Seppeltsfield),
  523–524
Serpentine Gorge, 395
Serviced apartments, 80–81
    Sydney, 121, 129, 133
75-Mile Beach, 355
Shark Bay (Monkey Mia
  Reserve), 479–483
Sharks
    around Sydney, 163–164
    diving/snorkeling with,
      162, 216
        Great Barrier Reef, 278,
          279, 280, 282
        Northwest Cape, 480
        the Northwest Cape, 485
        Perth, 453
Shell Beach, 482
Shelly Beach, 165

Shipping your luggage, 57
Shipwreck Coast, 600
Shipwreck Galleries (Perth),
  17, 458
Shotover (catamaran), 482
Shrine of Remembrance
  (Melbourne), 574
Silvertip City, 279
Silverton, 236
Simpson's Gap, 395
Single travelers, 49
Sir Thomas Brisbane Planetar-
  ium & Cosmic Skydome,
  258–259
Skiing
    Snowy Mountains, 232
    Victoria, 609–611
    the Victorian Alps, 9
Skyrail Rainforest Cableway,
  293–294
Skytour (Sydney), 1
Skywalk (Dorrigo National
  Park), 217
Skyway (the Blue Mountains),
  196
Smoking, 2, 87–88
Snake bites, 43
Snorkeling. See also Sharks,
  diving/snorkeling with
    best sites for, 13–14
    Lady Elliot Island, 352
    Magnetic Island, 328–329
    the Northwest Cape, 485
    Perth, 460
    Rottnest Island, 464
The Snowy Mountains,
  8, 231–233
Snowy River National Park,
  607–608
South Australia, 28, 501–545
    exploring, 501
    Outback, 538–544
    transportation, 502
South Australian Maritime
  Museum (Adelaide), 516–517
South Australian Museum
  (Adelaide), 517
South Bank Parklands
  (Brisbane), 259
South Head (Sydney), 169
South Stradbroke Island,
  266–267
Sovereign Hill (Ballarat),
  596–597
Space Theatre 3D Ride
  (Sydney), 166
Special events and festivals,
  39–41
Spider bites, 43

Standley Chasm, 395
Stanley, 661
Star City (Sydney), 189
State Houses of Parliament
  (Melbourne), 573
State Library of New South
  Wales (Sydney), 167
State Theatre (Melbourne),
  580
Steve's Bommie, 278
Stingers, 163–164
Story Bridge Adventure Climb
  (Brisbane), 2, 261
Strahan, 659–661
The Strand (Townsville), 325
Student travelers, 48–49
Sublime Point Lookout, 199
Summer Cloud Bay, 226
Sun-Herald City to Surf, 40
Sun Pictures (Broome), 498
Sun protection, 44
Sunshine Beach, 358, 360
The Sunshine Coast, 357–365
Super Pit (Kalgoorlie), 478
Surfers Paradise Beach, 12, 366
Surfing, 68
    Broome, 496
    Byron Bay, 220
    Margaret River, 9, 473
    Perth, 460
    Rottnest Island, 464
    the Sunshine Coast, 360
    Sydney, 174–175, 176
Surfworld Museum (West
  Torquay), 599
Swan Lake, 589
The Swan Valley, 465–467
Swimming
    Canberra, 629
    Kakadu National Park,
      429–430
    Sydney, 175
Sydney, 4, 103–189
    accommodations, 1, 120–136
    American Express, 116
    arriving in, 104, 106–107
    Balmain, 111
    bar scene, 187–189
    beaches, 163–165
    Bondi, accommodations,
      132–134
    Bondi and the southern
      beaches, 110
    Bondi Beach, restaurants,
      151–152
    business hours, 116
    cafes, 149–150
    casino, 189
    Central, 110

Circular Quay, 108
  accommodations,
    121–126
  restaurants, 137–141
City Center, accommodations,
  126–128
club and music scene,
  185–187
consulates, 118
currency exchange, 116
Darling Harbour, 108
  accommodations,
    128–129
  restaurants, 146–147
  sights and attractions,
    159–160
Darlinghurst, 110
  accommodations, 131
  restaurants, 147–149
doctors and dentists, 116, 118
emergencies, 118
eyeglass repair, 118
gay and lesbian clubs,
  186–187
Glebe, 110
  accommodations, 132
  restaurant, 149
harbor cruises and organized
  tours, 171–173
Homebush Bay, 111
hospitals, 118
for kids, 171
Kings Cross and the suburbs
  beyond, 108–109
  accommodations,
    129–131
  restaurants, 147–149
layout of, 107
lost property, 118
luggage storage, 118
main arteries and streets,
  107–108
Manly and the northern
  beaches, 111, 164
  accommodations,
    134–135
  restaurants, 152
movies, 189
neighborhoods in brief,
  108–111
newspapers, 119
Newtown, 110
  accommodations,
    131–132
  restaurants, 150–151
nightlife, 183–189
The North Shore, 111
North Sydney, 110–111
outdoor activities, 173–176

Paddington/Oxford Street,
  109–110
  accommodations, 131
  restaurant, 149
  shopping, 177
parks and gardens, 168–170
picnic fare, 140
post offices, 119
restaurants, 136–152
  surcharges, 141
restrooms, 119
The Rocks, 108, 171
  accommodations, 121–126
  restaurants, 141–145
safety, 119
shopping, 176–183
sights and attractions,
  153–171
spectator sports, 176
in suggested itineraries, 94,
  95, 97–98
telephones, 119
Town Hall, 108
  restaurants near,
    145–146
transportation, 111–116
visitor information, 107
Watsons Bay, 110
weather forecasts, 120
what's new in, 1
Sydney Airport Train Link,
  104, 106
Sydney AMP Tower, 160–161
Sydney Aquarium, 160
Sydney Aquatic Centre, 175
Sydney Festival, 39, 184
Sydney Film Festival, 40
Sydney Fishmarket, 148, 181
Sydney Gay & Lesbian Mardi
  Gras, 39, 186
Sydney Harbour, 153, 156
Sydney Harbour Bridge, 156–157
Sydney Harbour National Park,
  156, 168–169
Sydney International Airport,
  104
  accommodations, 136
Sydney International Aquatic
  Centre, 161
Sydney Jewish Museum, 167
Sydney Olympic Park, 161
Sydney Opera House,
  157–159, 183–184
SydneyPass, 112
Sydney Symphony Orchestra,
  184
Sydney-to-Hobart Yacht
  Race, 41
Sydney Visitor Centre, 107

Tamarama, 164
Tamborine, Mount, 374–376
Tamburlaine Winery, 205
Tamworth Country Music
  Festival, 39
Tandanya Aboriginal Cultural
  Institute (Adelaide), 16, 517
Tangalooma, 10
Tanunda, 522, 523
Tanunda Cellars, 523
Taronga Zoo (Sydney),
  162–163, 171
Tasmania, 2–3, 29, 630–661
  exploring, 630–634
  west coast of, 659
Tasmanian Devil Park Wildlife
  Rescue Centre, 648
Tasmanian devils, 661
Tasmanian Expeditions, 68
Tasmanian Museum and Art
  Gallery (Hobart), 639
Taxes, 88
Telephones, 89
Telopea Gallery (Sydney), 179
Telstra Stadium (Sydney), 161
Telstra Tower (Canberra), 627
Tennis
  Canberra, 629
  Melbourne, 575, 576
  Sydney, 175
Territory Craft (Alice Springs),
  386
Territory Wildlife Park (Darwin),
  415–416
Tesselaar's Bulbs and Flowers
  (Silvan), 586
Theater
  Brisbane, 263–264
  Melbourne, 580–581
  Sydney, 184–185
Theatre Royal (Hobart), 645
Thredbo Village, 231
Three Brothers, 200
Three Sisters, 196
Ticks, 43
Tidbinbilla Nature Reserve
  (Canberra), 628
Tinklers, 205–206
Tipping, 89–90
Titzs, 89
The Tiwi Islands, 428
Tjapukai Aboriginal Cultural
  Park (Cairns), 15, 95, 289–290
Tolmer Falls, 423
The Top End, 27, 409–435
  exploring, 409–412
  tour operators, 412
Torquay, 599

Tours, package, 60–62
Townsville, 316, 323–327
    day trips to Great Barrier Reef
        from, 281, 323, 324
    diving the Great Barrier Reef
        from, 283
Trailer (caravan) parks, the
    Hunter Valley, 207
Train travel, 71–72
Transportation, 68–80
Traveler's checks, 36
Travel insurance, 41–42
Treasury Casino (Brisbane),
    264
Treasury Gardens (Melbourne),
    574
Trephina Gorge Nature Park,
    397
Trevallyn State Recreation
    Area, 652
Trigg, 456
Trip-cancellation insurance, 41
Tropical Fruit World (near
    Murwillumbah), 223
Tully River, 68, 296, 316, 318
Turquoise Bay, 485
Turtles, sea, 278, 280, 341, 350
    the Northwest Cape, 485
The Tweed Valley, 223, 224
Twelve Apostles, 600
Tyrell's, 206

Ubirr Rock, 428–429
Ulladulla, 227–228
Uluru (Ayers Rock), 5, 403–405
    in suggested itineraries, 96
Uluru–Kata Tjuta National Park
    (Ayers Rock/The Olgas),
    11, 399–408
The Umbarra Aboriginal
    Cultural Centre (Wallaga
    Lake), 15, 230
Underwater World
    (Mooloolaba), 361
Upolu Cay, 280

Valley of the Waters, 199
Vaucluse House (Sydney),
    167–168
Victoria, 28–29, 593–614
Victorian Arts Centre
    (Melbourne), 580
Victoria's Open Range Zoo at
    Werribee, 591
Video, flying with, 60
Vincentia, 226
Visitor information, 29–30

Voyager Estate (Margaret
    River), 471
Voyage to Discovery (Ballarat),
    597

Waddy Point, 356
Wait-a-While Rainforest
    Tours, 10
Walcott Inlet, 499
Walls of Jerusalem National
    Park, 656
WA Museum Kalgoorlie-
    Boulder, 478
Wangi Falls, 423
Warner Bros. Movie World
    (Oxenford), 370
Warning, Mount, 223
Warradjan Aboriginal Cultural
    Centre, 17, 429
Warrawong Sanctuary (Mylor),
    526–527
Watego Beach, 220
Water, drinking, 90
Watersports. See also specific
    sports
    Four Mile Beach, 310
    the Sunshine Coast, 360
Wave Rock, 440
Websites, 29–30
Wellington, Mount, 637
Wentworth Falls, 199
Werribee, 591
The West Coast (Tasmania),
    659–661
West Coast Wilderness Railway,
    2–3
Western Australia, 27–28,
    436–500
    exploring, 438
    midwest and northwest
        coasts of, 479–486
    tour operators, 438
    transportation, 438
Western Australian Maritime
    Museum (Perth), 17, 458
Western Australian Museum
    (Perth), 455
West MacDonnell National
    Park, 395–396
Wet 'n' Wild Water World
    (Oxenford), 371
Wet Tropics Rainforest, 5
Whales and whale-watching
    Eden Killer Whale Museum,
        230–231
    Margaret River, 473
    Narooma, 229
    Perth, 459

Port Stephens, 212
    the Whitsundays, 338
Wharf Theatre (Sydney), 185
Wheelchair accessibility, 45–46
White Cliffs, 100, 237
Whitehaven Beach, 12, 337
White-water rafting, 68
    Cairns, 296
    Tully River, 8, 318
The Whitsunday Coast and
    Islands, 13, 14, 330–343
    choosing a base in, 333
    day trips to Great Barrier Reef
        from, 281–282, 333–335
    diving the Great Barrier Reef
        from, 283
    exploring, 333–337
    fishing, 337
    island hopping, 336
    kayaking, 338
    resorts, 340–343
    sailing and snorkeling trips,
        335–336
    scenic flights, 337
    seasons, 336
    transportation, 333
    traveling to, 332
    visitor information,
        332–333
The Whitsundays Great Walk,
    339
Wi-Fi connections, 52–53
Wilcannia, 100
Wildflowers, 5, 8, 101
    Perth, 454
    Western Australia, 439
Wildlife and wildlife viewing.
    See also Aquariums and
    marine-life parks; Bird-
    watching; Dolphins and
    dolphin-watching; Whales
    and whale-watching; Zoos;
    and specific wildlife
    Alice Springs Desert Park, 386
    Alice Springs Reptile Centre,
        386
    best places for, 9–11
    Billabong Sanctuary
        (Townsville), 325
    Cleland Wildlife Park (Mount
        Lofty), 528–529
    Currumbin Wildlife Sanctuary,
        371
    Darwin, 415–416
    David Fleay Wildlife Park
        (West Burleigh), 371–372
    Kakadu National Park, 424
    Kangaroo Island, 534
    safety tips, 319

Sydney, 161–163
Tasmanian Devil Park Wildlife Rescue Centre, 648
William Ricketts Sanctuary (Mt. Dandenong), 586
Willie Creek Pearl Farm (near Broome), 497
Wilpena Pound, 539
Windjana Gorge, 499
Window on the Wetlands Visitor Centre (Beatrice Hill), 426
Windsurfing, Sydney, 176
Wineglass Bay, 648, 649
Wineglass Bay Lookout, 649
Wineries and vineyards
   the Barossa, 523–524
   the Hunter Valley, 204–206
   Margaret River, 471
   Milawa, 605
   The National Wine Centre of Australia (Adelaide), 516
   the Swan Valley, 465–466
Wines, Sydney, 183
Wolf Blass (Nuriootpa), 524
WOMADelaide Festival, 506
Women travelers, 48
Woodbridge (West Midland), 466
Woongarra Marine Park, 282
Woongarra Marine Park (Bundaberg), 352
World Expeditions, 68
The World Outdoors, 68
World War II oil storage tunnels (Darwin), 417

Yachting. See Sailing
Yalumba (Angaston), 524
Yamatji Bitja Aboriginal Bush Tours, 16, 478
Yarra Valley, 587–588
Yellow Water Billabong, 427–428
Yongala, SS (wreck dive), 13, 281, 324, 325
Yulara, 405–408

Zenbar (Brisbane), 265
Zoos
   Adelaide, 517
   Australia Zoo (Beerwah), 361
   Cairns Tropical Zoo, 291
   Caversham Wildlife Park & Zoo, 466
   Coffs Harbour Zoo, 216
   Melbourne, 571

Perth Zoo, 455
Victoria's Open Range Zoo at Werribee, 591

ACCOMMODATIONS

Adelaide City Park Motel, 511
Adelaide Hills Country Cottages (Oakbank), 528
Adelphi Court YHA Hostel (Hobart), 643
Adelphi Hotel (Melbourne), 557
Albert Heights Executive Apartments (Melbourne), 559
Alice on Todd (Alice Springs), 392
Alice's Cottages & Spa Hideaways (Launceston), 653
Alice Springs Resort, 391
Alinga Longa Lodge (Bright), 607
Alishan International Guest House (Sydney), 132
All Seasons Plaza Hotel Kalgoorlie, 479
Andu Lodge (Quorn), 540–541
The Ansonia (Ballarat), 597
Archipelago Studio Apartments (Port Douglas), 20, 312
Arts Factory Lodge (Byron Bay), 220–221
Atlantic Tower Motor Inn (Glenelg), 513
Aurora Alice Springs, 392
Avocado Grove Bed & Breakfast (Flaxton, Montville), 364
Ayers Rock Resort, 405–406
The Backpacker's Inn at Radeka's Downunder Motel (Coober Pedy), 543
Ballarat Heritage Homestay, 597
Barossa Valley (SA) Tourist Park (Nuriootpa), 524
Barrington Guest House (Salisbury), 21, 209–210
Basildene Manor (Margaret River), 474
Bayside Gardens (Apollo Bay), 601
The Bay Soldiers Esplanade Motor Inn (Batemans Bay), 229
Bedarra Island, 18, 322
Bernly Private Hotel (Sydney), 130
Best Western (Canberra), 622
Best Western Elkira Motel (Alice Springs), 392–393

Billabong Gardens (Sydney), 131–132
Binna Burra Mountain Lodge (Beechmont), 20, 377–378
Black Prince (Hobart), 642
Bondi Beachside Inn (Sydney), 133
Bondi Serviced Apartments (Sydney), 133
Bond Springs Outback Retreat (Alice Springs), 391
The Brassey of Canberra, 621
Broken Hill Overlander Motor Inn, 237–238
Byron at Byron, 1–2
The Byron Bay Waves Motel (The Waves), 221
Byron Central Apartments, 221
Cable Beach Club Resort Broome, 19, 498
Cairns Plaza Hotel, 298
Caribbean Motel (Coffs Harbour), 218
Carriages Guest House (Pokolbin), 208
The Carrington Hotel (Katoomba), 197–198
Casuarina Coastal Units (Kangaroo Island), 536
Casuarina Restaurant and Country Inn (Pokolbin), 207
Central City Backpackers (Hobart), 643
Cessnock Heritage Inn, 206–207
City Walk Hotel (Canberra), 622
Coffs Harbour Motor Inn, 218
Collingrove Homestead (Angaston), 22, 524
Colonial Cottages of Ross, 650
Coral Sea Resort (Airlie Beach), 339
Coral Tree Inn (Cairns), 298–299
Country Club Hotel (Kununurra), 493–494
Country Plaza International (Gladstone), 349
Couran Cove Island Resort (South Stradbroke Island), 268
Cradle Mountain Lodge, 21, 657
Crowne Plaza Canberra, 621
Crown Towers (Melbourne), 554, 556
Crystal Creek Rainforest Retreat (Murwillumbah), 224

Cumberland Lorne Conference & Leisure Resort, 600–601

Customs House Hotel (Hobart), 643

Daintree Eco Lodge & Spa, 314–315

Daydream Island Resort, 342

The Desert Cave Hotel (Coober Pedy), 543

Desert Gardens Hotel (Yulara), 407

Desert Palms Resort (Alice Springs), 393

DeVere Hotel (Sydney), 130

Dunk Island, 321–322

Duxton Hotel Perth, 447

Echoes Hotel & Restaurant, Blue Mountains (Katoomba), 21, 197

Echo Point Holiday Villas (Katoomba), 198

Echuca Gardens B&B and YHA, 606

Ellis Beach Oceanfront Bungalows, 300–301

The Elms of Hobart, 641

El Paso Motor Inn (Port Macquarie), 215

El Questro Homestead, 19, 492–493

Emma Gorge Resort (The Kimberley), 20–21, 493

Emu Walk Apartments (Yulara), 407

Enderley Gardens (Surfers Paradise), 373

Equinox Resort (Surfers Paradise), 373–374

Esplanade Hotel Fremantle, 449–450

Eton (Brisbane), 251

Explorers Inn Hotel (Brisbane), 19, 251–252

Feathertop Alpine Lodge (Falls Creek), 611

Fitzroy Island Resort, 302–303

Forrest Inn and Apartments (Canberra), 621

Fountain Terrace (Melbourne), 560

Franklin Manor (Strahan), 660

Fraser Island Retreat, 356

Freycinet Lodge, 21, 649

Frueauf Village (Falls Creek), 611

Gagudju Crocodile Holiday Inn (Jabiru), 431

Gagudju Lodge Cooinda (Jim Jim), 431

The Gatehouse Jenolan (Jenolan Caves Village), 202

Georgian Court Guest House (Melbourne), 559–560

Glen Helen Resort, 396

Gordon Gateway Chalets, 660

The Grace Hotel Sydney, 126

Grahams Castle Resort (Goolwa), 545

Grand Hotel (Melbourne), 557–558

Grand Hyatt Melbourne, 556

Great Ocean Road Cottages (Lorne), 601

Green Island Resort, 301

The Hahndorf Resort, 527–528

Hamilton Island, 342–343

Hanson Bay Cabins (Kangaroo Island), 537–538

Hansons Swan Valley (near Perth), 22, 466

Hayman, 19, 340

Heritage Trail Lodge (Margaret River), 22, 474

Hermitage Lodge (Pokolbin), 208–209

The Hermitage of Marananga, 525

Heron Island Resort, 350–351

Hillview House (Launceston), 654

Hilton Adelaide, 509–510

Holiday Inn Townsville, 325–326

Holiday Village Backpackers (Byron Bay), 221

Hook Island Wilderness Resort, 343

The Horizon (Mission Beach), 320

Hotel Claremont (Melbourne), 562

The Hotel Como (Melbourne), 19, 562

Hotel 59 (Sydney), 130

Hotel George Williams (Brisbane), 19, 252

Hotel Grand Chancellor (Hobart), 640

Hotel Grand Chancellor Launceston, 653

Hotel Ibis Brisbane, 251

Hotel Lindrum (Melbourne), 556

Hotel Rendezvous Observation City Perth, 449

Hotel Sofitel Reef Casino (Cairns), 297

Hotel Tasmania (Launceston), 654–655

Hotel Tolarno (Melbourne), 560, 562

Huskisson Beach Tourist Resort (Jervis Bay), 226

Hyatt Hotel Canberra, 19, 620–621

Hyatt Regency Adelaide, 510

Hyatt Regency Coolum, 362–363

Ibis Melbourne, 558

Indy's (Sydney), 132–133

Innkeepers Colonial Motor Inn (Launceston), 654

Islington Elegant Private Hotel (Hobart), 641

Jenolan Caves House, 202

Jervis Bay Guest House, 226–227

Kangaroo Island Lodge, 537

Katoomba Mountain Lodge, 198

Keppel Haven (Great Keppel Island), 347–348

Kingfisher Bay Resort (Fraser Island), 20, 356–357

Kings Canyon Resort, 399

Kingsgate Hotel (Melbourne), 558–559

Kingston Court Apartments (Canberra), 621–622

The Kirketon, 129

Knotts Crossing Resort (Katherine), 435

Lady Elliot Island Resort, 353

Lightning Ridge Hotel/Motel, 239–240

Lilianfels Blue Mountains (Katoomba), 197

Lilybank Bed & Breakfast (Cairns), 21, 299

Lizard Island, 18, 301–302

The Lodge on Elizabeth (Hobart), 641

Longitude 131 (Red Centre), 19, 406

The Lord Nelson Brewery Hotel (Sydney), 126

The Lost Camel (Yulara), 407

Macka's Farm (Port Campbell), 601

Mackays (Mission Beach), 320–321

Macquarie Manor (Hobart), 641–642

Mangrove Resort Hotel (Broome), 498–499

Manly Backpackers Beachside (Sydney), 134
Manly Lodge (Sydney), 134–135
Manly Pacific Parkroyal (Sydney), 134
Manly Paradise Motel and Beach Plaza Apartments (Sydney), 135
Marae (near Port Douglas), 21, 313
Marble Lodge, 525
Mario the Palace Hotel (Broken Hill), 238
Martinique Whitsunday Resort (Airlie Beach), 339–340
Medina Grand, Harbourside (Sydney), 128
Melba Lodge (Yarra Glen), 588
The Melbourne Hotel (Perth), 447
Mercure Grand Hydro Majestic Hotel (Medlow Bath), 200
Mercure Hotel Brisbane, 251
Mercure Hotel Perth, 448–449
Mercure Resort Great Keppel Island, 2, 347, 348
Mercure Resort Surfers Paradise (Surfers Paradise), 372–373
Mildura Grand Hotel, 606
Mirambeena Tourist Resort (Darwin), 419
Miss Maud Swedish Hotel (Perth), 20, 447–448
Monkey Mia Dolphin Resort, 483
Moore's Brecknock Hotel, 511
The Mountain Grand Guesthouse (Grampians), 613–614
Mt. Buffalo Chalet, 612
Mt. Cockburn Lodge, 2
National Park Hotel, 646
New Norcia Hotel, 469
Ningaloo Reef Resort (Coral Bay), 486
Noah's (Sydney), 133
The Noble Grape (Cowaramup), 475
Nomads Backpackers, 511
Noosa Village Motel, 363–364
North Adelaide Heritage Group, 20, 512
Novotel Adelaide on Hindley, 510
Novotel Vines Resort (near Upper Swan), 467
The Nunnery Guesthouse (Melbourne), 560

Oakford/Somerset Executive Apartments (Melbourne), 558
Oasis Resort Cairns, 297–298
Observatory Hotel (Sydney), 121
Ocean View Motor Inn (Merimbula), 231
The Old Cable Station (Stanley), 661
Old Lion Apartments (North Adelaide), 512
Olembia Private Hotel (Melbourne), 562
The Open House (Kangaroo Island), 537
O'Reilly's Rainforest Guesthouse (Lamington National Park), 20, 378
Ormiston House (Strahan), 660–661
Orpheus Island Resort, 18–19, 330
Outback Pioneer Hotel and Lodge (Yulara), 408
Outrigger Beach Club & Spa (Palm Cove), 300
Ozone Seafront Hotel (Kangaroo Island), 536
Palazzo Versace (Main Beach), 372
Park Hyatt Sydney, 18, 124
Park Regis Sydney, 127
Pelican Beach Resort Australis (Coffs Harbour), 218
Penguin Hill Country House B&B (Phillip Island), 590
Penneshaw Youth Hostel (Kangaroo Island), 536
Peppers Anchorage Port Stephens, 212–213
Peppers Convent Hunter Valley (Pokolbin), 207–208
Peppers Guest House (Pokolbin), 208
Peppers Palm Bay (Long Island), 341
Peppers Seaport Hotel (Launceston), 653
Periwinkle–Manly Cove Guesthouse (Sydney), 135
Poltalloch, 545
Port Arthur Motor Inn, 648
Port Douglas Peninsula Boutique Hotel, 311–312
Port Douglas Retreat, 312
Port O'Call Lodge (Port Douglas), 313
The Portsea Hotel, 592

Port Stephens Motor Lodge, 213
Potshot Hotel Resort (Exmouth), 486
Prairie Hotel (Flinders Ranges), 21, 23, 541
Princes Lodge Motel (North Adelaide), 512–513
Quay Grand Suites Sydney, 124
Quokka Arms (Rottnest Island), 465
Ramada Melbourne, 558
Ravesi's on Bondi Beach (Sydney), 134
The Reef Retreat (Cairns), 19, 301
Riverside Cabins (Thredbo), 233
River View on Mount Street (Perth), 449
Rockford Adelaide (The Townhouse), 510–511
The Rocks (Townsville), 21–22, 326
The Ross Village Bakery and Inn, 650
Rothsaye on Lovers Walk (Cowes), 590
Rottnest Lodge, 465
The Russell (Sydney), 21, 125
Russell Falls Holiday Cottages (National Park), 646
Rydges Capricorn Resort (Yeppoon), 346
Rydges Esplanade Resort Cairns, 298
Rydges Plaza Resort Alice Springs, 392
Sails in the Desert (Yulara), 406–407
Salamanca Inn (Hobart), 642
Salamander Shores, 213
Sanctuary House Motel Healesville, 588
Sanctuary Motor Inn Resort (Coffs Harbour), 218
Saville Park Suites Adelaide, 511
Saville Park Suites Darwin, 418–419
Seagulls Resort (Townsville), 326
The Sebel Pier One Sydney, 125
The Sebel Reef House & Spa Palm Cove (Cairns), 18, 299–300
The Sebel Residence East Perth, 448
Shangri-la Hotel Sydney, 124

Shangri-La Hotel, The Marina (Cairns), 297

Sheraton Mirage Port Douglas, 311

Sheraton Noosa Resort & Spa, 363

Silky Oaks Lodge & Healing Waters Spa (Mossman), 313–314

Sir Stamford at Circular Quay, Sydney, 18, 125

Skycity Darwin, 2, 418

Sofitel Melbourne, 556

South Long Island Nature Lodge, 20, 341

The Sovereign Hill Lodge (Ballarat), 597

The Stafford (Sydney), 126

Stamford Grand Adelaide, 513

Stamford Plaza Brisbane, 250

Stamford Sydney Airport, 136

Star City Hotel (Sydney), 128

Station Township Bungalows (El Questro), 493

Station Township Riverside Camping (El Questro), 493

Sullivans Hotel (Sydney), 131, 448

The Summer House (Darwin), 22, 419–420

Summit Ridge Alpine Lodge (Falls Creek), 611

Sun City Motel (Bundaberg), 352

Swiss-Grand Hotel (Sydney), 133

Sydney Central YHA, 127–128

Tamborine Mountain Bed & Breakfast (Eagle Heights), 376

Tangalooma Wild Dolphin Resort (Moreton Island), 269

Taylor's Guest House (Byron Bay), 222

Thala Beach Lodge (near Port Douglas), 314

Thornbury House Bed & Breakfast (Brisbane), 252

Thredbo Alpine Apartments, 233

Toad Hall (Melbourne), 559

Top End Hotel (Darwin), 420

Travelodge Hotel Sydney, 127

Tricketts Luxury Bed & Breakfast (Sydney), 132

Ulladulla Guest House, 21, 228

Underground Motel (White Cliffs), 20, 238

University House (Canberra), 622

Value Inn (Darwin), 420

Victoria Court Sydney, 130–131

Victor Lodge (Canberra), 622

Vineyard Hill Country Motel (Pokolbin), 209

Waldheim Cabins, 657

The Wallangulla Motel (Lightning Ridge), 240

Wanderers Rest (Kangaroo Island), 537

Waratah on York (Launceston), 654

Wattle Private Hotel (Sydney), 131

Waverley (Brisbane), 21, 252–253

Wellington Lodge (Hobart), 642

Westin Sydney, 126–127

Whale Motor Inn (Narooma), 230

Wilpena Pound Resort, 541

The Windsor (Melbourne), 556–557

Wisteria Lodge (Kangaroo Island), 536

Wool Brokers Arms (Sydney), 129

Woolmers Inn (Hobart), 642–643

Wrest Point Casino (Hobart), 640–641

Wrest Point Motor Inn (Hobart), 640–641

York Mansions (Launceston), 20, 653–654

RESTAURANTS

Akudjura (Kalgoorlie), 479

Amalfi (Adelaide), 514

Amicos (Cessnock), 210

Antibar (Sydney), 141

Ashiana (Sydney), 152

Asturiana (Sydney), 146

Austral Hotel (Adelaide), 514

Babka Bakery (Melbourne), 567

Balmoral Boatshed Kiosk (Sydney), 149–150

Bamboo House (Melbourne), 24, 564

Bar Coluzzi (Sydney), 150

Bar Doppio (Alice Springs), 394

Basil Leaves Café (Perth), 451

Beach Hotel Barbecue (Byron Bay), 222

Becco (Melbourne), 564

bel mondo (Sydney), 141

Bill's (Sydney), 150

Bistro Lulu (Sydney), 149

Blaxland's Restaurant (Pokolbin), 210

The Blue Duck (Perth), 452

The Boat House by the Lake, 623

Bojangles Saloon and Restaurant (Alice Springs), 394

Bondi Icebergs/Icebergs Dining Room & Bar (Sydney), 151

Botanic Gardens Restaurant (Sydney), 137

Bourbon & Beefsteak Bar (Sydney), 147–148

Breakfast Creek Hotel (Brisbane), 255

Bridgewater Mill (Hahndorf), 528

Brunetti (Melbourne), 566

Buzz Café (Darwin), 420–421

Café Enzo (Pokolbin), 210

Café Hernandez (Sydney), 150

Café Segovia (Melbourne), 565

Café Sydney (Sydney), 141

Caffe Della Piazza (Canberra), 624

Cape Willoughby Café (Kangaroo Island), 538

Capitan Torres (Sydney), 146

Casa Nostra (Alice Springs), 394–395

Casuarina Restaurant and Country Inn (Pokolbin), 207, 210–211

Chairman and Yip (Canberra), 623

Chinta Blues (Melbourne), 567

Chinta Ria (The Temple of Love; Sydney), 147

Chocolate Buddha (Melbourne), 565

Chork Dee Thai Restaurant (Katoomba), 199

Churinga Café (Mt. Dandenong), 587

City Extra (Sydney), 140

Colonies (Palm Cove), 304

Conservation Hut Café (Wentworth Falls), 199

Croplines Coffee Bar (Launceston), 656

Crystal Creek Rainforest Retreat (Murwillumbah), 224

Cumquat on Criterion (Hobart), 645

Dolphin Rock Café (Kangaroo Island), 538

DOME chain of cafes (Perth), 450

Donovans (Melbourne), 567

Doyles at the Quay (Sydney), 142

Doyles Fisherman's Wharf (Sydney), 142–143

Doyles on the Beach (Sydney), 142

Drunken Admiral Restaurant (Hobart), 644

Earth 'n' Sea (Byron Bay), 222

e'cco bistro (Brisbane), 22, 253

Explorers Cafe (Brisbane), 254

Far Horizons (Palm Cove), 304

Fast Eddy's Café (Perth), 451

Fee & Me Restaurant (Launceston), 655

Fishlips Bar & Bistro (Cairns), 22, 303

Flower Drum (Melbourne), 23, 563–564

44 King Street (Perth), 450–451

Forty One (Sydney), 137

Fraser's (Perth), 22, 450

Friends (Mission Beach), 322–323

G'Day Café (Sydney), 145

Govindas (Sydney), 148–149

The Grange (Adelaide), 514

Green Papaya (East Brisbane), 23, 255

Green's Eatery (Sydney), 152

Grossi Florentino (Melbourne), 564

Guillaume at Bennelong (Sydney), 137

The Gumnut Café (Sydney), 144

Hansons (Henley Brook), 23–24, 467

Hanuman (Darwin), 421

Hard Rock Cafe (Sydney), 148

Hopetoun Tearooms (Melbourne), 565–566

Hursey Seafoods (Stanley), 661

Il Bacaro (Melbourne), 564–565

Il Primo (Melbourne), 566

Il Solito Posto (Melbourne), 565

Indiana Tea House (Perth), 452

Irish Times (Melbourne), 565

The Italian Village (Sydney), 144

Jasmin Indian Restaurant (Adelaide), 514–515

Jo Jo's (Brisbane), 254

Jolleys Boathouse Restaurant (Adelaide), 515

Kanpai (Melbourne), 568

Koko (Melbourne), 564

Konditorei Cafe Manfred (Launceston), 655–656

Lamont Winery Cellar Door (near Upper Swan), 467

La Pizzeria (Perth), 452–453

La Porchetta Pizza Restaurant (Melbourne), 567

Leeuwin Estate's restaurant (Margaret River), 475

Le Kilimanjaro (Sydney), 150

Level One (Sydney), 145

Level Two Revolving Restaurant (Sydney), 145

Lindsay's (Katoomba), 198

Little Saigon (Canberra), 624

The Löwenbräu Keller (Sydney), 143

Malathi's Restaurant & Sean's Irish Bar (Alice Springs), 393–394

Mangrove Jack's Café Bar (Airlie Beach), 340

The Manse (North Adelaide), 515–516

Mario's (Melbourne), 567

Marks of Lorne, 602

Matsuri (Adelaide), 515

Meccabah (Melbourne), 568

Mekong Thai (Adelaide), 515

Mezzaluna (Sydney), 22, 147

Michel's Cafe and Bar (Townsville), 327

Miss Maud Swedish Restaurant (Perth), 451

Mit Zitrone (Hobart), 644

Mount Street Café and Food Store (Perth), 451

Mures Upper Deck (Hobart), 24, 643–644

Nautilus (Port Douglas), 315

Newtown House (near Margaret River), 23, 475

Nina's Ploy Thai Restaurant (Sydney), 151

Nudel Bar (Melbourne), 565

O'Keefe's Hotel (Launceston), 655

The Old Coffee Shop (Sydney), 150

Old Ghan Restaurant (Hawker), 541

Old Saigon (Sydney), 150–151

Otto Ristorante (Sydney), 147

Overlanders Steakhouse (Alice Springs), 393

Ozone Milk Bar (Port Campbell), 602

The Palette Café (Canberra), 623

Palms Restaurant (Alice Springs), 393

Pancakes Licensed Café (Sydney), 144

Paragon Café (Katoomba), 199

The Pass Café (Byron Bay), 222

Pee Wee's at The Point (Darwin), 421–422

Peppers Convent Hunter Valley (Pokolbin), 207–208

Perrotta's (Cairns), 303–304

Phillip's Foote (Sydney), 23, 144

Pier Nine (Brisbane), 253

The Point Revolving Restaurant (Hobart), 644

Pompei's (Sydney), 151–152

Portia's Place (Canberra), 624

Portobello Caffé (Sydney), 140–141

Port O'Call Bistro (Port Douglas), 315

Prairie Hotel (Flinders Ranges), 23, 541

Quay (Sydney), 22, 141–142

Rae's Restaurant and Bar (Byron Bay), 222–223

Raving Prawn (Byron Bay), 223

Red Ochre Grill (Alice Springs), 23, 394

Red Ochre Grill (Cairns), 303

Ricky Ricardo's (Noosa Sound), 23, 364

Rigoni's Bistro (Adelaide), 515

Robert's Restaurant (Pokolbin), 211

Robin Hood Family Bistro (Ballarat), 598

Rob's on the Boardwalk (Port Stephens), 213

Rockpool (Sydney), 22, 142

Roma Bar Cafe (Darwin), 420

Rossini (Sydney), 140

Sailors Thai (Sydney), 142

Salsa Bar & Grill (Port Douglas), 23, 315

Salters (Angaston), 525

Seafood Mama's (Coffs Harbour), 218

Season (Noosa Heads), 23, 364–365

The Seasons of the Valley (Angaston), 525

Shakahari (Melbourne), 566

Shenanigan's Irish Pub, Restaurant & Bar (Darwin), 422

Sheni's Curries (Melbourne), 566

Shrimps (Launceston), 655

Simone's of Bright, 607
Sisco's on the Pier (Hobart), 644
Standpipe Motor Inn (Port Augusta), 541
Star Bar Cafe (Launceston), 655
The Summit (Brisbane), 255
The Summit (Mount Lofty), 529
Supper Inn (Melbourne), 566
Supreme View Café (Sydney), 146
Sushi Roll (Sydney), 146
Sydney Cove Oyster Bar, 140
Tandoor Indian Restaurant (Melbourne), 568
Tetsuya's (Sydney), 22, 145
Thai Terrific (Sydney), 151

Tim's Surf 'n' Turf (Darwin), 422–423
Tognini's BistroCafeDeli (Brisbane), 254
Tosolini's (Canberra), 623
TrisElies (Katoomba), 198–199
The Tryst (Canberra), 23, 623–624
Turenne's at Bondi (Sydney), 152
Vanidol's Asian Cuisine (Hobart), 644–645
Vat 107 (Margaret River), 475–476
Vintner's Bar & Grill (Angaston), 525

Vue du Monde (Melbourne), 566–567
Vulture's Restaurant & Café (Perth), 452
Waterfront Restaurant (Sydney), 144
Watt Modern Dining (Brisbane), 254
Wild Oak Café (Mt. Dandenong), 587
Wino's, 476
Wolfie's Grill (Sydney), 144
Zaaffran (Sydney), 146–147
Zia Pina (Sydney), 145
Zouí Alto (Townsville), 23, 327

HE NEW TRAVELOCITY GUARANTEE

EVERYTHING YOU BOOK WILL BE RIGHT, OR WE'LL WORK WITH OUR TRAVEL PARTNERS TO MAKE IT RIGHT, RIGHT AWAY.

To drive home the point, we're going to use the word "right" in every single sentence.

Let's get right to it. Right to the meat! Only Travelocity guarantees everything about your booking will be right, or we'll work with our travel partners to make it right, right away. Right on!

Here's a picture taken smack dab right in the middle of Antigua, where the guarantee also covers you.

The guarantee covers all but one of the items pictured to the right.

Now, you may be thinking, "Yeah, right, I'm so sure." That's OK; you have the right to remain skeptical. That is until we mention help is always right around the corner. Call us right off the bat, knowing that our customer service reps are there for you 24/7. Righting wrongs. Left and right.

For example, what if the ocean view you booked actually looks out at a downright ugly parking lot? You'd be right to call – we're there for you. And no one in their right mind would be pleased to learn the rental car place has closed and left them stranded. Call Travelocity and we'll help get you back on the right track.

Now if you're guessing there are some things we can't control, like the weather, well you're right. But we can help you with most things – to get all the details in righting,* visit **travelocity.com/guarantee**.

*Sorry, spelling things right is one of the few things not covered under the guarantee.

I'd give my right arm for a guarantee like this, although I'm glad I don't have to.

You'll never roam alone.

IF YOU BOOK IT, IT SHOULD BE THERE.

Only Travelocity guarantees it will be, or we'll work
with our travel partners to make it right, right away.
So if you're missing a balcony or anything else you
booked, just call us 24/7. **1-888-TRAVELOCITY.**

travelocity
You'll never roam alone